SECOND EDITION

THE MAKING OF THE WEST

PEOPLES AND CULTURES

A CONCISE HISTORY

N
W   E
S

NORWAY

SWEDEN

Bergen

Oslo

Stockholm

Göteborg

Baltic Sea

SCOTLAND

Glasgow   Edinburgh

NORTHERN
IRELAND

Belfast

North Sea

Aarhus

DENMARK   Copenhagen

RUSSIA

Kaliningrad

Gdańsk

Dublin   UNITED

IRELAND

Liverpool

KINGDOM

Birmingham

Cork

WALES   ENGLAND

Thames R.

London

NETHERLANDS

Amsterdam

Berlin

Elbe R.

POLAND

Vistula R.

Oder R.

Prague

Cracow

CZECH REP.

Brno

Antwerp   Rotterdam

Brussels

BELGIUM

GERMANY

Frankfurt

Rhine R.

Paris

Luxembourg

LUXEMBOURG

Seine R.

SLOVAKIA

Bratislava

Miskolc

Vienna

Munich

Loire R.

LIECHTENSTEIN

Danube R.

AUSTRIA

Budapest

HUNGARY

A T L A N T I C
O C E A N

Bay of
Biscay

FRANCE

Lyon

Zürich   Vaduz

Bern

SWITZERLAND

Innsbruck

Graz

A
L
P
S

Milan

SLOVENIA

Ljubljana

Rhône R.

Po R.

CROATIA

Zagreb

Belgrade

San
Marino   SAN
MARINO

BOSNIA AND
HERZEGOVINA

Split   Sarajevo

Oporto

PORTUGAL

PYRENEES

ANDORRA

Andorra
la Vella

Ebro R.

MONACO

Marseille

A P E N N I N E S

Adriatic Sea

SERBIA AND
MONTENEGRO

Lisbon

Madrid

SPAIN

Barcelona

Corsica

Rome   ITALY

Naples

Tirana

ALBANIA

Seville

BALEARIC IS.

Sardinia

Tyrrhenian
Sea

Ionian
Sea

Gibraltar
(Br.)

Algiers

Tunis

Palermo

Sicily

Rabat

Valletta

MALTA

MOROCCO

TUNISIA

M e d i t e r r a n e a n

Tripoli

ALGERIA

LIBYA

English Channel

0   150   300 miles
0   150   300 kilometers

SECOND EDITION

THE MAKING OF THE WEST

PEOPLES AND CULTURES

A CONCISE HISTORY

LYNN HUNT
University of California at Los Angeles

THOMAS R. MARTIN
College of the Holy Cross

BARBARA H. ROSENWÉIN
Loyola University Chicago

R. PO-CHIA HSIA
Pennsylvania State University

BONNIE G. SMITH
Rutgers University

BEDFORD/ST. MARTIN'S   Boston   ◆   New York

FOR BEDFORD/ST. MARTIN'S

Publisher for History: Mary Dougherty
Executive Editor for History: Katherine Meisenheimer
Director of Development for History: Jane Knetzger
Developmental Editor: Sara Wise
Production Editor: Deborah Baker
Senior Production Supervisor: Dennis Conroy
Executive Marketing Manager: Jenna Bookin Barry
Editorial Assistant: Kate Macmillan
Copyeditor: Susan Free
Proofreaders: Lisa Wehrle, Jan Cocker
Text Design: Wanda Kossak, Joan O'Connor
Indexer: EdIndex
Cover Design: Donna Lee Dennison
Composition: Techbooks
Cartography: Mapping Specialists Limited
Printing and Binding: R.R. Donnelley & Sons Company

President: Joan E. Feinberg
Editorial Director: Denise B. Wydra
Director of Marketing: Karen Melton Soeltz
Director of Editing, Design, and Production: Marcia Cohen
Managing Editor: Elizabeth M. Schaaf

Library of Congress Control Number: 2005938009

Manufactured in the United States of America.

1   0   9
f

For information, contact: Bedford/St. Martin's, 75 Arlington Street, Boston, MA 02116 (617-399-4000)
bedfordstmartins.com

ISBN-10: 0–312–43937–7 (paperback complete edition)   ISBN-13: 978–0–312–43937–8
        0–312–43945–8 (paperback Volume I)   978–0–312–43945–3
        0–312–43946–6 (paperback Volume II)   978–0–312–43946–0

Cover and Title Page Art: Henri Rousseau. *A Centennial of Independence*, 1892 (detail). The J. Paul Getty Museum, Los Angeles.

Preface

THE IDEA OF "THE WEST" is now urgently under discussion. The end of the cold war after 1989 presented new challenges for historical interpretation, but these had hardly been digested when the shock of September 11, 2001, reverberated throughout the world. Conflict now takes place on a global stage, and globalization of the economy and culture has become a subject of passionate debate. These momentous issues and events present extraordinary challenges for authors of Western civilization textbooks. We welcome the challenges, for they have deepened our commitment to our project's basic goal and approach. From the very beginning, we have insisted on an expanded vision of the West that includes the United States, fully incorporates eastern Europe, and emphasizes Europe's relationship with the rest of the world, whether through trade, colonization, migration, cultural exchange, or religious and ethnic conflict.

Every generation of students needs new textbooks that synthesize recent findings. Textbooks conceived during the era of the cold war are, of course, oriented toward explaining the clash between a West unquestionably identified as western Europe and the United States and its eastern-bloc opponents, eastern Europe and the Soviet Union. Since much of eastern Europe has now joined the European Union, the notion of Europe—and the West—has to change. New histories must reflect these dramatic changes. We feel confident that ours meets the challenge. Our post–cold war conception applies not only to our coverage of recent events, but informs our entire treatment of Western Civilization—from antiquity to the present. By adopting a wider view of the West from the start, our book offers a more coherent and convincing view of the important issues in the making of the West to help students understand the world in which they live.

Central Themes and Approach

Our title—*The Making of the West: Peoples and Cultures, A Concise History*—makes three enduring points about our themes and approach: (1) that the history of the West is the story of a process that is still ongoing, not a finished result with only one fixed meaning; (2) that "the West" includes many different peoples and cultures; that is, that there is no one Western people or culture that has existed from the beginning until now. To understand the historical development of the West and its position in the world today, it is essential to place the West's emergence in a larger, global context that reveals the cross-cultural interactions fundamental to the shaping of the Western identity. Finally, (3), that a "concise" approach is ideally suited to meet the needs of instructors who wish to assign additional supplementary readings, who need to cover the entire introduction to Western civilization in a single semester, or who find a comprehensive textbook too detailed and daunting for their students. By reworking, condensing, and combining thematically related sections throughout the text ourselves, we've created a brief edition that preserves the narrative flow, balance, and power of our full-length work.

Our task as authors, moreover, is to integrate the best of social and cultural history with the enduring developments of political, military, and diplomatic history, offering a clear, compelling narrative that sets all the key events and stages of the West's evolution in a broad, meaningful context.

We know from our own teaching that introductory students need a solid chronological framework, one with enough familiar benchmarks to make the material readily digestible, but also one with enough flexibility to incorporate the new varieties of historical research. That is one reason we present our account in a straightforward, chronological manner. Each chapter treats all the main events, people, and themes of a period together; thus students are not required to learn about political events in one chapter, and then backtrack to concurrent social and cultural developments in the next. The chronological organization also accords with our belief that it is important, above all else, for students to see the interconnections among varieties of historical experience— between politics and cultures, between public events and private experiences, between wars and diplomacy and everyday life. Our chronological synthesis allows students to appreciate these relationships while it, we hope, captures the spirit of each age and sparks students' historical imaginations. For teachers, our chronological approach ensures a balanced account, allows the flexibility to stress themes of one's own choosing, and perhaps best of all, provides a text that reveals history not as a settled matter but as a process that is constantly alive, subject to pressures, and able to surprise us.

In writing *The Making of the West: Peoples and Cultures, A Concise History*, it has been our aim to communicate the vitality and excitement as well as the fundamental importance of history. If we have succeeded in conveying some of the vibrancy of the past and the thrill of historical investigation, we will be encouraged to start rethinking and revising—as historians always must—once again.

Textual Changes

Unlike most scholarly books, a textbook offers historians the rare chance to revise the original work, to keep it fresh, and to make it better. It has been a privilege to bring our own scholarship and teaching to bear on this rewriting. In this second edition, we have kept our emphasis on a strong central story line that incorporates the best of new research, but we have worked to make the narrative even more focused and accessible by reviewing every line of text and recrafting the headings to provide better signposts for readers.

To illustrate our conception of the history of the West as an ongoing process, the first chapter opens with a new discussion of the origins and contested meaning of "Western civilization." In this conversation, we emphasize our theme of cultural borrowing between the peoples of Europe and their neighbors that has characterized Western civilization from the beginning. We continue to incorporate the experiences of borderland regions and the importance of global interactions into the historical narrative and in many of our new art selections.

Of course, the recent past is the most pressing arena in which to examine the West as an evolving construct. The impact of recent events is reflected most dramatically in the last two chapters, which have been completely rewritten and now divide at 1989, the year that marks the beginning of a new era after the cold war.

Throughout each chapter, we've added new material and drawn on new scholarship on topics such as Zoroastrianism and the influence of Persian religion on later faiths (Chapter 1); criticisms of radical democracy (Chapter 2); the origins of Islam (Chapter 7); Byzantine court culture (Chapter 8); the prominence of the flagellant movement (Chapter 11); sugar grinding in the colonies (Chapter 14); the role of peasants in the French Revolution (Chapter 16); nineteenth-century French efforts to transform Saigon (Chapter 18); Japan's imperialist activity in the 1920s (Chapter 20); discontent in the colonies during the depression (Chapter 21); postwar recovery in Scandinavia and the contributions of immigrants to postwar European economies (Chapter 22); the rise in the study of social sciences (Chapter 23); and the impact of global outsourcing (Chapter 24).

Pedagogy and Features

More and more is required of students these days, and not just in Western Civilization courses. We know from our own teaching that students need all the help they can get in assimilating information, acquiring skills, and learning about historical debate. With these goals in mind, we retained the class-tested learning and teaching aids that contributed to the first edition, but we have also added more such features.

Each chapter begins with a *vivid anecdote* that draws readers into the atmosphere and issues of the period and raises the chapter's main themes, supplemented by a full-page illustration that echoes the anecdote and similarly reveals the temper of the times. To help students check their comprehension of main ideas, we have added new *review questions* strategically placed at the end of each major section. Bolded *key terms* in the text are defined in a new *Glossary of Key Terms* at the end of the book. Each chapter closes with a list of *important date*s and a strong *chapter conclusion* that reviews main topics and ties together the chapter's thematic strands. Two new *Making Connections questions* at the end of each chapter encourage students to analyze chapter material or make comparisons within or beyond the chapter.

To reflect the richness of the themes in the text and to enliven the past with many more original sources, in the second edition we have greatly expanded the companion sourcebook that accompanies this textbook, *Sources of THE MAKING OF THE WEST: A CONCISE HISTORY.* There are now five documents per chapter, which vary in length to offer instructors the flexibility to use them in the classroom or for outside assignments. Nothing can give a more direct experience of the past than original voices, and we have endeavored to let those voices speak in the sourcebook, whether it is Seneca describing everyday life in the Roman Empire (Chapter 3), student impressions of university life in the twelfth and early thirteenth centuries (Chapter 9), or a child's view of war-torn Sarajevo in the early 1990s (Chapter 24). *Sources of THE MAKING OF THE WEST* is available free when packaged with *A Concise History,* or at a nominal charge if purchased separately.

The map program of the first edition was widely praised as the most comprehensive in any brief survey text. In each chapter we offer a set of three types of maps, each with a distinct role in conveying information to students. On average, three to four *full-size maps* show major developments, one to three *"spot" maps*—small maps that emphasize a detailed area from the discussion—aid students' understanding of specific but crucial issues, and *Mapping the West* summary maps at the end of each chapter provide a snapshot of the West at the close of a transformative period and help students visualize the West's changing contours over time. For this edition, we have carefully considered each map, improved the colors for better contrast, and clarified and updated borders and labels where needed. In addition to the *more than 160 maps,* numerous charts and graphs visually support the narrative, including innovative *Taking Measure* features, which highlight a chart, table, graph, or map of historical statistics that illuminates an important political, social, or cultural development.

It has been our intention to integrate art as fully as possible into the narrative and to show its value for teaching and learning. *Over 260 illustrations,* carefully chosen to reflect this edition's broad topical coverage and geographic inclusion, reinforce the text and show the varieties of visual sources from which historians build their narratives and interpretations. All artifacts, illustrations, paintings, and photographs are contemporaneous with the chapter; there are no anachronistic illustrations—no fifteenth-century peasants tilling fields in a chapter on the tenth century! We know that today's students are very attuned to visual sources of information, yet they do not always receive systematic instruction in how to "read" or think critically about such visual sources. Our substantive captions for the maps and art help them learn how to make the most of these informative materials, and new to the second edition, we have frequently included specific questions or suggestions for comparisons that might be developed. Specially designed visual exercises in the Online Study Guide supplement this approach.

Supplements

Because textbook supplements take on special importance in classrooms in which a brief survey text is assigned, we have taken care in revising and augmenting the comprehensive and well-integrated set of print and electronic resources for students and instructors that support the second edition of *The Making of the West: A Concise History.*

For Students

Sources of THE MAKING OF THE WEST: A CONCISE HISTORY, Second Edition— Volumes I (to 1740) and II (since 1340)—by Katharine J. Lualdi, University of Southern Maine. For each chapter in *The Making of the West,* this companion sourcebook now features five important political, social, and cultural documents that reinforce or extend discussions in the textbook, encouraging students to make connections between narrative history and primary sources. The second edition provides instructors with even more flexibility with 35 percent more documents and the addition of visual sources. This edition also pays more attention to geographic areas beyond Europe and includes an improved balance between traditional documents and selections that provide a fresh perspective. Short chapter summaries and document headnotes contextualize the wide array of sources and perspectives represented, while discussion and new comparative questions guide students' reading and promote historical thinking skills. *Available free when packaged with the text.*

Online Study Guide at bedfordstmartins.com/huntconcise.   The popular Online Study Guide for *The Making of the West: A Concise History* is a free and uniquely personalized learning tool to help students master themes and information in the textbook and improve their historical skills. Assessment quizzes let students evaluate their comprehension and provide them with customized plans for further study through a variety of activities. Instructors can monitor students' progress through the online Quiz Gradebook or receive e-mail updates.

NEW The Bedford Glossary for European History.   This handy supplement for the European history survey course provides students with clear, concise definitions of the political, economic, social, and cultural terms used by historians and contemporary media alike. All terms are placed within their historical context to aid comprehension. *Available free when packaged with the text.*

The Bedford Series in History and Culture—Advisory Editors Lynn Hunt, University of California, Los Angeles; David W. Blight, Yale University; Bonnie G. Smith, Rutgers University; Natalie Zemon Davis, Princeton University; and Ernest R. May, Harvard University. European titles in this highly praised series combine first-rate scholarship, historical narrative, and important primary documents for undergraduate courses. Each book is brief, inexpensive, and focused on a specific topic or period. To see a complete list of titles in this series, please go to bedfordstmartins.com/wwbshc. *Package discounts are available.*

NEW Trade Books.   Titles published by our sister companies Farrar, Straus and Giroux; Henry Holt and Company; Hill and Wang; Picador; and St. Martin's Press are available at a discount when packaged with the text. For a list of titles, please see bedfordstmartins.com/tradeup.

A Student's Online Guide to History Reference Sources at bedfordstmartins.com/benjamin.   This Web site provides links to history-related databases, indexes, and journals, plus contact information for state, provincial, local, and professional history organizations.

Research and Documentation Online at bedfordstmartins.com/resdoc.   This Web site provides clear advice on how to integrate primary and secondary sources into research papers, how to cite sources correctly, and how to format in MLA, APA, *Chicago,* or CBE style.

The St. Martin's Tutorial on Avoiding Plagiarism at bedfordstmartins.com/plagiarismtutorial.   This online tutorial reviews the consequences of plagiarism and explains what sources to acknowledge, how to keep good notes, how to organize research, and how to integrate sources appropriately. The tutorial includes exercises to help students practice integrating sources and recognize acceptable summaries.

Bedford Research Room at bedfordstmartins.com/researchroom.   The Research Room, drawn from Mike Palmquist's *The Bedford Researcher,* offers a wealth of resources—including interactive tutorials, research activities, student writing samples, and links to hundreds of other places online—to support students in courses across the disciplines. The site also offers instructors a library of helpful instructional tools.

For Instructors

Instructor's Resource Manual to Accompany THE MAKING OF THE WEST, A CONCISE HISTORY, Second Edition, by Dakota Hamilton, Humboldt State University. This helpful manual offers both first-time and experienced teachers a wealth of tools for structuring and customizing Western Civilization history courses of different sizes. For each chapter in the textbook, the *Instructor's Resource Manual* includes an outline of chapter themes; a chapter summary; lecture and discussion topics; film and literature suggestions; writing and class-presentation assignments; research topic suggestions; and in-class exercises for working with maps, illustrations, and sources. The new edition includes a chapter-by-chapter guide to all of the supplements available with *The Making of the West: A Concise History,* answers to the new in-text Review questions and Making Connections questions, and a brief guide for using the book companion site.

Transparencies.   A set of over 200 full-color acetate transparencies of maps and images in the parent text broaden the art program in *A Concise History* to help instructors present images and teach students important map-reading skills. A correlation guide that shows how the transparencies align with the brief text appears in the *Instructor's Resource Manual* and on the book companion Web site.

Book Companion Web site at **bedfordstmartins.com/huntconcise**.   The companion Web site for *The Making of the West: A Concise History* gathers all the electronic resources for the text—including the Online Study Guide and related Quiz Gradebook—at a single Web address, providing convenient links, and lecture, assignment, and research materials such as PowerPoint chapter outlines and the digital libraries at Make History.

Computerized Test Bank by Joseph Coohill, Pennsylvania State University at New Kensington, and Frances Mitilineos, Loyola University Chicago. This fully updated test bank offers over 80 exercises per chapter, including multiple-choice, identification, timelines, map labeling and analysis, and full-length essay questions. Instructors can customize quizzes and add or edit both questions and answers, as well as export questions and answers to a variety of formats, including WebCT and Blackboard. The disc includes answer keys and essay outlines.

Instructor's Resource CD-ROM.   This disc provides instructors with ready-made and easily customized PowerPoint multimedia presentations built around chapter outlines, maps, figures, and selected images from the textbook. The disc also includes selected images from the textbook in JPEG format, an electronic version of the *Instructor's Resource Manual,* outline maps in PDF format for quizzing or handouts, and a quick-start guide to the Online Study Guide.

NEW Make History at bedfordstmartins.com/makehistory.   Comprising the content of our acclaimed online libraries—Map Central, DocLinks, and HistoryLinks—Make History provides one-stop access to relevant digital content including maps, documents, and Web links. Students and instructors can search this free, easy-to-use database by keyword, topic, date, or specific chapter of *The Making of the West: A Concise History* and can download any content they find. Instructors using *The Making of the West: A Concise History* can also create entire collections of content and store them online for later use or post their collections to the Web to share with students.

Using the Bedford Series in History and Culture with THE MAKING OF THE WEST: A CONCISE HISTORY, Second Edition at bedfordstmartins.com/usingseries.   This online guide helps instructors integrate volumes from the highly regarded Bedford Series in History and Culture into their Western Civilization survey course. The guide correlates themes from each series book with relevant chapters in *A Concise History.*

Course Management Content.   E-content is available for this book in Blackboard, WebCT, Angel, and Desire2Learn. This e-content includes nearly all of the offerings in the book's Online Study Guide, as well as the book's test bank.

Videos and Multimedia.   A wide assortment of videos and multimedia CD-ROMs on various topics in European history is available to qualified adopters. Contact your Bedford/St. Martin's sales representative for more information.

Acknowledgments

In the vital process of revision, the authors have benefited from repeated critical readings by many talented scholars and teachers. Our sincere thanks go to the following instructors, as well as three anonymous reviewers, whose comments often challenged us to rethink or justify our interpretations and who always provided a check on accuracy down to the smallest detail: Michael Anderson, George Mason University; Marjorie Berman, Red Rocks Community College; Stephen Bourque, California State University, Northridge; Scott Bruce, University of Colorado at

Boulder; Elspeth Carruthers, University of Illinois at Chicago; Elizabeth Dennison, University of Alaska Anchorage; Constantina Scourtis Gaddis, Onondaga Community College; Richard Golden, University of North Texas; Richard Jobs, Pacific University; Bill Kamil, Sinclair Community College; Joseph Lepore, University of South Alabama; Steven Marks, Clemson University; John Moser, Ashland University; Larry Ping, Southern Utah University; Jana Pisani, Ferris State University; Jennifer Popiel, St. Louis University; Mark Potter, University of Wyoming; Thomas Saylor, Concordia University, St. Paul; Barbara Shepard, Longwood University; Heath Spencer, Seattle University; Daniel Thiery, Iona College; and William Virden, University of Northern Colorado.

Many colleagues, friends, and family members have helped us develop this work as well. They know how grateful we are. We also wish to acknowledge and thank the publishing team at Bedford/St. Martin's who did so much to bring this revised edition to completion: Joan Feinberg, Denise Wydra, Elizabeth Welch, Mary Dougherty, Jane Knetzger, Sara Wise, Deborah Baker, Jenna Bookin Barry, Katherine Meisenheimer, Kate Macmillan, Danielle Slevens, and Gillian Speeth. Our students' questions and concerns have shaped much of this work, and we welcome all our readers' suggestions, queries, and criticisms. Please contact us at our respective institutions or via history@bedfordstmartins.com.

L. H.   T. R. M.   B. H. R.   R. P. H.   B. G. S.

Brief Contents

1   Foundations of Western Civilization, to 500 B.C.E.   3

2   The Greek Golden Age, c. 500–400 B.C.E.   51

3   From the Classical to the Hellenistic World, c. 400–30 B.C.E.   91

4   The Rise of Rome, c. 753–44 B.C.E.   129

5   The Roman Empire, c. 44 B.C.E.–284 C.E.   171

6   The Transformation of the Roman Empire, c. 284–c. 600 C.E.   213

7   The Heirs of the Roman Empire, 600–750   259

8   Unity and Diversity in Three Societies, 750–1050   295

9   Renewal and Reform, 1050–1200   339

10 An Age of Confidence, 1200–1340   385

11 Crisis and Renaissance, 1340–1500   425

12 Struggles over Beliefs, 1500–1648   473

13 State Building and the Search for Order, 1648–1690   523

14 The Atlantic System and Its Consequences, 1690–1740   567

15 The Promise of Enlightenment, 1740–1789   609

16   The French Revolution and Napoleon, 1789–1815   *651*

17   Industrialization and Social Ferment, 1815–1850   *699*

18   Constructing the Nation-State, c. 1850–1880   *747*

19   Empire, Modernity, and the Road to War, c. 1880–1914   *797*

20   War, Revolution, and Reconstruction, 1914–1929   *851*

21   An Age of Catastrophes, 1929–1945   *899*

22   Remaking Europe in the Shadow of Cold War, c. 1945–1965   *945*

23   Postindustrial Society and the End of the Cold War Order,
      1965–1989   *987*

24   The New Globalism: Opportunities and Dilemmas,
      1989 to the Present   *1029*

Contents

Preface   *vii*

Brief Contents   *xvii*

Maps and Figures   *xliv*

Authors' Note: The B.C.E./C.E. Dating System   *l*

About the Authors   *liii*

Foundations of Western Civilization, to 500 B.C.E.   3

Making Civilization, to 1000 B.C.E.   5

Paleolithic and Neolithic Life, c. 400,000–4000 B.C.E.   5 ◆ The Birth of Cities and Empire in Mesopotamia, c. 4000–1000 B.C.E.   8 ◆ Mesopotamian Legacies: Commerce, Law, and Learning, c. 2200–1000 B.C.E.   13

Early Civilizations in Egypt, the Levant, and Anatolia, c. 3100–1000 B.C.E.   15

Religion and Rule in Egypt, c. 3100–2190 B.C.E.   16 ◆ Life in the Egyptian and Hittite Kingdoms, 2190–1000 B.C.E.   21

Shifting Empires in the Ancient Near East, to 500 B.C.E.   25

From Neo-Assyrian to Babylonian to Persian Empire, c. 900–500 B.C.E.   26 ◆ Creating Hebrew Monotheism, c. 1000–539 B.C.E.   30

Greek Civilization, to 750 B.C.E.   33

Minoan and Mycenaean Civilization, c. 2200–1000 B.C.E.   33 ◆ The Greek Dark Age, c. 1000–750 B.C.E.   36

Remaking Greek Civilization, c. 750–500 B.C.E.   38

Citizenship and Freedom in the City-State   39 ◆ New Ways of Thought and Expression   45

Conclusion   48

The Greek Golden Age, c. 500–400 B.C.E. 51

The Persian Wars, 499–479 B.C.E. *52*

The Ionian Revolt and the Battle of Marathon, 499–490 B.C.E. *52*
◆ Xerxes' Invasion of 480–479 B.C.E. *54*

Athenian Confidence in the Golden Age, 479–431 B.C.E. *56*

The Establishment of the Athenian Empire, 479–c. 460 B.C.E. *56*
◆ Radical Democracy and Pericles' Leadership, 461–445 B.C.E. *59*
◆ The Urban Landscape of Golden Age Athens *61*

Tradition and Innovation in Athens's Golden Age *65*

Religious Tradition in a Period of Change *66* ◆ Women, Slaves, and
Metics in Traditional Society *68* ◆ Education and Intellectual Innovation
73 ◆ The Development of Tragedy and Comedy *79*

The End of the Golden Age, 431–403 B.C.E *83*

The Peloponnesian War, 431–403 B.C.E. *84* ◆ The Rule of the Thirty
Tyrants, 404–403 B.C.E. *86*

Conclusion *88*

From the Classical to the Hellenistic World, c. 400–30 B.C.E.   91

Disunity in Classical Greece, c. 400–350 B.C.E.   *93*

The Aftermath of War and the Trial of Socrates   *93*   ◆   The Philosophy of Plato and Aristotle   *95*   ◆   The Fracturing of Greece   *98*

The Rise of Macedonia, 359–323 B.C.E.   *99*

Philip II and the Background of Macedonian Power   *99*   ◆   Exploits of Alexander the Great, 336–323 B.C.E.   *102*

The Hellenistic Kingdoms, 323–30 B.C.E.   *106*

The Structure of Hellenistic Kingdoms   *106*   ◆   Hierarchy in Hellenistic Society   *110*

Hellenistic Culture   *112*

The Arts under Royal Support   *112*   ◆   Philosophy for a New Age   *115*   ◆   Innovation in the Sciences   *118*   ◆   A New East-West Culture   *120*

Conclusion   *125*

The Rise of Rome, c. 753–44 B.C.E.   129

Social and Religious Traditions   *131*

Roman Values   *131*   ◆   The Patron-Client System   *132*   ◆   The Roman
Family   *134*   ◆   Education for Public Life   *136*   ◆   Religion for Public
and Private Interests   *137*

From Monarchy to Republic, c. 753–287 B.C.E.   *139*

Rule by Kings, c. 753–509 B.C.E.   *140*   ◆   The Early Roman Republic,
509–287 B.C.E.   *142*

Consequences of Roman Imperialism, Fifth to Second Centuries B.C.E.   *146*

Roman Expansion in Italy   *147*   ◆   Wars with Carthage   *148*   ◆   Greece's
Influence on Rome's Literature, Philosophy, and Art   *152*   ◆   Imperialism's
Effects on Republican Society   *156*

The Destruction of the Republic, c. 133–44 B.C.E.   *158*

The Gracchus Brothers and Political Rupture   *159*   ◆   Gaius Marius and
the First Client Armies   *160*   ◆   Sulla and Civil War   *161*   ◆   Pompey,
Caesar, and the End of the Republic   *163*

Conclusion   *168*

The Roman Empire, c. 44 B.C.E.–284 C.E.   171

Creating "Roman Peace"   *173*

From Republic to Principate, 44–27 B.C.E.   *173* ◆ Augustus's "Restoration,"
27 B.C.E.–14 C.E.   *174* ◆ Life in Augustan Rome   *177* ◆ Art and
Literature to Please the Emperor   *182*

Maintaining "Roman Peace"   *184*

Making Monarchy Permanent, 14–180 C.E.   *185* ◆ Life under the Five
Good Emperors, 96–180 C.E.   *189*

The Emergence of Christianity   *195*

The Teachings of Jesus   *196* ◆ Growth of a New Religion   *199*
 ◆ Competing Beliefs   *202*

The Crisis of the Third Century   *205*

Defending the Frontiers   *205* ◆ The Severan Emperors and
Catastrophe   *206*

Conclusion   *210*

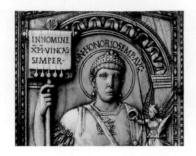

The Transformation of the Roman Empire, c. 284–c. 600 C.E.

213

Reorganizing the Empire   *214*

Imperial Reform and Fragmentation   *215*   ◆   Financial Reform and Social Consequences   *219*   ◆   Religious Reform: From Persecution to Conversion   *220*

Christianizing the Empire   *222*

The Spread of Christianity   *222*   ◆   Competing Visions of Religious Truth *227*   ◆   The Beginning of Christian Monasticism   *232*

Non-Roman Kingdoms in the West   *235*

Migrations into the Empire   *235*   ◆   Mixing Traditions   *243*

The Byzantine Empire in the East   *245*

Byzantine Society   *245*   ◆   The Reign of Justinian, 527–565   *249* ◆   Preserving Classical Literature   *252*

Conclusion   *255*

The Heirs of the Roman Empire, 600–750   259

Byzantium: A Christian Empire under Siege   *260*

Wars on the Frontiers, c. 570–750   *261*   ◆   From an Urban to a Rural Way of Life   *263*   ◆   Religion, Politics, and Iconoclasm   *266*

Islam: A New Religion and a New Empire   *268*

The Rise and Development of Islam, c. 610–632   *268*   ◆   Muhammad's Successors, 632–750   *273*   ◆   Peace and Prosperity in Islamic Lands   *274*

The Western Kingdoms   *275*

Frankish Kingdoms with Roman Roots   *276*   ◆   Economic Activity in a Peasant Society   *280*   ◆   The Powerful in Merovingian Society   *282*   ◆   Christianity and Classical Culture in the British Isles   *286*   ◆   Unity in Spain, Division in Italy   *288*

Conclusion   *292*

CHAPTER 8

Unity and Diversity in Three Societies, 750–1050

Byzantium: Renewed Strength and Influence   *296*

Imperial Might   *297*   ◆   The Macedonian Renaissance, c. 870–c. 1025   *299*
◆   New States under the Influence of Byzantium   *301*

From Unity to Fragmentation in the Islamic World   *303*

The Abbasid Caliphate, 750–c. 950   *304*   ◆   Regional Diversity   *305*
◆   The Islamic Renaissance, c. 790–c. 1050   *307*

The Creation and Division of a New Western Empire   *309*

The Rise of the Carolingians   *310*   ◆   Charlemagne and His Kingdom,
768–814   *311*   ◆   The Carolingian Renaissance   *314*   ◆   Charlemagne's
Successors, 814–911   *315*   ◆   Land and Power   *317*   ◆   Vikings, Muslims,
and Magyars Invade   *318*

The Emergence of Local Rule in the Post-Carolingian Age   *323*

Public Power and Private Relationships   *323*   ◆   War and Peace   *327*
◆   Political Communities in Italy, England, and France   *329*   ◆   Emperors
and Kings in Central and Eastern Europe   *332*

Conclusion   *336*

Renewal and Reform, 1050–1200   339

The Commercial Revolution   *340*

Centers of Commerce and Commercial Life   *340*   ◆   Business Arrangements   *343*   ◆   Self-Government for the Towns   *345*

Church Reform and Its Aftermath   *346*

Beginnings of the Reform Movement   *346*   ◆   Gregorian Reform and the Investiture Conflict, 1073–1085   *349*   ◆   The Sweep of Reform   *351* ◆   Early Crusades and Crusader States   *352*   ◆   The Jews as Strangers   *356*

The Revival of Monarchies   *358*

Byzantium in Its Prime   *359*   ◆   Norman and Angevin England   *360* ◆   Praising the King of France   *365*   ◆   Remaking the Empire   *366* ◆   The Courtly Culture of Europe   *367*

New Forms of Scholarship and Religious Experience   *369*

Schools, Scholars, and the New Learning   *370*   ◆   Benedictine Monks and Artistic Splendor   *373*   ◆   New Monastic Orders of Poverty   *375* ◆   Religious Fervor and Dissent   *377*

Conclusion   *382*

An Age of Confidence, 1200–1340

385

War, Conquest, and Settlement *386*

The Northern Crusades *386* ◆ The Capture of Constantinople *387*
◆ The Spanish Reconquista Advances *390* ◆ Putting Down the Heretics
in Their Midst *391* ◆ The Mongol Takeover *396*

Politics of Control *398*

France: From Acorn to Oak *398* ◆ England: Crisis and Consolidation
401 ◆ Papal Monarchy *402* ◆ Power Shifts in the Italian Communes
406 ◆ New-Style Associations amid the Monarchies *406* ◆ The Birth
of Representative Institutions *407*

Religious and Cultural Life in an Age of Expansion *409*

Lay Religious Fervor *409* ◆ Scholastics and Scholasticism *411* ◆ New
Syntheses in Writing and Music *413* ◆ The Order of High Gothic *415*

Conclusion *422*

Crisis and Renaissance, 1340–1500   425

A Multitude of Crises   *426*

Economic Contraction and the Black Death   *426*   ◆   The Hundred Years' War, 1337–1453   *430*   ◆   Ottoman Conquest and New Political Configurations in Eastern Europe   *436*   ◆   Hard Times   *439*   ◆   The Crisis of the Papacy   *440*   ◆   Stamping Out Dissenters, Heretics, Jews, and Muslims   *444*   ◆   End of the Reconquista and Expulsion of the Jews from Spain, 1492   *447*

New Forms of Thought and Expression: The Renaissance   *448*

Renaissance Humanism   *448*   ◆   New Perspectives in Art and Music   *452*   ◆   Republics and Principalities in Italy   *457*   ◆   The Intersection of Private and Public Lives   *459*

On the Threshold of World History   *463*

The Divided Mediterranean   *463*   ◆   Portuguese Confrontations   *465*   ◆   The Voyages of Columbus   *466*   ◆   A New Era in Slavery   *467*   ◆   Europeans in a New World   *468*

Conclusion   *471*

Struggles over Beliefs, 1500–1648   473

The Protestant Reformation   *474*

Popular Piety and Christian Humanism   *474*   ◆   Martin Luther and the German Nation   *476*   ◆   Huldrych Zwingli and John Calvin   *479*   ◆   Reshaping Society through Religion   *481*   ◆   Catholic Renewal and Missionary Zeal   *484*

State Power and Religious Conflict, 1500–1618   *486*

Wars among Habsburgs, Valois, and Ottomans   *487*   ◆   French Wars of Religion   *489*   ◆   Challenges to Habsburg Power and the Rise of the Dutch Republic   *491*   ◆   England Goes Protestant   *494*

The Thirty Years' War and the Balance of Power, 1618–1648   *498*

Origins and Course of the War   *498*   ◆   The Effects of Constant Fighting   *500*   ◆   The Peace of Westphalia, 1648   *501*   ◆   Growth of State Authority   *503*

From Growth to Recession   *504*

Causes and Consequences of Economic Crisis   *505*   ◆   The Economic Balance of Power   *507*

A Clash of Worldviews   *509*

The Arts in an Age of Religious Conflict   *509*   ◆   The Natural Laws of Politics   *512*   ◆   Origins of the Scientific Revolution   *514*   ◆   Magic and Witchcraft   *517*

Conclusion   *520*

State Building and the Search for Order, 1648–1690   523

Louis XIV: Model of Absolutism   *524*

The Fronde, 1648–1653   *525*   ◆   Court Culture as an Element of
Absolutism   *526*   ◆   Enforcing Religious Orthodoxy   *528*   ◆   Extending
State Authority at Home and Abroad   *529*

Absolutism in Central and Eastern Europe   *532*

Brandenburg-Prussia and Sweden: Militaristic Absolutism   *533*   ◆   An
Uneasy Balance: Austrian Habsburgs and Ottoman Turks   *535*   ◆   Russia:
Foundations of Bureaucratic Absolutism   *537*   ◆   Poland-Lithuania
Overwhelmed   *539*

Constitutionalism in England   *540*

England Turned Upside Down, 1642–1660   *541*   ◆   The "Glorious
Revolution" of 1688   *545*

Other Outposts of Constitutionalism   *548*

The Dutch Republic   *548*   ◆   Freedom and Slavery in the New World   *551*

The Search for Order in Elite and Popular Culture   *552*

Social Contract Theory: Hobbes and Locke   *553*   ◆   Newton and the
Consolidation of the Scientific Revolution   *554*   ◆   Freedom and Order in
the Arts   *556*   ◆   Women and Manners   *559*   ◆   Reforming Popular
Culture   *561*

Conclusion   *565*

The Atlantic System and Its Consequences, 1690–1740   567

The Atlantic System and the World Economy   *569*

Slavery and the Atlantic System   *569*   ◆   World Trade and Settlement   *574*
◆   The Birth of Consumer Society   *577*

New Social and Cultural Patterns   *578*

Agricultural Revolution   *578*   ◆   Social Life in the Cities   *581*   ◆   The
Growing Public for Culture   *582*   ◆   Religious Revivals   *586*

Consolidation of the European State System   *586*

The Limits of French Absolutism   *587*   ◆   British Rise and Dutch Decline
589   ◆   Russia's Emergence as a European Power   *592*   ◆   The Balance of
Power in the East   *594*   ◆   The Power of Diplomacy and the Importance of
Numbers   *597*   ◆   Public Hygiene and Health Care   *598*

The Birth of the Enlightenment   *600*

Popularization of Science and Challenges to Religion   *600*   ◆   Travel
Literature and the Challenge to Custom and Tradition   *602*   ◆   Raising the
Woman Question   *604*

Conclusion   *606*

The Promise of Enlightenment, 1740–1789   609

The Enlightenment at Its Height   *610*

The Men and Women of the Republic of Letters   *611*   ◆   Conflicts with Church and State   *613*   ◆   The Individual and Society   *615*   ◆   Spreading the Enlightenment   *618*   ◆   The Limits of Reason: Roots of Romanticism and Religious Revival   *619*

Society and Culture in an Age of Enlightenment   *621*

The Nobility's Reassertion of Privilege   *621*   ◆   The Middle Class and the Making of a New Elite   *623*   ◆   Life on the Margins   *627*   ◆   Roots of Industrialization   *629*

State Power in an Era of Reform   *632*

War and Diplomacy   *632*   ◆   State-Sponsored Reform   *636*   ◆   Limits of Reform   *638*

Rebellions against State Power   *640*

Food Riots and Peasant Uprisings   *640*   ◆   Public Opinion and Political Opposition   *642*   ◆   Revolution in North America   *644*

Conclusion   *647*

The French Revolution and Napoleon, 1789–1815   651

The Revolution of Rights and Reason   *653*

Protesters in the Low Countries and Poland   *653*   ◆   Origins of the French Revolution, 1787–1789   *655*   ◆   From Monarchy to Republic   *659*

Terror and Resistance   *665*

Robespierre and the Committee of Public Safety   *665*   ◆   The Republic of Virtue, 1793–1794   *667*   ◆   Resisting the Revolution   *669*   ◆   The Fall of Robespierre and the End of the Terror, 1794–1799   *671*

The Directory and the Rise of Napoleon Bonaparte   *674*

Revolution on the March   *675*   ◆   Revolution in the Colonies   *678*   ◆   The End of the French Republic   *680*

Emperor Napoleon I, r. 1804–1814   *683*

The Authoritarian State   *683*   ◆   The New Paternalism   *685*   ◆   "Europe Was at My Feet": Napoleon's Military Conquests   *688*   ◆   Napoleon's Fall   *691*

Conclusion   *695*

Industrialization and Social Ferment, 1815–1850   699

The "Restoration" of Europe   *700*

The Congress of Vienna, 1814–1815   *700*   ◆   The Revival of Religion   *703*
◆   Political Challenges to the Vienna Settlement   *704*

The Advance of Industrialization and Urbanization   *707*

Engines of Change   *708*   ◆   Formation of the Working Class   *709*
◆   Urbanization and Its Consequences   *712*

New Ideologies   *714*

Conservatism   *714*   ◆   Liberalism   *715*   ◆   Socialism and the Early Labor
Movement   *717*   ◆   Nationalism   *720*   ◆   Romanticism   *723*

Reform or Revolution?   *726*

Depicting and Reforming the Social Order   *726*   ◆   Abuses and Reforms
Overseas   *731*   ◆   The Revolutions of 1830 and 1848   *732*   ◆   Aftermath
to 1848   *739*

Conclusion   *745*

Constructing the Nation-State, c. 1850–1880   747

The End of the Concert of Europe   749

Napoleon III and the Quest for French Glory   *749*   ◆   The Crimean War, 1853–1856: Turning Point in European Affairs   *751*   ◆   Spirit of Reform in Russia   *752*

War and Nation Building   755

Cavour, Garibaldi, and the Process of Italian Unification   *755*   ◆   Bismarck and the Realpolitik of German Unification   *758*   ◆   Francis Joseph and the Creation of the Austro-Hungarian Monarchy   *762*   ◆   Political Stability through Gradual Reform in Great Britain   *763*   ◆   Civil War and Nation Building in the United States and Canada   *764*

Industry and Nation Building   766

Industrial Innovation   *766*   ◆   Facing Economic Crisis   *768*   ◆   Revolution in Business Practices   *770*

Establishing Social Order   772

Bringing Order to the Cities   *772*   ◆   Expanding the Reach of Bureaucracy   *774*   ◆   Schooling and Professionalizing Society   *775*   ◆   Spreading Western Order beyond the West   *778*   ◆   Contesting the Nation-State at Home   *781*

The Culture of Social Order   785

The Arts Confront Social Reality   *785*   ◆   Religion and Secular Order   *789*   ◆   From Natural Science to Social Science   *791*

Conclusion   794

Empire, Modernity, and the Road to War, c. 1880–1914   797

The Challenge of Empire   *799*

Scramble for Africa   *799*   ◆   Imperial Newcomers   *804*   ◆   Growing Resistance to Colonial Domination   *806*

Modern Life in an Age of Empire   *809*

Life in the "Best Circles"   *809*   ◆   The "Best Circles" Transformed   *811* ◆   Working People's Strategies   *816*   ◆   Toward National Fitness: Reforming the Working Class, Expanding Sports and Leisure   *818* ◆   Sciences of the Modern Self   *820*

Modernity and the Revolt in Ideas   *822*

The Challenge to Positivism   *823*   ◆   Revolutionizing Science   *824* ◆   Modern Art   *825*   ◆   Musical Iconoclasm   *827*

The Birth of Mass Politics   *829*

Mass Politics and the Growing Power of Labor   *829*   ◆   Rights for Women and the Battle for Suffrage   *833*   ◆   Liberalism Modified   *835*   ◆   Anti-Semitism, Nationalism, and Zionism in Mass Politics   *836*   ◆   Threats to Russian Empire   *841*

Roads to World War I   *843*

Competing Alliances and Clashing Ambitions   *843*   ◆   The Race to Arms *846*

Conclusion   *849*

War, Revolution, and Reconstruction, 1914–1929   851

The Great War, 1914–1918   *852*

War Erupts   *853*   ◆   The Conflict Widens   *854*   ◆   Battlefronts   *855*
◆   The Home Front   *860*

Protest, Revolution, and War's End: 1917–1918   *863*

War Protest   *863*   ◆   Revolution and Civil War in Russia   *864*   ◆   Ending
the War: 1918   *869*

The Search for Peace in an Era of Revolution   *870*

Europe in Turmoil   *870*   ◆   The Paris Peace Conference, 1919–1920   *871*
◆   Economic and Diplomatic Consequences of the Peace   *874*

A Decade of Recovery: Europe in the 1920s   *876*

Changes in the Political Landscape across Europe   *877*   ◆   Reconstructing
the Economy   *881*   ◆   Restoring Society   *882*

Mass Culture and the Rise of Modern Dictators   *885*

Culture for the Masses   *885*   ◆   Cultural Debates over the Future   *886*
◆   The Communist Utopia   *889*   ◆   Fascism on the March in Italy   *892*

Conclusion   *896*

An Age of Catastrophes, 1929–1945   899

The Great Depression   *900*

Economic Disaster Strikes   *900*   ◆   Social Effects of the Depression   *902* ◆   Global Dimensions of the Crash   *903*

Totalitarian Triumph   *905*

The Rise of Stalinism   *906*   ◆   Hitler's Rise to Power   *909*   ◆   The Nazification of German Politics   *911*   ◆   Nazi Racism   *913*

Democracies on the Defensive   *914*

Confronting the Economic Crisis   *914*   ◆   Cultural Visions in Hard Times   *918*

The Road to Global War   *920*

A Surge in Global Imperialism   *921*   ◆   The Spanish Civil War, 1936–1939   *923*   ◆   Hitler's Conquest of Central Europe, 1938–1939   *925*

World War II, 1939–1945   *927*

The German Onslaught   *927*   ◆   War Expands: The Pacific and Beyond   *929*   ◆   The War against Civilians and the Holocaust   *930*   ◆   Societies at War   *932*   ◆   From Resistance to Allied Victory   *933*   ◆   An Uneasy Postwar Settlement   *938*

Conclusion   *942*

Remaking Europe in the Shadow of Cold War, c. 1945–1965 945

World Politics Transformed *946*

Europe Prostrate *947* ◆ New Superpowers: The United States and the Soviet Union *949* ◆ Origins of the Cold War *950* ◆ The Division of Germany *953*

Political and Economic Recovery in Europe *955*

Dealing with the Nazi Past *955* ◆ Rebirth of the West *957* ◆ The Welfare State: Common Ground East and West *961* ◆ Recovery in the East *963*

Decolonization in a Cold War Climate *966*

The End of Empire in Asia *967* ◆ The Struggle for Identity in the Middle East *968* ◆ New Nations in Africa *970* ◆ The Arrival of New Europeans *973*

Cultural Life on the Brink of Nuclear War *974*

Restoring "Western" Values *975* ◆ Rising Consumerism and Shifting Gender Norms *977* ◆ The Culture of Cold War *979* ◆ Kennedy, Khrushchev, and the Atomic Brink *981*

Conclusion *984*

Postindustrial Society and the End of the Cold War Order, 1965–1989

987

The Revolution in Technology   988

The Information Age: Television and Computers 988 ◆ The Space Age 991 ◆ Revolutions in Biology, Reproductive Technology, and Sexual Behavior 993

Postindustrial Society and Culture   995

The New Worker 996 ◆ The Boom in Education and Research 997 ◆ A Redefined Family and a Generation Gap 998 ◆ Art, Ideas, and Religion in a Technocratic Society 1000

Protesting Cold War Conditions   1003

Cracks in the Cold War Order 1004 ◆ The Explosion of Civic Activism 1006 ◆ 1968: Year of Crisis 1010

The Erosion of Superpower Mastery Ends the Cold War   1013

The West, the World, and the Politics of Energy 1013 ◆ The Western Bloc Meets Challenges with Reform 1016 ◆ Collapse of Communism in the Soviet Bloc 1020

Conclusion   1026

The New Globalism: Opportunities and Dilemmas, 1989 to the Present

The New Globalism: Opportunities and Dilemmas, 1989 to the Present   1029

Soviet Collapse Releases Global Forces   *1031*

The Breakup of Yugoslavia *1032* ◆ The Soviet Union Comes Apart *1034* ◆ An Elusive Market Economy *1036* ◆ Chechnya and Post-Soviet States: The Quest for Independence and Influence *1038*

Global Opportunities Transcend the Nation-State   *1040*

Europe Looks beyond the Nation-State *1040* ◆ Globalizing Cities and Fragmenting Nations *1043* ◆ Global Organizations *1045*

Global Challenges and Discontents   *1047*

Pollution and Population *1047* ◆ Population and Disease *1049* ◆ North versus South? *1051* ◆ Islam Confronts the West *1052* ◆ The Rise of the Pacific Economy *1055*

Global Culture and Society in the New Millennium   *1057*

Redefining the West: The Impact of Global Migration *1057* ◆ Global Networks and the Economy *1059* ◆ The Global Diffusion of Culture *1060*

Conclusion: The Making of the West Continues   *1067*

Suggested References   *SR-1*

Glossary of Key Terms   *G-1*

Index   *I-1*

Maps and Figures

M A P S

Chapter 1

The Ancient Near East   *7*

SPOT MAP   The Ancient Levant   *16*

Ancient Egypt   *17*

Expansion of the Neo-Assyrian
Empire, c. 900–650 B.C.E.   *26*

Expansion of the Persian Empire,
c. 550–490 B.C.E.   *29*

Greece and the Aegean Sea,
c. 1500 B.C.E.   *33*

Archaic Greece, c. 750–500 B.C.E.   *39*

SPOT MAP   Sparta and the Peloponnese,
c. 750–500 B.C.E.   *43*

SPOT MAP   Ionia and the Aegean,
c. 750–500 B.C.E.   *46*

MAPPING THE WEST   Mediterranean
Civilizations, c. 500 B.C.E.   *47*

Chapter 2

The Persian Wars, 499–479 B.C.E.
53

SPOT MAP   The Delian and
Peloponnesian Leagues   *57*

Fifth-Century B.C.E. Athens   *62*

The Peloponnesian War,
431–404 B.C.E.   *86*

MAPPING THE WEST   Greece, Europe,
and the Mediterranean, c. 400 B.C.E.
88

Chapter 3

SPOT MAP   Expansion of Macedonia
under Philip II, r. 359–336 B.C.E.
101

Conquests of Alexander the Great,
336–323 B.C.E.   *103*

Hellenistic Kingdoms, c. 240 B.C.E.
107

MAPPING THE WEST   The Fall of the
Hellenistic Kingdoms, to 30 B.C.E.
124

Chapter 4

Ancient Italy, c. 500 B.C.E.   *141*

SPOT MAP   Rome and Central Italy,
Fifth Century B.C.E.   *147*

SPOT MAP   Roman Roads, c. 110 B.C.E.
148

Roman Expansion, c. 500–44 B.C.E.
153

MAPPING THE WEST   The Roman World
at the End of the Republic,
c. 44 B.C.E.   *168*

Chapter 5

The Expansion of the Roman Empire,
30 B.C.E.–117 C.E.   *188*

Natural Features and Languages of the
Roman World   *191*

SPOT MAP   Palestine in the Time of
Jesus, 30 C.E.   *197*

Christian Populations in the Late Third
Century C.E.   *201*

MAPPING THE WEST   The Roman
Empire in Crisis, c. 284 C.E.   *209*

Chapter 6

Diocletian's Reorganization of 293
217

SPOT MAP   The Division of the Empire,
c. 395   *218*

The Spread of Christianity, 300–600
226

Migrations and Invasions of the Fourth
and Fifth Centuries   *236*

Peoples and Kingdoms of the Roman
World, c. 526   *243*

MAPPING THE WEST   The Byzantine
Empire and Western Europe, c. 600
254

Chapter 7

Byzantine and Sassanid Empires, c. 600
261

SPOT MAP   The Byzantine Empire,
c. 700   *263*

SPOT MAP   Arabia in Muhammad's
Lifetime   *269*

Expansion of Islam to 730   *272*

The Merovingian Kingdoms in the
Seventh Century   *276*

SPOT MAP   The British Isles   *286*

SPOT MAP   Lombard Italy, Early Eighth
Century   *289*

MAPPING THE WEST   Europe and the
Mediterranean, c. 750   *291*

Chapter 8

The Expansion of Byzantium,
860–1025   *298*

SPOT MAP   The Balkans, c. 850–950
302

Islamic States, c. 1000   *306*

Expansion of the Carolingian Empire
under Charlemagne   *312*

Viking, Muslim, and Magyar Invasions
of the Ninth and Tenth Centuries
319

SPOT MAP   The Fragmentation of
France, c. 1000   *326*

SPOT MAP   England in the Age of King
Alfred, r. 871–899   *330*

SPOT MAP   The Ottonian Empire,
936–1002   *332*

MAPPING THE WEST   Europe and the
Mediterranean, c. 1050   *335*

Chapter 9

Medieval Trade Routes in the Eleventh
and Twelfth Centuries   *341*

SPOT MAP   The World of the Investiture
Conflict, c. 1070–1122   *349*

The First Crusade, 1096–1098   *353*

SPOT MAP   The Crusader States in 1109
355

SPOT MAP   Norman Conquest of
England, 1066   *360*

Europe in the Age of Frederick
    Barbarossa and Henry II, 1150–1190
    363

MAPPING THE WEST   Major Religions in
    the West, c. 1200   *380*

Chapter 10

Crusades and Anti-Heretic Campaigns,
    1150–1204   *388*

The Reconquista Triumphs, 1212–1275
    391

Europe in the Time of Frederick II,
    r. 1212–1250   *394*

SPOT MAP   Italy at the End of the
    Thirteenth Century   *395*

The Mongol Invasions to 1259   *397*

SPOT MAP   The Consolidation of
    France under Philip Augustus,
    r. 1180–1223   *398*

France under Louis IX, r. 1226–1270
    400

SPOT MAP   Growth of the Swiss
    Confederation to 1353   *407*

MAPPING THE WEST   Europe, c. 1340
    420

Chapter 11

Advance of the Plague   *427*

The Hundred Years' War, 1337–1453
    432

Ottoman Expansion in the Fourteenth
    and Fifteenth Centuries   *436*

Eastern Europe in the Fifteenth
    Century   *438*

The Great Schism, 1378–1417   *442*

SPOT MAP   Unification of Spain, Late
    Fifteenth Century   *447*

Exploitation and Exploration in the
    Sixteenth Century   *464*

MAPPING THE WEST   Renaissance
    Europe, c. 1500   *469*

Chapter 12

SPOT MAP   The Peasants' War of 1525
    478

Spread of Protestantism in the
    Sixteenth Century   *482*

Habsburg-Valois-Ottoman Wars,
    1494–1559   *487*

SPOT MAP   Protestant Churches in
    France, 1562   *490*

The Empire of Philip II, r. 1556–1598
    493

SPOT MAP   The Netherlands during the
    Revolt, c. 1580   *494*

The Thirty Years' War and the Peace of
    Westphalia, 1648   *502*

MAPPING THE WEST   The Religious
    Divisions of Europe, c. 1648   *519*

Chapter 13

SPOT MAP   The Fronde, 1648–1653
    525

Louis XIV's Acquisitions, 1668–1697
    531

State Building in Central and Eastern
    Europe, 1648–1699   *535*

SPOT MAP   England during the Civil
    War   *542*

Dutch Commerce in the Seventeenth
    Century   *549*

MAPPING THE WEST   Europe at the End
    of the Seventeenth Century   *564*

Chapter 14

European Trade Patterns, c. 1740
    570

Europe, c. 1715 *588*

Russia and Sweden after the Great
Northern War, 1721 *595*

SPOT MAP Austrian Conquest of
Hungary, 1657–1730 *596*

MAPPING THE WEST Europe in
1740 *605*

Chapter 15

The War of the Austrian Succession,
1740–1748 *633*

The Seven Years' War, 1756–1763 *635*

SPOT MAP The First Partition of
Poland, 1772 *636*

SPOT MAP The Pugachev Rebellion,
1773 *641*

MAPPING THE WEST Europe and the
World, c. 1780 *648*

Chapter 16

Revolutionary Paris, 1789 *658*

Redrawing the Map of France,
1789–1791 *661*

The Second and Third Partitions of
Poland, 1793 and 1795 *675*

SPOT MAP St. Domingue on the Eve of
the Revolt, 1791 *678*

SPOT MAP France's Retreat from
America *688*

SPOT MAP Consolidation of German
and Italian States, 1812 *689*

MAPPING THE WEST Europe under
Napoleonic Domination, 1812 *696*

Chapter 17

Europe after the Congress of Vienna,
1815 *702*

SPOT MAP Nationalistic Movements in
the Balkans, 1815–1830 *705*

Latin American Independence,
1804–1830 *707*

Languages of Nineteenth-Century
Europe *721*

SPOT MAP The First Opium War,
1839–1842 *732*

SPOT MAP The Divisions of Italy,
1848 *736*

SPOT MAP The German States,
1848 *738*

MAPPING THE WEST Industrialization
in Europe, c. 1850 *744*

Chapter 18

The Crimean War, 1853–1856 *751*

The Unification of Italy, 1859–1870
756

Unification of Germany, 1862–1871
760

SPOT MAP The Austro-Hungarian
Monarchy, 1867 *762*

U.S. Expansion, 1850–1870 *765*

SPOT MAP Indian Resistance, 1857
779

MAPPING THE WEST Europe and the
Mediterranean, c. 1880 *793*

Chapter 19

Africa, c. 1890 *800*

Africa in 1914 *803*

Imperialism in Asia, 1894–1914
805

SPOT MAP Principal Ethnic Groups in
Austria-Hungary, c. 1900 *839*

SPOT MAP Russian Revolution of 1905
842

The Balkans, 1908–1914   *845*

MAPPING THE WEST   Europe at the Outbreak of World War I, August 1914   *848*

Chapter 20

The Fronts of World War I, 1914–1918   *857*

The Russian Civil War, 1917–1922   *867*

Europe and the Middle East after the Peace Settlements of 1919–1920   *873*

SPOT MAP   National Minorities in Postwar Poland   *878*

SPOT MAP   The Irish Free State and Ulster, 1921   *880*

MAPPING THE WEST   Europe and the World in 1929   *895*

Chapter 21

SPOT MAP   The Ethiopian War, 1935–1936   *922*

The Spanish Civil War, 1936–1939   *923*

The Growth of Nazi Germany, 1933–1939   *925*

SPOT MAP   The Division of France, 1940   *928*

World War II in Europe and North Africa   *935*

World War II in the Pacific   *937*

MAPPING THE WEST   Europe at War's End, 1945   *941*

Chapter 22

The Impact of World War II on Europe   *948*

SPOT MAP   Yugoslavia after the Revolution, 1948   *952*

Divided Germany and the Berlin Airlift, 1946–1949   *953*

European NATO Members and the Warsaw Pact in the 1950s   *954*

SPOT MAP   The Korean War, 1950–1953   *967*

SPOT MAP   Indochina, 1954   *968*

The Partition of Palestine and the Creation of Israel, 1947–1948   *969*

The Decolonization of Africa, 1951–1990   *971*

MAPPING THE WEST   The Cold War World, c. 1960   *983*

Chapter 23

The Vietnam War, 1954–1975   *1007*

SPOT MAP   Israel after the Six-Day War, 1967   *1014*

SPOT MAP   Nationalist Movements of the 1970s   *1016*

MAPPING THE WEST   The Collapse of Communism in Europe, 1989–1990   *1025*

Chapter 24

The Former Yugoslavia, c. 2000   *1033*

Countries of the Former Soviet Union, c. 2000   *1035*

The European Union in 2004   *1042*

Eastern Europe, c. 2000   *1045*

The Middle East, c. 2003   *1053*

SPOT MAP   Tigers of the Pacific Rim, c. 1995   *1056*

MAPPING THE WEST   The World in the New Millennium   *1066*

FIGURES

Cuneiform Writing   13

Egyptian Hieroglyphs   18

Triremes, the Foremost Classical Greek Warships   58

Styles of Greek Capitals   64

TAKING MEASURE   Military Forces of Athens and Sparta at the Beginning of the Peloponnesian War   84

TAKING MEASURE   Census Records of Adult Male Roman Citizens during the First and Second Punic Wars   151

Cutaway Reconstruction of the Forum of Augustus   176

TAKING MEASURE   The Falling Value of Roman Imperial Coinage, 27 B.C.E.–300 C.E.   207

TAKING MEASURE   Viking Coin Hoards, c. 865–895   321

Floor Plan of a Romanesque Church   375

Floor Plan of a Cistercian Monastery   376

TAKING MEASURE   Sentences Imposed by an Inquisitor, 1308–1323   393

Elements of a Gothic Cathedral   417

TAKING MEASURE   Population Losses and the Plague, 1340–1450   429

TAKING MEASURE   The Rise and Fall of Silver Imports to Spain, 1550–1660   504

TAKING MEASURE   The Seventeenth-Century Army   534

African Slaves Imported into American Territories, 1701–1810   571

TAKING MEASURE   Relationship of Crop Harvested to Seed Used, 1400–1800   579

TAKING MEASURE   Railroad Lines, 1830–1850   708

TAKING MEASURE   Decline of Illiteracy, 1850–1900   776

TAKING MEASURE   Population Growth Worldwide, 1890–1910   812

European Emigration, 1881–1910   817

TAKING MEASURE   The Growth of Radio, 1924–1929   887

TAKING MEASURE   World Manufacturing Output, 1950–1970   959

Fluctuating Oil Prices, 1955–1985   1015

TAKING MEASURE World Population Growth, 1950–2004   1050

AUTHORS' NOTE

The B.C.E./C.E. Dating System

"**W**HEN WERE YOU BORN?" "What year is it?" We customarily answer questions like these with a number, such as "1987" or "2006." Our replies are usually automatic, taking for granted the numerous assumptions Westerners make about how dates indicate chronology. But to what do numbers such as 1987 and 2006 actually refer? In this book the numbers used to specify dates follow a recent revision of the system most common in the Western secular world. This system reckons the dates of solar years by counting backward and forward from the traditional date of the birth of Jesus Christ, over two thousand years ago. Using this method, numbers followed by the abbreviation B.C.E., standing for "before the common era" (or, as some would say, "before the Christian era"), indicate the number of years counting backward from the assumed date of the birth of Jesus Christ. B.C.E. therefore indicates the same chronology marked by the traditional abbreviation B.C. ("before Christ"). The larger the number following B.C.E. (or B.C.), the earlier in history is the year to which it refers. The date 431 B.C.E., for example, refers to a year 431 years before the birth of Jesus and therefore comes earlier in time than the dates 430 B.C.E., 429 B.C.E., and so on. The same calculation applies to numbering other time intervals calculated on the decimal system: those of ten years (a decade), of one hundred years (a century), and of one thousand years (a millennium). For example, the decade of the 440s B.C.E. (449 B.C.E. to 440 B.C.E.) is earlier than the decade of the 430s B.C.E. (439 B.C.E. to 430 B.C.E.). "Fifth century B.C.E." refers to the fifth period of 100 years reckoning backward from the birth of Jesus and covers the years 500 B.C.E. to 401 B.C.E. It is earlier in history than the fourth century B.C.E. (400 B.C.E. to 301 B.C.E.), which followed the fifth century B.C.E. Because this system has no year "zero," the first century B.C.E. covers the years 100 B.C.E. to 1 B.C.E. Dating millennia works similarly: the second millennium B.C.E. refers to the years 2000 B.C.E. to 1001 B.C.E., the third millennium to the years 3000 B.C.E. to 2001 B.C.E., and so on. To indicate years counted

1

forward from the traditional date of Jesus' birth, numbers are followed by the abbreviation C.E., standing for "of the common era" (or "of the Christian era"). C.E. therefore indicates the same chronology marked by the traditional abbreviation A.D., which stands for the Latin phrase *anno Domini* ("in the year of the Lord"). A.D. properly comes before the date being marked. The date A.D. 1492, for example, translates as "in the year of the Lord 1492," meaning 1,492 years after the birth of Jesus. Under the B.C.E./C.E. system, this date would be written as 1492 C.E. For dating centuries, the term "first century C.E." refers to the period from 1 C.E. to 100 C.E. (which is the same period as A.D. 1 to A.D. 100). For dates C.E., the smaller the number, the earlier the date in history. The fourth century C.E. (301 C.E. to 400 C.E.) comes before the fifth century C.E. (401 C.E. to 500 C.E.). The year 312 C.E. is a date in the early fourth century C.E., while 395 C.E. is a date late in the same century. When numbers are given without either B.C.E. or C.E., they are presumed to be dates C.E. For example, the term *eighteenth century* with no abbreviation accompanying it refers to the years 1701 C.E. to 1800 C.E. No standard system of numbering years, such as B.C.E./C.E., existed in antiquity. Different people in different places identified years with varying names and numbers. Consequently, it was difficult to match up the years in any particular local system with those in a different system. Each city of ancient Greece, for example, had its own method for keeping track of the years. The ancient Greek historian Thucydides, therefore, faced a problem in presenting a chronology for the famous Peloponnesian War between Athens and Sparta, which began (by our reckoning) in 431 B.C.E. To try to explain to as many of his readers as possible the date the war had begun, he described its first year by three different local systems: "the year when Chrysis was in the forty-eighth year of her priesthood at Argos, and Aenesias was overseer at Sparta, and Pythodorus was magistrate at Athens." A Catholic monk named Dionysius, who lived in Rome in the sixth century C.E., invented the system of reckoning dates forward from the birth of Jesus. Calling himself *Exiguus* (Latin for "the little" or "the small") as a mark of humility, he placed Jesus' birth 754 years after the foundation of ancient Rome. Others then and now believe his date for Jesus' birth was in fact several years too late. Many scholars today calculate that Jesus was born in what would be 4 B.C.E. according to Dionysius's system, although a date a year or so earlier also seems possible. Counting backward from the supposed date of Jesus' birth to indicate dates earlier than that event represented a natural complement to reckoning forward for dates after it. The English historian and theologian Bede in the early eighth century was the first to use both forward and backward reckoning from the birth of Jesus in a historical work, and this system gradually gained wider acceptance because it provided a basis for standardizing the many local calendars used in the Western Christian world. Nevertheless, B.C. and A.D. were not used regularly until the end of the eighteenth century. B.C.E. and C.E. became common in the late twentieth century. The system of numbering years from the birth of Jesus is far from the only one in use today.

The Jewish calendar of years, for example, counts forward from the date given to the creation of the world, which would be calculated as 3761 B.C.E. under the B.C.E./C.E. system. Under this system, years are designated A.M., an abbreviation of the Latin *anno mundi,* "in the year of the world." The Islamic calendar counts forward from the date of the prophet Muhammad's flight from Mecca, called the *Hijra,* in what is the year 622 C.E. The abbreviation A.H. (standing for the Latin phrase *anno Hegirae,* "in the year of the Hijra") indicates dates calculated by this system. Anthropology commonly reckons distant dates as "before the present" (abbreviated B.P.). History is often defined as the study of change over time; hence the importance of dates for the historian. But just as historians argue over which dates are most significant, they disagree over which dating system to follow. Their debate reveals perhaps the most enduring fact about history—its vitality.

About the Authors

LYNN HUNT, Eugen Weber Professor of Modern European History at the University of California, Los Angeles, received her B.A. from Carleton College and her M.A. and Ph.D. from Stanford University. She is the author of *Revolution and Urban Politics in Provincial France* (1978); *Politics, Culture, and Class in the French Revolution* (1984); and *The Family Romance of the French Revolution* (1992). She is also the coauthor of *Telling the Truth about History* (1994); coauthor of *Liberty, Equality, Fraternity: Exploring the French Revolution* (2001, with CD-ROM); editor of *The New Cultural History* (1989); editor and translator of *The French Revolution and Human Rights* (1996); and coeditor of *Histories: French Constructions of the Past* (1995), *Beyond the Cultural Turn* (1999), and *Human Rights and Revolutions* (2000). She has been awarded fellowships by the Guggenheim Foundation and the National Endowment for the Humanities and is a fellow of the American Academy of Arts and Sciences. She served as president of the American Historical Association in 2002.

THOMAS R. MARTIN, Jeremiah O'Connor Professor in Classics at the College of the Holy Cross, earned his B.A. at Princeton University and his M.A. and Ph.D. at Harvard University. He is the author of *Sovereignty and Coinage in Classical Greece* (1985) and *Ancient Greece* (1996, 2000) and one of the originators of *Perseus 1.0: Interactive Sources and Studies on Ancient Greece* (1992, 1996, and www.perseus.tufts.edu), which, among other awards, was named the EDUCOM Best Software in Social Sciences (History) in 1992. He also wrote the lead article on ancient Greece for the revised edition of the *Encarta* electronic encyclopedia. He serves on the editorial board of STOA (www.stoa.org) and as codirector of its DEMOS project (online resources on ancient Athenian democracy). A recipient of fellowships from the National Endowment for the Humanities and the American Council of Learned Societies, he is currently conducting research on the comparative historiography of ancient Greece and ancient China.

BARBARA H. ROSENWEIN, professor of history at Loyola University Chicago, earned her B.A., M.A., and Ph.D. at the University of Chicago. She is the author of *Rhinoceros Bound: Cluny in the Tenth Century* (1982); *To Be the Neighbor of Saint Peter: The Social Meaning of Cluny's Property, 909–1049* (1989); *Negotiating Space: Power, Restraint, and Privileges of Immunity in Early Medieval Europe* (1999); and *A Short History of the Middle Ages* (2001). She is the editor of *Anger's Past: The Social Uses of an Emotion in the Middle Ages* (1998) and coeditor of *Debating the Middle Ages: Issues and Readings* (1998) and *Monks and Nuns, Saints and Outcasts: Religion in Medieval Society* (2000). A recipient of Guggenheim and National Endowment for the Humanities fellowships, she is currently working on a history of emotions in the early Middle Ages.

R. PO-CHIA HSIA, Edwin Erle Sparks Professor of History at Pennsylvania State University, received his B.A. from Swarthmore College and his M.A. and Ph.D. from Yale University. He is the author of *Society and Religion in Münster, 1535–1618* (1984); *The Myth of Ritual Murder: Jews and Magic in Reformation Germany* (1988); *Social Discipline in the Reformation: Central Europe 1550–1750* (1989); *Trent 1475: Stories of a Ritual Murder Trial* (1992); and *The World of the Catholic Renewal* (1997). He has edited *The German People and the Reformation* (1988); *In and Out of the Ghetto: Jewish-Gentile Relations in Late Medieval and Early Modern Germany* (1995); *Calvinism and Religious Toleration in the Dutch Golden Age* (2002); and *A Companion to the Reformation World* (Blackwell Companion Series, 2004). An academician at the Academia Sinica, Taiwan, he has also been awarded fellowships by the Woodrow Wilson International Society of Scholars, the National Endowment for the Humanities, the Guggenheim Foundation, the Davis Center of Princeton University, the Mellon Foundation, the American Council of Learned Societies, and the American Academy in Berlin. Currently he is working on the cultural contacts between Europe and Asia between the sixteenth and eighteenth centuries.

BONNIE G. SMITH, Board of Governors Professor of History at Rutgers University, earned her B.A. at Smith College and her Ph.D. at the University of Rochester. She is the author of *Ladies of the Leisure Class* (1981); *Confessions of a Concierge: Madame Lucie's History of Twentieth-Century France* (1985); *Changing Lives: Women in European History Since 1700* (1989); *The Gender of History: Men, Women and Historical Practice* (1998); and *Imperialism* (2000). She is also the coauthor and translator of *What Is Property?* (1994); editor of *Global Feminisms Since 1945* (2000) and *Women's History in Global Perspective* (3 vols. 2004–2005); coeditor of *History and the Texture of Modern Life: Selected Writings of Lucy Maynard Salmon* (2001), *Gendering Disability* (2004), and *Sources of the Medieval and Early Modern World* (2005); and general editor of the forthcoming *Oxford Encyclopedia of Women in World History*. She has received fellowships from the Guggenheim Foundation, the National Endowment for the Humanities, the National Humanities Center, the Davis Center of Princeton University, and the American Council of Learned Societies. Currently she is studying the globalization of European culture since the seventeenth century.

SECOND EDITION

THE MAKING OF THE WEST

PEOPLES AND CULTURES

A CONCISE HISTORY

Foundations of Western Civilization

To 500 B.C.E.

ACCORDING TO THE MESOPOTAMIAN *EPIC OF CREATION*, the gods created the universe in a violent struggle. The goddess Tiamat, furious over her husband's murder, threatened to destroy the other gods. In response, they pledged to make the male god Marduk their king if he protected them. The fierce Marduk—"four were his eyes, four were his ears; when his lips moved, fire blazed forth"—crushed Tiamat and her army of snaky monsters in a gory battle. He then created human beings from the blood of her fiercest monster to be the gods' servants.

This myth showed how important it was for people to please the gods, who could crush them if humans made them angry. The precariousness of life implied by this story was real. Before civilization, in the Stone Age, tens and tens of thousands of years ago, people hunted and gathered food in the wild, using tools that they made from stone, bone, and wood. They roamed constantly to find enough food for their families and still have some left over for offerings to the gods that they believed controlled nature. Around ten or twelve thousand years ago, this way of life slowly began to change when people living in southwestern Asia began to cultivate wild plants and domesticate wild animals to become farmers and herders. The

■ **Gold Bull's Head Decoration for a Musical Instrument from Ancient Iraq**
This bull's head, made of gold leaf and lapis lazuli (a semiprecious stone prized for its vivid blue color), decorated a lyre—a stringed instrument similar to a harp. It was found in a tomb in the royal cemetery at Ur in what is today Iraq and was probably made in the period 2650–2550 B.C.E. The scenes below the beard, carved from mother of pearl, show animals walking upright like human beings and a mythological figure who appears to be a combination of a man and perhaps a scorpion. The donkey shown just above him is playing a lyre like this one. The meaning of the bull's head and the scenes remains a mystery. (© University of Pennsylvania Museum [neg. S4=142913].)

invention of agriculture and the domestication of animals made life in permanent settlements possible and produced surpluses of grain, fruit, vegetables, and meat that allowed people to do jobs besides farming. Some settlements gradually grew larger, until by 4000–3000 B.C.E., the first cities developed in Mesopotamia, the region between the Euphrates and Tigris Rivers (today southern Iraq). This was the start of civilization: life based in cities operating as political states, each having its own territory, ruler, taxes, and sense of local identity. Religion was the center of Mesopotamian civilization. Remembering the Marduk myth, rulers believed that the gods held them responsible for maintaining order on earth and for making sure that people honored the gods. The Egyptians, whose civilization emerged about 3100–3000 B.C.E., also held strong religious beliefs. Religion, combined with extraordinary architectural skills, inspired them to build fabulous temples and the pyramids.

Civilizations arose at different times in different places. Starting about 2500 B.C.E., they emerged in India, China, and the Americas. By 2000 B.C.E., civilizations had appeared in Anatolia (today Turkey), on islands in the eastern Mediterranean Sea, and in Greece. The early civilizations of Mesopotamia, Egypt, the eastern Mediterranean, and Greece began the history of Western civilization by interacting with each other. Building on concepts they took from their Near Eastern neighbors, the Greeks passed on to us today the idea of the West as a region with its own type of civilization. They identified Europe as the West (where the sun sets) and different from the East (where the sun rises).

The Greeks also inherited from their Near Eastern neighbors the idea that regional differences meant that one people's way of life was better than another's. This ancient dispute continues today in ongoing arguments about whether Western, Eastern, or some other civilization is best. One point is clear: the story of Western civilization is the story of cultural borrowings between the peoples of Europe and their neighbors near and far. That borrowing involved ideas, technologies, and goods. In short, the story of Western civilization concerns cultural, political, and economic interchange both among the West's diverse peoples and between them and other peoples around the globe. The West is a constantly evolving concept, not a fixed region with unchanging borders or members. It is wrong to take the word *Western* in Western civilization to mean "fenced off in the West from the rest of the world."

Early Western civilization developed when trade and war brought peoples in the Near East and Europe into contact. This cultural interaction provided opportunities for different people to learn from one another and to adapt for their own use the traditions, beliefs, and technology of others. These exchanges generated intended and unintended consequences. Metallurgical technology, for example, created ever better tools and weapons but also increased social differences among people. Just as the gods insisted on their superiority to human beings, people also developed **hierarchy**, or status differences, among themselves.

Making Civilization, to 1000 B.C.E.

The background of the story of civilization reaches far back into time. About four hundred thousand years ago, people whose brains and bodies resembled ours appeared first in Africa. These people, called *Homo sapiens*, or "wise human beings" by scientists, were the immediate ancestors of modern human beings. They spread out from there and gradually populated the rest of the earth. Anthropologists call this time the "Stone Age" because people made tools and weapons from stone; these early humans did not yet know how to work metals. The Stone Age is divided into two parts to mark an enormous transformation in the way people lived: the earlier part is the Paleolithic ("Old Stone") period, and the later part is the Neolithic ("New Stone"), which began about ten to twelve thousand years ago (c. 10,000–8000 B.C.E.). At this time, many human populations gradually transformed their ways of acquiring food by learning to farm—with enormous consequences for later history. This change was so radical that historians call it the "Neolithic Revolution."

Eventually, the Neolithic Revolution led to what historians traditionally identify as the features of **civilization**: cities with large buildings for community purposes (especially religion); political systems; production of textiles, pottery, and other crafts for local use and trade; and writing. In Mesopotamia, where the first cities arose about 4000 to 3000 B.C.E., the invention of bronze, an alloy of copper and tin used to make tools, weapons, and jewelry, led archaeologists to call the period from approximately 4000 to 1000 B.C.E. the "Bronze Age." The rulers of Bronze Age cities battled one another for glory, territory, and, especially, access to copper and tin. The drive to acquire metal ores pushed the Akkadians (named after Akkad, their capital city on the Tigris River) to create the first **empire**, a political unit controlling formerly independent territories subjected to a single ruler.

Paleolithic and Neolithic Life, c. 400,000–4000 B.C.E.

Paleolithic peoples lived as hunter-gatherers, meaning they roamed around looking for food; they did not know how to farm and did not live in settled communities. They probably banded together in groups of twenty to fifty, frequently changing their location to hunt animals and gather plants, fruits, and nuts. Finding food was the responsibility of both men and women. Women of childbearing age had to nurse their young, so they usually stayed close to camp; the food they gathered provided the group's most reliable supply of nourishment. Women beyond childbearing age, unburdened by infants, performed many different tasks for the group. Men probably did most of the hunting of dangerous wild animals far from camp, although recent archaeological evidence shows that women also participated, especially in hunting with nets.

Hunter-gatherer societies perhaps started out as egalitarian (meaning all adults enjoyed a rough equality in making decisions for the group), but hierarchy eventually developed. Men could acquire prestige from hunting large beasts and bringing back meat. Older women and men earned respect because of their wisdom from long experience and because their age set them apart at a time when illness and accidents killed most people before age thirty. Some Paleolithic graves contain weapons, tools, animal figurines, seashells, ivory beads, and bracelets. These individuals probably were especially prestigious members of their group. The care with which the dead were buried, decorated with red paint, flowers, and seashells, indicates concern with the mystery of death and perhaps some belief in an afterlife. Paleolithic artists also sculpted statuettes of human figures, probably for religious purposes.

Items found in burials indicate that hunter-gatherer bands traded energetically with one another. Trade spread knowledge—especially technological advances, such as ways to start fires or make tools, and artistic techniques for creating beauty and expressing beliefs—that changed lives. The use of fire for cooking was a far-reaching technological innovation because cooking made it possible for people to eat plants, such as wild grain, that they could not digest raw.

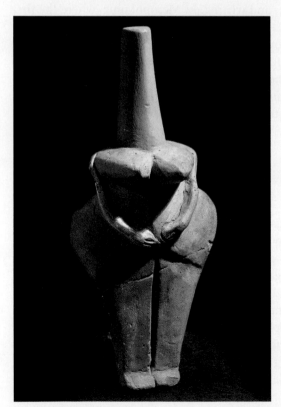

The Neolithic Revolution took place when people learned to farm and to domesticate animals about ten to twelve thousand years ago. The first farms emerged in the foothills of the Near East's Fertile Crescent, an arc of territory that curved up from what is today the

■ **Prehistoric Venus Figurine**
Archaeologists have discovered small female figures, like this one from Romania, at many late Paleolithic and Neolithic sites in Europe. They predate writing, so we cannot be sure of their significance, but many scholars assume that their hefty proportions are meant to signal a special concern for fertility. These female figures may represent prehistoric people's vision of rare good fortune: having enough food to become fat and produce healthy children. The statuettes are called Venus figurines after the Roman goddess of love.
(Erich Lessing/Art Resource, NY.)

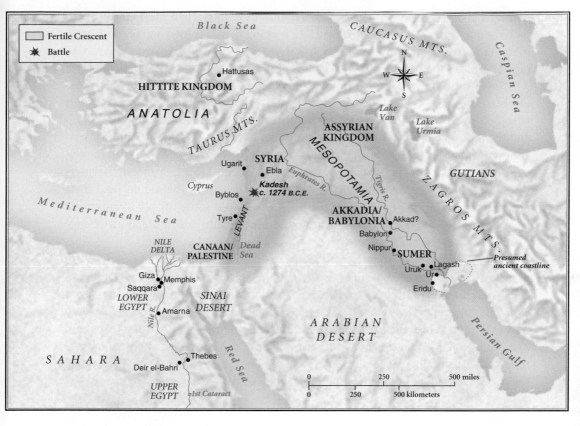

■ MAP 1.1 The Ancient Near East

The large region we call the ancient Near East included a variety of landscapes, climates, peoples, and languages; monarchy was the usual form of government. Trade by land and sea for natural resources, especially metals, kept the peoples of the region in constant contact with one another, as did the wars of conquest that the region's kings regularly launched.

Jordan Valley in Israel, through eastern Turkey, and down into the foothills and plains of Iraq and Iran (Map 1.1).[*] The revolution started when a climate change brought more rainfall and increased the amount of wild grains to gather. This larger food supply meant people could support more children, but, the more hungry mouths were born, the greater became people's need for food. After thousands of years of trial and error, people in the Fertile Crescent invented agriculture by sowing seeds from one crop to produce another. Since women had more experience foraging for plants, they probably played the major role in developing farming, while men continued to hunt.

---

[*]The meanings of the terms *Near East* and *Middle East* have changed over time. Both originally reflected a European geographic point of view. During the nineteenth century, *Middle East* usually meant the area from Iran to Burma, especially the Indian subcontinent (then part of the British Empire); *Near East* meant the Balkan peninsula (today the countries of Croatia, Slovenia, Bosnia-Herzegovina, Macedonia,

During this same period, people learned to domesticate animals for meat, starting with sheep about 8500 B.C.E. By about 7000 B.C.E., keeping herds for food had become common in the Near East, which was home to various kinds of wild animals such as goats, pigs, and cattle, that turned out to be suitable for domestication.

Some bands moved around to find grazing land for their animals, living as pastoralists, but farmers had to reside in a permanent location to raise crops year after year. Settling down marked a turning point in the relation between human beings and the natural environment. Farmers cut down trees and diverted streams for irrigation. By 4000 B.C.E., people migrating from the Fertile Crescent had spread knowledge of agriculture to the European shores of the Atlantic Ocean. Eventually, farmers were able to produce more food than they needed to feed themselves and their families. The creation of agricultural surpluses allowed some people to specialize in architecture, art, crafts, metalwork, textile production, and trade. This change opened the way for cities to develop.

The Neolithic Revolution created greater social hierarchy because new levels of management were needed to supervise irrigation. Greater economic activity also created a new division of labor by gender. Men began to dominate agriculture when heavy wooden plows pulled by oxen were invented, sometime after 4000 B.C.E. Not having to bear and nurse babies, men also took over long-distance trade. Women and older children took on new domestic labor as they turned milk into cheese and yogurt and made their families' clothing. This gendered division of labor arose as an efficient response to the conditions and technologies of the time, but it also increased men's status.

The Birth of Cities and Empire in Mesopotamia, c. 4000–1000 B.C.E.

The first cities emerged in Mesopotamia by about 4000 B.C.E. in the plains between and around the Tigris and Euphrates Rivers (Map 1.1). Agriculture had begun in the Fertile Crescent's well-watered hills, but there was not enough good farmland to support large settlements. The flatland bordering the rivers was huge but hard to farm: temperatures soared to 120 degrees Fahrenheit and little rain fell, yet the rivers flooded unpredictably. Mesopotamians transformed this harsh environment into lush farmland by irrigating the plains with water channeled from the rivers. A vast

---

Yugoslavia, Albania, Greece, Bulgaria, Romania, and the European portion of Turkey) and the eastern Mediterranean. The term *Far East* referred to the Asian lands that border the Pacific Ocean. Today, *Middle East* usually refers to the area encompassing the Arabic-speaking countries of the eastern Mediterranean region, Israel, Iran, Turkey, Cyprus, and much of North Africa. Ancient historians, by contrast, commonly use the term *ancient Near East* to designate Anatolia (often called Asia Minor, today occupied by the Asian portion of Turkey), Cyprus, the lands around the eastern end of the Mediterranean, the Arabian peninsula, Mesopotamia (the lands north of the Persian Gulf, today Iraq and Iran), and Egypt. Some historians exclude Egypt from this group on strict geographic grounds because it is in Africa (the rest of the region lies in Asia). In this book, we observe the common usage of the term *Near East* to mean the lands of southwestern Asia and Egypt.

system of canals allowed farmers to turn the desert green with crops and controlled flooding. The increase in food production created surpluses, which allowed the population to swell and nonagricultural occupations to flourish. Thus city life began.

The need to construct and maintain irrigation canals promoted centralization in Mesopotamian cities, which controlled the farmland lying outside their fortified walls. This arrangement—an urban center exercising political and economic control over the nearby countryside—is called a **city-state**. Mesopotamian city-states were independent communities competing with each other for land and resources. Travelers from one to another would first come to irrigated fields on a city's outskirts, then villages housing agricultural workers, and finally the city's walls. Ships transporting grain and goods would be docked nearby on the riverbank. Inside the walls were private houses and apartments, the huge royal palace, and immense temples.

The people of Sumer, the name for southern Mesopotamia, built the earliest cities. Unlike other Mesopotamians, the Sumerians did not speak a Semitic language (the group of languages from which Hebrew and Arabic came); the origins of their language remain a mystery. By 3000 B.C.E., the Sumerians had created twelve independent city-states, such as Uruk, Eridu, and Ur, which repeatedly fought each other over territory. By 2500 B.C.E., these cities had each expanded to twenty thousand residents or more. The rooms in Sumerians' mud-brick houses surrounded open courts. Large homes had a dozen rooms or more. Everyone was in danger from contaminated water because no sewerage system existed. Pigs and dogs scavenged in the garbage dumped in the streets.

Agriculture and trade made these cities prosperous. Sumerians bartered grain, vegetable oil, woolens, and leather with one another, and they acquired metals, timber, and precious stones from foreign trade. Traders traveled as far as India, where the cities of Indus civilization emerged about 2500 B.C.E. Technological innovation also strengthened the Mesopotamian economy, especially around 3000 B.C.E., when Sumerians invented a wheel for use on wagons. Temples and the rulers' families dominated the Sumerian economy because they both controlled large farms and gangs of laborers, but some private households also amassed wealth.

Hierarchy, which had initially emerged from the organization of irrigation during the Neolithic Revolution, dominated Sumerian society. Slaves, owned by temples and by individuals, had the lowest status. People became slaves by being captured in war, by being born to slaves, by voluntarily selling themselves or their children (usually to escape starvation), or by being sold by their creditors when they could not repay loans (known as "debt slavery"). Children whose parents dedicated them as slaves to the gods could rise to prominent positions in the temple administrations. In general, however, slaves existed in near-total dependency on other people and were excluded from normal social relations. They usually worked without pay and lacked almost all legal rights. They could be bought, sold, beaten, or even killed by their masters because they were considered property.

Slaves worked in domestic service, craft production, and farming, but scholars dispute whether they or free laborers were more important to the economy. Free persons performed most government labor, paying their taxes with work rather than with money, which was measured in amounts of food or precious metal (coins were not invented until about 700 B.C.E., in Anatolia). Most slaves had little chance of gaining freedom. Masters' wills could liberate them, or they could purchase their freedom from earnings that some owners would let them keep.

Hierarchy became so strong in Mesopotamian society that its most powerful man became a king—a sole ruler whose son inherited his father's position. To display their exalted status, royal families lived in elaborate palaces that served as administrative centers and treasure-houses. Archaeologists excavating royal graves in Ur have revealed the rulers' dazzling riches—spectacular possessions crafted in gold, silver, and precious stones. These burials also yielded grisly evidence of the top-ranking status of the king and queen: servants sacrificed to look after their royal masters after death.

Patriarchy—domination by men in political, social, and economic life— already existed in Mesopotamian city-states. A Sumerian queen was respected because she was the king's wife and the mother of the royal children, but her husband held supreme power. The king formed a council of older men as his advisers, but he publicly acknowledged the gods as his rulers; this concept made the state a theocracy (government by gods) and gave priests and priestesses public influence. The king's greatest responsibility was to keep the gods happy and to defeat attacks from rival cities. The king demanded taxes from the working population to support his family, court, palace, army, and officials. The kings, along with the priests of the large temples, regulated most of the economy in their kingdoms by controlling the exchange of food and goods between farmers and crafts producers in a system known as a **redistributive economy**.

Mesopotamians practiced **polytheism**: they worshipped many gods whom they believed controlled different aspects of life, such as the weather, fertility, and war. They believed that their safety depended on the goodwill of the gods, and each city-state honored one deity as its special protector. To please their gods, city dwellers offered sacrifices and built ziggurats (temple towers) soaring as high as ten stories. Mesopotamians believed that if human beings angered the gods, divinities such as the sky-god Enlil and Inanna (also called Ishtar), goddess of love and war, would punish them by sending disease, floods, famine, and defeats in war.

Mythical stories such as the *Epic of Creation* and the *Epic of Gilgamesh* described the unbridgeable gap between gods and human beings. Gilgamesh was a legendary king of Uruk, who lusted to cheat death. He forced the young men of Uruk to toil like slaves and the young women to sleep with him. When his mistreated subjects begged Aruru, mother of the gods, to grant them a protector, she created a man of nature, Enkidu, "hairy all over . . . dressed as cattle are."

A week of sex with a prostitute tamed this brute, preparing him for civilization: "Enkidu was weaker; he ran slower than before. But he had gained judgment, was wiser." After wrestling Gilgamesh to a draw, he and the king became friends and conquered Humbaba (or Huwawa), the ugly giant of the Pine Forest, and the Bull of Heaven. The gods doomed Enkidu to die soon after these triumphs. Depressed about the human condition, Gilgamesh sought the secret of immortality, but a thieving snake ruined his quest. He decided that the road to immortality for mortals was to win fame for deeds. Only memory and gods could live forever.

A late version of the Gilgamesh story recounted how the gods sent a huge flood over the earth. They warned one man, Utnapishtim, telling him to build a boat. He loaded his vessel with his relatives, workers, possessions, domesticated and wild animals, and "everything there was." After a week of torrential rains, they left the boat to repopulate the earth. This story recalled the devastating floods of Mesopotamia and looked ahead to the later biblical account of the flood and Noah's ark. Mesopotamian myths, living on in poetry, song, and art, greatly influenced Greek mythology.

The invention of writing helped these stories live on. Sumerians originally invented this new technology to do accounting. Before writing, people drew small pictures on clay tablets to keep count of objects or animals. Writing started when people created symbols instead of pictures to represent the sounds of speech. Sumerian writing did not use an alphabet (a system in which each symbol represents the sound of a letter), but rather a system of wedge-shaped marks pressed into clay tablets to represent the sounds of syllables and entire words (see Figure 1.1, page 13). Other Mesopotamians adopted this form of writing, which is today called **cuneiform** (from *cuneus*, Latin for "wedge"). For a long time, writing was a professional skill for accounting mastered by only a few men and women, known as scribes.

■ **The Ziggurat of Ur in Sumer**
King Ur-Nammu and his son Shulgi built this huge temple to honor the gods in their city of Ur (in what is today southern Iraq) in the early twenty-first century B.C.E. It had three massive terraces, one above another, connected by stairways. The mud-brick core of the structure was covered with baked bricks held in place with tar. The walls were more than seven feet thick to support the enormous weight of the terraces. The total height is uncertain, but the first terrace alone soared some forty-five feet above ground level.

(Hirmer Fotoarchiv,
Munich, Germany.)

■ **A Cuneiform Letter in Its Envelope**
Written about 1900 B.C.E., this cuneiform text records a merchant's complaint that a shipment of copper contained less metal than he had expected. His letter, written on a clay tablet several inches long, was enclosed in an outer clay shell marked with the sender's private seal. This envelope protected the inner text from tampering or breakage. (© Copyright The Trustees of The British Museum.)

Eventually, scribes began to record nature lore, mathematics, foreign languages, and literature. Written poems and stories then provided a powerful new way to pass on traditions. The world's oldest written poetry by a known author was composed in the twenty-third century B.C.E. by Enheduanna, the daughter of King Sargon of the city of Akkad. Written in Sumerian, her poetry praised the life-giving goddess of love, Inanna: "the great gods scattered from you like fluttering bats, unable to face your intimidating gaze . . . knowing and wise queen of all the lands, who makes all creatures and people multiply." Later princesses who wrote love songs, lullabies, dirges, and prayers continued the Mesopotamian tradition of royal women becoming authors.

Metallurgy was another influential technology that developed in this period; its invention indirectly helped produce the world's first empire, in Akkadia (see Map 1.1). After figuring out how to smelt ore and forge metal alloys, Bronze Age smiths could make new luxury goods, such as jewelry, as well as better tools and weapons. Bronze, a copper-tin alloy hard enough to hold a razor edge, produced durable swords and spearheads. Rich men found a new way to display their status by paying artisans to decorate their weapons with ornate engravings and inlays, as on costly guns today. Metal weapons also emphasized the differences between men's and women's roles in society because they marked the masculine roles of hunter and warrior that had emerged long ago in the division of labor among hunter-gatherers. The development of metallurgy helped lead to the first empires because Mesopotamian kings craved a reliable supply of metals to support their royal status: those who had no ore in their territory had to get it by trade or by conquest.

The first empire arose about 2350 B.C.E., when Sargon, king of the city of Akkad, launched invasions north and south of his homeland in mid-Mesopotamia seeking metals and glory. His violent campaigns conquered lands from Sumer all the way to the Mediterranean Sea. Sargon's grandson Naram-Sin continued this foreign conquest. By 2250 B.C.E., he had attacked Ebla, a large city whose site was recently discovered in modern Syria. Archaeologists at Ebla have unearthed many cuneiform tablets, some in multiple languages, suggesting Ebla thrived as a center for learning.

The conquests that created empire also spread Mesopotamian literature and art throughout the Near East. Although the Akkadians spoke a Semitic language, not Sumerian, after conquering Sumer they adopted much of the defeated land's

					SAG Head
					NINDA bread
					GU$_7$ eat
					AB$_2$ cow
					APIN plough
					SUHUR carp
c. 3100 B.C.E.	c. 3000 B.C.E.	c. 2500 B.C.E.	c. 2100 B.C.E.	c. 700 B.C.E. (Neo- Assyrian)	Sumerian reading + meaning

■ **FIGURE 1.1 Cuneiform Writing**

*The earliest known form of writing developed in different locations in Mesopotamia in the late
3000s B.C.E., when meaning and sound were associated with signs such as these. The scribes who
mastered the system used sticks or reeds to press dense rows of small wedge-shaped marks into damp
clay tablets or chisels to engrave them on stone. Cuneiform was used for at least fifteen Near Eastern
languages and continued to be written for three thousand years.*

religion, literature, and culture. Other peoples later conquered by the Akkadians
were thus exposed to Sumerian beliefs and traditions, which they in turn adapted to
their own purposes. In this way, war indirectly promoted cultural interaction
between peoples.

Neighboring hill peoples, the Gutians, defeated the Akkadian empire around
2200 B.C.E. A Mesopotamian poet gave a religious explanation for this catastrophe:
King Naram-Sin, enraged at the god Enlil when his capital's prosperity waned,
reduced Enlil's temple to "dust like a mountain mined for silver." Enlil then punished the Akkadians by sending the Gutians swooping down from their "land that
rejects outside control, with the intelligence of human beings but with the form and
stumbling words of a dog." This account reflected the Mesopotamians' deep-seated
belief that the gods held ultimate power over human destiny.

Mesopotamian Legacies: Commerce, Law, and Learning, c. 2200–1000 B.C.E.

Two kingdoms, Assyria and Babylonia, emerged in the second millennium B.C.E. to
replace the Akkadian Empire. Their innovations in private commerce, law, and

learning influenced later Western civilization. The Assyrians, a Semitic people descended from the Akkadians, lived in northern Mesopotamia (see Map 1.1). By becoming middlemen in the long-distance trade between Anatolia and southern Mesopotamia, the Assyrians became the Near East's leading merchants. They produced woolen textiles to exchange for Anatolian copper, silver, and gold, which they sold throughout Mesopotamia. In earlier Mesopotamian societies, the kings and priests had directed a largely state-run redistributive economy. This tradition never totally disappeared, but by 1900 B.C.E., the Assyrian kings were allowing private individuals to trade with other city-states and regions on their own. Assyrian investors sought profits by financing donkey caravans to travel hundreds of rocky and dangerous miles to Anatolia.

The expansion of profit-based commerce created a demand for the enforcement of contracts, which required law. It was the king's sacred duty to render justice to his subjects in commercial disputes as well as for crimes. The record of the king's decisions is today called a law code. King Hammurabi (r. c. 1792–1750 B.C.E.) of Babylon, a great city on the Euphrates River, instituted the most famous set of early laws. Hammurabi proclaimed he was showing Shamash, the Babylonian sun-god and god of justice, that he was fulfilling a king's responsibility imposed on him by the gods—to ensure justice and the moral and material welfare of his people: "So that the powerful may not oppress the powerless, to provide justice for the orphan and the widow . . . let the victim of injustice see the law which applies to him, let his heart be put at ease."

Hammurabi's code divided society into three categories: free persons, commoners, and slaves. We do not know what made the first two categories different, but free persons outranked commoners in the hierarchy of Babylonian society. An attacker who caused a pregnant woman of the free class to miscarry, for example, paid twice the fine levied for the same offense against a woman of the commoner class. A member of the free class who killed a commoner was fined instead of executed. For social equals, the code specified "an eye for an eye."

The people themselves assembled in courts to determine most cases. The laws primarily concerned the king's interests as a property owner who leased innumerable tracts of land to tenants in return for rent or services. For offenses against property, the laws imposed severe penalties, including mutilation or a gruesome death for crimes as varied as theft, wrongful sales, and careless construction. In this patriarchal society, women had limited legal rights, but they could make business contracts and appear in court. A wife could divorce her husband for cruelty; a husband could divorce his wife for any reason. Since, however, divorced wives were entitled to recover the property they had brought to the marriage, husbands had to think twice before ending their marriages.

Hammurabi's laws reveal much about urban life in Bronze Age Mesopotamia. Burglary and assault apparently plagued city dwellers. Marriages were arranged by the groom and the bride's father, who sealed the agreement with a legal contract.

Laws about surgery inform us about the work of doctors. Because people believed that angry divinities caused many diseases, Mesopotamian medicine included magic as well as potions and specific diets. Magicians treated illness by interpreting signs, such as the patient's dreams or hallucinations, and casting spells.

Archaeological excavations and cuneiform records reveal that Mesopotamian cities had numerous wine shops, often run by women proprietors, offering drinks and a place to relax. Residents also found relief from the odors and crowding in the streets in open spaces set aside as parks. The world's oldest known map, an inscribed clay tablet showing the outlines of the Babylonian city of Nippur about 1500 B.C.E., indicates that a sizeable section of the city was parkland.

Mapmaking required sophisticated calculations and spatial knowledge, which point to Mesopotamia's most influential achievements: knowledge in mathematics and astronomy. Mathematicians used algebra to solve complex problems and knew how to derive the roots of numbers. They invented place-value notation and a system of reckoning based on sixty, still used in our division of a circle into hours, minutes, and degrees. Mesopotamians' skill in describing the paths of the stars and planets probably arose from a desire to make predictions about the future, based on the astrological belief that the movements of celestial objects affect human life. The charts and tables compiled by Mesopotamian stargazers laid the foundation for later advances in astronomical knowledge.

■ **REVIEW:** *How did life change for people in Mesopotamia when they began to live in cities?*

Early Civilizations in Egypt, the Levant, and Anatolia, c. 3100–1000 B.C.E.

Africa was home to the second great civilization to shape the West: Egypt. It lay close enough to Mesopotamia to learn from that culture but was geographically set apart enough to develop its own distinct culture. Egyptians created a wealthy, deeply religious, and strongly traditional civilization ruled by kings. Unlike Mesopotamia, Egypt was politically united under a strong central authority. The Egyptian kings' desire for immortality in the afterlife led them to build some of the largest tombs in history, the pyramids. Egyptian architecture and art inspired later Mediterranean peoples, especially the Greeks.

The height of Egyptian power came under the New Kingdom (c. 1569–1081 B.C.E.*); the Hittite kingdom in Anatolia was then Egypt's most aggressive rival

---

*Every date in Egyptian history is approximate and controversial, and different scholars use different dates because the evidence is often contradictory. Those used here are taken from the articles and "Egyptian King List" in *The Oxford Encyclopedia of Ancient Egypt*, edited by Donald B. Redford (2001).

The Ancient Levant

(see Map 1.1). The Hittites had become a powerful people by about 1750 B.C.E. They flourished because they inhabited a fertile, upland region and controlled trade there and southward into the Levant[*] (modern Jordan, Syria, Lebanon, and Israel), the commercial crossroads of the eastern Mediterranean and the persistent site of conflict among Near Eastern powers.

Religion and Rule in Egypt, c. 3100–2190 B.C.E.

The first large-scale Egyptian state emerged about 3100–3000 B.C.E., when King Menes united Upper (southern) Egypt and Lower (northern) Egypt. (*Upper* and *Lower* refer to the direction in which the Nile River flows—from south of Egypt northward to the Mediterranean Sea.) By around 2687 B.C.E., the kings following Menes had forged a centralized state, today known as the Old Kingdom, which lasted until around 2190 B.C.E. (Map 1.2). Egypt's people lived mainly in farming villages in a narrow band of land along the Nile. Their irrigated farms extended several miles away from the river's banks on both sides. The Nile overflowed its banks once every year for several weeks, when melting snow from the mountains of central Africa gradually swelled its flow. This predictable and gentle flood enriched the soil near the river with nutrients from silt and diluted harmful deposits of mineral salts. Unlike the random deluges in Mesopotamia, the Nile's flood recurred at the same season every year and benefited the land. Trouble came only if dry weather in the mountains kept the river from overflowing.

Deserts east and west of the Nile protected Egypt from invasion, except through the Nile delta in the north and on the southern frontier with Nubia. Deposits of metal ores, trade by sea, and lush agriculture made Egypt prosperous, but it had fewer and smaller cities than in Mesopotamia. From their ample supplies of grain, the Egyptians made bread and beer, the most common beverage. Egypt's population included a diversity of people, whose skin color ranged from light to very dark. Many ancient Egyptians would be regarded as black by modern racial classification (unknown to ancient peoples). The modern controversy over whether Egyptians were people of color is anachronistic; ancient Egyptians presumably identified themselves by geography, language, religion, and social traditions. Later peoples, especially the Greeks, admired Egyptian civilization for its great antiquity and religious devotion. Some nineteenth-century historians minimized the Egyptian contribution to Western civilization, but ancient peoples did not.

---

[*]The name *Levant*, French for "rising (sun)"—that is, the East—reflects the European perspective on the area's location.

■ MAP 1.2 Ancient Egypt
The Nile River, closely embraced by arid deserts, provided Egyptians with water to irrigate their fields and a highway for traveling north to the Mediterranean Sea and south to Nubia. The only easy land route into and out of Egypt lay through the Nile delta region into the northern Sinai peninsula and on into the coastal area of the Levant; Egyptian kings therefore always fought to control these areas to secure the safety of their land.

Like everyone else in history, Egyptians learned from other peoples. For example, they probably learned the technology of writing from the Sumerians, but they developed their own scripts rather than adopting cuneiform. To write formal and official texts, they used an ornate, picture-based script known as hieroglyphs (see Figure 1.2 on page 18). Looking southward, Egyptians saw that the Nubians had already built extensive settlements and produced complex art by Menes' time. At places such as Afyeh near the Nile's First Cataract, a Nubian social elite lived in dwellings much grander than the small huts housing most of the population. Egyptians constantly interacted with Nubians while trading for raw materials such as gold, ivory, and animal skins, and Nubia's hierarchical organization perhaps influenced the development of centralized authority in Egypt's Old Kingdom. Eventually, however, Egypt's power overshadowed that of its southern neighbor.

The strength or weakness of the central authority determined Egyptian political history. When the kings were strong, as during the Old Kingdom, the country was stable, and trade flourished with the Levant and other Mediterranean areas.

Hieroglyph	Meaning	Sound value
	vulture	glottal stop
	flowering reed	consonantal I
	forearm and hand	ayin
	quail chick	W
	foot	B
	stool	P
	horned viper	F
	owl	M
	water	N
	mouth	R
	reed shelter	H
	twisted flax	slightly guttural
	placenta (?)	H as in "loch"
	animal's belly	slightly softer than h
	door bolt	S
	folded cloth	S
	pool	SH
	hill	Q
	basket with handle	K
	jar stand	G
	loaf	T

■ **FIGURE 1.2 Egyptian Hieroglyphs**

Ancient Egyptians developed their own system of writing about 3100 B.C.E., using pictures such as these. Because this formal script was used mainly for religious inscriptions on buildings and sacred objects, Greeks referred to it as ta hieroglyphica *("the sacred carved letters"), from which comes the modern term* hieroglyphs. *Egyptian hieroglyphs employ around seven hundred pictures in three categories: ideograms (signs indicating things or ideas), phonograms (signs indicating sounds), and determinatives (signs clarifying the meaning of the other signs). Eventually (the chronology is unsure), Egyptians also developed the handwritten cursive script called* demotic *(Greek for "of the people"), a much simpler and quicker form of writing.*

However, when regional governors or prominent priests, whose status was second only to that of the royal family, refused to support the king, political instability resulted.

The king's success depended on his properly fulfilling his religious duties. Egyptians worshiped many gods, often depicted as creatures with both human and animal features such as the head of a jackal or a bird atop a human body. They did not worship animals; rather, they believed that each god had a particular animal to serve as the bearer of the god's divine soul. A picture or statue of a divinity had to include the animal so the image would include the soul. Egyptian religion told lively stories about the passion-filled lives of the gods to explain their powers. Deities were associated with powerful natural objects, emotions, qualities, and technologies, such as the sun-god Re; Isis, goddess of love and fertility; and Thoth, god of wisdom and the inventor of writing.

Egyptians regarded their king as a god in human form, but they recognized that the man on the throne was mortal. That is, they saw a difference between the individual king's human existence and the divine origin of his rule. The monarchy as a system was divine because it represented on earth the supernatural, eternal force that created harmony and stability in the universe. This force was called Maat, often translated as "truth" or "justice" or "correct balance." The king had to rule according to Maat by keeping the forces of nature in balance for the benefit of his people. The Egyptian kings' religious identity made them different from Sumerian kings, who ruled only as men, though their kingdoms were devoted to the gods.

An Egyptian king ensured his people's safety and prosperity by strictly observing ritual. For example, he had to keep to a specific time for taking a bath, going for a walk, or having sex with his wife. Above all, the king was responsible for summoning the divine power that made the Nile overflow. If he failed to make the flood occur, he gravely weakened his authority. If he could not produce annual floods and keep the people well fed, then he had lost his Maat—and might lose his kingdom.

Old Kingdom rulers used expensive building programs to demonstrate their devotion to the gods and proclaim their status atop the social hierarchy. Their great buildings were mainly the temples or tombs that were constructed outside their cities. In the suburbs of Memphis, the first capital (south of modern Cairo), these kings erected the most stunning proofs of their piety and status—huge tombs in the form of pyramids. These monuments formed the centerpieces of groups of buildings for royal funerals and religious ceremonies. Although the pyramids were not the first monuments built from enormous, worked stones (that title goes to temples on the Mediterranean island of Malta), they rank as the grandest.

The Old Kingdom rulers spent vast sums of money on these huge complexes because they cared so much about protecting their mummified bodies for the afterlife. In the twenty-sixth century b.c.e., King Cheops commissioned the biggest of them all—the so-called Great Pyramid at Giza. At about 480 feet high, it stands taller than a forty-story skyscraper. Covering over thirteen acres and extending 760 feet on each side, it required more than two million blocks of limestone, some of which weighed fifteen tons apiece. Quarried in the desert, the stone was floated to the site on river barges and dragged on rollers and sleds up earthen ramps into position.

The kings' lavish preparations for death reflect the strong Egyptian belief in life after death. A prayer from about 2300 B.C.E. expresses that idea: "O divine Atum, put your arms around King Neferkare Pepy II, around this construction work, around this pyramid. . . . May you guard lest anything evil happen to him throughout the course of eternity." So they would be comfortable in their new existence, the royal family packed their tombs with gilded furniture, sparkling jewelry, and luxury goods of all kinds. Archaeologists have uncovered two full-size cedar ships buried next to the Great Pyramid, meant to carry King Cheops on his voyage into eternity.

Their need to direct the labor and expenses for their mammoth projects led Old Kingdom rulers to centralize their administration and strengthen the social hierarchy. The king and queen topped the social order. Brothers and sisters in the royal family could marry each other, perhaps because such matches were believed necessary to preserve the purity of the royal line or to imitate the marriages of the gods. The priests, royal administrators, regional governors, and commanders of the army ranked next in the hierarchy. The common people, who did all the manual labor, made up the great majority of free people in Egypt. (Slaves became more common after the Old Kingdom.) Free workers had heavy obligations to the state. For example, although they were not slaves, they were required to work on the pyramids. On occasion they received wages, but mostly their labor was a

■ **The Pyramids at Giza in Egypt**
The kings of Old Kingdom Egypt constructed enormous stone pyramids for their tombs. Pyramids were the centerpieces of large complexes of temples and courtyards stretching to the banks of the Nile or along a canal leading to the river. The burial chambers lay at the end of long, narrow tunnels snaking through the pyra-   mids' interiors. The largest pyramid shown here is the nearly five-hundred-foot high   Great Pyramid of King Cheops, erected in the twenty-sixth century B.C.E.   (© John Lawrence/SuperStock.)

way of paying taxes. Rates of taxation reached 20 percent on the produce of free farmers.

Women generally had the same legal rights as men. They could own land and slaves, inherit property, pursue lawsuits, transact business, and initiate divorces. Old Kingdom portrait statues display the equal status of wife and husband: each figure is the same size and sits on the same kind of chair. Men dominated public life, while women devoted themselves mainly to private life, managing their households and property. When their husbands went to war, however, women often took on men's work. As a result, some women held government posts, served as priestesses, managed farms, and practiced medicine.

The formal, even rigid appearance of Egypt's art illustrates how much its people valued religion, order, and predictability. Almost all sculptures and paintings belonged to tombs or temples, testimony to the desire to please the gods. Old Kingdom artists excelled in stonework, from carved ornamental jars to massive portrait statues of kings and queens. These statues represent the person either standing stiffly with the left leg advanced or sitting on a chair or throne, stable and poised. Concern for appropriate behavior also appears in the Old Kingdom literature the Egyptians called instructions, known today as wisdom literature. These texts instructed high officials how to act. In the *Instruction of Ptahhotep,* for example, the king advises his minister Ptahhotep to tell his son, who will follow him in office, not to be arrogant or overconfident just because he is well educated and to seek advice from ignorant people as well as from the wise.

Life in the Egyptian and Hittite Kingdoms, 2190–1000 B.C.E.

The Old Kingdom's stability disintegrated when climate change shrank the annual Nile flood. This disaster caused starvation, which caused civil unrest, which discredited the kings. By 2190 B.C.E., regional governors seized and held onto power until King Mentuhotep II finally restored central authority, initiating what historians call the Middle Kingdom (c. 2061–1665 B.C.E.). This restoration of the monarchy gave Egyptians pride in their homeland, to judge from the period's vigorous literature. The Egyptian narrator of *The Story of Sinuhe,* for example, reports that he lived luxuriously during a forced stay in Syria but still pined to return: "Whichever deity you are who ordered my exile, have mercy and bring me home! Please allow me to see the land where my heart dwells! Nothing is more important than that my body be buried in the country where I was born!" The Middle Kingdom fell apart, however, around 1665 B.C.E., when irregular Nile floods again undermined royal power.

A foreign invasion worsened the situation when a Semitic people from the Syria-Palestine region, whom the Egyptians called the Hyksos, took over Lower Egypt around 1664 B.C.E. (see Map 1.2). Recent archaeological discoveries have revealed the Hyksos transplanted elements of foreign culture to Egypt. The invaders brought bronze-making technology, horses and war chariots, more powerful bows, new musical instruments, hump-backed cattle, and olive trees, and they promoted contact with other Near Eastern states. As with the foreign wars of the Akkadians, so, too, the Hyksos invasion generated cultural interchange.

The leaders of Thebes in southern Egypt eventually reunited Egypt by defeating the Hyksos around 1569 B.C.E. and starting the New Kingdom (c. 1569–1081 B.C.E.). Its kings, known as pharaohs (meaning "the Great House," that is, the royal palace and estate), rebuilt central authority by restricting the power of regional governors. Recognizing that knowledge about the world was important for safety, they established diplomatic contacts with foreign states, such as the Hittite kingdom in Anatolia.

The New Kingdom pharaohs also used war to promote Egypt's interests. They earned the title "warrior pharaohs" by invading Nubia and the Sudan to the south, seeking gold and other precious materials, and by fighting in Palestine and Syria to control trade routes. As in the earlier kingdoms, religion remained the kings' most important activity. The principal festivals of the gods, for example, involved lavish public celebrations. A calendar based on the moon governed the dates of religious ceremonies. (The Egyptians also developed a calendar for administrative and fiscal purposes that had 365 days divided into twelve months of thirty days each, with the extra five days added before the start of the next year. Our modern calendar comes from it.) The royal family in the New Kingdom also built most of Egypt's magnificent temples, whose sculpted columns set a precedent for later Greek architecture. Queen Hatshepsut in the fifteenth century B.C.E., for example, erected a massive sanctuary at Deir el Bahri near Thebes. After her husband (who was also her half-brother) died, Hatshepsut proclaimed herself "female king" as co-ruler with her young stepson. To observe Egyptian political traditions, which did not include a queen ruling on her own, she had official artists portray her as a man, sporting a king's beard and male clothing.

So intense were Egyptians' religious feelings that they threatened the stability of the New Kingdom in the fourteenth century B.C.E., when the pharaoh Akhenaten reformed official religion. He made the cult of Aten, the shining disk of the sun, the centerpiece of royal worship and excluded other deities and their supporters. Akhenaten's reforms did not aim at pure **monotheism** (belief in the existence of only one god, as in Judaism, Christianity, and Islam) because they did not change the divine status of the king. His wife, Queen Nefertiti, tried to restrain him when she realized the hostility that his changes were generating in the priesthood and the general population, but he kept on, even neglecting the defense of Egypt to devote himself to religion. His religious reform died with him; during the reign of his successor Tutankhamun (r. 1355–1346 B.C.E.), famous today through the discovery in 1922 of his unlooted tomb, the traditional solar cult of Amun-Re reclaimed its leading role.

Whether Egypt was at peace or in turmoil, Egyptians' daily lives focused on work (mainly farming and craft production) and religion. Ordinary people devoted much attention to deities outside the royal cults, especially to gods they believed protected them. They venerated Bes, for instance, a dwarf with the features of a lion, as a protector of the household. They carved his image on amulets, beds, headrests, and the handles of mirrors. Magic also played a large role in people's lives. They used spells and charms to ward off demons, smooth the course of love, take revenge on enemies, and find relief from disease and injury. Egyptian doctors made medicinal use of herbs, knowledge that was passed on to later civilizations, and they could perform surgeries, including opening the skull.

Like royalty, ordinary people prepared for the afterlife. Those who could afford it arranged to have their bodies mummified and their tombs outfitted with all the goods needed for the journey to their new existence. A mummy's essential equipment included a copy of the *Book of the Dead*—a collection of magic spells to ward off danger and gain a successful verdict from the divine jury that put every

■ **The "Opening of the Mouth" Ceremony in an Egyptian Funeral**
This picture from a papyrus scroll containing the Egyptian Book of the Dead, *instructions for the afterlife, shows priests, mourners, and the god Anubis performing the Opening of the Mouth funeral ceremony. In this ritual, the deceased's mummy was touched on the mouth by sacred instruments that released the person's individual personality* (ba) *to join the rest of his or her spirit for a happy new existence in the afterlife.* (© Copyright The Trustees of The British Museum.)

soul on trial. To avoid experiencing death a second time, the *Book* instructed, dead people had to convince the jury of gods by sworn statements such as "I have not committed crimes against people; I have not mistreated cattle; I have not robbed the poor; I have not caused pain; I have not caused tears." Souls who received positive judgments experienced a mystical union with the god Osiris, the head judge of the dead.

The greatest external threat to the safety of New Kingdom Egyptians came from the aggressive wars of the Hittite kingdom in Anatolia (see Map 1.1). Unrelated to the Egyptians, the Hittites spoke an Indo-European language from the family of languages that eventually spread over most of Europe. The original Indo-European speakers had migrated as separate groups into Anatolia and Europe from somewhere in western Asia. Recent archaeological discoveries there of graves of women buried with weapons suggest that Indo-European women originally occupied positions of leadership alongside men; the prominence of Hittite queens in official documents perhaps sprang from that tradition.

Hittite kingship was based on religion—the worship of Indo-European gods and local Anatolian deities. The king served as high priest of the storm-god and had to maintain strict purity. His drinking water, for example, was always strained, and his water carrier was executed if so much as a hair was found in a drink. Like Egyptian kings, Hittite rulers felt responsible for maintaining divine goodwill toward their subjects. One of them, King Mursili II (r. 1321–1295 B.C.E.), issued a set of prayers begging the gods to end a plague: "What is this, o gods, that you have done? Our land is dying. . . . We have lost our wits, and we can do nothing right. O gods, whatever sin you behold, either let a prophet come forth to identify it . . . or let us see it in a dream!"

The Hittite rulers launched long-range military campaigns to acquire metals and control trade routes. The Hittites did not owe their success in war to a special knowledge of making weapons from iron, as once thought, because iron weapons did not become common until well after 1200 B.C.E. They did excel in the use of war chariots, however. Hittite kings particularly wanted to dominate the lucrative trade from Mesopotamia and Egypt. In 1595 B.C.E., therefore, their army raided as far as Babylon, overthrowing that kingdom.

They also invaded the Levant, the principal trade highway to Egypt. Previously, independent Canaanite city-states, such as the bustling ports of Ugarit, Byblos, and Tyre, had dominated the Levant. There, the interaction of traders and travelers from different cultures created about 1600 B.C.E. a supremely important innovation in writing technology: the alphabet. In this new system, a simplified picture—that is, a letter—stood for only one sound in the language. This offered a dramatic improvement in ease of writing over cuneiform and hieroglyphic scripts. The Canaanite alphabet later became the basis for the Greek and Roman alphabets, from which came modern Western alphabets.

The New Kingdom pharaohs fiercely resisted Hittite expansion in the Levant, but they could not defeat the Hittites at the climactic battle of Kadesh in Syria about 1274 B.C.E. Diplomacy finally created a balance of power between the kingdoms when, around 1259 B.C.E., the Hittite king Hattusili III signed a treaty with the Egyptian king Ramesses II and gave Ramesses his daughter in marriage to seal the agreement. Remarkably, both Egyptian and Hittite copies of this landmark in diplomatic history survive. In it the two monarchs pledged to be "at peace and brothers forever."

■ **REVIEW:** *How did religion guide the lives of people in the early civilizations of Egypt, the Levant, and Anatolia?*

Shifting Empires in the Ancient Near East, to 500 B.C.E.

A widespread spasm of attacks, apparently generated by invasions of separate bands of shipborne raiders known to us as the "Sea Peoples" (their history remains mysterious), afflicted the eastern Mediterranean region from about 1200 to 1000 B.C.E. The turmoil wiped out many communities, producing what scholars call a "Dark Age" because economic conditions became gloomy for many people, and because our view of what happened is so dim. In the Near East, recent archaeological excavation suggests that this Dark Age lasted about a century. Egypt lost its international power forever during this troubled period when the New Kingdom fell apart about 1081 B.C.E.

By 900 B.C.E., a powerful Assyrian kingdom had reemerged from the Near East's Dark Age. From their Mesopotamian homeland, these Assyrians ruthlessly carved out a centralized empire even larger than the one their ancestors had created. The riches and power of this Neo-Assyrian ("New Assyrian") Empire later inspired the Babylonians and then the Persians to create their own empires when the Assyrians lost their power. This constant striving for imperial wealth and territory kept the Near East on the same violent political and military path—monarchy and empire—that the region had followed in the past.

Hebrew (or Israelite) civilization, centered in the southern Levant, lost its independence to these Near Eastern empires, but its religion—Judaism—became influential in Western civilization. The Hebrews' religion, originally reflecting influences from their polytheistic Canaanite neighbors, took a long time to develop into monotheism. Eventually, however, the Hebrew ideas of belief in one god and basing a religion on scripture became essential concepts for major religions that deeply influenced Western civilization.

From Neo-Assyrian to Babylonian to Persian Empire, c. 900–500 B.C.E.

The collapse of the Egyptian and Hittite kingdoms by around 1000 B.C.E. allowed the aggressive warriors of Assyria to seize supplies of metal and control land and sea trade routes. By about 900 B.C.E., the armies of the Neo-Assyrian kingdom were relentlessly driving westward against the Aramaean states in Syria until they punched through to the Mediterranean coast (Map 1.3). Neo-Assyrian monarchs constantly pursued foreign expansion, and for the first time, their armies made foot soldiers the principal striking force instead of cavalry. Trained infantrymen excelled in the use of military technology such as siege towers and battering rams; archers rode in chariots. Campaigns against foreign lands brought back plunder to supplement the kingdom's agriculture and long-distance trade. Conquered peoples had to pay annual tribute to the Assyrians, supplying raw materials and luxury goods such as incense, wine, dyed linens, glass, and ivory.

Neo-Assyrian kings treated conquered peoples brutally to keep order. They herded large numbers of people from their homelands to Assyria, forcing them to build temples and palaces. One unexpected consequence of this merciless policy was that the kings undermined their native language: so many Aramaeans were deported from Canaan to Assyria that Aramaic largely replaced Assyrian as Assyria's everyday language by the eighth century B.C.E.

When not waging war, Neo-Assyrian men loved to hunt—the more dangerous the animal, the better. The king hunted lions as proof of his vigor and power. Royal lion hunts provided a favorite subject for sculptors, who carved long relief sculptures

■ **MAP 1.3 Expansion of the Neo-Assyrian Empire, c. 900–650 B.C.E.**
Like their Akkadian, Assyrian, and Babylonian predecessors, the Neo-Assyrian kings dominated a vast region of the Near East to secure a supply of metals, access to trade routes on land and sea, and imperial glory. They built the largest empire the world had yet seen. Also like their predecessors, they treated disobedient subjects harshly and intolerantly to try to prevent their diverse territories from rebelling.

telling a connected story. Although the Neo-Assyrian imperial administration pre-served countless documents in its archives, literacy apparently mattered less to the kingdom's males than war, hunting, and practical technology. King Sennacherib (r. 704–681 B.C.E.), for example, boasted that he invented new irrigation equipment and a novel method of metal casting. Ashurbanipal (r. 680–626 B.C.E.) is the only king to proclaim his scholarly accomplishments: "I have read complicated texts, whose versions in Sumerian are obscure and in Akkadian hard to understand. I do research on the cuneiform texts on stone from before the Flood." Women of the social elite probably learned to read, but they were excluded from the male domin-ions of hunting and war. Public religion, which included deities adopted from Babylonia, also reflected the prominence of war in Assyrian culture: even the Assyrian cult of Ishtar (the Babylonian name for Inanna), the goddess of love and fertility, glorified warfare.

The Neo-Assyrian kings' harshness made their own people dislike their rule, especially the social elite. Rebellions were common, and in the seventh century B.C.E., they crippled the kingdom. The Medes, an Iranian people, and the Chaldeans, a Semitic people who had driven the Assyrians from Babylonia, combined forces to invade. They destroyed the Neo-Assyrian capital at Nineveh in 612 B.C.E. and ended its kings' imperial power.

Sprung from seminomadic herders along the Persian Gulf, the Chaldeans estab-lished the Neo-Babylonian Empire, which became the most powerful empire in Babylonian history. King Nebuchadnezzar II (r. 605–562 B.C.E.) drove the Egyptian army from Syria at the battle of Carchemish in 605 B.C.E. Nebuchadnezzar spent lav-ishly to turn Babylon into an architectural showplace, rebuilding the great temple of its chief god, Marduk; creating the famous Hanging Gardens (so named because lush plants drooped over its terraced sides); and constructing a dazzling city gate dedicated to the goddess Ishtar. Blue-glazed bricks and lions molded in yellow, red, and white decorated the gate's walls, which soared thirty-six feet high.

The Chaldeans adopted traditional Babylonian culture and preserved much ancient Mesopotamian literature, such as the *Epic of Gilgamesh.* They also created many new works of prose and poetry, which the few educated people often read aloud publicly for the enjoyment of the many illiterate members of the population. Particularly popular were fables, proverbs, essays, and prophecies that taught moral-ity and proper behavior. This so-called wisdom literature, a Near Eastern tradition going back at least to the Egyptian Old Kingdom, greatly influenced the later reli-gious writings of the Hebrews.

The Chaldeans' advances in astronomy became so influential in the ancient Mediterranean world that the word *Chaldean* became the Greeks' word for "astronomer." People's main reason for observing the stars was the belief that the gods communicated their will to humans through events in nature, such as eclipses and the movements of the stars and planets, abnormal births, smoke curling upward from a fire, and the trails of ants. The interpretation of these events as messages from the gods was characteristic of the mixture of science and religion in ancient Near Eastern thought, which so deeply influenced the Greeks.

The Persian kingdom, the Near East's last and greatest empire, began when Cyrus (r. 559–530 B.C.E.) overthrew Median rule in Persia (today Iran). Relying on his skills as a general and a diplomat who respected others' religious beliefs, he conquered Babylon in 539 B.C.E. A rebellion there had weakened the Chaldean dynasty when King Nabonidus (r. c. 555–539 B.C.E.) provoked a revolt among Marduk's priests by promoting a different deity. Cyrus profited from this religious crisis by promising to restore traditional Babylonian religion, thereby winning local support. According to an ancient inscription, he proclaimed: "Marduk, the great lord, caused Babylon's generous residents to adore me."

Later Persian kings expanded their rule by following Cyrus's principles of military strength and cultural tolerance. Darius I (r. 522–486 B.C.E.) vastly extended Cyrus's conquests by pushing Persian power eastward to the Indus Valley and westward to Thrace (Map 1.4). Organizing this vast territory into provinces, he assigned each region taxes payable in the form best suited to its local economy—precious metals, grain, horses, or slaves. He required each region to send soldiers to staff the royal army. A network of roads and a courier system for royal mail aided contact among the far-flung provincial centers. The Greek historian Herodotus reported that neither snow, rain, heat, nor darkness slowed the couriers from completing their routes as swiftly as possible (an achievement later transformed into the U.S. Postal Service motto). The kings' belief in their divine right to rule everyone, everywhere would provoke great conflicts—above all, the war between Persians and Greeks that would break out around 500 B.C.E.

The revenues flowing into the imperial treasury made the Persian king wealthy beyond imagination and supported his exalted status. So special was the monarch that servants held their hands before their mouths in his presence so that he would not have to breathe the same air as they. In sculpture adorning the immense palace at Persepolis, artists carved royal figures larger than other people. The king's purple robes were more splendid than anyone else's, and no other person could walk on the red carpets spread before him. To show that he used his gargantuan resources to help his loyal subjects, the king often provided meals for fifteen thousand nobles, courtiers, and other followers at one sitting—although he himself ate hidden from the view of his guests. Lawbreakers or rebels the king punished harshly, mutilating their bodies and executing their families. Greeks, in awe of the Persian monarch's power and luxury, referred to him as "The Great King."

So long as his subjects—numbering in the millions and of many different ethnicities—remained peaceful, the king left them alone to live and worship as they pleased. The empire's smoothly functioning administrative structure sprang from Assyrian precedents: provincial governors (satraps) ruled enormous territories with little interference from the king. In this decentralized system, the governors' duties included keeping order, enrolling troops, and sending revenues to the royal treasury.

■ **MAP 1.4 Expansion of the Persian Empire, c. 550–490 B.C.E.**
*Cyrus (r. 559–530 B.C.E.) founded the Persian Empire, which his successors expanded to be even
larger than the Neo-Assyrian Empire, which it replaced. By the later years of Darius's reign
(r. 522–486 B.C.E.), the Persian Empire had expanded east as far as the western edge of India; to the
west, it reached Thrace, the eastern edge of Europe. Persian kings, unlike their imperial predecessors,
won their subjects' loyalty with tolerance and religious freedom, although they treated rebels
harshly.* **For more help analyzing this map,** *see the map activity for this chapter in the* ONLINE
STUDY GUIDE *at* bedfordstmartins.com/huntconcise.

Ruling as absolute autocrats and therefore possessing the power to make the
rules for everyone else, the Persian kings believed they were superior to all humans.
They regarded themselves not as gods but as the agents of Ahura Mazda, the
supreme god of Persia. As Darius said in his autobiography that was carved into a
mountainside in three languages, "Ahura Mazda gave me kingship . . . by the will of
Ahura Mazda the provinces respected my laws."

■ The Great King of Persia

Like their Assyrian predecessors, the Persian kings decorated their palaces with large relief sculptures emphasizing royal dignity and success. This one from Persepolis shows officials and petitioners giving the king proper respect when entering his presence. To symbolize their elevated status, the king and his son, who stands behind the throne, are depicted as larger than everyone else. **For more help analyzing this image,** see the visual activity for this chapter in the ONLINE STUDY GUIDE at bedfordstmartins.com/huntconcise. (Courtesy of the Oriental Institute of the University of Chicago.)

Persian religion, based on the teachings of the legendary prophet Zarathustra (and called Zoroastrianism from the Greek name for this holy man), made the god Ahura Mazda the center of worship. It seems, however, not to have been pure monotheism. Its most important doctrine was a moral dualism: perceiving the world as the arena for an ongoing battle between the opposing forces of good and evil. Ahura Mazda's two children, according to Persian belief, made different moral choices: one chose the way of the truth, but the other chose the way of the lie. Humans, too, could freely decide between purity and impurity, and their judgment had consequences: Zoroastrianism promised that salvation awaited those following the way of the truth, while damnation would strike those electing the way of the lie. The Persian religious emphasis on ethical behavior had a lasting influence on others, especially the Hebrews.

Creating Hebrew Monotheism, c. 1000–539 B.C.E.

The Hebrews' enduring impact on Western civilization comes from the book that became their sacred scripture, the Hebrew Bible (known to Christians as the Old Testament). It deeply affected the formation of not only Judaism but also Christianity and, later, Islam. Unfortunately, no source provides clear information on the origins of the Hebrews or their religion. The Bible tells stories to explain

God's moral plan for the universe, not the full history of the Hebrews, and archaeology has not yielded a clear picture.

The Hebrew Bible reports that the patriarch Abraham led his followers from the Mesopotamian city of Ur to ancient Palestine, at the southeast corner of the Mediterranean Sea where the Canaanites ruled (see Map 1.1). Traditionally said to have been divided into twelve tribes, the Hebrews never formed a political state in this period, about 1900 B.C.E. The biblical story of Joseph bringing Hebrews to Egypt may belong between 1600 and 1400 B.C.E., during the time of Hyksos rule. By the thirteenth century B.C.E., the pharaohs had conscripted the male Hebrews into labor gangs for farming and construction work.

According to the book of Exodus, around 1250 B.C.E. the Hebrew deity Yahweh instructed Moses to lead the Hebrews out of bondage in Egypt against the will of the king. The biblical narrative then relates the central event in Hebrew history: the sealing of a covenant between the Hebrews and Yahweh at Mount Sinai. This agreement declared that, if the Hebrews promised to worship Yahweh as their only God and to live by his laws, Yahweh would make them his chosen people and lead them into a promised land of safety and prosperity. This binding arrangement demanded human obedience to divine law and promised punishment for unrighteousness. As God described himself, he was "compassionate and gracious, patient, ever constant and true . . . forgiving wickedness, rebellion, and sin, and not sweeping the guilty clean away; but one who punishes sons and grandsons to the third and fourth generation for their fathers' iniquity" (Exodus 34:6–7). The religious and moral code that bound the Hebrews was written down in the Ten Commandments and the Pentateuch (the first five books of the Hebrew Bible), or Torah.

Many of the laws in the Pentateuch recalled earlier Mesopotamian rules, such as those of Hammurabi, but Hebrew law differed because it applied the same rules and punishments to everyone, regardless of their social position. Hebrew law also ruled out vicarious punishment—a Mesopotamian tradition ordering, for example, that a rapist's wife be raped. Hebrew women had less extensive legal rights than men, such as in seeking a divorce. Crimes against property never carried the death penalty, as they frequently did in other Near Eastern societies, and Hebrew laws protected slaves against glaring mistreatment.

The earliest parts of the Hebrew Bible were probably composed about 950 B.C.E., some three centuries after the exodus from Egypt. Many uncertainties cloud our understanding of how the Hebrews acquired their monotheism. It seems that it took much longer to evolve than the biblical account suggests. In the time of Moses, Yahweh-religion was not yet monotheistic because it did not deny the existence of other gods, such as Baal of Canaan. Fully developed Hebrew monotheism did not emerge until well after 1000 B.C.E., by which time the first Hebrew kingdom had formed. Solomon (r. c. 961–922 B.C.E.) brought the united nation to the height of its prosperity, largely from trade. He displayed his wealth by building in Jerusalem a temple to Yahweh richly decorated with gold leaf; it became the center of Hebrew religion.

After Solomon, the monarchy split into two kingdoms: Israel in the north and Judah in the south. The Assyrian king Tiglath-pileser III conquered Israel in 722 B.C.E. and deported its population to Assyria. In 597 B.C.E., the Neo-Babylonian king Nebuchadnezzar II conquered Judah; ten years later he destroyed Solomon's temple and sent most of the Hebrews into exile in Babylon. When the Persian king Cyrus overthrew the Babylonians in 539 B.C.E., he permitted the Hebrews to return to Palestine, which was called *Yehud* from the name of the southern Hebrew kingdom, Judah. From this geographical term came the name *Jews,* a designation for the Hebrews after their Babylonian exile. Cyrus allowed them to rebuild their Jerusalem temple and practice their religion. After returning from exile, the Jews in the ancient world remained a people subject to the political domination of various Near Eastern powers, except for a period of independence during the second and first centuries B.C.E.

Jewish prophets, both men and women, preached that the Hebrews' defeats were divine punishment for neglecting the Sinai covenant and mistreating the poor. Some prophets also predicted the coming end of the present world following a great crisis, a judgment by Yahweh, and salvation leading to a new and better world. Yahweh would save the Hebrew nation, the prophets thundered, only if Jews learned to observe divine law strictly. This **apocalypticism** ("uncovering" of the future), which recalled Babylonian prophetic wisdom literature, would later influence Christianity.

Jewish religious leaders developed strict regulations requiring people to maintain ritual and ethical purity in all aspects of life. Ethics applied not only to obvious crimes but also to financial dealings. Jews had to pay taxes and offerings to support Yahweh's temple, and they had to forgive debts every seventh year. Jews therefore created laws based on ethics as the focus of the world's first complete monotheism. They retained their cultural identity by following their religious laws, regardless of where they lived. In this way, Jews who did not return to their homeland could maintain their identity while living among foreigners. Over time, the Diaspora ("dispersion of population") came to characterize the history of the Jewish people.

Hebrew monotheism made the preservation and understanding of a sacred text, the Hebrew Bible, the key to a religious life. Making scripture important to religion became a crucial development for the history not only of Judaism but also of Christianity and Islam because these later religions placed their own sacred texts, the Christian Bible and the Qur'an, respectively, at the centers of their belief and practice. The Hebrews thus passed on ideas that have endured to this day, such as the belief in monotheism, the importance of scripture in religion, and a commitment to a covenant between God and a people who are promised salvation if they obey divine will.

■ **REVIEW:** *How did religion affect the history of the Near East from c. 1000 B.C.E. to c. 500 B.C.E.?*

Greek Civilization, to 750 B.C.E.

Neolithic settlements of Indo-European speakers dotted the mountainous Greek mainland and the islands of the Aegean Sea by 8000 B.C.E. By 6000 B.C.E., Anatolian peoples had migrated to the large island of Crete, southeast of the Greek mainland. The type of language spoken by these early Cretans, called *Minoans,* remains uncertain, but they created the first civilization in this part of the world in the late third millennium B.C.E. Eventually, they lost their preeminence and power to their warlike northern neighbors, the Mycenaean Greeks.

When Mycenaean civilization was destroyed during the tumult that affected the entire eastern Mediterranean from about 1200 to 1000 B.C.E., the aftermath—a prolonged Dark Age of depopulation and poverty—threatened doom for Greek civilization.

Minoan and Mycenaean Civilization, c. 2200–1000 B.C.E.

With its fertile plains, adequate rainfall, and sheltered ports for fishing and seaborne trade, Crete offered a fine home for settlers (Map 1.5). By 2200 B.C.E., the inhabitants

■ **MAP 1.5 Greece and the Aegean Sea, c. 1500 B.C.E.**
Mountains, islands, and sea defined the geography of Greece. The rough terrain and seasonally stormy sailing made travel a chore. The distance from the mainland to the largest island in this region, Crete, where Minoan civilization arose, was sufficiently long to keep Cretans isolated from the turmoil of most of later Greek history.

of Crete created what scholars have named a palace society, referring to the sprawling, many-chambered buildings that seem to have been both the residences of the rulers and centers of political, economic, and religious administration. The palaces seem to have been independent; no one ruler controlled Crete. We call this civilization Minoan because a famous archaeologist, Arthur Evans (1851–1941), believed that one of its rulers was King Minos, renowned in Greek myth because his wife gave birth to the half-man, half-bull Minotaur ("Minos's bull").

Minoan farmers developed Mediterranean polyculture—growing olives, grapes, and grain all on the same farm. This innovation made the best use of agricultural labor because these crops' different growing cycles allowed the same laborers to take care of them all. Farmers could thus produce valuable and versatile products such as olive oil and wine. This combination of crops provided a healthy diet that stimulated population growth.

The storage areas in the Cretan palaces, such as the vast one at Knossos, suggest that Minoan rulers enforced a redistributive economic system. The Knossos palace, for example, held hundreds of gigantic jars holding 240,000 gallons of olive oil and wine. The rulers evidently decided how much each farmer or crafts producer had to contribute to the palace storehouse and how much of those contributions would then be redistributed to each person in the community for basic subsistence or as an extra reward.

Greek civilization on the mainland also had a redistributive economy controlled by independent rulers. Emerging about the same time as the Hittite kingdom, in the early second millennium B.C.E., this civilization derives its modern designation—Mycenaean—from the hilltop site of Mycenae in the Peloponnese (the large peninsula forming southern Greece), which by 1400 B.C.E. had a fortified settlement dominated by a palace and dotted with rich tombs (see Map 1.5). Because mountainous Greece had little fertile land but many useful ports, settlements tended to arise near the coast. Greeks always depended on the sea: for food, for trade with one another and with foreign lands, and for naval raids on rich targets.

Seaborne commerce involved Greeks with the rest of the eastern Mediterranean region and promoted cultural interaction, as underwater archaeology reveals. Off Uluburun in Turkey, for example, divers discovered a late-fourteenth-century B.C.E. ship carrying such a mixed cargo and varied personal possessions—from Greece, Egypt, Canaan, Cyprus, Babylon, and elsewhere in the Near East—that attaching a single "nationality" to this vessel makes no sense.

The sea brought Mycenaeans and Minoans into close contact. Many objects found on the mainland display designs clearly inspired by Cretan traditions. At the same time, the two civilizations remained different in important ways. The Mycenaeans burned offerings to the gods; the Minoans did not. The Minoans scattered sanctuaries across the landscape in caves, on mountaintops, and in country villas; the Mycenaeans kept their sanctuaries inside their palaces. When the Mycenaeans

■ Minoan Wall Painting from the Island of Thera

Minoan artists painted with vivid colors on plaster to enliven the walls of buildings. They depicted a wide variety of subjects, from lively animals and flowering plants to young boxers and women of the court in splendid dress. Unfortunately, time and earthquakes have severely damaged most Minoan wall paintings, and the versions we see today are largely reconstructions, painted around surviving fragments of the originals. This wall painting was found on the island of Thera (or Santorini), whose volcano exploded in the seventeenth century B.C.E., blowing out the entire center of the island and burying its Minoan settlements. Some scholars think the explosion of Santorini was the inspiration for the story of the lost land of Atlantis. (Julia M. Fair.)

started building palaces in the fourteenth century B.C.E., unlike the Minoans, they designed them around megarons—rooms with prominent ceremonial hearths and thrones for the rulers. Some Mycenaean palaces had more than one megaron, which could tower two stories high with columns to support a roof above the second-floor balconies.

A cache of clay tablets discovered in the Knossos palace shows that Mycenaeans achieved dominance over Crete, possibly in a war over international trade. These documents were written in a script that archaeologists call Linear B, a picture-based script that evolved from an earlier script called Linear A. Linear B, we now know, was used to write the Mycenaeans's language: Greek. Because the Linear B tablets date from before the final destruction of Knossos in about 1370 B.C.E., they reveal that the palace administration had been keeping its records in this non-Minoan language for some time and therefore that Mycenaeans controlled Crete well before the end of Minoan civilization.

Later Greeks recalled this conquest of Crete with the myth describing how Theseus of Athens defeated the Minotaur monster: when Minos forced the Athenians to send youths for the creature to devour in his labyrinth, Theseus slew the brute and found his way out of the maze by backtracking along the thread that the king's daughter Ariadne, who had fallen in love with the handsome hero, told him to leave to mark his path.

By the time Mycenaeans ruled Crete, war at home and abroad was the principal concern of well-off Mycenaean men. Contents of Bronze Age tombs in Greece reveal that no wealthy man went to his grave without his war equipment. The expense of these grave goods shows that armor and weapons were so central to a Mycenaean male's identity that he could not leave them behind even in death.

Their warlike spirit, however, probably ruined the Mycenaeans during the Sea Peoples period (c. 1200–1000 B.C.E.). At this time, the palace settlements of eastern Greece constructed such massive defensive walls that later Greeks believed giants had built them. These fortifications would have protected coastal palaces against invading Sea Peoples, so these marauders most likely did not destroy Mycenaean civilization. The great wall around the palace at Gla, far inland where foreign sea raiders could not easily reach, suggests instead a land-based threat; that is, the Mycenaeans at Gla and elsewhere were defending themselves against other Mycenaeans. Archaeologists therefore speculate that internal turmoil, made worse by earthquakes, destroyed the order and prosperity of Mycenaean civilization by about 1000 B.C.E.

The loss of their redistributive economies devastated most Mycenaeans, who depended on their rulers' system for their subsistence. The catastrophic fall of Mycenaean civilization led to the Greek Dark Age.

The Greek Dark Age, c. 1000–750 B.C.E.

Greek culture came close to vanishing in the Dark Age (c. 1000–750 B.C.E.). Political organization faded, the economy collapsed, and the population dwindled. Conditions were so depressed that Greeks even lost the technologies of writing and of illustrating people and animals in art.

When the powerful rulers of Mycenaean Greece disappeared, competition for leadership in Dark Age society was wide open. The men and women who proved themselves excellent in action, words, and religious knowledge became the new social elite. Excellence—*aretê* in Greek—became a competitive value: men and women earned high social status by outdoing others. Men displayed aretê through prowess in war and persuasiveness in speech; women, through savvy management of a bustling household of children, slaves, and the family's storerooms. Members of the elite accumulated wealth by controlling agricultural land, which people of lower status worked for them as tenants or slaves.

The rebuilding of Greek social and political life after the Dark Age required the reestablishment of values. The poetry of Homer and Hesiod provided the elite with its ideals. Greeks believed that Homer was a blind poet from Ionia (today Turkey's western coast) who composed the epics the *Iliad* and the *Odyssey*, whose stories explore the consequences of making excellence the principal social value. Homer probably lived in the eighth century B.C.E. and belonged to a long line of poets who, influenced by Near Eastern mythology, had been singing these stories for centuries. The *Iliad* tells the story of the Greek army in the Trojan War (one of the many wars of the Sea Peoples period). The manliest Greek hero is Achilles, who displays his surpassing excellence by choosing to die gloriously in battle rather than return home safely but without glory. The *Odyssey* describes the hero Odysseus's ten-year adventure finding his way home to his family after the fall of Troy, and the struggle of his wife, Penelope, to protect their household from schemes and threats while her husband is missing. Penelope proves herself the best of women, showing her aretê by outwitting treacherous neighbors and thereby preserving her family's prosperity.

The *Iliad* and *Odyssey* reveal how the quest for excellence could produce both wondrous deeds and brutal inhumanity. As Achilles prepares to duel with Hector, the prince of Troy, he coldly rejects the Trojan's proposal for the winner to return the loser's corpse to his family and friends: "Do wolves and lambs agree to cooperate? No, they hate each other to the roots of their being." After Achilles kills Hector, he mutilates his body. When Hecuba, the queen of Troy and Hector's mother, sees this outrage, she bitterly shouts, "I wish I could sink my teeth into his liver in his guts to eat it raw." Homer's poems suggest that the gods could promote reconciliation, but they also reveal that the level of suffering in the human condition means excellence comes at a supremely high price.

Hesiod's poetry stressed the human need for justice. Like Homer a poet of the eighth century B.C.E., Hesiod told stories influenced by Near Eastern myths, such as the Mesopotamian *Epic of Creation*. His poems explain that existence, even for deities, entails sorrow and violence. They also show that justice is part of the divine order of the universe. In *Works and Days*, Hesiod identifies Zeus, king of the gods, as the source of justice: "Zeus ordained that fishes and wild beasts and birds should eat each other, for they have no justice; but to human beings he has given justice, which is far the best." Hesiod emphasizes that men from the social elite should demonstrate excellence by promoting justice through persuasion instead of force: "When his people in their assembly get on the wrong track, [a good leader] gently sets matters right, persuading them with soft words." Hesiod proclaims that the divine origin of justice should be a warning to "bribe-devouring chiefs" who impose "crooked judgments." By the end of the Dark Age, the outrage that ordinary people felt at not receiving just treatment was producing pressure for a new form of social and political organization in Greece.

During the Dark Age, the Greeks remained in contact with the Near East, and about 800 B.C.E., they learned to write again in a new way when Phoenician traders from Canaan taught them their alphabet. Eastern art inspired Greeks once more to include lively figures in their paintings. Most important, trade brought to Greece the new technology of iron metallurgy. Because iron ore was available in Greece, iron was cheaper than bronze. The relatively low cost of iron tools helped revive farming, which in turn rebuilt the population. By the eighth century B.C.E., Greece was emerging from its Dark Age.

■ **REVIEW:** *What factors contributed to the onset of the Greek Dark Age?*

Remaking Greek Civilization, c. 750–500 B.C.E.

The Greeks' ties with Egypt and the Near East had kept them going economically and culturally during their Dark Age; beginning in the eighth century B.C.E., they gradually remade their civilization on new social and political principles, inventing citizenship based on freedom and sharing power in government. In doing so, they created their version of the city-state complete with new directions in politics, art, literature, philosophy, and science.

The best evidence of Greece's revival is the founding of the Olympic Games, traditionally dated to 776 B.C.E. Every four years, the games took place during a religious festival at Olympia, in the northwest Peloponnese, in a huge sanctuary dedicated to Zeus. There, male athletes from elite families competed in sports based on activities needed for war: running, wrestling, jumping, and throwing. Horse and chariot racing were added to the program later, but the main event remained a two-hundred-yard sprint, the *stadion*. Women were barred on pain of death, but they had their own separate Olympic festival on a different date in honor of Hera, queen of the gods; only unmarried women could compete.

Athletes competed as individuals, not on national teams as in the modern Olympic Games. Only first prizes were awarded; winners received no financial rewards, only a garland made from wild olive leaves that signified the prestige of victory. Later, full-time athletes dominated the Olympics, earning their living from appearance fees and prizes at games held throughout the Greek world. The most famous winner was Milo, from Croton in Italy. Six-time Olympic wrestling champion, he stunned audiences with demonstrations of strength such as holding his breath until his veins expanded so much that they snapped a cord tied around his head.

Historians date the end of the Dark Age and the beginning of the Archaic Age (c. 750–500 B.C.E.) near the time when the Olympics began. The Archaic Age gave birth to the Greek **polis** as an independent community of citizens inhabiting a city and the countryside around it. Greece's geography, dominated by mountains and islands, promoted the creation of city-states that remained fiercely independent communities (Map 1.6). The ancient Greeks never constituted a united nation.

During the Archaic Age, Greeks established settlements around the Mediterranean in a process traditionally called Greek colonization. This modern

■ MAP 1.6 Archaic Greece, c. 750–500 B.C.E.
*The Greek heartland lay in and around the Aegean Sea, in what is today the nation of Greece
and the western edge of the nation of Turkey (ancient Anatolia). The "mainland," where Athens,
Corinth, and Sparta are located, is the southernmost tip of the mountainous Balkan peninsula. The
many islands of the Aegean area were home mainly to small city-states, with the exception of the
large islands just off the western Anatolian coast, which were home to populous ones.*

term, however, is misleading because it implies that governments originated and
administered foreign colonies. In truth, individuals' desire for profit from trade,
especially in raw materials such as metals, and from acquiring farmland on foreign
shores drove the founding of most new settlements. By about 580 B.C.E., Greeks had
settled in Spain, present-day southern France, southern Italy and Sicily, North
Africa, and along the Black Sea coast. Greek settlements in the east were fewer, perhaps because the monarchies there restricted foreign immigration.

Citizenship and Freedom in the City-State

Greeks lived in more than a thousand separate city-states, most no larger than several hundred to a thousand or so in population. The Greek city-state was a new form
of political organization because all free inhabitants were considered citizens and,

usually, all free men could participate in governance. Some historians argue that the Greeks modeled their city-states on the older city-states on the island of Cyprus and in Phoenicia in the Levant, but this conclusion seems flawed because those city-states were ruled by kings and were not based on the concept of free citizens sharing power in governing, which was a defining characteristic of most Greek city-states. The most famous ancient analyst of Greek politics and society, the philosopher Aristotle (384–322 B.C.E.), insisted that the city-state was natural: "Humans are beings who by nature live in a city-state." Anyone who existed outside such a community, Aristotle concluded, must be either a simple fool or superhuman.

Citizenship was a new concept because it assumed a basic level of political and legal equality—above all, the expectation of equal treatment under the law for citizens regardless of their social status or wealth. Women had the protection of the law, but they were barred from participation in politics on the assumption that female judgment was inferior to male. The most dramatic indication of political equality in a Greek city-state was the right of all free, adult male citizens to vote on laws and policies in a political assembly. Not all city-states reached this level of power sharing and participation, however. In some, the social elite kept a stranglehold on politics, with a small group or, more rarely, a single person or family dominating. Rule by a small elite group is called oligarchy. Rule by one person is called tyranny.

Even if the Greeks' implementation of citizenship and equality before the law remained imperfect, the fact that they developed these concepts at all is remarkable because legal inequality between rich and poor in the free population was the rule in the ancient Near East and in Greece itself before the polis came into existence. Given the lack of precedent, how and why the poor in Greece gained citizenship and equality before the law remains a mystery. The greatest population increase in the late Dark Age and in the Archaic Age occurred in the ranks of the poor. These families raised more children to help farm more land, which otherwise would have lain idle because of the depopulation brought on by the worst of the Dark Age. There was no precedent for extending even limited political and legal power to this growing segment of the population, but most Greek city-states did so.

For a long time, historians attributed the general widening of political and legal rights to a so-called hoplite revolution, but recent research undermines this theory. Hoplites were infantrymen who wore metal body armor, carried a large shield in one hand, and wielded a spear with the other. They constituted the main strike force of the volunteer militia that defended each city-state. In the eighth century B.C.E., a growing number of men could afford to buy hoplite equipment (the use of iron had cut its cost). It seems likely that the new hoplites believed they were entitled to a say in politics because they bought their own equipment and voluntarily trained hard to defend their community. According to the hoplite revolution theory, the new hoplites forced the social elite to share political power by threatening to refuse to serve in the militia. The problem with that theory is that hoplites were not poor. How, then, did poor men, too, win political rights, especially the vote in the

■ A Hoplite's Breastplate
This bronze armor protected the chest of a sixth-century B.C.E. hoplite. It had to be fitted to his individual body; the design is meant to match the musculature of his chest and symbolize his manliness. The Greek soldier would have worn a cloth or leather shirt underneath to prevent the worst chafing, but such a heavy and hot device could never be comfortable, and soldiers often removed them despite the danger. A slave would have carried the soldier's armor for him until the moment of battle, when he would have donned his protective gear just before facing the enemy. (Olympia Museum © Archaeological Receipts Fund.)

assembly? The answer is unknown. Perhaps poor men earned respect and political rights by fighting as lightly armed fighters, disrupting the enemy's infantry by hurling barrages of rocks. Whatever the reason for the designation of poor men as citizens with roughly the same rights as the rich, this unprecedented decision constituted the most innovative feature of the transformation of Greek society in the Archaic Age.

The inclusiveness of the Greek city-state did not extend to slaves. As the notion of freedom became stronger, the practice of slavery—the opposite of freedom—became ever more widespread in Archaic Age Greece. Individual Greeks and the city-states themselves owned slaves. Public slaves sometimes lived on their own, performing specialized tasks such as detecting counterfeit coins. Temple slaves "belonged" to the deity of the temple, for whom they worked as servants. Private slaves totaled perhaps a third of the population by the fifth century B.C.E. They did all sorts of jobs, from household chores to crafts production to farm labor. Their masters controlled their lives and could punish them or demand sexual favors at will. Most owners did not brutalize their slaves because that damaged their human property. Lacking any right to family life and having no property or legal rights, slaves were completely alienated from polis society. As Aristotle put it, slaves were "living tools." Sometimes owners let slaves earn money to purchase their freedom, or promised freedom at a future date to encourage hard work. Slaves who gained their freedom did not become citizens but instead joined the population of noncitizens

■ A Greek Woman at an Altar

This vase painting from the center of a large drinking cup shows a woman in rich clothing pouring a libation to the gods onto a flaming altar. In her other arm, she carries some sort of religious object. This scene illustrates the most important and frequent role of women in Greek public life: participating in religious ceremonies, both at home and in community festivals. This painting style is called red figure because the picture's details are painted over the reddish color of the baked clay, which shows through to depict the surfaces of the figures, such as skin or clothing.

(The Toledo Museum of Art, Toledo, Ohio. Purchased with funds from the Libbey Endowment, Gift of Edward Drummond Libbey [1972.55].)

(metics) officially allowed to live in the city-state. Despite the bitter nature of their existence, Greek slaves rarely revolted on a large scale except in Sparta, perhaps because elsewhere they were of too many different origins and nationalities to organize. No Greek is known to have called for the abolition of slavery.

Women, like slaves, lacked the right of political participation in the city-state. Freeborn women, however, did count as citizens, enjoyed the protection of the laws, and—in a crucial role respected by everyone—performed numerous religious functions. Citizen women had recourse to the courts in disputes over property, although they usually had to have a man speak for them. Before marriage, a woman's father served as her legal guardian; after marriage, her husband did. The paternalism of Greek society—men acting as "fathers" to regulate the lives of women and safeguard their interests as men defined them—demanded that all women have male guardians to protect them physically and legally.

The expansion of slavery in the Archaic Age increased the size of households and added new responsibilities for women. While their husbands farmed, participated in politics, and met with their male friends, wives managed the household: raising children, supervising the cooking, keeping the family's financial accounts, making clothing, directing the slaves, and tending them and other family members when they were ill. Poor women worked outside the home, tilling gardens and selling produce and small goods such as ribbons and trinkets in the market found at the center of every settlement. Women rich and poor attended funerals, state festivals, and public rituals, and they controlled cults reserved exclusively for female worshippers. Their religious functions gave them freedom of movement and prestige. At Athens, for example, by the fifth century B.C.E. they officiated as priest-esses for more than forty different deities and enjoyed benefits such as salaries paid by the state.

Greek paternalism allowed men to control human reproduction and therefore the inheritance of property. Families arranged marriages, and everyone was expected to marry and produce children. The bride brought to the marriage a dowry of property (land yielding an income, if she was wealthy) that her children would inherit. Her husband was legally obligated to preserve this dowry and to return it to his wife if they divorced. A husband could divorce his wife at will. Legally, a wife could leave her husband on her own initiative to return to the guardianship of her male relatives, but her husband could force her to stay if her family refused to help her. Except in certain cases in Sparta, monogamous marriage was the rule in Greece, as was a nuclear family (that is, husband, wife, and children living together without other relatives in the same house). Citizen men could have sexual relations without penalty with slaves, foreign concubines, female prostitutes, or willing pre-adult citizen males. Citizen women, single or married, had no such freedom. Sex between a married woman and anyone other than her husband carried harsh penalties for both parties.

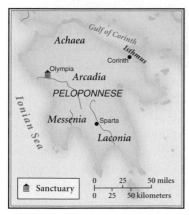

Sparta and the Peloponnese, c. 750–500 B.C.E.

Sparta differed from other city-states because it ranked regimentation and obedience as the highest social values. Spartans placed military readiness above personal concerns because Sparta's survival was threatened by its economic foundation: the great mass of slaves called helots, who were owned by the community and did almost all the work. Helots were Greeks from neighboring towns and regions that the Spartans had conquered, especially Messenia, a fertile region to the west that Sparta captured by about 700 B.C.E. The helots greatly outnumbered Sparta's citizens. They toiled as farmers and servants so that Spartans would not have to stoop to ordinary tasks. Spartan men wore their hair very long to show that they were "gentlemen," not laborers.

The helots faced constant humiliation and violence. Every year Spartan officials formally declared war on them so that a citizen could kill without penalty any helot thought to be disobedient or dangerous. To control the helots and intimidate other city-states, Spartans devoted their lives to constant preparation for war. Boys left home at age seven to live in barracks, drilling and eating together to learn discipline. Any youth unable to complete the harsh training fell into disgrace and lost citizen rights.

Adolescent boys in Sparta often were involved in homosexual relationships with older men. A boy would be chosen as a special favorite by the man to promote love for a fellow soldier at whose side he would one day march into battle; their relationship could include sex. The elder partner was supposed to help educate the young man in politics and community values and not just exploit him for physical pleasure. Both were expected to marry. Homoerotic sex between adult males was considered disgraceful, as it was between women of all ages (at least according to the reports of men).

Spartan women were known throughout the Greek world for the freedom of their lives, especially being able to exercise in public in short outfits. (Greek women elsewhere lacked exercise facilities and had to keep their bodies modestly covered.) Citizen women were expected to use their liberty from labor, which helots provided, to stay fit so they could bear healthy children to sustain the Spartan population. They could own property, including land. Women also were expected to teach their children Spartan values. One mother became legendary for handing her son his shield on the eve of battle and sternly telling him, "Come back with it—or on it!"

Athens differed from Sparta politically, socially, and economically. During the Archaic Age, it took the first steps toward democracy, a new system of government that gave equal political and legal rights to all male citizens, and toward an economy based on international trade by sea. In 594 B.C.E., an economic crisis that pitted rich against poor unexpectedly promoted change when Solon, appointed as a mediator, outlawed debt slavery and created a council to guide the legislative work of the assembly. The council's members were chosen by lottery and could serve only two annual terms (not in succession), ensuring wide participation. Equally important was Solon's decision to empower any citizen to bring charges in court on behalf of any victim and to appeal any magistrate's judgments to the assembly. These reforms gave ordinary citizens a real share in the administration of justice. Finally, Solon convinced the Athenians to improve the economy by exporting olive oil.

Some elite Athenians vehemently opposed Solon's political reforms because they wanted oligarchy. The unrest they caused opened the door temporarily to tyranny at Athens, and the family of Peisistratus held power from 546 to 510 B.C.E. by championing the interests of the poor. A rival elite family finally got the tyranny overthrown by denouncing it as unjust and inducing the Spartans, the self-proclaimed defenders of Greek freedom, to "liberate" Athens. Cleisthenes, an ambitious politician, found that he could win prominence only by promising greater democracy to the masses. Beginning in 508 B.C.E., he delivered on his promises and came to be remembered as the "father of Athenian democracy" for his reforms. His complex political reorganization achieved its goal of promoting participation in governance by as many male citizens as possible. It would take another fifty years of controversy before Athens's democracy reached its fullest form, but Cleisthenes' changes opened the way to an unprecedented way of life based on people persuading, not compelling, each other to achieve common goals. Athenian citizens believed in the rule of law, but they chose personal freedom and responsibility for themselves (though not for their slaves) over forced social regimentation like that at Sparta.

New Ways of Thought and Expression

The political idea that people should make decisions based on persuasion, rather than force or social status, matched the spirit of intellectual change rippling through Greece in the late Archaic Age. In city-states all over the Greek world, new ways of thought were inspiring artists, poets, and philosophers. Ongoing contacts with the Near East exposed the Greeks to traditions from which to learn and create something new. Artists became expert at rendering fully three-dimensional figures—whether goddesses, warriors, or monsters from myth—in an increasingly realistic style. Sculptors made their statues less stiff and more varied, from gracefully clothed young women to muscular male nudes, and made them come alive with gleaming paint.

Poets expanded the Near Eastern tradition of expressing personal emotions in poetry by developing lyric, a new type of verse similar to popular songs. Composed in diverse rhythms and performed to the music of a lyre (a kind of harp that gives

■ Archaic Age Sculpture of a Dead Athenian Warrior

This Athenian marble statue dating from about 530–520 B.C.E. shows the stiff posture and smiling expression that Archaic Age Greek sculptors used for "heroic nudes" depicting dead young men. These kouros ("young male") statues had a striding stance recalling the style of Egyptian art and were painted in bright colors; this one retains traces of red paint. A base probably belonging to this six-feet four-inch tall statue bore an inscription addressed to people passing by: "Stand and mourn at this monument of Croesus, now dead; raging Ares [the Greek war god] destroyed him as he battled in the front ranks."

(The Art Archive/National Archeological Museum Athens/Dagli Orti.)

its name to the poetry), Greek lyric poems could be short and for one singer or long and for a chorus. Archilochus of Paros, who lived in the early 600s B.C.E., became infamous for his unheroic lines about throwing down his shield in battle so he could run away to save his life: "Oh, the hell with it; I can get another one just as good." Sappho, a lyric poet from Lesbos born about 630 B.C.E., became famous for her love poems, writing, "Some would say the most beautiful thing on our dark earth is an army of cavalry, others of infantry, others of ships, but I say it's whatever a person loves." In this poem Sappho was expressing her longing for a woman she loved, who was far away.

Ionia and the Aegean, c. 750–500 B.C.E.

Greek philosophers in the Archaic Age developed radically new explanations of the nature of the universe and its relation to the gods. Most of these thinkers came from Ionia. This location placed them in close contact with Near Eastern knowledge, especially astronomy, mathematics, and myth. Because there were no formal schools, pupils who studied privately with these philosophers helped spread the new ideas. Inspired by Babylonian astronomy, Ionian Greek philosophers such as Thales (c. 625–545 B.C.E.) and Anaximander (c. 610–540 B.C.E.) of Miletus expressed the bold idea that laws of nature, not the whims of gods, governed the universe. Pythagoras, who emigrated from the island of Samos to the Greek city-state Croton in southern Italy about 530 B.C.E., taught that patterns and relationships of numbers explained the entire world and promoted the systematic study of mathematics and its relation to music.

Ionian philosophers insisted that they could discover the workings of the universe because nature was not random but rather determined by what we today call the laws of physics. They named the universe *cosmos*, meaning an orderly arrangement that is beautiful. The order of the cosmos encompassed not only the motions of stars and planets but also the weather, the growth of plants and animals, human health, and so on. Because the universe was ordered, it could be understood; because it could be understood, its events could be explained by thought and research. Early Greek philosophers therefore looked for the first or universal cause of things, a problem that scientists still pursue. The philosophers who taught these ideas about the cosmos believed they needed to give reasons for their conclusions and to persuade others by arguments based on evidence. That is, they used logic. This mode of thought, called **rationalism**, was a crucial first step toward science and philosophy as these disciplines endure today. This rule-based explanation of the causes of things developed by these philosophers contrasted sharply with the traditional mythological explanation that the gods controlled the universe. Naturally, many people had difficulty accepting such a

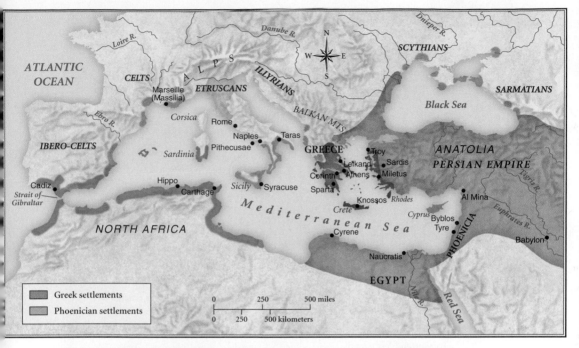

■ **MAPPING THE WEST** Mediterranean Civilizations, c. 500 B.C.E.

At the end of the sixth century B.C.E., the Persian Empire was far and away the most powerful civilization touching the Mediterranean. Its vast territory and riches gave it resources that no Phoenician or Greek city could match. The Phoenicians dominated economically in the western Mediterranean, while the Greek city-states in Sicily and southern Italy rivaled the power of those in the heartland. In Italy, the Etruscans were the most powerful civilization; the Romans were still a small community struggling to replace monarchy with a republic.

startling change in their understanding of the world, and the older tradition explaining events as the work of gods lived on alongside the new idea.

The idea that people must give reasons to explain their beliefs, rather than just make assertions that others must believe without evidence, was the Ionian philosophers' most important achievement. This insistence on logic, coupled with the belief that the world could be understood through logic, gave people hope that they could improve their lives through their own efforts. As Xenophanes from Colophon (c. 580–480 B.C.E.) put it, "The gods have not revealed all things from the beginning to mortals, but, by seeking, human beings find out, in time, what is better." This saying well expressed the value Archaic Age Greek philosophers attached to intellectual freedom, a new idea corresponding to the value given to the new idea of a citizen's freedom and legal equality in the city-state, however imperfect it may have been in reality.

■ **REVIEW:** *How did the Greeks recover from their Dark Age?*

IMPORTANT DATES

c. 10,000– 8000 B.C.E.	The "Neolithic Revolution" (the development of agriculture and domestication of animals)	c. 1400 B.C.E.	Mycenaeans take over Minoan Crete
c. 4000– 1000 B.C.E.	Bronze Age in southwestern Asia, Egypt, and Europe	c. 1200– 1000 B.C.E.	The Sea Peoples period
		c. 1000– 750 B.C.E.	Greece's Dark Age
c. 4000– 3000 B.C.E.	First cities established and writing developed in Mesopotamia	c. 950 B.C.E.	Earliest Hebrew scripture composed
2500s B.C.E.	The Great Pyramid is built in Egypt	c. 900 B.C.E.	Neo-Assyrians create an empire
		776 B.C.E.	Traditional date of first Olympic Games in Greece
c. 2350 B.C.E.	Sargon establishes the first empire in Akkadia in Mesopotamia	775–500 B.C.E	Greeks establish many new settlements around the Mediterranean
c. 2200 B.C.E.	Earliest Minoan palaces on Crete	c. 750 B.C.E.	Greeks begin to create city-states
c. 1792– 1750 B.C.E.	Reign of Hammurabi, king of Babylon, in Mesopotamia	559 B.C.E.	Cyrus founds the Persian Empire
c. 1750 B.C.E.	Beginning of Hittite kingdom in Anatolia	508 B.C.E.	Cleisthenes strengthens Athenian democracy

Conclusion

Fundamental characteristics of Western civilization slowly emerged as human life changed in the lengthy period from the Stone Age to 1000 B.C.E. The Neolithic Revolution turned many people into farmers living in settled communities; from these, the first cities arose in Mesopotamia by 4000 to 3000 B.C.E. International trade and wars of conquest generated cultural interaction. The development of metallurgy, large-scale architecture, mathematics, and the alphabet in the eastern Mediterranean region during the Bronze Age deeply influenced later ages.

After the devastation wrought by the Sea Peoples (1200–1000 B.C.E.), the traditional political pattern of empire under a strong central authority revived in the Near East. The Neo-Assyrians, then the Neo-Babylonians, and then the Persians succeeded one another as rulers of enormous empires. The moral dualism of Persian Zoroastrianism influenced later religions, most importantly Hebrew monotheism, whose expression in the Torah created the first religion based on scripture.

The destruction of the Mycenaean palaces about 1000 B.C.E. opened the way to remaking Greek civilization after the Dark Age. Recovering from economic and population decline, Greeks in the Archaic Age invented the polis (city-state) as a new form of social and political organization based on the notions of citizenship and equal protection of the laws as essential components of justice. The Greek city-state treasured the notion of personal freedom for men, but only in limited ways for women and not at all for slaves. Equally revolutionary were new ways of thought. By arguing that the universe was based on laws of nature that humans could discover through reason and research, Greek philosophers established rationalism as the basis for science and philosophy.

In this way, ideals with a lasting significance for Western civilization began to emerge in Greece. But the Greek world and its new values would soon face a grave threat from the awesome empire of Persia.

■ MAKING CONNECTIONS

1. *How did the Greek city-state differ from the political and social organizations of earlier civilizations?*

2. *How were the ideas of Ionian philosophers different from mythic traditions?*

■ FOR FURTHER EXPLORATION

For further reading and online research ideas, see the Suggested References on page SR-1 at the back of the book.

For practice quizzes, a customized study plan, and other study tools, see the ONLINE STUDY GUIDE at **bedfordstmartins.com/huntconcise**.

For primary-source material from this period, see Chapter 1 in *Sources of THE MAKING OF THE WEST: A CONCISE HISTORY*, Second Edition.

The Greek Golden Age

c. 500–400 B.C.E.

FAILED DIPLOMACY IGNITED THE GREATEST DANGER ever to threaten ancient Greece. In 507 B.C.E., the Athenians, fearing a Spartan invasion, sent ambassadors to the Persian king, Darius I (r. 522–486 B.C.E.), to request a protective alliance. The Persian Empire was then the greatest power in the ancient world. The diplomats met with one of the king's governors at Sardis, the Persian regional headquarters in western Anatolia (modern Turkey). After the royal administrator heard their plea, he reportedly replied, "But who in the world are you and where do you live?"

This incident reveals the background to the wars that would dominate the military and political history of mainland Greece during the fifth century B.C.E. First, the two major powers of mainland Greece—Athens and Sparta—distrusted each other. Second, the Persian kingdom had taken over Ionia (today western Turkey), including the Greek city-states there. Yet neither the Persians nor the mainland Greeks knew much about each other. Their mutual ignorance sparked a bloody conflict.

Although the fifth century B.C.E. saw almost continuous warfare, first between Greeks and Persians and then between Greek city-states themselves, it was also the period of Greece's most enduring cultural and artistic achievements. Athenian accomplishments in the fifth century B.C.E. had such a lasting impact that historians call this period a Golden Age. This Golden Age opens the Classical Age of Greek

■ **A Greek Warrior Leaves Home for Battle**

This vase, made about 450 B.C.E. to hold wine, shows a well-armed Greek infantryman (hoplite) leaving for battle. The vase painter portrayed the warrior in full armor to make the scene more dramatic; in real life, a slave would have carried the nearly seventy pounds of metal armor to the battlefield, where the soldier would put it on at the last minute. The warrior holds a thrusting spear, his main battle weapon, but also wears a sword for close-in fighting. The man on the left is probably the warrior's father, his age indicated by his cane. The woman is probably his wife, who is ready both to pour a libation to the gods for her husband's safety and give him a last drink before he leaves home on his dangerous mission. (© Copyright The Trustees of The British Museum.)

history, a modern title that covers the period from about 500 B.C.E. to the death of Alexander the Great in 323 B.C.E.

Despite the pressures of war, Athenians in the Golden Age created Greece's leading state, developing a "radical" democracy at home while establishing an empire abroad. They generated enormous prosperity and artistic and cultural accomplishments that dazzled the Greek world. More than any other city-state, Golden Age Athens was home to innovations in drama, art, architecture, and thought that have deeply influenced Western civilization. Some of these changes angered Greeks at the time, however, because they conflicted with ancient traditions, especially people's religious fear that abandoning their ancestors' beliefs and practices would offend the gods and bring disaster.

The Peloponnesian War, a bitter struggle between Athens and Sparta that dragged on from 431 to 404 B.C.E., ended the Golden Age in the closing decades of the fifth century B.C.E. This period of cultural blossoming therefore both began and finished with destructive wars, with Greeks standing together in the first one and tearing each other apart in the concluding one.

The Persian Wars, 499–479 B.C.E.

The most famous series of wars in ancient Greek history had its roots in the Athenian-Persian meeting at Sardis in 507 B.C.E. There the Athenian ambassadors accepted the customary Persian terms for an alliance: admitting Persian superiority by presenting symbolic tokens of earth and water to the king's representative. Although the Athenian assembly expressed outrage when they learned that their diplomats had submitted to a foreign power, they never informed King Darius that they were rejecting the alliance. He therefore continued to believe that Athens remained an obedient ally. This misunderstanding started a chain of events that led to two Persian invasions of Greece, the so-called Persian Wars.

The Persian kingdom surpassed Greece in every category of material resources, from precious metals to soldiers. The clash between Persia and Greece pitted the equivalent of an elephant against a pack of undersized dogs. Greek victory in such a mismatch seemed unthinkable. Making the situation gloomier was the habit of the Greek city-states of quarreling with one another. Their usual lack of unity made it seem unlikely that they could work together to fight the Persians.

The Ionian Revolt and the Battle of Marathon, 499–490 B.C.E.

War broke out in 499 B.C.E., when the Ionian Greek city-states rebelled against their Persian-installed tyrants. Athenian troops sent to aid the rebels burned Sardis, but a Persian counterattack sent them fleeing and crushed the revolt by 494 B.C.E. (Map 2.1).

Greek states allied against Persia

Persian Empire

States capitulating to Persia
or remaining neutral

Areas of Ionian revolt, 499–494 B.C.E.

Route of Ionian Greek city-states'
rebel army in 498 B.C.E.

Route of expedition sent
by Darius in 490 B.C.E.

Route of Xerxes' army in 480 B.C.E.

Route of Xerxes' navy in 480 B.C.E.

Battle

■ **MAP 2.1 The Persian Wars, 499–479 B.C.E.**

*The Persian Wars originated in the failed revolt (499–494 B.C.E.) of the Greek city-states in Ionia
against Persian control. To punish the Greeks, the Persian king Darius (r. 522–486 B.C.E.) first sent
an expedition by sea whose infantry the Athenians defeated on the Marathon plain in 490 B.C.E.
Darius's son Xerxes (r. 486–465 B.C.E.) then led a mammoth invasion of Greece, starting from
Sardis in Ionia. The Persians' unexpected defeats at sea at Salamis (480 B.C.E.) and on land at
Plataea and Mycale (479 B.C.E.) ended the Persians' attempt to extend their empire into Europe.
Compare the relative sizes of Greece and the Persian Empire to get an idea of how bold an idea it
was for Greeks to attack Persians in Asia.*

King Darius erupted when he learned that the Athenians had aided the Ionian revolt: not only had they dared attack his kingdom, but they had done it after, as far as he knew, pledging loyalty to him. To remind himself to punish this betrayal, Darius ordered a slave to say to him three times at every meal, "Sire, remember the Athenians." In 490 B.C.E., he launched a fleet with orders to punish them by installing their exiled tyrant, Hippias, as his puppet ruler, who would force the Athenians to pay heavy taxes and obey the king's orders.

The Persians expected Athens to surrender without a fight. The Athenians, however, met the fearsome invaders at Marathon, on the northeastern coast of Athenian territory. The Athenian soldiers, who had never before seen Persians, grew nervous just seeing their strange (to Greek eyes) outfits—pants instead of the short tunics and bare legs that Greeks regarded as manly dress. The Athenian generals never let their men lose heart. Planning their tactics to shorten the time their men would be exposed to Persian arrows, the commanders sent their hoplites against the enemy at a dead run. The Greeks dashed across the Marathon plain in their clanking metal armor (seventy pounds per man) under a hail of missiles to engage the Persians in hand-to-hand combat. The hoplites' heavier weapons gave them the edge. After a furious struggle, they drove their opponents backward into a swamp; the Persians who failed to splash their way to their ships were slaughtered.

The Athenian army then hurried the twenty-six miles from Marathon to Athens to guard the city against a Persian naval attack. (Today's marathons recall the legendary run of a messenger who raced ahead to announce the victory, after which he dropped dead from the exertion.) The Persians then sailed home, leaving the Athenians to rejoice in disbelief at their victory. For decades thereafter, the greatest honor a family could claim was that one of its men had once been a "Marathon fighter."

The symbolic importance of the battle of Marathon far outweighed its military significance. His expedition's defeat enraged Darius because it injured his prestige, not because it threatened his kingdom's security. The Athenians' success demonstrated the depth of their commitment to preserve their freedom. The unexpected victory at Marathon boosted Athenian self-confidence, and the city-state's citizens ever after boasted that they had withstood the feared Persians on their own, without Sparta's help.

Xerxes' Invasion of 480–479 B.C.E.

The Marathon victory encouraged Greeks to resist the gigantic Persian invasion of Greece that Darius's son and successor, Xerxes (r. 486–465 B.C.E.) led in 480 B.C.E. So immense was Xerxes' army, the Greeks claimed, that it took seven days and seven nights of continuous marching to cross a pontoon bridge over the Hellespont strait, the narrow passage of sea between Anatolia and mainland Greece. Xerxes expected the Greek city-states to surrender immediately once they learned the size of his forces.

Some did, but thirty-one city-states united to fight the Persians. This alliance, known as the Hellenic League, accomplished the incredible: protecting their

■ **Greek against Persian in Hand-to-Hand Combat (detail)**

This red-figure painting appears on the inside a Greek wine cup. Painted during the Persian Wars (about 480 B.C.E.), it shows a hoplite about to kill a Persian warrior at the ultimate moment in battle— hand-to-hand combat with swords. The Greek has lost his principal weapon, a spear, and the Persian can no longer shoot his weapon, the bow and arrow. The scene expresses multiple messages: the realistic rendering of the Persian's colorful outfit with sleeves and pants stresses the "otherness" of the enemy in Greek eyes; representing the fighters with bare feet is an artistic convention to make the scene more heroic; and their serene expressions at a moment of extreme stress dignify the horror of killing in war. (© The Trustees of the National Museums of Scotland.)

independence from the world's strongest power. They succeeded without the aid of the city-states in Italy and Sicily, such as Syracuse, the powerful ruler of a regional empire. Those western Greeks refused to join the league because they were occupied fighting Carthage, a Phoenician settlement in North Africa that was aggressively trying to monopolize commerce in the west.

The united Greeks chose Sparta as their leader because of its famous hoplite army. The Spartans demonstrated their courage when three hundred of their men held off Xerxes' huge army for several days at the narrow pass called Thermopylae ("warm gates") in central Greece. A hoplite summed up the Spartans' bravery with his response to a remark that the Persian archers were so numerous that their arrows darkened the sky in battle. "That's good news," said the Spartan warrior. "We'll fight in the shade." They all died fighting.

When the Persians marched south, the Athenians evacuated their city instead of surrendering. They believed their city-state and its freedom would survive so long as its people survived, regardless of what happened to their property. The Persians promptly burned the empty city. In the summer of 480 B.C.E., Themistocles of Athens tricked the other, less aggressive Greek leaders into facing the larger Persian navy in a sea battle in the narrow channel between the island of Salamis and the west coast of Athenian territory. The narrowness of the channel prevented the Persians from using all their ships at once and let the heavier Greek ships win victory by ramming the flimsier Persian vessels. When Xerxes observed that his most aggressive naval commander appeared to be the one woman among his admirals, Artemisia, ruler of

Caria (the southwest corner of Anatolia), he shouted, "My men have become women, and my women, men." In 479 B.C.E., the Greek infantry headed by the Spartans defeated the remaining Persian land forces at Plataea (see Map 2.1).

The Greeks' superior weapons and clever use of Greece's geography to overcome the Persians' greater numbers help explain their military victories. But most remarkable is the decision of the thirty-one Greek city-states to unite in a coalition. They could easily have agreed to become Persian subjects to save themselves; for most of them, Persian rule would have imposed little interference in their internal affairs. Instead, they chose to fight for absolute independence against seemingly overwhelming odds. Because the Greek forces included not only the social elite and hoplites but also thousands of poorer men who rowed the warships, the effort against the Persians cut across social and economic divisions. The Hellenic League's decision to fight the Persian Wars demonstrated both courage and a commitment to the ideal of political freedom that had emerged in the Archaic Age.

■ **REVIEW:** *How did differences in Persian and Greek political and military organization determine the course of the Persian Wars?*

Athenian Confidence in the Golden Age, 479–431 B.C.E.

Victory ruptured the alliance that the Persian threat had forged between Sparta and Athens. Out of this fractured partnership arose the so-called Athenian Empire, a modern label to describe the Athenians' new vision of grander international power that emerged following the Persian Wars. The growth of Athens's power internationally went hand in hand with more democracy and vast spending on public buildings, art, and festivals.

The Establishment of the Athenian Empire, 479–c. 460 B.C.E.

After the Persian Wars, Sparta and Athens both built up their own alliances to strengthen their positions against each other. Relying on long-standing treaties with city-states located mainly in the Peloponnese, Sparta headed forces stronger in infantry than in warships, with the notable exception of Corinth, a naval power. The Spartan allies, called the Peloponnesian League, met in a representative assembly, but no action could be taken unless the Spartan leaders approved.

By 477 B.C.E., under the leadership of the Athenian upper-class leader Aristides (c. 525–465 B.C.E.), Athens allied with city-states exposed to possible Persian retaliation— in northern Greece, on the islands of the Aegean Sea, and along the western coast of Anatolia. Most Athenian allies had strong navies, and all solemnly swore never to desert the coalition. This alliance, called the **Delian League** because its treasury was original-ly located on the island of Delos, also had an assembly. Supposedly, every ally had an equal say in making decisions, but in practice Athens was in charge.

The Delian and Peloponnesian Leagues

The special arrangements for financing the alliance's naval operations allowed the Athenians to dominate. Each ally paid annual "dues" based on its size and prosperity. Because they were required, these dues were actually "tribute." Larger member states supplied entire triremes (warships) complete with crews and their pay (Figure 2.1); smaller states could share the cost of a ship and crew or contribute cash instead.

Over time, more and more members paid cash. It proved beyond their capaci-ties to build warships and to train crews (170 rowers each); the recent reconstruction of a full-size trireme has shown how difficult it was to build one and train an effective crew. Athens, far larger than most league members, possessed the necessary shipyards as well as many men eager to earn pay as rowers. Many oarsmen came from Athens's poor, and they earned not only money but also political influence in Athenian democracy, as naval strength became the city-state's principal source of military power. Without them, Athens had no navy.

The decision of many Delian League allies to let Athens supply warships eventual-ly left them without any navies of their own. Therefore, they had no power if they disagreed with Athens's policy. The Athenian assembly could simply order its fleet to compel discontented allies to comply and continue paying their tribute. As the Athenian historian Thucydides observed, rebellious allies "lost their independence," and the Athenians became "no longer as popular as they used to be." This unpopular-ity was the price Athenians paid for making themselves the leading naval power in the eastern Mediterranean. They insisted that their dominance of the Delian League was justified because it kept the alliance strong enough to protect Greece from the Persians.

By about 460 B.C.E., their fleet had expelled almost all the Persian garrisons that had held out along the northeastern Aegean coast. The alliance drove the enemy fleet from the Aegean Sea, quashing any Persian threat to Greece for the next fifty years. Athens meanwhile grew rich off spoils captured from Persian outposts and the league's tribute.

The Athenian assembly decided how to spend this revenue. Rich and poor alike had a stake in keeping the fleet active and the league members paying for it. The poor men who rowed the ships came to depend on the pay they earned on league expedi-tions. Members of the social elite enhanced their social status by commanding cam-paigns and spending their portion of the plunder on public festivals and buildings.

■ FIGURE 2.1 Triremes, the Foremost Classical Greek Warships

Innovations in military technology and training fueled a naval arms race in the fifth century B.C.E., when Greek shipbuilders devised larger and faster ramming ships called triremes. The boats were powered by 170 rowers seated in three rows, one above each other as shown in the illustration of the rowers from behind (top). These ships' radical new design with triple banks of oars made them expensive to build and required extensive crew training. Only wealthy and populous city-states such as Athens could afford to maintain large fleets of triremes. No ancient trireme survives to show exactly how such a warship was built, but this relief sculpture (bottom) found on the Athenian acropolis and dating from about 400 B.C.E. gives a glimpse of what a trireme looked like from the side when being rowed into battle. Sails were used to power the ship only when not in combat.
(The Art Archive/Acropolis Museum Athens/Dagli Orti.)

Wealthy Athenians were expected to make financial contributions for public works and festivals to win popular support. They did not form political parties but gathered informal circles of friends and followers to support their agendas. Arguments about policy tended to revolve around how Athens should exercise its growing power internationally, not whether it was right to treat allies as subjects.

Radical Democracy and Pericles' Leadership, 461–445 B.C.E.

As the Delian League grew, the poorer men who powered the Athenian fleet came to recognize that they provided a cornerstone of Athenian security and prosperity. They felt the time had come to increase their political power by making the judicial system of Athens just as democratic as the process of passing laws in the assembly, which was open to all male citizens over eighteen years of age. The leaders of this initiative were members of the elite, who competed for popular support to win elective office. One of Athens's most socially prominent citizens, Pericles (c. 495–429 B.C.E.), became the leading Golden Age politician by supporting the masses' desire for greater democracy.

Golden Age Athenian democracy gradually became so sweeping, compared with most ancient governments, that today it is called **radical democracy**. Its principles were clear: direct and widespread participation by male citizens in the assembly to make laws and policy by majority rule; random selection and rotation for members of the Council of 500 (which prepared the agenda for the assembly), most magistrates, and jurors; elaborate precautions to prevent corruption; and equal protection under the law for citizens regardless of wealth. At the same time, excellence was recognized by making the top public offices—the board of ten "generals," who managed the city-state's military and financial affairs—elective annually and without limits on how many terms a man could serve.

Reforming the judicial system was essential to radical democracy. Ever since Cleisthenes' reforms at the end of the sixth century B.C.E, most judicial verdicts had been rendered by archons (magistrates) and the Areopagus Council of exarchons (separate from the Council of 500). Although archons were now chosen annually by lottery to make their selection democratic, they and the Areopagus members were still susceptible to bribery and pressure from the social elite. Since even democratically enacted laws meant little if applied unfairly, the masses demanded reforms to halt corruption in trials.

The opportunity for change arose in 461 B.C.E., when a prominent member of the elite, Ephialtes, sought the people's political support by sponsoring a reformed court system. Ephialtes' reforms made it nearly impossible to bribe or pressure jurors. They were selected by lottery from male citizens over thirty years old, the selection was made only on the day of the trial, all trials were concluded in one day, and juries were large (from several hundred to several thousand). No judges presided; only one official was present—to stop fistfights. Jurors voted after hearing speeches from the accuser and the accused, who had to speak for themselves although they might pay someone else to compose their speeches and ask others to speak in support. A majority vote of the jurors ruled, and no appeals were allowed.

Majority rule was the operative principle for enforcing accountability in Athenian radical democracy. Any citizen could call for a trial to judge an official's conduct in office, but the most striking example of this principle was the procedure called **ostracism** (from *ostracon*, meaning a "piece of broken pottery," the material used for casting ballots). Once a year, all male citizens could scratch on a ballot the name of one man they thought should be ostracized (exiled for ten years). If at least six thousand ballots were cast, the man who received the most "votes" was expelled from Athenian territory. He suffered no other penalty, and his family and property remained behind undisturbed. Ostracism was not a criminal penalty, and ostracized men recovered their citizen rights after their exile.

This process was meant to protect radical democracy; a man therefore could be ostracized if the majority perceived his prominence as a threat to their interests. An anecdote about the politician Aristides illustrates this possibility. He was nicknamed "the Just" because he had proved himself so fair-minded in setting the dues for Delian League members. On the day of the balloting, an illiterate farmer handed Aristides a pottery fragment and asked him to scratch the name of the man's choice for ostracism on it.

> *"Certainly," said Aristides. "Which name shall I write?"*
> *"Aristides," replied the countryman.*
> *"Very well," remarked Aristides as he proceeded to inscribe his own name.*
> *"But tell me, why do you want to ostracize Aristides? What has he done to you?"*
> *"Oh, nothing. I don't even know him," sputtered the man. "I just can't stand hearing everybody refer to him as 'the Just.'"*

True or not, this tale demonstrates that Athenians assumed that the right way to protect democracy was always to trust the majority vote of freeborn, adult male citizens, without any restrictions on a man's ability to decide what he thought was best for democracy. It also shows that men seeking political success in Athenian democracy had to be ready to pay the price that jealousy or spite could exact.

Like his distant relative Cleisthenes before him, Pericles became the most influential Athenian politician of his era by devising innovations to strengthen the egalitarian tendencies of Athenian democracy. The Golden Age's most spellbinding public speaker, Pericles repeatedly persuaded the assembly to pass laws increasing its political power. In return, he gained such popularity that he was regularly elected as a general.

Pericles' most important democratic innovation was pay for service in public jobs filled by lottery. This allowed poorer men to leave their regular work to serve in government. Early in the 450s B.C.E., he convinced the assembly to use state revenues to pay a daily stipend to men who served in the Council of 500, on juries, and in numerous other posts. The amount was approximately what an unskilled worker could earn in a day. The generals received no pay because the prestige of their position was considered its own reward.

In 451 B.C.E., Pericles strengthened citizen identity, which even the poor possessed under democracy, by sponsoring a law making citizenship more exclusive and enhancing the status of Athenian mothers. This law mandated that citizenship would be given only to children whose mother and father were both Athenian by birth. Thereafter, men avoided seeking wives outside the citizen body.

Finally, Pericles supported the interests of poorer men by recommending frequent naval campaigns against Spartan and Corinthian interests in Greece and against Persian control of Cyprus, Egypt, and the eastern Mediterranean. The assembly's confidence reached such a fever pitch that they voted to carry on as many as three different major expeditions simultaneously. The Athenians' ambitions at last exceeded their resources, however, and by 450 B.C.E., they had to pull back from the eastern Mediterranean and stop fighting against the Peloponnesian League. In the winter of 446–445 B.C.E., Pericles engineered a peace treaty with Sparta designed to freeze the balance of power in Greece for thirty years and thus preserve Athenian control of the Delian League. Pericles dropped his aggressive foreign policy because he realized that preserving radical democracy at home depended on Athens not losing its power over its allies.

The Urban Landscape of Golden Age Athens

The Delian League's fleet protected seaborne trade, and Athens became a flourishing commercial center for traders, merchants, and crafts producers from around the Mediterranean world. The city's new riches flowed mainly into public building projects, art, and festivals rather than private luxury. People's homes in the city and the countryside remained modest. Farmhouses usually clustered in villages, while homes in the city wedged tightly against one another along narrow, winding streets. Houses grouped bedrooms, storerooms, and dining rooms around small, open-air courtyards. People only rarely decorated their rooms with paintings or art, and their furniture was kept to a minimum. Toilets usually consisted of a pit dug outside the front door, which was emptied by collectors paid to dump the excrement outside the city at a distance set by law. Poorer people rented small apartments.

Generals who became rich plundering Persian outposts in the eastern Mediterranean used this wealth to beautify the city, not to build themselves mansions. They paid for public landscaping that included shade trees, running tracks for exercise, and gathering places such as the colorful Painted Stoa. A stoa was a narrow building open along one side whose purpose was to provide shelter from sun or rain. One successful general's family built the Painted Stoa in the heart of the city, on the edge of the central market square, the **agora**. The crowds who came to the agora daily to shop and chat about politics would cluster inside this shelter. There they could gaze at its bright paintings, which depicted the glorious exploits of the general's family and thus publicized its dedication to the city-state. Wealthy citizens also paid for other major public expenses, such as equipment for warships and entertainment at city festivals. This custom was essential because Athens, like most Greek city-states, had no regular direct taxes on income or property.

Huge buildings paid for by public funds were the most prominent new architecture in Golden Age Athens. In 447 B.C.E., Pericles persuaded the assembly to fund

■ **MAP 2.2 Fifth-Century B.C.E. Athens**
The urban center of Athens with the agora and acropolis at its heart measured about one square mile, surrounded by a stone wall with a perimeter of some four miles. Fifteen large gates flanked by towers and various smaller doors allowed traffic in and out of the city; much of the Athenian population lived in the many villages (demes) of the surrounding countryside. Most of the city's water supply came from wells and springs inside the walls, but, unusually for a Greek city, Athens also had water piped in from outside. The Long Walls provided a protected corridor connecting the city to its harbor at Piraeus, where the Athenian navy was anchored and grain was imported to feed the people.

the city's greatest building project ever, on the rocky hill at the center of the city called the *acropolis* (Map 2.2). The project's centerpieces were a mammoth gate building with columns straddling the western entrance of the acropolis and a new temple of Athena housing a huge statue of the goddess. Comparing the value of a day's wage then and now, we can calculate that these buildings easily cost more than the modern equivalent of a billion dollars, a phenomenal sum for a Greek city-state. Pericles' political rivals denounced him for squandering public funds. Scholars disagree about whether the assembly spent Delian League dues to help finance the program; it is certain that substantial funds were taken from sales taxes, harbor taxes, and the financial reserves of the sanctuaries of the goddess Athena, which derived from private donations and public support.

The vast new temple built for Athena—the Parthenon ("the house of the virgin goddess")—became Greece's most famous building. As the patron goddess of Athens, Athena had long had another sanctuary on the acropolis. Its focus was an olive tree regarded as the goddess's sacred symbol as protector of the city-state's economic health. The Parthenon honored her in a different capacity: as the divine

■ **The Acropolis of Athens**

Like most Greek city-states, Athens grew up around a prominent hill (acropolis) whose summit served as a special sanctuary for the gods and as a fortress to which the population could retreat when an enemy attacked. The invading Persians burned the buildings on the Athenian acropolis in 480 B.C.E. The Athenians left the charred remains in place for thirty years to remind themselves of the sacrifice they had made for their freedom. In the 440s B.C.E., they began erecting the magnificent temples and other public buildings that have made the city famous for its monumental marble architecture. (© AKG-Images, London/John Hios.)

champion of Athenian military power. Inside the temple stood a gold and ivory statue nearly forty feet high depicting the goddess in battle armor, holding in her outstretched hand a six-foot statue of Victory (*Nike* in Greek).

Like all Greek temples, the Parthenon was built to be a house for its divinity, not as a gathering place for worshipers. Its design followed standard temple architecture: a rectangular box on a raised platform, a plan the Greeks probably derived from Egyptian temples. Columns on a raised porch surrounded the box on all sides. The Parthenon's columns were carved in the simple style called Doric, in contrast to the more elaborate Ionic and Corinthian styles, often imitated in modern buildings (see Figure 2.2 on page 64). Only priests and priestesses could enter the temple usually; public religious ceremonies took place out front.

DORIC   IONIC   CORINTHIAN

■ **FIGURE 2.2 Styles of Greek Capitals**
The Greeks decorated the capitals, or tops, of columns in these three styles to fit the different architectural "canons" (their word for precise mathematical systems of proportions) that they devised for designing buildings. The "pillow" atop Doric columns evolved into the Ionic style sporting "ears" (volutes). Corinthian capitals with their elaborately carved leaves were a later outgrowth of Ionic. These styles were widely imitated in later times, as on many U.S. state capitols and the U.S. Supreme Court Building in Washington, D.C.

The Parthenon proclaimed the self-confidence of Golden Age Athens. Constructed from twenty thousand tons of Attic marble, it stretched nearly 230 feet in length and 100 feet wide, with eight columns across the ends instead of the six normally found in Doric style and seventeen instead of thirteen along the sides. Its massive size conveyed an impression of power. The temple's sophisticated architecture demonstrated Athenian ability to construct order that was both apparent and real: because perfectly rectangular shapes in large-scale architecture appear curved to the human eye, subtle curves and inclines were built into the Parthenon to produce an illusion of completely straight lines and emphasize its massiveness.

The elaborate sculptural frieze of the Parthenon announced the temple's most innovative and confident message: Athens's citizens possessed the special goodwill of the gods. The frieze, a continuous band of figures, was carved in relief around the top of the walls inside the porch that ran along all four sides of the building. This sort of decoration usually appeared only on Ionic-style buildings. Adding it to a Doric-style temple was a striking departure meant to attract attention. The Parthenon's frieze portrayed Athenian men, women, and children in a parade in the presence of the gods. Depicting the procession in motion, like a filmstrip in stone, the frieze included youths riding spirited horses and women carrying sacred implements. As usual on Greek temples, brightly colored paint and shiny metal attachments enlivened the figures of people and animals.

No other city-state had ever gone beyond the traditional function of temples— glorifying and honoring the community's protector gods—by adorning a temple with representations of its citizens. The Parthenon frieze made a unique statement about how Athenians perceived their relationship to the gods. A temple adorned with pictures of citizens being viewed by the gods amounted to a claim of special closeness between the city-state and the gods. This assertion reflected the Athenians' interpretation of their success in helping turn back the Persians, in achieving leadership of a powerful naval alliance, and in amassing wealth that made Athens richer than all its neighbors in mainland Greece. Their success, the Athenians believed, proved that the gods were on their side.

Like the Parthenon frieze, the changes that Golden Age artists made in freestanding sculpture broke with tradition. Archaic male statues had only one pose: arms pressed to their sides and left leg striding forward, imitating the unchanging posture of Egyptian statuary. This style gave them an appearance of stability; even a hard shove seemed unlikely to budge them. By the time of the Persian Wars, Greek sculptors began to express motion in their art. Male statues could have bent arms and the body's weight on either leg. Female statues, too, had more relaxed poses and clothing that hung in a way that hinted at the shape of the curves underneath. The faces of Golden Age sculptures were self-confidently calm rather than smiling like Archaic Age figures. This spirited new style suggested the confident energy of the times but also hinted at the possibility of instability: Golden Age sculptors took more chances with the balance of their statues.

Statues were meant to be displayed in public to broadcast a message, regardless of whether private individuals or the city-state paid for them. Art was not yet used to decorate homes. Instead, wealthy families would pay for statues of gods to be housed in a sanctuary as symbols of devotion. They also placed statues of their deceased members above their graves as memorials of their virtue, especially if they had died young in war or in childbirth.

■ **REVIEW:** *What factors prompted political change in fifth-century B.C.E. Athens?*

Tradition and Innovation in Athens's Golden Age

Fifth-century B.C.E. Athens generated unprecedented accomplishments in architecture, art, drama, and ways of thought, but many central aspects of its social and religious life remained unchanged. Conflicts between innovation and tradition created social tensions, especially concerning religion. Women's roles in public life did not change, and they continued to make essential contributions by managing the household, participating in religious ceremonies, and, if they were poor, working in commerce and agriculture to help support their families. The greatest tension arose from the startling ideas of teachers called **sophists** and the ethical views of the philosopher Socrates. The most visible reflection of the tension was the growing popularity of state-funded theater: plays—both tragedies and comedies—whose plots explored problems in city-state life.

Religious Tradition in a Period of Change

Greeks maintained their polytheistic religious traditions with sacrifices and public festivals and by seeking a personal relationship with the gods in the rituals of hero cults and **mystery cults**. City-states were officially religious communities: each honored a particular god or goddess, such as Athena at Athens, as its protector and patron, while also worshiping many other deities. The twelve most important gods were envisioned assembling for banquets atop Mount Olympus, the highest peak in mainland Greece. Zeus headed this immortal pantheon; joining him were Hera, his wife; Aphrodite, goddess of love; Apollo, sun god; Ares, war god; Artemis, moon goddess; Athena, goddess of wisdom and war; Demeter, goddess of agriculture and fertility; Dionysus, god of pleasure, wine, and disorder; Hephaestus, god of fire and technology; Hermes, messenger god; and Poseidon, sea god.

Like the peoples of the ancient Near East, the Greeks believed that humans, as individuals and as communities, must honor the gods to thank them for blessings received and to receive blessings in return. This idea of reciprocity between gods and humans underlay the Greeks' understanding of the nature of the gods. Deities did not love humans, though in some mythological stories they took earthly lovers and produced half-divine children. Rather, they supported humans who paid them honor and did not anger them. Gods offended by humans could punish them by sending calamities such as famine, earthquake, epidemic disease, or defeat in war. The Greeks did not expect to achieve paradise on earth at some future time when evil forces would finally be vanquished forever.

Each god's cult—the set of prayers and rituals for worshiping a particular divinity—had its own practices, but sacrifice provided the focus. Sacrifices ranged from bloodless offerings—fruits, vegetables, and small cakes—to large animals roasted for eating. The speechwriter Lysias (c. 445–380 B.C.E.), a Syracusan who lived in Athens, explained the importance of state-sponsored sacrifices in a speech composed for an Athenian official: "Our ancestors handed down to us the most powerful and prosperous community in Greece by performing the prescribed sacrifices. It is therefore fitting for us to offer the same sacrifices they did, for the sake of the success that those rites have brought us." Sacrificing large animals, such as cattle and sheep, provided occasions for the community to assemble and reaffirm its ties to the divine world and for the worshippers, by sharing the roasted meat from the sacrifice, to benefit personally from their relationship with the gods. People who were not rich— the great majority of the population—particularly loved the feasting that followed a large-animal sacrifice because meat was too costly for them to buy regularly.

The bloody killing of the animal followed strict rules to prevent ritual contamination. The victim had to be an unblemished domestic animal, specially decorated with garlands and made to approach the altar as if willing to be sacrificed. The assembled crowd maintained strict silence to avoid possibly impure remarks. The official in charge of the sacrifice sprinkled water on the animal's head so it would shake its head and appear to consent to die. After washing his hands, the official scattered barley grains on the altar fire and on the animal's head and then cut a lock of the animal's hair and threw it on the fire. Following a prayer, he swiftly cut the animal's throat while musicians played flutelike pipes and female worshipers screamed, presumably to express the group's ritual sorrow at the victim's death. The carcass was then butchered, and some portions of it were thrown on the altar fire so that the aromatic smoke could waft its way upward to the cult's god. The rest of the meat was cooked for the worshipers to eat.

Public festivals featured not just sacrifices but also elaborate ceremonies, such as parades and musical performances. Athens boasted of having the most festivals, with nearly half the days of the year featuring one. Its biggest festival, the Panathenaia, honored Athena with sacrifices, parades, and contests with valuable prizes for music, dancing, poetry, and athletics. Some occasions were for women only, such as the three-day festival for married women in honor of Demeter.

Greek religion included many activities besides the civic cults of the twelve Olympian gods. People took a keen interest in religious actions meant to improve their personal relations with the divine. Families marked significant moments such as birth, marriage, and death with prayers, rituals, and sacrifices. They honored their ancestors with offerings made at their tombs, consulted seers about the meanings of dreams and omens, and sought out magicians for spells to improve their love lives or curses to harm their enemies.

Hero cults and mystery cults had special appeals. The former were rituals performed at the tomb of an extraordinarily famous man or woman. Local heroes' remains were thought to retain special power to reveal the future through oracles, to heal illnesses and injuries, and to provide protection in battle. The only hero to whom cults were established all over

■ Cup with Symbols to Avert Evil

Ancient Greeks had a healthy respect for the ability of nature and their fellow human beings to do them harm. Like prayer, magical symbols were thought to have power to ward off bad luck and other evils. Sometimes items from everyday life, such as this cup, were decorated with these symbols as a way of providing the object's owner with some hope of averting evil fortune both large and small. Here the god Dionysus is seated between two large eyes as sources of magical power. What objects do people use for similar purposes today?

(Kanellopoulos Museum © Archaeological Receipts Fund.)

the Greek world was the strongman Heracles (or Hercules, as his name was later spelled by the Romans). His superhuman feats gave him an appeal as a protector in many city-states.

The Athenian mystery cult of Demeter and her daughter Kore (also called Persephone), headquartered in the village of Eleusis, attracted men and women from all over the Mediterranean world because it offered the hope of protection in this life and the afterlife. The central rite of this cult was the Mysteries: a series of initiation ceremonies into the secret knowledge of the cult. The main initiation occurred during an annual festival lasting nearly two weeks, which built up to the revelation of Demeter's central secret, after a day of fasting. The most eloquent proof of how seriously people took these Mysteries is that no one ever revealed the secret throughout the thousand years during which the rites were celebrated; some hints reveal that it promised initiates a better life on earth and a happier fate in the afterlife.

Other mystery cults also emphasized protection for initiates in their current lives, whether against ghosts, illness, poverty, shipwrecks, or the countless other dangers of life. People received divine protection as a reward for appropriate worship, not for abstract faith. The ancient Greeks believed that the gods expected visible honors and rites, and their religion required action from worshipers. Greeks had to pray and sing hymns praising the gods, perform sacrifices, and undergo ritual purification. Preserving religious tradition mattered deeply to most people because it offered a safeguard against the precarious conditions of human life in a world in which early death from disease, accident, or war was commonplace.

Women, Slaves, and Metics in Traditional Society

The power and status of Athenian women came from their roles in the family and in religion. Upper-class women devoted their lives to running their households, meeting female friends, and participating in the city-state's religious cults. Poorer women helped support themselves and their families, often as small-scale merchants and crafts producers.

Women's exclusion from politics meant that men might overlook women's contributions to the city-state. In his play *Medea* of 431 B.C.E., the Athenian dramatist Euripides had his heroine insist that women who bear children are owed at least as much respect as are hoplites, a plausible claim given the high risks of childbirth under the medical conditions of antiquity:

> *People say that we women lead a safe life at home, while men have to go to war. What fools they are! I would much rather fight in the army three times than give birth to a child even once.*

Women, like men, could own property, including land (the most valued possession in Greek society), and they were supposed to preserve it to hand down to their

■ Vase Painting of a Woman Buying Shoes

Greek vases were frequently decorated with scenes from daily life instead of mythological stories. Here, a woman is being fitted for a pair of custom-made shoes by a craftsman and his apprentice. Her husband has accompanied her on the expedition and, to judge from his gesture, is participating in the discussion of the purchase. This vase was painted in so-called black-figure technique, in which the figures are rendered as black outlines, with their details incised into a background of red clay. Painters later reversed this technique on red-figure vases so that they could draw pictures with greater precision and elegance of line. **For more help analyzing this image,** see the visual activity for this chapter in the ONLINE STUDY GUIDE at bedfordstmartins.com/huntconcise.

(Museum of Fine Arts, Boston. Henry Lillie Pierce Fund. Photograph © 2007 Museum of Fine Arts, Boston [01.8035].)

children. A daughter's share in her father's estate usually came to her as her dowry (the money and property a woman brought to her marriage). Husband and wife co-owned the household's common property. The husband was legally responsible for preserving the dowry and using it for the support and comfort of his wife and any children she bore. Upon her death, her children inherited the dowry. In a divorce, the wife got her property back.

Athenian laws concerning heiresses reveal the society's goal of enabling males to establish and maintain households. If a father died leaving only a daughter, his property went to her, but she could not dispose of it as she pleased. Instead, the law required her father's closest male relative—her official guardian after her father's death—to marry her, with the aim of producing a son. This child inherited the property when he reached adulthood. This law applied regardless of whether the heiress was already married (without any sons) or whether the male relative already had a wife. The heiress and the male relative were both supposed to divorce their present spouses and marry each other (although in practice the rule could be circumvented by legal subterfuge) to preserve the father's line and keep the property in his family.

Athenian women from the urban propertied class were expected to avoid close contact with men who were not family members or good friends. They were supposed to spend much of their time in their own homes or the homes of women friends. Women dressed and slept in rooms set aside for them, which opened onto a walled courtyard where they could walk in the open air, talk, supervise the family's slaves, and interact with other members of the household and visitors, male and female. Here in her "territory" a woman would spin wool for clothing, converse with friends, play with her children, and give her opinions on various matters to the men of the house as they came and went. Poor women had little time for such activities because they, like their husbands, sons, and brothers, had to leave their homes, usually crowded rental apartments, to work. They often set up small stalls to sell bread, vegetables, simple clothing, or trinkets.

A woman with servants who answered the door herself would be reproached as careless of her reputation. A proper woman left her home only for an appropriate reason, but Athenian life offered many occasions for women to get out: religious festivals, funerals, childbirths at the houses of relatives and friends, and trips to workshops to buy shoes or other domestic articles. Sometimes her husband escorted her, but more often a woman was accompanied only by a servant and could act independently. Social tradition required men not to speak the names of respectable women in public conversations or in court speeches unless absolutely necessary.

Rich women maintained pale complexions because they stayed out of the sun. This paleness was much admired as a sign of an enviable life of leisure and wealth. Women regularly used powdered white lead to give themselves a suitably pallid look. Many upper-class women most likely viewed their limited contact with men outside the household as a badge of superior social status. In a gender-segregated society such as that of upper-class Athens, a woman's primary personal relationships were probably with her children and other women.

Men restricted women's freedom of movement partly to reduce uncertainty about the paternity of their children and to protect their daughters' virginity from seducers and rapists. Since citizenship guaranteed the city-state's political structure and a man's personal freedom, Greeks felt it crucial to ensure that a boy truly was his father's son and not the child of a foreigner or a slave. Women who bore legitimate children earned higher status and greater freedom in the family, as an Athenian man explained in this excerpt from a court case:

> When I decided to marry and had brought a wife home, at first my attitude towards her was this: I did not wish to annoy her, but neither was she to have too much of her own way. . . . I kept an eye on her as was proper. But later, after my child had been born, I came to trust her, and I handed all my possessions over to her, believing that this was the greatest possible proof of affection.

Bearing male children brought special honor to a woman because sons meant security for parents. Sons could appear in court in support of their parents in lawsuits and protect them in the streets of Athens, which for most of its history had no police force. By law, sons were required to support elderly parents. So intense was the pressure to produce sons that stories were common of women who smuggled in male babies born to slaves and passed them off as their own. Such tales, whose truth is hard to gauge, were credible because husbands customarily stayed away at childbirth.

A small number of Athenian women were able to ignore traditional restrictions because they gave up the usual expectations of marrying or were too rich to care what others thought. The most talked-about of the former group were called companions. Often foreigners, they were physically attractive, witty in conversation, and able to sing and play musical instruments. They often entertained at a **symposium** (a male dinner party without wives), and sometimes they sold sexual favors for a high price. Their independent lives set companions apart from citizen women, as did the freedom to control their own sexuality. Equally distinctive was their skill in conversing with men in public. Companions charmed men with their witty, joking conversation. Their characteristic skill at clever remarks and verbal jabs allowed companions a freedom of speech denied to "proper" women.

■ **Vase Painting of a Symposium**

Upper-class Greek men often spent their evenings at a symposium, a drinking party that always included much conversation and usually featured music and entertainers; wives were not included. The discussions could range widely, from literature to politics to philosophy. Here, a female musician, whose nudity shows she is a hired prostitute, entertains the guests, who recline on couches, as was customary. The man on the right is about to fling the dregs of his wine, playing a messy game called kottabos.

(Reproduction by permission of the Syndics of the Fitzwilliam Museum, Cambridge. Master and Fellows of Corpus Christi College, Cambridge, The Parker Library.)

Some companions lived precarious lives subject to exploitation and even violence at the hands of their male customers, but the most skillful could attract lovers from the highest levels of society and live in luxury on their own. The most famous companion was Aspasia from Miletus, who became Pericles' lover and bore him a son. She dazzled Athens's upper-class males with her brilliant conversation and confidence. Ironically, Pericles' own law of 451 B.C.E. restricting citizenship to children of two Athenian parents meant that their child was not a citizen.

Only the wealthiest citizen women could speak to men openly with the frankness of companions. One such was Elpinike, a member of a super-rich Athenian family of great military distinction. She once publicly criticized Pericles for having boasted about the Athenian conquest of a rebellious ally. When some other Athenian women praised Pericles for his success, Elpinike sarcastically remarked, "This really is wonderful, Pericles, . . . that you have caused the loss of many good citizens, not in battle against Phoenicians or Persians, like my brother Cimon, but in suppressing an allied city of fellow Greeks." Ancient sources confirm that ordinary women, too, remained engaged and interested in issues affecting the city-state as a whole. They often had strong opinions on politics and public policy, but they had to express their views privately to their husbands, children, and relatives.

In contrast to citizen women, slaves and **metics** (immigrants who were granted permanent residency in Athens in exchange for paying taxes and serving in the military) had no political influence because they were "outsiders" living inside Greek society. Individuals and the city-state alike owned slaves, who could be purchased from traders or bred in the household. Unwanted newborns abandoned by their parents (a practice called infant exposure) were often picked up by others and raised as slaves. Athens's commercial growth in this period increased the demand for slaves to provide manual labor. Although no reliable statistics survive, slaves probably made up 100,000 or more of the city-state's estimated 250,000 residents in Pericles' time. (This population made Athens an extraordinarily large city-state.) Slaves worked in homes, on farms, in crafts shops, and, if they were truly unfortunate, in the cramped and dangerous silver mines whose riches boosted Athens's prosperity. Unlike Sparta's helots, Athens's slaves never rebelled, probably because they originated from too many different places to be able to unite.

Golden Age Athens's wealth and cultural vitality attracted numerous metics who worked in Athens as traders, crafts producers, entertainers, and laborers. By the start of the Peloponnesian War in 431 B.C.E., these immigrants made up perhaps half the free population. Metics had to pay for the privilege of working in Athens through a special foreigners' tax and military service. Citizens valued metics' contributions to the city's prosperity but only rarely offered them citizenship.

Metics sometimes found themselves forced into making a living outside the mainstream, especially as prostitutes. Men, unlike women, were not penalized for sexual activity outside marriage. "Certainly you don't think men beget children out of sexual desire?" wrote the upper-class author Xenophon. "The streets and the brothels are swarming with ways to take care of that." Men could have sex with female or male slaves, who could not refuse their masters, or they could have sex with various classes of prostitutes, depending on how much money they wanted to spend.

Education and Intellectual Innovation

Education was privately funded in Golden Age Athens; public schools did not yet exist. Well-to-do families paid private tutors to teach their sons to read, write, and perhaps sing or play a musical instrument, and trainers to instruct them in athletics. Physical fitness was considered vital for men because it was thought to be disgraceful not to be in shape and because all male citizens and metics could be called up for military service from ages eighteen to sixty. Therefore, men exercised daily in public, open-air facilities paid for by wealthy families. Men frequently discussed politics and exchanged news at these gymnasia. The daughters of wealthy families usually learned to read, write, and do arithmetic; a woman with these skills would be better prepared to manage a household and help her future husband run their estate.

Poorer girls and boys learned a trade and perhaps a bit of reading and arithmetic by assisting their parents in their daily work; if they were fortunate, they would become apprentices learning from skilled crafts producers. Scholars disagree about how many people could read and write, but most likely they were a small minority. The predominance of oral rather than written communication meant that people usually absorbed information by ear: songs, speeches, narrated stories, and lively conversation were central to Greek life.

Young men from prosperous families traditionally acquired the skills to participate successfully in the public life of Athenian democracy by observing their fathers, uncles, and other older men as they debated in the Council of 500 and the assembly, served as public officials, and made speeches in court. In many cases, an older man would choose an adolescent male as his special favorite to educate. The younger man would learn about public life by spending his time in the company of the older man and his adult friends. During the day, the youth would observe his mentor talking politics in the agora, help him perform his duties in public office, and work out with him in a gymnasium. Their evenings would be spent at a symposium, where the entertainment ranged from serious political and philosophical discussion to riotous partying fueled by endless cups of wine.

This type of relationship could lead to sexual relations between the youth and the older male, who would normally be married. Although both male homosexuality between adults and female homosexuality in general were regarded as wrong throughout the Greek world, sexual relations between older mentors and younger favorites were considered acceptable in many, though not all, city-states. These differing attitudes about homosexual behavior reflected the complexity of Greek ideas of masculinity, about what made a man a man and what unmade him. In any case, a mentor was never supposed to exploit his younger partner physically or neglect his political education. If this ideal was observed, Athenian society accepted the relationship as part of a complicated range of bonds among males, from political and military activity to training of mind and body to sexual relations.

By the time democracy at Athens had become "radical," young men eager to become skilled political speechmakers could study with a new kind of expert. These teachers of public speaking and clever arguments were called *sophists* ("wise men"), a label that later became an insult (preserved in the English word *sophistry*) because ordinary people thought sophists were dangerously persuasive in making misleading arguments. Sophists created bitter controversy because they taught unprecedented skills in public speaking, but also because they expressed ideas about the nature of human existence and religion that challenged traditional beliefs. The earliest sophists were foreigners who began moving to Athens about 450 B.C.E., at the height of the city-state's prosperity, to attract pupils who could pay the high tuition that sophists charged.

Sophists primarily taught what every ambitious young man needed to learn to gain power in Athens's radical democracy: techniques for persuasive public speaking for the political debates in the assembly and the councils or lawsuits in court. Wealthy men therefore flocked to the dazzling demonstrations these foreign teachers put on to showcase their new methods of persuasion. In some cases, the sophists charged stiff fees to write speeches that customers could deliver as their own compositions.

The sophists alarmed traditionalists, who feared this new and seductive eloquence would undermine communal social and political traditions in favor of individual interests. In ancient Greek culture, where codes of proper behavior, moral standards, and religious ideals were handed down in speech from generation to generation, a persuasive and charismatic speaker could potentially wield as much power as an army of warriors. Sophists made people anxious because political leaders, such as Pericles, flocked to hear them. Many citizens feared that selfish politicians would use the silver-tongued style of the sophists to mislead the assembly and the councils.

The sophists' innovative ideas about human existence and religion deeply upset many people. One especially controversial sophist was Protagoras, a contemporary of Pericles from Abdera in northern Greece. He immigrated to Athens around 450 B.C.E., when he was about forty, and spent most of his career there. His views proved extremely controversial, especially his agnosticism (the belief that human beings cannot know anything about the supernatural): "Whether the gods exist I cannot discover, nor what their form is like, for there are many barriers to knowledge, [such as] the difficulty of the subject and the short span of human life." Ideas like this implied that traditional religion had no meaning, and people worried that they might provoke divine anger.

Equally controversial was Protagoras's denial of any absolute standard of truth: he asserted that every issue had two, irreconcilable sides. For example, he argued, if one person feeling a breeze thinks it warm, whereas another person thinks it cool, neither judgment can be absolutely correct because the wind simply is warm to one and cool to the other. Protagoras summed up his **subjectivism**—the belief that there is no absolute reality behind and independent of appearances—in the much-quoted opening of his work *Truth*: "Man is the measure of all things, of the things that are that they are, and of the things that are not that they are not." *Man* (*anthropos* in Greek, hence our word *anthropology*) in this passage refers to the individual human, male or female, whom Protagoras makes the sole judge of his or her own impressions.

These ideas and other similarly unsettling ones taught by sophists deeply worried many people. They feared that sophists would convince others that human institutions and values were only matters of convention, custom, or law (*nomos*) and not products of nature (*physis*), and that because truth was subjective, speakers should be able to argue either side of a question with equal persuasiveness. The first view implied that traditional human institutions were arbitrary rather than grounded in nature, and the second made morality irrelevant to politics. The combination of the two ideas amounted to moral relativism, the idea that there were no absolute moral values, which threatened the shared public values of the democratic city-state.

Protagoras tried to meet such objections by insisting that his doctrines were not hostile to democracy, arguing that every person had an innate capability for "excellence" and that human survival depended on the rule of law based on a sense of justice. Members of the community, he explained, must be persuaded to obey the laws not because they are based on absolute truth, which does not exist, but because it was advantageous for people to live by them. A thief, for example, would have to be persuaded that the law forbidding theft was to his advantage because it protected his own property and the city-state in which he, like others, had to live in order to survive.

Other sophists taught other disturbing ideas. Anaxagoras of Clazomenae, for example, offended believers in traditional religion by arguing that the sun was nothing more than a lump of flaming rock, not a deity. Leucippus of Miletus, whose doctrines were made famous by his pupil Democritus of Abdera, invented an atomic theory of matter to explain how change was constant. Everything, he argued, consisted of tiny, invisible particles in eternal motion. Their random collisions caused them to combine and recombine in an infinite variety of forms. This physical explanation of the source of change, like Anaxagoras's theory about the sun, implied that traditional religion, which explained events as the outcome of divine forces, was invalid.

Because only wealthy men could afford instruction from sophists, this new education worked against the egalitarian principles of Athenian democracy by giving an advantage to the rich. In addition, moral relativism and the physical explanation of the universe struck many Athenians as dangerous: they feared that the teachings of the sophists could bring divine punishment on the whole community.

The ideas of Socrates of Athens (469–399 B.C.E.), the most famous philosopher of the Golden Age, added to the tension that the sophists provoked. He was not a sophist and offered no courses, but his views became well known because his lifestyle was so distinctive. Socrates devoted his life to conversation combating the notion that justice should be equated with the power to impose one's will on others. His passionate concern to discover valid guidelines for leading a just life and to prove that justice is better than injustice under all circumstances gave a new direction to Greek philosophy: an emphasis on individual ethics. Although other thinkers before him

■ **Statuette of the Philosopher Socrates**

The controversial Socrates, the most famous philosopher of Athens in the fifth century B.C.E., joked that he had a homely face and a bulging stomach. This small statue is an artist's impression of what Socrates looked like; we cannot be sure of the truth. Socrates was famous for his irony, and he may have purposely exaggerated his physical unattractiveness to show his disdain for ordinary standards of beauty, which valued a fit body, and his own emphasis on the quality of one's soul as the true measure of a person's worth.

(© Copyright The Trustees of The British Museum.)

had dealt with moral issues, especially poets and dramatists, Socrates was the first to make the ethics and morality of the individual a central concern for philosophy.

Socrates lived a life that attracted attention. He paid so little notice to his physical appearance and clothes that he seemed eccentric. Sporting a stomach, in his words, "somewhat too large to be convenient," he wore the same cheap cloak summer and winter and went barefoot in all weather. His tirelessness as a hoplite and his ability to outdrink anyone at a symposium amazed his companions. Unlike the sophists, he lived in poverty and disdained material possessions, somehow managing to support a wife and several children. He may have inherited some money, but he certainly received gifts from wealthy admirers.

Socrates spent his time in conversations: participating in a symposium, strolling in the agora, or watching young men exercise in a gymnasium. He wrote nothing; our knowledge of his ideas comes from others' writings, especially those of his pupil Plato (c. 428–348 B.C.E.). Plato portrays Socrates as a relentless questioner of his fellow citizens, foreign friends, and leading sophists. Socrates' questions aimed at making his conversational partners examine the basic assumptions of their way of life. Giving few answers, Socrates never directly instructed anyone; instead, he led them to draw conclusions in response to his asking probing questions that picked apart their unexamined assumptions. Teaching this way is today called the **Socratic method**.

This indirect method of searching for the truth often left people uncomfortably baffled because they were forced to conclude that they were ignorant of what they had assumed they knew very well. Socrates' questions showed that normal careers—pursuing success in politics or business or art—were excuses for avoiding genuine virtue. Socrates insisted that he was ignorant of the best definition of virtue but that his wisdom consisted of knowing that he did not know. He vowed that he was trying to improve, not undermine, people's beliefs in morality, even though, as a friend put it, a conversation with Socrates made a man feel numb—just as if he had been stung by a stingray. Socrates especially wanted to use reasoning to discover universal standards justifying individual morality. He fiercely attacked the sophists, who dismissed traditional morality as "chains that bind nature." This idea, he protested, equated human happiness with power and "getting more."

Socrates passionately believed that just behavior was better for people than injustice and that morality was priceless because it guaranteed happiness. Essentially, he argued that just behavior, or virtue, was identical to knowledge and that true knowledge of justice would inevitably lead people to choose good over evil. They would therefore live truly happy lives, regardless of how rich or poor they were. Since Socrates believed that moral knowledge was all a person needed for the good life, he argued that no one knowingly behaved unjustly and that behaving justly was always in the individual's interest. It was simply ignorant to believe that the best life was the life of unlimited power to pursue whatever one desired. The most desirable human life was focused on virtue and guided by reason, not by dreams of personal gain.

Socrates' effect on many people was as disturbing as the sophists' doctrines that questioned traditional morality. Socrates' attacks on his fellow citizens' ideas about the importance of wealth and public success made some men extremely upset because his ideas seemed to mean that people should not bother thinking about the community, only about their individual virtue. Unhappiest of all were the fathers whose sons, after listening to Socrates reduce someone to utter bewilderment, came home to try the same technique on their parents by arguing that the public accomplishments their family held dear were old-fashioned, even worthless. Men who experienced this reversal of the traditional educational hierarchy—fathers were supposed to educate sons—felt that Socrates was undermining the stability of society by making young men question Athenian traditions. The ancient sources fail to reveal what Athenian women thought of Socrates, or he of them. His thoughts about human capabilities and behavior could be applied to women as well as to men, and he probably believed that women and men both had the same basic capacity for justice.

People's worry that Socrates presented a danger to traditional society inspired playwright Aristophanes to write his comedy *Clouds* (423 B.C.E.). He portrayed Socrates as a cynical sophist operating a Thinking Shop who, for a fee, offered instruction in Protagoras-like techniques of making the weaker argument the stronger.

When Socrates' curriculum transforms a youth into a public speaker arguing that a son has the right to beat his parents, his father burns down Socrates' school. None of these plot details was real; what was genuine was the fear that Socrates' uncompromising views on individual morality endangered the traditional practices of the community at a time when new ways of thought were angering many Athenians.

One especially significant intellectual innovation that emerged in the Golden Age was historical writing as a critical vision of the past. Herodotus of Halicarnassus (c. 485–425 B.C.E.) and Thucydides of Athens (c. 455–399 B.C.E.) became Greece's most famous historians and established Western civilization's tradition of history writing. By 428–425 B.C.E., Herodotus had finished his groundbreaking work called *Histories* (meaning "inquiry" in Greek) to explain the Persian Wars as a clash between East and West; by Roman times he had been christened "Father of History." Herodotus achieved an unprecedented depth for his book by giving it a wide geographical scope, an investigative approach to evidence, and a lively story. Herodotus searched for the origins of the Persian-Greek conflict both by delving deep into the past and by examining the cultural traditions of all the peoples involved. He recognized the relevance and the delight of studying other cultures as a component of historical investigation.

Thucydides took another giant step in this process by writing contemporary history influenced by what today is called political science. His *History of the Peloponnesian War* made power politics, not divine intervention, the primary force in history. Deeply affected by the war's brutality, he used his personal experiences as a politician and military commander to make his history vivid and frank in describing human moral failings. His insistence that historians should spare no effort in seeking out the most reliable sources and evaluating their testimony with objectivity set a high standard for later writers.

Equally innovative were the medical doctrines of Hippocrates of Cos, a fifth-century B.C.E. contemporary of Thucydides, who became Greece's most famous physician. He is remembered today in the oath bearing his name that doctors swear at the beginning of their professional careers. Hippocrates made great strides in putting medical diagnosis and treatment on a scientific basis. Earlier medicine had depended on magic and ritual. Hippocrates viewed the human body as an organism whose parts must be understood in relation to the whole. Some attributed to him the view, profoundly influential in later times, that four humors (fluids) made up the human body: blood, phlegm, black bile, and yellow bile. Health depended on keeping the proper balance among them; being healthy was to be in "good humor." This intellectual system corresponded to philosophers' division of the physical world into four parts: the elements earth, air, fire, and water. Hippocrates taught that the physician's most important duty was to base his knowledge on careful observation of patients and their response to remedies. Clinical experience, not theory, he insisted, was the best guide to effective treatments. Although various cults in Greek religion offered healing to worshippers, Hippocratic medical doctrine apparently made little or no mention of any role for the gods in illnesses and their treatments.

The Development of Tragedy and Comedy

The complex relationship between gods and humans formed the basis of Golden Age Athens's most influential cultural innovation: tragic drama. Greek plays, still read and produced onstage today, were presented over three days at the major annual festival of the god Dionysus, which was held in the spring. They were staged in a drama contest with prizes for the best plays, in keeping with the competitive spirit characteristic of many events honoring the gods. By presenting shocking stories exploring tensions in the city-state, tragedy inspired its large audiences to ponder the danger that ignorance, arrogance, and violence presented to Athens's democratic society. Following the tradition of Homer and Hesiod, Golden Age playwrights treated themes ranging from individual freedom and responsibility in the polis, to the underlying nature of good and evil.

Every year, Athens's government held a competition to choose three authors to present four plays each: three tragedies in a row (a trilogy), followed by a semicomic play featuring satyrs (mythical half-man, half-animal beings) to end the day on a lighter note. The term *tragedy*—derived for reasons now lost from the Greek words for "goat" and "song"—referred to plays with plots that presented fierce conflicts among characters representing powerful forces. Tragedies were written in verse and used solemn language; they were often based on stories about the violent consequences of interaction between gods and humans told in myth. The plots often ended with a resolution to the trouble—but only after great suffering.

The performance of Athenian tragedies took place during the daytime in an outdoor theater sacred to Dionysus, built into the southern slope of Athens's acropolis. This theater held about fifteen thousand spectators overlooking an open, circular area in front of a slightly raised stage. Every tragedy had to have eighteen cast members, all of whom were men: three actors to play the speaking roles (both male and female characters) and fifteen chorus members. Although the chorus leader sometimes engaged in dialogue with the actors, the chorus primarily performed songs and dances in the circular area in front of the stage, called the *orchestra*.

A successful tragedy presented a vivid spectacle. The chorus wore decorative costumes and performed intricate dance routines. The actors wore masks and used broad gestures and booming voices to reach the upper tier of seats. A powerful voice was crucial to a tragic actor because words represented the heart of a tragedy, in which dialogue and long speeches were far more common than physical action. Special effects, however, were part of the spectacle. For example, a crane allowed actors playing the roles of gods to fly suddenly onto the stage. The actors playing lead roles, called the *protagonists* ("first competitors"), competed against one another to win an award for best actor. So important was a first-rate protagonist to a successful tragedy that actors were assigned by lottery to the playwrights to give all three an equal chance to have the finest cast. Great protagonists became international celebrities.

■ **Theater of Dionysus at Athens**
Tragedies, satyr plays, and comedies produced at this theater in daytime festivals riveted the
attention of the city. The theater held about fifteen thousand spectators. In the Classical period, the
seating, the stage, and scenery were not yet permanent installations. The seating and stone stage
building foundations are remnants of much later changes. What qualities in an actor do you think
would be most important under these conditions? (John Elk III/Bruce Coleman, Inc.)

Most playwrights came from the social elite because only men of property
could afford the amount of time and learning their work demanded; they served as
author, director, producer, musical composer, choreographer, and sometimes even
actor. The prizes awarded in the tragedy competition were modest, but the fame was
enormous. As citizens, playwrights also fulfilled the normal military and political
obligations of Athenian men. The best-known Athenian tragedians—Aeschylus
(525–456 B.C.E.), Sophocles (c. 496–406 B.C.E.), and Euripides (c. 485–406 B.C.E.)—
all served in the army, held public office at some point in their careers, or did both.

Athenian tragedy was a public art form. Its performances were subsidized with
public funds, and its plots explored the ethical problems of humans in conflict with
the gods and with one another in a city-state. Even though most tragedies were
based on stories that referred to a legendary time before city-states existed, such as
tales of the Trojan War, the moral issues the plays explored always concerned the
society and obligations of citizens in a city-state. To take only a few examples: in his
trilogy *Oresteia* (458 B.C.E.), Aeschylus explains the importance of democratic

Athens's court system by reworking the story of how the gods stopped the murderous violence in the family of Orestes, son of the Greek leader against Troy. The plays suggest that human beings have to learn by suffering but that the gods will provide justice in the long run. Sophocles' *Antigone* (441 B.C.E.) presents the sad story of the family of Oedipus of Thebes as a drama of harsh conflict between a courageous woman, Antigone, who insists on her family's moral obligation to bury its dead in obedience to divine command, and her uncle Creon, the city-state's stern male leader, who defends the need to preserve order and protect community values by prohibiting the burial of traitors. In a horrifying story of anger and suicide centered on one of the most famous heroines of Western literature, Sophocles deliberately exposes the right and wrong on each side of the conflict. His play offers no easy resolution to the possible conflict between divine and human laws. Euripides' *Medea* (431 B.C.E.) implies that the political order of a city-state depends on men treating their wives and families with honor and trust: when Medea's husband betrays her for a younger woman, she takes revenge by destroying their children and the community's political leadership with her magical power.

We cannot reconstruct precisely how the audiences of the drama competition of the Dionysian festival understood the messages of tragedies. At the very least, however, they must have been aware that the central characters of the plays were figures who fell into disaster from positions of power and prestige. The characters' reversals of fortune came about not because they were absolute villains but because, as humans, they could fail through a lethal combination of error, ignorance, and **hubris** (violent arrogance). The Athenian Empire was at its height when audiences at Athens attended the tragedies of these three great playwrights. Thoughtful spectators may have reflected on the possibility that Athens's current power and prestige, managed as they were by humans, remained hostage to the same forces that controlled the fates of the heroes and heroines of tragedy. Tragedies certainly appealed to audiences because they were entertainment, but they also had an educational function: to remind male citizens, who made policy for the city-state, that success created complex moral problems that could not be solved casually or arrogantly.

Athens also developed theatrical comedy as another innovative form of public art. Like tragedies, comedies were written in verse, were performed in a competition in the city's large outdoor theater during festivals honoring the god Dionysus, and were subsidized with public funds. Unlike tragedies, comedies made direct comments about public policy, criticized current politicians and intellectuals by name, and devised plots of outrageous fantasy to make their points. Comic choruses of twenty-four actors, for example, could feature characters colorfully dressed as talking birds or dancing clouds.

The immediate goal of a comic playwright was to win the award for the festival's best comedy by creating beautiful poetry, raising laughs with constant jokes and puns, and mocking prominent men. Much of the humor concerned sex and bodily functions, delivered in a stream of imaginative profanity. Well-known male

citizens were targeted for insults as cowardly or sexually effeminate. Women characters who were made fun of, however, seem to have been fictional.

Comedy's remarkable freedom of speech promoted frank, even brutal, commentary on current issues and personalities. Even during the Peloponnesian War,
comic playwrights presented plays that criticized the city-state's policy, for example
by recommending an immediate peace settlement. It was no accident that this energetic, critical drama emerged in Athens at the same time as radical democracy, in
the mid-fifth century B.C.E. The principle that all voters should have a stake in determining government policies evidently fueled a passion for using biting humor to
keep the community's leaders from becoming arrogant and aloof.

Athenian comedies often blamed particular political leaders for government
policies that had been approved by the assembly, similar to the way ostracism singled out individuals for punishment. As the leading politician of radical democracy, Pericles came in for fierce criticism in comedy. Comic playwrights mocked his
policies, his love life, and his looks ("Old Turnip Head" was a favorite insult). Cleon,
the most prominent politician after Pericles, was so outraged by the way that he was
parodied on stage by Aristophanes (c. 455–385 B.C.E.), Athens's most famous comic
playwright, that he sued him. When Cleon lost the case, Aristophanes responded by
pitilessly mocking him as a slavish foreign slob in *The Knights* (424 B.C.E.).

The most remarkable of Aristophanes' comedies are those in which the main
characters are powerful women who force the men of Athens to change their policy to preserve family life and the city-state. Most famous is *Lysistrata* (411 B.C.E.),
named after the female lead character of the play. In it, the women of Athens and
Sparta unite to force their husbands to end the Peloponnesian War. To make the
men agree to a peace treaty, they first seize the acropolis, where Athens's financial
reserves are kept, to prevent the men from spending them on the war. They then
beat back an attack on their position by the old men who have remained in Athens
while the younger men are out on campaign. When their husbands return from battle, the women refuse to have sex with them. This strike, which is portrayed in a
series of risqué episodes, finally coerces the men of Athens and Sparta to agree to
a treaty.

Lysistrata presents women acting bravely and aggressively against men who
seem bent on destroying their traditional family life—they are staying away from
home for long stretches while on military campaigns and are ruining the city-state
by prolonging a pointless war. Lysistrata insists that women have the intelligence
and judgment to make political decisions: "I am a woman, and, yes, I have brains.
And I'm not badly off for judgment. Nor has my education been bad, coming as it
has from my listening often to the conversations of my father and the elders among
the men." Her old-fashioned training and good sense allow her to see what needs to
be done to protect the community. Like the heroines of tragedy, Lysistrata is a reactionary; she wants to put things back the way they were. To do that, however, she has
to act like an impatient revolutionary. That irony well sums up the challenge that

■ **Statuettes of Comic Actors**
These little statues portray comic actors wearing the kinds of masks and costumes that became popular after Aristophanes and his contemporaries wrote their comedies in the fifth century B.C.E., and they give a vivid sense of the slapstick acting that characterized Greek comedy. In Aristophanes' day, the grotesque unreality of comic costumes would have been even more striking because attached below the waists of the male actors were large leather phalluses that were props for all sorts of sex-related jokes.
(Bildarchiv Preussischer Kulturbesitz/ Art Resource, NY.)

Golden Age Athens faced in trying to balance its reliance on tradition with the energy of the period's innovation in so many fields.

■ **REVIEW:** *How did new ways of thinking in the Golden Age threaten cherished traditions?*

The End of the Golden Age, 431–403 B.C.E.

A war between Athens and Sparta that lasted a generation (431–404 B.C.E.) ended the Athenian Golden Age. Called Peloponnesian today because it pitted Sparta's Peloponnese-based alliance against Athens's alliance, the war arose at least in part as a result of Pericles' policies. The most powerful politician in Athens—he won election as a general for fifteen years in a row beginning in 443 B.C.E.—Pericles nevertheless had to withstand severe criticism of the huge public spending on his building program and harsh measures against Delian League allies; his rivals said these policies soiled Athens's reputation. He faced his greatest challenge, however, when relations with Sparta worsened in the mid-430s B.C.E. over Athenian actions against Corinth and Megara, crucial Spartan allies. Finally, Corinth told Sparta to attack Athens, or Corinth would change sides to the Athenian alliance. Sparta's leaders therefore gave Athens an ultimatum—stop mistreating our allies—which Pericles convinced the Athenian assembly to reject as unfair because Sparta was refusing arbitration of the disputes. In this way, the relations of Athens and Sparta with lesser city-states propelled the two powers over the brink into war. Pericles' critics claimed he was insisting on war against Sparta to revive his popularity. By 431 B.C.E., the thirty-year peace made in 446–445 B.C.E. had been shattered beyond repair.

The Peloponnesian War, 431–403 B.C.E.

Dragging on longer than any previous war in Greek history, the Peloponnesian War took place above all because Spartan leaders feared that the Athenians would use their superior long-distance offensive weaponry—the naval forces of the Delian League—to destroy Spartan control over the Peloponnesian League. (See "Taking Measure," below.) The duration of the struggle reflects the unpredictability of war

■ **TAKING MEASURE** **Military Forces of Athens and Sparta at the Beginning of the Peloponnesian War**
These figures give estimates of the comparative strengths of the military forces of the Athenian side and the Spartan side when the Peloponnesian War broke out in 431 B.C.E. The numbers come from ancient historical sources— above all, the Athenian general and historian Thucydides, who fought in the war. The bar graphs reveal the different characteristics of the competing forces: Athens relied on its navy of triremes and its archers (the fifth-century B.C.E. equivalent of artillery and snipers). Sparta was preeminent in the forces needed for land battles—hoplites (heavily armed infantry) and cavalry (shock troops used to disrupt opposing infantry). These differences dictated the strategies and tactics of each side. Athens tried to launch surprise raids from the sea, and Sparta tried to force decisive confrontations on the battlefield.

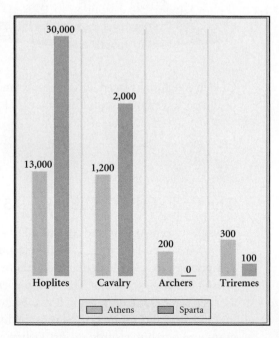

and the consequences of the repeated refusal of the Athenian assembly to negotiate lasting peace terms.

Thucydides dramatically revealed the absolute refusal of the Athenians to find a compromise solution with these words of Pericles to the assembly:

> If we do go to war, harbor no thought that you went to war over a trivial affair. For you this trifling matter is the assurance and the proof of your determination. If you yield to their demands, they will immediately confront you with some larger demand, since they will think that you only gave way on the first point out of fear. But if you stand firm, you will show them that they have to deal with you as equals. . . . When our equals, without agreeing to arbitration of the matter under dispute, make claims on us as neighbors and state those claims as commands, it would be no better than slavery to give in to them, no matter how large or how small the claim may be.

Pericles advised Athens to use its superior navy to raid enemy lands while avoiding battles with the Spartan infantry, even when they invaded the Athenian countryside and destroyed citizens' property there. In the end, he predicted, the superior resources of Athens would enable it to win a war of attrition. With his unyielding leadership, this strategy might have prevailed, but unexpected trouble struck. From 430 to 426 B.C.E., an epidemic disease ravaged Athens's population, killing thousands—including Pericles in 429 B.C.E. The Athenians fought on, but they lost the clear direction that Pericles' costly strategy had required. The generals after him followed increasingly risky plans, culminating in an overambitious campaign against Sparta's allies in Sicily, far to the west. Dazzling the assembly in 415 B.C.E. with the dream of conquering that rich island, Alcibiades, the most innovative and brashest commander of the war, persuaded the Athenians to launch their largest naval expedition ever. His political rivals got him recalled from his command, however, and the invasion force suffered a catastrophic defeat in 413 B.C.E. (see Map 2.3 on page 86).

The Spartans then launched the final phase of the war by establishing a permanent base of operations in the Athenian countryside for year-round raids. The agricultural economy was devastated, and revenues fell drastically when twenty thousand slave workers crippled production in Athens's publicly owned silver mines by deserting to the enemy. Distress over the war's losses led to a group of antidemocratic citizens briefly overturning the democracy in 411 B.C.E., but other citizens soon restored democratic government. Athens fought on. The end came when Persia sent money to help the Spartans finally build a strong navy.

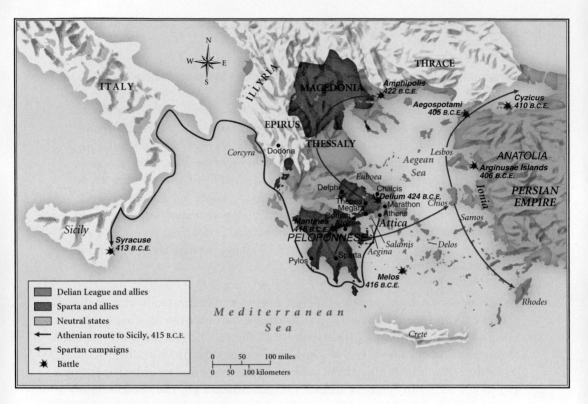

■ MAP 2.3 The Peloponnesian War, 431–404 B.C.E.

During the first ten years of the war, most of the battles took place in mainland Greece. Sparta, whose armies usually avoided long-distance campaigns, shocked Athens when its general Brasidas led successful attacks against Athenian forces in northeast Greece. In the war's next phase, Athens stunned the Greek world by launching a naval expedition against Spartan allies in Sicily. In the last ten years of the war, the action moved to the east, on and along the western coast of Anatolia and its islands; this was the western boundary of the Persian Empire, which helped the Spartans build a navy to defeat the Athenian fleet and win the war. **For more help analyzing this map**, see the map activity for this chapter in the ONLINE STUDY GUIDE at bedfordstmartins.com/huntconcise.

Aggressive Spartan action at sea forced Athens to surrender in 404 B.C.E. After twenty-seven years of near-continuous war, the Athenians were at the mercy of their enemies.

The Rule of the Thirty Tyrants, 404–403 B.C.E.

The victorious Spartans installed a regime of antidemocratic Athenians, members of the social elite who became known as the Thirty Tyrants. Brutally suppressing democratic opposition, these rulers embarked on an eight-month period of terror in 404–403 B.C.E. The speechwriter Lysias, for example, reported that

IMPORTANT DATES			
c. 499–494 B.C.E.	Ionian revolt against Persian control	446–445 B.C.E.	Athens and Sparta sign a peace treaty meant to last thirty years
490 B.C.E.	Battle of Marathon		
480 B.C.E.	Battles of Thermopylae and Salamis	431 B.C.E.	Peloponnesian War between Athens and Sparta begins
477 B.C.E.	Athens forms the Delian League	c. 428–425 B.C.E.	Herodotus finishes the *Histories*
469–399 B.C.E.	Life of Socrates	411 B.C.E.	Aristophanes presents the comedy *Lysistrata*
461 B.C.E.	Ephialtes' political and judicial reforms strengthen Athenian democracy	404 B.C.E.	Athens surrenders to Sparta, ending the Peloponnesian War
458 B.C.E.	Aeschylus presents the trilogy *Oresteia*	404–403 B.C.E.	Thirty Tyrants suspend democracy at Athens but are soon overthrown; Athenian democracy is restored but weakened economically
450 B.C.E.	The sophist Protagoras comes to Athens		
447 B.C.E.	Construction begins on the Parthenon in Athens		

the tyrants' thugs seized his brother for execution as a way of stealing the family's valuables, down to the gold earrings ripped from the ears of his brother's wife. An Athenian democratic resistance movement soon arose and expelled the Thirty Tyrants in 403 B.C.E. with a series of bloody street battles. Fortunately for the democrats, a split in the Spartan leadership, propelled by the competing ambitions of its two most prominent men, prevented Spartan military support for the tyrants.

This civil war made Athenians so angry at each other that internal strife threatened to tear the community apart even after democracy was restored. The assembly therefore proclaimed the first known amnesty in Western history, a truce forbidding any official charges or revenge for crimes committed during the rule of the Thirty Tyrants. Athens's government was once again a functioning democracy, but its financial and military strength was shattered. Worse, its society harbored bitterness that no amnesty could fully dissolve. The end of the Golden Age left Athenians worriedly wondering how to remake their lives and restore the luster that their city-state's innovative accomplishments had produced in that wondrous period.

■ **REVIEW:** *How did unexpected events contribute to the outcome of the Peloponnesian War?*

■ **MAPPING THE WEST Greece, Europe, and the Mediterranean, c. 400 B.C.E.**
No single power controlled the Mediterranean region at the end of the fifth century B.C.E. In the west, the Phoenician city of Carthage and the Greek cities of Sicily and southern Italy were rivals for the riches to be won by trade. In the east, the Spartans, made ambitious by their victory over Athens in the Peloponnesian War, tried to become an international power outside the mainland for the first time in their history by sending campaigns into Anatolia and, they hoped, further east still. This aggressive action aroused stiff opposition from the Persians because it was a threat to their western-most imperial provinces.

Conclusion

Athens's Golden Age in the fifth century B.C.E. was a time of prosperity, political sta-bility, international power, and artistic and cultural accomplishment. Its citizens had won great glory in the unexpected victory of the Greek alliance against the Persians at the beginning of the century. This stunning triumph occurred, the Athenians believed, because the gods smiled upon them with special favor and because they displayed superior courage, intelligence, and virtue.

Athens soon rivaled Sparta for the leadership of the Greek world, and by the mid-fifth century B.C.E. it was enjoying unprecedented confidence and prosperi-ty. As the money poured in, the city-state built glorious temples, instituted pay for service in many government offices, and assembled the Mediterranean's most powerful navy. The poorer men who rowed the ships demanded greater democracy, leading to a judicial system guaranteeing fair treatment for all. Pericles became the most famous politician of the Golden Age by leading the drive for radical democracy.

Traditional boundaries remained in place for women and for religious worship, but the scale of intellectual change was as dramatic as that in politics. Art and architecture broke out of old forms, promoting an impression of precarious motion rather than stability. Tragedy and comedy developed at Athens as public art forms commenting on contemporary social and political issues. Sophists' new ideas about the nature of the universe and morality disturbed traditionally minded people, as did Socrates' strict ethics denying the value of the ordinary pursuit of wealth and success.

Wars framed the Golden Age. The Persian Wars sent the Athenians soaring to imperial power and prosperity, but their high-handed treatment of allies and enemies helped bring on the disastrous Peloponnesian War. Nearly three decades of battle brought the stars of the Greek Golden Age thudding back to earth: the Athenians by 400 B.C.E. found themselves in the same situation as in 500 B.C.E., fearful of Spartan power and worried whether the world's first democracy could survive. As it turned out, the next great threat to Greek stability and independence would once again come from outside, not from the east this time but from the north.

■ **MAKING CONNECTIONS**

1. *What were the most significant differences between Greece in the Archaic Age and in the Golden Age?*

2. *What did Greeks in the Golden Age believe it was worth spending public funds to pay for and why?*

■ **FOR FURTHER EXPLORATION**

For further reading and online research ideas, see the Suggested References on page SR-1 at the back of the book.

For practice quizzes, a customized study plan, and other study tools, see the ONLINE STUDY GUIDE at bedfordstmartins.com/huntconcise.

For primary-source material from this period, see Chapter 2 in *Sources of THE MAKING OF THE WEST: A CONCISE HISTORY*, Second Edition.

From the Classical to the Hellenistic World

c. 400–30 B.C.E.

ABOUT 255 B.C.E., AN EGYPTIAN CAMEL TRADER in Syria paid a bilingual scribe to write a letter to his Greek employer, Zeno, back in Egypt, to complain about his treatment by Zeno's Greek assistant, Krotos: "You know that when you left me in Syria with Krotos I followed all your instructions concerning the camels and behaved blamelessly towards you. But Krotos has ignored your orders to pay me my salary; I've received nothing despite asking him for my money over and over. He just tells me to go away. I waited a long time for you to come, but when I no longer had enough to live on and couldn't get help anywhere, I had to run away to keep from starving to death. . . . I am desperate summer and winter. . . . They have treated me with contempt because I am not a Greek. I therefore beg you, please, command them to pay me my salary so that I won't go hungry just because I don't know how to speak Greek."

The camel trader's name has been lost, but his desperate plea reveals that not being Greek contributed to his mistreatment. His difficult situation—having to

■ **Solving the Mystery of Egyptian Writing**
The three kinds of writing on this stone found by Napoleon's army in 1799 C.E. near Rosetta in Egypt's Nile River delta unlocked the thousand-year mystery of how to read ancient Egyptian hiero- glyphs. The three bands of text repeat the same message (praise for King Ptolemy V of Egypt decreed by priests in 196 B.C.E.) in three different scripts: at the top, hieroglyphs (Egypt's oldest writing system, c. 3100–3000 B.C.E.), then demotic (a cursive form of Egyptian invented around 600 B.C.E.), and finally a translation in Greek. Scholars in the nineteenth century C.E. deciphered the hiero- glyphs by comparing them to the Greek version, which they could read. Most Egyptians, like the mistreated camel trader stranded in Syria, could not read Greek, and most Greeks living in Egypt under the rule of the Ptolemaic kings could not read Egyptian, so bilingual texts such as the Rosetta Stone were necessary to reach the widest possible audience in Hellenistic Egypt. (Art Resource, NY.)

communicate persuasively with a foreigner holding power in his homeland—reveals the challenges facing the eastern Mediterranean world as it moved from the Classical period (500–323 B.C.E.) to the Hellenistic period (323–30 B.C.E.). These challenges were created by the large-scale movement of Greeks into the Near East and the resulting interaction between the local cultures and the culture of the newcomers. War brought these changes. The Peloponnesian War (431–404 B.C.E.) had accustomed many Greeks to making a living as soldiers, and after the war thousands of them became mercenaries serving Near Eastern rulers. The migration of Greeks to the Near East accelerated when the Macedonian king Alexander the Great (356–323 B.C.E.) conquered the Persian Empire and left behind colonies of Greeks from Egypt and the Near East to present-day Afghanistan.

Nineteenth-century scholars coined the term **Hellenistic** to designate the period of Greek and Near Eastern history from Alexander's death in 323 B.C.E. to the death of Cleopatra VII, the last Macedonian queen of Egypt, in 30 B.C.E. The term expresses the idea that a mixed, more international form of social and cultural life, combining Hellenic (that is, Greek) and local, Near Eastern traditions, emerged in the aftermath of Alexander's conquest of the Persian Empire.

The kings who followed Alexander revived monarchy in the Greek world by carving Macedonian and Near Eastern territory into kingdoms whose wealth made them dominant and reduced Greece's city-states to second-rate powers. The city-states retained their local political and social institutions but lost their independence in foreign policy: Hellenistic kings decided international politics. The kings hired Greeks to fill royal offices, man their armies, and run businesses throughout their Near Eastern territories; this policy created tension with their non-Greek subjects. Immigrant Greeks, such as Zeno in Egypt, formed a social and political elite dominating the kingdoms' local populations. Egyptians, Syrians, or Mesopotamians who wanted to rise in society had to win the support of these Greeks and learn their language. Otherwise, they might find themselves as powerless as the hungry camel trader.

Over time, however, the local cultures in the Near East interacted with the culture of the Greek overlords. The result was a new, multicultural mixture. Locals married Greeks, shared their religious traditions with the newcomers, taught them their agricultural and scientific knowledge, and sometimes learned Greek to win administrative jobs. The social tension between Greeks and non-Greeks never disappeared in the Hellenistic kingdoms, but their blending of Greek and Near Eastern traditions nevertheless promoted innovations in art, science, philosophy, and religion.

The Hellenistic kingdoms ended during the second and first centuries B.C.E., when the Romans overpowered all of them. The complex mixing of peoples and ideas that occurred in the Hellenistic period greatly influenced Roman civilization and thus later Western civilization. Hellenistic religious developments, for example, provided the background for Christianity. The period's cultural achievements remained influential long after the glories of Greece's Golden Age had faded away.

Disunity in Classical Greece, c. 400–350 B.C.E.

Sparta's victory over Athens in the Peloponnesian War brought a violent end to the Golden Age of Greece in the fifth century B.C.E. Once the Athenians had restored their democracy following the fall of the Thirty Tyrants, their city-state's economy gradually recovered, but the stability of daily life did not remove the hatred that democratic Athenians felt toward their fellow citizens whom they blamed for the Tyrants' violent rule. This bitterness led to the execution of Socrates in 399 B.C.E. Outraged at Socrates' fate, Plato and Aristotle created Greece's most famous philosophies about right and wrong and how human beings should live.

The Spartans tried to use their victory to turn their city-state into an international power, but their harsh leadership and collaboration with the Persian king stirred up fierce resistance from Greek city-states, especially Thebes and Athens. By the 350s B.C.E., the Greeks had become so disunited by their bloody battles with one another that they were too weak to prevent the expansion of their ambitious northern neighbors, the Macedonians.

The Aftermath of War and the Trial of Socrates

Spartan invaders during the Peloponnesian War had wrecked the homes of many Athenians living in the countryside and devastated Athens's agriculture and trade. Especially hard hit were moderately well-off women whose husbands and brothers died in the war. These women traditionally did weaving at home and supervised household slaves while the men earned the family's income by farming or commerce. Without male providers, many war widows had to find work outside the home. The jobs open to them were low-paying occupations, some traditional for women, such as wet nurses or weavers, or some for which there were not enough men, such as vineyard laborers.

Some Athenian families found ways to profit from women's skills. Socrates' friend Aristarchus, for example, became poverty-stricken supporting several widowed sisters, nieces, and female cousins. Socrates reminded his friend that his relatives knew how to make cloaks, shirts, capes, and smocks, "the work considered the best and most fitting for women." The women had been making clothing only for family members. Socrates suggested that they sell it for profit. The plan succeeded financially, but the women complained that Aristarchus was the only member of the household who ate without working. Socrates advised his friend to reply that the women should think of him as sheep viewed a guard dog—earning his food by keeping the wolves away.

■ Vase Painting of Women Fetching Water

This painting shows a scene from everyday life in a Greek city-state: women filling water jugs at a covered public fountain to take back to their homes. Few Greek homes had running water, so it was the duty of freeborn and slave women in a household to gather water for drinking, cooking, washing, and cleaning. Prosperous cities built attractively decorated fountain houses, such as the one shown here, where a regular supply of fresh water was available from springs or was piped in through aqueducts. These fountains were popular spots for women's conversations outside the house. The women in this scene wear the long robes and hair coverings characteristic of the time.

(Museum of Fine Arts, Boston. William Francis Warden Fund. Photograph © 2004 Museum of Fine Arts, Boston [61.195].)

Economic recovery stumbled when revenue fell in Athens's biggest enterprise— the state-owned silver mines, which were leased to private citizens who owned crews of slave miners. Economic conditions gradually improved as households and business owners revived trade and the production of goods in their homes and in small shops, such as metal foundries and pottery workshops. Businesses, usually family run, were small; the largest known was a shield-making company owning 120 slaves. The return of prosperity, coupled with the more flexible work roles that war had created, apparently led to changes in gender-defined occupations. The earliest evidence for men working alongside women in cloth production occurs in this postwar period, when commercial weaving shops sprang up for the first time. Previously, only women made cloth and did so at home. Later in the fourth century B.C.E., there is also evidence that women made careers in the arts, especially painting and music, which men traditionally dominated.

Even in the improved postwar economy, most workers earned just enough to feed and clothe their families. They customarily ate two meals a day, a light lunch in midmorning and a heavier evening meal. Bread baked from barley provided the main part of their diet; only rich people could afford wheat bread. A family bought its bread from small bakery stands, often run by women, or made it at home. Most people ate greens, beans, onions, garlic, olives, fruit, and cheese with their bread;

they had meat only at animal sacrifices paid for by the state. Everyone drank wine, diluted with water. Water was fetched from public fountains in jugs by women or slaves. All but the poorest families owned at least one or two slaves to do household chores and to look after the children.

The restored stability in the everyday lives of Athenians did not erase their memories of the murderous rule of the Thirty Tyrants and the civil war of 404–403 B.C.E. Socrates became the best-known victim of this lingering bitterness dividing Athenians when he was blamed for the violent crimes of his follower Critias, one of the Thirty. In fact, Socrates had put himself at risk by refusing to cooperate with the tyrants, but some prominent Athenians believed his philosophy had turned Critias into a traitor. Since the amnesty blocked prosecution for offenses during the civil war, Socrates' opponents indicted him on a charge of impiety in 399 B.C.E. At his trial they accused him of not believing in the city-state's gods and of introducing new divinities, and also of turning young men away from Athenian moral traditions. When Socrates spoke in his own defense, he repeated his unyielding dedication to goading his fellow citizens into examining their unexamined assumptions about individual virtue. He vowed to remain their stinging gadfly.

After the jury narrowly voted to convict, the prosecutors proposed death. In such a case, the defendant was then expected to propose exile as an alternative, which the jury usually accepted. Socrates, however, said that he deserved a reward rather than a punishment, until his friends at the trial made him propose a fine as his penalty. The jury, however, chose death. Socrates accepted his sentence calmly because, as he put it, "nothing evil can happen to a good man, either in life or in death." He was executed in the customary way, with a poisonous drink concocted from powdered hemlock. Later sources report that many Athenians soon came to regret the execution of Socrates as a tragic mistake and a severe blow to their reputation.

The Philosophy of Plato and Aristotle

Socrates' trial and execution turned the world upside down for his most famous follower, Plato (c. 429–348 B.C.E.). Tormented by anger and grief, Plato turned his back on marriage and a public career and devoted himself to thinking about the nature of a world in which an evil fate could befall such a good man as Socrates. He established a philosophical "school," the Academy, in Athens around 386 B.C.E. The Academy was an informal association of educated people—mostly men but also some women—who studied philosophy, mathematics, and theoretical astronomy; it attracted intellectuals to Athens for the next nine hundred years.

Plato's ideas on ethics and politics have remained central to philosophy and political science since his day. He presented his ideas in written dialogues that read like plays instead of philosophy textbooks; he wanted them to make readers reflect thoughtfully on difficult philosophical questions. His views apparently changed

■ **Mosaic of Plato's Academy**
*This mosaic from the Roman period portrays philosophers—identified by their beards—at Plato's
school in Athens, called the Academy, holding discussions among themselves. Founded around
386 B.C.E., the Academy became one of Greece's most famous and long-lasting organizations,
attracting scholars and students until it closed around 530 C.E. The columns and tree express the
Academy's harmonious blend of the natural and built environments, a setting meant to promote
pleasant and productive discussions.* (Erich Lessing/Art Resource, NY.)

over time—nowhere did he present a fully worked out list of doctrines.
Nevertheless, he always maintained one essential idea: moral qualities in their ultimate reality are universal and absolute, not relative.

To support this idea, Plato argued that absolute virtues, such as Goodness,
Justice, Beauty, and Equality, existed as metaphysical realities he called Forms (or
Ideas). He explained that the Forms are invisible, invariable, and eternal entities
located in a higher realm beyond the daily world. According to Plato, the Forms are
the only true reality; what we experience through our senses in everyday life are only
dim and imperfect representations of these flawless realities, as if, he said, we were
watching their shadows cast on the wall of a cave. His theory of Forms made
metaphysics—the consideration of the ultimate nature of reality beyond the reach
of the human senses—into a central issue for philosophers.

Plato's idea that humans possess immortal souls distinct from their bodies
established the concept of **dualism**, a separation between spiritual and physical

being. This notion influenced much of later philosophical and religious thought. Plato believed the proper goal for humans is to seek order and purity in their own souls by using reason to control their irrational desires, which are harmful. The desire to drink wine to excess, for example, is irrational because the drinker fails to consider the hangover to come the next day. Finally, because the soul is immortal and the body is not, our present, impure existence is only one part of our true existence.

Plato presented the most famous version of his utopian political ideas in his dialogue *The Republic*. This work, whose Greek title means "system of government," primarily concerns the nature of justice and the reasons people should be just. According to Plato, justice is impossible in a democracy and requires hierarchy. The trial of Socrates convinced him that most citizens were incapable of rising above self-interest. He therefore ranked people in his ideal society by their ability to grasp the truth of the Forms.

Women could rank as high as men because they possess the same virtues. To minimize distraction, the highest-ranking members of Plato's utopia are to have neither private property nor individual families. These men and women are to live together in barracks, eat in mess halls, and exercise in the same gymnasiums. They are to have sexual relations with various partners so that the best women can mate with the best men to produce the best children, who will be raised in a common environment by special caretakers. Those who achieve the highest level of knowledge in Plato's ideal society qualify to rule over it as philosopher-kings. Plato did not think such a society was truly possible, but he did believe that imagining it was important in teaching people to live justly. For this reason above all, he passionately believed the study of philosophy mattered to human life.

Plato was also influential because he trained an extremely famous pupil, Aristotle (384–322 B.C.E.). From 342 to 335 B.C.E., Aristotle tutored the young Alexander the Great in Macedonia. He then created his own practical philosophy for living a happy life and founded his own "school" in Athens, the Lyceum, in 335 B.C.E. Later called the Peripatetic School after the covered walkway (*peripatos*) where students conversed protected from the sun, Aristotle's Lyceum became world famous. He lectured with dazzling intelligence on nearly every branch of learning: biology, medicine, anatomy, psychology, meteorology, physics, chemistry, mathematics, music, metaphysics, rhetoric, political science, ethics, and literary criticism.

Aristotle's vast writings made him one of the most influential scientists and philosophers in Western history. His great reputation rests on his development of rigorous systems of logical argument and his scientific investigation of the natural world. Creating a sophisticated system of logic to identify the forms of valid arguments, Aristotle established rules to tell the difference between a logically proven case and a merely persuasive one. Furthermore, Aristotle insisted on explanations based on common sense rather than metaphysics. He denied the validity of Plato's theory of Forms, for example, on the grounds that the separate, unverifiable existence Plato asserted for them did not make sense. As for scientific investigation, Aristotle believed that the best way to understand objects and beings was to observe them in their natural settings. The first scientist to try to collect all available information on animals, Aristotle recorded facts about more than five hundred different species, including insects. His recognition that whales and dolphins are mammals, which later writers on animals overlooked, was not rediscovered for another two thousand years.

Like Plato, Aristotle criticized democracy because it allowed uneducated instead of "better" people to control politics. Some of Aristotle's views justified inequalities characteristic of his time. He regarded slavery as natural, arguing that some people were by nature meant to be slaves because their souls lacked the rational part that should rule in a human. He also concluded, based on faulty notions of biology, that women were by nature inferior to men, a conclusion with disastrous influence on later thought.

In ethics, Aristotle emphasized the need to develop habits of just behavior and not just good intentions. People should achieve self-control by training their minds to win out over instincts and passions. Self-control did not mean denying human desires and appetites; rather, it meant striking a balance between suppressing and heedlessly indulging physical yearnings, of finding "the mean." Aristotle claimed that the mind should rule in finding this balance because the intellect is the finest human quality and the mind is the true self—indeed, the godlike part of a person.

The Fracturing of Greece

During the fifty years following the Peloponnesian War, Sparta, Thebes, and Athens each in turn tried to dominate Greece. None succeeded. Their struggles with one another left Greece too weak to prevent outside interference and undermined the political independence of the Classical city-states. In the 390s to 370s B.C.E., the Spartans did the most to provoke this fatal disunity by trying to conquer other city-states. Thebes, Athens, Corinth, and Argos responded by forming an anti-Spartan coalition because Spartan aggression threatened their interests at home and abroad. The Spartans counterbalanced the alliance by making a treaty with the Persian king. Blatantly renouncing their commitment to defend Greek freedom, the Spartans acknowledged the Persian ruler's right to control the Greek city-states of Anatolia—in return for permission to pursue their own interests in Greece without Persian interference. This treaty of 386 B.C.E., called the *King's Peace*, deprived the Anatolian Greeks of the freedom won in the Persian Wars. The Athenians rebuilt their military strength to combat Sparta. By 377 B.C.E., Athens had again become the leader of a naval alliance. This time, league members insisted that their rights be specified in writing to prevent any imperialistic Athenian behavior.

The Thebans became Greece's main land power in the 370s B.C.E. Attacking the Spartan homeland, they destroyed Sparta's power forever by freeing many helots.

This Theban success so frightened the Athenians, whose city lay only forty miles from Thebes, that they made a temporary alliance with the Spartans. Their combined armies confronted the Thebans in the battle of Mantinea in the Peloponnese in 362 B.C.E. Thebes won the battle but lost the war when its best general was killed and no capable replacement could be found.

The battle of Mantinea left the Greek city-states in impotent disunity. As the contemporary historian Xenophon said: "Everyone had supposed that the winners of this battle would be Greece's rulers and its losers their subjects; but there was only more confusion and disturbance in Greece after it than before." By the 350s B.C.E., then, the Greek city-states' struggle for supremacy over one another had left them in a stalemate of exhaustion. Failing to cooperate, they opened the way for the rise of a new power—the kingdom of Macedonia, which would threaten their cherished independence.

■ **REVIEW:** *What were the major philosophical ideas of Plato and Aristotle?*

The Rise of Macedonia, 359–323 B.C.E.

The rulers of Macedonia took advantage of the Greek city-states' disunity to make their kingdom an international superpower. That this previously weak kingdom would seize the leadership of Greece and conquer the Persian Empire ranks as one of the greatest surprises in ancient political and military history. Two aggressive and charismatic kings produced this amazing transformation: Philip II (r. 359–336 B.C.E.) and his son Alexander the Great (r. 336–323 B.C.E.). Their conquests marked the end of the Classical period and set in motion the cultural interactions of the Hellenistic age.

Philip II and the Background of Macedonian Power

The Macedonians' power sprang from the characteristics of their society and their ethnic pride. The Macedonian people demanded the freedom to tell their monarchs what needed to be improved, and a king could govern effectively only as long as he maintained the support of the other Macedonian men heading powerful families, who were the king's social equals and controlled large bands of followers. Fighting, hunting, and heavy drinking were these men's favorite pastimes. The king was expected to excel in these activities to prove he was capable of ruling. Queens and royal mothers received respect in this male-dominated society because they came from powerful Macedonian families or the ruling houses of lands bordering Macedonia.

■ Dancing Figures on a Gilded Bowl from Macedonia
Archaeologists discovered this large metal wine bowl, made of bronze plated with gold, at Derveni in Macedonia. Its artistic style dates it to the 330s B.C.E. Wealthy Macedonian men at a Greek-style drinking party (symposium) used these expensive bowls to dilute wine so they could drink large amounts of it. The excited conditions of the two figures—a satyr and a female worshipper of Dionysus, the god of wine and pleasure—expressed the ecstasy that the partygoers hoped to achieve. Since erect penises were shown frequently in Greek and Macedonian art associated with Dionysus, representing hopes for fertility and sexual pleasure, pictures like this were not regarded as obscene.
(Thessalonike, Archaeological Museum, © Archaeological Receipts Fund.)

Macedonians thought of themselves as Greek by blood and took pride in their identity. They had their own language, but wealthy Macedonians routinely learned to speak Greek. Macedonians looked down on their southern relatives as being too soft for the adversities of northern life. The Greeks returned this scorn. The famed Athenian orator Demosthenes (384–322 B.C.E.) lambasted Philip II as "not only not a Greek nor related to the Greeks, but not even a barbarian from a land worth mentioning; no, he's a plague from Macedonia, a region where you can't even buy a slave worth his salt."

Until Philip II's reign, rivalry between the king and the other leading families kept Macedonia from mobilizing its full military strength. Indeed, kings so feared violence from their own countrymen that they stationed bodyguards outside the royal bedroom. A military disaster brought Philip to the throne at a desperate moment. The Illyrians, hostile neighbors to the north, had slaughtered the previous Macedonian king and four thousand troops. Philip restored the army's confidence by teaching the infantry an unstoppable new tactic. Arming his infantry with long thrusting spears that extended fourteen to sixteen feet and took two hands to wield, and arranging these troops in a phalanx formation, he created deep blocks of soldiers bristling with outstretched spears like a lethal porcupine. Using cavalry to disrupt the enemy's battle line and protect his own infantry's flanks, Philip smashed the Illyrians with his revived army.

Philip soon embarked on a whirlwind of diplomacy, bribery, and military action that turned Macedonia into an international power. A Greek contemporary, the historian Theopompus of Chios, labeled Philip "never satisfied, extravagant—he did everything in a hurry . . . he never spared the time to reckon up his income and expenses." By the late 340s B.C.E., Philip had persuaded or forced most of northern Greece to follow his lead in foreign policy. Seeking the glory of avenging Greece and fearing the potentially destabilizing effect his victorious army would have on his kingdom if the soldiers had nothing to do, Philip planned to lead a united Macedonian and Greek army against the Persian Empire. To launch this grandiose invasion, he needed to control the forces of southern Greece.

Expansion of Macedonia under Philip II, r. 359–336 B.C.E.

Philip found in Greek history the justification for attacking Persia: revenge for the Persian Wars. But some Greeks remained unconvinced. Demosthenes used stirring rhetoric to criticize Greeks for their failure to resist Philip. They stood by, he thundered, "as if Philip were a hailstorm, praying that he would not come their way, but not trying to do anything to head him off." Finally, Athens and Thebes headed an alliance of southern Greek city-states to try to block Philip, but in 338 B.C.E. the king and his Greek allies trounced the coalition's forces at the battle of Chaeronea in Boeotia. The defeated city-states retained their internal freedom, but Philip forced them to form a league under his leadership. The course of later history showed the battle of Chaeronea to be a turning point in Greek history: although Philip promised the league city-states freedom from interference in their internal affairs, they had to yield to him their power to decide foreign policy. As it turned out, the Greeks would never again regain the freedom to make such decisions on their own without some outside ruler looking over their shoulder.

Exploits of Alexander the Great, 336–323 B.C.E.

Alexander III stepped onto center stage in 336 B.C.E., when a Macedonian assassinated his father. Unconfirmed rumors speculated that Alexander's mother, Olympias, had arranged the murder to seize the throne for her twenty-year-old son. Alexander soon murdered potential rivals for the crown and, in several lightning-fast wars, subdued Macedonia's enemies on the west and north. Then Alexander compelled the southern Greeks, who had defected from the Macedonian-led league after Philip's death, to rejoin. To demonstrate the price of disloyalty, in 335 B.C.E. he destroyed Thebes for rebelling.

The following year Alexander embarked on the most astonishing military campaign in ancient history by leading a Macedonian and Greek army against the Persian Empire to fulfill his father's dream of avenging Greece. Alexander's astounding success in conquering everything from Turkey to Egypt to Uzbekistan while still in his twenties earned him the title "the Great" in later ages and inspired countless legends. His greatness came from his ability to inspire his men to follow him into unknown lands and to lead daring cavalry charges to disrupt the enemy's infantry. Alexander regularly rode his warhorse Bucephalus ("Oxhead") into the heart of the enemy's front line, sharing the danger of the common soldier. No one could miss him in his plumed helmet, vividly colored cloak, and armor polished to reflect the sun. He alarmed his principal adviser by giving away nearly all his property to create new landowners who would furnish troops. "What," the adviser asked, "do you have left for yourself?" "My hopes," Alexander replied. Those hopes centered on being a warrior as splendid as the matchless Achilles of Homer's *Iliad*; he always slept with a copy of the *Iliad* and a dagger under his pillow.

Alexander displayed his heroic ambitions as his army advanced relentlessly eastward through Persian territory (Map 3.1). In Anatolia, he visited Gordion, where an oracle had promised the lordship of Asia to whoever could loosen a seemingly impenetrable knot of rope tying the yoke of an ancient chariot preserved in the city. The young king, so the story goes, cut the knot with his sword. When his army later forced the Persian king, Darius III, to abandon his wives and daughters, Alexander treated the captured women with honor. His polite behavior toward the royal women won him respect from the peoples of the Persian Empire.

Alexander complemented his bravery and courtesy toward women with a keen eye for innovative military technology. When Tyre, a fortified city on an island off the coast of the Levant, refused to surrender in 332 B.C.E., he built a massive stone pier as a platform for armored battering rams and catapults flinging boulders to breach the walls of the city. The capture of Tyre demonstrated to walled city-states that they could no longer expect to hold out indefinitely in a siege; this awareness that a well-equipped army could penetrate fortification walls made it difficult for cities to remain united in the face of attacks and easier for Alexander to convince them to surrender.

■ **MAP 3.1 Conquests of Alexander the Great, 336–323 B.C.E.**

The huge extent of Alexander's military campaigns in Asia made him a legend. From the time he led his army out of Macedonia and Greece in 334 B.C.E. until his death in Babylon in 323 B.C.E., he never stopped fighting. His careful intelligence gathering combined with his charismatic and brilliant generalship produced an unbroken string of victories. His skillful choice of regional administrators, founding of garrison cities and colonies, and preservation of local governing structures kept his conquests stable after he moved on. **For more help analyzing this map,** *see the map activity for this chapter in the* ONLINE STUDY GUIDE *at* bedfordstmartins.com/huntconcise.

After conquering Egypt and the Persian heartland, Alexander revealed his strategy for ruling a vast empire: establish colonies of Greeks and Macedonians in conquered territory but keep the area's traditional administrative system. The first new colony he established, in 331 B.C.E., was a city in Egypt on the Mediterranean coast to the west of the Nile River. He named it Alexandria, after himself. In Persia, he proclaimed himself king of Asia but left the existing Persian administrative system in place, even retaining some high-ranking Persian officials. That a Macedonian became Persian king hardly changed the lives of the local populations of the Persian Empire. They continued to send the same taxes to a still remote master, whom they rarely if ever saw.

Alexander's goal seems to have been to outdo even the heroes of legend by marching to the end of the world. Reducing his army to lessen the need for supplies, he led his forces northeast into lands previously unknown to Greeks, Bactria and

Sogdiana (modern Afghanistan and Uzbekistan). On the Jaxartes River (Syr Darya), he founded a city called Alexandria the Furthest to show that he had penetrated deeper into this region than even Cyrus, founder of the Persian Empire. When it proved impossible to pin down the fast-moving locals, however, Alexander settled for an alliance sealed by his marriage to the Bactrian princess Roxane. He then headed east into India. Seventy days of marching through monsoon rains extinguished his soldiers' fire for conquest. In the spring of 326 B.C.E., they mutinied on the banks of the Hyphasis River in western India and forced Alexander to turn back. A difficult march brought him back to Persia by 324 B.C.E.; he immediately began planning an invasion of the Arabian peninsula and, after that, North Africa.

His conquests changed Alexander. He was no longer keeping the promise to the league city-states to respect their internal freedom. He ordered them to restore citizenship to the many war-created exiles whose status as wandering, stateless

■ **Mosaic of Alexander the Great at the Battle of Issus**
This large mosaic, which served as a floor in an upscale Roman house, was a copy of a famous earlier painting of the battle of Issus of 333 B.C.E. It shows Alexander the Great on his warhorse Bucephalus (at left) confronting the Persian king Darius in his chariot. Darius reaches out in compassion for his warriors, who are sacrificing themselves to protect him. The original artist was an extremely skilled painter. Notice the dramatic foreshortening of the horse directly in front of Darius and the startling effect of the face of the dying warrior reflected in the polished shield just to the right of the horse. Alexander usually wore a helmet; why do you think the artist portrayed him bareheaded? (Erich Lessing/Art Resource, NY.)

persons was creating unrest. Even more startling was his announcement that he wished to receive the honors due a god. At first bewildered by these instructions, most Greek city-states soon complied by sending honorary religious delegations to him. The Spartan Damis expressed the only prudent position on Alexander's deification: "If Alexander wishes to be a god, then we'll agree that he be called a god." Personal rather than political motives best explain Alexander's wish. He almost certainly had come to believe he was actually the son of Zeus; after all, Greek mythology contained many stories of Zeus mating with a human female and producing children. Alexander's feats exceeded the bounds of human possibility, demonstrating that he had achieved godlike power and therefore must be a god himself.

Alexander's plans for more conquest ended when he unexpectedly died of an illness, made worse by heavy drinking, in Babylon in 323 B.C.E. Roxane gave birth to a child a few months after Alexander's death, but, like Pericles, Alexander had made no plans about who should rule in his place if he suddenly disappeared. The story goes that when his commanders asked him on his deathbed to whom he bequeathed his kingdom, he replied, "To the most powerful."

Modern scholars disagree on almost everything about Alexander. They offer varying judgments on his character, ranging from bloodthirsty monster interested only in endless conquest to romantic dreamer aiming to create a multiethnic world open to all cultures. The ancient sources suggest that Alexander had interlinked goals: the conquest and rule of the known world and the exploration and possible colonization of new territory beyond. Conquest through military action was a time-honored pursuit for Macedonian leaders like Alexander and suited his restless, ruthless, and incredibly energetic nature. He included non-Macedonians in his administration and army because he needed their skills. Alexander's explorations benefited numerous scientific fields, from geography to botany, because he took along scientifically minded writers to collect and catalog the new knowledge they acquired; he regularly sent reams of new scientific information to his old tutor Aristotle. The far-flung cities that Alexander founded served as outposts to warn headquarters about local uprisings. They also created new opportunities for trade in valuable goods such as spices that were not produced in the Mediterranean region.

The Athenian orator Aeschines (c. 397–322 B.C.E.) summed up the stunned reaction of many people to Alexander's deeds: "What strange and unexpected event has not occurred in our time? The life we have lived is no ordinary human one, but we were born to be an object of wonder to later ages." Aeschines predicted correctly. Stories of fabulous deeds attributed to Alexander became popular folktales throughout the world, reaching even distant regions where Alexander had never set foot, such as southern Africa. The popularity of his legend as a warrior-hero lasted into later ages because his achievements seemed incredible. That the worlds of Greece and the Near East had been brought into closer contact than ever before represented another long-lasting effect of his astonishing career, which drew the curtain on the Classical period and opened the next act in the drama of Western history, the Hellenistic period.

> ■ **REVIEW:** *How were Philip II and his son Alexander able to establish such a powerful empire?*

The Hellenistic Kingdoms, 323–30 B.C.E.

The innovative political, cultural, and economic developments of the Hellenistic period arose from the interaction of Greek and Near Eastern civilizations. War set this process in motion, and its changes created tension between conquerors and subjects and produced uneven results. Greek ideas and practices had their greatest impact on the urban populations of Egypt and southwestern Asia. The many people who farmed in the countryside had much less contact with Greek ways of life. Later on, the Hellenistic world's cultural achievements greatly influenced the Romans.

The dominant Hellenistic political structures were new kingdoms, which reintroduced monarchy into Greek history; kings had been rare in Greece since the fall of Mycenaean civilization nearly a thousand years earlier. Commanders from Alexander's army created the new kingdoms by seizing portions of his empire for themselves after his death and declaring themselves kings. Between 306 and 304 B.C.E., after more than twenty years of struggle, their families established themselves as dynasties ruling Hellenistic kingdoms.

The Structure of Hellenistic Kingdoms

Alexander's commanders divided his conquests into three major parts (Map 3.2): Antigonus (c. 382–301 B.C.E.) took over in Anatolia, the Near East, Macedonia, and Greece; Seleucus (c. 358–281 B.C.E.), in Babylonia and the East as far as India; and Ptolemy (c. 367–282 B.C.E.), in Egypt. These new rulers—historians call them **successor kings** because they succeeded Alexander—had to create their own form of kingship because they did not inherit their positions legitimately: they were self-declared monarchs with neither blood ties to any traditional royal family line nor any personal relationship to a particular territory. For this reason, historians often characterize their type of rule as "personal monarchy."

By the middle of the third century B.C.E., the three major Hellenistic kingdoms had reached a balance of power that prevented them from expanding much beyond their core territories. The Antigonids had been reduced to a kingdom in Macedonia, but they also controlled mainland Greece, whose city-states had to follow royal foreign policy even though they retained much internal freedom. The Seleucids ruled in Syria and Mesopotamia, but they had been forced to yield their easternmost

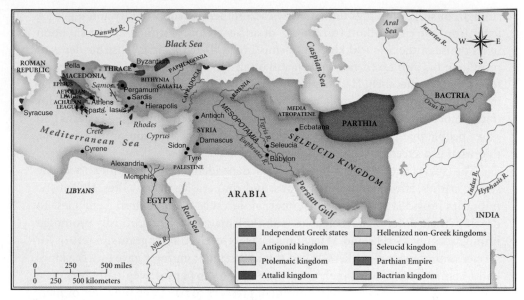

■ MAP 3.2 Hellenistic Kingdoms, c. 240 B.C.E.

Although the traditional Greek city-states kept their internal independence in the Hellenistic period, monarchy became the dominant political system in the areas of Alexander's former conquests. By about eighty years after his death in 323 B.C.E., the most striking changes to the three major kingdoms originally established by his successors were that the Seleucids had given up their easternmost territories and the Attalid kingdom had carved out an independent local reign in western Anatolia.

territory to the Indian king Chandragupta (r. 323–299 B.C.E.), founder of the Mauryan dynasty. They also lost most of Persia to the Parthians, a northern Iranian people. The Ptolemies retained control of the rich land of Egypt.

Conflicts frequently arose over contested border areas. The armies of the Ptolemaic and Seleucid kingdoms, for example, periodically battled over the lands of the Levant, just as the Egyptians and Hittites had done a thousand years earlier. Sometimes the struggles between the major kingdoms left openings for smaller, regional kingdoms to establish themselves. The most famous of these was the kingdom of the Attalids in western Anatolia, with the wealthy city of Pergamum as its capital. In Central Asia (in modern Afghanistan), Greek colonists settled by Alexander broke off from the Seleucid kingdom in the mid–third century B.C.E. to found their own regional kingdom in Bactria. Between 239 and 130 B.C.E., it flourished from the trade in luxury goods between India and China and the Mediterranean world.

The Hellenistic kings realized that establishing the legitimacy of their rule was essential if their royal lines were to endure. To gain it, they tried to incorporate local traditions into their rule. For the Seleucids, this meant combining Macedonian with Near Eastern royal customs; for the Ptolemies, Macedonian with Egyptian. The strength of successor kings ultimately rested on their personal ability and power. A letter from the city of Ilion (on the site of ancient Troy) summed up the situation in its praise of the Seleucid king Antiochus I (c. 324–261 B.C.E.): "His rule depends mostly on his own excellence [*aretê*], and on the goodwill of his friends and on his forces." In the end, then, Hellenistic monarchy amounted to foreign rule over original local populations by kings and queens of Macedonian descent. Seleucus, for one, claimed this right as a universal truth: "It is not the customs of the Persians and other people that I impose upon you, but the law which is common to everyone, that what is decreed by the king is always just."

The survival of Hellenistic dynasties depended on their ability to create strong armies, effective administrations, and cooperative urban elites. Hellenistic militaries provided security against internal unrest as well as external enemies. To develop their forces, the Seleucid and Ptolemaic kings vigorously promoted immigration by Greeks and Macedonians, who received land grants in return for service as professional soldiers. When this source of manpower gave out, the kings had to employ more local men as troops. Military expenses eventually became a problem because the kings faced continual pressure to pay large numbers of mercenaries and because military technology had become so expensive. To compete effectively, a Hellenistic king had to provide giant artillery, such as catapults capable of flinging a projectile weighing 170 pounds a distance of nearly two hundred yards.

Hellenistic kings had to create large administrations to collect the revenues they needed. They recruited immigrant Greeks and Macedonians to be their top officials. Local men who wanted a job as a lower official bettered their chances if they learned to read and write Greek in addition to their native language. This bilingualism qualified them to communicate official orders, especially tax laws, to farmers and crafts producers. Greeks and Macedonians generally saw themselves as too superior to mix with the locals, so Greeks and non-Greeks tended to live in separate communities.

Agriculture and trade generated the wealth of the kingdoms, and cities old and new were their economic and social hubs. Many Greeks and Macedonians lived in new cities founded by Alexander and his successors in Egypt and the Near East, and they also moved to old cities. Hellenistic kings promoted this urban emigration to build communities supportive of their rule. These rulers adorned their new cities with the traditional features of classical Greek city-states, such as gymnasiums and theaters. Although these cities often had the political institutions of the polis, such as councils and assemblies for citizen men, the requirement to follow royal policy limited their freedom. The kings treated the cities considerately because they needed the Greek and Macedonian urban elites to keep order and ensure a steady flow of tax revenues. Wealthy people had the crucial responsibility of collecting taxes from the surrounding countryside, as well as from their city, and sending the money

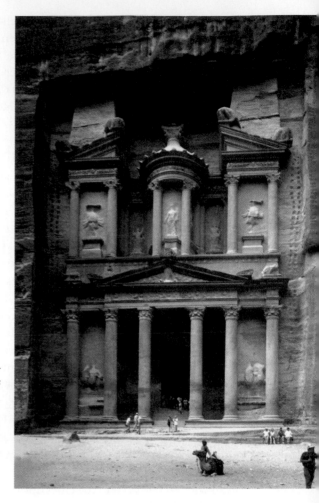

■ Hellenistic Architecture in the Jordanian Desert

This decorative front for a structure carved into a sheer rock cliff in probably the first century B.C.E. stands at the entrance to the ancient settlement of Petra, the capital of the Nabatean Arabs (in what is today Jordan). This desert people grew rich by controlling caravan trade from Asia across the deserts to the Mediterranean coast. In true Hellenistic spirit, they took Greek architectural models and adapted them to express their own style. For example, this carved front has Greek triangular pediments but also makes a break in the upper pediment to include a round gazebo. What do you think the visual effect of this innovation would be as the sunlight moves during the day?
(Z. Radovan, www.BibleLandPictures.com.)

on to the royal treasury. In turn, the kings honored and flattered members of the cities' social elites.

The kings' reliance on local elites led them to establish close relationships with well-to-do non-Greeks living in the old cities of Anatolia and the Near East, such as Sardis, Tyre, and Babylon. In addition, non-Greeks and non-Macedonians from eastern regions began moving westward to the new Hellenistic Greek cities in increasing numbers. Jews in particular moved from Palestine to Anatolia, Greece, and Egypt. The Jewish community eventually became an influential minority in Egyptian Alexandria, the most important Hellenistic city.

All the Hellenistic kingdoms eventually fell to the Romans. The Ptolemaic kingdom survived the longest. The end came when Queen Cleopatra VII, a descendant of Ptolemy and the last Macedonian to rule Egypt, chose the losing side in the Roman civil war between Mark Antony, her lover at that time, and the future emperor Augustus in the late first century B.C.E. In 30 B.C.E., an invading Roman army ended her reign and three centuries of Hellenistic monarchy.

Hierarchy in Hellenistic Society

People in the eastern Mediterranean Hellenistic world lived in a social hierarchy with the royal family and the king's friends ranking highest. The Greek and Macedonian elites of the major cities ranked next. Just under them came the non-Greek wealthy elites of the cities, the leaders of large minority urban populations, and the traditional lords and princes of local groups who maintained their ancestral domains in rural regions. Lowest of the free population were the masses of small merchants, artisans, and laborers. Slaves had no social standing.

The growth of the kingdoms apparently increased the demand for slave labor throughout the eastern Mediterranean. The centrally located island of Delos established a market where up to ten thousand slaves were bought and sold daily. The fortunate ones would become servants at court and live physically comfortable lives; the luckless ones would toil, and soon die, in the mines. Enslaved children often were taken far from home and put to work. A sales contract from 259 B.C.E. shows that Zeno, to whom the camel trader wrote, bought a girl about seven years old named Sphragis ("Gemstone") to work in an Egyptian textile factory. This was not her first job. Originally from Sidon in the Levant, she had previously been the slave of a Greek mercenary soldier employed by Toubias, a Jewish cavalry commander in the Transjordan region.

Even with power based in the cities, most of the population continued to live in small villages. Most farmers were forced tenants on royal land who were not allowed to move away or stop working. Free peasants still worked their own small plots as well as the farms of wealthy landowners. Perhaps 80 percent of all adult men and women had to work the land to produce enough food to sustain the population. In the cities, the poor worked as small merchants, peddlers, and artisans. Men could sign on as deckhands on the merchant ships that sailed the Mediterranean Sea and Indian Ocean.

Women's status in the Hellenistic world depended on the social layer to which they belonged. Like their Macedonian predecessors, Hellenistic queens enjoyed enormous riches and high honor. Because the Ptolemaic royal family observed the Egyptian royal tradition of brother-sister marriage, daughters could rule alongside sons. For example, Arsinoe II (c. 316–270 B.C.E.), the daughter of Ptolemy I, first married the Macedonian successor king Lysimachus, who gave her four towns as her personal domain. After Lysimachus's death she married her brother Ptolemy II and exerted at least as much influence on Egyptian policy as he did. The virtues publicly praised in a queen reflected traditional Greek values for women. When the city of Hierapolis around 165 B.C.E. passed a decree honoring Queen Apollonis of Pergamum, for example, it praised her piety toward the gods, her reverence toward her parents, her distinguished conduct toward her husband, and her harmonious relations with her "beautiful children born in wedlock."

Elite women continued to live separated from nonfamily males; poor women still worked in public. Greeks continued to abandon infants they could not or would not raise—girls more often than boys. Other populations, such as the Egyptians and the Jews, did not practice abandonment, or exposure, as it is called. Exposure differed from infanticide because the parents expected someone else to find the child and raise it, albeit usually as a slave.

In some limited ways, women achieved greater control over their own lives in the Hellenistic period. A woman of exceptional wealth could enter public life by making donations or loans to her city and being rewarded with an official post in local government. Such positions were less prestigious than in the days of the independent city-states because the king and his top administrators now controlled the real power. In Egypt, women acquired greater say in the family because marriage contracts, the standard procedure, gradually evolved from an agreement between the groom and the bride's parents to one in which the bride made her own arrangements with the groom.

■ **Egyptian-Style Statue of Queen Arsinoe II**
Arsinoe II (c. 316–270 B.C.E.), daughter of Ptolemy I and widow of the Macedonian "successor" king Lysimachus, married her brother Ptolemy II to unify the monarchy. Hailed as Philadelphoi *("Brother-Loving"), the couple set a precedent for brother-sister marriages in the Ptolemaic dynasty. One of the most remarkable women of the Hellenistic period, Arsinoe was the first Ptolemaic ruler whose image was placed in Egyptian temples as a "temple-sharing goddess." This eight-foot-tall, red granite statue portrays her in the traditional sculptural style of the pharaohs.* (Vatican Museums.)

During this period, it became more common for the wealthy to follow the example of royalty and show concern for the poor. On the island of Samos, for example, prosperous citizens funded a foundation to distribute free grain. Donor-sponsored schools sprang up in various cities, and sometimes girls as well as boys could attend. Many cities also began sponsoring doctors. Donors were repaid by the respect and honor they earned from their fellow citizens. In this system, the welfare of the masses depended on the generosity of the rich; without democracy, the poor had no political power to demand reforms. This strongly hierarchical arrangement reflected the top-down structure of Hellenistic society.

■ **REVIEW:** *What were the biggest challenges faced by the Hellenistic kings?*

Hellenistic Culture

Hellenistic culture reflected three principal characteristics of the age: the effects of royal wealth, ordinary people concentrating on private matters more than public life, and the increased interaction of diverse peoples. In keeping with the era's hierarchical trends, the kings almost single-handedly determined developments in literature, art, science, and philosophy by deciding which fields and which scholars and artists to support financially. The kings' status as sole rulers and the source of law meant that authors and artists did not have freedom to criticize public policy and thus concentrated on individual emotions and aspects of private life. Nevertheless, royal support did produce an expansion and diversification of knowledge. Cultural interaction between Greek and Near Eastern traditions happened most prominently in language and religion. These developments eventually became extremely influential in Roman culture; in this way, "captive Greece captured its fierce victor," as the Roman poet Horace (65–8 B.C.E.) expressed the effect of Hellenistic culture on his own.

The Arts under Royal Support

The Hellenistic kings supported scholarship and the arts on a vast scale, competing with one another to lure the best scholars and artists to their capitals with magnificent salaries and benefits. They paid for many intellectual innovations but for little applied technology except for military use. The Ptolemies assembled the Hellenistic world's most intellectually distinguished court by turning Alexandria into the Mediterranean's leading center of the arts. There they established the first scholarly research institute. Its massive library had the ambitious goal of trying to collect all the books (that is, manuscripts) in the world; it grew to hold a half-million scrolls, an enormous number for the time. Linked to it was a building in which the hired scholars dined together and produced encyclopedias of knowledge such as

The Wonders of the World and *On the Rivers of Europe* by Callimachus, a learned prose writer as well as a poet. The name of this building, the Museum (meaning "place of the Muses," the Greek goddesses of learning and the arts), is still used to designate institutions that preserve and promote knowledge. The output of the Alexandrian scholars was huge. Their champion was Didymus (c. 80–10 B.C.E.), nicknamed "Brass Guts" for his tireless writing of nearly four thousand books of research; it is a sad commentary on the preservation of ancient sources that not a single one has survived.

The writers and artists whom Hellenistic kings paid had to please their employers with their works. The poet Theocritus (c. 300–260 B.C.E.), for example, relocated from his home in Syracuse to the Ptolemaic court. In a poem expressly praising his employer, Ptolemy II, he spelled out their professional relationship: "The spokesmen of the Muses [that is, poets] celebrate Ptolemy in return for his benefactions." Theocritus and other poets succeeded by avoiding political subjects and stressing the division in society between the intellectual elite—to which the kings belonged—and the uneducated masses. Their poetry centered on individual emotions and broke new ground in demanding great intellectual effort as well as emotional engagement from the audience. Only people with a deep literary education could appreciate the allusions and complex references to mythology that these poets employed in their elegant poems.

Theocritus was the first Greek poet to express the divide between town and countryside that was becoming a Hellenistic reality. The *Idylls*, his pastoral poems, emphasized the discontinuity between the elegant environment of the city and the simple life in the country, reflecting the fundamental social division of the Ptolemaic kingdom between the food consumers of the town and the food producers of the countryside. He presented a city dweller's idealized dream that country life must be peaceful and stress free; this fiction deeply influenced later literature.

Women poets made important contributions to literature in the Hellenistic period, apparently without any royal support. They excelled in writing **epigrams**, a style of short poem originally meant for tombstones. Elegantly worded poems written by women from diverse regions of the Hellenistic world—Anyte of Tegea in the Peloponnese, Nossis of Locri in southern Italy, Moero of Byzantium—still survive. Women, from "companions" to respectable matrons, figured as frequent subjects in their work and expressed a wide variety of personal feelings, love above all. Nossis's poem on the power of Eros (Greek for "Love"), for example, proclaimed, "Nothing is sweeter than Eros. All other delights are second to it—from my mouth I spit out even honey. And this Nossis says: whoever Aphrodite has not kissed knows not what sort of flowers are her roses." No Hellenistic literature better conveys the depth of human emotion than the epigrams of women poets.

The Hellenistic theater also presented stories of individual emotion; no longer did dramatists offer open criticism of politics or contemporary leaders as they had in Golden Age comedy. Comic playwrights such as Menander (c. 342–289 B.C.E.)

composed plays with timeless plots concerning the trials and tribulations of fictional lovers. These comedies of manners, as they are called, proved enormously popular because, like modern situation comedies, they offered a humorous view of situations and feelings that occur in daily life and cleverly made fun of social conditions. Recent papyrus finds have allowed us to recover almost complete plays of Menander, the most famous Hellenistic playwright, and to appreciate his subtle skill in depicting personality. He presented his first comedy at Athens in 324 or 323 B.C.E. No tragedies written in this period have survived intact, but we know that they could involve the interaction among peoples and cultures at this time. Ezechiel, for example, a Jew living in Alexandria, wrote *Exodus*, a tragedy in Greek about Moses leading the Hebrews out of captivity in Egypt.

Like poet and dramatists, Hellenistic sculptors and painters featured human emotions prominently in their works. Classical-era artists had given their subjects' faces a serenity that represented an ideal rather than reality. Numerous examples, usually surviving only in later copies, show that Hellenistic artists portrayed individual emotions more naturally in a variety of types. In portrait sculpture, Lysippus's widely copied bust of Alexander the Great captured the young commander's passionate dreaminess. A sculpture from Pergamum by an unknown artist commemorated the third-century B.C.E. Attalid victory over the plundering Gauls (one of the Celtic peoples, called *Galatians*) by showing a defeated Gallic warrior stabbing himself after killing his wife to prevent her enslavement by the victors. A large-scale painting of Alexander battling the Persian king Darius (see page 104) portrayed Alexander's intense concentration and Darius's horrified expression. The artist, probably either Philoxenus of Eretria or a Greek woman from Egypt named Helena (one of the first female artists known), used foreshortening and strong contrasts between shadows and highlights to increase the picture's emotional impact.

To appreciate fully the appeal of Hellenistic sculpture, we must remember that, like earlier Greek sculpture, it was painted in bright colors. But Hellenistic art differed from classical art in its social context. Works of classical art had been paid for by the city-states for public display or by wealthy individuals to donate to their city-state as a work of public art. Now sculptors and painters created their works primarily for royalty and the urban elites who wanted to show they had artistic taste like the royal family. The increasing diversity of subjects that emerged in Hellenistic art presumably represented a trend approved by kings, queens, and the elites. Sculpture best reveals this new preference for showing humans in a wide variety of poses, mostly from private life (in contrast with classical art). Hellenistic sculptors portrayed subjects never before shown: foreigners, drunkards, battered athletes, wrinkled old people. The female nude became a particular favorite. A statue of Aphrodite, which Praxiteles sculpted completely nude as an innovation in portraying this goddess, became so famous as a religious object and tourist attraction in the city of Cnidos that the king of Bithynia later offered to pay off the citizens' entire public debt if they would give him this work of art. They refused.

■ Dying Celts

Hellenistic artists excelled in portraying deeply emotional scenes such as this scene of a Celtic warrior, who is committing suicide after killing his wife to prevent their capture by the enemy after defeat in battle. Celtic women followed their men to the battlefield and willingly exposed themselves to the same dangers. The original statues (these are Roman imitations) were in bronze, forming part of a large sculptural group that Attalus I, king of Pergamum from 241 to 197 B.C.E., set up on his acropolis to commemorate his defeat around 230 B.C.E. of the Celts, called Galatians, who had moved into Anatolia in the 270s B.C.E. in order to conduct raids throughout the area. Why do you think that Attalus celebrated his victory by erecting a monument that portrayed the defeated enemy as brave and noble? **For more help analyzing this image,** see the visual activity for this chapter in the ONLINE STUDY GUIDE at **bedfordstmartins. com/ huntconcise.**

(Erich Lessing/Art Resource, NY.)

Philosophy for a New Age

New philosophies arose in the Hellenistic period, all asking the same question: what is the best way for humans to live? They recommended different paths to the same answer: individual humans must find personal serenity, to achieve freedom from the turbulence of outside forces, especially chance. For Greeks in particular, the changes in political and social life accompanying the rise to dominance of the Macedonian and, later, the Hellenistic kings made this focus necessary. Outside forces—aggressive kings—had robbed the city-states of their freedom of action internationally, and the fates of entire communities as well as individuals rested in the hands of distant, unpredictable monarchs. More than ever before, human life and opportunities for free choice seemed out of individuals' control. It therefore made sense, at least for those wealthy enough to spend time philosophizing, to look for personal, private solutions to the unsettling new conditions of life in the Hellenistic Age. More women than ever before joined in this quest.

Few Hellenistic thinkers concentrated on metaphysics. Instead they focused on philosophical **materialism,** a doctrine asserting that only things made up of matter truly exist. It denied the concept of soul that Plato described and ignored any suggestion that nonmaterial phenomena could exist. Hellenistic philosophy was regularly divided into three related areas: *logic,* the process for discovering truth; *physics,* the fundamental truth about the nature of existence; and *ethics,* the way humans should achieve happiness and well-being as a consequence of logic and physics. The era's philosophical thought greatly influenced Roman thinkers and many important Western philosophers who followed them.

One of the two most significant new philosophical schools of thought was **Epicureanism**. It took its name from its founder, Epicurus (341–271 B.C.E.), who settled his followers in Athens in a house about 307 B.C.E. amid a shady park (hence "The Garden" as his school's name). Under Epicurus the study of philosophy broke with tradition because he admitted not only women but also slaves as regular members of his group. His lover, the "companion" Leontion, became well known for her treatise criticizing the views of Theophrastus (c. 370–285 B.C.E.), Aristotle's most famous pupil.

People should above all be free of worry about death, Epicurus taught, because all matter consists of microscopic atoms in random movement and death is nothing more than the painless separating of the body's atoms. Moreover, all human knowledge must be empirical—that is, derived from experience and perception. Despite the common belief, the gods do not cause thunder, drought, and other natural events. The gods live far away in perfect peacefulness, paying no attention to human affairs. People therefore have nothing to fear from the gods, in life or in death.

Epicurus believed people should pursue pleasure, but his notion of true pleasure had a special definition: he insisted that it consists of the "absence of disturbance" from pain and everyday troubles, passions, and desires. A sober life spent with friends apart from the cares of the world could best provide this essential peace of mind. His teaching represented a serious challenge to the traditional ideal of Greek citizenship, which required men of means to participate in local politics and citizen women to engage in public religious cults.

The other important new Hellenistic philosophy, Stoicism, did not call for people to retire from public life. Its name derived from the Painted Stoa in Athens, where Stoic philosophers discussed their doctrines. Zeno (c. 333–262 B.C.E.) from Citium on Cyprus founded **Stoicism**, but Chrysippus (c. 280–206 B.C.E.) from Cilicia in Anatolia did the most to make it a complete guide to life. Stoics believed that life is fated but that people should still pursue virtue as their goal. Virtue, they said, consists of putting oneself in harmony with the divine, rational force of universal Nature by developing the virtues of good sense, justice, courage, and moderation. These doctrines applied to women as well as men. In fact, the Stoics advocated equal citizenship for women and doing away with marriage and families as the Greeks knew them. Zeno even proposed unisex clothing as a way to obliterate unnecessary distinctions between women and men.

The belief that fate determines everything created the question of whether humans truly have free will. Employing some of the subtlest reasoning ever applied to this fundamental issue, Stoic philosophers concluded that purposeful human actions do have significance. Nature, itself good, does not prevent evil from occurring because virtue would otherwise have no meaning. What matters in life is the striving for good, not the result. A person should therefore take action against evil by, for example, participating in politics. To be a Stoic also meant to shun desire and anger while enduring pain and sorrow calmly, an attitude that yields the modern meaning of the word *stoic*. Through endurance and self-control, followers of Stoic philosophy attained personal serenity. They did not fear death because they believed that people live over and over again infinitely in identical fashion to their present lives.

Numerous other philosophies emerged in the Hellenistic period to compete with Epicureanism and Stoicism. Some of them carried on the work of famous earlier thinkers such as Plato and Pythagoras. Still others struck out in new directions. Skeptics, for example, aimed at the same state of personal serenity as did Epicureans and Stoics, but from a completely different assumption about reality. Pyrrho (c. 360–270 B.C.E.) of Elis in the Peloponnese established the principles of Skepticism; his ideas were influenced by the Indian ascetic wise men (the magi) he met while a member of Alexander the Great's expedition. Skeptics believed that secure knowledge about anything is impossible because the human senses yield contradictory information about the world. All that people can do, they insisted, is depend on appearances while withholding judgment about their reality.

The philosophers called *Cynics* boastfully rejected every convention of ordinary life, especially wealth and material comfort. They believed that humans should aim for complete self-sufficiency. Whatever is natural is good, they said, and can be done without shame before anyone. According to this idea, public defecation and fornication were acceptable, and women and men alike were free to have sex however and whenever they pleased. Above all, Cynics rejected traditional human behavior as ridiculous. The most famous early Cynic, Diogenes (d. 323 B.C.E.) from Sinope on the Black Sea, had a reputation for wearing borrowed clothes and sleeping in a giant storage jar. Almost as notorious was Hipparchia, a Cynic of the late fourth century B.C.E. She once bested an obnoxious philosophical opponent named Theodorus the Atheist with the following argument: "That which would not be considered wrong if done by Theodorus would also not be considered wrong if done by Hipparchia.

Now if Theodorus strikes himself, he does no wrong. Therefore, if Hipparchia strikes Theodorus, she does no wrong." The name *Cynic*, which meant "like a dog," reflected the ancient evaluation of this unconventional way of life; our word *cynical* recalls the Cynics' biting criticism of what others regarded as normal.

In the Hellenistic period, Greek philosophy reached a wider audience than ever before. Although the working poor had neither the leisure nor the money to attend philosophers' lectures, affluent members of society studied philosophy in growing numbers. Theophrastus lectured to crowds of up to two thousand in Athens. Most philosophy students continued to be men, but women could join the groups attached to certain philosophers. Kings competed to attract famous thinkers to their courts, and Greek settlers took their interest in philosophy with them, even to the most remote Hellenistic cities. Archaeologists excavating a Hellenistic city located thousands of miles from Greece on the Oxus River in Afghanistan, for example, turned up a Greek philosophical text as well as inscriptions of moral advice imputed to Apollo's oracle at Delphi.

Innovation in the Sciences

Science first became an activity separated from philosophy during the Hellenistic period. Scientific investigation of the physical world so benefited from this divorce that historians have dubbed this era the Golden Age of ancient science. Various factors contributed to this flourishing of thought and discovery: the expeditions of Alexander had encouraged curiosity and increased knowledge about the extent and differing features of the world, royal wealth supported scientists financially, and the concentration of scientists in Alexandria promoted an exchange of ideas that could not have taken place otherwise.

The greatest advances came in geometry and mathematics. Euclid, who taught at Alexandria around 300 B.C.E., made revolutionary progress in the analysis of two- and three-dimensional space. The usefulness of Euclidean geometry continues today. Archimedes of Syracuse (287–212 B.C.E.) was a mathematical genius who calculated the approximate value of *pi* and devised a way to manipulate very large numbers. He also invented hydrostatics (the science of the equilibrium of a fluid system) and mechanical devices such as a screw for lifting water to a higher elevation. Archimedes' shout of delight "I have found it" (*heureka* in Greek) when he solved a problem while soaking in his bathtub lives on in the modern expression "Eureka!"

The sophistication of Hellenistic mathematics affected other fields that also required complex computation. Aristarchus of Samos early in the third century B.C.E. became the first to propose the correct model of the solar system: the earth revolves around the sun, which is far larger and far more distant than it appears. Later astronomers rejected Aristarchus's heliocentric model in favor of the traditional geocentric one (with the earth at the center) because calculations based on

■ Bronze Astronomical Calculator

Underwater archaeologists found these fragments in an ancient shipwreck off Anticythera, south of the Peloponnese. This bronze object, which its discoverers at first could not identify, was being transported to Italy in the early first century B.C.E. as part of a shipment of metalwork and other valuable objects. Historians of science have figured out that it was a calculator to determine the position of stars and planets. Its intermeshed gears controlled rotating dials. The sophisticated applied engineering and astronomical knowledge necessary to design and build this machine reveal the high level of achievement of Hellenistic science. (National Archaeological Museum, Athens. Archaeological Receipts Fund.)

the orbit he calculated for the earth failed to correspond to the observed positions of the planets. Aristarchus had made an unfortunate mistake: assuming a circular orbit instead of an elliptical one. Eratosthenes of Cyrene (c. 275–194 B.C.E.) pioneered mathematical geography. He calculated the circumference of the earth with astonishing accuracy by simultaneously measuring the length of the shadows of widely separated but identically tall structures. The ideas and procedures of these Hellenistic researchers gave Western scientific thought an important start toward the principle scientists now take for granted: the need to verify theory through observation and measurement in experiments.

Hellenistic science maintained a spirit of discovery despite the enormous difficulties imposed by technical limitations. Many experiments were not possible because no technology existed for the precise measurement of very short intervals of time. Measuring tiny quantities of matter was also next to impossible. The science of the age was as quantitative as it could be given these limitations. Ctesibius of Alexandria (b. c. 310 B.C.E.), a contemporary of Aristarchus, invented the scientific field of pneumatics by creating machines operated by air pressure. He also built a working water pump, an organ powered by water, and the first accurate water clock. A later Alexandrian, Hero, continued the Hellenistic tradition of mechanical ingenuity by building a rotating sphere powered by steam. As in most of Hellenistic science, these inventions did not lead to uses in daily life. The scientists and their royal supporters were more interested in new theoretical discoveries than in practical results, and the metallurgical technology to produce the pipes, fittings, and screws needed to build powerful machines did not yet exist.

Military technology was the one area in which Hellenistic science produced practical inventions. The kings hired engineers to design powerful catapults and wheeled siege towers many stories high to batter down the defenses of walled cities. The most famous large-scale application of technology for nonmilitary purposes was the construction of a lighthouse three hundred feet tall (the Pharos) for the harbor at Alexandria. Using polished metal mirrors to reflect the light from a large bonfire, it shone many miles out over the sea. Grateful sailors regarded it as one of the wonders of the world.

Medicine also benefited from the thirst for new knowledge characteristic of Hellenistic science. The increased contact between Greeks and people of the Near East in this period made the medical knowledge of the ancient civilizations of Mesopotamia and Egypt better known in the West and promoted study of human health and illness. Around 325 B.C.E., Praxagoras of Cos discovered the value of measuring the pulse in diagnosing illness. A bit later, Herophilus of Chalcedon (b. c. 300 B.C.E.), working in Alexandria, became the first scientist in the West to study anatomy by dissecting human cadavers and, it was rumored, the bodies of condemned criminals while they were still alive; he had this gruesome opportunity because the king authorized his research. Some of the anatomical terms Herophilus invented are still used. Other Hellenistic advances in understanding anatomy included the discovery of the nerves and nervous system.

As in science, however, Hellenistic medicine was limited by its inability to measure and observe things not visible to the naked eye. Unable to see what really occurred under the skin in living patients, for example, doctors thought many illnesses in women were caused by displacements of the womb, which they wrongly believed could move around in the body. These mistaken ideas could not be corrected because the technology to evaluate them did not yet exist.

A New East-West Culture

Wealthy non-Greeks increasingly adopted Greek ways as they adapted to the new social hierarchy of the Hellenistic world. To give only one example: Diotimus of Sidon in the Levant adopted a Greek name and pursued the premier Greek sport, chariot racing. He traveled to Nemea in the Peloponnese to enter his chariot in the race at the prestigious festival of Zeus. He announced his victory in an inscription written in Greek, which had become the language of international commerce and culture in the Hellenistic world. The explosion in the use of a simplified version of Greek called **Koine** ("shared" or "common") reflected the emergence of an international culture based on Greek models; this was why the Egyptian camel trader stranded in Syria had to communicate in Greek with a high-level official such as Zeno.

The most striking evidence of this cultural development comes from Afghanistan. There, King Ashoka (r. c. 268–232 B.C.E.), who ruled most of the Indian subcontinent, used Greek as one of the languages in his public inscriptions to announce his efforts to introduce his subjects to Buddhist traditions of self-control, such as not eating meat. Local languages did not disappear in the Hellenistic kingdoms, however. In one region of Anatolia, people spoke twenty-two different languages.

The diversity of Hellenistic religion matched the variety of many other areas of life in this period of cultural interaction. The traditional cults of Greek religion remained very popular, but new cults, such as those that made gods of ruling kings, responded to changing political and social conditions. Preexisting cults that previously had only local significance, such as that of the Greek healing god Asclepius or the mystery cult of the Egyptian goddess Isis, grew prominent all over the Hellenistic world. In many cases, Greek cults and local cults from the eastern Mediterranean influenced each other. Their beliefs meshed well because these cults shared many assumptions about how to remedy the troubles of human life. In other instances, local cults and Greek cults existed side by side, with some overlap. The inhabitants of villages in the Fayum district of Egypt, for example, continued worshiping their traditional crocodile god and mummifying their dead according to the old ways but also worshiped Greek deities. In the tradition of polytheistic religion, people could worship in both old and new cults.

New cults picked up a prominent theme of Hellenistic thought: anxiety about the relationship between individuals and the unpredictable power of the divinities Luck and Chance. Although Greek religion had always been concerned with the unpredictability of life, the chaotic course of Greek history since the Peloponnesian War had made human existence seem more uncertain than ever. Since advances in astronomy revealed the mathematical precision of the heavens, religion now had to address the seeming disconnect between that celestial uniformity and the shapeless chaos of life on earth. One increasingly popular approach to bridging that gap was to rely on astrology for guidance derived from the movement of the stars and planets, thought of as divinities. Another very common choice was to worship Tyche (Chance) as a god in the hope of securing good luck in life.

The most revolutionary approach in seeking protection from the unpredictable tricks of Chance or Luck was to pray for salvation from a king regarded as a god, worshiped in what are known as **ruler cults**. Various populations established these cults to honor royal benefactors. The Athenians, for example, deified the Macedonians Antigonus and his son Demetrius as savior gods in 307 B.C.E., when these commanders liberated the city and bestowed magnificent gifts on it. Like most ruler cults, this one expressed both spontaneous gratitude and a desire to flatter the rulers in the hope of obtaining additional favors. Many cities in the Ptolemaic and Seleucid kingdoms created ruler cults for their kings and queens. An inscription put up by Egyptian priests in 238 B.C.E. described the qualities appropriate to a divine king and queen:

> King Ptolemy III and Queen Berenice, his sister and wife, the Benefactor Gods, . . . have provided good government . . . and [after a drought] sacrificed a large amount of their revenues for the salvation of the population, and by importing grain . . . they saved the inhabitants of Egypt.

As these words make clear, the Hellenistic rulers' tremendous power and wealth gave them the status of gods to the ordinary people who depended on their generosity and protection in times of danger. The idea that a human being could be a god, present on earth to be a "savior" delivering people from evils, was firmly established and would prove influential later in Roman imperial religion and Christianity.

Healing divinities offered another form of protection to anxious individuals. Scientific Greek medicine had rejected the notion of supernatural causes and cures for disease ever since Hippocrates had established his medical school on the Aegean island of Cos in the late fifth century B.C.E. Nevertheless, the cult of the god Asclepius, who offered cures for illness and injury at his many shrines, grew popular during the Hellenistic period. Suppliants seeking Asclepius's help would sleep in special dormitories at his shrines to await dreams in which he prescribed healing treatments. These prescriptions emphasized diet and exercise, but numerous inscriptions set up by grateful patients also testified to miraculous cures and surgery performed while the sufferer slept. The following example is typical:

> Ambrosia of Athens was blind in one eye. . . . She . . . ridiculed some of the cures [described in inscriptions in the sanctuary] as being incredible and impossible. . . . But when she went to sleep, she saw a vision; she thought the god was standing next to her. . . . He split open the diseased eye and poured in a medicine. When day came she left cured.

People's faith in divine healing gave them hope that they could overcome the constant, unpredictable danger of illness.

Mystery cults promised secret knowledge as a key to salvation during life and after death. The cults of the Greek god Dionysus and, in particular, the Egyptian goddess Isis gained many followers in this period. The popularity of Isis, whose powers extended over every area of human life, received a boost from King Ptolemy I, who established a headquarters for her cult in Alexandria. He also promoted the cult of the Egyptian deity Sarapis, Isis's consort, as his dynasty's protector; Sarapis reportedly performed miracles of rescue from shipwreck and illness. The cult of Isis, who became the most popular female divinity in the Mediterranean, involved

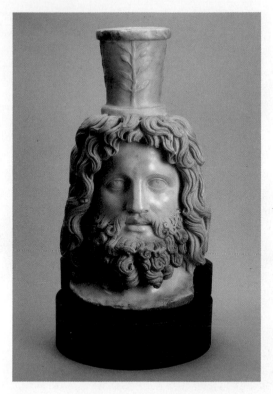

■ **Marble Head of the Greco-Egyptian God Sarapis**

Sarapis was originally an Egyptian god incorporating aspects of Osiris, the consort of Isis, and the sacred Apis bull. In the early Hellenistic period, the Ptolemaic royal family adopted Sarapis as its divine protector. Eventually, worshippers spread the cult of Sarapis around the Hellenistic world. They identified Sarapis as a transcendent god combining the powers of Zeus with those of other divinities, and they looked to him for miracles. He was commonly portrayed with a food container or measure on his head, as here, to signify his concern for human prosperity in this world and in the afterlife. That this head was found in a Roman-era temple in Britain indicates the long-lasting and widespread appeal of this deity.

(Museum of London Photographic Library.)

extensive rituals and festivals mixing features of Egyptian and Greek religion. Followers of Isis hoped, in return for a virtuous life, to gain the goddess's help against the demonic influence of Chance; they also expected she would reward them with a happier fate after death. That an Egyptian deity like Isis could achieve enormous popularity among Greeks (and Romans in later times) alongside the traditional gods of Greek religion is the best evidence of the cultural cross-fertilization of the Hellenistic world.

The history of Judaism in the Hellenistic period shows especially strong evidence of cultural interaction. King Ptolemy II had the Hebrew Bible translated into Greek (the Septuagint) in Alexandria in the early third century B.C.E. Many Jews, especially those living in the large Jewish communities that had grown up in Hellenistic cities outside Palestine, adopted the Greek language and many aspects of Greek culture. Nevertheless, these Hellenized Jews largely retained the ritual practices and habits of life that defined traditional Judaism, and they did not worship Greek gods. Hellenistic politics also affected the Jewish community in Palestine, which was controlled militarily and politically first by the Ptolemies and then by the Seleucids. Both allowed the Jews to live according to their ancestral tradition under the political leadership of a high priest in Jerusalem.

■ **MAPPING THE WEST The Fall of the Hellenistic Kingdoms, to 30 B.C.E.**
By 30 B.C.E. (the death of Cleopatra VII, the last Ptolemaic monarch of Egypt), the Roman republic had conquered or absorbed the Hellenistic kingdoms of the eastern Mediterranean. Competition for the tremendous wealth that Romans captured in this expansion helped fuel bitter and divisive feuds between Rome's most ambitious generals and political leaders. The territories of the former Hellenistic kingdoms became the main part of the eastern half of the Roman Empire.

Internal conflicts among Jews erupted in second-century B.C.E. Palestine over the amount of Greek influence that traditional Judaism could accept. The Seleucid king Antiochus IV (r. 175–163 B.C.E.) intervened in the conflict in support of the Jerusalem Jews who were most Greek-like in their ways. In 167 B.C.E., Antiochus converted the main Jewish temple there into a Greek temple and outlawed the practice of Jewish religious customs, such as observing the Sabbath and circumcision. A revolt led by Judah the Maccabee eventually won Jewish independence from the Seleucids after twenty-five years of war. The most famous episode of this revolt was the retaking of the Jerusalem temple and its rededication to the worship of the Jewish god Yahweh—a triumphant moment celebrated by Jews ever since on the holiday of Hanukkah. That Greek culture attracted some Jews in the first place, however, provides a striking example of the transformations that affected many—though far from all—people of the Hellenistic world. By the time of the Roman Empire, one of those transformations would be Christianity, whose beliefs had roots in the cultural interaction of Hellenistic Jews and Greeks and their ideas on religion.

■ **REVIEW:** *How did political changes in the Hellenistic period affect art and science?*

IMPORTANT DATES

399 B.C.E.	Trial and execution of Socrates at Athens	**331 B.C.E.**	Alexander founds Alexandria in Egypt
386 B.C.E.	Sparta makes a peace with Persia ceding control over the Anatolian Greek city-states; Plato founds the Academy in Athens	**324 or 323 B.C.E.**	Menander presents his first comedy at Athens
		323 B.C.E.	Alexander dies in Babylon
362 B.C.E.	Greek city-states weakened by fighting one another at battle of Mantinea	**c. 307 B.C.E.**	Epicurus founds "The Garden" in Athens
		306–304 B.C.E.	Alexander's successors declare themselves kings
338 B.C.E.	Philip II, Macedonian king, defeats Greek alliance at Chaeronea to become the leading power in Greece	**239–130 B.C.E.**	Independent Greek kingdom in Bactria (Afghanistan)
		167 B.C.E.	Jewish revolt in Jerusalem
336 B.C.E.	Philip II is murdered; Alexander becomes king	**30 B.C.E.**	Death of Cleopatra VII and takeover of the Ptolemaic kingdom by Rome
335 B.C.E.	Aristotle founds the Lyceum in Athens		
334 B.C.E.	Alexander leads an army of Greeks and Macedonians against the Persian Empire		

Conclusion

Greece's Classical period came to an end in the fourth century B.C.E. The violence and bitterness of the Peloponnesian War and its aftermath led ordinary people as well as philosophers to question the basis of morality. The characteristic disunity of Greek international politics proved disastrous because the

Macedonian kingdom developed aggressive leaders, Philip II and Alexander the Great, who made themselves masters of the quarreling city-states to their south. Inspired by Greek heroic ideas, Alexander conquered the entire Persian Empire and set in motion the great political, social, and cultural changes of the Hellenistic period.

When Alexander's generals transformed themselves into Hellenistic kings, they made use of the governmental structures they found already established in the lands they conquered, but they also added an administrative staff of Greeks and Macedonians. Local elites as well as Greeks and Macedonians cooperated with the Hellenistic monarchs in governing and financing their society, which was divided into a hierarchy along ethnic lines. To enhance their image of magnificence, the kings and queens of the Hellenistic world supported writers, artists, scholars, philosophers, and scientists, thereby encouraging Hellenistic intellectual innovation. The traditional city-states continued to exist in Hellenistic Greece, but their freedom extended only to local affairs; they lost their independence in foreign policy to the period's powerful kings.

The diversity of the Hellenistic world included much that was new, especially because cultural interaction between different peoples became more common than ever before. An outgrowth of the greater opportunities created by this interaction and change was anxiety about the role of chance in life. In response, people looked to new religious experiences to satisfy their yearning for protection from dangers. In the midst of so much novelty, however, the most fundamental elements of the ancient world remained unchanged—the labor, the poverty, and the limited opportunities for the mass of ordinary people working in fields, vineyards, and pastures.

In the end, the longest lasting effect of the Hellenistic period came in the changes it brought to Roman society and culture; Romans had increasingly close contact with the multicultural traditions of the Hellenistic kingdoms as they gradually rose to become the Mediterranean's dominant political state. That rise to power, however, took centuries because Rome originated as a tiny, insignificant place that no one except Romans ever expected to amount to anything on the world stage.

■ MAKING CONNECTIONS

1. *What were the central political, economic, and social developments of the Hellenistic world?*

2. *Compare life for people of all social classes in the Hellenistic kingdoms with that of people living in the Classical Greek city-state.*

■ **FOR FURTHER EXPLORATION**

For further reading and online research ideas, see the Suggested References on page SR-2 at the back of the book.

For practice quizzes, a customized study plan, and other study tools, see the ONLINE STUDY GUIDE at **bedfordstmartins.com/huntconcise**.

For primary-source material from this period, see Chapter 3 in *Sources of THE MAKING OF THE WEST: A CONCISE HISTORY*, Second Edition.

The Rise of Rome

c. 753–44 B.C.E.

R OMANS TREASURED THE LEGENDS describing their state's slow, violence-plagued transformation from a tiny village to a world power. They especially loved stories about their legendary first king, Romulus, because they remembered him as a passionate leader. According to the legend later known as the "Rape of the Sabine Women," Romulus's Rome was a small settlement without enough women to bear children to increase the population and defend the community in war. The king therefore begged the nearby peoples of central Italy to allow Romans to intermarry with them. Everyone turned him down, out of contempt for Rome's poverty and weakness. Enraged, Romulus hatched a plan: he invited the neighboring Sabines to a festival honoring the gods and had his Roman men kidnap the unmarried Sabine women and fight off their relatives' frantic attempts to rescue them. The kidnappers immediately married the women, persuading them of their good intentions by promising to cherish them as beloved wives and new citizens. When the Sabine men returned to attack Rome, the newly married women rushed into the bloody battle, yelling at their brothers, fathers, and new husbands to stop the slaughter either by laying down their weapons or killing all the women. The men immediately made peace and agreed to unite their populations under Roman rule.

■ **Temple of Castor and Pollux in the Roman Forum**
From the time of Romulus, Rome's first king, Romans believed that the gods supported their city and that citizens needed to show their gratitude in visible ways. These columns belonged to one of Rome's most prominent temples, originally constructed at the heart of the city in the forum in the fifth century B.C.E. to honor the divine twins Castor and Pollux for their help in battle. It was rebuilt several times; the remains seen today date to the time of Augustus (c. 27 B.C.E.–14 C.E.). The temple served important state functions: the Senate often met inside, and it held the official standards for weights and measures as well as treasuries for the emperors and wealthy individuals. Its architectural detail is famous for its elegance. Notice the sculpted capitals atop the forty-foot-high columns.
(Sonia Halliday Photographs.)

129

This legend emphasizes that Rome, unlike the city-states of Greece, expanded by absorbing outsiders into its citizen body, sometimes violently, sometimes peacefully. Rome's growth became the ancient world's largest expansion of population and territory, as a people originally housed in a few huts slowly created a state that, after centuries of war, came to control most of Europe, North Africa, Egypt, and the eastern Mediterranean. The social, cultural, political, legal, and economic traditions that the Romans developed in ruling this vast area created closer connections among its diverse peoples than ever before or since. Unlike the Greeks and Macedonians, the Romans maintained the unity of their state for centuries. Alexander the Great's conquests won him everlasting fame as the ancient world's most fearless hero, but not even he equaled the Romans in affecting the course of Western civilization: the history of Europe and its colonies, including the United States, has deep roots in Rome.

Roman culture sprang from the traditions of ancient Italy's many peoples, but Greek literature, art, and thought deeply influenced Romans as they gained international power. Of course, they did not just passively absorb other civilizations' traditions or change them only in superficial ways, such as giving Latin names to Greek gods. Whatever Romans took over from others they adapted to their own purposes in complex ways. The cross-cultural contact that so greatly influenced Rome was a kind of competition in innovation rather than an "advanced" Greek culture improving a "primitive" Roman culture.

The kidnapping legend belongs to the earliest period of Rome, when kings ruled (c. 753–509 B.C.E.), but the majority of Roman history comes in two later periods of about five hundred years each—the republic and the empire. These terms refer to the system of government in each period: under the republic (founded 509 B.C.E.), an oligarchy (the social elite) governed; under the empire (founded at the end of the first century B.C.E.), monarchs (the Roman emperors) once again ruled.

Rome's greatest expansion came during the republic. The confidence that fueled this amazing growth sprang from Romans' faith that the gods wanted them to rule the world by military might and law and improve it through social and moral values. The foundation legend illustrates Romans' faith in their divine destiny: Romulus employs a religious festival as a cover for kidnapping. Romans' firm belief that values should drive politics showed in their using persuasion to convince the captive women that loyalty and love would wipe out the crime that had forcibly turned them into wives and Romans.

In addition to the devotion to family that the legend implied, Roman values under the republic emphasized selfless service to the community, individual honor and public status, the importance of laws, and shared decision making. By the first century B.C.E., however, tension between these values had erupted into open conflict because powerful individuals were placing their personal and family interests ahead of the common good. Blinded by ambition, Rome's politician-generals began a civil war that destroyed the republic.

Social and Religious Traditions

Romans regulated their lives by traditional values stressing personal connections, education for public service, religious duties, and hierarchy. Just as Greeks had emphasized excellence as a social value, Romans believed that men and women should show courage in all aspects of life. In public life, Roman men connected with one another as patron or client, each with obligations to the other. In private life, men as the heads of households held power over their children and slaves, but most wives lived independent of their husband's control. In religion, the gods' power over human life meant that everyone had to pray for divine favor to protect the family and the community.

Roman Values

Romans believed that their ancestors had handed down their values from ancient times. They therefore referred to their values as **mos maiorum**, "the way of the ancestors." The Romans treasured their ancient values because, for them, "old-fashioned" meant "good because tested by long experience," while "new" suggested "dangerous because not tested by any experience." Roman morality made honor the reward for right conduct, which required uprightness, faithfulness, and respect for others. Uprightness defined how a person related to others. In the second century B.C.E., the poet Lucilius defined it as virtue:

> *Virtue is to know the human relevance of each thing,*
> *To know what is humanly right and useful and honorable,*
> *And what things are good and what are bad, useless, shameful,*
>   *and dishonorable. . . .*
> *Virtue is to pay what in reality is owed to honorable status,*
> *To be an enemy and a foe to bad people and bad values*
> *But a defender of good people and good values. . . .*
> *And, in addition, virtue is putting the country's interests first,*
> *Then our parents' interests, with our own third and last.*

Faithfulness (*fides*, from which the English word *fidelity* derives) had many forms, for women as well as for men. Basically, it meant to keep one's obligations, no matter the cost. Failing to meet an obligation offended the community and the gods. Faithful women remained virgins before marriage and avoided adultery afterward. Faithful men kept their word, paid their debts, never had sex with another man's wife, and treated everyone justly—which did not mean treating everyone the same, but rather treating people appropriately according to whether they were equals, superiors, or inferiors.

Faithfulness was one aspect of respect, a very complex value. Respect's supreme form was devotion to the gods, to one's own dignity, and to one's family, especially elders. Honoring the gods required carefully planned worship, prayers, and sacrifices performed in a state of strict purity. Respect for one's self meant maintaining self-control and displaying only limited emotion. So strict was this expectation that not even wives and husbands could kiss in public without seeming emotionally out of control. Respect also required never giving up, regardless of difficulties. Standing firm and overcoming all obstacles to do one's duty were thus fundamental Roman values.

Honor was the Romans' reward for living by these values. Women earned honor—a good reputation—especially by bearing legitimate children and educating them morally. Honor for upper-class men brought concrete rewards: election to government office and public recognition of their military bravery and other contributions to the common good. A man who had gained the status bestowed by honor commanded so much respect that others would obey him regardless of whether he exercised formal power over them. A man earning this much prestige was said to possess "authority."

Finally, Romans believed that family background influenced a person's values. Being born in an elite family was therefore a two-edged sword. It automatically carried greater status, but at the same time it imposed a stricter demand to behave morally. Originally, wealth had nothing to do with Roman moral virtue. Over time, however, it became overwhelmingly important to the elite to spend money in displays of conspicuous consumption, social entertainments, and gifts to the community. By the later centuries of the Roman republic, ambitious men required vast fortunes to buy honor, and they became willing to abandon other values to acquire riches.

The Patron-Client System

The hierarchy of Roman society was rooted in the **patron-client system**, an interlocking network of personal relationships linking Romans to one another morally and legally. A patron was a man of superior status who was obliged to provide benefits to certain men of lower status, who paid special attention to him. These were his clients, who in return owed him duties. Both sets of obligations centered on financial and political help. The system had multiple levels: a patron of others was often himself the client of a more distinguished man. The Romans called this hierarchy "friendship"—with clearly defined roles for each party. A sensitive patron would greet a social inferior as "my friend," not as "my client." A client, however, showed respect by addressing his superior as "my patron."

■ **Sculpted Tomb of a Family of Ex-Slaves**
*The husband and wife depicted on this tomb, which perhaps dates to the first century B.C.E., started
life as slaves but gained their freedom and thus became Roman citizens. Their son, in the background holding a pet pigeon, was a free person. One of the remarkable features of Roman civilization, and a source of its demographic strength, was that it granted citizenship to ex-slaves. This
family had done well enough financially to afford a sculpted tomb. The tablets the man is holding
and the carefully groomed hairstyle of the woman are meant to show that their family was educated
and stylish. What do you think it means that the couple are shown holding hands?*
(German Archeological Institute/Madeline Grimoldi.)

Benefits and duties took various forms. A patron benefited his clients by
providing gifts or loans in hard times, supporting them when they started
political careers, and speaking for them in lawsuits. Clients' duties included
lending money when patrons needed it to pay for public works or their daughters' expensive dowries, or aiding their campaigns for public office by soliciting
votes. Furthermore, because it was a mark of great status for a man to have
numerous clients thronging around like a swarm of bees, a patron expected them
to gather at his house early in the morning and accompany him to the forum, the
city's public center. A Roman leader needed a large, fine house to accommodate
this throng and to entertain his social equals; a crowded house signified social
success.

These mutual obligations endured over generations. Ex-slaves, for example,
who automatically became the clients of the masters who freed them, passed on this

relationship to their children. Wealthy Romans could acquire clients among foreigners, sometimes even entire communities. With its emphasis on duty and permanence, the system epitomized the Roman view that social stability and well-being were achieved by faithfully maintaining people's obligations to one another.

The Roman Family

The family was the bedrock institution of Roman society because it taught values and determined the ownership of property. Men and women shared the duty of teaching values to their children, though by law the father possessed the **patria potestas** ("power of a father") over his children of any age and over his slaves. This power gave him legal ownership of all the property acquired by his dependents. As long as he was alive, no son or daughter could own anything, accumulate money, or possess any independent legal standing—in theory at least. In practice, adult children controlled personal property and money, and favored slaves might accumulate savings. Fathers also held legal power of life and death over these members of their households, but they rarely exercised it on anyone except unwanted or deformed newborns. Abandoning babies so that they would die, be adopted, or be raised as slaves by strangers was an accepted practice to control the size of families and dispose of physically imperfect infants. Baby girls probably suffered this fate more often than boys—a family enhanced its power by investing its resources in its sons.

As the emphasis in Roman values on shared decision making required, fathers regularly conferred with others on important family issues. Each Roman man identified a circle of friends and relatives, his "council," whom he always consulted before making important decisions. A man brooding over the drastic decision to execute an adult member of his household, for example, would never have made the decision on his own. His council would recommend this violent exercise of a father's power only in the most extreme circumstances, as in 63 B.C.E. when a father had his son executed because the youth had committed treason by joining a conspiracy to overthrow the government.

Patria potestas did not allow a husband to control his wife because "free" marriages—in which the wife formally remained under her father's power for as long as he lived—eventually became common. Many Roman wives were relatively independent because their fathers were dead, and their husbands did not legally control their lives (four out of five parents died before their children reached thirty). Legally, a woman needed a male guardian to conduct business for her, but guardianship became an empty formality by the first century B.C.E. As one legal expert said about Roman women's freedom of action: "The common belief, that because of their instability of judgment women are often deceived and that it is only fair to have them controlled by the authority of guardians, seems more specious than true. For women of full age manage their affairs themselves." Upper-class women could express their opinions publicly. In 195 B.C.E., for example, they blocked Rome's streets for days until the men ended a wartime law meant to reduce tensions between rich and poor by limiting the amount of gold jewelry and fine clothing women could wear and where they could ride in carriages.

Roman women had to grow up fast to assume their duties as teachers of values to children and managers of their household's resources. Tullia (c. 79–45 B.C.E.), daughter of the renowned politician and orator Marcus Tullius Cicero (106–43 B.C.E.), was engaged at twelve, married at sixteen, and widowed by twenty-two. As a married Roman woman of wealth, she oversaw the household slaves, including wet nurses for infants, kept account books for the property she personally owned, and accompanied her husband to dinner parties—something Greek wives never did.

Roman mothers won public honor for managing their households well and shaping their children's moral outlook. Cornelia, an aristocrat of the second century B.C.E., won extraordinary fame after her husband died by refusing an offer of marriage from the Ptolemaic king of Egypt so she could instead oversee the family estate and educate her surviving daughter and two sons. (Her other nine children had died.) The boys, Tiberius and Gaius Gracchus, grew up to be among the most influential and controversial officials of the late republic. Wealthy women such as Cornelia wielded political influence, if only indirectly, by expressing their opinions to the male members of their families. Marcus Porcius Cato (234–149 B.C.E.), a famous politician and author, hinted at the behind-the-scenes reality of women's

■ **Sculpture of a Woman Running a Store**
This relief sculpture shows a woman selling food from behind the counter of a small shop, while customers make purchases or converse with each other. Roman women could own property, so the woman may be the store owner. The man immediately to her right behind the counter could be her husband or a servant. Market areas in Roman towns were packed with small family-run stores like this that sold everything imaginable, much like the malls of today. (Art Resource, NY.)

power with a biting comment directed at his fellow leaders: "All mankind rule their wives, we rule all mankind, and our wives rule us."

Women accumulated property in many ways, from inheritance to entrepreneurship. Recent archaeological discoveries suggest that by the late republic some women owned large businesses. Poor women, like poor men, toiled to help support their families by selling vegetables or charms or colorful ribbons from stands. Slightly more prosperous families crafted furniture or clothing at home, the location of most Roman production, with the men cutting, fitting, and polishing the wood, leather, and metal. The poorest women could earn money only as prostitutes, which was legal but considered disgraceful. Prenuptial agreements to outline the rights of both partners in marriage were common, and divorce was a simple matter, with fathers usually keeping the children.

Education for Public Life

Education for both women and men aimed to make them supporters of traditional values and, for different purposes, effective speakers. As in Greece, most children received their education in the family; only the rich could afford to pay teachers. Wealthy parents bought literate slaves to tend and teach their children. By the late republic, they often chose Greek slaves so their children could be taught to speak Greek and read Greek literary classics, which most Romans regarded as the world's best. Parents might also send their children, from about seven years old, to classes offered by independent schoolmasters in their lodgings. Repetition was the usual teaching technique. Teachers slapped and hit students to keep them attentive.

In upper-class families, both daughters and sons learned to read. The girls were also taught literature, perhaps some music, and, especially, how to make educated conversation at dinner parties. Another principal aim of women's education was to prepare them for the important role of teaching their children traditional social and moral values.

Fathers taught their sons a man's life, especially physical training, fighting with weapons, and courage, but the crown of an upper-class boy's education was rhetoric—skill in persuasive public speaking. Rhetorical training was crucial to a successful public career. A boy would accompany his father to public meetings and court sessions. By listening to speeches, he would learn to imitate winning techniques. Cicero, Rome's most famous orator, agreed with his brother's advice that a young man must learn "to become an excellent public speaker. This is the way to control men at Rome, winning them over to your side and keeping them from harming you. You really have power when you are a man who can cause your rivals the greatest fears of meeting you [as a speaker] in a trial." Roman rhetoric owed much to Greek techniques. This was only one of the crucial ways in which Greek culture influenced Rome.

Religion for Public and Private Interests

Romans followed Greek models in religion, too, worshiping many divinities that corresponded directly with Greek gods. Romans viewed their chief god, Jupiter, who corresponded to the Greek god Zeus, as a powerful, stern father. Juno (Greek Hera), queen of the gods, and Minerva (Greek Athena), goddess of wisdom, joined Jupiter as the three central gods of the state cults. This divine triad shared Rome's most revered temple on its acropolis, the Capitoline hill.

The goal of Roman religion was to preserve Rome's safety and prosperity; above all, people prayed to the gods for victory in war and fertility in agriculture. Many official prayers implored divine aid for growing crops, preventing disease, and spurring healthy reproduction for animals and people. In times of crisis, Romans sought foreign gods to protect them, such as when the government brought the cult of the healing god Asclepius from Greece in 293 B.C.E. to fight a plague. In 204 B.C.E., officials imported the pointed black stone representing Cybele ("the Great Mother"), whose chief sanctuary was in Phrygia in Asia Minor (the Roman term for Anatolia), to promote fertility.

Romans supported many other cults with special guardian responsibilities. The shrine of Vesta, goddess of the hearth and a protector of the family, housed the official eternal flame of Rome, which guaranteed the state's permanent existence. Vestal Virgins, six unmarried women who were sworn to chastity at age six to ten for terms of thirty years, tended Vesta's shrine. Their chastity symbolized Roman family values and thus the preservation of the republic itself. As Rome's only female priesthood, the Vestals earned high status and freedom from their fathers' control by performing their most important duty: keeping the flame from going out. As the Greek historian Dionysius of Halicarnassus reported in the first century B.C.E., "The Romans dread the extinction of the fire above all misfortunes, looking upon it as an omen which means the destruction of the city." Should the flame go out, the Romans assumed that one of the women had broken her vow of chastity and that this Vestal had to be buried alive as punishment.

At home, families maintained a sacred space for small shrines housing statuettes of their Penates (spirits of the household) and Lares (spirits of the ancestors), protectors of their well-being and moral traditions. Upper-class families hung death masks of famous ancestors in the main room in their homes and wore them at funerals to express the current generation's responsibility to live up to the family's virtuous past. In sum, tradition represented the main source of Roman morality. The shame of losing status by tarnishing one's reputation, not the fear of divine punishment, was the strongest deterrent to immoral behavior.

Romans performed many rituals to combat life's uncertainty, in activities as diverse and commonplace as breast-feeding babies and fertilizing crops. Many public religious gatherings promoted the community's health and stability. For example, during the February 15 Lupercalia festival (whose name recalled the wolf, *luper*

■ Household Religious Shrine from Pompeii

This colorfully painted shrine stood inside the entrance to a house at Pompeii known as the House of the Vettii, from the name of its owners. Successful businessmen, they spared no expense in decorating their home: with 188 frescoes (paintings done by applying pigments to damp plaster) adorning its walls, the interior blazed in a riot of color. This type of shrine for family religion, found in every Roman home, is called a lararium because it housed the Lares (spirits of the ancestors), who are shown here flanking a central figure, who represents the spirit (genius) of the father of the family. The snake, poised to drink from a bowl probably holding milk set out for it, also symbolizes a protective force, as it did for Greeks as well. The scene sums up the role Romans expected their gods to play: staving off harm and bad luck. Why do you think these ancient peoples regarded snakes as symbols of divine protection? (Scala/Art Resource, NY.)

in Latin, which legend said had reared Romulus), naked young men streaked around the Palatine hill, lashing any woman they met with strips of goat skin. Women who had not yet borne children would run out to be struck, believing this would make them fertile. The December 17 Saturnalia festival, honoring the Italian god of liberation, Saturnus, temporarily turned the social order upside down to release tensions caused by the inequalities between masters and slaves. As the playwright and scholar Accius (c. 170–80 B.C.E.) described the occasion, "People joyfully hold feasts all through the country and the towns, each owner acting as a waiter to his slaves." This reversal of roles reinforced slaves' ties to their owners by symbolizing patrons' benefits, which slaves were expected to repay with faithful service.

Roman tradition did not regard the gods as the guarantors of the Romans' moral code. Like the Greek gods, Roman gods were more connected to national security and prosperity than to human morality, as Cicero explains: "We call Jupiter the Best (*Optimus*) and Greatest (*Maximus*) not because he makes us just or sober or wise but, rather, healthy, unharmed, rich, and prosperous." Therefore, every official action was preceded by "taking the auspices"—seeking Jupiter's approval by observing natural "signs" such as the direction of the flights of birds, their eating habits, or the presence of thunder and lightning. Romans gave human moral actions a religious dimension by hailing their values, such as faithfulness, as divine forces. Also regarded as divine was piety (*pietas*), the sense of devotion and duty to family, friends, and the republic. Rome's temple to pietas housed a statue personifying it as a female divinity. The religious importance attached to the cults of moral qualities emphasized that they were supreme human values that all Romans should practice.

Roman government and public religion had a common goal: to preserve the community. Priests were supposed to ensure the gods' goodwill toward the state, a crucial relationship the Romans called the *pax deorum* ("peace of/with the gods"). Men from the top of the social hierarchy served as priests by conducting sacrifices, and presiding at festivals and other rituals conforming strictly to ancestral tradition. They were not professionals devoting their lives solely to religious activity but, rather, citizens performing public service. The most important official, the *pontifex maximus* ("highest priest"), served as the head of state religion and the ultimate authority on religious matters affecting government; Rome's most prominent men sought this priesthood for its political influence.

Disrespect for religious tradition brought punishment. Naval commanders, for example, took the auspices by feeding sacred chickens on their ships: if the birds ate energetically before a battle, Jupiter favored the Romans and an attack could begin. In 249 B.C.E., the commander Publius Claudius Pulcher grew frustrated when his chickens, probably seasick, refused to eat. Determined to attack, he finally hurled them overboard in a rage, sputtering, "Well then, let them drink!" When he suffered a huge defeat, he was fined very heavily.

■ **REVIEW:** *What role did family and values play in Roman society?*

From Monarchy to Republic, c. 753–287 B.C.E.

Rome's community-focused values provided the unity necessary for its astounding growth from a tiny settlement into the Mediterranean's greatest power. This process took centuries, while the Romans reinvented their government and expanded their territory and population. Rome's first government was a monarchy, the most common type of government in the ancient world. This rule by kings lasted from 753 to

509 B.C.E, when members of the social elite overthrew it in anger at the royal family's violent behavior. The elite then created a new political system—the republic—that lasted until almost the end of the first century B.C.E. The **Roman republic**, from the Latin *res publica* ("the people's matter" or "the public business"), was based on shared political decision making and the election of officials in assemblies of male citizens organized by social hierarchy. Rome acquired land and population by winning aggressive wars and by absorbing other peoples. Its economic and cultural growth depended on contact with peoples around the Mediterranean.

Rule by Kings, c. 753–509 B.C.E.

Legend taught that Rome's original government had seven kings in succession from 753 (the most commonly given date for the city's founding) to 509 B.C.E.; in truth, little reliable evidence exists for this period. The kings probably created the Senate, a body of advisers chosen from the city's leading men to serve as the ruler's council, in keeping with the Roman principle that decisions should be made by consensus. This institution advised government leaders for two thousand years, as Rome changed from a monarchy to the republic and back to a monarchy under the empire.

Rome's policy of making conquered outsiders into citizens or allies produced tremendous expansion, promoted ethnic diversity, and contrasted sharply with the exclusionary citizenship policies of Greek city-states. Another important Roman policy—also different from Greek tradition—was to grant citizenship to freed slaves. These freedmen and freedwomen, as ex-slaves were called, became clients of their former owners. They were barred from elective offices or military service but in all other ways possessed full civil rights, such as legal marriage. Their children enjoyed citizenship without any limitations. By the late republic, many Roman citizens were descendants of freed slaves.

By around 550 B.C.E., the Romans controlled three hundred square miles of the area around Rome, called Latium—enough agricultural land to support a population of thirty thousand to forty thousand people. Geography and contact with other cultures, especially Greek, drove Rome's growth. The city lay at the natural center of both Italy and the Mediterranean world. As the historian Livy (59 B.C.E.–17 C.E.), our source for the heroic legends of early Rome, expressed it, "Gods and men chose this site for good reasons: all its advantages make it the best place in the world for a city destined to grow great." Those advantages were fertile farmland, control of a river crossing on the major north-south route in the peninsula, a nearby harbor on the Mediterranean Sea, and easy access to the surrounding areas in Italy. Most important, Rome was ideally situated for contact with the outside world. The Italian peninsula stuck out so far into the Mediterranean that east-west ship traffic naturally stopped in its ports (Map 4.1).

Ancient Italy was home to a diverse population, and contact with their neighbors profoundly influenced the Romans' cultural development. The people of

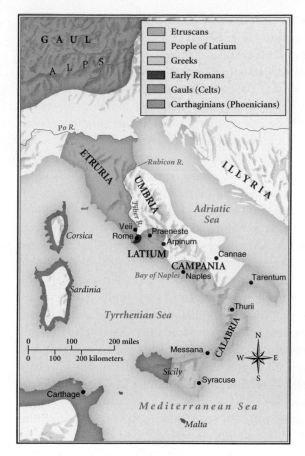

■ MAP 4.1 Ancient Italy, c. 500 B.C.E.

When the Romans ousted the monarchy to found a republic in 509 B.C.E., they inhabited a relatively small territory in central Italy between the western coast and the mountain range that runs down the peninsula from north to south. Numerous different peoples lived in Italy at this time. The most prosperous occupied fertile agricultural land and sheltered harbors on the peninsula's west side. The early republic's most urbanized neighbors were the Etruscans to the north and the Greek city-states to the south and on the island of Sicily.

Latium were poor villagers like the Romans and spoke the same Indo-European language, an early form of Latin. Flourishing Greek city-states dotted Italy to the south, however, and contact with them had the greatest effect on Rome. Greeks had established colonies in the Campanian plain, such as Naples, from the 700s B.C.E. These settlements grew rich thanks to their ideal location for participating in international trade. Romans developed a love-hate relationship with Greeks, admiring their literature and art but despising their lack of military unity. They adopted many elements from Greek culture—from ethical values to gods, from the model for their poetry and prose to architectural design and style.

The Etruscans, a people north of the Tiber River, also influenced the Romans. They lived in prosperous, independent towns nestled on central Italian hilltops. Vividly colored wall paintings, which survive in some tombs, portray funeral banquets and games testifying to their society's splendor. Etruscans crafted fine artwork, jewelry, and sculpture, but they also loved importing luxury objects from Greece and other

Mediterranean lands. Most of the intact Greek vases known today, for example, were found in Etruscan tombs. The Etruscans' international contacts encouraged cultural interaction: gold tablets inscribed in Etruscan and Phoenician and discovered in 1964 at the port of Pyrgi (thirty miles northwest of Rome) reveal that at about 500 B.C.E., the Etruscans dedicated a temple to the Phoenician goddess Astarte, whom they had learned about by trading with Carthage. That rich city, founded in western North Africa (modern Tunisia) by Phoenicians around 800 B.C.E., dominated seaborne commerce in the western Mediterranean and would later become the Romans' most feared rival.

The extent of Etruscan influence on Rome remains controversial. Until recently, scholars speculated that the Etruscans conquered Rome and dominated it political-ly in the sixth century B.C.E. The Etruscans were also seen as more culturally refined, mainly because so much Greek art has been found at Etruscan sites; they were there-fore assumed to have reshaped Roman culture during this period of supposed domination. New scholarship, however, stresses the independence of Romans in developing their own cultural traditions: they borrowed from Etruscans, as from Greeks, whatever appealed to them and adapted it to fit their local circumstances. Romans took over the Etruscans' procedures for religious rituals, and adopted their magistrates' elaborate garments and musical instruments. They also learned Etruscan divination techniques for discovering the gods' will by identifying clues in the shapes of the internal organs of slaughtered animals. Romans may also have adopted from Etruscan society the tradition of wives joining husbands at dinner parties.

Many features of Roman culture formerly seen as examples of Etruscan influ-ence were probably part of the ancient Mediterranean's shared cultural environ-ment. The organization of the Roman army, a citizen militia of heavily armed infantry troops fighting in formation, reflected not just Etruscan precedent but that of other peoples. The Romans' alphabet, which they first learned from the Etruscans, was Greek; the Greeks had acquired it through their contact with the Levant. The engineering necessary to urbanize Rome has been said to have been done by the Etruscans, but it is too simplistic to assume that cultural developments of this size resulted from one superior culture "instructing" another, less-developed one. Rather, at this time in Mediterranean history, similar cultural developments were under way in many places. The Romans, like so many others, found their own way in navigating through this common cultural sea.

The Early Roman Republic, 509–287 B.C.E.

The social elite's hatred of kings created the Roman republic. Their belief that monarchy always turned into tyranny was expressed in Livy's story of the rape of Lucretia, the most famous legend about the creation of the republic. Like most of Livy's stories, it stressed the role of moral virtue in Roman history. The assault on

■ Banquet Scene Painted in an Etruscan Tomb
Painted about 480–470 B.C.E., this brightly colored fresco at Tarquinia decorated a wall in an Etruscan tomb (known today as the "Tomb of the Leopards," from the animals painted just above this scene). Wealthy Etruscan men and women filled their tombs with pictures such as these, which simultaneously represented the funeral feasts held to celebrate the life of the dead person and the social pleasures experienced in this life and expected in the next. The banqueters recline on their elbows in Greek style. (Scala/Art Resource, NY.)

Lucretia, a chaste wife in the social elite, took place when the swaggering son of King Tarquin the Proud violently raped her to demonstrate his superior power. Despite pleas from her husband and father not to blame herself, she committed suicide after identifying her attacker.

Declaring themselves Rome's liberators from tyranny, her relatives and friends, led by Lucius Junius Brutus, expelled Tarquin in 509 B.C.E. They then created a new political system—the republic—to ensure the sharing of power by the elite and to block rule by one man or family. Thereafter, the Romans prided themselves on living under a freer political system than that of their neighbors. The legend of the warrior Horatius at the bridge, for example, advertised the republic's dedication to national freedom. As Livy told the story, Horatius single-handedly blocked the Etruscan army's march on Rome when they wanted to put a king back in charge of the city. While hacking at his opponents, Horatius cursed them as slaves who had lost their freedom because they were ruled by arrogant kings. Horatius's legend made clear that Romans created the republic to prevent a leader from abusing power by ruling alone.

Conflict over how to achieve this goal persisted for over two hundred years after 509 B.C.E., a period called the **struggle of the orders**. Bitter turmoil between a closed circle of elite families (called the patricians) and the rest of Rome's citizen population (the plebeians), the two "orders" of the republic's social hierarchy, centered on social and economic issues. The patricians inherited their status by being born into one of the about 130 wealthy families controlling important religious activities. Some plebeians, however, were also rich, and they resented the patricians' arrogance in monopolizing political elections, banning intermarriage with plebeians, and advertising their social superiority by wearing special red shoes (later they changed to black footwear adorned with a shiny metal crescent).

Poor plebeians demanded relief from crushing debts and a fairer distribution of farmland. To pressure the patricians, plebeians periodically took the extreme step of leaving the city (secession) for a temporary settlement and refusing to serve in the army. This tactic worked because they made up the majority of Rome's military. A secession provoked by a patrician's violence against a plebeian woman led to the earliest Roman laws, called the Twelve Tables from the bronze tablets on which they were engraved for display between 451 and 449 B.C.E. In Livy's words, these laws prevented the patrician government officials who judged most legal cases from "arbitrarily giving the force of law to their own preferences." So important did the Twelve Tables become as a symbol of the Roman commitment to justice for all citizens that for the next four hundred years children were required to memorize them.

These laws were, however, only a first step toward greater sharing of political power; that process occurred mainly through hammering out the different and sometimes overlapping responsibilities of Rome's assemblies. At these outdoor meetings, adult male citizens elected officials, passed laws, decided government policies, and held some trials. Assemblies were only for voting, not discussion, but every session was preceded by a public gathering to hear speeches. Everyone, including women and noncitizens, could listen to these addresses. The crowd loudly expressed its agreement or disagreement by applauding or hissing. Speakers therefore had to pay close attention to public opinion in forming the proposals that they put before the male citizens who then voted them up or down in the assemblies.

A significant restriction on the democratic aspect of assemblies was that each one was divided into groups according to the social hierarchy determined by status and wealth. Voting took place by groups. Each group, not each individual, had a vote, and a small group had the same vote as a large group. The hierarchy of the voting groups in the Centuriate Assembly, which elected the major officials (consuls and praetors), reflected the organization of the army: it confined the huge population of men too poor to afford military weapons, the **proletarians**, to one group that cast only one out of the total of 193 votes. The Plebeian Assembly excluded patricians and grouped itself into thirty-five tribes based on where voters lived; it elected special officials (tribunes) responsible for protecting plebeians, and it passed resolutions called **plebiscites**, which were originally not recognized as law by patricians. The conflict of the orders finally ended in 287 B.C.E., when patricians conceded that plebiscites had the status of laws. In a third grouping, the Tribal Assembly, patricians joined plebeians as voters grouped by residence. This assembly, in which plebeians greatly outnumbered patricians, eventually became the republic's most important institution for making policy, passing laws, and, until separate courts were created in the second century B.C.E., conducting judicial trials.

Annually elected officials ran the republic's government; they served in groups, numbering from two to more than a dozen, to ensure shared rule. The highest officials were consuls; two were elected each year, and their most important duty was commanding Rome's army legions. Winning a consulship was the greatest political honor a Roman man could achieve, and it bestowed high status on his descendants forever, entitling them to be called nobles. To be elected consul, a man traditionally had to work his way up a **ladder of offices**. After ten years of military service beginning about age twenty, he would seek election as a quaestor, a financial administrator. Continuing to climb the ladder, he would next be elected to the board of aediles, officials overseeing the city's streets, sewers, aqueducts, temples, and markets. Each rung up the ladder was more competitive, and few men reached the next office, that of praetor, which performed judicial and military command duties. The most successful praetors then reached for the gold ring of Roman public office, the consulship.

Ex-consuls could also compete to become one of the censors, prestigious senior officials elected every five years to conduct censuses of the citizen body and select new members of the three-hundred-man Senate, which advised the consuls (as it had the kings). The special role of the Senate in the republic's government made clear the Roman principle of making decisions by consensus. The Senate had no authority to pass laws; it could only give advice. But its prestige was so enormous that no high official or assembly would disregard the senators' advice, unless they wished to start a political crisis. Following the Roman tradition that status should be visible, the senators wore special black high-top shoes and robes embroidered with a broad purple stripe.

The struggle of the orders extended to control of the elective offices. The patricians tried to monopolize the highest ones, but the plebeians resisted fiercely. Through violent struggle from about 500 to 450 B.C.E., the plebeians forced the patricians to yield another important concession besides the Twelve Tables: the creation of a special panel of ten annually elected officials, called tribunes. Their responsibility was to stop actions that would harm the plebeians and their property. The tribunate's purpose made it stand apart from regular ladder offices. Tribunes, who had to be plebeians, based their power on the sworn oath of the other plebeians to protect them against all attacks; this protected status, called sacrosanctity, allowed tribunes the right to use a veto (Latin, meaning "I forbid") to block the actions of officials, suspend elections, and even counter the advice of the Senate. The tribunes' extraordinary power to halt government action sometimes made them the sources of bitter political disputes.

Roman values motivated men to compete for honor, not money, in pursuing a public career. By 367 B.C.E., the plebeians had pushed their way fully into this competition by requiring that at least one consul every year must be a plebeian. Only well-off men could run for election because officials earned no salaries. On the contrary, they were expected to spend large sums to win popular support by entertaining the electorate with, for example, spectacles featuring gladiators (trained fighters) and wild beasts, such as lions imported from Africa. Once elected, a magistrate had to benefit the people by paying for public works, such as roads, aqueducts, and temples.

When Rome later won control of more and more overseas territory through warfare, the desire for the status that money could buy in financing successful election campaigns overcame the values of faithfulness and honesty. By the second century B.C.E., military officers could enrich themselves by seizing booty from enemies in successful foreign wars and by extorting bribes from the local people while administering conquered territory. They could then use these profits of war to finance their political careers at home. In this way, acquiring money became more important in the late republic than winning honor through honest public service.

Outrage over corrupt officials dismissing complaints about each other's conduct led to the creation of a court system with jury trials in the second century B.C.E. Since most officials were also senators, the Senate self-interestedly tried to have these juries be manned only by its members, while nonsenators agitated to be included. Both accusers and accused had to speak for themselves in court or have friends speak for them. Prominent men, usually senators with legal knowledge, played a central role as advisers in the Roman judicial system. These jurists, as they were called (from the Latin *jus, juris,* "law"), operated as private citizens, not official judges, in providing legal advice. This reliance on jurists reflected the Roman tradition of consulting councils of advisers to reach decisions. Roman law developed over centuries, sometimes adapting laws from other peoples, and became the basis for many later European legal codes still in use today.

These centuries of conflict over how to organize the republic did not produce coordinated political and judicial systems. Republican Rome had a jumbled network of overlapping institutions. Several different assemblies voted on laws or, in the Senate's case, opinions that guided lawmaking. Legal cases could be decided by magistrates, assemblies, or juries. Rome had no highest judicial authority, such as the U.S. Supreme Court, to resolve disputes about conflicting laws or verdicts. The republic's stability therefore depended on observing tradition, the mos maiorum. This reliance on tradition ensured that the most socially prominent and the richest Romans dominated government and society—because they defined the "way of the ancestors."

■ **REVIEW:** *What issues fueled the struggle of the orders?*

Consequences of Roman Imperialism, Fifth to Second Centuries B.C.E.

Expansion through war made military service and conquest central to the lives of Romans under the republic. During the fifth, fourth, and third centuries B.C.E., they fought war after war in Italy until they became the most powerful state on the peninsula. In the third and second centuries B.C.E., they began warring far from home in the west, the north, and the east, but above all they battled Carthage to the south. Their success in these campaigns made Rome the premier power in the Mediterranean.

Fear and ambition motivated this imperialism. Worries about national security made the senators recommend preemptive attacks against others perceived as enemies of Rome, and everyone longed to capture wealth on foreign military campaigns. Poorer soldiers hoped their gains would pull their families out of poverty. The elite longed to increase their riches and acquire glory as commanders, to promote their public careers.

The consequences of repeated wars in Italy and abroad transformed Romans culturally and socially. Astonishingly, they had no literature before about 240 B.C.E. Cultural interaction with others during overseas expansion stimulated Romans to write their first history and poetry and deeply influenced their art, especially portraits. Endless military campaigns far from home created stresses on family life and small farmers in the army, while the novel demands of ruling conquered territory undermined the government's stability. The importation of huge numbers of war captives to work as slaves on the estates of the rich put free laborers out of work. The conquests and spoils of war from Rome's great victories in the third and second centuries B.C.E. thus turned out to be a two-edged sword: they brought expansion and wealth, but their unexpected social and political consequences disrupted traditional values and the community's stability.

Roman Expansion in Italy

The Romans believed they were successful militarily because they respected the will of the gods. Cicero claimed, "We have defeated all the nations of the world, because we have realized that the world is directed and governed by the gods." Believing that the gods supported defensive wars as just, the Romans always insisted they fought only in self-defense, even when they attacked first. After a victory over their Latin neighbors in the 490s B.C.E., the Romans spent the next hundred years warring with the Etruscan town of Veii, a few miles north of the Tiber River. Their 396 B.C.E. victory doubled Roman territory. A devastating sack of Rome in 387 B.C.E. by Gauls (a Celtic group) from beyond the Alps proved only a temporary military setback, but it made Romans forever fearful of foreign invasion. By around 220 B.C.E., Rome controlled all of the peninsula south of the Po River.

Rome and Central Italy, Fifth Century B.C.E.

The Romans sometimes forced defeated opponents to give up large amounts of land or even enslaved them, yet they also often struck generous peace terms with former enemies. Some defeated Italians immediately became Roman citizens; others gained limited citizenship without the right to vote; still other communities received treaties of alliance. No conquered Italian peoples had to pay taxes to Rome. All, however, had to send soldiers for future wars. These new allies then received a share of the booty, chiefly slaves and land, from victorious campaigns against a new crop of enemies. In this way, the Romans used the sharing of the profits of conquest to turn former opponents into partners, an arrangement that only made Rome more powerful.

Roman Roads, c. 110 B.C.E.

To strengthen Italy's security, the Romans planted colonies of citizens and constructed roads up and down the peninsula to allow troops to march faster. These roads also connected the diverse peoples of Italy, speeding the creation of a more unified culture dominated by Rome. Latin, for example, came to be the common language, although local tongues lived on, especially Greek in the south. The wealth flowing from Rome's first two centuries of expansion in Italy attracted hordes of people to the city because these riches financed new aqueducts to provide fresh, running water—a rarity in the ancient world—and a massive building program employing poor laborers. By around 300 B.C.E., perhaps 150,000 people lived within Rome's walls. Outside the city, about 750,000 free Roman citizens inhabited various parts of Italy on land taken from local peoples. Much conquered territory was declared public land, open to any Roman to use for grazing herds of cattle.

Rich patricians and rich plebeians cooperated to exploit the expanding Roman territories; the old hierarchy separating the orders had become a technicality for the wealthy. This merged elite derived its wealth mainly from agricultural land and plunder acquired during military service. Since Rome levied no regular income or inheritance taxes, families could pass down their assets from generation to generation.

Wars with Carthage

Rome fought three wars against the powerful and wealthy North African city of Carthage. Also governed as a republic, Carthage by the third century B.C.E. controlled an empire stretching across the northwest African coast, part of Libya, Sardinia, Corsica, Malta, and the southern portion of Spain. Geography therefore ensured that an expanding Rome would sooner or later bump up against Carthage's

■ **Aqueduct at Nîmes in France**

Like the Greeks, the Romans supplied fountains and public baths in their towns with water by constructing aqueducts. They excelled at building complex systems of tunnels, channels, and bridges to move water over great distances. One of the best-preserved sections of a major aqueduct is the so-called Pont-du-Gard near present-day Nîmes in France, erected in the late first century B.C.E. to serve the flourishing town of Nemausus. Built of stones fitted together without clamps or mortar, the span soars 160 feet high and is 875 feet long, carrying water from 35 miles away in a channel constructed to fall only 1 foot in height for every 3,000 feet in length, so that the flow would remain steady but gentle. What sort of social and political organization would be necessary to construct such a system? **For more help analyzing this image,** see the visual activity for this chapter in the ONLINE STUDY GUIDE at bedfordstmartins.com/huntconcise. (© Hubertus Kanus/Photo Researchers, Inc.)

interests, which depended on the sea; the Carthaginians fielded a strong fleet but had to hire mercenaries to field a sizable infantry. To Romans, remembering the invasion by the Gauls, Carthage seemed a dangerous rival, as well as a fine prize because of its riches. Roman hostility was also fueled by horror at the Carthaginian tradition of sacrificing infants in times of trouble in the belief that this would placate their gods.

A coincidence ignited open conflict with Carthage, taking Roman troops outside Italy and across the sea for the first time; the three wars that followed are called the Punic Wars, from the Roman term *Punici,* meaning "Phoenicians" (the ancestors of the Carthaginians). The First Punic War (264–241 B.C.E.) began when a band of mercenaries stranded in a local war at Messana, on Sicily's northeastern tip, appealed for help to Rome and Carthage simultaneously. Both states sent troops. The Carthaginians wanted to protect the profits they earned from Sicilian trade; the Romans wanted to keep Carthaginian troops from moving close to their territory and to win plunder. The clash between their forces exploded into a war that lasted a generation. Its bloody battles revealed why the Romans so consistently conquered their rivals. In addition to being able to draw on the Italian population for reserves of manpower, they were prepared to lose as many troops, vote as much money, and fight as long as necessary to win. Previously unskilled at naval warfare, they spent vast sums to build warships to combat Carthage's experienced navy; they lost more than five hundred ships and 250,000 men while learning how to win at sea. (See "Taking Measure," page 151.)

Victory in the First Punic War made the Romans masters of Sicily, where they set up their first province (a foreign territory ruled and taxed by Roman officials). This innovation proved so profitable that they created another province by seizing the islands of Sardinia and Corsica from Carthage's control. Acquiring these foreign territories whetted the Romans' appetite for more, and they also feared a renewal of Carthage's power (Map 4.2). Pressing their advantage, they next made alliances with local peoples in Spain, where the Carthaginians were expanding from their original trading posts in the south.

The Senate's harsh warning to Carthage not to expand any further convinced the Carthaginians that another war was inevitable, so they decided to strike back. In the Second Punic War (218–201 B.C.E.), the daring Carthaginian general Hannibal (247–182 B.C.E.) shocked the Romans by marching troops and war elephants over the snowy Alps into Italy. After slaughtering a Roman army at the battle of Cannae in 216 B.C.E.—thirty thousand men died in the bloodiest defeat in Roman history—Hannibal tried to convince Rome's Italian allies to come over to his side. Disastrously for him, most Italians remained loyal to Rome. Hannibal's alliance in 215 B.C.E. with King Philip V of Macedonia (238–179 B.C.E.) forced the Romans to fight on a second front in Greece (their first presence in that region), but they refused to crack despite Hannibal's ravaging Italy for fifteen years before retreating to Africa in 203 B.C.E. The Romans finally won by turning the tables and invading the Carthaginians' homeland. Their general Scipio trained his soldiers to keep formation and then swivel out of the way of Hannibal's war elephants, even when facing dozens of the beasts charging so hard they shook the earth. At the decisive battle of Zama in 202 B.C.E., Scipio crushed Carthage's forces. The Senate imposed a punishing settlement on the Carthaginians in 201 B.C.E., forcing them to eliminate their navy, pay huge fines for fifty years, and hand over their rich territory in Spain, which Rome made into provinces famous for their mines.

The Third Punic War (149–146 B.C.E.) broke out when the Carthaginians, who had revived financially, struck back against an aggressive African neighbor and Roman ally. After defeating Carthage for a third time, the Romans followed the advice of the tough-minded senator Cato: "We must destroy Carthage." They destroyed the city and converted its territory into a province. This disaster did not obliterate Carthaginian language and culture, however, and under the Roman

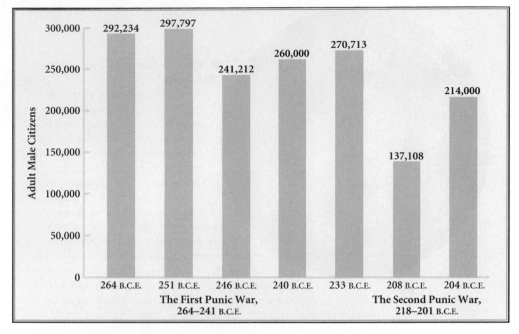

■ **TAKING MEASURE** Census Records of Adult Male Roman Citizens during the First and Second Punic Wars

Livy (59 B.C.E.–17 C.E.) and Jerome (c. 347–420 C.E.) provide these numbers from Roman censuses conducted during and between the first two wars against Carthage. Only adult male citizens (the men eligible for Rome's regular army) were counted. The drop in the total for 246 B.C.E., compared with the total for 264 B.C.E., reflects losses in the First Punic War. The low total for 208 B.C.E. reflects losses in battle and defections by communities such as Capua in 216 B.C.E. Because the censuses did not include the Italian allies fighting on Rome's side, the numbers understate the wars' total casualties. Scholars estimate that the first two Punic Wars took the lives of nearly a third of Italy's adult male population—perhaps a quarter of a million soldiers killed.

Empire this part of North Africa became renowned for its economic and intellectual vitality, which emerged from a combination of Roman and Punic traditions.

Rome's conquests in the Punic Wars led to the extension of Roman power to Macedonia, Greece, and part of Asia Minor. After defeating Philip in Macedonia for revenge and to prevent any threat of his invading Italy, the Roman commander Flamininus proclaimed the "freedom of the Greeks" in 196 B.C.E. to show respect for Greece's tradition of fighting for independence. The Greek cities and federal leagues naturally interpreted the proclamation to mean they could behave as they liked. They misunderstood. The Romans meant them to behave as clients and follow their new patrons' advice; the Greeks thought, as "friends" of Rome, that they were truly independent. Trouble then developed because the two sides failed

■ **Plate Decorated with a War Elephant**

This third-century B.C.E. plate from southern Italy depicts an Indian elephant followed by her calf. The adult animal carries on its back a fortified compartment for holding archers. War elephants were introduced to the Mediterranean after Alexander the Great fought them in his campaigns in India. Commanders used them to frighten and confuse the enemy with their size and loud bellowing. The Carthaginian general Hannibal shocked the Romans by bringing elephants over the treacherous passes of the Alps to invade Italy, but most of them died on the way. In the long run, however, armies gave up on elephants because they were too expensive to feed and too difficult to control when panicked or wounded in battle. (Scala/Art Resource, NY.)

to realize that common and familiar words such as *freedom* and *friendship* could carry very different meanings in different societies. To make the kingdom of Macedonia and the Greeks observe their obligations as clients, the Romans repeatedly sent armies. Frustrated by continuing Greek resistance, the Senate in 146 B.C.E. ordered the destruction of Corinth for asserting its independence and converted Macedonia and Greece into a province. In 133 B.C.E., the Attalid king of Pergamum boosted Roman power with an astonishing gift: he left his rich Asia Minor kingdom to Rome in his will. In 121 B.C.E., when the Greek city of Massilia on the southern coast of Gaul asked for protection against local tribes, the Romans made the lower part of Gaul across the Alps (modern France) into a province. By this date, then, Rome governed and profited from two-thirds of the Mediterranean region; only the easternmost Mediterranean lay outside its control (see Map 4.2).

Greece's Influence on Rome's Literature, Philosophy, and Art

Although Romans looked down on Greeks for their military weakness, they admired their literature, philosophy, and art. The wars that brought Roman armies to Greece also brought increased Greek cultural influence on Romans. In about 200 B.C.E., the first Roman historian, Fabius Pictor, wrote in Greek to compose his account of Rome's foundation and the Punic War. Greece also directly inspired the earliest literature in Latin: an adaptation of Homer's

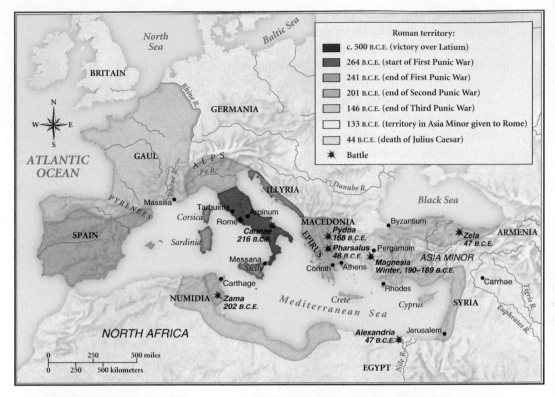

■ MAP 4.2 Roman Expansion, c. 500–44 B.C.E.

During the first two centuries of its existence, the Roman republic used war and diplomacy to extend its power north and south on the Italian peninsula. In the third and second centuries B.C.E., conflict with Carthage to the south and west and with the Hellenistic kingdoms to the east extended Roman power far outside Italy and led to the creation of provinces from Spain to Greece. The first century B.C.E. saw the conquest of the Levant by Pompey and of Gaul by Julius Caesar. **For more help analyzing this map,** see the map activity for this chapter in the ONLINE STUDY GUIDE at bedfordstmartins.com/huntconcise.

Odyssey by a Greek ex-slave, Livius Andronicus, written sometime after the First Punic War.

Like Livius, many of the most famous early Latin authors were not native Romans. Their widespread origins reveal the mixing of cultures under the republic. The poet Naevius (d. 201 B.C.E.) came from Campania in southern Italy; the poet Ennius (d. 169 B.C.E.) from even farther south, in Calabria; the comic playwright Plautus (d. 184 B.C.E.) from north of Rome, in Umbria; his fellow comedy writer Terence (c. 190–159 B.C.E.) from North Africa. They all found inspiration in Greek literature. Roman comedies, for example, took their plots and standard characters from Hellenistic Greek comedy, which raised laughs from family life and stereotyped personalities, such as the boastful warrior and the obsessed lover.

Not all Romans applauded Greek influence. Cato, although he studied Greek himself, insisted that the "feeble" Greeks were corrupting the "sturdy" Romans. He established Latin as an appropriate language for prose by publishing a history of Rome, *The Origins* (written between 168 and 149 B.C.E.), and instructions for running a large farm, *On Agriculture* (published about 160 B.C.E.). He glumly predicted that if the Romans ever became infected with Greek literature, they would lose their power. In fact, as usual in cultural interactions, early Roman authors employed foreign models to express their own values in new ways. Ennius, for example, was inspired by Greek epic poetry to compose his own Latin epic *Annals,* a poetic version of Roman history, but he praised ancestral Roman tradition, as a much-quoted line demonstrated: "On the ways and the men of old rests the Roman commonwealth."

Later Roman writers also took inspiration from Greek literature. Lucretius (c. 94–55 B.C.E.), for example, published a long poem entitled *On the Nature of Things* to argue that people should have no fear of death, which only inflamed "the running sores of life." His work's content followed closely the "atomic theory" of the nature of existence of the Greek philosopher Epicurus (341–270 B.C.E.) and described matter as composed of tiny, invisible particles. The poem explained that death meant only that the atoms temporarily forming a person's body once again separated, without pain or suffering. There could be no eternal punishment—or reward—after death, indeed no afterlife at all, because a person's soul, itself made up of atoms, dissolved along with the body.

Hellenistic Greek authors inspired Catullus (c. 84–54 B.C.E.), whose witty poems satirized prominent politicians for their sexual behavior and revealed his own disastrous love life. His most notorious erotic poems detailed his passion for a married woman named Lesbia, whom he begged to think only of immediate pleasures: "Let us live, my Lesbia, and love; the gossip of stern old men is not worth a cent. Suns can set and rise again; we, when once our brief light has set, must sleep one never-ending night. Give me a thousand kisses, then a hundred, then a thousand more."

The orator Cicero wrote not only speeches and letters but also many essays on philosophy, ethics, theology, and political science that built on the work of Greek philosophers. He adapted Greek ideas to Roman life—above all expressing the value of appreciating the uniqueness of each human personality. He wrote his most influential philosophical works in one period of furious activity while in political exile in 45 and 44 B.C.E. His doctrine of **humanitas** ("humanness, the quality of humanity") combined various ideas from Greek philosophy, especially Stoicism, to express an ideal for human life based on generous and honest treatment of others and an abiding commitment to morality derived from natural law

■ **Actors in a Comedy**

This relief sculpture dating to the first century B.C.E. shows actors portraying characters in one of the various kinds of comedy popular during the Roman republic. In this variety, which derived from Greek New Comedy of the Hellenistic period, the actors wore exaggerated masks designating stock personality types and strove for broad, slapstick comedy. The plots ranged from burlesques of famous mythological stories to stereotypes of common family problems. Here, on the right, an irresponsible son returns home after a night of drinking, supported by his slave and preceded by a hired female musician. On the left, his enraged father is restrained by a friend from beating the prodigal son with his cane. (Scala/Art Resource, NY.)

(the right that exists for all people by nature, independent of the differing laws and customs of different societies). The spirit of humanitas that Cicero passed on to later ages was perhaps the most attractive ideal to emerge from republican Rome.

Greece influenced Rome not only in literature but also in art and architecture, from the style of sculpture and painting to the design of public buildings. As usual, Romans adapted Greek models to their own purposes, most strikingly in portrait sculpture. Hellenistic artists had pioneered the sculpting of realistic statues that showed the damage old age and stress did to the human body. These Greek statues, however, portrayed human stereotypes (the "old man," the "drunken woman"), not specific people; Greek portrait sculpture, by contrast, presented real individuals in the best possible light, much like a retouched photograph today.

Roman artists in the later republic transferred the Greek tradition of realistic sculpture to portrait statues. Roman sculptures of specific men did not conceal unflattering features: protruding noses, receding chins, deep wrinkles, bald heads, careworn eyes. Portraits of women, however, were more idealized, perhaps to represent the traditional vision of a happy marriage. Portraits of children were not popular during the republic, perhaps because offspring were not seen as contributing to public life until they were grown. Because either the men shown in the portraits or their families paid for their statues, they must have wanted the faces sculpted realistically—showing the toll of age and effort—to emphasize how hard the men had worked to serve "the people's matter" that was the republic.

Imperialism's Effects on Republican Society

Before the long campaigns required to defeat Carthage, Macedonia, and Greece in the third and second centuries B.C.E., Roman warfare, like Greek, had followed a pattern of short campaigns timed not to interfere with the labor needs of farming. Rome's long wars abroad had the unintended consequence of disrupting the traditional rhythm of Roman agricultural life and forcing many poor people to move to the capital. Furthermore, the years of conquest led to hard times for the poorer families in Italy, who constituted the principal source of soldiers. A farmer absent on prolonged military expeditions had two choices: relying on a hired hand or slave to manage his crops and animals or having his wife take on what was traditionally man's work in the fields in addition to her usual domestic tasks. The story of the consul Regulus, who led a Roman army to victory in Africa in 256 B.C.E., revealed the severe problems a man's absence could cause. When the man who managed his 4⅓-acre farm died while the consul was away fighting Carthage, a hired hand ran off with all the farm's tools and livestock. Regulus begged the Senate to send a general to replace him so he could return home to save his wife and children from starving. The senators saved Regulus's family and property from ruin because they wanted to retain him as a commander in the field.

Ordinary soldiers could expect no such special aid, and these troubles hit poorer families particularly hard when in the second century B.C.E., for reasons that remain unclear, there was not enough farmland to support their children from generation to generation. Scholars have usually concluded that the rich had deprived the poor of land, but recent research suggests that the problem stemmed from an astonishing growth in the number of young people in the population. Not all regions of Italy suffered as severely as others, and some impoverished farmers and their families managed to remain in the countryside by working as day laborers for others. In any case, the number of poor people without a way to make a living had created a social crisis by the late second century B.C.E. Many homeless people migrated to Rome, where the men looked for work as menial laborers and women sought piecework making cloth but often were forced into prostitution.

This influx of desperate, landless people swelled the poverty-level urban population. The difficulty they experienced just surviving made them an important factor in Roman politics, as ambitious politicians competed for their support by promising welfare benefits. The state had to feed them to avert riots, and by the late second century B.C.E., Rome was importing food to support this swollen population of urban poor. Their demand for rations of low-priced (and eventually free) grain distributed at the state's expense became one of the most explosive issues in late republican politics.

At the other end of the social hierarchy, Rome's elite reaped abundant rewards from imperialism. The increased need for commanders to lead military campaigns

■ Wall Painting of a Woman Playing a Lyre

This painting done in about 40–30 B.C.E. covered part of a wall in a rich family's house at Boscoreale, near Pompeii in southern Italy. Wealthy Romans loved brightly colored rooms elaborately decorated on every wall. This painting shows an unnamed woman playing a kind of concert lyre or harp known as a kithara. The gilding on her instrument and her gold jewelry identify her as a wealthy person. She and the young girl stare out into the room in a style popular at the time. What effect do you think this pose was meant to have on spectators?

(The Metropolitan Museum of Art, Rogers Fund, 1903 [03.14.5]. Photograph © 1986 The Metropolitan Museum of Art.)

overseas created opportunities for successful generals to enrich themselves and their families. By using their gains to finance public buildings, the elite built up their reputations while benefiting the general population. Building new temples, for example, was thought to increase everyone's security by pleasing the gods. In 146 B.C.E., a victorious general paid for Rome's first temple built of marble, finally bringing this Greek style to the capital city.

The financial troubles of small farmers suited rich landowners because they could buy bankrupt plots to create large estates. They further increased their holdings by illegally occupying public land carved out of the territory of defeated peoples. The rich worked their large estates, called latifundia, with slaves as well as free laborers. Many free but poor Romans now found it hard to get work as laborers because the rich had bought workers from the many slaves taken captive during the foreign wars. The growing size of the slave crews working on latifundia was a mixed blessing for their wealthy owners because the presence of so many slave workers in one place led to periodic revolts that required the army to suppress.

The elite also profited from Rome's expansion by filling government offices in the new provinces; they could enrich themselves if they ignored the traditional value of uprightness. Since Roman provincial officials ruled by martial law, no one in the provinces could curb a greedy governor's appetite for graft, extortion, and plunder. Not all governors were corrupt, but some did use their unsupervised power to extort everything they could from the provincials. Until jury trials were created, such offenders faced little or no punishment because in the Senate they and their colleagues would routinely excuse one another's crimes.

The new desire for luxury, financed by the fruits of expansion abroad, fractured the traditional values of moderation and frugality. Before, a general like Manius Curius (d. 270 B.C.E.) represented the ideal: despite his glorious military victories, he was said to have boiled turnips for his meals in a humble hut. Now, the elite acquired showy luxuries, such as large country villas for entertaining friends and clients, to proclaim their social superiority. Money had become more valuable to them than the good of "the people's matter."

▪ **REVIEW:** *What were some of the unintended consequences of Rome's victories over foreign peoples?*

The Destruction of the Republic, c. 133–44 B.C.E.

Placing their own interests ahead of the traditional values of community service, ambitious leaders from the Roman elite destroyed the republic in civil war. When the tribunes Tiberius and Gaius Gracchus agitated for reforms to help poor

Romans, their opponents in the Senate resorted to murder to curb them. When a would-be member of the elite, Gaius Marius, opened army service to the poor to boost his personal status, his creation of "client armies" undermined faithfulness to the republic. When the people's unwillingness to share citizenship with Italian allies sparked a war in Italy and the clashing ambitions of the "great men" Sulla, Pompey, and Julius Caesar burst into civil war, the republic shattered beyond repair.

The Gracchus Brothers and Political Rupture

The aristocratic brothers Tiberius and Gaius Sempronius Gracchus won election as tribunes by advocating a much higher level of financial help for poor citizens. This policy set them at odds with many of the elite, into whose order they had been born: their grandfather Scipio had defeated Hannibal, and their mother was the Cornelia whom the king of Egypt had courted after their father died. Tiberius, the elder brother, spoke bluntly about the horrible lives of the landless poor, according to the biographer Plutarch (c. 50–120 C.E.):

> The wild beasts that roam over Italy have their dens. . . . But the men who fight and die for Italy enjoy nothing but the air and light; without house or home they wander about with their wives and children. . . . They fight and die to protect the wealth and luxury of others; they are styled masters of the world, and have not a clod of earth they call their own.

In 133 B.C.E., when the Senate blocked Tiberius's proposed reforms, he outflanked his opponents by having the Plebeian Assembly pass laws redistributing public land to landless Romans. He further shattered tradition by defying the Senate in financing his land reform: before the Senate could decide whether to accept the gift of the Attalid kingdom from the ruler of Pergamum, Tiberius had the plebeians pass another law specifying that the kingdom's riches be distributed to the poor so they could buy equipment and livestock to start a farm.

Tiberius then announced his intention to run for reelection as tribune, violating the tradition against consecutive terms. His senatorial enemies boiled over: Tiberius's own cousin led a band of senators and their clients in an ambush against him to, as they shouted, "save the republic." Pulling their togas up over their left arms so they would not trip in the attack, they clubbed to death the tribune and many of his followers. Their assault marked a turning point in the republic's history: murder now became a political tool.

Gaius, elected tribune for 123 B.C.E. and, contrary to tradition, elected again the next year, followed his brother's lead by pushing measures that outraged the elite: more land reform, greatly subsidized prices for grain, public works projects throughout Italy to provide employment for the poor, and colonies abroad with farms for the landless. His most revolutionary proposals were to grant Roman citizenship to many Italians and to establish new courts that would try senators accused of corruption as provincial governors. The new juries would be manned not by senators but by *equites* ("equestrians" or "knights"). These were landowners from outside the city, wealthy businessmen whose choice of commerce over a public career set them apart from senators. Because they did not serve in the Senate, equestrians could convict corrupt senators without fear of peer pressure. Gaius's proposal marked the emergence of the equestrians as a political force in Roman politics and angered the Senate. When the senators blocked his plans, Gaius in 121 B.C.E. assembled an armed group to threaten them. They responded by instructing the consuls "to take all measures necessary to defend the republic," meaning the use of force. To escape arrest and certain execution, Gaius had one of his slaves cut his throat; hundreds of his supporters were then murdered by the senators and their supporters.

The violent deaths of the Gracchus brothers and so many of their followers introduced a deep rupture in Roman elite politics. From now on, members of the elite divided themselves either as "supporters of the common people" (*populares*), or "supporters of the best people" (*optimates*). Some identified with one side or the other from genuine allegiance to its policies; others based their choice on self-interest, supporting whichever side better promoted their own political advancement. This split in the elite made political cooperation in service of the republic a lost cause.

Gaius Marius and the First Client Armies

The rupture in the elite broke the nobles' stranglehold on political power, allowing a new kind of leader to arise: men from the elite but with no consul among their ancestors. These men relied on sheer ability to force their way to fame, fortune, influence, and—their ultimate goal—election as consul. The most controversial of them was Gaius Marius (c. 157–86 B.C.E.), an equestrian from Arpinum in central Italy. Ordinarily, a man from this background had no chance of cracking the nobles' hold on the consulships. When Marius succeeded as a general against a rebel in Africa where nobles had failed, however, the people's enthusiasm powered him to election as consul for 107 B.C.E. In Roman terms, this election made him a "new man"—that is, the first man in the history of his family to become consul. Marius's further successes in great crises, especially against German tribes who attacked southern France and then Italy, led the people to elect him consul for six terms, including consecutive service, by 100 B.C.E. This overturned Roman political tradition.

Marius became so famous that the Senate voted him a triumph, Rome's highest—and rarest—military honor. On the day of the ceremony, the general paraded through Rome in a chariot. His face was painted red for reasons Romans no longer remembered. Huge crowds cheered him, while his army teased him with off-color jokes to avert the evil eye at this moment of supreme glory. For a similar reason, a slave rode with him to keep whispering in his ear, "Look behind you, and remember that you are a mortal."

The optimates never accepted Marius, despising him as a dangerous upstart. His support came mainly from the common people, who loved him for his reform of military service. Previously, only men with property could enroll as soldiers. Marius opened enlistment to proletarians, men who owned almost nothing. For them, serving in the army meant an opportunity to better their lot by acquiring plunder and a grant of land to retire on.

This change had a consequence fatal to the republic: creating armies more loyal to their commander than to the community. Proletarian troops felt tremendous goodwill toward a commander who led them to victory and then divided the loot with them generously. Poor soldiers thus began to behave like an army of clients following their general as their patron. They naturally supported his personal ambitions. Marius was the first to promote his own career in this way, but he lost his political importance after 100 B.C.E. because he stopped commanding armies and tried to gain acceptance from the optimates. When later generals used client armies to advance their political careers more violently than Marius ever had, the republic's doom was sealed.

Sulla and Civil War

Taking Marius's lesson to heart, a noble named Lucius Cornelius Sulla (c. 138–78 B.C.E.) exploited the dirty secret of politics in the late republic: traditional values no longer restrained commanders who prized their own advancement and the enrichment of their troops above peace and the good of the community. Sulla wielded his client army as a weapon to extort the consulship and dominate the Senate, perverting the Roman notion of honor. His opportunity came when Rome's Italian allies rebelled in frustration at their being denied citizenship. The Italians' discontent finally erupted in 91–87 B.C.E. in the Social War (so named because the Latin word for "ally" is *socius*). The allies lost the war and 300,000 men, but they won the political battle: Romans granted citizenship to all freeborn peoples of Italy south of the Po River. Most important, their men were now entitled to vote in Rome's assemblies.

Sulla's successful command in the Social War won him election as consul for 88 B.C.E. His luck continued when, in that same year, the king of Pontus on the southern coast of the Black Sea, Mithridates VI (120–63 B.C.E.), organized a murderous rebellion against Rome's control of Asia Minor, especially its greedy tax collectors, who squeezed provincials to pay much more than they owed. Denouncing Romans as "the common enemies of all mankind," Mithridates persuaded the locals to slaughter all the Italians they could locate—tens of thousands of them—in a single day. As retaliation for this treachery, the Senate advised a military expedition;

victory would mean unimaginable plunder because Asia Minor held many wealthy cities.

Born to a patrician family that had lost most of its status and all of its money, Sulla craved the command against Mithridates. When the Senate advised giving Sulla the appointment, his jealous rival Marius, now an old man, immediately plotted to have it transferred to himself by plebiscite. Outraged, Sulla marched his client army against Rome itself. All his officers except one deserted him in horror at this unthinkable outrage. But common soldiers united behind him; neither they nor their commander shrank from civil war. Capturing Rome, Sulla murdered or exiled his opponents and let his men rampage through the city. He then led them off to fight Mithridates, ignoring a summons to stand trial and sacking Athens on the way to Asia Minor.

Sulla's violence generated more violence from his rivals. In Sulla's absence, Marius and his friends embarked on their own reign of terror in Rome. In 83 B.C.E., Sulla returned after defeating Mithridates and allowing his soldiers to plunder Asia Minor. Civil war began again for two years until Sulla crushed his enemies and their Italian allies. The climactic battle took place in 82 B.C.E. before the gates of Rome. An Italian general whipped his troops into a frenzy by shouting, "The last day is at hand for the Romans! These wolves that have made such ravages upon our liberty will never vanish until we have cut down the forest that harbors them."

This passionate cry for freedom failed. Sulla won and destroyed everyone who had opposed him. To speed the extermination, he devised a merciless procedure called proscription—posting a list of those supposedly guilty of treasonable crimes so that anyone could kill them without a trial. Because the property of those proscribed was confiscated, the victors listed the name of anyone whose wealth they desired. The Senate in terror appointed Sulla dictator—an emergency office supposed to be held only temporarily—without any limitation of term. He reorganized the government in the interest of "the best people"—his social class—by making senators the only ones allowed to judge cases against their colleagues and forbidding tribunes to offer legislation on their own or hold any other office after their term.

Convinced by an old prophecy that he had only a short time to live, Sulla surprised everyone by retiring to private life in 79 B.C.E. and indeed dying the next year. His bloody career revealed the sad fate of the traditional values of the republic. First, success in war had long ago changed its meaning from defense of the community to acquiring profits for commanders and common soldiers alike. Second, the patron-client system had mutated to make poor soldiers feel stronger ties of obligation to their generals than to the republic; Sulla's men obeyed his order to attack Rome because they owed obedience to him as their patron and could expect benefits from him in return. He fulfilled his obligations to them by permitting the plundering of Roman and foreign opponents alike.

Finally, the traditional desire to win honor now worked both for and against political stability. So long as that value motivated men from leading families to seek office to promote the welfare of the population as well as the status of their families—the traditional ideal of a public career—it exerted a powerful force for social peace and general prosperity. But pushed to its extreme, the concern for prestige and wealth could overshadow all considerations of public service, even to the point of unleashing civil war. The republic was doomed once its leaders and followers abandoned the "way of the ancestors" that valued respect for the peace, prosperity, and traditions of the republic above personal gain.

Pompey, Caesar, and the End of the Republic

The generals whose names dominate the history of the republic after Sulla all took him as their model: while claiming to be serving the community, in truth they cared most about their own careers. Their motivation—the belief that a Roman noble could never have too much glory or too much wealth—was a corruption of the republic's finest ideals of public service. Two Roman nobles, Pompey and Julius Caesar, fanned the flames of political conflict more than anyone else. They ended up fighting a civil war that ended the republic: for peace to revive, monarchy had to return to Rome after an absence of nearly five hundred years.

The career of Gnaeus Pompey (106–48 B.C.E.) shows how weak the traditional restraints on an individual's power became after Sulla. At only twenty-three years of age, Pompey gathered a private army from his father's clients to fight for Sulla in 83 B.C.E. So splendid were his victories that his shameless demand for a triumph could not be refused. Awarding the supreme honor to such a young man, who had not held a single public office, shattered tradition, but Pompey's personal power was too great to refuse. As he told Sulla, "People worship the rising, not the setting, sun."

Pompey won victory after victory. In 71 B.C.E., he claimed the credit for stopping a massive slave rebellion led by Spartacus, a fugitive gladiator who had terrorized southern Italy for two years and defeated consuls with his army of 100,000 escaped slaves. Stealing the glory from the real victor, the commander Marcus Licinius Crassus (c. 115–53 B.C.E.), Pompey demanded and won election to the consulship in 70 B.C.E., without climbing the ladder of offices or reaching the legal age of forty-two. Three years later, he received unlimited powers to eradicate the pirates infesting the Mediterranean. He smashed them in a matter of months. This success made him wildly popular with the urban poor, who depended on a steady flow of imported grain; with wealthy shippers, who depended on safe sea lanes; and with coastal communities that had suffered from the pirates' raids. Next he won the first Roman victories in the Levant and made Syria a province in 64 B.C.E., thereby ending the Seleucid kingdom and extending Rome's power to the eastern edge of the Mediterranean. He marched as far south as Jerusalem, capturing it in 63 B.C.E. Jews had lived in Rome since the second century B.C.E., but most Romans knew little about their religion; Pompey inspected the Jerusalem temple to satisfy his curiosity and remove its treasures.

Pompey's victories were so spectacular that people compared him to Alexander the Great and referred to him as *Magnus* ("the Great"). No fan of modesty, he boasted that he had increased Rome's provincial revenues by 70 percent and distributed plunder equal to twelve and a half years' pay to his soldiers. He treated foreign policy as his personal business: in the east he operated on his own and ignored the tradition of commanders consulting the Senate to decide on new political arrangements for conquered territories. For all practical purposes, he behaved abroad more like an independent king than a Roman officer. He explained his attitude when replying to some foreigners after they objected to his actions as unjust: "Stop quoting the laws to us," he told them. "We carry swords."

Fearing his power, Pompey's enemies at Rome tried to strengthen their own positions by proclaiming their concern for the common people. By the 60s B.C.E., Rome's population had soared to over half a million people. Hundreds of thousands of them lived crowded together in shabby, multistory apartment buildings no better than slums and depended on subsidized food. Work was hard to find. Danger haunted the crowded streets because the city had no police force. Even the propertied class was in trouble: Sulla's confiscations had produced a credit crunch by flooding the real estate market with properties for sale and caused land values to crash. Overextended investors were trying to borrow their way back to financial health, with no success.

Pompey's return to Rome in 62 B.C.E. lit the fuse to this political powder keg. The Senate, eager to bring "the Great" down a notch, refused to approve his arrangements in the Levant or his grants of land to his veterans. This setback forced Pompey to negotiate with his fiercest political rivals, Crassus and Julius Caesar (100–44 B.C.E.). In 60 B.C.E., these three joined in an unofficial power-sharing arrangement called the **First Triumvirate** ("coalition of three men"). Their combined power proved unstoppable: Pompey rammed through laws confirming his eastern arrangements and guaranteeing land for his troops, thus affirming his status as a generous patron; Caesar gained the consulship for 59 B.C.E. along with a special command in Gaul, allowing him to build his own client army financed with plunder; and Crassus received financial breaks for the Roman tax collectors in Asia Minor, whose support gave him political clout and in whose business he had invested.

This alliance of former political enemies shared no common philosophy of governing; its only cohesion came from personal connections. To cement his bond with Pompey, Caesar married his daughter, Julia, to Pompey in 59 B.C.E., even though she had been engaged to another man. Pompey soothed Julia's jilted fiancé by having him marry his own daughter, who had been engaged to yet somebody else. Through these marital connections, the two powerful rivals now had a common interest: the well-being of Julia, Caesar's only daughter and Pompey's new wife. (Pompey had earlier divorced his second wife after Caesar allegedly seduced her.) Pompey and Julia apparently fell deeply in love in their arranged marriage. As long as Julia lived, Pompey's affection for her restrained him from an outright break with her father.

■ **Coin Portrait of Julius Caesar**

Julius Caesar (100–44 B.C.E.) was the first living Roman to have his portrait appear on a Roman coin. Roman republican coinage had annually changing types—the images and words stamped on the front and back of coins—chosen by the officials in charge of minting. Tradition mandated that only persons who had died could be shown (the same rule applies to U.S. currency), but after Caesar won the civil war in 45 B.C.E., he broke that tradition, as he did many others, to show that he was Rome's supreme leader. Here, he wears the laurel wreath of a conquering general. The realistic portrait conforms to late republican style. Caesar's wrinkled neck and careworn expression emphasize the suffering he endured—and imposed on others—to reach the pinnacle of success. Do you think a portrait is more impressive if it shows the person's blemishes or if it is idealized? (Bibliothèque nationale de France.)

Caesar won the loyalty of his client army with years of victories and plunder in central and northern Gaul, which he added to the Roman provinces; he awed his troops with his daring by crossing the channel to campaign in Britain. His political enemies at Rome dreaded him even more as his military successes mounted, and the bond linking him to Pompey vanished in 54 B.C.E. when Julia died in childbirth. With Caesar's followers agitating to win the masses' support for his return to the capital, the two sides' rivalry exploded into violence. By the mid-50s B.C.E., political gangs of young men roamed the alleys of Rome in search of opponents to assault or murder. Street fighting reached such a level of violence in 53 B.C.E. that it prevented elections; no consuls could be chosen until the year was half over. The triumvirate completely dissolved that same year with the death of Crassus in battle against the Parthians at Carrhae in northern Mesopotamia. Feeling inferior to Pompey and Caesar in military glory, Crassus—without the Senate's authorization—had taken a Roman army across the Euphrates River to fight the Parthians, an Iranian people who ruled a vast territory stretching from the Euphrates to the Indus River. A year later, Caesar's enemies took the extraordinary step of having Pompey appointed sole consul. The traditions of republican government had crumbled.

When the Senate ordered Caesar to surrender his command and thus open himself to prosecution by his enemies, he led his army against Rome. As he crossed the Rubicon River, the official northern boundary of Italy, in early 49 B.C.E., he uttered the famous words signaling that he had chosen civil war: "The die is cast." His troops followed him without hesitation, and the people of Italy cheered him on enthusiastically. He had many backers in Rome, too, from the masses who looked forward to his legendary generosity and from poverty-stricken members of the elite hoping to make money through proscriptions.

The enthusiasm for Caesar led Pompey and most senators to flee to Greece to prepare to fight back. Caesar entered Rome peacefully but soon departed to defeat the army his enemies had raised in Spain; he then sailed to Greece in 48 B.C.E. There he nearly lost the war when his supplies ran out, but his soldiers remained loyal even when they were reduced to eating bread made from roots. When Pompey saw what his opponent's troops were willing to live on, he cried, "I am fighting wild beasts." Pompey's weak generalship gave Caesar a decisive victory at the battle of Pharsalus in 48 B.C.E. Pompey fled to Egypt, where the ministers of the boy-king Ptolemy XIII (63–47 B.C.E.) murdered him, mistakenly thinking this would please Caesar.

Caesar then invaded Egypt, winning a difficult campaign that ended when the young pharaoh drowned in the Nile. Caesar restored Cleopatra VII (69–30 B.C.E.) to the Egyptian throne. As intelligent as she was ruthless, Cleopatra charmed the invader into sharing her bed and supporting her rule. This attachment shocked Caesar's friends and enemies alike: they believed Rome should seize power from foreigners, not yield it to them. Still, so effective were Cleopatra's powers of persuasion that Caesar maintained the love affair and guaranteed her rule over a rich land that his army otherwise would have plundered.

By 45 B.C.E., Caesar had won the civil war but faced the problem of how to govern a shattered republic: only a strong, sole ruler seemed capable of ending the cycle of violence, but the oldest tradition of the republic's elite was its hatred of monarchy. The second-century B.C.E. senator Cato, notorious for his advice in favor of destroying Carthage, had best expressed this feeling: "A king," he said, "is an animal that feeds on human flesh." Caesar's solution was to rule as king in everything but name. First, he had himself appointed dictator in 48 B.C.E.; his term in this temporary office was extended to a lifetime tenure around 44 B.C.E. "I am not a king," he insisted, but the distinction was hard to see. As dictator, he controlled the government despite the appearance of normal procedures. Elections for offices continued, for example, but Caesar controlled the results by recommending candidates to the assemblies, which his supporters dominated. Naturally his recommendations were followed.

Caesar introduced changes that he hoped would strengthen Rome: a moderate cancellation of debts; a limitation on the number of people eligible for subsidized grain; a large program of public works, including the construction of public libraries; colonies for his veterans in Italy and abroad; the rebuilding of Corinth and Carthage as commercial centers; and a revival of the ancient policy of giving citizenship to non-Romans, such as the Cisalpine Gauls (those on the Italian side of the Alps). He also admitted non-Italians to the Senate when he expanded its membership from six hundred (the size established by Sulla) to nine hundred.

Unlike Sulla, Caesar did not proscribe his enemies. Instead he prided himself on his clemency, the recipients of which were, by Roman custom, bound to be his grateful clients. In return, he received unprecedented honors, such as a special golden seat in the Senate house and the renaming of the seventh month of the year after him (July). He also regularized the Roman calendar by having each year include 365 days, a calculation based on an ancient Egyptian calendar that formed the basis for our modern one.

His rule pleased most Romans but outraged the optimates. They resented being dominated by one of their own, a "traitor" who had deserted to the people's side. A band of senators formed a conspiracy, led by Caesar's former close friend Marcus Junius Brutus and inspired by the legend about Brutus's ancestor Lucius Junius Brutus having led the violent expulsion of Rome's original monarchy. They cut Caesar to pieces with daggers in the Senate house on March 15 (the Ides of March on the Roman calendar), 44 B.C.E. When his friend Brutus stabbed him, Caesar, according to some ancient reports, gasped his last words—in Greek: "You, too, my son?"

The "liberators," as they called themselves, had no concrete plans for reviving the republic. They apparently believed that it would automatically spring back to life, overlooking the horrible political violence of the previous forty years and the distortion of Roman values that it brought, with ambitious individuals honoring their own interests and those of their clients above those in the community. Panicked by the loss of their patron, the masses rioted at Caesar's funeral to vent their anger against the elite that had robbed them of their benefactor. Failing to form a united front, the elite resumed their feuds with one another over personal political power. By 44 B.C.E., the republic was lost beyond recovery.

■ **REVIEW:** *How did the actions and policies of individual leaders destroy the republic?*

IMPORTANT DATES

753 B.C.E.	Traditional date of Rome's founding	**133 B.C.E.**	Tiberius Gracchus elected tribune and then assassinated
509 B.C.E.	Roman republic established	**91–87 B.C.E.**	Social War between Rome and its Italian allies
509–287 B.C.E.	Struggle of the orders		
451–449 B.C.E.	Creation of the Twelve Tables, Rome's first written law code	**60 B.C.E.**	First Triumvirate (Caesar, Pompey, and Crassus)
264–241 B.C.E.	First Punic War	**49–45 B.C.E.**	Civil war, with Caesar the victor
218–201 B.C.E.	Second Punic War	**45–44 B.C.E.**	Cicero writes his philosophical works on humanitas
168–149 B.C.E.	Cato writes The Origins, the first history of Rome in Latin	**44 B.C.E.**	Caesar appointed dictator for life and then assassinated
149–146 B.C.E.	Third Punic War		
146 B.C.E.	Destruction of Carthage and Corinth		

■ MAPPING THE WEST The Roman World at the End of the Republic, c. 44 B.C.E.

Upon Julius Caesar's assassination in 44 B.C.E., the territory that Rome would control during the coming centuries was almost complete. Caesar's young relative Octavian (the future Augustus) would conquer and add Egypt in 30 B.C.E. Geography and distance were the primary factors preventing further expansion, which Romans never stopped thinking of as desirable even when practical difficulties made this goal only a dream. The deserts of Africa and the Near East worked against expansion southward or eastward against the powerful peoples located beyond, and trackless forests and fierce resistance from local inhabitants made expansion into central Europe and the British Isles impossible to sustain.

Conclusion

From its beginnings in 509 B.C.E., Rome's republic flourished because its values stressed the common good, it incorporated outsiders, and its small farmers produced agricultural surpluses. These surpluses supported a growing population to supply soldiers for a strong army. Romans' willingness to endure tremendous losses of life and property—the proof that they valued faithfulness—helped make them unbeatable: Rome might lose battles but never wars. Because warfare brought profits, peace seemed a wasted opportunity. Elite commanders craved victories because they brought glory and riches to raise their status in Rome's social hierarchy.

The long wars against Carthage, Macedonia, and Greece, however, had unexpected and harmful consequences. In ways still hard to determine, they created a shortage of farmland for Italy's rural poor. When landless people flocked to Rome, they created an unstable political force: the urban mob demanding subsidized food. Members of the elite upped their competition with each other for the increased career opportunities presented by constant war. These rivalries became unmanageable when successful generals began to extort advantages for themselves by acting as patrons to their client armies of poor troops. In this hypercompetitive environment, force became the preferred means of settling political disputes. But violent actions provoked violent responses; community values were drowned in the blood of civil war. No reasonable Roman could have been optimistic about the chances for an enduring peace in the aftermath of Caesar's assassination in 44 B.C.E. That another "great man" would forge such a peace less than fifteen years later would have seemed an impossible dream.

■ **MAKING CONNECTIONS**

1. *Compare the political and social values of the Roman republic with those of the Classical Greek city-state.*

2. *What were the positive and negative consequences of war for the Roman republic?*

■ **FOR FURTHER EXPLORATION**

For further reading and online research ideas, see the Suggested References on page SR-2 at the back of the book.

For practice quizzes, a customized study plan, and other study tools, see the ONLINE STUDY GUIDE at bedfordstmartins.com/huntconcise.

For primary-source material from this period, see Chapter 4 in *Sources of THE MAKING OF THE WEST: A CONCISE HISTORY*, Second Edition.

The Roman Empire

c. 44 B.C.E.–284 C.E.

IN 203 C.E., VIBIA PERPETUA, wealthy and twenty-two years old, nursed her infant in a Carthage jail while awaiting execution. She had received a death sentence for refusing to offer a sacrifice to the gods for the Roman emperor's health and safety. One morning, the jailer dragged her off to the city's main square, where a crowd gathered. Perpetua described in her journal what happened next when the local governor attempted to persuade her to save her life:

> *My father came carrying my son, crying "Perform the sacrifice; take pity on your baby!" Then the governor pleaded, "Think of your old father; show pity for your little child! Offer the sacrifice for the health of the emperor's family." "I refuse," I answered. "Are you a Christian?" asked the governor. "Yes." When my father would not stop trying to change my mind, the governor ordered him thrown to the ground and whipped with a rod. I felt sorry for my father; it seemed they were beating me. I pitied his pathetic old age.*

Nevertheless, she did not give in. Later, gored by a bull and stabbed by a gladiator, she died still proclaiming her faith.

■ **Executing a Criminal in Public**
This mosaic shows a convicted criminal being killed by a leopard at a public execution. Romans believed that serious criminals deserved disgraceful deaths before crowds of spectators. Martyrs charged with treason, like Perpetua, often were executed by "being condemned to the beasts." Here the prisoner is tied to a stake on a chariot so the handlers can push him into the face of the leopard to provoke an angry leap; wild animals frequently would not attack without such provocation. Dated to about Perpetua's time, c. 200 C.E., the mosaic covered a villa floor in North Africa in what is today Libya. The villa's owner perhaps ordered this subject for his floor to show visitors that he had paid for the expensive spectacle that included this grisly execution. (© Roger Wood/Corbis.)

The clash of traditional Roman values of faithfulness and loyalty doomed Perpetua: she believed that her faith in Christ required her to refuse the state's demand for loyalty to the "way of the elders" in public religion and her father's pleas to preserve her family. Her refusal to observe traditional values in traditional ways echoed the refusal of ambitious Roman commanders in the late republic to value the community's interests over their own private ambitions. The civil wars they fought ended the republic. A bloodbath followed Julius Caesar's assassination in 44 B.C.E.: seventeen more years of Roman fighting Roman. Augustus (63 B.C.E.–14 C.E.) finally restored peace in 27 B.C.E. by inventing a special kind of monarchy—the **principate**—that claimed to restore traditional values. His new political and social system opened the pivotal period in Western civilization known to us as the Roman Empire.

Augustus disguised his government as a restoration of the republic so that he could seem to satisfy the Roman elite's insistence of maintaining the tradition of shared political decision making. He retained old institutions—the Senate, the consuls and other officials, the courts—while reshaping political power by making himself a sole ruler who was not called a king. He masked his monarchy by taking the title "first man" (*princeps*, hence the term *principate* for his new system of government), a traditional honorary title for the leading senator. Princeps was therefore the actual title for the ruler today we call "the Roman emperor" (from Latin *imperator*, "commander").

The principate transformed Rome into a disguised monarchy with a fundamental weakness: since the ruler was officially not a king, he could not automatically pass on his rule to a son as his successor and legitimate ruler. In traditional, acknowledged monarchies, the king's son inherited his father's position and political legitimacy. Augustus had to create a new process to try to ensure a peaceful succession that everyone would regard as legitimate: the princeps would train a successor to be approved by the Senate. If that approved successor just happened to be the princeps's son, so be it. This new system of government brought stability for two hundred years, except during a few brief struggles over who, with the Senate's approval, should become the next princeps. This stability came at a price: since Augustus's successors did not have automatic, inherited legitimacy as rulers, they were always quick to try to suppress any sign of disloyalty or rebellion. Perpetua's refusal to sacrifice, for example, was considered treason and impiety, which was punishable by death because it disrespected the princeps and angered the gods, thereby threatening the safety of the entire community.

Romans welcomed the principate's peacefulness, which historians call the **Pax Romana** ("Roman peace"). In the third century C.E., however, rivalry over the succession reignited civil war, leading to economic crisis. By the 280s, Roman imperial government again desperately needed to transform its political system to restore traditional values of loyalty and public service. Diocletian, a military commander from the provinces, would begin that process by winning rule over the Roman world in 284 C.E.

Creating "Roman Peace"

Inventing tradition takes time. Augustus developed his new political system gradually; as the biographer Suetonius (c. 70–130) expressed it, Augustus "made haste slowly." The principate produced an extended period of peace, although its rulers periodically fought to expand imperial territory, suppress rebellions, and repel invaders. Augustus succeeded in reinventing monarchy as an effective form of Roman government because he won the civil war and, during his long rule, found new ways to inspire loyalty by promoting an image of himself as a dedicated leader.

From Republic to Principate, 44–27 B.C.E.

The principate was born in blood. Julius Caesar's assassination in 44 B.C.E. set off another civil war between generals. The leading opponents were Mark Antony and Octavian (the future Augustus), Caesar's eighteen-year-old grandnephew, who by Caesar's will became his adopted son and heir. Despite his limited military experience, Octavian won the loyalty of Caesar's soldiers by taking his new father's name and promising them rewards from their murdered general's wealth. Marching these veterans to Rome, in 43 B.C.E. the teenager forced his election as consul without, like Pompey before him, ever having been elected to any post on the ladder of offices.

Octavian, Antony, and a general named Lepidus then joined forces to eliminate rivals, especially Caesar's assassins. In late 43 B.C.E., the three formed the so-called Second Triumvirate, which they forced the Senate to recognize as an official emergency panel for "rebuilding the state." With no checks on their power, they began to murder their enemies and confiscate their property. Octavian and Antony soon forced Lepidus into retirement and, too ambitious to cooperate, began civil war with each other.

Antony made the eastern Mediterranean his base, joining forces with Cleopatra VII (69–30 B.C.E.), the Ptolemaic queen of Egypt who had earlier allied with Caesar. Enchanted by Cleopatra's wit and intelligence, Antony became her ally and lover. Skillfully playing on Romans' fear of foreign attack, Octavian rallied support by claiming that Antony planned to make Cleopatra queen of Rome. He persuaded the residents of Italy and the western provinces to swear a personal oath of loyalty to him, making them all his clients. Octavian's victory at the naval battle of Actium in northwest Greece in 31 B.C.E. won the war (see Map 5.1). Cleopatra and Antony fled to Egypt, where they both committed suicide in 30 B.C.E., choosing their own deaths to rob their enemy of celebrity hostages. The general first stabbed himself, bleeding to death in his lover's embrace. The queen then ended her life by letting a poisonous snake, a symbol of Egyptian royal authority, bite her. Octavian's capture of Egypt made him Rome's richest citizen and its unrivaled leader.

Augustus's "Restoration," 27 B.C.E.–14 C.E.

After distributing land to his soldiers and creating colonies in the provinces, Octavian announced in 27 B.C.E. that he had restored the republic. It was now, he proclaimed, the duty of the Senate and the Roman people to preserve it. Awed by Octavian's power, the Senate begged him to do whatever was necessary to safeguard the restored republic, granted him special civil and military powers, and gave him the honorary name **Augustus**, meaning "favored by the gods." Octavian had considered changing his name to Romulus, after Rome's legendary first king, but as the historian Cassius Dio (c. 164–230) later wrote, "When he realized people thought this idea meant he wanted to be their king, he accepted the other title instead, as if he were more than human; for everything that is most treasured and sacred is called *augustus.*"

■ **Priests on the Altar of Augustan Peace**
After four years of construction, Augustus dedicated the Altar of Augustan Peace in northwest Rome on his wife's birthday in 9 B.C.E. The altar stood inside four walls measuring about thirty-four feet long, thirty-eight feet wide, and twenty-three feet high and was open to the sky. Relief sculptures covered the walls. This section shows a religious procession. The figures wearing leather caps with spikes are priests called flamines, *who had to wear this headgear whenever they went outside; the man holding a staff is their attendant. The hooded man at the right is probably Marcus Agrippa, Augustus's greatest general. The laurel wreaths worn on bare heads signify both religious devotion and victory; as Augustus commented in his* Res Gestae *("Accomplishments") 13, "Peace was achieved through victories." The altar can be seen today in its original form because it was reconstructed by Benito Mussolini, Fascist dictator of Italy from 1926 to 1943, who wanted to associate his regime with Augustus's glory.* (Scala/Art Resource, NY.)

In the years following 27 B.C.E., Augustus maintained the appearance of republican government by continuing the annual election of consuls and other officials, the passing of legislation in public assemblies, and respect for the Senate. He served several times as consul, the republic's premier official. To preserve the tradition that no official should hold more than one post at a time, he had the Senate grant him the powers of a tribune without his holding the office. He possessed the authority to act and to compel citizens as if he were a tribune protecting the rights of the people, but he left the posts open for members of the plebeian elite to occupy, as they had done under the republic. Augustus also kept his own appearance "republican" instead of royal: he dressed and acted like a regular citizen, not an aloof king.

Augustus's taking *princeps* as his only title of office was a cleverly calculated move. In the republic, the "first man" had guided Rome because of the respect (***auctoritas***) he had earned; he had no more formal power (*potestas*) than any other leader. By choosing the title *princeps*, Augustus appeared to carry on this valued tradition, but in fact he revised the basic power structure. Previously, no one could have exercised the powers of both consul and tribune simultaneously. The reality of the principate was that it was a monarchy masked as a restored and improved republic, headed by an emperor cloaked as the princeps.

Augustus and his successors exercised supreme power because they controlled the army and the treasury. Augustus made the military the basis for his moral authority as restorer of the republic by turning the republican army—a part-time militia—into a full-time professional force. He completed the transformation of the princeps into the troops' patron by establishing set lengths of service, regular pay, and substantial benefits upon retirement. To cover the added costs, Augustus imposed an inheritance tax on citizens. The rich hated this innovation, but the grateful army obeyed and protected the emperor. Another change Augustus made was to station soldiers—the **praetorian guard**—in Rome itself for the first time. These troops prevented rebellion in the capital and provided an imperial bodyguard, a visible reminder of the emperor's dominance.

To broadcast the political legitimacy he claimed, Augustus communicated his image as protector and patron using objects from coins to buildings. As the only mass-produced source of official messages, coins functioned like modern political advertising. They proclaimed slogans such as "Father of his Country" to remind Romans of their emperor's moral authority over them, or "Roads have been built" to emphasize his personal generosity in paying for highway construction.

To fulfill the tradition that rich politicians and generals should spend money for the public good, Augustus erected huge buildings in Rome paid for by the fortune he had inherited from Caesar and then increased in war. The huge Forum of Augustus best illustrates his skill at communicating through bricks and stone (Figure 5.1). Its plaza centered on a temple to Mars, the Roman god of war. Two-story colonnades stretched out from the temple like wings, sheltering statues of famous Roman heroes as inspirations to future leaders. Augustus's Forum provided gathering space for religious rituals

Temple of Mars Ultor   Colonnades (porches)   Statues of
                        lined with columns   Roman heroes

Unroofed area

■ **FIGURE 5.1 Cutaway Reconstruction of the Forum of Augustus**
*Augustus built this large forum (120 × 90 yards) to commemorate his victory over the assassins
of his adoptive father, Julius Caesar. Dedicated in 2 B.C.E., its centerpiece was a marble temple
dedicated to the god Mars Ultor ("The Avenger"). Inside the temple he placed statues of Mars,
Venus (the divine ancestor of Julius Caesar), and Julius Caesar (as a god), as well as Caesar's sword
and works of art. The two curved spaces flanking the temple featured statues of Aeneas and Romulus,
Rome's founders. The porches stretching along the open courtyard housed other statues of Roman
heroes. The ceremony marking teenaged boys' passage into adulthood took place here, where they
were surrounded by images of the valorous and glorious men whom they were expected to imitate.*

and ceremonies marking the passage into adulthood of upper-class boys, but it also
stressed the themes Augustus wanted to communicate about his new system: peace
restored through victory, the foundation of a new age, devotion to the gods who led
Rome to victory, respect for tradition, and unselfishness in spending money for the
community. These messages communicated Augustus's justification for his rule.

Augustus never revealed his deepest motives in establishing the principate.
Was he a cynical tyrant working to destroy the freedoms of the republic? Did he
have no choice but to impose a disguised monarchy to reunite a society ripped
apart by civil war? Or did his motives lie somewhere in between? Perhaps it is best
to see him as a revolutionary bound by tradition. His problem had been the one
always facing Roman politicians—how to balance his own personal ambitions, the
need for peace, and Rome's tradition of shared rule. Augustus's goals were stability, order, and legitimacy for his system, not political freedom for citizens; his
strategy was to employ traditional values to justify changes, as in his reinventing
the meaning of the title "first man." Above all, he extended the patron-client system to politics by making the emperor everyone's most important patron, possessing the moral authority to guide the lives of all. This process reached its peak

when the Senate proclaimed him "Father of his Country" in 2 B.C.E. Declaring that this title was the greatest honor Rome could grant, he treasured it because it agreed with his image of himself as princeps: a leader governing Romans like a father, stern but caring, requiring obedience and loyalty from his children but dedicated to taking care of them in return.

Despite frequent illnesses, Augustus ruled until he died at age seventy-five in 14 C.E. The length of his rule—forty-one years—gave his innovations time to become traditions. As the Roman historian Tacitus (c. 56–120) remarked, by the time Augustus died, "almost no one was still alive who had seen the republic." Augustus transformed republican Rome into imperial Rome by his long life, his military and financial innovations, his care for the capital's poor people, and his manipulation of the traditional vocabulary of politics to disguise his power and proclaim his legitimacy.

Life in Augustan Rome

A crucial factor in Augustus's success was trying to better the lives of ordinary people. Their problems were most serious in Rome. Archaeology and literature let us sketch a picture of life in Augustus's Rome. Although some of the sources refer to times after Augustus and to cities other than the capital, they nevertheless help us understand this period; economic and social conditions were essentially the same in all larger cities throughout the early centuries of the empire.

The population of Augustan Rome—probably far over half a million—was vast for the ancient world. Indeed, no European city would have nearly as many people again until London in the 1700s. The streets were packed: "One man jabs me with his elbow, another whacks me with a pole; my legs are smeared with mud, and from all sides big feet step on me" was the poet Juvenal's description of walking in Rome in the early second century C.E. To ease congestion in the narrow streets, wagon traffic was banned in the daytime. This regulation made nights noisy with the creaking of axles and the shouting of drivers caught in traffic jams.

Most urban residents lived in small apartments in multistoried buildings called islands (so named because originally each building had an open strip around it). Outnumbering private houses by more than twenty to one, apartment buildings usually housed shops, bars, and simple restaurants on the first floor. Graffiti—political endorsements, personal insults, advertising, messages of all kinds—covered many outside walls. The higher the floor, the cheaper were the apartments; the poorest people lived on the top floors in single rooms that they rented by the day. Aqueducts delivered fresh water to public fountains, but because apartments had no plumbing, residents had to lug buckets up the stairs. The wealthy few had piped-in water at ground level. Most tenants lacked bathrooms and had to use public latrines or pots for toilets at home. Some buildings had cesspits, or buckets could be carried down to the streets to be emptied by people who made their living collecting excrement. Lazy tenants flung the foul-smelling contents of these containers out the window.

Because the city generated about sixty tons of human waste every day, sanitation presented an ongoing problem that Roman officials constantly worked to overcome. By 33 B.C.E., Augustus's general Marcus Agrippa had improved the city's main sewer, but its untreated contents emptied directly into the Tiber River, which ran through the city. The technology for sanitary disposal of waste simply did not exist. People sometimes left human and animal corpses in the streets, to be gnawed by vultures and dogs until the city's officials had them removed. The poor were not the only people affected by such conditions: a stray mutt once brought a human hand to the table where Vespasian, who would be emperor from 69 to 79, was eating lunch. Flies buzzing everywhere and a lack of mechanical refrigeration contributed to frequent digestive illness: the most popular jewelry of the time was supposed to ward off stomach trouble. Although the wealthy could not eliminate such discomforts, they made their lives more pleasant with luxuries such as snow rushed from the mountains to ice their drinks and slaves to clean their houses, which were built around courtyards and gardens to let in air and sunshine.

Public baths helped residents keep clean. Because admission fees were low, almost everyone could afford to go daily. Many baths dotted the city, serving like modern health clubs as centers for exercising and socializing as well as washing. Bathers progressed through a series of increasingly warm, humid areas until they reached a sauna-like room. They swam naked in their choice of hot or cold pools. Women went to the public baths, but the genders bathed apart, either in separate rooms or at different times of the day. Since bathing was thought to help sick people but doctors did not yet understand the danger of infections, the untreated pools could spread disease.

City residents faced hazards beyond infectious disease. Tenants routinely threw broken dishes and other trash out their apartment windows, to fall like missiles onto the streets below. "If you are walking to a dinner party in Rome," Juvenal warned, "you would be foolish not to make out your will first. For every open window is a source of potential disaster." The apartment buildings could also be dangerous because they sometimes collapsed. Roman engineers, despite their skill in using concrete, brick, and stone as building materials, lacked the technology to calculate precisely how much weight their constructions could stand. Builders trying to cut costs paid little attention to engineering safeguards in any case. Augustus upgraded public safety by imposing a height limit of seventy feet on new apartment buildings. Fire presented the greatest risk; one of Augustus's most important innovations to improve people's lives was to provide Rome with the first public fire department in Western history. He also established the first permanent police force, despite his fondness for stopping to watch the fistfights that often broke out in Rome's crowded streets.

Many city dwellers had too little to eat and few chances for jobs. Augustus aided them by guaranteeing an adequate food supply. This service was his responsibility as Rome's supreme patron, and he freely drew upon his personal fortune to pay for

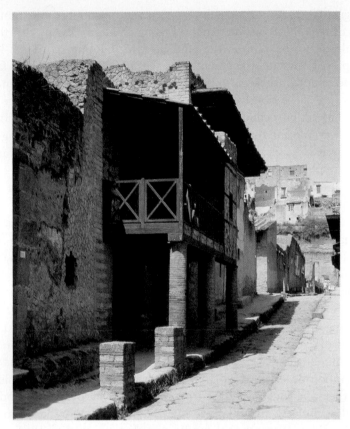

■ **Downtown Street in Herculaneum**

Like Pompeii, the prosperous town of Herculaneum on the shore of the Bay of Naples was frozen in time by the massive eruption of the neighboring volcano, Mount Vesuvius, in 79 C.E. A flood of mud from the eruption buried the town and preserved its buildings until they were excavated beginning in the eighteenth century. Typical of a Roman town, it had straight roads paved with large, flat stones and flanked by sidewalks. Balconies jutted from the upper stories of houses, offering residents a shady viewing point for the lively traffic in the urban streets. Instead of having yards in front or back, houses often enclosed a garden courtyard that was open to the sky. Why do you think urban homes were arranged in this way? (Scala/Art Resource, NY.)

imported grain. Distributing grain at public expense to the capital's poor citizens had been a tradition for decades, but Augustus's welfare system reached the unprecedented size of 250,000 recipients, plus their families. This statistic suggests that between 600,000 and 700,000 people depended on the government for food to survive. Poor Romans usually boiled this grain to make a sticky soup, which they washed down with cheap wine. If they were lucky, they might have some beans, onions, or cheese on the side. The rich, as we learn from an ancient cookbook, ate costlier foods, such as roast pork or shellfish, served very spicy with pepper, a salty condiment, or sweet-and-sour sauce made from honey and vinegar.

By Augustus's time, many wealthy Romans were spending more money on luxuries and costly political careers than on raising children. Fearing that this decline in the birthrate would destroy the elite on which Rome relied for leadership, Augustus passed laws to strengthen marriage and encourage larger families by granting special legal privileges to the parents of three or more children. He made adultery a crime. So seriously did Augustus back these reforms that he exiled his own daughter—his only child—and a granddaughter for sex scandals. His laws had little effect, however, and the old elite families dwindled over the coming centuries. Recent research suggests that up to three-fourths of senatorial-rank families lost their official status (by losing the wealth required for that designation) or died out every generation. Equestrians and men from the provinces who won the ruler's favor took their places in the social hierarchy and in the Senate.

Slaves occupied the lowest rung in society's hierarchy. Unlike Greece, however, Rome gave citizenship to freed slaves, a policy meaning, over the long term, that many Romans were the descendants of slaves. All slaves could hope to acquire the rights of a free citizen, and their descendants, if they became wealthy, could become members of the social elite. This possibility gave slaves reason to work harder and cooperate with their masters. Conditions of slavery varied widely according to occupation. Slaves in agriculture and manufacturing had harsh lives. Most such workers were men, although women might assist the foremen who managed gangs of rural laborers. The second-century novelist Apuleius wrote this grim description of slaves at work in a flour mill: "Through the holes in their ragged clothes you could see scars from whippings all over their bodies. Some wore only loincloths. Letters had been branded on their foreheads and shackles bound their ankles." Worse than the mills were the mines, where the foremen constantly flogged the miners to keep them digging out metal ores in dangerous conditions.

Household slaves had an easier physical existence. Most Romans owned slaves to work in their homes, from one or two in modestly well-off families to large numbers in rich houses and, above all, the imperial palace. Domestic slaves were often women, working as nurses, maids, kitchen help, and clothes makers. Some male slaves ran businesses for their masters, and, to encourage them to work hard, they were allowed to keep part of the profits to save toward purchasing their freedom someday. Women had less opportunity to earn money. Masters sometimes granted tips for sexual favors, and female prostitutes (many of whom were slaves) could earn money for themselves. Slaves who managed to earn money would sometimes buy slaves themselves, thereby creating their own hierarchy. A male slave might buy a woman for a mate. They could then have an imitation of normal family life, though a legal marriage was impossible because they remained their master's property, as did their children. If truly fortunate, slaves could slowly accumulate enough to buy themselves from their masters or could be freed by their masters' wills. Some inscriptions on tombs testify to masters' affectionate feelings for slaves, but even household servants had to endure violent treatment if their masters were cruel. If they attacked their owners because of brutal treatment, the punishment was death.

While slaves always faced potential violence, actual violence was common in Roman public entertainment. The emperors regularly provided mass spectacles featuring hunters killing fierce beasts, wild African animals such as lions mangling condemned criminals, mock naval battles in flooded arenas, gladiatorial combats, and chariot races. Spectators jammed stadiums for these shows, seated according to their social rank and gender following an Augustan law; the emperor and senators sat close to the action, while women and the poor sat in the upper tiers. These spectacles communicated a political message claiming legitimacy for the new system of government by showing that the emperors were generous in providing expensive entertainment for their subjects, powerful enough to command life-and-death exhibitions, and dedicated to preserving the social hierarchy.

Gladiators were men and, rarely, women, who underwent long and expensive training; war captives, criminals, slaves, and free volunteers performed as gladiators. Gladiatorial combats, which originated under the republic as part of the ceremony at extravagant funerals, became so popular under Augustus that they attracted crowds in the tens of thousands. Gladiatorial fights were bloody but usually fought to the death only for captives and criminals; professional fighters could have extended careers. To make the fights more exciting, gladiators used a variety of weapons. One favorite bout pitted a lightly armored fighter, called a net man because he used a net and a trident, against a more heavily armored fish man, so named from the design of his helmet crest. Betting was a great attraction, and spectators could be rowdy. As the Christian theologian Tertullian (c. 160–240) complained: "Look at the mob coming to the show—already they're out of their minds! Aggressive, mindless, already in an uproar about their bets! They all share the same suspense, the same madness, the same voice."

Champion gladiators won riches and celebrity but not social respectability. Early in the first century C.E., the senators became alarmed at what they regarded as the disgrace caused by members of the upper class fighting as gladiators. They therefore banned the elite and all freeborn women under twenty from appearing in gladiatorial shows. Daughters trained by their gladiator fathers had first competed during the republic, and women continued to compete until the emperor Septimius Severus (r. 193–211) banned them.

Gladiatorial shows, chariot races, and theater productions became an opportunity for ordinary citizens to express their feelings on civic conditions to the emperors, who were expected to attend. On more than one occasion, for example, poorer Romans rioted at shows to protest a shortfall in the free grain supply. In this way, public entertainment served as a two-way form of communication between ruler and ruled.

■ Gladiators Sculpted on a Tomb

This relief sculpture, which adorned a tomb near Rome dating to about 30–10 B.C.E., shows gladiators competing in games held to honor the deceased. Gladiatorial combats originated as part of funeral ceremonies because they portrayed with dramatic energy the violent and inevitable struggle to avoid death. Only the very wealthy could afford to have gladiators perform at their funerals or in spectacles meant to win the people's favor. These gladiators represent a traditional form of fighting called provocator ("challenger"). A challenger, who fought gladiators only of the same type, used a short sword, a curved shield, a metal belt cinching up a loincloth, forearm and lower-leg guards, a partial chest protector, and a plumed helmet. These men's muscular bodies show the great strength required to be a successful fighter. (© Alinari/Art Resource, NY.)

Art and Literature to Please the Emperor

Elite culture changed under Augustus to serve the same goal as public entertainment: to express the legitimacy of his transformed system of government. In particular, oratory—the highest attainment of Roman education—lost its bite. Under the republic, rhetorical skill in making stinging speeches to criticize political opponents had been such a powerful weapon that it could catapult a "new man" like Cicero, who lacked social and military distinction, to international fame. Under the principate, the emperor's supremacy ruled out freewheeling debate and open decision making; political criticism was now out of bounds. Speakers now turned their rhetorical skills to praising the emperor at public festivals meant to advance his image as a competent, compassionate, and legitimate ruler.

Education for oratory remained a privilege of wealthy men. Rome had no free public schools, so the poor had to get basic learning from their parents. Most people had time only for training in practical skills. A character in *Satyricon*, a satirical literary work of the first century by Petronius, expressed this hardheaded attitude toward education: "I didn't study geometry and literary criticism and worthless junk like that. I just learned how to read the letters on signs and how to work out percentages, and I learned weights, measures, and the values of the different kinds of coins."

Although Roman tradition called for mothers to teach children right from wrong, servants usually looked after the offspring of rich families. These children attended private elementary schools from age seven to eleven to learn reading, writing, and basic arithmetic. Teachers used rote methods in the classroom and physical punishment for mistakes. Some children went on to the next three years of school, in which they were introduced to literature, history, and grammar. Only a few boys then proceeded to the study of oratory.

Advanced studies for men covered literature, history, ethical philosophy, law, and dialectic (reasoned argument). Mathematics and science were rarely studied as separate subjects, but engineers and architects learned to calculate. Much reading was done aloud. The rich owned educated slaves who would read to them. Books consisted of continuous scrolls made from papyrus or animal skin, not bound pages.

So much new literature emerged at this time that modern scholars call Augustus's reign the Golden Age of Latin literature. The emperor himself composed verse and prose and served as the patron of a circle of writers and artists. His favorites were Horace (65–8 B.C.E.) and Virgil (70–19 B.C.E.). Horace delighted audiences with the rhythms and wit of his short poems on public and private subjects. His poem celebrating Augustus's victory over Antony and Cleopatra at Actium became famous for its opening line, "Now it's time to drink!"

Virgil later became the most popular poet of Augustus's time for his epic poem, the *Aeneid*, in which he mixed praise and subtle criticism of Augustus. Virgil took great pains with his poem, and it remained unfinished at his death. He wanted it burned, but Augustus preserved it. Inspired by Homer's *Iliad* and *Odyssey*, the *Aeneid* told the legend of the Trojan Aeneas, the most distant ancestor of the Romans. Virgil mixed his praise of the principate with recognition of the pain that success required. The *Aeneid* therefore spoke to the complex mix of gain and loss that followed Augustus's transformation of politics and society. Above all, it expressed a moral code for all Romans: no matter how tempting the emotional pull of revenge and pride, be merciful to the conquered but destroy the arrogant.

Authors had to be careful not to anger the ruler. Livy (54 B.C.E.–17 C.E.) composed a lengthy history of Rome in which he recorded the ruthless actions of Augustus and his supporters. The emperor was unhappy, but he did not punish Livy because his history did explain that success and stability depended on traditional values of loyalty and self-sacrifice. Ovid (43 B.C.E.–17 C.E.) was punished. In his poems *Art of Love* and *Love Affairs*, he mocked the emperor's laws on marriage and adultery with tongue-in-cheek tips for conducting secret love affairs and picking up other men's wives at festivals. His *Metamorphoses* ("Transformations") undermined the idea of hierarchy as natural by telling bizarre stories of supernatural shape changes, with people becoming animals and confusion between the human and the divine. In 8 C.E., Augustus exiled Ovid to a bleak town on the Black Sea after the poet became mixed up in a scandal involving the emperor's granddaughter.

■ **Marble Statue of Augustus from Prima Porta**

At six feet eight inches high, this statue stood a foot taller than its subject, Augustus, Rome's first emperor. Found at his wife's country villa at Prima Porta ("First Gate") just outside the capital, the statue was probably a copy of a bronze original sculpted about 20 B.C.E., when Augustus was in his early forties. The sculptor showed him as a younger man, using the idealizing techniques of Greek art of the fifth and fourth centuries B.C.E. to emphasize the emperor's dignity. The sculpture is crowded with symbols that express the image of Augustus that he wanted to communicate. His bare feet hint that he is a near-divine hero, and the statue of Cupid refers to the Julian family's descent from the goddess Venus. The carving on the breastplate shows a Parthian surrendering to a Roman soldier under the gaze of personified cosmic forces basking in the peace of Augustus's reign. **For more help analyzing this image**, see the visual activity for this chapter in the ONLINE STUDY GUIDE at bedfordstmartins.com/huntconcise.

(Scala/Art Resource, NY.)

The style of public sculpture clearly reflected the emperor's wishes. When Augustus was growing up, portraits were starkly realistic, portraying the strain of human experience. The sculpture that Augustus ordered displayed a more idealized style, recalling classical Greek portraiture. In famous works of art such as the *Prima Porta* ("First Gate") statue of himself or the sculpted frieze on his Altar of Peace (finished in 9 B.C.E.), Augustus had himself portrayed as serene and dignified, not careworn and sick as he often was. As with his monumental architecture, Augustus used sculpture to project a calm and competent image of himself as "restorer of the world" and founder of a new age for Rome.

■ **REVIEW:** *How did Augustus bring peace to Rome and transform its political system?*

Maintaining "Roman Peace"

A serious problem confronted Augustus's "restored republic": how to prevent the violent struggles for power that ruined the republic. His solution was to train an heir to take over as princeps at his death after receiving the Senate's approval and the same powers conferred on Augustus. This strategy kept the throne in his family, called the Julio-Claudians, until the death of Nero in 68, and it established the tradition that family dynasties ruled imperial Rome.

Under Augustus's system, the ruler's goals were building loyalty, preventing unrest, and financing the administration while governing a vast territory of diverse provinces. Augustus set a pattern for effective rule that some of his successors followed more successfully than others: taking special care of the army, communicating the image of the princeps as a just and generous ruler, and promoting Roman law and culture as universal standards while allowing as much local freedom in the provinces as possible. The citizens, in return for their loyalty, expected the emperors to be generous patrons, but the difficulties of long-range communication imposed practical limits on the government's intervention in the lives of the empire's residents, for better or worse.

Making Monarchy Permanent, 14–180 C.E.

Augustus wanted to make monarchy the permanent government to avoid civil war, but he needed the Senate's cooperation to give legitimacy to what he called his restoration of the republic. During the 20s B.C.E., he began looking for a male relative to name as his heir (he had no son), but one after another the young men he chose died before he did. Finally, in 4 C.E., he adopted someone who would outlive him, his stepson Tiberius (42 B.C.E.–37 C.E.). Because Tiberius had a fine record as a general, the army supported recommending him to the Senate as the next "first man." The senators approved Tiberius in this role after Augustus died in 14 C.E.; the Julio-Claudian dynasty thus began.

Tiberius's sour personality made him unpopular, but he ruled for twenty-three years (r. 14–37) because he had the most important qualification for succeeding as princeps: the army's loyalty. His long reign provided the stable transition period that the principate needed to establish the compromise between the elite and the emperor that made the monarchy workable. On the one hand, the traditional offices of consul, senator, and others continued, filled by the elite; on the other hand, the emperor decided who held office and determined law and policy. In doing this, everyone claimed that the government was still a republic.

Tiberius's reign also revealed the problems that an unhappy emperor could create. Tiberius paid a steep personal price for becoming "first man" because, to strengthen their family ties, Augustus had forced him to divorce his beloved wife Vipsania and marry Augustus's daughter, Julia. This marriage became a disaster. Tiberius's unhappiness and fear of rivals led him to spend the last decade of his rule away from Rome as a recluse on an island. His withdrawal from governing opened the way for abuses by his officials in Rome and kept him from training his successor.

Tiberius named Gaius (12–41), better known as Caligula, to be the next princeps because he was Augustus's great-grandson, despite Caligula's lack of the personal qualities and training that a worthy ruler needed. Still, the young emperor

(r. 37–41) might have been successful because he knew about soldiering. *Caligula* means "baby boots." Soldiers gave him that nickname as a child because he wore little leather shoes like theirs while growing up in the military bases his father commanded. Unfortunately, he paid attention only to his personal desires. Ruling through cruelty and violence, Caligula drained the treasury to humor his whims. Suetonius labeled him a "monster." He frequently outraged the elite by fighting mock gladiatorial combats and appearing in public in women's clothing or costumes imitating gods. Two praetorian guard commanders murdered him in 41 to avenge personal insults.

After Caligula's assassination, the Senate debated the possibility of refusing to choose a new "first man" and restoring a true republic. They gave in, however, when Claudius (r. 41–54), Augustus's grandnephew and Caligula's uncle, bought the praetorian guard's support with money and the soldiers threatened the senators. Claudius becoming princeps by threat of force made it clear that the genuine republic would never return because the soldiers would always insist on having an emperor—a patron—to promote their interests. Claudius won wider support for his rule by making men from Gaul (today France), a province outside Italy, members of the Senate. This change signaled that provincial elites would be the emperor's partners in governing. In return for their help in keeping their regions peaceful and prosperous, they received offices at Rome and the emperor as patron. Claudius also changed imperial government by employing freed slaves as top administrators. Because these men owed their positions to the emperor, they could be expected to be loyal.

Nero (r. 54–68) succeeded Claudius, whom his mother probably poisoned. Only sixteen when he became "first man," Nero loved music and theater, not governing. The spectacular public festivals he sponsored and the cash he distributed to the poor in Rome kept him popular with the masses. A giant fire in 64 (the incident that led to the legend of Nero "fiddling while Rome burned") made the elite suspect that he had ordered the blaze to clear space for an enormous new palace. Nero outraged the senators by making them attend his singing performances and by bankrupting the treasury to pay for his building project and a trip to sing all over Greece. He raised money by faking charges of treason against senators and equestrians to seize their property. When military commanders in the provinces rebelled at his abuses, he had a servant help him cut his own throat, after wailing, "To die! And such a great performer!"

A year of civil war followed in 69; four generals warred to become princeps in this "Year of the Four Emperors." Vespasian (r. 69–79) won and began the dynasty of the Flavian family. The new emperor took two steps to minimize resistance. First, he had the Senate publicly recognize him as "first man" even though he was not a Julio-Claudian. Second, he encouraged the spread of the imperial cult (worship of the emperor as a living god and sacrifices for the welfare of the emperor's household) in the provinces outside Italy, where most of the empire's population lived.

In promoting emperor worship, Vespasian was building on local traditions. In the eastern provinces, the Hellenistic kingdoms had long before established the tradition of worshiping royalty; provincials there had treated Augustus as a living god. The imperial cult communicated the same image of the emperor to people in the provinces as Rome's architecture and sculpture did to people in the city: he was larger than life, deserved loyalty, and provided aid and gifts as a patron. Because emperor worship was already well established in Greece and the ancient Near East, Vespasian concentrated on spreading it in the provinces of Spain, southern France, and North Africa. Italy, however, still had no temples to the living emperor. Traditional Romans looked down on the imperial cult as a provincial tradition. Vespasian, known for his wit, even muttered as he lay dying in 79, "Oh me! I think I'm becoming a god."

Vespasian's sons Titus (r. 79–81) and Domitian (r. 81–96) strengthened the principate with hardheaded financial policy, professional administration, and high-profile, preemptive military campaigns on the frontiers. Titus sent relief to the populations of Pompeii and Herculaneum after a giant volcanic eruption of Mount Vesuvius buried their towns in 79, and he provided a fifty-thousand seat stadium for public entertainments by finishing Rome's **Colosseum**, built on arches and outfitted with giant awnings to shade the crowd. This multistory amphitheater was deliberately constructed on the site of the former fish pond in Nero's Golden House to demonstrate the public-spiritedness of the new Flavian dynasty. Domitian balanced the budget and led the army north to hold the line against Germanic tribes threatening the empire's frontier regions along the Rhine and Danube Rivers—an area of wars for centuries to come.

Domitian handled his success poorly, and his arrogance inspired hatred among the senators, to whom he once sent a letter announcing, "Our lord god, myself, orders you to do this." Embittered by the rebellion of a general in Germany, he executed numerous upper-class citizens as conspirators. From fear Domitian would kill them, his wife and members of his court murdered him in 96. As Domitian's murder revealed, the principate had not solved monarchy's enduring weakness: rivalry for rule that was likely to explode into murderous conspiracy and destabilize the succession. The danger of civil war always existed, whether generated by ambitious generals or by competition among the emperor's heirs. As Tacitus commented, emperors became like the weather: "We just have to wait for bad ones to pass and hope for good ones to appear."

Fortunately for Rome, politically better weather came with the next five emperors—Nerva (r. 96–98), Trajan (r. 98–117), Hadrian (r. 117–138), Antoninus Pius (r. 138–161), and Marcus Aurelius (r. 161–180). Historians call them "The Five Good Emperors" because they provided peaceful transfers of power for nearly a century (the first four of these men, lacking surviving sons, used adoption to pick capable successors). This period, however, remained full of war and strife, as Roman history always was. Trajan fought fierce campaigns expanding Roman power northward across the Danube River into Dacia (today Romania) and eastward into Mesopotamia (see Map 5.1 on page 188). Hadrian earned the hatred of the Senate by executing several senators as alleged conspirators and punished a Jewish revolt by

■ **MAP 5.1 Expansion of the Roman Empire, 30 B.C.E.–117 C.E.**
*When Octavian (the future Augustus) captured Egypt in 30 B.C.E. after the suicides of Mark Antony
and Cleopatra, he made a significant contribution to the economic strength of Rome because the land
of the Nile provided huge amounts of grain and gold. Roman power now encircled the Mediterranean
Sea (except for Mauretania, which remained technically under the rule of local kings with Roman
approval until c. 44 C.E.). When the emperor Trajan took over the southern part of Mesopotamia in
114–117 C.E., imperial conquest reached its height: Rome's control had never before extended so far
east. Hadrian, Trajan's successor, abandoned Mesopotamia, probably because it seemed too far away
from Rome to defend. Egypt remained part of the empire until the Arab conquest in 642 C.E.*

turning Jerusalem into a military colony. Aurelius spent many miserable years at war
protecting the Danube region from outside attacks.

Still, it makes sense to speak of these five rulers as "good emperors." They succeeded one another without murder or conspiracy, the economy continued strong,
and the army remained obedient. Their reigns marked the longest stretch in Roman
history without a civil war since the second century B.C.E.

Life under the Five Good Emperors, 96–180 *C.E.*

The peace and prosperity of the second century C.E. cause historians to call it Rome's Golden Age. Imperial rule remained strong because it had a loyal military, public-spirited provincial elites, common laws and culture spreading through the provinces, and a healthy population reproducing itself.

In theory, Rome's military goal remained unlimited expansion because conquest brought glory to the emperor. Virgil in the *Aeneid* had expressed this ambition by portraying Jupiter, king of the gods, as promising "imperial rule without limit." In reality, the emperors were usually satisfied if neighboring peoples left the frontier regions undisturbed. Imperial territory never expanded permanently much beyond the area that Augustus had controlled. Stable and peaceful in the first two centuries after Augustus, most provinces had no need for garrison troops during this era; soldiers were a rare sight in many places. Even Gaul, which had bitterly resisted the Roman takeover, was now, according to a contemporary witness, "kept in order by 1,200 troops—hardly more soldiers than it has towns." Most legions (a legion was a unit of five thousand to six thousand troops) were stationed on the empire's northern and eastern frontiers, where hostile neighbors threatened and the distance from the capital weakened the provincials' loyalty.

The policy of not conquering new lands made paying for the army difficult. In the past, victories abroad had brought in huge amounts of booty, prisoners of war sold into slavery, and additional taxes from conquered peoples. These sources of money had now dried up, but the army—no longer a part-time militia—still had to be paid to maintain discipline. To fulfill their obligations as the military's patrons, emperors on their accession and on other special occasions supplemented soldiers' regular pay with large bonuses. These rewards made a legionary career desirable, and enlistment counted as a privilege restricted to free male citizens. The army, however, also included auxiliary units of noncitizens from the provinces. Serving under Roman officers, they could pick up some Latin and Roman customs, and they improved life in the provinces by constructing public works. Upon discharge, they received Roman citizenship. In this way, the army served as an instrument for spreading a common way of life.

The Roman peace guaranteed by the army allowed commerce to operate smoothly in imperial territory. The Golden Age's prosperity promoted long-distance trade for luxury goods, such as spices and silk, from as far away as India and China. Still, taxation of agricultural land in the provinces (Italy was exempt) provided the government's principal source of revenue. The administration itself cost relatively little because it was small compared with the size of the population it governed: several hundred top officials governed about fifty million people. Most taxes collected in the provinces stayed there to pay for local projects. Senatorial and equestrian governors with small staffs ran the provinces, which eventually numbered about forty. In Rome, the emperor employed a substantial palace staff, but equestrian officials called prefects managed the city itself.

The decentralized tax system required public service by the provincial elites; the government's financial well-being absolutely depended on it. Local officials called decurions (members of a municipal senate, later called curiales) collected taxes and personally guaranteed that their town's expenses were covered. If there was a shortfall in tax collection or local finances, these wealthy men had to make up the difference from their own pockets. Most emperors under the early principate attempted to keep taxes low. As Tiberius put it when refusing a request for tax increases from provincial governors, "I want you to shear my sheep, not skin them alive."

The financial obligations of civic office could make public service expensive, but the status that the positions brought made the elite willing to take the risk. Some received priesthoods in the imperial cult as a reward, an honor open to both men and women. All could hope to catch the emperor's ear for special help for their area—for example, after an earthquake or a flood. The system worked because it sprang from Roman tradition: the local social elites were the patrons of their communities but the clients of the emperors. As long as there were enough rich, public-spirited provincials participating in this system for its nonmonetary rewards, the principate could function effectively by relying on the old republic's tradition of public service.

The principate changed the Mediterranean world deeply but not evenly. Within the provinces lived a wide diversity of peoples speaking different languages, observing different customs, dressing in different styles, and worshiping different gods (Map 5.2). In the remote countryside, Roman conquest had only a modest effect on local customs. Where new cities sprang up, however, Roman influence increased. These communities sprouted around Roman forts or grew from the settlements of army veterans the emperors had sprinkled throughout the provinces. They became especially influential in western Europe, permanently rooting Latin (and the languages that would emerge from it) and Roman law and customs there. Modern cities such as Trier and Cologne in Germany started as Roman towns. As time passed, status gaps between the provinces and Italy lessened. Eventually, emperors came from the provinces; Trajan, from Spain, was the first.

Romanization, as historians call the spread of Roman culture in the provinces, raised people's standard of living as roads and bridges improved, trade increased, and agriculture flourished under the peaceful conditions provided by the army. Selling supplies to the troops brought new business to farmers and merchants. Greater prosperity under Roman rule made Romanization easier for provincials to accept. In addition, Romanization was not a one-way process of cultural change. In western areas as different from each other as Gaul, Britain, and North Africa, interactions among the local people and Romans produced new, mixed cultural traditions, especially evident in religion and art. Romanization led not to the imposition of the conquerors' way of life but to the gradual merging of Roman and local western cultures.

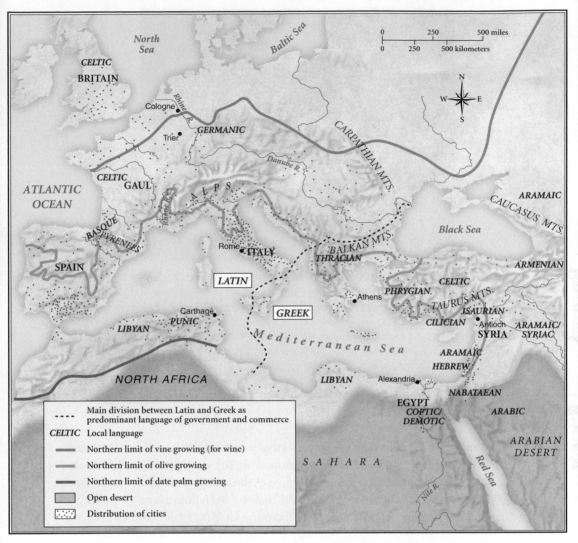

■ **MAP 5.2 Natural Features and Languages of the Roman World**

The Roman world had great variety in land, languages, and climate. People living there, estimated to have numbered as many as 55 million, spoke dozens of languages, many of which survived until the last years of the empire. The two predominant languages spoken by Roman citizens were Latin in the western part of the empire and Greek in the eastern. Latin remained the language of law even in the eastern empire. Fields suitable for growing grain were the most valuable land feature because wheat and barley were the basis of the ancient diet. Vineyards and olive groves also were important. Wine was regarded as an essential beverage, and olive oil was the main source of fat in the diets of most people and the principal ingredient in soap, perfume, and other products for daily life.

■ The Arch at Thamugadi, a Roman Military Colony in North Africa
The emperors fueled the process of Romanization in the provinces by building new settlements for military veterans. The best preserved such town is Thamugadi (today Timgad in Algeria). Founded by Emperor Trajan in 100 C.E., it was laid out like a Roman military camp, a perfect square with a grid of straight streets and rectangular houses. The new town's architecture imitated that of Rome. A spacious theater provided room for public entertainments, and this mammoth arch, probably built toward the end of the second century C.E., provided a spectacular entrance to a boulevard lined with columned porches. Romanization was a two-way process: local peoples influenced the Roman settlers and vice versa. At Thamugadi, local African religious cults, lightly adapted to Roman traditions, flourished alongside ancient Roman cults and attracted worshipers of all kinds. (SEF/Art Resource, NY.)

Romanization affected the eastern provinces less; they retained their Greek and Near Eastern character. In much of this region, daily life continued to follow traditional Greek models. When the Romans took over these areas during the second and first centuries B.C.E., they found urban cultures that had been flourishing for hundreds of years. Huge Hellenistic cities such as Alexandria in Egypt and Antioch in Syria rivaled Rome in size and splendor (see Map 5.1). In fact, compared with Rome, they boasted more single-family houses, fewer blocks of high-rise apartments, and equally magnificent temples. While retaining their local languages and customs, the eastern social elites easily accepted the nature of Roman governance: the emperor was their patron, and they were his clients, with the mutual obligations this traditional relationship required. Provincial elites were long accustomed to such a system because of the paternalistic rule of Hellenistic kingdoms. Their willing cooperation in the task of governing the provinces was crucial for imperial stability and prosperity.

The continuing vitality of Greek culture and language in prosperous eastern cities contributed to the flourishing of literature. New forms of literature blossomed in Greek. Authors of the second century, such as Chariton and Achilles Tatius, wrote romantic adventure novels, making that literary form popular. Lucian (c. 117–180) composed satirical dialogues fiercely mocking both stuffy people and religious superstition. As part of his enormous literary output, the essayist and philosopher Plutarch (c. 50–120) wrote *Parallel Lives*, paired biographies of illustrious Greek and Roman men. His moral sense and taste for anecdotes made his works favorite reading for centuries; the English dramatist William Shakespeare (1564–1616) based several of his plays on Plutarch's biographies.

Latin literature thrived, too; in fact, scholars rank the late first and early second centuries C.E. as its Silver Age, second only to the masterpieces of Augustan literature. Its most famous authors wrote with acid wit, verve, and imagination. Tacitus (c. 56–120) composed his *Annals* as a biting narrative of the Julio-Claudians, laying bare the ruthlessness of Augustus and the personal weaknesses of his successors. The satiric poet Juvenal (c. 65–130) skewered pretentious Romans and greedy provincials while hilariously describing the problems of being broke in the city. Apuleius (c. 125–170) intrigued readers with *The Golden Ass*, a sex-filled novel about a man turned into a donkey who regains his body and his soul through the power of the Egyptian goddess Isis.

Unlike Augustus, later emperors never worried that sexy literature posed a threat to social order. They did, however, share his belief that law was essential. Indeed, Romans prided themselves on their ability to order their society through law. As Virgil said, their mission was "to establish law and order within a framework of peace." Even today, the influence of Roman law is still evident in most systems of law in Europe. One distinctive characteristic of Roman law was its recognition of the principle of equity, which meant accomplishing what was "good and fair" even if the letter of the law had to be disregarded. This principle led legal thinkers to insist, for example, that the intent of parties in a contract outweighed the words of their agreement and that the burden of proof lay with the accuser rather than the accused. The emperor Trajan ruled that no one should be convicted without clear evidence because it was better for a guilty person to go unpunished than for an innocent person to be condemned.

Roman notions of fairness required formal ranking of the "orders" in which it was believed people naturally belonged. As always, the elites made up a tiny portion of the population. Only about one person in fifty thousand had enough money to qualify for the senatorial order, the highest-ranking class, while about one in a thousand belonged to the equestrian order, the second-ranking class. Different purple stripes on clothing identified these orders. The third-highest order consisted of decurions, the local officials in provincial towns.

Those outside the social elite faced greater disadvantages than just snobbery. An old republican distinction between the "better people" and the "humbler people" hardened under the principate, and by the third century it spread throughout Roman law. Law protected such distinctions because social order was thought to depend on them. The "better people" included senators, equestrians, decurions, and retired army veterans. Everybody else—except slaves, who counted as property, not people—made up the vastly larger group of "humbler people." The latter faced their worst disadvantage in court: the law imposed harsher penalties on them than were imposed on the "better people" who committed the same crimes. "Humbler people" convicted of capital crimes were regularly executed by being crucified or torn apart by wild animals before a crowd of spectators. "Better people" rarely suffered the death penalty. But if they were condemned, they received a quicker and more dignified execution by the sword. "Humbler people" could also be tortured in criminal investigations, even if they were citizens. Romans regarded these differences as fair on the grounds that a person's higher status created a higher level of responsibility for the common good. As one provincial governor expressed it, "Nothing is less equitable than mere equality itself."

Law was crucial for maintaining order, but nothing mattered more to the stability and prosperity of the empire than steady population levels. Keeping up the birthrate was difficult because medicine could do little to help pregnant women or infants. The upper-class government official Pliny, for example, sent the following report to the grandfather of his third wife, Calpurnia: "You will be very sad to learn that your granddaughter has suffered a miscarriage. She is a young girl and did not realize she was pregnant. As a result she was more active than she should have been and paid a high price." Complications at birth could easily lead to the mother's death because doctors could not stop internal bleeding or cure infections. They possessed carefully made instruments for surgery and physical examinations but were seriously misinformed about reproduction. Gynecologists such as Soranus, who practiced in Rome during the reigns of Trajan and Hadrian, mistakenly recommended the days just after menstruation as the best time to become pregnant, when the woman's body was "not congested." As in Hellenistic medicine, treatments were mainly limited to potions, herbs, and bleeding; Soranus recommended treating exceptionally painful menstruation by drawing blood "from the bend of the arm." Doctors, often freedmen from Greece and other provinces, were considered of low status, unless they served the upper class.

As in earlier times, girls often wed in their early teens to have as many years as possible to bear children; their husbands would typically be around age thirty. Because so many babies died, families had to produce numerous offspring to keep from disappearing. The tombstone of Veturia, a soldier's wife married at eleven, tells a typical story: "Here I lie, having lived for twenty-seven years. I was married to the same man for sixteen years and bore six children, five of whom died before I did." Richer families usually arranged marriages between spouses who hardly knew each other, although they could grow to love each other in a partnership devoted to family.

The emphasis on childbearing in marriage brought many health hazards to women, but to remain single and childless represented social failure for Romans. Once children were born, they were cared for by their mothers and by servants. Wealthy women routinely hired "wet nurses" to attend to and breast-feed their babies. When Romans wanted to control family size, they used female contraception by obstructing the female organs or by administering drugs. Like the Greeks, they practiced exposure,

■ **Midwife's Sign Depicting Childbirth**
Childbirth was a dangerous experience for women because of the chance of dying from internal bleeding. This terra-cotta sign from Ostia, the ancient port city of Rome, probably hung outside a midwife's rooms to announce her skill in aiding women in giving birth. It shows a pregnant woman clutching the sides of her chair and supported by another woman while the midwife crouches in front to help deliver the baby. The meaning of the sign was clear to people who were illiterate; a person did not have to be able to read to understand the services that the specialist inside could provide. (Scala/Art Resource, NY.)

more frequently for infant girls than for boys because sons were considered more valuable than daughters as future supporters and protectors of families.

The emperors and some members of the social elite did their best to support reproduction. The emperors aided needy children to encourage larger families, and wealthy people often adopted children in their communities. One North African man gave enough money to support three hundred boys and three hundred girls each year until they grew up. The differing value afforded male and female children was also evident in these humanitarian programs: boys often received more aid than girls.

■ **REVIEW:** *What distinguished the rule of "bad" and "good" emperors?*

The Emergence of Christianity

Christianity began as a splinter group within Judaism in Judaea, where, as elsewhere under Roman rule, Jews were allowed to practice their ancestral religion. The new faith did not soon attract many converts; three centuries after the death

of Jesus, Christians remained a small minority. Christianity grew, if only gradually, because it had an appeal based on the career of Jesus, its message of salvation,
its believers' sense of mission, the democratic openness of its early congregations,
and the strong bonds of community it inspired. Ultimately, the emergence of
Christianity proved the most significant and enduring development during the
Roman Empire.

The Teachings of Jesus

The new religion sprang from the life and teachings of Jesus (c. 4 B.C.E.–30 C.E.; see
"The B.C.E./C.E. System for Dates" at the beginning of this book for an explanation
of the date given for Jesus' birth). Christianity's background lay in Jewish history. By
the time of Jesus' boyhood, some of his fellow Jews in Judaea were agitating for
independence from Roman rule, making provincial officials fear rebellion. Jesus'
career, therefore, took place in a troubled region. His execution was the typical
Roman response to anyone they believed threatened peace and social order. In the
two decades after his crucifixion, his devoted followers, particularly Paul of Tarsus,
developed a new religion—Christianity—that expanded beyond the Jewish community in Palestine.

Christianity offered an answer to a troubling question about divine justice
raised by the Jews' long history of defeat and exile: how could a just God allow the
wicked to prosper and the righteous to suffer? The question had become pressing
some two centuries before Jesus' birth, when persecution by the Seleucid king
Antiochus IV (r. 175–164 B.C.E.) had provoked the Jews into a bloody revolt. This
war gave birth to a complex of ideas called apocalypticism (from the Greek for
"uncovering the future"). According to this worldview, evil powers, divine and
human, controlled the present world. Their rule would soon end, however, when
God and his agents revealed their plan to conquer the forces of evil by sending a
Christ (Greek for "anointed one"; in Hebrew, *Mashia*, or in English *Messiah*) to
win the great battle. A final judgment would follow, bringing eternal punishment
for the wicked and eternal reward for the righteous. The apocalypticism that first
inspired Jews living in Judaea under Roman rule later motivated Christians and
Muslims.

Apocalyptic ideas became controversial around the time of Jesus' birth
because most Judaean Jews were angry about Rome's control but disagreed about
what form Judaism should take in response. Some cooperated with their overlords, while others preached rejection of the non-Jewish world and its spiritual
corruption. Their local ruler, installed by the Romans, was Herod the Great
(r. 37–4 B.C.E.). His Greek style of life broke Jewish law, making him unpopular
with his subjects despite his magnificent rebuilding of the holiest Jewish shrine,
the great temple in Jerusalem. When a decade of unrest followed Herod's death,
Augustus installed a provincial government to oversee the region. The imposition

of direct Roman government made many Judaeans unhappy because they were used to living under Jewish rulers.

Jesus began his career as a teacher and healer in his native Galilee, the northern region of Palestine, during the reign of Tiberius. The books that would later become the Gospels, or the first four books of the Christian New Testament, offer the earliest accounts of his life and teachings; they were composed between about 70 and 90, decades after Jesus' death. Jesus himself wrote nothing down, and others' accounts of his words and deeds do not always agree on what he said or did. He taught mostly by telling parables, stories with a moral or religious message that challenged his followers to figure out what he meant.

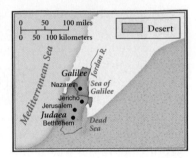

Palestine in the Time of Jesus, 30 C.E.

All of the Gospels begin the story of his career with his baptism by John the Baptist, a prophet who urged people to repent before God's final judgment, which John preached was coming soon. John was executed by the Jewish ruler Herod Antipas, a son of Herod the Great whom the Romans supported; Herod feared that John's apocalyptic preaching might set off riots. After John's death, Jesus continued his mission by traveling around Judaea's countryside warning people to prepare spiritually for the coming of God's kingdom. Many saw Jesus as the Messiah, but his apocalypticism did not preach immediate revolt against the Romans. Instead, he taught that God's true kingdom was to be sought not on earth but in heaven. He stressed that this kingdom was open to believers regardless of their social status or sinfulness. His emphasis on God's love for humanity and people's responsibility to love one another reflected Jewish religious teachings, as in the first-century scholar Hillel's interpretation of the Hebrew Bible.

An educated Jew who perhaps knew Greek as well as Aramaic, the local language, Jesus realized that he had to reach the urban crowds to make an impact. Therefore, leaving the Galilean villages where he had started, he took his message to the Jewish population of Jerusalem, the region's main city. His miraculous healings and exorcisms and his powerful preaching created a sensation. His popularity attracted the attention of the Jewish authorities, who automatically assumed he aspired to political power. Fearing he might ignite a Jewish revolt, the Roman governor Pontius Pilate (r. 26–36) ordered his crucifixion, the usual punishment for rebellion, in Jerusalem in 30.

After Jesus' death, his followers reported that they had seen him in person. They proclaimed that God had miraculously raised him from the dead, and they set about convincing other Jews that Jesus was the promised savior and would soon return to judge the world and impose God's kingdom. His closest disciples, twelve Apostles (Greek for "messengers"), still considered themselves faithful Jews and continued to follow the commandments of Jewish law.

A radical change took place with the conversion of Paul of Tarsus (c. 10–65), a pious Jew of the Diaspora and a Roman citizen who had violently opposed those who accepted Jesus as the Messiah. Around three years after Jesus' death, Paul experienced a spiritual vision on the road to Damascus in Syria, which he interpreted as a divine revelation. It inspired him to become a follower of Jesus as the Messiah or Christ—a Christian, as members of the movement came to be known. Paul taught that belief in the divinity of Jesus and that his crucifixion was the ultimate sacrifice for the sins of humanity was the only way of becoming righteous in the eyes of God. In this way alone, Paul said, could people expect to win salvation in the world to come.

Seeking to win converts outside Judaea, in about 46 Paul began to travel to preach to Jews of the Diaspora and to Gentiles (non-Jews) who had adopted some Jewish customs in Syria, Asia Minor, and Greece (see Map 5.3). Although Paul stressed the necessity of ethical behavior along traditional Jewish lines, especially the rejection of sexual immorality and polytheism, he also taught that converts did not need to obey all of Jewish law. To make conversion easier, Paul did not require men who became Christians to undergo the Jewish initiation rite of circumcision. This view, combined with his teachings that his congregations did not have to observe Jewish dietary restrictions or festivals, created great controversy and led to tensions with Jewish authorities in Jerusalem as well as with the followers of Jesus living there, who still believed that Christians had to follow Jewish law. Roman authorities then arrested Paul as a criminal troublemaker; he was executed in about 65.

Paul's mission was only one part of the unrest in the Jewish community in this period; hatred of Roman rule in Palestine finally pushed the Jews to revolt in 66. When they were defeated in 70, the Roman victors destroyed the Jerusalem temple and sold most of the city's population into slavery. This catastrophe meant that the Jewish community lost its religious center, and the separation of Christianity from Judaism begun by Paul gained momentum. In this way Christianity became a separate religion.

Paul's impact on early Christianity can be seen in the number of letters—thirteen—attributed to him in the twenty-seven writings brought together as the New Testament by around 200. Followers of Jesus came to regard the New Testament as having equal authority with the Hebrew Bible, which they then called the Old Testament. Because teachers like Paul preached mainly in the cities to reach large crowds, congregations of Christians mostly sprang up in urban areas. Originally these groups had a democratic organization without much hierarchy. Women could be leaders in this early stage of Christianity, though not without controversy; many people believed that men should teach and women only listen. Still, early Christianity was diverse enough that a woman could found a congregation, such as Lydia at Philippi in Greece, or earn respect as a "deacon," such as Phoebe at Cenchreae, also in Greece.

Growth of a New Religion

Christianity faced serious obstacles in developing as a new religion separate from Judaism. Roman officials, suspecting Christians of political disloyalty, sometimes persecuted them as traitors, especially for refusing to participate in the imperial cult (as happened to Perpetua). Christian leaders had to build an organization from scratch to administer their growing congregations. Also, they had to address the controversial question of whether women could be Christian leaders.

Most Romans found early Christians puzzling and irritating. First, in contrast to Jews, Christians proclaimed a new faith rather than a traditional religion handed down from their ancestors; they therefore enjoyed no special treatment under Roman law. Next, people feared that tolerating Christians would offend the gods of official religion; Christians' denial of the old gods and of the emperor's cult seemed sure to provoke natural catastrophes. Christians furthermore aroused contempt because they proclaimed as their divine king a man whom the imperial government had crucified as a criminal. Finally, Christians' secret rituals led to accusations of

■ **Painting of a Sacred Banquet from a Roman Catacomb**
This banquet scene appears on a wall of a Rome catacomb (catacombs were the underground chambers Christians used for burials and meetings before their religion was officially recognized). Such scenes seem simultaneously to represent actual meals held to remember the dead, heavenly banquets that the blessed dead were thought to have in their heavenly life, and symbolic gatherings expressing a sense of community and mutual affection among believers. Seven people were usually shown, for reasons still not clear to historians. Women are prominently depicted here in the middle and at either end of the table. The woman at the left is presenting a goblet of wine to the banqueters. As the inscription suggests, she may be a personification of agape, *the shared love that such sacred banquets commemorated.* (Held Collection/Bridgeman Art Library.)

cannibalism and sexual promiscuity because they symbolically ate the body and drank the blood of Jesus during communal dinners called Love Feasts, which men and women attended together. In short, Christians seemed a threat to social order and peace with the gods.

Not surprisingly, then, Romans were quick to blame Christians for disasters. When a large portion of Rome burned in 64, Nero punished them for arson. As Tacitus reports, the emperor had innocent Christians "covered with the skins of wild animals and torn to death by dogs, or fastened to crosses and set on fire to provide light at night." The cruelty of their punishment reportedly earned these Christians sympathy from Rome's population. After Nero, the government did not persecute Christians regularly or as a policy because no law specifically banned their religion. Nevertheless, Christians made easy prey for officials looking for people to blame for crimes or disruptions in public order.

In response to persecution, defenders of Christianity, such as Tertullian (c. 160–240) and Justin (c. 100–165), argued that Romans had nothing to fear from Christianity. Far from spreading disloyalty and immorality, these writers insisted, their faith taught respect for authority and a strict morality. It was not a foreign superstition but the true philosophy that combined the best features of Judaism and Greek thought and was thus a fitting religion for their diverse world. Tertullian pointed out that, although Christians could not worship the emperors, they did "pray to the true God for their [the emperors'] safety. We pray for a fortunate life for them, a secure rule, . . . a courageous army, a loyal Senate, a virtuous people, a world of peace."

Persecution did not stop Christianity. Tertullian indeed claimed that "the blood of the martyrs is the seed of the Church." Christians like Perpetua regarded public trials and executions as an opportunity to become a **martyr** (Greek for "witness") to their faith and thus to strengthen Christians' sense of identity. Their belief that their deaths would lead directly to happiness in heaven allowed them to face painful tortures with courage; some even became martyrs on purpose. For example, Ignatius (c. 35–107), bishop of Antioch, begged Rome's congregation, which was becoming the most prominent Christian group, not to ask the emperor to show him mercy after his arrest: "Let me be food for the wild animals [in the arena] through whom I can reach God," he pleaded. "I am God's wheat, to be ground up by the teeth of beasts so that I may be found pure bread of Christ." Most Christians tried their best to avoid becoming martyrs, but stories recording the martyrs' courage shaped the identity of this new religion as a faith that gave its believers the spiritual strength to endure great suffering.

Many first-century Christians expected their troubles would end during their lifetime because Jesus would return to pass judgment on the world and overturn the Roman Empire. When this expectation did not come true, believers began transforming their faith into a religion organized to survive indefinitely, instead of an apocalyptic offshoot of Judaism predicting the immediate end of the world. To make this change, they tried to achieve unity in their beliefs and created a hierarchical organization to impose order on congregations.

Unity was impossible, however, because early Christians constantly and fiercely disagreed about what they should believe, how they should live, and who had the authority to decide these questions. Some Christians believed they could observe Christ's teachings while keeping their jobs and regular lives. Others insisted that it was necessary to withdraw from the everyday world to escape its evil, even abandoning their families, sex, and reproduction. Many Christians believed they should not serve in the army because, as soldiers required to worship in the imperial cult, they would betray their faith. Controversy over such questions raged in the numerous congregations that arose in the early empire around the Mediterranean, from Gaul to Africa to the Near East (Map 5.3).

Creating bishops as religious officials with authority to specify true doctrine and proper conduct for Christian believers was the most important development in organizing the new religion to live on indefinitely. Bishops received their positions through the principle later called **apostolic succession**, which declares that

■ **MAP 5.3 Christian Populations in the Late Third Century C.E.**
Christians remained a minority in the Roman world three hundred years after the crucifixion of Jesus. Certain areas of the empire, however, especially Asia Minor (western Turkey), where Paul had preached, had a concentration of Christians. Most Christians lived in cities and towns, where missionaries had gone to spread their message to crowds of curious listeners. Paganus, a Latin word for "country person" or "rural villager," came to mean a believer in traditional polytheistic cults—hence the term pagan, meaning "non-Christian," often found in modern works on this period.

Jesus' Apostles appointed the first bishops as their successors, granting these new officials the powers Jesus had originally given to the Apostles. Those men named as bishops by the Apostles in turn appointed their own successors, and so on. Bishops had authority to ordain priests with the holy power to administer the sacraments, above all baptism and communion, which believers regarded as necessary for achieving eternal life. Bishops also controlled their congregations' memberships and finances (the money financing early churches came from members' gifts).

The bishops had authority to define what was true doctrine (orthodoxy) and what was false (heresy), but Christians' disagreements over doctrine were too strong for the bishops to overcome and impose unity of belief. In this early stage, the occasional meetings of the bishops of different cities constituted the church's organization. Today it is common to refer to this loose organization as the early Catholic ("universal") church, but even the bishops disagreed among themselves on what beliefs were proper.

A particularly bitter disagreement concerned women's roles in the church. In the first congregations, women sometimes held leadership positions. When bishops were established atop the hierarchy, however, women usually were kept in inferior posts. This demotion reflected the view that in Christianity, as in Roman imperial society, women should be subordinate to men. Some congregations took a long time to accept this change, however, and some women still occupied leadership positions during the second and third centuries.

When leadership roles were closed off to them, many women chose not to marry to demonstrate their devotion to Christ. This commitment to celibacy and chastity gave them the power to control their own bodies by removing their sexuality from the domination of men. Women choosing this special closeness to God were judged holy and socially superior by other Christians. By rejecting the traditional functions of wife and mother in favor of spiritual excellence, celibate Christian women achieved an independence and authority denied them in the outside world.

Competing Beliefs

Three centuries after Jesus' death, a large majority of the population still believed in polytheistic religion. Polytheists never sought a unity of beliefs (despite the implication to the contrary of the modern term *paganism*, which actually refers to diverse cults). They did agree, however, that the old gods favored and protected them and that the imperial cult added to their safety; the success and prosperity of the principate was the proof. Even people who found a more intellectually satisfying understanding of the world in philosophies, such as Stoicism, respected the traditional cults as symbols of divine protection for Rome.

Polytheistic worship therefore had as its goal gaining the favor of all the divinities who could affect human life. Its deities ranged from the traditional gods of the state cults, such as Jupiter and Minerva, to spirits thought to inhabit local groves and springs. Famous old cults, such as the initiation rituals of Demeter and Persephone at Eleusis outside Athens, remained popular; the emperor Hadrian was initiated at Eleusis in 125.

The cult of the Egyptian goddess Isis in its Hellenistic form reveals how polytheism could provide believers with a religious experience arousing strong personal emotions and demanding a moral way of life. Her cult had already attracted Romans by the time of Augustus. He tried to suppress it because it was Cleopatra's religion, but Isis's reputation as a kind, compassionate goddess who relieved her followers' suffering made her cult too popular to crush. The Egyptians believed that her tears for starving people caused the Nile to flood every year and bring them good harvests. Her image was that of a loving mother, and in art she is often shown nursing her son. A central doctrine of her cult concerned the death and resurrection of her husband, Osiris; Isis promised her followers a similar hope for life after death.

Isis required her worshipers to behave righteously. Inscriptions put up by believers declared the goddess's standards for them by quoting her on her own work for justice: "I broke down the rule of tyrants; I put an end to murders; I caused what is right to be mightier than gold and silver." The main character of Apuleius's novel *The Golden Ass*, whom Isis rescues from his mistaken transformation into a donkey, expresses his intense joy after being spiritually reborn: "O holy and eternal guardian of the human race, who always cherishes mortals and blesses them, you care for the troubles of miserable humans with a sweet mother's love. Neither day nor night, nor any moment of time, ever passes by without your blessings." Other cults also required their believers to lead just lives. Inscriptions from remote villages in Asia Minor, for example, record the confessions of peasants to sexual sins for which their local god had imposed severe penance.

Many upper-class Romans found moral guidance in philosophy. Stoicism, derived from the teachings of the Greek Zeno (335–263 B.C.E.), was the most popular. Stoics believed in self-discipline above all, and their code of personal ethics left no room for immoral conduct. As the philosopher Seneca (4 B.C.E.–65 C.E.) explained, "It is easier to prevent harmful emotions from entering the soul than it is to control them once they have entered." Stoicism taught a creative force combining reason, nature, and divinity directs the universe. Humans share in the essence of this universal force and find happiness and patience by living in harmony with it and always doing their duty. The emperor Marcus Aurelius, in his book entitled *Meditations*, emphasized the Stoic belief that people exist for each other: "Either make them better, or just put up with them," he advised.

Christian and polytheist scholars argued over the merits of Christianity compared to traditional Greek philosophy. The theologian Origen (c. 185–255), for example, argued that Christianity, because it was true, was a better guide to correct living than were Greek philosophical ideas. At about the same time, however, the

■ **Mithras Slaying the Bull**

Hundreds of shrines to the mysterious god Mithras have been found in the Roman Empire, but the cult remains poorly known because almost no texts exist to explain it. To judge from the many representations in art, such as this wall painting of about 200 C.E. from the shrine at Marino south of Rome, the story of Mithras slaying a bull was a central part of the cult's identity. Scholars debate the symbolic meaning of the bull slaying shown here, in which a snake and a dog lick the animal's blood while a scorpion pinches its testicles. Most agree, however, that Mithras was derived, perhaps as late as the early imperial period, from the ancient Persian divinity Mithra. Only men could be worshipers, and many were soldiers. Earlier scholarly claims of the cult's popularity were exaggerated; its members numbered no more than 1 or 2 percent of the population. Mithraism probably involved complex devotion to astrology, with devotees ranked in grades, each grade protected by a different celestial body. (Scala/Art Resource, NY.)

philosopher Plotinus (c. 205–270) gave Greek ideas new strength with his books on spiritual philosophy. These ideas, called **Neoplatonism** because their doctrines sprang from Plato's philosophy, influenced many educated Christians as well as polytheists. Neoplatonic religious ideas centered on a human longing to return to the universal Good from which human existence comes. By turning away from the life of the body through the study of philosophy, individual souls could rise to the level of the universal soul, becoming the whole of what as individuals they formed a potential part. This mystical union with what the Christians would call God could be achieved only through strenuous self-discipline in personal morality as well as intellectual life. Neoplatonism's stress on spiritual purity gave it a powerful appeal to educated Christians. Like the cult of Isis or Stoicism, Neoplatonism provided guidance, comfort, and hope through good times or bad.

■ **REVIEW:** *What beliefs and actions made Roman officials suspicious of Christians?*

The Crisis of the Third Century

Bad times arrived for the empire in the middle of the third century. War, money troubles, and natural disasters combined to create a crisis. Attacks by outsiders on the northern and eastern frontiers forced the emperors to expand the army for defense. The rulers' attempts to find money to pay for these wars fueled inflation and crippled the economy. The public's outrage at these developments encouraged ambitious generals to seek power by commanding personal armies, once again plunging Rome into civil war in a bloody replay of the destruction of the republic. Earthquakes and epidemics added to the crisis. By the end of the third century, this combination of troubles had shredded the "Roman peace."

Defending the Frontiers

Emperors since Domitian (r. 81–96) had been fighting wars to repel invaders from the frontier regions. The most aggressive attackers were loosely organized Germanic bands that often crossed the Danube and Rhine Rivers for raiding. Their constant fighting against Roman troops turned these raiders into powerful armies, and they launched dangerous invasions during the reign of Marcus Aurelius (r. 161–180). A major threat also emerged at the empire's eastern edge when a new dynasty, the Sassanids, defeated the Parthian Empire and reenergized the ancient Persian kingdom. By 227, Persia's military power forced the emperors to bring in legions to protect the rich eastern provinces, at the expense of the defense of the northern frontiers.

Recognizing the courage of Germanic warriors, Domitian and his successors began hiring them as auxiliary soldiers for the Roman army and settling them on the frontiers as buffers against invasion. By around 200, the army had enrolled perhaps as many as 450,000 legionary and auxiliary troops (the size of the navy remains unknown). As always, Roman military life was hard. Training constantly, soldiers had to be fit enough to carry forty-pound packs up to twenty miles in five hours, swimming rivers on the way. Since the reign of Hadrian (r. 117–138), the emperors had built many permanent bases for garrisons, but an army on the march constructed its own fort every night. Soldiers transported all the materials for a wooden-walled camp everywhere they went. As one ancient commentator noted during the republic, "Infantrymen were little different from loaded pack mules." At one camp in a frontier area, archaeologists found a supply of a million iron nails— ten tons in all. The same fort required seventeen miles of timber for its barracks walls. To outfit a legion with tents required 54,000 calves' hides.

These defensive wars strained imperial finances because they did not bring in much plunder, unlike the republic's wars of conquest. The army had become a source of negative instead of positive cash flow to the treasury, and the economy had not expanded sufficiently to make up the difference. To make matters worse, inflation had driven up prices. A main cause of inflation under the principate may have been, ironically, the long period of peace that promoted increased demand for the economy's relatively static production of goods and services.

In desperation at their financial problems, some emperors responded to rising prices by debasing imperial coinage in a vain attempt to cut government costs. **Debasement of coinage** meant putting less silver in each coin (there was no paper money) without changing its face value and therefore creating more cash with the same amount of precious metal. (See "Taking Measure," page 207.) Merchants, however, raised prices to make up for the reduced value of the debased coins. By 200, the debased coinage and inflation were ruining the imperial balance sheet and undermining public confidence in the imperial currency. As the soldiers kept demanding that their patrons, the emperors, pay them well, the situation only grew worse. The financial system fell into full collapse in the 250s and 260s.

The Severan Emperors and Catastrophe

Decisions by the emperor Septimius Severus (r. 193–211) and his sons did the most to bring on the crisis: the father drained the treasury to satisfy the army, and his sons' murderous rivalry and reckless spending destroyed the government's stability. A soldier's soldier who came from the large North African city of Leptis Magna in what is today Libya, Severus became ruler in 193 after waging a civil war to get rid of the incompetent emperor currently holding power. To restore imperial prestige and acquire money through foreign conquest, Severus fought successful campaigns beyond the frontiers of the provinces, in Mesopotamia and northern Britain.

By this time, the soldiers were angry because inflation had eroded the value of their wages to practically nothing after they bought themselves basic supplies and clothing. They therefore expected the emperors to favor them with gifts of extra money. Severus spent large sums on such gifts, but then he decided to try improve the situation by raising the soldiers' pay by one-third. The expanded size of the army made this raise more expensive than the treasury could afford and made inflation worse. The financial consequences of his policy, however, concerned Severus not at all. His deathbed advice to his sons in 211 was to "stay on good terms with each other, be generous to the soldiers, and pay no attention to anyone else."

27 B.C.E. — 6%, 94%

100 C.E. — 11%, 89%

150 C.E. — 16%, 84%

200 C.E. — 36%, 64%

250 C.E. — 40%, 60%

300 C.E. — 4%, 96%

Silver content (%)　　Other metals (%)

■ **TAKING MEASURE** The Falling Value of Roman Imperial Coinage, 27 B.C.E.–300 C.E.

Ancient silver coinage derived its value from its metallic content; the less silver a coin had, the less it was worth. Emperors facing rising government and military expenses but flat or falling revenues tried to cut costs by debasing the coinage: they reduced the amount of silver in each coin and increased the amount of other, cheaper metals. These pie charts reveal the gradual debasement of the Roman imperial coinage until the third century, when military expenses apparently skyrocketed. By 300 C.E., coins contained only trace amounts of silver. Merchants and producers had to raise their prices for goods and services when they were being paid with currency that was increasingly less valuable. Thus debasement fueled inflation.

Severus's sons undermined the principate's stability by following only the last two points of his advice. Caracalla (r. 211–217) seized the throne for himself by murdering his brother Geta; his violent reign and limitless spending ended the peace and prosperity of the Roman Golden Age. He increased the soldiers' pay by another 40 to 50 percent and spent gigantic sums on building projects to display his glory, including the largest public baths Rome had ever seen, covering blocks and blocks of the city. The need for money to pay his out-of-control expenses put unbearable pressure on the provincial elites responsible for collecting taxes and on the citizens whom they squeezed for ever greater amounts.

In 212, Caracalla took his most famous step to try to fix the budget crisis: he granted Roman citizenship to almost every man and woman in imperial territory except slaves. His goal was to increase revenues from inheritance taxes and from fees for freeing slaves, which only citizens paid (noncitizens paid other taxes): the more citizens, the more money (most of it earmarked for the army). Caracalla, who contemporaries whispered was insane, wrecked the imperial budget, setting in motion the ruinous inflation of the coming decades. Once when his mother criticized him for his excesses, he replied as he drew his sword, "Never mind, we shall not run out of money as long as I have this."

The empire's financial troubles created political instability. When Macrinus, commander of the praetorian guard, murdered Caracalla in 217 to make himself emperor, Caracalla's female relatives bribed the army to overthrow Macrinus in favor of a young male relative. The restored Severan dynasty did not last long, however, and the assassination of the last Severan emperor in 235 began a half-century of civil wars that, compounded by natural disasters, destroyed the principate. For the next fifty years, emperors and generals constantly fought to rule. During this period of near anarchy, over two dozen men, often several at a time, held or claimed the throne. Their only qualification was their ability to lead an army and reward the troops for loyalty to their commander instead of to Rome.

The violence and financial distress caused by the third century's civil wars made life miserable in many regions. Battling armies trampled farmers' fields searching for food, making it impossible to keep up normal agricultural production. City council members faced constantly rising demands for tax revenues from every new emperor; this financial pressure destroyed their commitment to serving their communities.

Foreign enemies took advantage of the Roman civil wars, invading from the east and north. Roman fortunes hit bottom in 260 when Shapur I, king of the Sassanid Empire of Persia, captured the emperor Valerian (r. 253–260) while attacking the province of Syria. Imperial territory was in danger of splintering into breakaway regions. Even the tough and competent emperor Aurelian (r. 270–275) could do no more to reduce the danger than to recover Egypt and Asia Minor from Zenobia, the warrior queen of Palmyra in Syria. He also had to encircle Rome with a massive wall to ward off surprise attacks by Germanic tribes smashing their way into Italy from the north.

Historians dispute how severely these troubles were worsened by natural disasters, but strong earthquakes and epidemics did strike some of the provinces around the middle of the century. The population declined significantly as food supplies became less dependable, civil war killed soldiers and civilians alike, and infection flared over large regions. The loss of population meant fewer soldiers for the army, whose efficiency as a defense and police force had already declined because of the political and financial chaos. More frontier areas became vulnerable to raids, and roving bands of robbers became increasingly common within the imperial borders.

Polytheists explained these horrible times in the traditional way: the state gods were angry. But why? The obvious answer seemed to be the presence of Christians, who denied the existence of the Roman gods and refused to participate in their worship. The emperor Decius (r. 249–251) conducted systematic persecutions to

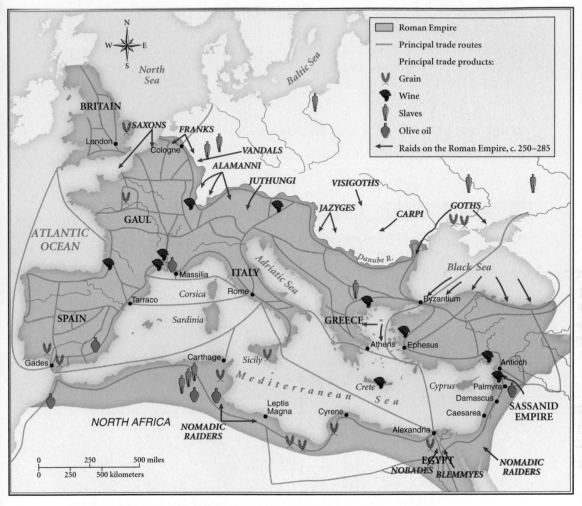

■ **MAPPING THE WEST** The Roman Empire in Crisis, c. 284 C.E.
By the early 280s, the principate had been torn apart by the fifty years of civil war that followed the end of the Severan dynasty. Imperial territory remained the same as in the time of Augustus (see Map 5.1), except for the loss of Dacia during the reign of Aurelian (r. 270–275). Attacks from the north and east had repeatedly penetrated the frontier regions, however. The Sassanid king Shapur I (r. c. 240–270), for example, temporarily held Antioch and captured the emperor Valerian in 260. The public humiliation and death in captivity of the elderly imperial ruler indicate the depths to which Roman fortunes sank in the third century. **For more help analyzing this map,** *see the map activity for this chapter in the* ONLINE STUDY GUIDE *at* bedfordstmartins.com/huntconcise.

eliminate Christians as a way to regain the goodwill of the gods. He justified the violence by calling himself "Restorer of the Cults," proclaiming, "I would rather see a rival to my throne than another bishop of Rome." He ordered all inhabitants of the empire to prove their loyalty to the state by participating in a sacrifice to its gods. Christians who refused to join in were killed.

These new persecutions did not end the civil war, economic failure, or the diseases that brought on the crisis. By the early 280s, the empire was in danger of fragmenting. Remarkably, in 284 Diocletian would drag it back to safety in the same way Augustus had begun the principate: by creating a new form of authoritarian leadership.

■ **REVIEW:** *What factors provoked the crisis in Roman government and society in the third century C.E.?*

IMPORTANT DATES

44 B.C.E.	Julius Caesar's assassination reignites civil war	**69 C.E.**	Civil war in the "Year of the Four Emperors"
27 B.C.E. –14 C.E.	Augustus's principate	**70 C.E.**	Titus captures Jerusalem and destroys the Jewish temple
19 B.C.E.	The poet Virgil dies, leaving the *Aeneid* unfinished	**161–180 C.E.**	Germanic bands attack northern frontiers during reign of Marcus Aurelius
2 B.C.E.	Senate proclaims Augustus "Father of his Country"	**212 C.E.**	Caracalla extends Roman citizenship to almost all free inhabitants of the provinces
8 C.E.	Augustus exiles the poet Ovid		
30 C.E.	Jesus of Nazareth crucified in Jerusalem	**250s–260s C.E.**	Imperial finances collapse from civil war, debased coinage, and inflation
c. 33 C.E.	Paul of Tarsus becomes a Christian	**284 C.E.**	Diocletian becomes emperor
64 C.E.	Nero blames Christians for great fire in Rome		

Conclusion

Augustus created the principate by installing a monarchy while insisting that he was restoring the Roman republic. He succeeded because he kept the loyalty of the army and extended the patron-client system. The principate made the emperor the patron of the army and, indeed, of everyone else. Most provincials, especially in the eastern Mediterranean, found this arrangement acceptable because it aligned with the familiar relationship between ruler and ruled in the Hellenistic kingdoms.

Stability endured as long as the emperors had enough money to keep their millions of clients satisfied. They provided food to the poor, built baths and arenas for public entertainment, and paid for a permanent army. The emperors of the first and second centuries enlarged the military to protect distant territories stretching from Britain to North Africa to Syria. By the second century, peace and prosperity had created an imperial Golden Age. Long-term money trouble set in, however, because the army, concentrating on defense rather than conquest, no longer brought money into the treasury. Severe inflation and debasement of the currency worsened the situation. The wealthy elites found they could no longer meet the demand for increased taxes without draining their personal fortunes, and they lost their public-spiritedness and avoided their communal responsibilities. Loyalty to the state became too expensive.

The emergence of Christians added to the uncertainty. Roman officials worried that some citizens placed their loyalty to their divinity ahead of their loyalty to the state. Their new religion evolved from Jewish apocalypticism to a hierarchical organization of bishops. Christians disputed with each other and with the authorities; martyrs such as Perpetua worried the imperial government with the depth of their convictions.

When financial ruin, civil war, and natural disasters struck the empire in the mid-third century, the emperors lacked the money and the popular support to end the crisis. Not even the persecution of Christians could convince the gods to restore Rome's good fortunes. The empire instead had to be transformed politically and religiously. Against all expectations, Diocletian began that process in 284.

■ MAKING CONNECTIONS

1. *Compare the crisis in the first century B.C.E. that undermined the republic with the crisis of the third century C.E. that undermined the principate.*

2. *If you had been a first-century emperor, what would you have done about the Christians and why? What if you had been a third-century emperor?*

■ FOR FURTHER EXPLORATION

For further reading and online research ideas, see the Suggested References on page SR-3 at the back of the book.

For practice quizzes, a customized study plan, and other study tools, see the ONLINE STUDY GUIDE at bedfordstmartins.com/huntconcise.

For primary-source material from this period, see Chapter 5 in *Sources of THE MAKING OF THE WEST: A CONCISE HISTORY*, Second Edition.

INNOMINE
XPI·VINCAS
SEMPER·

DN·HONORIOSEMPER·AVG

DN·HONORIOSEMPER·AVG

PROBVS·FAMVLVSV·C·CONS·ORD·

PROBVS·FAMVLVSV·C·CONS·ORD·

The Transformation of the Roman Empire

c. 284–c. 600 C.E.

A N EGYPTIAN WOMAN NAMED ISIS wrote a letter to her mother in the third century that modern archaeologists found at the site of a village near the Nile River. Written in Greek on papyrus, the letter hints at the problems and worries many people experienced during this troubled time:

> Every day I pray to the lord Sarapis and his fellow gods to watch over you. I want you to know that I have arrived in Alexandria safely after four days. I send fond greetings to my sister and the children and Elouath and his wife and Dioscorous and her husband and children and Tamalis and her husband and son and Heron and Ammonarion and . . . Sanpat and her children. And if Aion wants to be in the army, let him come. For everybody is in the army.

The letter leaves us with puzzling questions unanswered: What was the relationship between Isis and most of the people she mentions, with their mixture of Greek and

■ **Emperor Honorius as Christian Victor, c. 406 C.E.**
Both sides of this ivory diptych ("folding tablet") depict Honorius, emperor of the western Roman empire, as a military victor who credits Christ for his success. Petronius Probus presented this gift to the emperor to show his gratitude for being awarded the consulship, the empire's highest honor. On the left, Honorius holds a sign that says, "You will always conquer, in the name of Christ"; a statuette of Victory standing on a globe offers him a victor's wreath. On the right, he holds a shield and a scepter. His clothing and armor identify him as a military leader; the inscription above his head proclaims him "Our Master, Always Augustus," while the circle around his head testifies to his special holiness. As this carving shows, Honorius, like other emperors, believed that he had divine backing for his army. In his case, it was not enough: the Goths sacked Rome only four years later.
(© Alinari/Art Resource, NY.)

Semitic names? Did Isis know how to write or, as was common, had she hired a scribe? Why had she gone to Alexandria? Why did Aion want to become a soldier? Why was "everybody" in the army?

These questions relate to the crisis that had struck the Roman Empire in the third-century C.E. Perhaps financial troubles forced Isis to leave her village to seek work in the city. Perhaps Aion wanted to join the army to earn wages; the emperors, like Honorius (r. 395–423) shown in the chapter-opening illustration dressed as a general, were always looking for more soldiers. Perhaps everybody seemed to be in the army because there was continuous civil war. These answers reflect the challenge facing imperial government by the 280s, after half a century of Roman armies fighting Roman armies over who should be emperor: how to reorganize the empire to restore peace and order through military force, government administration, ancestral religion, and economic prosperity. Diocletian, emperor beginning in 284 C.E., turned out to be a leader tough enough to meet this challenge and delay the political fragmentation of the empire.

Restoring peace and order proved difficult because religious tensions were growing between Christians and followers of traditional polytheistic cults like Isis the letter writer, named after the famous Egyptian goddess. Polytheist emperors, believing that Christians angered the gods, conducted brutal persecutions. Then, unexpectedly, early in the fourth century the emperor Constantine stopped the violence by converting to Christianity and officially favoring it. By the end of the fourth century, the new faith had become the state religion. The persistence of pre-Christian traditions and Christians' fierce disputes over doctrine kept this transformed Roman world in a state of religious tension.

Ending the civil wars postponed but did not prevent the break up of imperial territory. At the end of the fourth century, Honorius's father split the empire permanently into western and eastern sections. In the west, non-Roman peoples began migrating into the region, transforming it—and themselves—socially, culturally, and politically by replacing Roman provincial government with their own new kingdoms. They lived side by side with Romans, the different groups often merging their customs. By the fifth century, the loss of Roman control had transformed western Europe politically into different states, anticipating its modern divisions. In the east, the Roman provinces remained economically vibrant and politically united, becoming (in modern terminology) the Byzantine Empire in the sixth century. Despite financial pressures and shrinking territory, the Roman Empire would endure under Christian rule for centuries, until Turkish invaders finally conquered it in 1453.

Reorganizing the Empire

During the third-century crisis, attacks by foreign enemies had weakened the Roman Empire's defenses and hurt tax collection. The emperors also faced a significant religious problem: the growing influence of the Christian church. Diocletian

■ **Miniature Portrait of Emperor Constantine**

This eight-inch-high bust of Constantine is carved from chalcedony, a crystalline mineral prized for its milky look. The first Christian emperor is shown gazing upward, imitating his hero and model Alexander the Great, who had ordered his portrait to show him in this way. Constantine does not have a beard, a style made popular by Alexander and imitated by Augustus and Trajan, successful emperors to whom Constantine also wished to be linked. The cross in the center of Constantine's breastplate makes this one of the relatively few pieces of fourth-century Roman art to display Christian symbols. The position of this unmistakable sign of the emperor's religious choice recalls the sculpture on the armor on the Prima Porta statue of Augustus (see page 184); like the founder of the principate, Constantine communicated his image through art. What do you think Constantine hoped to gain by doing this?
(Bibliothèque nationale de France.)

(r. 284–305) and Constantine (r. 306–337) met these challenges by restoring strong central authority to the empire.

Imperial Reform and Fragmentation

Diocletian was an uneducated military man from outside Italy (Dalmatia, in what is now Croatia), but his exceptional leadership and intelligence propelled him through the ranks until the army made him emperor in 284. He ended the third-century crisis by imposing the strongest form of monarchy in Roman history. With the military's support, Diocletian proclaimed himself *dominus*—"master," what slaves called their owners—to replace Augustus's republican title, *princeps* ("first man"). Roman imperial rule from Diocletian onward is therefore called the **dominate**. Senators, consuls, and other traditional republican offices continued to exist, but the emperors held all the power. They therefore reigned as autocrats—true sole rulers.

The emperors of the dominate emphasized their supremacy by placing their throne on a raised platform, wearing jeweled robes, and surrounding themselves with attendants and ceremony. Constantine wore a diadem—a purple headband sparkling with gems, a symbol of kingship that earlier emperors had avoided. To demonstrate the ruler's superiority, a series of veils separated palace waiting rooms from the inner space where the emperor listened to people's pleas for help. High-ranking officials received showy titles such as "most perfect" and wore special shoes and belts. The court of the dominate resembled the splendid court of the Great King of Persia a thousand years earlier (see photo on page 30). The emperors of the dominate abandoned the first Roman emperors' claim that the ruler was merely the princeps, the "first man" but still just a citizen. Diocletian and his successors instead believed that citizens were their subjects. The architecture of the dominate reflected its rulers' all-powerful status. Diocletian's public bath in Rome rivaled earlier emperors' buildings in the capital; its soaring vaults and domes covered a space more than three thousand feet long on each side.

The dominate also used religious language to mark the emperor's special status. The emperors added *et deus* ("and God") to *dominus* as their title. Diocletian also adopted the title *Jovius*, claiming Jupiter (Jove), the chief Roman god, as his ancestor. His titles signaled the elevated respect he now demanded from his subjects because he expected to be honored as magnificently as the gods.

The emperors alone made law and did not consider themselves bound by earlier rulers' decisions. Relying on a loyal personal staff that isolated them from the outside world, they rarely asked for advice from the elite, as the first emperors had done. Their desire to maintain order led them to impose brutal punishments for crimes. For example, Constantine punished officials who did not keep what he called their "greedy hands" off bribes by having their hands "cut off by the sword"; the guardians of a young girl who allowed a lover to seduce her were punished by having molten lead poured into their mouths. The emperors of the dominate also widened the divide between poor and rich by making punishments even more harsh for the large segment of the population legally known as "humbler people"; their laws excused the "better people" from most of the harshest penalties for the same crimes.

Diocletian decided that the empire could not be administered and defended from a single center (that is, Rome). In 293, he therefore divided imperial territory into four administrative districts, two in the west and two in the east (Map 6.1). Having no sons, he appointed three "partners" so he and they could govern cooperatively in two pairs, both consisting of a senior "Augustus" with a junior "Caesar" as his adopted son and designated successor. Each emperor controlled one of the four districts. To prevent disunity, the most senior partner—in this case Diocletian—served as supreme ruler and was supposed to receive the loyalty of the others. This **tetrarchy** ("rule by four"), as modern scholars call it, was Diocletian's attempt to keep imperial government from being isolated at the center and to prevent civil war over who should be the next emperor.

Diocletian also subdivided the provinces, nearly doubling their number to almost a hundred. He grouped them into twelve dioceses under the jurisdiction of

■ MAP 6.1 Diocletian's Reorganization of 293

To try to prevent civil war and tighten imperial control, Emperor Diocletian reorganized the Roman Empire. He created four administrative districts, each one governed by a different ruler. He also sub-divided the preexisting provinces into smaller units and grouped them into twelve dioceses, each overseen by a regional administrator. This map shows the four districts as the imperial official Sextus Aurelius Victor described them in his book On the Caesars, *a biographically oriented history of the empire inspired by the famous biographies of Suetonius from the early second century. Victor published his book around 360.*

regional administrators, who reported to the four emperors' first assistants, the praetorian prefects. To try to keep provincial governors from becoming powerful enough to threaten the emperors, Diocletian began to separate their civil from their military authority, restricting administrators to control only of legal and financial affairs and restricting generals only to defense. Constantine completed this process.

Although later emperors abandoned the tetrarchy, Diocletian's reform of provincial administration into a hierarchy continued. He also ended Rome's thousand years as the empire's capital city. Diocletian lived in Nicomedia, in Asia Minor, and did not even visit Rome until 303, nearly twenty years after becoming emperor. He chose four new capitals for their usefulness as military command posts closer to the frontiers: Milan in northern Italy, Sirmium near the Danube River border, Trier near the Rhine River border, and Nicomedia. Italy became just another region in the empire, on an equal footing with the other provinces and subject to the same taxation system, except for the tax-free district of Rome itself—the last trace of the city's former superiority.

Despite Diocletian's reforms, civil war broke out soon after he retired in 305. It took Constantine (r. 306–337) until 324 to eliminate rivals. Near the end of his reign, he named his three sons as joint heirs, ordering them to rule as co-emperors. They failed as bloodily as had the sons of Septimius Severus a century earlier, plunging into war with one another. This civil war informally split the empire on a north-south line along the Balkan peninsula. In 395, Honorius and Arcadius divided the empire into western and eastern halves, ruling as co-emperors. The co-emperors were supposed to cooperate, but this division launched the two parts of the empire toward different fates.

Each half of the empire had its own capital. Constantinople, near the mouth of the Black Sea, was the eastern capital. Originally Byzantium (today Istanbul, Turkey), Constantinople had been reconstructed and renamed by Constantine in 324 as his "new Rome." He had chosen it for its geography, on an easily fortified peninsula controlling routes for trade and troop movements. To recall the glory of Rome, Constantine had given his refounded city a forum, an imperial palace, a hippodrome for chariot races, and huge statues of the traditional gods. The eastern emperors inherited Constantine's "new" city as their capital; from its ancient name modern historians call the eastern section of the old Roman Empire the **Byzantine Empire**.

The Division of the Empire, c. 395

Geography determined the site of the western capital as well. The western emperor Honorius (r. 395–423) wanted to keep the Alps mountains between his territory and the raiders living to the north. In 404, he made Ravenna, a port on Italy's northeastern coast, the western capital because it was a naval base and an important commercial city. Walls and marshes protected it from attack by land, while its harbor kept it from being starved out in a siege. Ravenna never rivaled Constantinople in size or riches, but the emperors did build churches gleaming with multicolored mosaics.

Financial Reform and Social Consequences

Diocletian's rescue of the empire required vast amounts of money, which the inflation of the third century had made hard to find. He tried to improve imperial finances by issuing new money, price controls, and a new taxation system. Unfortunately, Diocletian miscalculated in setting values for his new coins and set off a financial panic that increased inflation in many regions after 293. High prices caused people to hoard whatever goods they could buy, and hoarding drove prices ever higher. "Hurry and spend all my money you have; buy me any kinds of goods at whatever prices they are available," wrote one official to his servant, fearing yet another decline in the value of the currency.

In 301, Diocletian tried to stop inflation by imposing price and wage controls in the worst-hit regions. His Edict on Maximum Prices blamed high prices on profiteers' "unlimited and crazed avarice," banned hoarding, and set limits on the prices that could legally be charged for about a thousand goods and services. The edict soon became ineffective because merchants refused to cooperate and government officials were unable to enforce it despite the threat of death or exile as the penalty for violations. In his final years, Diocletian revalued the currency to restore sound money and stable prices, but the civil war under Constantine again weakened it.

With the currency losing value, the emperors began collecting taxes not only in coins but also in goods. Recent research disputes whether this form of revenue actually replaced taxes paid in coin, as previous scholars believed, or only served as a way to impose higher property taxes, which had to be paid in coin as much as possible. By the end of the fourth century, it is clear that the government expected payment in gold and silver, and that taxes rose, especially on the local elites. Taxes went mostly to support the army, which required enormous amounts of grain, meat, wine, horses, camels, and mules. The major sources of revenue were a tax on land, assessed according to its productivity, and a head tax on individuals.

The empire was too large to enforce consistency in tax rates. In some areas, both men and women from about the age of twelve to sixty-five paid the full tax; in others, women paid only one-half the tax assessment or none at all. Workers in cities probably owed taxes only on their property. They periodically paid "in kind"— laboring without pay on public works projects such as cleaning municipal drains or repairing buildings. Urban businesspeople, from shopkeepers to prostitutes, paid taxes in money. Members of the senatorial class were exempt from ordinary taxes but had to make other payments when the emperor demanded them.

The new tax system would work only if agricultural production remained stable and the government controlled the people liable for the head tax. Diocletian therefore restricted the movement of tenant farmers (*coloni*), who formed the empire's economic base. Coloni had traditionally been free to move to different farms under different landlords. Now tenant farmers were increasingly tied to a particular plot, and their children were required to remain farmers.

The government also restricted workers in other essential occupations. Bakers, for example, could not leave their jobs, and anyone who acquired a baker's property had to assume that occupation. The bakers were essential in producing free bread for Rome's poor, a tradition begun under the republic to prevent food riots. Also, from Constantine's reign on, military service became a lifetime career that sons of soldiers inherited: they had to serve in the army.

The emperors announced equally oppressive regulations for the propertied class in the empire's towns, the **curials**. Almost all men in the curial class were obliged sooner or later to serve as unsalaried city council members, who had to use their own funds if necessary to support the community. Their financial responsibilities ranged from maintaining the water supply to feeding troops, but their most expensive duty was covering shortfalls in tax collection. The emperors' demands for increased revenue made this a crushing burden, compounding the damage to the curials that the third-century crisis had begun.

For centuries, the empire's welfare had depended on a steady supply of public-spirited members of the social elite enthusiastically filling these crucial posts to win the admiration of their neighbors. Now this tradition broke down as wealthy people avoided public service to escape financial ruin. So distorted was the situation that forced service on a city council became one of the punishments for a minor crime. Eventually, to prevent curials from escaping their obligations, the emperors ordered them not to move away from the town where they had been born; they even had to ask official permission to travel. These laws made members of the elite try to win exemptions from public service by begging the emperor, bribing high-ranking officials, or taking up an occupation that freed them from such obligations (such as being a soldier, an imperial administrator, or a church official). The most desperate simply fled, abandoning home and property.

The restrictions on freedom caused by the pressure for higher taxes thus eroded wealthy Romans' long-standing commitment to public service. The emperors' attempt to stabilize the empire by increasing its revenues also hurt nonelite citizens. The tax rate on land eventually reached one-third of its gross yield. This burden crushed poor farmers. They had to eat most of what they produced just to survive, save enough seed to plant the next crop, and then pay the high tax out of what was left. A bad harvest meant starvation. Conditions became so bad in fifth-century Spain, for example, that peasants openly revolted against imperial control. Financial troubles, especially severe in the west, kept the empire from ever regaining the prosperity of its Golden Age and worsened the friction between government and citizens.

Religious Reform: From Persecution to Conversion

Traditional belief required religious explanations for disasters. Diocletian therefore concluded that the gods' anger had caused the third-century crisis. To restore divine goodwill, he instructed citizens to follow the traditional gods who had guided Rome to power and virtue: "The providence of the immortal gods has allowed superior, wise, and upright men in their wisdom to establish good and true principles. It is wrong to oppose these principles or to abandon the ancient religion for some new one." Christianity was the new religion Diocletian had in mind.

Blaming Christians for the empire's troubles, Diocletian in 303 launched the **Great Persecution**. He expelled Christians from his administration, seized their property and tore down their churches, and executed them for refusing to participate in official religious rituals. As was often true, policy was applied differently in different regions. In the western empire, the violence stopped after about a year; in the east, it continued for a decade. So gruesome were the public executions of martyrs that they aroused the sympathy of some polytheists.

Constantine changed the empire's religious history forever by converting to Christianity. He chose the new faith for the same reason that Diocletian had persecuted it: in the belief that he would receive divine protection for himself and the empire. During the civil war that he fought to succeed Diocletian, Constantine experienced a dream vision promising him the support of the Christian God. His biographer, Eusebius (c. 260–340), later reported that Constantine had also seen a vision of Jesus' cross in the sky surrounded by the words "In this sign you shall be the victor." When Constantine defeated his main rival at the Battle of the Milvian Bridge in Rome in 312, he proclaimed that God's miraculous power and goodwill had brought him the victory. He therefore declared himself a Christian emperor.

After his conversion, Constantine did not outlaw polytheism or make Christianity the official religion. Instead, he announced religious toleration. The best statement of his new policy survives in the **Edict of Milan** of 313. It proclaimed free choice of religion for everyone and referred to the empire's protection by "the highest divinity"—an imprecise term meant to satisfy both polytheists and Christians.

Constantine wanted to avoid angering polytheists because they still greatly outnumbered Christians, but he nevertheless did all he could to promote his newly chosen religion. These goals called for a careful balancing act. For example, he returned all property seized during the Great Persecution to its Christian owners, but he had the treasury pay back those who had bought the confiscated property at auction. When in 321 he made Lord's Day a holy occasion each week on which no official business or manufacturing work could be performed, he called it Sunday to blend Christian and traditional notions in honoring two divinities, God and the sun. To beautify his new capital, Constantinople, he erected numerous statues of traditional gods around the city. He also respected Roman tradition by holding the office of *pontifex maximus* ("chief priest"), which emperors had filled ever since Augustus.

■ **REVIEW:** *What changes did Diocletian and his successors make in their reorganization of the empire?*

■ **Relief Sculpture of Saturn from North Africa**

This pillar shows the god known to the Romans as Saturn and to the Carthaginians as Ba'al Hammon (one of the gods of the Phoenician founders of Carthage). This syncretism (identifying gods as the same even though they carried different names in different places) was typical of ancient polytheism and allowed Roman and non-Roman cults to merge. The smaller figure below the god is sacrificing a sheep before an altar. The inscription dates the pillar to 323, a decade later than Constantine's conversion to Christianity. Such objects testifying to the continuing existence of polytheistic cults remained common until the end of the fourth century, when the Christian emperors succeeded in suppressing most public activities of traditional religion.
(© Copyright Martha Cooper/Peter Arnold, Inc.)

Christianizing the Empire

Constantine's religious policy of toleration and compromise set the empire on the path to Christianization. The process proved to be slow and sometimes violent. Not until the end of the fourth century did the emperors close the traditional gods' temples. Even after the vast majority of people in the empire had become Christians, some polytheists long kept worshiping in private. From the perspective of later history, however, the transformation from polytheist empire into Christian state became by far the most enduring influence of Greco-Roman antiquity.

The Spread of Christianity

The empire's Christianization generated passionate disputes because ordinary people cared deeply about religion. It provided their best hope for private salvation in a dangerous world over which they had little control. On this point, polytheists and Christians held some similar beliefs. Both believed spirits and demons had powerful influences on daily life. For some, it seemed safest to believe in all religions. For example, a silver spoon used in the worship of the polytheist forest spirit Faunus has been found engraved with a fish, the common symbol whose Greek spelling (*ichthys*) was an abbreviation for the Greek words "Jesus Christ the Son of God, the Savior."

Nevertheless, the differences between polytheists' and Christians' beliefs were much greater than their similarities. People disagreed on whether there was one God or many, and about what effect God or the gods had on the human world. Polytheists still participated in festivals and sacrifices to many different gods. Why, they asked, did these joyous occasions not satisfy Christians' desires for contact with divinity?

Polytheists also could not understand why Christians believed in a savior who had not established a new kingdom on earth and been executed as a common criminal. The traditional gods, they insisted, had given a world empire to their worshipers. Moreover, they told Christians, cults such as that of the goddess Isis, after whom the worried Egyptian letter writer had been named, and philosophies such as Stoicism insisted that only the pure of heart could be their followers. Christianity, by contrast, took in sinners. Why, puzzled polytheists wondered, would any righteous person want to associate with wrongdoers? In short, as the Greek philosopher Porphyry (c. 234–305) remarked, Christians had no right to claim that only they had a true religion, for no one had ever found one single doctrine providing "a universal path to the liberation of the soul."

The slow pace of religious change revealed how strong polytheism remained in the fourth century, especially in the social elite. In fact, the emperor Julian (r. 361–363) rebelled against his family's Christianity and tried to impose his philosophical brand of polytheism as Rome's official religion. This rejection of Christianity earned him the name Julian the Apostate (someone who turns against an established faith is called an **apostate**). Deeply religious, he believed in a supreme deity corresponding to the ideas of Greek philosophers: "This divine and completely beautiful universe, from heaven's highest sky to earth's lowest limit, is tied together by the continuous providence of god, has existed forever, and will last forever." Julian's restoration of the traditional gods ended with his unexpected death while invading Persia.

The Christian emperors who followed Julian worked to end polytheism through various restrictions. In 382, Gratian (r. 375–383 in the west) removed from the Senate in Rome the Altar of Victory, which Augustus had placed there to remind senators of Rome's success under its ancestral religion; most importantly, Gratian stopped public funding for traditional sacrifices. Aurelius Symmachus (c. 340–402), a polytheist senator who served as prefect ("mayor") of Rome, objected to what he saw as an outrage against Rome's tradition of religious diversity. Protesting the emperors' moves against polytheism, he argued: "We all have our own way of life and our own way of worship. . . . So vast a mystery [as religious truth] cannot be approached by only one path."

■ **Mosaic of Christ as Sun God**
This mosaic comes from a burial chamber in Rome that is now in the Vatican, under the basilica of St. Peter built by Constantine. It perhaps dates to the mid-third century. Christ appears here similar to a traditional polytheistic representation of the Sun god, especially the Greek Apollo: with rays of light shining forth around his head as he rides in a chariot pulled by horses. This symbolism —God is light—reached back to ancient Egypt. Christian artists showed Jesus in this way because he had said, "I am the light of the world" (John 8:12). The cloak flaring from Christ's shoulder suggests the spread of his motion across the sky. **For more help analyzing this image**, see the visual activity for this chapter in the ONLINE STUDY GUIDE at bedfordstmartins.com/ huntconcise. (Scala/Art Resource, NY.)

Christianity finally replaced traditional polytheism as the state religion in 391 when the emperor Theodosius (r. 379–395 in the east) successfully banned all polytheist sacrifices, even if private individuals paid for the animals. He also made divination (predicting the future) by the inspection of animal entrails punishable as high treason and ordered that all polytheist temples be closed. Many shrines, however, such as the Parthenon in Athens, remained in use for a long time because the empire was too large for the emperors to control at the local level. Temples were only gradually converted to churches during the fifth and sixth centuries. Non-Christian schools were not forced to close—the Academy, founded by Plato in Athens in the early fourth century B.C.E., endured for 140 years after Theodosius's reign—but Christians received advantages in government careers. Over time, non-Christians became outsiders in an empire ruled by Christian emperors.

Jews posed a special problem for the Christian emperors. Like polytheists, Jews rejected the new state religion. Yet they seemed entitled to special treatment because Jesus had been a Jew and because previous emperors had allowed Jews to practice their religion, even when Hadrian refounded Jerusalem as a Roman colony after putting down a fierce revolt there (132–135). Fourth-century and later emperors placed legal restrictions on Jews. For example, they banned Jews from holding government jobs but still required them to take on the financial burdens of curials—without receiving the honor of curial status. By the late sixth century, they increased the pressure on Jews to convert to Christianity by barring them from making wills, receiving inheritances, or testifying in court.

Although these developments began the long process that made Jews into second-class citizens in later European history, they did not destroy Judaism. Synagogues continued to exist in Palestine, where a few Jews still lived (most had been dispersed throughout the cities of the empire and the lands beyond the eastern border). The study of Jewish law and traditions flourished in this period, leading to the creation of books known as the Palestinian and the Babylonian Talmuds (collections of scholars' interpretations of Jewish law) and the scriptural commentaries of the Midrash (an explanation of the meaning of the Hebrew Bible). These works of religious scholarship provided guidance on how to live according to God's will and greatly influenced later Judaism.

Christianity's status as the state religion aided its spread by encouraging new believers to adopt the emperor's religion. Soldiers, for example, now found it possible to convert to Christianity and still serve in the army. Previously, Christian soldiers had sometimes created disciplinary problems. As one senior infantryman had said in 298 at his court-martial for abandoning his duties, "A Christian serving the Lord Christ should not serve the affairs of this world." Once the emperors had become Christians, however, soldiers could more easily justify military duty as supporting Christ.

Christianity's spread also depended on the appeal of its religious and social values. Christianity offered believers a strong sense of community in this world as well as the promise of salvation in the next. Wherever they went, they could find a warm welcome in the local congregation (see Map 6.2 on page 226). The new religion also won converts by performing charitable works—in the tradition of Jews and some polytheist cults—especially for the poor, widows, and orphans. By the mid-third century, for example, Rome's congregation was supporting fifteen hundred widows and other poor people. Christianity's emphasis on taking care of others was especially important because people at that time had to depend mostly on friends and relatives for help; state-funded social services were rare.

Although scholars continue to debate the role of women in early Christianity, it is clear they were a major force in spreading the new religion. Augustine (354–430), bishop of Hippo in North Africa and perhaps the most influential theologian in Western history, recognized women's contribution to the strengthening of Christianity in a letter he wrote to the unbaptized husband of a baptized woman: "O you men, who fear all the burdens imposed by baptism. The women are far better than you. Chaste and devoted to the faith, it is their presence in large numbers that causes the church to grow." Some women earned high status by giving their property to their congregation or by refusing marriage to dedicate themselves to Christ. Life-long virgins and widows who chose not to remarry thus joined large

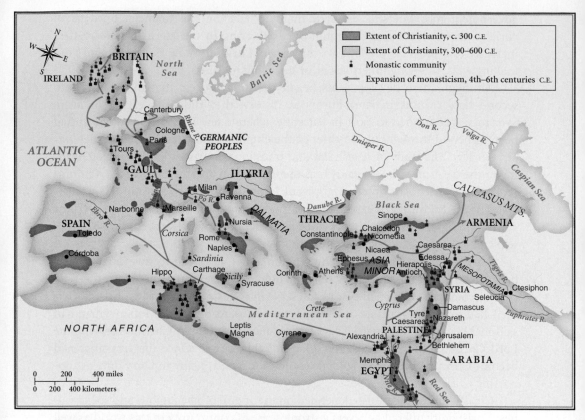

■ **MAP 6.2 The Spread of Christianity, 300–600**

Christians were still a minority in the population of the Roman Empire in 300, although congregations existed in many cities and towns, especially in the eastern provinces. The emperor Constantine's conversion to Christianity in the early fourth century gave a boost to the new religion; it gained further strength during that century as the Christian emperors provided financial support and eliminated payments for the polytheist cults that had previously made up the religion of the state. By 600, the preaching of the church's missionaries and the money of the emperors had spread Christianity from one end of the empire to the other.

(Adapted from Henry Chadwick and G. R. Evans, *Atlas of the Christian Church* [Oxford: Andromeda Oxford Ltd., 1987], 28. Reproduced by permission of Andromeda Oxford Limited.)

donors as especially respected women. These women rejected the traditional social order, in which women were supposed to devote themselves to raising families. But even these holy women were excluded from leadership positions once the church's organization became a hierarchy of bishops matching the male-dominated hierarchy of the Roman world.

The final development that promoted the spread of Christianity was the creation of a hierarchical organization in which male bishops became Christianity's official leaders. The bishops replaced early Christianity's more democratic organization in which women could be leaders. Bishops had the authority to certify priests to conduct the church's sacraments, above all baptism and communion—rituals guaranteeing eternal life. Bishops also controlled their congregations' memberships and finances; much of the funds came from believers' donations and gifts in their wills. Over time, bishops became the emperors' partners in local rule, replacing the curials, whose numbers had shrunk drastically from the financial pressures the government had imposed on them but not on bishops. The bishops gained power because they could influence the emperor to direct money back to their region. Regional councils of bishops appointed new bishops and tried to settle disputes over Christian doctrine. The bishops in the largest cities became the most powerful leaders in the church. The main bishop of Carthage, for example, supervised at least one hundred local bishops in the surrounding area. The bishop of Rome, however, became the church's supreme leader in the western empire. The eastern church never agreed that he controlled the entire Christian world, but his dominance in the west won him the title previously applied to many bishops: pope (from *pappas,* Greek for "father"), the name still used for the head of the Roman Catholic church.

The bishops of Rome quoted the New Testament to establish their leadership over other bishops. In the book of Matthew (16:18–19), Jesus speaks to the Apostle Peter: "You are Peter, and upon this rock I will build my church. . . . I will entrust to you the keys of the kingdom of heaven. Whatever you bind on earth shall be bound in heaven. Whatever you loose on earth shall be loosed in heaven." Because Peter's name in Greek means "rock" and because Peter was believed to have been the first bishop of Rome, later bishops in Rome, believing they inherited Peter's power, used this passage to justify their command over the church.

Competing Visions of Religious Truth

The spread of Christianity was not a calm and peaceful process because Christians had angry conflicts about what they should believe. The church's hierarchy of bishops struggled to create uniformity in belief and worship to ensure its members' spiritual purity and to maintain its authority over them. These leaders clashed over theology, however, and Christians never achieved unity on what was religious truth.

Disputes flared over what was orthodoxy (the official doctrines determined by councils of bishops, from the Greek for "correct thinking") as opposed to heresy (deviation from official doctrines, from the Greek for "private choice"). After Christianity became the state religion, the emperor became the top official responsible for enforcing orthodox creed (a summary of beliefs); he used force against believers who persisted in their heresy.

Questions about the nature of the Trinity of Father, Son, and Holy Spirit—which orthodoxy defined as a unified, co-eternal, and identical divinity—caused the worst conflict. **Arianism**, for example, generated fierce controversy for centuries. Named after its founder, Arius (c. 260–336), a priest from Alexandria in Egypt, this doctrine maintained that Jesus as God's son had not existed eternally; rather, God the Father had "begot" (created) his son from nothing and given him his special status. Thus Jesus was not co-eternal with God and not identical in nature with his father. This view implied that the Trinity was divisible and that Christianity's monotheism was not absolute. Arianism found widespread support, perhaps because it eliminated the difficulty of understanding how a son could be as old as his father and also because its making the son inferior to the father corresponded to regular family life. Arius used popular songs to make his views known, and people everywhere argued about the controversy. "When you ask for your change from a shopkeeper," one observer remarked in describing Constantinople, "he lectures you about the Begotten and the Unbegotten. If you ask how much bread costs, the reply is that 'the Father is superior and the Son inferior.' "

Many Christians became so angry about Arius's position on Jesus that Constantine had to intervene. In 325, he assembled 220 bishops at the Council of Nicaea to settle the dispute. The majority of bishops voted to crack down on Arianism: they banished Arius to the Balkan Mountains and declared that the Father and the Son were "of one substance" and co-eternal. So complicated were the issues, however, that Constantine later changed his mind twice, first recalling Arius from exile and then punishing him again not long after. The doctrine lived on: Constantine's third son, Constantius II (r. 337–361), favored Arianism, and his missionaries converted many of the immigrants who later came to live in the empire.

Nestorius, who became bishop of Constantinople in 428, disagreed with the orthodox doctrine of how Jesus' human and divine natures were related to his birth, insisting that his mother Mary gave birth to the human that became the temple for the divine. Nestorianism enraged orthodox Christians by rejecting Mary's title as *theotokos* (Greek for "bearer of God"). The bishops of Alexandria and Rome had Nestorius deposed and his doctrines officially rejected at councils held in 430 and 431; they condemned his writings in 435. Nestorian bishops in the eastern empire refused to accept these decisions, however, and they formed a separate church centered in Persia, where for centuries Nestorian Christians flourished under the tolerance of non-Christian rulers. They later became important agents of cross-cultural interaction by establishing communities that still endure in Arabia, India, and China.

No heresy better illustrates the bitterness of Christian conflicts over religious truth than Donatism. Following the Great Persecution, a dispute arose in North Africa in the fourth century over whether to readmit to their old congregations those Christians who had cooperated with imperial authorities to avoid persecution. Some

■ Mosaic of a Family from Edessa in the Middle East

This mosaic, found in a cave tomb, depicts an upper-class family of Edessa in the late Roman imperial period. Their names are given in Syriac, the dialect of Aramaic spoken in their region, and their colorful clothing reflects local traditions. Edessa was the capital of the small kingdom of Osrhoëne, which lay on the east bank of the Euphrates River between the Taurus Mountains and the Syrian desert. Rome took over the kingdom in 216, and it became famous in Christian history because its king, Abgar (r. 179–216), was remembered as the first ruler to convert to Christianity, well before Constantine. By the early fourth century, the story had emerged that after Jesus' death and resurrection, he sent one of his disciples to Edessa, where the disciple painted a picture of Jesus that protected the city from its enemies. The Byzantine emperors proclaimed themselves the heirs of King Abgar and of Jesus' grant to the city of special divine protection.

(Photo courtesy Thames & Hudson Ltd., London, from *Vanished Civilizations*, ed. Edward Bacon.)

North African Christians felt these lapsed members should be forgiven, but the Donatists (followers of the North African priest Donatus) insisted that the church should not be polluted with such "traitors." Most important, Donatists insisted, unfaithful priests and bishops could not administer the sacraments. So bitter was the clash that it even split Christian families. As one son threatened his mother, "I will join Donatus's followers, and I will drink your blood."

These fiery emotions made it difficult for bishops to enforce orthodoxy as religious truth. The Council of Chalcedon (an outskirt of Constantinople), at which the empress Pulcheria and her consort Marcian brought together more than five hundred bishops in 451, was the most important attempt to forge agreement. Its conclusions on correct doctrine form the basis of what many Christians still accept as doctrine: Jesus' divine and human natures were mixed within his person but nevertheless remained distinct. Monophysites (a Greek term for "single-nature believers") refused to agree, however, arguing that Jesus had only a single, divine nature. They split from the orthodox hierarchy in the sixth century to found independent churches in Egypt (the Coptic church), Ethiopia, Syria, and Armenia.

No one person had a stronger impact on the establishment of the western church's orthodoxy and therefore on later Catholicism than Augustine (354–430). Born in North Africa to a Christian mother and a polytheist father, he began his career by teaching rhetoric at Carthage, where he fathered a son by a mistress; he was later befriended by the prominent polytheist noble Aurelius Symmachus after moving to Italy. In 386, he converted to Christianity under the influence of his mother and Ambrose (c. 339–397), the powerful bishop of Milan. In 395, he himself was appointed bishop of Hippo, but his reputation rests on his writings. By around 500, Augustine and other influential theologians such as Ambrose and Jerome (c. 345–420) had earned the informal title "church fathers" because their views were quoted as authoritative in disputes over orthodoxy. Augustine became the most famous of this group of patristic (from the Greek for "father," *pater*) authors, and for the next thousand years his works would be the most influential texts in western Christianity besides the Bible. He wrote so much about religion and philosophy that a later scholar was moved to declare: "The man lies who says he has read all your works."

Augustine's most influential book on Christianity's role in the world was *City of God*, a "large and difficult work," as he called it, written between 413 and 426. In this book he knocked down the idea that Christianity, like the traditional cults it had replaced, guaranteed earthly success to Christians. Most importantly, he said, Christians were not responsible for Alaric's sacking of Rome in 410, a disaster that polytheists claimed was the gods' punishment for Romans' abandoning their traditional religion. Like other Christian thinkers, Augustine worried that Christianity would be blamed for Rome's loss of power. In addition, Augustine redefined the ideal state as a society of Christians. Not even Plato's doctrines offered a true path to purity, Augustine insisted, because the true struggle for individuals was not between their emotions and reason, but between their desire for earthly pleasures and spiritual purity. Emotions, especially love, were natural and desirable, but only when directed toward God. Humans were wrong to look for value in life on earth. Only life in God's city had meaning.

Nevertheless, Augustine wrote, earthly law and government were required because humans are by nature imperfect. God's original creation in the Garden of Eden was full of goodness, but humans lost their original perfection by inheriting a permanently sinful nature after Adam and Eve had disobeyed God. This doctrine of original sin—a subject of theological debate since at least the second century—meant that people suffered from a hereditary moral disease that turned the human will into a corrupting force. This corruption required governments to use force to combat vice. Although far inferior to the divine ideal, civil government was necessary to impose moral order on the chaos of human life after the fall from grace in the Garden of Eden. The government therefore had a right to force people to remain united to the church, by violence if necessary.

Order in society was essential, Augustine argued; it even justified the naturally evil practice of slavery because it was, in his view, a lesser evil than the violent troubles that would follow from overturning social traditions. Moreover, it was Christians' duty to obey the emperor and participate in political life. Soldiers, too, had to follow their orders. Augustine ruled out torture and capital punishment, however, because the purpose of government was to maintain a social order based on a moral order.

In *City of God*, Augustine tried to uncover a divine purpose in the events of history that humans found hard to understand, such as why God allowed Alaric to sack Rome. All that Christians could know with certainty was that history progressed toward an ultimate goal, but only God could know the meaning of each day's events. What could not be doubted was God's guiding power:

> *To be truthful, I myself fail to understand why God created mice and frogs, flies and worms. Nevertheless, I recognize that each of these creatures is beautiful in its own way. For when I think about the body and limbs of any living creature, where do I not find proportion, number, and order showing the unity of concord? Where one discovers proportion, number, and order, one should look for the craftsman.*

The repeated *I* in this passage reveals the intense personal commitment Augustine brought to matters of faith and doctrine.

Next to the nature of Christ, the question of how to understand and control sexual desire presented Christians with the toughest problem in the search for religious truth. Augustine became the most influential source of the doctrine that sex automatically involved human beings in evil and that they should therefore practice **asceticism**, self-denial of all pleasures (from the Greek *askesis*, meaning "training"). Augustine knew from personal experience how difficult it was to accept this doctrine. In fact, he revealed in his autobiographical work *Confessions*, written about 397, that he felt a deep conflict between his sexual desire and his religious doctrines. Only after a long period of doubt, he explained, did he find the inner strength to pledge future chastity as part of his conversion to Christianity.

He advocated no sex as the purest choice for Christians because he believed that Adam and Eve's disobedience in the Garden of Eden had forever ruined the original harmony God created between human will and human passions. According to Augustine, God punished his disobedient children by making sexual desire a corrupting force that humans could never completely control through will. Although he declared the value of marriage in God's plan, he added that sexual intercourse even between loving spouses carried the sad reminder of humanity's fall from grace. A married couple should "lie down with a certain sadness" to the task of starting a pregnancy, the only acceptable reason for sex; sexual pleasure could never be a human good.

This doctrine made virginity and avoidance of sex high virtues; in the words of Jerome, they counted as "daily martyrdom." This self-chosen holiness proved especially valuable for women in boosting their status in Christian society; their sexual abstinence earned them such respect that they could demand privileges usually reserved for men, such as more education in Hebrew and Greek to read the Bible. By the end of the fourth century, sexual purity had become so significant for Christian virtue that congregations began to expect celibate male priests and bishops.

The Beginning of Christian Monasticism

Christian asceticism reached its peak in monasticism. The word *monk* (from Greek *monos*, "single, solitary") described the basis of monasticism: men and women withdrawing from society to live a life of extreme self-denial imitating Jesus' suffering, demonstrating their devotion to God, and praying for divine mercy on the world. The earliest monks lived alone, but soon they formed communities for mutual support in the pursuit of ascetic holiness (see Map 6.2).

Polytheist and Jewish ascetics, motivated by philosophy and religion, had long existed. What made Christian monasticism different were the huge numbers of people it attracted and the high status that monks earned. Leaving their families and congregations, they gave up sex, worshiped frequently, wore the roughest clothes, and ate barely enough to survive, aiming to win an inner peace isolated from daily concerns. They reported, however, that they constantly struggled against fantasies of earthly delights, dreaming of plentiful, tasty food more often than of sex.

The earliest Christian ascetics appeared in the late third century in Egypt. Antony (c. 251–356), from a well-to-do family, was among the first. One day, he abruptly abandoned all his property after hearing a sermon based on Jesus' advice to a rich young man to sell his possessions and give the proceeds to the poor (Matt. 19:21). Putting aside his duty to see his sister married, he placed her in a home for unmarried women and spent his life alone in a barren region, demonstrating his excellence through worshiping God.

Monasticism to people appealed for many reasons, but above all because it gave ordinary people a way to achieve excellence and recognition. This opportunity seemed all the more valuable after Constantine's conversion and the end of the persecutions. Becoming a monk—a living martyrdom—served as the substitute for a martyr's death and imitated the sacrifice of Christ. Individual—or eremetic (hence "hermit")—monks went to great lengths to win fame. In Syria, for example, "holy women" and "holy men" attracted great attention by their feats of endurance. Symeon the Stylite (390–459) lived atop a tall pillar (*stylos* in

Greek) for thirty years, preaching to people gathered below his perch. Egyptian Christians believed that their monks' religious devotion made them living heroes ensuring the annual flooding of the Nile, the duty once linked to the pharaohs' divine power. Exceptionally famous ascetics had even greater influence after death. Their relics—body parts or clothing—became treasured sources of protection and healing. Relics gave believers faith in God's favor by expressing the power of saints (people receiving special honor after their deaths as reward for their special holiness).

The earliest monks followed the example of Antony in living alone. In about 323, Pachomius in Upper Egypt organized the first monastic community. In this "coenobitic" (seen-uh-BIT-ick), or "life in common," monasticism, men or women monks formed single-gender settlements to encourage one another along the hard road to holiness. Coenobitic monasticism became the primary form of Christian

■ **Monastery of St. Catherine at Mount Sinai**
The Byzantine emperor Justinian (r. 527–565) built a wall to enclose the building of this monastery in the desert at the foot of Mount Sinai (on the peninsula between Egypt and Arabia). Jews and Christians regarded this spot as holy because Moses had received the Ten Commandments there during the Hebrews' wanderings after their exodus from Egypt. Justinian supported the monastery to promote orthodoxy in a region dominated by Monophysite Christians. The monks at St. Catherine's gained a reputation for exceptional religious devotion: they spent much of their time repeating a simple prayer to Jesus over and over. The monastery gained its name in the ninth century from a story about angels bringing the body of Catherine of Alexandria there. Catherine was said to have been martyred in the fourth century for refusing to marry the emperor because, in her words, she was the bride of Christ. (Erich Lessing/ Art Resource, NY.)

asceticism. Monasteries were often built close together to divide their labor, with women making clothing, for example, while men farmed.

All monasteries imposed military-style discipline, but they differed in the harshness of their rules and amount of contact with the outside world. The most isolationist groups arose in the eastern empire, but the followers of Martin of Tours (c. 316–397), an ex-soldier famed for his religious deeds, founded communities in the west as harsh as any eastern ones. Basil ("the Great") of Caesarea in Asia Minor (c. 330–379) started a different tradition: monasteries serving society. He required monks to perform charitable deeds, leading to the foundation of the first hospitals attached to monasteries.

A milder, but still strict, code telling monks how to live became the standard in the west, influencing almost every area of Catholic worship. Called the Benedictine rule after its creator, Benedict of Nursia in central Italy (c. 480–553), this code prescribed a daily routine of prayer, scriptural readings, and manual labor. The rule divided the day into seven parts, each with a compulsory service of prayers and lessons, called "the office." Unlike harsher codes, Benedict's did not isolate the monks from the outside world or deprive them of sleep, adequate food, or warm clothing. Although his code gave the abbot (the head monk) full authority, it instructed him to listen to what every member of the community, even the youngest monk, had to say before he decided important matters. He was not allowed to beat them severely as punishment for breaking the rules, as sometimes happened under other, harsher systems. Communities of women, such as those founded by Basil's sister Macrina and Benedict's sister Scholastica, usually followed the rules of the male monasteries, with an emphasis on the modesty thought necessary for women.

The thousands of Christians who became monks from the fourth century onward joined monasteries for social as well as theological reasons. Some had been given as babies to monasteries by parents who could not raise them or were fulfilling religious vows, a practice called oblation. Jerome once gave this advice to a mother about her daughter:

> Let her be brought up in a monastery, let her live among virgins, let her learn to avoid swearing, let her regard lying as a sin against God, let her be ignorant of the world, let her live the angelic life, while in the flesh let her be without the flesh, and let her suppose that all human beings are like herself.

When she reaches adulthood as a virgin, he added, she should avoid the baths so she would not be seen naked or give her body pleasure by dipping in the warm pools. Jerome expressed traditional Roman values favoring males when he promised that God would reward the mother with the birth of sons to compensate for her dedicating her daughter to God. But he also said, "[As monks] we evaluate people's virtue not by their gender but by their character, and judge those to be worthy of the greatest glory who have given up both status and riches."

The monasteries' independence threatened the power of the church's hierarchy. Bishops did not like devoted members of their congregations withdrawing into monasteries, not least because they then gave their donations to their new community rather than to their local churches. Moreover, monks challenged bishops' authority because holy men and women earned their special status not by having it awarded by the church's leaders but by earning it through their own actions. Bishops and monks did share a spiritual goal—salvation and service to God. While polytheists had enjoyed immediate access to their gods, who were thought to visit the earth constantly, Christians worshiped a God outside this world. Monks bridged the gap between the human and the divine by asking God to be merciful to faithful believers.

■ **REVIEW:** *What were the major disputes among early Christians, and why were they so fierce?*

Non-Roman Kingdoms in the West

Just as western and eastern monasticism differed in the harshness of their rules, the western and eastern regions of the empire grew increasingly different in their social and political arrangements. The western part underwent the biggest changes. The migrations of non-Roman peoples into western Europe transformed politics, society, and the economy there. Two strong motives drove these diverse groups into Roman territory: to flee the brutal attacks of the Huns (nomads from the steppes of central Asia) and to benefit from the empire's prosperity. By the 370s, their presence was provoking much violence in the western empire. As the imperial government's ability to maintain order weakened, these immigrants experienced great changes themselves, transforming from vaguely defined and organized tribes into kingdoms with separate ethnic identities. By the 470s, one of their commanders ruled Italy. That political change has been said to mark the "fall of the Roman Empire." In fact, the lasting effects of the interactions of these non-Roman peoples with the diverse peoples of western Europe and North Africa are better understood as a political, social, and cultural transformation that made them the heirs of the western Roman Empire and led to the formation of medieval Europe.

Migrations into the Empire

At first, the fourth-century emperors encouraged the migrations. Like the earlier emperors, they recruited foreign warriors for the Roman army. By the late fourth century, crowds of women and children had followed these warriors into the empire

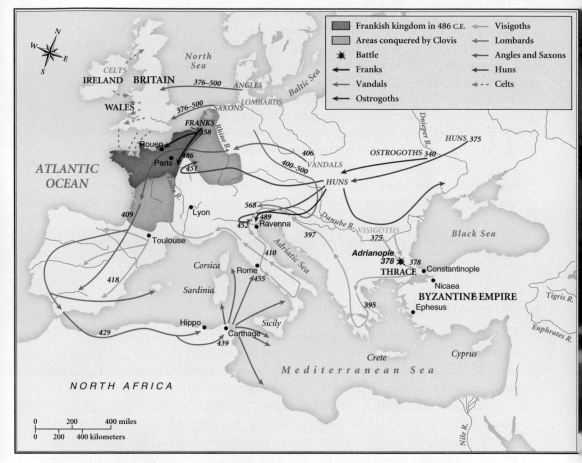

■ MAP 6.3 Migrations and Invasions of the Fourth and Fifth Centuries

The movements of non-Roman peoples into imperial territory transformed the Roman Empire. These migrations began as early as the reign of Domitian (r. 81–96), but in the fourth century, they became a pressing problem for the emperors when the Huns' attacks pushed many multiethnic bands from their homelands in eastern Europe into the empire's northern provinces. Maps cannot really show dynamic processes such as migrations and invasions, and the arrows on this one do not mean that the newcomers came in an unbroken stream. The map does indicate, however, the variety of peoples involved, the wide extent of imperial territory that they affected, and the concentration of their effects in the western section of the empire.

(Map 6.3). The western Roman government regarded them as barbarians; the emperors' failure either to absorb the newcomers or expel them led to the "Fall of the Roman Empire."

Economic weakness stemming from the third-century crisis hindered the emperors' ability to react to the migrations. They had demanded higher taxes during the crisis, forcing landowners to demand higher payments from their coloni.

Many of these tenants responded by illegally running away. Eventually, landowners also had to run away if they could not pay their taxes. This flight left farms deserted; as much as 20 percent of agricultural land lay unfarmed in the most seriously affected areas. The government pressed the farmers who remained to pay even more, but this only made more of them abandon their farms. In the end, the emperors' financial problems meant they could not hire enough soldiers to stop non-Roman peoples from immigrating into the empire.

Non-Roman groups crossed into Roman territory not in carefully planned invasions but often fleeing for their lives. Fourth-century raids by the Huns drove them from their homelands east of the Rhine and north of the Danube. Mostly small groups of men, women, and children crossed the Roman border as refugees. Their future looked grim because they came with no political or military unity, no clear plan, and not even a shared sense of identity.

Loosely organized in democratic groups and often warring with one another, these diverse bands or tribes originally shared only similar languages and their terror of the Huns. The migrating groups developed different ethnic identities only because the Roman government refused to accept them into Roman society. The newcomers therefore created their own kingdoms inside the imperial frontiers. Their desire for security forced them to develop a more tightly structured society to govern their new lands and gave them new identities.

Previously, these peoples lived in their homelands in small settlements as farmers, herders, and ironworkers; they had no experience running kingdoms. Most of these bands operated as chiefdoms, whose members could only be persuaded, not forced, to follow the chief. Chiefs maintained their leadership by leading warriors on successful raids to seize cattle and slaves and then giving gifts to their followers.

Family life was patriarchal: men headed households and exercised authority over women, children, and slaves. Women earned respect by bearing children, and rich men could have more than one wife and perhaps concubines as well. A clear division of labor made women responsible for agriculture, pottery making, and the production of textiles, while men worked iron and herded cattle. Fighting and raiding meant so much to the men that they packed graves with weapons, which archaeologists have found in northern European swamps. Women had some rights of inheritance and could control property, and married women received a marriage gift of one-third of their husbands' property.

Households were grouped into clans based on kinship through mothers as well as fathers. The members of a clan were supposed to keep peace among themselves, and violence against another clan member was the worst possible crime. Clans in turn grouped themselves into tribes, multiethnic coalitions that anyone could join. Different tribes identified themselves by their clothing, hairstyles, jewelry, weapons, religious cults, and oral stories.

Assemblies of free male warriors provided the tribes' only political organization. Tribal leaders' functions were mostly religious and military. Tribes tended to be unstable groupings with frequent bloody feuds between clans. Tribal law tried to set limits to the violence permitted in seeking revenge, but laws were oral, not written, and thus open to wide dispute.

Migrations into Roman territory surged when the Huns invaded eastern Europe in the fourth century. Related to the Hiung-nu people who had attacked China and Persia, these Turkish-speaking nomads arrived on the Russian plains shortly before 370. They excelled as raiders, launching cavalry attacks far and wide. With elongated skulls (from having been bound between boards in infancy), faces grooved with decorative scars, and their arms bristling with elaborate tattoos, they terrified their victims. Their skill as horsemen made them legendary. They could shoot their powerful bows while riding full speed, and they could remain on horseback for days, sleeping atop their horses and holding snacks of raw meat between their thighs and the animal's back.

The eastern emperors in Constantinople bribed the Huns not to attack their territory. The Huns then abandoned their nomadic lifestyle and became landlords, cooperating among themselves to create an empire north of the Danube that forced local farmers to support these new masters. The Huns' most ambitious leader, Attila (r. c. 440–453), extended their domains from the Caspian Sea to the Alps and even farther west. He led his forces as far as Paris in 451 and into northern Italy the next year. At Attila's death in 453, the Huns lost their unity and faded from history. By this time, however, the terror that they inspired in the people living in eastern Europe had already started the migrations that transformed the western empire.

The people who, after entering imperial territory, created a new identity as Visigoths were the first to experience what became the common pattern of the migrations: some desperate and poorly organized group would plead with the emperor for protection from the Huns, and the empire would accept them in return for military service. Shredded by constant raids by the Huns, in 376 the Visigoths begged the eastern emperor Valens (r. 364–378) to let them migrate into the Balkans. They received permission on condition that their warriors enlist in the Roman army to help drive away the Huns.

As the story of the Visigoths shows, the final part of the pattern was for these deals to fall apart. When greedy and incompetent Roman officers ordered to help the refugee Visigoths instead mistreated them, they starved; the officials forced them to sell some of their own people into slavery in return for dogs to eat. The hungry Visigoths rebelled. In 378, they defeated and killed Valens in battle at Adrianople in Thrace (see Map 6.3). The next eastern emperor, Theodosius I (r. 379–395), then had to renegotiate the deal from a position of weakness. His concessions to the Visigoths established the terms that other bands would seek for themselves and that would create new, self-conscious identities for them: permission to settle permanently inside the imperial borders, freedom to establish a kingdom under their own

■ **Eagle Brooches (*Fibulae*) from Visigothic Spain**

Visigothic women in their new kingdom in Spain showed their new ethnic identity by their style of dress, in particular through the tradition of fastening their clothing at the shoulders with brooches. These expensive examples, fashioned from gold inlaid with semi-precious stones, also expressed elite status. The choice of eagles as a Gothic brooch design reveals how ethnic identity can be constructed through cultural inter-action: Goths probably adopted the eagle as a symbol of power from Hunnic and Roman traditions.
(The Walters Art Museum, Baltimore.)

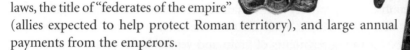

laws, the title of "federates of the empire" (allies expected to help protect Roman territory), and large annual payments from the emperors.

The eastern emperors soon realized, however, that they could not afford to keep such agreements. They therefore forced the migrating bands westward by cutting off the payments and threatening full-scale war unless the refugees left. With no army blocking them from moving westward, the Visigoths moved in that direction; neither the western empire nor they would ever be the same. In 410, they shocked the world by sacking Rome itself when the emperor Honorius in Ravenna botched negotiations. When their commander Alaric demanded all the city's gold, silver, movable property, and foreign slaves, the Romans asked, "What will be left to us?" "Your lives," he replied.

Too weak to defeat the invaders, the western emperor Honorius (r. 395–423) in 418 reluctantly agreed to settle the Visigoths in southwestern Gaul (present-day France), saving face by calling them federates. The Visigoths then completed their transition from tribal society to new kingdom by doing what no non-Roman group had done before: establishing an ethnic identity and organizing a state. They followed the model of Roman emperors by building mutually beneficial relations with local elites, including Romans. Romans in that elite could use time-tested ways of flattering their superiors to gain advantages. Sidonius Apollinaris, for example, a noble from Lyon (c. 430–479), once purposely lost a backgammon game to the Visigothic king as a way of gaining a favor from the ruler. Honorius tried, without much success, to limit what he saw as "barbarian" influence on Roman citizens by ordering them not to adopt Visigothic clothing styles.

How the new non-Roman kingdoms such as that of the Visigoths financed their states is a much-debated question. The older view is that the newcomers became landowners by forcing Romans to turn over some of their land, slaves, and movable property to them. Recent scholarship argues that Roman taxpayers in the kingdoms did not have to give up land but were instead made directly responsible for paying the expenses of the non-Roman soldiers, who lived mostly in city garrisons. Whatever the new arrangements were, the Visigoths found them so profitable that they later expanded into Spain.

The western emperor's deal with the Visigoths motivated other groups to enter Roman territory to create kingdoms and identities (see Map 6.4). The process was often violent. In 406, the Vandals, fleeing the Huns, fought their way all through Gaul to the Spanish coast. (The modern word *vandal*, meaning "destroyer of property," preserves their reputation for destruction.) In 429, eighty thousand Vandals crossed to North Africa, where they broke their agreement to become federates and captured the region. Their new kingdom caused tremendous hardship for local Africans by confiscating property rather than allowing owners to make regular payments to the occupiers. The Vandals further weakened the western emperors by seizing North Africa's tax payments of grain and vegetable oil and disrupting the importation of grain to Rome; they also built a navy strong enough to threaten the eastern empire. In 455, they plundered Rome, proving the western imperial government was powerless.

Other small groups also managed to break off distant pieces of the weakened western empire. The most significant small band for later history was the Anglo-Saxons. Composed of Angles from what is now Denmark and Saxons from northwestern Germany, this group invaded Britain in the 440s after the Roman army had been recalled from the province to defend Italy against the Visigoths. They established their kingdoms by taking territory away from the local Celtic peoples and the remaining Roman inhabitants. Gradually, Anglo-Saxon culture replaced the local traditions of the island's eastern regions: the Celts there lost most of their language, and Christianity survived only in Wales and Ireland.

The western empire's military weakness led to a change in leadership in 476 that has traditionally, but simplistically, been called the "fall of Rome." In that year a non-Roman commander replaced the Roman emperor in the west, and no Roman would rule there ever again. The idea of a "fall" comes from the best-selling, multivolume work that made it famous—*The Decline and Fall of the Roman Empire* by the English historian Edward Gibbon (1737–1794). The real story's details, however, reveal the complexity of the political transformation of the western empire under the pressure of the external migrations. The weakness of the imperial army in the west had forced the western emperors to employ non-Roman officers to lead the defense of Italy. By the middle of the fifth century, one general after another decided who would serve as puppet emperor under his

■ Mosaic of Upper-Class Country Life

This fourth-century mosaic, measuring fourteen-by-eighteen feet, covered a floor in a country villa at Carthage in North Africa. It shows the life of an elite couple on their estate at different seasons of the year. Their house, so large it had towers and a second-story colonnade, stands as a fortified compound at the center. The top third of the mosaic shows the lady of the house sitting in park-like surroundings while her servants and tenants tend to animals; winter activities are shown at the left, summer activities at the right. In the middle third, hunters pursue game. The bottom third shows the lady in a springtime setting (on the left) and her husband sitting (on the right) among characteristic fall activities. A servant hands the husband a roll addressed "to the master Julius." Such estates provided security and prosperity for their owners but also made desirable targets for the Vandal invaders of North Africa. (Le Musée du Bardo, Tunis.)

control. The last such unfortunate "emperor" was a usurper; his father, Orestes, a former aide to Attila, had rebelled against the emperor Julius Nepos in 475 and raised his young son to the throne. He gave the boy emperor the name Romulus Augustulus, meant to recall both Rome's founder and its first emperor. In 476, after a dispute over pay, soldiers murdered Orestes and deposed the boy; pitied as an innocent child, Romulus was given a safe home and a generous pension. The rebels' leader, Odoacer, did not choose another emperor. Instead, seeking to block Nepos's campaign to regain the throne, he had the Roman Senate ask Zeno, the eastern emperor, to recognize his leadership in return for his recognizing Zeno as sole emperor. Odoacer thereafter led Italy supposedly as the eastern emperor's assistant, but in fact, he ruled as he liked.

In 488, Zeno plotted to rid himself of Theodoric, a Germanic general living in Constantinople, by sending him to fight Odoacer, whom the emperor had found too independent. Eliminating Odoacer by 493, Theodoric (r. 493–526) established the Ostrogothic kingdom to rule Italy from the capital at Ravenna. He built legitimacy for his new state by preserving traditional Roman institutions, especially the Senate and the office of consul. An Arian Christian, Theodoric followed Constantine's example by announcing a policy of religious toleration: "No one can be forced to believe against his will." Many members of the Roman elite, such as the famous scholars Boethius and Cassiodorus, cooperated with Theodoric to try to establish stable government. Unfortunately, the Ostrogothic emperor showed that he was just as suspicious as any Roman emperor had ever been by imprisoning and executing Boethius, whom he had made a consul but later accused of disloyalty with other senators. While in prison, Boethius wrote the *Consolation of Philosophy*, a book that explained divine providence according to the ideas of Stoic and Neoplatonic philosophy as well as those of Augustine. Boethius's scholarship became vastly influential in medieval Europe.

As in the other kingdoms, the Ostrogoths took over the Roman traditions that supported their new state's legitimacy and stability. Theodoric and his Ostrogothic nobles wanted to enjoy the empire's luxury and prestige, not destroy them. For this reason, modern scholars consider it more accurate to speak of the western empire's "transformation" than its "fall" (Map 6.4), even though the process was often violent.

The Franks were the Germanic people who transformed Roman Gaul into Francia (from which the name *France* comes). They first moved into that region with the permission of the western emperor in the early fourth century. In 507, their king, Clovis (r. 485–511), overthrew the Visigothic king in southern Gaul with support from the eastern emperor. When the emperor named him an honorary Roman consul, Clovis celebrated this ancient honor by having himself crowned with a diadem in the style of the dominate's emperors. He carved out western Europe's largest new kingdom in what is today mostly France, growing larger than the neighboring and rival kingdoms of the Burgundians and Alemanni in eastern Gaul. Probably persuaded by his Christian wife Clotilda to believe that God had helped him defeat the Alemanni, Clovis proclaimed himself an orthodox Christian. To build stability, he forged good relations with Gaul's bishops, who helped him control the people in their regions.

Clovis's dynasty, called Merovingian after the legendary Frankish ancestor Merovech, lasted for another two hundred years, far longer than most other non-Roman royal families in the west. The Merovingian state anticipated the kingdom that emerged later as the forerunner of modern France. The Merovingians survived so long because their new state combined barbarian military might with Roman social and legal traditions.

■ MAP 6.4 Peoples and Kingdoms of the Roman World, c. 526

The provinces of the Roman Empire had always been home to a population diverse in language and ethnicity. By the early sixth century, the territory of the western empire had fragmented into diverse political units as well. Italy and most of the former western provinces were kingdoms created and ruled by non-Roman peoples who had moved into former Roman territory over the past several centuries. The eastern empire (the Byzantine Empire) remained under the political control of the emperor in Constantinople. Justinian, who became Byzantine emperor in 527, made it his mission to try to reunite the eastern and western halves of the empire by force. How much do these states correspond to the modern boundaries of states in Europe? **For more help analyzing this map,** *see the map activity for this chapter in the* ONLINE STUDY GUIDE *at* **bedfordstmartins.com/huntconcise.**

Mixing Traditions

The political transformation of the western Roman empire—the replacement of imperial government by non-Roman kingdoms—fueled innovative social and cultural transformations in Europe. Newcomers and long-time Roman inhabitants combined their traditions to create new ways of life, above all law codes, but they failed to build a strong economy.

The memory of Rome's glory persisted through these changes. Visigoth king Athaulf (r. 410–415), having married a Roman noblewoman, explained his goals in this way:

> At the start I wanted to erase the Romans' name and turn their land into a Gothic empire, myself doing what Augustus had done. But I have learned that the Goths' freewheeling wildness will never accept the rule of law, and that a state with no law is no state. Thus, I have more wisely chosen another path to glory: reviving the Roman name with Gothic strength. I pray that future generations will remember me as the founder of a Roman restoration.

Roman law greatly influenced the new kings in their efforts to organize new states. They had never before had written laws; now that they had transformed themselves into kings ruling Romans as well as their own people, they wanted legal codes to establish justice and order. The Visigothic kings were the first non-Roman leaders to create a written law code. Composed in Latin and dependent on Roman legal tradition, it made the payment of fines and compensation the primary method for resolving disputes.

Clovis also relied on written law in his Merovingian kingdom. His code, published in Latin, supported social order by setting clear penalties for specific crimes. In particular, he established a system of payments intended to defuse feuds between individuals and between clans. This system of penalties included **wergild**, the payment a murderer had to make as compensation for his crime. Most of the money was paid to the victim's kin, but the king received perhaps one-third of the amount.

Because law codes correspond to social values, the differing payments offer a glimpse of the relative social value of different categories of people in Clovis's kingdom. The penalty for murdering a woman of childbearing age, a boy under twelve, or a man in the king's service was a massive fine of six hundred gold coins, enough to buy six hundred cattle. The fine for murdering a woman past childbearing age (specified as sixty years), a young girl, or a freeborn man was two hundred gold coins; for murdering ordinary slaves, thirty-five.

The migrations that transformed the west harmed its already weak economy. The Vandals damaged many towns in Gaul. In the countryside, now outside the control of any central government, wealthy Romans from the social elite built villas on large estates staffed by tenants bound to the land like slaves. The owners of these estates operated them as self-sufficient units by producing all they needed, defending themselves against raids, and keeping their distance from any authorities. Craving isolation, the owners shunned membership on city councils and tax collection—the public services that had supplied the lifeblood of Roman administration—although the wealthiest boasted an annual income rivaling that of an entire region in the old western empire. The elites' withdrawal from public service withered Roman provincial government, and the new kingdoms never matured sufficiently to replace its services to the population.

A few provincial Romans helped transmit ancient learning to later ages. Cassiodorus, one of the scholars who had worked for Theodoric, founded a monastery on his ancestral estate in Italy in the 550s following his career in imperial administration. He gave the monks the task of copying manuscripts to keep their contents alive as old texts disintegrated. His own book *Institutions*, composed in the 550s to guide his monks, explained the respect for tradition that kept classical traditions alive: in prescribing the works a person of superior education should read, it included ancient secular texts as well as Scripture and Christian literature. The most energetic effort to perpetuate the Roman past, however, came from the eastern empire.

> ■ **REVIEW:** *What societal changes took place among non-Romans who came to the Roman Empire from around 370 to the 550s?*

The Byzantine Empire in the East

The eastern Roman Empire avoided the transformations that reshaped western Europe. Trade routes and diverse agriculture kept the east richer than the west, and the eastern emperors minimized the effect of the foreign migrations on their territory and blunted the aggression of the Sassanid kingdom in Persia with force, diplomacy, and bribery. By the early sixth century, the empire's eastern half had achieved such power, riches, and ambition that historians have given it a new name, the Byzantine Empire; its emperors held power until 1453.

The Byzantine emperors saw themselves as continuing the Roman Empire and guarding its culture against barbarians. Justinian (r. 527–565), the most famous of the early Byzantine emperors, took this mission so seriously that he nearly bankrupted his treasury with wars to recover the western empire; he tried to impose religious orthodoxy to win God's will for his projects. One especially significant contribution of the early Byzantine Empire to later history was its crucial role in preserving classical literature and learning, which nearly disappeared in the west.

Byzantine Society

The sixth-century Byzantine Empire enjoyed a prosperity that western Europe had lost. Members of the elite spent freely on luxury goods imported from China and India: silk, precious stones, and expensive spices such as pepper. People of all kinds flocked to the empire's largest cities—Constantinople, Damascus, and Alexandria. There, churches with soaring domes testified to the Byzantines' confidence in God's power and favor.

■ Justinian and His Court in Ravenna

This mosaic scene centered on the Byzantine emperor Justinian (r. 527–565) is opposite Theodora's mosaic in San Vitale's Church in Ravenna. Justinian and Theodora had finished building the church, which the Ostrogothic king Theodoric had started, to celebrate their successful campaign to restore Italy to the Roman Empire and retake control of the western capital, Ravenna. The soldiers at left remind viewers of the rulers' aggressive military policy in service of imperial unity. The presence of Maximianus, bishop of Ravenna, standing on Justinian's left and identified by name, stresses the theme of cooperation between bishops and emperors in ruling the world. (Scala/Art Resource, NY.)

Continuing a Roman imperial tradition, the Byzantine emperors sponsored costly religious festivals and entertainments to rally public support. Rich and poor alike crowded city squares, theaters, and racetracks on these spirited occasions; chariot racing aroused the hottest passions. Constantinople's residents, for example, divided themselves into competitive factions—called Blues and Greens after the racing colors of their favorite charioteers—that combined religious and sports rivalries: orthodox Christians became Blues, Monophysites Greens. They clashed as frequently over theological arguments as over race results.

The eastern emperors did everything they could to preserve "Romanness." They feared that contact with non-Roman peoples would make their empire "barbarian,"

■ Theodora and Her Court in Ravenna

This mosaic shows the empress Theodora (c. 500–548) and her court. It was placed on one wall of the church of San Vitale in Ravenna, facing the matching scene of her husband, Justinian, and his attendants. Theodora wears the jewels, pearls, and rich robes characteristic of Byzantine rulers. She extends in her hands a gem-encrusted bowl, evidently a present to the church; her gesture imitates the gift-giving of the Magi to the baby Jesus, the scene illustrated on the hem of her garment. Like Honorius on page 212, a circle around her head indicates special holiness. (Scala/Art Resource, NY.)

as in the west. Like the western emperors, they employed foreign mercenaries, but they tried to keep foreign customs from influencing the empire's residents. They paid special attention to clothing styles. Like the western emperor Honorius in the early fifth century, eastern emperors banned Constantinople's residents from wearing barbarian-style outfits (especially heavy boots and clothing made from animal furs) instead of traditional Roman clothes (sandals or light shoes and robes).

The Byzantines referred to themselves as "the Romans" because they saw themselves as the heirs and protectors of ancient Roman culture. At the same time, they spoke Greek as their native language and used Latin only for government and military communication. (The Latin-speaking western empire referred to them as

"Greeks.") Since Byzantine society was deeply multilingual and multiethnic, preserving an unchanging Roman identity was a hopeless goal. Many people spoke their traditional languages, such as Phrygian and Cappadocian in western Asia Minor, Armenian farther east, and Syriac and other Aramaic dialects in the Levant. Travelers around the empire heard countless languages, saw varying styles of dress, and encountered numerous ethnic groups.

For the Byzantines, Romanness included Christianity, but their theological diversity rivaled their ethnic variety. Bitter controversies over doctrine divided eastern Christians, and emperors joined forces with bishops to impose orthodoxy. They generally preferred words to swords to pressure heretics to accept orthodox theology, but they used violence when persuasion failed. Resorting to such extreme measures against fellow Christians was necessary, they believed, to save lost souls and preserve God's goodwill toward the empire. The persecution of nonorthodox Christian subjects by Christian emperors demonstrated the depth of passion created by the desire for a unitary identity.

In patriarchal Byzantine society, most women followed ancient Mediterranean tradition by focusing their lives on their households and minimizing contact with men outside that circle. Law barred women from fulfilling many public functions, such as witnessing wills. Subject to the authority of their fathers and husbands, women veiled their heads (though not their faces) to show modesty. Christian theology made divorce more difficult than under Roman law and discouraged remarriage, even for widows. Stiffer legal penalties for sexual offenses also developed. Female prostitution remained legal, but emperors raised the penalties for people forcing women (children or slaves) to become prostitutes.

As always, women in the imperial family lived by different rules than ordinary women and could directly influence government. Theodora (c. 500–548), wife of the emperor Justinian, became the most influential and talked about of all Byzantine empresses. Using her brains and beauty to overcome her low social status (she was the daughter of a bear trainer and then an actress accused of performing pornographic scenes), she married Justinian and advised him in every part of his rule. She helped him make personnel choices for his administration, strongly pushed her religious views in the continuing disputes over Christian doctrine, and rallied her husband's courage in time of crisis. John Lydus, a high-ranking administrator, judged her "superior in intelligence to any man."

Byzantine government made the social hierarchy more rigid than ever because it provided services according to people's wealth. It required piles of paperwork and fees for official transactions, from commercial permits to legal complaints. Without bribery, nothing got done. This arrangement benefited people with status and money: they used their social connections to get a hearing from the right official and used their wealth to pay bribes to get fast action.

The poor, by contrast, could not afford the large bribes that government officials expected. Since interest rates were high, they had to take on backbreaking debt to raise the cash to pay officials to help them. This system saved the emperors money: they paid civil servants small salaries because bribes from the public supplemented their incomes. John Lydus, for example, reported that he earned thirty times his annual salary in bribes during his first year in office. To keep unlimited extortion from destroying the system, the emperors published an official list of the maximum bribes that employees could demand. Overall, however, this kind of government generated enormous hostility among poorer subjects and did nothing to encourage public support for the emperors' plans for glory and conquest.

The Reign of Justinian, 527–565

Justinian dreamed of reuniting the empire as it had been under Augustus. Born to a Latin-speaking family in a small Balkan town, he rose rapidly in imperial service until 527, when he succeeded his uncle as emperor. During his reign, he launched military expeditions to try to win back western Europe and North Africa from the non-Roman kingdoms. His desire to build imperial glory led him to decorate Constantinople with magnificent and costly buildings. He was also an intellectual—the first on the throne since Julian in the 360s—whose passion for the law and theology drove him to push reforms with the same goals cherished by all previous emperors, whether Christian or polytheist: to preserve social order based on hierarchy and maintain divine favor for himself and his subjects.

Unfortunately for Justinian's dream, the huge expense of his plans created social unrest. His taxes became so heavy and his chief tax collector so violent that they provoked a major riot in 532. Known as the "Nika Riot," it erupted when the Blue and Green factions gathering in Constantinople's hippodrome to watch chariot races united against the emperor, shouting "Nika! Nika!" ("Win! Win!"). After nine days of violence that left much of the capital in ashes, a panicky Justinian prepared to abandon his throne and flee. Theodora, however, showed the steel in her soul by telling him: "Once born, no one can escape dying, but for one who has held imperial power it would be unbearable to be a fugitive. May I never take off my imperial robes of purple, nor live to see the day when those who meet me will not greet me as their ruler." Shamed, Justinian called out his guard, who crushed the rebellion by slaughtering thirty thousand rioters trapped in the racetrack.

Justinian's most ambitious plan was to reunite the eastern and western empires. His generals defeated the Vandals and Ostrogoths after campaigns that in some cases took decades to complete. At enormous expense, imperial armies reoccupied Italy, the Dalmatian coast, Sicily, Sardinia, Corsica, part of southern Spain, and western North Africa by 562. These successes temporarily restored the old empire's geography: Justinian's territory stretched from the Atlantic to the western edge of Mesopotamia (see "Mapping the West," page 254).

These triumphs carried a tragic price: inflicting horrible damage on Europe and emptying Justinian's treasury. Italy endured the greatest damage; the war there against the Goths inflicted death and destruction on a massive scale. The east suffered as Justinian squeezed ever more taxes out of his already overburdened population to finance the western wars and bribe the Sassanids in Mesopotamia not to attack while his eastern defenses were weak. The tax burden crippled the economy, leading to constant banditry in the countryside. Crowds poured into the capital from rural areas, seeking relief from poverty and robbers.

Natural disasters added to Justinian's troubles. In the 540s, an epidemic killed a third of the empire's inhabitants; a quarter of a million died in Constantinople alone, half the capital's population. This was only the first in a long series of diseases that erased millions of people in the eastern empire over the next two centuries. The loss of so many people created a shortage of army recruits, forced the emperors to hire expensive mercenaries, and left many farms vacant, thus hurting tax revenues.

The wars and the resulting financial pressures made Justinian crave stability; to strengthen his authority, he emphasized the emperor's closeness to God and his authority over the people. He had his artists portray the symbols of rule in a Christian context. A gleaming mosaic in his church at San Vitale in Ravenna, for example, displayed a dramatic vision of the emperor's role: Justinian standing at the center of the universe shoulder to shoulder with both the ancient Hebrew leader Abraham and Christ. In legal matters, Justinian proclaimed the emperor the "living law," reviving a Hellenistic royal doctrine.

Justinian's building program in Constantinople expressed his religious devotion and worldly power. Most spectacular of all was his magnificent reconstruction of Constantine's Church of the Holy Wisdom (Hagia Sophia). Its location facing the palace matched Justinian's emphasis on combining imperial and Christian authority. Creating a new design for churches, his architects erected a huge building on a square plan capped by a dome 107 feet across and soaring 160 feet above the floor. Its interior walls glowed like the sun from the light reflecting off their four acres of gold mosaics. Imported marble of every color added to the sparkling effect. When he first entered his masterpiece, dedicated in 538, Justinian exclaimed, "Solomon, I have outdone you," boasting that he had bested the glorious temple the ancient king built for the Hebrews.

Justinian's building up of the emperor's power made Constantinople still more important and reduced the local independence of the empire's other cities. Their councils ceased to govern; imperial officials took over instead. Provincial elites still had to ensure full payment of their area's taxes, but they lost the compensating reward of deciding local matters. Now the imperial government made all decisions and determined people's social status. Men of property from the provinces who wanted a public career knew they could satisfy their ambitions only by joining the imperial administration.

■ **The Soaring Architecture of Hagia Sophia**

Golden mosaics originally reflected a dazzling light from the interior of Hagia Sophia ("Holy Wisdom"), the enormous church that the Byzantine emperor Justinian built in the 530s C.E. near his palace in Constantinople. A central dome, 184 feet high and supported by four arches resting on massive piers, capped the church's vast interior; the ring of windows at the base of the dome is just visible at the top of the picture. Hagia Sophia became a mosque after the Turks captured the city in 1453; the large medallions contain religious quotations in Arabic. Now a museum, Hagia Sophia continues to host people offering prayers. (© Adam Woolfitt/Corbis.)

To strengthen his control, Justinian had the empire's laws codified to bring uniformity to the inconsistent decisions of earlier emperors; the final edition of his *Codex* (set of laws) appeared in 534. A team of scholars also condensed millions of words to produce the *Digest* in 533, a collection of past decisions intended to make legal cases go faster and provide class materials for law schools. This collection, written like the others in Latin and therefore readable in the western empire, influenced legal scholars for centuries. Justinian's experts also wrote a textbook for students in 533, the *Institutes*, which proclaimed the principles of a just life: "live honorably, harm no one else, and give to each his own"; it remained on law school reading lists until modern times.

To fulfill his sacred duty to protect the empire, Justinian enacted reforms to guarantee religious orthodoxy. Like the emperors before him, he believed his world would suffer if its divine protector became angered by the presence of religious offenders. Harshly enforcing laws against polytheists, he ordered them to be baptized or else lose their lands and official positions. Three times he purged Christians whom he could not convince to accept his version of orthodoxy. In pursuit of sexual purity, his laws made sex between men illegal for the first time in Roman history. Homosexual marriage, apparently not uncommon earlier, had been officially prohibited in 342, but penalties had never before been imposed on men engaging in homosexual activity. All the previous emperors, for example, had simply taxed male prostitutes. The legal status of homosexual activity between women is unclear; it probably counted as criminal adultery for married women.

A brilliant theologian, Justinian tried to unite orthodox and Monophysite Christians by revising the creed of the Council of Chalcedon. But church leaders in Rome and Constantinople had become too bitterly divided to agree on a unified church. The church's eastern and western divisions were by now launched on the diverging courses that would climax in a formal schism five hundred years later. Perhaps no emperor could have done better, but Justinian's drive for religious orthodoxy only drove Christians further apart and worked against his dream of a reunited Roman world.

Preserving Classical Literature

The empire's Christianization endangered classical literature—from plays and histories to speeches and novels—because these works were polytheist, and therefore many Christians thought they were the work of the devil. The real danger to the survival of pre-Christian literature, however, stemmed less from active censorship than from simple neglect. As Christians became authors in great numbers, their works displaced the ancient texts of Greece and Rome as the most important literature of the age. Fortunately for later times, however, the Byzantine Empire helped preserve at least part of the famous works of the past.

Classical texts survived because elite Christian culture was rooted in traditional polytheist learning, both Greek and Roman. Latin literature continued to be read in the eastern empire because the administration was bilingual; official documents were published in Rome's original language along with Greek translations. Latin scholarship in the east received a boost when Justinian's wars sent Latin-speaking scholars fleeing from Italy for safety to Constantinople. Their work there helped conserve many works that might otherwise have disappeared in the destruction in the west.

Byzantine scholars valued classical literature because they regarded it as the basis of a high-level education. Many of the classical works available today survived because they served as school texts in the eastern empire. A basic knowledge of famous pre-Christian classics was a requirement for a good career in government service, the goal of most ambitious students. In the words of an imperial decree from 360, "No person shall obtain a post of the first rank unless it shall be shown that he excels in long practice of liberal studies, and that he is so polished in literary matters that words flow from his pen faultlessly."

IMPORTANT DATES

284	Diocletian becomes Roman emperor	c. 413–426	Augustine writes *City of God*
303	Diocletian begins Great Persecution of Christians	418	Western emperor settles Visigoths in southwestern Gaul
312	Constantine wins the Battle of the Milvian Bridge in Rome and converts to Christianity	429	Vandals capture Roman North Africa after invading Spain
c. 323	Pachomius in Upper Egypt establishes the first monasteries for men and women	440s	Anglo-Saxons take over Roman Britain
324	Constantine refounds Byzantium as Constantinople, the "new Rome"	451	Council of Chalcedon
325	Council of Nicaea	476	"Fall of the Roman Empire" when German commander Odoacer deposes the final western emperor, Romulus Augustulus
361–363	Julian attempts to restore polytheism as the state religion	c. 480–553	Life of Benedict of Nursia, who devises the Benedictine rule
391	Theodosius bans polytheist sacrifice and closes the temples of traditional Roman religion	493–526	Theodoric establishes Ostrogothic kingdom in Italy
395	Roman Empire is split into western and eastern sections	507	Clovis establishes Frankish kingdom in Gaul
410	Visigoths sack Rome	c. 530	Plato's Academy in Athens closes
		538	Justinian dedicates Church of the Holy Wisdom

What also helped classical literature survive was the use of the principles of ancient rhetoric for effective presentation of Christian theology. When Ambrose, bishop of Milan from 374 to 397, composed the first systematic description of Christian ethics for young priests, he imitated the great classical orator Cicero. Theologians employed the dialogue form pioneered by Plato to refute Christian heresies, and polytheist traditions in writing biography influenced the hugely popular Christian literature of saints' lives. Similarly, Christian artists used polytheist traditions to communicate their beliefs in paintings, mosaics, and carved reliefs. Artists showing Christ with a sunburst surrounding his head, for example, took their inspiration from polytheist depictions of the radiant Sun as a god (see page 224).

Ironically, a technological innovation related to the growth of Christian literature also helped preserve classical polytheist texts. Previously, scribes had written

■ **MAPPING THE WEST The Byzantine Empire and Western Europe, c. 600**
Justinian employed brilliant generals and spent huge sums of money to reconquer Italy, North Africa, and part of Spain to reunite the western and eastern halves of the old Roman Empire. His wars to regain Italy and North Africa eliminated the Ostrogothic and Vandal kingdoms, respectively, but at a huge cost in effort, time—the war in Italy took twenty years—and expense. The resources of the eastern empire were so exhausted that following emperors could not maintain the reunification. By the early seventh century, the Visigoths had taken back all of Spain. Africa, despite serious revolts by local Berber tribes, remained under imperial control until the Arab conquest of the seventh century, but within five years of Justinian's death, the Lombards set up a new kingdom that controlled a large section of Italy. Never again would anyone attempt to reestablish a universal Roman Empire. Compare the political divisions on this map with the one at the end of Chapter 5 (page 209) showing Roman territory more than two centuries earlier.

books on sheets made from thin animal skin or paper made from papyrus, gluing the sheets together and attaching rods at both ends to form a scroll. Readers had to unroll the books to read them. For ease of use, Christians produced their literature in the form of the codex—a book with bound pages. Eventually the codex became the standard form of book production in the Byzantine world. Because the codex was less subject to damage from rolling and unrolling and could contain text more efficiently than scrolls, which were inefficient for long works, this invention aided the preservation of all forms of literature.

Despite the continuing importance of classical Greek and Latin literature in Byzantine education and rhetoric, its survival remained uncertain in a war-torn world governed by Christians. Knowledge of Greek in the transformed west faded so drastically that almost no one could read the original versions of Homer's *Iliad* and *Odyssey*, the traditional foundations of a polytheist literary education. Latin fared better, and scholars such as Augustine and Jerome knew Rome's ancient literature extremely well. But they also saw its classics as too seductive because the pleasure of reading them could distract Christians from worshiping God. Jerome once had a nightmare of being condemned on Judgment Day for having been a Ciceronian instead of a Christian.

The closing around 530 of Plato's Academy, founded in Athens more than nine hundred years earlier, demonstrated the dangers for classical learning in the Byzantine world. This most famous of classical schools finally shut its doors when many of its scholars moved to Persia to escape restrictions on polytheists and its revenues dwindled because the Athenian elite, its traditional supporters, were increasingly Christianized. The Neoplatonist school at Alexandria, by contrast, continued; its leader John Philoponus (c. 490–570) was a Christian. In addition to Christian theology, Philoponus wrote commentaries on Aristotle's works; some of his ideas anticipated those of Galileo a thousand years later. John's work achieved the kind of blending of old and new that was one fruitful possibility of the transformation of the late Roman world—that is, he was a Christian subject of the Byzantine Empire in Egypt, heading a school founded long before by polytheists, studying the works of an ancient Greek philosopher as the inspiration for his innovative scholarship. The strong possibility that the present could learn from the past would continue as Western civilization once again remade itself in medieval times.

■ **REVIEW:** *What role did the emperor Justinian see himself playing in Roman history?*

Conclusion

Tension between unity and division characterized the late Roman Empire. Diocletian's reorganization delayed the empire's fragmentation but opened the way to its eventual separation in 395 into western and eastern halves. From then on, Roman history increasingly divided into two regional streams, even though emperors as late as Justinian in the sixth century clung to the dream of reuniting the empire and restoring the glory of Rome's Golden Age.

Multiple causes interacted to destroy the Roman Empire's unity, beginning with the catastrophic losses of property and people during the third-century crisis, which hit the west harder than the east. The late-fourth-century migrations of non-Roman peoples fleeing the Huns further weakened centralized rule. When Roman authorities failed to absorb these tribes peacefully, the newcomers violently created kingdoms that replaced imperial government in the west. This change transformed not only the west's politics, society, and economy but also the tribes themselves, who developed ethnic identities while organizing themselves into new political states. The economic troubles accompanying these transformations destroyed the elite's commitment to public office and public service, which had been essential to imperial government. Wealthy nobles in the west retreated to self-sufficient country estates and avoided local politics.

The eastern empire fared better economically and avoided the worst of the violent effects from the foreign migrations, as the Byzantine emperors sought to preserve an idealized "Romanness" that they believed would strengthen their rule. The financial drain of pursuing unity through war against the new kingdoms, however, fueled social unrest by raising tax rates to punishing levels, while the concentration of power in the capital weakened other cities, the traditional centers for collecting taxes and maintaining social order.

In religion, the emperor Constantine's conversion to Christianity in 312 marked a turning point in Western civilization. Nevertheless, Christianization of the Roman world proceeded slowly because many polytheists were reluctant to abandon their traditional religion. Christians fiercely disagreed among themselves over doctrine, to the point of violence. Some of them abandoned everyday society to live as monks, to come closer to God personally and to pray for mercy for the world. Monastic life redefined the meaning of holiness by creating communities of God's heroes who withdrew from this world to devote their service to glorifying the next.

In the end, the emperor's dream of political and religious unity faded before the divisive forces of the human spirit combined with the unpredictable effects, especially economic, of political and social transformation. Nevertheless, the memory of Roman power, culture, and glory remained potent and present, providing an influential inheritance to the peoples and states that would become Rome's heirs.

■ MAKING CONNECTIONS

1. *What similarities existed between traditional Roman religion and Christianity as official state religion?*

2. *Compare the fates of the eastern and western empires after they split apart.*

■ **FOR FURTHER EXPLORATION**

For further reading and online research ideas, see the Suggested References on page SR-3 at the back of the book.

For practice quizzes, a customized study plan, and other study tools, see the ONLINE STUDY GUIDE at bedfordstmartins.com/huntconcise.

For primary-source material from this period, see Chapter 6 in *Sources of THE MAKING OF THE WEST: A CONCISE HISTORY*, Second Edition.

The Heirs of
the Roman Empire
600–750

ACCORDING TO A WRITER who was not very sympathetic to the Byzantines, one night Emperor Heraclius (r. 610–641) had a dream: "Verily [he was told] there shall come against thee a circumcised nation, and they shall vanquish thee and take possession of the land." Heraclius thought the vision foretold an uprising of the Jews, and he ordered mass baptisms into the Christian faith in all his provinces. "But," continued the story,

> *after a few days there appeared a man of the Arabs, from the southern districts, that is to say, from Mecca or its neighborhood, whose name was Muhammad; and he brought back the worshipers of idols to the knowledge of the One God. . . . And he took possession of Damascus and Syria, and crossed the Jordan and dammed it up. And the Lord abandoned the army of the Romans before him.*

This tale, however fanciful, recalls the most astonishing development of the seventh century: the Arabs conquered much of the Roman Empire and became one of its heirs. The western and eastern parts of the empire, both diminished, were now joined by yet a third power—Arab and Muslim. The resulting triad has endured in

■ **Mosque at Damascus (detail)**
Islam conquered the Byzantines; then Islam was "conquered" in turn by Byzantine culture. For the grand mosque at Damascus, his capital city, the Umayyad caliph al-Walid employed Byzantine-trained mosaicists, who depicted classical motifs—buildings, animals, vegetation—in a style that harked back to the classical past. However, the artists scrupulously avoided depicting human beings, in this way conforming to one strain of Islamic thought that argued against figural representations.
(The Bridgeman Art Library.)

various forms to the present day: the western third of the old Roman Empire became western Europe; the eastern third, occupying what is now Turkey, Greece, and some of the Balkans, became part of eastern Europe and helped to create Russia; and North Africa, together with the ancient Near East (now called the Middle East), remains the Arab world.

As diverse as these cultures are today, they share many of the same roots. All were heirs of Hellenistic and Roman traditions. All adhered to monotheism. The western and eastern halves of the empire had Christianity in common, although they differed at times in interpreting it. The Arab world's religion, Islam, accepted the same one God that Christians did but considered Jesus a prophet of God rather than his son.

The history of the seventh and eighth centuries is a story of adaptation and transformation. Historians consider the changes important enough to signal the end of one era—antiquity—and the beginning of another—the Middle Ages.* During this period, all three heirs of the Roman Empire combined elements of their heritage with new values, interests, and conditions. The divergences among them resulted from disparities in geographical and climatic conditions, material and human resources, skills, and local traditions. But these differences should not obscure the fact that the Byzantine, Muslim, and western European worlds were sibling cultures.

Byzantium: A Christian Empire under Siege

Emperor Justinian (r. 527–565) had tried to re-create the old Roman Empire. On the surface he succeeded. His empire once again included Italy, North Africa, and the Balkans. Vestiges of old Roman society persisted: an educated elite maintained its prestige, town governments continued to function, and old myths and legends were retold in poetry and depicted on silver plates and chests. By 600, however, the eastern empire began to undergo a transformation as striking as the one that had earlier remade the western half. Historians call this reorganized empire the Byzantine Empire, or Byzantium, after the Greek name for the city of Constantinople. From the last third of the sixth century, Byzantium was almost constantly at war, and its territory shrank drastically. Cultural and political change came as well. Cities—except for a few such as Constantinople—decayed, and the countryside became the focus of government and military administration. Following these shifts, the old elite largely disappeared, and classical learning gave way to new forms of education, mainly religious in content. The traditional styles of urban life, dependent on public gathering places and community spirit, faded away.

---

*The term *Middle Ages* was coined in the sixteenth century to refer to the period "in between"—in the middle of—the ancient and modern periods.

■ MAP 7.1 Byzantine and Sassanid Empires, c. 600

Justinian hoped to re-create the old Roman Empire, but just a century after his death Italy was largely conquered by the Lombards. Meanwhile, the Byzantine Empire had to contend with the Sassanid Empire to its east. In 600, these two major powers faced each other uneasily. Three years later, the Sassanid king attacked Byzantine territory. The resulting wars, which lasted until 627, exhausted both empires and left them open to invasion by the Arabs.

Wars on the Frontiers, c. 570–750

From about 570 to 750, the Byzantine Empire waged war against invaders on all fronts. Its first major challenge came from the east, from the **Sassanid Empire** of Persia. Its second came from new groups—Lombards, Slavs, Avars, Bulgars, and Muslims—who pushed into the empire. In the wake of these onslaughts, Byzantium was transformed.

The Persian challenge was the most predictable: since the third century, the Sassanid kings and Roman emperors had fought sporadically but never with decisive effect on either side. But in the middle of the sixth century, the Sassanids chose to concentrate their activities on their western half, Mesopotamia (today Iraq), nearer the Byzantine border (Map 7.1). Reforming the army, which previously had depended on nobles who could provide their own arms, the Sassanid kings began to pay and arm new warriors drawn from the lower nobility. With the army more fully their

■ A Sassanid King

His head topped by a mighty horned headdress, this sixth- or seventh-century representation of a Sassanid ruler evokes the full majesty of a king of kings. A glance at "The Great King of Persia" on page 30 shows that traditional Persian sculpture was not, as here, three dimensional. The new style is explained by the influence of Greek and Roman sculpture, despite the enmity between Sassanid Persia and Byzantium (heir of Greece and Rome) at the time.
(Réunion des Musées Nationaux/Art Resource, NY.)

own, the Sassanid kings tried to re-create the Persian Empire of Xerxes and Darius (see page 104). Under Chosroes II (r. 591–628), the Persians invaded the Byzantine Empire in 603. By 613, they had taken Damascus; by 619, they dominated Egypt. But after reorganizing his own army, Byzantine emperor Heraclius regained all of Byzantium's lost territory by 627. The chief outcome of these confrontations was the exhaustion of both sides.

The Byzantines could ill afford this weakness. From every side, new groups were pushing into their empire. The Lombards, a Germanic people, arrived in northern Italy in 568 and by 572 were masters of the Po valley and some inland regions in Italy's south, leaving the Byzantines only Bari, Calabria, and Sicily as well as Rome and a narrow swath of land through Italy's middle called the Exarchate of Ravenna.

The Byzantines were equally weak in the face of the Slavs, Bulgars, and Avars just beyond the Danube River. The Slavs conducted lightning raids on the Balkan countryside (part of Byzantium at the time) and, joined by the Avars—nomadic pastoralists and warriors—they attacked Byzantine cities as well. The Bulgars, entering what is now Bulgaria in the 670s, defeated the Byzantine army and in 681 forced the emperor to recognize the state they carved out of formerly Byzantine territory. This Bulgar state crippled Byzantine influence in the Balkans and helped isolate them from western Europe. Avar and Slavic control of the Balkans effectively cut off trade and travel between Constantinople and the cities of the Dalmatian coast, and the Bulgar state threw a political barrier across the Danube River. Perhaps as a result of this physical separation, Byzantine historians ceased to be interested in the West, and eastern scholars no longer bothered to learn Latin. The two halves of the Roman Empire, once united, communicated very little in the seventh century.

While fighting these groups on their northern frontier, the Byzantines at the same time had to contend with the Arabs, whose military prowess was creating a new empire and spreading a new religion, Islam. In the hundred years between 630 and 730, the Muslim Arabs succeeded in conquering much of the Byzantine Empire, at times attacking the walls of Constantinople itself. No wonder the patriarch of Jerusalem, chief bishop of the entire Levant, saw in the Arab onslaught the impending end of the world: "Behold," he said, "the Abomination of Desolation, spoken of by the Prophet Daniel, that standeth in the Holy Place."

From an Urban to a Rural Way of Life

As Byzantine borders shrank, Byzantines confronted new rulers and learned to accommodate them. Slavs and Avars settling in the Balkans intermingled with the indigenous population, gradually absorbing local agricultural techniques and burial practices while contributing the Slavic language and religious cults. When Byzantine subjects in Syria and Egypt found themselves under Arab rule, they learned to adjust, paying a special tax to their conquerors but continuing to practice their Christian and Jewish religions in peace. In the countryside they were permitted to keep and farm their lands, and their cities remained centers of government, scholarship, and business. For these former Byzantines, daily life remained essentially unchanged.

Ironically, the most radical transformations in seventh- and eighth-century Byzantine life occurred not in the territories conquered but in the shrunken empire itself. Under the ceaseless barrage of invaders, many towns, formerly bustling hubs of trade and centers of the imperial bureaucratic network, vanished or became unrecognizable in their changed way of life. The public activity of marketplaces, theaters, and town squares gave way to the private pursuits of table and hearth. City baths, once places where

The Byzantine Empire, c. 700

people gossiped, made deals, and talked politics and philosophy, disappeared in most Byzantine towns—with the significant exception of Constantinople. Warfare reduced some cities to rubble, and when they were rebuilt, the limited resources available went to construct thick city walls and solid churches instead of large open marketplaces and baths. Markets moved to overcrowded streets that looked much like the open-air bazaars of the modern Middle East. People under siege sought protection rather than community pastimes. In the Byzantine city of Ephesus, for example, the citizens who built the new walls in the seventh century enclosed not the old public edifices but rather their homes and churches. Despite the new emphasis on church buildings, many cities were too impoverished even to repair their churches.

■ The Walls of Constantinople

The thick walls and stone forts built by Emperor Theodosius II (r. 408–450) are still visible at Istanbul. The walls enclosed not only the urban center but rural fields and gardens as well, ensuring that the city could support and feed itself even when under siege. For over a thousand years, the walls helped protect Constantinople from the onslaughts of invaders. (Sonia Halliday Photographs.)

The pressures of war against the Arabs brought a change in Byzantine society parallel to the change in the West a few centuries before, spelling the end of the class of *curiales* (town councilors), the elite that for centuries had mediated between the emperor and the people. But an upper class nevertheless remained: as in the West, bishops and their clergy continued to form a rich and powerful upper stratum even within the declining cities.

In spite of the general urban decay, Constantinople and a few other urban centers retained much of their old vitality. Some industry and trade continued, particularly the manufacture of silk textiles. These were the prestige items of the time, and their production and distribution were monitored by the government. State-controlled factories produced the finest fabrics, which legally could be worn only by the emperor, his court, and his friends. In private factories, merchants, spinners, and weavers turned raw silk into slightly less luxurious cloth for both internal consumption and foreign trade. Even though Byzantium's economic life became increasingly rural and barter-based in the seventh and eighth centuries, the skills, knowledge, and institutions of urban workers made possible long-distance trade and the domestic manufacture of luxury goods.

As urban life declined, agriculture, always the basis of the Byzantine economy, became the center of its social life as well. But unlike the West, where an extremely rich and powerful elite dominated the agricultural economy, the Byzantine Empire of the seventh century was principally a realm of free and semi-free peasant farmers who grew food, herded cattle, and tended vineyards on small plots of land. In the shadow of decaying urban centers, the social world of the farmer was narrow. Two or three neighbors were enough to witness a land transfer. Farmers interacted mostly with their families or with local monasteries. The buffer once provided by the curial class was gone; these families now felt directly the impact of imperial rule.

Eager to strengthen these social developments, the emperors of the seventh and eighth centuries tried to give ordinary family life new institutional importance. Imperial legislation narrowed the grounds for divorce and set new punishments for marital infidelity. Husbands and wives who committed adultery were whipped and fined, and their noses were slit. Abortion was prohibited, and new protections were set in place against incest with children. Mothers were given equal power with fathers over their offspring and, if widowed, became the legal guardians of their minor children and controlled the household property.

The transformations of the countryside went hand in hand with military, political, and cultural changes. On the military front, the Byzantine navy found a potent weapon in "Greek fire," a combustible oil that floated on water and burst into flames upon hitting its target. Determined to win wars on land as well, the imperial government exercised greater autocratic control, hastening the decline of the curial class, wresting power from other elite families, and encouraging the formation of a middle class of farmer-soldiers.

In the seventh century, an emperor, possibly Heraclius, divided the army into region-based regiments called *themes*. Soon the regions (also called *themes*) came to be dominated by the army general, a *strategos* (plural, *strategoi*), who took over civilian as well as military administration. Landless men were lured to join the army with the promise of land and low taxes; they fought side by side with local farmers, who provided their own weapons and horses. The new organization effectively countered frontier attacks.

Military reorganization was matched by a new educational curriculum emphasizing piety over the classics. The old curial elite had studied classical literature and sent their children (above all, their sons) to city schools or tutors to learn to read the works of Greek poets and philosophers. In the face of Islam's challenge, however, eighth-century parents wanted to give their children, both sons and daughters, a Christian religious education. Even with the decay of urban centers, cities and villages often retained an elementary school. There teachers used the Book of Psalms (the Psalter) as their primer. Throughout the seventh and eighth centuries, secular, classical learning remained decidedly out of favor, while dogmatic writings, saints' lives, and devotional works took center stage.

Religion, Politics, and Iconoclasm

The importance placed on religious learning and piety complemented both the autocratic imperial ideal and the powers of the bishops in the seventh century. Since the spiritual and secular realms were understood to be inseparable, the bishops wielded political power in their cities, while Byzantine emperors ruled as religious as well as political figures. In theory, imperial and church power were separate but interdependent. In fact, the emperor exercised considerable power over the church: he influenced the appointment of the chief religious official, the patriarch of Constantinople; he called church councils to determine dogma; and he regularly used bishops as local governors.

Because of this, bishops functioned as administrators, acting as judges and tax collectors in their cities. They distributed food in times of famine or siege, provisioned troops, and set up military fortifications. As part of their charitable work, they cared for the sick and the needy. In theory, they controlled the monasteries in their region (diocese) as well. However, in fact, monasteries were enormously powerful institutions that often defied the authority of bishops and even emperors. Monks commanded immense prestige as the holiest of God's faithful, and they were the chief sponsors of icons.

Icons were (and are) images of holy people—Christ, the Virgin, and the saints. To many Byzantine Christians, they were far more than mere representations: they were believed to possess holy power that directly affected people's daily lives as well as their chances for salvation. Many seventh-century Byzantines followed the monks in making icons the focus of their religious devotion. To them, icons were like the incarnation of Christ; they turned

■ **Icon of Virgin and Child**
With two angels behind them and a saint at either side, the Virgin Mary and the Christ Child display a still, otherworldly dignity. Working with hot pigmented beeswax, the sixth-century artist gave the angels transparent halos to emphasize their spiritual natures but depicted the saints as earthly men, with hair and beard, feet planted firmly on the ground. Icons such as this were used in private worship as well as in the religious life of Byzantine monasteries. **For more help analyzing this image,** *see the visual activity for this chapter in the* ONLINE STUDY GUIDE *at* bedfordstmartins.com/ huntconcise.

spirit into material substance. Thus an icon manifested in physical form the holy person it depicted. As the monk St. John of Damascus put it, in his vigorous defense of holy images, "I do not worship matter, I worship the God of matter, who became matter for my sake, and deigned to inhabit matter, who worked out my salvation through matter."

Other Byzantines, however, abhorred icons. Most numerous of these were soldiers on the frontiers. Shocked by Arab triumphs, they thought that the cause of their misfortunes was the biblical injunction against graven images. When they compared their defeats to Muslim successes, they could not help but notice that Islam prohibited all representations of the divine. To these soldiers and others who shared their view, icons revived pagan idolatry and desecrated Christian divinity. As iconoclastic ("anti-icon" or, literally, "icon-breaking") feeling grew, some churchmen became outspoken in their opposition to icons.

Byzantine emperors shared these religious objections, and they also had important political reasons for opposing icons. In fact, the issue of icons became a test of their authority. Icons represented intermediaries between worshipers and God; they undermined the emperor's exclusive place in the divine and temporal order. In addition, the emphasis on icons in monastic communities made the monks potential threats to imperial power; the emperors hoped to use this issue to break the power of the monasteries. Above all, though, the emperors opposed icons because the army did, and they needed the support of their troops.

The controversy climaxed in 726, after Emperor Leo III the Isaurian (r. 717–741) had defeated the Arabs besieging Constantinople in 718 and turned his attention to consolidating his political position. In the wake of the victory, officers of the imperial court tore down the great golden icon of Christ at the gateway of the palace and replaced it with a cross. In protest, a crowd of women went on a furious rampage in support of icons. This event marked the beginning of the period of **iconoclasm**; soon afterward, Leo ordered all icons destroyed, a ban that remained in effect, despite much opposition, until 787. A modified ban would be revived in 815 and last until 843. Thereafter, icons again became an important part of Byzantine Christianity.

Iconoclasm had an enormous impact on daily life. At home, where people had their own portable icons, it forced changes in private worship: the devout had to destroy their icons or venerate them in secret. Many women were devoted to icons— it was an empress who overturned the ban (temporarily, however) in 787. Iconoclasm also meant ferocious attacks on the monasteries: splendid collections of holy images were destroyed, vast properties were confiscated, and monasteries were disbanded. With their power now consolidated, Byzantine rulers were able to maintain themselves against the onslaught of the Arabs, who attacked under the banner of Islam.

■ **REVIEW:** *What stresses did the Byzantine Empire endure in the seventh and eighth centuries, and how was iconoclasm a response to those pressures?*

Islam: A New Religion and a New Empire

Islam, which means "submission to God" in Arabic, called for all to submit to the will of one God. It demanded a revolutionary change—the conversion to one community—of the many tribes who lived on the Arabian peninsula. The first to teach Islam was Muhammad, a merchant turned holy man from the Arabian city of Mecca, a major oasis near the Red Sea. He recognized only one God, that of the Jews and the Christians. He saw himself as God's last prophet, receiving and in turn repeating God's final words to humans. Invited by the city of Medina to come and mediate disputes there, Muhammad exercised the powers of both a religious and a secular leader. This dual role became the model for his successors (the caliphs) as well. Through a combination of persuasion and force, Muhammad and his coreli-gionists, the Muslims, converted most of the Arabian peninsula. By the time he died in 632, Islamic conquest and conversion had begun to move northward, into Byzantine and Persian territories. In the next generation, the Muslims took over most of Persia and all of Egypt and were on their way across North Africa to Spain. Yet within the territories they conquered with such lightning speed, daily life went on much as before.

The Rise and Development of Islam, c. 610–632

In the seventh century, the Arabian peninsula was populated by both sedentary and nomadic peoples. By far the largest group was made up of those who lived in one place (the sedentary), some making a living by farming, others living in oases, where they raised dates (a highly prized food). Some oases were prosperous enough to support merchants and artisans. By contrast, the nomads and seminomads (called Bedouins) lived in the desert. They herded goats, sheep, or camels, surviving large-ly from the products (leather, milk, meat) of their animals. Warriors, the Bedouins raided one another, valuing their honor highly and prizing bravery and generosity as well. Lacking written literature, they were proud of their oral culture of story-telling and poetry.

   Islam began as a religion of the sedentary, but it soon found support and mili-tary strength among the nomads. It began in Mecca, a major oasis and commercial center. More important, Mecca was a religious center because it contained a shrine, the Ka'ba, which served as a sacred place within which war and violence among all tribes were prohibited. The tribe that dominated Mecca, the Quraysh, controlled access to the shrine and was able to tax the pilgrims who flocked there as well as sell them food and drink. Plunder from raids was transformed into trade as the visitors bartered on the sacred grounds, assured of their security.

   Mecca was the birthplace of Muhammad (c. 570–632). His early years were unpromising: orphaned at the age of six, he spent two years with his grandfather and then came under the care of his uncle, a leader of the Quraysh tribe. Eventually, Muhammad became a trader. At the age of twenty-five, he married Khadija, a rich widow who had once employed him. They had at least four daughters and lived (to all appearances) happily and comfortably. Yet Muhammad sometimes left home and spent a few days in a nearby cave in prayer and contemplation, practicing a type of piety similar to that of early Christians.

In about 610, on one such retreat, Muhammad heard a voice calling on him to worship Allah, the God of the Jews and Christians. (*Allah* means "the God" in Arabic.) He accepted the call as coming from God. Over the next years he received mes-

Arabia in Muhammad's Lifetime

sages that he understood to be divine revelation. Later, when they had been written down and arranged—a process that was completed in the seventh century, but after Muhammad's death—these messages became the Qur'an, the holy book of Islam. The Qur'an, which means "recitation," is understood to be God's revelation as told to Muhammad by the angel Gabriel, then recited in turn by Muhammad to others. Its first chapter—or *sura*—is the Fatihah, which begins: "In the name of Allah, most benevolent, ever-merciful. All praise be to Allah." The Qur'an continues with 114 suras that are vaguely equivalent to (but generally much shorter than) books of the Bible. For Muslims (literally, "those who submit to Islam") the Qur'an addresses all of human experience—the sum total of history, prophecy, and the legal and moral code by which men and women should live—and the life to come.

The Qur'an emphasizes the nuclear family—a man, his wife, and children— as the basic unit of Muslim society. With the family given new importance, larger tribal affiliations were downgraded. However, all Muslims did have a wider identity as part of the **ummah**, the community of believers, who shared both a belief in one God and a set of religious practices. Islam stresses individual belief and adherence to the Qur'an. Thus Muslims have no priests, no mass, and no intermediaries between the divine and the individual. However, Islam does recognize authorities whose interpretations of the Qur'an and related texts are considered decisive. The Ka'ba, with its many idols, had attracted tribes from the surrounding vicinity. Muhammad, with his beliefs in one God, forged an even more universal religion.

■ **Qur'an**

More than a "holy book," the Qur'an represents the very words of God. Usually the text appeared on pages wider than they were long, perhaps to differentiate the Qur'an from other books. This particular example dates from the seventh or eighth century. It is written in Kufic script, a formal and majestic form of Arabic that scribes used for the Qur'an until the eleventh century. The round floral decoration on the right-hand page marks a new section of the text.

First to convert to Muhammad's faith were his wife, Khadija, and a few friends and members of his immediate family. However, Muhammad's insistence that all polytheistic cults be abandoned in favor of his one faith brought him into conflict with leading members of the Quraysh tribe, whose positions of leadership and livelihood were tied to the Ka'ba. Lacking political means to expel him, they insulted Muhammad and harassed his adherents.

Disillusioned and angry with his own tribe and with Mecca, where he had failed to make much of an impact, Muhammad tried to find a place and a population receptive to his message. Most important, he expected support from Jews, whose monotheism, in Muhammad's view, prepared them for his own faith. When a few of Muhammad's converts from Medina promised to protect him if he would join them there, he eagerly accepted the invitation, in part because Medina had a significant Jewish population. In 622, Muhammad emigrated to Medina, an oasis about two hundred miles north of Mecca. This journey, known as the Hijra, proved a crucial event for the fledgling movement. At Medina, Muhammad found followers ready to listen to his religious message and to regard him as the leader of their community. They expected him to act as a neutral and impartial judge in their interclan disputes. Muhammad's political position in the community set the pattern by which Islamic society would be governed afterward; rather than add a church to political and cultural life, Muslim political and religious institutions were inseparable. After Muhammad's death, the year of the Hijra was named the first year of the Islamic calendar; it marked the beginning of the new Islamic era.*

Although successful at Medina, the Muslims felt threatened by the Quraysh at Mecca, who actively opposed the public practice of Islam. For this reason, Muhammad led raids against them. At the battle of Badr in 624, Muhammad and his followers killed forty-nine of the Meccan enemy, took numerous prisoners, and confiscated rich booty. Thus traditional Bedouin plundering was grafted onto the Muslim duty of jihad.†

The battle of Badr was a great triumph for Muhammad, who was now able to consolidate his position at Medina, gaining new adherents and silencing all doubters. When Jews at Medina remained unreceptive to his message, Muhammad attacked them, expelling, executing, or enslaving many. At the same time Muhammad instituted new practices to define Islam as a unique religion. Among these were the *zakat*, a tax on possessions to be used for alms; the fast of Ramadan, which took place during the ninth month of the Islamic year, the month in which the battle of Badr had been fought; the *hajj*, an annual pilgrimage to Mecca that each Muslim was to try to accomplish at least once in his or her lifetime; and the *salat*, formal worship at least three times a day (later increased to five), which could include the *shahadah*, or profession of faith—"There is no god but God, and Muhammad is his Messenger." Soon Muhammad had Muslims direct their prayer away from Jerusalem, the center of Jewish worship, toward Mecca and the Ka'ba. Detailed regulations for these practices, sometimes called the "five pillars of Islam," were worked out in the eighth and early ninth centuries.

Meanwhile, the fierce rivalry between Mecca's tribes and Medina's Muslims began to spill over into the rest of the Arabian peninsula as both sides strove to win converts. Muhammad sent troops to subdue Arabs north and south. In 630, he entered Mecca with ten thousand men and took over the city, assuring the Quraysh of leniency and offering alliances with tribal leaders. By this time the prestige of Islam was enough to convince tribes elsewhere to convert. Through a combination of force, conversion, and negotiation, Muhammad was able to unite many, though

---

*Thus 1 A.H. (1 *anno Hegirae*, "year of the Hijra") on the Muslim calendar is equivalent to A.D. 622 (*anno Domini*, "year of the Lord," 622) on the Christian calendar.

†*Jihad* means "striving" and is used in particular in the context of striving against unbelievers. In that sense, it is often translated as "holy war." But it can also mean striving against one's own worst impulses.

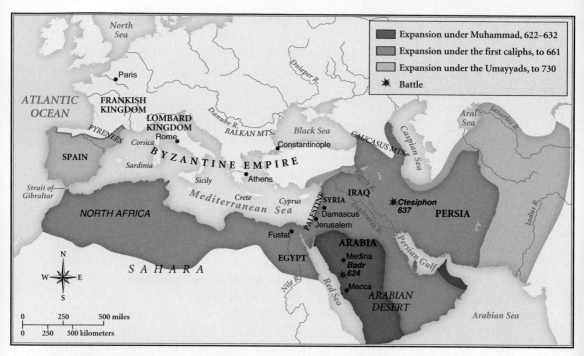

■ **MAP 7.2 Expansion of Islam to 730**

In little more than a century, Islamic armies conquered a vast region that included numerous differ-
ent peoples, cultures, climates, and living conditions. Under the Umayyads, these disparate territo-
ries were administered by one ruler from his capital city at Damascus. The uniting force was the
religion of Islam itself, which gathered all believers into one community, the ummah.

by no means all, Arabic-speaking tribes under his leadership by the time of his death
two years later (Map 7.2).

In so doing, Muhammad transformed Arab society. As Muhammad's converts
"submitted" to Islam, they formed not a tribe but rather a community bound
together by the worship of God. Women were accepted into this community, and
their status was enhanced. Islam prohibited all infanticide, a practice that had long
been used largely against female infants. Men were allowed to have up to four wives
at one time, but they were obliged to treat them equally; wives received dowries and
had certain inheritance rights. At first, Muslim women joined men during the salat,
the prayer periods that punctuated the day. Beginning in the eighth century, however, women began to pray apart from the men. Like Judaism and Christianity,
Islam retained the practices of a patriarchal society in which women's participation
in community life was circumscribed.

Even though Islamic society was a new sort of community, in many ways it functioned as a tribe, or rather a "supertribe," obligated to fight common enemies, share
plunder, and resolve peacefully any internal disputes. Muslims participated in group

rituals, such as the salat and public recitation. The Qur'an was soon publicly sung by professional reciters, much as the old tribal poetry had been. Most significant for the eventual spread of Islam, Muslim men were warriors, and their armies reaped profits at the point of a sword. But this differed from intertribal fighting; it was the "striving" (jihad) of people who were carrying out the injunction of God against unbelievers. "Strive, O Prophet," says the Qur'an, "against the unbelievers and the hypocrites, and deal with them firmly. Their final abode is Hell: And what a wretched destination!"

Muhammad's Successors, 632–750

Following his death, Muhammad's successors, the caliphs, conquered much of the Roman and Persian world. To the west, the Muslims attacked Byzantine territory in Syria with ease and moved into Egypt in the 640s (see Map 7.2). To the east, they invaded the Sassanid Empire, defeating the Persians at the gates of their capital, Ctesiphon, in 637. All of Persia was in Muslim hands by 661. During the last half of the seventh and the beginning of the eighth century, Islamic rule extended from Spain to India.

How were such conquests possible, especially in so short a time? First, the Islamic forces came up against weakened empires. The Byzantine and Sassanid states were exhausted from fighting each other. The cities of the Middle East that had been taken by the Persians and retaken by the Byzantines were depopulated, their few survivors burdened with heavy taxes. Second, the Muslims were welcomed into both Byzantine and Sassanid territories by discontented groups. Many Monophysite Christians in Syria and Egypt, for example, had suffered persecution by the Byzantines and were glad to have new, Islamic overlords.

These were the external reasons for Islamic success. There were also internal reasons. Arabs had long been used to intertribal warfare; now, under the banner of jihad, Muslims exercised their skills as warriors not against one another but rather against unbelievers. Fully armed, on horseback, and employing camels in convoys, they seemed almost a force of nature. Where they conquered, the Muslims built garrison cities from which soldiers requisitioned taxes and goods. Sometimes whole Arab tribes, including women and children, were imported to settle conquered territory, as happened in parts of Syria. In other regions, such as Egypt, a small Muslim settlement at Fustat sufficed to gather the spoils of conquest.

These successes hid tensions that developed within the Muslim leadership. Muhammad's death in 632 marked a crisis in the government of the new Islamic state, as different groups sought to promote their own successor. The first caliphs came not from the traditional tribal elite but rather from a new inner circle of men close to Muhammad and participants in the Hijra. The first two caliphs ruled without serious opposition, but the third, Uthman (r. 644–656), a member of the Umayyad family and one of Muhammad's sons-in-law, aroused discontent among other clan members of the inner circle and soldiers unhappy with his distribution of high offices and revenues. Accusing Uthman of favoritism, they supported his rival,

■ Arab Coin

The Arabs learned coinage and minting from peoples whom they conquered—the Persians and the Byzantines. Although one branch of Islam barred depicting the human form, others were less condemning. Thus the Umayyads saw nothing wrong with imitating traditional coinage. The ruler depicted on this silver coin is wearing a headdress that echoes the one worn by the Sassanid ruler depicted on page 262. But dirham, *the word for this type of coin, was not Persian but rather Greek, from* drachma. *The Umayyad Islamic fiscal system retained the old Roman land tax and was administered by Syrians who had served Byzantine rulers in the same capacity.* (© Copyright The Trustees of the British Museum.)

Ali, a member of the Hashim clan (to which Muhammad had belonged) and the husband of Muhammad's only surviving child, Fatimah. After a group of discontented soldiers murdered Uthman, civil war broke out between the Umayyads and Ali's faction. It ended in 661 when Ali was killed by one of his own former supporters, and the caliphate remained in Umayyad hands from 661 to 750.

Nevertheless, the *Shi'at Ali*, the faction of Ali, did not fade away. Ali's memory lived on among groups of Muslims, Shi'ites, who saw in him a symbol of justice and righteousness. For them, Ali's death was the martyrdom of the only true successor to Muhammad. They remained faithful to his dynasty, shunning the caliphs of the other Muslims (Sunni Muslims, from Arabic *sunna*, "custom" or "the way"). The Shi'ites awaited the arrival of the true leader—the imam—who in their view could come only from the house of Ali. The Sunni–Shi'ite split remains a political fact even today.

Under the **Umayyad caliphate**, the Muslim world became a state with its capital at Damascus. Borrowing from the institutions well known to the civilizations they had just conquered, the Muslims issued coins and hired former Byzantine and Persian officials. They made Arabic a tool of centralization, imposing it as the language of government on regions not previously united linguistically. For Byzantium this period was one of unparalleled military crisis, the prelude to iconoclasm. For the Islamic world, now a diverse society of Muslim Arabs, Syrians, Egyptians, Iraqis, and other peoples, it was a period of settlement, new urbanism, and literary and artistic flowering.

Peace and Prosperity in Islamic Lands

Ironically, the Islamic warriors brought peace. While the conquerors stayed within their fortified cities or built magnificent hunting lodges in the deserts of Syria, the conquered went back to work, to study, to play, and—in the case of Christians and

Jews, who were considered "protected subjects"—to worship as they pleased in return for the payment of a special tax. At Damascus, local artists and craftspeople worked on the lavish decorations for a mosque in a neoclassical style at the very moment Muslim armies were storming the walls of Constantinople (see page 264). Leaving the Byzantine institutions in place, the Muslim conquerors allowed Christians and Jews to retain their posts and even protected dissidents.

During the seventh and eighth centuries, Muslim scholars wrote down the hitherto largely oral Arabic literature. They determined the definitive form for the Qur'an and compiled pious narratives about Muhammad (hadith literature). Scribes composed these works in exquisite calligraphy, handwriting that was also an art form. A literate class, composed mainly of the old Persian and Syrian elite now converted to Islam, created new forms of prose writing in Arabic—official documents as well as essays on topics ranging from hunting to ruling. Umayyad poetry explored new worlds of thought and feeling. Patronized by the caliphs, who found in written poetry an important source of propaganda and a buttress for their power, the poets also reached a wider audience that delighted in their clever use of words, their satire, and their invocations of courage, piety, and sometimes erotic love:

> I spent the night as her bed-companion, each enamored of the other,
> And I made her laugh and cry, and stripped her of her clothes.
> I played with her and she vanquished me;
> I made her happy and I angered her.
> That was a night we spent, in my sleep, playing and joyful,
> But the caller to prayer woke me up.

Such poetry scandalized conservative Muslims, brought up on the ascetic tenets of the Qur'an. But this love poetry was a product of the new urban civilization of the Umayyad period, where wealth, cultural mix, and the confidence born of conquest inspired diverse and experimental literary forms. By the close of the Umayyad era in 750, Islamic civilization was multiethnic, urban, and sophisticated—a true heir of Roman and Persian traditions.

■ **REVIEW:** *How and why did the Muslims conquer so many lands in the relatively short period from 632 to 750?*

The Western Kingdoms

With the demise of Roman imperial government in the West, the primary foundations of power and stability in Europe were kinship networks, church patronage, royal courts, and wealth derived from land and plunder. In contrast to Byzantium, where an emperor still ruled as the successor to Augustus and Constantine, drawing

■ MAP 7.3 The Merovingian Kingdoms in the Seventh Century
By the seventh century, there were three powerful Merovingian kingdoms: Neustria, Austrasia, and Burgundy. The important cities of Aquitaine were assigned to one or another of these major kingdoms, while Aquitaine as a whole was assigned to a duke or other governor. Kings did not establish capital cities; they did not even stay in one place. Rather, they continually traveled throughout their kingdoms, making their power felt in person.

upon an unbroken chain of Roman legal and administrative traditions, political power in the West was more diffuse. Churchmen and rich magnates, sometimes one and the same person, held sway. Power derived as well from membership in royal dynasties, such as that of the Merovingian kings of the Franks. In addition, people believed that power lodged in the tombs and relics of saints, who represented and wielded the divine forces of God. Although the patterns of daily life and the procedures of government in the West remained recognizably Roman, they were undergoing change, borrowing from and adapting local traditions.

Frankish Kingdoms with Roman Roots

The core of the Frankish kingdoms was Roman Gaul. During the sixth century, the Franks had established themselves as dominant in Gaul, and by the seventh century

■ **Stadium and Amphitheater at Arles**

In what is today the south of France, the ruins of an amphitheater built by the Romans still dwarf the surrounding buildings of the modern city of Arles. This huge stadium was even more striking in the seventh century, when the city was impoverished and depopulated. Plague, war, and the dislocation of Roman trade networks forced most people to abandon the cities to live on the land. Only the bishop and his clergy—and individuals who could make a living servicing them—stayed in the cities. At Arles there were monasteries as well, and some of them were thriving. In the mid-sixth century there were perhaps two hundred nuns at one of the female convents there.
(Bridgeman-Giraudon/Art Resource, NY.)

the limits of their kingdoms roughly approximated the eastern borders of present-day France, Belgium, Switzerland, and Luxembourg (Map 7.3). Moreover, their kings, the Merovingians (c. 485–751), had conquered many of the peoples beyond the Rhine, foreshadowing the contours of modern Germany. These northern and eastern regions were little Romanized, but the inhabitants of the rest of the Frankish kingdoms lived with bits and pieces of the ancient Roman Empire at their front door.

Travel was difficult in this world of decaying roads and few amenities. Yet there were many travelers, such as pilgrims on their way to Rome and traders with slaves—precious human cargo captured on the borders of the Christian world and sold to wealthy aristocrats within. Most seventh-century voyagers would have relied on river routes, for land travel was very slow, and even large groups of travelers on the roads were vulnerable to attacks by robbers. Such travelers would have seen a very diverse landscape. Imagine pilgrims returning north from a pious trip to Rome. They might take the Rhône River, in which case they would pass Roman amphitheaters and farmland neatly and squarely laid out by Roman land surveyors. The great stone palaces of villas still dotted the countryside of southern Gaul. All this would have seemed quite classical and Roman. But if the travelers had been very observant, they would have noticed what was missing: thriving cities. By the seventh century, Roman cities were mere shells, serving as the centers of church administration but no longer boasting commercial or cultural vitality. Depopulated, many survived as mere skeletons, with the exception of such busy commercial centers as Arles and Marseille.

Continuing their journey north along the Moselle River, our travelers would pass through dense, nearly untouched forests and land more often used as pasture for animals than for cereal cultivation. Not much influenced by the Romans, these areas represented far more the farming and village settlement patterns of the Germans. Yet even here some structures of the Roman Empire remained. Fortresses were still standing at Trier, and large stone villas, such as the one excavated by archaeologists near Douai, loomed over the humble wooden dwellings of the countryside.

In the south, gangs of slaves still might occasionally be found cultivating the extensive lands of wealthy estate owners, as they had done since the days of the late Roman Republic. Scattered here and there, independent peasants worked their own small plots as they had for centuries. But for the most part, seventh-century travelers would find semifree peasant families settled on small holdings, their manse—including a house, a garden, and cultivable land—for which they paid dues and owed labor services to a landowner. Some of these peasants were descendants of the *coloni* (tenant farmers) of the late Roman Empire; others were the sons and daughters of slaves, now provided with a small parcel of land; and a few were people of free Germanic origin who for various reasons had come down in the world. At the lower end of the social scale, the status of Germans and Romans had become identical.

At the upper end of the social scale, Romans (or, more precisely, Gallo-Romans) and Germans had also merged. Although people south of the Loire River continued to be called "Romans" and people to the north "Franks," their cultures were strikingly similar: they shared languages, settlement patterns, and religious sensibilities. Many dialects were spoken in the western kingdoms in the seventh century, many deriving from Latin, though no longer the Latin of Cicero. "Though my speech is rude," Gregory, bishop of Tours (r. 573–c. 594), wrote at the end of the sixth century,

> I have been unable to be silent as to the struggles between the wicked and the upright; and I have been especially encouraged because, to my surprise, it has often been said by men of our day, that few understand the learned words of the rhetorician but many the rude language of the common people.

Thus Gregory began his *Histories,* a valuable source for the Merovingian period (c. 485–751). He was trying to evoke the sympathies of his readers, a traditional Roman rhetorical device; but he also expected that his "rude" Latin—the plain Latin of everyday speech—would be understood and welcomed by the general public.

In the fourth and fifth centuries Gallo-Roman aristocrats had lived in isolated villas with their *familia*—family members, slaves, and servants. In the seventh century, aristocrats lived in more populous settlements: in small villages surrounded by the huts of peasants, shepherds, and artisans. The early medieval village, constructed mostly out of wood or baked clay, was generally built near a waterway or forest or around a church for protection.

The cities, too, were transformed. At Tours, Bishop Gregory and his household and clerics still lived in the old Roman city center. But Tours's main focus was now outside the city walls, where a church had been built. The population of the surrounding countryside was pulled to this church as if to a magnet, for it housed the remains of the most important and venerated person in the locale: St. Martin. This saint, a fourth-century soldier-turned-monk, was long dead, but his relics—his bones, teeth, hair, and clothes—could be found at Tours, where he had served as bishop. There, in succeeding centuries, he remained a supernatural force: a protector, healer, and avenger through whom God manifested divine power. In Gregory's view, for example, Martin's relics (or rather God *through* Martin's relics) had prevented armies from plundering local peasants. Martin was not the only human thought to have great supernatural power; all of God's saints were miracle workers.

In the classical world, the dead had been banished from the presence of the living; in the medieval world, the holy dead held the place of highest esteem. The church had no formal procedures for proclaiming saints in the early Middle Ages, but influential

■ Reliquary

The cult of relics necessitated housing the precious parts of the saints in equally precious containers. This reliquary, made of cloisonné enamel (bits of enamel framed by metal), garnets, glass gems, and a cameo, is in the shape of a miniature sarcophagus. On the back is the inscription "Theuderic the priest had this made in honor of Saint Maurice." Theuderic must have given the reliquary to the monastery of Saint-Maurice d'Agaune (today in Switzerland), which was renowned for its long and elaborate liturgy—its daily schedule of prayer—in the late seventh century. (Photo courtesy Thames and Hudson Ltd., London, from *The Dark Ages,* ed. David Talbot Rice.)

community leaders, including the local bishop, "recognized" holiness. When, for example, miracles were observed at the site of a tomb in Dijon, the common people went there regularly to ask for help. The nearby bishop, however, was convinced that St. Benignus inhabited the tomb only after the martyr himself visited the bishop in a vision. At St. Illidius's tomb in Clermont, it was reported that "the blind are given light, demons are chased away, the deaf receive hearing, and the lame the use of their limbs." Even a few women were so esteemed: "[Our Savior] gave us as models [of sanctity] not only men, who fight [against sinfulness] as they should, but also women, who exert themselves in the struggle with success," wrote Gregory as a preface to his story of the nun Monegund, who lived with a few other ascetic women and whose miracles included curing tumors and prompting paralyzed limbs to work again. No one at Tours doubted that Martin was a saint, and to tap into the power of his relics one of Gregory's predecessors as bishop had constructed his church in the cemetery directly over Martin's tomb. For a man like Gregory of Tours and his flock, the church building was above all a home for the relics of the saints.

Economic Activity in a Peasant Society

As a bishop, Gregory was aware of some of the sophisticated forms of economic activity in seventh- and eighth-century Europe, such as long-distance trade. Yet most people lived on the edge of survival. Studies of Alpine peat bogs show that from the fifth to the mid–eighth century glaciers advanced and the average temperature in Europe dropped. This climatic change spelled shortages in crops. Chronicles, histories, and saints' lives also describe crop shortages, famines, and diseases as a normal part of life. For the year 591 alone, Gregory reported that

> a terrible epidemic killed off the people in Tours and in Nantes. . . . In the town of Limoges a number of people were consumed by fire from heaven for having profaned the Lord's day by transacting business. . . . There was a terrible drought which destroyed all the green pasture. As a result there were great losses of flocks and herds.

An underlying reason for these calamities was the weakness of the agricultural economy. The dry, light soil of the Mediterranean region was easy to till, and wooden implements were no liability there. But in the north of Europe, where the soil was heavy, wet, and difficult to turn, the limitations of wooden implements meant a meager food supply. At the same time, agricultural work was not equitably or efficiently allocated and managed. A leisure class of landowning warriors and churchmen lived off the work of peasant men, who tilled the fields, and peasant women, who gardened, brewed, baked, and wove cloth.

Occasionally surpluses developed, either from peaceful agriculture or plunder in warfare, and these were traded, though rarely in an impersonal, commercial manner. Most economic transactions of the seventh and eighth centuries were part of a **gift economy**, a system of give-and-take: booty was taken, tribute was demanded, harvests were hoarded, and coins were minted, all to be redistributed to friends, followers, and dependents. Kings and other rich and powerful men and women amassed gold, silver, ornaments, and jewelry in their treasuries and grain in their storehouses to mark their power, add to their prestige, and demonstrate their generosity. Those benefiting from this bounty included religious people and institutions: monks, nuns, and bishops, monasteries and churches. We still have a partial gift economy today. At holidays, for example, goods change hands for social purposes: to consecrate a holy event, to express love and friendship, to show off wealth and status. In the Merovingian world, the gift economy was the dynamic behind most of the moments when goods and money changed hands.

Some economic activity in the seventh century was purely commercial and impersonal. In the north of Europe, a thriving North Sea trade was beginning. Older networks still tied the West—which supplied slaves and raw materials such as furs and honey—to the East, which provided luxuries and manufactured goods such as silks and papyrus. Trade was a way for the Byzantine, Islamic, and western European descendants of the Roman Empire to keep in tenuous contact with one another. Seventh- and eighth-century sources speak of Byzantines, Syrians, and Jews as the chief intermediaries, many of them living in the still-thriving port cities of the Mediterranean. Gregory of Tours associated Jews with commerce, complaining that they sold things "at a higher price than they were worth."

Contrary to Gregory's view, Jews were not involved only, or even primarily, in trade but were almost entirely integrated into every aspect of secular life in many regions of Europe. They used Hebrew in worship, but otherwise they spoke the same languages as Christians and used Latin in their legal documents. Their children were often given the same names as Christians (and, in turn, Christians often took Old Testament biblical names); they dressed like everyone else; and they engaged in the same occupations. Many Jews planted and tended vineyards, in part because of the importance of wine in synagogue services, in part because the surplus could easily be sold. Some Jews were rich landowners, with slaves and dependent peasants working for them; others were independent peasants of modest means. Some Jews lived in towns with a small Jewish quarter where their homes and synagogues were located. However, most Jews, like their Christian neighbors, lived on the land. Only much later, in the tenth century, would their status change as they were driven off of the land.

Women were also more fully integrated into the society of Merovingian Gaul than had been the case in the ancient world. Like Islamic women, those of the West received dowries and could inherit property. In the West, they could be entrepreneurs as well: documents reveal at least one enterprising peasant woman who sold wine at Tours to earn additional money.

The Powerful in Merovingian Society

Monarchs and aristocrats were the powerful people in Merovingian society. Aristocrats included monks and bishops as well as laypeople. Holding power through hereditary wealth, status, and political influence, they lived in leisurely abundance. At the end of the sixth century, for example, one of them, Bishop Nicetius, inhabited a palace that commanded a view of his estates overlooking the Moselle River:

> From the top [of the palace] you can see boats gliding by on the surface of the river in summertime; orchards with fruit-trees growing here and there fill the air with the perfume of their flowers.

Besides tending their estates, male aristocrats of the period spent their time honing their skills as warriors. To be a great warrior in Merovingian society, as in the otherwise very different world of the Bedouin, meant more than just fighting: it meant perfecting the virtues necessary for leading armed men. Aristocrats affirmed their skills and comradeship in the hunt; they proved their worth in the regular taking of booty; and they rewarded their followers afterward at generous banquets. At these feasts, following the dictates of the gift economy, the lords combined fellowship with the redistribution of wealth, as they gave abundantly to their retainers.

Merovingian aristocrats also spent a good deal of time in bed. The bed—and the production of children—was the focus of their marriage. Because of its importance to the survival of aristocratic families and to the transmission of their property and power, marriage was an expensive institution, especially the most formal kind, in which the husband paid a dowry to his bride—a generous gift of livestock and land—and gave her a smaller morning gift after the marriage was consummated. Very wealthy men might also support "lesser wives," to whom they gave a morning gift but no dowry. In this period, churchmen had many ideas about the value of marriages, but in practice they had little to do with the matter: no one was married in a church.

Sixth-century aristocrats with wealth and schooling like Nicetius patterned their lives on those of Romans, teaching their children Latin poetry and writing to one another in phrases borrowed from the classical poet Virgil. Less than a century later, however, aristocrats no longer adhered to the traditions of the classical past. Some still learned Latin, but they cultivated it mainly to read the Psalms. A religious culture emphasizing Christian piety over the classics was developing in the West at the same time as in Byzantium.

The new religious sensibility was given powerful impetus by the arrival (c. 591) on the European continent of the Irish monk St. Columbanus (d. 615). The Merovingian aristocracy, by now highly Christianized and anxious about the afterlife, was much taken by Columbanus's brand of monasticism, which stressed prayer, penance, and discipline. The numerous monasteries that St. Columbanus established from Gaul to Italy attracted local recruits from the aristocracy, some of them grown men and women. Others were young children, given to the monastery by their parents. This practice, called oblation, was not only accepted but also often considered essential for the spiritual well-being of both the children and their families. Irish monasticism introduced aristocrats on the continent to a deepened religious devotion. Those aristocrats who did not join or patronize a monastery still often read (or listened to others read) books about penitence, and they chanted the Psalms.

Bishops, generally aristocrats, ranked among the most powerful men in Merovingian society. Gregory of Tours, for example, considered himself the protector of "his citizens" at Tours. When representatives of the king came to collect taxes, Gregory stopped them in their tracks, warning them that St. Martin would punish anyone who tried to tax his people. "That very day," Gregory reported, "the man who had produced the tax rolls caught a fever and died." Gregory then obtained a letter from the king, "confirming the immunity from taxation of the people of Tours, out of respect for Saint Martin."

Like other aristocrats, many bishops were married. Church councils demanded celibacy, however, and as the overseers of priests, bishops were expected to be moral supervisors and refrain from sexual relations with their wives. Since bishops were ordinarily appointed late in life, long after they had raised a family, this restriction did not get in the way of their founding a family and fathering heirs.

Because unions bound together extended families rather than simply husbands and wives, noble parents determined whom their daughters were to marry. But women had some control over their lives. If they were widowed without children, they were allowed to sell, give away, exchange, or rent out their dowry estates as they wished. Moreover, men could give their women kinfolk property outright in written testaments. Fathers so often wanted to share their property with their daughters that an enterprising author created a formula for scribes to follow when drawing up such wills. It began:

> For a long time an ungodly custom has been observed among us that forbids sisters to share with their brothers the paternal land. I reject this impious law: I make you, my beloved daughter, an equal and legitimate heir in all my patrimony [inheritance].

Because of such bequests, dowries, and other gifts, many aristocratic women were very rich. Childless widows frequently gave grand and generous gifts to the church from their vast possessions. But a woman need not have been a widow to control enormous wealth: in 632, for example, the nun Burgundofara, who had never married, drew up a will giving her monastery the land, slaves, vineyards, pastures, and forests she

■ **Relic of Queen Balthild**
The slave Balthild, purchased in England by a Frankish mayor of the palace, caught the eye of the Frankish king himself, who made her his queen. This seventh-century Cinderella story did not end with marriage. When her husband died, Balthild played an important role as regent (caretaker ruler) for her young son. Later, she retired to a monastery, where she was revered as a saint. This shirt is one of her relics. Tradition has it that instead of wearing real jewels, Balthild distributed them to the poor and contented herself with their images in embroidery.
(Musée Alfred Bonno, Chelles, France. Photographers: E. Mittard and N. Georgieff.)

had received from her two brothers and her father. In the same will, she gave other properties near Paris to her brothers and sister. Aristocratic women maintained close ties with their relatives. They tried to find powerful husbands for their sisters and prestigious careers for their brothers; in turn, they relied on their relatives for support.

Though legally under the authority of her husband, a Merovingian woman often found ways to assert control over her life and her husband's life as well. Tetradia, wife of Count Eulalius, left her husband, taking all his gold and silver, because

> he was in the habit of sleeping with the women-servants in his household . . . *[and] neglected his wife. . . . As a result of his excesses, he ran into serious debt, and to meet this he stole his wife's jewelry and money.*

In a court of law, Tetradia was sentenced to repay Eulalius four times the amount she had taken from him, but she was allowed to keep and live on her own property. Other women were able to exercise behind-the-scenes control through their sons. Nicetius's mother, Artemia, used the prophecy that her son would become a bishop to prevent her husband from taking the bishopric himself. The prophecy took some time to be fulfilled, so Nicetius remained at home with his mother well into his thirties, working alongside the servants and teaching the younger children of the household to read the Psalms.

Occasionally women exercised direct power. Some women were abbesses, rulers in their own right over female monasteries and sometimes over "double monasteries," with separate facilities for men and women. These could be very substantial centers of population: the convent at Laon, for example, had three hundred nuns in the seventh century. Because women lived in populous convents or were monopolized by rich men able to support several wives or mistresses at one time, unattached aristocratic women were scarce in society and therefore valuable.

Atop this aristocracy of men and women were the Merovingian kings, rulers of the Frankish kingdoms from about 485 to 751. The **Merovingian dynasty** owed its longevity to good political sense: it had allied itself with local lay aristocrats and ecclesiastical authorities. The kings relied on these men to bolster their power, which was largely based on their tribal war leadership and access to the lion's share of plunder as well as their takeover of the taxation system, public lands, and the legal framework of Roman administration. The kings' courts functioned as schools for the sons of the aristocracy, tightening the bonds between royal and aristocratic families and loyalties. And when kings sent officials—counts and dukes—to rule in their name in various regions of their kingdoms, these regional governors worked with and married into the aristocratic families who had long controlled local affairs.

Aristocrats as well as kings had good reason to want a powerful royal authority. The king acted as arbitrator and intermediary for the competing interests of the aristocrats while taking advantage of local opportunities to appoint favorites and garner prestige by giving out land and privileges to supporters and religious institutions. Gregory of Tours's history of the sixth century is filled with stories of bitter battles between Merovingian kings, as royal brothers fought continuously over territories, wives, and revenues. Yet what seemed like royal weakness and violent chaos to the bishop was in fact one way the kings focused local aristocratic enmities, preventing them from spinning out of royal control. By the beginning of the seventh century, three relatively stable kingdoms had emerged: Austrasia to the northeast; Neustria to the west, with its capital city at Paris; and Burgundy, incorporating the southeast (see Map 7.3). These divisions were so useful to local aristocrats and to the Merovingian dynasty alike that even when royal power was united in the hands of one king, Clothar II (r. 584–629), he made his son the independent king of Austrasia.

The very power of the kings in the seventh century, however, gave greater might to their chief court official, the mayor of the palace. In the following century, allied with the Austrasian aristocracy, one mayoral family would displace the Merovingian dynasty and establish a new royal line, the Carolingians.

Christianity and Classical Culture in the British Isles

The Frankish kingdoms exemplify some of the ways in which Roman and non-Roman traditions combined. **Anglo-Saxon England** shows still another blending in its formation of a learned monastic culture. The impetus for this culture came not from native traditions but from Rome and Ireland. After the Anglo-Saxon conquest (440–600), England gradually emerged politically as a mosaic of about a dozen kingdoms ruled by separate kings. They were surrounded by Christian cultures in the rest of the British Isles (Wales, Scotland, and Ireland), and slowly the quadrant conquered by the Anglo-Saxons became Christian as well.

In the north of England, Irish monks brought their own brand of Christianity. Converted in the fifth century by St. Patrick and other missionaries, the Irish had rapidly evolved a church organization that corresponded to its rural clan organization. Abbots and abbesses, generally from powerful dynasties, headed monastic *familiae*, communities composed of blood relatives, servants, and slaves as well as monks or nuns. Bishops were often under the authority of abbots, and the monasteries rather than cities were the centers of population settlement in Ireland. The Irish missionaries to England were monks, and they set up monasteries on the model of those at home.

The British Isles

In the south of England, Christianity came by way of missionaries sent by Pope Gregory the Great (r. 590–604) in 596 to 597. The missionaries, under the leadership of Augustine (not the same Augustine as the bishop of Hippo), intended to convert the king and people of Kent, the southernmost kingdom, and then work their way northward. But Augustine and his party brought with them Roman practices at odds with those of Irish Christianity, stressing ties to the pope and the organization of the church under bishops rather than abbots. Using the Roman model, they divided England into dioceses, territorial units headed by an archbishop and bishops. Augustine, for example, became archbishop of Canterbury. Because he was a monk, he set up a monastery right next to his cathedral, and it became a unique characteristic of the English church to have a community of monks attached to the bishop's church.

A major bone of contention between the Roman and Irish churches involved the calculation of the date of Easter. The Roman church insisted that Easter fall on the first Sunday following the first full moon after the spring equinox. The Irish had a different method of determining Easter's date, and therefore they celebrated on a different day. As everyone agreed that believers could not be saved unless they observed Christ's resurrection properly and on the right day, the conflict over dates was bitter. It was resolved by Oswy, king of Northumbria. In 664, he organized a meeting of churchmen, the Synod of Whitby, which chose the Roman calculation. Oswy was convinced that Rome spoke with the voice of St. Peter, who, according to the New Testament, held the keys of the Kingdom of Heaven. Oswy's decision paved the way for the triumph of the Roman brand of Christianity in England.

St. Peter was not the only reason the Anglo-Saxons favored Rome. To many English churchmen, Rome had great prestige because it was a treasure trove of knowledge, piety, and holy objects. Benedict Biscop (c. 630–690), the founder of two important English monasteries, made many arduous trips to Rome, bringing back relics, liturgical vestments, and even a cantor to teach his monks the proper melodies in a time before written musical notation. Above all, he went to Rome to get books. At his monasteries in the north of England, he built up a grand library. In Anglo-Saxon England as in Ireland, both of which lacked a strong classical tradition from Roman times, a book was considered a precious object, to be decorated as finely as a garnet-studded brooch.

The Anglo-Saxons and Irish Celts had a thriving oral culture but extremely limited uses for writing. The ability to write and read became valuable only when these societies converted to Christianity. Just as Islamic reliance on the Qur'an made possible a literary culture under the Umayyads, so Christian dependence on the Bible, written liturgy, and the ideas of "church fathers" such as Jerome and Augustine helped make England and Ireland centers of literature and learning in the seventh and eighth centuries. Archbishop Theodore (r. 669–690), who had

■ Page from the Lindisfarne Gospels

The lavishly illuminated manuscript known as the Lindisfarne Gospels, of which this is one page, was probably produced in the first third of the eighth century. For the monks at Lindisfarne and elsewhere in the British Isles, books were precious objects, to be decorated much like pieces of jewelry. To introduce each of the four Gospels of the New Testament, the artist—who was also the scribe—produced three elaborate pages: the first was a "portrait" of the evangelist, the second a decorative "carpet" page, and the third the beginning of the text itself. The page depicted here is the beginning of the Gospel according to St. Matthew, which opens with the words "Liber generationis." Note how elaborately the first letter, L, is treated and how the decoration gradually recedes, so that the last line, though still very embellished, is quite plain in comparison with the others. In this way, the very layout of the book led the reader slowly and reverently into the text of the Gospels itself. (By permission of the British Library.)

studied at Constantinople and was one of the most learned men of his day, founded a school at Canterbury where students mined Latin and even some Greek manuscripts to comment on biblical texts. Men like Benedict Biscop soon sponsored other centers of learning, using texts from the classical past. Although women did not establish famous schools, many abbesses ruled over monasteries that stressed Christian learning. Here as elsewhere, Latin writings, even pagan texts, were studied diligently, in part because Latin was so foreign a language that mastering it required systematic and formal study. One of Benedict Biscop's pupils was Bede (673–735), an Anglo-Saxon monk and a historian of extraordinary breadth. Bede in turn taught a new generation of monks who became advisers to eighth-century rulers.

Unity in Spain, Division in Italy

In contrast to England, southern Gaul, Spain, and Italy had long been part of the Roman Empire and preserved many of its traditions. Nevertheless, as new peoples settled and fought over them, their histories diverged dramatically. When the Merovingian king Clovis defeated the Visigoths in 507, their vast kingdom, which had sprawled across southern Gaul and into Spain, was dismembered. By midcentury, the Franks came into possession of most of the Visigothic kingdom in southern Gaul.

In Spain the Visigothic king Leovigild (r. 569–586) established territorial control by military might. But no ruler could hope to maintain power there without the support of the Hispano-Roman population, which included both the great landowners and the leading bishops. Their backing was unattainable while the Visigoths remained Arian Christians, but in 587 Leovigild's son Reccared (r. 586–601) took the necessary step, converting to Catholic Christianity. Two years later, at the Third Council of Toledo, most of the Arian bishops followed their king by announcing their conversion to Catholicism, and the assembled churchmen enacted decrees for a united church in Spain.

Thereafter the bishops and kings of Spain cooperated to a degree unprecedented in other regions. The king gave the churchmen free rein to set up their own hierarchy (with the bishop of Toledo at the top) and to meet regularly at synods to regulate and reform the church. The bishops in turn supported their Visigothic king, who ruled as a minister of the Christian people. Rebellion against him was considered equivalent to rebellion against Christ. The Spanish bishops reinforced this idea by anointing the king, daubing him with holy oil in a ritual that paralleled the ordination of priests and demonstrated divine favor. Toledo, the city where the highest bishop presided, was also where the kings were "made" through anointment. While the bishops in this way adopted the king's cause as their own, their lay counterparts, the great landowners, helped supply the king with troops, allowing him to maintain internal order and repel his external enemies.

Ironically, it was precisely the centralization and unification of the Visigothic kingdom that proved its undoing. When the Arabs arrived in 711, they needed only to kill the king, defeat his army, and capture Toledo to deal it a crushing blow.

By contrast, in Italy the Lombard king constantly faced a hostile papacy in the center of the peninsula and virtually independent dukes in the south. Theoretically royal officers, in fact the dukes of Benevento and Spoleto ruled on their own behalf.

Lombard Italy, Early Eighth Century

Although many Lombards were Catholics, others, including important kings and dukes, were Arian. The official religion varied with the ruler in power. Rather than signal a major political event, the conversion of the Lombards to Catholic Christianity occurred gradually, ending only around the mid-seventh century. Partly as a result of this slow development, the Lombard kings, unlike the Visigoths, Franks, or even the Anglo-Saxons, never enlisted the wholehearted support of any particular group of churchmen.

Lacking a strong and united church to back them up, Lombard kings still had important sources of power. Chief among these were the traditions of leadership associated with the royal dynasty and the kings' military role. In addition, the crown controlled large estates in northern Italy and made use of surviving Roman urban institutions. Although the Italian peninsula had been devastated by the wars between the Ostrogoths and the Byzantine Empire, the Lombard kings took advantage of the still-urban organization of Italian society and economy, assigning dukes to city bases and setting up a royal capital at Pavia. Recalling emperors like Constantine and Justinian, the kings built churches, monasteries, and other places of worship in the royal capital, maintained the walls, and minted coins.

Revenues from tolls, sales taxes, port duties, and court fines filled their coffers. Like other Germanic kings, the Lombards issued law codes that revealed a great debt to Roman legal collections, such as those commissioned by Justinian. While individual provisions of the law code promulgated by King Rothari (r. 636–652), for example, reflected Lombard traditions, the code also suggested the Roman idea that the law should apply to all under his rule, not just Lombards. "We desire," Rothari wrote,

> that these laws be brought together in one volume so that everyone may lead a secure life in accordance with the law and justice, and in confidence thereof will willingly set himself against his enemies and defend himself and his homeland.

Unfortunately for the Lombard kings, the "homeland" that they hoped to rule was fractured, not only by the duchies of Spoleto and Benevento but, more importantly, by the papacy, which dominated central Italy.

By 600, the pope's position was ambiguous: he was both a ruler and a subordinate. On the one hand, believing he was the successor of St. Peter and head of the church, he wielded real secular power. Pope Gregory the Great (r. 590–604) in many ways laid the foundations for the papacy's later spiritual and temporal ascendancy. During his tenure, the pope became the greatest landowner in Italy; he organized the defenses of Rome and paid for its army; he heard court cases, made treaties, and provided welfare services. The missionary expedition he sent to England was only a small part of his involvement in the rest of Europe. For example, Gregory maintained close ties with the churchmen in Spain who were working to convert the Visigoths from Arianism to Catholicism. A prolific author of spiritual works and biblical commentaries, Gregory digested and simplified the ideas of church fathers like St. Augustine of Hippo, making them accessible to a wider audience. His practical handbook for the clergy, *Pastoral Rule*, was matched by practical reforms within the church: in Italy, he tried to impose regular elections of bishops and to enforce clerical celibacy.

On the other hand, the pope was not independent. He was only one of many bishops in the Roman Empire, which was now ruled from Constantinople; and he was therefore subordinate to the emperor and Byzantium. Imperial authority did not begin to unravel in Rome until the late seventh century. In 691, Emperor Justinian II convened a council that determined 102 rules for the church, and he sent them to Rome for papal endorsement. Most of the rules were unobjectionable, but Pope Sergius I (r. 687–701) was unwilling to agree to the whole because it permitted priestly marriages (which the Roman church did not want to allow) and it prohibited fasting on Saturdays in Lent (which the Roman church required). Outraged by Sergius's refusal, Justinian tried to arrest the pope, but Italian armies (theoretically under the emperor) came to the pontiff's aid, while Justinian's arresting officer cowered under the pope's bed. The incident reveals that some local forces were already willing to rally to the side of the pope against the emperor. By now Constantinople's influence and authority over Rome was tenuous at best. Sheer distance, as well as diminishing imperial power in Italy, meant the popes were in effect the leaders of the parts of Italy not controlled by the Lombards.

The gap between Byzantium and the papacy widened in the early eighth century as Emperor Leo III tried to increase the taxes on papal property to pay for his all-consuming war against the Arab invaders. The pope responded by leading a general tax revolt. Meanwhile, Leo's fierce policy of iconoclasm collided with the pope's tolerance of images. In the West, Christian piety focused not so much on icons as on relics, but the papacy was not willing to allow sacred images and icons to be destroyed. The pope argued that holy images could and should be venerated—but not worshiped. His support of images reflected popular opinion as well. A later

■ **MAPPING THE WEST Europe and the Mediterranean, c. 750**

The major political event of the period 600–750 was the emergence of Islam and the conquest of an Islamic state that reached from Spain to the Indus River. The Byzantine Empire, once a great power, was dwarfed—and half swallowed up—by its Islamic neighbor. To the west were fledgling barbarian kingdoms, mere trifles on the world stage. The next centuries, however, would prove their resourcefulness and durability. **For more help analyzing this map,** *see the map activity for this* chapter in the ONLINE STUDY GUIDE *at* **bedfordstmartins.com/huntconcise.**

commentator wrote that iconoclasm so infuriated the inhabitants of Ravenna and Venice that "if the pope had not prohibited the people, they would have attempted to set up a [different] emperor over themselves."

These difficulties with the emperor were matched by increasing friction between the pope and the Lombards. The Lombard kings had gradually managed to bring under their control the duchies of Spoleto and Benevento as well as part of the Exarchate of Ravenna. By the mid-eighth century, the popes feared that Rome would fall to the Lombards, and Pope Zachary (r. 741–752) looked northward for friends. He created an ally by sanctioning the deposition of the last Merovingian king and his replacement by the first Carolingian king, Pippin III the Short (r. 751–768). In 753,

Zachary's successor, Pope Stephen II (r. 752–757), called on Pippin to march to Italy with an army to fight the Lombards. Thus events at Rome had a major impact on the history not only of Italy but of the Frankish kingdom as well.

■ **REVIEW:** *How important was the papacy in early medieval Europe?*

IMPORTANT DATES			
c. 570–632	Life of Muhammad, prophet of Islam	630–730	Period of Islamic conquests
590–604	Papacy of Gregory the Great	661	Death of Ali; origins of Sunni–Shi'ite split
c. 591	Columbanus, an Irish monk, arrives on the European continent	661–750	Umayyad caliphate
		664	Synod of Whitby; English king opts for Roman Christianity
596–597	Augustine sent to England by Pope Gregory the Great to convert the Anglo-Saxons	718	Major Arab attack on Constantinople repulsed
610–641	Reign of Emperor Heraclius	726–843	Period of iconoclasm at Byzantium
622	Muhammad's Hijra to Medina and beginning of Islamic calendar		

Conclusion

The three heirs of the Roman Empire—Byzantines, Muslims, and the peoples of western Europe—built upon three distinct legacies. Byzantium directly inherited the central political institutions of Rome; its people called themselves Romans; its emperor was the Roman emperor; and its capital, Constantinople, was the new Rome. Sixth-century Byzantium also inherited the cities, laws, and religion of Rome. The changes of the seventh and eighth centuries—contraction of territory, urban decline, disappearance of the old elite, a ban on sacred images—whittled away at this Roman character. By 750, Byzantium was less Roman than it was a new, resilient political and cultural entity, a Christian community on the borders of the new Muslim Empire.

Muslims were the newcomers to the Roman world, with Islam influenced by Jewish monotheism and only indirectly by Roman Christianity. Under the guidance of the Prophet Muhammad, Islam became both a coherent theology and a tightly structured way of life with customs based on Bedouin tribal traditions and defined in the Qur'an. But once the Muslim Arabs embarked on military conquests, they, too, became heirs of Rome, preserving its cities, hiring its civil servants, and adopting its artistic styles. Drawing upon Roman and Persian traditions, the Muslims created a powerful Islamic state, with a capital city in Syria, regional urban centers elsewhere, and a culture that tolerated a wide variety of economic, religious, and social institutions so long as the conquered paid taxes to their Muslim overlords.

Western Europe also inherited Roman institutions but changed them in many diverse ways. Merovingian Gaul built on Roman traditions that had long been transformed by provincial and Germanic customs. In Italy and at Rome itself, the traditions of the classical past remained living parts of the fabric of life. The roads remained, the cities of Italy (though depopulated) survived, and both the popes and the Lombard kings ruled in the traditions of Roman government. In Spain, the Visigothic kings allied themselves with a Hispano-Roman elite that maintained elements of the organization and vigorous intellectual traditions of the late empire. However, in England, once the far-flung northern summit of the Roman Empire, the Roman legacy had to be "re-imported" in the seventh century by Anglo-Saxon churchmen seeking what they took to be a more authentic Christianity.

All three heirs to Rome suffered the ravages of war. In all three societies the social hierarchy became simpler, with the loss of "middle" groups like the *curiales* at Byzantium, the decline of city dwellers in western Europe, and the near suppression of tribal affiliations among Muslims. As each of the three heirs shaped Roman institutions to its own uses and advantages, each also strove to create a state founded on religion. In Byzantium, the emperor was a religious force, presiding over the destruction of images. In the Islamic world, the caliph was the successor to Muhammad, a religious and political leader. In the West, the kings allied with churchmen in order to rule. Despite their many differences, all these leaders had a common understanding of their place in a divine scheme: they were God's agents on earth, ruling over God's people.

■ **MAKING CONNECTIONS**

1. *What were the similarities and what were the differences between the three heirs of the Roman Empire?*

2. *Which of the heirs seemed best poised for economic, political, and cultural success around the year 750 and why?*

■ **FOR FURTHER EXPLORATION**

For further reading and online research ideas, see the Suggested References on page SR-4 at the back of the book.

For practice quizzes, a customized study plan, and other study tools, see the ONLINE STUDY GUIDE at bedfordstmartins.com/huntconcise.

For primary-source material from this period, see Chapter 7 in *Sources of THE MAKING OF THE WEST: A CONCISE HISTORY,* Second Edition.

Unity and Diversity in Three Societies

750–1050

I N 841, A FIFTEEN-YEAR-OLD BOY NAMED WILLIAM went to serve at the court of Charles the Bald, king of the Franks. William's father was Bernard, an extremely powerful noble. His mother was Dhuoda, a well-educated, pious, and able woman who administered the family's estates in the south of France while her husband occupied himself in court politics and royal administration. In 841, however, politics had become a dangerous business. King Charles, named after his grandfather Charlemagne, was fighting with his brothers over his portion of the Carolingian Empire, and Bernard (who had been a supporter of Charles's father, Louis the Pious) held a precarious position at the young king's court. In fact, William was sent to Charles's court as a kind of hostage, to ensure Bernard's loyalty. Anxious about her son, Dhuoda wanted to educate and counsel him, so she wrote a handbook of advice for William, outlining what he ought to believe about God, about politics and society, about obligations to his family, and, above all, about his duties to his father, which she emphasized even over loyalty to the king:

> *In the human understanding of things, royal and imperial appearance and power seem preeminent in the world, and the custom of men is to account those men's actions and their names ahead of all others. . . . But despite all*

■ **Carolingian Mother**

This depiction of a nursing mother is a detail from a full-page illustration of the biblical story of the Creation and Fall in a Carolingian Bible manuscript made in the ninth century. The mother is Eve, cast out of the Garden of Eden and suckling her firstborn, Cain. Christian mothers had an important model in Mary, the mother of Jesus, and Eve's dignified placement within a bower of garlands may reflect this association. (By permission of the British Library.)

this . . . I caution you to render first to him whose son you are special, faithful, steadfast loyalty as long as you shall live.

William heeded his mother's words, with tragic results: when Bernard ran afoul of Charles and was executed, William died in a failed attempt to avenge his father.

Dhuoda's handbook reveals the volatile political atmosphere of the mid-ninth century, and her advice to her son points to one of its causes: a crisis of loyalty. Loyalty to emperors, caliphs, and kings—all of whom were symbols of unity cutting across regional and family ties—competed with allegiances to local authorities; those, in turn, vied with family loyalties. The period 600–750 had seen the startling rise of Islam, the whittling away of Byzantium, and the emergence of stable political and economic institutions in an impoverished West. The period 750–1050 would see all three societies contend with internal issues of diversity even as they became increasingly conscious of their unity and uniqueness. At the beginning of this period, rulers built up and dominated strong and united polities. By the end, these realms had fragmented into smaller, more local units. Although men and women continued to feel some loyalty toward faraway kings, caliphs, or emperors, their most powerful allegiances often focused on authorities closer to home.

At Byzantium, military triumphs brought the emperors enormous prestige. A renaissance of culture and art took place at Constantinople. Yet at the same time newly powerful families began to dominate the Byzantine countryside. In the Islamic world, a dynastic revolution in 750 ousted the Umayyads from the caliphate and replaced them with a new family, the **Abbasids**. The new caliphs moved their capital eastward—shifting from Damascus to Baghdad—and adopted some elements of the persona of the Sassanid king of kings of Persia. Yet their power, too, began to ebb as regional Islamic rulers came to the fore. In the West, Charlemagne—a Frankish king from a new dynasty, the Carolingians—forged an empire that embraced most of Europe. But this new state, like the others, turned out to be fragile, disintegrating within a generation of Charlemagne's death. Indeed, in the West even more than in the Byzantine and Islamic worlds, power fell into the hands of local strongmen.

All along the fringes of these realms, new political entities began to develop, conditioned by the religion and culture of their more dominant neighbors. Russia grew up in the shadow of Byzantium, as did Bulgaria and Serbia. The West was more crucial in the development of central Europe. By the year 1050, the contours of modern Europe and the Middle East were dimly visible.

Byzantium: Renewed Strength and Influence

In the hundred years between 750 and 850, Byzantium staved off Muslim attacks in Asia Minor and began to rebuild itself. After 850 it went on the attack, and by 900 it had reconquered some of the territory it had lost. Military victory brought new wealth

and power to the imperial court, and the emperors supported a vast program of literary and artistic revival—the Macedonian renaissance—at Constantinople. But while
the emperor dominated at the capital, a new landowning elite began to control the
countryside. On its northern front, Byzantium helped create new Slavic realms.

Imperial Might

The seventh-century imperial reorganization of the Byzantine army into *themes*—
regiments based in particular regions—proved effective against Islamic armies.
Avoiding battles in the field, the Byzantines allowed Muslim warriors to enter their
territory, but they evacuated the local populations and burned any extra food. Then
they waited in their fortified strongholds for the Muslims to attack. In this way they
fought from a position of strength. If the Muslims decided to withdraw, other
Byzantine troops were ready at the border to ambush them.

Beginning around 850 and lasting until 1025, the Byzantines turned the tables.
They began advancing on all fronts, employing new mobile forces along with the
theme soldiers. By the 1020s, they had regained Antioch, Crete, and Bulgaria (see
Map 8.1 on page 298). They had not controlled so much territory since their wars
with the Sassanid Persians four hundred years earlier.

Victories such as these gave new prestige to the army and the imperial court.
New wealth matched this prestige. The emperors drew revenues from vast and
growing imperial estates. They could tax and demand services from the general
population at will—requiring them to build bridges and roads, to offer lodging to
the imperial retinue, and to pay taxes in cash. These taxes increased over time, partly
because of fiscal reforms and partly because of population increases (the approximately seven million people who lived in the empire in 780 had swelled to about
eight million less than a century later).

The emperor's power extended over both civil administration and military
command. Fearing potential rivals, whether from the court or in the army, emperors surrounded themselves with eunuchs—castrated men who were believed unfit
to rule as emperors themselves and who were unable to have sons to challenge the
imperial dynasty. Eunuchs were employed in the civil service; they held high positions in the army; and they were important palace officials.

Supported by their wealth and power, emperors negotiated with other rulers
from a position of strength. Ambassadors were exchanged, and the Byzantine court
received and entertained diplomats with elaborate ceremonies. One such diplomat,
Liutprand, bishop of the northern Italian city of Cremona, reported on his audience
with Emperor Constantine VII Porphyrogenitos (r. 913–959):

> *Leaning upon the shoulders of two eunuchs I was brought into the emperor's
> presence. At my approach [mechanical] lions began to roar and birds to cry
> out, each according to its kind. . . . After I had three times made obeisance to*

■ **MAP 8.1 The Expansion of Byzantium, 860–1025**

In 860, the Byzantine Empire was only a fraction of its former size. To the west, it had lost most of Italy; to the east, it held only part of Asia Minor. On its northern flank, the Bulgarians had set up an independent state. By 1025, however, it had ballooned, its western half embracing all of the Balkans, its eastern arm reaching around the Black Sea, and its southeastern fringe reaching nearly to Tripoli. The year 1025 marked the Byzantine Empire's greatest size after the rise of Islam.

> the emperor with my face upon the ground, I lifted my head, and behold! the man whom just before I had seen sitting on a moderately elevated seat had now changed his raiment and was sitting on the level of the ceiling. How it was done I could not imagine, unless perhaps he was lifted up by some such sort of device as we use for raising the timbers of a wine press.

Although this elaborate court ceremonial clearly amused Liutprand, its real function was to express the serious, sacred, concentrated power of imperial majesty. Liutprand missed the point because he was a westerner unaccustomed to such displays.

The emperor's wealth relied on the prosperity of an agricultural economy organized for trade. State regulation and entrepreneurial enterprise were delicately balanced in Byzantine commerce. Although the emperor controlled craft and commercial guilds (such as those of the silk industry) to ensure imperial revenues and a stable supply of valuable and useful commodities, entrepreneurs organized most of the fairs held throughout the empire. Foreign merchants traded within the empire, either at Constantinople or in some border cities. Because this international trade intertwined with foreign policy, the Byzantine government considered trade a political as well as an economic matter. Emperors issued privileges to certain "nations" (as such groups as the Venetians, Russians, and Jews were called), regulating the fees they were obliged to pay and the services they had to render. At the end of the tenth century, for example, the Venetians bargained to reduce their customs dues per ship from thirty *solidi* (coins) to two; in return they promised to transport Byzantine soldiers to Italy whenever the emperor wished.

Imperial authority was not absolute, however. In the countryside, particularly in Anatolia, powerful families—often army generals but also members of the civil service and the church—bought and dominated huge tracts of land. Many peasants became dependents of these great landlords, tilling the soil without owning it. Although the new magnates were a potential counterweight to imperial power, they ordinarily considered their interests to coincide with that of the emperor. They were glad to profit from imperial victories and the expansion of Byzantine territory.

The Macedonian Renaissance, c. 870–c. 1025

Flush with victory, which reminded them of Rome's glory, the emperors revived classical intellectual pursuits. Basil I (r. 867–886) from Macedonia founded the imperial dynasty that presided over the so-called Macedonian renaissance (c. 870–c. 1025). The *renaissance* (French for "rebirth")* was made possible by an intellectual elite, members of families who, even in the anxious years of the eighth century, had persisted in studying the classics despite the trend toward a simple religious education.

Now, with the empire slowly regaining its military eminence and with icons permanently restored in 843, this scholarly elite thrived again. Emperors and other members of the new court society, liberated from sober taboos, sponsored sumptuous artistic productions. Emperor Constantine Porphyrogenitos wrote books of geography and history and financed the work of other scholars and artists. He even supervised the details of his craftspeople's products, insisting on

---

*The word *renaissance* is commonly used in connection with a revival of classical art, languages, and culture in Italy during the period c. 1350–1500. However, it is also used for *any* artistic, intellectual, or cultural flowering nourished by classical traditions. It has both meanings in this book.

■ The Crowning of Constantine Porphyrogenitos

This ivory plaque was carved at Constantinople in the middle of the tenth century. The artist wanted to emphasize hierarchy and symbolism, not nature. Christ is shown placing the imperial crown on the head of Emperor Constantine Porphyrogenitos (r. 913–959). What message do you suppose the artist wanted to convey by placing Christ higher than the emperor and by having the emperor slightly incline his head to receive the crown? **For more help analyzing this image**, see the visual activity for this chapter in the ONLINE STUDY GUIDE at bedfordstmartins. com/huntconcise.

(Hirmer Fotoarchiv, Munich, Germany.)

exacting standards: "Who could enumerate how many artisans the Porphyrogenitos corrected? He corrected the stonemasons, the carpenters, the goldsmiths, the silversmiths, and the blacksmiths," wrote a historian supported by the same emperor's patronage.

Other members of the imperial court also sponsored writers, philosophers, and historians. Scholars wrote summaries of classical literature, encyclopedias of ancient knowledge, and commentaries on classical authors. Others copied manuscripts of religious and theological commentaries, such as homilies, liturgical texts, Bibles, and Psalters. They hoped to revive the intellectual and artistic achievements of the heyday of imperial Roman rule. But the Macedonian renaissance could not possibly succeed in this endeavor: too much had changed since the time of Justinian. Nevertheless, the renaissance permanently integrated classical forms into Byzantine political and religious life.

■ The Macedonian Renaissance

This manuscript illumination, made at Constantinople in the mid-ninth century, combines Christian and classical elements in a harmonious composition. David, author of the Psalms, sits in the center. Like the classical Orpheus, he plays music that attracts and tames the beasts. In the right-hand corner a figure labeled "Bethlehem" is modeled on a lounging river or mountain god. Compare this image with the crowning of Constantine Porphyrogenitos on page 300 and describe, using these two objects, the various styles and subject matters of the Macedonian renaissance.

(Bibliothèque nationale de France.)

New States under the Influence of Byzantium

The shape of modern eastern Europe—formed around Bulgaria, Serbia, and Russia—grew out of the Slavic states created during the period 850–950. By 800, Slavic settlements dotted the area from the Danube River down to Greece and from the Black Sea to Croatia. The Bulgar khagan ruled over the largest realm, populated mostly by Slavic peoples and situated northwest of Constantinople. Under Khagan Krum (r. c. 803–814) and his son, Slavic rule stretched west all the way to the Tisza River in modern Hungary. At about the same time as Krum's triumphant expansion, however, the Byzantine Empire began its own campaigns to conquer, convert, and control these Slavic regions.

The Byzantine offensive began under Emperor Nicephorus I (r. 802–811), who waged war against the Slavs of Greece in the Peloponnese, set up a new Christian diocese there, organized it as a new military theme, and forcibly resettled Christians in the area to counteract Slavic paganism. The Byzantines followed this pattern of conquest as they pushed northward. By 900, Byzantium ruled all of Greece.

Still under Nicephorus, the Byzantines launched a massive attack against the Bulgarians, took the chief city of Pliska, plundered it, burned it to the ground, and then marched against Krum's encampment in the Balkan mountains. Krum took advantage of his position, however, attacked the imperial troops, killed Nicephorus,

The Balkans, c. 850–950

and brought home the emperor's skull in triumph. Cleaned out and lined with silver, the skull served as the victorious Krum's drinking goblet. In 816, the two sides agreed to a peace that lasted for thirty years. But hostility remained, and wars between the Bulgarians and Byzantines broke out with increasing intensity. Intermittent skirmishes gave way to longer wars throughout the tenth century. The Byzantines advanced, at first taking Bulgaria's eastern territory. Then, in a slow and methodical conquest (1001–1018) led by Emperor Basil II (r. 963–1025), aptly called the "Bulgar-Slayer" (Bulgaroctonos), they subjected the entire region to Byzantine rule and forced its ruler to accept the Byzantine form of Christianity. Similarly the Serbs, encouraged by Byzantium to oppose the Bulgarians, began to form the state that would become Serbia, in the shadow of Byzantine interest and religion.

Religion played an important role in the Byzantine offensive. In 863, two brothers, Cyril and Methodius, were sent as missionaries from Byzantium to the Slavs. Well-educated Greeks, they spoke one Slavic dialect fluently and devised an alphabet for Slavic (until then an oral language) based on Greek forms. It was the ancestor of the modern Cyrillic alphabet used in Bulgaria, Serbia, and Russia.

Russia in the ninth and tenth centuries lay outside the sphere of direct Byzantine rule, but like Serbia and Bulgaria, it came under increasingly strong Byzantine cultural and religious influence. Vikings—Scandinavian adventurers who ranged over vast stretches of ninth-century Europe seeking trade, booty, and land—had penetrated Russia from the north and imposed their rule over the Slavs inhabiting the broad river valleys connecting the Baltic Sea with the Black Sea and thence with Constantinople. Like the Bulgars in Bulgaria, the Scandinavian Vikings gradually blended into the larger Slavic population. At the end of the ninth century, one Dnieper valley chief, Oleg, established control over most of the tribes in southwestern Russia and forced peoples farther away to pay tribute. The tribal association he created formed the nucleus of Kievan Russia, named for the city that had become the commercial center of the region and is today the capital of Ukraine (see "Mapping the West," page 335).

Kievan Russia and Byzantium began their relationship with war, developed it through trade agreements, and finally sustained it by religion. Around 905, Oleg launched a military expedition to Constantinople, forcing the Byzantines to pay a large fee and open their doors to Russian traders in exchange for peace. At the time only a few Christians lived in Russia, along with Jews and probably some Muslims. The Russians' conversion to Christianity was spearheaded by a Russian ruler later in the century. Vladimir (r. c. 980–1015), the grand prince of Kiev and all Russia, saw great military, cultural, and economic advantages in allying with the Byzantines. He and the Byzantine emperor Basil II agreed that Vladimir should adopt the Byzantine form of Christianity. Vladimir took a variant of the name Basil in honor of the emperor and married the emperor's sister Anne; then he reportedly had all the people of his state baptized in the Dnieper River.

Vladimir's conversion represented a wider pattern. Along with the Christianization of Slavic realms such as Old Moravia, Serbia, and Bulgaria under the Byzantine church, the rulers and peoples of Poland, Hungary, Denmark, and Norway were converted under the auspices of the Roman church. Russia's conversion to Christianity was especially significant, however, because Russia was geographically as close to the Islamic world as to the Christian and could conceivably have become an Islamic land. By converting to Byzantine Christianity, Russians made themselves heirs to Byzantium and its church, customs, art, and political ideology. Adopting Christianity linked Russia to the Christian world, but choosing Byzantine rather than Roman Christianity served to isolate Russia later from western Europe because in time the Greek and Roman churches would become estranged.

Under Prince Iaroslav the Wise (r. 1019–1054), Russia forged links through Iaroslav's own marriage and the marriages of his sons and daughters to rulers and princely families in France, Hungary, and Scandinavia. His ideal of rulership came directly from Roman traditions; he encouraged intellectual and artistic developments that would connect Russian culture to the classical past. But after his death, civil wars broke out, shredding what unity Russia had known. Massive invasions by outsiders, particularly from the east, further weakened Kievan rulers, who were eventually displaced by princes from northern Russia. At the crossroads of East and West, Russia could meet and adopt a great variety of traditions; but its situation also opened it to unremitting military pressures.

■ **REVIEW:** *How did Byzantium's expansion affect the power of its emperor?*

From Unity to Fragmentation in the Islamic World

A new dynasty of caliphs—the Abbasids—first brought unity and then, in their decline, fragmentation to the Islamic world. Caliphs continued to rule in name only, while regional rulers took over the real business of governing Islamic lands. Local traditions based on religious and political differences played an increasingly important role in people's lives. Yet even in the eleventh century, the Islamic world had a clear sense of its own unity, based on language, commercial life, and vigorous intellectual give-and-take across regional boundaries.

The Abbasid Caliphate, 750–c. 950

In 750, a civil war ousted the Umayyads and raised the Abbasids to the caliphate. The Abbasids found support in an uneasy coalition of Shi'ites (the faction loyal to Ali's memory) and non-Arabs who had been excluded from Umayyad government and now demanded a place in political life. The new regime signaled a revolution. The center of the Islamic state shifted from Damascus, with its roots in the Roman tradition, east to Baghdad, a new capital city built by the Abbasids right next to Ctesiphon, which had been the Sassanid capital. At first the caliphs were powerful: commanding a large centralized civil service, they also controlled the appointment of regional governors.

The Abbasid caliph Harun al-Rashid (r. 786–809), for example, presided over a flourishing empire from Baghdad. (He and his court are immortalized in some of the stories of *A Thousand and One Nights*, as for example "Sindbad the Sailor," in which a merchant's seagoing adventures bring him fabulous wealth.) Charlemagne, Harun's contemporary, was very impressed with the elephant Harun sent him as a gift, along with monkeys, spices, and medicines. But these items were mainstays of everyday commerce in Harun's Iraq. For example, a mid-ninth-century list of imports inventoried "tigers, panthers, elephants, panther skins, rubies, white sandal, ebony, and coconuts" from India and "silk, chinaware, paper, ink, peacocks, racing horses, saddles, felts, [and] cinnamon" from China.

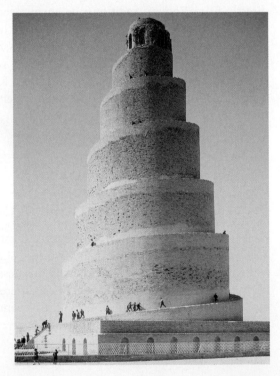

■ **Minaret of the Great Mosque at Samarra**
From 836 to 892, the Abbasid caliphs had their capital at Samarra, about seventy miles north of Baghdad. In part, the choice of this location was a response to the very tensions that eventually produced the separate Islamic states of the tenth century. At Samarra itself, the Abbasid court created a cultural center. The Great Mosque, begun in 847, is the largest mosque ever built. Shown here is its minaret (the tower from which Muslims are summoned to prayer), which looms over the mosque some distance from its outer wall. Scholars still debate the reasons for its spiral shape.
(Bildarchiv Preußischer Kulturbesitz/Art Resource, NY.)

The Abbasid dynasty began to decline after Harun's death, mostly due to economic problems. Obliged to support a huge army and an increasingly complex civil service, the Abbasids found their tax base inadequate. They needed to collect revenues from their provinces, such as Syria and Egypt, but the governors of those regions often refused to send the revenues. After Harun's caliphate, ex-soldiers, seeking better salaries, recognized different caliphs and fought for power in savage civil wars. The caliphs tried to bypass the regular army, made up largely of free Muslim foot soldiers, by turning to Turkish slaves—Mamluks—bought and armed to serve as mounted cavalry. But the caliphate's dwindling revenues could not sustain a loyal or powerful military force, and in the tenth century the caliphs became figureheads only, as independent rulers established themselves in the various Islamic regions. To support themselves militarily, many of these new rulers turned to independent military commanders who led Mamluk troops. Well paid to maintain their mounts and arms, many Mamluks gained renown and, after being freed by their masters, high positions at the courts of regional rulers. In the thirteenth century, some of them became rulers themselves.

Regional Diversity

A faraway caliph could not command sufficient allegiance from local leaders once he demanded more in taxes than he gave back in favors. The forces of fragmentation were strong in the Islamic world: it was, after all, based on the conquest of many diverse regions, each with its own deeply rooted traditions and culture. The Islamic religion, with its Sunni–Shi'ite split, also became a source of polarization. Western Europeans knew almost nothing about Muslims and ordinarily called them all Saracens (from the Latin for "Arabs") without distinction. But, in fact, Muslims were of different ethnicities, practiced different customs, and identified with different regions. With the fragmentation of political and religious unity, each of the tenth- and early-eleventh-century Islamic states built on local traditions under local rulers (see Map 8.2 on page 306).

The most important and successful of these new states was formed by the Fatimids, a group of Shi'ites who took their name after Fatimah, wife of Ali and Muhammad's only surviving child. Allying with the Berbers in North Africa, the Fatimids established themselves in 909 as rulers in the region now called Tunisia. The Fatimid Ubayd Allah claimed to be not only the true imam, descendant of Ali, but also the *mahdi*, the "divinely guided" messiah, come to bring justice on earth. In 969, the Fatimids declared themselves rulers of Egypt, and eventually they controlled North Africa, Arabia, and even southern Syria. Their dynasty lasted for about two hundred years.

While the Shi'ite Fatimids were dominating Egypt, Sunni Muslims ruled al-Andalus, the Islamic central and southern heart of Spain. Unlike the other independent Islamic states forged during the ninth and tenth centuries, the Spanish

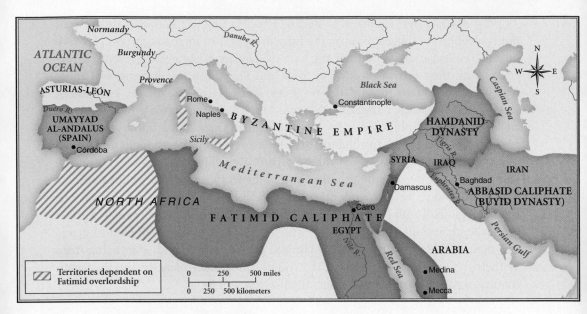

■ MAP 8.2 Islamic States, c. 1000

A glance back at Map 7.2 (see page 272) quickly demonstrates the fragmentation of the once united Islamic caliphate. In 750, one caliph ruled territory stretching from Spain to India. In 1000, there was more than one caliphate as well as several other ruling dynasties. The most important were the Fatimids, who began as organizers of a movement to overthrow the Abbasids. By 1000, they had conquered Egypt and controlled all of North Africa and even Sicily.

emirate of Córdoba (so called because its ruler took the secular title *emir*, "commander," and fixed his capital at Córdoba) was created near the start of the Abbasid caliphate, in 756. During the Abbasid revolution, Abd al-Rahman—a member of the Umayyad family—fled to North Africa, gathered an army, invaded Spain, and was declared emir after only one battle. He and his Umayyad successors ruled a broad range of peoples, including many Jews and Christians. After the initial Islamic conquest of Spain, the Christians adopted so much of the new language and so many of the customs that they were called Mozarabs, "would-be Arabs," by Christians elsewhere. Their rulers allowed them freedom of worship and let them live according to their own laws. Some Mozarabs were content with their status; others converted to Islam; still others intermarried—most commonly, Christian women married Muslim men and raised their children as Muslims.

Under Abd al-Rahman III (r. 912–961), who took the title caliph ("successor" to Muhammad) in 929, members of all religious groups in al-Andalus were given absolute freedom of worship and equal opportunity to rise in the civil service. Abd al-Rahman initiated important diplomatic contacts with Byzantine and European rulers. He felt strong enough not to worry much about the weak and tiny Christian kingdoms squeezed into northern Spain. Yet al-Andalus, too, experienced the same political fragmentation that was occurring everywhere else. In 1031, the caliphate of Córdoba broke up, as rulers of small, independent regions, called *taifas*, took power.

The regional diversity exemplified by the Fatimids and rulers of Islamic Spain did not prevent a measure of unity through trade networks and language. The principal bond of all Islamic lands was Arabic, the language of the Qur'an. At once poetic and sacred, Arabic was also the language of commerce and government from Baghdad to Córdoba. Moreover, despite political differences, borders were open: an artisan could move from Córdoba to Cairo; a landowner in North Africa might very well own property in al-Andalus; a young man from North Africa would think nothing of going to Iran to find a wife; a young girl purchased as a slave in Mecca might become part of a prince's harem in Baghdad. With no national barriers to trade and few regulations (though every city and town had its own customs dues), traders regularly dealt in far-flung, various, and often exotic goods.

Although the primary reason for this internationalism was Islam itself, open borders extended to non-Muslims as well. The Tustari brothers, Jewish merchants from southern Iran, typified the commercial activity in the Arabic-speaking world. By 1026, they had established a flourishing business in Egypt. The Tustaris did not have "branch offices," but informal contacts allowed them many of the same advantages and much flexibility: friends and family in Iran shipped them fine textiles to sell in Egypt, and the Tustaris exported Egyptian fabrics to sell in Iran. But the sophisticated Islamic society of the tenth and eleventh centuries supported networks even more vast than those represented by the Tustari family. Muslim merchants brought tin from England; salt and gold from Timbuktu in west-central Africa; amber, gold, and copper from Russia; and slaves from every region.

The Islamic Renaissance, c. 790–c. 1050

The dissolution of the caliphate into separate political entities multiplied the centers of learning and intellectual productivity. Unlike the Macedonian renaissance of Byzantium, which was concentrated in Constantinople, a "renaissance of Islam" occurred throughout the Islamic world. It was particularly dazzling in urban court centers such as Córdoba, where tenth-century rulers presided over a brilliant court culture. They patronized scholars, poets, and artists, and their library at Córdoba contained the largest collection of books in Europe.

Elsewhere, already in the eighth century, the Abbasid caliphs endowed research libraries and set up centers for translation where scholars culled the writings of the ancients, including the classics of Persia, India, and Greece. Scholars read, translated, and commented on the works of Neoplatonists and Aristotle. Others worked on mathematical matters. Al-Khwarizmi wrote a book on equation theory in about 825 that became so well known in the West that the word *al-jabr* in the title of his book became the English word *algebra*. Other scholars, such as Ali al-Hasan

■ **Andromeda**
The study of medicine, physics, astronomy, and other sciences flourished in the tenth and eleventh centuries in the cosmopolitan Islamic world. This whimsical depiction of Andromeda, a constellation visible in the Northern Hemisphere, illustrates the Book of Images of the Fixed Stars *(c. 965), an astronomical treatise written by al-Sufi at the request of his "pupil," the ruler of Iran. Knowledge of astronomy was important for both secular and religious reasons: the Muslim calendar was lunar, and the times of Muslim prayer were calculated from the movement of the sun. Al-Sufi drew from classical treatises, particularly the* Almagest *by Ptolemy. This copy of the* Book of Images, *probably made by al-Sufi's son in 1009, also draws on classical models for the illustrations, although instead of Greek clothing, Andromeda wears the pantaloons and skirt of an Islamic dancer.*
(Bodleian Library, University of Oxford.)

(d. 1038) (known as "Alhazen" in the West), wrote studies on cubic and quadratic equations. Muhammad ibn Musa (d. 850) used a numeral system devised in India in his treatise on arithmetical calculations, introducing as well the crucial number zero. No wonder that the numbers 1, 2, 3, and so on were known as "Arabic numerals" when they were introduced into western Europe in the twelfth century.

The newly independent Islamic rulers supported science as well as mathematics. Unusual because she was a woman was al-Asturlabi, who followed her father's profession as a maker of astrolabes for the Syrian court. Astrolabes measured the altitude of the sun and stars to calculate time and latitude. More typical were men like Ibn Sina (980–1037), known in the West as Avicenna, who wrote books on logic, the natural sciences, and physics. His *Canon of Medicine* systematized earlier treatises and reconciled them with his own experience as a physician. Active in the centers of power, he served as vizier (prime minister) to various rulers.

Long before there were universities in the West, there were important institutions of higher learning in the Islamic world. In Islam all law and literature was understood to derive from God's commands as contained in the Qur'an or as revealed to the ummah, the community of believers. For this reason, the study of the Qur'an and related texts held a central place in Islamic life. In the tenth and eleventh centuries, rich Muslims, generally of the ruling elite, demonstrated their piety and charity by establishing schools for professors and their students. Each school, or **madrasa**, was located within or attached to a mosque. Visiting scholars often arrived at the madrasas to dispute, in a formal and rational way, with the professors there. Such events of intellectual sparring attracted huge audiences. On ordinary days, though, the professors held regular classes. A professor might begin his day with a class interpreting the Qur'an, following it with a class on other interpretations, and ending with a class on literary or legal texts. Students, all male, attended the classes that suited their achievement level and interest. Most students paid a fee for learning, but there were also scholarship students, such as one group of lucky students who were given annual funds by a vizier. This official was so solicitous for the welfare of all scholars that each day he set out for them iced refreshments, candles, and paper in his own kitchen.

The use of paper, made from flax and hemp or rags and vegetable fiber, points to a major difference among the Islamic, Byzantine, and (as we shall see) Carolingian renaissances. Byzantine scholars worked to enhance the prestige of the ruling classes. Using expensive parchment, their manuscripts could serve only the very rich. This was true of scholarship in the West as well. By contrast, Islamic scholars had goals that cut across all classes: to be physicians to the rich, teachers to the young, and contributors to passionate religious debates. Their writings, on less expensive paper, were widely available.

■ **REVIEW:** *What forces led to the fragmentation of the Islamic world in the tenth and eleventh centuries?*

The Creation and Division of a New Western Empire

Just as in the Byzantine and Islamic worlds, so, too, in the West, the period 750–1050 saw first the formation of a strong empire, ruled by one man, and then its fragmentation, as local rulers took power into their own hands. A new dynasty, the Carolingians, came to rule in the Frankish kingdom at almost the very moment that the Abbasids gained the caliphate. Charlemagne, the most powerful Carolingian monarch, conquered new territory, took the title of emperor, and initiated the revival of Christian classical culture known as the "Carolingian renaissance" (c. 790–c. 900). He ruled at the local level through counts and other military men who were faithful to him—he called them his *fideles*, or "loyal men." Nevertheless, the unity of this empire, based largely on conquest, a measure of prosperity, and personal allegiance to Charlemagne, was shaky. Its weaknesses were exacerbated by attacks from invaders—Vikings, Muslims, and Magyars. Charlemagne's successors divided his empire among themselves and saw it divided further as local strongmen took over the defense—and rule—of the land.

The Rise of the Carolingians

The Carolingians were among many aristocratic families on the rise during the Merovingian period. Like the others, they were important landowners, but unlike the others they gained exceptional power by monopolizing the position of "palace mayor" in the kingdom of Austrasia and, after 687, the kingdom of Neustria as well (see Map 7.3 on page 276). As mayors, the Carolingians traveled with the Merovingian kings, signed their documents, and helped them formulate and carry out policies. They also cemented alliances with other aristocrats on their own behalf and, by patronizing monasteries and supporting churchmen in key positions, they garnered additional prestige and influence. In the first half of the eighth century, many of the Merovingian kings were children, and the mayors took over much of the responsibility and power of kings themselves.

Charles Martel gave the name "Carolingian" (from *Carolus*, Latin for "Charles") to the dynasty. As palace mayor from 714 to 741, Charles Martel spent most of his time fighting vigorously against opposing aristocratic groups, although later generations would recall with nostalgia his defeat of a contingent of Muslims between Poitiers and Tours in 732. In contending against regional aristocrats who were trying to carve out independent lordships for themselves, Charles Martel and his successors turned aristocratic factions against one another, rewarded supporters while crushing enemies, and brought both lay and clerical aristocrats into alliance with him.

The Carolingians chose their allies well. One was the Anglo-Saxon monk Boniface (680–754), who wanted the continental church to have the same close relations with Rome as the English church had had with the papacy since the time of Gregory the Great. With Carolingian support Boniface went as a missionary to Frisia (today the Netherlands) and Germany, converting the population as a prelude to conquest. Many of the areas he reached had long been Christian, but the churches there had followed local or Irish models rather than Roman. Boniface, who came to Germany from England as the pope's ambassador, set up a hierarchical church organization and founded monasteries dedicated to the rule of St. Benedict. His newly appointed bishops were loyal to Rome and the Carolingians, not to regional aristocracies. They knew that their power came from papal and royal fiat rather than from local power centers.

Charles Martel's son Pippin III (d. 768) and his supporters cemented the Carolingian partnership with the pope by deposing the Merovingian king in 751 and petitioning Pope Zachary to legitimize their actions. He agreed. The Carolingians readily returned the favor a few years later when the pope asked for their help in defense against hostile Lombards. The request signaled a major shift. Before 754, the papacy had been part of the Byzantine Empire; after that it turned to the West. Pippin launched a successful campaign against the Lombard king that ended in 756 with the so-called Donation of Pippin, a peace accord between the

Lombards and the pope. The treaty gave back to the pope cities that had been ruled by the Lombard king. The new arrangement recognized what the papacy had long ago created: a territorial "republic of St. Peter" ruled by the pope, not by the Byzantine emperor. Henceforth the fate of Italy would be tied largely to the policies of the pope and the Frankish kings to the north, not to the emperors of the East.

The Carolingian partnership with the Roman church gave the dynasty a Christian aura, expressed in symbolic form by anointment. Carolingian kings, as Visigothic kings had been, were rubbed with holy oil on their foreheads and on their shoulders in a ceremony that to contemporaries harked back to the Old Testament kings who had been anointed by God.

Charlemagne and His Kingdom, 768–814

The most famous Carolingian king was Charles (r. 768–814), called "the Great" (*le Magne* in Old French) by his contemporaries. Epic poems portrayed Charlemagne as a just, brave, wise, and warlike king. In a biography written by Einhard, his friend and younger contemporary, Charlemagne was the model of a Roman emperor. Some scholars at his court described him as another David, the anointed Old Testament king. Modern historians are less dazzled than his contemporaries were, noting that he was complex, contradictory, and sometimes brutal. He loved listening to St. Augustine's *City of God* and supported major scholarly enterprises, yet he never learned to write. He was devout, building a beautiful chapel at his major residence at Aachen in Austrasia, yet he flouted the advice of churchmen when they told him to convert pagans rather than force baptism on them. He waged many successful wars, yet he thereby destroyed the buffer states surrounding the Frankish kingdoms, unleashing a new round of invasions even before his death.

Behind these contradictions, however, lay a unifying vision. Charlemagne dreamed of an empire that would unite the military and learned traditions of the Roman and Germanic worlds with the legacy of Christianity. In the early years of his reign, he emphasized the military tradition, conquering lands in all directions and subjugating the conquered peoples (see Map 8.3 on page 312). He invaded Italy, seizing the crown of the Lombard kings and annexing northern Italy in 774. He then moved northward and began a long and difficult war against the Saxons, concluded only after more than thirty years of fighting, during which he forcibly annexed Saxon territory and converted the Saxon people to Christianity through mass baptisms at the point of the sword. To the southeast, Charlemagne waged a campaign against the Avars, the people who had fought the Byzantines almost two centuries before. To the southwest, Charlemagne led an expedition to Spain, setting up a march, or military buffer region, between al-Andalus and his own realm. By the 790s, Charlemagne's kingdom stretched eastward to the Saale River (today in eastern Germany), southeast to what is today Austria, and south to Spain and Italy.

■ **MAP 8.3 Expansion of the Carolingian Empire under Charlemagne**

The conquests of Charlemagne temporarily united almost all of western Europe under one government. Although this great empire broke apart (the inset shows the divisions resulting from the Treaty of Verdun), the legacy of that unity remained, even serving as one of the inspirations behind today's European Union.

Such hegemony in the West was unheard of since the time of the Roman Empire, and Charlemagne began to act according to the old Roman imperial model. He sponsored building programs to symbolize his authority, standardized weights and measures, and became a patron of intellectual and artistic efforts, building at Aachen a capital city that included a church patterned on one built by Justinian at Ravenna. To discourage corruption, Charlemagne appointed special officials, called *missi dominici* (meaning "those sent out by the lord king"), to oversee his regional governors—the counts—on the king's behalf. The missi—lay aristocrats or bishops—traveled in pairs to make a circuit of regions of the kingdom. As one of Charlemagne's capitularies (summaries of royal decisions) put it, the missi "are to make diligent inquiry wherever people claim that someone has done them an injustice, so that the missi fully carry out the law and do justice for everyone everywhere, whether in the holy churches of God or among the poor, orphans, or widows."

While Charlemagne was busy imitating Roman emperors through his conquests, his building programs, his legislation, and his efforts at church reform, the papacy was beginning to claim imperial power for itself. At some point, perhaps in the 760s, members of the papal chancery, or writing office, forged a document, called the Donation of Constantine, that declared the pope the recipient of the fourth-century emperor Constantine's crown, cloak, and military rank along with "all provinces, palaces, and districts of the city of Rome and Italy and of the regions of the West." The tension between the imperial claims of the Carolingians and those of the pope was heightened by the existence of an emperor at Constantinople who also had rights in the West.

Pope Hadrian I (r. 772–795) maintained a balance among these three powers. But Hadrian's successor, Leo III (r. 795–816), tipped the balance. In 799, accused of adultery and perjury by a faction of the Roman aristocracy, Leo narrowly escaped being blinded and having his tongue cut out. He fled northward to seek Charlemagne's protection. Charlemagne had him escorted back to Rome and arrived there himself in late November 800 to an imperial welcome orchestrated by Leo. On Christmas Day of that year, Leo put an imperial crown on Charlemagne's head, and the clergy and nobles who were present acclaimed the king *Augustus*, the title of the first Roman emperor. The pope hoped in this way to exalt the king of the Franks, to downgrade the Byzantine ruler, and to enjoy the role of "emperor maker" himself.

About twenty years later, when Einhard wrote about this coronation, he said that the imperial title at first so displeased Charlemagne "that he stated that, if he had known in advance of the pope's plan, he would not have entered the church that day." In fact, Charlemagne did not use any title but king for more than a year afterward. But it is unlikely that he was completely surprised by the imperial title; his advisers certainly had been thinking about claiming it. He might have hesitated adopting it because he feared the reaction of the Byzantines, as Einhard went on to suggest, or he might well have objected to the papal role in his crowning rather than to the crown itself. When he finally did call himself emperor, after establishing a peace with the Byzantines, he used a long and revealing title: "Charles, the most serene Augustus, crowned by God, great and peaceful Emperor who governs the Roman Empire and who is, by the mercy of God, king of the Franks and the Lombards." According to this title, Charlemagne was not the Roman emperor crowned by the pope but rather God's emperor, who governed the Roman Empire along with his many other duties.

The Carolingian Renaissance

Charlemagne inaugurated—and his successors continued to support—a revival of learning designed to enhance the glory of the kings, educate their officials, reform the liturgy, and purify the faith. Like the renaissances of the Byzantine and Islamic worlds, the Carolingian renaissance resuscitated the learning of the past. Scholars studied Roman imperial writers such as Suetonius and Virgil; they read and commented on the works of the church fathers; and they worked to establish complete and accurate texts of everything they read and prized.

The English scholar Alcuin (c. 732–804), a member of the circle of scholars whom Charlemagne recruited to form a center of study, brought with him the traditions of Anglo-Saxon scholarship that had been developed by men such as Benedict Biscop and Bede. Invited to Aachen, Alcuin became Charlemagne's chief adviser, writing letters on the king's behalf, counseling him on royal policy, and tutoring the king's household, including the women. Charlemagne's sister and daughter, for example, often asked Alcuin to explain passages from the Gospel to them. Charlemagne entrusted Alcuin with the task of preparing an improved edition of the Vulgate, the Latin Bible read in all church services.

■ **St. Matthew**
The Carolingian renaissance produced art of extraordinary originality. Although the artist of this picture was inspired by classical models, his frenetic, emotional lines and uncanny colors are something new. This illustration, a depiction of St. Matthew writing (with an ink horn in his left hand and a quill in his right hand), precedes the text of St. Matthew's Gospel in a book of Gospels made around 820. Compare it to the Psalter illumination from Constantinople on page 301. What does this comparison tell you about the similarities and differences between the Macedonian and Carolingian renaissances? (La Médiathèque, Ville d'Epernay.)

The Carolingian renaissance depended on an elite staff of scholars such as Alcuin, yet its educational program had broader appeal. In one of his capitularies, Charlemagne ordered that the cathedrals and monasteries of his kingdom teach reading and writing to all who were able to learn. Some churchmen expressed the hope that schools for children (perhaps they were thinking of girls as well as boys) would be established even in small villages and hamlets. Although this dream was never realized, it shows that even before the Islamic world was organizing the madrasa system of schools, the Carolingians were thinking about the importance of religious education for more than a small elite.

Scholarship complemented the alliance between the church and the king symbolized by Charlemagne's anointment. In the Carolingian world, much as in the Islamic and Byzantine, there was little distinction between politics and religion: kings considered themselves appointed by the grace of God, often based their laws on biblical passages, involved themselves in church reform, appointed churchmen on their own initiative, and believed their personal piety a source of power.

Art, like scholarship, served Carolingian political and religious goals. Just as in the Byzantine renaissance, Carolingian artists illuminated texts—often lavish Gospels meant for the royal family or liturgical books commissioned by bishops and abbots—using earlier pictures as models. But their imitation was not slavish. To their models Carolingian artists added exuberant decoration and design, often rendering architectural elements as bands of color and portraying human figures with great liveliness. Some models came from Byzantium, and perhaps some Carolingian artists themselves came from there, refugees from Byzantium during its iconoclastic period. Pictorial models from Italy provided the kings' artists with examples of the sturdy style of the late Roman Empire.

The Carolingian program was ambitious and lasting, even after the Carolingian dynasty had faded to a memory. The work of locating, understanding, and transmitting models of the past continued in a number of monastic schools. In the materials they studied, the questions they asked, and the answers they suggested, the Carolingians offered a mode of inquiry fruitful for subsequent generations. In the twelfth century, scholars would build on the foundations laid by the Carolingian renaissance. The very print of this textbook depends on one achievement of the period: modern letter fonts are based on the clear and beautiful letter forms, called Caroline minuscule, invented in the ninth century to standardize manuscript handwriting and make it more readable.

Charlemagne's Successors, 814–911

Charlemagne's son Louis the Pious (r. 814–840) was also crowned emperor, and he took his role as guarantor of the Christian empire even more seriously. He brought the monastic reformer Benedict of Aniane to court and issued a capitulary in 817 imposing on all the monasteries of the empire a uniform way of life based on the rule of St. Benedict. Although some monasteries opposed this legislation, and in the years to come the king was unable to impose his will directly, this moment marked the effective adoption of the Benedictine rule as the monastic standard in the West. Louis also standardized the practices of his notaries, who issued his documents and privileges, and he continued to use missi to administer justice throughout the realm.

In a new development of the coronation ritual, Louis's first wife, Ermengard, was crowned empress by the pope in 816. In 817, their firstborn son, Lothar, was given the title emperor and made coruler with his father. Their other sons, Pippin and Louis (later called "the German"), were made subkings under imperial rule. Louis the Pious hoped in this way to ensure the unity of the empire while satisfying the claims of his and Ermengard's three sons. But Louis's plans were thwarted by events.

Ermengard died, and Louis married Judith, the daughter of one of the most powerful families in the kingdom. In 823, Judith and Louis had a son, Charles (later known as "the Bald," to whose court Dhuoda's son William was sent). The three sons of Ermengard, bitter over the birth of another royal heir, rebelled against their father and fought one another. A chronicle written during this period suggests that nearly every year was filled with family tragedies. In 830, for example, Pippin and his brother Lothar plotted to depose their father and shut Judith up in a convent. Louis the Pious regained control, but three years later his sons by Ermengard once again banded together and imprisoned him. Louis was lucky that the brothers began quarreling among themselves. Their alliance broke apart, and he was released.

Family battles such as these continued, both during Louis's lifetime and, with great vigor, after his death in 840. In 843, the Treaty of Verdun divided the empire among the three remaining brothers (Pippin had died in 838) in an arrangement that would roughly define the future political contours of western Europe (see Map 8.3, inset). The western third, bequeathed to Charles the Bald (r. 840–877), would eventually become France; the eastern third, handed to Louis the German (r. 840–876), would become Germany. The "Middle Kingdom," which was given to Lothar (r. 817–855) along with the imperial title, had a different fate: parts of it were absorbed by France and Germany, and the rest eventually formed the modern states of the Netherlands, Belgium, Luxembourg, Switzerland, and Italy.

In 843, the European-wide empire of Charlemagne dissolved. Forged by conquest, it had been supported by a small group of privileged aristocrats with lands and offices stretching across the entire realm. Their loyalty, based on shared values, real friendship, expectations of gain, and sometimes formal ties of vassalage and fealty (see pages 324–25), was crucial to the success of the Carolingians. The empire had also been supported by an ideal, shared by educated laymen and churchmen alike, of Christian belief and imperialism working together to bring good order to the earthly state. But powerful forces operated against the Carolingian Empire. Once the empire stopped expanding, the aristocrats could no longer hope for new lands and offices. They put down roots in particular regions and began to gather their own followings. Powerful local traditions such as different languages also undermined imperial unity. Finally, as Dhuoda revealed, some people disagreed with the imperial ideal. Asking her son to put his father before the emperor, she demonstrated her belief in the primacy of the family and the intimate and personal ties that bound it together. Dhuoda's ideal did not eliminate the emperor (European emperors would continue to reign until World War I), but it represented a new sensibility that saw real value in the breaking apart of Charlemagne's empire into smaller, more intimate local units.

Land and Power

The Carolingian economy, based on trade and agriculture, contributed to both the rise and the dissolution of the Carolingian Empire. At the onset, its wealth came from land and plunder. After the booty from war ceased to pour in, the Carolingians still had access to money and goods. To the north, in Viking trading stations such as Haithabu (today Hedeby, in northern Germany), archaeologists have found Carolingian glass and pots alongside Islamic coins and cloth, which tells us that the Carolingian economy intermingled with that of the Abbasid caliphate. Silver from the Islamic world probably came north up the Volga River through Russia to the Baltic Sea. There the coins were melted down, the silver traded to the Carolingians in return for wine, jugs, glasses, and other manufactured goods. The Carolingians turned the silver into coins of their own, to be used throughout the empire for small-scale local trade. The weakening of the Abbasid caliphate in the mid-ninth century, however, disrupted this far-flung trade network and contributed to the weakening of the Carolingians at about the same time.

Land provided the most important source of Carolingian wealth and power. Like the landholders of the late Roman Empire and the Merovingian period, Carolingian aristocrats held many estates, scattered throughout the Frankish Empire. But in the Carolingian period these estates were reorganized, and their productivity was carefully calculated. Modern historians often call these estates **manors.**

Typical was the manor called Villeneuve St.-Georges, which belonged to the monastery of St.-Germain-des-Prés (today in Paris) in the ninth century. Villeneuve consisted of arable fields, vineyards, meadows where animals could roam, and woodland, all scattered about the countryside rather than connected in a compact unit. The land was not tilled by slave gangs, as had been the custom on great estates of the Roman Empire, but rather by peasant families, each one settled on its own manse, consisting of a house, a garden, and small pieces of the arable land. The peasants farmed the land that belonged to them and also worked the demesne, the very large manse of the lord (in this case, the abbey of St.-Germain). These peasant farms marked a major social and economic development. Slaves had not been allowed to live in family units. By contrast, the peasants on Villeneuve and on other Carolingian estates could not be displaced from their manses or separated involuntarily from their families. In this sense, the peasant household of the Carolingian period was the precursor of the modern nuclear family.

Peasants at Villeneuve practiced the most progressive sort of plowing, known as the three-field system. At any one time, they farmed two-thirds of the arable land. They plowed one-third and planted winter wheat; they plowed another third and planted summer crops; and they plowed the final third but left the land fallow, to restore its fertility. The fields sown with crops and the field left fallow were then rotated so that land use was repeated only every three years. Because two-thirds of the arable land was cultivated each year, this system produced larger yields than did the still prevalent two-field system, in which only one-half of the arable land was cultivated in any one year.

All the peasants at Villeneuve were dependents of the monastery and owed dues and services to St.-Germain. Peasants' obligations varied enormously, depending on their status and on the manse they held. One family, for example, owed four silver coins, wine, wood, three hens, and fifteen eggs every year, and the men had to plow the fields of the demesne land. Another family owed the intensive labor of working the vineyards. One woman was required to weave cloth and feed the chickens. Peasant women spent much time at the lord's house in the *gynaeceum*—the women's workshop, where they made and dyed cloth and sewed garments—or in the kitchens as cooks. Peasant men spent most of their time in the fields.

Like other lords, the Carolingians benefited from their extensive estates. Nevertheless, farming was still too primitive to return great surpluses. Further, as the lands belonging to the king were divided up in the wake of the partitioning of the empire and new invasions, Carolingian dependence on manors scattered throughout the kingdom proved to be a source of weakness.

Vikings, Muslims, and Magyars Invade

Like the Roman emperors they emulated, Carolingian kings and counts confronted new groups along their borders (Map 8.4). The new peoples—Vikings to the north, Muslims to the south, and Magyars to the east—were feared and hated; but like the Germanic tribes that had entered the Roman Empire earlier, they also served as military allies. As royal sons fought one another and as counts and other powerful men sought to carve out their own principalities, their alliances with the newcomers helped integrate the outsiders swiftly into European politics. The impact of these foreign groups hastened, but did not cause, the dissolution of the empire. The Carolingian kings could not muster troops quickly or efficiently enough to counter

MAP 8.4 Viking, Muslim, and Magyar Invasions of the Ninth and Tenth Centuries

Bristling with multicolored arrows, this map suggests that western Europe was continually and thoroughly pillaged by outside invaders for almost two centuries. That impression is only partially true; it must be offset by several factors. First, not all the invaders came at once. The Viking raids were about over when the Magyar attacks began. Second, the invaders were not entirely unwelcome. The Magyars were for a time enlisted as mercenaries by the king of Italy, and some Muslims were allied to local lords in Provence. Third, the invasions, though widespread, were local in effect. Note, for example, that the Viking raids were largely limited to rivers and coastal areas.

319

the lightning attacks of the raiders. Defense fell into the hands of local authorities who, building on their new prestige and the weakness of the king, became increasingly independent rulers themselves.

The first of the new groups to attack the Carolingian Empire was the Vikings. The Franks called them "Northmen"; the English called them "Danes." They were, in fact, much less united than their victims thought. When they began their voyages at the end of the eighth century, they did so in independent bands. Merchants and pirates at the same time, Vikings followed a chief, seeking profit, prestige, and land. Many traveled as families: husbands, wives, children, and slaves.

The Vikings perfected the art of navigation. In their longships they crossed the Atlantic, settling Iceland and Greenland and (about 1000 C.E.) landing on the coast of North America. Other Viking bands navigated the rivers of Europe. The Vikings were pagans, and to them monasteries and churches—with their reliquaries, chalices, and crosses—were storehouses of booty. "Never before," wrote Alcuin, who experienced one attack, "has such terror appeared in Britain as we have now suffered from a pagan race. . . . Behold the church of St. Cuthbert spattered with the blood of the priests of God, despoiled of all its ornaments."

The British Isles confronted sporadic invasions by the Vikings from the eighth to the tenth century. From their fortified bases along the coast of Ireland the Vikings attacked and plundered churches and monasteries. But they also established Dublin as a commercial center and, in the tenth century, began to intermarry with the Irish and convert to Christianity. In Scotland, the Scandinavians settled on the west coast. Meanwhile, by the 870s, they had settled the east coast of England, plowing the land and preparing to live on it. The

■ **Viking Picture Stone**
Picture stones, some very elaborate, others with simple incisions, were made on the island of Gotland, today part of Sweden, from the fifth to the twelfth century. This one, dating from the eighth or ninth century, has four interrelated scenes. At the bottom is a battle between people defending a farm (note the cattle tied to the walls of the enclosure) and archers outside. Above is another enclosure with a woman at its wall. She is either Gudrun mourning her brother Gunnar, who was thrown into a snake pit, or Sigyn, the faithful wife of the god Loke, catching in a bowl the venom that a snake pours down on her chained husband. Next comes a ship, a typical picture stone motif; it is the ship of death that takes heroes to heaven. At the very top is heaven, or Valhalla, itself, where the heroes hunt and feast for all eternity. (Photo: Raymond Hejdstrom.)

0   50   100 miles

0   50   100 kilometers

Coins
● 1–119
● 120 or more

North Sea

DANELAW

London

■ TAKING MEASURE Viking Coin Hoards, c. 865–895

From chronicles and other texts, we know that the Vikings invaded and settled in England. But from such sources it is very hard to know exactly where they settled and how many Vikings there were. Counting buried coins from the period can help answer these questions. Before safe-deposit boxes and banks, people buried their money in times of trouble. Archaeologists counting Viking coin hoards in England believe that the area called Danelaw was fairly thickly populated by Vikings, with a scattering in other regions as well. The Viking impact on England was not so much political—no Viking king took it over—as demographic. After 900, England was as much Scandinavian as it was Anglo-Saxon.

region where they settled and imposed their own laws was later called the *Danelaw*. (See "Taking Measure," above.)

In Wessex, the southernmost kingdom of England, King Alfred the Great (r. 871–899) bought time and peace by paying tribute and giving hostages. Such tribute, later called *Danegeld*, was collected as a tax that eventually became the basis of a relatively lucrative taxation system in England. Then in 878, Alfred led an army that, as his biographer put it, "gained the victory through God's will. He destroyed the Vikings with great slaughter and pursued those who fled . . . hacking them down." Thereafter, the pressures of invasion eased as Alfred reorganized his army, set up strongholds, and deployed new warships.

On the continent of Europe, too, the invaders set up trading emporia and set-tled where originally they had raided. Beginning about 850, their attacks became well-organized expeditions for regional control. At the end of the ninth century, one contingent settled in the region of France that soon took the name Normandy, land of the Northmen. The new inhabitants converted to Christianity during the tenth century. Rollo, the Viking leader in Normandy, accepted Christianity in 911 when the Frankish king Charles the Simple (or Straightforward) formally ceded Normandy to him.

Normandy was not the only new Christian state formed in the north during the tenth and eleventh centuries. Scandinavia itself was transformed with the creation of the powerful kingdom of Denmark. There had been kings in Scandinavia before the tenth century, but they had been weak, their power challenged by nearby chieftains. The Vikings had been led by these chieftains, each competing for booty to win prestige, land, and power back home. During the course of their raids, they and their followers came into contact with new cultures and learned from them. Meanwhile the Carolingians and the English supported missionaries in Scandinavia. By the middle of the tenth century, the Danish kings and their people had become Christian. Following the model of the Christian kings to their south, the Danish kings built up an effective monarchy, with a royal mint and local agents who depended on them. By about 1000, the Danes had extended their control to parts of Sweden, Norway, and even, under King Cnut (r. 1017–1035), England.

Far from Denmark, Muslims were taking advantage of Byzantium's early weakness. In 827 one group unconnected to the caliphate began the slow conquest of Sicily, which took nearly one hundred years. During the same century, Muslim pirates set up bases on Mediterranean islands and strongholds in Provence (in southern France) and near Naples (in southern Italy). Liutprand of Cremona reported on the activities of one such group:

> [Muslim pirates from al-Andalus], disembarking under cover of night, entered the manor house unobserved and murdered—O grievous tale!—the Christian inhabitants. They then took the place as their own ... [fortified it, and] started stealthy raids on all the neighboring country.

The Muslims at this base, set up in 891, robbed, took prisoners, and collected ransoms. But they were so useful to their Christian neighbors, who called on them to support their own feuds, that they were not ousted until 972. Only then, when they caused a scandal by capturing the holiest man of his era, Abbot Maieul of Cluny, did the count of Provence launch a successful attack against their lair.

Farther to the east, the Magyars, latecomers to the West, arrived around 899 in the Danube basin. Until then, the region had been predominantly Slavic, but the Magyars came from the East and spoke a language unrelated to any other in Europe (except Finnish). Their entry drove a wedge between the Slavs near the Frankish kingdom and those bordering on Byzantium; those near Byzantium, such as the Bulgarians, Serbs, and Russians, were driven into the Byzantine orbit, while those nearer the Frankish kingdom came under the influence of Germany.

From their bases in present-day Hungary, the Magyars raided far to the west, attacking Germany, Italy, and even southern Gaul frequently between 899 and 955. Then in the summer of 955, one marauding party of Magyars was met at the Lech River by the German king Otto I (r. 936–973), whose army decimated them in the battle of Lechfeld. Otto's victory, his subsequent military reorganization of his eastern frontiers, and the cessation of Magyar raids around this time made Otto a great hero to his contemporaries. Today, however, historians think the containment of the Magyars had more to do with their internal transformation from nomads to farmers than with their military defeat.

The Viking, Muslim, and Magyar invasions were the final onslaught western Europe experienced from outsiders. In some ways they were a continuation of the invasions that had rocked the Roman Empire in the fourth and fifth centuries. Loosely organized in warbands, the new groups entered western Europe looking for wealth but, apart from the Muslims, stayed on to become absorbed in its new post-invasion society.

■ **REVIEW:** *What were the strengths and weaknesses of the Carolingian institutions of government, warfare, and defense?*

The Emergence of Local Rule in the Post-Carolingian Age

The Carolingian Empire was too diverse to cohere. Latin was a universal language, but few people spoke it; instead they used a wide variety of languages and dialects. The king demanded loyalty from everyone, but most people knew only his representative, the local count. As the empire ceased to expand and was instead attacked by outsiders, the counts and other powerful men stopped looking to the king for new lands and offices and began to develop and exploit what they already had. They became powerful lords, commanding warriors and peasants, building castles, setting up markets, collecting revenues, keeping the peace, and seeing themselves as independent regional rulers. In this way, a new warrior class of lords and vassals came to dominate post-Carolingian society.

Yet it would be wrong to imagine that all of Europe came under the control of rural warlords. In Italy, where cities had never lost their importance, urban elites ruled over the surrounding countryside. Everywhere, kings retained a certain amount of power; indeed, in some places, such as Germany and England, they were extremely effective. Central European monarchies formed under the influence of Germany.*

Public Power and Private Relationships

The key way in which both kings and less powerful men commanded others was by ensuring personal loyalty. In the ninth century, the Carolingian kings had their

---

*Terms such as *Germany*, *France*, and *Italy* are used here for the sake of convenience. They refer to regions, not to the nation-states that would eventually become associated with those names.

fideles, their "faithful men." Among these were the counts. In addition to a share in the revenues of their administrative district, the county, the counts received benefices, later also called fiefs, which were temporary grants of land given in return for service. These short-term arrangements often became permanent, however, once a count's son inherited the job and the fiefs of his father. By the end of the ninth century, fiefs were often properties that could be passed on to heirs.

In the wake of the invasions, more and more warriors were drawn into similar networks of dependency, but not with the king: they became the faithful men—the **vassals**—of local lords. From the Latin word for fief comes the word *feudal,* and historians often use the term *feudalism* to describe the social and economic system created by the relationship among vassals, lords, and fiefs.*

It was frequently said by medieval people that their society consisted of three groups: those who prayed, those who fought, and those who worked. All of these people were involved in hierarchies of dependency and were linked by personal bonds, but the upper classes—the prayers (monks) and the fighters (the knights)— were free. Their brand of dependency was honorable, whether they were vassals, lords, or both. In fact, a typical warrior was lord of several vassals and the vassal of another lord. Monasteries normally had vassals to fight for them, and their abbots in turn were likely to be vassals of a king or other powerful lord.

Vassalage grew up as an alternative to public power and at the same time as a way to strengthen what little public power there was. Given the impoverished economic conditions of the West, its primitive methods of communication, and its lack of unifying traditions, kings came to rely on vassals personally loyal to them to muster troops, collect taxes, and administer justice. When in the ninth century the Frankish Empire broke up politically and power fell into the hands of local lords, they, too, needed "faithful men" to protect them and carry out their orders. And vassals needed lords. At the low end of the social scale, poor vassals looked to their lords to feed, clothe, house, and arm them. They hoped that they would be rewarded for their service with a fief of their own, with which they could support themselves and a family. At the upper end of the social scale, vassals looked to lords to enrich them further.

A few women were vassals and some were lords (or, rather, "ladies," the female counterpart); many upper-class laywomen participated in the society of fighters and prayers as wives and mothers of vassals and lords. Other aristocratic women entered convents and became members of the social group that prayed. Through its abbess or a man standing in for her, a convent was likely to have vassals as well.

---

*Many historians, however, regard *feudalism* as a problematic term. Does it mean "anarchy"? Some historians have used it that way. Does it mean "a hierarchical scheme of lords and knights"? This is another common definition. And there are others as well. This imprecision has led some historians to drop the word altogether. Moreover, feudalism implies that one way of life dominated the Middle Ages, when in fact, there were numerous social, political, and economic arrangements. For these reasons, *feudalism* rarely appears in *The Making of the West.*

Becoming the vassal of a lord often involved both ritual gestures and verbal promises. In a ceremony witnessed by others, the vassal-to-be knelt and, placing his hands between the hands of his lord, said, "I promise to be your man." This act, known as homage, was followed by the promise of **fealty**—fidelity, trust, and service—which the vassal swore with his hand on relics or a Bible. Then the vassal and the lord kissed. In an age when many people could not read, a public ceremony such as this represented a visual and verbal contract. Vassalage bound the lord and vassal to one another with reciprocal obligations, usually military. Knights, as the premier fighters of the day, were the most desirable vassals.

At the bottom of the social scale were those who worked—the peasants. In the Carolingian period, many peasants were free; they did not live on a manor, or if they did, they owed very little to its lord. But as power fell into the hands of local rulers, fewer and fewer peasants remained free. Rather, they were made dependent on lords, not as vassals but as **serfs**. Serfdom was a dependency separate from and completely unlike that of a vassal. It was not voluntary but inherited. No serf did homage or fealty to his lord; no serf kissed his lord as an equal. And the serf's work as a laborer was not considered honorable. Unlike knights, who were celebrated in songs and stories, peasants, who constituted the majority of the population, were nevertheless barely noticed by the upper classes—except as a source of revenue.

New methods of cultivation and a burgeoning population helped transform the rural landscape and make it more productive. With a growing number of men and women to work the land, the lower classes now had more mouths to feed and faced the hardship of food shortage. Landlords began reorganizing their estates to run more efficiently. In the tenth century, the three-field system became more prevalent; heavy plows that could turn the heavy northern soils came into wider use; and horses (more effective than oxen) were harnessed to pull the plows. The result was surplus food and a better standard of living for nearly everyone.

In search of greater profits, some lords lightened the dues and services of peasants temporarily to allow them to open up new lands by draining marshes and cutting down forests. Some landlords converted dues and labor services into money payments, a boon for both lords and peasants. Lords now had money to spend on what they wanted rather than hens and eggs they might not need or want. Peasants benefited because their tax was fixed despite inflation. Thus, as the prices of their hens and eggs went up, they could sell them, reaping a profit in spite of the dues they owed their lords.

By the tenth century, many peasants lived in populous rural settlements, true villages. In the midst of a sea of arable land, meadow, wood, and wasteland, these villages developed a sense of community. Boundaries—sometimes real fortifications, sometimes simple markers—told nonresidents to keep out and to find shelter in huts located outside the village limits.

The church often formed the focal point of local activity. There people met, received the sacraments, drew up contracts, and buried their parents and children.

Religious feasts and festivals joined the rituals of farming to mark the seasons. The church dominated the village in another way: men and women owed it a tax called a **tithe** (equivalent to one-tenth of their crops or income, paid in money or in kind), which was first instituted on a regular basis by the Carolingians.

Village peasants' sense of common purpose grew out of their practical interdependence, as they shared oxen or horses for the teams that pulled the plow or turned to village craftsmen to fix their wheels or shoe their horses. Their feeling of solidarity sometimes encouraged villagers to band together to ask for privileges as a group. Near Verona, in northern Italy, for example, twenty-five men living around the castle of Nogara in 920 joined together to ask their lord, the abbot of Nonantola, to allow them to lease plots of land, houses, and pasturage there in return for a small yearly rent and the promise to defend the castle. The abbot granted their request.

Village solidarity could be compromised, however, by conflicting loyalties and obligations. A peasant in one village might very well have one piece of land connected with a certain manor and another bit of arable field on a different estate, and he or she might owe several lords different kinds of dues. Even peasants of one village working for one lord might owe him varied services and taxes.

Layers of obligations were even more striking across the regions of Europe than in particular villages. The principal distinction was between free peasants, such as small landowners in Saxony and other parts of Germany, and unfree peasants, who were especially common in France and England. In Italy, peasants ranged from small independent landowners to leaseholders (like the tenants at Nogara); most were both, owning a parcel in one place and leasing another nearby.

Once the power of kings began to weaken, this system of peasant obligations became part of a larger system of local rule. As landlords consolidated their power over their manors, they collected not only dues and services but also fees for the use of their flour mills, bake houses, and breweries. Some built castles, fortified strongholds, and imposed the even wider powers of the **ban**: the rights to collect taxes, hear court cases, levy fines, and muster men for defense.

The Fragmentation of France, c. 1000

In France, for example, as the king's power waned, political control fell into the hands of counts and other princes. By 1000, castles had become the key to their power. In the south of France, power was so fragmented that each man who controlled a castle—a **castellan**—was a virtual ruler, although often with a very limited reach. In northwestern France, territorial princes, basing their rule on the control of *many* castles, dominated much broader regions. For example, Fulk Nera, count of Anjou (r. 987–1040), built more than thirteen castles and captured others from rival counts. By the end of his life, he controlled a region extending from Blois to Nantes along the Loire valley.

Castellans extended their authority by subjecting everyone near their castle to their ban. Peasants, whether or not they worked on a castellan's estates, had to pay him a variety of dues for his "protection" and judicial rights over them. Castellans also established links with the better-off landholders in the region, tempting or coercing them to become vassals. Lay castellans often supported local monasteries and controlled the appointment of local priests. But churchmen themselves sometimes held the position of territorial lord: a good example is the archbishop of Milan in the eleventh century.

The development of nearly independent local political units, dominated by a castle and controlled by a military elite, marked an important turning point for western Europe. Although this development did not occur everywhere simultaneously (and in some places it hardly occurred at all), the social, political, and cultural life of the West was now dominated by landowners who saw themselves as military men and regional leaders.

War and Peace

All warriors were not alike. At the top of the elite were the kings, counts, and dukes. Below them, but "on the rise," were ordinary castellans. Still farther down the social scale were knights. Yet all shared in a common lifestyle.

Knights and their lords fought on horseback. High astride his steed, wearing a shirt of chain mail and a helmet of flat metal plates riveted together, the knight marked a military revolution. The war season started in May, when the grasses were high enough for horses to forage. Horseshoes allowed armies to move faster than ever before and to negotiate rough terrain previously unsuitable for battle. Stirrups, probably invented by Asiatic nomadic tribes, allowed the mounted warrior to hold his seat. This made it possible for knights to thrust at their enemy with heavy lances. The light javelin of ancient warfare was abandoned.

Lords and their vassals often lived together. In the lord's great hall they ate, listened to entertainment, and bedded down for the night. They went out hunting together and went off to the battlefield as a group as well. More powerful vassals— counts, for example—lived on their own fiefs and hardly ever saw their lord (probably the king), except when doing homage and fealty—once in their lifetime—or serving him in battles, for perhaps forty days a year. But they themselves were lords of knightly vassals who were not married and who lived and ate and hunted with them.

No matter how old they might be, unmarried knights who lived with their lords were called youths by their contemporaries. Such perpetual bachelors were something new, the result of a profound transformation in the organization of families and inheritance. Before the eleventh century, noble families had recognized all their children as heirs and had divided their estates accordingly. In the mid-ninth century, Count Everard and his wife, for example, willed their large estates, scattered from Belgium to Italy, to their four sons and three daughters (although they gave the boys far more than they gave the girls, and the oldest boy far more than the others).

By around the year 1000, however, adapting to diminished opportunities for land and office and wary of fragmenting the estates they had, French nobles changed both their conception of their families and the way property passed to the next generation. Recognizing the overriding claims of one son, often the eldest, they handed down their entire inheritance to him. In cases where the heir is indeed the eldest son, this system of inheritance is called **primogeniture**. The heir, in turn, traced his lineage only through the male line, backward through his father and forward through his own eldest son. Such patrilineal families left many younger sons without an inheritance and therefore without the prospect of marrying and founding families; instead, the younger sons lived at the courts of the great as youths or they joined the church as clerics or monks. The development of territorial rule and patrilineal families went hand in hand, as fathers passed down to one son undiminished not only manors but titles, castles, and the authority of the ban.

Patrilineal inheritance tended to bypass daughters and so tended to work against the interests of aristocratic women. In families without sons, however, widows and daughters did inherit property. And wives often acted as lords of estates when their husbands were at war. Moreover, all aristocratic women played an important role in this warrior society, whether in the monastery (where they prayed for the souls of their families) or through their marriages (where they helped forge alliances between their own families and the families of their husbands).

This highly militarized society was almost constantly at war. Warfare benefited territorial rulers in the short term, but in the long run their revenues suffered as armies plundered the countryside and sacked walled cities. Bishops, who were themselves from the class of lords and warriors, worried about the dangers to church property. Peasants cried out against wars that destroyed their crops or forced them to join regional infantries. Monks and religious thinkers were appalled at violence that was not in the service of an anointed king. By the end of the tenth century, all classes clamored for peace.

Sentiment against local violence was united in a movement called the **Peace of God**, which began in the south of France and by 1050 had spread over a wide region. Meetings of bishops, counts, and lords and often crowds of lower-class men and women set forth the provisions of this peace: "No man in the counties or bishoprics shall seize a horse, colt, ox, cow, ass, or the burdens which it carries. . . . No one shall seize a peasant, man or woman," ran the decree of one council held in 990. Anyone who violated this peace was to be excommunicated: cut off from the community of the faithful, denied the services of the church and the hope of salvation.

The peace proclaimed at local councils like this limited some violence but did not address the problem of conflict between armed men. A second set of agreements, the Truce of God, soon supplemented the Peace of God. The truce prohibited fighting between warriors at certain times: on Sunday because it was the Lord's Day, on Saturday because it was a reminder of Holy Saturday, on Friday because it symbolized Good Friday, and on Thursday because it stood for Holy Thursday. Enforcement of the truce fell to the local knights and nobles, who swore over saints' relics to uphold it and to fight anyone who broke it.

The Peace of God and Truce of God were only two of the mechanisms that attempted to contain or defuse violent confrontations in the tenth and eleventh centuries. At times, lords and their vassals mediated wars and feuds in assemblies called *placita*. In other instances, monks or laymen tried to find solutions to disputes that would leave the honor of both parties intact. Rather than try to establish guilt or innocence, winners or losers, these methods of adjudication often resulted in compromises on both sides.

Political Communities in Italy, England, and France

The political systems that emerged in the wake of the breakup of the Carolingian Empire were as varied as the regions of Europe. In Italy, cities were the centers of power, still reflecting, though feebly, the political organization of ancient Rome. In England, strong kings came to the fore. In France, as we have seen, great lords dominated the countryside; there the king was relatively weak.

Whereas in France great landlords built their castles in the countryside, in Italy they often constructed their family seats within the walls of cities such as Milan and Lucca. Churches, as many as fifty or sixty, were also built within the city walls, the proud work of rich laymen and laywomen or of bishops. From their perches within the cities, the great landholders of Italy, both lay and religious, dominated the countryside.

Italian cities also functioned as important marketplaces. Peasants sold their surplus goods there; artisans and merchants lived within the walls; foreign traders offered their wares. These members of the lower classes were supported by the noble rich, who in Italy even more than elsewhere depended on cash to satisfy their desires. In the course of the ninth and tenth centuries, both servile and free tenants became renters who paid in currency.

Social and political life in Italy favored a familial organization somewhat different from the patrilineal families of France. To stave off the partitioning of their properties among heirs, families organized themselves by formal contract into *consorteria*, in which all male members shared the profits of the family's inheritance and all women were excluded. The consorterial family became a kind of blood-related corporation, a social unit on which early Italian businesses and banks would later be modeled.

Where Italy was urban, England was rural. In the face of the Viking invasions in England, King Alfred of Wessex (r. 871–899) developed new mechanisms of royal government, instituting reforms that his successors continued. He fortified settlements throughout Wessex and divided the army into two parts. The duty of one was to defend the fortifications (or *burhs*); the other operated as a mobile unit. Alfred also started a navy. These military innovations cost money, and the assessments fell on peasants' holdings.

England in the Age of King Alfred, r. 871–899

Alfred sought to strengthen his kingdom's religious integrity as well as its regional fortifications. In the ninth century, people interpreted invasions as God's punishment for sin, which therefore was the real culprit. Thus Alfred began a program of religious reform by bringing scholars to his court to write and to educate others. Above all, Alfred wanted to translate key religious works from Latin into Anglo-Saxon (or Old English). He was determined to "turn into the language that we can all understand certain books which are the most necessary for all men to know." Alfred and scholars under his guidance translated works by church fathers such as Gregory the Great and St. Augustine. Even the Psalms, until now sung only in Hebrew, Greek, and Latin, were rendered into Anglo-Saxon. In most of ninth- and tenth-century Europe, Latin remained the language of scholarship and writing, separate from the language people spoke. In England, however, the vernacular—the common spoken language—was also a literary language. With Alfred's work giving it greater legitimacy, Anglo-Saxon came to be used alongside Latin for both literature and royal administration.

Alfred's reforms strengthened not only defense, education, and religion but also royal power. He consolidated his control over Wessex and fought the Danish kings, who by the mid-870s had taken Northumbria, northeastern Mercia, and East Anglia. Eventually, as he harried the Danes who were pushing south and westward, he was recognized as king of all the English not under Danish rule. He issued a law code, the first by an English king since 695. Unlike earlier codes, drawn up for each separate kingdom of England, Alfred drew up his laws from and for all of the English kingdoms. In this way, Alfred became the first king of all the English.

Alfred's successors rolled back Danish rule in England. "Then the Norsemen departed in their nailed ships, bloodstained survivors of spears," wrote one poet about a battle the Vikings lost in 937. But many Vikings remained. Converted to Christianity, their great men joined Anglo-Saxons in attending the English king at court. As peace returned, new administrative subdivisions—shires (counties) and

■ The Alfred Jewel

About two and a half inches long, this jewel consists of a gold drop-shaped frame surrounding an enamel plaque that depicts a man enthroned and holding two flowering rods. Rock crystal encloses the plaque within the frame. Along the side of the frame are gold letters in Anglo-Saxon that say: "Alfred had me made." The snout of the beast at the bottom was hollowed out, probably to hold a wooden or ivory pointer. If this jewel belonged to King Alfred, as is likely, it may be like the pointers that Alfred wanted distributed to all the bishops in his kingdom along with the Anglo-Saxon translation of Gregory the Great's Pastoral Care. *Such pointers were used to point to passages in manuscripts. Why did Alfred have the* Pastoral Care *translated? Why did he want copies sent to the bishops? And why did he want the bishops to have pointers?*
(Ashmolean Museum, Oxford.)

hundreds (districts)—were established throughout England for judicial and taxation purposes. The powerful men of the kingdom swore fealty to the king, promising to be enemies of his enemies, friends of his friends. England was united and organized to support a strong ruler.

Alfred's grandson Edgar (r. c. 959–975) commanded all the possibilities early medieval kingship offered. He was the sworn lord of all the great men of the kingdom. He controlled appointments to the English church and sponsored monastic reform. In 973, following the continental fashion, he was anointed. The fortifications of the kingdom were in his hands, as was the army, and he took responsibility for keeping the peace by proclaiming certain crimes—arson and theft—to be under his special jurisdiction and mobilizing the machinery of the shire and the hundred to find and punish thieves.

Despite its apparent centralization, England was not a unified state in the modern sense, and the king's control was often tenuous. Many royal officials were great landowners who (as on the continent) worked for the king because doing so was in their best interest. When it was not, they allied with different claimants to the throne. This political fragility may have helped the Danish king Cnut (or Canute) to conquer England. King there from 1017 to 1035, Cnut reinforced the already strong connections between England and Scandinavia while keeping intact much of the administrative, ecclesiastical, and military apparatus already established in England by the Anglo-Saxons. By Cnut's time Scandinavian traditions had largely merged with those of the rest of Europe, and the Vikings were no longer an alien culture.

French kings had a harder time than the English coping with the invasions because their realm was much larger. They had no chance to build up their defenses slowly from one powerful base. During most of the tenth century, Carolingian kings alternated on the throne with kings from a family that would later be called "Capetian." As the Carolingian dynasty waned, the most powerful men of the kingdom—dukes, counts, and important bishops—came together to elect as king Hugh Capet (r. 987–996), a lord of considerable prestige yet relatively little power. His choice marked the end of Carolingian rule and the beginning of the new Capetian dynasty, which would hand down the royal title from father to son until the fourteenth century.

In the eleventh century, the reach of the Capetian kings was limited by territorial lordships in the vicinity. The king's scattered but substantial estates lay in the north of France, in the region around Paris—the Île-de-France (literally, "island of France"). His castles and his vassals were there. Independent castellans, however, controlled areas nearby. In the sense that he was a neighbor of castellans and not much more powerful militarily than they, the king of the Franks—who would only later take the territorial title of king of France—was just another local strongman. Yet the Capetian kings enjoyed considerable prestige. They were anointed with holy oil, and they represented the idea of unity inherited from Charlemagne. Most of the counts, at least in the north of France, became their vassals. They did not promise to obey the king, but they did vow not to try to kill or depose him.

Emperors and Kings in Central and Eastern Europe

In contrast with the development of territorial lordships in France, Germany's fragmentation hardly began before it was reversed. Five duchies (regions dominated by dukes) emerged in Germany in the late Carolingian period, each much larger than the counties and castellanies of France. With the death in 911 of the last Carolingian king in Germany, Louis the Child, the dukes elected one of themselves as king. Then, as the Magyar invasions increased, the dukes gave the royal title to the duke of Saxony, Henry I (r. 919–936), who proceeded to set up fortifications and reorganize his army, crowning his efforts with a major defeat of a Magyar army in 933.

Otto I (r. 936–973), the son of Henry I, was an even greater military hero. His defeat of the Magyar forces in 955 gave him prestige and helped solidify his dynasty. In 951, he marched into Italy and took the Lombard crown. Against the Slavs, with whom the Germans shared a border, Otto set up marches from which he could make expeditions and stave off counterattacks.

The Ottonian Empire, 936–1002

After the pope crowned him emperor in 962, he claimed the Middle Kingdom carved out by the Treaty of Verdun and cast himself as the agent of Roman imperial renewal.

Otto's victories brought tribute, plunder, plum positions to disburse, and lands to give away, ensuring him a following among the great men of the realm. His successors, Otto II (r. 961–983), Otto III (r. 983–1002)—not surprisingly, the dynasty is called the "Ottonian"—and Henry II (r. 1002–1024), built on his achievements. Granted power by the magnates, they gave back in turn: they gave away lands and appointed their aristocratic supporters to duchies, counties, and bishoprics. Always, however, their decisions were tempered by hereditary claims and plenty of lobbying by influential men at court and at the great assemblies that met with the king to hammer out policies. The role of kings in appointing bishops and archbishops was particularly important because these positions, unlike counties and duchies, could not be inherited. Otto I created new eastern bishoprics, endowing them with extensive lands and subjecting the local peasantry to their overlordship. In some areas of Germany, bishops gained the power of the ban: they collected revenues, gained rights of justice, and called men to arms. Answering to the king and furnishing him with troops, the bishops became royal officials while also carrying out their pastoral and religious duties. German kings claimed the right to select bishops (usually with the consent of the cathedral clergy) and to "invest" them by participating in the ceremony that installed them in office. The higher clergy joined the king at court, gaining their schooling there in their youth and, in their more mature years, teaching the kings, princes, and noblewomen there.

Like all the strong rulers of the day, whether in the West or in the Byzantine and Islamic worlds, the Ottonians presided over a renaissance of learning. For example, the tutor of Otto III was Gerbert (d. 1003) (later Pope Sylvester II), the best-educated man of his time. Gerbert knew how to use the abacus and to calculate with Arabic numerals. He spent "large sums of money to pay copyists and to acquire copies of authors," as he put it. He studied the classics as models of rhetoric and argument, and he reveled in logic and debate. Not only did churchmen and kings support Ottonian scholarship, but to an unprecedented extent, noblewomen in Germany also acquired an education and participated in the intellectual revival. Aristocratic women spent much of their wealth on learning. Living at home with their kinfolk and servants or in convents that provided them with comfortable private apartments, noblewomen wrote books and occasionally even Roman-style plays. They also supported other artists and scholars.

The German kings' policies played a crucial role in the political communities on its eastern border. Hand in hand with the papacy, the Ottonians fostered the emergence of Christian monarchies aligned with the Roman church in the regions that today constitute the Czech and Slovak Republics, Poland, and Hungary.

The Czechs, who lived in the region of Bohemia, converted under the rule of Václav (r. 920–929), who thereby gained recognition in Germany as the duke of Bohemia. He and his successors did not become kings, remaining politically within

■ Otto III Receiving Gifts

This triumphal image is in a book of Gospels made for Otto III. The crowned women on the left are personifications of the four "parts" of Otto's empire: Sclavinia (the Slavic lands), Germania (Germany), Gallia (Gaul), and Roma (Rome). Each holds a gift in tribute and homage to the emperor, who sits on a throne, holding the symbols of his power (orb and scepter) and flanked by representatives of the church (on his right) and of the army (on his left). Why do you suppose the artist separated the image of the emperor from that of the women? What does the body language of the women tell you about the relations that Otto wanted to portray between himself and the parts of his empire? Can you relate this manuscript, which was made in 997–1000, to Otto's conquest over the Slavs in 997? (Bayerische Staatsbibliothek, Munich.)

the German sphere. Václav's murder by his younger brother made him a martyr and the patron saint of Bohemia, a symbol around which later movements for independence rallied.

The Poles gained a greater measure of independence than the Czechs. In 966, Mieszko I (r. 963–992), the leader of the Slavic tribe known as the Polanians, accepted baptism to forestall the attack that the Germans were already mounting against pagan Slavic peoples along the Baltic coast and east of the Elbe River. Busily engaged in bringing the other Slavic tribes of Poland under his control, he adroitly shifted his alliances with various German princes to suit his needs. In 991, Mieszko placed his realm under the protection of the pope, establishing a tradition of Polish loyalty to the Roman church. Mieszko's son Boleslaw the Brave (r. 992–1025) greatly extended Poland's boundaries, at one time or another holding sway from the Bohemian border to Kiev. In 1000, he gained a royal crown with papal blessing.

■ **MAPPING THE WEST** Europe and the Mediterranean, c. 1050

The clear borders and bright colors of the "states" on this map distort an essential truth: none of them had centralized governments that controlled whole territories, as in modern states. Instead, there were numerous regional rulers within each, and there were numerous overlapping claims of jurisdiction. The next centuries would show both the weaknesses and surprising strengths of this fragmentation. **For more help analyzing this map,** see the map activity for this chapter in the ONLINE STUDY GUIDE at bedfordstmartins.com/huntconcise.

Hungary's case was similar to that of Poland. The Magyars settled in the region known today as Hungary. They became landowners, using the native Slavs to till the soil and imposing their language. At the end of the tenth century, the Magyar ruler Stephen I (r. 997–1038) accepted Christianity. In return, German knights and monks helped him consolidate his power and convert his people. According to legend, the crown placed on Stephen's head in 1001, like Boleslaw's crown, was sent to him by the pope. To this day, the crown of St. Stephen remains the most hallowed symbol of Hungarian nationhood.

Symbols of rulership such as crowns, consecrated by Christian priests and accorded a prestige almost akin to saints' relics, were among the most vital institutions of royal rule in central Europe. The economic basis for the power of central European rulers gradually shifted from slave raids to agriculture. This change encouraged a proliferation of regional centers of power that challenged monarchical rule. From the eleventh century onward, all the medieval Slavic states would face a constant problem of internal division.

■ **REVIEW:** *How did power over people and land shift from kings and emperors to local rulers between 800 and 1050?*

IMPORTANT DATES

750	Abbasid caliphate begins	843	End of iconoclasm at Byzantium; Treaty of Verdun divides Frankish kingdom
751	Pippin III deposes the last Merovingian king; Carolingian monarchy begins		
		c. 870–c. 1025	Macedonian renaissance at Byzantium
756	Spanish emirate at Córdoba begins	871–899	Reign of King Alfred the Great in England
768–814	Charlemagne rules as king of the Franks	955	Otto I defeats Magyars
786–809	Caliphate of Harun al-Rashid	969–1171	Fatimid dynasty in Egypt
c. 790–c. 900	Carolingian renaissance	963–1025	Reign of Byzantine emperor Basil II Bulgaroctonos
c. 790–c. 1050	Islamic renaissance		
800	Charlemagne crowned emperor by Pope Leo III	c. 1000	Age of the castellans in France

Conclusion

In 800, the three heirs of the Roman Empire all appeared to be organized like their "parent": centralized, monarchical, imperial. Byzantine emperors writing their learned books, Abbasid caliphs holding court in their resplendent new palace at Baghdad, and Carolingian emperors issuing their directives for reform to the *missi dominici* all mimicked the Roman emperors. Yet they confronted tensions and regional pressures that tended to decentralize political power. Byzantium felt this fragmentation least, yet even there the emergence of a new elite led to decentralization and the emperor's loss of control over the countryside. In the Islamic world, economic crisis, religious tension, and the ambitions of powerful local rulers decisively weakened the caliphate and opened the way to separate successor states. In the West, powerful independent landowners strove with greater or lesser success (depending on the region) to establish themselves as effective rulers. By 1050, the states that would become those of modern Europe began to form.

In Europe, local conditions determined political and economic organizations. Between 900 and 1000, for example, French society was transformed by the development of territorial lordships, patrilineal families, and ties of vassalage. These factors figured less prominently in Germany, where a central monarchy remained, buttressed by churchmen and conquests to the east. We shall see in the next chapter, however, how fragile this centralization was to be.

■ MAKING CONNECTIONS

1. *How were the Byzantine, Islamic, and European economies similar? How did they differ? How did these economies interact?*

2. *Compare the effects of the barbarian invasions into the Roman Empire with the effects of the Viking, Muslim, and Magyar invasions into the Carolingian Empire.*

■ FOR FURTHER EXPLORATION

For further reading and online research ideas, see the Suggested References on page SR-4 at the back of the book.

For practice quizzes, a customized study plan, and other study tools, see the ONLINE STUDY GUIDE at bedfordstmartins.com/huntconcise.

For primary-source material from this period, see Chapter 8 in *Sources of THE MAKING OF THE WEST: A CONCISE HISTORY*, Second Edition.

Renewal and Reform

1050–1200

B RUNO OF COLOGNE WAS AN ESTEEMED TEACHER at the prominent French cathedral school of Reims and the likely choice for promotion to bishop or even
archbishop. But around 1084, outraged by a new archbishop of Reims who had
purchased his office and cared nothing about religion, Bruno abandoned his
promising career and left the city. He did not do what ethical and morally outraged men of the time were expected to do—join a monastery. Instead, he set up
a hermitage—an isolated retreat—in an Alpine valley. The hermits who gathered
there lived in poverty. One of Bruno's contemporaries marveled: "They do not take
gold, silver, or ornaments for their church from anyone." This unworldliness was
matched, however, by keen interest in learning: for all its poverty, Bruno's community had a rich library.

Thus began La Chartreuse, the chief house of the Carthusian order, an order
still in existence. The Carthusian monks lived as hermits, rejected material wealth,
and emphasized learning. In some ways their style of life was a reaction against
the monumental changes rumbling through their age: their solitude countered
newly bustling cities, and their austerity contrasted sharply with the opulence and
power of princely courts. Their reverence for the written word, however, reflected
the growing interest in scholarship and learning.

The most salient feature of the period 1050–1200 was increasing wealth. Cities,
trade, and agricultural production swelled. The resulting worldliness met with a

■ **La Chartreuse**
*The impulse behind the foundation of La Chartreuse was withdrawal from the world. Yet the
world came to the Carthusians' high perch. One of the abbots of the Cluny made it his custom
to visit every year. He said that the new monks reminded him of the desert hermits. He did not
mean that the Alps looked liked Egypt but rather that the monks, living in separate cells,
practiced the heroically ascetic life of the first monks.* (Bridgeman Art Library.)

wide variety of responses. Some people, like Bruno, fled the world; others tried to reform it; and still others embraced, enjoyed, or tried to understand it. Within one century, the development of a profit economy transformed western European communities. Many villages and fortifications became cities where traders, merchants, and artisans conducted business. Although most people still lived in less-populated, rural areas, their lives were touched in many ways by the new cash economy. Economic concerns drove changes within the church, where a movement for reform gathered steam. Money helped redefine the role of the clergy, while popes, kings, and princes came to exercise new forms of power. At the same time, city dwellers began to demand their own governments. Monks and clerics reformulated the nature of their communities and, like Bruno of Cologne, sought intense spiritual lives. All of these developments inspired (and in turn were inspired by) new ideas, new forms of scholarship, and new methods of inquiry. The rapid pace of religious, political, and economic change was matched by new developments in thought, learning, and artistic expression.

The Commercial Revolution

As the population of Europe continued to expand in the eleventh century, cities, long-distance trade networks, local markets, and new business arrangements meshed to create a profit-based economy. With improvements in agriculture and more land in cultivation, the great estates of the eleventh century produced surpluses that helped feed—and therefore made possible—a new urban population. The result was the **commercial revolution** of the Middle Ages, which produced the institutions that would be the direct ancestors of modern business and commerce.

Centers of Commerce and Commercial Life

The new commercial centers developed around castles and monasteries and within the walls of ancient towns. Great lords in the countryside—including monasteries—were eager to take advantage of the profits generated by their estates. In the late tenth century, they had reorganized their lands for greater productivity, encouraged their peasants to cultivate new land, and converted services and dues to money payments. Now with ready cash, they not only fostered the development of temporary markets where they could sell their surpluses and buy luxury goods, but even encouraged traders and craftspeople to settle down near them. The lords gained at each step: their purchases brought them an enhanced lifestyle and greater prestige, while they charged merchants tolls and sales taxes, in this way profiting even more from trade. At Besalú (Spain), for example, the count's castle was a magnet for artisans and food purveyers. Sometimes markets formed just outside the walls of older cities; these gradually merged into new and enlarged urban communities as town walls were built around them to protect the inhabitants. At other times informal country markets came to be

■ MAP 9.1 Medieval Trade Routes in the Eleventh and Twelfth Centuries

In the medieval world, bulk goods from the north (furs, fish, and wood) were traded for luxury goods from the south (ivory, spices, medicines, perfumes, and dyes). Already regions were beginning to specialize. England, for example, supplied raw wool, and Flanders (Ypres, Ghent) specialized in turning that wool into cloth and shipping it farther south, to the fairs of Champagne (whose capital was Troyes) or Germany. Italian cities channeled goods from the Muslim and Byzantine worlds northward and exported European goods south and eastward.

housed in permanent structures. Along the Rhine and in other river valleys, cities sprang up to service the merchants who traversed the route between Italy and the north (Map 9.1).

By the mid-twelfth century even rural life was increasingly organized for the marketplace in many regions of western Europe. The commercialization of the countryside opened up opportunities for both peasants and lords, but it also burdened

■ **Medieval Besalú**
The bridge leading to Besalú, a town in Catalonia (Spain), was constructed, like the town's walls and many of its other buildings, during the eleventh and twelfth centuries. The high fortified entrance was added in the fourteenth century. Already in the ninth century, Besalú was the center of a county, and in the eleventh century, it briefly became the seat of a bishopric. At the same time, it was home to a thriving Jewish population, whose mikvah, or ritual bath house, still stands today. (AKG Images/Schütze/Rodemann.)

some with unwelcome obligations. Great lords hired trained, literate agents to administer their estates, calculate profits and losses, and make marketing decisions. Aristocrats needed money not only because they relished luxuries such as fine wines, spices, and soft, glowing fabrics, but also because their honor and authority continued to depend on their personal generosity, patronage, and displays of wealth. In the late twelfth century, when some townsmen could boast fortunes that rivaled the riches of the landed aristocracy, economic pressures on the nobles increased as their extravagance exceeded their income. Many went into debt.

The lord's need for money changed peasant life, as peasants, too, became more integrated into the developing commercial economy. The population continued to increase in the twelfth century, and the greater demand for food required more farmland. By the middle of the century, isolated and sporadic attempts to cultivate new land had become a regular and coordinated activity. Great lords offered special privileges to peasants who would do the backbreaking work of plowing marginal land. In Flanders, where land was regularly inundated by seawater, the great monasteries sponsored drainage projects, and newly dug canals linking the cities to the agricultural regions let boats ply the waters to nearly every nook and cranny of the region.

On old estates the rise in population strained the manse organization that had developed in Carolingian Europe, where each household was settled on the land that supported it. In the twelfth century, twenty peasant families might live on what had been, in the tenth century, the manse of one family. With the manse supporting so many more people, labor services and dues had to be recalculated, and peasants and their lords often turned services and dues into money rents, payable once a year. With this change, peasant men gained more control over their plots— they could sell them, will them to their sons, or even designate a small portion for their daughters. However, for these privileges, they had to pay high fees. In addition, the revived monarchies of the twelfth century required taxes that were passed along to the lowest classes either directly or indirectly. In Italy the cities themselves often imposed and enforced dues on the peasants, normally tenant farmers who leased their plots in the *contado*, the countryside surrounding each city. Thus peasants' gains from rising prices, access to markets, greater productivity, and increased personal freedom were partially canceled out by their cash burdens.

Business Arrangements

The development of commercial centers reflected changing attitudes toward money. The new mode of commerce transformed the social relations involved in economic transactions. In the gift economy, exchanges of coins, gold, and silver were components of ongoing relationships. Kings offered treasures to their followers, peasants gave dues to their lords, and pious donors presented land to the saintly patrons of churches, all in the expectation of long-term relationships. In the new market economy, which thrived on the profit motive, arrangements were less personal. They often relied on written contracts and calculations of the profitability of a particular business venture.

Although the new business agreements took many forms, they had the common purpose of bringing people together to pool their resources and finance larger enterprises. The *commenda*, for example, an Italian invention, was a partnership established for commerce by sea. In a common arrangement, one or more investors furnished the money, and the other partners undertook the risks of the actual voyage. If a trip proved successful, the investors received three-quarters of the profit and the travelers the rest. But if the voyage failed, the investors lost their outlay, and the travelers expended their time and labor for no profit. The impermanence of such partnerships (they lasted for only one voyage) meant that capital could be shifted easily from one venture to another and could therefore be used to support a variety of enterprises.

Land trade often involved a more enduring partnership. In Italy this took the form of a *compagnia*, formed when family property was invested in trade. Unlike the *commenda*, in which the partners could lose no more than they had put into the enterprise, the compagnia left its members with joint and unlimited liability for all losses and debts. This provision enhanced family solidarity, as each member was responsible for the debts of all the others; but it also risked bankrupting entire households.

The commercial revolution also fostered the development of contracts for sales, exchanges, and loans. Loans were the most problematic. In the Middle Ages, as now, interest payments were the chief inducement for an investor to supply money. To circumvent the church's ban on usury (profiting from loans), interest was often disguised as a penalty for "late payment" under the rules of a contract. The new willingness to finance business enterprises with loans signaled a changed attitude toward credit: risk was acceptable if it brought profit.

Contracts and partnerships made large-scale productive enterprises possible. In fact, light industry began in the eleventh century. Just as in the Industrial Revolution of the eighteenth and nineteenth centuries, one of the earliest products to benefit from new industrial technologies was cloth. Water mills powered machines such as flails to clean and thicken cloth and presses to extract oil from fibers. Machines were also used to exploit raw materials more efficiently: new deep-mining technology provided Europeans with hitherto untapped sources of metals. At the same time, forging techniques improved, and iron was for the first time regularly used for agricultural tools and plows. This, in turn, made for better farming, and better farming fed the commercial revolution. Metals were also used for weapons, armor, and coins.

Whether fashioned by machines or handworkers, production relied on the expertise of artisans able to finish the cloth, mint the coins, and forge the weapons. To regulate and protect their products and trades, craftspeople and others involved in commerce formed **guilds**: local social, religious, and economic associations whose members plied the same trade. By the late twelfth century, they had become corporations defined by statutes and rules. They controlled their membership and determined dues, working hours, wages, and standards for materials and products.

Guilds often had to cooperate with one another. Producing wool cloth involved numerous guilds—shearers, weavers, fullers (people who beat the cloth to make it bulkier), dyers—generally working under the supervision of the merchant guild that imported the raw wool. Some guilds were more prestigious than others: in Florence, for example, professional guilds of notaries and judges ranked above craft guilds.

Within each guild of artisans or merchants existed another kind of hierarchy. Apprentices were at the bottom, journeymen and -women in the middle, and masters at the top. Apprentices were boys and occasionally girls placed under the tutelage of a master for a number of years to learn a trade. For example, in Paris a baker's apprenticeship took four years, while it took eleven years to train a harness maker. Once trained, the worker became a journeyman or -woman—a simple day laborer working for a wage. Only a few would become masters, the men (but almost never women) who dominated the offices and policies of the guild, hired journeymen, and recruited and educated apprentices. The masters drew up the guild regulations and served as chief overseers, inspectors, and treasurers.

During the late twelfth century, women's labor in some trades gradually declined in importance. In Flanders, for example, as the manufacture of woolen cloth shifted from rural areas to cities, women participated less in the process. In cities like Ypres and Ghent, men working in pairs ran new-style large looms, producing a heavyweight cloth superior to the fabric that women could make on lighter looms. Similarly, water mills and animal-powered mills gradually took over the grinding of grain, formerly women's work. Most millers who ran the new machinery were male. Some women were certainly artisans and traders, and their names occasionally appeared in guild memberships. But they did not become guild officers, and they played no official role in town government.

Self-Government for the Towns

Guilds were one way townspeople expressed their mutual concerns and harnessed their collective energies. Movements for self-government were another. Townspeople banded together for protection and freedom.

Both to themselves and to outsiders, townspeople seemed different. Tradespeople, artisans, ship captains, innkeepers, and moneychangers did not fit into the old categories of medieval types—those who pray, those who fight, and those who labor. Just knowing they were different gave townspeople a sense of solidarity with one another. But practical reasons also contributed to their feeling of common purpose: they lived in close quarters with one another, and they shared a mutual interest in reliable coinage, laws to facilitate commerce, freedom from servile dues and services, and independence to buy and sell as the market dictated. Already in the early twelfth century, the king of England granted to the citizens of Newcastle-upon-Tyne the privilege that any unfree peasant who lived there unclaimed by his lord for a year and a day would thereafter be a free person. To townspeople, freedom meant having their own officials and law courts. They petitioned the political powers that ruled them— bishops, kings, counts, castellans—for the right to govern themselves. Often they formed **communes**, sworn associations of townspeople that generally cut across the boundaries of rich and poor, merchants and craftspeople, clergy and laity.

Collective movements for urban self-government emerged especially in Italy, France, and Germany. Italian cities were centers of regional political power even before the commercial revolution. Castellans constructed their fortifications, and bishops ruled the countryside from such cities. The commercial revolution swelled the Italian cities with tradespeople, whose interest in self-government was often fueled by religious as well as economic concerns. At Milan in the second half of the eleventh century, popular discontent with the archbishop, who effectively ruled the city, led to numerous armed clashes. In 1097, the Milanese succeeded in transferring political power from the archbishop and his clergy to a government of leading men of the city who called themselves "consuls." The title recalled the government of the ancient Roman republic, affirming the consuls' status as representatives of the people. Like the archbishops' power before, the consuls' rule extended beyond the town walls, into the contado, the outlying countryside.

Outside of Italy, movements for city independence took place within the framework of larger kingdoms or principalities. Such movements were sometimes violent, as at Milan, but at other times they were peaceful. For example, William Clito, who claimed the county of Flanders (today in Belgium), willingly granted the citizens of Saint-Omer the rights they asked for in 1127 in return for their support of his claims: he recognized them as legally free, gave them the right to mint coins, allowed them their own laws and courts, and lifted certain tolls and taxes.

■ **REVIEW:** *What new professions and institutions arose as a result of the commercial revolution?*

Church Reform and Its Aftermath

The commercial revolution affected the church because the church, too, was part of the world. Bishops ruled over many cities. Kings appointed many bishops. Local lords installed priests in their parish churches. Churchmen gave gifts and money to these secular powers for their offices. The impulse to free the church from "the world" was as old as the origins of monasticism, but, beginning in the tenth century and increasingly insistent in the eleventh, reformers demanded that the church as a whole remodel itself and become free of secular entanglements.

This freedom was from the start as much a matter of power as of religion. Most people had long believed that their ruler—whether king, duke, count, or castellan—reigned by the grace of God and had the right to control the churches in his territory. But by the second half of the eleventh century, more and more people saw a great deal wrong with secular power over the church. They looked to the papacy to lead the movement of church reform. The most important moment came in 1075, when Pope Gregory VII called on the emperor, Henry IV, to end his appointment of churchmen. This request brought about a major civil war in Germany and a great upheaval in the distribution of power everywhere. By the early 1100s, a reformed church—with the pope at its head—had become institutionalized, penetrating into areas of life never before touched by churchmen. Church reform began as a way to free the church from the world; but in the end, the church was equally involved in the new world it had helped to create.

Beginnings of the Reform Movement

The idea of freeing the church from the world began in the tenth century with no particular program and only a vague idea of what it might mean. At the Benedictine

monastery of Cluny, for example, which was founded in 910, there was no organized program of reform. Nevertheless, the founders of the monastery, the duke and
duchess of Aquitaine, wanted to "free" it from the world. They achieved this goal
by endowing the monastery with property but then giving it and its worldly possessions to Saints Peter and Paul. In this way, they put control of the monastery
into the hands of the two most powerful heavenly saints. They designated the pope,
as the successor of St. Peter, to be the monastery's worldly protector if anyone
should bother or threaten it. The whole notion of "freedom" at this point was very
vague. But Cluny's prestige was great because of its status as St. Peter's property
and because of the elaborate round of prayers that its monks carried out with
scrupulous devotion. The Cluniac monks fulfilled the role of "those who pray" in
a way that dazzled their contemporaries. Through their prayers they seemed to
guarantee the salvation of all Christians. Rulers, bishops, rich landowners, and even
serfs (if they could) gave Cluny donations of land, joining their contributions to
the land of St. Peter. Powerful men and women called on the Cluniac monks to
reform new monasteries along the Cluniac model.

The abbots of Cluny came to see themselves as reformers of the world as well.
They believed in clerical celibacy, preaching against the prevailing norm that let
parish priests and even bishops marry. They also thought that the laity could be
reformed, become more virtuous, and cease its oppression of the poor. In the
eleventh century, the Cluniacs began to link their program of internal monastic
and external worldly reform to the papacy. They asked the popes to help them
when Cluniac lands were encroached upon by bishops and laypeople at the same
time as the papacy itself was becoming interested in reform.

Around the time when the Cluniacs were joining their fate to that of the popes,
a small group of clerics and monks in the empire began calling for systematic reform
within the church. They buttressed their arguments with new interpretations of
canon law—the laws decreed over the centuries at church councils and by bishops
and popes. They concentrated on two breaches of those laws: nicolaitism (clerical
marriage) and **simony** (buying church offices). Most of the men who promoted these
ideas lived in the most commercialized regions of the empire: the Rhineland (the
region along the northern half of the Rhine River) and Italy. Their familiarity with
the impersonal practices of a profit economy led them to interpret as crass purchases
the gifts that churchmen were used to giving in return for their offices.

Emperor Henry III (r. 1039–1056) supported the reformers. Taking seriously
his position as the anointed of God, Henry felt responsible for the well-being of
the church in his empire. He denounced simony and personally refused to accept
money or gifts when he appointed bishops to their posts. When in 1046 three men,
each representing a different faction of the Roman aristocracy, claimed to be pope,
Henry, as ruler of Rome, traveled to Italy to settle the matter. The Synod of Sutri
(1046), over which he presided, deposed all three popes and elected another. In
1049, Henry appointed Leo IX (r. 1049–1054), a bishop from the Rhineland, to the

papacy. This appointment marked an unanticipated turning point for the emperor when Leo set out to reform the church under papal, rather than imperial, control. He traveled to France and Germany, holding councils to condemn simoniac bishops. He sponsored the creation of a canon law textbook—the *Collection in 74 Titles*—that emphasized the pope's power. To the papal court, Leo brought the most zealous reformers of his day: Humbert of Silva Candida, Peter Damian, and Hildebrand (later Pope Gregory VII).

At first, Leo's claims to new power over the church hierarchy were complacently ignored by clergy and secular rulers alike. The Council of Reims, which he called in 1049, for example, was attended by only a few bishops and boycotted by the king of France. Nevertheless, Leo made it into a forum for exercising his authority. Placing the relics of St. Remegius (the patron saint of Reims) on the altar of the church, he demanded that the attending bishops and abbots say whether or not they had purchased their offices. A few confessed that they had; some did not respond; others gave excuses. The new and extraordinary development was that all present felt accountable to the pope and accepted his verdicts.

In 1054, Leo sent Humbert of Silva Candida to Constantinople on a diplomatic mission to argue against the patriarch of Constantinople on behalf of the new, lofty claims of the pope. Furious at the contemptuous way he was treated by the patriarch, Humbert ended his mission by excommunicating the patriarch. In retaliation, the Byzantine emperor and his bishops excommunicated Humbert and his party, threatening them with eternal damnation. Clashes between the two churches had occurred before and had been patched up, but this one, called the **Great Schism** (1054), proved insurmountable.* Thereafter, the Roman Catholic and the Greek Orthodox churches were largely separate.

The popes who followed Leo continued his program to expand papal power. When military adventurers from Normandy began carving out states for themselves in southern Italy, the popes in nearby Rome felt threatened. After waging unsuccessful war against the interlopers, the papacy made the best of a bad situation by granting the Normans Sicily and parts of southern Italy as a fief, turning its former enemies into vassals. Similarly, the papacy participated in wars in Spain, where it supported Christians against the dominant Muslims. The political fragmentation of al-Andalus into small and weak *taifas* (see page 307) made it seem fair game to the Christians to the north. Slowly the idea of the *reconquista*, the Christian reconquest of Spain, took shape, fed by religious fervor as well as worldly ambition.

---

*Despite occasional thaws and liftings of the sentences, the mutual excommunications of pope and patriarch largely remained in effect until 1965, when Pope Paul VI and the Greek Orthodox patriarch, Athenagoras I, publicly deplored them.

Gregorian Reform and the Investiture Conflict, 1073–1085

The papal reform movement is above all associated with Pope Gregory VII (r. 1073–1085) and is therefore often called the **Gregorian reform**. Gregory began as a lowly Roman cleric—Hildebrand—with the job of administering the papal estates and rose slowly in the hierarchy. A passionate advocate of papal primacy (the theory that the pope was head of the church), he was not afraid to clash with Emperor Henry IV (r. 1056–1106) over leadership of the church. In his view—and it was astonishing at the time, given the religious and spiritual roles associated with rulers—the emperor was just a layman who had no right to meddle in church affairs.

Gregory was and remains an extraordinarily controversial figure. He certainly thought that he was acting as the vicar, or representative, of St. Peter on earth. Describing himself, he declared, "I have labored with all my power that Holy Church, the bride of God, our Lady Mother, might come again to her own splendor and might remain free, pure, and Catholic." He thought the reforms he advocated and the upheavals he precipitated were necessary to free the church from the Satanic rulers of the world. His great nemesis, Henry IV, had a very different view. He considered Gregory an ambitious and evil man who "seduced the world far and wide and stained the Church with the blood of her

The World of the Investiture Conflict, c. 1070–1122

sons." Not surprisingly, modern historians are only a bit less divided in their assessment of Gregory. Few deny his sincerity and deep religious devotion, but many speak of his pride, ambition, and single-mindedness. He was not an easy man.

Henry IV was less complex. He was brought up in the traditions of his father, Henry III, a pious church reformer who considered it part of his duty to appoint bishops and even popes to ensure the well-being of church and state together. The emperor believed that he and his bishops—who were, at the same time, his most valuable supporters and administrators—were the rightful leaders of the church. He had no intention of allowing the pope to become head of the church.

The great confrontation between Gregory and Henry began over the appointment of the archbishop of Milan. Gregory disputed Henry's right to "invest" the archbishop (put him into office). In the investiture ritual, the emperor or his representative symbolically gave the church and the land that went with it to the priest or bishop or archbishop chosen for the job. When, in 1075, Henry invested his own candidate as archbishop of Milan, Gregory called on Henry to "give more respectful attention to the master of the Church"; he meant St. Peter and his living representative, Gregory himself. In reply, Henry and the German bishops called on Gregory to resign from the papacy. This was the beginning of what historians delicately call the **Investiture Conflict** or "Investiture Controversy." In fact, it was war. In February 1076, Gregory called a synod that both excommunicated and suspended Henry from office, authorizing anyone in Henry's kingdom to rebel against him. Henry's enemies, mostly German princes (as German aristocrats were called), now threatened to elect another king.

His fortunes low, Henry traveled to intercept Gregory, who was journeying northward to visit the rebellious princes. In early 1077, the king and pope met at Canossa, high in central Italy's Apennine Mountains. Gregory was inside a fortress there; Henry stood outside as a penitent—barefoot in the cold and snow. The gesture was an astute move by Henry because no priest could refuse absolution to a penitent; Gregory had to lift the excommunication and receive Henry back into the church. But Gregory had the advantage of making the king humble himself before the majesty of the pope.

Although Henry was technically back in the fold, nothing of substance had been resolved, and civil war began. The princes elected an antiking (a king chosen illegally), and Henry and his supporters elected an antipope. From 1077 until 1122, papal and imperial armies waged intermittent war. Long after the original antagonists Gregory and Henry had died, the Concordat of Worms of 1122 ended the fighting with a compromise that relied on a conceptual distinction between two parts of the investiture ceremony—the spiritual (in which a man received the symbols of his clerical office) and the secular (in which he received the symbols of the material goods that would allow him to function). Under the terms of the concordat, the ring and staff, the symbols of church office, would be given by a churchman in the first part of the ceremony. In the second part, the emperor or his representative would touch the bishop with a scepter, a symbolic gesture that stood for the land and other possessions that went with his office. Elections of bishops in Germany would take place "in the presence" of the emperor—that is, under his influence. In Italy, the pope would have a comparable role.

Superficially, nothing much had changed; secular rulers would continue to have a part in choosing and investing churchmen. In fact, however, almost no one any longer would claim that the king was head of the church. Just as the new investiture ceremony broke the ritual into spiritual and secular parts, so too, it implied a new notion of kingship that separated it from priesthood. The Investiture Conflict did not produce the modern distinction between church and state—that would develop only very slowly—but it set the wheels in motion.

The most important changes brought about by the Investiture Conflict, however, were on the ground: the political landscape in both Italy and Germany was irrevocably transformed. In Germany, the princes consolidated their lands and their positions at the expense of royal power. They gradually became virtual monarchs within their own principalities; the emperor, though retaining his title, eventually became a figurehead. In Italy, the emperor lost power to the cities. The Italian communes were formed in the crucible of the war between the pope and the emperor. In fierce communal struggles, city factions, motivated in part by local grievances but often claiming to fight on behalf of the papal or the imperial cause, created their own governing bodies. In the course of the twelfth century, northern Italian cities became used to self-government.

The Sweep of Reform

Church reform involved much more than the clash of popes, emperors, and their supporters. It penetrated deeply into the daily lives of ordinary Christians, in part through the church's new emphasis on the sacraments—the regular means (according to the Catholic church) by which God's heavenly grace infused mundane existence. But this did not mean that Christians were clear about how many sacraments there were, how they worked, or even their significance. Eleventh-century church reformers began the process—which continued into the thirteenth century—of emphasizing the importance of the sacraments and the special nature of the priest, whose chief role was to administer them.

In the sacrament of marriage, for example, the effective involvement of the church in the wedding of man and woman came only after the Gregorian reform. Not until the twelfth century did people regularly come to be married by a priest, and only then did churchmen assume jurisdiction over marital disputes, not simply in cases involving royalty but also in those of lesser aristocrats. At the same time, churchmen began to stress the sanctity of marriage. Hugh of St. Victor, a twelfth-century scholar, dwelled on the sacramental meaning of marriage:

> Can you find anything else in marriage except conjugal society which makes it sacred and by which you can assert that it is holy? . . . Each shall be to the other as a same self in all sincere love, all careful solicitude, every kindness of affection, in constant compassion, unflagging consolation, and faithful devotedness.

Hugh saw marriage as a matter of love.

The reformers also proclaimed the special importance of the sacrament of the Mass, holy communion through the body and blood of Christ. Gregory VII called the Mass "the greatest thing in the Christian religion." No layman, no matter how powerful, and no woman of any sort at all could perform anything equal to it, for the Mass was the key to salvation.

The new emphasis on the difference between the priest (who could celebrate Mass) and the laity (who could not) led to vigorous enforcement of an old element of church discipline: the celibacy of priests. The demand for a celibate clergy had far-reaching significance for the history of the church. It distanced western clerics even further from their eastern Orthodox counterparts (whose priests did not practice celibacy), exacerbating the Great Schism of 1054. It also broke with traditional local practices, for clerical marriage was customary in many places in the West. Gregorian reformers exhorted every cleric in higher orders, from the humble parish priest to the exalted bishop, to refrain from marriage or to abandon his wife. In 1123 the pope proclaimed all clerical marriages invalid.

The rule about clerical marriages was only one in a veritable explosion of canon law. Canon law had begun simply as rules determined at church councils. These were then coupled with papal declarations. Some attempts to gather together and organize these laws had been made before the eleventh century. But the proliferation of rules during that century, along with the desire of Gregorians to clarify church law as they saw it, made a systematic collection even more necessary. This was supplied in about 1140 by a landmark work in canon law: the *Concordance of Discordant Canons*, also known as the *Decretum*, by Gratian, a monk who taught law at Bologna in northern Italy. Gratian gathered thousands of passages from the decrees of popes and councils with the intention of showing their harmony. If he found any "discord," he strove to show how they applied to different situations. A bit later a different legal scholar revised and expanded the *Decretum*, adding Roman law to the mix. Meanwhile the papacy itself was gradually developing its own court of law to hear cases and rule on petitions. These services were expensive, and the papacy made the petitioners and litigants pay. Before the Gregorian reform the papacy had been relatively powerless and much loved; afterward, it was very powerful and often resented. A satire written about 1100, in the style of the Gospels, made bitter fun of papal greed:

> There came to the court a certain wealthy clerk, fat and thick, and gross, who in the sedition [rebellion] had committed murder. He first gave to the dispenser, second to the treasurer, third to the cardinals. But they thought among themselves that they should receive more. The Lord Pope, hearing that his cardinals had received many gifts, was sick, nigh unto death. But the rich man sent to him a couch of gold and silver and immediately he was made whole.

With his law courts, bureaucracy, and financial apparatus, the pope had become a monarch.

Early Crusades and Crusader States

Asserting itself as head of the Christian church and leader of its reform movement, the papacy sometimes supported and proclaimed holy wars to advance the cause of Christianity. The most important of these were the crusades. Combinations of war and pilgrimage—the popular practice of making a pious voyage to a sacred shrine to petition for help or cure—the early crusades sent armed European Christians into

■ MAP 9.2 The First Crusade, 1096–1098

The First Crusade was a major military undertaking that required organization, movement over both land and sea, and enormous resources. Four main groups were responsible for the conquest of Jerusalem. One set out from Cologne, in northern Germany; a second group started from Blois, in France; the third originated to the west of Provence; and the fourth launched ships from Brindisi, at the heel of Italy. All joined up at Constantinople, where their leaders negotiated with Alexius for help and supplies in return for a pledge of vassalage to the emperor.

battle against Muslims in the Holy Land, the place where Christ had lived and died. The crusaders established several tiny states in the Levant, holding on to them precariously until 1291. Although the crusades ultimately "failed," in the sense that the crusaders did not succeed in permanently retaining the Holy Land for Christendom, they were a pivotal episode in Western civilization. They marked the first stage of European overseas expansion, of what later would become imperialism.

The First Crusade began with the entry of the **Seljuk Turks** in Asia Minor (Map 9.2). In the 1050s, taking advantage of the political fragmentation of the Muslim world, the Seljuks, converts to Sunni Islam, captured Baghdad, subjugated the caliphate, and began to threaten Byzantium. The difficulties the Byzantine emperor Romanus IV had in pulling together an army to attack the Turks in 1071 reveal how weak his position had become. Unable to muster Byzantine troops—the generals (*strategoi*) were busy defending their own districts, and provincial nobles were wary of sending support to the emperor—Romanus had to rely on a mercenary army made up of Normans, Franks, Slavs, and even Turks. In 1071, this motley force met the Seljuks under Sultan Alp Arslan at Manzikert, in what is today eastern Turkey. The battle was a disaster for Romanus: the Seljuks routed his army and captured him. Manzikert marked the end of Byzantine domination in the region.

The Turks, gradually settling in Asia Minor, extended their control across the empire and beyond, all the way to Jerusalem, which had been under Muslim control since the seventh century. In 1095, the Byzantine emperor Alexius I appealed for help to Pope Urban II (r. 1088–1099), hoping to get new mercenary troops for a fresh offensive.

Urban II chose to interpret the request in his own way. At the Council of Clermont (in France) in 1095, Urban moved outside the church and addressed an already excited throng:

> Oh, race of Franks, race from across the mountains, race beloved and chosen by God. . . . Let hatred depart from among you, let your quarrels end, let wars cease, and let all dissensions and controversies slumber. Enter upon the road to the Holy Sepulcher; wrest that land from the wicked race, and subject it to yourselves.

The crowd reportedly responded with one voice: "God wills it." Urban's call placed the papacy in a new position of leadership, one that complemented in a military arena the position the popes had gained in the church hierarchy.

■ A Crusader and His Wife

How do we know that the man on the left is a crusader? On his shirt is a cross, the sign worn by all men going on the crusades. In his right hand is a pilgrim's staff, a useful reminder that the crusades were sometimes considered less a matter of war than of penance and piety. What does the embrace of the crusader's wife imply about marital love in the twelfth century?

(© Musée Lorrain, Nancy/Photo: P. Mignot.)

Men and women, rich and poor, young and old, heeded Urban's call. They abandoned their homes and braved the rough journey to the Holy Land to fight for their God. They also went—especially younger sons of aristocrats, who could not expect an inheritance because of the practice of primogeniture—because they wanted land and booty. Some knights went on the expedition because in addition to their pious duty, they were obligated to follow their lord. Although women were discouraged from going on the crusades, some crusaders were accompanied by their wives. Other women went as servants; a few may have been fighters. Children, old men, and women, not able to fight, made the cords for siege engines—giant machines used to hurl stones at enemy fortifications. As more crusades were undertaken during the twelfth century, the transport and supply of these armies became a lucrative business for the commercial classes of maritime Italian cities such as Venice.

The main objective of the First Crusade—to wrest the Holy Land from the Muslims and subject it to Christian rule—was accomplished largely because of Muslim disunity. After nearly a year of ineffectual attacks, the crusaders took Antioch on June 28, 1098; on July 15, 1099, they seized Jerusalem. By 1109 they had carved out several tiny states in the Holy Land.

Because the crusader states were created by conquest, they were treated as lordships. The rulers granted fiefs to their own vassals, and some of these men in turn gave portions of their holdings as fiefs to some of their own vassals. Since most Europeans went home after the First Crusade, the rulers who remained learned to coexist with the indigenous population, which included Muslims, Jews, and Greek Orthodox Christians. They encouraged a lively trade at their ports, which received merchants from Italy, Byzantium, and Islamic cities.

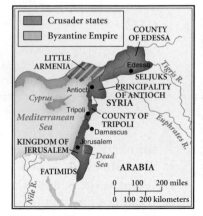

The Crusader States in 1109

The main concern of these rulers, however, was military. They set up castles and recruited knights from Europe. So organized for war was this society that it produced a new and militant kind of monasticism: the Knights Templar. Like Bruno's Carthusians, the Templars vowed themselves to poverty and chastity. But rather than withdraw to a hermitage on a mountaintop, the Templars, whose name came from their living quarters in the area of the former Jewish Temple at Jerusalem, devoted themselves to warfare. Their first mission—to protect the pilgrimage routes from Palestine to Jerusalem—soon diversified. They manned the town garrisons of the crusader states, and they transported money from Europe to the Holy Land. In this way the Templars became enormously wealthy, with branch "banks" in major cities across Europe.

The presence of the Templars did not prevent a new Seljuk chieftain, Zengi, from taking the city of Edessa in 1144. The event marked the slow but steady

■ **Krak-des-Chevaliers**

The Hospitallers, a religious military order much like the Templars, built this imposing castle in 1142 on the site of a Muslim fortification in Syria. A large community of perhaps fifty monk-knights and their hired mercenaries lived there. To the northeast (in back of the complex seen here) was a fortified village that served the needs of the castle. Peasants raised grain, which was ground by a windmill on one wall of the castle. For water, there were reservoirs to catch the rain, wells, and an aqueduct (visible on the right). Twelve toilets connected to a common drain. The monks worshiped in a chapel within the inner walls. The outer walls, built of masonry, completely enclosed the inner buildings, making Krak one of the most important places for refuge and defense in the crusader states.

(Maynard Owen Williams/National Geographic Image Collection.)

shrinking of the crusader states. New crusades were called, but none was successful. The Second Crusade (1147–1149) came to a disastrous end. After besieging the walls of Damascus for only four days, the crusaders, whose leaders could not keep the peace among themselves, gave up and went home. Soon the Muslim hero Nur al-Din united Syria under his command and presided over a renewal of Sunni Islam. His successor, Saladin (1138–1193), took Jerusalem in 1187, galvanizing the pope to call the Third Crusade (1189–1192). Led by the greatest rulers of Europe—Emperor Frederick I Barbarossa, Philip II of France, Leopold of Austria, and Richard I of England—the Third Crusade nevertheless accomplished little, and the crusader states were reduced to a few tiny outposts.

The Jews as Strangers

The same militant piety that inspired the crusades was turned against the Jews. Sentiment against Jews grew over time. Ever since the Roman Empire had become Christian, Jews had been seen as separate from Christians. Imperial law, for example, prohibited them from owning Christian slaves or marrying Christian women. Church laws added to these restrictions. Socially isolated and branded as outcasts,

Jews served as scapegoats who helped define the larger society as orthodox. But only at the end of the eleventh century did severe persecution begin.

Forced out of the countryside during the eleventh century by castellans and other regional rulers, most Jews ended up in the cities as craftsmen or merchants. But they were not allowed into guilds, and many were thus pushed into the one profession that Christians could not have: moneylending. Jews thus provided capital for the developing commercial society, whose Christian members were prohibited from charging interest by the Bible's constraints against usury. Many Jews lived in the flourishing commercial region of the Rhineland. Under Henry IV, the Jews in Speyer and elsewhere in the empire gained a place within the government system by receiving protection from the local bishop (an imperial appointee) in return for paying a tax. Within these cities, the Jews lived in their own neighborhoods, their tightly knit communities focused on local synagogues, which served as schools and community centers as well as places of worship. Nevertheless, Jews also participated in the life of the larger Christian community. Archbishop Anno of Cologne dealt with Jewish moneylenders, and other Jews in Cologne were allowed to trade their wares at the fairs there.

It was against these Rhineland Jews that some of the earliest anti-Jewish attacks were directed. Some of the crusaders of the First Crusade declared it ridiculous to attack Muslims when other infidels lived in their own backyards: "That's doing our work backward," they said, as they moved into the Rhineland to force conversions or to kill. Some Jews found refuge with bishops or in the houses of Christian friends, but in many cities—Metz, Speyer, Worms, Mainz, and Cologne—they were massacred.

In the course of the twelfth century, Jews were attacked elsewhere as well. European rulers claimed the Jews as their serfs and Jewish property as their own. King Henry II of England (r. 1154–1189) imposed new and arbitrary taxes on the Jewish community. In France, persecuting Jews and confiscating

■ **The Jew as the Other**
Medieval artists often portrayed people not as individuals but rather as "types" that could be identified by physical markers. In the second half of the twelfth century, Jews were increasingly portrayed as looking different from Christians. This illustration shows clerics borrowing money from a Jew. What physical features do all the clerics have in common? (Be sure to look at the clothes as well as the hairstyle.) What distinguishes the layman from the clerics? How do you know who is meant to be the Jew? In fact, Jews did not regularly wear this type of pointed hat until they were forced to do so in some regions of Europe in the late thirteenth century.
(Bayerische Staatsbibliothek, Munich.)

their property benefited both the treasury and the authoritative image of the king. Early in the reign of the French king Philip II—known as Philip Augustus (r. 1180–1223)—royal agents surprised Jews at Sabbath worship in their synagogues and seized their goods, demanding that they redeem their own property for a large sum of money. Shortly thereafter, Philip canceled 80 percent of all debts owed to Jews; the remaining 20 percent was to be paid directly to the king. About a year later, in 1182, Philip expelled the Jews from the Île-de-France. When he allowed them to return in 1198, he permitted them to be moneylenders or moneychangers only, taxed and monitored by royal officials.

Limiting Jews to moneylending in an increasingly commercial economy, then persecuting them, served the interests of lords in debt to Jewish creditors. For example, in 1190, local nobles orchestrated a brutal attack on the Jews of York (in England). Their purpose was to rid themselves of their debts—and of the Jews to whom they owed money. Churchmen, too, used credit in a money economy but resented the fiscal obligations it imposed. With their drive to create centralized territorial states and their desire to make their authority known and felt, powerful rulers of Europe—churchmen and laymen alike—exploited and coerced the Jews while drawing upon and encouraging widespread anti-Jewish feeling. Although Jews must have looked exactly like Christians in reality, Jews now became clearly identified in sculpture and in drawings by markers such as conical hats and, increasingly, by demeaning features.

Attacks against Jews were inspired by more than resentment against Jewish money and the desire for power and control. They also grew out of the codification of Christian religious doctrine and Christians' anxiety about their own institutions. For example, in the twelfth century, church leaders promulgated a newly rigorous definition of the Eucharist, declaring that when the bread and wine were blessed by the priest during Mass, they became the true body and blood of Christ. For some believers this meant that Christ, wounded and bleeding, lay on the altar. Miracle tales sometimes reported that the elements of the Eucharist bled. Reflecting Christian anxieties about the presence of real flesh on the altar, sensational stories—originating in clerical circles but soon widely circulated—told of Jews who secretly sacrificed Christian children in a morbid revisiting of the crucifixion of Jesus. This charge, called "blood libel" by historians, led to massacres of Jews in cities in England, France, Spain, and Germany. Jews had no rituals involving blood sacrifice at all, but they were convenient and vulnerable scapegoats for Christian guilt and anxiety.

■ **REVIEW:** *What were the causes and consequences of the Gregorian reform?*

The Revival of Monarchies

Attacks on the Jews reveal the ugly side of a wider development: kings and other rulers were enhancing and consolidating their power. They created new and revived old ideologies to justify their power; they hired officials to work for them;

and they found vassals and churchmen to support them. The money that flowed into their treasuries from the new urban economy increased their effectiveness.

Byzantium in Its Prime

The First Crusade was an unanticipated result of a monarchical revival at Byzantium. In 1081, ten years after the disastrous battle at Manzikert, the energetic soldier Alexius Comnenus (r. 1081–1118) seized the throne. He faced considerable unrest in Constantinople, whose populace suffered from a combination of high taxes and rising living costs. In addition, the empire was under attack on every side—by Normans in southern Italy, Seljuk Turks in Asia Minor, and new groups in the Balkans. But, Alexius managed to turn actual and potential enemies against one another, staving off immediate defeat.

When Alexius asked Pope Urban II to supply him with some western troops to fight his enemies, he was shocked and disappointed to learn that crusaders rather than mercenaries were on the way. His daughter Anna Comnena (1083–c. 1148) later wrote an account of the crusades from the Byzantine perspective in a book about her father, the *Alexiad*. To her, the crusaders were barbarians and her father the consummate statesman and diplomat:

> *The emperor sent envoys to greet them as a mark of friendship. . . . It was typical of Alexius: he had an uncanny prevision [foresight] and knew how to seize a point of vantage before his rivals. Officers appointed for this particular task were ordered to provide victuals on the journey—the pilgrims must have no excuse for complaint for any reason whatever.*

To wage all the wars he had to fight, Alexius relied less on the peasant farmers and the *theme* system than on mercenaries and great magnates armed and mounted like western knights and accompanied by their own troops. In return for their services he gave these nobles *pronoia* grants, lifetime possession of large imperial estates and their dependent peasants. The theme system, under which peasant soldiers in earlier centuries had been settled on imperial lands, gradually disappeared. Alexius conciliated the great families by giving the provincial nobility pronoia grants and satisfied members of the urban elite by granting them new offices. The emperor normally got on well with the patriarch and Byzantine clergy, for emperor and church depended on each other to suppress heresy and foster orthodoxy. The emperors of the Comnenian dynasty (1081–1185) thus gained a measure of increased imperial power, but at the price of important concessions to the nobility.

In the eleventh and twelfth centuries, Constantinople remained a rich, sophisticated, and highly cultured city. Sculptors and other artists strove to depict ideals of human beauty and elegance. Churches built during the period were decorated with elaborate depictions of the cosmos. Significant innovations occurred in Byzantine scholarship and literature. The Neoplatonic tradition of late antiquity had always influenced Byzantine religious and philosophical thought, but now scholars renewed their interest in the wellsprings of classical Greek philosophy, particularly Plato and Aristotle. The rediscovery of ancient culture inspired Byzantine writers to reintroduce old forms into the grammar, vocabulary, and rhetorical style of Greek literature. Anna Comnena wrote her *Alexiad* in this newly learned Greek and prided herself on "having read thoroughly the treatises of Aristotle and the dialogues of Plato." The revival of ancient Greek writings, especially those of Plato, in eleventh- and twelfth-century Byzantium would have profound consequences for both eastern and western European civilization in centuries to come as their ideas slowly penetrated European culture.

Norman Conquest of England, 1066

Norman and Angevin England

In Europe, the twelfth-century kings of England were the most powerful monarchs before 1200 because they ruled the whole kingdom by right of conquest. When the Anglo-Saxon king Edward the Confessor (r. 1042–1066) died childless in 1066, the duke of Normandy, William (1027–1087), claimed the throne of England. Gathering a force recruited from many parts of France, he launched an invasion. His armies clashed with those of another claimant to the throne, Harold, at Hastings on October 14, 1066. In one of history's rare decisive battles, William won and took over the realm.

Some people in England gladly supported William, considering his victory a verdict from God and hoping to be granted a place in the new order themselves. But William—known to posterity by the epithet "the Conqueror"—wanted to replace, not assimilate, the Anglo-Saxons. In the course of William's reign, families from continental Europe almost totally supplanted the English aristocracy. And although the English peasantry remained—now with new lords—the peasants were severely shaken. A twelfth-century historian claimed to record William's deathbed confession:

> I have persecuted [England's] native inhabitants beyond all reason. Whether gentle or simple, I have cruelly oppressed them; many I unjustly disinherited; innumerable multitudes, especially in the county of York, perished through me by famine or the sword.

Modern historians estimate that one out of five people in England died as a result of the Norman conquest and its immediate aftermath.

Although the Normans destroyed a generation of English men and women, they preserved and extended some Anglo-Saxon institutions, retaining the old

■ **Bayeux "Tapestry"**
This famous "tapestry" is misnamed; it is really an embroidery, 231 feet long and 20 inches
wide, created to tell the story of William's conquest of England from his point of view. In this
detail, Norman archers are lined up at the bottom. Above them, Norman knights on horseback
attack English foot soldiers wielding long battle-axes. Who seems to be winning? **For more help**
analyzing this image, see the visual activity for this chapter in the ONLINE STUDY GUIDE at
bedfordstmartins.com/huntconcise. (Tapisserie de Bayeux. By special permission of the City of Bayeux, France.)

administrative divisions and legal system of shires (counties) and hundreds (see
pages 330–31). The Normans also, of course, drew from continental institutions.
They set up a political hierarchy, culminating in the king and buttressed by his
castles, just as French kings were trying to do at about the same time (see page 366).
But because all of England was the king's by conquest, he could treat it as his
booty; William kept about 20 percent of the land for himself and divided the rest,
distributing it in large but scattered fiefs to a relatively small number of his barons
and family members, lay and ecclesiastical, as well as to some lesser men, such as
personal servants and soldiers. In turn, these men and their vassals owed the king
military service along with certain dues, such as reliefs (money paid upon inheriting a fief) and aids (payments made on important occasions).

Those were the revenues expected from the nobles, but the king of England
commanded the peasantry as well. In 1086, twenty years after his conquest,
William ordered a survey and census of England, popularly called "Domesday"
because, like the records of people judged at doomsday, it provided facts that could
not be appealed. It was the most extensive inventory of land, livestock, taxes, and
population that had ever been compiled in Europe. The king

> *sent his men over all England into every shire and had them find out how*
> *many hundred hides [a measure of land] there were in the shire, or what*
> *land and cattle the king himself had in the country, or what dues he ought*

to receive every year from the shire. . . . So very narrowly did he have the
survey to be made that there was not a single hide or yard of land, nor
indeed . . . an ox or a cow or a pig left out.

The Norman conquest tied England to the languages, politics, institutions, and culture of France and Flanders. Modern English is an amalgam of Anglo-Saxon and Norman French, the language spoken by the Normans. English commerce was linked to the wool industry in Flanders. St. Anselm (1033–1109), the archbishop of Canterbury (England), was born in Italy and was the abbot of a monastery in Normandy before crossing the Channel. The barons of England retained their estates in Normandy and elsewhere, and the kings of England often spent more time on the continent than they did on the island. When William's son Henry I (r. 1100–1135) died without male heirs, civil war soon erupted: the throne of England was fought over by two French counts—one married to Henry's daughter, the other to his sister.

The outcome of that civil war was the accession to the English throne of Henry II (r. 1154–1189).* He was not only count of Anjou but also, by an astute marriage to Eleanor of Aquitaine in 1152, duke of Aquitaine. His father, who had conquered Normandy, named him duke there, and he also exercised hegemony over Poitou and Brittany. Although technically a vassal of the king of France for his continental lands, in effect, Henry ruled a territory that stretched from England to the south of France (Map 9.3).

The marriage to Eleanor brought Henry both a huge duchy and a feisty queen, who, however, bore him the sons he needed to maintain his dynasty. Before her marriage to Henry, Eleanor was married to King Louis VII of France. Louis had the marriage annulled because she bore him only daughters. Nevertheless, as queen of France, Eleanor enjoyed an important position: she disputed with St. Bernard, the Cistercian abbot who was the most renowned churchman of the day; and she accompanied her husband on the Second Crusade, bringing more troops than he did. She determined to separate from Louis even before he considered leaving her. Married to Henry, she had much less power, for he dominated her as he dominated his barons. Turning to her offspring in 1173, Eleanor, disguised as a man, tried to join her eldest son, Henry the Younger, in a plot against his father. But the rebellion was put down, and she spent most of her years thereafter, until her husband's death in 1189, confined under guard at Winchester Castle.

As king of England, Henry immediately set to work to undo the damage to the monarchy caused by the civil war of 1139–1153, during which the English barons and high churchmen had gained new privileges and powers, building

---

*Henry II is known as the first Angevin (from *Anjou*) king of England because by inheritance, he was count of Anjou. But he also has another name: his father, Count Geoffrey of Anjou, was nicknamed *Plantagenet*, from *genet*, a shrub that he liked, and historians sometimes use that name to refer to the entire dynasty. Thus Henry II was the first Plantagenet as well as the first Angevin king of England.

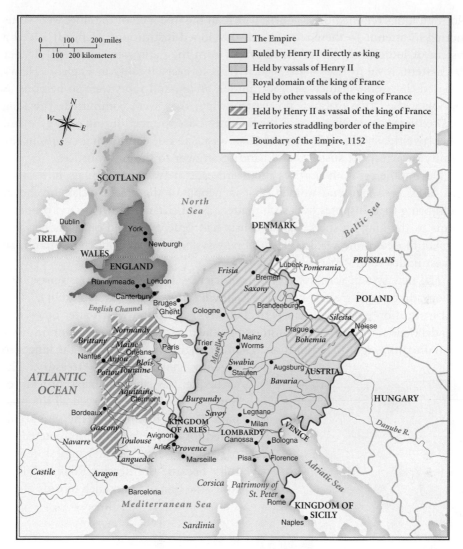

The Empire
Ruled by Henry II directly as king
Held by vassals of Henry II
Royal domain of the king of France
Held by other vassals of the king of France
Held by Henry II as vassal of the king of France
Territories straddling border of the Empire
Boundary of the Empire, 1152

■ **MAP 9.3 Europe in the Age of Frederick Barbarossa and Henry II, 1150–1190**
The second half of the twelfth century was dominated by two men, Emperor Frederick Barbarossa and King Henry II. Not just king of England, Henry also held northwestern France by inheritance and southwestern France through his wife, Eleanor of Aquitaine. A few hundred miles to the east were the borders of Frederick Barbarossa's empire, a huge territory—much of it held by him only weakly. Only the Staufen lands were directly under his control.

private castles as symbols of their strength. Henry destroyed or confiscated the new castles and regained crown lands. Then he proceeded to further extend monarchical power, above all by imposing royal justice.

Henry's judicial reforms built on an already well-developed English system. The Anglo-Saxon kings had established royal district courts and appointed sheriffs to police the shires, call up men to fight, and haul criminals into court. The

Norman kings retained these courts, which all the free men of the shire were summoned to attend. To these already well-developed institutions, Henry II added a system of judicial visitations called eyres (from the Latin *iter*, "journey"). Under this system, royal justices made regular trips to every locality in England. Henry declared that some crimes, such as murder, arson, and rape, were so heinous as to violate the "king's peace," no matter where they were committed. The king required local representatives of the knightly class to meet during each eyre and either give the sheriff the names of those suspected of committing crimes in the vicinity or arrest the suspects and hand them over to the royal justices.

During the eyres, the justices also heard cases between individuals, now called civil cases. Free men and women (that is, people of the knightly class or above) could bring their disputes over such matters as inheritance, dowries, and property claims to the king's justices. Earlier courts had generally relied on duels between litigants to determine verdicts. Henry's new system offered a different option, an inquest under royal supervision.

The new system was praised for its efficiency, speed, and conclusiveness by a contemporary legal treatise known as *Glanvill* (after its presumed author): "This legal institution emanates from perfect equity. For justice, which after many and long delays is scarcely ever demonstrated by the duel, is advantageously and speedily attained through this institution." *Glanvill* might have added that the king also speedily gained a large treasury. The exchequer, as the financial bureau of England was called, recorded all the fines paid for judgments and the sums collected for writs. The amounts, entered on parchment sewn together and stored as rolls, became the Receipt Rolls and Pipe Rolls, the first of many such records of the

■ **Hanging Thieves**

The development of common law in England meant mobilizing royal agents to bring charges and make arrests. In 1124, the royal justice Ralph Basset hanged forty-four thieves. This miniature from around 1130 shows the hanging of eight thieves for breaking into the shrine of St. Edmund. Under Henry II, all cases of murder, arson, and rape were considered crimes against the king himself. The result, in addition to the enhancement of the king's power, was new definitions of crime, more thorough policing, and more systematic punishments.

(Pierpont Morgan Library/Art Resource, NY.)

English monarchy and an indication that writing had become a mechanism for institutionalizing royal power in England.

The stiffest opposition to Henry's extension of royal courts came from the church, where a separate system of trial and punishment had long been available to the clergy and to others who enjoyed church protection. The punishments that these courts meted out were generally quite mild. Jealous of their prerogatives, churchmen refused to submit to the jurisdiction of Henry's courts, and the ensuing contest between Henry II and his appointed archbishop, Thomas Becket (1118–1170), became the greatest battle between the church and the state in the twelfth century. The conflict over jurisdiction simmered for six years, until Henry's henchmen murdered Thomas, unintentionally turning him into a martyr. Although Henry's role in the murder remained ambiguous, he had to do public penance for the deed largely because of the general outcry. In the end, both church courts and royal courts expanded to address the concerns of an increasingly litigious society.

Praising the King of France

The twelfth-century kings of France were much less obviously powerful than their English and Byzantine counterparts. Yet they too took part in the monarchical revival. Louis VI the Fat (r. 1108–1137), so heavy that he had to be hoisted onto his horse by a crane, was a tireless defender of royal power. We know a good deal about him because a contemporary and close associate, Suger (1081–1152), abbot of St. Denis, wrote Louis's biography. When Louis set himself the task of consolidating his rule in the Île-de-France, Suger portrayed the king as a righteous hero. He thought of the king as the head of a political hierarchy in which Louis had rights over the French nobles because they were his vassals or because they broke the peace.

Suger also believed that Louis had a religious role: to protect the church and the poor. He viewed Louis as another Charlemagne, a ruler for all society, not merely an overlord of the nobility. Louis waged war to keep God's peace. Of course, the Gregorian reform had made its mark: Suger did not claim Louis was head of the church. Nevertheless, he emphasized the royal dignity and its importance to the papacy. When a pope happened to arrive in France, Louis, not yet king, and his father, Philip I (r. 1052–1108), bowed low, but (recalled Suger) "the pope lifted them up and made them sit before him like devout sons of the apostles. In the manner of a wise man acting wisely, he conferred with them privately on the present condition of the church." Here, the pope was shown needing royal advice. Meanwhile, Suger stressed Louis's piety and active defense of the faith:

> *Helped by his powerful band of armed men, or rather by the hand of God, he abruptly seized the castle [of Crécy] and captured its very strong tower as if it were simply the hut of a peasant. Having startled those criminals, he piously slaughtered the impious.*

When Louis VI died in 1137, Suger's notion of the might and right of the king of France reflected reality in an extremely small area. Nevertheless, Louis laid the groundwork for the gradual extension of royal power in France. As the lord of vassals, the king could call upon his men to aid him in times of war (though the great ones sometimes disregarded his wishes and chose not to help). As a king and landlord, he could obtain many dues and taxes. He also drew revenues from Paris, a thriving city not only of commerce but also of scholarship. Officials enforced his royal laws and collected taxes. With money and land, Louis could dispense the favors and give the gifts that added to his prestige and his power. Louis VI and Suger together created the territorial core and royal ideal of the future French monarchy. Louis's grandson Philip Augustus would build on this foundation, greatly expanding the territory of the French monarchy in the thirteenth century.

Remaking the Empire

The Investiture Conflict and the civil war it generated (1075–1122) strengthened the German princes and weakened the emperors. For decades, the princes enjoyed near independence, building castles on their properties and establishing control over whole territories. To ensure that the emperors who succeeded Henry V (r. 1106–1125) would be weak, the princes supported only rulers who agreed to give them new lands and powers. A ruler's success depended on his ability to juggle the many conflicting interests of his own royal and imperial offices, his family, and the German princes. He also had to contend with the increasing influence of the papacy and the Italian communes, which were forging alliances with one another and with the German princes, preventing the consolidation of power under a strong German monarch during the first half of the twelfth century.

Weakness at the top, however, meant constant warfare among princely factions. Eventually the German princes became exhausted by conflict and in 1152 elected Frederick I Barbarossa (r. 1152–1190) as the first Hohenstaufen king of Germany. He was an impressive man with a striking red-blond beard (hence *Barbarossa*, or "red-beard") and a firm sense of his position. Frederick affirmed royal rights even when he handed out duchies and allowed others to name bishops, because in return for these political powers he required the princes to concede formally and publicly that they held their rights and territories from him as their lord. By making them his vassals, though with nearly royal rights within their principalities, Frederick defined the princes' relationship to the German king: they were powerful yet personally subordinate to him. In this way, Frederick hoped to save the monarchy and to coordinate royal and princely rule, thus ending Germany's chronic civil wars. Frederick used the lord–vassal relationship to give himself a free hand to rule while placating the princes.

Since the Investiture Conflict, the emperor had ruled Italy in name only. The communes of the northern cities guarded their liberties jealously, and the pope considered Italy his own sphere of influence. Frederick's territorial base north of Italy (in Swabia) and his designs on northern Italy threatened those interests (see Map 9.3). Some historians have criticized Frederick for "entangling" himself in Italy, but Frederick's title was *emperor*, a position that demanded he intervene there. To fault him for not concentrating on Germany is to blame him for lacking modern wisdom, which knows from hindsight that European polities developed into nation-states, such as France, Germany, and Italy. There was nothing inevitable about the development of nation-states, however, and Frederick should not be condemned for failing to see into the future. In addition, control of Italy made sense even for Frederick's effectiveness in Germany. His base in Swabia together with northern Italy would give him a compact and central territory. Moreover, the flourishing commercial cities of Italy would make him rich. Taxes on agricultural production there alone would yield thirty thousand silver talents annually, an incredible sum.

By alternately negotiating with and fighting against the great cities of northern Italy, especially Milan, Frederick achieved military control there in 1158. No longer able to make Italian bishops royal governors, as German kings had done earlier—the Investiture Conflict had effectively ended that practice—Frederick insisted that the communes be governed by magistrates (called *podestà*) from outside the commune who were appointed (or at least authorized) by the emperor and who would collect revenues on his behalf. Here is where Frederick made his mistake: the heavy hand of these officials, many of them from Germany, created enormous resentment. By 1167, most of the cities of northern Italy had joined with Pope Alexander III (r. 1159–1181) to form the Lombard League against Frederick. Defeated at the battle of Legnano (near Milan) in 1176, Frederick made peace with Alexander and withdrew most of his forces from Italy. The battle marked the triumph of the city over the crown in Italy, which would not have a centralized government until the nineteenth century; Italy's political history would instead be that of its various regions and their dominant cities.

The Courtly Culture of Europe

With the consolidation of territory, wealth, and power in the last half of the twelfth century, kings, barons, princes, and their wives and daughters created a newly opulent court culture. For the first time on the European continent, poems and songs were written in the vernacular, the spoken language, rather than in Latin. They celebrated the lives of the nobility and were meant to be read aloud or sung as entertainment. Already at the beginning of the twelfth century, Duke William IX of Aquitaine (1071–1126), the grandfather of Eleanor of Aquitaine, had written lyric poems in Occitan, the vernacular spoken in southern France. Perhaps influenced by love poetry in Arabic and Hebrew from al-Andalus, his own poetry in

■ Troubadour Song

Raimon de Miraval flourished between 1191 and 1229, very late for a troubadour. He was a petty knight who became a poet and was welcomed at the courts of rulers such as those of Toulouse, Aragon, and Castile. More than forty of his poems have survived, twenty-two with written music. The song here, beginning "A penas," is set to music with a five-line staff. Notice that some of the notes (called neumes*) are single and others are in groups. The grouped notes are to be sung, one right after the other, on the same syllable or word.*

turn provided a model for poetic forms that gained great popularity. The final four-line stanza of one such poem demonstrates the composer's skill with words:

> *Per aquesta fri e tremble,*   For this one I shiver and tremble,
> *quar de tan bon' amor l'am;*   I love her with such a good love;
> *qu'anc no cug qu'en nasques*   I do not think the like of her was ever
>   *semble*   born
> *en semblan de gran linh*   in the long line of Lord Adam.
>   *n'Adam.*

The rhyme scheme of this poem appears to be simple—*tremble* rhymes with *semble*, *l'am* with *n'Adam*. But the poem has five earlier verses, all six lines long and all containing the *-am, -am* rhyme in the fourth and sixth lines, while every other line within each verse rhymes as well. The whole scheme is dazzlingly complex.

William was followed by other troubadours—lyric poets who wrote in Occitan. Whether male or female, their subject was love. The Contessa de Dia, probably the wife of the lord of Die in France, wrote about her unrequited love for a man:

> *So bitter do I feel toward him*
> *whom I love more than anything.*
> *With him my mercy and fine manners [*cortesia*] are in vain.*

The key to troubadour verse was the notion of *cortesia*—courtesy—which referred to the refinement of people living at court and to their struggle to achieve an ideal of virtue.

Historians and literary critics used to use the term *courtly love* to emphasize one of the themes of courtly literature: the poet expresses overwhelming love for a beautiful married noblewoman who is far above him in status and utterly unattainable. But this was only one of many aspects of love that the troubadours sang about. Some boasted of sexual conquests; others played with the notion of equality between lovers; still others preached that love was the source of virtue. The real overall theme of this literature was not courtly love but the power of women. No wonder Eleanor of Aquitaine and other aristocratic women patronized the troubadours: they enjoyed the image that the poetry gave them of themselves. Nor was that image a delusion. There were many powerful female lords in southern France. They owned property, had vassals, led battles, decided disputes, and entered into and broke political alliances as their advantage dictated. Both men and women appreciated troubadour poetry, which recognized and praised women's power even as it eroticized it.

From southern France the lyric love song spread to Italy, northern France, England, and Germany—regions where Occitan was a foreign language. Similar poetry appeared in other vernacular languages: the *minnesingers* (literally, "love singers") sang in German; the *trouvères* sang in the Old French of northern France.

Some poets wrote much longer works—long heroic poems focused on war (later called epics) or equally long romantic poems about love (later called romances). Romances, often inspired by the legend of King Arthur, reached the zenith of their popularity during the late twelfth and early thirteenth centuries. A good example is *Lancelot* by Chrétien de Troyes (c. 1150–1190). The hero, in love with Queen Guinevere, the wife of his lord, King Arthur, will do anything for her. When she sees him—the greatest knight in Christendom—fighting in a tournament, she tests his love for her by asking him to do his "worst." The poor knight is obliged to lose all his battles until she changes her mind.

Lancelot was the perfect chivalric knight. The word **chivalry** derives from the French word *cheval* ("horse"); the fact that the knight was a horseman marked him as a warrior of the most prestigious sort. Perched high on his mount, his heavy lance couched in his right arm, the knight was an imposing and menacing figure. Chivalry made him gentle—except to his enemies on the battlefield. The chivalric hero was a knight constrained by a code of refinement, fair play, piety, and devotion to an ideal. Historians debate whether real knights lived up to the codes implicit in epics and romances. But there is no doubt that real knights liked to imagine themselves that way.

■ **REVIEW:** *What new sources and institutions of power became available to rulers in the twelfth century?*

New Forms of Scholarship and Religious Experience

The commercial revolution, the newly organized church, and the revived monarchies of the twelfth century set the stage for the growth of schools and for new forms of scholarship. Money and career opportunities attracted unheard-of numbers of young men to city schools. Worldly motivations, however, were equaled by spiritual ones. The movement for church reform stressed the importance of the church and its beliefs. Many students and teachers in the twelfth century sought knowledge to make their faith clearer and deeper. "Nothing can be believed unless it is first understood," said one of the period's greatest scholars, Peter Abelard (1079–1142).

Other people in the twelfth century, however, sought to avoid the cities and the schools. Some found refuge in the measured ceremonies and artistic splendor of Benedictine monasteries such as Cluny. Others considered these vast monastic complexes to be ostentatious and worldly. Rejecting the opulence of cities and the splendor of well-endowed monasteries alike, some pursued a monastic life of poverty, while others, like St. Francis, rejected even the shelter of the cloister.

Schools, Scholars, and the New Learning

Schools had been connected to monasteries and cathedrals since the Carolingian period. They served to train new recruits to become either monks or priests. Some were better endowed with books and masters (or teachers) than others; a few developed a reputation for a certain theological approach or specialized in a certain branch of learning, such as literature, medicine, or law. By the end of the eleventh century, the best schools were generally in the larger cities: Reims, Paris, Bologna, Montpellier.

Eager students sampled nearly all of them. The young monk Gilbert of Liège was typical: "Instilled with an insatiable thirst for learning, whenever he heard of somebody excelling in the arts, he rushed immediately to that place and drank whatever delightful potion he could draw from the master there." For Gilbert and other students, a good lecture had the excitement of theater. Teachers at cathedral schools found themselves forced to find larger halls to accommodate the crush of students. Other teachers simply declared themselves "masters" and set up shop by renting a room. If they could prove their mettle in the classroom, they had no trouble finding paying students.

"Wandering scholars" like Gilbert were probably all male, and because schools had hitherto been the training ground for clergymen, all students were considered clerics, whether or not they had been ordained. Wandering became a way of life as the consolidation of castellanies, counties, and kingdoms made violence against travelers less frequent. Urban centers soon responded to the needs of transients with markets, taverns, and lodgings. Using Latin, Europe's common language, students could drift from, say, Italy to Spain, Germany, England, and France, wherever a noted master had settled. Along with crusaders, pilgrims, and merchants, students made the roads of Europe very crowded indeed.

What the students sought, above all, was knowledge of the seven liberal arts. Grammar, rhetoric, and logic (or dialectic) belonged to the "beginning" arts, the so-called trivium. Logic, involving the technical analysis of texts as well as the application and manipulation of mental constructs, was a transitional

■ A Teacher and His Students

*This miniature expresses the hierarchical relation-
ship between students and teachers in the twelfth
century. But there is more. The miniature
appears in a late-twelfth-century manuscript of a
commentary written by Gilbert (d. 1154), bishop
of Poitiers. Gilbert's ideas in this commentary provoked the ire of St. Bernard, who accused Gilbert
of heresy. But Gilbert escaped condemnation.
Here, in pictorial form, the artist asserts Gilbert's
orthodoxy by depicting him with a halo, in the
full dress of a bishop, speaking from his throne.
Below Gilbert are three of his disciples, also with
halos. The artist's positive view of Gilbert is
echoed by modern historians, who recognize
Gilbert as a pioneer in his approach to scriptural
commentary.* (Bibliothèque municipale de Valenciennes.)

subject leading to the second, higher part of the liberal arts, the quadrivium. This comprised four areas of study that we might call theoretical math and science: arithmetic, geometry, music (theory rather than practice), and astronomy. Of all these subjects, logic excited the most intense interest. Medieval students and masters were convinced that logic clarified every issue, even questions about the nature of God. With logic, they thought, one could prove that what one believed on faith was in fact true. At the end of the twelfth century, some western scholars took advantage of Islamic achievements; they traveled to Islamic centers in Spain and Sicily, where the Greek texts of Aristotle, with their sophisticated logic, had already been translated into Arabic and closely commented on. Translating these Arabic texts into Latin, western scholars made Aristotle their own.

After studying the liberal arts, students went on to study medicine, theology, or law. At Bologna, for example, students studied Lombard, Roman, and canon law. Men skilled in canon law served popes and bishops; popes, kings, princes, and communes all found that Roman law, which claimed the emperor as its fount, justified their claims to power. The University of Paris, established at the very end of the twelfth century, concentrated on theology. Montpellier, in the south of France, was noted for its medical education. With books expensive and hard to find, lectures were the chief method of communication. These were centered on important texts: the master read an excerpt aloud, delivered his commentary on it, and disputed any contrary commentaries that rival masters might have proposed. Student committed the lectures to memory.

Universities functioned as guilds, with the teachers in the role of the masters and the students the apprentices (except at Bologna, where the students, usually older men experienced in administration, had their own guild). Like guilds, they set prices (in this case, fees), determined standards (in this case, the knowledge that had to be learned), and regulated discipline. Given generous privileges by both popes and kings, who valued the services of scholars, the universities were sometimes at odds with the townspeople. It is common to speak of "town against gown"—the "gown" referring to the garb worn by the students and masters (and imitated by the American graduation gown). Students could be rowdy and worse; and townspeople resented a self-governing body of transients—the university—in their midst. On the other hand, pub owners, innkeepers, food purveyors, and landlords benefited from the patronage of students and masters, and generally town–gown relations were good.

The remarkable renewal of scholarship in the twelfth century had an unexpected benefit: we know a great deal about the men involved in it—and a few of the women—because they wrote so much, often about themselves. Three important figures typify the scholars of the period: Abelard and Heloise, who embraced the new learning wholeheartedly and retired to monasteries only when forced to do so, and Hildegard of Bingen, who spent most of her life happily in a cloister yet wrote knowingly about the world.

Peter Abelard (1079–1142) was one of the twelfth century's greatest thinkers. Turning his back on an expected career as a warrior and lord, he studied in Paris and soon began to write influential works on ethics, logic, and theology. Around 1122–1123, he prepared a textbook for his students, the *Sic et Non* (*Yes and No*), unusual because it arranged side-by-side opposing positions on various subjects without reconciling them. Instead, Abelard challenged his students to make sense of the conflicts and resolve the contradictions themselves. In Abelard's view, the inquiring student would follow the model of Christ himself, who as a boy sat among the rabbis, questioning them.

Abelard's fame as a teacher was such that a Parisian cleric named Fulbert gave him room and board and engaged him as tutor for Heloise (c. 1100–c. 1163/1164), Fulbert's niece. Brought up under her uncle's guardianship, Heloise had been sent as a young girl to a convent school, where she received a thorough grounding in literary skills. Her uncle hoped to continue her education at home by hiring Abelard. Abelard, however, became her secret lover as well as her tutor. "Our desires left no stage of love-making untried," wrote Abelard in his *Historia calamitatum* (*Story of My Calamities*), his autobiographical account. When Heloise became pregnant, Abelard insisted they marry. They did so clandestinely, informing only a very few, such as Fulbert, for the new emphasis on clerical celibacy meant that Abelard's professional success and prestige would have been compromised if news of his marriage were made public. After they were married, Heloise and Abelard rarely saw one another. Suspecting that Abelard had abandoned his niece, Fulbert plotted a cruel punishment: he paid a servant to castrate Abelard. Soon after, husband and wife entered separate monasteries.

For Heloise, separation from Abelard was a lasting misfortune. For Abelard, however, the loss of Heloise and even his castration were not the worst disasters of his life. The cruelest blow came later, and it was directed at his intellect. He wrote a book that applied "human and logical reasons" (as he put it) to the Trinity; the book was condemned at the Council of Soissons in 1121, and he was forced to throw it, page by page, into the flames. Bitterly weeping at the injustice, Abelard lamented, "This open violence had come upon me only because of the purity of my intentions and love of our Faith which had compelled me to write."

Abelard had written the treatise on the Trinity for his students, maintaining that "words were useless if the intelligence could not follow them, [and] that nothing could be believed unless it was first understood." For Abelard, logic was the key to knowledge, and knowledge the key to faith.

Unlike Abelard and Heloise, Hildegard of Bingen (1098–1179) did not attend the city schools or learn under one of their scholars. Placed in a German convent at age eight, she received her schooling there and took vows as a nun. In 1136, she was elected abbess of the convent. Shortly thereafter, very abruptly, she began to write and to preach. She was probably the only woman authorized by the church to preach in her day.

Writing and preaching were the sudden external manifestations of an inner life that had been extraordinary from the beginning. Even as a child, Hildegard had experienced visions—of invisible things, of the future, and (always) of a special kind of light. These visions were intermingled with pain and sickness. Only in her forties did Hildegard interpret her sickness and her visions as gifts from God. In her *Scivias* ("Know the Ways of the Lord," 1151), Hildegard described some of her visions and explained their meaning. She interpreted them as containing nothing less than the full story of creation and redemption, a summa, or compendium, of church doctrine.

Benedictine Monks and Artistic Splendor

Hildegard's contentment within the confines of her cloister was characteristic of many. Known as "black monks"—so called because they dyed their robes black—the Benedictines reached the height of their popularity in the eleventh century. Monasteries often housed hundreds of monks; convents for nuns were usually less populated. Cluny was one of the largest monasteries, with some four hundred brothers in the mid-eleventh century.

The chief occupation of the monks, as befitted (in their view) citizens of heaven, was prayer. The black monks and nuns devoted themselves to singing Psalms and other prayers specified in the rule of St. Benedict, adding to them still more Psalms. The rule called for chanting the entire Psalter—150 psalms—over the course of a week, but some monks, like those at Cluny, chanted that number in a day. Such prayer was neither private nor silent. Black monks had to know not only the words but also the music that went with their prayers; they had to be

■ **Eve**

The Romanesque sculptor of this depiction of Eve delighted in her sinuous curves, which he por-
trayed as a continuation of the snake from which Eve accepted the apple. Compare this seductive
view of Eve with the motherly Eve on page 294. Sculptural figures such as this one, which once
adorned the church at Autun, France, were typical of the inventive variety of the Romanesque
style. (© Musée Rolin, Autun, France/Peter Willi/SuperStock.)

musicians. The music of the Benedictine monastery was plainchant, also known
as Gregorian chant, which consisted of melodies, each sung in unison, without
accompaniment. Although chant was rhythmically free, lacking a regular beat, its
melodies ranged from extremely simple to highly ornate and embellished. By the
twelfth century, a large repertoire of melodies had grown up—at first through oral
composition and transmission and then in written notation, which was first
invented in the ninth century.

The **Romanesque** church (so called because its round arches and other
architectural elements reminded modern art historians of Roman buildings)
was the place in which black monks spent most of their day chanting the
psalms. It was ideally quite large, finely decorated with inventive sculpture and
wall paintings, and built of stone. The various parts of the church—the chapels
in the *chevet*, or apse (at the east end of the building), for example—were
treated as discrete units, retaining the forms of cubes, cones, and cylinders
(Figure 9.1).

In such a setting, gilded reliquaries and altars made of silver, precious gems,
and pearls were the fitting accoutrements of worship. Prayer, liturgy, and music
in this way complemented the gift economy: richly clad in vestments of the finest
materials, intoning the liturgy in the most splendid of churches, monks and
priests offered up the gift of prayer to God; in return they begged for the gift
of salvation of their souls and the souls of all the faithful.

New Monastic Orders of Poverty

Not everyone agreed that such opulence pleased God. At the end of the eleventh century, the new commercial economy and the profit motive that fueled it led many to reject wealth and to embrace poverty as a key element of religious life. The Carthusian order founded by Bruno of Cologne was one such group. Each monk took a vow of silence and lived as a hermit in his own small hut. Monks occasionally joined others for prayer in a common prayer room, or oratory. When not engaged in prayer or meditation, the Carthusians copied manuscripts. They considered this task part of their religious vocation, a way to preach God's word with their hands rather than their mouths. The Carthusian order grew slowly. Each monastery was limited to only twelve monks, the number of the Apostles.

The Cistercians, by contrast, expanded rapidly. Rejecting even the conceit of blackening their robes, they left them the original color of wool (hence their nickname, "white monks"). The Cistercian order began as a single monastery, Cîteaux (in Latin, *Cistercium*) in France, founded in 1098. It grew rapidly under the leadership of St. Bernard (c. 1090–1153), abbot of the important Cistercian monastery Clairvaux. Despite the Cistercian order's official repudiation of female houses,

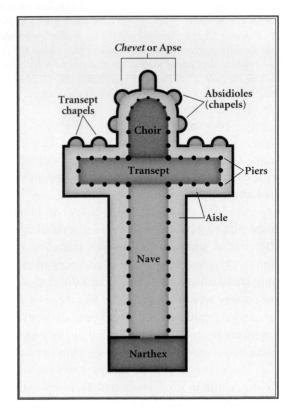

■ FIGURE 9.1 Floor Plan of a Romanesque Church

As churchgoers entered a Romanesque church, they passed through the narthex, an anteroom decorated with sculptured depictions of important scenes from the Bible. Walking through the portal of the narthex, they entered the church's nave, at the east end of which—just after the crossing of the transept and in front of the choir—was the altar, the focus of the Mass. Walking down the nave, they passed massive and tall piers leading up to the vaulting (the roof) of the nave. Each of these piers was decorated with sculpture, and the walls were brightly painted. Romanesque churches were both lively and colorful (because of their decoration) and solemn and somber (because of their heavy stones and massive scale).

■ FIGURE 9.2 Floor Plan of a Cistercian Monastery
*Cistercian monasteries seldom deviated much from this standard plan, which perfectly suited
their double lifestyle: one half for the lay brothers, who worked in the fields, the other half for the
monks, who performed the prayers. This plan shows the first floor. Above were dormitories: the
lay brothers slept above their cellar and refectory; the monks slept above their chapter-house
(where the rule of St. Benedict was read to them), common room, and room for novices. No one
had a private bedroom, just as the rule prescribed.*

many convents followed its lead and adopted its customs. Women were as eager
as men to live the life of simplicity and poverty that they believed the Apostles
had enjoyed and endured.

Although they held up the rule of St. Benedict as the foundation of their customs, the Cistercians elaborated a style of life all their own, largely governed by
the goal of simplicity. Cistercian churches, though built of stone, were initially
unlike the great Romanesque churches of the Benedictines. They were remarkably standardized; the church and the rest of the buildings of any one Cistercian
monastery were almost exactly like those of any other (Figure 9.2). The churches
were small, made of smoothly hewn, undecorated stone. Wall paintings and sculpture were prohibited. Illuminated by the pure white light that came through clear
glass windows, Cistercian houses were luminous, cool, and serene.

There were two sorts of white monks: *conversi* or "lay brothers" toiled in the
fields; "choir monks" dedicated themselves to private prayer and contemplation
and to monastic administration. By the end of the twelfth century, the Cistercians
had a closely monitored network of houses, and each year the Cistercian abbots

met to hammer out legislation for all of them. The abbot of the mother house (or founding house) visited the daughter houses annually to make sure the legislation was being followed. Each house, whether mother or daughter, had large and highly organized farms and grazing lands called granges. Cistercian monks spent much of their time managing their estates and flocks, both of which were yielding handsome profits by the end of the twelfth century. Clearly part of the agricultural and commercial revolutions of the Middle Ages, the Cistercian order made managerial expertise a part of the monastic life.

At the same time, the Cistercians elaborated a spirituality of intense personal emotion. As Bernard said:

> *Often enough when we approach the altar to pray our hearts are dry and lukewarm. But if we persevere, there comes an unexpected infusion of grace, our breast expands as it were, and our interior is filled with an overflowing love.*

The Cistercians emphasized not only human emotion but also Christ's and Mary's humanity. While pilgrims continued to stream to the tombs and reliquaries of saints, the Cistercians dedicated all their churches to the Virgin Mary (for whom they had no relics) because for them she signified the model of a loving mother. Indeed, the Cistercians regularly used maternal imagery (as Bernard's description invoking the metaphor of a flowing breast illustrates) to describe the nurturing care provided to humans by Jesus himself. The Cistercians' God was approachable, human, protective, even mothering.

Similar views of God were held by many who were not members of the Cistercian order; their spirituality signaled wider changes. For example, around 1099, St. Anselm wrote a theological treatise entitled *Why God Became Man*, in which he argued that since man had sinned, only a sinless man could redeem him. St. Anselm's work represented a new theological focus on the redemptive power of human charity, including that of Jesus as a human being.

Religious Fervor and Dissent

The emphasis on a common humanity in Christ beckoned to men and women of every age and every walk of life. Fervent piety spread beyond the convent, punctuating the routines of daily life with scriptural reading, fasting, and charity. The new religious groups of the late twelfth century embraced urban populations. Rich and poor, male and female joined these movements. Many criticized the existing church as too wealthy, ritualistic, and impersonal. Intensely and personally focused on the life of Christ, men and women in the late twelfth century made his childhood, agony, death, and presence in the Eucharist—the bread and wine that became the body and blood of Christ in the Mass—the most important experiences of their own lives. Some of this intense religious response developed into official, orthodox movements within

■ **St.-Savin-sur-Gartempe**

The nave of the church of St.-Savin was built between 1095 and 1115. Its barrel (or tunnel) vault is typical of Romanesque churches, as is its sense of liveliness, variety, and color. The columns, decorated with striped or wavy patterns, are topped by carved capitals, each one different from the next. The entire vault is covered with frescoes painted in shades of brown, ocher, and yellow depicting scenes from the Old Testament. What were the purposes of such decorations?

(Bridgeman-Giraudon/Art Resource, NY.)

■ **Eberbech**

Compare the nave of Eberbech, a Cistercian church built between 1170 and 1186, with the nave of St.-Savin. What at St.-Savin appears full of variety and color is here subdued by order and calm. There are no wall paintings in a Cistercian church, no variegated columns— nothing that might distract the worshiper. Yet a close look reveals subtle points of interest. How has the architect played with angles, planes, and light in the vaulting? Are the walls utterly smooth? What decorative elements can you see on the massive piers between the arches?

(AKG London/Stefan Drechsel.)

the church; other religious movements so threatened established doctrine that church leaders declared them heretical.

St. Francis (c. 1182–1226) founded the most famous orthodox religious movement—the Franciscans. Francis was a child of the commercial revolution. Expected to follow his well-to-do father in the cloth trade at Assisi in Italy, Francis experienced doubts, dreams, and illnesses, which spurred him to religious self-examination. In time, he renounced his family's wealth, dramatically marking the decision by casting off all his clothes and standing naked before his father, a crowd of spectators, and the bishop of Assisi. Francis then put on a simple robe and went about preaching penance to anyone who would listen. Adopting the life of a mendicant (one who begs for his livelihood), he accepted no money (only hospitality), walked without shoes, wore only one coarse tunic, and refused to be cloistered. Intending to follow the model of Christ, he received, as his biographers put it, a miraculous gift of grace: the stigmata, bleeding sores corresponding to the wounds Christ suffered on the cross.

By all accounts Francis was a spellbinding speaker, and he attracted many followers. Recognized as a religious order by the pope, the Brothers of St. Francis (or **friars**, from the Latin term for "brothers") spent their time preaching, ministering to lepers, and doing manual labor. Eventually they dispersed, setting up fraternal groups throughout Italy and then in France, Spain, the Holy Land, Germany, and England. Unlike Bruno of Cologne and the Cistercians, who had rejected cities, the friars sought town life, preaching to urban crowds and begging for their daily bread. St. Francis converted both men and women. In 1212, a young noblewoman named Clare formed the nucleus of a community of pious women, which became the Order of the Sisters of St. Francis. At first the women worked alongside the friars; but the church disapproved of their activities in the world, and soon Franciscan sisters were confined to cloisters under the rule of St. Benedict.

Clare was one of many women who sought a new kind of religious expression. In northern Europe at the end of the twelfth century, laywomen who lived together in informal pious communities were called Beguines. Without permanent vows or an established rule, the Beguines chose to be celibate (though they were free to leave and marry) and often made their living by weaving cloth or working with the sick and old. Although their daily occupations were ordinary, the Beguines' private, internal lives were often emotional and ecstatic, infused with the combined imagery of love and religion so pervasive in both monasteries and courts. One renowned Beguine, Mary of Oignies (1177–1213), who like St. Francis was said to have received the very wounds of Christ (the stigmata), felt herself to be a pious mother entrusted with the Christ child. As her biographer, Jacques de Vitry, wrote:

> *Sometimes it seemed to her that for three or more days she held [Christ] close to her so that He nestled between her breasts like a baby, and she hid Him there lest He be seen by others.*

■ **MAPPING THE WEST** Major Religions in the West, c. 1200

The broad washes of color on this map tell a striking story: by 1150, there were three major religions, each corresponding to a broad region. To the west, north of the Mediterranean Sea, Catholic Christianity held sway; to the east, the Greek Orthodox church was ascendant; all along the southern Mediterranean, Islam triumphed. Only a few places defied this logic: one was the crusader states, a tiny outpost of Catholics who ruled over a largely Muslim population. What this map does not show, however, are the details: Jewish communities in many cities; lively varieties of Islamic beliefs within the Muslim world; communities of Coptic Christians in Egypt; and scattered groups of heretics in Catholic lands. **For more help analyzing this map,** *see the map activity for this chapter in the* ONLINE STUDY GUIDE *at* bedfordstmartins.com/huntconcise.

More hardheaded was St. Dominic (1170–1221), founder of an order of friars—the Dominicans—that was patterned very closely on the Franciscans. Like Francis, Dominic and his followers rejected material riches and instead went about on foot, preaching and begging. Their initial audience was not the men and women of the Italian cities, however, but rather the people of southern France, where new doctrines that contradicted those officially accepted by the church—and were therefore labeled "heretical"—had become very popular.

Dominic and his friars were responding to an unprecedented explosion of heresies, part of the ferment of ideas and experiments in social life that were characteristic of medieval city growth. Among the most visible of the heretics were dualists, who saw the world torn between two great forces—one good, the other evil. Dualism became a prominent ingredient in religious life in Italy and the Rhineland by the end of the twelfth century. Another center of dualism was Languedoc, an area of southern France; there the dualists were called Albigensians, a name derived from the Languedoc town of Albi.

Described collectively as Cathars, or "Pure Ones," these dualists believed that the devil had created the material world. Therefore they renounced the world, abjuring wealth, sex, and meat. Their repudiation of sex reflected some of the attitudes of eleventh-century church reformers (whose orthodoxy, however, was never in doubt); their rejection of wealth echoed the same concerns that moved Bruno of Cologne to abandon city life and St. Francis to embrace poverty. In many ways the dualists simply took these attitudes to an extreme; but unlike orthodox reformers, they also challenged the efficacy and value of the church hierarchy. Cathars considered themselves followers of Christ's original message. But the church called them heretics.

The church also condemned other, nondualist groups as heretical, not on doctrinal grounds but because these groups allowed their lay members to preach, challenging the authority of the church hierarchy. In Lyon (in southeastern France) in the 1170s, for example, a rich merchant named Waldo decided to take literally the Gospel message "If you wish to be perfect, then go and sell everything you have, and give to the poor" (Matt. 19:21). The same message had inspired countless monks and would worry the church far less several decades later, when St. Francis established his new order. But when Waldo went into the street and gave away his belongings, announcing, "I am not really insane, as you think," he scandalized not only the bystanders but the church as well. Refusing to retire to a monastery, Waldo and his followers, men and women called Waldensians, lived in poverty and went about preaching, quoting the Gospel in the vernacular so that everyone would understand. But the papacy rebuffed Waldo's bid to preach freely, and the Waldensians—denounced, excommunicated, and expelled from Lyon—wandered to Languedoc, Italy, northern Spain, and the Moselle valley (in Germany).

■ **REVIEW:** *How and to what degree was religious life and thought influenced by the new learning of the schools?*

IMPORTANT DATES

1054	Great Schism between Roman Catholic and Greek Orthodox churches	c. 1122	Abelard writes *Sic et Non*
		1139–1153	Civil war in England
1066	Norman conquest of England; battle of Hastings	c. 1140	Gratian's *Decretum* published
1077	Emperor Henry IV does penance before Pope Gregory VII at Canossa	1151	Hildegard of Bingen's *Scivias* published
		1152–1190	Reign of Emperor Frederick Barbarossa
1086	Domesday survey commissioned by William I of England	1154–1189	Reign of Henry II of England
c. 1090–1153	Life of St. Bernard, leader of Cistercian order	1176	Battle of Legnano; Frederick Barbarossa defeated in northern Italy
1095	Urban II preaches the First Crusade at Clermont	1182–1226	Life of St. Francis
1122	Concordat of Worms ends the Investiture Conflict		

Conclusion

The commercial revolution and the building boom it spurred profoundly changed the look of Europe. Thriving cities of merchants and artisans brought trade, new wealth, and new institutions to the West. Mutual and fraternal organizations like the commune, the compagnia, and the guilds expressed and reinforced the solidarity and economic interest of city dwellers.

Political consolidation accompanied economic growth, as kings and popes exerted their authority and tested its limits. The Gregorian reform pitted the emperor against the pope, and two separate political hierarchies emerged: the secular and the ecclesiastical. The two might cooperate, as Suger and Louis VI showed in their mutual respect, admiration, and dependence. But they might also clash, as Becket did with Henry II. Secular and religious leaders developed new and largely separate systems of administration, reflecting in political life the new distinctions that separated clergy from laity, such as clerical celibacy and allegiance to the pope. Although in some ways growing apart, the two groups never worked together so closely as in the crusades, military pilgrimages inspired by the pope and led by lay lords.

The commercial economy, political stability, and ecclesiastical needs fostered the growth of schools and the achievements of new scholarship. Young men sought learning to enhance their careers and bring personal fulfillment; women gained excellent educations in convents. Logic fascinated some students because it seemed to clarify the nature of both the world and God. But others, such as St. Bernard, felt that faith could not be analyzed.

While Benedictine monks added to their hours of worship, built lavish churches, and devoted themselves to the music of the plainchant, the white monks insisted on an intense, interior spiritual life in a monastery shorn of decoration. Other reformers, such as Bruno of Cologne, sought isolation and hardship. These reformers repudiated urban society yet unintentionally reflected it: the Cistercians were as anxious as any tradesman about the success of their granges, and the Carthusians were dedicated to their books. With the Franciscans and Dominicans—as well as heretical groups such as the Cathars—laypeople were drawn to participate actively in a deeply felt imitation of Christ's life and sufferings. Yet this new piety, paired with new power, contributed to the persecution of Jews and the periodic call for Crusades against the Muslims.

■ MAKING CONNECTIONS

1. *What were the similarities and differences between the powers wielded by the Carolingian kings and those wielded by twelfth-century rulers?*

2. *Contrast the purposes and the institutions of the gift economy discussed in Chapter 8 with those of the new profit economy.*

■ FOR FURTHER EXPLORATION

For further reading and online research ideas, see the Suggested References on page SR-5 at the back of the book.

For practice quizzes, a customized study plan, and other study tools, see the ONLINE STUDY GUIDE at bedfordstmartins.com/huntconcise.

For primary-source material from this period, see Chapter 9 in *Sources of THE MAKING OF THE WEST: A CONCISE HISTORY*, Second Edition.

An Age of Confidence

1200–1340

I N ABOUT 1220, CHINGIZ KHAN (c. 1162–1227), leader of a confederation of horseback warriors in Mongolia, conquered northern China. By 1240, his successors had conquered Russia and were attacking Poland and Hungary. Europeans were galvanized. Some considered the Mongols a new incarnation of the Devil. Others looked forward to converting the newcomers to Christianity and hoped for new ports of call for their ships, caravans, and traders. The brothers Niccolò and Maffeo Polo, merchants from Venice, were among the first Western adventurers who saw an opportunity to make a profit. According to Niccolò's son Marco, early in their travels the brothers met the Mongol ruler of the Volga region in Russia, "gave him all the jewels they had brought; and [the ruler] took [the jewels] willingly . . . and gave them goods of fully twice the value in return." After making a tidy profit, the brothers moved on, eventually finding their way to China. On a second trip, they brought with them the young Marco, whose later account of his travels dazzled his contemporaries.

Niccolò and Maffeo's fearless self-confidence in the face of the "inhuman Tartars," as Pope Alexander IV called the Mongols in 1260, was characteristic of an age in which participants in emerging institutions of government, commerce, and religion were unafraid to assert themselves, their rights, and their interests. In the

■ **Pietro Vesconte's World Map (c. 1320)**
The Polo brothers knew perfectly well how to travel from Venice to China, but not because they were guided by maps. Most of the maps available in their day were symbolic rather than accurate. Pietro Vesconte's world map is partly in that old style. But it also shows a growing interest in precision. Note, for example, the "rhumb lines" that crisscross the map. These were carefully constructed as a series of equidistant spokes radiating from a point, each indicating a wind direction. Vesconte was here copying "portolan charts"—the most scientific maps of his day—which gave accurate indications of land and water shapes to help sailors navigate. (By permission of the British Library.)

thirteenth century, merchants, kings, princes, popes, city dwellers, and even heretics were acutely conscious of themselves as individuals and as members of like-minded groups with identifiable objectives and plans to promote and perpetuate their aims. Staffs of literate government officials now preserved official documents and other important papers; lords calculated their profits with the help of accountants; craft guilds and religious associations defined and regulated their membership with increased precision.

The period 1200–1340 was characterized by confidence bolstered by new organizations and institutions. Well-prepared rulers exercised control over whole territories through organs of government that could—if need be—function without them. As monarchs gained power, so, too, did the popes, and this period witnessed the height of the medieval church. In the cultural arena, vernacular poets wrote literature of astonishing beauty and increasing complexity and sophistication. Musicians, like poets, developed forms that bridged sacred and secular subjects, and Gothic churches sprang up in cities throughout Europe, dazzling observers with their light-filled expression of a universe of order and harmony.

With greater confidence and more clearly defined group and individual identities came conflict as well as unity. Kings and popes disputed about the limits of their power, while theologians fought over the place of reason in matters of faith. The church created tribunals of inquisition to root out religious dissidents, and kings and other rulers extended their influence over their subjects. Yet these tribunals did not end heresy, and kings did not gain all the power that they wanted. Diversity and opposition continually threatened expectations of harmony and order.

War, Conquest, and Settlement

In the thirteenth and early fourteenth centuries, Europeans aggressively moved outward in nearly all directions. While one group of armies pushed north and east on the Baltic coast, another was attacking Constantinople itself, while still a third was pursuing the *reconquista* of Spain. In the south of France and in Sicily, crusaders, with the pope's blessing, waged war against people whom the church declared to be heretics, including a Christian king. Far beyond Europe's eastern fringes, merchants like Marco Polo traveled to and settled in lands ruled by the Mongols.

The Northern Crusades

Long before the twelfth century, the peoples living along the Baltic coast—partly pagan, mostly Slavic- or Baltic-speaking—had learned to glean a living and a profit from the inhospitable soil and climate. Through fishing and trading, they supplied the rest of Europe and Russia with slaves, furs, amber, wax, and dried fish. Like the Vikings, they combined commercial competition with outright raiding. The Danes and the Saxons (that is, the Germans in Saxony) both benefited and suffered from their presence.

When St. Bernard began to preach the Second Crusade in Germany, he discovered that the Germans were indeed eager to attack the infidels—the ones right next door to them. St. Bernard pressed the pope to add these northern heathens to the list of those against whom holy war should be launched, and he urged their conversion or extermination. Thus began the Northern Crusades, which continued intermittently until the early fifteenth century.

The king of Denmark and the duke of Saxony launched the first phase of the Northern Crusades. Their initial attacks were uncoordinated—in some instances they even fought each other. Then, in key raids in the 1160s and 1170s, the two leaders worked together briefly to bring much of the region west of the Oder River under their control. They took some land outright—the Saxon duke apportioned conquered territory to his followers, for example—but more often the Slavic princes surrendered and had their territories reinstated once they became vassals of the Christian rulers.

In 1198, Pope Innocent III (r. 1198–1216) declared a crusade against the Livs, even farther to the north and east. A military order—the Order of Sword Brothers, later supplanted by the Teutonic Knights—was set up to lead crusading armies, and a bishopric, the "see of Riga," was established at the mouth of the Dvina River. The native populations were obliged to submit, whether by material inducements (the crusaders helped the Livs raid the Estonians, for example) or by sheer force. Repeatedly they agreed to truce and baptism, and just as repeatedly they rebelled. In some areas, the crusaders resorted to scorched-earth tactics. By 1300, they had secured Livonia, Prussia, Estonia, and Finland. Only Lithuania managed to resist conquest and conversion (see Map 10.1 on page 388).

Though less well known than the crusades to the Holy Land, the Northern Crusades had far more lasting effects: they settled the Baltic region with German-speaking lords and peasants, and they forged a permanent relationship between the very north of Europe and its neighbors to the south and west. With the Baltic dotted with churches and monasteries and its peoples dipped into baptismal waters, the region would gradually adopt the institutions of western medieval society—cities, guilds, universities, castles, and manors.

The Capture of Constantinople

Four years after calling for the crusade against the Livs, Pope Innocent III declared the Fourth Crusade (1202–1204) to the Holy Land. He hoped to reverse the failures of the Second and Third Crusades, but attitudes and circumstances beyond his control took over the new enterprise. Prejudices, religious zeal, and self-confidence had become characteristic of western European dealings with the Byzantine Greeks.

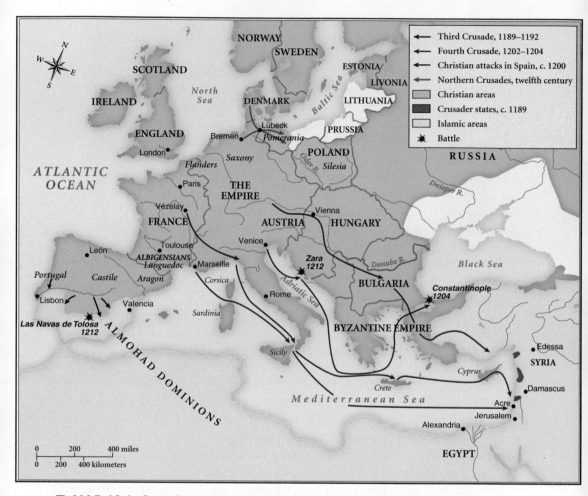

■ MAP 10.1 Crusades and Anti-Heretic Campaigns, 1150–1204

Europeans aggressively expanded their territory during the second half of the twelfth century. To the north, German knights pushed into the lands bordering the Baltic Sea; to the south, Spanish warriors moved into most of Islamic Iberia; to the east, new crusades were undertaken to shore up the tiny European outpost in the Holy Land. Although most of these aggressive activities had the establishment of Christianity as at least one motive, the conquest of Constantinople in 1204 had no such justification. It occurred in part because of general European hostility toward Byzantium but mainly because of Venice's commercial ambitions.

These attitudes help explain what happened from 1202 to 1204. The crusading army turned out to be far smaller than had been expected. Its leaders could not pay the Venetians, who had fitted out a large fleet of ships in anticipation of carrying multitudes of warriors across the Mediterranean to Jerusalem. The Venetians seized the opportunity to exact a different form of payment by convincing the crusade's

■ Innocent III

Pope Innocent III appears young, aristocratic, and impassive in this thirteenth-century fresco in the lower church of Sacro Speco, Subiaco, about thirty miles east of Rome and not far from Innocent's birthplace. Innocent claimed full power over the whole church, in any region. Moreover, he thought the pope had the right to intervene in any issue where sin might be involved—and that meant most matters. Although these were only theoretical claims, difficult to put into practice given his meager resources and inefficient staff, Innocent was a major force through his calls for crusade and through the Fourth Lateran Council, which set the standard for Catholic belief and worship. (Scala/Art Resource, NY.)

leaders to attack Zara, a Christian city that was Venice's competitor in the Adriatic (see Map 10.1). The Venetians then turned their sights toward Constantinople, hoping to control it and gain a commercial monopoly there. They persuaded the crusaders to join them on behalf of Alexius, a member of the ousted imperial family. Alexius claimed the Byzantine throne and promised the crusaders that he would reunite the eastern with the western church and fund the expedition to the Holy Land. Most of the crusaders convinced themselves that the cause was noble. "Never," wrote a contemporary, "was so great an enterprise undertaken by any people since the creation of the world."

The siege of Constantinople lasted nearly a year. Finally, on April 12, 1204, the city fell to the crusaders. Their deal with Alexius had broken down, and the crusaders brutally sacked Constantinople, killing residents and plundering treasure and relics. When one crusader discovered a cache of relics, a chronicler recalled, "he plunged both hands in and, girding up his loins, he filled the folds of his gown with the holy booty of the Church." The loss of that "holy booty" was, for the Byzantines, a great tragedy. The bishop of Ephesus wrote:

> And so the streets, squares, houses of two and three stories, sacred places, nunneries, houses for nuns and monks, sacred churches, even the Great Church of God and the imperial palace, were filled with men of the enemy, all of them

*maddened by war and murderous in spirit. . . . [T]hey tore children from their
mothers and mothers from their children, and they defiled the virgins in the
holy chapels, fearing neither God's anger nor man's vengeance.*

Pope Innocent decried the looting of Constantinople but also took advantage
of it, ordering the crusaders to stay there for a year to consolidate their gains.
The crusade leaders chose one of themselves—Baldwin of Flanders—to be
Byzantine emperor, and he, the other princes, and the Venetians parceled out the
empire among themselves. This new Latin empire of Constantinople lasted until
1261, when the Byzantines recaptured the city and some of its outlying territory. No
longer a strong heir to the Roman Empire, Byzantium in 1204 became overshadowed and hemmed in by the military might of the Muslims and the Europeans.

Popes continued to call crusades to the Holy Land until the mid-fifteenth century,
but the Fourth Crusade marked the last major mobilization of men and leaders.
Working against these expeditions were the new values of the late twelfth century,
which placed a premium on the *interior* pilgrimage of the soul and valued rulers who
stayed home to care for their people. The crusades to the Holy Land served as an outlet for religious fervor, self-confidence, ambition, prejudice, and aggression. But they
had very little lasting positive effect. They managed to stimulate the European economy slightly, and they inspired a vast literature of songs and chronicles. Such achievements must be weighed against the lives lost on both sides and the religious polarization and prejudices that the crusades fed upon and fortified. The bitterest fruit of the
crusades was the destruction of Byzantium. The Latin conquest of Constantinople in
1204 irrevocably weakened the one buffer state standing between Europe and Islam.

The Spanish Reconquista Advances

By 1200, Christian Spain had achieved the political configuration that would last
for centuries: to the east was the kingdom of Aragon; to the west was Portugal;
and in between was Castile, which in 1230 merged with León (see Map 10.2). The
leaders of these kingdoms competed for territory and power, but above all, they
sought an advantage against the Muslims who still ruled a strip of southern Spain.

The reconquista, which had begun against the Muslim *taifas* (small, independent
Muslim states) continued in full force, aided by Muslim disunity. The taifas not only
were in competition with one another but were beset from the south by the Almoravids
and, after 1147, the Almohades, Muslims from North Africa. Claiming religious purity, these Berber groups declared their own holy war against the Andalusians. These
simultaneous threats caused alliances within Spain to be based on political as well as
religious considerations. The Muslim ruler of Valencia, for example, declared himself a
vassal of the king of Castile and bitterly opposed the Berber expansion.

The crusading ideal, however, held no room for such subtleties. During the 1140s,
armies under the command of the Christian kings of Portugal, Castile, and Aragon
scored resounding victories against Muslim cities. Enlisting the aid of crusaders on

■ **MAP 10.2 The Reconquista Triumphs, 1212–1275**

A major turning point in the reconquista was the battle of Las Navas de Tolosa (1212). This marked not only the defeat of the Muslims but also the triumph of Castile, which had originally been a tributary of León. In the course of the twelfth century, Castile became a power in its own right; in 1230, León and Castile merged into one kingdom. During the thirteenth century, Castile-León (and, to a lesser extent, Portugal and Aragon) conquered most of the rest of the Iberian peninsula, leaving only Granada under Islamic rule.

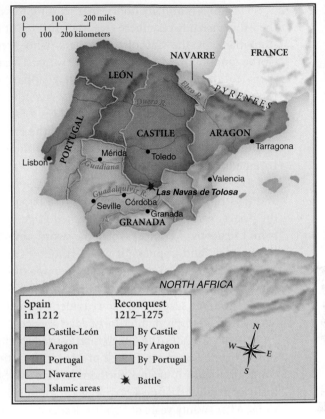

their way to the Holy Land in 1147, the king of Portugal promised land, plunder, and protection to all who would help him attack Muslim-controlled Lisbon. His efforts succeeded, and Lisbon's Muslim inhabitants fled or were slain, its Mozarabic bishop (the bishop of the Christians living under Muslim rule) was killed, and a crusader from England was set up as bishop.

In the 1170s, the Almohades conquered the Muslim south and advanced toward the cities taken by the Christians, but their exertions had no lasting effect. In 1212, a Christian crusading army of Spaniards led by the kings of Aragon and Castile defeated the Almohades decisively at Las Navas de Tolosa. "On their side 100,000 armed men or more fell in the battle," the king of Castile wrote afterward, "but of the army of the Lord . . . incredible though it may be, unless it be a miracle, hardly 25 or 30 Christians of our whole army fell. O what happiness! O what thanksgiving!" The turning point in the reconquista had been reached (Map 10.2). The Almohades continued to lose strength, and Christian armies marched from victory to victory. Mérida fell in 1230. Córdoba was taken six years later, Seville in 1248. All that remained of Muslim-controlled Spain was a thin wedge of territory around Granada.

Putting Down the Heretics in Their Midst

In the thirteenth century, the church and secular powers combined not only to conquer pagans and Muslims on the borders of Europe but also to stamp out heresy in their midst. The papacy declared crusades against the dualist Albigensians of southern France and even against a reigning emperor, Frederick II.

The church initially hoped that sending missionaries to Languedoc would end the Albigensian heresy there (see Map 10.1). But it did not bargain for the impression made by the Catholic preachers, who arrived on horseback, wearing fine clothes and followed by a crowd of servants. These men had no moral leverage with their audience. This was immediately apparent to St. Dominic (1170–1221), founder of the Dominican order. Like his adversaries the Albigensians, Dominic rejected material riches. Instead he and his followers went about on foot, preaching and begging. The Dominicans resembled the Franciscans both organizationally and spiritually; they, too, were called friars. But their first calling was to the heretics of Languedoc rather than to the city dwellers of Italy.

Even with St. Dominic's preachers at the forefront, missionary work was slow and frustrating. In 1208, the murder of a papal legate (an official representative of the pope) in southern France prompted Pope Innocent III to demand that princes from the north of France take up the sword, invade Languedoc, wrest the land from the heretics, and populate it with orthodox Christians. This Albigensian Crusade (1209–1229) marked the first time the pope offered warriors fighting an enemy in Christian Europe all the spiritual and temporal benefits of a crusade to the Holy Land. Innocent suspended the crusaders' monetary debts and promised that their sins would be forgiven after forty days' service.

Like all crusades, the Albigensian Crusade had political as well as religious dimensions. It pitted southern French princes with Cathar connections, like Raymond VI, count of Toulouse, against northern leaders like Simon IV de Montfort l'Amaury, a castellan from the Île-de-France eager to demonstrate his piety and win new possessions. After twenty years of fighting, leadership of the crusade was taken over in 1229 by the Capetian kings of France. Southern resistance was broken, and Languedoc was brought under the French crown.

Meanwhile, the papacy set up the Inquisition in southern France to discover undetected heretics. The **Inquisition** was a legal proceeding. First the inquisitors typically called the people of a district to a "preaching," where they gave a sermon and promised clemency to those who confessed their heresy promptly. Then, at a general inquest, they questioned each man and woman who seemed to know something about heresy: "Have you ever seen any heretics . . . ? Have you heard them preach? Attended any of their ceremonies? Adored heretics?" The judges assigned relatively lenient penalties to those who were not aware that they held heretical beliefs and to heretics who quickly recanted. But unrepentant heretics were punished, because the church believed that such people threatened the salvation of all. Anyone who died while still a heretic could not be buried in consecrated ground. Raymond VII, count of Toulouse, saw the body of his father—who died excommunicated—rot in its coffin as the pope denied all requests for its burial. Houses where heretics had resided or even simply entered were burned, and the sites were turned into garbage dumps. Children of heretics could not inherit any property or become priests, even if they adopted orthodox views.

In the thirteenth century, for the first time, long-term imprisonment became a tool to repress heresy, even if the heretic confessed. "It is our will," wrote one tribunal, "that [Raymond Maurin and Arnalda, his wife,] because they have rashly transgressed against God and holy church . . . be thrust into perpetual prison to do [appropriate] penance, and we command them to remain there in perpetuity." The inquisitors also used imprisonment to force people to recant, to give the names of other heretics, or to admit a plot. Guillaume Agasse, for example, confessed to participating in a wicked (and imaginary) meeting of lepers who planned to poison all the wells. As the quest for religious control spawned wild fantasies of conspiracy, the inquisitors pinned their paranoia on real people.

The Inquisition also created a new group—penitent heretics—who lived on the margins of Christian society. Forced to wear huge yellow fabric crosses sewn on the front and back of their shirts, they were publicly disgraced. Moreover, every Sunday and every feast day penitent heretics had to attend church twice; and during religious processions these men and women were required to join with the clergy and the faithful, carrying large branches in their hands as a sign of their penance. (See "Taking Measure," below.)

One "heretic" was an emperor. Innocent III—the pope who called the Fourth Crusade, the crusade against the Livs, and the Albigensian Crusade—had given the imperial crown to Frederick II (r. 1212–1250). Innocent's successors would rue the day. Like his grandfather Frederick Barbarossa, Frederick II, who was king of Sicily as well as Germany, sought to control Italy. This policy was intolerable to the papacy, which had its own ambitions on the peninsula.

■ TAKING MEASURE
Sentences Imposed by an Inquisitor, 1308–1323

How harsh was the Inquisition? Did its agents regularly burn people alive? How frequently did they imprison people or order them to wear crosses on their clothing? Statistical data to answer these sorts of questions are normally lacking for the medieval period. But there are exceptions. One comes from a register of offenses and punishments kept by the Languedocian inquisitor Bernard Gui from 1308 to 1323. Of 633 punishments handed down by Gui's tribunal, only a relatively small number of people were burned alive. (Those "burned posthumously" would have been burned alive, but they died before that could happen.) Nearly half of

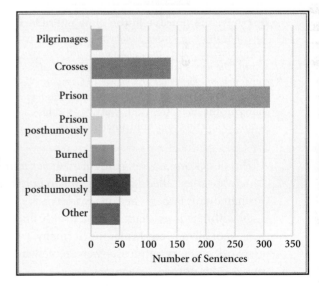

the guilty were sentenced to prison, usually for life. (Some were sent to prison posthumously—that is, they would have gone to prison had they not died in the meantime.) Many historians conclude that the Inquisition was not particularly harsh, for capital punishment at the time was regularly meted out to criminals under secular law.

■ MAP 10.3 Europe in the Time of Frederick II, r. 1212–1250

King of Sicily and Germany and emperor as well, Frederick ruled over territory that encircled—and threatened—the papacy. Excommunicated several times, Frederick spent much of his career fighting the pope's forces. In the process, he conceded so many powers to the German princes that the emperor thenceforth had little power in Germany. Meanwhile, rulers of smaller states, such as England, France, and Castile-León, were increasing their power and authority. **For more help analyzing this map,** see the map activity for this chapter in the ONLINE STUDY GUIDE at bedfordstmartins.com/huntconcise.

Frederick was an amazing ruler: *stupor mundisli* —"wonder of the world"—his contemporaries called him. Heir to two cultures, Sicilian on his mother's side and German on his father's, he cut a worldly and sophisticated figure. In Sicily, he moved easily within a diverse culture of Jews, Muslims, and Christians. There he could play the role of all-powerful ruler. In Germany, where Christian princes—often churchmen with military retinues—were acutely aware of their rights and privileges, he was less at home.

Frederick had a three-pronged imperial strategy. First, to ensure that opponents in Germany would not hound him, he granted the princes important concessions, finalized in 1232. These privileges allowed the German princes to turn their principalities into virtually independent states. Second, Frederick revamped the government of Sicily to give himself more control and yield greater profits. His *Constitutions of Melfi* (1231), an eclectic body of laws, called for nearly all court cases to be heard by royal courts, regularized commercial privileges, and set up a system of taxation. Third, Frederick sought to enter Italy through Lombardy, as his grandfather had done (Map 10.3).

The papacy followed Frederick's every move, excommunicating the emperor a number of times. The most serious of these came in 1245, when the pope and other churchmen, assembled at the Council of Lyon, excommunicated and deposed Frederick, absolving his vassals and subjects of their fealty to him and, indeed, forbidding anyone to support him. "He has deservedly become suspect of heresy," the council intoned, explaining that "he has despised and continues to despise the keys of the church [the symbol of St. Peter and thus of the pope], causing the sacred rites to be celebrated or rather . . . to be profaned. . . . Besides, he is joined in odious friendship with the Saracens [Muslims]." By 1248, papal legates were preaching a crusade against Frederick and all his followers. Two years later, Frederick died.

The fact that Frederick's vision of the empire failed is of less long-term importance than the way it failed. His concessions to the German princes meant that Germany would remain divided under numerous regional princes until the nineteenth century. Between 1254 and 1273, the princes kept the German throne empty. Splintered into factions, they elected two different foreigners, who spent their time fighting each other. In one of history's strange twists, it was during this low point of the German monarchy that the term *Holy Roman Empire* was coined. In 1273, the princes at last united and elected a German, Rudolph (r. 1273–1291), whose family, the Habsburgs, was new to imperial power. Rudolf used the imperial title to help him gain Austria for his dynasty, but he did not try to fulfill the meaning of the imperial title in Italy. For the first time, the word *emperor* was freed from its association with Italy and Rome. For the Habsburgs, the title Holy Roman Emperor was prestigious but otherwise meaningless. In 1356 the reigning emperor published the Golden Bull—so called because of its golden seal—which delared the seven German princes who henceforth were to be the electors of the emperor. They included three churchmen (the archbishop of Mainz was one) and four laymen (for example, the duke of Saxony). The office of "king of the Romans"—

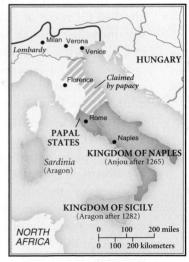

Italy at the End of the Thirteenth Century

as the Bull called the emperor—was completely divorced from papal power, and Germany was henceforth to be ruled by the princes.

As for Italy, Frederick's failure meant that the cities of northern Italy would continue their independent course, while the papacy ensured that the heirs of Frederick would not continue to rule in Sicily. The popes called successively on other rulers to take over the island—first Henry III of England and then Charles of Anjou. Forces loyal to Frederick's family turned to the king of Aragon (Spain). That move left two enduring claimants to Sicily's crown: the kings of Aragon and the house of Anjou. And it spawned a long war impoverishing the region.

In the struggle between pope and emperor, the pope had clearly won. The moment marked a high point in the political power of the medieval papacy. Nevertheless, some agreed with Frederick II's view that by tampering with secular matters the popes had demeaned and sullied their office: "These men who feign holiness," Frederick sneered, referring to the popes, are "drunk with the pleasures of the world." Scattered throughout Germany were people who believed that Frederick was a divine scourge sent to overpower a materialistic papacy. The papacy won the war against Frederick, but at a cost. Even the king of France criticized the popes for doing "new and unheard of things." By making its war against Frederick part of its crusade against heresy, the papacy came under attack for using religion as a political tool.

The Mongol Takeover

Europeans were not the only warring society in the thirteenth century: to the east, the Mongols (sometimes called Tatars or Tartars) created an aggressive army under the leadership of Chingiz Khan and his sons. In part, economic necessity impelled them out of Mongolia: climatic change had reduced the grasslands that sustained their animals and their nomadic way of life. But they were also inspired by Chingiz's hope of conquering the world. In the 1230s, the Mongols began concerted attacks in Europe—in Russia, Poland, and Hungary—where weak native princes were no match for the Mongols' formidable armies and tactics. Only the death of their Great Khan, Chingiz's son Ogodei (1186–1241)—styled the *khagan*, or khan of khans—and disputes over his succession prevented a concentrated assault on Germany. In the 1250s, the Mongols took Iran, Baghdad, and Damascus.

The Mongols' sophisticated and devastating military tactics contributed to their overwhelming success. Organizing their campaigns at meetings held far in advance of a planned attack, they devised two- and three-flank operations. The invasion of Hungary, for example, was two-pronged: one division of the Mongol army arrived from Russia while the other moved through Poland and Germany. Many Hungarians perished in the assault as the Mongols, fighting mainly on horseback and wielding heavy lances and powerful bows whose arrows traveled far and penetrated deeply, crushed the Hungarian force of mixed infantry and cavalry (Map 10.4).

The Mongols' attacks on Russia had the most lasting impact. At Vladimir, in the north, they broke through the walls of the city and burned the people huddled for protection in the cathedral. The Mongols' most important victory in Russia was the capture of Kiev in 1240. Making the mouth of the Volga River the seat of their power in Russia, the Mongols dominated Russia's principalities for about two hundred years.

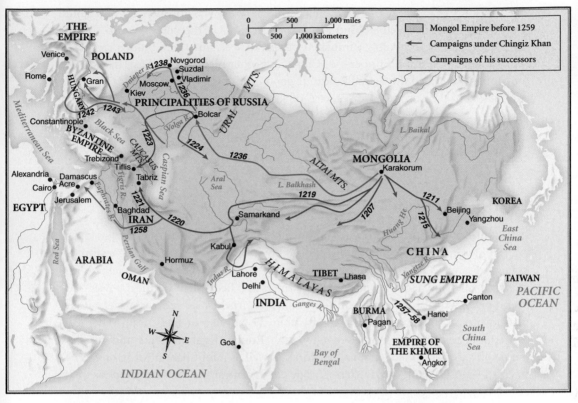

■ MAP 10.4 The Mongol Invasions to 1259

The Mongols were the first people to tie the eastern world to the west. Their conquest of China, which took place at about the same time as their invasions of Russia and Iran, opened up trade relations across regions formerly separated by language, religion, and political regimes.

The Mongol Empire in Russia, later called the **Golden Horde** (*golden* probably from the color of their leader's tent; *horde* from a Turkish word meaning "camp"), adopted much of the local government apparatus. The Mongols standardized the collection of taxes and the recruitment of troops by basing them on a population census, and they allowed Russian princes to continue ruling as long as they paid homage and tribute to the khan. Mongol overlords even exempted the Russian church from taxes.

The Mongol invasion changed the political configuration of Europe and Asia. Because the Mongols were willing to deal with westerners such as the Polo family, one effect of their conquests was to open China to Europeans for the first time. For example, an entire community of Venetian traders—women, men, and children—lived in the city of Yangzhou in the mid-fourteenth century. Some missionaries, diplomats, and merchants traveled overland to China; others made the difficult journey from the Persian Gulf (controlled by the Mongols), rounding India before arriving in China.

The long-term effect of the Mongols on the West was to open up new land routes to the East that helped bind together the regions of the known world. Travel stories such as Marco Polo's stimulated others to seek out the fabulous riches—textiles, ginger, ceramics, copper—of China and other places in the East. In a sense, the Mongols initiated the search for exotic goods and missionary opportunities that culminated in the European "discovery" of a new world, the Americas.

■ **REVIEW:** *In what ways did the secular rulers of the period 1200–1340 cooperate with the church? In what ways did they not—and why?*

Politics of Control

In the thirteenth century, Europeans for the first time spoke of their rulers not as kings of a people (for example, king of the Franks) but as kings of a territory (for example, king of France). This new designation reflected an important new element in medieval rulership. However strong earlier rulers had been, their political power had been only personal (depending on ties of kinship, friendship, and vassalage) rather than territorial (touching all who lived within the borders of their state). The new conception, reinforced by renewed interest in Roman legal concepts and supplemented by old-fashioned personal networks, served as a foundation for strong, central rule—most strikingly in western Europe but in central and eastern Europe as well.

France: From Acorn to Oak

Even with the achievements of Louis VI, the French monarchy remained weak, a realm surrounded by powerful neighbors. This changed under Philip Augustus (r. 1180–1223), whose acquisitive policies toward the Jews (see page 358) were matched by his territorial ambitions. When Philip first came to the throne, the royal domain, the Île-de-France, was sandwiched between territory controlled by the counts of Flanders, Champagne, and Anjou. By far the most powerful ruler on the European continent was King Henry II of England, who was both count of Anjou and duke of Normandy and also held the duchy of Aquitaine through his wife while exercising hegemony over Poitou and Brittany.

Henry and the counts of Flanders and Champagne vied to control the young king of

Consolidation of France under Philip Augustus, r. 1180–1223

France. Philip, however, quickly learned to play them off against one another. Contemporaries were astounded when Philip successfully gained territory: he wrested Vermandois and Artois from Flanders in the 1190s and Normandy, Anjou, Maine, Touraine, and Poitou from Henry II's son King John of England in 1204, making good his claim at the decisive battle of Bouvines in 1214.

Pivotal forces led to the extension of the French king's power and the territorial integrity of France. The Second Crusade (1147–1149) had brought together many French lords as vassals of the king and united them against a common foe. The language they spoke was becoming increasingly uniform and "French." Nevertheless, this in itself did not create a larger French kingdom. That came about through royal strategy. Rather than give his new territories out as fiefs, Philip determined to govern them himself.[*] In Normandy, for example, he demanded that the aristocrats become his vassals, and he sent his officials to collect taxes and hear cases. Philip also instituted a new kind of French administration, based on writing. Before his day, most royal arrangements were committed to memory rather than to parchment. If decrees were written at all, they were saved by the recipient, not by the government. For example, when a monastery wanted a confirmation of its privileges from the king, its own scribes wrote the document for its archives to preserve the monastery against possible future challenges. The king did keep some documents, which generally followed him in his travels like personal possessions. But in 1194, in a battle with the king of England, Philip lost his meager cache of documents along with much treasure when he had to abandon his baggage train. After 1194, the king had all his decrees written down, and he established permanent repositories in which to keep them.

To do the daily work of government, Philip relied on members of the lesser nobility—knights and clerics, many of whom were "masters" educated in the city schools of France. They served as officers of his court; as *prévôts* (provosts), who oversaw the king's estates and collected his taxes; and as *baillis* (bailiffs; *sénéchaux* in the south), who supervised the provosts and functioned as regional judges, presiding over courts that met monthly and making the king's power felt locally as never before.

Under Philip's grandson, Louis IX (r. 1226–1270), the Capetian monarchy reached the height of its prestige if not its power. Louis was revered, not because he was a military leader but because he was an administrator, judge, and "just father" of his people. On warm summer days, he would sit under a tree in the woods near his castle at Vincennes on the outskirts of Paris, hearing disputes and dispensing justice personally. He used his administrators to impose royal law and justice throughout his kingdom. Over the city of Paris he appointed a salaried officer who could be supervised and fired if necessary. During his reign, the influence of the parlement of Paris, the royal court of justice, increased significantly. Originally a changeable and movable body, part of the king's personal entourage when he dealt

---

[*]Philip was particularly successful in imposing royal control in Normandy; later French kings gave most of the other territories to collateral members of the royal family.

English Channel

Flanders
Artois
Vermandois
Picardy
Normandy
Paris
Champagne
Brittany
Chartres
Maine
Île-de-France
(Royal Domain)
Blois
Orléans
Anjou
Tours
Touraine
Poitiers
Poitou
Bourges
Bourbonnais
Cluny

THE
EMPIRE

Rhine R.

Seine R.

Loire R.

Burgundy

Lyon

Nantes

Bay of
Biscay

Aquitaine

Bordeaux

Garonne R.

Rhône R.

Gascony

Languedoc

Toulouse

Avignon

Montpellier

Marseille

SPAIN

0 100 200 miles	
0 100 200 kilometers	

☐ Louis IX's kingdom

☐ English possessions
in France in 1259

■ **MAP 10.5 France under Louis IX, r. 1226–1270**
Louis IX did not expand his kingdom as dramatically as his grandfather Philip Augustus had done. He was greatly admired nevertheless, for he was seen by contemporaries as a model of Christian charity, piety, and justice. After his death, Louis IX was recognized as a saint and thus posthumously enhanced the prestige of the French monarchy in a new way.

with litigation, it was now permanently housed in Paris and staffed by professional judges who heard cases and recorded their decisions.

Unlike his grandfather Philip Augustus, Louis did not try to expand his territory. He inherited a large kingdom that included Poitou and Languedoc (Map 10.5), and he was content. Although the king of England attacked him continually to try to regain territory lost under Philip Augustus, Louis remained unprovoked. Rather than prolong the fighting, he conceded a bit and made peace in 1259. At the same time, Louis was a zealous crusader. He took seriously the need to defend the Holy Land when most of his contemporaries were weary of the idea.

Louis was respectful of the church and the pope; he accepted limits on his authority in relation to the church and never claimed power over spiritual matters. Nevertheless, Louis vigorously maintained the dignity of the king and his rights. He expected royal and ecclesiastical power to work in harmony, and he refused to let the church dictate how he should use his temporal authority. For example, French bishops wanted royal officers to support the church's sentences of excommunication. But Louis declared that he would authorize his officials to do so only if he were able to judge each case for himself, to see whether the excommunication had been justly pronounced. The bishops refused, but Louis held his ground. Royal and ecclesiastical power would work side by side, neither subservient to the other.

Many modern historians fault Louis for his policies toward the Jews. His hatred of them was well known. He did not exactly advocate violence against them, but he sometimes subjected them to arrest, canceling debts owed to them (but collecting part into the royal treasury) and confiscating their belongings. In 1253, he ordered them to live "by the labor of their hands" or leave France. He meant that they should no longer lend money, in effect taking away their one means of livelihood. Louis's contemporaries did not criticize him for his Jewish policies. If anything, his hatred of Jews enhanced his reputation.

In fact, many of Louis's contemporaries considered him a saint, praising his care for the poor and sick, the pains and penances he inflicted on himself, and his regular participation in church services. In 1297, Pope Boniface VIII canonized him as St. Louis. The result was enormous prestige for the French monarchy. This prestige, joined with the renown of Paris as the center of scholarship and the repute of French courts as the hubs of chivalry, made France the cultural model of Europe.

England: Crisis and Consolidation

What the French king gained the English king lost. Henry II had been very strong, and his son Richard I (r. 1189–1199) was called "Lion-Hearted" for his boldness. Under these men, the English monarchy was omnipresent and rich. Its omnipresence derived largely from its judicial and administrative apparatus. Its wealth came from court fees, income from numerous royal estates both in England and on the continent, taxes from cities, and customary feudal dues (called aids) collected from barons and knights. These aids were paid on such occasions as the knighting of the king's eldest son and the marriage of the king's eldest daughter. Enriched by the commercial economy of the late twelfth century, the English kings encouraged their knights and barons not to serve them personally in battle but instead to pay the king a tax called scutage in lieu of service. The monarchs preferred to hire mercenaries both as troops to fight external enemies and as policemen to enforce the king's will at home.

But Richard died young, and his brother and heir, John (r. 1199–1216), lost badly to Philip Augustus. John was widely disliked by his contemporaries, who accused him of asserting his will in a high-handed way. But to understand John, it is necessary to appreciate how desperate he was to keep his continental possessions. After he lost his northern French territories to Philip, John did everything he could to add to the crown revenues so he could pay for an army to fight the French. He forced his vassals to pay ever-increasing scutages and extorted money in the form of new feudal aids. He compelled the widows of his vassals to marry men of his choosing or pay him a hefty fee if they refused. John's heavy investment in this war effort, however, could not prevent defeat of his army in 1214 at the battle of Bouvines, and this defeat caused discontented English barons to rebel openly against the king. At Runnymede in June 1215, John was forced to agree to the charter of baronial liberties that has come to be called Magna Carta, "Great Charter."

The English barons intended Magna Carta (so named to distinguish it from a smaller charter issued around the same time concerning the royal forests) to be a conservative document defining the "customary" obligations and rights of the

■ **John's Seal on Magna Carta**

When the rebels at Runnymede got John to assent to their charter, later known as Magna Carta, he did not sign it; he sealed it. From the thirteenth through the fifteenth century, kings, queens, aristocrats, guilds, communes, and many other people at all levels of society used seals to authenticate their charters, or legal documents. The seal itself was made of melted wax or lead, which was dropped onto the document and pressed with a gold or brass matrix carved with an image in the negative. These images reminded the public of the status as well as the name of the sealer. Notice the image that John chose to place on his seal. (© Copyright The Trustees of The British Museum.)

nobility and forbidding the king to break from these customs without consulting his barons. "No widow shall be forced to marry so long as she wishes to live without a husband," it declares, continuing:

No scutage or aid shall be imposed in our kingdom unless by common counsel of our kingdom, except for [the customary purposes:] ransoming our person, for making our eldest son a knight, and for once marrying our eldest daughter.

In its most famous clause, Magna Carta provided that

No free man shall be arrested or imprisoned or disseised [deprived of his property] or outlawed or exiled or in any way victimized, neither will we attack him or send anyone to attack him, except by the lawful judgment of his peers or by the law of the land.

Thus Magna Carta established that all free men in the land had certain customs and rights in common and that the king had to uphold those customs and rights. In this way, it documented the subordination of the king to custom; it implied that the king was not above the law. Magna Carta shows that the growth of royal power was matched by the self-confidence of the English barons, certain of their rights and eager to articulate them. Although in the thirteenth century the "free men" of the realm were a tiny elite, in time, as the definition of *free men* expanded to include all the king's subjects, Magna Carta came to be seen as a guarantee of the rights of Englishmen in general.

Papal Monarchy

As the kings of France and England were gaining newly precise roles, so, too, were the popes. Innocent III was the most powerful, respected, and prestigious of the medieval popes. The first pope to be trained at the city schools, Innocent had studied theology at Paris and law at Bologna. From theology, he learned to tease new meaning out of the pope's position: he thought of himself as ruling in the place of Christ the King. In his view, secular kings and emperors existed to help the pope. From law, Innocent gained his conception of the pope as lawmaker and of law as an instrument of moral reformation.

Utilizing the traditional method of declaring church law, Innocent convened and presided over a council in 1215 at the pope's Lateran Palace in Rome. Known as the Fourth Lateran Council, it aimed to reform not only the clergy but also the laity. Innocent and the other assembled churchmen hoped to create a society united under the authority of the church.

For laymen and laywomen, perhaps the most important canons of the Fourth Lateran concerned the sacraments, the rites the church believed Jesus had instituted to confer sanctifying grace. One canon required Christians to attend Mass and confess their sins to a priest at least once a year. At the same time, the council explained with new precision the transformation of bread and wine (the Eucharist) in the Mass. In the twelfth century, a newly rigorous understanding of this transformation had already been publicized, according to which Christ's body and blood were truly contained in the sacrament that looked like bread and wine on the altar. The Fourth Lateran Council not only declared this to be dogma (authoritative) but also explained it by using a technical term coined by twelfth-century scholars. The bread and wine were *transubstantiated*: although the Eucharist continued to *look* like bread and wine, with its consecration during the Mass the bread became the actual flesh and the wine the real blood of Christ. The council's emphasis on this potent event strengthened the role of the priesthood, for only a priest could celebrate this mystery (that is, transform the bread and wine into Christ's body and blood) through which God's grace was transmitted to the faithful.

Innocent III wanted the council to condemn Christian men who had intercourse with Jewish women and then claimed "ignorance" as their excuse. But the council went even further, requiring all Jews to advertise their religion by some outward sign: "We decree that [Jews] of either sex in every Christian province at all times shall be distinguished from other people by the character of their dress in public." Like all church rules, this canon took effect only when local rulers enforced it. In many instances, they did so with zeal, not so much because they were eager to humiliate Jews but rather because they could make money selling exemptions to Jews who were willing to pay to avoid the requirements. Nonetheless, sooner or later Jews almost everywhere had to wear a badge as a sign of their second-class status. In southern France and in a few places in Spain, Jews were supposed to wear round badges. In England, the city of Salisbury demanded that they wear special clothing. In Vienna, they were told to put on pointed hats.

The Fourth Lateran Council's longest decree blasted heretics: "Those condemned as heretics shall be handed over to the secular authorities for punishment." If the secular authority did not "purge his or her land of heretical filth," the heretic was to be excommunicated. If he had vassals, they were to be released from their oaths of fealty, and the heretic's land was to be taken over by orthodox Christians. Rulers heeded these rules. Already some had taken up arms against heretics in the Albigensian Crusade (1209–1229). The Fourth Lateran Council was also responsible for setting up the Inquisition.

The Fourth Lateran was the high-water mark of the medieval papacy. However, the growing prestige and actual jurisdiction of secular rulers changed the balance of power between church and state in the course of the thirteenth century. At the end of that century, when the pope clashed with the kings of France and England, the kings were the clear winners, and the papacy lost both prestige and power.

The clash began over taxing the clergy. The French king Philip IV (r. 1285–1314), known as Philip the Fair, and the English king Edward I (r. 1272–1307) financed their wars (mainly against one another) by taxing the clergy along with everyone else. The new principle of national sovereignty that they were claiming led them to assert jurisdiction over all people, even churchmen, who lived within their borders. For the pope, however, the principle at stake was his role as head of the clergy. In response to clerical taxation, Boniface VIII (r. 1294–1303) declared that only the pope could authorize such taxes. Threatening to excommunicate kings who taxed prelates without papal permission, he called upon clerics to disobey any such royal orders.

Edward and Philip reacted swiftly. Taking advantage of the important role that English courts played in protecting the peace, Edward

■ **Boniface VIII**

For the sculptor who depicted Pope Boniface VIII, Arnolfo di Cambio (d. 1302), not much had changed since the time of Innocent III. Look at the picture of Innocent on page 389 and compare the two popes: both are depicted as young, majestic, authoritative, sober, and calm. Yet Boniface could not have been very calm, for his authority was challenged at every turn. He was forced to withdraw his opposition to royal taxation of the clergy. He tried to placate the French king, Philip the Fair, by canonizing Philip's grandfather, Louis IX. Even so, Philip arrested the bishop of Pamiers and brought him to trial. When Boniface protested, he was proclaimed a heretic by the French. A few months later he was dead. (Scala/Art Resource, NY.)

declared that all clerics who refused to pay their taxes would be considered outlaws—literally, "outside the law." Clergymen who were robbed, for example, would have no recourse against their attackers; if accused of crimes, they would have no defense in court. Relying on a different strategy, Philip forbade the exportation of precious metals, money, or jewels, effectively sealing the French borders. Immediately the English clergy cried out for legal protection, while the papacy itself clamored for the revenues it had long enjoyed from French pilgrims, litigants, and travelers. Boniface was forced to back down, conceding in 1297 that kings had the right to tax the clergy of their kingdoms in emergencies.

But the crisis was not over. In 1301, Philip the Fair tested his jurisdiction in southern France by arresting Bernard Saisset, the bishop of Pamiers, on a charge of treason for slandering the king by comparing him with an owl, "the handsomest of birds which is worth absolutely nothing." Saisset's imprisonment violated the principle, maintained both by the pope and by French law, that a clergyman was not subject to lay justice. Boniface reacted angrily, and Philip seized the opportunity to deride and humiliate the pope, orchestrating a public relations campaign against him. Boniface's reply, the bull* *Unam Sanctam* (1302), intensified the situation by declaring bluntly "that it is altogether necessary to salvation for every human creature to be subject to the Roman Pontiff." At meetings of the king's inner circle, Philip's agents declared Boniface a false pope, accusing him of sexual perversion, various crimes, and heresy. In 1303, royal agents, acting under Philip's orders, invaded Boniface's palace at Anagni (southeast of Rome) to capture the pope, bring him to France, and try him. Fearing for the pope's life, however, the people of Anagni joined forces and drove the French agents out of town. Yet even after such public support for the pope, the king made his power felt. Boniface died shortly thereafter, and the next two popes quickly pardoned Philip and his agents for their actions.

Just as Frederick II's defeat showed the weakness of the empire, so Boniface's humiliation showed the limits of papal control. The two powers that claimed "universal" authority had little weight in the face of the new, limited, but tightly controlled national states. After 1303, popes continued to criticize kings, but their words had less and less impact. In the face of newly powerful medieval states such as France, Spain, and England—supported by vast revenues, judicial apparatuses, representative institutions, and even the loyalty of churchmen—the papacy could make little headway. The delicate balance between church and state, a hallmark of the years of Louis IX, broke down by the end of the thirteenth century.

In 1309, forced from Rome by civil strife, the papacy settled at Avignon, a city technically in the Holy Roman Empire but very close to, and influenced by, France (see Map 10.5). Here the popes remained until 1378. The period from 1309 to 1378 came to be called the "Babylonian Captivity" by Europeans sensitive to having the popes live far from Rome, on the Rhône River. The Avignon popes, many of them

---

*An official papal document is called a *bull*, from the *bulla*, or seal, that was used to authenticate it.

French, established a sober and efficient organization that took in regular revenues and gave the papacy more say than ever before in the appointment of churchmen. They would, however, slowly abandon the idea of leading all of Christendom and would tacitly recognize the growing power of the secular states to regulate their internal affairs.

Power Shifts in the Italian Communes

During the thirteenth century, the Italian communes continued to extend their control over the surrounding countryside as independent city-states. While generally presenting a united front to outsiders, factions within the communes fought for control and its spoils. In the early thirteenth century, these factions represented noble families. However, in the course of the century, newer groups, generally— though not exclusively—from the non-noble classes, attempted to take over the reins of power in the communes. The *popolo* ("people"), as such groups were called, incorporated members of city associations such as craft and merchant guilds, parishes, and the commune itself. In fact, the popolo was a kind of alternative commune, a sworn association in each city that dedicated itself to upholding the interests of its members. Armed and militant, the popolo demanded a share in city government, particularly to gain a voice in matters of taxation. In 1222 at Piacenza, for example (see Mapping the West, page 420), the popolo's members won half the government offices; a year later, they and the nobles worked out a plan to share the election of their city's *podestà*, or chief executive. Such power sharing often resulted from the popolo's struggle, though in some cities, nobles overcame and dissolved the popolo, while in others, the popolo virtually excluded the nobles from government. Constantly confronting one another, quarreling, feuding, and compromising, such factions turned Italian cities into centers of civil discord.

Weakened by this constant friction, the communes were tempting prey for great regional nobles who, allying with one or another faction, established themselves as *signori* (singular *signore*, "lord") of the cities, keeping the peace at the price of repression. In these circumstances, the commune gave way to the *signoria* (a state ruled by a signore), and one family began to dominate the government. The communes ceased to exist, and many Italian cities fell under control of despots. The fate of Piacenza over the course of the thirteenth century was typical. First dominated by nobles, its commune granted the popolo a voice by 1225; but then by mid-century the signore's power eclipsed both the nobles and the popolo.

New-Style Associations amid the Monarchies

Although the thirteenth century was the age of newly strong signori or monarchs, there were some exceptions. Under the leadership of the city of Lübeck, the cities of northern Germany trading between the Baltic and the North Seas banded together to form the Hanseatic League (or Hanse). It was one fruit of the Northern Crusades: even the Teutonic Knights were members. Merchants in these cities dominated the northern grain trade, and their control over this commodity gave them power. They were able to declare embargoes against enemies and monopolies for themselves. Throughout the thirteenth and fourteenth centuries, the Hanse dominated the Baltic region.

Similarly independent were the self-governing peasant and town communes in the high Alpine valleys that became a united Swiss Confederation. In 1291, the peasants of Uri, Schwyz, and Unterwalden swore a perpetual alliance against their oppressive Habsburg overlord. After defeating a Habsburg army in 1315, these free peasants took the name "Confederates" and developed a new alliance that would become Switzerland. In the process, the Swiss enshrined their freedom in the legend of William Tell, their national hero, who was forced by a Habsburg official to prove his archery skills by shooting an apple placed on the head of his own son. This act so outraged the

Growth of the Swiss Confederation to 1353

citizens that they rose up in arms against Habsburg rule. By 1353, the important cantons of Lucerne, Zurich, and Bern had joined the confederation. The Swiss Confederation continued to acquire new members into the sixteenth century, defeating armies sent by different princes to undermine its liberties.

The Birth of Representative Institutions

Even monarchies found it useful to embrace groups beyond the narrow elite of the aristocracy. One of the ways in which Philip the Fair orchestrated his public relations campaign against Pope Boniface was to convene representatives of the clergy, nobles, and townspeople to explain, justify, and propagandize his position. This new assembly, which met at Paris in 1302, was the ancestor of the Estates General, which would meet sporadically for centuries thereafter—for the last time in 1789, at the beginning of the French Revolution. (In France, the various orders—clergy, nobles, and commoners—were called estates.) After Philip's agents declared Boniface a false pope, the king sent his commissioners to the various provinces of France to convene local meetings to popularize his charges against Boniface and gain support. Clergy, local nobles, townspeople, and even villagers attending these meetings almost unanimously denounced the pope.

As in France, representative institutions elsewhere began as political tools with which rulers hoped to broaden their support. All across Europe—from Spain to Poland, from England to Hungary—rulers summoned parliaments. These assemblies grew out of the ad hoc advisory sessions kings customarily held with their nobles and clergy, men who informally represented the two most powerful classes, or "orders," of medieval society. Although these bodies differed from place to place, the impulse behind their creation was similar. They began (as in France) as assemblies where kings celebrated their royal power and prestige and where the "orders" simply assented to royal policy. In the thirteenth century, the advisory sessions became solemn, formal meetings of representatives of the "orders" to the kings' chief councils—the precursor of parliamentary sessions. Eventually these bodies became organs through which people not ordinarily at court could articulate their wishes.

In practice, thirteenth-century kings did not so much command representatives of the orders to come to court as they simply summoned the most powerful members of their realm—whether clerics, nobles, or important townsmen—to support their policies. In thirteenth-century León (part of present-day Spain), for example, the king sometimes called only the clergy and nobles; sometimes he sent for representatives of the towns, especially when he wanted the help of town militias. As townsmen gradually began to participate regularly in advisory sessions, kings came to depend on them and their support. In turn, commoners became more fully integrated into the work of royal government.

The *cortes* of Castile-León were among the earliest representative assemblies called to the king's court and the first to include townsmen. Enriched by plunder from the reconquista, fledgling villages soon turned into major commercial centers. Like the cities of Italy, Spanish towns dominated the countryside. Their leaders—called *caballeros villanos*, or "city horsemen," because they were rich enough to fight on horseback—monopolized municipal offices. In 1188, when King Alfonso IX (r. 1188–1230) summoned townsmen to the cortes, the city caballeros served as their representatives, agreeing to Alfonso's plea for military and financial support and for help in consolidating his rule. Once convened at court, these wealthy townsmen joined bishops and noblemen in formally counseling the king and assenting to royal decisions. Beginning with Alfonso X (r. 1252–1284), Castilian monarchs regularly called on the cortes to participate in major political and military decisions and to assent to new taxes to finance them.

The English Parliament* also developed as a new tool of royal government. In this case, however, the king's control was complicated by the power of the barons, manifested, for example, in Magna Carta. In the twelfth century, King Henry II had consulted prelates and barons at Great Councils, using these parliaments as his tool to ratify and gain support for his policies. Although Magna Carta had nothing to do with such councils, the barons thought the document gave them an important and permanent role in royal government as the king's advisers and a solid guarantee of their customary rights and privileges. When Henry III (r. 1216–1272) was crowned at the age of nine, he was king in name only for the first sixteen years of his reign. During that period, England was governed by a council consisting of a few barons, professional administrators, and a papal legate. Though not quite "government by Parliament," this council set a precedent for baronial participation in government.

---

*Although *Parliament* and *Parlement* are very similar words, both deriving from the French word *parler* ("to speak"), the institutions they named were very different. The Parlement of France was a law court, whereas the English Parliament, although beginning as a court to redress grievances, had by 1327 become above all a representative institution. The major French representative assembly, the Estates General, first convened at the beginning of the fourteenth century.

An English parliament that included commoners came into being in the midst of war and as a result of political weakness. Henry so alienated nobles and commoners alike by his wars, debts, choice of advisers, and demands for money that the barons threatened to rebel. At a meeting at Oxford in 1258, they forced Henry to dismiss his foreign advisers; to rule with the advice of a Council of Fifteen chosen jointly by the barons and the king; and to limit the terms of his chief officers. However, this new government itself was riven by strife among the barons, and civil war erupted in 1264. At the battle of Lewes in the same year, the leader of the baronial opposition, Simon de Montfort (c. 1208–1265), routed the king's forces, captured the king, and became England's de facto ruler. Because only a minority of the barons followed Simon, he sought new support by convening a parliament in 1265. He summoned not only the earls, barons, and churchmen who backed him but also representatives from the towns—the "commons"—and he appealed for their help. Thus, for the first time, the commons were given a voice in government. Simon's brief rule ended that very year, and Henry's son Edward I (r. 1272–1307) became a rallying point for royalists (backers of the king). Yet the idea of representative government in England had emerged, born out of the interplay between royal initiatives and baronial revolts. Edward's constant need for new revenues led him to call regular sessions of Parliament. Without meaning to do so, he solidified its role as a regular institution of royal government in England.

■ **REVIEW:** *Compare the institutions of papal monarchy with those of secular monarchies in France and England.*

Religious and Cultural Life in an Age of Expansion

In the course of the thirteenth century, the religious life, originally associated with monks, nuns, priests, and bishops, became possible—and officially recognized—for laypeople as well. There was a clear connection between this development and the rise of universities, for the ethical teachings of "scholastics" (the scholars of medieval universities) were preached to the people. But the scholastics were also occupied with subjects that ranged far beyond ethics. Outside of the schools, poets well aware of scholastic teachings wrote vernacular works of great sophistication. And architects and artists elaborated the soaring structures of "Gothic" style in which much of this activity took place.

Lay Religious Fervor

The Fourth Lateran's mission to regulate and Christianize lay behavior was carried forward by the friars. Both the Dominican and Franciscan orders insisted on travel, preaching, and poverty—vocations that brought friars into cities and towns. Soon

■ **A Lady and Her Loving Falcon**
This sumptuous velvet-and-silk pouch, made by an embroideress in about 1320, shows a lady in the position of falconer. The falcon—a bird ordinarily used as an aid in hunting—is here depicted as her lover. He is flying toward her to place a crown of greenery on her head while she touches him tenderly on the shoulder. In her other hand she holds the leash with which she trained him. (© Musée de Tissus, Lyon.)

their members dominated the fledgling city universities and were sending into the community friar-preachers trained by the scholastics. Townspeople flocked to such preachers because they wanted to know how the Christian message applied to their daily lives. They were concerned, for example, about the ethics of moneymaking, sex in marriage, and family life. In turn, the preachers represented the front line of the church. They met the laity on their own turf and taught them to bend their activities to church teachings.

The friars further tied their members to the lay community through **tertiaries**, affiliated laymen and -women who adopted many Franciscan practices—prayer and works of charity, for example—while continuing to live in the world, raising families and tending to the normal tasks of daily life, whatever their occupation. Even kings became tertiaries.

All across Europe, women, too, sought outlets for their piety. As in previous centuries, powerful families founded new nunneries, especially within towns and cities. On the whole, these were set up for the daughters of the wealthy, while ordinary women found different modes of religious expression. Some sought the lives of quiet activity and rapturous mysticism of the Beguines; others found comfort in the lives of charity and service of women's mendicant orders, such as those connected to the Franciscans; and still others lived happily as wives and mothers, punctuating their domestic duties with religious devotions. Elisabeth of Hungary, who married a German prince at the age of fourteen, raised three children. At the same time, she devoted her life to fasting, prayer, and service to the poor.

Of course, many women were not as devout as Elisabeth. In the countryside, they cooked their porridge, brewed their ale, and raised their children. They attended church regularly, on major feast days or for churching—the ritual of purification after a pregnancy—but not extravagantly. In the cities, workingwomen scratched out a meager living. They sometimes made pilgrimages to relic shrines to seek help or cures.

■ Friars and Usurers

As the illustration on page 357 indicates, clerics sometimes borrowed money. The friars had a different attitude. St. Francis, son of a merchant, refused to touch money altogether. Franciscans begged for food and shelter. Even when their numbers grew and they began forming communities and living in monasteries, the friars still insisted on personal poverty while ministering to city dwellers, who had to deal with money in some way to make a living. In this illumination from about 1250, a Franciscan (in light-colored robes) and a Dominican (in black) reject offers from two usurers, whose profession they are thus shown to condemn. Other friars, including Thomas Aquinas, worked out jus-tifications for some kinds of moneymaking professions. (Bibliothèque nationale de France.)

Religion was part of these women's lives but did not dominate them.

For some women, however, religion was the focus of life, and the church's attempt to define and control the Eucharist had some unintended results. The new emphasis on the holiness of the transformed wine and bread induced some of these pious women to eat nothing but the Eucharist. One such woman, Angela of Foligno, reported that the consecrated bread swelled in her mouth, tasting sweeter than any other food. In the minds of these holy women, Christ's crucifixion was the literal sacrifice of his body, to be eaten by sinful men and women as the way to redeem themselves. Renouncing all other foods became part of a life of service to others, because many of these devout women gave to the poor the food that they refused to eat. Even if not engaged in community service, holy women felt their suffering itself was a work of charity, helping to release souls from purgatory, the place where (the church taught) souls were cleansed of their sins.

Scholastics and Scholasticism

Purgatory was a doctrine first elaborated in the universites by "scholastics"—scholars who used a form of inquiry and exposition called **scholasticism**. It was a method based on the logical analysis of contradictory points, pioneered by Abelard in his *Sic et Non* and extended by other twelfth-century teachers. In the thirteenth century, the method was used to summarize and reconcile all knowledge. Many of the thirteenth-century scholastics were members of the Dominican and Franciscan orders, who dominated some of the faculties of the universities. Most were sure that knowledge obtained through the senses and by logical reasoning was compatible with the knowledge known through faith and revelation. One of their goals was to demonstrate this harmony. The scholastic ***summa***, or summary of knowledge, was a systematic exposition of the answer to every possible question about human morality, the physical world, society, belief, action, and theology.

The summa was an orderly presentation of various positions that were then "reconciled" by the author. Both the presentation and the arguments borrowed much of the vocabulary and rules of logic long ago outlined by Aristotle. Even though Aristotle was a pagan, scholastics considered his coherent and rational body of thought the most perfect that human reason alone could devise. Because they had the benefit of Christ's revelations, the scholastics considered themselves able to take Aristotle's philosophy one necessary step further and reconcile human reason with Christian faith. Full of confidence in their method and conclusions, scholastics embraced the world and its issues.

Some scholastics considered questions about the natural world. Albertus Magnus (c. 1200–1280), a major theologian, also contributed to the fields of biology, botany, astronomy, and physics. His reconsideration of Aristotle's views on motion led the way to distinctions that helped scientists in the sixteenth and seventeenth centuries arrive at the modern notion of inertia.

One of Albertus's students was St. Thomas Aquinas (c. 1225–1274), perhaps the most famous scholastic. Huge of build, renowned for his composure in debate, Thomas came from a noble Neapolitan family that had hoped to see him become a powerful bishop rather than a poor university professor. When he was about eighteen years old, he thwarted his family's wishes and joined the Dominicans. Soon he was studying at Cologne with Albertus. At thirty-two he became a master at the University of Paris.

Like many other scholastics, Thomas considered Aristotle "the Philosopher," the authoritative voice of human reason, which he sought to reconcile with divine revelation in a universal and harmonious scheme. In 1273, he published his monumental *Summa Theologiae* (sometimes called the *Summa Theologica*), which covered all important topics, human and divine. He divided these topics into questions, exploring each one thoroughly and systematically, and concluding each question with a decisive position and a refutation of opposing views.

Many of Thomas's questions spoke to the keenest concerns of his day. He asked, for example, whether it was lawful to sell something for more than its worth. Thomas arranged his argument systematically, quoting first authorities that seemed to declare every sort of selling practice, even deceptive ones, to be lawful. This was the *sic* (or "yes") position. Then he quoted an authority who opposed selling something for more than its worth. This was the *non*. Following that, he gave his own argument, prefaced by the words *I answer that*. Unlike Abelard, whose method left differences unresolved, Thomas wanted to harmonize the two points of view, so he pointed out that price and worth depended on the circumstances of the buyer and seller, and he concluded that charging more than a seller had originally paid could be legitimate at times.

For townspeople engaged in commerce and worried about biblical prohibitions on moneymaking, Thomas's ideas about selling practices addressed burning questions. Hoping to go to heaven as well as reap the profits of their business ventures, laypeople listened eagerly to preachers who delivered their sermons in the vernacular but who based their ideas on the Latin *summae* of Thomas and other scholastics. Thomas's conclusions aided townspeople in justifying their worldly activities.

In his own day, Thomas Aquinas was a controversial figure, and his ideas, emphasizing reason, were by no means universally accepted. In Thomas's view, God, nature, and reason were in harmony, so Aristotle's arguments could be used to explore both the human and the divine orders. The work of the thirteenth-century scholastics to unite the secular with the sacred continued for another generation after Thomas. Yet at the beginning of the fourteenth century, fissures began to appear. In the summae of John Duns Scotus (c. 1266–1308), for example, the world and God were less compatible. John, whose name "Duns Scotus" betrays his Scottish origin, was a Franciscan who taught at both Oxford and Paris. For John, human reason could know truth only through the "special illumination of the uncreated light"—that is, by divine illumination. But unlike his predecessors, John believed that this illumination came not as a matter of course but only when God chose to intervene. John—and others—now sometimes experienced God as willful rather than reasonable. Human reason could not soar to God; God's will alone determined whether a person could know God. In this way, John separated the divine and secular realms.

Like John, William of Ockham (c. 1285–1349), an English Franciscan who was one of the most eminent theologians of his age, rejected any confident synthesis of Christian doctrine and Aristotelian philosophy. Ockham believed that universal concepts had no reality in nature but instead existed only as mere representations, names in the mind—a philosophy that came to be called nominalism. Perceiving and analyzing such concepts as "man" or "papal infallibility" offered no assurance that the concepts expressed truth. Observation and human reason were limited as the means to understand the universe and to know God. Ockham's insistence that the simplest explanation is the best came to be known as "Ockham's razor." Where human reason left off, God's covenant with his faithful took over.

New Syntheses in Writing and Music

Thirteenth-century writers and musicians, as confident in their powers as any king or scholastic, presented complicated ideas and feelings as harmonious and unified syntheses. Writers explored the relations between this world and the next; musicians found ways to bridge sacred and secular forms of music.

Dante Alighieri (1265–1321), perhaps the greatest vernacular poet of the Middle Ages, harmonized the scholastic universe with the mysteries of faith and the poetry of love. Born in Florence in a time of political turmoil, Dante incorporated the heroes and villains of his day into his most famous poem, the *Commedia*, written between 1313 and 1321. Later known as the *Divine Comedy*, Dante's poem describes the poet taking an imaginary journey from Hell to Purgatory and finally to Paradise.

The poem is an allegory in which every person and object must be read at more than one level. At the most literal level, the poem is about Dante's travels. At a deeper level, it is about the soul's search for meaning and enlightenment and its ultimate discovery of God in the light of divine love. Just as Thomas Aquinas thought that Aristotle's logic could lead to important truths, so Dante used the pagan poet Virgil as his guide through Hell and Purgatory. And just as Thomas believed that faith went beyond reason to even higher truths, so Dante found a new guide representing earthly love to lead him through most of Paradise. This guide was Beatrice, a Florentine girl with whom Dante had fallen in love as a boy and whom he never forgot. But only the Virgin Mary, representing faith and divine love, could bring Dante to the culmination of his journey—a blinding and inexpressibly awesome vision of God:

> *What I then saw is more than tongue can say.*
> *Our human speech is dark before the vision.*
> *The ravished memory swoons and falls away.*

Dante's poem electrified a wide audience. By elevating one dialect of Italian—the language that ordinary Florentines used in their everyday life—to a language of exquisite poetry, Dante was able to communicate the scholastics' harmonious and optimistic vision of the universe in an even more exciting and accessible way. So influential was his work that it is no exaggeration to say that modern Italian is based on Dante's Florentine dialect.

Other writers of the period used different methods to express the harmony of heaven and earth. The anonymous author of *Quest of the Holy Grail* (c. 1225), for example, wrote about the adventures of the knights of King Arthur's Round Table to convey the doctrine of transubstantiation and the wonder of the vision of God.

In *The Romance of the Rose*, begun by one author (Guillaume de Lorris, a poet in the romantic tradition) and finished by another (Jean de Meun, a poet in the

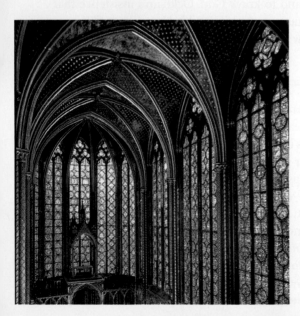

■ **French Gothic: Ste.-Chapelle**

Gothic architecture opened up the walls of the church to windows. Filled with "stained" glass—actually, the colors were added to the ingredients of the glass before they were heated, melted, and blown—the windows glowed like jewels. Moreover, each had a story to tell: the life of Christ, major events from the Old Testament, the lives of saints. Ste.-Chapelle, commissioned by King Louis IX (St. Louis) and consecrated in 1248, was built to house Christ's crown of thorns and other relics of the Passion. Compare the use of windows, walls, vault, and piers here with that of a Romanesque church such as St.-Savin (see page 378).

(Bridgeman-Giraudon/Art Resource, NY.)

scholastic tradition), a lover seeks the rose, his true love. In the long dream that the poem describes, the narrator's search for the rose is thwarted by personifications of love, shame, reason, abstinence, and so on. They present him with arguments for and against love, not incidentally commenting on people of the poets' own day. In the end, sexual love is made part of the divine scheme—and the lover plucks the rose.

Musicians, like poets, developed new forms that bridged sacred and secular subjects in the thirteenth and fourteenth centuries. This connection appears in the most distinctive musical form of the thirteenth century, the **motet** (from the French *mot*, meaning "word"). The motet is an example of **polyphony**, music that consists of two or more melodies performed simultaneously. Before about 1215, most polyphony was sacred; purely secular polyphony was not common before the fourteenth century. The motet, a unique merging of the sacred and the secular, evidently originated in Paris, the center of scholastic culture as well.

The typical thirteenth-century motet has three melody lines (or "voices"). The lowest, usually from a liturgical chant melody, has no words and may have been played on an instrument rather than sung. The remaining melodies have different texts, either Latin or French (or one of each), which are sung simultaneously. Latin texts are usually sacred, whereas French ones are secular, dealing with themes such as love and springtime. In one example, the top voice chirps in quick rhythm about a lady's charms ("Fair maiden, lovely and comely; pretty maiden, courteous and pleasing, delicious one"); the middle voice slowly and mournfully laments the "malady" of love; and the lowest voice sings a liturgical melody. The motet thus weaves the sacred (the chant melody in the lowest voice) and the secular (the French texts in the upper voices) into a sophisticated tapestry of music. Like the scholastic summae, the motets were written by and for a clerical elite. Yet, they incorporated the music of ordinary people, such as the calls of street vendors and the boisterous songs of students. In turn, they touched the lives of everyone, for polyphony influenced every form of music, from the Mass to popular songs that entertained and diverted laypeople and churchmen alike.

Complementing the motet's complexity was the development of a new notation for rhythm. Until the thirteenth century, musical notation could indicate pitch but had no way to denote the duration of the notes. In that century, music theorists developed increasingly precise methods to indicate rhythm. Franco of Cologne, for example, in his *Art of Measurable Song* (c. 1280), used different shapes to mark the number of beats each note should be held. His system became the basis of modern musical notation. Because each note could now be allotted a specific duration, written music could express new and complicated rhythms. The music of the thirteenth century reflected both the melding of the secular and the sacred and the possibilities for greater order and control.

The Order of High Gothic

Just as polyphonic music united the sacred with the secular, so Gothic architecture, sculpture, and painting expressed the order and harmony of the universe. The term

Gothic was originally used to belittle medieval art and architecture, but it now refers with admiration to a particular syle used in the twelfth to fifteenth centuries. Its chief characteristic is the use of pointed arches, which began as architectural motifs but were soon adopted in every art form. Gothic churches appealed to the senses the way that scholastic argument appealed to human reason: both were designed to lead people to knowledge that touched the divine. Being in a Gothic church was a foretaste of heaven.

Gothic architecture began around 1135, with the project of Abbot Suger, the close associate of King Louis the Fat (see page 365), to remodel portions of the church of St. Denis. Suger's rebuilding of St. Denis was part of the fruitful melding of royal and ecclesiastical interests and ideals in the north of France. At the west end of his church, the point where the faithful entered, Suger decorated the portals with figures of Old Testament kings, queens, and patriarchs, signaling the links between the present king and his illustrious predecessors. Within the church, Suger rebuilt the *chevet*, or choir area, using pointed arches and stained glass to let in light, which Suger believed would transport the worshiper from the "slime of earth" to the "purity of Heaven." Suger thought that the Father of lights, God himself, "illuminated" the minds of the beholders via the light that filtered through the stained-glass windows.

Soon the style that Suger pioneered was taken up across northern France and then, in the 1250s, as French culture gained enormous prestige under Louis IX, all across Europe. Gothic was an urban architecture, reflecting—in its towering heights, jewel-like windows, and bright ornaments—the aspirations, pride, and confidence of rich and powerful merchants, artisans, and bishops. A Gothic church, usually a cathedral (the bishop's principal church), was the focal point of a city.

Building Gothic cathedrals was a community project, enlisting the labor and support of an entire urban center. New cathedrals required a small army of quarrymen, builders, carpenters, and glass cutters. Bishops, papal legates, and clerics planned and helped pay for these grand churches, but townspeople also generously financed them and filled them to attend Mass and visit relics. Guilds raised money to pay for stained-glass windows that depicted and celebrated their own patron saints. In turn, towns made money when pilgrims came to visit relics, and sightseers arrived to marvel at their great churches. At Chartres, near Paris, for example, which had the relic of the Virgin's robe, crowds thronged the streets, the poor buying small lead figures of the Virgin, the rich purchasing wearable replicas of her robe. Churches were centers of commercial activity. In their basements, wine merchants plied their trade, while other vendors sold goods outside.

The technologies that made Gothic churches possible were all known before the twelfth century. But Suger's church showed how they could be used together to achieve a particularly dazzling effect. Gothic techniques included ribbed vaulting, which gave a sense of precision and order; pointed arches, which produced a feeling of soaring height; and flying buttresses, which took the weight of the vault off the walls (Figure 10.1). The buttresses permitted much of the wall to be cut away and the open spaces to be filled with glass.

■ FIGURE 10.1 Elements of a Gothic Cathedral

Bristling on the outside with stone flying buttresses, Gothic cathedrals were lofty and serene on the inside. The buttresses, which held the weight of the vault, allowed Gothic architects to pierce the walls with windows running the full length of the church. Within, thick piers anchored on sturdy bases became thin columns as they mounted over the triforium and clerestory, blossoming into ribs at the top. Whether plain or ornate, the ribs gave definition and drew attention to the high pointed vault.

■ **German Gothic: Strasbourg**

The Virgin is mourned in this tympanum over the portal of the Strasbourg cathedral's south transept (the arm that crosses the church from north to south). Here, in German Gothic, the emphasis is on emotion and expressivity. Notice the depiction of Mary, with her bedclothes agitated and her body contorted. Why do you suppose that Christ stands in the center of the tympanum, as if he is one of the mourners? What is he holding in the crook of his arm? (Hint: The souls of the dead are often shown as miniature people.) **For more help analyzing this image,** see the visual activity for this chapter in the ONLINE STUDY GUIDE at bedfordstmartins.com/huntconcise.

(Foto Marburg/Art Resource, NY.)

Unlike Romanesque churches, whose exteriors prepare visitors for what they will see within, Gothic cathedrals surprise. The exterior of a Gothic church has an opaque, bristling, and forbidding look owing to the dark surface of its stained glass and its flying buttresses. The interior, however, is just the opposite. It is all soaring lightness, harmony, and order. Just as a scholastic presented his argument with utter clarity, so the interior of a Gothic church revealed its structure through its skeleton of ribbed vaults and piers. And just as a scholastic bridged the earthly and celestial realms, so the cathedral elicited a response beyond reason, evoking a sense of awe.

By the mid-thirteenth century, Gothic architecture had spread from France to other European countries. Yet the style varied by region, most dramatically in Italy. The outer walls of the cathedral at Orvieto, for example, alternate bricks of light and dark color, providing texture instead of glass and light; and the vault over the large nave is round rather than pointed, recalling the Roman aqueducts that could still be seen in Italy when the builders were designing the cathedral. With no flying buttresses and relatively little portal sculpture, Italian Gothic churches convey a spirit of austerity.

Gothic art, both painting and sculpture, echoed and decorated the Gothic cathedral. Gothic sculpture differed from earlier church sculpture by its naturalism and monumentality. Romanesque sculpture played upon a flat surface; Gothic figures were liberated from their background. Sculpted in the round, they turned,

■ Mocking of Christ

Like the artist who portrayed "A Teacher and His Students" on page 371, Giotto, too, used decorative bands to frame his subject. But, within the frame, the conception of the human body and the human interaction is entirely different. On page 371, the four figures are elongated to express their elegance and unworldliness; they interact via scrolls. Gilbert is clearly the oldest: he wears a beard. But the three students look almost exactly the same. By contrast, in the "Mocking of Christ" the figures are heavy and fleshy, emphasizing their presence in a real world. They poke and stare and converse with one another. Each torturer around Christ takes individual delight in his particular cruelty, while a group of elders a bit apart shows weighty concern. Giotto was here portraying factions as well as individuals. (Scala/Art Resource, NY.)

■ MAPPING THE WEST Europe, c. 1340

The empire, now called the Holy Roman Empire, still dominated the map of Europe in 1340, but the emperor himself had power only in his own principality. Each region—and sometimes each city—was ruled separately and independently. To the east, the Ottoman Turks were beginning to make themselves felt. In the course of the next century, they would disrupt Mongol hegemony and become a great power.

moved, and interacted with one another. The positions of the figures, the people they represented, and the ways in which they interacted were meant to be "read" like a scholastic summa, for Gothic sculpture often depicted complex stories or scenes. The south portal complex of Chartres cathedral is a good example. Each massive doorway tells a separate story through sculpture: the left depicts the martyrs, the right the confessors, and the center the Last Judgment. Like Dante's *Divine Comedy,* these portals taken together show the soul's pilgrimage from the suffering of this world to eternal life.

Gothic sculpture began in France and was adopted, with many variations, elsewhere in Europe during the thirteenth century. The German sculptor who carved the tympanum (the half-circle form over the portal) over the south portal of

Strasbourg's cathedral was particularly interested in emotional expression. As the Virgin Mary dies, the figures around her bend and gesture, showing their grief with their hands and faces. The Italian sculptor Nicola Pisano (c. 1220–1278?), by contrast, was very interested in classical forms.

By the early fourteenth century, the expressive sculptures so prominent in architecture were reflected in painting as well. This new style is evident in the work of Giotto (1266–1337), a Florentine artist who helped change the emphasis of painting, which had been predominantly symbolic, decorative, and intellectual. For example, Giotto filled the walls of a private chapel at Padua with paintings depicting scenes of Christ's life. Here he experimented with the illusion of depth. Giotto's figures, appearing weighty and voluminous, express a range of emotions as they seem to move across interior and exterior spaces. In bringing sculptural realism to a flat surface, Giotto stressed three-dimensionality, illusional space, and human emotion. By melding earthly sensibilities with religious themes, Giotto found yet another way to bring together the natural and divine realms.

■ **REVIEW:** *How did artists, architects, musicians, and scholastics try to link this world with the divine?*

IMPORTANT DATES

1180–1223	Reign of Philip II ("Philip Augustus") of France	1265	English Parliament called by Simon de Montfort includes representatives of the commons
1198–1216	Papacy of Innocent III		
1202–1204	Fourth Crusade; sack of Constantinople	1265–1321	Life of Dante Alighieri
		1273	*Summa Theologiae* of Thomas Aquinas
1209–1229	Albigensian Crusade		
1212–1250	Reign of Frederick II	1285–1314	Reign of Philip IV ("the Fair") of France
1215	Magna Carta; Fourth Lateran Council	1294–1303	Papacy of Boniface VIII
		1302	Meeting of the Estates at Paris; Boniface issues *Unam Sanctam*
1216–1272	Reign of Henry III of England		
c. 1225–1274	Life of Thomas Aquinas	1309–1378	Avignon papacy ("Babylonian Captivity")
1226–1270	Reign of Louis IX ("St. Louis") of France		
1230s	Mongols begin attacks on the West	1313–1321	Dante's *Divine Comedy*
1250s	Gothic becomes a European-wide style		

Conclusion

In the thirteenth and early fourteenth centuries, western Europeans aggressively expanded outward, from the Baltic to the Strait of Gibraltar. When they sacked Constantinople in 1204, they joined the Muslims as the dominant political forces in the West. They treated the Mongol hegemony in the East as an opportunity for trade and missionary work.

Powerful territorial kings and princes expressed their new self-confidence through bureaucratic institutions. They hired staffs to handle their accounts, record acts, collect taxes, issue writs, and preside over courts. Flourishing cities, a growing money economy, and trade and manufacturing provided the finances necessary to support the personnel now used by medieval governments. The universities became the training grounds for the new administrators as well as for urban preachers.

Both the church and the state became more assertive. The Fourth Lateran Council was an attempt to regulate intimate aspects of the lives of all, even laypeople and non-Christians. The conflict between Boniface and Philip showed how the French king could galvanize his subjects—even his clergy—on behalf of the interests of the state. In England, where John agreed to Magna Carta, it was the barons who helped forge a notion of government that transcended the king. On the other hand, the artists and architects of the time sought to bring together two separate entities—the worldly and the divine.

New power, new piety, and new exclusivity arose in a society both more confident and less tolerant. Crusaders fought against an increasing variety of foes, not only in the Holy Land but in Spain, in southern France, and on Europe's northern frontiers. With heretics voicing criticisms and maintaining their beliefs, the church, led by the papacy, now defined orthodoxy and declared dissenters its enemies. The Jews, who had once been fairly well integrated into the Christian community, were treated ambivalently, alternately used and abused. Balts became targets for new evangelical and armed zeal; the Greeks became the butt of envy, hostility, and finally enmity.

Confident and aggressive, the leaders of Christian Europe in the thirteenth and early fourteenth centuries attempted to impose their rule, legislate morality, and create a unified worldview impregnable to attack. But their drive for order would be countered by economic and political crises and epidemic disease.

■ MAKING CONNECTIONS

1. *Why was Innocent III more successful than Boniface VIII in carrying out his objectives?*

2. *What impact did the Mongolian invasion have on the medieval economy?*

■ **FOR FURTHER EXPLORATION**

For further reading and online research ideas, see the Suggested References on page SR-5 at the back of the book.

For practice quizzes, a customized study plan, and other study tools, see the ONLINE STUDY GUIDE at bedfordstmartins.com/huntconcise.

For primary-source material from this period, see Chapter 10 in *Sources of THE MAKING OF THE WEST: A CONCISE HISTORY*, Second Edition.

11

Crisis and Renaissance

1340–1500

W HEN, IN 1453, THE CANNONS OF OTTOMAN RULER MEHMED II breached the walls of Constantinople, the whole Christian world shuddered. Yet a very few years later, Mehmed was writing to the lord of the Renaissance Italian city of Rimini, asking for the Rimini court painter and architect Matteo de Pasti to come help him build a new palace. The Ottoman sultan considered himself a Renaissance prince and expected cooperation from his European counterparts. Pasti's lord accepted the invitation, but on his way to Istanbul, Pasti was waylaid by the Venetians, who wanted no city but theirs to have relations with the sultan. Mehmed didn't give up; he simply called upon several Venetian painters to come instead. The palace came to be called the Topkapi Saray and still stands today looking across the Bosporus, the strait that divides European and Asian Turkey.

Mehmed sums up in one personage the twin themes of the period 1340–1500. His conquest of Constantinople was one of many crises that rocked the West from the Bosporus to the Atlantic: his age saw disease, war, economic contraction, and religious upheaval. At the same time, his tastes and culture aligned him with the Renaissance, a movement that was rediscovering the arts and worldview of classical antiquity. His interest in Italian art reflected the connection between power and

■ **The Siege of Constantinople**
Bertrandon de la Broquière wrote his Overseas Voyage *in the 1430s for the Duke of Burgundy, who was contemplating a new crusade against the Turks. "I will discuss the means and the men necessary to break their power and defeat them in battle and gain their territory," he wrote, adding: "I don't think it would be very hard to break and defeat them, given their lack of arms." Within two decades, however, the Turks had taken Constantinople. When an artist was commissioned around 1455 to illustrate Bertrandon's work, he or she chose to show the siege. In this picture, you can see the tents of the Turkish captains, their cannons and cannonballs just behind them, and, across the water, the city of Constantinople with its doomed defenders.*
(Bibliothèque Nationale, Paris/Bridgeman Art Library.)

culture characteristic of his era. In the fourteenth and fifteenth centuries, much new artistic, architectural, and musical work was created in praise of personal and public lives. Portraits, palaces, and poetry commemorated the glory of the rich and powerful, while a new cultural movement called humanism advocated classical learning and argued for the active participation of the individual in civic affairs. Family, honor, social status, and individual distinction—these were the goals that fueled the ambitions of Renaissance men and women.

Their quest for glory duplicated on a smaller scale the enhanced power of the state, shored up by new military technologies—firearms, siege equipment, fortifications, and well-equipped soldiers. Commoners, criminals, and adventurers often joined the ranks of the fighters. To maintain their social eminence, many nobles were forced to take on new roles as officials or officers in the service of the state. By appointing nobles to the royal household, as military commanders and councilors, kings and princes consolidated their power.

Like individuals, these states, too, competed for wealth, glory, and honor. While warfare and diplomacy channeled the restless energy of the Italian states, monarchies and empires outside of Italy also expanded their power through conquests and institutional reforms. The European world changed dramatically as new powers such as the Ottoman Empire and Muscovy rose to prominence in the east, while the Iberian kingdoms of Portugal and Spain expanded European domination to Africa, Asia, and the Americas.

A Multitude of Crises

Beginning in the fourteenth century and extending to the middle of the fifteenth, Europeans confronted crises of both nature and human design. The plague wracked the cities and hurt the countryside. The Hundred Years' War devastated France. To the east, the rise of the Ottomans had a cataclysmic impact on the politics of eastern and central Europe. Everywhere, economic contraction made for material hard times, while spiritual well-being seemed threatened by a long papal schism. Minorities—religious dissenters, heretics, Jews, and Muslims in Spain—suffered the effects of pent-up anxieties.

Economic Contraction and the Black Death

Bad weather and overpopulation contributed to a series of famines at the beginning of the fourteenth century. Having cleared forests and drained swamps, peasants divided their plots into ever smaller parcels and farmed marginal land; their income and the quality of their diet eroded. In the great urban centers, where thousands depended on steady employment and cheap bread, a bad harvest, always followed by sharply rising food prices, meant hunger and eventual famine. A cooling of the European climate also contributed to the crisis in the food supply.

■ MAP 11.1 Advance of the Plague
The gradual but deadly spread of the plague followed the roads and rivers of Europe. Note the earlier transmission by sea from the Crimea to the ports of the Mediterranean before the general spread to northern Europe.

Modern studies of tree rings (dendrochronology) indicate that fourteenth-century Europe entered a colder period, with a succession of severe winters beginning in 1315 and extending to 1317. Crop failures were widespread. In many cities of northwestern Europe, the price of bread tripled, and thousands starved to death. Some Flemish cities, for example, lost 10 percent of their population. Many who survived were badly weakened and vulnerable to disease.

In midcentury, the bubonic plague passed from its breeding ground in central Asia eastward into China, where it decimated the population and wiped out the remnants of the tiny Italian merchant community in Yangzhou. Bacteria-carrying fleas living on black rats transmitted the disease. They traveled back to Europe alongside valuable cargoes of silk, porcelain, and spices. In 1347, the Genoese colony in Caffa in the Crimea contracted the plague (Map 11.1). Fleeing by ship in a desperate but futile attempt to escape the disease, the Genoese in turn communicated the plague to other Mediterranean seaports. By January 1348, the plague had infected Sicily, Sardinia, Corsica, and Marseille. Six months later, it had spread to Aragon, all of Italy, the Balkans, and most of France. The disease then crept northward to Germany, England, and Scandinavia, reaching the Russian city of Novgorod in 1351.

Nothing like the Black Death, as this epidemic came to be called, had struck Europe since the great plague of the sixth century. The Italian writer Giovanni Boccaccio (1313–1375) reported that the plague

> *first betrayed itself by the emergence of certain tumors in the groin or the armpits, some of which grew as large as a common apple, others as an egg. . . . From the two said parts of the body this . . . began to propagate and spread itself in all directions indifferently; after which the form of the malady began to change, black spots or livid making their appearance in many cases on the arm or the thigh or elsewhere, now few and large, now minute and numerous.*

Inhabitants of cities, where crowding and filth increased the chances of contagion, died in massive numbers. Florence lost almost two-thirds of its population of ninety thousand; Siena, like most cities visited by the plague, lost half its people. Rural areas suffered fewer deaths, but regional differences were pronounced. (See "Taking Measure," page 429.) Nor was the danger over after 1350. Further outbreaks of the plague occurred in Europe in 1361, 1368–1369, 1371, 1375, 1390, and 1405; they continued, with longer dormant intervals, into the eighteenth century.

Although the Black Death took a horrible human toll, the disaster actually profited some people. In an overpopulated society with limited resources, massive death opened the ranks for advancement. For example, after 1350, landlords had difficulty acquiring new tenant farmers without making concessions in land contracts, fewer priests competed for the same number of benefices (ecclesiastical offices funded by an endowment), and workers received much higher wages because the supply of laborers had plummeted. The Black Death and the resulting decline in urban population meant there was less demand for grain relative to the supply and thus brought about a drop in cereal prices.

All across Europe noble landlords, whose revenues fell as prices dropped, had to adjust to these new circumstances. Some revived seigneurial demands for labor services. Others looked to their central government for legislation to regulate wages. Still others granted favorable terms to peasant proprietors, often after bloody peasant revolts. Many noblemen lost a portion of their wealth and a measure of their autonomy and political influence. Consequently, European nobles

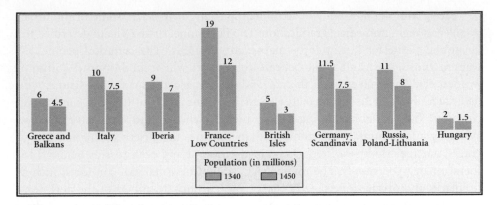

■ **TAKING MEASURE** Population Losses and the Plague, 1340–1450
The bar chart represents dramatically the impact of the Black Death and the recurrent plagues between 1340 and 1450. More than a century after the Black Death, none of the regions of Europe had made up for the losses of population. The population of 1450 stood at between 75 and 80 percent of the preplague population. The hardest-hit areas were France and the Low Countries, which also suffered from the devastations of the Hundred Years' War.

became more dependent on their monarchs and on war to supplement their incomes and enhance their power.

For the peasantry and the urban working population, higher wages generally meant an improvement in living standards. To compensate for the lower demand and price for grain, many peasants and landlords turned to stock breeding and grape and barley cultivation. As European agriculture diversified, peasants and artisans consumed more beer, wine, meat, cheese, and vegetables, a better and more varied diet than their thirteenth-century forebears had eaten.

Because of the shrinking population and decreased demand for food, cultivating marginal fields was no longer profitable, and many settlements were simply abandoned. By 1450, for example, some 450 large English villages and many small hamlets had disappeared. In central Europe east of the Elbe River, where German peasants had migrated, large tracts of cultivated land reverted to forest. Estimates suggest that some 80 percent of all villages in parts of Thuringia (Germany) vanished.

In the cities, production shifted from manufacturing for a mass market to a highly lucrative, though small, luxury market. The drastic loss in urban population had reduced the demand for such mass-manufactured goods as cloth. Fewer people now possessed proportionately greater concentrations of wealth. In the southern French city of Albi, for example, the proportion of citizens possessing more than 100 livres in per capita income doubled between 1343 and 1357, while the number of poor people, those with less than 10 livres, declined by half.

Faced with the possibility of imminent and untimely death, some of the urban populace sought immediate gratification. The Florentine Matteo Villani described the newfound desire for luxury in his native city in 1351. "The common people . . . wanted the dearest and most delicate foods . . . while children and common women clad themselves in all the fair and costly garments of the illustrious who had died." Those with means increased their consumption of luxuries such as silk clothing, hats, doublets (snug-fitting men's jackets), and expensive jewelry. Whereas agricultural prices continued to decline, the prices of manufactured goods, particularly luxury items, remained constant and even rose as demand for them outstripped supply. The middle class sought new material comforts, such as fireplaces and private toilets, beds, chests, and curtains. Members of the new peasant elite must have lived in simpler style, but perhaps they no longer shared their house with animals, as they had in the thirteenth century.

The long-term consequences of this new consumption pattern spelled the end for the traditional woolen industry that had produced for a mass market. Diminishing demand for wool caused hardships for woolworkers, and social and political unrest shook many older industrial centers dependent on the cloth industry, such as Flanders. At Ypres, for example, production figures fell from a high of ninety thousand pieces of cloth in 1320 to fewer than twenty-five thousand by 1390. In Ghent, where 44 percent of all households were woolworkers and where some 60 percent of the working population depended on the textile industry, the woolen market's slump meant constant labor unrest.

The new labor market tended to undermine women's economic position. In the German city of Cologne, for example, more and more artisan guilds excluded women from their ranks. Everywhere, fathers favored sons and sons-in-law to succeed them in their crafts. Daughters and widows resisted this patriarchal regime in the urban economy, but they were most successful in industries with the least regulations, such as beer brewing.

The Hundred Years' War, 1337–1453

In France, the misery wrought by the plague was compounded by the devastation of war. The English and French kings had long sparred over control of territories in France. In 1337, as part of the French royal policy to centralize its jurisdiction, Philip VI confiscated the southwestern province of Aquitaine, which had been held by the English monarchs as a fief of the French crown. To recover his lands, Edward III of England in turn laid claim to the French throne. Thus the Hundred Years' War began. It satisfied the interests of many groups, especially on the English side: nobles and knights hoped to demonstrate their chivalric valor on the battlefield; English yeomen (free farmers) were eager for booty, hostages, and amorous conquests. Mercenary companies hired by the English were glad to make money; when not employed in war, they remained to wreak havoc on the French countryside.

Ruling over a more populous realm and commanding far larger armies than the English, the French kings were nevertheless hindered in the war by the independent actions of their powerful barons. Against the accurate and deadly English freemen archers, the French knights met repeated defeats. Yet the French nobility despised their own peasants, perhaps fearing them and the urban middle classes more than they feared their noble English adversaries.

The war may be divided into three periods: the first was marked by English triumphs, the second saw France slowly gaining the upper hand, and the third ended in the English expulsion from France (see Map 11.2 on page 432). The final, most important phase saw two key developments: the rise of Burgundy, a hodgepodge of territories held together only by the political machinations of its dukes; and the rise of France as a distinct nation. This phase began when the English king Henry V (r. 1413–1422) launched a full-scale invasion of France and crushed the French at Agincourt (1415). Three parties then struggled for domination in France. Henry occupied Normandy and claimed the French throne; the dauphin (heir apparent to the French throne), Charles VII of France (r. 1422–1461),* ruled central France; and the duke of Burgundy held a vast territory in the northeast that included the Low Countries. Burgundy was thus able to broker war or peace by shifting support first to the English and then to the French. But even with Burgundian support, the English could not establish firm control. In Normandy, a savage guerrilla war harassed the English army. Driven from their villages by pillaging and murdering soldiers, Norman peasants retreated into forests, formed armed bands, and attacked the English. The miseries of war inspired prophecies of miraculous salvation; among the predictions was that a virgin would deliver France from the English invaders.

At the court of the dauphin, in 1429, a sixteen-year-old peasant girl presented herself and her vision to save France. Born in a village in Lorraine, Joan of Arc, La Pucelle ("the Maid"), as she always referred to herself, grew up in a war-ravaged country that longed for divine deliverance. She had first presented herself as God's messenger to the local noble, who was sufficiently impressed to equip Joan with horse, armor, and a retinue to send her to the dauphin's court. Joan of Arc's extraordinary appearance inspired the beleaguered French to trust in divine providence. In 1429, she accompanied the French army that laid a prolonged but successful siege on Orlèans, was wounded, and showed great courage in battle. Upon her urging, the dauphin traveled deep into hostile Burgundian territory to be anointed King Charles VII of France at Reims cathedral, thus strengthening his legitimacy by following the traditional ritual of coronation.

---

*Although the dauphin was not crowned until 1429, he assumed the title Charles VII in 1422, after the death of his father.

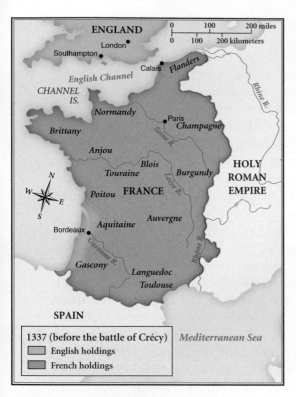

1337 (before the battle of Crécy)
- English holdings
- French holdings

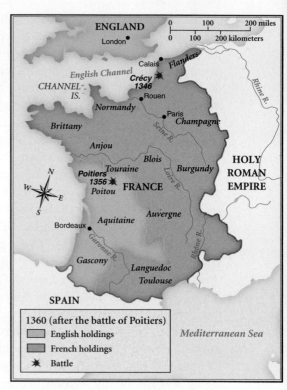

1360 (after the battle of Poitiers)
- English holdings
- French holdings
- ✳ Battle

c. 1429 (after the Siege of Orléans)
- English holdings
- French holdings
- Burgundian lands allied with England to 1435
- ✳ Battle
- ← Route taken by Joan of Arc, 1429–1431

1453 (end of war)
- English holdings
- French holdings
- Burgundian lands reconciled with France after 1435

■ **The Spoils of War**
This illustration from Jean Froissart's Chronicles *depicts soldiers pillaging a conquered city. During the Hundred Years' War, looting became the main source of income for mercenary troops and contributed to the general misery of late-medieval society. Food, furniture, and even everyday household items were taken.* (Bibliothèque nationale de France.)

Although Joan's fortunes declined after Reims and she was burned as a heretic by the English in 1431, she had helped undermine the English position, which slowly crumbled thereafter. The duke of Burgundy recognized Charles VII as king of France, and Charles entered Paris in 1437. Skirmish by skirmish, the English were driven from French soil.

The Hundred Years' War profoundly altered the economic and political landscape of western Europe. It aggravated the demographic and economic crises of the fourteenth century by further ravaging the countryside. Constant insecurity

■ **MAP 11.2 The Hundred Years' War, 1337–1453**
As rulers of Aquitaine and claimants to the throne of France, English kings contested the French monarchy for domination of France. Squeezed between England and Burgundy, the holdings of the French kings were vastly reduced after the battle of Poitiers in 1356. Then the fortune of war changed, and slowly France emerged as an intact nation.

■ Joan of Arc, c. 1430
Painted in the style of the French-Flemish school, this manuscript illustration contrasts the metallic hardness of Joan's armor and sword with the soft fluttering banner depicting God and two angels. With her right hand upturned clasping a sword and her left turned down to support the banner, Joan strikes a perfect pose as a messenger of God, similar to the angels depicted above. **For more help analyzing this image,** see the visual activity for this chapter in the ONLINE STUDY GUIDE at **bedfordstmartins.com/huntconcise.** (© AKG-Images, London.)

caused by marauding bands of soldiers prevented the cultivation of fields even in times of truce. City and countryside united in 1358, unhappy with the heavy war taxes and the incompetence of the warrior nobility. The movement, called the Jacquerie, began when the townspeople of Paris, led by Étienne Marcel, the provost of the merchants there, sought to take over control of the city. His rebellion was put down and Marcel was killed, but meanwhile rebels in the countryside began their own revolt, destroying manor houses and castles near Paris and massacring entire noble families in a savage class war. The chronicler Jean Froissart, sympathetic to the nobility, reflected the views of the ruling class in describing the rebels as "small, dark, and very poorly armed." Repression by nobles was swift, as thousands of rebels died in battles or were executed.

In England, the war brought discontent to the rural and urban classes as well. The trigger for outright rebellion by the peasantry was the imposition of a poll tax passed by Parliament in 1377 to raise money for the war against France, a war that peasants believed benefited only the king and the nobility. Unlike traditional subsidies to the king, the poll tax was levied on everyone. In May 1381, a revolt broke out to protest the taxes. Rebels in Essex and Kent joined bands in London to confront the king. The famous couplet of the radical preacher John Ball, who was executed after the revolt, expresses the rebels' egalitarian, anti-noble sentiment:

> When Adam delved [dug] and Eve span [spun]
> Who was then the gentleman?

Forced to address the rebels, young King Richard II (r. 1377–1399) agreed to abolish serfdom and impose a ceiling on land rent, but he immediately rescinded these concessions after the rebels' defeat.

Richard was not the only monarch to pay little attention to the pains of the war. In France, the ruler benefited from it: under Charles VII, a standing army was established to supplement the feudal noble levies, an army financed by increased taxation and expanded royal judicial claims. Steadily increasing in power and pretensions, in the 1470s the French monarchy dismantled and absorbed Burgundy, and in the 1490s it entered Italy with conquest in mind. By 1500, it was clear that the French monarchy was one of the leading powers of Europe.

Defeated in war, the English monarchy suffered more. From the 1460s to 1485, England was torn by civil war—the War of the Roses between the red rose of Lancaster and the rival white rose of York. A deposed king (Henry VI), a short reign (Edward IV), and the murder of two princes by their uncle (Richard III) followed in quick succession in a series of conflicts that decimated the leading noble families of England. When Henry Tudor succeeded to the throne as Henry VII in 1485, England was tired of civil war. Henry ended the fighting and united the houses of Lancaster and York. By the early sixteenth century, the English monarchy was poised to take advantage of the general prosperity and war-weariness to enhance its position and power.

When the Hundred Years' War began, there were still knights who thought they could achieve valorous deeds of chivalry for their own glory and on behalf of their lord. By its end, chivalry was clearly a dreamy fantasy: cannons and gunpower had been added to the arsenal of European weapons, and many soldiers were mercenaries who hired themselves out to whichever ruler would pay. Equipment and fortifications counted more than valor in the outcome of battles.

■ **MAP 11.3 Ottoman Expansion in the Fourteenth and Fifteenth Centuries**
The Balkans were the major theater of expansion for the Ottoman Empire, whose conquests also included Egypt and the North African coast. The Byzantine Empire was long reduced to the city of Constantinople and surrounded by the Ottomans before its final fall in 1453.

Ottoman Conquest and New Political Configurations in Eastern Europe

The rise of the Ottoman Turks was the most astonishing development of the late thirteenth century, when the Islamic Ottomans began a holy war against Byzantium. Under Osman I (r. 1280–1324), who gave the dynasty its name, and his successors, the Ottomans became a formidable force in Anatolia and the Balkans, where political disunity opened the door for their advances (Map 11.3). By the end of the fourteenth century, they had reduced the Byzantine Empire to the city of Constantinople, Thessalonika, and a narrow strip of land in modern-day Greece. Further to the west, the Ottomans defeated a joint Hungarian-Serbian army at the Maritsa River (1364), alerting Europe for the first time to the threat of an Islamic invasion. Pope Urban V called vainly for a crusade. In the Balkans, the Ottomans skillfully exploited Christian disunity, playing local interests against one another. An Ottoman army allied with the Bulgarians and some Serbian princes won the battle of Kosovo (1389), destroying the last organized Christian resistance south of the Danube. Even today the battle remains a rallying cry for Serbian nationalists. The Ottomans secured control of southeastern Europe after 1396, when at Nicopolis they crushed a crusading army summoned by Pope Boniface IX.

When Mehmed II (r. 1451–1481) ascended the Ottoman throne, he proclaimed a holy war and laid siege to Constantinople in 1453. A city of 100,000, the Byzantine capital could muster only 6,000 defenders (including a small contingent of Genoese) against an Ottoman force estimated at between 200,000 and 400,000 men. The city's fortifications, many of which dated from Emperor

Justinian's rule in the sixth century, were no match for fifteenth-century cannons. The defenders held out for fifty-three days. While the Christians confessed their sins and prayed for divine deliverance in desperate anticipation of the Second Coming, the Muslim besiegers pressed forward, urged on by the certainty of rich spoils and Allah's promise of a final victory over the infidel Rome. Finally the defenders were overwhelmed, and the last Byzantine emperor, Constantine XI Palaeologos, died in battle. Some 60,000 residents were carried off into slavery, and the city was sacked. Mehmed entered Constantinople in triumph and rendered thanks to God in Justinian's Church of the Holy Wisdom (Hagia Sophia), which became a mosque.

Mehmed wanted to be the new ruler of the Roman Empire—a Muslim Roman Empire. We have seen that he asked Italian court painter Matteo de Pasti to help create his Topkapi palace, intended to communicate Ottoman power. The Ottoman conquest was more than a continuation of the struggle between Christendom and Islam. The battle for territory transcended the boundaries of faith. Christian princes also served the Ottoman Empire as vassals to the sultan. The Janissaries, Christian slave children raised by the sultan as Muslims, constituted the fundamental backbone of the Ottoman army. They formed a service class that was both dependent on and loyal to the ruler. At the sultan's court, Christian women were prominent in the harem; thus many Ottoman princes had Greek or Serbian mothers. In addition to the Janissaries, Christian princes and converts to Islam served in the emerging Ottoman administration. In areas conquered, existing religious and social structures remained intact when local people accepted Ottoman overlordship and paid taxes. Only in areas of persistent resistance did the Ottomans drive out or massacre the inhabitants, settling Turkish tribes in their place. A distinctive pattern of Balkan history was therefore established at the beginning of the Ottoman conquest: the extremely diverse ethnic and religious communities were woven together into the fabric of an efficient central state.

The rise of strong, new monarchies—represented by France, England, and the Ottoman sultanate—contrasted sharply with the weakness of state authority in central and eastern Europe, where Hungary, Bohemia, and Poland were held together, like Burgundy, by personal dynastic authority alone (see Map 11.4 on page 438). Under Matthias Corvinus (r. 1456–1490), the Hungarian king who briefly united the Bohemian and Hungarian crowns, a central-eastern European empire seemed to be emerging. A patron of the arts and a humanist, Matthias created a great library in Hungary. He repeatedly defeated the encroaching Austrian Habsburgs and even occupied Vienna in 1485. However, his empire did not outlast his death in 1490. The powerful Hungarian magnates, who enjoyed the constitutional right to elect the king, ended it by refusing to acknowledge his son's claim to the throne.

In the mid-fourteenth century, two large monarchies—Poland and Lithuania—began to take shape in northeastern Europe. King Casimir III (r. 1333–1370)

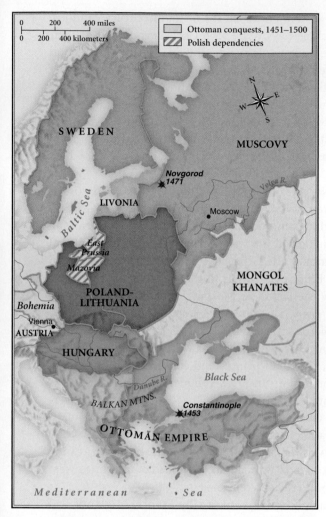

The following labels appear on the map:

- Ottoman conquests, 1451–1500
- Polish dependencies
- 0   200   400 miles
- 0   200   400 kilometers
- SWEDEN
- MUSCOVY
- Novgorod 1471
- Volga R.
- Baltic Sea
- LIVONIA
- Moscow
- East Prussia
- Mazovia
- MONGOL KHANATES
- POLAND-LITHUANIA
- Bohemia
- Vienna
- AUSTRIA
- HUNGARY
- Danube R.
- Black Sea
- BALKAN MTNS.
- Constantinople 1453
- OTTOMAN EMPIRE
- Mediterranean   Sea

■ **MAP 11.4 Eastern Europe in the Fifteenth Century**

The rise of Muscovy and the Ottomans shaped the map of eastern Europe. Some Christian monarchies, such as Serbia, lost their independence. Others, such as Hungary, held off the Ottomans until the early sixteenth century.

won recognition in most of Poland's regions. A problem that persisted throughout his reign, however, was conflict with the neighboring princes of Lithuania, Europe's last pagan rulers, who for centuries had fiercely resisted the Christianization demanded by the German crusading order, the Teutonic Knights. After the Mongols conquered Russia, Lithuania extended its rule southward, offering western Russian princes protection against Mongol and Muscovite rule. By the late fourteenth century, a vast Lithuanian principality had arisen, embracing modern Lithuania, Belarus, and Ukraine.

Casimir III died in 1370 without a son; the failure of a new dynasty to take hold opened the way for the unification of Poland and Lithuania. In 1386, the Lithuanian prince Jogaila (Jagiellon) accepted Roman Catholicism, married the young queen of Poland, and assumed the Polish crown as Wladyslaw II. Under the Jagiellonian dynasty, Poland and Lithuania kept separate legal systems. Catholicism and Polish culture prevailed among the principality's upper class, while most native Lithuanian village folk remained pagan for several centuries. With only a few interruptions, the Polish-Lithuanian federation would last for five centuries.

North of the Black Sea and east of Poland-Lithuania, a different polity was taking shape. In the second half of the fifteenth century, the princes of Muscovy embarked on a spectacular path of success that would make their state the largest on earth. Subservient to the Mongols in the fourteenth century, the Muscovite princes began to assert their independence with the collapse of Mongol power. Ivan III (r. 1462–1505) was the first Muscovite prince to claim an imperial title, referring to himself as **tsar** (or "czar," from the name *Caesar*). Expanding his power to Novgorod in 1471, Ivan then moved to the south and east, pushing back the Mongols to the Volga River. Unlike monarchies in western and central-eastern Europe, whose powers were bound by collective rights and laws, Ivan's Russian monarchy claimed absolute property rights over all lands and subjects.

The expansionist Muscovite state was shaped by two traditions: religion and service. After the fall of the Byzantine Empire, the tsar was the Russian Orthodox church's only defender of the faith against Islam and Catholicism. Orthodox propaganda thus legitimized the tsar's rule by proclaiming Moscow the "Third Rome" (the first two being Rome and Constantinople) and praising the tsar's autocratic power as essential to protect the faith. The Mongol system of service to rulers also deeply informed Muscovite statecraft. Ivan III and his descendants considered themselves heirs to the empire of the Mongols. In their conception of the state as private dominion, their emphasis on autocratic power, and their division of the populace into a landholding elite in service to the tsar and a vast majority of taxpaying subjects, the Muscovite princes created a state more in the despotic political tradition of the central Asian steppes and the Ottoman Empire than of western Europe.

Hard Times

The wars of the fourteenth and fifteenth centuries brought hard times to many members of the commercial classes. During the Hundred Years' War, the English king Edward III borrowed heavily from the largest Italian banking houses, the Bardi and Peruzzi of Florence. With many of their assets tied up in loans to the English monarchy, the Italian bankers had no choice but to extend new credits, hoping vainly to recover their initial investments. In the early 1340s, however, Edward defaulted, and the once-illustrious houses went bankrupt. Meanwhile, diminished production and trade eventually caused turmoil in northern Europe and a crisis for financiers in the Low Countries. Bruges, the financial center for northwestern Europe, saw its power fade during the fifteenth century when a succession of its money changers went bankrupt.

This breakdown in the most advanced economic sector reflected the general recession in the European economy. Merchants were less likely to take risks and more willing to invest their money in government bonds than in production and commerce. Fewer merchants traveled to Asia, partly because of the danger of attack by Ottoman Turks on the overland routes that had once been protected by the Mongols. Italians, while still exporting luxuries north and obtaining raw materials and silver in return, now tended to invest in the arts rather than in trade and industry. The Medici, who dominated Florence in the fifteenth century, are good examples. They stayed close to home, investing part of their banking profits in art and politics and relying on business agents to conduct their affairs in other European cities.

At the lower end of the economic ladder, this war-torn society rested on a broad base of underclass—poor peasants and laborers in the countryside, workers and servants in the cities. Lower still were the marginal elements of society. Organized gangs prowled the larger cities, their members mostly artisans vacillating between work and crime. Paris, for example, teemed with thieves, thugs, beggars, prostitutes, and vagabonds. Some disguised themselves as clerics to escape the law, and others were bona fide clerics who turned to crime to make ends meet during an age of steadily declining clerical income.

Often the underclass served as soldiers as well. War was no longer mainly for knights; it absorbed young men from poor backgrounds. Initiated into a life of plunder and killing, soldiers adjusted poorly to civilian life after discharge; between wars, these men turned to crime, adding to the misery.

Women featured prominently in the underclass, reflecting the unequal distribution of power between the sexes. Urban domestic service was the major employment for girls from the countryside, who worked to save money for their dowries. In addition to the usual household chores, women also worked as wet nurses (women hired to nurse other people's children). Some women, unable to find other means of support, became prostitutes. In Mediterranean Europe, some 90 percent of slaves were women in domestic servitude. They came from Muslim or Greek Orthodox countries and usually served in upper-class households in the great commercial city republics of Venice, Florence, and Ragusa. Their actual numbers were small—several hundred in fourteenth-century Florence, for example—because only rich households could afford slaves.

The Crisis of the Papacy

In the early years of the fourteenth century, the papacy moved from Rome to Avignon, just outside the borders of France. It had a markedly French character: all five popes elected between 1305 and 1378 were natives of southern France. Subjected to pressure from the French monarchy and turning increasingly secular in its opulence and splendor, the papacy was lambasted by the Italian poet Francesco Petrarch as being "in Babylonian Captivity," like the Jews of ancient Israel who were exiled by their Babylonian conquerors.

The popes did not see themselves as captives. Lawyers by training, they concentrated on consolidating the financial and legal powers of the church, mainly through appointments and taxes. Claiming the right to assign all benefices (the properties or income that supported clerical positions), the popes gradually secured authority over the clergy throughout western and central Europe. Under the skillful guidance of John XXII (r. 1316–1334), papal rights increased incrementally without causing much protest. By 1350, the popes had secured the right to grant all major benefices and many minor ones. To gain these lucrative positions, potential candidates often made gifts to the papal court. The imposition of papal taxes on all benefice holders originated in taxes to finance the crusades. Out of these precedents, the papacy instituted a regular system of papal taxation that produced the money it needed to consolidate papal government.

That government—the curia—consisted of the pope's personal household, the College of Cardinals, and the church's financial and judicial apparatuses. Combining elements of monarchy and oligarchy, the curia developed a bureaucracy that paralleled the organization of secular government. The pope's relatives often played a major role in his household; many popes came from extended noble lineages, and they often gave their family members preferential treatment.

After the pope, the cardinals as a collective body were the most elevated entity in the church. Like great nobles in royal courts, the cardinals, many of them nobles themselves, advised and aided the pope. They maintained their own households, employing scores of scribes, servants, and retainers. The papal army also expanded at the same time, as the popes sought to restore and control the Papal States in the region around Rome.

This growing papal monarchy was sharply criticized by some members of the Franciscan and Dominican orders, who denounced the papal pretension to worldly power and wealth. The scholastic William of Ockham, for example, believed that church power derived from the congregation of the faithful, both laity and clergy, not from the pope or church councils. Imprisoned by Pope John XXII for heresy, Ockham escaped in 1328 and found refuge with Emperor Louis of Bavaria.

Another antipapal refugee at the imperial court was Marsilius of Padua, a citizen of an Italian commune, a physician and lawyer by training, and rector of the University of Paris. Marsilius attacked the very basis of papal power in *The Defender of the Peace* (1324). The true church, Marsilius argued, was constituted by the people, who had the right to select the head of the church, either through the body of the faithful or through a "human legislator." Papal power, Marsilius asserted, was the result of historical usurpation, and its exercise represented tyranny. In 1327, John XXII, the living target of the treatise, decreed the work heretical.

Greater stability in Italy emboldened Gregory XI, elected pope in 1371, to return to Rome. When he died in 1378, sixteen cardinals—one Spanish, four Italian, and eleven French—met in Rome to elect the new pope. Although many in the curia were homesick for Avignon, the Roman people, determined to keep the papacy and its revenues in Rome, clamored for the election of a Roman. An unruly crowd rioted outside the conclave, drowning out the cardinals' discussions. Fearing for their lives, the cardinals elected the archbishop of Bari, an Italian, who took the title Urban VI. If the cardinals thought they had elected a weak man who

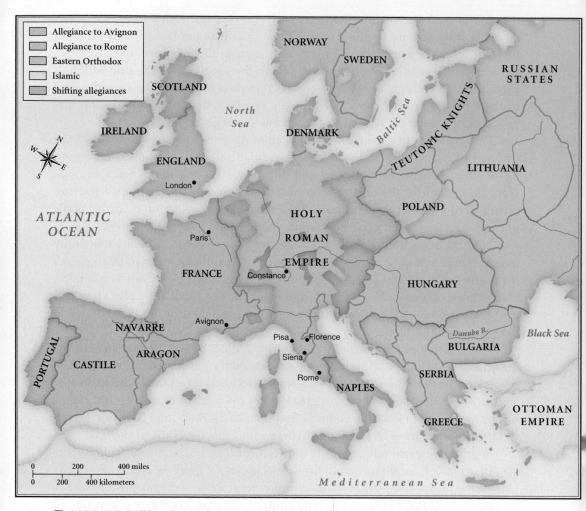

■ **MAP 11.5 The Great Schism, 1378–1417**
Allegiance to Roman and Avignon popes followed the political divisions among the European monarchs. The Great Schism weakened the Latin West during a period of Islamic expansion through the Ottoman Empire.

would do their bidding and satisfy the Romans, they were wrong: Urban immediately tried to curb the cardinals' power. In response, thirteen cardinals elected another pope, Clement VII, and returned to Avignon.

Thus began the **Great Schism** of the papacy, which was perpetuated by political divisions in Europe (Map 11.5). Charles V of France, who did not want the papacy to return to Rome, immediately recognized Clement, his cousin, as did several other rulers, including those of Sicily, Scotland, and Castile. An enemy of

Charles V, Richard II of England professed allegiance to Urban, as did the rulers of other areas, including most of the Holy Roman Empire, central and northern Italy, and Hungary and Poland. Faithful Christians were equally divided in their loyalties. Even the greatest mystic of the age—Catherine of Siena (1347–1380), who told of her mystical unions with God and spiritual ecstasies in more than 350 letters and was later canonized a saint—found herself forced to take sides. Catherine supported Urban. But another holy man, Vincent Ferrer (1350–1419), a popular Dominican preacher, supported Clement. All Christians theoretically found themselves deprived of the means of salvation, as bans from Rome and Avignon each placed part of Christian Europe under interdict, which deprived them of most sacraments and Christian burial.

Because neither pope would step down willingly, the leading intellectuals in the church tried to end the schism another way. Many of them became "conciliarists." According to canon law, only a pope could summon a general council of the church—a sort of parliament of all Christians. But given the state of confusion in Christendom, many intellectuals argued that the crisis justified calling a general council to represent the body of the faithful, over and against the head of the church. Jean Gerson, chancellor of the University of Paris, asserted that "the pope can be removed by a general council celebrated without his consent and against his will."

In 1409 the Council of Pisa asserted its supremacy and declared both popes deposed. It then elected a new pontiff, Alexander V. When the popes at Rome and Avignon refused to yield to the authority of the council, Christian Europe found itself in the embarrassing position of having three popes. Pressure to hold another council then came from central Europe, where a new heretical movement, ultimately known as Hussitism, undermined orthodoxy from Bohemia to central Germany. Threatened politically by challenges to church authority, Emperor Sigismund pressed Pope John XXIII, the successor to Alexander (who had died ten months after being elected), to convene a church council at Constance in 1414.

The cardinals, bishops, and theologians assembled in Constance felt compelled to combat heresy, heal the schism, and reform the church. They ordered Jan Hus, the Prague professor and inspiration behind the Hussite movement, burned at the stake despite an imperial safe conduct he had been promised, but this act failed to suppress dissent. They deposed John XXIII, the "Pisan pope," because of tyrannical behavior, condemning him as an antipope. The Roman pope, Gregory XII, accepted the council's authority and resigned in 1415 (having been elected in 1406). At its closing in 1417, the council also deposed Benedict XIII (Clement's successor), the "Spanish mule," who refused to abdicate the Avignon papacy and lived out his life in a fortress in Spain, still regarding himself as pope and surrounded by his own curia. The rest of Christendom, however, hailed Martin V, the council's appointment, as the new pope, thus ending the Great Schism. The council had taken a stand against heresy and had achieved unity under one pope. But the papacy's prestige had suffered a lasting blow.

▪ The Burning of Jews

While knights and noblewomen watch, an executioner carries more firewood to the pyre of Jews,
an example of the horrible persecutions against Jewish communities during the plague years from
1348 to 1350. This religious violence, arising out of the confrontation between Christianity and
Judaism, had the opposite effect to that intended by Christians. Instead of converting, most Jews
honored their martyrs and felt less incentive to accept the faith of their oppressors.
(Copyright, Bibliothèque royale de Belgique, Brussels.)

Stamping Out Dissenters, Heretics, Jews, and Muslims

The Council's burning of Hus was part of a wider movement. Everywhere church
and state moved to stamp out groups that, in their view, did not fit within the
established church. The church condemned the Free Spirits, for example. These
groups, found mostly in northern Europe, practiced an extreme form of mysticism, asserting that humans and God were of the same essence and that individual believers could attain salvation, even sanctity, without the church and its
sacraments. In the 1360s, Emperor Charles IV and Pope Urban V extended the
Inquisition to Germany in a move to crush this heresy. In the cities of the Rhineland,
fifteen mass trials took place, most around the turn of the fifteenth century.

   In England, intellectual dissent, social unrest, and nationalist sentiment combined to create a powerful movement that the church hierarchy labeled Lollardy
(from *lollar*, meaning "idler"). It was inspired by John Wycliffe (c. 1330–1384), an
Oxford professor who challenged the very foundations of the Roman church. His
treatise *On the Church*, composed in 1378, advanced the view that the true church

was a community of believers rather than a clerical hierarchy. In other writings, Wycliffe repudiated monasticism, excommunication, the Mass, and the priesthood, substituting reliance on Bible reading and individual conscience in place of the official church as the path to salvation. Responsibility for church reform, Wycliffe believed, rested with the king, whose authority (in his view) exceeded that of the pope. Despite persistent persecutions, Lollardy survived underground during the fifteenth century, to resurface during the convulsive religious conflict of the early sixteenth century known as the Reformation.

The most profound challenge to papal authority in the later Middle Ages came from Bohemia. Here the spiritual, intellectual, political, and economic criticisms of the papacy that sprang up in other countries fused in one explosive spark. Religious dissent quickly became the vehicle for a nationalist uprising and a social revolution: the Hussite movement.

Under Emperor Charles IV, the pace of economic development and social change in the Holy Roman Empire had quickened in the mid-fourteenth century. Prague, the capital of Bohemia, became one of Europe's great cities: the new silver mine at Kutnà Hora boosted Prague's economic growth, and the first university in the empire was founded there in 1348. Bohemia, a part of the Holy Roman Empire, had been settled by a Slavic people, the Czechs, since the early Middle Ages. Later, many German merchants and artisans migrated to Bohemian cities, and Czech peasants, uprooted from the land, flocked to the cities in search of employment. This diverse society became a potentially explosive mass when heightened expectations of commercial and intellectual growth collided with the grim realities of the plague and economic problems in the late fourteenth century. Tax protests, urban riots, and ethnic conflicts signaled growing unrest, but it was religious discontent that became the focus for popular revolt.

Critics of the clergy, often clergy themselves, decried the moral conduct of priests and bishops, accusing them of holding multiple benefices, leading dissolute lives, and ignoring their pastoral duties. How could the clergy, living in a state of mortal sin, legitimately perform the sacraments? critics asked. Advocating greater lay participation in the Mass and in the reading of Scripture, religious dissenters drew some of their ideas from the writings of Wycliffe. Among those influenced by Wycliffe's ideas were Jan Hus (d. 1415) and his follower Jerome of Prague (d. 1416), both Prague professors, ethnic Czechs, and leaders of a reform party in Bohemia. Although the reform party attracted adherents from all Czech-speaking social groups, the German minority, who dominated the university and urban elites in Prague, opposed it out of ethnic rivalry. The Bohemian nobility protected Hus; the common clergy rebelled against the bishops; and the artisans and workers in Prague were ready to back the reform party by force. These disparate social interests all focused on one symbolic but passionately felt religious demand: the right to receive the Eucharist as both bread and wine at Mass. In traditional Roman liturgy, the chalice was reserved for the clergy; the Utraquists, as their opponents called them (from *utraque*, Latin for "both"), wanted to drink wine from the chalice as well, to achieve a measure of equality between laity and clergy.

When Hus was burned at the stake by the Council of Constance in 1415, his death caused a national uproar. The reform movement, which had thus far focused only on religious issues, burst forth as a national revolution. Sigismund's initial repression of the revolt in the provinces was brutal, and many dissenters were massacred. To organize their defense, the Hussites gathered at a mountain in southern Bohemia, which they called Mount Tabor after the mountain in the New Testament where the transfiguration of Christ took place. Now called Taborites, they began to restructure their community according to biblical injunctions. Like the first Christian church, they initially practiced communal ownership of goods and thought of themselves as the only true Christians awaiting the return of Christ and the end of the world. As their influence spread, the Taborites compromised with the surrounding social order, collecting tithes from peasants and retaining magistrates in towns under their control. Taborite leaders were radical priests who ministered to the community in the Czech language, exercised moral and judicial leadership, and even led the people into battle. Resisting all attempts to crush them, the Czech revolutionaries eventually gained the right from the papacy to receive the Eucharist as both bread and wine, a practice that continued until the sixteenth century.

A still different group of heretics grew out of the anguish of the Black Death. Believing that the plague was God's way of chastising a sinful world, bands of men and women sought to save themselves by repenting their sins in a dramatic manner: wearing tattered clothes, they visited local churches and sang hymns while publicly whipping themselves until blood flowed. The **flagellants**, as they soon came to be called, cried out to God for mercy and called upon the congregation to repent their sins. But the clergy distrusted this lay movement that did not originate within the church hierarchy.

In some communities, the religious fervor aroused by the flagellants spawned violence against Jews. From 1348 to 1350, anti-Semitic persecutions, beginning in southern France and spreading through Savoy to the Holy Roman Empire, destroyed many Jewish communities in central and western Europe. Sometimes the clergy incited the attacks against the Jews, calling them Christ-killers, accusing them of poisoning wells and kidnapping and ritually slaughtering Christian children. In towns throughout Europe, economic resentment fueled anti-Semitism as those in debt turned on creditors, often Jews who had become rich from the commercial expansion of the thirteenth century.

Many anti-Semitic incidents were spontaneous, with mobs plundering Jewish quarters and killing anyone who refused baptism. But it is equally true that at times civic authorities orchestrated the violence. For example, the magistrates of Nuremberg obtained approval from Emperor Charles IV before organizing the 1349 persecution directed by the city government. Thousands of German Jews were slaughtered. Many fled to Poland, where the incidence of plague was low and where the authorities welcomed Jews as productive taxpayers. In western and central Europe, however, the persecutions destroyed the financial power of the Jews.

End of the Reconquista and Expulsion of the Jews from Spain, 1492

Like France and England, war wracked Spain as dynasties fought over the royal succession in the various kingdoms. But again, as in France and England, the result was a strengthened monarchy. In 1469, Queen Isabella of Castile and King Ferdinand of Aragon married. Retaining their separate titles, the two monarchs ruled jointly over their dominions, each of which adhered to its traditional laws and privileges. Their union represented the first step toward the creation of a unified Spain out of two medieval kingdoms. Isabella and Ferdinand limited the privileges of the nobility and allied themselves with the cities, relying on urban militias to enforce justice and on professional lawyers to staff the royal council.

Unification of Spain, Late Fifteenth Century

The reconquista, the slow "reconquest" of Muslim Spain by the Christian north, came to a close under the united strength of Castile and Aragon. In 1478 war broke out between Granada, the last Iberian Muslim state, and Catholic royal forces. Weakened by internal strife, Granada finally fell in 1492. Two years later, in recognition of that crusade, Pope Alexander VI bestowed the title "Catholic monarchs" on Isabella and Ferdinand.

In this climate, it no longer seemed possible for Iberian Muslims, Jews, and Christians to live side by side. The practice of Catholicism became a test of one's loyalty to the church and to the Spanish monarchy. In 1478, the king and queen introduced the Inquisition into Spain, primarily as a means to control the *conversos* (Jewish converts to Christianity), whose elevated positions in the economy and the government aroused widespread resentment from the so-called Old Christians. Conversos often were suspected of practicing Judaism, their ancestral religion, in secret while pretending to adhere to their new Christian faith. Appointed by the monarchs, the inquisitors presided over tribunals set up to investigate those suspected of religious deviancy. The accused, who were arrested on charges often based on anonymous denunciations and information gathered by the inquisitors, could defend themselves but not confront their accusers. The wide spectrum of punishments ranged from monetary fines to the **auto da fé** (a ritual of public confession) to burning at the stake. After the fall of Granada, many Muslims were forced to convert or resettle. At the same time, Ferdinand and

Isabella ordered all Jews in their kingdoms to choose between exile and conversion. Many chose exile.

The expulsion of the Jews from Spain had far greater consequences than their earlier banishments from France and England. Spain had had the largest and most vibrant Jewish communities of Europe. On the eve of the expulsion, approximately 200,000 Jews and 300,000 conversos were living in Castile and Aragon. Faced with the choice to convert or leave, well over 100,000 Jews dispersed, some settling in North Africa, more in Italy, and many in the Ottoman Empire, Greek-speaking Thessalonika, and Palestine. Conversant in two or three languages, these Jews often served as intermediaries between the Christian West and Muslim East.

■ **REVIEW:** *What central factors contributed to the crises of the fourteenth and mid-fifteenth centuries?*

New Forms of Thought and Expression: The Renaissance

The Renaissance had its medieval roots in vernacular literature like Dante's *Divine Comedy* and the humanism of the Gothic sculptors who portrayed figures in the round. But it grew far beyond those roots, to discover and embrace the classical past and to use classical themes to celebrate human glory. Fostered by the printing press, Renaissance writings spread far and wide to a literate middle class eager to absorb every sort of text. Meanwhile, Renaissance artists celebrated the newly powerful republics, principalities, and kingdoms of their age. Flush with power, these states intruded into the most intimate personal matters, such as sexuality, marriage, and childbirth.

Renaissance Humanism

From the epics and romances of the twelfth and thirteenth centuries, vernacular writings blossomed into a full-blown literature in the fourteenth. Poetry, stories, and chronicles composed in Italian, French, English, and other national languages helped redefine style and beauty. The great writers of late medieval Europe were of urban middle-class origins, from families that had done well in government, church service, or commercial enterprises. Unlike the medieval troubadours, with their aristocratic backgrounds, the men and women who wrote vernacular literature in this age typically came from the cities, and their audience was the literate laity. Francesco Petrarch (1304–1374), the poet laureate of Italy's vernacular literature, and his younger contemporary and friend Giovanni Boccaccio (1313–1375) were both from the Florentine professional classes. Geoffrey Chaucer (c. 1342–1400), an important vernacular poet of medieval England, came from a family of wine

■ Poet and Queen

Christine de Pisan, kneeling, presents a manuscript of her poems to Isabella of Bavaria, the queen of France. Isabella's royal status is indicated by the royal French emblem, the fleur-de-lis, which decorates the bedroom walls. The sumptuous interior (chairs, cushions, tapestry, paneled ceiling, glazed and shuttered windows) was typical of aristocratic domestic architecture. Even in the intimacy of her bedroom, Queen Isabella, like all royal personages, was constantly attended and almost never alone (notice her ladies-in-waiting).
(The British Library.)

merchants. Even writers who celebrated the life of the nobility were children of commoners. Though born in Valenciennes to a family of moneylenders and merchants, Jean Froissart (c. 1333–c. 1405), whose chronicle vividly describes the events of the Hundred Years' War, was an ardent admirer of chivalry. Christine de Pisan (1364–c. 1430), a poet and prose writer of great range, was the daughter of a Venetian municipal counselor who spent most of her life in France. Widowed early in life, she made a living and supported her children by writing books.

Life in all its facets found expression in the new vernacular literature, as writers told of love, greed, and salvation. Boccaccio's *Decameron* popularized the short story, as the characters in this novella tell sensual and bizarre tales in the shadow of the Black Death. Members of different social orders parade themselves in Chaucer's *Canterbury Tales*, journeying together on a pilgrimage. Christine de Pisan celebrated womanhood—and refuted misogynists (women-haters)—in *The Book of the City of Ladies* (1405); she populated her city with all the heroines of the past, present, and future. At the end of her book she turned to her readers, inviting them into the city:

> *My most honored ladies, may God be praised, for now our City is entirely finished and completed, where all of you who love glory, virtue, and praise may be lodged in great honor . . . for it has been built and established for every honorable lady.*

Noble patronage was crucial to the growth of vernacular literature. Christine often found wealthy female patrons within the royal French household. Even

Petrarch, perhaps closest to the model of an independent man of letters, relied on powerful patrons at various times. His early career began at the papal court in Avignon, where his father worked as a notary; during the 1350s, Petrarch enjoyed the protection and patronage of the Visconti duke of Milan. Boccaccio started out in the Neapolitan world of commerce. The court of King Robert of Naples initiated him into the realm of letters. Chaucer served in administrative posts and on many diplomatic missions. Noble patronage also shaped the literary creations of Froissart.

Vernacular literature blossomed not at the expense of Latin but alongside a classical revival. Despite the renown of their Italian writings, Petrarch and Boccaccio, for example, took great pride in their Latin works. In the second half of the fourteenth century, writers began to imitate the antiquated "classical" Latin of Roman literature. In the forefront of this literary and intellectual movement, Petrarch traveled to many monasteries in search of long-ignored Latin manuscripts. Writers like Petrarch considered medieval church Latin an artificial, awkward language, whereas classical Latin and classical Greek they believed the mother tongues of the ancients, even more authentic, vivid, and glorious than the poetry and prose written in Italian and other contemporary European languages. Classical allusions and literary influences abound in the works of Boccaccio, Chaucer, Christine de Pisan, and others. The new intellectual fascination with the ancient past also stimulated translations of classical works into the vernacular.

The attempt to emulate the virtues and learning of the ancients gave impetus to an intellectual movement: **humanism**. Humanists believed that a person could develop his or her full human potential only by studying the "humanities"—the liberal arts, and in particular literature and its subgenre history. They absorbed the eloquence of a Cicero with gusto, finding in it a source of virtue as well as style. "For what," the humanist Poggio Bracciolini asked his friend Guarino of Verona,

is there that could be more delightful, more pleasant, and more agreeable to you and the rest of the learned world than the knowledge of those things whose acquaintance makes us more learned and, what seems even more important, stylistically more polished? . . . For it is speech alone which we use to express the power of our mind and which separates us from the other beings.

Gradually the imitation of ancient style led to the adoption of ancient ideas. In the writings of Roman historians such as Livy and Tacitus, fifteenth-century Italian civic elites (many of them lawyers) found echoes of their own devout patriotism. Between 1400 and 1430 in Florence, a time of war and crisis, the study of the humanities evolved into a republican ideology that historians call "civic humanism." In the early fifteenth century, the Florentines waged a highly successful propaganda war on behalf of virtuous republican Florence against tyrannical

Milan, invoking the memory of the overthrow of Etruscan tyrants by the first Romans. Thus, the study of ancient civilization was not only an antiquarian quest but also a call to public service and political action.

The fall of Constantinople in 1453 sent Greek scholars to Italy for refuge, giving extra impetus to the revival of Greek learning in the West. Venice and Florence assumed leadership in this new field—the former by virtue of its commercial and political ties to the eastern Mediterranean, the latter thanks to the patronage of Cosimo de' Medici, who sponsored the Platonic Academy, a discussion group dedicated to the study of Plato and his followers under the intellectual leadership of Marsilio Ficino (1433–1499).

Humanists did not consider the study of ancient cultures to be in conflict with their Christian faith. In "returning to the sources"—a famous slogan of the time— philosophers attempted to harmonize the disciplines of Christian faith and ancient learning. Ficino, the foremost Platonic scholar of the Renaissance, was also a priest. He argued that the immortality of the soul, a Platonic idea, was perfectly compatible with Christian doctrine and that much of ancient wisdom actually foreshadowed later Christian teachings.

Through their activities as educators and civil servants, professional humanists gave new vigor to the humanist curriculum of grammar, rhetoric, poetry, history, and moral philosophy. By the end of the fifteenth century, European intellectuals considered a good command of classical Latin, with perhaps some knowledge of Greek, as one of the requirements of an educated person.

The invention of mechanical printing aided greatly in making the classical texts widely available. Printing from movable type—a revolutionary departure from the old practice of copying by hand—was invented in the 1440s by Johannes Gutenberg, a German goldsmith. Mass production of identical books and pamphlets made the world of letters more accessible to a literate audience.

The advent of mass-printed books depended on paper production. The art of papermaking came to Europe from China via Arab intermediaries. By the fourteenth century, paper mills were operating in Italy, producing paper that was more fragile but much cheaper than parchment or vellum, the animal skins that Europeans had previously used for writing. To produce paper, old rags were soaked in a chemical solution, beaten by mallets into a pulp, washed with water, treated, and dried in sheets—a method that still produces good-quality paper today.

Even before the printing press, a brisk industry in manuscript books had been flourishing in Europe's university towns and major cities. Production was in the hands of stationers, who organized workshops known as *scriptoria*, where the manuscripts were copied, and acted as retail booksellers. Demand was high. The stationer for Cosimo de' Medici, for example, employed forty-five copyists to complete two hundred volumes in twenty-two months.

Nonetheless, bookmaking in scriptoria was slow and expensive, and the invention of movable type was an enormous technological breakthrough. It took bookmaking out of the hands of human copyists. Movable type consisted of reusable metal molds of letters, numbers, and various other characters. The typesetter arranged the characters by hand, page by page, to create a printable text. The surface of the type was inked, and sheets of paper pressed against the type picked up an impression of the text. Numerous copies could be made with only a small amount of human labor.

After the 1440s, printing spread rapidly from Germany to other European countries. In Germany, Cologne, Strasbourg, Nuremberg, and Augsburg all had major presses. In 1467, two German printers established the first press in Rome and produced twelve thousand volumes in five years, a feat that in the past would have required a thousand scribes working full-time. By 1480, many Italian cities had established their own presses. In the 1490s, the German city of Frankfurt-am-Main became an international meeting place for printers and booksellers. The Frankfurt Book Fair, where printers from different nations exhibited their newest titles, represented a major international cultural event and remains an unbroken tradition to this day.

The invention of mechanical printing gave rise to a "communications revolution" as significant as the widespread use of the personal computer today. The multiplication of standardized texts altered the thinking habits of Europeans by freeing individuals from having to memorize everything they learned; it made possible the relatively speedy and inexpensive dissemination of knowledge; and it created a wider community of scholars, no longer dependent on personal patronage or church sponsorship for texts. Printing facilitated the free expression and exchange of ideas, and its disruptive potential did not go unnoticed by political and ecclesiastical authorities. Emperors and bishops in Germany, the homeland of the printing industry, moved quickly to issue censorship regulations.

New Perspectives in Art and Music

New techniques in painting, architecture, and musical performance fostered original styles and subjects. Artists paid close attention to the human figure and strove to depict the world from nature rather than from pictorial models. Musicians enhanced polyphony with new harmonies and more versatile instruments.

As individual talent and genius were recognized by a society hungry for culture, artists themselves gained prestige. In exalting the status of the artist, Leonardo da Vinci (1452–1519), painter, architect, and inventor, described himself as a creative genius. He was not alone; Renaissance artists intended to convince society that their works were unique and their talents priceless. They exalted the artist above the "mere artisan," claiming to be independent of the blueprints of a patron. During the fifteenth century, as artists began to claim the respect and recognition of society, however, the reality was that most relied on wealthy patrons for support. And although they wished to create as their genius dictated, not all patrons of the arts allowed artists to work without restrictions. While the duke of Milan appreciated Leonardo's genius, the duke of Ferrara paid for his art by the square foot.

A successful artist who did fit the new vision of unfettered genius was the Florentine sculptor Donatello (1386–1466). Not only did Donatello's sculptures evoke classical Greek and Roman models, but the grace and movement of his work inspired Cosimo de' Medici, the ruler of Florence, to excavate antique works of art and put them on display. Donatello was one artist who enjoyed the long-term, high-status patronage of a prince. Others, like Andrea Mantegna (1431–1506), worked more precariously. Treated more as a skilled worker in service to the prince than as an independent artist, he was once even required to adorn his majestic Gonzaga tapestries with life sketches of farm animals.

The workshop—the normal place of production in Renaissance Italy and in northern European cities such as Nuremberg and Antwerp—afforded the artist greater autonomy. As heads of workshops, artists trained apprentices and negotiated contracts with clients. The most famous artists fetched good prices for their work. These artists developed followings, and wealthy consumers were willing to pay a premium for work done by a master instead of apprentices. Studies of art contracts show that in the course of the fifteenth century artists gained greater control over their work. Early in the century, clients routinely stipulated detailed conditions for works of art—specifying, for instance, gold paint or "ultramarine blue," which were among the most expensive pigments. Clients might also determine the arrangement of figures in a picture, leaving to the artist little more than the execution. After midcentury, such specific directions became less common. In 1487, for example, the Florentine painter Filippo Lippi (1457–1504), in his contract to paint frescoes in the Strozzi chapel, specified that the work should be "all from his own hand and particularly the figures." The shift underscores the increasing recognition of the unique skills of individual artists.

A market system for the visual arts emerged during the Renaissance, initially in the Low Countries. In the fifteenth century, most large-scale work was commissioned by specific patrons, but the art market, for which artists produced works without prior arrangement for sale, was to develop into the major force for artistic creativity, a force that prevails in contemporary society. The commercialization of art celebrated the new context of artistic creation itself: artists working in an open, competitive, urban civilization.

If the individual artist was a man of genius, what greater subject for the expression of beauty was there than the human body itself? Taking their cue from fourteenth-century painters such as Giotto (see page 421), Renaissance artists learned to depict ever more expressive human emotions and movements. The work of the short-lived but brilliant painter Masaccio (1401–1428) exemplifies this development. His painting *St. Peter Baptizing* shows the recipient of the baptism trembling in the cold water. In addition to rendering homage to classical and

■ **Masaccio's St. Peter Baptizing**
*This detail from a cycle of frescoes
about the life of St. Peter painted by
Masaccio in the church of Santa Maria
del Carmine in Florence shows the
artist's interest in the nude body. The
man receiving baptism is portrayed in
the round, light playing on his flesh and
revealing its contours. This emphasis on
human nakedness may have reflected
an egalitarian strain in republican
Florence. It also echoes what Masaccio
found in ancient art and sculpture.*
(Erich Lessing/Art Resource, NY.)

biblical figures, Renaissance artists painted their contemporaries as well. For the first time after classical antiquity, sculptors again cast the human body in bronze, in life-size or bigger freestanding statues. Free from fabric and armor, the human body was idealized in the eighteen-foot marble sculpture *David*, the work of the great Michelangelo Buonarroti (1475–1564).

The increasing number of portraits in Renaissance painting illustrates the new, elevated view of human existence. Portraiture initially was limited to representations of pontiffs, monarchs, princes, and patricians, but soon portraits of middle-class people became more widespread. Painters from the Low Countries such as Rogier van der Weyden (c. 1400–1464) distinguished themselves in this genre; their portraits achieved a sense of detail and reality unsurpassed until the advent of photography.

All of this art was distinguished from its predecessors by its depiction of the world as the eye perceives it. The use of *visual perspective*—an illusory three-dimensional space on a two-dimensional surface and the ordered arrangement of painted objects from one viewpoint—became one of the distinctive features of Western art. Underlying the idea of perspective was a new Renaissance worldview: humans asserting themselves over nature in painting and design by controlling space. Optics became the organizing principle of the natural world in that it detected the "objective" order in nature. The Italian painters were keenly aware of their new technique, and they criticized the Byzantine and the northern Gothic stylists for "flat" depictions of the human body and the natural world. The highest accolade for a Renaissance artist was to be described as an "imitator of nature": this epithet meant that the artist's teacher was nature, not design books or master painters. For the frescoes of the bridal chamber of the Gonzaga palace (executed 1465–1474), Mantegna created an illusory extension of reality: the actual living space in the chamber "opened out" to the painted landscape on the walls.

Perhaps even more than visual artists, fifteenth-century architects fulfilled the Renaissance ideals of uniting artistic creativity and scientific knowledge. The Florentine architect Leon Battista Alberti (1404–1472) made such ideas explicit in *On Architecture* (1415). Alberti argued for large-scale urban planning, with monumental buildings set on open squares, harmonious and beautiful in their proportions. His ideas were put into action by Pope Sixtus IV (r. 1471–1484) and his successors in the urban renewal of Rome, and they served to transform the city into a geometrically constructed monument to architectural brilliance by recalling the grandeur of its ancient origins.

Musicians and composers, too, worked for wealthy patrons at court. Developments in polyphony were led by Guillaume Dufay (1400–1474), whose musical training began in the cathedral choir of his hometown, Cambrai, in the Low Countries. His successful career took him to all the cultural centers of the Renaissance, where nobles sponsored new compositions and maintained a corps of

■ **Michelangelo's *David***

Michelangelo realized a synthesis of the ancient nude statue and the biblical figure of David in this larger-than-life sculpture of the young David, his body poised for action against the giant Goliath. The figure's easy slouch recalls depictions of Greek athletes, but this sculpture was commissioned by the administrators of the cathedral at Florence and was placed in front of the Florentine town hall. Both church and state thus garnered prestige from the artist and his work.
(Nimatallah/Art Resource, NY.)

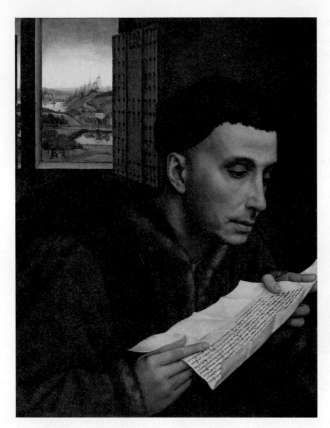

■ **St. Ivo by
Rogier van der Weyden**
*This painting of St. Ivo of
Chartres (c. 1040–1116) by
Rogier van der Weyden
(c. 1400–1464) exemplifies the
Flemish School style of detailed
realistic human portraits shown
against the backdrop of a landscape or city scene. Born in
Tournai, Weyden spent most of
his life as the official city painter
of Brussels. The Flemish School
exerted a significant influence on
painting in France, Portugal, and
Castile in the fifteenth century.*
(© National Gallery Collection; by kind
permission of the Trustees of the
National Gallery/CORBIS.)

musicians for court and religious functions. In 1438, Dufay composed festive music
to celebrate the completion of the cathedral dome in Florence designed by Filippo
Brunelleschi (1377–1446). Dufay expressed the harmonic relationship among four
voices in ratios that matched the mathematically precise dimensions of
Brunelleschi's architecture. After a period of employment at the papal court, Dufay
returned to his native north and composed music for the Burgundian and French
courts.

    Josquin des Prez (1440–1521), another Netherlander, wrote music in Milan,
Ferrara, Florence, Paris, and at the papal court. Music was an integral part of
courtly life: Lorenzo de' Medici sent Dufay a love poem to set to music, and the
great composer maintained a lifelong relationship with the Medici family.
Composers often adapted familiar folk melodies for sacred music, expressing
religious feeling primarily through human voices instead of instruments. The
tambourine and the lute were indispensable for dances, however, and small en-
sembles of wind and string instruments with contrasting sounds performed with

singers in the fashionable courts of Europe. Also in use in the fifteenth century were new keyboard instruments—the harpsichord and clavichord—which could play several harmonic lines at once.

Republics and Principalities in Italy

In his book *The Prince*, the Florentine political theorist Niccolò Machiavelli (1469–1527) argued that the state was an artifice of human creation to be conquered, shaped, and administered by princes according to the principles of power politics. Whether a republic—which preserved the traditional institutions of the medieval commune by allowing a civic elite to control political and economic life—or a principality, ruled by one dynasty, each Italian Renaissance state was as centralized and controlling as the new monarchies of France and England.

Venice and Florence were republics. Venice, built on a lagoon, ruled an extensive colonial empire that extended from the Adriatic to the Aegean Sea. Venetian merchant ships sailed the Mediterranean, the Black Sea, and, increasingly, the Atlantic coast. Whether threatened by competing Italian states or by the Turks, Venice drew strength from its internal social cohesion. Under the rule of an oligarchy of aristocratic merchants, Venice enjoyed stability. Its maritime empire benefited citizens of all social classes, who joined efforts to defend the interests of the "Most Serene Republic," a contemporary name that reflected Venice's lack of social strife.

Compared with serene Venice, the republic of Florence was in constant agitation, as social classes and political factions engaged in ongoing conflict. By 1434, a single family had emerged dominant in this fractious city: the Medici. Cosimo de' Medici (1388–1464), head of the family, "disposed of his rivals, proceeded to administer the state at his pleasure and amassed wealth. . . . In Florence he built a palace fit for a king," as Pope Pius II put it. Head of one of the largest banks of Europe, Cosimo de' Medici used his immense wealth to influence politics. Even though he did not hold any formal political office, he wielded influence in government through business associates and clients indebted to him for loans, political appointments, and other favors. Cosimo became the arbiter of war and peace, the regulator of law, more master than citizen. Yet the prosperity and security that Florence enjoyed made him popular as well. At his death, Cosimo was lauded as "father of his country."

Cosimo's grandson Lorenzo (called "the Magnificent"), who assumed power in 1467, bolstered the regime's legitimacy with his lavish patronage of the arts. But opponents were not lacking. In 1478, Lorenzo narrowly escaped an assassination attempt. Two years after Lorenzo's death in 1494, partisans who opposed the Medici drove them from Florence. The Medici returned to power in 1512, only to be driven out again in 1527. In 1530, the republic fell and the Medici once again seized control, declaring themselves dukes of Florence.

Milan had been a principality long before then. Since the fourteenth century, it had been a military state, relatively uninterested in supporting the arts but with first-class armaments and textile industries in the capital city and rich farmlands in Lombardy. Until 1447, the duchy was ruled by the Visconti dynasty, a group of powerful lords whose plans to unify all of northern and central Italy failed from the combined opposition of Venice, Florence, and other Italian powers. After a brief republican interlude (1447–1450) during which Milan fought against its neighbors, its ruling nobility appointed Francesco Sforza, who had married the illegitimate daughter of the last Visconti duke, to the post of general. Sforza promptly turned against his employers, claiming the duchy as his own. A bitter struggle between the nobility and the townspeople in Milan further undermined the republican cause, and in 1450 Sforza entered Milan in triumph.

The power of the Sforza dynasty reached its height during the 1490s. In 1493, Duke Ludovico married his niece Bianca Maria to Maximilian, the newly elected Holy Roman Emperor, promising an immense dowry in exchange for the emperor's legitimization of his rule. But the newfound Milanese glory was soon swept aside by France's invasion of Italy in 1494, and the duchy itself eventually came under Spanish rule.

In the violent arena of Italian politics, the papacy, an uneasy mixture of worldly splendor and religious authority, was a player like the other states. The popes' concern with politics stemmed from their desire to restore papal authority, greatly undermined by the Great Schism and the conciliar movement. To that end, the popes used both politics and culture. Politically, they curbed local power, expanded papal government, increased taxation, enlarged the papal army and navy, and cultivated diplomacy. Culturally, the popes renovated churches, created the Vatican Library, sponsored artists, and patronized writers to glorify their role and power. In undertaking these measures, the Renaissance papacy merely exemplified the larger trend toward the centralization of power evident everywhere else.

Concentrated power, competition between states, and the extension of warfare all raised the practice of diplomacy to nearly an art form. The first diplomatic handbook, composed in 1436, emphasized ceremonies, elegance, and eloquence. These masked the complex game of diplomatic intrigue and spying. In the fifteenth century, a resident ambassador was expected to keep a continuous stream of foreign political news flowing to the home government, not just to conduct temporary diplomatic missions, as earlier ambassadors had done. In some cases, the presence of semiofficial agents developed into full-fledged ambassadorships: the Venetian embassy to the sultan's court in Constantinople developed out of the merchant-consulate that had represented all Venetian merchants, and Medici Bank branch managers eventually acted as political agents for the Florentine republic.

Foremost in the development of diplomacy was Milan. Under the Visconti dukes, Milan sent ambassadors to Aragon, Burgundy, the Holy Roman Empire, and the Ottoman Empire. Under the Sforza dynasty, Milanese diplomacy continued to function as a cherished form of statecraft. For generations, Milanese diplomats at the French court sent home an incessant flow of information on the rivalry between France and Burgundy. Francesco Sforza, founder of the dynasty, also used his diplomatic corps to extend his political patronage. In letters of recommendation to the papacy, Francesco commented on the political desirability of potential ecclesiastical candidates by using code words, sometimes supplemented with instructions to his ambassador to indicate his true intent regardless of the coded letter of recommendation. Ciphers were used in more sensitive diplomatic reports to hide their real meaning from hostile powers.

The most outstanding achievement of Italy's Renaissance diplomacy was the negotiation of a general peace treaty that settled the decades of warfare engendered by Milanese expansion and civil war. The Treaty of Lodi (1454) established a complex balance of power among the major Italian states and maintained relative stability on the peninsula for half a century. Renaissance diplomacy eventually failed, however, when more powerful northern European neighbors invaded in 1494, bringing on the collapse of the whole Italian state system.

The Intersection of Private and Public Lives

To deal with a mounting fiscal crisis, in 1427 the government of Florence ordered that a comprehensive tax record of households in the city and territory be compiled. Completed in 1430, this survey (called a *catasto*) represented the most detailed population census then taken in European history. From the resulting mass of fiscal and demographic data, historians have been able to reconstruct a picture of Florentine society.

The state of Florence, roughly the size of Massachusetts, had a population of more than 260,000. Tuscany, the area in which the Florentine state was located, was one of the most urbanized regions of Europe. With 38,000 inhabitants, the capital city of Florence claimed 14 percent of the total population and an enormous 67 percent of the state's wealth. Straddling the Arno River, Florence was a beautiful, thriving city with a defined social hierarchy. In describing class divisions, the Florentines themselves referred to the "little people" and the "fat people." Some 60 percent of all households belonged to the "little people"—workers, artisans, small merchants. The "fat people" (roughly our middle class) made up 30 percent of the urban population and included the wealthier merchants, the leading artisans, notaries, doctors, and other professionals. At the very bottom of the hierarchy were slaves and servants, most of them women employed in domestic service. Whereas the small number of slaves were of Balkan origin, the much larger population of domestic servants came to the city from the surrounding countryside as contracted wage earners. At the top, a tiny elite of patricians, bankers, and wool merchants controlled the state with their enormous wealth. In fact, the richest 1 percent of urban households (approximately one hundred families) owned more than one-quarter of the city's wealth and one-sixth of Tuscany's total wealth. The patricians in particular owned almost all government bonds, a lucrative investment guaranteed by a state they dominated.

Surprisingly, men seem to have outnumbered women in the 1427 survey. For every 100 women there were 110 men, unlike most past and present populations, in which women are the majority. In addition to female infanticide, which was occasionally practiced, the survey itself reflected the society's bias against women: persistent underreporting on women probably explained the statistical abnormality; and married daughters, young girls, and elderly widows frequently disappeared from the memories of householders. Most people, men and women alike, lived in households with at least six inhabitants, although the form of family unit—nuclear or extended—varied, depending mainly on wealth. Poor people rarely were able to support extended families. Among the urban rich and landowning peasants, the extended family held sway. The number of children in a family, it seems, reflected class differences as well. Wealthier families had more children; childless couples existed almost exclusively among the poor.

■ **Renaissance "Birth Tray" (c. 1450)**

Scenes from the story of David and Goliath decorate this round tray, which was used to bring sweets to a well-to-do Florentine mother who had just given birth. Such trays were relatively common in fifteenth-century Florence. They were commissioned by husbands, and after their initial presentation, they were hung on a wall in the family's home. This one shows David (in red) flinging a stone at Goliath with his slingshot; cutting off Goliath's head; and, in the center, holding up Goliath's head as a trophy. Such scenes were meant to inspire the young child to be brave, like David.

(Courtesy of The Loyola University Museum of Art, Martin D'Arcy Collection, Chicago.)

Wealth and class clearly determined family structure and the pattern of marriage and childbearing. In a letter to her eldest son, Filippo, dated 1447, Alessandra Strozzi announced the marriage of her daughter Caterina to the son of Parente Parenti. She described the young groom, Marco Parenti, as "a worthy and virtuous young man, and . . . the only son, and rich, 25 years old, and keeps a silk workshop; and they have a little political standing." The dowry was set at one thousand florins, a substantial sum—but for four to five hundred florins more, Alessandra admitted to Filippo, Caterina would have fetched a husband from a more prominent family.

The Strozzi belonged to one of Florence's most distinguished traditional families, but at the time of Caterina's betrothal the family had fallen into political disgrace. Alessandra's husband, an enemy of the Medici, was exiled in 1434; Filippo, a rich merchant in Naples, lived under the same political ban. Although Caterina was clearly marrying beneath her social station, the marriage represented an alliance in which money, political status, and family standing all balanced out. More an alliance between families than the consummation of love, an Italian Renaissance marriage was usually orchestrated by the male head of a household. In this case, Alessandra, as a widow, shared the matchmaking responsibility with her eldest son and other male relatives. Eighteen years later, when it came time to find a wife for Filippo, who had by then accumulated enough wealth to start his own household, Marco Parenti, his brother-in-law, would serve as matchmaker.

The upper-class Florentine family was patrilineal, tracing descent and determining inheritance through the male line. Because the distribution of wealth depended on this patriarchal system, women occupied an ambivalent position in the household. A daughter could claim inheritance only through her dowry, and she often disappeared from family records after her marriage. A wife seldom emerged from the shadow of her husband, and consequently the lives of many women have been lost to history.

Women's subordination in marriages often reflected the age differences between spouses. The Italian marriage pattern, in which young women married older men, contrasted sharply with the northern European model, in which partners were much closer in age. Significant age disparity also left many women widowed in their twenties and thirties, and remarriage often proved a hard choice. A widow's father and brothers frequently pressed her to remarry to form a new family alliance. A widow, however, could not bring her children into her new marriage because they belonged to her first husband's family. Faced with the choice between her children and her paternal family, not to mention the question of her own happiness, a widow could hope to gain greater autonomy only in her old age, when, like Alessandra, she might assume matchmaking responsibilities to advance her family's fortunes.

In northern Europe, however, women enjoyed a relatively more autonomous position. In England, the Low Countries, and Germany, for example, women played a significant role in the economy—not only in the peasant household, in which everyone worked, but especially in the town, serving as peddlers, weavers, seam-stresses, shopkeepers, midwives, and brewers. In Munich, for example, they ranked among some of the richest brewers. Women in northern Europe shared inheritances with their brothers, retained control of their dowries, and had the right to repre-sent themselves before the law. Italian men who traveled to the north were appalled at the differences in gender relations, criticizing English women as violent and brazen and disapproving of the mixing of the sexes in German public baths.

Child care and attitudes toward sexuality also reflected class differences in Renaissance life. Florentine middle- and upper-class fathers arranged business con-tracts with wet nurses to breast-feed their infants; babies thus spent prolonged peri-ods of time away from their families. Such elaborate child care was beyond the reach of the poor, who often abandoned their children to strangers or to public charity.

By the beginning of the fifteenth century, Florence's two hospitals were accept-ing large numbers of abandoned children in addition to the sick and infirm. In 1445, the government opened the Ospedale degli Innocenti to deal with the large number of abandoned children from poor families or from women who had given birth out of wedlock. Many of the latter were domestic slaves or servants impreg-nated by their masters; in 1445, one-third of the first hundred foundlings at the new hospital were children of the unequal liaisons between masters and women slaves. For some women, the foundling hospital provided an alternative to infanti-cide. Over two-thirds of abandoned infants were girls. Although Florence's government employed wet nurses to care for the foundlings, the large number of abandoned infants overtaxed the hospital's limited resources. The hospital's death rate for infants was much higher than the already high infant mortality rate of the time.

Illegitimacy in itself did not necessarily carry a social stigma in fifteenth-century Europe. Most upper-class men acknowledged and supported their illegitimate chil-dren as a sign of virility, and illegitimate children of noble lineage often rose to social and political prominence. Any social stigma was borne primarily by the woman, whose ability to marry became compromised. Shame and guilt drove some poor sin-gle mothers to kill their infants, a crime for which they paid with their own lives.

In addition to prosecuting infanticide, the public regulation of sexuality focused on prostitution and homosexuality. Intended "to eliminate a worse evil by a lesser one," a 1415 statute established government brothels in Florence. Concurrent with its higher tolerance of prostitution, the Renaissance state had a low tolerance of homosexuality. In 1432, the Florentine state appointed magistrates "to discover—whether by means of secret denunciation, accusations, notification, or any other method—those who commit the vice of sodomy, whether actively or passively." The government set fines for homosexual acts and carried out death sentences against pederasts (men who have sex with boys).

Fifteenth-century European magistrates took violence against women less seri-ously than illegal male sexual behavior, as the different punishments indicate. In Renaissance Venice, for example, the typical jail sentence for rape and attempted rape was only six months. Magistrates often treated noblemen with great leniency and handled rape cases according to class distinctions. For example, Agneta, a young girl living with a government official, was abducted and raped by two millers, who were sentenced to five years in prison; several servants who abducted and raped a slave woman were sentenced to three to four months in jail; and a nobleman who abducted and raped Anna, a slave woman, was freed. Whether in marriage, inheritance, illicit sex, or sexual crime, the Renaissance state regulated the behavior of men and women according to differing concepts of gender. The brilliant civilization of the Renaissance was experienced quite differently by men and women.

■ **REVIEW:** *How did the Renaissance encompass both arts and conceptions of the state?*

On the Threshold of World History

The fifteenth century constituted the first time that Europe was a major player in world history. Before the maritime explorations of Portugal and Spain, Europe had remained at the periphery of world events. Fourteenth-century Mongols had been more interested in conquering China and Persia—lands with sophisticated cultures—than in invading Europe; Persian historians of the early fifteenth century dismissed Europeans as "barbaric Franks"; and China's Ming dynasty rulers, who sent maritime expeditions to Southeast Asia and East Africa around 1400, seemed unaware of the Europeans, even though Marco Polo and other Italian merchants had appeared at the court of the preceding Mongol Yuan dynasty. In the fifteenth century, Portuguese and Spanish vessels, followed a century later by English, French, and Dutch ships, sailed across the Atlantic, Indian, and Pacific Oceans, bringing with them people, merchandise, crops, and diseases in a global exchange that would shape the modern world. For the first time, the people of the Americas were brought into contact with a larger historical force that threatened to destroy not only their culture but their existence. European exploitation and conquest defined this historical era of transition from the medieval to the modern world, as Europeans left the Baltic and the Mediterranean for wider oceans.

The Divided Mediterranean

In the second half of the fifteenth century, the Mediterranean Sea, which had dominated medieval maritime trade, began to lose its preeminence to the Atlantic Ocean. To win control over the Mediterranean, the Ottomans embarked on an ambitious naval program to transform their empire into a major maritime power. War and piracy disrupted the flow of Christian trade: the Venetians mobilized all their resources to fight off Turkish advances, and the Genoese largely abandoned the eastern Mediterranean for trade opportunities presented by the Atlantic.

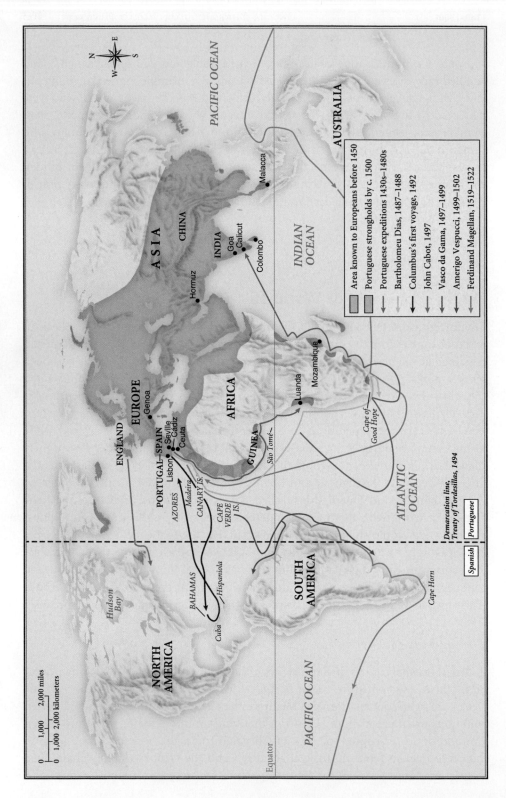

PACIFIC OCEAN

AUSTRALIA

N
W E
S

ASIA

CHINA

Malacca

INDIA
Goa
Calicut
Colombo

INDIAN OCEAN

Hormuz

Area known to Europeans before 1450
Portuguese strongholds by c. 1500
Portuguese expeditions 1430s–1480s
Bartholomeu Dias, 1487–1488
Columbus's first voyage, 1492
John Cabot, 1497
Vasco da Gama, 1497–1499
Amerigo Vespucci, 1499–1502
Ferdinand Magellan, 1519–1522

EUROPE
Genoa

AFRICA

Mozambique

ENGLAND

Luanda

PORTUGAL—SPAIN
Lisbon Seville Cadiz
Ceuta

Cape of
Good Hope

GUINEA
São Tomé

ATLANTIC OCEAN

AZORES
Madeira
CANARY IS.

CAPE
VERDE
IS.

Demarcation line,
Treaty of Tordesillas, 1494

Portuguese

Spanish

Hudson
Bay

BAHAMAS
Hispaniola
Cuba

SOUTH
AMERICA

Cape Horn

NORTH
AMERICA

0   1,000   2,000 miles
0 1,000 2,000 kilometers

Equator

PACIFIC OCEAN

Mediterranean trade used ships made with relatively backward naval technology. The most common ship, the galley—a flat-bottom vessel propelled mainly by oarsmen with the help of a sail—dated from the time of ancient Rome. Most galleys could not withstand open-ocean voyages, although Florentine and Genoese galleys did make long journeys to Flanders and England, hugging the coast for protection. The galley's dependence on human labor was a more serious handicap. Because prisoners of war and convicted criminals toiled as oarsmen in both Christian and Muslim ships, victory in war or the enforcement of criminal penalties was crucial to a state's ability to float large numbers of galleys. Slaves, too, sometimes provided the necessary labor.

Portuguese Confrontations

The exploration of the Atlantic began with the Portuguese (Map 11.6). By 1415, they had captured Ceuta on the Moroccan coast, establishing a foothold in Africa. Thereafter, Portuguese voyages sailed farther still down the West African coast. By midcentury, a chain of Portuguese forts reached Guinea, protecting the trade in gold and slaves. At home, the royal house of Portugal financed the fleets, with crucial roles played by Prince Peter, regent between 1440 and 1448; his more famous younger brother Prince Henry the Navigator; and King John II (r. 1481–1495). As a governor of the noble crusading Order of Christ, Henry financed many voyages out of the order's revenues. Private monies also helped, as leading Lisbon merchants participated in financing the gold and slave trades off the Guinea coast.

In 1455, Pope Nicholas V (r. 1447–1455) sanctioned Portuguese overseas expansion, commending King John II's crusading spirit and granting him and his successors the monopoly on trade with inhabitants of the newly "discovered" regions. In 1478–1488, Bartholomeu Dias took advantage of the prevailing winds in the South Atlantic to reach the Cape of Good Hope. A mere ten years later (1497–1499), under the captainship of Vasco da Gama, a Portuguese fleet rounded the cape and reached Calicut, India, center of the spice trade. By 1517, a chain of Portuguese forts dotted the Indian Ocean. In 1519, Ferdinand Magellan, a Portuguese sailor in Spanish service, led the first expedition to circumnavigate the globe.

■ **MAP 11.6 Exploitation and Exploration in the Sixteenth Century**
At the end of the fifteenth century, Europeans began moving aggressively across the globe. Beginning with initial forays along the African coast, their voyages soon widened out to transatlantic crossings and, by 1522, the circumnavigation of the world. The web of arrows on this map suggests an earth bound together by many threads, and this is partly true, for never again would the two halves of the globe be isolated. At the same time, the threads pulled in one direction only—toward the Europeans. Africa was exploited for gold and slaves, while the discovery of precious metals fueled the explorations and settlements of Central and South America. **For more help analyzing this map**, *see the map activity for this chapter in the* ONLINE STUDY GUIDE *at* bedfordstmartins.com/huntconcise.

In many ways a continuation of the struggle against Muslims on the Iberian peninsula, Portugal's maritime voyages displayed that country's mixed motives of piety, glory, and greed. The sailors dreamed of finding gold mines in West Africa and a mysterious Christian kingdom established by a mythical Prester John. The Portuguese hoped to reach the spice-producing lands of South and Southeast Asia by sea to bypass the Ottoman Turks, who controlled the traditional land routes between Europe and Asia.

The new voyages depended for their success on several technological break-throughs. The lateen (triangular) sail permitted ships to tack against headwinds. Light caravels and heavy galleons, however different in size, were alike in using more than one mast and sail, harnessing wind—rather than human—power to move them. Better charts, maps, and instruments made long-distance voyages less risky.

After the voyages of Christopher Columbus, Portugal's interests clashed with those of Spain. Mediated by Pope Alexander VI, the 1494 Treaty of Tordesillas rec-onciled Portugal and Spain by dividing the Atlantic world between the two royal houses. A demarcation 370 leagues west of the Cape Verde Islands divided the Atlantic Ocean, reserving for Portugal the western coast of Africa and the route to India and giving Spain the oceans and lands to the west (see Map 11.6). Unwittingly, this agreement also allowed Portugal to claim Brazil in 1500, which Pedro Álvares Cabral (1467–1520) accidentally "discovered" on his voyage to India.

The Voyages of Columbus

Historians agree that Christopher Columbus (1451–1506) was born of Genoese parents; beyond that, we have little accurate information about this man who brought together the history of Europe and the Americas. In 1476, he arrived in Portugal, apparently a survivor in a naval battle between a Franco-Portuguese and a Genoese fleet; in 1479, he married a Portuguese noblewoman. He spent the next few years mostly in Portuguese service, gaining valuable experience in regular voy-ages down the west coast of Africa. In 1485, after the death of his wife, Columbus settled in Spain.

Fifteenth-century Europeans already knew that Asia lay beyond the vast Atlantic Ocean, and *The Travels of Marco Polo*, written more than a century ear-lier, still exerted a powerful hold on European images of the East. Columbus read it many times, along with other travel books, and proposed to sail west across the Atlantic to reach the lands of the khan, unaware that the Mongol Empire had already collapsed in eastern Asia. Vastly underestimating the distances, he dreamed of finding a new route to the East's gold and spices and partook of the larger European vision that had inspired the Portuguese voyages. (His critics had a much more accurate idea of the globe's size and of the difficulty of the venture, but no one believed that the world was flat!) But after the Portuguese and French monarchs rejected his proposal, Columbus found royal patronage with the recently proclaimed Catholic monarchs Isabella of Castile and Ferdinand of Aragon.

In August 1492, equipped with a modest fleet of three ships and about ninety men, Columbus set sail across the Atlantic. His contract stipulated that he would claim Castilian sovereignty over any new land and inhabitants and share any profits with the crown. Reaching what is today the Bahamas on October 12, Columbus mistook the islands to be part of the East Indies, not far from Japan and "the lands of the Great Khan." As the Castilians explored the Caribbean islands, they encountered communities of peaceful Indians, the Arawaks, who were awed by the Europeans' military technology, not to mention their appearance. Exchanging gifts of beads and broken glass for Arawak gold—an exchange that convinced Columbus of the trusting nature of the Indians—the crew established peaceful relationships with many communities. Yet despite many positive entries in the ship's log referring to Columbus's personal goodwill toward the Indians, the Europeans' objectives were clear: find gold, subjugate the Indians, and propagate Christianity.

Excited by the prospect of easy riches, many flocked to join Columbus's second voyage. When Columbus departed Cádiz in September 1493, he commanded seventeen ships that carried between 1,200 and 1,500 men, many believing all they had to do was "to load the gold into the ships." Failing to find the imaginary gold mines and spices, however, the colonial enterprise quickly switched its focus to finding slaves. Columbus and his crew first enslaved the Caribs, enemies of the Arawaks; in 1494, Columbus proposed a regular slave trade based in Hispaniola. The Spaniards exported enslaved Indians to Spain, and slave traders sold them in Seville. Soon the Spaniards began importing sugarcane from the Portuguese island of Madeira, forcing large numbers of Indians to work on plantations to produce enough sugar for export to Europe. Columbus himself was edged out of this new enterprise. When the Spanish monarchs realized the vast potential for material gain that lay in their new dominions, they asserted direct royal authority by sending officials and priests to the Americas, which were later named after the Italian Amerigo Vespucci, who led a voyage across the Atlantic in 1499–1502.

Columbus's place in history embodies the fundamental transformations of his age. A Genoese in the service of Portuguese and Spanish employers, Columbus had a career illustrating the changing balance between the Mediterranean and the Atlantic. The voyages of 1492–1493 would eventually draw a triangle of exchange among Europe, the Americas, and Africa, an exchange gigantic in its historical impact and its human cost.

A New Era in Slavery

During the Middle Ages and Renaissance, female slaves served as domestic servants in wealthy Mediterranean homes, and male slaves toiled in the galleys of Ottoman and Christian fleets. Some were captured in war or by piracy; others—Africans—were

■ **Dürer's Engraving of Katharina, an African Woman**
Like other artists in early-sixteenth-century Europe, Albrecht Dürer would have seen in person Africans who went to Portugal and Spain as students, servants, and slaves. Notice Katharina's noble expression and dignified attire. Before the rise of the slave trade in the seventeenth century, most Africans in Europe were household servants of the aristocracy. Considered symbols of prestige, such servants generally were not used for economic production.
(Foto Marburg/Art Resource, NY.)

sold by other Africans and Bedouin traders to Christian buyers. In western Asia, parents sold their children into servitude out of poverty. Many people in the Balkans became slaves when their land was devastated by Ottoman invasions. Slaves were Greek, Slav, European, African, and Turk.

The Portuguese maritime voyages changed this picture. From the fifteenth century, Africans increasingly filled the ranks of slaves. Exploiting warfare in West Africa, the Portuguese traded in gold and "pieces," as African slaves were called, a practice condemned at home by some conscientious clergy. Critical voices, however, could not deny the enormous profits that the slave trade brought to Portugal. Most slaves toiled in the sugar plantations of the Portuguese Atlantic islands and in Brazil. A fortunate few labored as domestic servants in Portugal, where African freedmen and slaves, some 35,000 in the early sixteenth century, constituted almost 3 percent of the population, a percentage that was much higher than in other European countries. In the Americas, slavery would truly flourish as an institution of exploitation.

Europeans in a New World

In 1500, on the eve of European invasion, the native peoples of the Americas were divided into many sedentary and nomadic societies. Among the settled peoples,

■ MAPPING THE WEST Renaissance Europe, c. 1500

By 1500, the shape of early modern Europe was largely set. It would remain stable until the eighteenth century, except for the disappearance of an independent Hungarian kingdom, which was conquered by the Ottomans in 1529.

the largest political and social organizations centered in the Mexican and Peruvian highlands. The Aztecs and the Incas ruled over subjugated Indian populations in their respective empires. With an elaborate religious culture and a rigid social and political hierarchy, the Aztecs and Incas based their civilizations in large urban capitals.

The Spanish explorers organized their expeditions to the mainland from a base in the Caribbean (see Map 11.6). Two prominent leaders, Hernán Cortés (1485–1547) and Francisco Pizarro (c. 1475–1541), gathered men and arms and set off in search of gold. Catholic priests accompanied the fortune hunters to bring

Christianity to allegedly uncivilized peoples and thus to justify brutal conquests. His small band swelled by peoples who had been subjugated by the Aztecs, Cortés captured the Aztec capital, Tenochtitlán, in 1519. To the south, Pizarro conquered the Andean highlands, exploiting a civil war between rival Incan kings.

By the mid-sixteenth century, the Spanish Empire stretched unbroken from Mexico to Chile. Not to be outdone by the Spaniards, other European powers joined the scramble for gold in the New World. In 1500, a Portuguese fleet led by Pedro Álvares Cabral landed at Brazil, but Portugal did not begin colonizing there until 1532, when it established a permanent fort on the coast. In North America, the French went in search of a "northwest passage" to China. By 1504, French fishermen had appeared in Newfoundland. Thirty years later, Jacques Cartier led three voyages that explored the St. Lawrence River as far as Montreal. An early attempt in 1541 to settle Canada failed because of the harsh winter and Indian hostility, and John Cabot's 1497 voyage to find a northern route to Asia also failed. More permanent settlements in Canada and the present-day United States would succeed only in the seventeenth century.

■ **REVIEW:** *Which European countries led the way in maritime expansion, and what were their motives?*

IMPORTANT DATES

1337–1453	Hundred Years' War	1440s	Gutenberg introduces the printing press
1347–1350	First outbreak of the Black Death in Europe; anti-Jewish persecutions in the empire	c. 1450–1500	Height of the Florentine Renaissance
1358	Jacquerie uprising in France	1453	Fall of Constantinople; end of the Byzantine Empire
1378	Beginning of the Great Schism; John Wycliffe's treatise *On the Church*	1460s–1485	Wars of the Roses in England
		1462	Ivan III of Muscovy claims imperial title "tsar"
1381	English peasant uprising		
1389	Ottomans defeat Serbs at Kosovo	1478	Inquisition established in Spain
		1492	Columbus's first voyage; Christians conquer Muslim Granada and expel Jews from Spain
1414–1417	Council of Constance ends the Great Schism		
1415	Execution of Jan Hus; Portugal captures Ceuta, establishing foothold in Africa	1499	Vasco da Gama reaches India
		1500	Portugal claims Brazil

Conclusion

Confronted by war, plague, peasant uprisings, turbulence in the cities, anti-Jewish pogroms, and a disgraced papacy, Europe's ruling classes grasped the reins of power ever more tightly, creating more centralized and institutionalized states. Surrounding themselves with artists, musicians, and humanists, these new-style rulers supported the "Renaissance"—an attempt to resuscitate the classical past for the purposes of the present. The Renaissance, which emphasized human potential and achievement, was one of Europe's most brilliant periods in artistic activity, one that glorified both God and humanity. Overwhelming confidence spurred Renaissance artists to a new appreciation for the human body and a new visual perspective in art and to apply mathematics and science to architecture, music, and artistic composition.

This intense cultural production both resulted from and fueled the competition among the burgeoning Renaissance states and between Christian Europe and the Muslim Ottoman Empire. The competition also fostered an expansion of the frontiers of Europe first to Africa and then across the Atlantic Ocean to the Americas, ushering in the first period of global history. Few at the time would have guessed that Europe would soon enter yet another period of turmoil, one brought about not by demographic and economic collapse but by a profound crisis of conscience that the brilliance of Renaissance civilization had tended to obscure.

■ **MAKING CONNECTIONS**

1. *How did Renaissance states differ from medieval monarchies?*

2. *How did the impact of the Ottomans on Europe differ from the impact of the Mongols?*

■ **FOR FURTHER EXPLORATION**

For further reading and online research ideas, see the Suggested References on page SR-6 at the back of the book.

For practice quizzes, a customized study plan, and other study tools, see the ONLINE STUDY GUIDE at **bedfordstmartins.com/huntconcise**.

For primary-source material from this period, see Chapter 11 in *Sources of THE MAKING OF THE WEST: A CONCISE HISTORY*, Second Edition.

12

Struggles over Beliefs

1500–1648

H ILLE FEIKEN LEFT THE NORTHERN GERMAN CITY of Münster on June 16, 1534, elegantly dressed, bedecked with jewels, and determined to kill. Münster, which religious radicals had declared a holy city, lay under siege by armies loyal to the local Catholic bishop—her intended victim. Hille crossed enemy lines and tried to persuade the commander of the besieging troops to take her to the bishop, promising to reveal a secret means of recapturing the city. When a defector from her camp recognized Hille and betrayed her, she was beheaded.

Hille Feiken belonged to the religious group known as Anabaptists, who wanted to form a holy community separate from the rest of society. Anabaptists organized in response to the Protestant Reformation, which was set in motion by the German friar Martin Luther in 1517 and quickly became a sweeping movement to uproot church abuses and restore early Christian teachings. Supporters of Luther were called **Protestants**, those who protested. Inspired by Luther and then by other reformers, ordinary men and women across much of Europe attempted to remake their heaven and earth. Their stories intertwined with bloody struggles among princes for domination in Europe, an age-old conflict now complicated by the clash of rival faiths.

Struggles over religious beliefs frequently erupted into armed confrontation, culminating in the Thirty Years' War of 1618–1648, which devastated the lands of

■ **Vincenzo Catena, *Judith***

The Book of Judith tells the story of a beautiful young Israelite who presents herself to Holofernes, the general of an army besieging Jerusalem. His guard lowered by wine and Judith's charms, Judith assassinates Holofernes and cuts off his head, thus frightening off the enemy and saving her people. In this painting from the 1520s, Venetian artist Vincenzo Catena conveys Judith's strength, beauty, and commitment to her task—one that Hille Feiken sought to reenact so that she might free her own besieged city of Münster. (AKG Images/Cameraphoto.)

central Europe. The orgy of mutual destruction in the Thirty Years' War left no winners in the religious struggle, and the cynical manipulation of religious issues by both Catholic and Protestant leaders showed that political interests eventually outweighed those of religion. The extreme violence of religious conflict pushed rulers and political thinkers to seek other, nonreligious grounds for governmental authority. Few would argue for genuine toleration of religious differences, but many began to insist that the interests of states had to take priority over the desire for religious conformity.

Although particularly dramatic and deadly, the church-state crisis was only one of a series of upheavals that shaped this era. After decades of rapid economic and population growth in the sixteenth century, a major economic downturn led to food shortages, famine, and disease in the first half of the seventeenth century. An upheaval in worldviews was also in the making, catalyzed by increasing knowledge of the new worlds discovered overseas and in the heavens. The development of new scientific methods of research would ultimately reshape Western attitudes toward religion and state power, as Europeans desperately sought alternatives to wars over religious beliefs.

The Protestant Reformation

Since the mid-fifteenth century, many clerics had tried to reform the church from within, criticizing clerical abuses and calling for moral renewal, but their efforts came up against the church's inertia and resistance. At the beginning of the sixteenth century, widespread popular piety and anticlericalism existed side by side, fomenting a volatile mixture of need and resentment. A young German friar, tormented by his own religious doubts, was to become the spokesman for a generation. From its origins as a theological dispute, Martin Luther's reform movement sparked explosive protests. By the time he died in 1546, half of western Europe had renounced allegiance to the Roman Catholic church. Christian unity fractured, opening the way not only to widespread turmoil but also to a host of new attitudes about the nature of religious and political authority.

Popular Piety and Christian Humanism

Numerous signs pointed to an intense spiritual anxiety among the laity. New shrines sprang up, reports of miracles multiplied, and prayer books sold briskly. Critics complained that the church gave external behavior more weight than spiritual intentions. In receiving the sacrament of penance—one of the central pillars of the Roman church—sinners were expected to examine their consciences, sincerely confess their sins to a priest, and receive forgiveness. In practice, however, some priests abused their authority by demanding sexual or monetary favors in return for forgiveness. Priests also sold **indulgences**, which according to doctrine could alleviate suffering in purgatory after death. The faithful were supposed to earn indulgences by performing certain religious tasks—going on pilgrimage, attending mass, doing holy works. The sale of indulgences as a substitution for performing good works suggested that the church was more interested in making money than in saving souls.

Dissatisfaction with the official church prompted some Christian intellectuals to link their scholarship to the cause of social reform and to dream of ideal societies based on peace and morality. The Dutch scholar Desiderius Erasmus (c. 1466–1536) and the English lawyer Thomas More (1478–1535) stood out as representatives of these Christian humanists, who, unlike Italian humanists, placed their primary emphasis on Christian piety. Each established close links to the powerful. Erasmus was on intimate terms with kings and popes, and his fame spread across all Europe. More became lord chancellor to England's king Henry VIII.

Erasmus advocated a simple piety devoid of greed and the lust for power, but he also promoted the new humanist learning. To this end he devoted years to translating a new Latin edition of the New Testament from the original Greek. He argued ironically in *The Praise of Folly* (1509) that the wise appeared foolish, because modesty, humility, and poverty had few adherents in this world. Although Erasmus mocked the clergy's corruption and Christian princes' bloody ambitions, he emphasized the role of education in reforming individuals and through them society as a whole. Even ordinary table manners drew his attention. In the *Colloquies* (1523), a compilation of Latin dialogues intended as language-learning exercises, he advised his cultivated readers not to pick their noses at meals and not to speak while stuffing their mouths. He also advocated an end to wet nursing. Challenged by angry younger men and radical ideas once the Reformation took hold, Erasmus chose Christian unity over reform and schism. He died in the Swiss city of Basel, isolated from the Protestant community and condemned by many in the Catholic church, who found his writings too critical of the church's authority.

Erasmus's good friend Thomas More, to whom *The Praise of Folly* was dedicated,* met with even greater suffering for his beliefs. He would later pay with his life for upholding conscience over political expediency. Inspired by the recent voyages of discovery, More's best-known work, *Utopia* (1516), describes an imaginary ideal place that offered a stark contrast to his own society. Because Utopians enjoyed public schools, communal kitchens, hospitals, and nurseries, they had no need for money. Greed and private property disappeared in this world. Dedicated to the pursuit of knowledge and natural religion, with equal distribution of goods and few laws, Utopia knew neither crime nor war (*Utopia* means both "no place" and "best place" in Greek). More believed that politics,

---

*The Latin title *Encomium Moriae* ("The Praise of Folly") was a pun on More's name and the Latin word for *folly*.

property, and war fueled human misery, whereas for his Utopians, "fighting was a thing they absolutely loathe. They say it's a quite subhuman form of activity, although human beings are more addicted to it than any of the lower animals." Despite a few oddities—voluntary slavery, for instance, and strictly controlled travel—Utopia seemed a paradise compared with the increasing violence in a Europe divided by religion.

Martin Luther and the German Nation

Like Erasmus and More, Martin Luther (1483–1546) pursued a life of scholarship, but a personal crisis of faith led him to break with the Roman church and establish a competing one. The son of a miner, Luther abandoned his studies in the law to enter the Augustinian order. The choice of a monastic life did not resolve Luther's doubts about his own salvation. Appalled at his own sense of sinfulness and the weakness of human nature, he lived in terror of God's justice despite frequent confessions and penance. A pilgrimage to Rome only deepened his unease with the institutional church. Sent to study theology by a sympathetic superior, Luther gradually came to new insights through his study of Scripture. He later described his breakthrough experience:

> At last, by the mercy of God, meditating day and night, I gave heed to the context of the words [in Romans 1:17], namely, "In [the gospel] the righteousness of God is revealed, as it is written, 'He who through faith is righteous shall live.'" There I began to understand that the righteousness of God is that by which the righteous live by a gift of God, namely by faith.

Luther soon came into conflict with the church authorities. In 1516, the new archbishop ordered the sale of indulgences to help cover the cost of constructing St. Peter's Basilica in Rome and also to defray his expenses in pursuing his election. Such blatant profiteering outraged many, including Luther, who now served as professor of theology at the University of Wittenberg. In 1517, Luther composed ninety-five theses—propositions for an academic debate—that questioned indulgence peddling and the purchase of church offices. Once they became public, the theses unleashed a torrent of pent-up resentment and frustration among the laypeople. This apparently ordinary academic dispute soon engulfed the Holy Roman Empire in conflict.

As Luther developed his ideas more fully, rupture became inevitable. In 1520, he published three treatises that laid out his theological position, attacked the papacy in Rome as the embodiment of the Antichrist, and called upon the German princes to reform the church themselves. Luther insisted that faith alone, not good works or penance, could save sinners from damnation. Faith came from the believer's personal relationship with God, which he or she cultivated through

■ **Luther as Monk, Doctor, Man of the Bible, and Saint, 1521**
This woodcut by an anonymous artist appeared in a volume that the Strasbourg printer Johann Schott published in 1521. In addition to being one of the major centers of printing, Strasbourg was also a stronghold of the reform movement. Notice the use of traditional symbols to signify Luther's holiness: the Bible in his hands, the halo, the Holy Spirit in the form of a dove, and his friar's robes. Although monasticism and the cult of saints came under severe criticism during the Reformation, the representation of Luther with traditional symbols of sanctity stressed his conservative values instead of his radical challenge to church authorities.
(The Granger Collection, NY.)

individual study of Scripture. Ordinary laypeople thus made up "the priesthood of all believers," who had no need of a professional caste of clerics to show them the way to salvation. The attack on the church's authority could not have been more dramatic.

From Rome's perspective, the "Luther Affair," as church officials called it, was essentially a matter of clerical discipline. Rome ordered Luther to obey his superiors and keep quiet. But the church establishment had seriously misjudged the extent of Luther's influence. Luther's ideas, published in numerous German and Latin editions, spread rapidly throughout the Holy Roman Empire, unleashing forces that Luther himself could not control. Social, nationalist, and religious protests fused into an explosive mass very similar to the Czech revolution that Jan Hus had inspired a century earlier. Like Hus, Luther appeared before an emperor: in 1521, he defended his faith before Charles V (r. 1520–1558), the newly elected Holy Roman Emperor who at the age of nineteen was the ruler of the Low Countries, Spain, Spain's Italian and New World dominions, and the Austrian Habsburg lands. At the Imperial Diet of Worms, the formal assembly presided over by this powerful ruler, Luther shocked Germans by declaring his admiration for the Czech heretic. But unlike Hus, Luther did not suffer martyrdom because he enjoyed the protection of Frederick the Wise, the elector of Saxony (one of the seven German princes entitled to elect the Holy Roman Emperor) and Luther's lord.

Luther also had the support of many literate townspeople who were eager to read the Scriptures for themselves.

What began as an urban movement turned into a war in the countryside in 1525. Lutheran propaganda radiated outward from the German towns, where local officials had appointed clerics sympathetic to reform. Luther's anticlerical message struck home with merchants and artisans who resented the clergy's tax-exempt status, but peasants had even more reason for discontent because they paid taxes to both their lord and the church. The church was the largest landowner in the Holy Roman Empire: about one-seventh of the empire's territory consisted of ecclesiastical principalities in which bishops and abbots exercised both secular and churchly power. In the spring of 1525, many peasants in southern and central Germany rose in rebellion, sometimes inspired by wandering preachers. Urban workers and artisans joined the peasant bands, plundering monasteries, refusing to pay church taxes, and demanding village autonomy, the abolition of serfdom, and the right to appoint their own pastors. In Thuringia, the rebels were led by an ex-priest, Thomas Müntzer (1468?–1525), who promised to chastise the wicked and thus clear the way for the Last Judgment.

The uprising of 1525, known as the Peasants' War, split the reform movement. In Thuringia, Catholics and reformers joined hands to crush Müntzer and his supporters. All over the empire, princes rallied their troops to defeat the peasants and hunt down their leaders. By the end of 1525, more than 100,000 rebels had been killed and others maimed, imprisoned, or exiled. Luther had tried to mediate, criticizing the princes for their brutality toward the peasants but also warning the rebels against mixing religion and social protest. Luther believed that rulers were ordained by God and thus must be obeyed even if they were tyrants. The Kingdom of God belonged not to this world but to the next. When the rebels ignored Luther's appeal and continued to follow radical preachers like Müntzer, Luther called on the princes to destroy "the devil's work" and slaughter the rebels. Fundamentally conservative in its political philosophy, the Lutheran church would henceforth depend on established political authority for its protection.

The Peasants' War of 1525

Emerging as the champions of an orderly religious reform, many German princes eventually confronted Emperor Charles V, who supported Rome. In 1529, Charles declared the Roman Catholic faith the empire's only legitimate religion.

Proclaiming their allegiance to the reform cause, the Lutheran German princes protested and thus came to be called Protestants.

Huldrych Zwingli and John Calvin

While Luther provided the religious leadership for northern Germany, the south soon came under the influence of reformers based in Switzerland. In 1520, Huldrych Zwingli (1484–1531), the son of a Swiss village leader, broke with Rome and established his reform headquarters in German-speaking Zurich. In 1541, the Frenchman John Calvin (1509–1564) made French-speaking Geneva his center for reform campaigns in western Europe (see Map 12.1). Like Luther, Zwingli and Calvin began their careers as priests, but in contrast to their predecessor, they demanded an even more radical break with the Roman Catholic church.

Zwingli served as an army chaplain before declaring himself a reformer, and he brought to his version of church reform a stern disciplinarian's emphasis on a theocratic (church-directed) society in which religious values infused every aspect of politics and social life. Zwingli differed from Luther in his view of the role of the Eucharist, or holy communion. According to Catholic doctrine, during the mass officiated by a priest the bread and wine of holy communion changed into the body and blood of Christ. Luther believed that the body and blood were actually present in the bread and wine, but only because of the faith of the believer, not because a priest officiated. Zwingli took Luther's argument a step further and insisted that the bread and wine simply symbolized Christ's union with believers; the bread and wine did not change in substance. Efforts to mediate between Luther and Zwingli in this critical element of doctrine failed. The German and Swiss reform movements continued on separate paths.

In Zurich, Zwingli tolerated no dissent. When laypeople secretly set up their own new sect, called Anabaptists, Zwingli immediately attacked them. The **Anabaptists** believed that only adults had the free will to truly understand and accept baptism and therefore had to be rebaptized (*anabaptism* means "rebaptism"). How could a baby knowingly choose Christ? Rebaptism symbolized the Anabaptists' determination to withdraw from a social order corrupted, as they saw it, by power and evil. They therefore rejected the authority of courts and magistrates and refused to bear arms or swear oaths of allegiance. When persuasion failed to convince them, Zwingli urged Zurich magistrates to impose the death sentence.

Anabaptism spread quickly from Zurich to many cities in southern Germany, despite the Holy Roman Empire's general condemnation of the movement in 1529. In 1534, one incendiary Anabaptist group, believing that the end of the world was imminent, seized control of the northwestern German town of Münster. Proclaiming themselves a community of saints and imitating the ancient Israelites, they were initially governed by twelve elders and later by Jan of Leiden, a Dutch Anabaptist tailor who claimed to be the prophesied leader—a second "King David."

The Münster Anabaptists abolished private property and dissolved traditional marriages, allowing men, like Old Testament patriarchs, to have multiple wives, to the chagrin of many women. In 1535, Münster fell to a combined Protestant and Catholic army. Many Anabaptists died in battle or—like Hille Feiken—were executed. The remnants of the Anabaptist movement survived under the determined pacifist leadership of the Dutch reformer Menno Simons (1469–1561), whose followers were eventually named Mennonites.

Yet another wave of reform surged forward under the leadership of John Calvin. As a young priest, Calvin believed it might be possible to reform the Roman Catholic church from within, but gradually he came to share Luther and Zwingli's conviction that only fundamental change could reestablish the true religion. While Calvin moved toward the Protestant position, his homeland of France experienced increasing turmoil over religion. On Sunday, October 18, 1534, in the so-called Affair of the Placards, Parisians found church doors posted with ribald broadsheets denouncing the Catholic Mass. The government arrested hundreds of French Protestants and executed scores of them, precipitating the flight into exile of many others, including Calvin.

Calvin did not intend to settle in Geneva, but when he stopped there, a local reformer threatened him with God's curse if he did not stay and help organize reform in the city. After intense conflict between the supporters of reform, many of whom were French refugees, and the opposition, led by the traditional elite families, the Calvinists triumphed in 1541. Geneva soon followed the precepts laid out in Calvin's great work, *The Institutes of the Christian Religion*, first published in 1536. Calvin took the reform doctrines to their logical conclusion. If God is almighty and humans cannot earn their salvation by good works, as all Protestants argued, then no Christian can be certain of salvation. Developing the doctrine of **predestination**, Calvin insisted that God had foreordained every man, woman, and child to

The Progress of the Reformation	
1517	Martin Luther disseminates ninety-five theses attacking the sale of indulgences and other church practices
1520	Reformer Huldrych Zwingli breaks with Rome
1525	Radical reformer Thomas Müntzer killed in Peasants' War
1529	Lutheran German princes protest the condemnation of religious reform by Charles V; genesis of the term *Protestants*
1529	The English Parliament establishes King Henry VIII as head of the Anglican church, severing ties to Rome
1534–1535	Anabaptists control the city of Münster, Germany, in a failed experiment to create a holy community
1541	John Calvin and his followers take control in Geneva, making that city the center for Calvinist reforms

salvation or damnation—even before the creation of the world. Only God knew who was among the "elect."

In practice, however, Calvinist doctrine demanded rigorous discipline: the knowledge that a small group of "elect" would be saved should guide the actions of the godly in an uncertain world. Fusing church and society into what followers named the "Reformed church," Geneva became a single theocratic community, in which dissent was not tolerated. The Genevan magistrates arrested the Spanish physician Michael Servetus when he passed through in 1553 because he had published books attacking Calvin and questioning the doctrine of the Trinity, the belief shared by virtually all Christians that God exists in three persons—the Father, Son (Christ), and Holy Spirit. Calvin urged the authorities to execute him. Geneva quickly became the new center of the Reformation, sending out pastors trained for mission work and exporting books that taught Calvinist doctrines. The Calvinist movement spread to France, the Netherlands, England, Scotland, the German states, Poland, Hungary, and eventually New England, becoming the established form of the Reformation in many of these countries (Map 12.1).

Reshaping Society through Religion

For all their differences over doctrine and church organization, the Protestant reformers shared a desire to instill greater discipline in Christian worship and in social behavior. As a consequence, they advocated changes in education and marriage to create a God-fearing, pious, and orderly Christian society. Some of these efforts grew out of developments that stretched back to the Middle Ages, but others, such as an emphasis on literacy, appeared first in Protestant Europe.

Prior to the Reformation, the Latin Vulgate was the only Bible authorized by the church; as a result, priests interpreted the Bible for their parishoners. In 1522, Martin Luther translated Erasmus's Greek New Testament into German because he believed that everyone should read the Bible for him- or herself. Within twelve years, printers published more than 200,000 copies of it, an immense number for the time. In 1534, Luther completed a German translation of the Old Testament. In the same year that Luther's German New Testament appeared in print, the French humanist Jacques Lefèvre d'Étaples (c. 1455–1536) translated the Vulgate New Testament into French. Sponsored by the bishop of Meaux, who wanted to distribute free copies of the New Testament to the poor of the region, Lefèvre's translation represented an early attempt to reform the French church without breaking with Rome. By contrast, England's church hierarchy reacted swiftly against English-language Bibles, sensing in them the threat of heresy. Inspired by Luther's example during a visit to Wittenberg, the Englishman William Tyndale (1495–1536) translated the Bible into English. After he had his translation printed in Germany and the Low Countries, Tyndale smuggled copies into England. He paid for his boldness by being burned at the stake as a heretic.

■ **MAP 12.1 Spread of Protestantism in the Sixteenth Century**

The Protestant Reformation divided northern and southern Europe. From its heartland in the Holy Roman Empire, the Reformation won the allegiance of Scandinavia, England, and Scotland and made considerable inroads in the Low Countries, France, eastern Europe, the Swiss Confederation, and even parts of northern Italy. While the Mediterranean countries remained loyal to Rome, a vast zone of confessional divisions and strife characterized the religious landscape of Europe from Britain in the west to Poland in the east.

■ The Disciplined Home

Proper table manners reflected discipline and morality in the godly household, an ideal of the religious reformers of the sixteenth century. The householder, the father-patriarch, leads his wife and children in prayer before a meal. The orderly behavior parallels the comfort (oven, smoked glass windows, chandeliers, timber ceiling, and cabinets) of a well-off patrician family. **For more help analyzing this image,** see the visual activity for this chapter in the ONLINE STUDY GUIDE at **bedfordstmartins.com/huntconcise.**

(Staatsbibliothek Bamberg, Germany.)

Although the vernacular Bible was a prized possession in many Protestant households, Bible reading did not become widespread until the 1600s. To educate children in the new religious principles, and replace the late medieval church schools, the Protestant reformers set up state school systems. Luther urged the German princes to use the proceeds of confiscated church properties to establish primary schools in every parish for boys and girls between six and twelve. The Protestant churches also developed a secondary system of higher schools for boys, called gymnasia (from the Greek *gymnasion*), in which the study of Greek and Latin classics and religious instruction prepared future pastors, scholars, and officials for university study.

Like the reforms of education, Protestant efforts to reshape marriage reflected their concern to discipline individual behavior and institute an orderly Christian society. Protestant magistrates established marital courts, passed new marriage laws, closed brothels, and inflicted harsher punishments for sexual deviance. Under canon law, the Catholic church recognized any promise made between two consenting adults (with the legal age of twelve for females, fourteen for males) as a valid marriage. In rural areas and among the urban poor, most couples simply lived together as common-law husband and wife, and some couples never even registered with the church. Sometimes young men promised marriage in a moment of passion only to renege later. Protestant governments declared a marriage illegitimate if the partners failed to register their marriage with a local official and a pastor. They usually also required parental consent, thus giving parents immense power in regulating marriage and the transmission of family property.

Taught to become obedient spouses and affectionate companions in Christ, women approached this new sexual regime with ambivalence. The new laws stipulated that women could seek divorce for desertion, impotence, and flagrant abuse, although in practice the marital courts encouraged reconciliation. These improvements came at a price, however: Protestant women were expected to be obedient wives, helpful companions, and loving mothers, but they could no longer join the convent and pursue their own religious paths outside the family. Luther's wife, Katharina von Bora, typified the new ideal Protestant woman. A former nun, she accepted her prescribed role in a patriarchal household: once married, Katharina ran the couple's household, feeding their children, relatives, and student boarders. Although she deferred to Luther—she addressed him as "Herr Doktor"—she nonetheless defended a woman's right as an equal in marriage. Other Protestant women spoke out even more decisively. Katharina Zell, wife of the reformer Matthew Zell, wrote hymns, fed the sick and imprisoned, and denounced the intolerance of the new Protestant clergy. Rebuking one for his persecution of dissenters, she wrote, "You young fellows tread on the graves of the first fathers of this church in Strasbourg and punish all who disagree with you, but faith cannot be forced." She also insisted that women should have a voice in religious affairs.

Catholic Renewal and Missionary Zeal

Reacting to the waves of Protestant challenge, the Catholic church mobilized for defense in a movement that is called by some the Counter-Reformation and by others Catholic Reform. Pope Paul III (r. 1534–1549) convened a general church council to codify church doctrine, and he personally approved the founding of new religious orders to undertake aggressive missionary efforts. The Council of Trent (Trent sat on the border between the Holy Roman Empire and Italy) met intermittently between 1545 and 1563, when it concluded its work. Its decisions shaped the essential character of Catholicism until the 1960s. Emphatically rejecting the major Protestant positions, the council reasserted the supremacy of clerical authority over the laity and reaffirmed that the bread and wine of communion actually becomes Christ's body and blood. It required that all weddings take place in churches and be registered by the parish clergy and explicitly refused to allow for divorce. All hopes of reconciliation between Protestants and Catholics faded.

Most important of the new Catholic religious orders was the Society of Jesus. Its founder was Ignatius of Loyola (1491–1556), a Spanish nobleman and charismatic former military officer, who abandoned his quest for military glory in favor of serving the church. Ignatius soon attracted other young men to his side, and in 1540 the pope recognized his small band of "Jesuits." Over time, the Jesuits founded hundreds of colleges in Spain, Portugal, France, Italy, the German states, Hungary, Bohemia, and Poland. Among their alumni would be princes, philosophers, lawyers, churchmen, and officials—the elite of Catholic Europe. In 1544 the

■ The Portuguese in Japan

In this sixteenth-century Japanese black-lacquer screen painting of Portuguese missionaries, the Jesuits are dressed in black and the Franciscans in brown. At the lower right corner is a Portuguese nobleman depicted with exaggerated "Western" features. The Japanese considered themselves lighter in skin color than the Portuguese, whom they classified as "barbarians." In turn, the Portuguese classified Japanese (and Chinese) as "whites." The perception of ethnic differences in the sixteenth century depended less on skin color than on clothing, eating habits, and other cultural signals. Color classifications were unstable and changed over time: by the late seventeenth century, Europeans no longer regarded Asians as "white." (Laurie Platt Winfrey, Inc.)

pope recognized a new order for women, the Company of Saint Ursula, known as the "Ursulines," who devoted themselves to the education of girls. Together these new religious orders restored the confidence of the faithful in the dedication and power of the Catholic church.

Catholic missionaries set sail throughout the globe in order to bring Roman Catholicism to Africans, Asians, and native Americans. They saw their effort as proof of the truth of Roman Catholicism and the success of their missions as a sign of divine favor, both particularly important in the face of Protestant challenge. To ensure rapid Christianization, European missionaries focused initially on winning over local elites. A number of young African nobles went to Portugal to be trained in theology. Catholic missionaries preached the Gospel to Confucian scholar officials in China and to the samurai (the warrior aristocracy) in Japan. Measured in numbers alone, the missionary enterprise seemed highly successful: by the second half of the sixteenth century, vast multitudes of native Americans had become Christians at least in name, and thirty years after Francis Xavier's 1549 landing in Japan the Jesuits could claim over 100,000 Japanese converts.

After an initial period of relatively little racial discrimination, the Catholic church in the Americas and Africa adopted strict rules based on color. For example, the first Mexican Ecclesiastical Provincial Council in 1555 declared that holy orders were not to be conferred on Indians, mestizos (people of mixed European-Indian parentage), or mulattoes (people of mixed European-African heritage), groups deemed "inherently unworthy of the sacerdotal [priestly] office." Europeans reinforced their sense of racial superiority with their perception of the "treachery" that native Americans and Africans exhibited whenever they resisted domination. Frustrated in his efforts to convert Brazilian Indians, a Jesuit missionary wrote to his superior in Rome in 1563 that "for this kind of people it is better to be preaching with the sword and rod of iron." The Dominican Bartolomé de Las Casas (1474–1566) criticized the treatment of the Indians in Spanish America, yet even he argued that Africans should be imported in order to relieve the indigenous peoples, who were being worked to death.

■ **REVIEW:** *In what ways did Luther, Zwingli, and Calvin challenge the Roman Catholic church?*

State Power and Religious Conflict, 1500–1618

Even as religious disputes heightened the potential for conflict within Europe, the European powers continued to fight their traditional dynastic wars and still faced the military threat posed by the Muslim Ottoman Turks in the east. But these wars did not long deflect attention from increasing divisions within European countries. Rulers viewed religious divisions as a dangerous challenge to the unity of their realms and the stability of their regimes; a subject could very well swear greater allegiance to God than to his lord. Yet rulers often proved powerless to stem the rising tide of religious strife. Lutheranism flourished in the northern German states and Scandinavia; Calvinism spread from its headquarters in the Swiss city of Geneva all the way to England and Poland-Lithuania. The rapid expansion of Lutheranism and Calvinism created deadly political conflicts between Protestants and Catholics.

■ **MAP 12.2 Habsburg-Valois-Ottoman Wars, 1494–1559**
As the dominant European power, the Habsburg dynasty fought on two fronts: a religious war against the Islamic Ottoman Empire and a political war against the French Valois, who challenged Habsburg hegemony. The Mediterranean, the Balkans, and the Low Countries all became theaters of war.

Wars among Habsburgs, Valois, and Ottomans

While the Reformation was taking hold in the German states, the great powers of Spain and France fought each other for the domination of Europe (Map 12.2). French claims over Italian territories sparked conflict in 1494, but the ensuing Italian Wars soon involved most Christian monarchs and the Muslim Ottoman sultan as well. Despite some spectacular and bloody turns of fortune, no one power ultimately emerged victorious. In 1525, the troops of Habsburg Emperor Charles V crushed the French army at Pavia, Italy, and captured the French king, Francis I (r. 1515–1547). Charles treated Francis as an honored guest but held him in Spain until he agreed to renounce his claims to Italy. Furious at this humiliation, Francis repudiated the agreement the moment he returned to France, reigniting the conflict. In 1527, Charles's troops invaded and then pillaged Rome to punish the pope for allying with the French. Among the imperial troops were German Protestant mercenaries, who pillaged Catholic churches. The sack of Rome shocked the Catholic church hierarchy and helped turn it toward renewal.

Charles could not crush the French in one swift blow because he also had to counter the Muslim Ottomans in Hungary and along the Mediterranean coastline. The Ottoman Empire reached its height of power under Sultan Suleiman I, "the Magnificent" (r. 1520–1566). In 1526, a Turkish force destroyed the Hungarian army at Mohács. Three years later, the Ottoman army laid siege to Vienna; though unsuccessful, the siege shocked Christian Europe. In 1535, Charles V tried to capture Tunis, the lair of North African pirates under Ottoman rule. Desperate to overcome Charles's superior forces in Europe, Francis I eagerly forged an alliance with the Turkish sultan. The Turkish fleet besieged Nice, on the southern coast of France, to help the French wrest it from imperial occupiers. Francis even ordered all inhabitants of nearby Toulon to vacate their town so that he could turn it into a Muslim colony for eight months, complete with a mosque and slave market. The Franco-Turkish alliance, however brief, showed that the age-old idea of Christian crusade against Islam had to make way for a new political strategy that considered religion as but one factor in power politics.

In 1559, the French king finally acknowledged defeat and signed the peace treaty of Cateau-Cambrésis. By then, years of conflict had drained the treasuries of all monarchs. Fueled by warfare, all armies grew in size, firepower

■ **The Battle at Mohács**
This Ottoman painting shows the 1529 victory of the sultan's army over the Hungarians at Mohács. The battle resulted in the end of the Hungarian kingdom, which would be divided into three realms under Ottoman, Habsburg, and Transylvanian rule. Notice the prominence of artillery and the Ottoman fighting force (the Janissaries) with muskets. The Ottomans commanded a vast army with modern equipment, a key to their military prowess in the sixteenth century.
(Topkapi Palace Museum.)

became ever more deadly, and costs soared. For example, heavier artillery pieces meant that the rectangular walls of medieval cities had to be transformed into fortresses with jutting forts and gun emplacements. Charles V boasted the largest army in Europe—but he could not make ends meet with the proceeds from taxation, the sale of offices, and even outright confiscation.

Like other rulers, Charles V looked to private bankers for funds. Charles relied on the Fugger bank, based in the southern German imperial city of Augsburg. Jakob Fugger (1459–1525) had loaned money to Charles V's grandfather, Maximilian I, in exchange for mining and minting concessions as well as hefty interest payments. In 1519, Fugger assembled a consortium of German and Italian bankers to secure the election of Charles V as Holy Roman Emperor. The assets of the Fuggers more than doubled between 1527 and 1547; Charles V's debts nearly doubled, too. The French kings fared no better. On his death in 1547, Francis owed the bankers of Lyon nearly 7 million pounds—approximately the entire royal income for that year. As a result, the Valois and the Habsburgs had to pay 14 to 18 percent interest on their loans.

French Wars of Religion

During the 1540s and 1550s, one-third of the French nobles converted to Calvinism, usually influenced by noblewomen who protected pastors, provided money and advice, and helped found schools and establish relief for the poor. With this noble backing, the Reformed church organized openly and held synods (church meetings), especially in southern and western France. The Catholic Valois monarchy tried to maintain a balance of power between Catholics and Calvinists. Francis I and his successor, Henry II (r. 1547–1559), both succeeded to a degree. But when Henry was accidentally killed during a jousting tournament, the weakened monarchy could no longer hold together the fragile realm. Henry was succeeded first by his fifteen-year-old son Francis II, who died in 1560, and then by his ten-year-old son, Charles IX (r. 1560–1574).

Catherine de Medicis (1519–1589), the Italian wife of Henry II, acted as regent for her young son. She first urged limited toleration for the Calvinists—called **Huguenots** in France—in an attempt to maintain political stability, but she could not prevent the eruption of civil war between Catholics and Huguenots in 1562. Although a Catholic herself, Catherine desperately tried to play the Catholic and Huguenot factions off each other so that neither would dominate. To this end, she arranged the marriage of her daughter Marguerite to Henry of Navarre, head of the Bourbon family, which had converted to Calvinism. Just four days after the wedding in August 1572, assassins tried but failed to kill one of the Huguenot nobles allied with the Bourbons, Gaspard de Coligny. Panicked at the thought of Huguenot revenge and perhaps herself implicated in the botched plot, Catherine convinced her son to order the killing

Protestant Churches in France, 1562

of leading Huguenots. On St. Bartholomew's Day, August 24, a bloodbath began, fueled by years of growing animosity between Catholics and Protestants. In three days, Catholic mobs murdered three thousand Huguenots in Paris. Ten thousand died in the provinces over the next six weeks. The pope joyfully ordered the church bells rung throughout Catholic Europe; Spain's Philip II wrote Catherine that it was "the best and most cheerful news which at present could come to me." Protestants and Catholics alike now saw the conflict as an international struggle for survival that required aid to coreligionists in other countries. In this way, the French Wars of Religion paved the way for wider international conflicts over religion in the future.

The religious division in France grew even more dangerous when Charles IX died and his brother Henry III (r. 1574–1589) became king. Like his brothers before him, Henry III failed to produce an heir. Next in line to succeed the throne was none other than the Calvinist Bourbon leader Henry of Navarre. Because Henry III saw an even greater threat to his authority in a newly formed Catholic League, which had requested Spain's help in rooting out Protestantism in France, he took action against the league. In 1588, he summoned two prominent league leaders to a meeting and had his men kill them. A few months later a fanatical monk stabbed Henry III to death, and Henry of Navarre became Henry IV (r. 1589–1610), despite Spain's attempt to block his way with military intervention.

The new king soon concluded that to establish control over the war-weary country he had to place the interests of the French state ahead of his Protestant faith. In 1593, Henry IV publicly embraced Catholicism, reputedly explaining his conversion with the phrase "Paris is worth a Mass." In 1598, he made peace with Spain and issued the Edict of Nantes, in which he granted the Huguenots a large measure of religious toleration. The approximately 1.25 million Huguenots became a legally protected minority within an officially Catholic kingdom of some 20 million people. Protestants were free to worship in specified towns and were allowed their own troops, fortresses, and even courts. Few believed in religious toleration, but Henry IV followed the advice of those neutral Catholics and Calvinists called **politiques** who urged him to give priority to the development of a durable state. Although their opponents hated them for their compromising spirit, the politiques believed that religious disputes could be resolved only in the peace provided by strong government.

The Edict of Nantes ended the French Wars of Religion, but Henry still needed to reestablish monarchical authority. He used court festivities and royal processions to rally subjects around him, and he developed a new class of royal officials to counterbalance the fractious nobility. In exchange for an annual payment, officials who had purchased their offices could pass them on to heirs or sell them to someone else. By buying offices that eventually ennobled their holders, rich middle-class merchants and lawyers could become part of a new social elite known as the "nobility of the robe" (named after the robes that magistrates wore, much like those judges wear today). New income raised by the increased sale of offices reduced the state debt and helped Henry build the base for a strong monarchy. His efforts did not, however, prevent his own assassination in 1610 after nineteen unsuccessful attempts.

Challenges to Habsburg Power and the Rise of the Dutch Republic

Charles V proved more successful at fending off the Turks and subduing the French than he did at resolving growing religious conflicts inside his empire. After an Imperial Diet at Regensburg in 1541 failed to patch up the theological differences between Protestants and Catholics, Charles secured papal support for a war against the Schmalkaldic League, a powerful alliance of Lutheran princes and cities. Charles's army occupied the German imperial cities in the south, restoring Catholic patricians and suppressing the Reformation wherever they triumphed. In 1547, Charles defeated the Schmalkaldic League armies at Mühlberg and captured the leading Lutheran princes. Jubilant, Charles proclaimed a decree, the "Interim," which restored Catholics' right to worship in Protestant lands while still permitting Lutherans to celebrate their own services. Riots broke out in many cities as resistance to the Interim spread. Charles's victory proved ephemeral, for after one of his former allies, Duke Maurice of Saxony, joined the other side, the princes revived the war in 1552 and chased a surprised, unprepared, and practically bankrupt emperor back to Italy.

Forced to negotiate, Charles V agreed to the Peace of Augsburg in 1555. The settlement recognized the Lutheran church in the empire, accepted the secularization of church lands but kept the remaining ecclesiastical territories (mainly the bishoprics) for Catholics, and, most important, established the principle that all princes, whether Catholic or Lutheran, enjoyed the sole right to determine the religion of their lands and subjects. Significantly, the Peace excluded Calvinist, Anabaptist, and other dissenting groups from the settlement. The Peace of Augsburg preserved a fragile peace in central Europe until 1618, but the exclusion of Calvinists would plant the seeds for future conflict.

Exhausted by constant war and depressed by the disunity in Christian Europe, Charles V resigned his many thrones in 1555 and 1556, leaving his Netherlandish-Burgundian and Spanish dominions to his son, Philip II, and his Austrian lands to his brother, Ferdinand, who was also elected Holy Roman Emperor to succeed Charles. Retiring to a monastery in southern Spain, the once powerful Christian monarch spent his last years quietly seeking salvation. Although Philip II of Spain (r. 1556–1598) ruled over fewer territories than his father, his inheritance still left him the most powerful ruler in Europe (Map 12.3). In addition to the western Habsburg lands in Spain and the Netherlands, he had inherited all the Spanish colonies recently settled in the New World of the Americas. In 1580, when the king of Portugal died without a direct heir, Philip took over this neighboring realm with its rich empire in Africa, India, and the Americas. Gold and silver funneled from the colonies supported his campaigns against the Ottoman Turks and French and English Protestants.

A deeply devout Catholic, Philip II came to the Spanish throne at age twenty-eight determined to restore Catholic unity in Europe and lead the Christian defense against the Muslims. His brief marriage to Mary Tudor (Mary I of England) did not produce an heir, but it and his subsequent marriage to Elisabeth de Valois, the sister of Charles IX and Henry III of France, gave him reason enough to oppose the spread of Protestantism in England and France. In 1571, Philip joined with Venice and the papacy to defeat the Turks in a great sea battle off the Greek coast at Lepanto. But Philip could not rest on his laurels. Between 1568 and 1570, the Moriscos—Muslim converts to Christianity who remained secretly faithful to Islam—had revolted in the south of Spain, killing 90 priests and 1,500 Christians.

■ **Titian, *Gloria* (detail)**
All military glory and earthly power is doomed to fade away, as the Venetian painter Titian (1477–1576) vividly depicted in Gloria. Among the multitude turning to the Trinity in the heavens is the Emperor Charles V, dressed in a white robe. Painted after his abdication in 1556, Gloria is a reminder to Charles of the transience of earthly glory, for white is both the color of newborn innocence and that of the burial shroud. (Institut Amatller d'Art Hispanic.)

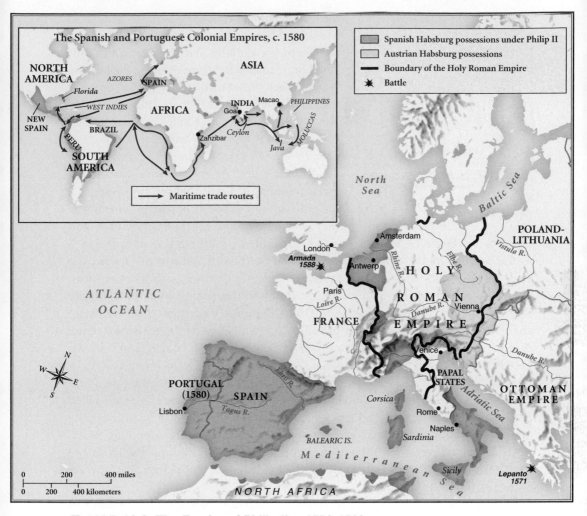

■ **MAP 12.3 The Empire of Philip II, r. 1556–1598**
Spanish king Philip II drew revenues from a truly worldwide empire. In 1580, he was the richest European ruler, but the demands of governing such far-flung territories eventually drained many of his resources. **For more help analyzing this map,** *see the map activity for this chapter in the* ONLINE STUDY GUIDE *at* bedfordstmartins.com/huntconcise.

The victory at Lepanto destroyed any prospect that the Turks might come to their aid, yet Philip nonetheless forced 50,000 Moriscos to leave their villages and resettle in other regions. In 1609, his successor, Philip III, ordered their expulsion, and by 1614 some 300,000 Moriscos had been forced to relocate to North Africa.

The Calvinists of the Netherlands were less easily intimidated than the Moriscos: they were far from Spain and accustomed to being left alone. In 1566, Calvinists in

The Netherlands during the Revolt, c. 1580

the Netherlands attacked Catholic churches, smashing stained-glass windows and statues of the Virgin Mary. Philip sent an army, which executed more than 1,100 people during the next six years. When resistance revived, the Spanish responded with more force, culminating in November 1576 when Philip's armies sacked Antwerp, then Europe's wealthiest commercial city. In eleven days of horror known as the Spanish Fury, the Spanish soldiers slaughtered seven thousand people. Shocked into response, the ten Catholic southern provinces joined with the seven Protestant northern provinces and expelled the Spaniards. In 1579, however, the Catholic southern provinces returned to the Spanish fold. Despite the assassination in 1584 of William of Orange, the leader of the anti-Spanish forces, Spanish troops never regained control in the north.

Spain would not formally recognize Dutch independence until 1648, but by the end of the sixteenth century the Dutch Republic was a self-governing state sheltering a variety of religious groups. The princes of Orange (whose name came from family lands in southern France) resembled a ruling family in the Dutch Republic, but their powers paled next to those of local interests. Urban merchant and professional families known as "regents" controlled the towns and provinces. Each province (Holland was the most populous of the seven provinces) governed itself and sent delegates to the one common institution, the States General. Well situated for maritime commerce, the Dutch Republic developed a thriving economy based on shipping and shipbuilding. By 1670, the Dutch commercial fleet was larger than the English, French, Spanish, Portuguese, and Austrian fleets combined.

Dutch society tolerated more religious diversity than the other European states. One-third of the Dutch population remained Catholic, and the secular authorities allowed Catholics to worship as they chose in private. Because Protestant sects could generally count on toleration from local regents, they remained peaceful. The Dutch Republic also had a relatively large Jewish population because many Jews had settled there after being driven out of Spain and Portugal; from 1597, Jews could worship openly in their synagogues. This openness to various religions helped make the Dutch Republic one of Europe's chief intellectual and scientific centers in the seventeenth and eighteenth centuries.

England Goes Protestant

Until 1527, England's king Henry VIII (r. 1509–1547) firmly opposed the Reformation, even receiving the title "Defender of the Faith" from Pope Leo X for a treatise Henry wrote against Luther. Henry's family problems changed his mind. Henry had married Catherine of Aragon (d. 1536), the daughter of Ferdinand and Isabella of Spain and the aunt of Charles V, and the marriage had produced a daughter, Princess Mary (known as Mary Tudor). Henry wanted a male heir to consolidate the rule of his Tudor dynasty, and he had fallen in love with Anne Boleyn, a lady-in-waiting at court and a strong supporter of the Reformation. In 1527, Henry asked the reigning pope, Clement VII, to declare his eighteen-year marriage to Catherine invalid on the grounds that she was the widow of his older brother, Arthur. Arthur and Catherine's marriage, which apparently was never consummated, had been annulled by Pope Julius II. When Henry failed to secure a papal dispensation for his divorce, he chose two Protestants as his new loyal servants: Thomas Cromwell (1485–1540) as chancellor and Thomas Cranmer (1489–1556) as archbishop of Canterbury. Under their leadership the English Parliament passed a number of acts that severed ties between the English church and Rome. The Act of Supremacy of 1529 established Henry as the head of the Anglican church (the Church of England), invalidated the claims of Catherine and Princess Mary to the throne, recognized Henry's marriage to Anne Boleyn, and allowed the English crown to confiscate the properties of the monasteries.

By 1536, Henry had grown tired of Anne Boleyn, who had given birth to the future Queen Elizabeth I but had produced no sons. The king, who would go on to marry four other wives but father only one son, Edward (by his third wife, Jane Seymour), had Anne beheaded on the charge of adultery, an act that he defined as treason. Thomas More, once Henry's chancellor, had been executed in 1535 for treason—in his case, for refusing to recognize Henry as "the only supreme head on earth of the Church of England"—and Cromwell suffered the same fate in 1540 when he lost favor. After Henry's death in 1547, the Anglican church, nominally Protestant, still retained much traditional Catholic doctrine and ritual. But the principle of royal supremacy in religious matters would remain a lasting feature of Henry's reforms.

When Henry's Protestant son Edward VI (r. 1547–1553) died at age 16, his half-sister Mary Tudor (r. 1553–1558) succeeded him. She restored Catholicism and executed three hundred Protestants. Hundreds more fled. Finally, after Anne Boleyn's daughter, Elizabeth, came to the throne in 1558, the Anglican cause again gained momentum. As Elizabeth I (r. 1558–1603) moved to solidify her personal power and the authority of the Anglican church, she had to squash uprisings by Catholics in the north and at least two serious plots against her life. She also had to hold off Calvinist Puritans who pushed for more reform and Spain's Philip II, who first wanted to be her husband then, failing that, planned to invade her country to restore Catholicism.

The **Puritans** were strict Calvinists who opposed all vestiges of Catholic ritual in the Church of England. After Elizabeth became queen, many Puritans returned

Elizabeth Regina.

2. PARALIPOM. 6.
Domine Deus Israel, non est similis tui Deus in cœlo & in ter-
ra,qui pacta custodis & misericordiam cum seruis tuis, qui
ambulant coram te in toto corde suo.

■ **Queen Elizabeth I of England**
*The Anglican (Church of England)
Prayerbook of 1569 included a hand-
colored print of Queen Elizabeth saying her prayers. As queen, Elizabeth
was also official head of the Church of
England (the scepter or sword at her
feet symbolizes her power). She named
bishops and made final decisions
about every aspect of church
governance.* **For more help analyzing
this image,** see the visual activity for
this chapter in the ONLINE STUDY
GUIDE at bedfordstmartins.com/
huntconcise. (Bridgeman Art Library.)

from exile abroad, but Elizabeth
resisted their demands for drastic
changes in Anglican ritual and
governance. She had assumed
control as "supreme governor"
of the Church of England,
replacing the pope as the ultimate religious authority, and
she appointed all bishops. The
Church of England's Thirty-Nine
Articles of Religion, issued in
1563, incorporated elements of
Catholic ritual along with
Calvinist doctrines. Puritan ministers angrily denounced the Church of England's
"popish attire and foolish disguising, . . . tithings, holy days, and a thousand more
abominations." Puritans tried to undercut the bishops' authority by placing control
of church administration in the hands of the local congregation. Elizabeth rejected
this Calvinist "presbyterianism." The Puritans nonetheless steadily gained influence.
Known for their emphasis on strict moral lives, the Puritans tried to close the theaters and Sunday fairs and insisted that every father "make his house a little church"
by teaching the children to read the Bible. At Puritan urging, a new translation of
the Bible, known as the King James Bible after Elizabeth's successor, James I, was
authorized in 1604. Believing themselves God's elect and England an "elect nation,"
the Puritans also urged Elizabeth to help Protestants in Europe.

Spain's Philip II had been married to Elizabeth's half-sister Mary Tudor and
had enthusiastically seconded Mary's efforts to return England to Catholicism.
When Mary died, Elizabeth rejected Philip's proposal of marriage and eventually
provided funds and troops to the Dutch rebels. Philip II bided his time as long as

she remained unmarried and her Catholic cousin Mary Stuart—better known as Mary, Queen of Scots—stood next in line to inherit the English throne. In 1568, Scottish Calvinists forced Mary to abdicate the throne of Scotland in favor of her year-old son James (eventually James I of England), who was then raised as a Protestant. The Scottish Calvinists feared Mary's connections to Catholic France; her mother was French and devoutly Catholic, and Mary Stuart had earlier been married to France's Francis II (he died in 1560). After her abdication, Mary spent nearly twenty years under house arrest in England, fomenting plots against Elizabeth. In 1587, when Mary's letter offering her succession rights to Philip was discovered, Elizabeth overcame her reluctance to execute a fellow monarch and ordered Mary's beheading.

In response, Pope Sixtus V decided to subsidize a Catholic crusade under Philip's leadership against the heretical queen. At the end of May 1588, Philip II sent his armada (Spanish for "fleet") of 130 ships from Lisbon toward the English Channel. The English scattered the Spanish Armada by sending blazing fire ships into its midst. A great gale then forced the Spanish to flee around Scotland. When the Armada limped home in September, half the ships had been lost and thousands of sailors were dead or starving. Protestants throughout Europe rejoiced. A Spanish monk lamented, "Almost the whole of Spain went into mourning."

By the time Philip II died in 1598, his great empire had begun to lose its luster. The costs of fighting the Dutch, the English, and the French mounted, and an overburdened peasantry could no longer pay the taxes required to meet rising expenses. In his novel *Don Quixote* (1605), the Spanish writer Miguel de Cervantes captured the sadness of Spain's loss of grandeur. Cervantes himself had been wounded at Lepanto, held captive in Algiers, and then served as a royal tax collector. His hero, a minor nobleman, reads so many romances and books of chivalry that he loses his wits and wanders the countryside hoping to re-create the heroic deeds of times past. He refuses to believe that these books are only fantasies: "Books which are printed under license from the king . . . can such be lies?" Don Quixote's futile adventures incarnated the thwarted ambitions of a declining military aristocracy.

England could never have defeated Spain in a head-to-head battle on land, but Elizabeth made the most of her limited means and consolidated the country's position as a Protestant power. In her early years, she held out the prospect of marriage to many political suitors but never married. She cajoled Parliament with references to her female weaknesses, but she showed steely-eyed determination in protecting the monarchy's interests. Her chosen successor, James I (r. 1603–1625), came to the throne as king of both Scotland and England. Elizabeth left James secure in a kingdom of growing weight in world politics.

■ **REVIEW:** *How did the power of states depend on unity in religion?*

The Thirty Years' War and the Balance of Power, 1618–1648

In 1618, a new series of violent conflicts between Catholics and Protestants erupted in the Holy Roman Empire. The final and most deadly of the wars of religion, the Thirty Years' War eventually drew in most European states. By the end of the war in 1648, many central European lands lay in ruins and many rulers were bankrupt. Reformation and Counter-Reformation had shattered the Christian humanist dream of peace and unity. The Thirty Years' War brought the preceding religious conflicts to a head and by its very violence effectively removed religion from future European disputes. Although religion still divided people *within* various states, after 1648 religion no longer provided the rationale for wars *between* European states. Out of the carnage would emerge centralized and powerful states that made increasing demands on ordinary people.

Origins and Course of the War

The fighting that devastated central Europe had its origins in religious, political, and ethnic divisions within the Holy Roman Empire. The Austrian Habsburg emperor and four of the seven electors who chose him were Catholic; the other three electors were Protestants. The Peace of Augsburg of 1555 was supposed to maintain the balance between Catholics and Lutherans, but it had no mechanism for resolving conflicts. Tensions rose as the Jesuits won many Lutheran cities back to Catholicism and as Calvinism, unrecognized under the Peace, made inroads into Lutheran areas. By 1613, two of the three Protestant electors had become Calvinists. When the Catholic Habsburg heir Archduke Ferdinand was crowned king of Bohemia in 1617, he began to curtail the religious freedom previously granted to Protestants. Protestants wanted to build new churches; Ferdinand wanted to stop them. Tensions boiled over when two Catholic deputy-governors tried to dissolve the meetings of Protestants.

On May 23, 1618, a crowd of angry Protestants surged up the stairs of the royal castle in Prague, trapped the two Catholic deputies, dragged them screaming for mercy to the windows, and hurled them to the pavement below. Because they landed in a dung heap, the Catholic deputies survived. Although no one died, this "defenestration" (from the French for "window," *la fenêtre*) of Prague touched off a new cycle of conflict. The Czechs, the largest ethnic group in Bohemia, established a Protestant assembly to spearhead resistance. A year later, when Ferdinand was elected emperor (as Ferdinand II, r. 1619–1637), the rebellious Bohemians deposed him and chose in his place the young Calvinist Frederick V of the Palatinate (r. 1616–1623). A quick series of clashes ended in 1620 when the imperial armies defeated the outmanned Czechs at the Battle of White Mountain, near Prague (see Map 12.4). Like the martyrdom of the religious reformer Jan Hus in 1415, White Mountain became an enduring symbol of the Czechs' desire for self-determination. They would not gain their independence until 1918.

White Mountain did not end the war. Private mercenary armies (armies for hire) began to form during the fighting, and the emperor had virtually no control over them. In 1625, a Czech Protestant, Albrecht von Wallenstein (1583–1634), offered to raise an army for the Catholic emperor and soon had in his employ 125,000 soldiers, who occupied and plundered much of Protestant Germany with the emperor's approval. In response, the Lutheran king of Denmark Christian IV (r. 1596–1648) invaded to protect the Protestants and to extend his own influence. Wallenstein's forces defeated him. Emboldened by his general's victories, Ferdinand issued the Edict of Restitution in 1629, which outlawed Calvinism in the empire and reclaimed Catholic church properties confiscated by the Lutherans.

With Protestant interests in serious jeopardy, Gustavus Adolphus (r. 1611–1632) of Sweden marched into Germany in 1630. A Lutheran by religion, he also hoped to gain control over trade in northern Europe, where he had already ejected the Poles from present-day Latvia and Estonia. Poland and Lithuania had joined in a commonwealth (common state) in 1569, and many Polish and Lithuanian nobles converted to Lutheranism or Calvinism, but this did not ensure common cause with Sweden. Gustavus's highly trained army of some 100,000 soldiers made Sweden, with a population of only one million, the supreme power of northern Europe, even more powerful than Russia, which had barely recovered from the "Time of Troubles" that followed on the rule of Tsar Ivan IV (r. 1533–1584). Ivan "the Terrible" initiated Russian expansion eastward into Siberia, but his moves westward ran up against the Poles and the Swedes.

Although Gustavus had religious motives for intervention in German affairs, events soon showed that power politics trumped religious interests. The Catholic French government under the leadership of Louis XIII (r. 1610–1643) and his chief minister Cardinal Richelieu (1585–1642) offered to subsidize Gustavus—and the Lutheran ruler accepted. The French hoped to counter Spanish involvement in the war and win influence and perhaps territory in the Holy Roman Empire. Gustavus defeated the imperial army and occupied the Catholic parts of southern Germany before he was killed at the battle of Lützen in 1632 (see Map 12.4). Once again the tide turned, but this time it swept Wallenstein with it. Because Wallenstein was rumored to be negotiating with Protestant powers, Ferdinand dismissed his general and had his henchmen assassinate him.

France openly joined the fray in 1635 by declaring war on Spain and soon after forged an alliance with the Calvinist Dutch to aid them in their struggle for independence from Spain. The two Catholic powers, France and Spain, pummeled each other. The Swedes kept up their pressure in Germany, the Dutch attacked the Spanish fleet, and a series of internal revolts shook the cash-strapped Spanish

Ic'y par vn effort facrilege et barbare   Pillent, et bruſlent tout, abattent les Autels ;   Et tirent des ſaincts lieux les Vierges deſolees
Ces Demons enragez, et d'vne humeur ouare   Se mocquent du reſpect qu'on doit aux Immortels,   Quils oſent enleuer pour eſtre violées .   6

■ **The Horrors of the Thirty Years' War**
The French artist Jacques Callot produced this engraving of the Thirty Years' War as part of a series called The Miseries and Misfortunes of War (1633). It shows soldiers burning down a church, pillaging the goods of local residents, and carrying off girls to rape them.
(Grosjean Collection, Paris/The Bridgeman Art Library.)

crown. In 1640, peasants in the rich northeastern province of Catalonia rebelled, overrunning Barcelona and killing the viceroy; the Catalans resented government confiscation of their crops and demands that they house and feed soldiers on their way to the French frontier. The Portuguese revolted in 1640 and proclaimed independence like the Dutch. In 1643, the Spanish suffered their first major defeat at French hands. Although the Spanish were forced to concede independence to Portugal (part of Spain only since 1580), they eventually suppressed the Catalan revolt.

France, too, faced exhaustion after years of rising taxes and recurrent revolts. In 1642, Richelieu died. Louis XIII followed him a few months later and was succeeded by his five-year-old son Louis XIV. With the queen mother, Anne of Austria, serving as regent and depending on the Italian cardinal, Mazarin, for advice, French politics once again moved into a period of instability, rumor, and crisis. All sides were ready for peace.

The Effects of Constant Fighting

When peace negotiations began in the 1640s, they did not come a moment too soon for the ordinary people of Europe. Some towns faced up to ten or eleven prolonged sieges during the fighting. In 1648, as negotiations dragged on, a

Swedish army sacked the rich cultural capital Prague, plundered its churches and castles, and effectively eliminated it as a center of culture and learning. Even worse suffering took place in the countryside. Peasants fled their villages, which were often burned down. War and intermittent outbreaks of plague cost some German towns one-third or more of their population. One-third of the inhabitants of Bohemia also perished.

Soldiers did not fare all that much better. Governments increasingly short of funds often failed to pay the troops, and frequent mutinies, looting, and pillaging resulted. Armies attracted all sorts of displaced people desperately in need of provisions. In the last year of the Thirty Years' War, the Imperial-Bavarian Army had 40,000 men entitled to draw rations—and more than 100,000 wives, prostitutes, servants, children, maids, and other camp followers forced to scrounge for their own food. The bureaucracies of early-seventeenth-century Europe simply could not cope with such demands: armies and their hangers-on had to live off the countryside.

The Peace of Westphalia, 1648

The comprehensive settlement finally provided by the Peace of Westphalia—named after the German province where negotiations took place—would serve as a model for resolving conflict among warring European states. For the first time, a diplomatic congress addressed international disputes, and the signatories to the treaties guaranteed the resulting settlement. A method still in use, the congress was the first to bring *all* parties together, rather than two or three at a time.

France and Sweden gained most from the Peace of Westphalia. Although France and Spain continued fighting until 1659, France replaced Spain as the prevailing power on the European continent and acquired parts of Alsace, a region on its eastern border that would remain a source of conflict between French and German rulers well into the twentieth century. Baltic conflicts would not be resolved until 1661, but Sweden took several northern territories from the Holy Roman Empire (see Map 12.4, on page 502).

The Habsburgs lost the most. The Spanish Habsburgs recognized Dutch independence after eighty years of war. The Swiss Confederation and the German princes demanded autonomy from the Austrian Habsburg rulers of the Holy Roman Empire. Each German prince gained the right to establish Lutheranism, Catholicism, or Calvinism in his state, a right denied to Calvinist rulers by the Peace of Augsburg in 1555. The independence ceded to German princes sustained political divisions that would remain until the nineteenth century and prepared the way for the emergence of a new power, the Hohenzollern Elector of Brandenburg, who increased his territories and developed a small but effective standing army. After losing considerable territory in the west, the Austrian

■ **MAP 12.4 The Thirty Years' War and the Peace of Westphalia, 1648**
*The Thirty Years' War involved many of the major continental European powers. The arrows
marking invasion routes show that most of the fighting took place in central Europe in the lands
of the Holy Roman Empire. The German states and Bohemia sustained the greatest damage during the fighting. None of the combatants emerged unscathed because even ultimate winners such
as Sweden and France depleted their resources of men and money.*

Habsburgs turned eastward to concentrate on restoring Catholicism to Bohemia
and wresting Hungary from the Turks.

The Peace of Westphalia permanently settled the distributions of the main religions in the Holy Roman Empire: Lutheranism would dominate in the north,
Calvinism in the area of the Rhine River, and Catholicism in the south (see
"Mapping the West," page 519). Most of the territorial changes in Europe remained
intact until the nineteenth century. In the future, warfare between European states
would be undertaken for reasons of national security, commercial ambition, or
dynastic pride rather than to enforce religious uniformity. As the politiques of the

late sixteenth century had hoped, state interests now outweighed motivations of faith in political affairs.

Growth of State Authority

Warfare increased the reach of states: as the size of armies increased, governments needed more men, more money, and more supervisory officials. Most armies in the 1550s had fewer than 50,000 men, but Gustavus Adolphus had 100,000 men under arms in 1631. In France, the rate of land tax paid by peasants doubled in the eight years after France joined the Thirty Years' War. In addition to raising taxes, governments deliberately depreciated the value of the currency, which often resulted in inflation and soaring prices; sold new offices; and manipulated the embryonic stock and bond markets. When all else failed, they declared bankruptcy. The Spanish government, for example, did so three times in the first half of the seventeenth century.

As the demand for soldiers and for the money to supply them rose, the number of state employees multiplied, paperwork proliferated, and appointment to office began to depend on university education in the law. Monarchs relied on advisers who began to take on the role of modern prime ministers. As French king Louis XIII's chief minister, Richelieu arranged support for the Lutheran Gustavus even though Richelieu was a cardinal of the Catholic church. His priority was **raison d'état** ("reason of state")—that is, the state's interest above all else. Richelieu silenced Protestants within France because they had become too independent, and he crushed noble and popular resistance to Louis's policies. He set up intendants— delegates from the king's council dispatched to the provinces—to oversee police, army, and financial affairs. Richelieu and his intendants still had to contend with the thousands of officials who had bought their offices and therefore owned them as personal property.

To justify the growth of state authority and the expansion of government bureaucracies, rulers carefully cultivated their royal images. James I of England explicitly argued that he ruled by divine right and was accountable only to God: "kings are not only God's lieutenant on earth, but even by God himself they are called gods." But words rarely sufficed to make the point, and rulers used displays at court to overawe their subjects. Already in the 1530s, the French court of Francis I numbered 1,600 people. Included were officials to handle finances, guard duty, clothing, and food as well as physicians, librarians, musicians, dwarfs, animal trainers, and a multitude of hangers-on. When the court changed residence, which it did frequently, no fewer than 18,000 horses were required to transport the people, furniture, and documents—not to mention the dogs and falcons for the royal hunt. Hunting and mock battles honed the military skills of the male courtiers. Francis once staged a mock combat at court involving 1,200 "warriors," and he led a party to lay siege to a model town during which several players were accidentally killed.

Just as soldiers had to learn new drills for combat, courtiers had to learn to follow precise rituals. In his influential treatise, *The Courtier* (1528), the Italian diplomat Baldassare Castiglione (1478–1529) depicted the ideal courtier as a gentleman who speaks in a refined language and carries himself with nobility and dignity in the service of his prince and his lady. Spain's king Philip IV (r. 1621–1665) translated this notion of courtesy into detailed regulations that set the wages, duties, and ceremonial functions of every courtier. State funerals, public festivities, and court display, like the acquisition of art and the building of sumptuous palaces, served to underline the power and glory of the ruler.

▪ **REVIEW:** *Why did a war fought over religious disputes result in stronger states?*

From Growth to Recession

A major economic shift occurred alongside the struggles over beliefs. The Protestant Reformation started in a period of economic growth, but by the time of the Thirty Years' War recession had set in. In the sixteenth century, despite religious and political turbulence, population grew, doubling in Spain and increasing 70 percent in England. The supply of precious metals swelled, too. In the 1540s new silver mines had been discovered in Mexico and Peru. Spanish gold imports peaked in the 1550s, silver in the 1590s. (See "Taking Measure," below.) The flood of gold and silver fueled an astounding inflation in food

▪ **TAKING MEASURE The Rise and Fall of Silver Imports to Spain, 1550–1660**

Gold and silver from the New World enabled the king of Spain to pursue aggressive policies in Europe and around the world. At what point did silver imports reach their highest level? Was the fall in silver imports precipitous or gradual? What can we conclude about the resources available to the Spanish king?

prices in western Europe—400 percent in the sixteenth century—and a more moderate rise in the cost of manufactured goods. When recession struck after 1600, all the economic indicators slumped. Silver imports to Spain declined. Textile production collapsed. Agricultural prices dropped. Overall, Europe's population may actually have declined, from 85 million in 1550 to 80 million in 1650.

Causes and Consequences of Economic Crisis

Historians have long disagreed about the causes of the early-seventeenth century recession. Some cite the inability of agriculture to support a growing population by the end of the sixteenth century; others blame the Thirty Years' War, the states' demands for more taxes, the irregularities in money supply resulting from rudimentary banking practices, or the waste caused by middle-class expenditures in the desire to emulate the nobility. To this list of causes, recent researchers have added climate change. Global cooling translated into advancing glaciers, falling temperatures, and great storms, like the one that blocked the escape of the Spanish Armada. Bad harvests, food shortages, and famine followed in short order.

Economic crisis dramatically altered the rural landscape. As prices began to stagnate and population growth slowed, farmers converted grain-growing land to pasture or vineyards. Interest in improvement of the land diminished. In some places, peasants abandoned their villages and left land to waste, as had happened during the plague epidemic of the late fourteenth century. The only country that emerged relatively unscathed from this downturn was the Dutch Republic, principally because it had long excelled in agricultural innovation. Inhabiting Europe's most densely populated area, the Dutch developed systems of field drainage, crop rotation, and animal husbandry that provided high yields of grain for both people and animals. After the Dutch, the English fared best; unlike the Spanish, the English never depended on New World gold and silver, and unlike most continental European countries, England escaped the direct impact of the Thirty Years' War.

When grain harvests fell short, peasants immediately suffered because outside of England and the Dutch Republic, grain had replaced more expensive meat as the essential staple of most Europeans' diets. Peasants lived on bread, soup with a little fat or oil, peas or lentils, garden vegetables in season, and only occasionally a piece of meat or fish. Usually the adverse years differed from place to place, but from 1594 to 1597 most of Europe suffered from shortages that triggered revolts from Ireland to Muscovy. To head off social disorder, the English government drew up a new Poor Law in 1597 that required each community to support its poor. Many other governments also increased relief efforts.

Most people, however, did not respond to their dismal circumstances by rebelling or mounting insurrections. They simply left their huts and hovels and took to the road in search of food and charity. Overwhelmed officials recorded pitiful tales of suffering. Women and children died while waiting in line for food at convents or churches. Husbands left their wives and families to search for better conditions in other parishes or even other countries. Those left behind might be reduced to eating chestnuts, roots, bark, and grass. In eastern France in 1637, a witness reported, "The roads were paved with people. . . . Finally it came to cannibalism." Eventually compassion gave way to fear as these hungry vagabonds, who sometimes banded together to beg for bread, became more aggressive, occasionally threatening to burn a barn if they were not given food.

Successive bad harvests led to malnutrition, which weakened people and made them more susceptible to such epidemic diseases as the plague, typhoid fever, typhus, dysentery, smallpox, and influenza. Disease did not spare the rich, although many epidemics hit the poor hardest. The plague was feared most: in one year it could cause the death of up to half of a town or village's population, and it struck with no discernible pattern. Nearly 5 percent of France's entire population died in the plague of 1628–1632.

Economic crisis heightened the contrast between prosperity and poverty. In England, the Dutch Republic, northern France, and northwestern Germany, the peasantry was disappearing: improvements gave some peasants the means to become farmers who rented substantial holdings, produced for the market, and in good times enjoyed relative comfort and higher status. Those who could not afford to plant new crops such as buckwheat or to use techniques that ensured higher yields became simple laborers with little or no land of their own. One-half to four-fifths of the peasants in Europe did not have enough land to support a family. They descended deeper into debt during difficult times and often lost their land to wealthier farmers or to city officials intent on developing rural estates.

Families reacted almost immediately to economic crisis. During bad harvests, they postponed marriages and had fewer children. When hard times passed, more people married and had more children. But even in the best of times, one-fifth to one-quarter of all children died in their first year, and half died before age twenty. Ten percent of women died in childbirth, and even in the richest homes childbirth often occasioned an atmosphere of panic. It might be assumed that families would have more children to compensate for high death rates, but from around 1600 to 1800, families in all ranks of society started to limit the number of children. Because methods of contraception were not widely known, they did this for the most part by marrying later; the average age at marriage during the seventeenth century rose from the early twenties to the late twenties. The average family had about four children. Poorer families seem to have had fewer children, wealthier ones more. Peasant couples, especially in eastern and southeastern Europe, had more children than urban couples because cultivation still required intensive manual labor.

The consequences of late marriage were profound. Young men and women were expected to put off marriage (*and* sexual intercourse) until their mid to late

■ The Life of the Poor
*This mid-seventeenth-century
painting by the Dutch artist
Adriaen Pietersz van de Venne
depicts the poor peasant weighed
down by his wife and child. An
empty food bowl signifies their
hunger. In retrospect, this painting
seems unfair to the wife of the
family; she is shown in clothes
that are not nearly as tattered as
her husband's and is portrayed
entirely as a burden, rather than
as a help in getting by in hard
times. In reality, many poor men
abandoned their homes in search
of work, leaving their wives behind
to cope with hungry children and
what remained of the family farm.*
(Allen Memorial Art Museum, Oberlin
College, Oberlin, Ohio, Mrs. F. F. Prentiss
Fund, 1960. Inv. #1960.94.)

twenties—if they were among the lucky 50 percent who lived that long and not
among the 10 percent who never married. Because both the Reformation and the
Counter-Reformation stressed sexual fidelity and abstinence before marriage, the
number of births out of wedlock was relatively small (2–5 percent of births);
premarital intercourse was generally tolerated only after a couple had announced
their engagement.

The Economic Balance of Power

Just as the recession produced winners and losers among ordinary people, so, too,
it created winners and losers among the competing states of Europe. The seventeenth-century downturn ended the dominance of Mediterranean economies,
which had endured since the time of the Greeks and Romans, and ushered in the
new powers of northwestern Europe with their growing Atlantic economies. With
expanding populations and geographical positions that promoted Atlantic trade,
England and the Dutch Republic vied with France to become the leading

mercantile powers. Northern Italian industries were eclipsed; Spanish commerce with the New World dropped. Amsterdam replaced Seville, Venice, Genoa, and Antwerp as the center of European trade and commerce. The plague also had differing effects. Whereas central Europe and the Mediterranean countries took generations to recover from its ravages, northwestern Europe quickly replaced its lost population, no doubt because this area's people had suffered less from the effects of the Thirty Years' War and from the malnutrition related to the economic crisis.

All but the remnants of serfdom had disappeared in western Europe, but in eastern Europe nobles reinforced their dominance over peasants, and the burden of serfdom increased. The price rise of the sixteenth century had prompted Polish and eastern German nobles to expand their holdings and step up their production of grain for western markets. Although noble landlords lost income in the economic downturn of the first half of the seventeenth century, their peasants gained nothing. Those who were already dependent became serfs—completely tied to the land. In Muscovy, the complete enserfment of the peasantry would eventually be recognized in the Code of Laws in 1649. Although enserfment produced short-term profits for landlords, in the long run it retarded economic development in eastern Europe and kept most of the population in a stranglehold of illiteracy and hardship.

Competition for colonies overseas intensified because many European states, including Sweden and Denmark, considered it a branch of mercantilist policy. According to the doctrine of mercantilism, governments should sponsor policies to increase national wealth. To this end, they chartered private joint-stock companies to enrich investors by importing fish, furs, tobacco, and precious metals, if they could be found, and to develop new markets for European products. Because Spain and Portugal had divided among themselves the rich spoils of South America, other prospective colonizers had to carve niches in seemingly less hospitable places, especially North America and the Caribbean. Eventually the English, French, and Dutch would dominate commerce with these colonies (see Map 14.1, page 570).

In establishing permanent colonies, the Europeans created whole new communities across the Atlantic. Originally, the warm climate of Virginia made it an attractive destination for the Pilgrims, a small English sect that, unlike the Puritans, attempted to separate from the Church of England. But the *Mayflower*, which sailed for Virginia with Pilgrim emigrants, landed far to the north in Massachusetts, where in 1620 the settlers founded New Plymouth Colony. As the religious situation for English Puritans worsened, wealthier people became willing to emigrate, and in 1629 a prominent group of Puritans incorporated themselves as the Massachusetts Bay Company. They founded a virtually self-governing colony headquartered in Boston.

Colonization gradually spread. Migrating settlers, including dissident Puritans, soon founded new settlements in Connecticut and Rhode Island. Catholic refugees from England established a much smaller colony in Maryland. By the 1640s, the British North American colonies had more than fifty thousand people—not including the Indians, whose numbers had been decimated in epidemics and wars—and the foundations of representative government in locally chosen colonial assemblies. By contrast, French Canada had only about three thousand European inhabitants by 1640. Because the French government refused to let Protestants emigrate from France and establish a foothold in the New World, it denied itself a ready population for the settling of permanent colonies abroad. Both England and France turned their attention to the Caribbean in the 1620s and 1630s when they occupied the islands of the West Indies after driving off the native Caribs. These islands would prove ideal for a plantation economy of tobacco and sugarcane.

■ **REVIEW:** *What were the consequences of economic recession in the early 1600s?*

A Clash of Worldviews

The countries that moved ahead economically in this period—England, the Dutch Republic, and to some extent France—turned out to be the most receptive to new secular worldviews. Although secularization did not entail a loss of religious faith, it did prompt a search for nonreligious explanations for political authority and natural phenomena. During the late sixteenth and early seventeenth centuries, art, political theory, and science all began to break some of their bonds with religion. A "scientific revolution" was in the making. Yet traditional attitudes such as belief in magic and witchcraft did not disappear. People of all classes accepted supernatural explanations for natural phenomena, a view only gradually and partially undermined by new ideas.

The Arts in an Age of Religious Conflict

A new form of artistic expression—professional theater—developed to express secular values in this age of conflict over religious beliefs. In previous centuries, traveling companies made their living by playing at major religious festivals. In London, Seville, and Madrid, the first professional acting companies performed before paying audiences in the 1570s. A huge outpouring of playwriting followed. The Spanish playwright Lope de Vega (1562–1635) alone wrote more than fifteen hundred plays. Between 1580 and 1640, three hundred English playwrights produced works for a hundred different acting companies. Theaters did a banner business despite Puritan opposition in England and Catholic objections in Spain. Shopkeepers, apprentices, lawyers, and court nobles crowded into open-air theaters to see everything from bawdy farces to profound tragedies.

The most enduring and influential playwright of the time was the Englishman William Shakespeare (1564–1616), son of a glovemaker, who wrote three dozen plays and acted in one of the chief troupes. Shakespeare never referred to religious disputes in his plays and did not set the action in contemporary England. Yet his works clearly reflected the political concerns of his age: the nature of power and the crisis of authority. Three of his greatest tragedies—*Hamlet* (1601), *King Lear* (1605), and *Macbeth* (1606)—show the uncertainty and even chaos that result when power is misappropriated or misused. In each play, family relationships are linked to questions about the legitimacy of government, just as they were for Elizabeth I herself. Hamlet's mother marries the man who murdered his royal father and usurped the crown; two of Lear's daughters betray him when he tries to divide his kingdom; Macbeth's wife persuades him to murder the king and seize the throne. One character in the final act describes the tragic story of Prince Hamlet as one "Of carnal, bloody, and unnatural acts; / Of accidental judgments, casual slaughters; / Of deaths put on by cunning and forced cause." Like many real-life people, Shakespeare's tragic characters found little peace in the turmoil of their times.

Although many rulers commissioned paintings on secular subjects for their own uses, religion still played an important role in painting, especially in Catholic Europe. The popes competed with secular rulers to hire the most talented painters and sculptors. Pope Julius II, for example, engaged the Florentine Michelangelo Buonarroti (1475–1564) to paint the walls and ceiling of the Sistine Chapel and to prepare a tomb and sculpture for himself. Michelangelo's talents served to glorify a papacy under siege, just as other artists burnished the image of secular rulers.

In the late sixteenth century, the artistic style known as mannerism departed abruptly from the Renaissance perspective of painters like Michelangelo. An almost theatrical style, **mannerism** allowed painters to distort perspective to convey a message or emphasize a theme. The most famous mannerist painter, El Greco, created new and often strange visual effects. The religious intensity of his pictures shows that faith still motivated many artists, as it did much political conflict.

The most important new style was the **baroque**, which featured exaggerated lighting, intense emotions, release from restraint, and even a kind of artistic sensationalism. Baroque was not used as a label by people living at the time; in the eighteenth century, art critics coined the word to mean shockingly bizarre, confused, and extravagant, and until the late nineteenth century, art historians and collectors largely disdained the baroque. Closely tied to the Counter-Reformation, the baroque melodramatically reaffirmed the emotional depths of the Catholic faith and glorified both church and monarchy. The first great baroque painter was Peter Paul Rubens (1577–1640). Born in the Spanish Netherlands and trained in Italy, Rubens painted vivid, exuberant pictures on religious themes. The style spread from Rome to other Italian states and then into central Europe, Spain, and the Spanish Netherlands. The Spanish built baroque churches in their American colonies as part of their massive conversion campaign. The great Dutch Protestant painters of the next generation, such as Rembrandt van Rijn (1606–1669), sometimes used biblical subjects, but their pictures were more realistic and focused on everyday scenes. Many of them suggested the Protestant concern for an inner life and personal faith rather than the public expression of religiosity.

Differences in musical style also reflected religious divisions. The new Protestant churches developed their own distinct music, which differentiated their worship from the Catholic Mass. Unlike Catholic services, for which professional musicians sang in Latin, Protestant services invited the entire congregation to sing, thereby encouraging participation. Martin Luther, an accomplished lute player, composed many hymns in German, including "Ein' feste Burg" ("A Mighty Fortress"). Protestants sang hymns before going into battle, and Protestant martyrs sang before their executions.

A new secular musical form, the opera, grew up parallel to the baroque style in the visual arts. First influential in the Italian states, opera combined music, drama, dance, and scenery in a grand sensual display, often with themes chosen to please the ruler and the aristocracy. Like Shakespeare, opera composers often turned to familiar

■ Mannerist Painting

With its distortion of perspective, crowding of figures, and mysterious allusions, El Greco's painting The Dream of Philip II *(1577) is a typical mannerist painting. Philip II can be seen in his usual black clothing with a lace ruffle as his only decoration. The painter Domenikos Theotokopoulos was called El Greco because he was of Greek origin. He trained in Venice and Rome before he moved to Spain in the 1570s.*

(© National Gallery, London.)

■ **Baroque Painting**
The baroque painter Peter Paul Rubens used monumental canvases like this one from the Antwerp cathedral to celebrate the Catholic religion. Known as The Elevation of the Cross, *this painting from 1610 to 1611 shows one of the most important moments in the story of the crucifixion of Jesus.*
(The Bridgeman Art Library.)

stories their audiences would recognize and readily follow. One of the most innovative composers of opera was Claudio Monteverdi (1567–1643), whose work contributed to the development of both opera and the orchestra. His earliest operatic production, *Orfeo* (1607), was the first to require an orchestra of about forty instruments and to include instrumental as well as vocal sections.

The Natural Laws of Politics

In reaction to the wars over religious beliefs, jurists and scholars not only began to defend the primacy of state interests over those of religious conformity but also insisted on secular explanations for politics. Machiavelli had pointed in this direction with his prescriptions for Renaissance princes in the early sixteenth century, but the intellectual movement gathered steam in the aftermath of the religious violence unleashed by the Reformation. Religious toleration could not take hold until government could be organized on some principle other than one king, one faith. The French *politiques* Michel de Montaigne and Jean Bodin and the Dutch jurist Hugo Grotius started the search for those principles.

Michel de Montaigne (1533–1592) was a French magistrate who resigned his office in the midst of the wars of religion to write about the need for tolerance and open-mindedness. Although himself a Catholic, Montaigne painted on the beams of his study the words "All that is certain is that nothing is certain." To capture this need for personal reflection in an age of religious turmoil, he invented the essay as a short and thoughtful form of expression. He revived the ancient doctrine of skepticism, which held that total certainty is never attainable—a doctrine, like toleration of religious differences, that was repugnant to Protestants and Catholics alike, both of whom were certain that their religion was the right one. Montaigne also questioned the common European habit of calling newly discovered peoples in the New World barbarous and savage: "Everyone gives the title of barbarism to everything that is not in use in his own country."

The French Catholic lawyer Jean Bodin (1530–1596) sought systematic secular answers to the problem of disorder in *The Six Books of the Republic* (1576). Comparing the different forms of government throughout history, he identified three basic types of sovereignty: monarchy, aristocracy, and democracy. Only strong monarchical power offered hope for maintaining order, he insisted. Bodin rejected any doctrine of the right to resist tyrannical authority: "I denied that it was the function of a good man or of a good citizen to offer violence to his prince for any reason, however great a tyrant he might be" (and, it might be added, whatever his ideas on religion). Bodin's ideas helped lay the foundation for absolutism, the idea that the monarch should be the sole and uncontested source of power. Nonetheless, the very discussion of types of governments in the abstract implied that they might be subject to choice rather than simply being God-given, as most rulers maintained.

During the Dutch revolt against Spain, the jurist Hugo Grotius (1583–1645) gave new meaning to the notion of "natural law"—laws of nature that give legitimacy to government and stand above the actions of any particular ruler or religious group. Grotius argued that natural law stood beyond the reach of either secular or divine authority; it would be valid even if God did not exist. Natural law should govern politics, by this account, not Scripture, religious authority, or tradition. Such ideas got Grotius into trouble with both Catholics and Protestants. When the Dutch Protestant government arrested him, his wife helped him escape prison by hiding him in a chest of books. Grotius was one of the first to argue that international conventions should govern the treatment of prisoners of war and the making of peace treaties.

At the same time that Grotius expanded the principles of natural law, many jurists worked on codifying the huge amount of legislation and jurisprudence devoted to legal forms of torture. Most states and the courts of the Catholic church used torture when the crime was serious and the evidence seemed to point to a particular defendant but no definitive proof had been established. The judges ordered torture—hanging the accused by the hands with a rope thrown over a beam, pressing the legs in a leg screw, or just tying the hands very tightly—to extract a confession, which had to be given with a medical expert and notary present and had to be repeated without torture. Children, pregnant women, the elderly, aristocrats, kings, and even professors were exempt.

Grotius's conception of natural law directly challenged the use of torture. To be in accord with natural law, Grotius argued, governments had to defend natural rights, which he defined as life, body, freedom, and honor. Grotius's ideas would influence John Locke and the American revolutionaries of the eighteenth century:

although Grotius did not encourage rebellion in the name of natural law or rights, he did hope that someday all governments would adhere to these principles and stop killing their own and one another's subjects in the name of religion. Natural law and natural rights would play an important role in the founding of constitutional governments from the 1640s forward and in the establishment of various charters of human rights in our own time.

Origins of the Scientific Revolution

Although the Catholic and Protestant churches encouraged the study of science and many prominent scientists were themselves clerics, the search for a secular, scientific method of determining the laws of nature eventually challenged the traditional accounts of natural phenomena. Christian doctrine had incorporated the scientific teachings of ancient philosophers, especially Ptolemy and Aristotle; now these came into question. A revolution in astronomy challenged the Ptolemaic view, endorsed by the Catholic church, which held that the sun revolved around the earth. Remarkable advances took place in medicine, too, which laid the foundations for modern anatomy and pharmacology. Conflicts between the new science and religion followed almost immediately.

The "new science" began with the first subject ever studied by scientists, astronomy. The traditional account of the movement of the heavens derived from the second-century Greek astronomer Ptolemy, who put the earth at the center of the cosmos. Above the earth were fixed the moon, the stars, and the planets in concentric crystalline spheres; beyond these fixed spheres dwelt God and the angels. The planets revolved around the earth at the command of God. In this view, the sun revolved around the earth; the heavens were perfect and unchanging, and the earth was "corrupted." Ptolemy insisted that the planets revolved in perfectly circular orbits (because circles were more "perfect" than other figures). To explain the actual elliptical paths that could be observed and calculated, he posited orbits within orbits, or epicycles.

In 1543, the Polish clergyman Nicolaus Copernicus (1473–1543) attacked the Ptolemaic account in his treatise *On the Revolution of the Celestial Spheres*. He argued that the earth and planets revolved around the sun, a view known as **heliocentrism** (a sun-centered universe). Copernicus discovered that by placing the sun instead of the earth at the center of the system of spheres, he could eliminate many epicycles from the calculations. In other words, he claimed that the heliocentric view simplified the mathematics.

Copernicus's views began to attract widespread attention in the early seventeenth century, when astronomers systematically collected evidence that undermined the Ptolemaic view. A leader among them was the Danish astronomer Tycho Brahe (1546–1601), whose observations of a new star in 1572 and a comet in 1577 called into question the Aristotelian view that the universe was unchanging. Brahe still rejected heliocentrism, but the assistant he employed when he moved to Prague in 1599, Johannes Kepler (1571–1630), was converted to the Copernican view. Kepler continued Brahe's collection of planetary observations and used the evidence to develop his three laws of planetary motion, published between 1609 and 1619. Kepler's laws provided mathematical backing for heliocentrism and directly challenged the claim long held, even by Copernicus, that planetary motion was circular. Kepler's first law stated that the orbits of the planets are ellipses, with the sun always at one focus of the ellipse.

The Italian Galileo Galilei (1564–1642) provided more evidence to support the heliocentric view and also challenged the doctrine that the heavens were perfect and unchanging. In 1609, he developed an improved telescope and then observed the earth's moon, four satellites of Jupiter, the phases of Venus (a cycle of changing physical appearances like that of the moon), and sunspots. The moon, the planets, and the sun were no more perfect than the earth, he insisted, and the shadows he could see on the moon could only be the product of hills and valleys like those on earth. Galileo portrayed the earth as a moving part of a larger system, only one of many planets revolving around the sun, not as the fixed center of a single, closed universe. Because he recognized the utility of the new science for everyday projects and hoped to appeal to a lay audience of merchants and aristocrats, Galileo was the first scientist to publish his studies in the vernacular (Italian) rather than in Latin.

Since his discoveries challenged the Bible as well as the commonsensical view that the sun rises and sets while the earth stands still, Galileo's work alarmed the Catholic church. In 1616, the church forbade Galileo to teach that the earth moves and in 1633 accused him of not obeying the earlier order. Forced to appear before the Inquisition, he agreed to publicly recant his assertion that the earth moves to save himself from torture and death. Afterward he lived under house arrest and could publish his work only in the Dutch Republic, which had become a haven for iconoclastic scientists and thinkers.

Startling breakthroughs took place in medicine, too. Until the mid-sixteenth century, medical knowledge in Europe had been based on the writings of the second-century Greek physician Galen, a contemporary of Ptolemy. In the same year that Copernicus challenged the traditions of astronomy (1543), the Flemish scientist Andreas Vesalius (1514–1564) did the same for anatomy. He published a new illustrated anatomical text, *On the Construction of the Human Body*, that revised Galen's work by drawing on public dissections in the medical faculties of European universities. Theophrastus Bombastus von Hohenheim, better known as Paracelsus (1493–1541), went even further than Vesalius. He burned Galen's text at the University of Basel, where he was a professor of medicine.

Paracelsus experimented with new drugs, performed operations (at the time most academic physicians taught medical theory, not practice), and pursued his interests in magic, alchemy, and astrology. He helped establish the modern science of pharmacology.

The Englishman William Harvey (1578–1657) also used dissection to examine the circulation of blood within the body, demonstrating how the heart worked as a pump. The heart and its valves were "a piece of machinery," Harvey claimed. They obeyed mechanical laws just as the planets and earth revolved around the sun in a mechanical universe. Nature could be understood by experiment and rational deduction, not by following traditional authorities.

In the 1630s, the European intellectual elite began to accept the new scientific views. Ancient learning, the churches and their theologians, and even cherished popular beliefs seemed to be undermined by a new standard of truth—**scientific method**, which was based on systematic experiments and rational deduction. Two men were chiefly responsible for spreading the prestige of scientific method, the English politician Sir Francis Bacon (1561–1626) and the French mathematician and philosopher René Descartes (1596–1650). Respectively, they represented the two essential processes of scientific method: (1) inductive reasoning through observation and experimental research and (2) deductive reasoning from self-evident principles.

In *The Advancement of Learning* (1605), Bacon attacked reliance on ancient writers and optimistically predicted that scientific method would lead to social progress. The minds of the medieval scholars, he said, had been "shut up in the cells of a few authors (chiefly Aristotle, their dictator) as their persons were shut up in the cells of monasteries and colleges." Knowledge, in Bacon's view, must be empirically based—that is, gained by observation and experiment. Bacon ardently supported the scientific method over popular beliefs, which he rejected as "fables and popular errors." Claiming that God had called the Catholic church "to account for their degenerate manners and ceremonies," Bacon looked to the Protestant English state, which he served as lord chancellor, for leadership on the road to scientific advancement.

Although Descartes agreed with Bacon's denunciation of traditional learning, he saw that the attack on tradition might only replace the dogmatism of the churches with the skepticism of Montaigne—that nothing at all was certain. A Catholic who served in the Thirty Years' War, Descartes insisted that human reason could not only unravel the secrets of nature but also prove the existence of God. He aimed to establish the new science on more secure philosophical foundations, those of mathematics and logic. Not coincidentally, Descartes invented analytic geometry. In his *Discourse on Method* (1637), he argued that mathematical and mechanical principles provided the key to understanding all of nature, including the actions of people and states. All prior assumptions must be repudiated in favor of one elementary principle: "I think, therefore I am." Everything else

■ **Persecution of Witches**
This engraving from a pamphlet account of witch trials in England in 1589 shows three women hanged as accused witches. At their feet are frogs and toads, which were supposed to be the witches' "familiars," sent by the devil to help them ruin the lives of their neighbors by causing disease or untimely deaths among people and livestock. The ferret on the woman's lap was reported to be the devil himself in disguise. (Lambeth Palace Library.)

could—and should—be doubted, but even doubt showed the certain existence of someone thinking. Begin with the simple and go on to the complex, he asserted, and believe only those ideas that present themselves "clearly and distinctly." Although Descartes hoped to secure the authority of both church and state, his reliance on human reason alone irritated authorities, and his books were banned in many places. He moved to the Dutch Republic to work in peace. Scientific research, like economic growth, became centered in the northern, Protestant countries, where it was less constrained by church control.

Magic and Witchcraft

Despite the new emphasis on clear reasoning, observation, and independence from past authorities, science had not yet become separate from magic. Paracelsus and other scholars studied alchemy alongside other scientific pursuits: magic and science were still closely linked. In a world in which most people believed in astrology, magical healing, prophecy, and ghosts, it is hardly surprising that many of Europe's learned people also firmly believed in witchcraft, the exercise of magical powers gained by a pact with the devil. The same Jean Bodin who argued against religious fanaticism insisted on death for witches—and for those magistrates who would not prosecute them. In France alone, 345 books and pamphlets on witchcraft appeared between 1550 and 1650. Trials of witches peaked in

Europe between 1560 and 1640, the very time of the celebrated breakthroughs of the new science. Montaigne was one of the few to speak out against executing accused witches: "It is taking one's conjectures rather seriously to roast someone alive for them," he wrote in 1580.

Belief in witches was not new in the sixteenth century. Witches had long been thought capable of almost anything: passing through walls, flying through the air, destroying crops, and causing personal catastrophes from miscarriage to demonic possession. What was new was the official persecution, justified by the notion that witches were agents of Satan whom the righteous must oppose. In a time of economic crisis, plague, warfare, and the clash of religious differences, witchcraft trials provided an outlet for social stress and anxiety, legitimated by state power. At the same time, the trials seem to have been part of the religious-reform movement itself. Denunciation and persecution of witches coincided with the spread of reform, both Protestant and Catholic. The trials concentrated especially in the German lands of the Holy Roman Empire, the boiling cauldron of the Thirty Years' War.

The victims of the persecution were overwhelmingly female: women accounted for 80 percent of the accused witches in about 100,000 trials in Europe and North America during the sixteenth and seventeenth centuries. About one-third were sentenced to death. Before 1400, when witchcraft trials were rare, nearly one-half of those accused had been men. Two Catholic clergymen compiled a guide for detecting witches, the *Malleus maleficarum* [Hammer of Witches], which was published in 1486 and reissued countless times in the sixteenth and seventeenth

IMPORTANT DATES

1517	Martin Luther criticizes sale of indulgences and other church practices, igniting the Reformation	1598	French Wars of Religion end with Edict of Nantes
		1618	Thirty Years' War begins
1529	Henry VIII is declared head of the Anglican church	1629	English Puritans set up the Massachusetts Bay Company and begin to colonize New England
1545–1563	Council of Trent		
1555	Peace of Augsburg	1633	Galileo Galilei is forced to recant his support of heliocentrism
1571	Battle of Lepanto marks victory of West over Ottomans at sea		
1572	St. Bartholomew's Day Massacre (August 24)	1648	Peace of Westphalia ends the Thirty Years' War
1588	Defeat of the Spanish Armada by England		

centuries. Official descriptions of witchcraft oozed lurid details of sexual orgies, incest, homosexuality, and cannibalism, in which women acted as the devil's sexual slaves. Social factors help explain the prominence of women among the accused. The poorest and most socially marginal people in most communities were elderly spinsters and widows. Because they were thought likely to hanker after revenge on those more fortunate, they were singled out as witches.

Witchcraft trials declined when scientific thinking about causes and effects raised questions about the evidence used in court: how could judges or jurors be

■ **MAPPING THE WEST The Religious Divisions of Europe, c. 1648**

The Peace of Westphalia recognized major religious divisions within Europe that have endured for the most part to the present day. Catholicism dominated in southern Europe, Lutheranism had its stronghold in northern Europe, and Calvinism flourished along the Rhine River. In southeastern Europe, the Islamic Ottoman Turks accommodated the Greek Orthodox Christians under their rule but bitterly fought the Catholic Austrian Habsburgs for control of Hungary.

certain that someone was a witch? The tide turned everywhere at about the same time, as physicians, lawyers, judges, and even clergy came to suspect that accusations were based on popular superstition and peasant untrustworthiness. In 1682, a French royal decree treated witchcraft as fraud and imposture, meaning that the law did not recognize anyone as a witch. In 1693, the jurors who had convicted twenty witches in Salem, Massachusetts, recanted, claiming: "We confess that we ourselves were not capable to understand. . . . We justly fear that we were sadly deluded and mistaken." The Salem jurors had not stopped believing in witches; they had simply lost confidence in their ability to identify them. When physicians and judges had believed in witches and persecuted them officially, with torture, witches had gone to their deaths in record numbers. But when the same groups distanced themselves from popular beliefs, the trials and the executions stopped.

■ **REVIEW:** *How could belief in witchcraft and the rising prestige of the scientific method coexist?*

Conclusion

The witchcraft persecutions reflected the traumas of these times of religious war and economic decline. Marauding armies combined with economic depression, disease, and the threat of starvation to shatter the lives of many ordinary Europeans, while religious conflicts shaped the destinies of every European power in this period. These conflicts began with the Protestant Reformation, which dispelled forever the Christian humanist dream of peace and unity, and came to a head from 1618 to 1648 in the Thirty Years' War, which cut a path of destruction through central Europe and involved most of the European powers. Shocked by the effects of religious violence, European rulers agreed to a peace that effectively removed disputes between Catholics and Protestants from the international arena.

The growing separation of political motives from religious ones did not mean that violence or conflict had ended, however. Struggles for religious uniformity within states would continue, though on a smaller scale. Bigger armies required more state involvement, and almost everywhere rulers emerged from these decades of conflict with expanded powers. The growth of state power directly changed the lives of ordinary people: more men went into the armies, and most families paid higher taxes. The constant extension of state power is one of the defining themes of modern history; religious warfare gave it a jump-start.

For all their increased power, rulers could not control economic, social, or intellectual trends, much as they often tried. The economic downturn of the seventeenth century produced unexpected consequences for European states even while it made life miserable for many ordinary people. Economic power and vibrancy shifted from the Mediterranean world to the northwest because the countries of northwestern Europe—England, France, and the Dutch Republic especially—suffered less from the fighting of the Thirty Years' War and recovered more quickly from the loss of population and production during bad times.

In the face of violence and uncertainty, some began to look for secular alternatives in art, politics, and science. Although it would be foolish to claim that everyone's mental universe changed because of the clash between religious and secular worldviews, a truly monumental shift in attitudes had begun. Secularization combined a growing interest in nonreligious forms of art, such as theater and opera, the search for nonreligious foundations of political authority, and the establishment of scientific method as the standard of truth. Proponents of these changes did not renounce their religious beliefs or even hold them less fervently, but they did insist that attention to state interests and scientific knowledge could serve as a brake on religious violence and popular superstitions. The search for order in the aftermath of religious warfare would continue in the decades to come.

■ MAKING CONNECTIONS

1. *How did the balance of power in Europe shift between 1500 and 1648? What were the main reasons for the shift?*

2. *Relate the new developments in the arts and sciences to the political and economic changes in this period of crisis.*

■ FOR FURTHER EXPLORATION

For further reading and online research ideas, see the Suggested References on page SR-6 at the back of the book.

For practice quizzes, a customized study plan, and other study tools, see the ONLINE STUDY GUIDE at bedfordstmartins.com/huntconcise.

For additional primary-source material from this period, see Chapter 12 in *Sources of THE MAKING OF THE WEST: A CONCISE HISTORY*, Second Edition.

A.F. VANDER. MEULEN. FE.

State Building and the Search for Order

1648–1690

IN ONE OF HER HUNDREDS OF LETTERS TO HER DAUGHTER, the French noblewoman Marie de Sévigné (1626–1696) told a disturbing story about a well-known cook. The cook got upset when he did not have enough roast for several unexpected guests at a dinner for King Louis XIV. Early the next morning, when the fish he had ordered did not arrive, the cook rushed up to his room, put his sword against the door, and, on the third try, ran it through his heart. The fish arrived soon after. The king regretted the trouble his visit had caused, but others soon filled in for the dead cook. That evening, Sévigné wrote, there was "a very good dinner, light refreshments later, and then supper, a walk, cards, hunting, everything scented with daffodils, everything magical."

It is difficult now for us to comprehend how anyone could care that much about a shipment of fish. The story nonetheless reveals an important aspect of state building in the seventeenth century: to extend state authority, which had been challenged during the wars over religion and threatened by economic recession, many rulers created an aura of overwhelming power and brilliance around themselves. Louis XIV, like many rulers, believed that he reigned by divine right. He served as God's lieutenant on earth and even claimed certain godlike qualities. The great gap between the ruler and ordinary subjects accounts for the extreme reaction of Louis's

■ **Louis XIV and His Bodyguards**
One of Louis XIV's court painters, Adam Frans van der Meulen, depicted the king arriving at the Palace of Versailles, still under construction (the painting dates from 1669). None of the gardens, pools, or statues had yet been installed. Louis is the only figure facing the viewer, and his dress is much more colorful than that of anyone else in the painting.
(Réunion des Musées Nationaux/Art Resource, NY.)

cook, and even leading nobles such as Sévigné came to see the king and his court as somehow "magical."

Louis XIV's model of state building was known as **absolutism**, a system of government in which the ruler claimed sole and uncontestable power. Although absolutism exerted great influence, especially in central and eastern Europe, it faced competition from **constitutionalism**, a system in which the ruler had to share power with parliaments made up of elected representatives. Constitutionalism led to weakness in Poland-Lithuania, but it provided a strong foundation for state power in England, the English North American colonies, and the Dutch Republic. Constitutionalism triumphed in England, however, only after one king had been executed as a traitor and another had been deposed.

Whether absolutist or constitutionalist, seventeenth-century states faced similar challenges to state building in the mid-seventeenth century. Competition in the international arena required resources, and all states raised taxes, provoking popular protests and even rebellions. The wars over religion that had culminated in the Thirty Years' War (1618–1648) left many economies in dire straits, and, even more significant, they created a need for new explanations of political authority. Monarchs still relied on religion to justify their divine right to rule, but they increasingly sought secular defenses of their powers, too. Absolutism and constitutionalism were the two main responses to the threat of disorder and breakdown left as a legacy of the wars over religion.

The search for order took place not only at the level of states and rulers but also in intellectual, cultural, and social life. In science, the Englishman Isaac Newton explained the regular movement of the universe with the law of gravitation and thereby consolidated the scientific revolution. Artists sought means of glorifying power and expressing order and symmetry in new fashion. As states consolidated their power, elites endeavored to distinguish themselves more clearly from the lower orders. The upper classes emulated the manners developed at court and tried in every way to distance themselves from anything viewed as vulgar or lower class. Officials, clergy, and laypeople all worked to reform the poor, now seen as a major source of disorder.

Louis XIV: Model of Absolutism

French king Louis XIV (r. 1643–1715) personified the absolutist ruler who in theory shared his power with no one. Louis personally made all important state decisions and left no room for dissent. In 1651, he reputedly told the Paris high court of justice, "*L'état, c'est moi*" ("I am the state"), emphasizing that state authority rested in him personally. Louis cleverly manipulated the affections and ambitions of his courtiers, chose as his ministers middle-class men who owed everything to him, built up Europe's largest army, and snuffed out every hint of religious or political opposition. Yet the absoluteness of his power should not be exaggerated.

Like all other rulers of his time, Louis depended on the cooperation of many others: local officials who enforced his decrees, peasants and artisans who joined his armies and paid his taxes, creditors who loaned crucial funds, and nobles who joined court festivities organized to glorify the king rather than stay home and cause trouble.

The Fronde, 1648–1653

Louis XIV built on a long French tradition of increasing centralization of state authority, but before he could extend it, he had to weather a series of revolts known as the **Fronde**. Derived from the French word for a child's slingshot, the term was used by critics to signify that the revolts were mere child's play. In fact, they posed an unprecedented threat to the French crown. Louis was only five when he came to the throne in 1643 upon the death of his father, Louis XIII. Louis XIV's mother, Anne of Austria, and her Italian-born adviser and rumored lover Cardinal Mazarin (1602–1661) ruled in the young monarch's name. To meet the financial pressure of fighting the Thirty Years' War and then even after the peace to keep up a draining war against Spain, Mazarin sold new offices, raised taxes, and forced creditors to extend loans to the government. In 1648, a coalition of his opponents presented him with a charter of demands that, if granted, would have given

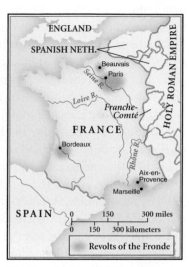

The Fronde, 1648–1653

the **parlements** (high courts) a form of constitutional power with the right to approve new taxes. Mazarin responded by arresting the coalition's leaders. He soon faced a series of revolts that at one time or another involved nearly every social group in France.

Faced with barricades in the streets of Paris, Anne took Louis and fled Paris. As civil war threatened, Mazarin and Anne agreed to compromise with the parlements. The nobles then tried to reassert their own claims to power by raising private armies. The middle and lower classes chafed at the constant tax increases and in some places organized revolts. Conflicts erupted throughout the kingdom, and rampaging soldiers devastated rural areas and disrupted commerce.

Neither the nobles nor the judges of the parlements really wanted to overthrow the king; they simply wanted a greater share in power. But Louis XIV never forgot the humiliation and uncertainty that marred his childhood. Years later he recalled an incident in which a band of Parisians invaded his bedchamber to determine whether he had fled the city, and he declared the event an affront not only to himself but also to the state. His own policies as ruler would be designed to prevent the repetition of any such revolts.

Court Culture as an Element of Absolutism

When Cardinal Mazarin died in 1661, Louis XIV decided to rule without a first minister. He described the dangers of his situation in memoirs he wrote later for his son's instruction: "Everywhere was disorder. My Court as a whole was still very far removed from the sentiments in which I trust you will find it." Typically quarrelsome, the French nobles had long exercised local authority by maintaining their own fighting forces, meting out justice on their estates, arranging jobs for underlings, and resolving their own conflicts through dueling.

Louis set out to domesticate the warrior nobles by replacing violence with court ritual. Using a systematic policy of bestowing pensions, offices, honors, gifts, and the threat of disfavor or punishment, he made himself the center of French power and culture. The aristocracy soon vied for his favor, attended the ballets and theatricals he put on, and learned the rules of etiquette he supervised. Great nobles competed for the honor of holding his shirt when he dressed; foreign ambassadors squabbled for places near him; and royal mistresses basked in the glow of his personal favor. In a typically acerbic comment, Louis de Rouvroy, duke of Saint-Simon (1675–1755), complained, "There was nothing he [Louis XIV] liked so much as flattery . . . the coarser and clumsier it was, the more he relished it." Madame de Lafayette described the effects on court life in her novel *The Princess of Clèves* (1678): "The Court gravitated around ambition. Nobody was tranquil or indifferent—everybody was busily trying to better his or her position by pleasing, by helping, or by hindering somebody else." Occasionally the results were tragic, as in the suicide of the cook recounted by Marie de Sévigné.

Louis XIV appreciated the political uses of every form of art. Mock battles, extravaganzas, theatrical performances, even the king's dinner—Louis's daily life was a public performance designed to enhance his prestige. Calling himself the Sun King, Louis adorned his court with statues of Apollo, Greek god of the sun, and emulated the style of ancient Roman emperors. Sculpture and paintings adorned his palace, commissioned histories vaunted his achievements, and coins and medals spread his likeness throughout the realm.

The king's officials treated the arts as a branch of government. Louis's ministers set up royal academies of dance, painting, architecture, and music and took control of the Académie Française (French Academy), which to this day decides on correct usage of the French language. A royal furniture workshop at the Gobelins tapestry works on the outskirts of Paris turned out the delicate and ornate pieces whose style bore the king's name. Louis's government also regulated the number and locations of theaters and closely censored all forms of publication.

■ **The Palace of Versailles**

This 1675 painting shows the central section of the newly reconstructed palace. The entire building was still not complete at this date, but some sense of King Louis XIV's emphasis on majesty and order is already apparent. (Réunion des Musées Nationaux/Art Resource, NY. Photo: Gérard Blot.)

Music and theater enjoyed special prominence. Louis commissioned operas to celebrate royal marriages, baptisms, and military victories. The king himself danced in ballets if a role seemed especially important. Playwrights presented their new plays directly to the court. Pierre Corneille and Jean-Baptiste Racine wrote tragedies set in Greece or Rome that celebrated the new aristocratic virtues that Louis aimed to inculcate: a reverence for order and self-control.

Louis glorified his image as well through massive public works projects. Military facilities, such as veterans' hospitals and new fortified towns on the frontiers, represented his military might. Urban improvements, such as the reconstruction of the Louvre palace in Paris, proved his wealth. But his most ambitious project was the construction of a new palace at Versailles, twelve miles from the turbulent capital. Building began in the 1660s, and by 1685, the frenzied effort engaged 36,000 workers, not including the thousands of troops who diverted a local river to supply water for pools and fountains. Even the gardens reflected the spirit of Louis XIV's rule: their geometrical arrangements and clear lines showed that art and design could tame nature and that order and control defined the exercise of power.

Versailles symbolized Louis's success in reining in the nobility and dominating Europe, and other monarchs eagerly mimicked French fashion and often conducted their business in French.

By the time Louis actually moved from the Louvre to Versailles in 1682, he had reigned as monarch for thirty-nine years. Fifteen thousand people crowded into the palace's apartments, including all the highest military officers, the ministers of state, and the separate households of each member of the royal family. After the death of his queen in 1683, Louis secretly married his mistress, Françoise d'Aubigné, marquise de Maintenon, and conducted most state affairs from her apartments at the palace. De Maintenon's opponents at court complained that she controlled all the appointments, but her efforts focused on her own projects, including her favorite: the founding in 1686 of a royal school for girls from impoverished noble families. She also inspired one of Louis XIV's most critical decisions—to pursue his devotion to Catholicism.

Enforcing Religious Orthodoxy

Louis believed that he ruled by divine right. As Bishop Jacques-Benigne Bossuet (1627–1704) explained, "We have seen that kings take the place of God, who is the true father of the human species. We have also seen that the first idea of power which exists among men is that of the paternal power; and that kings are modeled on fathers." The king, like a father, should instruct his subjects in the true religion, or at least make sure that others did so.

Louis's campaign for religious conformity first focused on the Jansenists, Catholics whose doctrines and practices resembled some aspects of Protestantism. Following the posthumous publication of the book *Augustinus* (1640) by the Flemish theologian Cornelius Jansen (1585–1638), the Jansenists stressed the need for God's grace in achieving salvation. They emphasized the importance of original sin and insisted on an austere religious practice. Prominent among the Jansenists was Blaise Pascal (1623–1662), a mathematician of genius, who wrote his *Provincial Letters* (1656–1657) to defend Jansenism against charges of heresy. Many judges in the parlements likewise endorsed Jansenist doctrine.

Some questioned Louis's understanding of the finer points of doctrine: according to his German-born sister-in-law, Louis himself "has never read anything about religion, nor the Bible either, and just goes along believing whatever he is told." But Louis rejected any doctrine that gave priority to considerations of individual conscience over the demands of the official church hierarchy. He preferred teachings that stressed obedience to authority. Therefore, in 1660 he began enforcing various papal bulls (decrees) against Jansenism and closed down Jansenist theological centers. Jansenists were forced underground for the rest of his reign.

After many years of escalating pressure on the Calvinist Huguenots, Louis revoked the Edict of Nantes in 1685 and eliminated all of the Calvinists' rights. Louis considered the edict (1598), by which his grandfather Henry IV granted the Protestants religious freedom and a degree of political independence, a temporary measure, and he fervently hoped to reconvert the Huguenots to Catholicism. He closed their churches and schools, banned all their public activities, and exiled those who refused to embrace the state religion. Thousands of Huguenots emigrated to England, Brandenburg-Prussia, or the Dutch Republic. Many now wrote for publications attacking Louis XIV's absolutism. Protestant European countries were shocked by this crackdown on religious dissent and would cite it when they went to war against Louis.

Extending State Authority at Home and Abroad

Louis XIV could not have enforced his religious policies without the services of a nationwide bureaucracy. **Bureaucracy**—a network of state officials carrying out orders according to a regular and routine line of authority—comes from *bureau*, the French word for "desk," which came to mean "office," in the sense of both a physical space and a position of authority. Louis extended the bureaucratic forms his predecessors had developed, especially the use of intendants, officials who held their positions directly from the king rather than owning their offices. Louis handpicked them to represent his will against entrenched local interests such as the parlements, provincial estates, and noble governors. The intendants reduced local powers over finances and insisted on more efficient tax collection. Despite the doubling of taxes in Louis's reign, the local rebellions that had so beset the crown from the 1620s to the 1640s subsided in the face of these better-organized state forces.

Louis's success in consolidating his authority depended on hard work, an eye for detail, and an ear to the ground. In his memoirs he explained his priorities:

> *to be well-informed on an infinite number of matters about which we are supposed to know nothing; to elicit from our subjects what they hide from us with the greatest care; to discover the most remote opinions of our courtiers and the most hidden interests of those who come to us with quite contrary professions [claims].*

To gather all this information, Louis relied on a series of talented ministers, usually of modest origins, who gained fame, fortune, and even noble status from serving the king. Most important among them was Jean-Baptiste Colbert (1619–1683), the son of a wool merchant turned royal official. Colbert had managed Mazarin's personal finances and worked his way up under Louis XIV to become controller general, the head of royal finances, public works, and the navy. He founded a family dynasty that eventually produced five ministers of state, an archbishop, two bishops, and three generals.

Colbert used the bureaucracy to establish a new economic doctrine, **mercantilism**. According to mercantilist policy, governments must intervene to increase national wealth by whatever means possible. Such government intervention inevitably increased the role and eventually the number of bureaucrats needed. Under Colbert, the French government established overseas trading companies, granted manufacturing monopolies, and standardized production methods for textiles, paper, and soap. A government inspection system regulated the quality of finished goods and compelled all craftsmen to organize into guilds, in which masters could supervise the work of the journeymen and apprentices. To protect French production, Colbert rescinded many internal customs fees while enacting high foreign tariffs, which effectively cut imports of competing goods. To compete more effectively with England and the Dutch Republic, Colbert also subsidized shipbuilding, a policy that dramatically expanded the number of seaworthy vessels. Such mercantilist measures aimed to ensure France's prominence in world markets and to provide the resources needed to fight wars against the increasingly long list of enemies. Although later economists questioned the value of this state intervention in the economy, nearly every government in Europe embraced mercantilism.

Colbert's mercantilist projects extended to Canada, where in 1663 he took control of the trading company that had founded New France. He transplanted several thousand peasants from western France to the present-day province of Quebec, which France had claimed since 1608, and he sent fifteen hundred soldiers to fend off the Iroquois, who regularly raided French fur-trading convoys. Shows of French military force, including the burning of Indian villages and winter food supplies, forced the Iroquois to make peace, and from 1666 to 1680 French traders moved westward with minimal interference. In 1672, fur trader Louis Jolliet and Jesuit missionary Jacques Marquette reached the upper Mississippi River and traveled downstream as far as Arkansas. In 1684, French explorer Sieur de La Salle ventured all the way down to the Gulf of Mexico, claiming a vast territory for Louis XIV and calling it Louisiana after him. Louis and Colbert encouraged colonial settlement as part of their rivalry with the English and the Dutch in the New World.

Colonial settlement occupied only a small portion of Louis XIV's attention, however, for his main foreign policy goal was to extend French power in Europe. In pursuing this purpose, he inevitably came up against the Spanish and Austrian Habsburgs, whose lands encircled his. To expand French power, Louis needed the biggest possible army. The ministry of war centralized the organization of French troops. Barracks built in major towns received supplies from a central distribution system. The state began to provide uniforms for the soldiers and to offer veterans some hospital care. A militia draft instituted in 1688 supplemented the army in times of war and enrolled 100,000 men. Louis's wartime army could field a force as large as that of all his enemies combined.

Louis gained new enemies as he tried to expand the territory under his rule. In 1667–1668, in the first of his major wars after assuming personal direction of French affairs, Louis defeated the Spanish armies but had to make peace when England, Sweden, and the Dutch Republic joined the war. In the Treaty of Aix-la-Chapelle in 1668, he gained control of towns on the border of the Spanish

■ MAP 13.1 Louis XIV's Acquisitions, 1668–1697

Every ruler in Europe hoped to extend his or her territorial control, and war was often the result. Louis XIV steadily encroached on the Spanish Netherlands to the north and the lands of the Holy Roman Empire to the east. Although coalitions of European powers reined in Louis's grander ambitions, he incorporated many neighboring territories into the French crown.

Netherlands. Pamphlets sponsored by the Habsburgs accused Louis of aiming for "universal monarchy," or domination of Europe.

In 1672, Louis XIV opened hostilities against the Dutch because they stood in the way of his acquisition of more territory in the Spanish Netherlands. He declared war again on Spain in 1673. By now the Dutch had allied themselves with their former Spanish masters to hold off the French. Louis also marched his troops into territories of the Holy Roman Empire, provoking many of the German princes to join with the emperor, the Spanish, and the Dutch in an alliance against Louis, now denounced as a "Christian Turk" for his imperialist ambitions. But the French armies more than held their own. Faced with bloody yet inconclusive results on the battlefield, the parties agreed to the Treaty of Nijmegen of 1678–1679, which ceded several Flemish towns and Franche-Comté to Louis (Map 13.1). These territorial additions were costly: French government deficits soared, and increases in taxes touched off the most serious antitax revolt of Louis's reign, in 1675.

Louis had no intention of standing still. Heartened by the Habsburgs' seeming weakness, he pushed eastward, seizing the city of Strasbourg in 1681 and invading the province of Lorraine in 1684. Lorraine would remain a subject of contention between France and its neighbors for nearly three centuries. In 1688, Louis attacked some of the small German cities of the Holy Roman Empire and was soon involved again in a long war against a Europe-wide coalition. Between 1689 and 1697, a coalition made up of England, Spain, Sweden, the Dutch Republic, the Austrian emperor, and various German princes fought Louis XIV to a stalemate. When hostilities ended in the Peace of Rijswijk in 1697, Louis returned many of his conquests made since 1678 with the exception of Strasbourg (see Map 13.1). Louis never lost his taste for war, but his enemies learned how to set limits on his ambitions.

Louis was the last French ruler before Napoleon to accompany his troops to the battlefield. In later generations, as the military became more professional, French rulers left the fighting to their generals. Although Louis had managed to suppress the private armies of his noble courtiers, he constantly promoted his own military prowess in order to keep his noble officers under his sway. He had miniature battle scenes painted on his high heels and commissioned tapestries showing his military processions into cities, even those he did not take by force. He seized every occasion to assert his supremacy, insisting that other fleets salute his ships first.

War required money and men, which Louis obtained by expanding state control over finances, conscription into the army, and military supply. Thus absolutism and warfare fed each other, as the bureaucracy created new ways to raise and maintain an army and the army's success in war justified the expansion of state power. But constant warfare also eroded the state's resources. Further administrative and legal reform, the elimination of the buying and selling of offices, and the lowering of taxes—all were made impossible by the need for more money.

The playwright Corneille wrote, no doubt optimistically, "The people are very happy when they die for their kings." What is certain is that the wars touched many peasant and urban families. The people who lived on the routes leading to the battlefields had to house and feed soldiers; only nobles were exempt from this requirement. Everyone, moreover, paid the higher taxes that were necessary to support the army. By the end of Louis's reign, one in six Frenchmen had served in the military.

■ **REVIEW:** *How "absolute" was the power of Louis XIV?*

Absolutism in Central and Eastern Europe

Central and eastern European rulers saw in Louis XIV a powerful model of absolutist state building. Yet they did not blindly emulate the Sun King, in part because they confronted conditions peculiar to their regions. The ruler of Brandenburg-Prussia had to rebuild lands ravaged by the Thirty Years' War and unite far-flung territories. The Austrian Habsburgs needed to govern a mosaic of ethnic and religious groups while fighting off the Ottoman Turks. The Russian tsars wanted to extend their power over a large but relatively impoverished empire. The great exception to absolutism in eastern Europe was Poland-Lithuania, where a long crisis virtually destroyed central authority and sucked much of eastern Europe into its turbulent wake.

Brandenburg-Prussia and Sweden: Militaristic Absolutism

Brandenburg-Prussia began as a puny state on the Elbe River, but it would have a remarkable future. In the nineteenth century, it would unify the disparate German states into modern-day Germany. The ruler of Brandenburg was an elector, one of the seven German princes entitled to select the Holy Roman Emperor. Since the sixteenth century, the ruler of Brandenburg had also controlled the duchy of East Prussia; after 1618, the state was called Brandenburg-Prussia. Despite meager resources, Frederick William of Hohenzollern, the Great Elector of Brandenburg-Prussia (r. 1640–1688), succeeded in welding his scattered lands into an absolutist state.

Pressured first by the necessities of fighting the Thirty Years' War and then by the demands of reconstruction, Frederick William determined to force his territories' estates (representative institutions) to grant him a dependable income. The Great Elector struck a deal with the Junkers (nobles) of each land: in exchange for allowing him to collect taxes, he gave them complete control over their enserfed peasants and exempted them from taxation. The tactic worked. By the end of his reign the estates met only on ceremonial occasions.

Supplied with a steady income, Frederick William could devote his attention to military and bureaucratic consolidation. Over forty years he expanded his army from eight thousand to thirty thousand men. (See "Taking Measure," page 534.) The army mirrored the rigid domination of nobles over peasants that characterized Brandenburg-Prussian society: peasants filled the ranks, and Junkers became officers. Nobles also took positions as bureaucratic officials, but military needs always had priority. The elector named special war commissars to take charge not only of military affairs but also of tax collection. To hasten military dispatches, he also established one of Europe's first state postal systems.

As a Calvinist ruler, Frederick William disdained the ostentation of the French court, even while following the absolutist model of centralizing state power. He boldly rebuffed Louis XIV by welcoming twenty thousand French Huguenot refugees after Louis's revocation of the Edict of Nantes. In pursuing policies that promoted state power, Frederick William adroitly switched sides in Louis's wars and would stop at almost nothing to crush resistance at home. In 1701, his son Frederick I (r. 1688–1713) persuaded Holy Roman Emperor Leopold I

State	Soldiers	Population	Ratio of soldiers/ total population
France	300,000	20 million	1:66
Russia	220,000	14 million	1:64
Austria	100,000	8 million	1:80
Sweden	40,000	1 million	1:25
Brandenburg-Prussia	30,000	2 million	1:66
England	24,000	10 million	1:410

*Figures for the end of the seventeenth century, ranging from 1688 for Prussia to 1710 for France

■ **TAKING MEASURE The Seventeenth-Century Army**

The figures in this chart are only approximate, but they tell an important story. What conclusions can be drawn about the relative weight of the military in the different European states? Why would England have such a smaller army than the others? Is the absolute or the relative size of the military the more important indicator?

to grant him the title "king in Prussia." Prussia had arrived as an important power (Map 13.2).

Across the Baltic, Sweden also stood out as an example of absolutist consolidation. In the Thirty Years' War, King Gustavus Adolphus's superb generalship and highly trained army had made Sweden the supreme power of northern Europe. The huge but sparsely populated state included not only most of present-day Sweden but also Finland, Estonia, half of Latvia, and much of the Baltic coastline of modern Poland and Germany. The Baltic, in short, was a Swedish lake. After Gustavus Adolphus died, his daughter Queen Christina (r. 1632–1654) conceded much authority to the estates. Absorbed by religion and philosophy, Christina eventually abdicated and converted to Catholicism. Her successors temporarily made Sweden an absolute monarchy.

In Sweden (as in neighboring Denmark-Norway), absolutism meant simply the estates standing aside while the king led the army on lucrative foreign campaigns. The aristocracy went along because it staffed the bureaucracy and reaped war profits. Intrigued by French culture, Sweden also gleamed with national pride. In 1668, the nobility demanded the introduction of a distinctive national costume: should Swedes, they asked, "who are so glorious and renowned a nation . . . let ourselves be led by the nose by a parcel of French dancing-masters"? Sweden spent the forty years after 1654 continuously warring with its neighbors. By the 1690s, war expenses

■ MAP 13.2 State Building in Central and Eastern Europe, 1648–1699
Brandenburg-Prussia emerged from relative obscurity after the Thirty Years' War to begin an aggressive program of expanding its military and its territorial base. The Austrian Habsburgs had long contested the Ottoman Turks for dominance of eastern Europe, and by 1699, they had pushed the Turks out of Hungary.

began to outrun the small Swedish population's ability to pay, threatening the continuation of absolutism.

An Uneasy Balance: Austrian Habsburgs and Ottoman Turks

Holy Roman Emperor Leopold I (r. 1658–1705) ruled over a variety of territories of different ethnicities, languages, and religions, yet in ways similar to his French and Prussian counterparts, he gradually consolidated his power. Like all the Holy Roman emperors since 1438, Leopold was an Austrian Habsburg. He was simultaneously duke of Upper and Lower Silesia, count of Tyrol, archduke of Upper and Lower Austria, king of Bohemia, king of Hungary and Croatia, and ruler of Styria and Moravia (see Map 13.2). Some of these territories were provinces in the Holy Roman Empire; others were simply ruled from Vienna as Habsburg family holdings.

■ The Siege of Vienna, 1683

This detail from a painting by Franz Geffels shows the camp of the Ottoman Turks. The Turkish armies had surrounded Vienna since July 14, 1683. Jan Sobieski led an army of Poles that joined with Austrians and Germans to beat back the Turks on September 12, 1683.

(© Archivo Iconografico, S.A. / CORBIS.)

Leopold needed to build up his armies and state authority in order to defend the Holy Roman Empire's international position, which had been weakened by the Thirty Years' War, and to push back the Ottoman Turks who steadily encroached from the southeast. The emperor and his closest officials took control over recruiting, provisioning, and strategic planning and worked to replace the mercenaries hired during the Thirty Years' War with a permanent standing army that promoted professional discipline. To pay for the army and to staff his growing bureaucracy, Leopold had to gain the support of local aristocrats and chip away at provincial institutions' powers. Intent on replacing Bohemian nobles who had supported the 1618 revolt against Austrian authority, the Habsburgs promoted a new nobility made up of Czechs, Germans, Italians, Spaniards, and even Irish, who used German as their common tongue, professed Catholicism, and loyally served the Austrian dynasty. Bohemia became a virtual Austrian colony. "You have utterly destroyed our home, our ancient kingdom," lamented a Czech Jesuit in 1670, addressing Leopold. "Woe to you! . . . The nobles you have oppressed, great cities made small. Of smiling towns you have made straggling villages." Austrian censors prohibited publication of this protest for over a century.

In addition to holding Louis XIV in check on his western frontiers, Leopold confronted the ever-present challenge of the Ottoman Turks to his east. In 1683, the

Turks pushed all the way to the gates of Vienna and laid siege to the Austrian capital; after reaching this high-water mark, however, Turkish power ebbed. With the help of Polish cavalry, the Austrians finally broke the siege and turned the tide in a major counteroffensive. By the Treaty of Karlowitz of 1699, the Ottoman Turks surrendered almost all of Hungary to the Austrians.

Hungary's "liberation" from the Turks came at a high price. The fighting laid waste vast stretches of Hungary's central plain, and the population may have declined as much as 65 percent since 1600. To repopulate the land, the Austrians settled large communities of foreigners: Romanians, Croats, Serbs, and Germans. Magyar (Hungarian) speakers became a minority, and the seeds were sown for the poisonous nationality conflicts in nineteenth- and twentieth-century Hungary, Romania, and Yugoslavia.

Once the Turks had been beaten back, Austrian rule over Hungary tightened. In 1687, the Habsburg dynasty's hereditary right to the Hungarian crown was acknowledged by the Hungarian diet, a parliament revived by Leopold in 1681 to gain the support of Hungarian nobles. The diet was dominated by nobles who had amassed huge holdings in the liberated territories. They formed the core of a pro-Habsburg Hungarian aristocracy that would buttress the dynasty until it fell in 1918. As the Turks retreated from Hungary, Leopold systematically rebuilt churches, monasteries, roadside shrines, and monuments in the flamboyant Austrian baroque style.

The Ottoman Turks also pursued state consolidation but in a very different fashion from the Europeans. The Ottoman state extended its authority through a combination of settlement and military control. Hundreds of thousands of Turkish families moved with Turkish soldiers into the Balkan peninsula in the 1400s and 1500s. As locals converted to Islam, administration passed gradually into their hands. In the Ottoman homeland of Anatolia, the sultans, the Ottoman rulers, were often challenged by mutinous army officers. Despite frequent palace coups and assassinations, the Ottoman state survived by hiring restive peasants as mercenaries and by playing bureaucratic elites off each other. This constantly shifting social and political system explains how the coup-ridden Ottoman state could appear "weak" in Western eyes and still pose a massive military threat on Europe's southeastern borders. In the end, the Ottoman state lasted longer than Louis XIV's absolute monarchy.

Russia: Foundations of Bureaucratic Absolutism

Seventeenth-century Russia seemed a world apart from the Europe of Louis XIV. Straddling Europe and Asia, it stretched across Siberia to the Pacific Ocean. Western visitors either sneered or shuddered at the "barbarism" of Russian life, and Russians reciprocated by nursing deep suspicions of everything foreign. But under the surface, Russia was evolving along paths much like the rest of absolutist Europe; the tsars increased their powers by surmounting internal disorder and coming to an accommodation with noble landlords.

When Tsar Alexei (r. 1645–1676) tried to extend state authority by imposing new administrative structures and taxes in 1648, Moscow and other cities erupted in bloody rioting. The government immediately doused the fire. In 1649, Alexei convoked the Assembly of the Land (consisting of noble delegates from the provinces) to consult on a sweeping law code to organize Russian society in a strict social hierarchy that would last for nearly two centuries. The code of 1649 assigned all subjects to a hereditary class according to their current occupation or state needs. Slaves and free peasants were merged into a serf class. As serfs they could not change occupations or move; they were tightly tied to the soil and to their noble masters. To prevent tax evasion, the code also forbade townspeople to move from the community where they resided. Nobles owed absolute obedience to the tsar and were required to serve in the army, but in return no other group could own estates worked by serfs. Serfs became the chattel of their lord, who could sell them like horses or land. Their conditions of life differed little from those of the slaves on the plantations in the Americas.

Some peasants resisted enserfment. In 1667, Stenka Razin led a huge rebellion in southern Russia that promised liberation from "the traitors and bloodsuckers of the peasant communes"—the great noble landowners, local governors, and Moscow courtiers. Razin was a Cossack, the name given to bandit gangs formed of runaway serfs and poor nobles in southern Russia and Ukraine. Captured four years later by the tsar's army, Razin was dismembered, his head and limbs publicly displayed, and his body thrown to the dogs. Thousands of his followers also suffered grisly deaths, but his memory lived on in folk songs and legends. Landlords successfully petitioned for the abolition of the statute of limitations on runaway serfs and for harsh penalties against those who harbored runaways. The increase in Russian state authority went hand in hand with the enforcement of serfdom.

To extend his power and emulate his western rivals, Tsar Alexei wanted a bigger army, exclusive control over state policy, and a greater say in religious matters. The size of the army increased dramatically from 35,000 in the 1630s to 220,000 by the end of the century (see "Taking Measure" on page 534). The Assembly of the Land, once an important source of noble consultation, never met again after 1653. In 1666, the Russian Orthodox church reaffirmed the tsar's role as God's direct representative on earth and took action against a religious group called the Old Believers, who rejected church efforts to bring Russian worship in line with Byzantine tradition. Whole communities of Old Believers starved or burned themselves to death rather than submit. Religious schism opened a gulf between the Russian people and the crown.

The tsar's emulation of western rivals extended to culture too. Alexei set up the first Western-style theater in the Kremlin, and his daughter Sophia

■ Stenka Razin in Captivity

After leading a revolt of thousands of serfs, peasants, and members of non-Russian tribes of the middle and lower Volga region, Razin was captured by Russian forces and led off to Moscow, as shown here, where he was executed in 1671. He has been the subject of songs, legends, and poems ever since. (Novosti Photo Library, London.)

translated French plays. Nobles and ordinary citizens commissioned portraits of themselves instead of buying only religious icons. The most adventurous nobles began to wear German-style clothing. A long struggle over Western influences had begun.

Poland-Lithuania Overwhelmed

Unlike the other eastern European powers, Poland-Lithuania did not follow the absolutist model. Decades of war weakened the monarchy and made the great nobles into practically autonomous warlords. They used the parliament and demands for constitutionalism to stymie monarchical power. The result was a precipitous slide into political disarray and weakness.

In 1648, Ukrainian Cossack warriors revolted against the king of Poland-Lithuania, inaugurating two decades of tumult known as the Deluge. In 1654, the Cossacks offered Ukraine to Russian rule, provoking a Russo-Polish war that ended in 1667 when the tsar annexed eastern Ukraine and Kiev. To profit from the chaos in Poland-Lithuania, Sweden, Brandenburg-Prussia, and Transylvania sent armies to seize territory. As much as a third of the Polish population eventually perished in the fighting. The once prosperous Jewish and Protestant minorities suffered great losses: some fifty-six thousand Jews were killed either by the Cossacks, Polish peasants, or Russian troops. One rabbi wrote, "We were slaughtered each day, in a more agonizing way than cattle: they are butchered quickly, while we were being executed slowly." Surviving Jews moved from towns to *shtetls* (Jewish villages), where they could survive only by petty trading, moneylending, tax gathering, and tavern leasing—activities that fanned peasant anti-Semitism. Desperate for protection amid the war, most Protestants backed the violently anti-Catholic Swedes, and the victorious Catholic majority branded them as traitors, forcing some Protestants to seek refuge as far away as the Dutch Republic and England. In Poland-Lithuania— once an outpost of religious toleration—it came to be assumed that a good Pole was a Catholic.

The commonwealth revived briefly when Jan Sobieski (r. 1674–1696) was elected king. He gained a reputation throughout Europe when he led twenty-five thousand Polish cavalrymen into battle in the siege of Vienna in 1683. His cavalry helped rout the Turks and turned the tide against the Ottomans. Married to a politically shrewd French princess, Sobieski openly admired Louis XIV's France. Despite his efforts to rebuild the monarchy, he could not halt Poland-Lithuania's decline into powerlessness.

Elsewhere the ravages of war had created opportunities for kings to increase their power, but in Poland-Lithuania the great nobles gained all the advantage. They dominated the Sejm (parliament), and to maintain an equilibrium among themselves, they each wielded an absolute veto power. This "free veto" constitutional system soon deadlocked parliamentary government. The monarchy lost its room to maneuver, and with it much of its remaining power. An appalled Croat visitor in 1658 commented, "Among the Poles there is no order in the state. . . . Everybody who is stronger thinks to have the right to oppress the weaker, just as the wolves and bears are free to capture and kill cattle. . . . Such abominable depravity is called by the Poles 'aristocratic freedom.'" The Polish version of constitutionalism fatally weakened the state and made it prey to its neighbors.

■ **REVIEW:** *Why did absolutism succeed everywhere in eastern Europe except Poland-Lithuania?*

Constitutionalism in England

In the second half of the seventeenth century, western and eastern Europe began to move in different directions. In general, the farther east one traveled, the more absolutist the style of government (with the exception of Poland-Lithuania) and the greater the gulf between landlord and peasant. In eastern Europe, nobles lorded over their serfs but owed almost slavish obedience in turn to their rulers. In western Europe, even in absolutist France, serfdom had almost entirely disappeared and nobles and rulers alike faced greater challenges to their control. The greatest challenges of all would come in England.

This outcome might seem surprising, for the English monarchs enjoyed many advantages compared with their continental rivals: they needed less money for their armies because they had stayed out of the Thirty Years' War, and their island kingdom was in theory easier to rule because they governed a relatively homogeneous population only one-fourth the size of France's with few regional institutions to block the ruler's will. Yet the English rulers failed in their efforts to install absolutist policies. The English revolutions of 1642–1660 and 1688–1689 overturned two kings, confirmed the constitutional powers of an elected parliament, and laid the foundation for the idea that government must guarantee certain rights under the law.

England Turned Upside Down, 1642–1660

Disputes about the right to levy taxes and the nature of authority in the Church of England had long troubled the relationship between the English crown and Parliament. For over a hundred years, wealthy English landowners had been accustomed to participating in government through Parliament and expected to be consulted on royal policy. Although England had no one constitutional document, a variety of laws, judicial decisions, charters, and petitions granted by the king, and customary procedures all regulated relations between king and Parliament. When Charles I tried to assert his authority over Parliament, a civil war broke out. It set in motion an unpredictable chain of events, which included an extraordinary ferment of religious and political ideas. Some historians view the English civil war of 1642–1646 as the last great war of religion because it pitted Puritans against those trying to push the Anglican church toward Catholicism, but it should be considered the first modern revolution because it gave birth to democratic political and religious movements.

Charles I (r. 1625–1649) inherited the problems that had been left by his father, James I, and James's predecessor, Elizabeth I. Elizabeth had defended the crown's right to regulate religion, but neither she nor James definitively reined in the Puritans. In addition, James antagonized Parliament by selling monopolies and titles to raise money and by relying increasingly on the advice of his personal favorite, George Villiers, on whom he bestowed the title of duke of Buckingham. Charles consequently faced an increasingly aggressive Parliament when he inherited the throne. In 1628, Parliament forced Charles to agree to a Petition of Right by which he promised not to levy taxes without its consent. Charles hoped to avoid further interference with his plans by simply refusing to call Parliament into session between 1629 and 1640.

Religious tensions brought conflicts over the king's authority to a head. The Puritans had long agitated for the removal of any vestiges of Catholicism, but

Charles, married to a French Catholic, moved in the opposite direction. With Charles's encouragement, the archbishop of Canterbury, William Laud (1573–1645), imposed increasingly elaborate ceremonies on the Anglican church. Angered by these moves toward "popery," the Puritans poured forth vituperative pamphlets and sermons. In response Laud hauled them before the feared Court of Star Chamber, which the king personally controlled. The court ordered harsh sentences for Laud's Puritan critics; they were whipped, pilloried, and branded, and even had their ears cut off and their noses split. When Laud tried to apply his policies to Scotland, however, they backfired completely: the stubborn Presbyterian Scots rioted against the imposition of the Anglican prayer book—the Book of Common Prayer—and in 1640 they invaded the north of England. To raise money to fight the war, Charles called Parliament into session and unwittingly opened the door to a constitutional and religious crisis.

England during the Civil War

Reformers in the House of Commons (the lower house of Parliament) seized the opportunity to undo what they saw as the royal tyranny of the 1630s. Parliament removed Laud from office, ordered the execution of an unpopular royal commander, abolished the Court of Star Chamber, repealed recently levied taxes, and provided for a parliamentary assembly at least once every three years, thus establishing a constitutional check on royal authority. Moderate reformers expected to stop there and resisted Puritan pressure to abolish bishops and eliminate the Anglican prayer book. But their hand was forced in January 1642, when Charles and his soldiers invaded Parliament and tried unsuccessfully to arrest those leaders who had moved to curb his power. Faced with mounting opposition within London, Charles withdrew from the city and organized an army.

The ensuing civil war between king and Parliament lasted four years (1642–1646) and divided the country. The king's army of royalists, known as Cavaliers, enjoyed the most support in northern and western England. The parliamentary forces, called Roundheads because they cut their hair short, had their stronghold in the southeast, including London. Although Puritans dominated on the parliamentary side, they were divided among themselves about the proper form of church government: the Presbyterians wanted a Calvinist church with some central authority, whereas the Independents favored entirely autonomous congregations free from other church government (hence the term *congregationalism*, often associated with the Independents). Putting aside their differences for the sake of military unity, the

Puritans united under an obscure member of the House of Commons, the country gentleman Oliver Cromwell (1599–1658), who sympathized with the Independents. After Cromwell skillfully reorganized the parliamentary troops, his New Model Army defeated the Cavaliers at the battle of Naseby in 1645. Charles surrendered in 1646.

Although the civil war between king and Parliament had ended in victory for Parliament, divisions within the Puritan ranks now came to the fore: the Presbyterians dominated Parliament, but the Independents controlled the army. The disputes between elites drew lower-class groups into the debate. When Parliament tried to disband the New Model Army in 1647, disgruntled soldiers protested. Called Levellers because of their insistence on leveling social differences, the soldiers took on their officers in a series of debates about the nature of political authority. The Levellers demanded that Parliament meet annually, that members be paid so as to allow common people to participate, and that all male heads of households be allowed to vote. Their ideal of political participation excluded servants, the propertyless, and women but offered access to artisans, shopkeepers, and modest farmers. Cromwell and other army leaders rejected the Levellers' demands as threatening to property owners. Cromwell insisted, "You have no other way to deal with these men but to break them in pieces. . . . If you do not break them they will break you."

Just as political differences between Presbyterians and Independents helped spark new political movements, so, too, their conflicts over church organization fostered the emergence of new religious doctrines. The new sects had in common only their emphasis on the "inner light" of individual religious inspiration and a disdain for hierarchical authority. Their emphasis on equality before God and greater participation in church governance appealed to the middle and lower classes. The Baptists, for example, insisted on adult baptism because they believed that Christians should choose their own church and that every child should not automatically become a member of the Church of England. The Quakers demonstrated their beliefs in equality and the inner light by refusing to doff their hats to men in authority. Manifesting their religious experience by trembling, or "quaking," the Quakers believed that anyone—man or woman—inspired by a direct experience of God could preach.

Parliamentary leaders feared that the new sects would overturn the whole social hierarchy. Rumors abounded, for example, of naked Quakers running through the streets waiting "for a sign." Some sects did advocate sweeping change. The Diggers promoted rural communism—collective ownership of all property. Seekers and Ranters questioned just about everything. A few men advocated free love. In keeping with their notions of equality and individual inspiration, many of the new sects provided opportunities for women to become preachers and prophets. Women also presented petitions, participated prominently in street demonstrations, distributed tracts, and occasionally even dressed as men, wearing swords and joining armies. The outspoken women in new sects like the Quakers underscored the threat of a social order turning upside down. These developments convinced the political elite that tolerating the new sects would lead to skepticism, anarchism, and debauchery.

At the heart of the continuing political struggle was the question of what to do with the king, who tried to negotiate with the Presbyterians in Parliament. In late 1648, Independents in the army purged the Presbyterians from Parliament, leaving a "rump" of about seventy members. This Rump Parliament then created a high court to try Charles I. The court found him guilty of attempting to establish "an unlimited and tyrannical power" and pronounced a death sentence. On January 30, 1649, Charles was beheaded before an enormous crowd, which reportedly groaned as one when the axe fell. Although many had objected to Charles's autocratic rule, few had wanted him killed. For royalists, Charles immediately became a martyr, and reports of miracles, such as the curing of blindness by the touch of a handkerchief soaked in his blood, soon circulated.

The Rump Parliament abolished the monarchy and the House of Lords (the upper house of Parliament) and set up a Puritan republic with Oliver Cromwell as chairman of the Council of State. Cromwell did not tolerate dissent from his policies. He saw the hand of God in events and himself as God's agent. Pamphleteers and songwriters ridiculed his red nose and accused him of wanting to be king, but few challenged his leadership. When his agents discovered plans for mutiny within the army, they executed the perpetrators; new decrees silenced the Levellers. Although Cromwell allowed the various Puritan sects to worship rather freely and permitted Jews with needed skills to return to England for the first time since the thirteenth century, Catholics could not worship publicly, nor could Anglicans use the Book of Common Prayer. The elites—many of whom were still Anglican— were troubled by Cromwell's religious policies but pleased to see some social order reestablished.

The new regime aimed to extend state power just as Charles I had before. Cromwell laid the foundation for a Great Britain made up of England, Wales, Ireland, and Scotland by reconquering Scotland and subduing Ireland. Anti-English rebels in Ireland had seized the occasion of troubles between king and Parliament to revolt in 1641. When Cromwell's position was secured in 1649, he went to Ireland with a large force and easily defeated the rebels, massacring whole garrisons and their priests. He encouraged expropriating the lands of the Irish "barbarous wretches," and Scottish immigrants resettled the northern county of Ulster. This seventeenth-century English conquest left a legacy of bitterness that the Irish even today call "the curse of Cromwell." In 1651, Parliament turned its attention overseas, putting mercantilist ideas into practice in the first Navigation Act, which allowed imports only if they were carried on English ships or came directly from the producers of goods. The Navigation Act was aimed at the Dutch, who dominated world trade; Cromwell tried to carry the policy further by waging naval war on the Dutch from 1652 to 1654.

■ **Oliver Cromwell**

In this painting of 1649, Robert Walker deliberately evokes previous portraits of English kings. Cromwell is shown preparing for battle in Ireland (note the shore and sea on Cromwell's left); he holds the baton of military command, and a young page is tying on a sash, symbol of his rank. Cromwell lived an austere life, and he is depicted here without any sign of luxury. When he died, he was buried in Westminster Abbey, but in 1661 his body was exhumed and hanged in its shroud. His head was cut off and displayed outside Westminster Hall for nearly twenty years.
(Courtesy of the National Portrait Gallery, London.)

At home, however, Cromwell faced growing resistance. His wars required a budget twice the size of Charles I's, and his increases in property taxes and customs duties alienated landowners and merchants. The conflict reached a crisis in 1653: Parliament considered disbanding the army, whereupon Cromwell abolished the Rump Parliament in a military coup and made himself Lord Protector. He now silenced his critics by banning newspapers and using networks of spies and mail readers to keep tabs on his enemies. Cromwell's death in 1658 revived the prospect of civil war and political chaos. In 1660, a newly elected, staunchly Anglican Parliament invited Charles II, the son of the executed king, to return from exile.

The "Glorious Revolution" of 1688

The traditional monarchical form of government was reinstated in 1660, restoring the king to full partnership with Parliament. Charles II (r. 1660–1685) promised to extend religious toleration, especially to Catholics, with whom he sympathized. Yet in the first years of his reign more than a thousand Puritan ministers lost their positions, and after 1664, attending a service other than one conforming with the Anglican prayer book was illegal. Natural disasters also marred the early years of Charles II's reign. The plague stalked London's rat-infested streets in May 1665 and claimed more than thirty thousand victims by September. Then in 1666, the Great Fire swept the city, causing cataclysmic destruction. The crown now had a city as well as a monarchy to rebuild.

■ **Great Fire of London, 1666**

This painting shows the three-day fire at its height. The writer John Evelyn described the scene in his diary: "All the sky was of a fiery aspect, like the top of a burning oven, and the light seen above 40 miles round about for many nights. God grant mine eyes may never behold the like, who now saw above 10,000 houses all in one flame; the noise and cracking and thunder of people, the fall of towers, houses, and churches, was like an hideous storm." Everyone in London at the time felt overwhelmed by the catastrophe, and many attributed it to God's punishment for the upheavals of the 1640s and 1650s. (Museum of London Photographic Library.)

The restoration of monarchy made some in Parliament fear that the English government would come to resemble French absolutism. This fear was not unfounded. In 1670, Charles II made a secret agreement, soon leaked, with Louis XIV in which he promised to announce his conversion to Catholicism in exchange for money for a war against the Dutch. Charles never proclaimed himself a Catholic, but in his Declaration of Indulgence (1673) he did suspend all laws against Catholics and Protestant dissenters. Parliament refused to continue funding the Dutch war unless Charles rescinded his Declaration of Indulgence. Asserting its authority further, Parliament passed the Test Act in 1673, requiring all government officials to profess allegiance to the Church of England and in effect disavow Catholic doctrine. Then in 1678, Parliament precipitated the so-called Exclusion Crisis by explicitly denying the throne to a Roman Catholic. This action was aimed at the king's brother and heir, James, an open convert to Catholicism. Charles refused to allow it to become law.

The dynastic crisis over the succession of a Catholic gave rise to two distinct factions in Parliament: the Tories, who supported a strong, hereditary monarchy and the restored ceremony of the Anglican church, and the Whigs, who advocated parliamentary supremacy and toleration for Protestant dissenters such as Presbyterians. Both labels were originally derogatory: *Tory* meant an Irish Catholic bandit; *Whig* was the Irish Catholic designation for a Presbyterian Scot. The Tories favored James's succession despite his Catholicism, whereas the Whigs opposed a Catholic monarch. The loose moral atmosphere of Charles's court also offended some Whigs, who complained tongue in cheek that Charles was father of his country in much too literal a fashion (he had fathered more than one child by his mistresses but produced no legitimate heir).

Upon Charles's death, James succeeded to the throne as James II (r. 1685–1688). James pursued pro-Catholic and absolutist policies even more aggressively than his brother. When a male heir—who would take precedence over James's two adult Protestant daughters and be reared a Catholic—was born, Tories and Whigs banded together. They invited the Dutch ruler William, prince of Orange and the husband of James's older daughter, Mary, to invade England. James fled to France, and hardly any blood was shed. Parliament offered the throne jointly to William (r. 1689–1702) and Mary (r. 1689–1694) on the condition that they accept a bill of rights guaranteeing Parliament's full partnership in a constitutional government.

In the Bill of Rights (1689), William and Mary agreed not to raise a standing army or to levy taxes without Parliament's consent. They also agreed to call meetings of Parliament at least every three years, to guarantee free elections to parliamentary seats, and to abide by Parliament's decisions and not suspend duly passed laws. The agreement gave England's constitutional government a written, legal basis by formally recognizing Parliament as a self-contained, independent body that shared power with the rulers. Victorious supporters of the coup declared it the **Glorious Revolution**. Constitutionalism had triumphed over absolutism in England.

The propertied classes who controlled Parliament prevented any resurgence of the popular turmoil of the 1640s. The Toleration Act of 1689 granted all Protestants freedom of worship, though non-Anglicans were still excluded from the universities; Catholics got no rights but were more often left alone to worship privately. When the Catholics in Ireland rose to defend James II, William and Mary's troops brutally suppressed them. With the Whigs in power and the Tories in opposition, wealthy landowners now controlled political life throughout the realm. Differences between the factions had become minor; the Tories simply enjoyed less access to the king's patronage.

■ **REVIEW:** *What differences over religion and politics caused the conflict between king and Parliament in England?*

Other Outposts of Constitutionalism

When William and Mary came to the throne in England in 1689, the Dutch and the English put aside the rivalries that had brought them to war against each other in 1652–1654, 1665–1667, and 1672–1674. Under William, the Dutch Republic and England together led the coalition that blocked Louis XIV's efforts to dominate continental Europe. The two states had much in common: oriented toward commerce, especially overseas, they were the successful exceptions to absolutism in Europe. Also among the few outposts of constitutionalism in the seventeenth century were the British North American colonies, which developed representative government while the English were preoccupied with their revolutions at home. Constitutionalism was not the only factor shaping this Atlantic world; as constitutionalism developed in the colonies, so, too, did the enslavement of black Africans as a new labor force.

The Dutch Republic

When the Dutch Republic gained formal independence from Spain in 1648, it had already established a decentralized, constitutional state. Rich merchants called *regents* effectively controlled the internal affairs of each province and through the Estates General (an assembly made up of deputies from each province) named the *stadholder*, the executive officer responsible for defense and for representing the state at all ceremonial occasions. They almost always chose one of the princes of the house of Orange, but the prince of Orange resembled a president more than a king.

The decentralized state encouraged and protected trade, and the Dutch Republic soon became Europe's financial capital. The Bank of Amsterdam offered interest rates less than half those available in England and France. Praised for their industriousness, thrift, and cleanliness—and maligned as greedy, dull "butterboxes"—the Dutch dominated overseas commerce with their shipping (Map 13.3). They imported products from all over the world: spices, tea, and silk from Asia; sugar and tobacco from the Americas; wool from England and Spain; timber and furs from Scandinavia; grain from eastern Europe. A widely reprinted history of Amsterdam that appeared in 1662 described the city as "risen through the hand of God to the peak of prosperity and greatness. . . . The whole world stands amazed at its riches and from east and west, north and south they come to behold it."

The Dutch rapidly became the most prosperous and best-educated people in Europe. Middle-class people supported the visual arts, especially painting, to an unprecedented degree. Artists and engravers produced thousands of works, and Dutch artists were among the first to sell to a mass market. Whereas in other countries, kings, nobles, and churches bought art, Dutch buyers were merchants, artisans, and shopkeepers. Engravings, illustrated histories, and oil paintings, even those of the widely acclaimed Rembrandt van Rijn (1606–1669), were relatively

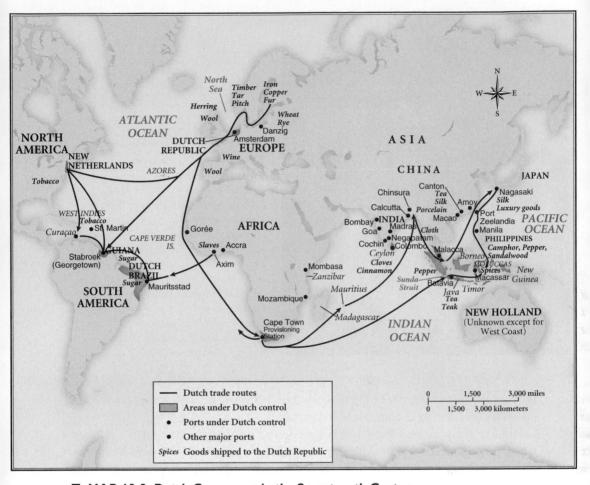

■ **MAP 13.3 Dutch Commerce in the Seventeenth Century**
Even before gaining formal independence from the Spanish in 1648, the Dutch had begun to com-
pete with the Spanish and Portuguese all over the world. In 1602, a group of merchants established
the Dutch East India Company, which soon offered investors an annual rate of return of 35 percent
on the trade in spices with countries located on the Indian Ocean. Global commerce gave the Dutch
the highest standard of living in Europe and soon attracted the envy of the French and the English.
For more help analyzing this map, see the map activity for this chapter in the ONLINE STUDY
GUIDE at bedfordstmartins.com/huntconcise.

inexpensive. The pictures reflected the Dutch interest in familiar daily details: children at play, winter landscapes, and ships in port.

The family household, not the royal court, determined the moral character of
this intensely commercial society. Dutch society fostered public enterprise in men
and work in the home for women, who were expected to filter out the greed and
materialism of commercial society by maintaining domestic harmony and virtue.

■ **A Typical Dutch Scene from Daily Life**
Jan Steen painted The Baker Arent Oostward and His Wife *in 1658. Steen ran a brewery and tavern in addition to painting, and he was known for his interest in the details of daily life. Dutch artists popularized this kind of "genre" painting, which showed ordinary people at work and play.* **For more help analyzing this image,** see the visual activity for this chapter in the ONLINE STUDY GUIDE at bedfordstmartins.com/huntconcise. (Rijksmuseum, Amsterdam.)

Relative prosperity decreased the need for married women to work, so Dutch society developed the clear contrast between middle-class male and female roles that would become prevalent elsewhere in Europe and in America more than a century later. As one contemporary Dutch writer explained, "The husband must be on the street to practice his trade; the wife must stay at home to be in the kitchen."

Extraordinarily high levels of urbanization and literacy created a large reading public. Dutch presses printed books censored elsewhere (printers or authors censored in one province simply shifted operations to another), and the University of Leiden attracted students and professors from all over Europe. Dutch tolerance extended to the works of Benedict Spinoza (1633–1677), a Jewish philosopher and biblical scholar who was expelled by his synagogue for alleged atheism but was left alone by the Dutch authorities. Spinoza strove to reconcile religion with science and mathematics, but his work scandalized many Christians and Jews because he seemed to equate God and nature. Like nature, Spinoza's God followed unchangeable laws and could not be influenced by human actions, prayers, or faith.

Dutch learning, painting, and commerce all enjoyed wide renown in the seventeenth century, but this luster proved hard to maintain. The Dutch lived in a world of international rivalries in which strong central authority gave their enemies an advantage. Though inconclusive, the naval wars with England drained the state's revenues. Even more dangerous were the land wars with France, which continued into the eighteenth century. The Dutch survived these challenges but increasingly depended on alliances with other powers, such as England. By the end of the seventeenth century, the regent elite had become more exclusive, more preoccupied with ostentation, less tolerant of deviations from strict Calvinism, and more concerned with imitating French styles than with encouraging their own.

Freedom and Slavery in the New World

The French and English also increasingly overshadowed the Dutch in the New World colonies. While the Dutch concentrated on shipping, including the slave trade, the seventeenth-century French and English established settler colonies that would eventually provide fabulous revenues to the home countries. Many European governments encouraged private companies to vie for their share of the slave trade, and slavery began to take clear institutional form in the New World in this period. While whites found in the colonies greater political and religious freedom than in Europe, they subjected black Africans to the most degrading forms of bondage.

After the Spanish and Portuguese had shown that African slaves could be transported and forced to labor in South and Central America, the English and French endeavored to set up similar labor systems in their new Caribbean island colonies. White planters with large tracts of land bought African slaves to work fields of sugarcane, and as they gradually built up their holdings, the planters displaced most of the original white settlers, who moved to mainland North American colonies. After 1661, when Barbados instituted a slave code that stripped all Africans of rights under English law, slavery became codified as an inherited status that applied only to blacks. The result was a society of extremes: the very wealthy whites, about 7 percent of the population in Barbados; and the enslaved, powerless black majority. The English brought little of their religious or constitutional practices to the Caribbean. Other Caribbean colonies followed a similar pattern of development. Louis XIV promulgated a "black code" in 1685 to regulate the legal status of slaves in the French colonies. Although one of his aims was to prevent non-Catholics from owning slaves in the French colonies, the code had much the same effect as the English codes on the slaves themselves: they had no legal rights.

The highest church and government authorities in Catholic and Protestant countries alike condoned the gradually expanding slave trade; the governments of England, France, Spain, Portugal, the Dutch Republic, and Denmark all encouraged private companies to traffic in black Africans. The Dutch West India Company was the most successful of them. In the early 1600s, about 9,500 Africans were exported from Africa to the New World every year; by 1700, this figure had increased nearly fourfold to 36,000 annually. Historians advance several different factors for the increase in the slave trade: some claim that improvements in muskets made European slavers more formidable; others cite the rising price for slaves, which made their sale more attractive for Africans; still others focus on factors internal to Africa, such as the increasing size of African armies and their use of muskets in fighting and capturing other Africans for sale as slaves. Whatever the reason, the way had been prepared for the development of an Atlantic economy based on slavery.

Virtually left to themselves during the upheavals in England, the fledgling English colonies in North America developed representative government on their own. Almost every colony had a governor and a two-house legislature. The colonial legislatures constantly sought to increase their power and resisted the efforts of Charles II and James II to reaffirm royal control. William and Mary reluctantly allowed emerging colonial elites more control over local affairs. The social and political elite among the settlers hoped to impose an English social hierarchy dominated by rich landowners. Ordinary immigrants to the colonies, however, took advantage of plentiful land to carve out their own farms using white servants and, later, in some colonies, African slaves.

For native Americans, the expanding European presence meant something else altogether. They faced death through unfamiliar disease and warfare and the accelerating loss of their homelands. Unlike white settlers, native Americans believed that land was a divine gift provided for their collective use and not subject to individual ownership. As a result, Europeans' claims that they owned exclusive land rights caused frequent skirmishes. In 1675–1676, for instance, three tribes allied under Metacomet (called King Philip by the English) threatened the survival of New England settlers, who savagely repulsed the attacks and sold their captives as slaves. Whites portrayed native Americans as conspiring villains and sneaky heathens, akin to Africans in their savagery.

■ **REVIEW:** *How could outposts of constitutionalism coexist with slavery?*

The Search for Order in Elite and Popular Culture

The early success of constitutionalism in England, the Dutch Republic, and the English North American colonies would help to shape a distinctive Atlantic world in the eighteenth century. Just how constitutionalism was linked to the growing commerce with the colonies remains open to dispute, however, because the constitutional governments, like the absolutist ones, avidly pursued profits in the burgeoning slave trade. Freedom did not mean liberty for everyone. One of the great debates of the time—and of much of the modern period that followed—concerned the meaning of freedom: for whom, under what conditions, and with what justifiable limitations could freedom be claimed?

There was no freedom without order to sustain it, and most Europeans feared disorder above all else. Political theories, science, poetry, painting, and architecture all reflected in some measure the attempts to ground authority—to define the relation between freedom and order—in new ways. Authority concerned not just rulers and subjects but also the hierarchy of groups in society. As European states consolidated their powers, elites worked to distinguish themselves from the lower classes. They developed new codes of correct behavior for themselves and tried to teach order and discipline to their social inferiors.

Social Contract Theory: Hobbes and Locke

The turmoil of the times prompted a major rethinking of the foundations of all authority. Two figures stood out prominently amid the competing voices: Thomas Hobbes and John Locke. Their writings fundamentally shaped the modern subject of political science. Hobbes justified absolute authority; Locke provided the rationale for constitutionalism. Yet both argued that all authority came not from divine right but from a **social contract** between citizens.

Thomas Hobbes (1588–1679) was a royalist who sat out the English civil war of the 1640s in France, where he tutored the future king Charles II. Returning to England in 1651, he published his masterpiece, *Leviathan* (1651), in which he argued for unlimited authority in a ruler. Absolute authority could be vested in either a king or a parliament; it had to be absolute, he insisted, in order to overcome the defects of human nature. Believing that people are essentially self-centered and driven by the "right to self-preservation," Hobbes made his case by referring to science, not religion. To Hobbes, human life in a state of nature—that is, any situation without firm authority—was "solitary, poor, nasty, brutish, and short." He believed that the desire for power and natural greed would inevitably lead to unfettered competition. Only the assurance of social order could make people secure enough to act according to law; consequently, giving up personal liberty, he maintained, was the price of collective security. Rulers derived their power, he concluded, from a contract in which absolute authority protects people's rights.

Hobbes's notion of rule by an absolute authority left no room for political dissent or nonconformity, and it infuriated both royalists and supporters of Parliament. He enraged royalists by arguing that authority came not from divine right but from the social contract between citizens. Parliamentary supporters resisted Hobbes's claim that rulers must possess absolute authority to prevent the greater evil of anarchy; they believed that a constitution should guarantee shared power between king and parliament and protect individual rights under the law. Like Machiavelli before him, Hobbes became associated with a cynical, pessimistic view of human nature, and future political theorists often began their arguments by refuting Hobbes.

Rejecting both Hobbes and the more traditional royalist defenses of absolute authority, John Locke (1632–1704) used the notion of a social contract to provide a foundation for constitutionalism. Locke experienced political life firsthand as physician, secretary, and intellectual companion to the earl of Shaftesbury, a leading English Whig. In 1683, Locke fled with Shaftesbury to the Dutch Republic when Charles II clamped down on those conspiring to prevent his Catholic brother from succeeding him. There Locke continued work on his *Two Treatises of Government*, which, when published in 1690, served to justify the Glorious Revolution of 1688. Locke's position was thoroughly anti-absolutist. He denied the divine right of kings and ridiculed the common royalist idea that political power in the state mirrored the father's authority in the family. Like Hobbes, he posited a state of nature that applied to all people. Unlike Hobbes, however, he thought people were reasonable and the state of nature peaceful.

Locke insisted that government's only purpose was to protect life, liberty, and property, a notion that linked economic and political freedom. Ultimate authority rested in the will of a majority of men who owned property, and government should be limited to its basic purpose of protection. A ruler who failed to uphold his part of the social contract between the ruler and the populace could be justifiably resisted, an idea that would become crucial for the leaders of the American Revolution a century later. For England's landowners, however, Locke helped validate a revolution that consolidated their interests and ensured their privileges in the social hierarchy.

Locke defended his optimistic view of human nature in the immensely influential *Essay Concerning Human Understanding* (1690). He denied the existence of any innate ideas and asserted instead that each human is born with a mind that is a *tabula rasa* (blank slate). Everything humans know, he claimed, comes from sensory experience, not from anything inherent in human nature. Locke's views promoted the belief that "all men are created equal," a belief that challenged absolutist forms of rule and ultimately raised questions about women's roles as well. Not surprisingly, Locke devoted considerable energy to rethinking educational practices; he believed that education crucially shaped the human personality by channeling all sensory experience. Although he himself owned shares in the Royal African Company and justified slavery, Locke's writings were later used by abolitionists in their campaign against slavery.

Newton and the Consolidation of the Scientific Revolution

New breakthroughs in science lent support to Locke's optimistic view of human potential and at the same time reaffirmed the underlying order of the natural world. Building on the work of Copernicus, Kepler, and Galileo (see Chapter 12), the English scientist Isaac Newton (1642–1727) finally synthesized astronomy and physics with his law of universal gravitation, further enhancing the prestige of the new science. A Cambridge University student at the time of Charles II's restoration, Newton was a pious Anglican who aimed to reconcile faith and science. By proving that the physical universe followed rational principles, Newton argued, scientists could prove the existence of God and so liberate humans from doubt and the fear of chaos. Newton applied mathematical principles to formulate three physical laws: (1) in the absence of external force, an object in motion continues in a straight line; (2) the rate of change in the motion of an object is a result of the forces acting on it; and (3) the action and reaction between two objects are equal and opposite. The basis of Newtonian physics thus required understanding mass, inertia, force, velocity, and acceleration—all key concepts in modern science.

Extending these principles to the entire universe in his masterwork, *Principia Mathematica* (1687), Newton united celestial and terrestrial mechanics—astronomy and physics—with his **law of universal gravitation**. This law held that every body in the universe exerts over every other body an attractive force directly proportional to the product of their masses and inversely proportional to the square of the distance between them. The law of gravitation explained Kepler's elliptical planetary orbits just as it accounted for the motion of ordinary objects on earth. Once set in motion, the universe operated like clockwork, with no need for God's continuing intervention. Gravity, though a mysterious force, could be expressed mathematically. In Newton's words, "From the same principles [of motion] I now demonstrate the frame of the System of the World." The English poet Alexander Pope later captured the intellectual world's appreciation of Newton's accomplishment:

> *Nature and Nature's laws lay hid in night*
> *God said, Let Newton be! and all was light.*

Newton's science was not just mathematical and deductive; he experimented with light and helped establish the science of optics. Even while making these fundamental contributions to scientific method, Newton carried out alchemical experiments in his rooms at Cambridge University and spent long hours trying to calculate the date of the beginning of the world and of the second coming of Jesus. Not all scientists accepted Newton's theories immediately, especially on the continent of Europe, but within a couple of generations his work was preeminent, partly because of experimental verification. His "frame of the System of the World" remained the basis for all physics until the advent of relativity theory and quantum mechanics in the early twentieth century.

Although not all Newton's peers immediately accepted the validity of his work, absolutist rulers quickly saw the potential of the new science for enhancing their prestige and glory. Frederick William, the Great Elector of Brandenburg-Prussia, for example, set up agricultural experiments in front of his Berlin palace, and various German princes supported the work of Gottfried Wilhelm Leibniz (1646–1716), one of the inventors of calculus. A lawyer, diplomat, and scholar who wrote about metaphysics, cosmology, and history, Leibniz helped establish scientific societies in the German states. Government involvement in science was greatest in France, where it became an arm of mercantilist policy; in 1666, Colbert founded the Royal Academy of Sciences, which supplied fifteen scientists with government stipends.

Constitutional states supported science less directly but nonetheless provided an intellectual environment that encouraged its spread. The English Royal Society, the counterpart to the Royal Academy of Sciences in France, grew out of informal meetings of scientists at London and Oxford rather than direct government involvement. It received a royal charter in 1662 but maintained complete independence. The society's secretary described its business to be "in the first place, to scrutinize the whole of Nature and to investigate its activity and powers by means of observations and experiments; and then in course of time to hammer out a more solid philosophy and more ample amenities of civilization." Whether the state was directly involved or not, thinkers of the day now tied science explicitly to social progress.

Because of their exclusion from most universities, women only rarely participated in the new scientific discoveries. In 1667, nonetheless, the English Royal Society invited Margaret Cavendish—a writer of poems, essays, letters, and philosophical treatises—to attend a meeting to watch the exhibition of experiments. She attacked the use of telescopes and microscopes because she detected in the new experimentalism a mechanistic view of the world that exalted masculine prowess and challenged the Christian belief in freedom of the will. She nonetheless urged the formal education of women, complaining that "we are kept like birds in cages to hop up and down in our houses." "Many of our Sex may have as much wit, and be capable of Learning as well as men," she insisted, "but since they want Instructions, it is not possible they should attain to it."

Freedom and Order in the Arts

Even though Newtonian science depicted an orderly universe, most artists and intellectuals had experienced enough of the upheavals of the seventeenth century to fear the prospect of chaos and disintegration. The French mathematician Blaise Pascal vividly captured their worries in his *Pensées* ("Thoughts") of 1660: "I look on all sides, and I see only darkness everywhere. Nature presents to me nothing which is not a matter of doubt and concern.... It is incomprehensible that God should exist, and incomprehensible that He should not exist." Poets, painters, and architects all tried to make sense of the individual's place within what Pascal called "the eternal silence of these infinite spaces."

The English Puritan poet John Milton (1608–1674) responded to the turmoil of the times by giving priority to individual liberty. In 1643, in the midst of the civil war between king and Parliament, he published writings in favor of divorce. When Parliament enacted a censorship law aimed at such literature, Milton countered in

1644 with one of the first defenses of freedom of the press, *Areopagitica* ("Tribunal of Opinion"). Forced into retirement after the restoration of the monarchy, Milton published in 1667 his epic poem *Paradise Lost.* He used Adam and Eve's Fall to meditate on human freedom and the tragedies of rebellion. Although Milton wanted to "justify the ways of God to man," his Satan, the proud angel who challenges God, is so compelling as to be heroic. In the end, Adam and Eve learn to accept moral responsibility. Individuals learn the limits to their freedom, yet personal liberty remains essential to their definition as human.

The dominant artistic styles of the time—the baroque and the classical—both submerged the individual in a grander design. The baroque style proved to be especially suitable for public displays of faith and power that overawed individual beholders. The combination of religious and political purposes in baroque art is best exemplified in the architecture and sculpture of Gian Lorenzo Bernini (1598–1680), the papacy's official artist. His architectural masterpiece was the gigantic square facing St. Peter's Basilica in Rome (1656–1671). His use of freestanding colonnades and a huge open space is meant to impress the individual observer with the power of the popes and the Catholic religion.

Bernini also sculpted tombs and statues for the popes and for private patrons too. In 1665, Louis XIV hired Bernini to plan the rebuilding of the Louvre palace in Paris but then rejected his ideas as incompatible with French tastes.

Although France was a Catholic country, French painters, sculptors, and architects, like their patron Louis XIV, preferred the standards of classicism to

■ **Gian Lorenzo Bernini,** *Ecstasy of St. Teresa of Ávila* **(c. 1650)**
In this baroque sculpture, Bernini captures the drama and sensationalism of a mystical religious faith. He based his figures on a vision of an angel reported by St. Teresa: "In his hands I saw a great golden spear, and at the iron tip there appeared to be a point of fire. This he plunged into my heart several times so that it penetrated my entrails. When he pulled it out I felt that he took them with it, and left me utterly consumed by the great love of God."
(Scala/Art Resource, NY.)

■ **French Classicism**

This painting by Nicolas Poussin, Discovery of Achilles on Skyros (1649–1650), shows the French interest in classical themes and ideals. In the Greek story, Thetis hid her son Achilles on the island of Skyros so he would not have to fight in the Trojan War. When a chest of treasures is offered to the women, Achilles reveals himself (he is the figure on the far right) because he cannot resist the sword. In telling the story, Poussin emphasizes harmony and almost a sedateness of composition, avoiding the exuberance and emotionalism of the baroque style.

(Photograph ©2006 Museum of Fine Arts, Boston.)

those of the baroque. French artists developed classicism to be a national style, distinct from the baroque style that was closely associated with France's enemies, the Austrian and Spanish Habsburgs. As its name suggests, **classicism** reflected the ideals of the art of antiquity; geometric shapes, order, and harmony of lines took precedence over the sensuous, exuberant, and emotional forms of the baroque. Rather than being overshadowed by the sheer power of emotional display, in classicism the individual could be found at the intersection of converging, symmetrical, straight lines. These influences were apparent in the work of the leading French painters of the period, Nicolas Poussin (1594–1665) and Claude Lorrain (1600–1682), both of whom worked in Rome and tried to re-create classical Roman values in their mythological scenes and Roman landscapes.

Art might also serve the interests of science. One of the most skilled illustrators of insects and flowers was Maria Sibylla Merian (1646–1717), a German-born

■ European Fascination with Products of the New World

In this painting of a banana plant, Maria Sibylla Merian offers a scientific study of one of the many exotic plants and animals found by Europeans who traveled to the colonies overseas. Merian was fifty-one when she traveled to the Dutch South American colony of Surinam.

(Courtesy of Hunt Institute for Botanical Documentation, Carnegie Mellon University, Pittsburgh, PA.)

painter-scholar whose engravings were widely celebrated for their brilliant realism and microscopic clarity. Merian eventually separated from her husband and joined a sect called the Labadists (after its French founder, Jean de Labadie), whose members did not believe in formal marriage ties and established a colony in the northern Dutch province of Friesland. After moving there with her daughters, Merian went with missionaries from the sect to the Dutch colony of Surinam in South America and painted watercolors of the exotic flowers, birds, and insects she found in the jungle around the cocoa and sugarcane plantations. In the seventeenth century, many women became known for their still lifes and especially their paintings of flowers. Paintings by the Dutch artist Rachel Ruysch, for example, fetched higher prices than works by Rembrandt.

Women and Manners

Poetry and painting imaginatively explored the place of the individual within a larger whole, but real-life individuals had to learn to navigate their own social worlds. Manners—the learning of individual self-discipline—were essential skills of social navigation, and women usually took the lead in teaching them. Under the tutelage of their mothers and wives, nobles learned to hide all that was crass and to maintain a fine sense of social distinction. In some ways, aristocratic men were expected to act more like women. Just as women had long been expected to please men, now aristocratic men had to please their monarch or patron by displaying proper manners and conversing with elegance and wit. Men as well as women had to master the art of pleasing—which included foreign languages (especially French), dance, a taste for fine music, and attention to dress.

As part of the evolution of new aristocratic ideals, nobles learned to disdain all that was lowly. The upper classes began to reject popular festivals and fairs in favor of private theaters, where seats were relatively expensive and behavior was formal. Clowns and buffoons now seemed vulgar; the last king of England to keep a court fool was Charles I. The greatest French playwright of the seventeenth century, Molière (the pen name of Jean-Baptiste Poquelin, 1622–1673), wrote sparkling comedies of manners that revealed much about the new aristocratic behavior. Molière's play *The Middle-Class Gentleman*, first performed at the royal court in 1670, revolves around the yearning of a rich, middle-class Frenchman, Monsieur Jourdain, to learn to act like a *gentilhomme* (meaning both "gentleman" and "nobleman" in French). By making fun of Jourdain's outlandish aspirations, the play seemed to reassure the nobles at court: only true nobles by blood can hope to act like nobles. But the play also showed how the middle classes were learning to emulate the nobility; if one could learn to *act* nobly through self-discipline, could not anyone with some education and money pass himself off as noble?

As Molière's play demonstrated, new attention to manners trickled down from the court to the middle class. A French treatise on manners from 1672 explained:

> If everyone is eating from the same dish, you should take care not to put your hand into it before those of higher rank have done so. . . . Formerly one was permitted . . . to dip one's bread into the sauce, provided only that one had not already bitten it. Nowadays that would be a kind of rusticity. Formerly one was allowed to take from one's mouth what one could not eat and drop it on the floor, provided it was done skillfully. Now that would be very disgusting.

The key words *rusticity* and *disgusting* reveal the association of unacceptable social behavior with the peasantry, dirt, and repulsion.

Courtly manners often permeated the upper reaches of society by means of the *salon*, an informal gathering held regularly in private homes and presided over by a socially eminent woman. In 1661, one French author claimed to have identified 251 Parisian women as hostesses of salons. Although the French government occasionally worried that these gatherings might be seditious, the three main topics of conversation were love, literature, and philosophy. Hostesses often worked hard to encourage the careers of budding authors. Before publishing a manuscript, many authors would read their compositions to a salon gathering. Corneille, Racine, and even Bishop Bossuet sought female approval for their writings.

Women who wrote on their own faced many obstacles. Marie-Madeleine de La Vergne, known as Madame de Lafayette, wrote several short novels that were published anonymously because it was considered inappropriate for aristocratic women to appear in print. After the publication of *The Princess of Clèves* in 1678, she denied having written it. Hannah Wooley, the English author of many books on domestic conduct, published under the name of her first husband. Women were known for writing wonderful letters (Marie de Sévigné was a prime example), many of which circulated in handwritten form; hardly any appeared in print during their authors' lifetimes. In the 1650s, despite these limitations, French women began to turn out best sellers in a new type of literature, the novel. Their success prompted the philosopher Pierre Bayle to remark in 1697 that "our best French novels for a long time have been written by women."

The new importance of women in the world of manners and letters did not sit well with everyone. Although the French writer François Poulain de la Barre (1647–1723), in a series of works published in the 1670s, used the new science to assert the equality of women's minds, most men resisted the idea. Clergy, lawyers, scholars, and playwrights attacked women's growing public influence. Women, they complained, were corrupting forces and needed restraint. Women were accused of raising "the banner of prostitution in the salons, in the promenades, and in the streets." Molière wrote plays denouncing women's pretension to judge literary merit. English playwrights derided learned women by creating characters with names such as Lady Knowall, Lady Meanwell, and Mrs. Lovewit. A real-life target of the English playwrights was Aphra Behn (1640–1689), one of the first professional woman authors, who supported herself by journalism and wrote plays and poetry. Her short novel *Oroonoko* (1688) told the story of an African prince mistakenly sold into slavery. The story was so successful that it was adapted by playwrights and performed repeatedly in England and France for the next hundred years. Behn responded to her critics by arguing that there was "no reason why women should not write as well as men."

Reforming Popular Culture

The illiterate peasants who made up most of Europe's population had little or no knowledge of the law of gravitation, upper-class manners, or novels, no matter who authored them. Their culture had three main elements: the knowledge needed to work at farming or in a trade; popular forms of entertainment such as village fairs and dances; and their religion, which shaped every aspect of life and death. In the seventeenth century the division between elite and popular culture widened as elites insisted on their difference from the lower orders and pushed forward the ongoing effort to instill religious and social discipline in their social inferiors.

Building upon campaigns against popular "paganism" that began during the sixteenth-century Protestant and Catholic reform movements, Protestant and Catholic churches alike pushed hard to change popular religious practices. Puritans in England tried to root out maypole dances, Sunday village fairs, gambling, taverns, and bawdy ballads because they interfered with sober observance of the Sabbath. In Lutheran Norway, pastors denounced a widespread belief in the miracle-working powers of St. Olaf. The word *superstition* previously meant "false religion" (Protestantism was a superstition for Catholics, Catholicism for Protestants). In the seventeenth century, it took on its modern meaning of irrational fears, beliefs, and practices, which anyone educated or refined would avoid. *Superstition* became synonymous with popular or ignorant beliefs.

The Catholic campaign against superstitious practices found a ready ally in Louis XIV. While he reformed the nobles at court through etiquette and manners, Catholic bishops in the French provinces trained parish priests to reform their flocks by using catechisms in local dialects and insisting that parishioners attend Mass. The church faced a formidable challenge. One bishop in France complained in 1671, "Can you believe that there are in this diocese entire villages where no one has even heard of Jesus Christ?" In some places, believers sacrificed animals to the Virgin, prayed to the new moon, and worshiped at the sources of streams as in pre-Christian times.

Like its Protestant counterpart, the Catholic campaign against ignorance and superstition helped extend state power. Clergy, officials, and local police worked together to limit carnival celebrations (festivities before the beginning of Lent that often had a riotous character), to regulate pilgrimages to shrines, and to replace "indecent" images of saints with more restrained and decorous ones. In Catholicism, the cult of the Virgin Mary and devotions closely connected with Jesus, such as the Holy Sacrament and the Sacred Heart, took precedence over the celebration of more popular saints who seemed to have pagan origins or were credited with unverified miracles. Reformers everywhere tried to limit the number of feast days on the grounds that they encouraged lewd behavior.

The campaign for more disciplined religious practices helped generate a new attitude toward the poor. Poverty previously had been closely linked with charity and virtue in Christianity: it was a Christian duty to give alms to the poor, and Jesus and many of the saints had purposely chosen lives of poverty. In the sixteenth and seventeenth centuries, the upper classes, the church, and the state increasingly regarded the poor as dangerous, deceitful, and lacking in character.

IMPORTANT DATES

1642–1646	Civil war between King Charles I and Parliament in England	1678	Marie-Madeleine de La Vergne (Madame de Lafayette) anonymously publishes *The Princess of Clèves*
1648	Peace of Westphalia ends Thirty Years' War; the Fronde revolt challenges royal authority in France; Ukrainian Cossack warriors rebel against the king of Poland-Lithuania	1683	Austrian Habsburgs break the Turkish siege of Vienna
1649	Execution of Charles I of England; new Russian legal code enacted	1685	Louis XIV revokes toleration for French Protestants granted by the Edict of Nantes
1651	Thomas Hobbes publishes *Leviathan*	1687	Isaac Newton publishes *Principia Mathematica*
1660	Monarchy restored in England	1688	Parliament deposes James II and invites his daughter, Mary, and her husband, William of Orange, to take the English throne
1661	Slave code set up in Barbados		
1667	Louis XIV begins the first of many wars that continue throughout his reign	1690	John Locke publishes *Two Treatises of Government* and *Essay Concerning Human Understanding*
1670	Molière publishes *The Middle-Class Gentleman*		

"Criminal laziness is the source of all their vices," wrote a Jesuit expert on the poor. The courts had previously expelled beggars from cities; now local leaders, both Catholic and Protestant, tried to reform their character. In the sixteenth century, local and state officials began to levy taxes for more organized poor relief; after the mid-seventeenth century officials began to transform hospitals into houses of confinement for beggars. In Catholic France, upper-class women's religious associations, known as confraternities, set up asylums that confined prostitutes (by arrest if necessary) and rehabilitated them. Confraternities also founded hospices where orphans learned order and respect. Such groups advocated harsh discipline as the cure for poverty.

Although hard times had increased the numbers of poor people and the rates of violent crime as well, the most important changes were attitudinal. The elites wanted to separate the very poor from society either to change them or to keep them from contaminating others. Hospitals became holding pens for society's unwanted members, where the poor joined the disabled, the incurably diseased, and the insane. The founding of hospitals demonstrates the connection between these

■ MAPPING THE WEST Europe at the End of the Seventeenth Century

A map can be deceiving. Although Poland-Lithuania looks like a large country on this map, it had been fatally weakened by internal conflicts. In the next century it would disappear entirely. The Ottoman Empire still controlled an extensive territory, but outside Anatolia its rule depended on intermediaries. The Austrian Habsburgs had pushed the Turks out of Hungary and back into the Balkans. At the other end of the scale, the very small Dutch Republic had become very rich through international commerce. Size did not always prove to be an advantage.

attitudes and state building. In 1676, Louis XIV ordered every French city to establish a hospital, and his government took charge of their finances. Other rulers soon followed the same path.

> **■ REVIEW:** *In what ways did elite and popular culture become more separate during the second half of the seventeenth century?*

Conclusion

The search for order in the wake of religious warfare and political upheaval took place on various levels, from the reform of the disorderly poor to the establishment of more regular bureaucratic routines in government. The biggest factor shaping the search for order was the growth of state power. Whether absolutist or constitutionalist in form, seventeenth-century states all aimed to penetrate more deeply into the lives of their subjects. They wanted more men for their armed forces, higher taxes to support their projects, and more control over foreign trade, religious dissent, and society's unwanted.

Some tearing had begun to appear, however, in the seamless fabric of state power. In England, the Dutch Republic, and the English North American colonies, property owners successfully demanded constitutional guarantees of their right to participate in government. In the eighteenth century, moreover, new levels of economic growth and the appearance of new social groups would exert pressures on the European state system. The success of seventeenth-century rulers created the political and economic conditions in which their critics would flourish.

■ MAKING CONNECTIONS

1. *What are the most important differences between absolutism and constitutionalism as political systems?*

2. *Why was the search for order a major theme in science, politics, and the arts during the second half of the seventeenth century?*

■ FOR FURTHER EXPLORATION

For further reading and online research ideas, see the Suggested References on page SR-7 at the back of the book.

For practice quizzes, a customized study plan, and other study tools, see the ONLINE STUDY GUIDE at bedfordstmartins.com/huntconcise.

For additional primary-source material from this period, see Chapter 13 in *Sources of THE MAKING OF THE WEST: A CONCISE HISTORY*, Second Edition.

14

The Atlantic System and Its Consequences

1690–1740

JOHANN SEBASTIAN BACH (1685–1750), composer of mighty organ fugues and church cantatas, was not above amusing his Leipzig audiences, many of them university students. In 1732 he produced a cantata about a young woman in love with coffee. Her old-fashioned father rages that he won't find her a husband unless she gives up the fad. She agrees, secretly vowing to admit no suitor who will not promise in the marriage contract to let her brew coffee whenever she wants. Bach offers this conclusion:

> *The cat won't give up its mouse,*
> *Girls stay faithful coffee-sisters*
> *Mother loves her coffee habit,*
> *Grandma sips it gladly too—*
> *Why then shout at the daughters?*

Bach's era might well be called the age of coffee. European travelers at the end of the sixteenth century had noticed Middle Eastern people drinking a "black drink," *kavah*. Few Europeans sampled it at first, and the Arab monopoly on its production kept prices high. This changed around 1700 when the Dutch East India

■ **London Coffeehouse**
This gouache (a variant on watercolor painting) from about 1725 depicts a scene from a London coffeehouse located in the courtyard of the Royal Exchange (merchants bank). Middle-class men (wearing wigs) read newspapers, drink coffee, smoke pipes, and discuss the news of the day. The coffeehouse draws them out of their homes into a new public space.
(British Museum/Bridgeman Art Library.)

Company introduced coffee plants to Java and other Indonesian islands. Coffee production then spread to the French Caribbean, where African slaves provided the plantation labor. In Europe, imported coffee spurred the development of a new kind of meeting place: London's first coffeehouse opened in 1652, and the idea spread quickly to other European cities. Coffeehouses became gathering places for men to drink, read newspapers, and talk politics. As a London newspaper commented in 1737, "There's scarce an Alley in City and Suburbs but has a Coffeehouse in it, which may be called the School of Public Spirit, where every Man over Daily and Weekly Journals, a Mug, or a Dram . . . devotes himself to that glorious one, his Country."

European consumption of coffee, tea, chocolate, and other novelties increased dramatically as European nations forged worldwide economic links. At the center of this new world economy was an **Atlantic system** that bound together western Europe, Africa, and the Americas. Europeans bought slaves in western Africa, transported and sold them in their colonies in North and South America and the Caribbean, bought the commodities such as coffee and sugar that were produced by the new colonial plantations, and then sold the goods in European ports for refining and reshipment. This Atlantic system first took clear shape in the early eighteenth century; it was the hub of European expansion all over the world.

Coffee drinking was one example among many of the new social and cultural patterns that took root between 1690 and 1740. Improvements in agricultural production at home reinforced the effects of trade overseas; Europeans now had more disposable income for "extras," and they spent their money not only in the new coffeehouses and cafés that sprang up all over Europe but also on newspapers, musical concerts, paintings, and novels. A new middle-class public began to make its presence felt in every domain of culture and social life.

Although the rise of the Atlantic system gave Europe new prominence in the global context, European rulers still focused most of their political, diplomatic, and military energies on their rivalries within Europe. A coalition of countries succeeded in containing French aggression, and a more balanced diplomatic system emerged. In eastern Europe, Prussia and Austria had to contend with the rising power of Russia under Peter the Great. In western Europe, both Spain and the Dutch Republic declined in influence but continued to vie with Britain and France for colonial spoils in the Atlantic. The more evenly matched competition among the great powers encouraged the development of diplomatic skills and drew attention to public health as a way of encouraging population growth.

In the aftermath of Louis XIV's revocation of the Edict of Nantes in 1685, a new intellectual movement known as the Enlightenment began to germinate. French Protestant refugees began to publish works critical of absolutism in politics and religion. Increased prosperity, the growth of a middle-class public, and the decline in warfare after Louis XIV's death in 1715 all fostered the development of this new critical spirit. Fed by the popularization of science and the growing interest in travel literature, the Enlightenment encouraged greater skepticism about religious and state authority. Eventually the movement would question almost every aspect of social and political life in Europe. The Enlightenment began in western Europe in those countries—Britain, France, and the Dutch Republic—most affected by the new Atlantic system. It, too, was a product of the age of coffee.

The Atlantic System and the World Economy

Although their ships had been circling the globe since the early 1500s, Europeans did not draw most of the world into their economic orbit until the 1700s. Western European trading nations sent ships loaded with goods to buy slaves from local rulers on the western coast of Africa; then transported the slaves to the colonies in North and South America and the Caribbean and sold them to the owners of plantations producing coffee, sugar, cotton, and tobacco; and bought the raw commodities produced in the colonies and shipped them back to Europe, where they were refined or processed and then sold to other parts of Europe and the world. The Atlantic system and the growth of international trade helped create a new consumer society.

Slavery and the Atlantic System

Spain and Portugal had dominated Atlantic trade in the sixteenth and seventeenth centuries, but in the eighteenth century European trade in the Atlantic rapidly expanded and became more systematically interconnected (Map 14.1, inset). By 1630, Portugal had already sent 60,000 African slaves to Brazil to work on the new **plantations** (large tracts of lands farmed by slave labor), which were producing some 15,000 tons of sugar a year. Realizing that plantations producing staples for Europeans could bring fabulous wealth, the European powers grew less interested in the dwindling trade in precious metals and more eager to colonize. Large-scale planters of sugar, tobacco, and coffee displaced small farmers who relied on one or two servants. Planters and their plantations won out because slave labor was cheap and therefore able to produce mass quantities of commodities at low prices.

State-chartered private companies from Portugal, France, Britain, the Dutch Republic, Prussia, and even Denmark exploited the 3,500-mile coastline of West Africa for slaves. Before 1675, most blacks taken from Africa had been sent to Brazil, but by 1700 half of the African slaves landed in the Caribbean (Figure 14.1). Thereafter, the plantation economy began to expand on the North American mainland. The numbers stagger the imagination. Before 1650, slave traders transported about 7,000 Africans each year across the Atlantic; this rate doubled between 1650 and 1675, nearly doubled again in the next twenty-five years, and kept going until the 1780s. In all, more than 11 million Africans, not counting those who died at sea or in Africa, were transported to the Americas before the slave trade began to wind down after 1850. Many traders gained spectacular wealth, but companies did not always make profits. The English Royal African

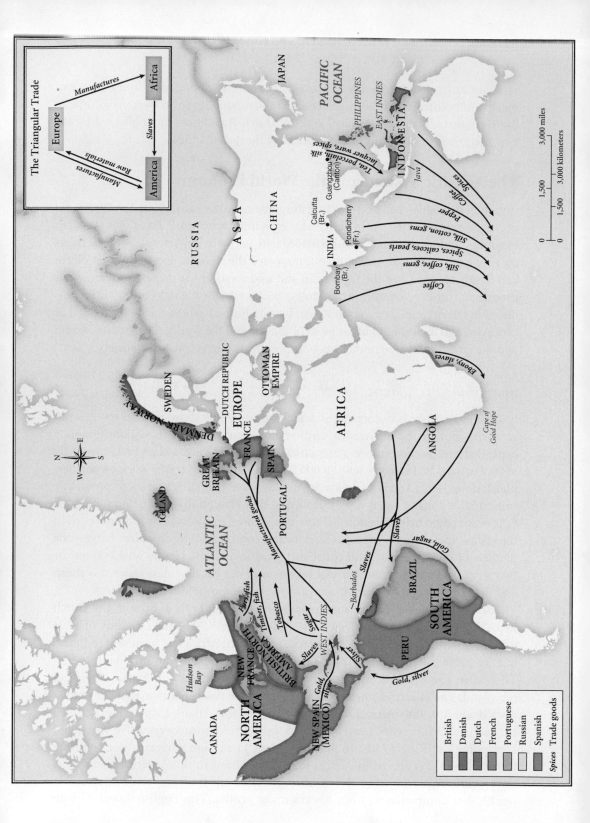

The Triangular Trade

Europe → Africa: Manufactures

Africa → America: Slaves

America → Europe: Raw materials

Europe → America: Manufactures

JAPAN

PACIFIC OCEAN

PHILIPPINES

EAST INDIES

INDONESIA

Tea, porcelain, silk, lacquer ware, spices

Guangzhou (Canton)

Java

Spices

Coffee

Pepper

Silk, cotton, gems

Spices, calicoes, pearls

Silk, coffee, gems

Coffee

Calcutta (Br.)

Pondicherry (Fr.)

INDIA

Bombay (Br.)

RUSSIA

ASIA

CHINA

OTTOMAN EMPIRE

AFRICA

Ebony, slaves

Cape of Good Hope

ANGOLA

SWEDEN

DENMARK-NORWAY

DUTCH REPUBLIC

EUROPE

FRANCE

GREAT BRITAIN

SPAIN

PORTUGAL

ICELAND

ATLANTIC OCEAN

N E S W

Slaves

Slaves

Gold sugar

BRAZIL

SOUTH AMERICA

PERU

Barbados

Slaves

WEST INDIES

Silver

Sugar

Gold, silver

Gold, silver

Manufactured goods

Tobacco

Timber, fish

Furs, fish

NEW SPAIN (MEXICO)

Gold, silver

BRITISH NORTH AMERICA

NEW FRANCE

NORTH AMERICA

Hudson Bay

CANADA

British
Danish
Dutch
French
Portuguese
Russian
Spanish

Spices Trade goods

3,000 miles
3,000 kilometers
1,500
1,500
0
0

570

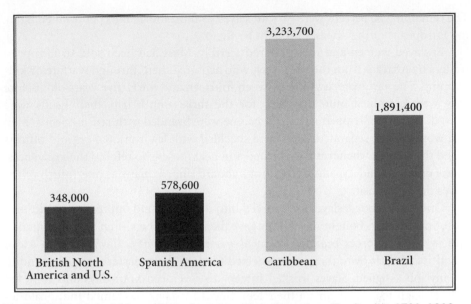

■ **FIGURE 14.1 African Slaves Imported into American Territories, 1701–1810**
During the eighteenth century, planters in the newly established Caribbean colonies imported millions of African slaves to work the new plantations. The vast majority of African slaves transported to the Americas ended up either in the Caribbean or in Brazil.

Company, for example, delivered 100,000 slaves to the Caribbean and imported 30,000 tons of sugar to Britain, yet lost money after the few profitable years following its founding in 1672.

The balance of white and black populations in the New World colonies was determined by the staples produced. New England merchants and farmers bought few slaves because they did not own plantations. Blacks—both slave and free—made up only 3 percent of the population in eighteenth-century New England, compared with 60 percent in South Carolina. On the whole, the British North American colonies contained a higher proportion of African Americans from 1730 to 1765 than at any other time in American history. The imbalance of whites and blacks was even more extreme in the Caribbean; in the early 1700s, the British sugar islands had a population of about 150,000 people, only 30,000 of them Europeans.

■ **MAP 14.1 European Trade Patterns, c. 1740**
By 1740, the European powers had colonized much of North and South America and incorporated their American colonies into a worldwide system of commerce centered on the slave trade and plantation production of staple crops. Europeans still sought spices and luxury goods in China and the East Indies, but outside of Java, few Europeans had settled permanently in these areas. **For more help analyzing this map,** *see the map activity for this chapter in the* ONLINE STUDY GUIDE *at* bedfordstmartins.com/huntconcise.

The remaining 80 percent were African slaves, as most indigenous people died fighting Europeans or the diseases brought by them.

Enslaved women and men suffered terribly. Most had been sold to European traders by Africans from the west coast who acquired them through warfare or kidnapping. The vast majority were between fourteen and thirty-five years old. Before they were crammed onto the ships for the three-month trip, their heads were shaved, they were stripped naked, and some were branded with red-hot irons. Men and women were separated. Men were shackled with leg irons. Sailors and officers raped the women whenever they wished and beat those who refused their advances. In the cramped and appalling conditions aboard ship, as many as one-fourth of the slaves died in transit.

Once they landed, slaves were forced into degrading and oppressive conditions. As soon as masters bought slaves, they gave them new names, often only first names, and in some colonies branded them as personal property. Slaves had no social identities of their own; they were expected to learn their master's language and to do any job assigned. Slaves worked fifteen- to seventeen-hour days and were fed only enough to keep them on their feet. Brazilian slaves consumed more calories than the poorest Brazilians do today, but that hardly made them well fed. The death rate among slaves was high, especially in Brazil, where quick shifts in the weather, lack of clothing, and squalid living conditions made them susceptible to a variety of deadly illnesses.

Not surprisingly, despite the threat of torture or death on recapture, slaves sometimes ran away. In Brazil, runaways hid in *quilombos* (hideouts) in the forests or backcountry. When it was discovered and destroyed in 1695, the quilombo of Palmares had thirty thousand fugitives who had formed their own social organization complete with elected kings and councils of elders. Outright revolt was uncommon, especially before the nineteenth century, but other forms of resistance included stealing food, breaking tools, and feigning illness or stupidity. Slaveholders' fears about conspiracy and revolt lurked beneath the surface of every slave-based society. In 1710, the royal governor of Virginia reminded the colonial legislature of the need for unceasing vigilance: "We are not to Depend on Either Their Stupidity, or that Babel of Languages among 'em; freedom Wears a Cap which Can Without a Tongue, Call Togather all Those who Long to Shake off the fetters of Slavery." Masters defended whipping and other forms of physical punishment as essential to maintaining discipline. Laws called for the castration of a slave who struck a white person.

Plantation owners often left their colonial possessions in the care of agents and collected the revenue to live as wealthy landowners back home, where they built opulent mansions and gained influence in local and national politics. William Beckford, for example, had been sent from Jamaica to school in England as a young boy. When he inherited sugar plantations and shipping companies from his father and older brother, he moved the headquarters of the family business to London in the 1730s to be close to the government and financial markets. His holdings formed

■ **Caribbean Sugar Mill**
This seventeenth-century engraving of a sugar mill or grinder makes the work seem much less diffi-
cult than it was in practice. Slaves cut the sugarcane and then hauled it from the fields to the mill,
where it was crushed. Many slaves lost fingers or hands in the process. The slaves then collected the
juice (bottom center) and carried it to the boilers, shown at the bottom left and right. The sap was
poured into molds and dried. Then the bricks of raw sugar were exported to Europe for refining.
(The Granger Collection, NY.)

the single most powerful economic interest in Jamaica, but he preferred to live in England, where he could collect art for his many luxurious homes, hold political office (he served as lord mayor of London and in Parliament), and even lend money to the government.

The slave trade permanently altered consumption patterns for ordinary people. Sugar had been prescribed as medicine before the end of the sixteenth century, but the development of plantations in Brazil and the Caribbean made it a standard food item. By 1700, the British sent home 50 million pounds of sugar a year, a figure that doubled by 1730. During the French Revolution of the 1790s, sugar shortages would become a cause for rioting in Paris. Equally pervasive was the spread of tobacco; by the 1720s, Britain imported two hundred shiploads of tobacco from Virginia and Maryland every year, and men of every country and class smoked pipes or took snuff.

The traffic in slaves disturbed many Europeans. As a government memorandum to the Spanish king explained in 1610: "Modern theologians in published books commonly report on, and condemn as unjust, the acts of enslavement which take place in provinces of this Royal Empire." Between 1667 and 1671, the French Dominican monk Father Du Tertre published three volumes in which he denounced the mistreatment of slaves in the French colonies.

In the 1700s, however, slaveholders began to justify their actions by demeaning the mental and spiritual qualities of the enslaved Africans. White Europeans and colonists sometimes described black slaves as animal-like, akin to apes. A leading New England Puritan asserted about the slaves: "Indeed their *Stupidity* is a *Discouragement.* It may seem, unto as little purpose, to *Teach*, as to *wash an Aethiopian* [Ethiopian]." One of the great paradoxes of this time was that talk of liberty and self-evident rights, especially prevalent in Britain and its North American colonies, coexisted with the belief that some people were meant to be slaves. Although Christians believed in principle in a kind of spiritual equality between blacks and whites, the churches often defended or at least did not oppose the inequities of slavery.

World Trade and Settlement

The Atlantic system helped extend European trade relations across the globe. The textiles that Atlantic shippers exchanged for slaves on the west coast of Africa, for example, were manufactured in India and exported by the British and the French East India Companies. As much as one-quarter of the British exports to Africa in the eighteenth century were actually re-exports from India. To expand its trade in the rest of the world, Europeans seized territories and tried to establish permanent settlements. The eighteenth-century extension of European power prepared the way for western global domination in the nineteenth and twentieth centuries.

In contrast to the sparsely inhabited trading outposts in Asia and Africa, the colonies in the Americas bulged with settlers. The British North American colonies, for example, contained about 1.5 million nonnative (that is, white settler and black slave) residents by 1750. While the Spanish competed with the Portuguese for control of South America, the French competed with the British for control of North America. Spanish and British settlers came to blows over the boundary between the British colonies and Florida, which was held by Spain.

Local economies shaped colonial social relations; men in French trapper communities in Canada, for example, had little in common with the men and women of the plantation societies in Barbados or Brazil. Racial attitudes also differed from place to place. The Spanish and Portuguese tolerated intermarriage with the native populations in both America and Asia. Sexual contact, both inside and outside marriage, fostered greater racial variety in the Spanish and Portuguese colonies than in the French or the English territories (though mixed-race people could be found everywhere). By 1800, **mestizos**, children of Spanish men and Indian women, accounted for more than a quarter of the population in the Spanish colonies, and many of them aspired to join the local elite. Greater racial diversity seems not to have improved the treatment of slaves, however, which was probably harshest in Portuguese Brazil.

Where intermarriage between colonizers and natives was common, conversion to Christianity proved most successful. Although the Indians maintained many of their native religious beliefs, the majority of Indians in the Spanish colonies had come to consider themselves devout Catholics by 1700. Indian carpenters and artisans in the villages produced innumerable altars, retables (painted panels), and sculpted images to adorn their local churches, and individual families put up domestic shrines. Yet the clergy remained overwhelmingly Spanish: the church hierarchy concluded that the Indians' humility and innocence made them unsuitable for the priesthood.

In the early years of American colonization, many more men than women emigrated from Europe. At the end of the seventeenth century, the sex imbalance began to decline but remained substantial; two and one-half times as many men as women were among the immigrants leaving Liverpool, England, between 1697 and 1707, for example. Women who emigrated as indentured servants ran great risks: if they did not die of disease during the voyage, they might end up giving birth to illegitimate children (the fate of at least one in five servant women) or being virtually sold into marriage.

The uncertainties of life in the American colonies provided new opportunities for European women and men willing to live outside the law, however. In the 1500s and 1600s, the English and Dutch governments had routinely authorized pirates to prey on the shipping of their rivals, the Spanish and Portuguese. Then, in the late 1600s, English, French, and Dutch bands made up of deserters and crews from wrecked vessels began to form their own associations of pirates, especially in the Caribbean. Called **buccaneers** from their custom of curing strips of beef, called *boucan* by the native Caribs of the islands, the pirates governed themselves and preyed on everyone's shipping without regard to national origin. After 1700, the colonial governments tried to stamp out piracy. As one British judge argued in 1705, "A pirate is in perpetual war with every individual and every state. . . . They are worse than ravenous beasts."

White settlements in Africa and Asia remained small and almost insignificant, except for their long-term potential. Europeans had little contact with East Africa and almost none with Africa's vast interior. A few Portuguese trading posts in Angola and Dutch farms on the Cape of Good Hope provided the only toeholds for future expansion. In China, the emperors had welcomed Catholic missionaries at court in the seventeenth century, but the priests' credibility diminished as they squabbled among themselves and associated with European merchants, whom the Chinese considered pirates. "The barbarians [Europeans] are like wild beasts," one Chinese official concluded. In 1720, only one thousand Europeans resided in Guangzhou (Canton), the sole place where foreigners could legally trade for spices, tea, and silk (see Map 14.1).

■ India Cottons and Trade with the East

This brightly colored cotton cloth was painted and embroidered in Madras in southern India in the late 1600s. The male figure with a mustache may be a European, but the female figures are clearly Asian. Europeans—especially the British—discovered that they could make big profits on the export of Indian cotton cloth to Europe. They also traded Indian cottons in Africa for slaves and sold large quantities in the colonies. (V&A Images/Victoria and Albert Museum.)

Europeans exercised more influence in Java in the East Indies and in India. Dutch coffee production in Java and nearby islands increased phenomenally in the early 1700s, and many Dutch settled there to oversee production and trade. In India, Dutch, English, French, Portuguese, and Danish companies competed for spices, cotton, and silk; by the 1740s the English and French had become the leading rivals in India, just as they were in North America. Both countries extended their power as India's Muslim rulers lost control to local Hindu princes, rebellious Sikhs, invading Persians, and their own provincial governors. A few thousand Europeans lived in India, though many thousands more soldiers were stationed there to protect them. The staple of trade with India in the early 1700s was calico—lightweight, brightly colored cotton cloth that caught on as a fashion in Europe.

Europeans who visited India were especially struck by what they viewed as exotic religious practices. In a book published in 1696 of his travels to western India, an Anglican minister described beggars of alms, "some of whom show their devotion by a shameless appearance, and walking naked." Such writings increased European interest in the outside world, but they also fed a European sense of superiority that helped excuse violent forms of colonial domination.

The Birth of Consumer Society

Worldwide colonization produced new supplies of goods, from coffee to calico, and population growth in Europe fueled demand for them. Beginning first in Britain, then in France and the Italian states, and finally in eastern Europe, population surged, growing by about 20 percent between 1700 and 1750. The gap between a fast-growing northwest and a more stagnant south and central Europe now diminished as regions that had lost population during the seventeenth-century downturn recovered. Cities, in particular, grew. Between 1600 and 1750, London's population more than tripled, and Paris's more than doubled.

Although contemporaries could not have realized it then, this was the start of the modern "population explosion." It appears that a decline in the death rate, rather than a rise in the birthrate, explains the turnaround. Three main factors contributed to this decline in the death rate: better weather and hence more bountiful harvests, improved agricultural techniques, and the plague's disappearance after 1720.

By the early eighteenth century, the effects of economic expansion and population growth brought about a **consumer revolution**. The British East India Company began to import into Britain huge quantities of calicoes. British imports of tobacco doubled between 1672 and 1700; at Nantes, the center of the French sugar trade, imports quadrupled between 1698 and 1733. Tea, chocolate, and coffee became virtual necessities. In the 1670s, only a trickle of tea reached London, but by 1720 the East India Company sent 9 million pounds to England—a figure that rose to 37 million pounds by 1750. By 1700, England had two thousand coffeehouses; by 1740, every English country town had at least two. Paris got its first cafés at the end of the seventeenth century; Berlin opened its first coffeehouse in 1714; Bach's Leipzig boasted eight by 1725.

The birth of consumer society did not go unnoticed by eyewitnesses. In the English economic literature of the 1690s, writers began to express a new view of humans as consuming animals with boundless appetites. Such opinions gained a wide audience with the appearance of Bernard Mandeville's poem *Fable of the Bees* (1705), which argued that private vices might have public benefits. Mandeville insisted that pride, self-interest, and the desire for material goods (all Christian vices) in fact promoted economic prosperity: "every part was full of Vice, Yet the whole mass a Paradise." Many authors attacked the new doctrine of consumerism, and the French government banned the poem's publication. But Mandeville had captured the essence of the emerging market for consumption.

■ **REVIEW:** *How is consumerism related to slavery?*

New Social and Cultural Patterns

The impact of the Atlantic system and world trade was most apparent in the cities, where people had more money for consumer goods. But rural changes also had significant long-term influence, as a revolution in agricultural techniques made it possible to feed more and more people with a smaller agricultural workforce. As population increased, more people moved to the cities, where they found themselves caught up in innovative urban customs such as attending musical concerts and reading novels. Along with a general increase in literacy, these activities helped create a public that responded to new writers and artists. Social and cultural changes were not uniform across Europe, however; as usual, people's experiences varied depending on whether they lived in wealth or poverty, in urban or rural areas, or in eastern or western Europe.

Agricultural Revolution

Although Britain, France, and the Dutch Republic shared the enthusiasm for consumer goods, Britain's domestic market grew most quickly. In Britain, as agricultural output increased 43 percent over the course of the 1700s, the population increased by 70 percent. The British imported grain to feed the growing population, but they also benefited from the development of techniques that together constituted an **agricultural revolution**. No new machinery propelled this revolution— just more aggressive attitudes toward investment and management. The Dutch and the Flemish had pioneered many of these techniques in the 1600s, but the British took them further.

Four major changes occurred in British agriculture that eventually spread to other countries. First, farmers increased the amount of land under cultivation by draining wetlands and by growing crops on previously uncultivated common lands (acreage maintained by the community for grazing). Second, farmers who could afford to do so consolidated smaller, scattered plots into larger, more efficient units. Third, livestock raising became more closely linked to crop growing, and the yields of each increased. (See "Taking Measure," page 579.) For centuries, most farmers had rotated their fields in and out of production to replenish the soil. Now farmers planted carefully chosen fodder crops such as clover and turnips that added nutrients to the soil, thereby eliminating the need to leave a field fallow (unplanted) every two or three years. With more fodder available, farmers could raise more livestock, which in turn produced more manure to fertilize grain fields. Fourth, selective breeding of animals combined with the increase in fodder to improve the quality and size of herds. New crops had only a slight impact; potatoes, for example, were introduced to Europe from South America in the 1500s, but because people feared they might cause leprosy, tuberculosis, or fevers, they were not grown in quantity until the late 1700s. By the 1730s and 1740s,

■ TAKING MEASURE
Relationship of Crop Harvested to Seed Used, 1400–1800
The impact and even the timing of the agricultural revolution can be determined by this figure, based on yield ratios (the number of grains produced for each seed planted). Britain, the Dutch Republic, and the Austrian Netherlands all experienced huge increases in crop yields after 1700. Other European regions lagged behind right into the 1800s.

Yield Ratios
—— A = Britain and the Low Countries
—— B = France, Spain, and Italy
—— C = Central Europe and Scandinavia
—— D = Eastern Europe

agricultural output had increased dramatically, and prices for food had fallen because of these interconnected innovations.

Changes in agricultural practices did not benefit all landowners equally. The biggest British landowners consolidated their holdings in the "enclosure movement." They put pressure on small farmers and villagers to sell their land or give up their common lands. The big landlords then fenced off ("enclosed") their property. Because enclosure eliminated community grazing rights, it frequently sparked a struggle between the big landlords and villagers, and in Britain it normally required an act of Parliament. Such acts became increasingly common in the second half of the eighteenth century, and by the century's end six million acres of common lands had been enclosed and developed. "Improvers" produced more food more efficiently and thus supported a growing population.

Contrary to the fears of contemporaries, small farmers and cottagers (those with little or no property) were not forced off the land all at once. But most villagers could not afford the litigation involved in resisting enclosure, and small landholders

■ **Treatment of Serfs in Russia**
Visitors from western Europe often remarked on the cruel treatment of serfs in Russia. This drawing by one such visitor shows the punishment that could be inflicted by landowners. Serfs could be whipped for almost any reason, even for making a soup too salty or neglecting to bow when the lord's family passed by. Their condition actually deteriorated in the 1700s, as landowners began to sell serfs much like slaves. New decrees made it illegal for serfs to contract loans, enter into leases, or work for anyone other than their lord. Some landlords kept harems of serf girls. Although the Russian landlords' treatment of serfs was more brutal than the treatment they experienced in the German states and Poland, upper classes in every country regarded the serfs as dirty, deceitful, brutish, and superstitious.
(New York Public Library/Art Resource, NY.)

consequently had to sell out to landlords or farmers with larger plots. Landlords with large holdings leased their estates to tenant farmers at constantly increasing rents, and the tenant farmers in turn employed the cottagers as salaried agricultural workers. In this way the English peasantry largely disappeared, replaced by a more hierarchical society of big landlords, enterprising tenant farmers, and poor agricultural laborers.

The new agricultural techniques spread slowly from Britain and the Low Countries (the Dutch Republic and the Austrian Netherlands) to the rest of western Europe. Outside a few pockets in northern France and the western German states, however, subsistence agriculture (producing just enough to get by rather than surpluses for the market) continued to dominate farming in western Europe and Scandinavia. In southwestern Germany, for example, 80 percent of the peasants produced no surplus because their plots were too small. Unlike the populations of the highly urbanized Low Countries (where half the people lived in towns and cities), most Europeans, western and eastern, eked out their existence in the countryside.

In eastern Europe, the condition of peasants worsened in the areas where landlords tried hardest to improve their yields. To produce more for the Baltic grain market, aristocratic landholders in Prussia, Poland, and parts of Russia drained wetlands, cultivated moors, and built dikes. They also forced peasants off lands the peasants worked for themselves, increased compulsory labor services (the critical element in serfdom), and began to manage their estates directly. Some eastern landowners grew fabulously wealthy. The Potocki family in the Polish Ukraine, for example, owned three million acres of land and had 130,000 serfs. In parts of Poland and Russia, the serfs hardly differed from slaves in status, and their "masters" ran their huge estates much like American plantations.

Social Life in the Cities

Because of emigration from the countryside, cities grew in population and consequently exercised more influence on culture and social life. Between 1650 and 1750, cities with at least 10,000 inhabitants increased in population by 44 percent. From the eighteenth century onward, urban growth would be continuous. Along with the general growth of cities, an important south-to-north shift occurred in the pattern of urbanization. Around 1500, half of the people in cities of at least 10,000 residents could be found in the Italian states, Spain, or Portugal; by 1700, the urbanization of northwestern and southern Europe was roughly equal. Eastern Europe, despite the huge cities of Istanbul and Moscow, was still less urban than western Europe. London was by far the most populous European city, with 675,000 inhabitants in 1750; Berlin had 90,000 people, Warsaw only 23,000.

Many landowners kept a residence in town, so the separation between rural and city life was not as extreme as might be imagined, at least not for the very rich. At the top of the ladder in the big cities were the landed nobles. Some of them filled their lives only with conspicuous consumption of fine food, extravagant clothing, coaches, books, and opera; others held key political, administrative, or judicial offices. However they spent their time, these rich families employed thousands of artisans, shopkeepers, and domestic servants. Many English peers (highest-ranking nobles) had thirty or forty servants at each of their homes.

The middle classes of officials, merchants, professionals, and landowners occupied the next rung down on the social ladder. London's population, for example, included about twenty thousand middle-class families (constituting, at most, one-sixth of the city's population). In this period, the middle classes began to develop distinctive ways of life that set them apart from both the rich noble landowners and the lower classes. Unlike the rich nobles, the middle classes lived primarily in the cities and towns, even if they owned small country estates. They ate more moderately than nobles but much better than peasants or laborers. For breakfast, the British middle classes ate toast and rolls and, after 1700, drank tea. Dinner, served midday, consisted of roasted or boiled beef or mutton, poultry or pork, and vegetables. Supper was a light meal of bread and cheese with cake or pie. Beer was the main drink in London, and many families brewed their own. Even children drank beer because of the lack of fresh water.

In contrast to the gigantic and sprawling country seats of the richest English peers, middle-class houses in town had about seven rooms, including four or five bedrooms and one or two living rooms, still many more than the poor agricultural worker. New household items reflected society's increasing wealth and its exposure to colonial imports: by 1700, the middle classes of London typically had mirrors in every room, a coffeepot and coffee mill, numerous pictures and ornaments, a china collection, and several clocks. Life for the middle classes on the European continent was quite similar, though wine replaced beer in France.

Below the middle classes came the artisans and shopkeepers (most of whom were organized in professional guilds), then the journeymen, apprentices, servants, and laborers. At the bottom of the social scale were the unemployed poor, who survived by intermittent work and charity. Women married to artisans and shopkeepers often kept the accounts, supervised employees, and ran the household as well. Every home from the middle classes to the upper classes employed servants; artisans and shopkeepers frequently hired them, too. Women from poorer families usually worked as domestic servants until they married. Four out of five domestic servants in the city were female. In large cities such as London, the servant population grew faster than the population of the city as a whole.

Social status in the cities was readily visible. Wide, spacious streets graced rich districts; the houses had gardens, and the air was relatively fresh. In poor districts, the streets were narrow, dirty, dark, humid, and smelly, and the houses were damp and crowded. The poorest people were homeless, sleeping under bridges or in abandoned homes. A Neapolitan prince described his homeless neighbors as "lying like filthy animals, with no distinction of age or sex." In some districts, rich and poor lived in the same buildings; the poor clambered up to shabby, cramped apartments on the top floors.

Like shelter, clothing was a reliable social indicator. The poorest workingwomen in Paris wore woolen skirts and blouses of dark colors over petticoats, bodice, and corset. They also donned caps of various sorts, cotton stockings, and shoes (probably their only pair). Workingmen dressed even more drably. Many occupations could be recognized by their dress: no one could confuse lawyers in their dark robes with masons or butchers in their special aprons, for example. People higher on the social ladder were more likely to sport a variety of fabrics, colors, and unusual designs in their clothing and to own many different outfits. Social status was not an abstract idea; it permeated every detail of daily life.

The Growing Public for Culture

The ability to read and write also reflected social differences. People in the upper classes were more literate than those in the lower classes; city people were more literate than peasants. Protestant countries appear to have been more successful at promoting education and literacy than Catholic countries, perhaps because of the

Protestant emphasis on Bible reading. Widespread popular literacy was first achieved in the Protestant areas of Switzerland and in Presbyterian Scotland, and rates were also very high in the New England colonies and the Scandinavian countries. In France, literacy doubled in the eighteenth century thanks to the spread of parish schools, but still only one in two men and one in four women could read and write. Despite the efforts of some Protestant German states to encourage primary education, primary schooling remained woefully inadequate almost everywhere in Europe: few schools existed, teachers received low wages, and no country had yet established a national system of control or supervision.

Despite the deficiencies of primary education, a new literate public arose, especially among the middle classes of the cities. More books and periodicals were published than ever before. Britain and the Dutch Republic led the way in this powerful outpouring of printed words. The trend began in the 1690s and gradually accelerated. In 1695, the British government allowed the licensing system, through which it controlled publications, to lapse, and new newspapers and magazines appeared almost immediately. The first London daily newspaper came out in 1702, and in 1709 Joseph Addison and Richard Steele published the first literary magazine, *The Spectator.* They devoted their magazine to the cultural improvement of the increasingly influential middle class. By the 1720s, twenty-four provincial newspapers were published in England. In the London coffeehouses, an edition of a single newspaper might reach ten thousand male readers. Women did their reading at home. Newspapers on the continent lagged behind and often consisted mainly of advertising with little critical commentary. France, for example, had no daily paper until 1777.

The new literate public did not just read newspapers; its members now pursued an interest in painting, attended concerts, and besieged booksellers in search of popular novels. Because increased trade and prosperity put money into the hands of the growing middle classes, a new urban audience began to compete with the churches, rulers, and courtiers as chief patrons for new work. As the public for the arts expanded, printed commentary on them emerged, setting the stage for the appearance of political and social criticism. New artistic tastes thus had effects far beyond the realm of the arts.

Developments in painting reflected the tastes of the new public. The **rococo** style challenged the hold of the baroque and classical schools, especially in France. Like the baroque, the rococo emphasized irregularity and asymmetry, movement and curvature, but it did so on a much smaller, subtler scale. Many rococo paintings depicted scenes of intimate sensuality rather than the monumental, emotional grandeur favored by classical and baroque painters. Personal portraits and pastoral paintings took the place of heroic landscapes and large ceremonial canvases. Rococo paintings adorned homes as well as palaces and served as a form of interior decoration rather than as a statement of piety. Its decorative quality made rococo art an ideal complement to newly discovered materials such as stucco and porcelain, especially the porcelain vases now imported from China.

■ Rococo Painting

In this painting, the Venetian artist Rosalba Carriera (1675–1757) reveals Europeans' growing interest in the outside world and their misunderstanding of the actual experience of colonized peoples. Africa (the title of the work) is represented by a young black woman wearing a bejewelled turban and calmly holding a handful of writhing snakes; the scorpion that dangles from her necklace competes with an enormous pearl earring for the fascinated viewer's attention. Known for her use of pastels, Carriera journeyed in 1720 to Paris, where she became an associate of Antoine Watteau and helped inaugurate the rococo style in painting. **For more help analyzing this image,** see the visual activity for this chapter in the ONLINE STUDY GUIDE at bedfordstmartins.com/ huntconcise.

(Staatliche Kunstsammlungen Dresden, Gemaldegalerie Alte Meister.)

Rococo, like *baroque,* was an invented word (from the French word *rocaille,* meaning "shellwork") and originally a derogatory label, meaning "frivolous decoration." But the great French rococo painters, such as Antoine Watteau (1684–1721) and François Boucher (1703–1770), were much more than mere decorators. Although both emphasized the erotic in their depictions, Watteau captured the melancholy side of a passing aristocratic style of life, and Boucher painted middle-class people at home during their daily activities. Both painters thereby contributed to the emergence of new sensibilities in art that increasingly attracted a middle-class public.

Music as well as art grew in popularity. The first public music concerts were performed in England in the 1670s, becoming much more regular and frequent in the 1690s. City concert halls typically seated about two hundred, but the relatively high price of tickets limited attendance to the better-off. Music clubs provided entertainment in smaller towns and villages. In continental Europe, Frankfurt organized the first regular public concerts in 1712; Hamburg and Paris began holding them within a few years. Opera continued to spread in the eighteenth century; Venice had sixteen public opera houses by 1700, and in 1732 Covent Garden opera house opened in London.

The growth of a public that appreciated and supported music had much the same effect as the extension of the reading public: like authors, composers could now begin to liberate themselves from court patronage and work for a paying audience. This development took time to solidify, however, and court or church patrons still commissioned much eighteenth-century music. Bach, a German Lutheran, wrote his *St. Matthew Passion* for Good Friday services in 1729 while he was organist and choirmaster for the leading church in Leipzig. He composed secular works (like the "Coffee Cantata") for the public and a variety of private patrons.

The composer George Frederick Handel (1685–1759) was among the first to grasp the new directions in music. He began his career playing second violin in the Hamburg opera orchestra and then moved to Britain in 1710, where he eventually turned to composing oratorios, a form he introduced in Britain. The oratorio combined the drama of opera with the majesty of religious and ceremonial music and featured the chorus over the soloists. Handel's most famous oratorio, *Messiah* (1741), reflected his personal, deeply felt piety but also his willingness to combine musical materials into a dramatic form that captured the enthusiasm of the new public. In 1740, a poem published in the *Gentleman's Magazine* exulted: "His art so modulates the sounds in all, / Our passions, as he pleases, rise and fall." Music had become an integral part of the new middle-class public's culture.

But nothing captured the imagination of the new public more than the novel, the literary genre whose very name underscored the eighteenth-century taste for novelty. Over three hundred French novels appeared between 1700 and 1730. During this unprecedented explosion, the novel took on its modern form and became more concerned with individual psychology and social description than with the picaresque adventures popular earlier (such as Cervantes's *Don Quixote*). The novel's popularity was closely tied to the expansion of the reading public, and novels were available in serial form in periodicals or from the many booksellers who popped up to serve the new market.

Women figured prominently in novels as characters, and women writers abounded. The English novel *Love in Excess* (1719) quickly reached a sixth printing, and its author, Eliza Haywood (1693?–1756), earned her living turning out a stream of novels with titles such as *Persecuted Virtue*, *Constancy Rewarded*, and *The History of Miss Betsy Thoughtless*—all showing a concern for the proper place of women as models of virtue in a changing world. Haywood had first worked as an actress when her husband deserted her and her two children, but she soon turned to writing plays and novels. In the 1740s, she began publishing a magazine, *The Female Spectator*, which argued in favor of higher education for women.

Haywood's male counterpart was Daniel Defoe (1660?–1731), a merchant's son who had a diverse and colorful career as a manufacturer, political spy, novelist, and social commentator. Defoe's novel about a shipwrecked sailor, *Robinson Crusoe* (1719), portrayed the new values of the time: to survive, Crusoe had to meet every challenge with fearless entrepreneurial ingenuity. He had to be ready for the unexpected and be able to improvise in every situation. He was, in short, the model for the new man in an expanding economy. Crusoe's patronizing attitude toward the black man Friday now draws much critical attention, but his discovery of Friday shows how the fate of blacks and whites had become intertwined in the new colonial environment.

Religious Revivals

Despite the novel's growing popularity, religious books and pamphlets still sold in huge numbers, and most Europeans remained devout, even as their religions were changing. In this period, a Protestant revival known as **Pietism** rocked the complacency of the established churches in the German Lutheran states, the Dutch Republic, and Scandinavia. Pietists believed in a mystical religion of the heart; they wanted a more deeply emotional, even ecstatic religion. They urged intense Bible study, which in turn promoted popular education and contributed to the increase in literacy. Many Pietists attended catechism instruction every day and also went to morning and evening prayer meetings in addition to regular Sunday services.

Catholicism also had its versions of religious revival. A Frenchwoman, Jeanne Marie Guyon (1648–1717), attracted many noblewomen and a few leading clergymen to her own Catholic brand of Pietism, known as Quietism. Claiming miraculous visions and astounding prophecies, she urged a mystical union with God through prayer and simple devotion. Despite papal condemnation and intense controversy within Catholic circles in France, Guyon had followers all over Europe.

Even more influential were the Jansenists, who gained many new adherents to their austere form of Catholicism despite Louis XIV's harassment and repeated condemnation by the papacy. Under the pressure of religious and political persecution, Jansenism took a revivalist turn in the 1720s. At the funeral of a Jansenist priest in Paris in 1727, the crowd who flocked to the grave claimed to witness a series of miraculous healings. Within a few years, a cult formed around the priest's tomb, and clandestine Jansenist presses reported new miracles to the reading public. When the French government tried to suppress the cult, one enraged wit placed a sign at the tomb that read "By order of the king, God is forbidden to work miracles here." Some believers fell into frenzied convulsions, claiming to be inspired by the Holy Spirit through the intercession of the dead priest. After midcentury, Jansenism became even more politically active as its adherents joined in opposition to crown policies on religion.

■ **REVIEW:** *What were the social and cultural consequences of the agricultural revolution?*

Consolidation of the European State System

The spread of Pietism and Jansenism reflected the emergence of a middle-class public that now participated in every new development, including religion. The middle classes could pursue these interests because the European state system gradually stabilized. Warfare settled three main issues between 1690 and 1740: a coalition of powers held Louis XIV's France in check on the continent; Great Britain emerged from the wars against Louis as the preeminent maritime power; and Russia defeated Sweden in the contest for supremacy in the Baltic. After Louis XIV's death in 1715, Europe enjoyed the fruits of a more balanced diplomatic system, in which warfare became less frequent and less widespread. States could then spend their resources establishing and expanding control over their own populations, both at home and in their colonies.

The Limits of French Absolutism

Lying on his deathbed in 1715, the seventy-six-year-old Louis XIV watched helplessly as his accomplishments continued to unravel. Not only had his plans for territorial expansion been thwarted, but his incessant wars had exhausted the treasury, despite new taxes. In 1689, Louis's rival, William III, prince of Orange and king of England and Scotland (r. 1689–1702), had set out to forge a European alliance that eventually included Britain, the Dutch Republic, Sweden, Austria, and Spain. The allies fought Louis to a stalemate in the War of the League of Augsburg, sometimes called the Nine Years' War (1689–1697), and when hostilities resumed four years later, they finally put an end to Louis's expansionist ambitions.

The War of the Spanish Succession (1701–1713) broke out when the mentally and physically feeble Charles II (r. 1665–1700) of Spain died without a direct heir. The Spanish succession could not help but be a burning issue. Even though Spanish power had declined steadily since Spain's golden age in the sixteenth century, Spain still had extensive territories in Italy and the Netherlands and colonies overseas. Before Charles died, he named Louis XIV's second grandson, Philip, duke of Anjou, as his heir, but the Austrian emperor Leopold I refused to accept Charles's deathbed will. In the ensuing war, the French lost several major battles and had to accept disadvantageous terms in the Peace of Utrecht of 1713–1714 (Map 14.2). Although Philip was recognized as king of Spain, he had to renounce any future claim to the French crown, thus barring unification of the two kingdoms. Spain surrendered its territories in Italy and the Netherlands to the Austrians and Gibraltar to the British; France ceded possessions in North America (Newfoundland, the Hudson Bay area, and most of Nova Scotia) to Britain. France no longer threatened to dominate European power politics.

At home, Louis's policy of absolutism had fomented bitter hostility. Nobles fiercely resented his promotions of commoners to high office. The duke of Saint-Simon complained that "falseness, servility, admiring glances, combined with a dependent and cringing attitude, above all, an appearance of being nothing without him, were the only ways of pleasing him." On his deathbed, Louis XIV gave his blessing and some sound advice to his five-year-old great-grandson and successor, Louis XV (r. 1715–1774): "My child, you are about to become a great King. Do not imitate my love of building nor my liking for war."

English and French Claims after the Peace of Utrecht, 1714

Newfoundland

Hudson Bay

English claim

French claim

Nova Scotia

English claim

0   500   1000 miles
0   500   1000 kilometers

0   200   400 miles
0   200   400 kilometers

SWEDEN

St. Petersburg

DENMARK–NORWAY

Baltic Sea

Moscow

SCOTLAND

Edinburgh

North Sea

POLAND-LITHUANIA

RUSSIA

IRELAND

Dublin

GREAT BRITAIN

ENGLAND

London

Utrecht

DUTCH REPUBLIC

Hanover

BRANDENBURG-PRUSSIA

Berlin

Warsaw

Kiev

English Channel

Austrian Neth.

Cologne

HOLY ROMAN EMPIRE

Rhine R.

Vistula R.

ATLANTIC OCEAN

Paris

Loire R.

FRANCE

SWISS CONFED.

AUSTRIA

Vienna

HUNGARY

Buda   Pest

Danube R.

Black Sea

SAVOY

MILAN   VENICE

GENOA

Marseille

TUSCANY   PAPAL STATES

Corsica

Rome

PORTUGAL

Madrid

SPAIN

Lisbon

Minorca (Gr. Br.)

Sardinia

KINGDOM OF NAPLES

Constantinople

OTTOMAN EMPIRE

BALEARIC IS.

Gibraltar (Gr. Br.)

Sicily

Mediterranean Sea

Territories gained after the Peace of Utrecht, 1714

- French Bourbon lands
- Spanish Bourbon lands
- Austrian Habsburg lands
- Prussian lands
- Great Britain
- To Great Britain
- To the Austrian Empire
- The Jacobite rising of 1715
- Main areas of fighting during the War of the Spanish Succession, 1701–1713
- Boundary of the Holy Roman Empire

■ **MAP 14.2 Europe, c. 1715**

Although Louis XIV succeeded in putting his grandson Philip on the Spanish throne, France emerged considerably weakened from the War of the Spanish Succession. France ceded large territories in Canada to Britain, which also gained key Mediterranean outposts from Spain as well as a monopoly on providing slaves to the Spanish colonies. Spanish losses were catastrophic: Philip had to renounce any future claim to the French crown and give up considerable territories in the Netherlands and Italy to the Austrians.

After being named regent, the duke of Orléans (1674–1723), nephew of the dead king, revived some of the parlements' powers and tried to give leading nobles a greater say in political affairs. Financial problems plagued the Regency as they would beset all succeeding French regimes in the eighteenth century. In 1719, the regent appointed the Scottish adventurer and financier John Law to the top financial position of controller-general. Law founded a trading company for North America and a state bank that issued paper money and stock (without them, trade depended on the available supply of gold and silver). The bank was supposed to offer lower interest rates to the state, thus cutting the cost of financing the government's debts. The value of the stock rose rapidly in a frenzy of speculation, only to crash a few months later. With it vanished any hope of establishing a state bank or issuing paper money for nearly a century.

France finally achieved a measure of financial stability under the leadership of Cardinal Hercule de Fleury (1653–1743), the most powerful member of the government after the death of the regent. Fleury aimed to avoid adventure abroad and keep social peace at home; he balanced the budget and carried out a large project for road and canal construction. Colonial trade boomed. Peace and the acceptance of limits on territorial expansion inaugurated a century of French prosperity.

British Rise and Dutch Decline

The British and the Dutch had formed a coalition against Louis XIV under their joint ruler William III, who was simultaneously stadtholder of the Dutch Republic and, with his English wife, Mary (d. 1694), ruler of England, Wales, and Scotland. After William's death in 1702, the British and Dutch went their separate ways. Over the next decades, England incorporated Scotland and subjugated Ireland, becoming "Great Britain." At the same time Dutch imperial power declined, even though Dutch merchants still controlled a substantial portion of world trade. English relations with Scotland and Ireland were complicated by the problem of succession: William and Mary had no children. To ensure a Protestant succession, Parliament ruled that Mary's sister, Anne, would succeed William and Mary and that the Protestant House of Hanover in Germany would succeed Anne if she had no surviving heirs. Catholics were excluded. When Queen Anne (r. 1702–1714) died leaving no children, the elector of Hanover, a Protestant great-grandson of James I, consequently became King George I (r. 1714–1727). The House of Hanover—renamed the House of Windsor during World War I in response to anti-German sentiment—still occupies the British throne.

Support from the Scots and Irish for this solution did not come easily because many in Scotland and Ireland supported the claims to the throne of the deposed Catholic king, James II, and, after his death in 1701, his son James Edward. Out of fear of this "Jacobitism" (from the Latin *Jacobus* for "James"), Scottish Protestant leaders agreed to the Act of Union of 1707, which abolished the Scottish Parliament and affirmed the Scots recognition of the Protestant Hanoverian succession. The

Scots agreed to obey the Parliament of Great Britain, which would include Scottish members in the House of Commons and the House of Lords. A Jacobite rebellion in Scotland in 1715, aiming to restore the Stuart line, was suppressed. The threat of Jacobitism nonetheless continued into the 1740s (see Map 14.2).

The Irish—90 percent of whom were Catholic—proved even more difficult to subdue. When James II had gone to Ireland in 1689 to raise a Catholic rebellion against the new monarchs of England, William III responded by taking command of the joint English and Dutch forces and defeating James's Irish supporters. James fled to France, and the Catholics in Ireland faced yet more confiscation and legal restrictions. By 1700, Irish Catholics, who in 1640 had owned 60 percent of the land in Ireland, owned just 14 percent. The Protestant-controlled Irish Parliament passed a series of laws limiting the rights of the Catholic majority: Catholics could not bear arms, send their children abroad for education, establish Catholic schools at home, or marry Protestants. Catholics could not sit in Parliament, nor could they vote for its members unless they took an oath renouncing Catholic doctrine. These and a host of other laws reduced Catholic Ireland to the status of a colony; one English official commented in 1745, "The poor people of Ireland are used worse than negroes." Most of the Irish were peasants who lived in primitive housing and subsisted on a meager diet that included no meat.

The Parliament of Great Britain was soon dominated by the Whigs. In Britain's constitutional system, the monarch ruled with Parliament. The crown chose the ministers, directed policy, and supervised administration, while Parliament raised revenue, passed laws, and represented the interests of the people to the crown. The powers of Parliament were reaffirmed by the Triennial Act in 1694, which provided that Parliaments meet at least once every three years (this was extended to seven years in 1716, after the Whigs had established their ascendancy). Only 200,000 propertied men could vote, out of a population of more than 5 million people, and not surprisingly, most members of Parliament came from the landed gentry. In fact, a few hundred families controlled all the important political offices.

George I and George II (r. 1727–1760) relied on one man, Sir Robert Walpole (1676–1745), to help them manage their relations with Parliament. From his position as First Lord of the Treasury, Walpole made himself into first or "prime" minister, leading the House of Commons from 1721 to 1742. Although appointed initially by the king, Walpole established an enduring pattern of parliamentary government in which a prime minister from the leading party guided legislation through the House of Commons. Walpole also built a vast patronage machine that dispensed government jobs to win support for the crown's policies. Walpole's successors relied more and more on the patronage system and eventually alienated not only the Tories but also the middle classes in London and even the North American colonists.

The partisan division between the Whigs, who supported the Hanoverian succession and the rights of dissenting Protestants, and the Tories, who had backed the Stuart line and the Anglican church, did not hamper Great Britain's pursuit of

■ Sir Robert Walpole at a Cabinet Meeting

Sir Robert Walpole and George II developed government by means of a cabinet, which consisted of Walpole as first lord of the treasury, the two secretaries of state, the lord chancellor, the chancellor of the exchequer, the lord privy seal, and the lord president of the council. Walpole's cabinet was the predecessor of modern cabinets in both Great Britain and the United States. Its similarities to modern forms should not be overstated, however. The entire staff of the two secretaries of state, who had charge of all foreign and domestic affairs other than taxation, numbered twenty-four in 1726.
(The Fotomas Index, U.K.)

economic, military, and colonial power. In this period, Great Britain became a great power on the world stage by virtue of its navy and its ability to finance major military involvement in the wars against Louis XIV. The founding in 1694 of the Bank of England—which, unlike the French bank, endured—enabled the government to raise money at low interest for foreign wars. By the 1740s, the government could borrow more than four times what it could in the 1690s.

By contrast, the Dutch Republic, one of the richest and most influential states of the seventeenth century, saw its power eclipsed in the eighteenth. When William of Orange (William III of England) died in 1702, he left no heirs, and for forty-five years the Dutch lived without a stadtholder. The merchant ruling class of some two thousand families dominated the Dutch Republic more than ever, but they presided over a country that counted for less in international power politics. In some areas, Dutch decline was only relative: the Dutch population was not growing as fast as populations elsewhere, for example, and the Dutch share of the Baltic trade decreased from 50 percent in 1720 to less than 30 percent by the 1770s. After 1720, the Baltic countries—Prussia, Russia, Denmark, and Sweden—began to ban imports of manufactured goods to protect their own industries, and Dutch trade in particular suffered. The output of Leiden textiles dropped to one-third of its 1700 level by 1740. Shipbuilding, paper manufacturing, tobacco processing, salt refining,

The army so dominated life in Prussia that the country earned the label "a large army with a small state attached." So obsessed was Frederick William with his soldiers that the five-foot-five-inch-tall king formed a regiment of "giants," the Grenadiers, composed exclusively of men over six feet tall. Royal agents scoured Europe trying to find such men and sometimes kidnapped them right off the street. Frederick William, the "Sergeant King," was one of the first rulers to wear a military uniform as his everyday dress. He subordinated the entire domestic administration to the army's needs. He also installed a system for recruiting soldiers by local district quotas. He financed the army growth by subjecting all the provinces to an excise tax on food, drink, and manufactured goods and by increasing rents on crown lands. Prussia was now poised to become one of the major players on the continent of Europe.

During the War of the Polish Succession (1733–1735), Prussia stood on the sidelines, content to watch the bigger powers fight each other. The war showed how the balance of power had changed since the heyday of Louis XIV: France had to maneuver within a complex great-power system that now included Russia, and Poland-Lithuania no longer controlled its own destiny. When the king of Poland-Lithuania died in 1733, France, Spain, and Sardinia went to war against Austria and Russia, each side supporting rival claimants to the Polish throne. After Russia drove the French candidate out of Poland-Lithuania, France agreed to accept the Austrian candidate; in exchange, Austria gave the province of Lorraine to the French candidate, the father-in-law of Louis XV, with the promise that the province would pass to France on his death. France and Britain went back to pursuing their colonial rivalries. Prussia and Russia concentrated on shoring up their influence within Poland-Lithuania.

Austrian Conquest of Hungary, 1657–1730

Legend:
- Habsburg dominions, 1657
- Habsburg Hungary, 1657
- Expansion to 1699
- Expansion to 1718
- Regained by Ottoman Empire
- ✳ Battle

POLAND-LITHUANIA

AUSTRIA
Vienna 1683
HUNGARY
Transylvania
Belgrade 1717
Adriatic Sea
OTTOMAN EMPIRE

0   250   500 miles
0   250   500 kilometers

Austria did not want to become mired in a long struggle in Poland-Lithuania because its armies still faced the Turks on its southeastern border. Even though the Austrians had forced the Turks to recognize their rule over all of Hungary and Transylvania in 1699 and occupied Belgrade in 1717, the Turks did not stop fighting. In the 1730s, the Turks retook Belgrade, and Russia now claimed a role in the struggle against the Turks. Moreover, Hungary, though "liberated" from Turkish rule, proved less than enthusiastic about submitting to Austria. In 1703, the wealthiest Hungarian noble landlord, Ferenc Rákóczi (1676–1735), raised an army of seventy thousand men who fought for "God, Fatherland, and Liberty" until 1711. They forced the Austrians to recognize local Hungarian institutions, grant amnesty, and restore confiscated estates in exchange for confirming hereditary Austrian rule.

The Power of Diplomacy and the Importance of Numbers

No single power emerged from the wars of the first half of the eighteenth century clearly superior to the others, and the idea of maintaining a balance of power guided both military and diplomatic maneuvering. The Peace of Utrecht had explicitly declared that such a balance was crucial to maintaining peace in Europe, and in 1720 a British pamphleteer wrote, "There is not, I believe, any doctrine in the law of nations, of more certain truth . . . than this of the balance of power." It was the law of gravity of European politics. This system of equilibrium often rested on military force, such as the leagues formed against Louis XIV or the coalition against Sweden. All states counted on diplomacy, however, to resolve issues even after fighting had begun.

To meet the new demands placed on it, the diplomatic service, like the military and financial bureaucracies before it, had to develop regular procedures. The French set a pattern of diplomatic service that the other European states soon imitated. By 1685, France had embassies in all the important capitals. Nobles of ancient families served as ambassadors to Rome, Madrid, Vienna, and London, whereas royal officials were chosen for Switzerland, the Dutch Republic, and Venice. Most held their appointments for at least three or four years, and all went off with elaborate written instructions that included explicit statements of policy as well as full accounts of the political conditions of the country to which they were posted. The ambassador selected and paid for his own staff. This practice could make the journey to a new post very cumbersome, because the staff might be as large as eighty people, and they brought along all their own furniture, pictures, silverware, and tapestries. It took one French ambassador ten weeks to get from Paris to Stockholm.

By the early 1700s, French writings on diplomatic methods were read everywhere. François de Callières's manual *On the Manner of Negotiating with Sovereigns* (1716) insisted that sound diplomacy was based on the creation of confidence, rather than deception: "The secret of negotiation is to harmonize the real interests of the parties concerned." Callières believed that the diplomatic service had to be professional— that young attachés should be chosen for their skills, not their family connections. These sensible views did not prevent the development of a dual system of diplomacy, in which rulers issued secret instructions that often negated the official ones sent by their own foreign offices. Secret diplomacy had some advantages because it allowed rulers to break with past alliances, but it also led to confusion and, sometimes, scandal, for the rulers often employed unreliable adventurers as their confidential agents. Still, the diplomatic system in the early eighteenth century proved successful enough to ensure a continuation of the principles of the Peace of Westphalia (1648); in the midst of every crisis and war, the great powers would convene and hammer out a written agreement detailing the requirements for peace.

Adroit diplomacy could smooth the road toward peace, but success in war still depended on sheer numbers—of men and muskets. Because each state's strength depended largely on the size of its army, the growth and health of the population increasingly entered into government calculations. The publication in 1690 of the Englishman William Petty's *Political Arithmetick* quickened the interest of government officials everywhere. Petty offered statistical estimates of human capital—that is, of population and wages—to determine Britain's national wealth. In 1727, Frederick William I of Prussia founded two university chairs to encourage population studies, and textbooks and handbooks advocated state intervention to improve the population's health and welfare.

Public Hygiene and Health Care

Physicians used the new population statistics to explain the environmental causes of disease, another new preoccupation in this period. Petty devised a quantitative scale that distinguished healthy from unhealthy places largely on the basis of air quality, an early precursor of modern environmental studies. Cities were the unhealthiest places because excrement (animal and human) and garbage accumulated where people lived densely packed together. Paris seemed to a visitor "so detestable that it is impossible to remain there" because of the smell; even the façade of the Louvre palace in Paris was soiled by the contents of night commodes that servants routinely dumped out of windows every morning. Only the wealthy could escape walking in mucky streets, by hiring men to carry them in sedan chairs or to drive them in coaches.

After investigating specific cities, medical geographers urged government campaigns to improve public sanitation. Everywhere, environmentalists gathered and analyzed data on climate, disease, and population, searching for correlations to help direct policy. As a result of these efforts, local governments undertook such measures as draining low-lying areas, burying refuse, and cleaning wells, all of which eventually helped lower the death rates from epidemic diseases.

Hospitals and medical care underwent lasting transformations. Founded originally as charities concerned foremost with the moral worthiness of the poor, hospitals gradually evolved into medical institutions that defined patients by their diseases. The process of diagnosis changed as physicians began to use specialized Latin terms for illnesses. The gap between medical experts and their patients increased, as physicians now also relied on postmortem dissections in the hospital to gain better knowledge, a practice most patients' families resented. Press reports of body snatching and grave robbing by surgeons and their apprentices outraged the public well into the 1800s.

Despite the change in hospitals, individual health care remained something of a free-for-all in which physicians competed with bloodletters, itinerant venereal disease doctors, bonesetters, druggists, midwives, and "cunning women," who specialized in home remedies. The medical profession, with nationwide organizations and licensing, had not yet emerged, and no clear line separated trained physicians from quacks. Physicians often followed popular prescriptions for illnesses because they had nothing better to offer. Patients were as likely to die of diseases caught in the hospital as to be cured there. Antiseptics were nearly unknown.

The various "medical opinions" about childbirth highlight the confusion people faced. Midwives delivered most babies, though they sometimes encountered criticism even from within their own ranks. One consulting midwife complained that ordinary midwives in Bristol, England, made women in labor drink a mixture of their husband's urine and leek juice. By the 1730s, female midwives faced competition from male midwives, who were known for using instruments such as forceps to pull the baby out of the birth canal. Women rarely sought a physician's help in giving birth, however; they preferred the advice and assistance of trusted local midwives. In any case, trained physicians were few in number and almost nonexistent outside cities.

Hardly any infectious diseases could be cured, though inoculation against smallpox spread from the Middle East to Europe in the early eighteenth century, thanks largely to the efforts of Lady Mary Wortley Montagu, who learned about the technique while living in Constantinople. After 1750, physicians developed successful procedures for wide-scale vaccination, although even then many people resisted the idea of inoculating themselves with a disease. Other diseases spread quickly in the unsanitary conditions of urban life. Ordinary people washed or changed clothes rarely, lived in overcrowded housing with poor ventilation, and got their water from contaminated sources, such as refuse-filled rivers.

Until the mid-1700s, most people considered bathing dangerous. Public bathhouses had disappeared from cities in the sixteenth and seventeenth centuries because they seemed a source of disorderly behavior and epidemic illness. In the eighteenth century, even private bathing came into disfavor because people feared the effects of contact with water. Fewer than one in ten newly built private mansions in Paris had baths. Bathing was hazardous, physicians insisted, because it opened the body to disease. One manners manual of 1736 admonished, "It is correct to clean the face every morning by using a white cloth to cleanse it. It is less good to wash with water, because it renders the face susceptible to cold in winter and sun in summer." The upper classes associated cleanliness not with baths but with frequently changed linens, powdered hair, and perfume, which was thought to strengthen the body and refresh the brain by counteracting corrupt and foul air.

■ **REVIEW:** *What were the consequences of the stabilization of the balance of power in Europe at the start of the eighteenth century?*

The Birth of the Enlightenment

Economic expansion, the emergence of a new consumer society, and the stabilization of the European state system all generated optimism about the future. The intellectual corollary was the **Enlightenment**, a term used later in the eighteenth century to describe the loosely knit group of writers and scholars who believed that human beings could apply a critical, reasoning spirit to every problem they encountered in this world. The new secular, scientific, and critical attitude first emerged in the 1690s, scrutinizing everything from the absolutism of Louis XIV to the traditional role of women in society. After 1740, criticism took a more systematic turn as writers provided new theories for the organization of society and politics, but even by the 1720s and 1730s, established authorities realized they faced a new set of challenges.

Popularization of Science and Challenges to Religion

The writers of the Enlightenment glorified the geniuses of the new science and championed scientific method as the solution for all social problems. One of the most influential popularizations was the French writer Bernard de Fontenelle's *Conversations on the Plurality of Worlds* (1686). Presented as a dialogue between an aristocratic woman and a man of the world, the book made the Copernican,

■ **A Budding Scientist**
In this engraving, Astrologia, *by the Dutch artist Jacob Gole (c. 1660–1723), an upper-class woman looks through a telescope to do her own astronomical investigations. Women were not allowed to attend university classes in any European country, yet the Italian Laura Bassi (1711–1778) still managed to become professor of physics at the University of Bologna. Because many astronomical observatories were set up in private homes rather than public buildings or universities, wives and daughters of scientists could make observations and even publish their own findings.*
(Bibliothèque nationale de France.)

sun-centered view of the universe available to the literate public. By 1700, mathematics and science had become fashionable pastimes in high society, and the public flocked to lectures explaining scientific discoveries. Journals complained that scientific learning had become the passport to female affection: "There were two young ladies in Paris whose heads had been so turned by this branch of learning that one of them declined to listen to a proposal of marriage unless the candidate for her hand undertook to learn how to make telescopes." Such writings poked fun at women with intellectual interests, but they also demonstrated that women now participated in discussions of science.

Interest in science spread in literate circles because it offered a model for all forms of knowledge. As the prestige of science increased, some developed a skeptical attitude toward attempts to enforce religious conformity. A French Huguenot refugee from Louis XIV's persecutions, Pierre Bayle (1647–1706), launched an internationally influential campaign against religious intolerance from his safe haven in the Dutch Republic. His *News from the Republic of Letters* (first published in 1684) bitterly criticized the policies of Louis XIV and was quickly banned in Paris and condemned in Rome. After attacking Louis XIV's anti-Protestant policies, Bayle took a more general stand in favor of religious toleration. No state in Europe officially offered complete tolerance, though the Dutch Republic came closest with its tacit acceptance of Catholics, dissident Protestant groups, and open Jewish communities. In 1697, Bayle published the *Historical and Critical Dictionary*, which cited all the errors and delusions that he could find in past and present writers of all religions. Even religion must meet the test of reasonableness: "Any particular dogma, whatever it may be, whether it is advanced on the authority of the Scriptures, or whatever else may be its origins, is to be regarded as false if it clashes with the clear and definite conclusions of the natural understanding [reason]." Although Bayle claimed to be a believer himself, his insistence on rational investigation seemed to challenge the authority of faith. As one critic complained, "It is notorious that the works of M. Bayle have unsettled a large number of readers, and cast doubt on some of the most widely accepted principles of morality and religion." Bayle asserted, for example, that atheists might possess moral codes as effective as those of the devout. Bayle's *Dictionary* became a model of critical thought in the West.

Other scholars challenged the authority of the Bible by subjecting it to historical criticism. Discoveries in geology in the early eighteenth century showed that marine fossils dated immensely farther back than the biblical flood. Investigations of miracles, comets, and oracles, like the growing literature against belief in witchcraft, urged the use of reason to combat superstition and prejudice. Comets, for example, should not be considered evil omens just because such a belief had been passed on from earlier generations. Defenders of church and state published books warning of the dangers of the new skepticism. The spokesman for Louis XIV's absolutism, Bishop Bossuet, warned that "reason is the guide of their choice, but reason only brings them face to face with vague conjectures and baffling perplexities." Human beings, the traditionalists held, were simply incapable of subjecting everything to reason, especially in the realm of religion.

State authorities found religious skepticism particularly unsettling because it threatened to undermine state power, too. The extensive literature of criticism was not limited to France, but much of it was published in French, and the French government took the lead in suppressing the more outspoken works. Forbidden books were then often published in the Dutch Republic, Britain, or Switzerland and smuggled back across the border to a public whose appetite was only whetted by censorship.

The most influential writer of the early Enlightenment was a Frenchman born into the upper middle class, François-Marie Arouet, known by his pen name, Voltaire (1694–1778). In his early years, Voltaire suffered arrest, imprisonment, and exile, but he eventually achieved wealth and acclaim. His tangles with church and state began in the early 1730s, when he published his *Letters Concerning the English Nation* (the English version appeared in 1733), in which he devoted several chapters to Newton and Locke and used the virtues of the British as a way to attack Catholic bigotry and government rigidity in France. Impressed by British toleration of religious dissent (at least among Protestants), Voltaire spent two years in exile in Britain when the French state responded to his book with yet another order for his arrest.

Voltaire also popularized Newton's scientific discoveries in his *Elements of the Philosophy of Newton* (1738). The French state and many European theologians considered Newtonianism threatening because it glorified the human mind and seemed to reduce God to an abstract, external, rationalistic force. So sensational was the success of Voltaire's book on Newton that a hostile Jesuit reported, "The great Newton, was, it is said, buried in the abyss, in the shop of the first publisher who dared to print him. . . . M. de Voltaire finally appeared, and at once Newton is understood or is in the process of being understood; all Paris resounds with Newton, all Paris stammers Newton, all Paris studies and learns Newton." The success was international, too. Before long, Voltaire was elected a fellow of the Royal Society in London and in Edinburgh, as well as to twenty other scientific academies. Voltaire's fame continued to grow, reaching truly astounding proportions in the 1750s and 1760s (see Chapter 15).

Travel Literature and the Challenge to Custom and Tradition

Just as scientific method could be used to question religious and even state authority, a more general skepticism also emerged from the expanding knowledge about the world outside of Europe. During the seventeenth and eighteenth centuries, accounts of travel to exotic places dramatically increased as travel writers used the contrast between their home societies and other cultures to criticize the customs of European society.

In their travels to the new colonies, visitors sought something resembling "the state of nature"—that is, ways of life that preceded sophisticated social and political organization—although they often misinterpreted different forms of society and politics as having no organization at all. Travelers to the Americas found "noble savages" (native peoples) who appeared to live in conditions of great freedom and equality; they were "naturally good" and "happy" without taxes, lawsuits, or much organized government. In China, in contrast, travelers found a people who enjoyed prosperity and an ancient civilization. Christian missionaries made little headway in China, and visitors had to admit that China's religious systems had flourished for four or five thousand years with no input from Europe or from Christianity. The basic lesson of travel literature in the 1700s, then, was that customs varied: justice, freedom, property, good government, religion, and morality all were relative to the place. One critic complained that travel encouraged free thinking and the destruction of religion: "Some complete their demoralization by extensive travel, and lose whatever shreds of religion remained to them. Every day they see a new religion, new customs, new rites."

Travel literature turned explicitly political in Montesquieu's *Persian Letters* (1721). Charles-Louis de Secondat, baron of Montesquieu (1689–1755), the son of an eminent judicial family, was a high-ranking judge in a French court. He published *Persian Letters* anonymously in the Dutch Republic, and the book went into ten printings in just one year—a best seller for the times. Montesquieu tells the story of two Persians, Rica and Usbek, who leave their country "for love of knowledge" and travel to Europe. They visit France in the last years of Louis XIV's reign, writing of the king: "He has a minister who is only eighteen years old, and a mistress of eighty. . . . Although he avoids the bustle of towns, and is rarely seen in company, his one concern, from morning till night, is to get himself talked about." Other passages ridicule the pope. Beneath the satire, however, was a serious investigation into the foundation of good government and morality. Montesquieu chose Persians for his travelers because they came from what was widely considered the most despotic of all governments, in which rulers had life-and-death powers over their subjects. In the book, the Persians constantly compare France to Persia, suggesting that the French monarchy itself might verge on despotism.

The paradox of a judge publishing an anonymous work attacking the regime that employed him demonstrates the complications of the intellectual scene in this period. Montesquieu's anonymity did not last long, and soon Parisian society lionized him. In the late 1720s, he sold his judgeship and traveled extensively in Europe, including an eighteen-month stay in Britain. In 1748, he published a widely influential work on comparative government, *The Spirit of Laws*. The Vatican soon listed both *Persian Letters* and *The Spirit of Laws* in its index of forbidden books.

Raising the Woman Question

Many of the letters exchanged in *Persian Letters* focused on women, marriage, and the family because Montesquieu considered the position of women a sure indicator of the nature of government and morality. Although he was not a feminist, his depiction of Roxana, the favorite wife in Usbek's harem, struck a chord with many women. Roxana revolts against the authority of Usbek's eunuchs and writes a final letter to her husband announcing her impending suicide: "I may have lived in servitude, but I have always been free, I have amended your laws according to the laws of nature, and my mind has always remained independent." Women writers used the same language of tyranny and freedom to argue for concrete changes in their status. Feminist ideas were not entirely new, but they were presented systematically for the first time and represented a fundamental challenge to the ways of traditional societies.

The most systematic of these women writers was the English author Mary Astell (1666–1731), the daughter of a businessman and herself a supporter of the Tory party and the Anglican religious establishment. In 1694, she published *A Serious Proposal to the Ladies*, in which she advocated founding a private women's college to remedy women's lack of education. Addressing women, she asked, "How can you be content to be in the World like Tulips in a Garden, to make a fine *shew* [show] and be good for nothing?" Astell argued for intellectual training based on Descartes's principles, in which reason, debate, and careful consideration of the issues took priority over custom or tradition. Her book was an immediate success: five printings appeared by 1701. In later works such as *Reflections upon Marriage* (1706), Astell criticized the relationship between the sexes within marriage: "If Absolute Sovereignty be not necessary in a State, how comes it to be so in a family? . . . *If all Men are born free*, how is it that all Women are born slaves?" Her critics accused her of promoting subversive ideas and of contradicting the Scriptures.

Astell's work inspired other women to write in a similar vein. The anonymous *Essay in Defence of the Female Sex* (1696) attacked "The Usurpation of Men; and the Tyranny of Custom," which prevented women from getting an education. In 1709, Elizabeth Elstob published a detailed account of the prominent role women played in promoting Christianity in English history. She criticized men who "would declare openly they hated any Woman who knew more than themselves."

Most male writers unequivocally stuck to the traditional view of women, which held that women were less capable of reasoning than men and therefore did not need systematic education. Such opinions often rested on biological suppositions. The long-dominant Aristotelian view of reproduction held that only the male seed carried spirit and individuality. At the beginning of the eighteenth century, however, scientists began to undermine this belief. More physicians and surgeons began to champion the doctrine of ovism—that the female egg was essential in making new

■ MAPPING THE WEST Europe in 1740

*By 1740 Europe had achieved a kind of diplomatic equilibrium in which no one power predomi-
nated. But the relative balance should not deflect attention from important underlying changes:
Spain, the Dutch Republic, Poland-Lithuania, and Sweden had all declined in power and influence
while Great Britain, Russia, Prussia, and Austria had solidified their positions, each in a different
way. France's ambitions had been thwarted, but the combination of a big army and rich overseas
possessions made France a major player for a long time to come.*

humans. During the decades that followed, male Enlightenment writers would continue to debate women's nature and appropriate social roles.

■ **REVIEW:** *What were the main issues in the early decades of the Enlightenment?*

IMPORTANT DATES

1690s	Beginning of rapid development of plantations in the Caribbean	**1715**	Death of Louis XIV
1694	Bank of England established; Mary Astell's *A Serious Proposal to the Ladies* argues for the founding of a private women's college	**1719**	Daniel Defoe publishes *Robinson Crusoe*
		1720	Last outbreak of bubonic plague in western Europe
1697	Pierre Bayle publishes *Historical and Critical Dictionary*, detailing errors of religious writers	**1721**	Treaty of Nystad; Montesquieu publishes *Persian Letters* anonymously in the Dutch Republic
1699	Turks forced to recognize Habsburg rule over Hungary and Transylvania	**1733**	War of the Polish Succession; Voltaire's *Letters Concerning the English Nation* attacks French intolerance and narrowmindedness
1703	Peter the Great of Russia begins construction of St. Petersburg, founds first Russian newspaper	**1741**	George Frederick Handel composes the *Messiah*
1713–1714	Peace of Utrecht		
1714	Elector of Hanover becomes King George I of England		

Conclusion

Europeans crossed a major threshold in the first half of the eighteenth century. They moved silently but nonetheless momentously from an economy governed by scarcity and the threat of famine to one of ever increasing growth and the prospect of continuing improvement. Expansion of colonies overseas and economic development at home created greater wealth, longer life spans, and higher expectations for the future. In these better times for many, a spirit of optimism prevailed. People could now spend money on newspapers, novels, and travel literature as well as on coffee, tea, and cotton cloth. The growing literate public avidly followed the latest trends in religious debates, art, and music. Everyone did not share equally in the benefits: slaves toiled in abjection in the Americas; serfs in eastern Europe found themselves ever more closely bound to their noble lords; and rural folk almost everywhere tasted few fruits of consumer society.

Politics, too, changed as population and production increased and cities grew. Experts urged government intervention to improve public health, and states found it in their interest to settle many international disputes by diplomacy, which itself became more regular and routine. The consolidation of the European state system allowed a tide of criticism and new thinking about society to swell in Great Britain and France and begin to spill throughout Europe. Ultimately, the combination of the Atlantic system and the Enlightenment would give rise to a series of Atlantic revolutions.

■ **MAKING CONNECTIONS**

1. *How did the rise of slavery and the plantation system change European politics and society?*

2. *Why did the Enlightenment begin just at the moment that the Atlantic system took shape?*

■ **FOR FURTHER EXPLORATION**

For further reading and online research ideas, see the Suggested References on page SR-7 at the back of the book.

For practice quizzes, a customized study plan, and other study tools, see the ONLINE STUDY GUIDE at **bedfordstmartins.com/huntconcise**.

For primary-source material from this period, see Chapter 14 in *Sources of THE MAKING OF THE WEST: A CONCISE HISTORY*, Second Edition.

The Promise of Enlightenment

1740–1789

I N THE SUMMER OF 1766, Empress Catherine II ("the Great") of Russia wrote to Voltaire, one of the leaders of the Enlightenment:

> It is a way of immortalizing oneself to be the advocate of humanity, the defender of oppressed innocence. . . . You have entered into combat against the enemies of mankind: superstition, fanaticism, ignorance, quibbling, evil judges, and the powers that rest in their hands. Great virtues and qualities are needed to surmount these obstacles. You have shown that you have them: you have triumphed.

Over a fifteen-year period Catherine corresponded regularly with Voltaire, a writer who, at home in France, found himself in constant conflict with church and state authorities. Her admiring letter shows how influential Enlightenment ideals had become by the middle of the eighteenth century.

Catherine's letter aptly summed up Enlightenment ideals: progress for humanity could be achieved only by rooting out the wrongs left by superstition, religious fanaticism, ignorance, and outmoded forms of justice. Enlightenment writers used

■ **Catherine the Great**

In this portrait by the Danish painter Vigilius Eriksen, the Russian empress Catherine the Great is shown on horseback (c. 1752), much like any male ruler of the time. Born Sophia Augusta Frederika of Anhalt-Zerbst in 1729, Catherine was the daughter of a minor German prince. When she married the future tsar Peter III in 1745, she promptly learned Russian and adopted Russian Orthodoxy. Peter, physically and mentally frail, proved no match for her; in 1762, she staged a coup against him and took his place when he was killed. (Bridgeman–Giraudon/Art Resource, NY.)

every means at their disposal—from encyclopedias to novels to personal interaction with rulers—to argue for reform. Everything had to be examined in the clear light of reason, and anything that did not promote the improvement of humanity was to be jettisoned. As a result, Enlightenment writers attacked the legal use of torture to extract confessions, favored the spread of education to eliminate ignorance, supported religious toleration, and criticized censorship by state or church. The book trade and new places for urban socializing, such as coffeehouses and Masonic lodges (social clubs organized around the rituals of masons' guilds), spread these ideas within a new elite of middle- and upper-class men and women.

The lower classes had little contact with Enlightenment ideas. Their lives were shaped more profoundly by the continuing rise in population, the start of industrialization, and wars among the great powers. States had to balance conflicting social pressures: rulers pursued Enlightenment reforms that they believed might enhance state power, but they feared changes that might unleash popular discontent. For example, Catherine aimed to bring Western ideas, culture, and reforms to Russia, but when faced with a massive uprising of the serfs, she not only suppressed the revolt but also increased the nobles' powers over their serfs. All reform-minded rulers faced similar potential challenges to their authority.

Even though the movement for reform had its limits, governments now needed to respond to a new force: public opinion. Rulers wanted to portray themselves as modern, open to change, and responsive to the segment of the public that was reading newspapers and closely following political developments. Enlightenment writers appealed to public opinion, but they still looked to rulers to effect reform. Writers such as Voltaire expressed little interest in the future of peasants or lower classes; they favored neither revolution nor political upheaval. Yet their ideas paved the way for something much more radical and unexpected. The American Declaration of Independence in 1776 showed how Enlightenment ideals could be translated into democratic political practice. After 1789, democracy would come to Europe as well.

The Enlightenment at Its Height

The Enlightenment emerged as an intellectual movement before 1740 but reached its peak only in the second half of the eighteenth century. The writers of the Enlightenment called themselves **philosophes** (French for "philosophers"), but that term is somewhat misleading. Whereas philosophers concern themselves with abstract theories, the philosophes were public intellectuals dedicated to solving the real problems of the world. They wrote on subjects ranging from current affairs to art criticism, and they wrote in every conceivable format. The Swiss philosophe Jean-Jacques Rousseau, for example, wrote a political tract, a treatise on education, a constitution for Poland, an analysis of the effects of the theater on public morals, a best-selling novel, an opera, and a notorious autobiography.

The philosophes wrote for a broad educated public of readers who snatched up every Enlightenment book they could find at their local booksellers, even when rulers or churches tried to forbid publication. Between 1740 and 1789, the Enlightenment acquired its name and, despite heated conflicts between the philosophes and state and religious authorities, gained support in the highest reaches of government.

The Men and Women of the Republic of Letters

Although *philosophe* is a French word, the Enlightenment was distinctly cosmo-politan; philosophes could be found from Philadelphia to Moscow. The philosophes considered themselves part of a grand "republic of letters" that transcended national political boundaries. They were not republicans in the usual sense, that is, people who supported representative government and opposed monarchy. What united them were the ideals of reason, reform, and freedom. In 1784, the German philosopher Immanuel Kant summed up the program of the Enlightenment in two Latin words: *sapere aude,* "dare to know"—have the courage to think for yourself.

The philosophes used reason to attack superstition, bigotry, and religious fanaticism, which they considered the chief obstacles to free thought and social reform. Voltaire took religious fanaticism as his chief target: "Once fanaticism has corrupted a mind, the malady is almost incurable. . . . The only remedy for this epidemic malady is the philosophical spirit." Enlightenment writers did not necessarily oppose organized religion, but they strenuously objected to religious intolerance. They believed that the systematic application of reason could do what religious belief could not: improve the human condition by pointing to needed reforms. Reason meant critical, informed, scientific thinking about social issues and problems. Many Enlightenment writers collaborated on a new multivolume *Encyclopedia* that aimed to gather together knowledge about science, religion, industry, and society. The chief editor of the *Encyclopedia,* Denis Diderot (1713–1784), explained the goal: "All things must be examined, debated, investigated without exception and without regard for anyone's feelings."

The philosophes believed that the spread of knowledge would encourage reform in every aspect of life, from the grain trade to the penal system. Chief among their desired reforms was intellectual freedom, the freedom to use one's own reason and to publish the results. The philosophes wanted freedom of the press and freedom of religion, which they considered "natural rights" guaranteed by "natural law." In their view, progress depended on these freedoms. As Voltaire asserted, "I quite understand that the fanatics of one sect slaughter the enthusiasts of another sect . . . [but] that Descartes should have been forced to flee to Holland to escape the fury of the ignorant . . . these things are a nation's eternal shame."

■ Madame Geoffrin's Salon in 1755

This 1812 painting by Anicet Charles Lemonnier claims to depict the best-known Parisian salon of the 1750s. Lemonnier was only twelve years old in 1755 and so could not have based his rendition on firsthand knowledge. Madame Geoffrin is the figure in blue on the right, facing the viewer. The bust is of Voltaire. Rousseau is the fifth person to the left of the bust (facing right) and behind him (facing left) is Raynal. (Bridgeman-Giraudon/Art Resource, NY.)

Most philosophes, like Voltaire, came from the upper classes, yet Rousseau's father was a modest watchmaker in Geneva, and Diderot was the son of a cutlery maker. The French noblewoman Émilie du Châtelet (1706–1749) was one of the rare female philosophes. She wrote extensively about the mathematics and physics of Leibniz and Newton. (Her lover Voltaire learned much of his science from her.) Few of the leading writers held university positions, except those who were German or Scottish. Universities in France were dominated by the clergy and unreceptive to Enlightenment ideals.

Enlightenment ideas developed instead through personal contacts; through letters that were hand copied, circulated, and sometimes published; through informal readings of manuscripts; and through letters to the editor and book reviews in periodicals. **Salons**—informal gatherings, usually sponsored by middle-class or aristocratic women—gave intellectual life an anchor outside the royal court and the church-controlled universities. Best known was the Parisian salon of Madame Marie-Thérèse Geoffrin (1699–1777), a wealthy middle-class widow who had been raised by her grandmother and married off at fourteen to a much older man. She brought together the most exciting thinkers and artists of the time; her social gatherings provided a forum for new ideas and an opportunity to establish new intellectual contacts. In the salon, the philosophes could discuss ideas they might hesitate to put into print and thus test public opinion and even push it in new directions. Madame Geoffrin corresponded extensively with influential people across Europe, including Catherine the Great. One Italian visitor commented, "There is no way to make Naples resemble Paris unless we find a woman to guide us, organize us, *Geoffrinize* us."

Women's salons helped galvanize intellectual life and reform movements all over Europe. Wealthy Jewish women created nine of the fourteen salons in Berlin at the end of the eighteenth century, and in Warsaw, Princess Zofia Czartoryska gathered around her the reform leaders of Poland-Lithuania. Middle-class women in London used their salons to raise money to publish women's writings. Salons could be tied closely to the circles of power: in France, for example, Louis XV's mistress, Jeanne-Antoinette Poisson, first made her reputation as hostess of a salon frequented by Voltaire and Montesquieu. When she became Louis XV's mistress in 1745, she gained the title Marquise de Pompadour and turned her attention to influencing artistic styles by patronizing architects and painters.

Conflicts with Church and State

Madame Geoffrin did not approve of discussions that attacked the Catholic church, but elsewhere voices against organized religion could be heard. Criticisms of religion required daring because the church, whatever its denomination, wielded enormous power in society, and most influential people considered religion an essential foundation of good society and government. Defying such opinion, the Scottish philosopher David Hume (1711–1776) boldly argued in *The Natural History of Religion* (1755) that belief in God rested on superstition and fear rather than on reason.

Before the scientific revolution, nearly every European believed in God. After Newton, however, and despite Newton's own deep religiosity, people could conceive of the universe as an eternally existing, self-perpetuating machine in which God's intervention was unnecessary. In short, such people could become either an **atheist**, who did not believe in any kind of God, or a **deist**, who believed in God but gave him no active role in earthly affairs. For the first time, writers claimed the label *atheist* and disputed the common view that atheism led inevitably to immorality.

Deists continued to believe in a benevolent, all-knowing God who had designed the universe and set it in motion. But deists usually rejected the idea that God directly intercedes in the functioning of the universe, and they often criticized the churches for their dogmatic intolerance of dissenters. Voltaire was a deist, and in his popular *Philosophical Dictionary* (1764) he attacked most of the claims of organized Christianity, both Catholic and Protestant. Christianity, he argued, had been the prime source of fanaticism and brutality among humans. Throughout his life, Voltaire's motto was *Écrasez l'infâme*—"Crush the infamous thing" (the "thing" being bigotry and intolerance). French authorities publicly burned his *Philosophical Dictionary.*

Criticism of religious intolerance involved more than simply attacking the churches. Critics also had to confront the states to which churches were closely tied. In 1761, a judicial case in Toulouse provoked throughout France an outcry that Voltaire soon joined. When the son of a local Calvinist was found hanged (he probably committed suicide), authorities accused the father, Jean Calas, of murdering him to prevent his conversion to Catholicism. (Since Louis XIV's revocation of the Edict of Nantes in 1685, it had been illegal to practice Calvinism publicly in France.) The all-Catholic parlement of Toulouse tried to extract a confession using torture—by systematically tightening cords on his wrists and then by pouring pitchers of water down his throat—and ordered that he be broken on the wheel: have all his bones broken one by one in order to maximize the pain of execution. Voltaire launched a successful crusade to rehabilitate Jean Calas's good name and to restore the family's properties, which had been confiscated after his death. Voltaire's efforts eventually helped bring about the extension of civil rights to French Protestants and encouraged campaigns to abolish the legal use of torture.

Critics also assailed state and church support for European colonization and slavery. One of the most popular books of the time was the *Philosophical and Political History of European Colonies and Commerce in the Two Indies*, published in 1770 by Abbé Guillaume Raynal (1713–1796), a French Catholic clergyman. Raynal and his collaborators described in excruciating detail the destruction of native populations by Europeans and denounced the slave trade. Raynal was forced into exile, and his work was banned by both the Catholic church and the French government, but the Enlightenment belief in natural rights led many others to denounce slavery. An article in the new *Encyclopedia* proclaimed, "There is not a single one of these hapless souls . . . who does not have the right to be declared free . . . since neither his ruler nor his father nor anyone else had the right to dispose of his freedom." Some Enlightenment thinkers, however, took a more ambiguous or even negative view. Hume judged blacks to be "naturally inferior to the whites," concluding, "There never was a civilized nation of any other complexion than white."

Enlightenment critics of church and state advocated reform, not revolution. Although he lived near the French-Swiss border in case he had to flee arrest, Voltaire, for example, made a fortune from financial speculations, wrote a glowing history called *The Age of Louis XIV* (1751), and lived to be celebrated in his last years as a national hero even by many former foes. Other philosophes also lived respectably, believing that published criticism, rather than violent action, would bring about necessary reforms. As Diderot said, "We will speak against senseless laws until they are reformed; and, while we wait, we will abide by them." Those few who lived long enough to see the French Revolution in 1789 resisted its radical turn, for the philosophes generally regarded the lower classes—"the people"—as ignorant, violent, and prone to superstition, hence in need of leadership from above. They pinned their hopes on educated elites and enlightened rulers.

Despite the philosophes' preference for reform, in the long run their books often had a revolutionary impact. For example, Montesquieu's widely reprinted *Spirit of the Laws* (1748) warned against the dangers of despotism, opposed the divine right of kings, and favored constitutional government. In his somewhat rosy view, Great Britain was "the one nation in the world which has political liberty as the direct object of its constitution." His analysis of British constitutionalism inspired French critics of absolutism and would greatly influence the American revolutionaries.

The Individual and Society

In previous centuries, questions of theological doctrine and church organization had been the main focus of intellectual and even political interest. The Enlightenment writers shifted attention away from religious questions toward the secular study of society and the individual's role in it. In this way, the Enlightenment advanced the secularization of European political life that had begun after the Wars of Religion of the sixteenth and seventeenth centuries. At the same time, it laid the foundations for the social sciences of the modern era.

Just as Newton had used his reason to penetrate the laws of nature, so too the philosophes hoped to use reason to discern the laws of social life. But they did not necessarily agree about the conclusions to be drawn. Among the many different approaches were two that proved enduringly influential, those of the Scottish philosopher Adam Smith and the Swiss writer Jean-Jacques Rousseau. Smith provided a theory of modern capitalist society and devoted much of his energy to defending free markets as offering the best way to maximize individual efforts. The modern discipline of economics took shape around the questions raised by Smith. Rousseau set out the principles of a more communitarian philosophy, one that emphasized the needs of the community over those of the individual. His work led both toward democracy and toward communism and continues to inspire heated debate in political science and sociology. A closer look at these two thinkers will demonstrate the breadth and depth of Enlightenment thought.

Adam Smith (1723–1790) optimistically believed that individual interests naturally harmonized with those of the whole society. To explain how this natural harmonization worked, he published *An Inquiry into the Nature and Causes of the Wealth of Nations* in 1776. Smith insisted that individual self-interest, even greed, was quite compatible with society's best interest: the market served as an "invisible hand" ensuring that individual interests would be synchronized with those of the whole society. "By pursuing his own interest," the merchant "frequently promotes that of the society more effectually than when he really intends to promote it."

Smith rejected the prevailing mercantilist views that the general welfare would be served by accumulating national wealth through agriculture or the hoarding of gold and silver. Instead, he argued that the division of labor in manufacturing would increase productivity and generate more wealth for society and well-being for the individual. To maximize the effects of market forces and the division of labor, Smith endorsed a concept called **laissez-faire** (that is, "to leave alone") to free the economy from government intervention and control. He insisted that governments eliminate all restrictions on the sale of land, remove restraints on the grain trade, and abandon duties on imports. He believed that free international trade would stimulate production everywhere and thus ensure the growth of national wealth. He argued:

> *The natural effort of every individual to better his own condition, when suffered to exert itself with freedom and security, is so powerful a principle, that it is alone, and without any assistance, not only capable of carrying the society to wealth and prosperity, but of surmounting a hundred impertinent obstructions with which the folly of human laws too often encumbers its operations.*

Governments should restrict themselves to providing "security"—that is, national defense, internal order and a secure framework for market activity, and public works.

Much more pessimistic about the relation between individual self-interest and the good of society was Jean-Jacques Rousseau (1712–1778). In Rousseau's view, society itself threatened natural rights or freedoms: "Man is born free, and everywhere he is in chains." Rousseau first gained fame by writing a prize-winning essay in 1749 in which he argued that the revival of science and the arts had corrupted social morals, not improved them. This startling conclusion seemed to oppose some of the Enlightenment's most cherished beliefs. Rather than improving society, he claimed, science and art raised artificial barriers between people and their natural state. Rousseau's works extolled the simplicity of rural life over urban society. Although he participated in the salons, Rousseau always felt ill at ease in high society, and he periodically withdrew to live in solitude far from Paris. Paradoxically, his "solitude" was often paid for by wealthy upper-class patrons, who lodged him on their estates, even as his writings decried the upper-class privilege that made his efforts possible.

Rousseau explored the tension between the individual and society in various ways, including his widely influential work on education, *Émile* (1762), in which a boy develops practical skills and independent thinking under the guidance of his tutor. In *The Social Contract* (1762), Rousseau proposed a political solution to the tension between the individual and society. Whereas earlier he had argued that society corrupted the individual by taking him out of nature, in this work Rousseau insisted that individual moral freedom could be achieved only by learning to subject one's individual interests to "the general will"—that is, to the good

■ Rousseau's Worries

Jean-Jacques Rousseau's novel The New Heloise *(1761) sold better than any other work in French in the second half of the eighteenth century. But Rousseau himself was deeply concerned about the effects of novel reading, especially on young women. The first of these illustrations for the novel (on the left) by Moreau the Younger, was rejected by Rousseau because the couple (Julie and Saint Preux) are shown in direct physical contact. He accepted the engraving on the right, by Gravelot, because it only hinted at passion.* (Bibliothèque nationale de France.)

of the community. Individuals did this by entering into a social contract, not with their rulers but with one another. If everyone followed the general will, then all individuals would be equally free and equally moral because they lived under a law to which they had all consented.

These arguments threatened the legitimacy of eighteenth-century governments. Rousseau derived his social contract from human nature, not from history, tradition, or the Bible. He implied that people would be most free and moral under a republican form of government with direct democracy, and his abstract model included no reference to differences in social status. He roundly condemned slavery: "To decide that the son of a slave is born a slave is to decide that he is not born a man." Not surprisingly, authorities in both Geneva and Paris banned *The Social Contract* for undermining political authority. Rousseau's works would become a kind of political bible for the French revolutionaries of 1789, and his attacks on private property would inspire the communists of the nineteenth century such as Karl Marx. Rousseau's rather mystical concept of the general will remains controversial. The "greatest good of all," according to Rousseau, was liberty and equality, but he also insisted that the individual could be "forced to be free" by the terms of the social contract. He provided no legal protections for individual rights. In other words, Rousseau's particular version of democracy did not guarantee the individual freedoms so important to Adam Smith.

Spreading the Enlightenment

The Enlightenment flourished in places where an educated middle class provided an eager audience for ideas of constitutionalism and reform. Where constitutionalism and the guarantee of individual freedoms were most advanced, as in Great Britain and the Dutch Republic, the movement had less of an edge because there was, in a sense, less need for it. Scottish and English writers concentrated on economics, philosophy, and history rather than politics or social relations. Dutch printers made money publishing the books that were forbidden in France. In British North America, Enlightenment ideas helped stiffen growing colonial resistance to British rule after 1763. In places with small middle classes, such as Spain, the Italian states, and Russia, governments successfully suppressed writings they did not like. Italian philosophes, such as the Milanese penal reformer Cesare Beccaria (1738–1794), got moral support from their French counterparts in the face of stern censorship at home.

The hot spot of the Enlightenment was France. French writers published the most daring critiques of church and state and suffered the most intense harassment and persecution. Voltaire, Diderot, and Rousseau all faced arrest, exile, or even imprisonment. The Catholic church and royal authorities routinely forbade the publication of their books, and the police arrested publishers who ignored their warnings. Yet the French monarchy was far from the most autocratic in Europe, and Voltaire, Diderot, and Rousseau all were revered as cultural heroes. France seems to have been curiously caught in the middle during the Enlightenment: with fewer constitutional guarantees of individual freedom than Great Britain, it still enjoyed much higher levels of prosperity and cultural development than most other European countries. In short, French elites had reason to complain, the means to make their complaints known, and a government torn between the desires to censor dissident ideas and to appear open to modernity and progress.

The government in France controlled publishing—all books had to get official permissions—but not as tightly as in Spain, where the Catholic Inquisition made up its own list of banned books, or in Russia, where Catherine the Great allowed no opposition. In the 1760s and 1770s, a growing flood of works printed abroad poured into France and circulated underground. In the Dutch Republic and Swiss cities, private companies made fortunes smuggling illegal books into France over mountain passes and back roads. Foreign printers provided secret catalogs of their offerings and sold their products through booksellers who were willing to market forbidden texts for a high price—among them, not only philosophical treatises of the Enlightenment but also pornographic works and pamphlets (some by Diderot) lampooning the Catholic clergy and leading members of the royal court.

Whereas the French philosophes often took a violently anticlerical and combative tone, their German counterparts avoided direct political confrontations with authorities. Gotthold Lessing (1729–1781) complained in 1769 that Prussia was still "the most slavish society in Europe" in its lack of freedom to criticize government policies. As a playwright, literary critic, and philosopher, Lessing promoted religious toleration for Jews and spiritual emancipation of Germans from foreign, especially French, models of culture, which still dominated. Lessing also introduced the German Jewish writer Moses Mendelssohn (1729–1786) into Berlin salon society. Mendelssohn labored to build bridges between German and Jewish culture by arguing that Judaism was a rational and undogmatic religion. He believed persecution and discrimination against the Jews would end as reason triumphed.

Reason was also the chief focus of the most influential German thinker of the Enlightenment, Immanuel Kant (1724–1804). A university professor who lectured on everything from economics to astronomy, Kant wrote one of the most important works in the history of Western philosophy, *The Critique of Pure Reason* (1781). He admired Adam Smith and especially Rousseau, whose portrait he displayed proudly in his lodgings. Just as Smith founded modern economics and Rousseau modern political theory, Kant in *Critique of Pure Reason* set the foundations for modern philosophy. In this complex book, Kant established the doctrine of *idealism*, the belief that true understanding can come only from examining the ways in which ideas are formed in the mind. Ideas are shaped, Kant argued, not just by sensory information (a position central to *empiricism*, a philosophy based on John Locke's writings) but also by the operation on that information of mental categories such as space and time. In Kant's philosophy, these "categories of understanding" were neither sensory nor supernatural; they were entirely ideal and abstract and located in the human mind. For Kant the supreme philosophical questions—Does God exist? Is personal immortality possible? Do humans have free will?—were unanswerable by reason alone. But like Rousseau, Kant insisted that people could achieve true moral freedom only by living in society and obeying its laws.

The Limits of Reason: Roots of Romanticism and Religious Revival

In reaction to what some saw as the Enlightenment's excessive reliance on the authority of human reason, a new artistic movement called **romanticism** took root.

Although it would not fully flower until the early nineteenth century, romanticism traced its emphasis on individual genius, deep emotion, and the joys of nature to thinkers like Rousseau who had scolded the philosophes for ignoring those aspects of life that escaped and even conflicted with the power of reason. Rousseau's autobiographical *Confessions*, published posthumously in 1782, caused an immediate sensation because it revealed so much about his inner emotional life, including his sexual longings and his almost paranoid distrust of other Enlightenment figures.

The appeal to feelings and emotions also increased interest in the occult. In the 1780s, a charismatic Austrian physician turned "experimenter," Franz Mesmer, awed crowds of aristocrats and middle-class admirers with his Paris demonstrations of "animal magnetism." He passed a weak electrical current through tubs filled with water or iron filings, around which groups of his disciples sat, holding hands; with this process of "mesmerism" he claimed to cure their ailments. (The word *mesmerize*, meaning "hypnotize" or "hold spellbound," is derived from Mesmer's name.)

A novel by the German writer Johann Wolfgang von Goethe (1749–1832) captured the early romantic spirit with its glorification of emotion. *The Sorrows of Young Werther* (1774) tells of a passionate youth who reveres nature and rural life and is unhappy in love. When the woman he loves marries someone else, he falls into deep melancholy and eventually kills himself. Reason cannot save him. The book spurred a veritable Werther craze: there were Werther costumes, Werther engravings and embroidery, Werther medallions, and a perfume called Eau de Werther. Tragically, there were even a few imitations of Werther's suicide. The young Napoleon Bonaparte, who was to build an empire for France, claimed to have read Goethe's novel seven times.

Religious revivals underlined the limits of reason in a different way. Much of the Protestant world experienced an "awakening" in the 1740s. In the German states, Pietist groups founded new communities; and in the British North American colonies, revivalist Protestant preachers drew thousands of fervent believers in a movement called the Great Awakening. In North America, bitter conflicts between revivalists and their opponents in the established churches prompted the leaders on both sides to set up new colleges to support their beliefs. These included Princeton, Columbia, Brown, and Dartmouth, all founded between 1746 and 1769.

Revivalism also stirred eastern European Jews at about the same time. Israel ben Eliezer (1698–1760) laid the foundation for Hasidism in the 1740s and 1750s. He traveled the Polish countryside offering miraculous cures and became known as the Ba'al Shem Tov (or the Besht from the initials, meaning "Master of the Good Name") because he used divine names to effect healing and bring believers into closer personal contact with God. He emphasized mystical contemplation of the divine, rather than study of Jewish law, and his followers, the **Hasidim** (Hebrew for "most pious" Jews), often expressed their devotion through music, dance, and fervent prayer. Their practices soon spread all over Poland-Lithuania.

Most of the waves of Protestant revivalism ebbed after the 1750s, but in Great Britain the movement known as **Methodism** continued to grow. John Wesley (1703–1791), the Oxford-educated son of an Anglican cleric, founded Methodism, a term evoked by Wesley's insistence on strict self-discipline and a methodical approach to religious study and observance. In 1738, Wesley began preaching a new brand of Protestantism that emphasized an intense personal experience of salvation and a life of thrift, abstinence, and hard work. Traveling all over the British Isles, Wesley would mount a table or a box to speak to the ordinary people of the village or town. He slept in his followers' homes and treated their illnesses with various remedies, including small electric shocks for nervous diseases (Wesley eagerly followed Benjamin Franklin's experiments with electricity). In fifty years, Wesley preached forty thousand sermons, an average of fifteen a week. When the Anglican authorities refused to let him preach in the churches, Wesley began to ordain his own clergy. Nevertheless, during Wesley's lifetime the Methodist leadership remained politically conservative; Wesley himself denounced political agitation in the 1770s because, he said, it threatened to make Great Britain "a field of blood" ruled by "King Mob."

■ **REVIEW:** *Why was France the center of the Enlightenment?*

Society and Culture in an Age of Enlightenment

Religious revivals and the first stirrings of romanticism show that all intellectual currents did not flow in the same channel. Similarly, some social and cultural developments manifested the influence of Enlightenment ideas, but others did not. The traditional leaders of European societies—the nobles—responded to Enlightenment ideals in contradictory fashion: many simply reasserted their privileges and resisted the influence of the Enlightenment, but an important minority embraced change and actively participated in reform efforts. The expanding middle classes saw in the Enlightenment a chance to make their claim for joining society's governing elite. They bought Enlightenment books, joined Masonic lodges, and patronized new styles in art, music, and literature. The lower classes were more affected by economic growth. Continuing population increases contributed to a rise in prices for basic goods, but the industrialization of textile manufacturing, which began in this period, made cotton clothing more accessible to those at the bottom of the social scale.

The Nobility's Reassertion of Privilege

Nobles made up about 3 percent of the European population, but their numbers and way of life varied greatly from country to country. At least 10 percent of the population in Poland was noble and 7 to 8 percent in Spain, in contrast to only 2 percent in Russia and between 1 and 2 percent in the rest of western Europe. Many Polish and Spanish nobles lived in poverty; titles did not guarantee wealth. The wealthiest European nobles luxuriated in almost unimaginable opulence. Many of the English peers, for example, owned more than ten thousand acres of land (the average western European peasant owned about five acres), invested widely in government bonds and trading companies, kept several country residences with scores of servants as well as houses in London, and occasionally even had their own private orchestras as well as libraries of expensive books, greenhouses for exotic plants, kennels of pedigree dogs, and collections of antiques, firearms, and scientific instruments.

In the face of the commercialization of agriculture and inflation of prices, European aristocrats converted their remaining legal rights (called *seigneurial dues*, from the French *seigneur*, for "lord") into money payments and used them to support an increasingly expensive lifestyle. Peasants felt the squeeze as a result. French peasants, for instance, paid a wide range of dues to their landlords—including payments to grind grain at the lord's mill, bake bread in his oven, and press grapes at his winepress—and various inheritance taxes on the land. In addition, peasants had to work on the public roads without compensation for a specified number of days every year. They also paid taxes to the government on salt, an essential preservative, and on the value of their land; customs duties if they sold produce or wine in town; and the tithe on their grain (one-tenth of the crop) to the church.

In Britain, the landed gentry could not claim these same onerous dues from their tenants, but they fiercely defended their exclusive right to hunt game. The game laws kept the poor from eating meat and helped protect the social status of the rich. The gentry enforced the game laws themselves by hiring gamekeepers who hunted down poachers and even set traps for them in the forests. According to the law, anyone who poached deer or rabbits while armed or disguised could be sentenced to death. After 1760, the number of arrests for breaking the game laws increased dramatically. In most other countries, too, hunting was the special right of the nobility and a cause of deep popular resentment.

Even though Enlightenment writers sharply criticized nobles' insistence on special privileges, most aristocrats maintained their marks of distinction. The male court nobility continued to sport swords, plumed hats, makeup, and powdered hair; middle-class men wore simpler and more somber clothing. Aristocrats had their own seats in church and their own quarters in the universities. Frederick II ("the Great") of Prussia (r. 1740–1786) made sure that nobles dominated both the army officer corps and the civil bureaucracy. Catherine II of Russia (r. 1762–1796) granted the nobility vast tracts of land, the exclusive right to own serfs, and exemption from personal taxes and corporal punishment. Her Charter of the Nobility of 1785 codified these privileges in exchange for the nobles' political subservience to the state. In many countries, including Spain and France, the law prohibited aristocrats from engaging directly in retail trade. In Austria, Spain, the Italian states, Poland-Lithuania, and Russia, most nobles consequently cared little about Enlightenment ideas; they did not read the books of the philosophes and feared reforms that might challenge their dominance of rural society.

In France, Britain, and the western German states, however, the nobility proved more open to the new ideas. Among those who personally corresponded with Rousseau, for example, half were nobles, as were 20 percent of the 160 contributors to the *Encyclopedia*. It had not escaped their notice that Rousseau had denounced inequality. In his view, it was "manifestly contrary to the law of nature . . . that a handful of people should gorge themselves with superfluities while the hungry multitude goes in want of necessities."

The Middle Class and the Making of a New Elite

The Enlightenment offered middle-class people an intellectual and cultural route to social improvement. The term *middle class* referred to the middle position on the social ladder; middle-class families did not have legal titles like the nobility above them but did not work with their hands like the peasants, artisans, or workers below them. Most middle-class people lived in towns or cities and earned their living in the professions—as doctors, lawyers, or lower-level officials—or through investment in land, trade, or manufacturing. In the eighteenth century, the ranks of the middle class—also known as the bourgeoisie, after *bourgeois*, the French word for "city dweller"—grew steadily in western Europe as a result of economic expansion. In France, for example, the overall population grew by about one-third in the 1700s, but the bourgeoisie nearly tripled in size. Although middle-class people had many reasons to resent the nobles, they also aspired to be like them.

Nobles and middle-class professionals mingled in Enlightenment salons and joined the new Masonic lodges and local learned societies. The members of Masonic lodges were known as **Freemasons** because that was the term given to apprentice masons when they were deemed "free" to practice as masters of their guild. Although not explicitly political in aim, the lodges encouraged equality among members, and both aristocrats and middle-class men could join. Members wrote constitutions for their lodges and elected their own officers, thus promoting a direct experience of constitutional government.

Freemasonry arose in Great Britain and spread eastward: the first French and Italian lodges opened in 1726; Frederick II of Prussia founded a lodge in 1740; and after 1750, Freemasonry spread in Poland, Russia, and British North America. In France, women set up their own Masonic lodges. Despite the papacy's condemnation of Freemasonry in 1738 as subversive of religious and civil authority, lodges continued to multiply throughout the eighteenth century because they offered a place for socializing outside of the traditional channels and a way of declaring one's interest in the Enlightenment and reform. In short, Freemasonry

■ **Neoclassical Style**
In this Georgian interior of Syon House on the outskirts of London, various neoclassical motifs are readily apparent: Greek columns, Greek-style statuary on top of the columns, and Roman-style mosaics in the floor. The Scottish architect Robert Adam created this room for the duke of Northumberland in the 1760s. Adam had spent four years in Italy and returned in 1758 to London to decorate homes in the "Adam style," meaning the neoclassical manner.
(Fotomas Index, UK.)

offered a kind of secular religion. After 1789 and the outbreak of the French Revolution, conservatives would blame the lodges for every kind of political upheaval, but in the 1700s many high-ranking nobles became active members and saw no conflict with their privileged status.

Shared tastes in travel, architecture, and the arts helped strengthen the links between nobles and members of the middle class. "Grand tours" of Europe often led upper-class youths to the recently discovered Roman ruins at Pompeii and Herculaneum in Italy. The excavations aroused enthusiasm for the neoclassical style in architecture and painting, which began pushing aside the rococo and the long dominant baroque. Urban residences, government buildings, furniture, fabrics, wallpaper, and even pottery soon reflected the neoclassical emphasis on purity and clarity of forms. The English potter Josiah Wedgwood (1730–1795) almost single-handedly created a mass market for domestic crockery by appealing to middle-class desires to emulate the rich and royal. His designs of special tea sets for the British queen, for Catherine the Great of Russia, and for leading aristocrats allowed him to advertise his wares as fashionable. By 1767, he claimed that his Queensware pottery had "spread over the whole Globe," and indeed by then his pottery was being marketed in France, Russia, Venice, the Ottoman Empire, and British North America.

This period also supported artistic styles other than neoclassicism. Frederick II of Prussia built himself a palace in the earlier rococo style, gave it a French name, Sans-souci ("worry-free"), and filled it with the works of French

■ **Jean-Baptiste Greuze, *Broken Eggs* (1756)**
Greuze made his reputation as a painter of moralistic family scenes. In this one, an old woman (perhaps the mother) confronts the lover of a young girl and points to the eggs that have fallen out of a basket. The broken eggs are a symbol of lost virginity. Diderot praised Greuze's work as "morality in paint," but the paintings often had an erotic subtext. **For more help analyzing this image**, see the visual activity for this chapter in the ONLINE STUDY GUIDE at bedfordstmartins.com/huntconcise. (© Francis G. Mayer/CORBIS.)

masters of the rococo. The new emphasis on emotion and family life was reflected in a growing taste for moralistic family scenes in painting. The paintings of Jean-Baptiste Greuze (1725–1805), much praised by Diderot, depicted ordinary families at moments of domestic crisis. Such subjects appealed in particular to the middle-class public, which now attended the official painting exhibitions in France that were held regularly every other year after 1737. Court painting nonetheless remained much in demand. Marie-Louise-Elizabeth Vigée-Lebrun (1755–1842), who painted portraits at the French court, reported that in the 1780s "it was difficult to get a place on my waiting list. . . . I was the fashion."

Although wealthy nobles still patronized Europe's leading musicians, music, too, began to reflect the broadening of the elite, and the spread of Enlightenment ideals as classical forms replaced the baroque style. Complex polyphony gave way to melody, which made music more accessible to the ordinary listener. Professional orchestras now played for large audiences of well-to-do listeners in sizable concert halls. The public concert gradually displaced the private recital, and a new attitude toward "the classics" developed: for the first time in the 1770s and 1780s, concert groups began to play older music rather than simply playing the latest commissioned works. This laid the foundation for what we still call classical music today, that is, a repertory of the greatest music of the eighteenth and early nineteenth centuries. Because composers now created works that would be performed over and over again as part of a classical repertory, rather than occasional pieces for the court or noble patrons, they deliberately attempted to write lasting works. As a result, the major composers began to produce fewer symphonies: the Austrian composer Franz Joseph Haydn (1732–1809) wrote more than one hundred symphonies, but his successor Ludwig van Beethoven (1770–1827) would create only nine.

The two supreme masters of the new musical style of the eighteenth century show that the transition from noble patronage to classical concerts was far from complete. The Austrians Haydn and Wolfgang Amadeus Mozart (1756–1791) both wrote for noble patrons, but by the early 1800s their compositions had been incorporated into the canon of concert classics all over Europe. Incredibly prolific, both excelled in combining lightness, clarity, and profound emotion. Both also wrote numerous Italian operas, a genre whose popularity continued to grow: in the 1780s, the Papal States alone boasted forty opera houses. Haydn spent most of his career working for a Hungarian noble family, the Eszterházys. Asked why he had written no string quintets (at which Mozart excelled), he responded simply: "No one has ordered any."

Interest in reading, like attending public concerts, took hold of the middle classes. Shaped by coffeehouses, Masonic lodges, and public concerts more than by formal schooling, the new reading public fueled a frenzied increase in publication. By the end of the eighteenth century, six times as many books were being published in the German states, for instance, as at the beginning. One Parisian author commented that "people are certainly reading ten times as much in Paris as they did a hundred years ago." Provincial towns in Britain, France, the Dutch Republic, and the German states published their own newspapers; by 1780, thirty-seven English towns had local newspapers. Newspapers advertised arithmetic, dancing, and drawing lessons—and potions to induce abortions and cures for venereal disease. Lending libraries multiplied, and, in England especially, even small villages housed book clubs. Women benefited as much as men from the spread of print. As one Englishman observed, "By far the greatest part of ladies now have a taste for books."

The novel had become a respectable and influential genre. Among the most widely read novels were those of the English printer and writer Samuel Richardson

(1689–1761). In *Clarissa Harlowe* (1747–1748), a long novel in eight volumes, Richardson tells the story of a young woman from a heartless upper-class family who is torn between her family's choice of a repulsive suitor and her attraction to Lovelace, an aristocratic rake. Although she runs off with Lovelace to escape her family, she resists his advances; after being drugged and raped by Lovelace— despite the frantic pleas of readers of the first volumes to spare her—Clarissa dies of what can only be called a broken heart. One woman complained to Richardson, "I verily believe I have shed a pint of tears, and my heart is still bursting." Richardson claimed that he wrote *Clarissa* as a kind of manual of virtuous female conduct, yet critics nonetheless worried that novels undermined morals with their portrayals of lowlife characters, the seductions of virtuous women, and other examples of immoral behavior.

Although he himself grew up reading novels with his father, Rousseau discouraged novel reading in *Émile*. Still, he helped change attitudes in the new elite toward children by offering an educational approach for gently drawing the best out of children rather than repressing their natural curiosity and love of learning. Paintings now showed individual children playing at their favorite activities rather than formally posed with their families. Books about and for children became popular. *The Newtonian System of the Universe Digested for Young Minds*, by "Tom Telescope," was published in Britain in 1761 and reprinted many times. Children's toys, jigsaw puzzles, and clothing designed for children all appeared for the first time in the 1700s. At the same time, however, the Enlightenment's emphasis on reason, self-control, and childhood innocence made parents increasingly anxious about their children's sexuality. Moralists and physicians wrote books about the evils of masturbation, "proving" that it led to physical and mental degeneration and even madness. One English writer linked masturbation to debility of body and of mind; infertility; epilepsy; loss of memory, sight, and hearing; distortions of the eyes, mouth, and face; a pale, sallow, and bluish complexion; wasting of the limbs; idiotism; and death itself. While the Enlightenment thus encouraged excessive concern about children being left to their own devices, it nevertheless taught the middle and upper classes to value their children and to expect their improvement through education.

Life on the Margins

Even more than worrying about their children, the upper and middle classes worried about the increasing numbers of poor people. Although booming foreign trade—French colonial trade, for example, increased tenfold in the 1700s—fueled a dramatic economic expansion, the results did not necessarily trickle all the way down the social scale. The population of Europe grew by nearly 30 percent, with especially striking gains in England, Ireland, Prussia, and Hungary. Even though food production increased, shortages and crises still occurred periodically. Prices went up in many countries after the 1730s and continued to rise gradually until the early nineteenth century; wages in many trades rose as well, though less quickly than prices. Peasants who produced surpluses to sell in local markets and shop-keepers and artisans who could increase their sales to meet growing demand prospered. But those at the bottom of the social ladder—day laborers in the cities and peasants with small holdings—lived on the edge of dire poverty, and when they lost their land or work, they either migrated to the cities or wandered the roads in search of food and work. In France alone, 200,000 workers left their homes every year in search of seasonal employment elsewhere. At least 10 percent of Europe's urban population depended on some form of charity.

The growing numbers of poor people overwhelmed local governments and created fears about rising crime. In some countries, officials sent beggars and vagabonds to workhouses. The expenses for running these overcrowded institutions increased 60 percent in England between 1760 and 1785. After 1740, most German towns began to set up workhouses that were part workshop, part hospital, and part prison. Such institutions also appeared for the first time in Boston, New York, and Philadelphia. To supplement the inadequate system of religious charity, offices for the poor, public workshops, and workhouse-hospitals, the French government created *dépôts de mendicité*, or beggar houses, in 1767. The government sent people to these new workhouses to labor in manufacturing, but most were too weak or sick to work, and 20 percent of them died within a few months of incarceration.

Those who were able to work or keep their land fared better: an increase in literacy, especially in the cities, allowed some lower-class people to participate in new tastes and ideas. One French observer insisted, "These days, you see a waiting-maid in her backroom, a lackey in an ante-room reading pamphlets. People can read in almost all classes of society." In France, however, only 50 percent of men and 27 percent of women could read and write in the 1780s (although that was twice the rate of a century earlier). Literacy rates were higher in England and the Dutch Republic, much lower in eastern Europe. About one in four Parisians owned books, but the lower classes overwhelmingly read religious books, as they had in the past.

Whereas the new elite might attend salons, concerts, or art exhibitions, peasants enjoyed their traditional forms of popular entertainment, such as fairs and festivals, and the urban lower classes relaxed in cabarets and taverns. Sometimes pleasures were cruel. In Britain, bullbaiting, bearbaiting, dogfighting, and cockfighting were all common forms of entertainment that provided opportunities for organized gambling. Even "gentle" sports frequented by the upper classes had their violent side, showing that the upper classes had not become so different as they sometimes thought. Cricket matches, whose rules were first laid down in 1744, were often accompanied by brawls among fans (not unlike soccer matches today, though on a much smaller scale). Many Englishmen enjoyed what one observer called a "battle royal with sticks, pebbles and hog's dung."

As population increased and villagers began to move to cities to better their prospects, sexual behavior changed, too. The rates of births out of wedlock soared, from less than 5 percent of all births in the seventeenth century to nearly 20 percent at the end of the eighteenth. Historians have disagreed about the causes and meaning of this change. Some detect in this pattern a sign of sexual liberation and the beginnings of a modern sexual revolution: as women moved out of the control of their families, they began to seek their own sexual fulfillment. Others view this change more bleakly, as a story of seduction and betrayal: family and community pressure had once forced a man to marry a woman pregnant with his child, but now a man could abandon a pregnant lover by simply moving away.

Increased mobility brought freedom for some women, but it also aggravated the vulnerability of those newly arrived in cities from the countryside. Desperation, not reason, often ruled their choices. Women who came to the city as domestic servants had little recourse against masters or fellow servants who seduced or raped them. The result was a startling rise in abandoned babies. Most European cities established foundling hospitals to care for abandoned children in the 1700s, but infant and child mortality was 50 percent higher in such institutions than for children brought up at home. Some women tried herbs, laxatives, or crude surgical means of abortion; a few, usually servants who would lose their jobs if their employers discovered they had borne a child, resorted to infanticide. Reformers criticized the harshness of laws against infanticide, but they showed no mercy for "sodomites" (as male homosexuals were called), who in some places, in particular the Dutch Republic, were systematically persecuted and imprisoned or even executed. Male homosexuals attracted the attention of authorities because they had begun to develop networks and special meeting places. The stereotype of the effeminate, exclusively homosexual male seems to have appeared for the first time in the eighteenth century, perhaps as part of a growing emphasis on separate roles for men and women.

Roots of Industrialization

Although it was only starting to take hold, **industrialization** would eventually transform European society. The process began in England in the 1770s and 1780s and included four interlocking trends: (1) population increased dramatically, by more than 50 percent in England in the second half of the eighteenth century; (2) manufacturers introduced steam-driven machinery to increase output; (3) they established factories to concentrate the labor of their workers; and (4) the production of cotton goods, which were lighter and more versatile than woolens, increased tenfold. Together these factors sparked the Industrial Revolution, which would change the face of Europe—indeed, of the entire world—in the nineteenth century.

Innovations in the technology of cotton production permitted manufacturers to make use of the growing supply of raw cotton shipped from the plantations of

■ **Spinning Jenny**

James Hargreaves invented the spinning jenny in the mid-1760s. It was capable of spinning eight threads off the motion of one wheel, thus increasing the output of a spinner who previously spun one thread at a time. (© Bettmann/CORBIS.)

North America and the Caribbean. In 1733, the Englishman John Kay patented the flying shuttle, which weavers operated by pulling a cord that drove the shuttle to either side, enabling them to "throw" yarn across the loom rather than draw it back and forth by hand. When the flying shuttle came into widespread use in the 1760s, weavers began producing cloth more quickly than spinners could produce the thread. The shortage of spun thread propelled the invention of machines to speed the process of spinning: the spinning jenny and the water frame (a power-driven spinning machine) were introduced in the 1760s. In the following decades, water frames replaced thousands of women hand-spinning thread at home. In 1776, the Scottish engineer James Watt developed an improved steam engine, and, in the 1780s, Edmund Cartwright, an English clergyman and inventor, designed a mechanized loom, which when perfected could be run by a small boy and yield fifteen times the output of a skilled adult weaver working a handloom. By the end of the century, all the new power machinery was assembled in large factories that hired semiskilled men, women, and children to replace skilled weavers.

Historians have no single explanation for why England led the Industrial Revolution. Some have emphasized England's large internal market, increasing population, supply of private investment capital from overseas trade and commercial profits, or natural resources such as coal and iron. Others have cited England's greater opportunities for social mobility, its relative political stability in the eighteenth century, or the pragmatism of the English and Scottish inventors who designed the necessary machinery. These early industrialists hardly had a monopoly on ingenuity, but they did come out of a tradition of independent capitalist enterprise. They also shared a culture of informal scientific education through learned societies and popular lectures (one of the prominent forms of the Enlightenment in Britain). For whatever reasons, the combination of improvements in agricultural production, growth in population and foreign trade, and willingness to invest in new machines and factories appeared first in this relatively small island.

Although the rest of Europe did not industrialize until the nineteenth century, textile manufacturing—long a linchpin in the European economy—expanded dramatically in the eighteenth century even without the introduction of new machines and factories. Textile production increased because of the spread of the "putting-out" or "domestic" system. Hundreds of thousands of families manufactured cloth in every country from Britain to Russia. Under the putting-out system, manufacturers supplied the families with raw materials, such as woolen or cotton fibers. Working at home in a dimly lit room, a whole family labored together. The mother and her children washed the fibers and carded and combed them. Then the mother and oldest daughters spun them into thread. The father, assisted by the children, wove the cloth. The cloth was then finished (bleached, dyed, smoothed, and so on) under the supervision of the manufacturer in a large workshop, located either in town or in the countryside. This system had existed in the textile industry for hundreds of years, but in the eighteenth century it expanded immensely; rural manufacturing began to displace urban workshops of skilled laborers because it was cheaper (women and children worked for far less than skilled men), required little capital investment, was not subject to urban guild restrictions, and could respond more quickly to growing—or falling—demand. The domestic system drew in thousands of peasants in the countryside, and it included not only textiles but also the manufacture of such products as glassware, baskets, nails, and guns.

All across Europe, thousands of people who worked in agriculture became part-time or full-time textile workers. Peasants turned to putting-out work because they did not have enough land to support their families. Men labored off-season and women often worked year-round to augment their meager incomes. At the same time, population growth and general economic improvement meant that demand for cloth increased because more people could afford it. Working-class men in Paris began to wear underclothes, something rare at the beginning of the century. Men and women now bought nightclothes; before, Europeans had slept naked except in cold weather. And white, red, blue, yellow, green, and even pastel shades of cotton now replaced the black, gray, or brown of traditional woolen dress.

■ **REVIEW:** *What were the major differences in the impact of the Enlightenment on nobles, the middle classes, and the lower classes?*

State Power in an Era of Reform

All rulers recognized that manufacturing created new sources of wealth, but the start of industrialization had not yet altered the standard forms of competition between states: commerce and war. The diffusion of Enlightenment ideas of reform had a more immediate impact on the ways European monarchs exercised power than did industrialization. Historians label many of the sovereigns of this time **enlightened despots** or "enlightened absolutists," for they aimed to combine Enlightenment reforms with absolutist powers. Implementation of reforms, such as improvements in the peasantry's condition in Austria, freer markets for grain in France, extension of education in Russia, and new law codes in almost every country, were directly affected by the success or failure in the competition for trade and territory. French losses in the Seven Years' War, for example, prompted the French crown to introduce far-reaching reforms that provoked violent resistance and helped pave the way for the French Revolution of 1789. Reform proved to be a two-edged sword.

War and Diplomacy

Europeans no longer fought devastating wars over religion that killed hundreds of thousands of civilians; instead, professional armies and navies battled for control of overseas empires and for dominance on the European continent. Rulers continued to expand their armies: the Prussian army, for example, nearly tripled in size between 1740 and 1789. Widespread use of flintlock muskets required deployment in long lines, usually three men deep, with each line in turn loading and firing on command. Military strategy became cautious and calculating, but this did not prevent the outbreak of hostilities. The instability of the European balance of power resulted in two major wars, a diplomatic reversal of alliances, and the partition of Poland-Lithuania among Russia, Austria, and Prussia.

The War of the Austrian Succession (1740–1748) broke out when Holy Roman Emperor Charles VI died in 1740 without a male heir. Most European rulers recognized the emperor's chosen heiress, his daughter Maria Theresa, because Charles's Pragmatic Sanction of 1713 had given a woman the right to inherit the Habsburg crown lands. The new king of Prussia, Frederick II, who had just succeeded his father a few months earlier in 1740, saw his chance to grab territory and immediately invaded the rich Austrian province of Silesia. France joined Prussia in an attempt to further humiliate its traditional enemy Austria, and Great Britain allied with Austria to prevent the French from taking the Austrian Netherlands (Map 15.1). French and British colonials in North America soon fought each other all along their boundaries, enlisting native American auxiliaries. Britain tried but failed to isolate the French Caribbean colonies during the war, and hostilities broke out in India, too. Maria Theresa

■ **MAP 15.1 The War of the Austrian Succession, 1740–1748**

The accession of a twenty-three-year-old woman, Maria Theresa, to the Austrian throne gave the new king of Prussia, Frederick II, an opportunity to invade the province of Silesia. France joined on Prussia's side, Great Britain on Austria's. In 1745, the French defeated the British in the Austrian Netherlands and helped instigate a Jacobite uprising in Scotland. The rebellion failed, and British attacks on French overseas shipping forced the French to negotiate. The peace treaties guaranteed Frederick's conquest of Silesia, which soon became the wealthiest province of Prussia. France came to terms with Great Britain to protect its overseas possessions; Austria had to accept the peace settlement after a formal public protest.

(r. 1740–1780) survived only by conceding Silesia to Prussia in order to split the Prussians off from France. The Peace of Aix-la-Chapelle of 1748 recognized Maria Theresa as the heiress to the Austrian lands, and her husband, Francis I, became Holy Roman Emperor, thus reasserting the integrity of the Austrian Empire.

In 1756, a major reversal of alliances reshaped relations among the great powers. Prussia and Great Britain signed a defensive alliance, prompting Austria to overlook two centuries of hostility and ally with France. Austrian and French willingness to put aside their longstanding dynastic rivalry in favor of more immediate strategic interests prompted some to call this a "diplomatic revolution." Russia and Sweden soon joined the Franco-Austrian alliance. When Frederick II invaded Saxony, an ally of Austria, with his bigger and better-disciplined army, the long-simmering hostilities between Great Britain and France over colonial boundaries flared into a general war that became known as the Seven Years' War (1756–1763).

Fighting soon raged around the world (Map 15.2). The French and British battled on land and sea in North America (where the conflict was called the French and Indian War), the West Indies, and India. The two coalitions also fought each other in central Europe. At first, in 1757, Frederick the Great surprised Europe with a spectacular victory at Rossbach in Saxony over a much larger Franco-Austrian army. But in time, Russian and Austrian armies encircled his troops. Frederick despaired: "I believe all is lost. I will not survive the ruin of my country." A fluke of history saved him. Empress Elizabeth of Russia (r. 1741–1762) died and was succeeded by the mentally unstable Peter III, a fanatical admirer of Frederick and things Prussian. Peter withdrew Russia from the war. (He was soon mysteriously murdered, probably at the instigation of his wife, Catherine the Great.) In separate peace treaties with Russia and Austria, Frederick kept all his territory, including Silesia.

The Anglo-French overseas conflicts ended more decisively than the continental land wars. British naval superiority, fully achieved only in the 1750s, enabled Great Britain to rout the French in North America, India, and the West Indies. In the Treaty of Paris of 1763, France ceded Canada to Great Britain and agreed to remove its armies from India, in exchange for keeping its rich West Indian islands. Eagerness to avenge this defeat would motivate France to support the British North American colonists in their War of Independence just fifteen years later.

Although Prussia suffered great losses in the Seven Years' War—some 160,000 Prussian soldiers died either in action or of disease—the army helped vault Prussia to the rank of leading powers. In 1733, Frederick II's father, Frederick William I, had instituted the "canton system," which enrolled peasant youths in each canton (or district) in the army, gave them two or three months of training annually, and allowed them to return to their family farms the rest of the year. They remained "cantonists" (reservists) as long as they were able-bodied. In this fashion, the Prussian military steadily grew in size; by 1740, Prussia had the third or fourth largest army in Europe even though it was tenth in population and thirteenth in land area. Under Frederick II, Prussia's military expenditures rose to two-thirds of the state's revenue. Almost every nobleman served in the army, paying for his own support as an officer and buying a position as company commander. Once retired, the officers returned to their estates, coordinated the canton system, and served as local officials. In this way, the military permeated every aspect of rural society, fusing army and agrarian organi-

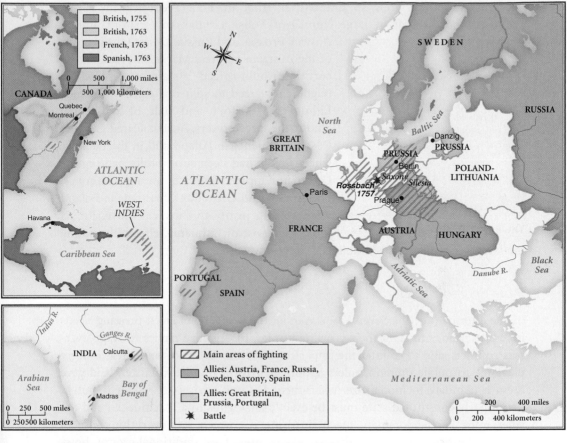

■ **MAP 15.2 The Seven Years' War, 1756–1763**

In what might justly be called the first worldwide war, the French and British fought each other on the European continent, in the West Indies, in the American colonies, and in India. Their international struggle coincided with a realignment of forces within Europe caused by the desire of Austria, France, and Russia to check Prussian growth. Fearing, with reason, a joint Austrian-Russian attack, Frederick II of Prussia invaded Saxony in August 1756. Despite overwhelming odds, Frederick managed time and again to emerge victorious, until the Russians withdrew and the coalition against Prussia fell apart. The treaty between Austria and Prussia simply restored the status quo. The changes overseas were much more dramatic. Britain gained control over Canada and India but gave back to France the West Indian islands of Guadeloupe and Martinique. Britain was now the dominant power on the seas. **For more help analyzing this map,** see the map activity for this chapter in the ONLINE STUDY GUIDE at bedfordstmartins.com/huntconcise.

zation. The army gave the state great power, but the militarization of Prussian society also had a profoundly conservative effect: it kept the peasants enserfed to their lords, and it blocked the middle classes from access to estates or high government positions.

Prussia's power grew so dramatically that in 1772 Frederick the Great proposed the division of large chunks of Polish-Lithuanian territory among

Austria, Prussia, and Russia. Despite the protests of the Austrian empress Maria Theresa that the partition would spread "a stain over my whole reign," she agreed to split one-third of Poland-Lithuania's territory and half of its people among the three powers. Austria feared growing Russian influence in Poland and in the Balkans, where Russia had been successfully battling the Ottoman Empire. Conflicts among Catholics, Protestants, and Orthodox Christians in Poland were used to justify this cynical move. Russia took over most of Lithuania, effectively ending the large but weak Polish-Lithuanian commonwealth.

The First Partition of Poland, 1772

State-Sponsored Reform

In the aftermath of the Seven Years' War, all the belligerents faced pressing needs for more money to fund their growing armies, to organize navies to wage over-seas conflicts, and to counter the impact of inflation. To make tax increases more palatable to public opinion, rulers appointed reform-minded ministers and gave them a mandate to modernize government. As one adviser to Joseph II put it, "A properly constituted state must be exactly analogous to a machine . . . and the ruler must be the foreman, the mainspring . . . which sets everything else in motion." Such reforms always threatened the interests of traditional groups, how-ever, and the spread of Enlightenment ideas aroused sometimes unpredictable desires for more change.

Legal reform, both of the judicial system and of the often disorganized and irregular law codes, was central to the work of many reform-minded monarchs. Although Frederick II favored all things French in culture—he insisted on speaking French in his court and prided himself on his personal friendship with Voltaire—he made Prussian justice the envy of Europe. His institution of a uniform civil justice system created the most consistently administered laws and efficient judi-ciary of the time. Joseph II of Austria (r. 1780–1790) also ordered the compilation of a unified law code, a project that required many years for completion. Catherine II of Russia began such an undertaking even more ambitiously. In 1767, she called together a legislative commission of 564 deputies and asked them to consider a long document called the *Instruction*, which represented her hopes for legal reform based on the ideas of Montesquieu and the Italian writer Cesare Beccaria. Montesquieu had insisted that punishment should fit the crime; he criticized the use of torture and brutal corporal punishment. In his influential book *On Crimes*

■ **Dividing Poland, 1772**
In this contemporary depiction, Catherine the Great, Joseph II, and Frederick II point on the map to the portion of Poland-Lithuania each plans to take. The artist makes it clear that Poland's fate rested in the hands of neighboring rulers, not its own people.
(Time Life Pictures/Getty Images.)

and Punishments (1764), Beccaria argued that laws should be printed for everyone to read and administered in rational procedures, that torture should be abolished as inhumane, and that the accused should be presumed innocent until proven guilty. Despite much discussion and hundreds of petitions and documents about local problems, little came of Catherine's commission because the monarch herself—despite her regard for Voltaire and his fellow philosophes—proved ultimately unwilling to see through far-reaching legal reform.

Rulers everywhere wanted more control over church affairs, and they used Enlightenment criticisms of the organized churches to get their way. In Catholic countries, many government officials resented the influence of the Jesuits, the major Catholic teaching order. The Jesuits trained the Catholic intellectual elite, ran a worldwide missionary network, enjoyed close ties to the papacy, and amassed great wealth. Critics mounted campaigns against the Jesuits in many countries, and by the early 1770s the Society of Jesus had been dissolved in Portugal, France, and Spain. In 1773, Pope Clement XIV (r. 1769–1774) agreed under pressure to disband the order, an edict that held until a reinvigorated papacy restored the society in 1814. Joseph II of Austria not only applauded the suppression of the Jesuits but also required Austrian bishops to swear fidelity and submission to him. Under Joseph, the Austrian state supervised seminaries, reorganized diocesan boundaries, abolished contemplative monastic orders, and confiscated their property to pay for education and poor relief.

Enlightened absolutists also tried to gain greater state authority over education, even while extending education to the lower classes. Joseph II launched the most ambitious educational reforms of the period. In 1774, once the Jesuits had been disbanded, a General School Ordinance in Austria ordered state subsidies for local schools, which the state would regulate. By 1789, one-quarter of the school-age children attended school. In Prussia, the school code of 1763 required all children between the ages of five and thirteen to attend school. Although not enforced uniformly, the Prussian law demonstrated Frederick II's belief that modernization depended on education. Catherine II of Russia also tried to expand elementary education—and the education of women in particular—and founded engineering schools.

No ruler pushed the principle of religious toleration as far as Joseph II of Austria, who became Holy Roman Emperor and co-regent with his mother, Maria Theresa, in 1765 and then ruled alone after 1780. In 1781, he granted freedom of religious worship to Protestants, Orthodox Christians, and Jews. For the first time, these groups were allowed to own property, build schools, enter the professions, and hold political and military offices. The efforts of other rulers to extend religious toleration proved more limited. Louis XVI signed an edict in 1787 restoring French Protestants' civil rights—but still they could not hold political office. Great Britain continued to deny Catholics freedom of open worship and the right to sit in Parliament. Most European states limited the rights and opportunities available to Jews. In Russia, only wealthy Jews could hold municipal office, and in the Papal States, the pope encouraged forced baptism. The leading philosophes opposed persecution of the Jews in theory but often treated them with undisguised contempt. Diderot's comment was all too typical: the Jews, he said, bore "all the defects peculiar to an ignorant and superstitious nation."

Limits of Reform

When enlightened absolutist leaders introduced reforms, they often faced resistance from groups threatened by the proposed changes. The most contentious area of reform was agricultural policy. Whereas Frederick II and Catherine II reinforced the authority of nobles over their serfs, Joseph II tried to remove the burdens of serfdom in the Habsburg lands. In 1781, he abolished the personal aspects of serfdom: serfs could now move freely, enter trades, or marry without their lords' permission. Joseph abolished the tithe to the church, shifted more of the tax burden to the nobility, and converted peasants' labor services into cash payments.

The Austrian nobility furiously resisted these far-reaching reforms. When Joseph died in 1790, his brother Leopold II had to revoke most reforms to appease the nobles. On his deathbed, Joseph recognized the futility of many of his efforts;

as his epitaph he suggested, "Here lies Joseph II, who was unfortunate in all his enterprises." Prussia's Frederick II, like Joseph, encouraged such agricultural innovations as planting potatoes and turnips (new crops that could help feed a growing population), experimenting with cattle breeding, draining swamplands, and clearing forests. But Prussia's noble landlords, the Junkers, continued to expand their estates at the expense of poorer peasants, and Frederick did nothing to ameliorate serfdom except on his own domains.

Reforming ministers also tried to stimulate agricultural improvement in France. Unlike most other western European countries, France still had about 100,000 serfs; though their burdens weighed less heavily than those in eastern Europe, serfdom did not entirely disappear until 1789. A group of economists called the **physiocrats** urged the French government to deregulate the grain trade and make the tax system more equitable to encourage agricultural productivity. In the interest of establishing a free market, they also insisted that urban guilds be abolished because they prevented free entry into the trades. Their proposed reforms applied the Enlightenment emphasis on individual liberties to the economy; Adam Smith took up many of the physiocrats' ideas in his writing in favor of free markets. The French government heeded some of this advice and gave up its system of price controls on grain in 1763, but it had to reverse this decision in 1770 when grain shortages caused a famine.

French reform efforts did not end there. To break the power of the parlements (the thirteen high courts of law that had led the way in opposing royal efforts to increase and equalize taxation), Louis XV appointed a reform-minded chancellor who in 1770 replaced the parlements with courts in which the judges no longer owned their offices and thus could not sell them or pass them on as an inheritance. Justice would then be more impartial. Nevertheless, the judges of the displaced parlements aroused widespread opposition to what they portrayed as tyrannical royal policy. The furor calmed down only when Louis XV died in 1774 and his successor, Louis XVI (r. 1774–1792), yielded to aristocratic demands and restored the old parlements. Louis XV died one of the most despised kings in French history, resented both for his high-handed reforms and for his private vices. Underground pamphlets lampooned him, describing his final mistress, Madame Du Barry, as a prostitute who pandered to the elderly king's well-known taste for young girls. This often pornographic literature linked despotism to the supposedly excessive influence of women at court.

Louis XVI tried to carry out part of the program suggested by the physiocrats, and he chose one of their disciples, Jacques Turgot (1727–1781), as his chief minister. Turgot pushed through several edicts that again freed the grain trade, suppressed many guilds, converted the peasants' forced labor on roads into a money tax payable by all landowners, and reduced court expenses. He also began making plans to introduce a system of elected local assemblies, which would have made government much more representative. Faced with broad-based resistance led by the parlements and his own courtiers, as well as with riots against rising grain prices, Louis XVI dismissed Turgot, and one of the last possibilities to overhaul France's monarchy collapsed.

The failure of reform in France paradoxically reflected the power of Enlightenment ideas; everyone now endorsed Enlightenment ideals but used them for different ends. The nobles in the parlements blocked the French monarchy's reform efforts using the very same Enlightenment language spoken by the crown's ministers. But unlike Austria, the other great power that faced persistent aristocratic resistance to reform, France had a large middle-class public that was increasingly frustrated by the failure to institute social change, a failure that ultimately helped undermine the monarchy itself. Where Frederick II, Catherine II, and even Joseph II used reform to bolster the efficiency of absolutist government, attempts at change in France backfired. French kings found that their ambitious programs for reform succeeded only in arousing unrealistic hopes.

■ **REVIEW:** *What prompted enlightened absolutists to undertake reforms in the second half of the eighteenth century?*

Rebellions against State Power

Although traditional forms of popular discontent had not disappeared, Enlightenment ideals and reforms changed the rules of the game in politics. Governments had become accountable for their actions to a much wider range of people than ever before. In Britain and France, ordinary people rioted when they perceived government as failing to protect them against food shortages. The growth of informed public opinion had its most dramatic consequences in the North American colonies, where a struggle over the British Parliament's right to tax turned into a full-scale war for independence. The American War of Independence showed that once put into practice, Enlightenment ideals could have revolutionary implications.

Food Riots and Peasant Uprisings

Population growth, inflation, and the extension of the market system put added pressure on the already beleaguered poorest classes of people. Seventeenth-century peasants and townspeople had rioted to protest new taxes. In the last half of the eighteenth century, the food supply became the focus of political and social conflict. Poor people living in the villages and the towns believed it was the government's responsibility to ensure that they had enough food, and many governments did stockpile grain to make up for the occasional bad harvest. At the same time, in keeping with Adam Smith's and the French physiocrats' free-market proposals, governments wanted to allow grain prices to rise with market demand, because higher profits would motivate producers to increase the supply of food.

Free trade in grain meant selling to the highest bidder even if that bidder was a foreign merchant. In the short run, in times of scarcity, big landowners and farmers could make huge profits by selling grain outside their hometowns or villages. This practice enraged poor farmers, agricultural workers, and city wage workers, who could not afford the higher prices. Lacking the political means to affect policy, they could enforce their desire for old-fashioned price regulation only by rioting. Most did not pillage or steal grain but rather forced the sale of grain or flour at a "just" price and blocked the shipment of grain out of their villages to other markets. Women often led these "popular price fixings," as they were called in France, in desperate attempts to protect the food supply for their children.

Such food riots occurred regularly in Britain and France in the last half of the eighteenth century. One of the most turbulent was the so-called Flour War in France in 1775. Turgot's deregulation of the grain trade in 1774 caused prices to rise in several provincial cities. Rioting spread from there to the Paris region, where villagers attacked grain convoys heading to the capital city. Local officials often ordered merchants and bakers to sell at the price the rioters demanded, only to find themselves arrested by the central government for overriding free trade. The government brought in troops to restore order and introduced the death penalty for rioting.

Frustrations with serfdom and hopes for a miraculous transformation provoked the Pugachev rebellion in Russia beginning in 1773. An army deserter from the southeast frontier region, Emelian Pugachev (1742–1775) claimed to be Tsar Peter III, the dead husband of Catherine II. Pugachev's appearance seemed to confirm peasant hopes for a "redeemer tsar" who would save the people from oppression. He rallied around him Cossacks like himself who resented the loss of their old tribal independence. Now increasingly enserfed or forced to pay taxes and endure army service, these nomadic bands joined with other serfs, rebellious mineworkers, and Muslim minorities. Catherine dispatched a large army to squelch the uprising, but Pugachev eluded them and the fighting spread. Nearly three million people eventually participated, making this the largest single rebellion in the history of tsarist Russia.

The Pugachev Rebellion, 1773

When Pugachev urged the peasants to attack the nobility and seize their estates, hundreds of noble families perished. Foreign newspapers called it "the revolution in southern Russia" and offered fantastic stories about Pugachev's life history. Finally,

■ **A Cossack**
*Pugachev and many of his
followers were Cossacks,
Ukrainians who set up nomadic
communities of horsemen to
resist outside control, whether
from Turks, Poles, or Russians.
This eighteenth-century engraving captures the common view of
Cossacks as horsemen always
ready for battle but with a
fondness for music too.*
(Bridgeman Art Library.)

the army captured the rebel leader and brought him in an iron cage to Moscow, where he was tortured and executed. In the aftermath, Catherine tightened the nobles' control over their serfs and harshly punished those who dared to criticize serfdom.

Public Opinion and Political Opposition

Peasant uprisings might briefly shake even a powerful monarchy, but the rise of public opinion as a force independent of court society caused more enduring changes in European politics. Across much of Europe and in the North American colonies, demands for broader political participation reflected Enlightenment notions about individual rights. Aristocratic bodies such as the French parlements, which had no legislative role like that of the British Parliament, insisted that the monarch consult them on the nation's affairs, and the new educated elite wanted more influence, too. Newspapers began to cover daily political affairs, and the public learned the basics of political life, despite the strict limits on political participation in most countries.

Monarchs turned to public opinion to seek support against aristocratic groups that opposed reform. Gustavus III of Sweden (r. 1771–1792) called himself "the first citizen of a free people" and promised to deliver the country from "insufferable aristocratic despotism." Shortly after coming to the throne, Gustavus proclaimed a new constitution that divided power between the king and the legislature, abolished the use of torture in the judicial process, and assured some freedom of the press.

In France, both the parlements and the monarch appealed to the public through the printed word. The crown hired writers to make its case; the magistrates of the parlements wrote their own rejoinders. French-language newspapers published in the Dutch Republic provided many people in France with detailed accounts of political news and also gave voice to pro-parlement positions. One of the new French-language newspapers printed inside France, *Le Journal des Dames* ("The Ladies' Journal"), was published by women and mixed short stories and reviews of books and plays with demands for more women's rights.

The Wilkes affair in Great Britain showed that public opinion could be mobilized to challenge a government. In 1763, during the reign of George III (r. 1760–1820), John Wilkes, a member of Parliament, attacked the government in his newspaper, *North Briton*, and sued the crown when he was arrested. He won his release as well as damages. When he was reelected, Parliament denied him his seat, not once but three times.

The Wilkes episode soon escalated into a major campaign against the corruption and social exclusiveness of Parliament, complaints the Levellers had first raised during the English Revolution of the late 1640s. Newspapers, magazines, pamphlets, handbills, and cheap editions of Wilkes's collected works all helped promote his cause. Those who could not vote demonstrated for Wilkes. In one incident, eleven people died when soldiers broke up a huge gathering of his supporters. The slogan "Wilkes and Liberty" appeared on walls all over London. Middle-class voters formed a Society of Supporters of the Bill of Rights, which circulated petitions for Wilkes; they gained the support of about one-fourth of all the voters. The more determined Wilkesites proposed sweeping reforms of Parliament, including more frequent elections, more representation for the counties, elimination of "rotten boroughs" (election districts so small that they could be controlled by one big patron), and restrictions of pensions used by the crown to gain support. These demands would be at the heart of agitation for parliamentary reform in Britain for decades to come.

Popular demonstrations did not always support reforms. In 1780, the Gordon riots devastated London. They were named after the fanatical anti-Catholic crusader Lord George Gordon, who helped organize huge marches and petition campaigns against a bill the House of Commons passed to grant limited toleration to Catholics. The demonstrations culminated in a seven-day riot that left fifty buildings destroyed and three hundred people dead. Despite the continuing limitation on voting rights in Great Britain, British politicians were learning that they could ignore public opinion only at their peril.

Political opposition also took artistic forms, particularly in countries where governments restricted organized political activity. A striking example of a play with a political message was *The Marriage of Figaro* (1784) by Pierre-Augustin Caron de Beaumarchais (1732–1799), a watchmaker, a judge, a gunrunner in the American War of Independence, and a French spy in Britain. *The Marriage of Figaro* was first a hit at court, when Queen Marie-Antoinette had it read for her friends. But when her husband, Louis XVI, read it, he forbade its production on the grounds that "this man mocks at everything that should be respected in government." When finally performed publicly, the play caused a sensation. The chief character, Figaro, is a clever servant who gets the better of his noble employer. When speaking of the count, he cries, "What have you done to deserve so many rewards? You went to the trouble of being born, and nothing more." Two years later, Mozart based an equally famous but somewhat tamer opera on Beaumarchais's story.

Revolution in North America

Oppositional forms of public opinion came to a head in Great Britain's North American colonies, where the result was American independence and the establishment of a republican constitution that stood in stark contrast to most European regimes. The successful revolution was the only blow to Britain's increasing dominance in world affairs in the eighteenth century, and as such it was another aspect of the power rivalries existing at that time. Yet many Europeans saw the American War of Independence, or the American Revolution (1775–1783), as a triumph for Enlightenment ideas. As one German writer exclaimed in 1777, American victory would give "greater scope to the Enlightenment, new keenness to the thinking of peoples and new life to the spirit of liberty."

The American revolutionary leaders had been influenced by a common Atlantic civilization; they participated in the Enlightenment and shared political ideas with the opposition Whigs in Britain. Supporters demonstrated for Wilkes in South Carolina and Boston, and the South Carolina legislature donated a substantial sum to the Society of Supporters of the Bill of Rights. In the 1760s and 1770s, both British and American opposition leaders became convinced that the British government was growing increasingly corrupt and despotic. British radicals wanted to reform Parliament so the voices of a broader, more representative segment of the population would be heard. The colonies had no representatives in Parliament, and colonists claimed that "no taxation without representation" should be allowed. Indeed, they denied that Parliament had any jurisdiction over the colonies, insisting that the king govern them through colonial legislatures and recognize their traditional British liberties. The failure of the "Wilkes and Liberty"

■ Overthrowing British Authority

The uncompromising attitude of the British government went a long way toward dissolving long-standing loyalties to the home country. During the American War of Independence, residents of New York City pulled down the statue of the hated George III. (Lafayette College Art Collection, Easton, PA.)

campaign to produce concrete results convinced many Americans that Parliament was hopelessly tainted and that they would have to stand up for their rights as British subjects.

The British colonies remained loyal to the crown until Parliament's encroachment on their autonomy and the elimination of the French threat at the end of the Seven Years' War transformed colonial attitudes. Unconsciously, perhaps, the colonies had begun to form a separate nation; their economies generally flourished in the eighteenth century, and between 1750 and 1776 their population almost doubled. With the British clamoring for lower taxes and the colonists paying only a fraction of the tax rate levied on the Britons at home, Parliament passed new taxes, including the Stamp Act in 1765, which required a special tax stamp on all legal documents and publications. After violent rioting in the colonies, the tax was repealed, but in 1773 a new Tea Act revived colonial resistance, which culminated in the so-called Boston Tea Party of 1773. Colonists dressed as Indians boarded British ships and dumped the imported tea (by this time an enormously popular beverage) into Boston's harbor. The British government tried to clamp down on the unrest, but British troops in the colonies soon found themselves fighting locally organized militias.

Political opposition in the American colonies turned belligerent when Britain threatened to use force to maintain control. In 1774, the First Continental Congress convened, composed of delegates from all the colonies, and unsuccessfully petitioned the crown for redress. The next year the Second Continental Congress organized an army with George Washington in command. After actual fighting had begun, in 1776, the congress proclaimed the Declaration of Independence. An eloquent statement of the American cause written by Thomas Jefferson, a delegate from Virginia, the Declaration of Independence was couched in the language of universal human rights, which enlightened Europeans could be expected to understand. George III denounced the American "traitors and rebels." But European newspapers enthusiastically reported on every American response to "the cruel acts of oppression they have been made to suffer." Two years after the Declaration was issued, France boosted the American cause by entering on the colonists' side in 1778. Spain, too, saw an opportunity to check the growing power of Britain, though without actually endorsing American independence out of fear of the response of its Latin American colonies. Spain declared war on Britain in 1779; in 1780, Great Britain declared war on the Dutch Republic in retaliation for Dutch support of the rebels. The worldwide conflict that resulted was more than Britain could handle. The American colonies achieved their independence in the peace treaty of 1783.

The newly independent states still faced the challenge of republican self-government. The Articles of Confederation, drawn up in 1777 as a provisional constitution, proved weak because they gave the central government few powers. In 1787, a constitutional convention met in Philadelphia to draft a new constitution. It established a two-house legislature, an indirectly elected president, and an independent judiciary. The Constitution's preamble insisted explicitly, for the first time in history, that government derived its power solely from the people and did not depend on divine right or on the tradition of royalty or aristocracy. The new educated elite of the eighteenth century had now created government based on a "social contract" among male, property-owning, white citizens. It was by no means a complete democracy, and women and slaves were excluded from political participation. But the new government represented a radical departure from European models. In 1791, the Bill of Rights was appended to the Constitution outlining the essential rights (such as freedom of speech) that the government could never overturn. Although slavery continued in the American republic, the new emphasis on rights helped fuel a movement for its abolition in both Britain and the United States.

Interest in the new republic was greatest in France. The U.S. Constitution and various state constitutions were published in French with commentary by leading thinkers. Even more important in the long run were the effects of the American war. Dutch losses to Great Britain aroused a widespread movement for political reform in the Dutch Republic, and debts incurred by France in supporting the

IMPORTANT DATES			
1740–1748	War of the Austrian Succession: France, Spain, and Prussia versus Austria and Great Britain	1776	American Declaration of Independence from Great Britain; James Watt improves the steam engine, making it suitable for new industrial projects; Adam Smith publishes *The Wealth of Nations*
1751–1772	*Encyclopedia* published in France		
1756–1763	Seven Years' War fought in Europe, India, and the American colonies		
		1781	Joseph II of Austria undertakes wide-reaching reform; Immanuel Kant publishes *The Critique of Pure Reason*
1762	Jean-Jacques Rousseau publishes *The Social Contract* and *Émile*		
1764	Voltaire publishes *Philosophical Dictionary*	1785	Catherine the Great's Charter of the Nobility grants nobles exclusive control over their serfs in exchange for subservience to the state
1770	Louis XV of France fails to break the power of the French law courts		
1772	First partition of Poland	1787	Delegates from the states draft a new U.S. Constitution
1773	Pugachev rebellion of Russian peasants		

American colonies would soon force the French monarchy to the edge of bank-ruptcy and then to revolution. Ultimately, the entire European system of royal rule would be challenged.

■ **REVIEW:** *Why did public opinion become a new factor in politics in the second half of the eighteenth century?*

Conclusion

The American Revolution was the most profound practical result of the general European movement known as the Enlightenment. When Thomas Jefferson looked back many years later on the Declaration of Independence, he said he hoped it would be "the signal of arousing men to burst the chains under which monkish ignorance and superstition had persuaded them to bind themselves." What began as a cosmopolitan movement of a few intellectuals in the first half of the eighteenth century reached a relatively wide audience among the educated elite of men and women. The spirit of reform swept from the salons and coffeehouses into the halls of government. Reasoned, scientific inquiry into the causes of social misery and laws defending individual rights and freedoms gained adherents everywhere.

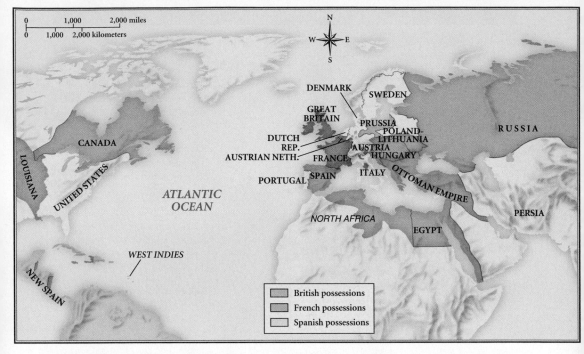

■ MAPPING THE WEST Europe and the World, c. 1780

Although Great Britain lost control over the British North American colonies, which became the new United States, European influence on the rest of the world grew dramatically in the eighteenth century. The slave trade linked European ports to African slave-trading outposts and to plantations in the Caribbean, South America, and North America. The European countries on the Atlantic Ocean benefited most from this trade. Yet almost all of Africa, China, Japan, and large parts of India still resisted European incursion, and the Ottoman Empire, with its massive territories, still towered over most European countries.

For most Europeans, however, Enlightenment remained a promise rather than a reality. Rulers such as Catherine the Great had every intention of retaining their full, often unchecked, powers, even as they corresponded with leading philosophes, announced support for their causes, and entertained them at their courts. Moreover, would-be reformers often found themselves thwarted by the resistance of nobles, by the priorities rulers gave to waging wars, or by popular resistance to deregulation of trade that stripped away protection against the uncertainties of the market. Yet even the failure of reform contributed to the ferment in Europe after 1770. Peasant rebellions in eastern Europe, the "Wilkes and Liberty" campaign in Great Britain, the struggle over reform in France, and the revolution in America all occurred at about the same time, and their conjunction convinced many Europeans that the world was in fact changing. Just how much it had changed, and whether the change was for better or for worse, would become more evident in the next decades.

■ MAKING CONNECTIONS

1. *Why would rulers feel ambivalent about the Enlightenment, supporting reform on the one hand, while clamping down on political dissent on the other?*

2. *Which major developments in the second half of the eighteenth century ran counter to the influence of the Enlightenment?*

■ FOR FURTHER EXPLORATION

For further reading and online research ideas, see the Suggested References on page SR-8 at the back of the book.

For practice quizzes, a customized study plan, and other study tools, see the ONLINE STUDY GUIDE at bedfordstmartins.com/huntconcise.

For primary-source material from this period, see Chapter 15 in *Sources of THE MAKING OF THE WEST: A CONCISE HISTORY*, Second Edition.

The French Revolution and Napoleon
1789–1815

O N OCTOBER 5, 1789, A CROWD OF SEVERAL THOUSAND WOMEN marched in a drenching rain twelve miles from the center of Paris to Versailles. They demanded the king's help in securing more grain for the hungry and his reassurance that he did not intend to resist the emerging revolutionary movement. Joined by thousands of men who came from Paris to reinforce them, the next morning they broke into the royal family's private apartments. To prevent further bloodshed—two of the royal bodyguards had already been killed and their heads paraded on pikes—the king agreed to move his family and his government back to Paris. A dramatic procession guarded by thousands of ordinary men and women made its slow way back to Paris. The people's proud display of cannons and pikes underlined the fundamental transformation that was occurring. Ordinary people had forced the king of France to respond to their grievances. The French monarchy was in danger, and if such a powerful and long-lasting institution could come under fire, then could any monarch of Europe rest easy?

Although even the keenest political observer did not predict its eruption in 1789, the French Revolution had its immediate origins in a constitutional crisis provoked by a growing government deficit, traceable to French involvement in the

■ **Women's March to Versailles**
Thousands of prints broadcast the events of the French Revolution to the public in France and elsewhere. They varied from fine art engravings signed by the artist to anonymous simple woodblock prints. This colored etching shows a crowd of armed women marching to Versailles on October 5, 1789, to confront the king. The sight of armed women frightened many observers and demonstrated that the Revolution was not only men's affair. (AKG-Images.)

651

American War of Independence. The constitutional crisis came to a head on July 14, 1789, when armed Parisians captured the Bastille, a royal fortress and symbol of monarchical authority in the center of the capital. The fall of the Bastille, like the women's march to Versailles three months later, showed the determination of the common people to put their mark on events.

The French Revolution first grabbed the attention of the entire world because it seemed to promise universal human rights, constitutional government, and broad-based political participation. In the words of its most famous slogan, it pledged "Liberty, Equality, and Fraternity" for all. The revolutionaries used a blueprint based on the Enlightenment idea of reason to remake all of society and politics: they executed the king and queen, established a republic for the first time in French history, abolished nobility, and gave the vote to almost all adult men. Even as the Revolution promised democracy, however, it also inaugurated a cycle of violence and intimidation. When the revolutionaries encountered resistance to their programs, they set up a government of terror to compel obedience. Some historians therefore see in the French Revolution the origins of modern totalitarianism—that is, governments that try to control every aspect of life, including daily activities, while limiting all forms of political dissent.

The Revolution might have remained a strictly French affair if war had not involved the rest of Europe. After 1792, huge French republican armies, fueled by patriotic nationalism, marched across Europe, promising liberation from traditional monarchies but often delivering old-fashioned conquest and annexation. French victories spread revolutionary ideas far and wide, from the colonies in the Caribbean, where the first successful slave revolt established the republic of Haiti, to Poland and Egypt. The army's success ultimately undermined the republic and made possible the rise of Napoleon Bonaparte, a remarkable young general from Corsica, an island off Italy, who brought France more wars, more conquests, and a form of military dictatorship.

Bonaparte ended the French Revolution even while maintaining some of its most important innovations. He transformed France from a democratically elected republic to an empire with a new aristocracy based on military service. Although he tolerated no opposition at home, he prided himself on bringing French-style liberation to peoples elsewhere. Yet he also continued the revolutionary policy of conquest and annexation; by 1812, he ruled over an empire bigger than any Europe had seen since Roman times. Eventually, resistance to the French armies and the ever-mounting costs of military glory toppled Napoleon I, but not before he had established himself as an almost mythic figure. Reformer, revolutionary, dictator, and empire-builder: Napoleon played all the roles and has remained a figure of controversy right down to the present. The French Revolution produced many surprises; Napoleon Bonaparte was the most astonishing of them.

The Revolution of Rights and Reason

Between 1787 and 1789, revolts in the name of liberty broke out in the Dutch Republic, the Austrian Netherlands (present-day Belgium and Luxembourg), and Poland as well as in France. At the same time, the newly independent United States of America prepared a new federal constitution. Historians have sometimes referred to these revolts as the "Atlantic revolutions" because so many protest movements arose in countries on both shores of the North Atlantic in the late 1700s. These revolutions were the product of long-term prosperity and high expectations: Europeans in general were wealthier, healthier, more numerous, and better educated than they had ever been before; and the Dutch, Belgian, and French societies were among the wealthiest and best educated within Europe. Most scholars agree, however, that the French Revolution differed greatly from the others. Not only was France the richest, most powerful, and most populous state in western Europe, but its revolution was also more violent, longer lasting, and ultimately more influential.

Protesters in the Low Countries and Poland

Political protests in the Dutch Republic attracted European attention because Dutch banks still controlled a hefty portion of the world's capital at the end of the eighteenth century, even though the Dutch Republic's role in international politics had diminished. Government-sponsored Dutch banks owned 40 percent of the British national debt; by 1796, they held the entire foreign debt of the United States. Relations with the British deteriorated during the American War of Independence, however, and by the middle of the 1780s, agitation in favor of the Americans had boiled over into an attack on the stadholder, the prince of Orange, who favored close ties with Great Britain.

Building on support among middle-class bankers, merchants, and writers who favored the American cause, the Dutch Patriots, as the protesters called themselves, demanded political reforms and organized armed citizen militias of men, called Free Corps. Parading under banners that read "Liberty or Death," they forced local officials to set up new elections to replace councils that had been packed with Orangist supporters through patronage or family connections. The future American president John Adams happened to be visiting Utrecht when such a revolt occurred. He wrote admiringly to Thomas Jefferson that "in no instance, of ancient or modern History, have the People ever asserted more unequivocally their own inherent and unalienable Sovereignty." When the Free Corps took on the troops of the prince of Orange in 1787, Frederick William II of Prussia, whose sister had married the stadholder, intervened with tacit British support. Thousands of Prussian troops soon occupied Utrecht and Amsterdam, and the House of Orange regained its former position.

Internal social divisions paved the way for successful outside intervention. Many of the Patriots from the richest merchant families feared the growing power of the Free Corps. The Free Corps wanted a more democratic form of government and encouraged the publication of pamphlets and cartoons attacking the prince and his wife, the rapid spread of clubs and societies made up of common people, and crowd-pleasing public ceremonies, such as parades and bonfires, which sometimes turned into riots. In the aftermath of the Prussian invasion in September 1787, the Orangists got their revenge: lower-class mobs pillaged the houses of prosperous Patriot leaders, forcing many to flee to the United States, France, or the Austrian Netherlands. Those Patriots who remained nursed their grievances until the French republican armies invaded in 1795.

The Austrian Netherlands experienced unrest, too. The Belgians of the ten provinces there might have remained tranquil if Austrian emperor Joseph II had not tried to introduce Enlightenment-inspired reforms. Joseph abolished torture, decreed toleration for Jews and Protestants (in this resolutely Catholic area), and suppressed monasteries. His reorganization of the administrative and judicial systems eliminated many offices that belonged to nobles and lawyers, sparking resistance among the upper classes in 1788. They claimed that they wanted only to defend historic local liberties against an overbearing government. Their resistance galvanized democrats, who wanted a more representative government and organized clubs to give voice to their demands. By late 1789, each province had separately declared its independence, and the Austrian administration had collapsed. Delegates from the various provinces declared themselves the United States of Belgium, a clear reference to the American precedent.

Once again, however, internal squabbling doomed the rebels. In the face of increasing democratic ferment, aristocratic leaders drew to their side the Catholic clergy and peasants, who had little sympathy for the democrats of the cities. Every Sunday in May and June 1790, thousands of peasant men and women, led by their priests, streamed into Brussels carrying crucifixes, nooses, and pitchforks to intimidate the democrats and defend the church. Faced with the choice between the Austrian emperor and "our current tyrants," the democrats chose to support the return of the Austrians under Emperor Leopold II (r. 1790–1792), who had succeeded his brother.

A reform party calling itself the Patriots also emerged in Poland, which had been shocked by the loss of a third of its territory in the First Partition of 1772. The Patriots looked to King Stanislaw August Poniatowski (r. 1764–1795) to lead them. Bogged down in war with the Ottoman Turks, Catherine the Great of Russia could not block the summoning in 1788 of a reform-minded parliament. Amid much oratory denouncing Russian overlordship, the parliament enacted the constitution of May 3, 1791, which at last freed the two-house legislature from the individual veto power of every aristocrat, granted townspeople limited political rights, and vaguely promised future Jewish emancipation. Abolishing serfdom was hardly mentioned. Catherine could not countenance the spread of revolution into eastern Europe and within a year engineered the downfall of the Patriots and further weakened the Polish state.

Origins of the French Revolution, 1787–1789

Many French enthusiastically greeted the American experiment in republican government and supported the Dutch, Belgian, and Polish patriots. But they did not expect the United States or the Dutch Republic to provide them a model. Montesquieu and Rousseau, the leading political theorists of the Enlightenment, taught that republics suited only small countries, not big ones like France. Moreover, the French monarchy on the surface seemed as strong as ever. After suffering humiliation at the hands of the British in the Seven Years' War (1756–1763), the French had regained international prestige by supporting the victorious Americans, and the monarchy had shown its eagerness to promote reforms. In 1787, for example, the French crown granted civil rights to Protestants. Yet by the late 1780s, the French monarchy faced a mounting deficit that before long provoked a political crisis of epic proportions.

France's fiscal problems stemmed from its support of the Americans against the British in the American War of Independence. About half of the French national budget went to paying interest on the debt that had accumulated. In contrast to Great Britain, which had a national bank to help raise loans for the government, the French government lived off relatively short-term, high-interest loans from private sources including Swiss banks, government annuities, and advances from tax collectors. For years the French government had been trying unsuccessfully to modernize the tax system to make it more equitable. The peasants bore the greatest burden of taxes and resented the exemptions enjoyed by the nobles and clergy. Private contractors collected many taxes and pocketed a large share of the proceeds. With the growing support of public opinion, the bond and annuity holders from the middle and upper classes now demanded a clearer system of fiscal accountability.

Faced with budget shortfalls and growing criticism of Queen Marie-Antoinette's personal spending, Louis XVI (r. 1774–1792) tried every available avenue to raise funds. In 1787, he submitted proposals for reform to an Assembly of Notables, a group of handpicked nobles, clergymen, and officials. When this group refused to cooperate, the king presented his plan for a more uniform land tax to his old rival, the parlement of Paris. When it too refused, he ordered the parlement judges into exile in the provinces. Overnight, the judges (members of the nobility because of the offices they held) became popular heroes for resisting the king's "tyranny"; in reality, however, the judges, like the notables, wanted reform only on their own terms. Louis finally gave in to demands that he call a meeting of the **Estates General**, which had last met 175 years before.

REVEIL DU TIERS ETAT.

Ma fainte, il étoit tems que je me réveillasse, car l'oppression de mes fers me donnoins le cochemar un peu trop fort.

▪ The Third Estate Awakens

This print, produced after the fall of the Bastille (notice the two heads raised on pikes outside the prison), shows a clergyman (First Estate) and a nobleman (Second Estate) alarmed by the awakening of the commoners (Third Estate). The Third Estate breaks the chains of oppression and arms itself to battle for its rights. The message is that social conflicts lay behind the political struggles in the Estates General. **For more help analyzing this image,** see the visual activity for this chapter in the ONLINE STUDY GUIDE at bedfordstmartins.com/huntconcise.
(Réunion des Musées Nationaux/Art Resource, NY.)

The calling of the Estates General electrified public opinion. Who would determine the fate of the nation? There were three estates, or orders, in the Estates General. The deputies in the First Estate represented some 100,000 clergy of the Catholic church, which owned about 10 percent of the land and collected its own taxes (the tithe) on peasants. The deputies of the Second Estate represented the nobility, about 400,000 men and women who owned about 25 percent of the land and collected seigneurial dues and rents from their peasant tenants. The deputies of the Third Estate represented everyone else, at least 95 percent of the nation. In 1614, at the last meeting of the Estates General, each order had voted separately, and either the clergy or the nobility could therefore veto any decision of the Third Estate. Before the elections to the Estates General in 1789, the king agreed to double the number of deputies for the Third Estate (making them equal in number to the other two combined), but he left it to the Estates General to decide whether the estates would continue to vote separately by order rather than by individual head. Voting by order would conserve the traditional powers of the clergy and nobility; voting by head would give the Third Estate an advantage because many clergymen and even some nobles sympathized with the Third Estate.

As the state's censorship apparatus broke down, pamphleteers by the hundreds denounced the traditional privileges of the nobility and clergy and called for voting by head rather than by order. In the winter and spring of 1789, thousands of men (and a few women by proxy) held meetings to elect deputies and write down their grievances. The effect was immediate. Although educated men dominated the meetings at the regional level, the humblest peasants also voted in their villages and burst forth with complaints, especially about taxes. As one villager lamented, "The last crust of bread has been taken from us." The grievance lists demanded fairer distribution of taxes, constitutional recognition of rights, revision of the law codes, and a variety of other reforms. The meetings and the compiling of grievances raised expectations that the Estates General would help the king to solve all the nation's ills.

These new hopes soared just at the moment France experienced an increasingly rare but always dangerous food shortage. Bad weather damaged the harvest of 1788, causing bread prices to rise in many places in the spring and summer of 1789 and threatening starvation for the poorest people. A serious slump in textile production had been causing massive unemployment since 1786. Hundreds of thousands of textile workers were out of work and hungry, adding another volatile element to an already tense situation.

When some twelve hundred deputies journeyed to the king's palace of Versailles for the opening of the Estates General in May 1789, many readers avidly followed the developments in newspapers that sprouted overnight. Although most nobles insisted on voting by order, the deputies of the Third Estate refused to proceed on that basis. After six weeks of stalemate, on June 17, 1789, the deputies of the Third Estate took unilateral action and declared themselves and whoever would join them the "National Assembly," in which each deputy would vote as an individual. Two days later, the clergy voted by a narrow margin to join them. Barred from their meeting hall on June 20, the deputies met on a nearby tennis court and swore an oath not to disband until they had given France a constitution that reflected their newly declared authority. This "tennis court oath" expressed the determination of the Third Estate to carry through a constitutional revolution.

At first Louis appeared to agree to the new representative assembly, but he also ordered thousands of soldiers to march to Paris. The deputies who supported

■ MAP 16.1 Revolutionary Paris, 1789

The French Revolution began with the fall of the Bastille on July 14, 1789. The huge fortified prison was located in a working-class neighborhood on the eastern side of the city. Before attacking the Bastille, crowds had torn down many of the customs booths located in the wall of the Farmers General (the private company in charge of tax collection) and had taken the weapons stored in the Hôtel des Invalides, a veterans' hospital on the western side of the city where the upper classes lived. In other words, the crowds had roamed throughout the city.

the new National Assembly feared a plot by the king and high-ranking nobles to arrest them and disperse the assembly. "Everyone is convinced that the approach of the troops covers some violent design," one deputy wrote home. Their fears were confirmed when on July 11 the king fired Jacques Necker, the Swiss Protestant finance minister and the one high official regarded as sympathetic to the deputies' cause.

The popular reaction in Paris to Necker's dismissal and the threat of military force changed the course of the French Revolution. When the news spread, the common people in Paris began to arm themselves and attack places where either grain or arms were thought to be stored (Map 16.1). A deputy in Versailles reported home: "Today all of the evils overwhelm France, and we are between despotism, carnage, and famine." On July 14, 1789, an armed crowd marched on the Bastille, the fortified prison that symbolized royal authority. After a chaotic battle in which one hundred armed citizens died, the prison officials surrendered.

The angry crowd shot and stabbed the governor of the prison and flaunted his head on a pike.

The fall of the Bastille (an event now commemorated as a French national holiday) set an important precedent. The common people showed themselves willing to intervene violently at a crucial political moment. All over France, food riots turned into local revolts. Local governments were forced out of power and replaced by committees of "patriots" loyal to the revolutionary cause. The patriots relied on newly formed National Guard units composed of civilians. One of their first duties was to calm the peasants in the countryside, who feared that the beggars and vagrants crowding the roads might be part of an aristocratic plot to starve the people by burning crops or barns. In some places, the **Great Fear** (the term used by historians to describe this rural panic) turned into peasant attacks on aristocrats or on seigneurial records of peasants' dues kept in the lord's château. The king's government began to crumble. One of Louis XVI's brothers and many other leading aristocrats fled into exile. In Paris, the Marquis de Lafayette, a hero of the American War of Independence and a noble deputy in the National Assembly, became commander of the new National Guard. The Revolution thus had its first heroes, its first victims, and its first enemies.

From Monarchy to Republic

Until July 1789, the French Revolution followed a course much like that of the protest movements in the Low Countries. Unlike the Dutch and Belgian uprisings, however, the French Revolution did not come to a quick end. The French revolutionaries first tried to establish a constitutional monarchy based on the Enlightenment principles of human rights and rational government. This effort failed when the king attempted to raise a counterrevolutionary army. When war broke out in 1792, new tensions culminated in a second revolution on August 10, 1792, that deposed the king and established a republic in which all power rested in an elected legislature.

Before drafting a new constitution, the deputies of the National Assembly had to confront growing violence in the countryside, as peasants refused to pay seigneurial dues to their landlords and in some places took matters into their own hands and attacked lords' castles and records. In response to peasant unrest, on the night of August 4, 1789, noble deputies announced their willingness to give up their tax exemptions and seigneurial dues. By the end of the night, amid wild enthusiasm, dozens of deputies had come to the podium to relinquish the tax exemptions of their own professional groups, towns, or provinces. The National Assembly decreed the abolition of what it called "the feudal regime"—that is, it freed the few remaining serfs and eliminated all special privileges in matters of taxation, including all seigneurial dues on the land (a few days later, the deputies insisted on financial compensation for some of these dues, but most peasants refused to pay). Peasants had achieved their goals. The Assembly also mandated equality of opportunity in access to official posts. Talent, rather than birth, was to be the key to success. Enlightenment principles were beginning to become law.

Three weeks later, the deputies drew up a **Declaration of the Rights of Man and of the Citizen** as a preamble to the constitution. In words reminiscent of the American Declaration of Independence, whose author Thomas Jefferson was in Paris at the time, it proclaimed, "Men are born and remain free and equal in rights." The Declaration granted freedom of religion, freedom of the press, equality of taxation, and equality before the law. By pronouncing all "men" free and equal, the Declaration immediately created new dilemmas. Did women have equal rights with men? What about free blacks in the colonies? How could slavery be justified if all men were born free? Did religious toleration of Protestants and Jews include equal political rights? Women never received the right to vote during the French Revolution, though Protestant and Jewish men did. Women were theoretically citizens under civil law but without the right to full political participation.

Some women did not accept their exclusion, viewing it as a betrayal of the promised new order. In addition to joining demonstrations, such as the march to Versailles in October 1789, women wrote petitions, published tracts, and organized political clubs to demand more participation. In her Declaration of the Rights of Women of 1791, Olympe de Gouges (1748–1793) played on the language of the official Declaration to make the point that women should also be included. In Article I, she announced, "Woman is born free and lives equal to man in her rights." Unresponsive to such calls for women's equality, the National Assembly gave voting rights only to white men who paid a minimum level of taxation. The Constitution defined them as the "active citizens"; all others were "passive."

Despite these limitations, France became a constitutional monarchy in which the king served simply as the leading state functionary. A one-house legislature was responsible for making laws. The king could hold up enactment of laws but could not veto them absolutely. The nobles not only lost their tax exemptions; on June 19, 1790, the Assembly abolished all titles of nobility. The deputies replaced the old administrative divisions of the provinces with a national system of eighty-three regional departments (*départements*) with identical administrative and legal structures (Map 16.2). All officials were elected; no offices could be bought and sold. The deputies also abolished the old taxes and replaced them with new ones that were supposed to be uniformly levied. The National Assembly had difficulty collecting taxes, however, because many people had expected a substantial cut in the tax rate. The new administrative system survived, nonetheless, and the departments are still the basic units of the French state today.

■ **MAP 16.2 Redrawing the Map of France, 1789–1791**

*Before 1789, France was divided into provinces, each with its own administration. Some
provinces had their own law codes. The new National Assembly determined to install uniform
administrations and laws for the entire country. Discussion of the administrative reforms began
in October 1789 and was completed on February 15, 1790, when the Assembly voted to divide
the provinces into eighty-three departments with names based on their geographical characteristics: Basses-Pyrénées for the Pyrenees mountains, Haute-Marne for the Marne River, and so on.
By eliminating the old names of provinces, with their historical associations, and supplanting
them with geographical ones, the Assembly aimed to show that reason would now govern all
French affairs.*

When the deputies turned to reforming the Catholic church, they created
enduring conflicts. Motivated partly by the ongoing financial crisis, the Assembly
confiscated all the church's property and promised to pay clerical salaries in return.
A Civil Constitution of the Clergy passed in July 1790 set pay scales for the clergy
and provided that the voters elect their own parish priests and bishops just as they
elected other officials. The impounded church property served as a guarantee for
the new paper money, called assignats, issued by the government. The government
began to sell the church lands to the highest bidders in state auctions. The sales
increased the landholdings of wealthy city dwellers and prosperous peasants
but cut the ground out from under the assignats. Convinced that monastic life

encouraged idleness and a decline in the nation's population, the deputies also outlawed any future monastic vows and encouraged monks and nuns to return to private life on state pensions.

Faced with resistance to these changes, in November 1790 the National Assembly required all clergy to swear an oath of loyalty to the Civil Constitution of the Clergy. Pope Pius VI in Rome condemned the constitution, and half of the French clergy refused to take the oath. The oath of allegiance permanently divided the Catholic population, which had to choose between loyalty to the old church and commitment to the Revolution with its "constitutional" church. The revolutionary government passed laws against the clergy who refused the oath, forcing some into exile and executing others as traitors. Riots and demonstrations led by women greeted many of the oath-taking priests who showed up to replace those who refused.

Louis XVI deeply resented the new limits on his powers and in particular the changes imposed on the Catholic church. On June 20, 1791, the royal family escaped in disguise from the Tuileries palace in Paris and fled to the eastern border of France, where they hoped to gather support from Austrian emperor Leopold II, the brother of Marie-Antoinette. The plans went awry when a postmaster recognized the king from his portrait on the new French money, and the royal family was arrested at Varennes, forty miles from the Austrian border. The National Assembly tried to depict this incident as a kidnapping, but the "flight to Varennes" touched off demonstrations in Paris against the royal family, whom some now regarded as traitors. Cartoons circulated depicting the royal family as animals being returned "to the stable."

The Constitution finally completed in 1791 provided for the immediate election of a new Legislative Assembly. The status of the king might have remained uncertain if war had not intervened, but by early 1792 everyone seemed intent on war with Austria. Louis and Marie-Antoinette hoped that war would lead to the definitive defeat of the Revolution, whereas the deputies in the new assembly who favored a republic believed that war would reveal the king's treachery and lead to his downfall. On April 20, 1792, Louis declared war on Austria. Prussia immediately entered on the Austrian side. Thousands of French aristocrats, including two-thirds of the army officer corps, had already emigrated, including both the king's brothers, and they were gathering along France's eastern border in expectation of joining Leopold's counterrevolutionary army.

When fighting broke out in 1792, all the powers expected a brief and relatively contained war. Instead, it would continue despite brief interruptions for the next twenty-three years. War had an immediate radicalizing effect on French politics. When the French armies proved woefully unprepared for battle, the authority of the Legislative Assembly came under fire. In June 1792, an angry crowd invaded the hall of the Assembly in Paris and threatened the royal family. When the Prussians crossed the border and advanced on Paris, the Prussian commander, the duke of Brunswick, issued a manifesto announcing that Paris would be totally destroyed if the royal family suffered any violence.

The ordinary people of Paris did not passively await their fate. Known as **sans-culottes** ("without breeches")—because men who worked with their hands wore long trousers rather than the knee breeches of the upper classes— they had followed every twist and turn in revolutionary fortunes. Political clubs had multiplied since the founding in 1789 of the first and most influential of them, the **Jacobin Club**, named after the former monastery in Paris where the club first met. Every local district in Paris had its club, where men and women listened to the news of the day and discussed their opinions. Faced with the threat of military retaliation and frustrated with the inaction of the Legislative Assembly, on August 10, 1792, the sans-culottes organized an insurrection and attacked the Tuileries palace, where the king resided. The Legislative Assembly ordered new elections, this time by universal male suffrage (no wealth qualifi- cations as in the Constitution of 1791), for a National Convention that would write a new constitution.

When it met, the Convention abolished the monarchy and on September 22, 1792, established the first republic in French history. The republic would answer only to the people, not to any royal authority. Violence soon exploded again early in September 1792 when the Prussians approached Paris. Hastily gathered mobs stormed the overflowing prisons to seek out traitors who might help the enemy. In an atmosphere of near hysteria, eleven hundred inmates were killed, including many ordinary and completely innocent people. The princess of Lamballe, one of the queen's favorites, was hacked to pieces and her mutilated body displayed beneath the windows where the royal family was kept under guard. These "September massacres" showed the dark side of popular revolution, in which the common people demanded instant revenge on supposed enemies and conspirators.

The National Convention faced a dire situation. It needed to write a new constitution for the republic while fighting a war with external enemies and con- fronting increasing resistance at home. The Revolution had divided the popula- tion: for some, it had not gone far enough toward providing food, land, and retribution against enemies; for others, it had gone too far by dismantling the church and the monarchy. The French people had never known any government other than monarchy. Only half the population could read and write at even a basic level. In this situation, symbolic actions became very important. Any public sign of monarchy was at risk, and revolutionaries soon pulled down statues of kings and burned reminders of the former regime.

The fate of Louis XVI and the future direction of the republic divided the deputies elected to the National Convention. Most of the deputies were middle- class lawyers and professionals who had developed their ardent republican beliefs in the national network of Jacobin Clubs. After the fall of the monarchy in

August 1792, however, the Jacobins divided into two factions. The Girondins (named after a department in southwestern France, the Gironde, which provided some of its leading orators) resented the growing power of Parisian militants and tried to appeal to the departments outside of Paris. The Mountain (so called because its deputies sat in the highest seats of the Convention), in contrast, was closely allied with the Paris militants.

The first showdown between the Girondins and the Mountain occurred during the trial of the king in December 1792. Although the Girondins agreed that the king was guilty of treason, many of them argued for clemency, exile, or a popular referendum on his fate. After a long and difficult debate, the Convention supported the Mountain and voted by a very narrow majority to execute the king. Louis XVI went to the guillotine on January 21, 1793, sharing the fate of Charles I of England in 1649. "We have just convinced

■ The Guillotine

Before 1789, only nobles were decapitated if condemned to death; commoners were usually hanged. J. I. Guillotin, a professor of anatomy and a deputy for the Third Estate in the National Assembly, first proposed equalization of the death penalty. He also suggested that a mechanical device be constructed for decapitation, leading to the instrument's association with his name. The Assembly decreed decapitation as the death penalty in June 1791. Another physician, A. Louis, actually invented the guillotine. Its use began in April 1792 and did not end until 1981, when the French government abolished the death penalty. Although it was invented to make death equal and painless, the guillotine disturbed many observers; its mechanical operation and efficiency—the executioner merely pulled up the blade by a cord and then released it—seemed somehow inhuman. Nonetheless, the guillotine fascinated as much as it repelled. Reproduced in miniature, painted onto snuffboxes and china, worn as jewelry, and even serving as a toy, the guillotine became a part of popular culture, celebrated as the people's avenger by supporters of the Revolution and vilified as the preeminent symbol of the Terror by opponents.
(Réunion des Musées Nationaux/Art Resource, NY.)

ourselves that a king is only a man," wrote one newspaper, "and that no man is above the law." The Girondins lasted only a few months longer. On June 2, 1793, twenty-nine Girondin deputies were arrested after militants in Paris organized an armed demonstration against them and invaded the National Convention. Dissent, even among republicans, could now prove fatal.

■ **REVIEW:** *In what ways did the beginning of the French Revolution resemble the other revolutions of 1787–1789?*

Terror and Resistance

The execution of the king and the arrest of the Girondins did not end the new regime's problems. The continuing war required ever more men and money, and the introduction of a national draft provoked massive resistance in some parts of France. In response to growing pressures, the National Convention set up a highly centralized government designed to provide food, direct the war effort, and punish counterrevolutionaries. Thus began the **Terror**, in which the guillotine became the most terrifying instrument of a government that suppressed almost every form of dissent. The leader of this government, Maximilien Robespierre, aimed to create a "Republic of Virtue," in which the government would teach, or force, citizens to become virtuous republicans through a massive program of political re-education. These policies only increased divisions, which ultimately led to Robespierre's fall from power and to a dismantling of government by terror.

Robespierre and the Committee of Public Safety

Setting the course for government and the war increasingly fell to the twelve-member Committee of Public Safety, set up by the Convention on April 6, 1793. When Robespierre (1758–1794) was elected to the committee three months later, he became in effect its guiding spirit and the chief spokesman of the Revolution. A lawyer from northern France known as "the incorruptible" for his stern honesty and fierce dedication to democratic ideals, Robespierre remains one of the most controversial figures in world history because of his association with the Terror. In September 1793, another demonstration organized by Parisian militants demanded that the Convention "put Terror on the agenda." Although he originally opposed the death penalty and the war, Robespierre took the lead in implementing emergency measures, including death for those, such as the Girondins, who opposed the committee's policies. At the same time, he maneuvered to clamp down on popular demonstrations.

Like many other educated eighteenth-century men, Robespierre read the classics of republicanism from the ancient Roman writers Tacitus and Plutarch to the Enlightenment thinkers Montesquieu and Rousseau. But he took them a step further. He spoke eloquently about "the theory of revolutionary government" as "the war of liberty against its enemies." He defended the people's right to democratic government, while in practice he supported many measures that restricted their liberties. He personally favored a free-market economy, as did almost all middle-class deputies, but in this time of crisis he was willing to enact price controls and requisitioning. The Convention had organized paramilitary bands called "revolutionary armies" to hunt down hoarders and political suspects, and on September 29, 1793, it established a General Maximum on the prices of thirty-nine essential commodities and on wages. In a speech to the Convention, Robespierre explained the necessity of a government by terror: "The first maxim of your policies must be to lead the people by reason and the people's enemies by terror ... without virtue, terror is deadly; without terror, virtue is impotent." *Terror* was not an idle term; it seemed to imply that the goal of democracy justified what we now call totalitarian means—that is, the suppression of all dissent.

The Committee of Public Safety did everything possible to ensure its control. It sent deputies out "on mission" to purge unreliable officials and organize the war effort. In the first universal draft of men in history, every unmarried man and childless widower between the ages of eighteen and twenty-five was declared eligible for conscription. Revolutionary tribunals set up in Paris and provincial centers tried political suspects. In October 1793, the Revolutionary Tribunal in Paris convicted Marie-Antoinette of treason and sent her to the guillotine. The Girondin leaders were also guillotined, as was Olympe de Gouges. The government confiscated all the property of convicted traitors.

The government won its greatest success on the battlefield. As of April 1793, France faced war with Austria, Prussia, Great Britain, Spain, Sardinia, and the Dutch Republic—all fearful of the impact of revolutionary ideals on their own populations. To face this daunting coalition of forces, the French republic tapped a new and potent source of power—nationalist pride—in decrees mobilizing young and old alike: "The young men will go to battle; married men will forge arms and transport provisions; women will make tents and clothing and serve in hospitals; children will make bandages." Forges were set up in the parks and gardens of Paris to produce thousands of guns, and citizens everywhere helped collect saltpeter, a rock salt used to make gunpowder. By the end of 1793, the French nation in arms had stopped the advance of the allied powers, and in the summer of 1794 it invaded the Austrian Netherlands and crossed the Rhine River. The army was ready to carry the gospel of revolution and republicanism to the rest of Europe.

The Republic of Virtue, 1793–1794

The program of the Terror went beyond pragmatic measures to fight the war and internal enemies to include efforts to "republicanize everything"—in other words, to effect a cultural revolution. Songs—especially the new national anthem, "La Marseillaise" (named after the soldiers from the city of Marseille who first sang it)—placards, posters, pamphlets, books, engravings, paintings, sculpture, even everyday crockery, chamberpots, and playing cards conveyed revolutionary slogans and symbols. Foremost among them was the figure of Liberty (an early version of the Statue of Liberty now in New York harbor), which appeared on coins and bills, on letterheads and seals, in engravings and paintings, and as statues in festivals. Hundreds of new plays were produced and old classics revised. To encourage the production of patriotic and republican works, the government sponsored state competitions for artists to "awaken the public spirit and make clear how atrocious and ridiculous were the enemies of liberty and of the Republic."

At the center of this elaborate cultural campaign were revolutionary festivals that first emerged in 1789 with the spontaneous planting of liberty trees in villages and towns. The Festival of Federation on July 14, 1790, marked the first anniversary of the fall of the Bastille. Under the Convention, the well-known painter Jacques-Louis David (1748–1825), who was a deputy and an associate of Robespierre, took over festival planning. David aimed to destroy the mystique of monarchy and to make the republic sacred. His Festival of Unity on August 10, 1793, for example, celebrated the first anniversary of the overthrow of the monarchy. In front of the statue of Liberty built for the occasion, a bonfire consumed the crowns and scepters of royalty while a cloud of three thousand white doves rose into the sky.

Some hoped the festival system would replace the Catholic church altogether. They initiated a campaign of **de-Christianization** that included closing churches (Protestant as well as Catholic), selling many church buildings to the highest bidder, and trying to force even those clergy who had taken the oath of loyalty to abandon their clerical vocations and marry. Great churches became storehouses for arms or grain, or their stones were sold off to contractors. The medieval statues of kings on the façade of Notre Dame cathedral were beheaded. Church bells were dismantled and church treasures melted down for government use. In the ultimate step in de-Christianization, extremists tried to establish a Cult of Reason to supplant Christianity. The Committee of Public Safety halted the de-Christianization campaign because the deputies feared it would turn rural, devout populations against the republic.

In principle, the best way to ensure the future of the republic was through the education of the young. The Convention voted to make primary schooling free and compulsory for both boys and girls. It took control of education away

■ Representing Liberty

Liberty was always represented by a female figure because in French the noun is gendered feminine (la liberté). *This painting by a woman, Jeanne-Louise Vallain, from 1793–1794, captures the usual attributes of liberty: she is soberly seated, wearing a Roman-style toga, and holding a pike with a Roman liberty cap on top. Her Roman appearance signals that she is not a contemporary French woman but rather the representation of an abstract quality. Yet the very fact that she holds an instrument of battle suggests that women might be active participants. Liberty is holding the Declaration of the Rights of Man and of the Citizen as it was revised in 1793. This painting was most likely hung in a central location in the Paris Jacobin Club.*

(Musée de la Révolution Française, Vizille.)

from the Catholic church and tried to set up a system of state schools at the primary and secondary levels, but it lacked trained teachers to replace those the Catholic religious orders provided. As a result, opportunities for learning how to read and write may have diminished. In 1799, only one-fifth as many boys enrolled in the state secondary schools as had studied in church schools ten years earlier.

Although many of the ambitious republican programs failed, almost all aspects of daily life became politicized, even colors. The tricolor—the combination of red, white, and blue that was to become the flag of France—was devised in July 1789, and by 1793, everyone had to wear a cockade (a badge made of ribbons) with the colors. Using formal forms of speech—*vous* for "you"—or the title *monsieur* or *madame* might identify someone as an aristocrat; true patriots used the informal *tu* and *citoyen* or *citoyenne* ("citizen") instead. Some people changed their names or gave their children new kinds of names. Biblical and saints' names, such as Jean, Pierre, Joseph, or Marie, gave way to names recalling heroes of the ancient Roman republic (Brutus, Gracchus, Cornelia), revolutionary heroes, or flowers and plants. Such changes symbolized adherence to the republic and to Enlightenment ideals rather than to Catholicism.

Even the measures of time and space were revolutionized. In October 1793, the Convention introduced a new calendar to replace the Christian one. Year I dated from the beginning of the republic on September 22, 1792. Twelve months of exactly thirty days each received new names derived from nature—for example, Pluviôse (roughly equivalent to February) recalled the rain (*la pluie*) of late winter. Instead of seven-day weeks, ten-day *décades* provided only one day of rest every ten days and pointedly eliminated the Sunday of the Christian calendar. The five days left at the end of the calendar year were devoted to special festivals called *sans-culottides*. The calendar remained in force for twelve years despite continuing resistance to it. More enduring was the new metric system based on units of ten that was invented to replace the hundreds of local variations in weights and measures. Other countries in Europe and throughout the world eventually adopted the metric system.

Successive revolutionary legislatures also changed the rules of family life. The state took responsibility for all family matters away from the Catholic church: birth, death, and marriage registration now happened at city hall, not the parish church. Marriage became a civil contract and as such could be broken. The new divorce law of September 1792 was the most far-reaching in Europe: a couple could divorce by mutual consent or for reasons such as insanity, abandonment, battering, or criminal conviction. Thousands of men and women took advantage of the law to dissolve unhappy marriages, even though the pope had condemned the measure. (In 1816, the government revoked the right to divorce.) In one of its most influential actions, the National Convention passed a series of laws that created equal inheritance among all children in a family, including girls. A father's right to favor one child, especially the oldest male, was considered aristocratic and hence antirepublican.

Resisting the Revolution

By intruding into religion, culture, and daily life, the republic inevitably provoked resistance. Shouting curses against the republic, uprooting liberty trees, carrying statues of the Virgin Mary in procession, hiding a priest who would not take the oath, singing a royalist song—all these actions expressed discontent with the new

■ **Anti-Robespierre Satire**

In The Purifying Pot of the Jacobins *(1793), the anonymous artist makes fun of the Jacobin Club's penchant for constantly examining the political correctness of its members. The Robespierre-like inquisitor uses a magnifying glass to check for loyalty, symbolized by the red cap of liberty worn by militant revolutionaries, and carries a knife in his pocket. Those who failed the test suffered harsh, sometimes fatal consequences.* (Art Resource, NY.)

symbols, rituals, and policies. Many women, in particular, suffered from the hard conditions of life that persisted in this time of war, and they had their own ways of dissenting. Long bread lines in the cities exhausted the patience of women, and police spies reported their constant grumbling, which occasionally turned into spontaneous demonstrations or riots over high prices or food shortages. Other forms of resistance were more individual. One young woman, Charlotte Corday, assassinated the outspoken deputy Jean-Paul Marat in July 1793. Corday fervently supported the Girondins, and she considered it her patriotic duty to kill the deputy who, in the columns of his paper *The Friend of the People*, had constantly demanded more heads and more blood.

Organized resistance broke out in many parts of France. The arrest of the Girondin deputies in June 1793 sparked in several departments insurrections that if coordinated might have threatened the central government in Paris. But the army promptly dispatched the rebels. After the government retook the city of Lyon, one of the centers of the revolt, the deputy on mission ordered sixteen hundred houses demolished. Special courts sentenced almost two thousand people to death. The name of the city was changed to Ville Affranchie (Liberated Town).

In the Vendée region of western France, resistance turned into full-scale civil war. Between March and December 1793, peasants, artisans, and weavers joined under noble leadership to form a "Catholic and Royal Army." One rebel group explained its motives: "They [the republicans] have killed our king, chased away our priests, sold the goods of our church, eaten everything we have and now they want to take our bodies [in the draft]." The uprising took two different forms: in the Vendée itself, a counterrevolutionary army organized to fight the republic; in nearby Brittany, resistance took the form of guerrilla bands, which united to attack a target and then quickly melted into the countryside. Great Britain provided money and underground contacts for these attacks.

For several months in 1793, the Vendée rebels stormed the largest towns in the region. Both sides committed atrocities. At the small town of Machecoul, for example, the rebels massacred more than a hundred republicans, including administrators and National Guard members; many were tied together, shoved into freshly dug graves, and shot. By the fall, however, republican soldiers had turned back the rebels. A republican general wrote to the Committee of Public Safety claiming, "There is no more Vendée, citizens, it has perished under our free sword along with its women and children. . . . Following the orders that you gave me I have crushed children under the feet of horses, massacred women who at least . . . will engender no more brigands." "Infernal columns" of republican troops marched through the region to restore control, military courts ordered thousands executed, and republican soldiers massacred thousands of others. In one especially gruesome incident, the deputy Jean-Baptiste Carrier supervised the drowning of some two thousand Vendée rebels, including a number of priests. Barges loaded with prisoners were floated into the Loire River near Nantes and then sunk. Controversy still rages about the rebellion's death toll. Estimates of rebel deaths alone range from about 20,000 to 250,000 and higher. Many thousands of republican soldiers and civilians also lost their lives. Even the low estimates reveal the carnage of this catastrophic confrontation between the republic and its opponents.

The Fall of Robespierre and the End of the Terror, 1794–1799

In an atmosphere of fear of conspiracy that these outbreaks fueled, Robespierre tried simultaneously to exert the Convention's control over popular political activities and to weed out opposition among the deputies. The Convention cracked down on popular clubs and societies in the fall of 1793. First to be suppressed were women's political clubs. Founded in early 1793, the Society of Revolutionary Republican Women played a very active part in sans-culottes politics. The society urged harsher measures against the republic's enemies and insisted that women have a voice in politics even if they did not have the vote. The Convention abolished women's political clubs in order to limit agitation in the streets. The deputies called on biological arguments about natural differences between the sexes to bolster their case. As one argued, "Women are ill suited for elevated thoughts and serious meditations."

In the spring of 1794, the Committee of Public Safety moved against its critics among leaders in Paris and deputies in the Convention itself. First, a handful of men labeled "ultrarevolutionaries"—in fact a motley collection of local Parisian politicians—were arrested and executed. Next came the other side, the "indulgents," so called because they favored moderation of the Terror. Included among them was the popular deputy Georges-Jacques Danton (1759–1794), once a member of the Committee of Public Safety and a friend of Robespierre despite the striking contrast in their personalities. Danton was the Revolution's most flamboyant orator and, unlike Robespierre, was a high-living, high-spending, excitable politician. At every turning point in national politics, his booming voice had swayed opinion in the National Convention. Now, under government pressure, the Revolutionary Tribunal convicted him and his friends of treason and sentenced them to death.

With the arrest and execution of these leaders in Paris, the prophecies of doom for the Revolution seemed about to be realized. "The Revolution," as one of the Girondin victims of 1793 had remarked, "was devouring its own children." Even after the major threats to the committee's power had been eliminated, the Terror continued and even worsened. A law passed in June 1794 denied the accused the right of legal counsel, reduced the number of jurors necessary for conviction, and allowed only two judgments: acquittal or death. The category of political crimes expanded to include "slandering patriotism" and "seeking to inspire discouragement." Ordinary people risked the guillotine if they expressed any discontent. The rate of executions in Paris rose from five a day in the spring of 1794 to twenty-six a day in the summer. The political atmosphere darkened even though the military situation improved. At the end of June, French armies decisively defeated the main Austrian army and advanced through the Austrian Netherlands to Brussels and Antwerp. The emergency measures for fighting the war were working, yet Robespierre and his inner circle had made so many enemies that they could not afford to loosen the grip of the Terror.

The Terror hardly touched many parts of France, but overall, the experience was undeniably traumatic. Across the country, the official Terror cost the lives of at least 40,000 French people, most of them living in the regions of major insurrections or near the borders with foreign enemies, where suspicion of collaboration ran high. As many as 300,000 people—one out of every fifty French people—went to prison as suspects between March 1793 and August 1794. The toll for the aristocracy and the clergy was especially high. Many leading nobles perished under the guillotine, and thousands emigrated. Thirty thousand to forty thousand clergy who refused the oath emigrated, at least two thousand (including many nuns) were executed, and thousands were imprisoned. The clergy were singled out in particular in the civil war zones: 135 priests were massacred at Lyon in November 1793 and 83 shot in one day during the Vendée revolt. Yet many victims of the Terror were peasants or ordinary working people.

Major Events of the French Revolution

1789

May 5	The Estates General opens at Versailles
June 17	The Third Estate renamed the National Assembly
June 20	"Tennis court oath" shows deputies will carry out a constitutional revolution
July 14	Fall of the Bastille
August 26	National Assembly passes Declaration of the Rights of Man and of the Citizen
October 5–6	Women march to Versailles and join with men in bringing the royal family back to Paris

1790

| July 12 | Civil Constitution of the Clergy |

1791

| June 20 | Louis and Marie-Antoinette try to flee in disguise and are captured at Varennes |

1792

April 20	Declaration of war on Austria
August 10	Insurrection in Paris and attack on Tuileries palace lead to suspension of the king
September 2–6	"September massacres" of prisoners in Paris
September 22	Establishment of the republic

1793

January 21	Execution of Louis XVI
March 11	Beginning of Vendée uprising
May 31–June 2	Insurrection leading to arrest of the Girondins
July 27	Robespierre named to the Committee of Public Safety
October 16	Execution of Marie-Antoinette

1794

February 4	Slavery abolished in the French colonies
March 13–April 5	Arrest, trial, and executions of so-called ultrarevolutionaries and arrest, trial, and executions of Danton and his followers
July 27–29	Arrest and execution of Robespierre and his supporters

1795

October 26	Directory government takes office
April 1796–October 1797	Succession of Italian victories by Bonaparte
May 1798–October 1799	Bonaparte goes to Egypt and Middle East

1799

| November 9 | Coup of 18 Brumaire establishes Bonaparte as First Consul |

The final crisis of the Terror came in July 1794. Conflicts within the Committee of Public Safety and the National Convention left Robespierre isolated. On July 27, 1794 (the ninth of Thermidor, Year II, according to the revolutionary calendar), Robespierre appeared before the Convention with yet another list of deputies to be arrested. Many feared they would be named, and they shouted him down and ordered him arrested along with his followers on the committee, the president of the Revolutionary Tribunal in Paris, and the commander of the Parisian National Guard. An armed uprising led by the Paris city government failed to save Robespierre when most of the National Guard took the side of the Convention. Robespierre tried to kill himself with a pistol but only broke his jaw. The next day, he and scores of followers went to the guillotine.

The men who led the attack on Robespierre in Thermidor (July 1794) did not intend to reverse all his policies, but that happened nonetheless because of a violent backlash known as the **Thermidorian Reaction**. Newspapers attacked the Robespierrists as "tigers thirsting for human blood." The new government released hundreds of suspects and arranged a temporary truce in the Vendée. It purged Jacobins from local bodies and replaced them with their opponents. It arrested some of the most notorious "terrorists" in the National Convention, such as Carrier, and put them to death. Within the year, the new leaders abolished the Revolutionary Tribunal and closed the Jacobin Club in Paris. Popular demonstrations met severe repression. In southeastern France, in particular, a "White Terror" replaced the Jacobins' "Red Terror." Former officials and local Jacobin leaders were harassed, beaten, and often murdered by paramilitary bands who had tacit support from the new authorities. Those who remained in the National Convention prepared yet another constitution in 1795, setting up a two-house legislature and an executive body—the Directory—headed by five directors.

■ **REVIEW:** *What factors can explain the Terror? To what extent was it simply a response to a national emergency or a reflection of deeper problems with the French Revolution?*

The Directory and the Rise of Napoleon Bonaparte

Between 1795 and 1799, the republic endured in France under a new government known as "the Directory," the name for its executive branch. The Directory kept power only by fending off challenges from the remaining Jacobins and the resurgent royalists. At the same time, it directed a war effort abroad that would ultimately bring to power the man who would dismantle the republic itself. The story of the rise of Napoleon Bonaparte (1769–1821) is one of the most remarkable in Western history. It would have seemed astonishing in 1795 that the twenty-six-year-old son of a Corsican noble would within four years become the

■ **MAP 16.3 The Second and Third Partitions of Poland, 1793 and 1795**

In 1793, after Russian armies invaded Poland, Russia and Prussia agreed to another partition of Polish territories. Prussia took over territory that included 1.1 million Poles while Russia gained 3 million new inhabitants. Austria gave up any claims to Poland in exchange for help from Russia and Prussia in acquiring Bavaria. When Kościuszko's nationalist uprising failed in 1794, Russia, Prussia, and Austria agreed to a final division. Prussia absorbed an additional 900,000 Polish subjects, including those in Warsaw; Austria incorporated 1 million Poles and the city of Cracow; Russia gained another 2 million Poles. The three powers determined never to use the term Kingdom of Poland *again.*

supreme ruler of France and one of the greatest military leaders in world history. In 1795, he was a penniless artillery officer, only recently released from prison as a presumed Robespierrist. Continuing warfare, the upheavals caused in the rest of Europe by the impact of the French Revolution, and political divisions within the republican leadership gave Bonaparte the opportunity to change the course of history.

Revolution on the March

The powers allied against France had squandered their best chance to defeat France in 1793, when the French armies verged on chaos because of the emigration of noble army officers and the problems of integrating new draftees. At that moment, Prussia, Russia, and Austria were preoccupied once again with Poland. "I shall fight Jacobinism, and defeat it in Poland," vowed Catherine the Great in 1792. She abolished Poland's constitution of May 3, 1791, and joined with Prussia in gobbling up generous new slices of Polish territory in the Second Partition of 1793 (Map 16.3). When Tadeusz Kościuszko (1746–1817), an officer who had been a foreign volunteer in the War of American Independence, tried to lead a nationalist uprising, Catherine's army struck again. This time, Russia, Prussia, and Austria wiped Poland completely from the map in the Third

Partition of 1795. "The Polish question" would plague international relations for more than a century as Polish rebels flocked to any international upheaval that might undo the partitions.

While Russia, Prussia, and Austria feasted on Poland, France regrouped. Because of the new national draft, the French had a huge fighting force of 700,000 men by the end of 1793. But the army faced many problems in the field. As many as a third of the recent draftees deserted before or during battle. Uniforms fashioned out of rough cloth constricted movements, tore easily, and retained the damp of muddy battlefields, exposing the soldiers to the elements and the spread of disease. At times, the soldiers were fed only moldy bread, and if their pay was late, they sometimes resorted to pillaging and looting. Generals might pay with their lives if they lost a key battle and their loyalty to the Revolution came under suspicion. France nevertheless had one overwhelming advantage: its soldiers, drawn largely from the peasantry and the lower classes of the cities, fought for a revolution that they and their brothers and sisters had helped make. The republic was their government, and the army was in large measure theirs, too; many officers had risen through the ranks by skill and talent rather than by inheriting or purchasing their positions. One young peasant boy wrote to his parents, "Either you will see me return bathed in glory, or you will have a son who is a worthy citizen of France who knows how to die for the defense of his country."

When French armies invaded the Austrian Netherlands and crossed the Rhine in the summer of 1794, they proclaimed a war of liberation. These promises profoundly divided European opinion. In 1789, many had greeted events with unabashed enthusiasm. The English Unitarian minister Richard Price had exulted, "Behold, the light . . . after setting AMERICA free, reflected to FRANCE, and there kindled into a blaze that lays despotism in ashes, and warms and illuminates EUROPE." Democrats and reformers from many countries flooded to Paris to witness events firsthand. Supporters of the French Revolution in Great Britain, like the earlier reformers of the 1760s and 1770s, joined constitutional and reform societies that sprang up in many cities. The most important of these societies, the London Corresponding Society, founded in 1792, corresponded with the Paris Jacobin Club and served as a center for reform agitation in England. Pro-French feeling ran even stronger in Ireland. Catholics and Presbyterians, both excluded from the vote, came together in 1791 in the Society of United Irishmen, which eventually pressed for secession from England.

European elites became alarmed when the French abolished monarchy and nobility and encouraged popular participation in politics. The British government, for example, quickly suppressed the corresponding societies and charged some of their leaders with sedition. In the United States, opinion fiercely divided on the virtues of the French Revolution. In Sweden, when Gustavus III (r. 1771–1792) was assassinated by a nobleman, the king's son and heir, Gustavus IV (r. 1792–1809),

■ The English Reaction to the French Revolution

In this caricature, James Gillray, a supporter of the Tories in Britain, satirizes the French version of liberty but also subtly mocks the British upper classes. He portrays French liberty as a creature (is it man or woman?) who has only onions to eat but still sings the praises of French freedom and plenty. The British figure is a fat magistrate who complains that high taxes will cause slavery and starvation, while he stuffs himself on the British national dish of roast beef. Gillray produced thousands of political caricatures. (© Copyright The Trustees of The British Museum.)

believed that the French Jacobins had sanctioned the killing. Spain's royal government suppressed all news from France, fearing that it might ignite the spirit of revolt. This fear was not misplaced because even in Russia, for instance, 278 outbreaks of peasant unrest occurred between 1796 and 1798. One Russian landlord complained, "This is the self-same . . . spirit of insubordination and independence, which has spread through all Europe."

Middle-class people near the northern and eastern borders of France reacted most positively to the French invasion. In the Austrian Netherlands, Mainz, Savoy, and Nice, French officers organized Jacobin Clubs that attracted middle-class locals. The clubs petitioned for annexation to France, and French legislation was then introduced, including the abolition of seigneurial dues. Despite resistance, especially in the Austrian Netherlands, these areas remained part of France until 1815, and the legal changes were permanent. Like Louis XIV a century before, most deputies in the National Convention considered the territories annexed in 1794 within France's "natural frontiers"—the Rhine, the Alps, and the Pyrenees.

The Directory government was torn between defending the new frontiers and launching a more aggressive policy of creating semi-independent "sister" republics wherever the armies succeeded. Aggression won out. When Prussia declared neutrality in 1795, French armies swarmed into the Dutch Republic, abolished the office of stadholder, and—with the revolutionary penchant for renaming—created the new Batavian Republic, a satellite of France. The French set up a Cisalpine Republic when Bonaparte defeated the Austrian armies in northern Italy in 1797. After the French attacked the Swiss cantons in 1798, they set up the Helvetic Republic and curtailed many of the Catholic church's privileges. They conquered the Papal States in 1798 and installed a Roman Republic; the pope fled to Siena. As the French conquered more and more territory, "liberated" people in many places began to view them as an army of occupation.

Revolution in the Colonies

The revolution that produced so much upheaval in continental Europe had repercussions in France's Caribbean colonies. These colonies were crucial to the French economy. Twice the size in land area of the neighboring British colonies, they also produced nearly twice as much revenue in exports. The slave population had doubled in the French colonies in the twenty years before 1789. St. Domingue (present-day Haiti) was the most important French colony. Occupying the western half of the island of Hispaniola, it was inhabited in 1789 by approximately 465,000 slaves, 30,000 whites, and 28,000 free people of color, whose primary job was to apprehend runaway slaves and ensure plantation security.

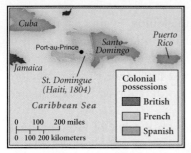

St. Domingue on the Eve of the Revolt, 1791

Despite the efforts of a Paris club called the Friends of Blacks, most French revolutionaries did not consider slavery a pressing problem. As one deputy explained, "This regime [in the colonies] is oppressive, but it gives a livelihood to several million Frenchmen. This regime is barbarous but a still greater barbarity will result if you interfere with it without the necessary knowledge."

In August 1791, slaves in northern St. Domingue organized a large-scale revolt. To restore authority over the slaves, the Legislative Assembly in Paris granted civil and political rights to the free people of color. This action infuriated white planters and merchants, and in 1793 they signed an agreement with Great Britain, now France's enemy in war, declaring British sovereignty over St. Domingue. To

■ **Toussaint L'Ouverture**
The leader of the St. Domingue slave uprising appears in his general's uniform, sword in hand. This portrait appeared in one of the earliest histories of the revolt, Marcus Rainsford's Historical Account of the Black Empire of Hayti *(London, 1805). Toussaint, a former slave who educated himself, fascinated many of his contemporaries in Europe as well as the New World by turning a chaotic slave rebellion into an organized and ultimately successful independence movement.*
(North Wind Picture Archives.)

complicate matters further, Spain, which controlled the rest of the island and had entered on Great Britain's side in the war with France, offered freedom to individual slave rebels who joined the Spanish armies as long as they agreed to maintain the slave regime for the other blacks.

The few thousand French republican troops on St. Domingue were outnumbered, and to prevent complete military disaster, the French commissioner freed all the slaves in his jurisdiction in August 1793 without permission from the government in Paris. In February 1794, the National Convention formally abolished slavery and granted full rights to all black men in France's colonies. These actions had the desired effect. One of the ablest black generals allied with the Spanish, the ex-slave François-Dominique Toussaint L'Ouverture (1743–1803), changed sides and committed his troops to the French. The French eventually appointed Toussaint governor of St. Domingue as a reward for his efforts.

The vicious fighting and flight of whites left the island's economy in ruins. In 1800, the plantations produced one-fifth of what they had in 1789. In the zones

Toussaint controlled, army officers or government officials took over the great estates and kept all the freed people working in agriculture under military discipline. The former slaves were bound to their estates like serfs and were forced to work the plantations in exchange for an autonomous family life and the right to maintain personal garden plots.

Toussaint remained in charge until 1802, when Napoleon sent French armies to regain control of St. Domingue. They arrested Toussaint and transported him to France, where he died in prison. His arrest prompted the English romantic poet William Wordsworth (1770–1850) to write of him:

> There's not a breathing of the common wind
> That will forget thee; thou hast great allies;
> Thy friends are exultations, agonies,
> And love, and man's unconquerable mind.

Toussaint became a hero to abolitionists everywhere, a potent symbol of black struggles to win freedom. Napoleon attempted to reimpose slavery, but the remaining black generals defeated his armies, which had been weakened by yellow fever, and in 1804 proclaimed the Republic of Haiti.

The End of the French Republic

Toussaint had followed with interest Napoleon's rise to power in France; he once wrote to Bonaparte, "From the First of the Blacks to the First of the Whites." Like Toussaint, Napoleon Bonaparte made the most of the opportunities afforded by war. The Directory regime faced a deeply divided populace at home while continuing to fight abroad. Constant elections meant constant upheaval as the government first arrested royalists, who won in 1797, and then Jacobins, who won in 1798. It never succeeded in establishing a firm center that could appeal to a majority of voters. In Paris bands of young dandies picked fights with known Jacobins and disrupted theater performances with loud antirevolutionary songs. All over France, people banded together and petitioned to reopen churches closed during the Terror. If necessary, they broke into a church to hold services with a priest who had been in hiding or with a lay schoolteacher who was willing to say Mass. Amid increasing political instability, generals in the field became practically independent, and the troops felt greater loyalty to their units and generals than to the republic. Military victories had made the army a parallel and rival force to the state.

Thanks to some early military successes and links to Parisian politicians, Bonaparte was named commander of the French army in Italy in 1796. His astounding success in the Italian campaigns of 1796–1797 launched his meteoric career. With an army of fewer than fifty thousand men, he defeated the Piedmontese and the Austrians. He negotiated with the Austrians himself, and in quick order he established client republics dependent on his own authority. He molded the army into his personal force by paying the soldiers in cash taken as tribute from the newly conquered territories. He mollified the Directory government by sending home wagonloads of Italian masterpieces of art, which were added to Parisian museum collections (most are still there) after being paraded in victory festivals.

In 1798, the Directory set aside its plans to invade England, gave Bonaparte command of the army raised for that purpose, and sent him across the Mediterranean Sea to Egypt, away from the Parisian centers of power. The French had encouraged the Irish to time a rebellion to coincide with their planned invasion, and when the French went elsewhere, the British mercilessly repressed the revolt. Thirty thousand people were killed. Twice as many regular British troops (seventy thousand) as fought in any of the major continental battles against Napoleon were required to put down the Irish rebellion.

The Directory government hoped that French occupation of Egypt would strike a blow at British trade by cutting the route to India and thus compensate France for its losses there years before. Once the army disembarked in Egypt, however, the British admiral Horatio Nelson destroyed the French fleet while it was anchored in Aboukir Bay. Unable to push further into Syria, the French nonetheless introduced Enlightenment-inspired legal reforms to largely Muslim Egypt: they abolished torture, introduced equality before the law, eliminated religious taxes, and proclaimed religious toleration.

Even the failures of the Egyptian campaign did not dull Bonaparte's luster. Bonaparte had taken France's leading scientists with him on the expedition, and his soldiers had discovered a slab of black basalt dating from 196 B.C.E. written in both hieroglyphic and Greek. Called the Rosetta stone after a nearby town, it enabled scholars to finally decipher the hieroglyphs used by the ancient Egyptians. When his army was pinned down after its initial successes, Napoleon slipped out of Egypt and made his way secretly across the Mediterranean to southern France.

In October 1799, Bonaparte arrived in Paris at just the right moment. The war in Europe was going badly. The departments of the former Austrian Netherlands had revolted against new conscription laws. Deserters swelled the ranks of the rebels in western France. A royalist army had tried to take the city of Toulouse in the southwest. And many government leaders wanted to revise the Constitution of 1795. Disillusioned members of the government saw in Bonaparte's return an occasion to overturn the Constitution of 1795.

On November 9, 1799 (18 Brumaire, Year VIII, by the revolutionary calendar), the conspirators within the Directory government persuaded the legislature to move out of Paris to avoid an imaginary Jacobin plot. But when Bonaparte stomped into the meeting hall the next day and demanded changes in the Constitution, he

■ **Napoleon as Military Hero**

In this painting from 1800–1801, Napoleon Crossing the Alps at St. Bernard, *Jacques-Louis David reminds the French of Napoleon's heroic military exploits. Napoleon is a picture of calm and composure while his horse shows the fright and energy of the moment. David painted this propagandistic image shortly after one of his former students went to the guillotine on a trumped up charge of plotting to assassinate the new French leader. The former organizer of republican festivals during the Terror had become a kind of court painter for the new regime.* (Réunion des Musées Nationaux/Art Resource, NY.)

was greeted by cries of "Down with the dictator." His quick-thinking brother Lucien, president of the Council of Five Hundred (the lower house), saved Bonaparte's coup by summoning troops guarding the hall and claiming that the deputies had tried to assassinate the popular general. The soldiers ejected the deputies, and a hastily assembled legislature voted to abolish the Directory and establish a new three-man executive called the consulate.

The deputies of the legislature who engineered the coup d'état of November 1799 picked Bonaparte as one of three provisional consuls only because he was a famous general. But under the new Constitution of 1799 he was named **First Consul**, a title revived from the ancient Roman republic, with the right to pick the Council of State, which drew up all laws. Millions had abstained from voting on the new Constitution, which eliminated direct elections for deputies and granted no independent powers to the three houses of the legislature. Bonaparte and his advisers chose the legislature's members out of a small pool of "notables." Inside France, political apathy had overtaken the original enthusiasm for revolutionary ideals. Bonaparte's coup d'état appeared to be just the latest in a long line of upheavals in revolutionary France. Within the year, however, Bonaparte had effectively ended the French Revolution and set France on a new course toward an authoritarian state.

■ **REVIEW:** *Why did some groups outside of France embrace the French Revolution while others resisted it?*

Emperor Napoleon I, r. 1804–1814

Napoleon left an indelible stamp on French institutions and political life. He reconciled with the Catholic church and with exiled aristocrats willing to return to France. He sped up the centralization of political power and ensured order by suppressing political dissent. He supervised the unification of France's many law codes into one Napoleonic Code that has remained in force to this day. Yet his fame and much of his power rested on his military conquests. His military prowess brought him to the heights of power, but as a consequence, he could not survive defeat on the battlefield.

The Authoritarian State

Bonaparte's most urgent task was to reconcile to his regime Catholics who had been alienated by revolutionary policies. Though nominally Catholic, Napoleon held no deep religious convictions. "How can there be order in the state without religion?" he asked cynically. "When a man is dying of hunger beside another who is stuffing himself, he cannot accept this difference if there is not an authority who tells him: 'God wishes it so.'" In 1801, a concordat with Pope Pius VII (r. 1800–1823) ended a decade of church-state conflict. The pope validated all sales of church lands, and Catholicism was officially recognized as the religion of "the great majority of French citizens." (The state continued to pay the salaries of clergymen, both Catholic and Protestant.) The pope thus brought the huge French Catholic population back into the fold, and Napoleon gained the pope's support for his regime.

Napoleon centralized state power more effectively than kings or revolutionaries had before him. He personally appointed prefects to directly supervise local affairs in every *département*, or region. He created the Bank of France to facilitate government borrowing and relied on gold and silver coinage rather than paper money. He severely limited political expression, refusing to allow those who opposed him to meet in clubs or influence elections. A decree reduced the number of newspapers in Paris from seventy-three to thirteen (and then finally to four), and the newspapers that remained became government mouthpieces. Government censors had to approve all operas and plays, and they banned "offensive" artistic works even more frequently than their royal predecessors. The minister of police, Joseph Fouché, a leading figure in the Terror of 1793–1794, kept political dissidents under constant surveillance. When a bomb attack on Napoleon's carriage failed in 1800, Fouché suppressed evidence of a royalist plot and instead arrested hundreds of former Jacobins. More than one hundred of them were deported and seven hundred imprisoned.

In 1802, once the republican opposition had been muzzled, Napoleon set up a referendum to approve him as First Consul for life, and then in 1804, with the pope's blessing, he crowned himself Emperor Napoleon I. Like the kings who preceded him, Napoleon cultivated personal symbolism. His face and name adorned coins, engravings, histories, paintings, and public monuments. His favorite painters embellished his legend by depicting him as a warrior-hero of mythic proportions. Believing that "what is big is always beautiful," Napoleon embarked on ostentatious building projects that would outshine even those of Louis XIV. Government-commissioned architects built the Arc de Triomphe, the Stock Exchange, fountains, and even slaughterhouses. In his imperial court, Napoleon staged his entrances carefully to maximize his personal presence: his wife and courtiers were dressed in regal finery, and he was announced with great pomp—but he usually arrived dressed in a simple military uniform with no medals.

Napoleon also worked hard at establishing his reputation as an efficient administrator with broad intellectual interests. He met frequently with scientists, jurists, and artists, and stories abounded of his unflagging energy. "Authority," declared his adviser Sieyès, "must come from above and confidence from below." To accomplish his aims, Napoleon relied on men who had served with him in the army. His chief of staff Alexandre Berthier, for example, became minister of war, and the chemist Claude Berthollet, who had organized the scientific part of the expedition to Egypt, became vice president of the Senate in 1804. Napoleon's bureaucracy was based on a patron-client relationship, with Napoleon as the ultimate patron. Some of Napoleon's closest associates married into his family.

Combining aristocratic and revolutionary values in a new social hierarchy that rewarded merit and talent, Napoleon used the Senate to dispense his patronage and personally chose as senators the nation's most illustrious generals, ministers, prefects, scientists, rich men, and former nobles. Intending to replace both the old nobility of birth and the republic's strict emphasis on equality, in 1802 he took a step toward creating a new nobility by founding a Legion of Honor, 95 percent of whose members in 1814 were military men. In 1808, Napoleon introduced a complete hierarchy of noble titles, ranging from princes down to barons and chevaliers. Titles could be inherited, but all Napoleonic nobles served the state in one way or another. To go along with their new titles, Napoleon gave his favorite generals huge fortunes, often in the form of estates in the conquered territories.

Napoleon's own family reaped the greatest benefits. He made his older brother, Joseph, ruler of the newly established kingdom of Naples in 1806; the same year he installed his younger brother Louis as king of Holland. He proclaimed his twenty-three-year-old stepson Eugène de Beauharnais viceroy of Italy in 1805 and established his sister Caroline and brother-in-law General Murat as king and queen of Naples in 1808, when he moved Joseph to the throne of Spain. Napoleon wanted to establish an imperial succession, but he lacked an heir. In thirteen years of marriage, his wife Josephine had borne no children, so in 1809 he divorced her and in 1810 married the eighteen-year-old Princess Marie-Louise of Austria. The next year she gave birth to a son to whom Napoleon immediately gave the title "king of Rome."

The New Paternalism

Napoleon believed that authority in the family and the workplace had to be reestablished in the same way that he had reasserted the authority of the state. The critical element in his vision of paternalism was the new **Civil Code** of 1804. Napoleon succeeded where previous governments had failed in unifying and standardizing France's local law codes. Called the Napoleonic Code as a way of further exalting his image, it defined and ensured property rights, guaranteed religious liberty, and provided equal legal treatment for all adult males. At the same time, however, the code sharply curtailed women's rights. The law obligated a husband to support his wife, but he alone controlled any property held in common. A wife could not sue in court, sell or mortgage her own property, or contract a debt without her husband's consent. Divorce was still possible, but a wife could petition for divorce only if her husband brought his mistress to live in the family home. In contrast, a wife convicted of adultery could be imprisoned for up to two years. The code's framers saw these discrepancies as a way to reinforce the family and make women responsible for private virtue, while leaving public decisions to men. The French code was imitated in many European and Latin American countries and in the French colony of Louisiana, where it had a similar negative effect on women's rights. Not until 1965 did French wives gain legal status equal to that of their husbands.

The Civil Code also insisted on a father's control over his children, which revolutionary legislation had limited. For example, children under age sixteen who refused to follow their fathers' commands could be sent to prison for up to a month with no hearing of any sort. At the same time, the code required fathers to provide for their children's welfare. Napoleon himself encouraged the foundation of private charities to help indigent mothers, and one of his decrees made it easier for women to abandon their children anonymously to a government foundling hospital. Napoleon hoped such measures would discourage abortion and infanticide, especially among the poorest classes in the fast-growing urban areas.

In periods of economic crisis, the government opened soup kitchens, but it also arrested beggars and sent them to newly established workhouses. For prostitutes, whose numbers had increased because of migration from the countryside to the cities and wartime upheavals, the Napoleonic state developed a novel paternalist approach. The authorities arrested prostitutes who worked on their own, but they tolerated brothels, which could be supervised by the police, and required the women working in them to have monthly medical examinations for venereal disease.

The new paternalism extended to relations between employers and employees. The state required all workers to carry a work card attesting to their good conduct, and it prohibited all workers' organizations. After 1806, arbitration boards settled labor disputes, but they took employers at their word while treating workers as minors, demanding that foremen and shop superintendents represent them. Occasionally strikes broke out, led by secret, illegal journeymen's associations, yet many employers laid off employees when times were hard, deducted fines from their wages, and dismissed them without appeal for being absent or making errors.

Napoleon continued the central government's patronage of science and intellectual life but once again put his own distinctive paternalist stamp on these activities. He closely monitored the research institutes established during the Revolution, sometimes intervening personally to achieve political conformity. An impressive outpouring of new theoretical and practical scientific work rewarded the state's efforts. Experiments with balloons led to the discovery of laws about the

■ Germaine de Staël

One of the most fascinating intellectuals of her time, Anne-Louise Germaine de Staël was the daughter of Louis XVI's Swiss Protestant finance minister, Jacques Necker, and wife of a Swedish diplomat. She published best-selling novels and influential literary criticism, and whenever allowed to reside in Paris, she encouraged the intellectual and political dissidents from Napoleon's regime. In this painting by François Gérard, de Staël is shown wearing a Turkish-style turban, fashionable in portraits of the era.

(Réunion des Musées Nationaux/Art Resource, NY.)

expansion of gases, and research on fossil shells prepared the way for new theories of evolutionary change later in the nineteenth century.

Napoleon aimed to modernize French society through science, but he could not tolerate criticism. He considered most writers useless or dangerous, "good for nothing under any government." Some of the most talented French writers of the time had to live in exile. The best known of them was Germaine de Staël (1766–1817). When explaining his desire to banish her, Napoleon exclaimed, "She is a machine in motion who stirs up the salons." While exiled in the German states, Madame de Staël wrote a novel, *Corinne* (1807), whose heroine is a brilliant woman thwarted by a patriarchal system, and *On Germany* (1810), an account of the important new literary currents east of the Rhine. Her books were banned in France.

Despite Napoleon's accommodation with the pope, many royalists and Catholics still criticized him as an impious usurper. François-René de Chateaubriand (1768–1848) admired Napoleon as "the strong man who has saved us from the abyss," but he preferred monarchy. In his view, Napoleon had not properly understood the need to defend Christian values against the Enlightenment's excessive reliance on reason. Chateaubriand wrote his *Genius of Christianity* (1802) to draw attention to the power and mystery of faith. He warned, "It is to the vanity of knowledge that we owe almost all our misfortunes. . . . The learned ages have always been followed by ages of destruction."

"Europe Was at My Feet": Napoleon's Military Conquests

Building on innovations introduced by the republican governments before him, Napoleon revolutionized the art of war with tactics and strategy based on a highly mobile army. Napoleon attributed his military success "three-quarters to morale" and the rest to leadership and superiority of numbers at the point of attack. Conscription provided the large numbers: 1.3 million men of ages twenty to twenty-four were drafted between 1800 and 1812, another million in 1813–1814. Military service was both a patriotic duty and a means of social mobility. The men who rose through the ranks to become officers were young, ambitious, and accustomed to the new ways of war. Consequently, the French army had higher morale than the armies of other powers, most of which rejected conscription as too democratic and continued to restrict their officer corps to the nobility. Only in 1813–1814 did French morale plummet, as the military tide turned against Napoleon.

When Napoleon came to power in 1799, desertion was rampant, and the generals competed with one another for predominance. Napoleon united all the armies into one Grand Army under his personal command. By 1812, he commanded 700,000 troops. In any given battle, between 70,000 and 180,000 men, not all of them French, fought for France. Life on campaign was no picnic, yet Napoleon inspired almost fanatical loyalty. A brilliant strategist who carefully studied the demands of war, he outmaneuvered nearly all his opponents. He gathered the largest possible army for one great and decisive battle and then followed with a relentless pursuit to break enemy morale altogether. He fought alongside his soldiers in some sixty battles and had nineteen horses shot from under him. One opponent said that Napoleon's presence alone was worth 50,000 men.

One of Napoleon's greatest advantages was the lack of coordination among his enemies. Britain dominated the seas but did not want to field huge land armies. On the European continent, the French republic had already established satellite regimes in the Netherlands and Italy, which served as a buffer against the big powers to the east—Austria, Prussia, and Russia. By maneuvering diplomatically and militarily, Napoleon could usually take these on one

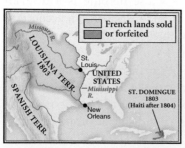

France's Retreat from America

by one. After reorganizing the French armies in 1799, for example, Napoleon won striking victories against the Austrians at Marengo and Hohenlinden in 1800, forcing them to agree to peace terms. Once the Austrians had withdrawn, Britain agreed to the Treaty of Amiens in 1802, effectively ending hostilities in Europe. Napoleon considered the peace with Great Britain merely a truce, however, and it lasted only until 1803. When the attempt to retake St. Domingue failed, Napoleon abandoned his plans to extend his empire to the Western Hemisphere and sold the Louisiana Territory to the United States in 1803.

When war resumed in Europe, the British navy once more proved its superiority by defeating the French and their Spanish allies in a huge naval battle at Trafalgar off the Spanish coast in 1805. France lost many ships; the British lost no vessels, but their renowned admiral Lord Horatio Nelson died in the battle. On land, however, Napoleon remained invincible. In 1805, Austria took up arms again when Napoleon demanded that it declare neutrality in the conflict with Britain. Napoleon promptly captured 25,000 Austrian soldiers at Ulm in Bavaria in 1805. After marching on to Vienna, he again trounced the Austrians, who had been joined by their new ally, Russia. The battle of Austerlitz, often considered Napoleon's greatest victory, was fought on December 2, 1805, the first anniversary of his coronation.

After maintaining neutrality for a decade, Prussia declared war on France. In 1806, the French promptly destroyed the Prussian army at Jena and Auerstadt. In 1807, Napoleon defeated the Russians at Friedland. Personal negotiations between Napoleon and the young tsar Alexander I (r. 1801–1825) resulted in a humiliating settlement imposed on Prussia, which paid the price for temporary reconciliation between France and Russia. The Treaties of Tilsit turned Prussian lands west of the Elbe River into the kingdom of Westphalia under Napoleon's brother Jerome, and Prussia's Polish provinces became the duchy of Warsaw. Alexander recognized Napoleon's conquests in central and western Europe and promised to help him against the British in exchange for Napoleon's support against the Turks. Neither party kept the bargain. Napoleon once again had turned the divisions among his enemies in his favor.

Wherever the Grand Army conquered, Napoleon's influence soon followed. By annexing some territories and setting up others as satellite kingdoms with much-reduced autonomy,

Consolidation of German and Italian States, 1812

Napoleon attempted to colonize large parts of Europe. He brought the disparate German and Italian states together to rule them more effectively and to exploit their resources for his own ends. In 1806, he established the Confederation of the Rhine, which soon included almost all the German states except Austria and Prussia. The Holy Roman Emperor gave up his title, held since the thirteenth century, and became simply the emperor of Austria. Napoleon established three units in Italy: the territories directly annexed to France and the satellite kingdoms of Italy and Naples. Italy had not been so unified since the Roman Empire.

Napoleon forced French-style reforms on both the annexed territories, which were ruled directly from France, and the satellite kingdoms, which were usually ruled by one or another of Napoleon's relatives but with a certain autonomy. Napoleon brought in French experts to work with handpicked locals to abolish serfdom, eliminate seigneurial dues, introduce the Napoleonic Code, suppress monasteries, subordinate church to state, and extend civil rights to Jews and other religious minorities. Reactions to these innovations were mixed. Napoleon's chosen rulers often made real improvements in roads, public works, law codes, and education. Yet tax increases and ever-rising conscription quotas also fomented discontent. The annexed territories and satellite kingdoms paid half the French war expenses. Napoleon's brother Louis would not allow conscription in his kingdom of the Netherlands because the Dutch had never had compulsory military service. In 1810, Napoleon annexed the satellite kingdom because his brother had become too sympathetic to Dutch interests.

Napoleon's victories forced defeated rulers to rethink their political and cultural assumptions. After suffering a crushing military defeat in 1806, Prussian king Frederick William III (r. 1797–1840) appointed a reform commission, and on its recommendation he abolished serfdom. Peasants gained their personal independence from their noble landlords, who could no longer sell them to pay gambling debts, for example, or refuse them permission to marry. Yet the lives of the former serfs remained bleak; they were left without land, and their landlords no longer had to care for them in hard times. The king's advisers also overhauled the army to make the high command more efficient and to open the way to the appointment of middle-class officers. Prussia instituted these reforms to try to compete with the French, not to promote democracy. As one reformer wrote to Frederick William, "We must do from above what the French have done from below."

Reform received lip service in Russia. Tsar Alexander I had gained his throne after an aristocratic coup deposed and killed his autocratic and capricious father, Paul (r. 1796–1801), and in the early years of his reign the remorseful young ruler created Western-style ministries, lifted restrictions on importing foreign books, and founded six new universities. There was even talk of drafting a constitution. But none of these efforts reached beneath the surface of Russian life, and by the second decade of his reign Alexander began to reject the Enlightenment spirit that his grandmother Catherine the Great had instilled in him.

Napoleon's Fall

Napoleon's empire ultimately failed because it was based on a contradiction: Napoleon tried to reduce almost all of Europe to the status of colonial dependents even though Europe had long consisted of independent states. His actions resulted instead in a great upsurge of the nationalist feeling that has dominated European politics to the present.

The one power always standing between Napoleon and total dominance of Europe was Great Britain. The British ruled the seas and financed anyone who would oppose Napoleon. In an effort to bankrupt this "nation of shopkeepers" by choking its trade, Napoleon inaugurated the **Continental System** in 1806. It prohibited all commerce between Great Britain and France as well as between Great Britain and France's dependent states and allies. After an initial decline in British exports and industrial production, the system proved impossible to enforce, and widespread smuggling brought British goods into the European market. British industrial growth resumed; calico-printing works, for example, quadrupled their production. The temporary protection from British competition could not make up for French losses in the port cities, whose trade with the Caribbean colonies had been disrupted by war and Haitian independence.

Smuggling British goods was only one way of opposing the French. Resistance to French demands for money or for draftees eventually prompted that patriotic defense of the nation known as nationalism. In southern Italy, opposition led to the formation of a network of secret societies, called the *carbonari* ("charcoal-burners"), which got its name from the practice of marking each new member's forehead with a charcoal mark. Throughout the nineteenth century, the carbonari played a leading role in Italian nationalism. In the German states, intellectuals wrote passionate defenses of the virtues of the German nation and of the superiority of German literature. A thriving press, the multiplication of Masonic lodges and literary clubs, and a resurgence of intellectual life in the German universities all eventually connected with anti-French nationalism.

No nations bucked under Napoleon's reins more than Portugal and Spain. In 1807, Napoleon sent 100,000 troops through Spain to invade Portugal, forcing the royal family to flee to the Portuguese colony of Brazil. But fighting continued, aided by a British army. When Napoleon got his brother Joseph named king of Spain in place of the senile Charles IV (r. 1788–1808), the Spanish clergy and nobles raised bands of peasants to fight the French occupiers. Peasants hated French requisitioning of their food supplies. Spanish nobles feared revolutionary reforms. The Spanish Catholic church spread anti-French propaganda that equated Napoleon with heresy. As the former archbishop of Seville wrote to the archbishop

■ Napoleon's Mamelukes Massacre the Spanish

In one of the paintings he produced to criticize Napoleon's occupation of Spain, Second of May 1808 at the Puerta del Sol *(1814), Francisco Goya depicts the brutal suppression of the Spanish revolt in Madrid against Napoleon. Napoleon used Mamelukes, Egyptian soldiers descended from freed Turkish slaves. For the Spanish Christians—and for European viewers of the painting—use of these mercenaries made the event even more horrifying. Europeans considered Muslims, and Turks in particular, as menacing because the Europeans had been fighting them for centuries.*
(Museo del Prado, Madrid.)

of Granada in 1808, "You realize that we must not recognize as king a free-mason, heretic, Lutheran, as are all the Bonapartes and the French nation." Even Napoleon's taking personal command of French forces failed to quell the Spanish. Germaine de Staël commented that Napoleon "never understood that a war might be a crusade. . . . He never reckoned with the one power that no arms could over-come—the enthusiasm of a whole people."

Despite opposition, by 1812 Napoleon controlled more territory than any European ruler had since Roman times (see "Mapping the West," page 696). Only two major European states remained fully independent—Great Britain and Russia—but once allied they would successfully challenge his dominion and draw many other states to their side. Britain sent aid to the Portuguese and Spanish rebels, while Russia once again prepared for war. Tsar Alexander I made peace with the Ottoman Turks and allied himself with Great Britain and Sweden. In 1812, Napoleon invaded Russia with 250,000 horses and 600,000 men, including contingents of Italians, Poles, Swiss, Dutch, and Germans. This daring move proved to be his undoing.

Napoleon followed his usual strategy of trying to strike quickly, but the Russian generals avoided confrontation and retreated eastward, destroying anything that might be useful to the invaders. In September, on the road to Moscow, Napoleon finally engaged the main Russian force in the gigantic battle of Borodino. French casualties were 30,000 men, including 47 generals; the Russians lost 45,000. Once again the Russians retreated, leaving Moscow undefended. Napoleon entered the deserted city, but the victory turned hollow when the departing Russians set the wooden city on fire. Within a week, three-fourths of it had burned to the ground. Alexander refused to negotiate, and French morale plunged with worsening problems of supply. Weeks of constant marching in the dirt and heat had worn down the foot soldiers, who were dying of disease or deserting in large numbers.

In October, Napoleon began his retreat; in November came the cold. Napoleon himself reported that on November 14 the temperature fell to 24 degrees Fahrenheit. A German soldier in the Grand Army described trying to cook fistfuls of raw bran with snow to make something like bread. For him the retreat was "the indescribable horror of all possible plagues." Within a week, the Grand Army lost 30,000 horses and had to abandon most of its artillery and food supplies. Russian forces harassed the retreating army, now more pathetic than grand. By December, only 100,000 troops remained, one-sixth the original number, and the retreat had turned into a rout: the Russians had captured 200,000 soldiers, including 48 generals and 3,000 other officers.

Napoleon had made a classic military mistake that would be repeated by Adolf Hitler in World War II: fighting a war on two distant fronts simultaneously. The Spanish war tied down 250,000 French troops and forced Napoleon to bully Prussia and Austria into supplying soldiers of dubious loyalty for the Moscow campaign. They deserted at the first opportunity. The fighting in Spain and Portugal also worsened the already substantial logistical and communications problems involved in marching to Moscow.

Napoleon's humiliation might have been temporary if the British and Russians had not successfully organized a coalition to complete the job. Napoleon still had resources at his command; by the spring of 1813 he had replenished his army with another 250,000 men. With British financial support, Russian, Austrian, Prussian, and Swedish armies met the French outside Leipzig in October 1813 and defeated Napoleon in the Battle of the Nations. One by one, Napoleon's German allies deserted him to join the German nationalist "war of liberation." The Confederation of the Rhine dissolved, and the Dutch revolted and restored the prince of Orange. Joseph Bonaparte fled Spain, and a combined Spanish-Portuguese army under British command invaded France. In only a few months, the allied powers crossed the Rhine and marched toward Paris. In March 1814, the French Senate deposed Napoleon, who abdicated when his remaining generals refused to fight.

Napoleon went into exile on the island of Elba off the Italian coast. His wife, Marie-Louise, refused to accompany him. The allies restored to the throne Louis XVIII (r. 1814–1824), the brother of Louis XVI (whose son was known as Louis XVII even though he died in prison in 1795 without ever ruling).

Napoleon had one last chance to regain power. Lacking a solid base of support, Louis XVIII tried to steer a middle course by granting a charter that established a British-style monarchy with a two-house legislature and guaranteed civil rights. But he was caught between returning émigré nobles who demanded a complete restoration of their lands and powers and those who had supported either the republic or Napoleon during the previous twenty-five years. Sensing an opportunity, Napoleon escaped from Elba in early 1815 and, landing in southern France, attracted cheering crowds and former soldiers to his side. The period known as the "Hundred Days" (the length of time between his escape and his final defeat) had begun. Louis XVIII fled across the border, waiting for help from France's enemies.

Napoleon quickly moved his reconstituted army into present-day Belgium. At first it seemed that he might succeed in separately fighting the two armies arrayed against him—a Prussian army and a joint force of Belgian, Dutch, German, and British troops led by Sir Arthur Wellesley (1769–1852), duke of Wellington. But the Prussians evaded him and joined with Wellington at Waterloo. Completely

IMPORTANT DATES

1787	Prussian invasion stifles Dutch Patriot revolt	1795	Third (final) Partition of Poland
1788	Resistance of Austrian Netherlands against reforms of Joseph II; opening of reform parliament in Poland	1799	Napoleon Bonaparte comes to power in a coup
		1801	Napoleon signs a concordat with the pope
1789	French Revolution begins	1804	Napoleon crowns himself emperor of France and issues new Civil Code
1791	Slave revolt in St. Domingue (Haiti)		
1792	Start of war between France and the rest of Europe; second revolution of August 10 overthrows French monarchy	1805	British naval forces defeat the French at the battle of Trafalgar; Napoleon wins his greatest victory at the battle of Austerlitz
		1812	Napoleon invades Russia
1793	Second Partition of Poland by Austria and Russia; Louis XVI of France executed for treason	1815	Napoleon defeated at Waterloo and exiled to island of St. Helena, where he dies in 1821
1794	France annexes the Austrian Netherlands; abolition of slavery in French colonies; Robespierre's government by terror falls		

routed, Napoleon had no choice but to abdicate again. This time the victorious allies banished him permanently to the remote island of St. Helena, far off the coast of West Africa, where he died in 1821 at the age of fifty-two.

■ **REVIEW:** *Why was Napoleon able to gain control over so much of Europe's territory?*

Conclusion

The cost of Napoleon's rule was high: 750,000 French soldiers and 400,000 others from annexed and satellite states died fighting for the French between 1800 and 1815. The losses among those attempting to stop Napoleon were at least as high, but no military figure since Alexander the Great in the fourth century B.C.E. had made such an impact on world history. Napoleon's plans for a united Europe, his insistence on spreading the legal reforms of the French Revolution, his model of an authoritarian state, and even his inadvertent awakening of national sentiment set the agenda for European history in the modern era.

The revolutionary cataclysm permanently altered the political landscape of Europe. The French executed their king as a traitor and set up Europe's first republic with universal male suffrage and a written guarantee of "the rights of man." Ordinary people marched in demonstrations, met in clubs, and in the case of men, voted in national elections for the first time. They got their first taste of democracy. But the ideals of universal education, religious toleration, and democratic participation could not prevent the institution of new forms of government terror to persecute, imprison, and kill dissidents. The French revolutionary experiment thus led to democracy *and* to a kind of totalitarianism. The French used the new spirit of national pride to inspire a huge citizen army, but the army conquered other peoples and gave a leading general the chance to take power for himself. Napoleon in turn created yet another new form of rule with a long history in the modern era: a police state in which the generals played a leading political role. Napoleon suppressed all other meaningful political participation and offered in its place law and order and modernization from above. Like many other authoritarian rulers after him, however, Napoleon could not maintain his position once he lost in battle.

As events unfolded between 1789 and 1815, the French Revolution became *the* model of modern revolution and in the process set the enduring patterns of all modern politics. Republicanism, democracy, terrorism, nationalism, and military dictatorship all took their modern forms during the French Revolution. Even the terms *left* and *right* got their political meaning in this period: "the left" was a reference to deputies who favored extensive change and sat together in seats to the speaker's left in 1789; deputies who preferred a more cautious and conservative stance sat as a group to the speaker's right. The breathtaking succession of regimes in France between 1789 and 1815 inevitably raised disturbing questions about the

■ **MAPPING THE WEST** Europe under Napoleonic Domination, 1812

In 1812, Napoleon had at least nominal control of almost all of western Europe. Even before he made his fatal mistake of invading Russia, however, his authority had been undermined in Spain and seriously weakened in the Italian and German states. His efforts to extend French power sparked resistance almost everywhere. As Napoleon insisted on French domination, local people began to think of themselves as Italian, German, or Dutch. Thus, Napoleon inadvertently laid the foundations for the nineteenth-century spread of nationalism. **For more help analyzing this map,** see the map activity for this chapter in the ONLINE STUDY GUIDE at bedfordstmartins.com/huntconcise.

relationship between rapid political change and violence. Do all revolutions in the name of democracy inevitably degenerate into wars of conquest or terror? Is a regime democratic if it does not allow poor men, women, or blacks to vote? Is a militaristic, authoritarian style of government the only answer to divisive political conflicts in a time of war? The French Revolution and its aftermath—the era of Napoleon—raised these questions and many more.

■ **MAKING CONNECTIONS**

1. *Why did the other rulers of Europe find the French Revolution so threatening?*

2. *What was the long-term significance of Napoleon for Europe?*

■ **FOR FURTHER EXPLORATION**

For further reading and online research ideas, see the Suggested References on page SR-8 at the back of the book.

For practice quizzes, a customized study plan, and other study tools, see the ONLINE STUDY GUIDE at bedfordstmartins.com/huntconcise.

For primary-source material from this period, see Chapter 16 in *Sources of THE MAKING OF THE WEST: A CONCISE HISTORY*, Second Edition.

17

Industrialization and Social Ferment

1815–1850

I N 1830–1832 AND AGAIN IN 1847–1851, devastating outbreaks of **cholera** swept across Asia and Europe, touching the United States as well in 1849–1850. Today we know that a waterborne bacterium causes cholera, but at the time no one understood the disease and everyone feared it. The usually fatal illness induced violent vomiting and diarrhea and left the skin blue, eyes sunken and dull, and hands and feet ice cold. While cholera particularly ravaged the crowded, filthy neighborhoods of rapidly growing cities, it also claimed many rural as well as some well-to-do victims. In Paris, 18,000 people died in the 1832 epidemic and 20,000 in that of 1849; in Russia, the epidemic claimed 250,000 victims in 1831–1832 and a million in 1847–1851. This British **lithograph** captures the fearsome and mysterious nature of the new epidemic disease. Mass-produced from inked stones, lithographs played a key role in social commentary and political discussion.

The picture might also stand for the continuing specter of revolution. Although many Europeans longed for peace and stability in the aftermath of the Napoleonic whirlwind, they lived in a world that was deeply unsettled by two parallel revolutions:

■ **The Threat of Cholera**
In this lithograph from 1831 by the British artist Robert Seymour, Cholera appears as a kind of monster that tramples everyone in its path. Lithography (from the Greek lithos, *"stone") was invented by a German engraver in 1798, but like the steam engine perfected in 1776, its use spread across Europe only in the nineteenth century. In lithography, an artist uses a greasy crayon to trace an image on a flat stone; the grease attracts the ink while the blank areas repel it. The inked stone is embedded in a printing press that can produce thousands of identical images. Designed for a mass audience, nineteenth-century lithographs helped ordinary people make sense of the changes taking place around them.* (National Library of Medicine.)

the French Revolution and the Industrial Revolution. Even as restored monarchs tried to limit challenges to their rule, political revolts broke out sporadically in the 1820s, again in 1830, and then over much of Europe in 1848. At the same time, the Industrial Revolution spread from Great Britain to continental Europe in the form of factories and railroads. Industrialization produced new social problems that reinforced demands for political change. Under the impact of the French and Industrial Revolutions, new ideologies emerged. Conservatism, nationalism, liberalism, socialism, and communism each offered their adherents a doctrine that explained social change and advocated a political program to confront it.

Social ferment appeared in a variety of forms. As industrialization spread across western Europe, peasants and workers streamed into the cities, raising fears of disease, crime, and social unrest. The population of Berlin, for example, more than doubled between 1819 and 1849, reaching 412,000. By 1840, more than half the residents of Berlin had been born outside the city. In response, middle-class men and women across Europe joined together in reform societies to urge specific programs for fighting prostitution, assisting poor mothers, encouraging temperance (abstention from alcohol), or abolishing slavery. Despite these efforts at reform, the most unfortunate sometimes pulled up stakes and emigrated to other places, such as the United States. Between 1815 and 1850, more than five million Europeans left their home countries for new lives overseas. For those who stayed behind, revolution remained an ever-present option.

The "Restoration" of Europe

When Napoleon went off to his permanent exile on St. Helena, those allied against him breathed a collective sigh of relief. Revolution, it seemed, had finally been defeated. Some of the returning rulers so detested French innovations that they tore French plants out of their gardens and threw French furniture out of their palaces. Even as Napoleon had made his last desperate bid for power in the Hundred Days between his escape from Elba and his final defeat, his enemies were meeting in the Congress of Vienna (1814–1815) to decide the fate of postrevolutionary Europe. Many of Europe's monarchs hoped to nullify revolutionary and Napoleonic reforms and "restore" their old regimes.

The Congress of Vienna, 1814–1815

Besides redrawing the boundaries of France, and determining who would rule each nation, the congress had to decide the fate of Napoleon's duchy of Warsaw, the German province of Saxony, the Netherlands, the states once part of the confederation of the Rhine, and various Italian territories. All had either changed hands or been created during the wars. These issues were resolved by face-to-face negotiations among representatives of the five major powers: Austria, Russia, Prussia,

■ The Congress of Vienna
An unknown French engraver caricatured the efforts of the diplomats at the Congress of Vienna, complaining that they used the occasion to divide the spoils of European territory. At the far left stands Metternich preparing to take Venice and Lombardy (northern Italy). (Historisches Museum der Stadt Wien.)

Britain, and France. With its aim to arrange a long-lasting, negotiated peace endorsed by all parties—both winners and losers—the Congress of Vienna produced a new equilibrium that relied on cooperation among the major powers while guaranteeing the status of smaller states. It also established a new framework for international relations based on periodic meetings—congresses—between the major powers. This congress system, or "concert of Europe," helped prevent another major war until the 1850s, and no conflict comparable to the Napoleonic wars would occur again until 1914.

Austria's chief negotiator, Prince Klemens von Metternich (1773–1859), took the lead in negotiations. A well-educated nobleman who spoke five languages, Metternich served as a minister in the Austrian cabinet from 1809 to 1848. Although his penchant for womanizing made him a security risk in the eyes of the British Foreign Office (he even had an affair with Napoleon's younger sister), he worked with the British prime minister Robert Castlereagh (1769–1822) to ensure a moderate agreement that would check French aggression yet maintain France's great-power status. Metternich and Castlereagh believed that France must remain a major player so that no one European power might dominate the others. In this way, France could help Austria and Britain counter the ambitions of Prussia and Russia. When the French army failed to oppose Napoleon's return to power in the Hundred

■ **MAP 17.1 Europe after the Congress of Vienna, 1815**

The diplomats meeting at the Congress of Vienna could not simply "restore" Europe to its prerevolutionary borders. Too much had changed since 1789. France was forced to return to its 1790 borders, and Spain and Portugal regained their former rulers. The Austrian Netherlands and the Dutch Republic were united in a new kingdom of the Netherlands, the German states were joined in a Germanic Confederation that built upon Napoleon's Confederation of the Rhine, and Napoleon's Grand Duchy of Warsaw became the kingdom of Poland with the tsar of Russia as king.

Days, the allies took away all territory conquered by France since 1790 and required France to pay an indemnity and support an army of occupation until it was paid.

The goal of the congress was to achieve postwar stability by establishing secure states with guaranteed borders (Map 17.1). Where possible, the congress simply restored traditional rulers, as in Spain and the Italian states. The great powers decided to turn Napoleon's duchy of Warsaw into a new Polish kingdom but made the tsar of Russia its king. (Poland would not regain its independence until 1918.) The former Dutch Republic and the Austrian Netherlands, both annexed to France, now united as the new kingdom of the Netherlands under the restored stadholder. Prussia gained territory in Saxony and on the left bank of the Rhine to compensate for its losses in Poland. To make up for its losses in Poland and Saxony, Austria reclaimed the Italian provinces of Lombardy and Venetia and the Dalmatian coast. Austria now presided over the German Confederation, which replaced the defunct Holy Roman Empire and also included Prussia.

The lesser powers were not forgotten. The kingdom of Piedmont-Sardinia took Genoa, Nice, and part of Savoy. Sweden obtained Norway from Denmark but had to accept Russia's conquest of Finland. Finally, various international trade issues were also resolved. At the urging of Great Britain, the congress agreed to condemn in principle the slave trade, abolished by Great Britain in 1807. In reality, however, the slave trade continued in many places until the 1840s.

To impart spiritual substance to this very calculated political settlement, Tsar Alexander proposed a Holy Alliance that would ensure divine assistance in upholding religion, peace, and justice. Prussia and Austria signed the agreement, but Great Britain refused to accede to what Castlereagh called "a piece of sublime mysticism and nonsense." Pope Pius VII also refused on the grounds that the papacy needed no help in interpreting Christian truth. Despite the reassertion of traditional religious principle, the congress had in fact given birth to a new diplomatic order: in the future, the legitimacy of states depended on the treaty system, not on divine right.

The Revival of Religion

Once peace returned, many Europeans renewed and reaffirmed their religious faith. In France, the Catholic church sent missionaries to hold open-air "ceremonies of reparation" to express repentance for the outrages of revolution. In Rome, the papacy re-established the Jesuit order, which had been disbanded during the Enlightenment. In the Italian states and Spain, governments used religious societies of laypeople to combat the influence of reformers and nationalists.

Revivalist movements, especially in Protestant countries, could on occasion challenge the status quo, not support it. In parts of the Protestant German states and Britain, religious revival had begun in the eighteenth century with the rise of Pietism and Methodism, movements that stressed individual religious experience rather than reason as the true path to moral and social reform. The English Methodists followed John Wesley (1703–1791), who preached an emotional, morally austere, and very personal "method" of gaining salvation. The Methodists, or Wesleyans, gradually separated from the Church of England and in the early decades of the nineteenth century attracted thousands of members in huge revival meetings that lasted for days. Shopkeepers, artisans, agricultural laborers, miners, and workers in cottage industry, both male and female, flocked to the new denomination. Even though Methodist statutes of 1792 had insisted that "none of us shall either in writing or in conversation speak lightly or irreverently of the government,"

Methodists fostered a sense of democratic community with their hostility to elaborate ritual and their encouragement of popular preaching. Methodist women traveled on horseback to preach in barns, town halls, and textile dye houses. Methodist Sunday schools that taught thousands of poor children to read and write eventually helped create greater demands for working-class political participation.

The religious revival was not limited to Europe. In the United States, the second "Great Awakening" began around 1790 with huge camp meetings that brought together thousands of people, many of them Methodist. (The original Great Awakening took place in the 1730s and 1740s, sparked by the preaching of George Whitefield, a young English evangelist and follower of John Wesley.) During this period, Protestant sects began systematic missionary activity in other parts of the world, with British and American missionary societies taking the lead in the 1790s and early 1800s. In the British colony of India, Protestant missionaries argued for the reform of Hindu customs. *Sati*—the burning of widows on the funeral pyres of their husbands—was abolished by the British administration of India in 1829. Protestant and Catholic missionary activity would become an arm of European imperialism and cultural influence in the nineteenth century.

Political Challenges to the Vienna Settlement

The decisions taken by the Congress of Vienna disappointed all those who dreamed of constitutional freedoms and national independence, and within a few years, discontent rose to the surface. The restored monarchy in France provided a major test because the returning Bourbons had to confront the legacy of twenty-five years of upheaval. Louis XVIII (r. 1814–1824) tried to ensure a measure of continuity by maintaining Napoleon's Civil Code. He also guaranteed the rights of ownership to church lands sold during the revolutionary period and created a parliament composed of a Chamber of Peers nominated by the king and a Chamber of Deputies elected by highly restricted suffrage (fewer than 100,000 voters in a population of 30 million, or about 3 percent). In making these concessions, the king tried to follow a moderate course of compromise, but the Ultras (ultraroyalists) pushed for complete repudiation of the revolutionary past. When Louis returned to power after Napoleon's final defeat, armed royalist bands attacked and murdered hundreds of Bonapartists and former revolutionaries. In 1816, the Ultras insisted on abolishing divorce and set up special courts to punish opponents of the regime. When an assassin killed Louis XVIII's nephew in 1820, the Ultras demanded even more extreme measures.

After Ferdinand VII regained the Spanish crown in 1814, he tried to restore the powers of the prerevolutionary nobility, church, and monarchy. He had foreign books and newspapers confiscated at the frontier and allowed the publication of only two newspapers. In 1820, disgruntled soldiers demanded that Ferdinand proclaim his adherence to the Constitution of 1812, which he had abolished in 1814.

Ferdinand stalled for time, and in 1823 a French army invaded with the consent of the other Vienna powers to support him. His government then tortured and executed hundreds of rebels; thousands were imprisoned or forced into exile.

Hearing of the Spanish uprising, rebellious soldiers in the kingdom of Naples joined forces with the carbonari and demanded a constitution. But when a new parliament met, it broke down over internal disagreements. The promise of reform sparked rebellion in the northern Italian kingdom of Piedmont-Sardinia, where rebels urged Charles Albert, the young heir to the Piedmont throne, to fight the Austrians for Italian unification. He vacillated, and in 1821, after the rulers of Austria, Prussia, and Russia met and agreed on intervention, the Austrians defeated the rebels in Naples and Piedmont (see Map 17.1). Despite the opposition of Great Britain, which condemned the "indiscriminate" suppression of revolutionary movements, Metternich convinced the other powers to agree to his muffling of the Italian opposition to Austrian rule.

Aspirations for constitutional government surfaced in Russia when Alexander I died suddenly in 1825. On the December day that the troops assembled in St. Petersburg to take an oath of loyalty to Alexander's brother Nicholas as the new tsar, rebel officers insisted that the crown belonged to another brother, Constantine, whom they hoped would be more favorable to constitutional reform. Constantine, though next in the line of succession after Alexander, had refused the crown. The soldiers nonetheless raised the cry "Long live Constantine, long live the Constitution." Soldiers loyal to Nicholas easily suppressed the outnumbered Decembrists (so called after the month of their uprising). The subsequent trial, however, made the rebels into legendary heroes. For the next thirty years, Nicholas I (r. 1825–1855) used a new political police to spy on potential opponents and stamp out rebelliousness.

The Ottoman Turks faced growing nationalist challenges in the Balkans, but the European powers feared that supporting them would encourage a rebellious spirit at home. The Serbs nonetheless revolted against Turkish rule and won virtual independence by 1817. An uprising by Greek peasants sparked a wave of mutual atrocities in 1821 and 1822. In retaliation for the killing of many Turks, the Ottoman authorities hanged the Greek patriarch (head of the Greek Orthodox church), and in the areas they still controlled the Turks pillaged churches, massacred thousands of men, and sold the women into slavery.

Nationalistic Movements in the Balkans, 1815–1830

■ **Greek Independence**
From 1836 to 1839, the Greek painter Panagiotis Zographos worked with his two sons on a series
of scenes depicting the Greek struggle for independence from the Turks. Response was so favorable
that one Greek general ordered lithographic reproductions for popular distribution. In this way,
nationalistic feeling could be encouraged even among people not directly touched by the struggle.
Here Turkish sultan Mehmet the Conqueror, exulting over the fall of Constantinople in 1453,
views a row of Greeks under the yoke, a sign of submission. (Collection, Visual Connection.)

Western opinion turned against the Turks; Greece, after all, was the home of
Western civilization. While the great powers negotiated, Greeks and pro-Greece committees around the world sent food and military supplies; a few enthusiastic European
and American volunteers even joined the Greeks. The Greeks held on until the great
powers were willing to intervene. In 1827, a combined force of British, French, and
Russian ships destroyed the Turkish fleet at Navarino Bay; and in 1828, Russia
declared war on the Turks and advanced close to Istanbul. The Treaty of Adrianople
of 1829 gave Russia a protectorate over the Danubian principalities in the Balkans and
provided for a conference among representatives of Britain, Russia, and France, all of
whom had broken with Austria in support of the Greeks. In 1830, Greece was declared
an independent kingdom under the guarantee of the three powers; in 1833, the son of
King Ludwig of Bavaria became Otto I of Greece. Nationalism, with the support of
European public opinion, had opened a hole in Metternich's system.

Across the Atlantic, national revolts also succeeded after a series of bloody wars
of independence. Taking advantage of the upheavals in Spain and Portugal that
began under Napoleon, restive colonists from Mexico to Argentina rebelled. Their
leader was Simon Bolívar (1783–1830), son of a slave owner, who was educated in

■ **MAP 17.2 Latin American Independence, 1804–1830**

The French lost their most important remaining American colony in 1804 when St. Domingue declared its independence as Haiti. But the impact of the French Revolution did not end there. Napoleon's occupation of Spain and Portugal seriously weakened the hold of those countries on their Latin American colonies. Despite the restoration of the Spanish and Portuguese rulers in 1814, most of their colonies successfully broke away in a wave of rebellions between 1811 and 1830. Meanwhile, a revolt in Spain in 1820–1823 led to a constitutional regime. The Spanish general sent to suppress the revolt in Mexico ended up joining the rebels' cause and helping them establish independence in 1821.

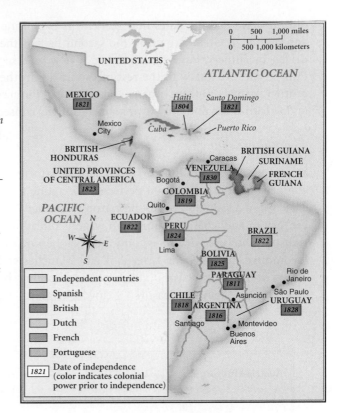

Europe on the works of Voltaire and Rousseau. Although Bolívar fancied himself a Latin American Napoleon, he had to acquiesce to the formation of a series of independent republics between 1821 and 1823, even in Bolivia, which is named after him. At the same time, Brazil (then still a monarchy) separated from Portugal (Map 17.2). The United States recognized the new states, and in 1823 President James Monroe (1758–1831) announced his Monroe Doctrine, closing the Americas to European intervention—a prohibition that depended on British naval power and British willingness to declare neutrality. The Vienna powers were only able to maintain their settlement in areas where they could intervene militarily.

■ **REVIEW:** *To what extent was the old order restored by the Congress of Vienna?*

The Advance of Industrialization and Urbanization

French and English writers of the 1820s introduced the term *Industrial Revolution* to capture the drama of contemporary economic change and to draw a parallel with the French Revolution. But unlike the French upheaval, the Industrial Revolution did not have definite dates that marked its beginning or ending. From their first appearance in Great Britain in the second half of the eighteenth century, steam-driven machinery, large factories, and a new working class spread fitfully across Europe and eventually to the rest of the world. In the first half of the nineteenth century many Europeans began to take notice of the acceleration of industrialization and urbanization and often complained of their consequences.

Engines of Change

Steam-driven engines took on a dramatic new form in the 1820s when the English engineer George Stephenson perfected an engine to pull wagons along rail tracks. The idea of a railroad was not new: iron tracks had been used since the seventeenth century to haul coal from mines in wagons pulled by horses. A railroad system of transport, however, developed only after Stephenson's invention of a steam-powered locomotive. In 1830, the Liverpool and Manchester Railway line opened to the cheers of British crowds. Suddenly, railroad building became a new industry every-where. (See "Taking Measure," below.) Belgium, newly independent in 1830,

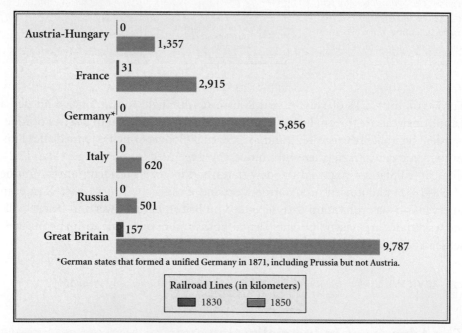

*German states that formed a unified Germany in 1871, including Prussia but not Austria.

Railroad Lines (in kilometers)
■ 1830   ▢ 1850

■ TAKING MEASURE Railroad Lines, 1830–1850

Great Britain quickly extended its lead in building railroads. The extension of commerce and, before long, the ability to wage war would depend on the development of effective rail networks. These statistics might be taken as predicting a realignment of power within Europe after 1850. What do the numbers say about the relative positions of Germany and Austria-Hungary and of Germany and France?

opened the first continental European railroad in 1835 with state bonds backed by British capital. Railroads grew spectacularly in the United States in the 1830s and 1840s, and the British also began to build railroads in India. In all, the world had 23,500 miles of track by midcentury, the vast majority of them in Europe.

Railroad building spurred both industrial development and state power (see "Mapping the West," page 744). Placed on the new tracks, steam-driven carriages could transport people and goods to the cities and link coal and iron deposits to the new factories. Canal building waned in the 1840s: the railroad had won out. Governments everywhere participated in the construction of railroads, which depended on private and state funds to pay for the massive amounts of iron, coal, heavy machinery, and human labor required to build and run them. One-third of all investment in the German states in the 1840s went into railroads. Some expected social and political change to follow. One German entrepreneur confidently predicted, "The locomotive is the hearse which will carry absolutism and feudalism to the graveyard." But the most obvious effects could be seen in the demand for iron products, which accelerated industrial development. Until the 1840s, cotton had led industrial production, but afterwards iron and coal began to count more and more.

Steam-powered engines made Britain the world leader in manufacturing. By midcentury, more than half of Britain's national income came from manufacturing and trade. The number of steamboats in Great Britain increased from two in 1812 to six hundred in 1840. Between 1840 and 1850, steam-engine power doubled in Great Britain and increased even more rapidly elsewhere in Europe, as those adopting British inventions strove to catch up. Although Great Britain consciously strove to protect its industrial supremacy, thousands of British engineers defied laws against the export of machinery or the emigration of artisans. The best known of them, John Cockerill, set up a machine works in Belgium that was soon selling its products as far east as Poland and Russia. Cockerill claimed to know about every innovation within ten days of its appearance in Britain.

Only slowly, thanks to such pirating of British methods and to new technical schools, did most continental European countries begin closing the gap. Belgium became the fastest-growing industrial power on the continent: between 1830 and 1844, the number of steam engines in Belgium quadrupled, and Belgians exported seven times as many steam engines as they imported. Even so, by 1850, continental Europe still lagged almost twenty years behind Great Britain in industrial development.

Formation of the Working Class

Steam-driven machines first brought workers together in factories in the textile industry. By 1830, more than one million people in Britain depended on the cotton industry for employment, and cotton cloth constituted 50 percent of the country's exports. The rapid expansion of the British textile industry had as its colonial corollary the destruction of the hand manufacture of textiles in India. The British put high import duties on Indian cloth entering Britain and kept such duties very low for British cloth entering India. The figures are dramatic: in 1813, the Indian city of Calcutta exported to England £2,000,000 of cotton cloth; by 1830, in contrast, Calcutta was importing from England £2,000,000 of cotton cloth. When Britain abolished slavery in its Caribbean colonies in 1833, British manufacturers began to buy raw cotton in the southern United States, where slavery still flourished.

Factories drew workers from the urban population surge, which had begun in the eighteenth century and now accelerated. The reasons for urban growth are not entirely clear. The population of such new industrial cities as Manchester and Leeds increased 40 percent in the 1820s alone. Historians long thought that factory workers came from the countryside, pushed off the land by the field enclosures of the 1700s. But recent studies have shown that the number of agricultural laborers actually increased during industrialization in Britain, suggesting that a growing birthrate created a larger population and fed workers into the new factory system. A system of employment that resembled family labor on farms or in cottage industry also developed in the new factories. Entire families came to toil for a single wage, although family members performed different tasks. Workdays of twelve to seventeen hours were typical, even for children, and the work was grueling.

As urban factories grew, their workers gradually came to constitute a new socioeconomic class with a distinctive culture and traditions. Like *middle class*, the term *working class* came into use for the first time in the early nineteenth century. It referred to the laborers in the new factories. In the past, workers had labored in isolated trades: water and wood carrying, gardening, laundry, and building. In contrast, factories brought people together with machines, under close supervision by their employers. They soon developed a sense of common interests and organized societies for mutual help and political reform. From these would come the first labor unions.

Fearing their displacement by machines, in 1811 and 1812 bands of handloom weavers wrecked factory machinery and burned mills in the Midlands, Yorkshire, and Lancashire. To restore order and protect industry, the British government sent in an army of twelve thousand regular soldiers and made machine wrecking punishable by death. The rioters were called Luddites after the fictitious figure Ned Ludd, whose signature appeared on their manifestos. (The term is still used to describe those who resist new technology.)

Other British workers focused their organizing efforts on reforming Parliament, whose members were chosen in elections dominated by the landowning elite. One reformer complained that the members of the House of Commons were nothing but "toad-eaters, gamblers, public plunderers, and hirelings." Reform clubs held large open-air meetings, and ordinary people eagerly bought cheap newspapers that clamored for change. In August 1819, sixty thousand people attended an illegal meeting held in St. Peter's Fields in Manchester. When the local authorities sent the cavalry to arrest the speaker, panic resulted; eleven people were killed and many hundreds injured. An alarmed government passed the Six Acts, which forbade large political meetings and restricted press criticism, suppressing the reform movement for a decade.

Despite increasing industrial growth, factory workers remained a minority everywhere. In the 1840s, factories in England employed only 5 percent of the workers; in France, 3 percent; in Prussia, 2 percent. Most workers, both men and women, continued to toil at home in putting-out, or cottage, industries. In the 1840s, for example, two-thirds of the manufacturing workers in Prussia and Saxony labored at home for contractors or merchants who supplied raw materials and then sold the finished goods. Some peasants kept their options open by combining factory work with agricultural labor. They worked in agriculture during the spring and summer and in manufacturing in the fall and winter. Unstable industrial wages made such arrangements essential. Some new industries idled periodically: for example, iron forges stopped for several months when the water level in streams dropped, and blast furnaces shut down for repairs several weeks every year. In hard times, factory owners simply closed their doors until demand for their goods improved.

Even though factories employed only a small percentage of the population, they attracted much attention because they created unheard-of riches and new forms of poverty all at once. "From this filthy sewer pure gold flows," wrote the French aristocrat Alexis de Tocqueville after visiting the new English industrial city of Manchester in the 1830s. "Here humanity attains its most complete development and its most brutish, here civilization works its miracles and civilized man is turned almost into a savage." Studies by physicians set the life expectancy of workers in Manchester at just seventeen years in 1840 (partly because of high rates of infant mortality), compared to the average in England of forty years. Visitors invariably complained about the smoke and soot. One American visitor to Britain in the late 1840s described how "in the manufacturing town, the fine soot or *blacks* darken the day, give white sheep the color of black sheep, discolor the human saliva, contaminate the air, poison many plants, and corrode monuments and buildings."

Authorities worried in particular about the effects on families. A doctor in the Prussian town of Breslau (population 111,000 in 1850), for example, reported that in working-class districts "several persons live in one room in a single bed, or perhaps a whole family, and use the room for all domestic duties, so that the air gets vitiated [polluted]. . . . Their diet consists largely of bread and potatoes." In Great Britain, the Factory Act of 1833 outlawed the employment of children under the age of nine in textile mills (except in the lace and silk industries) and limited the workdays of children ages nine to thirteen to nine hours a day and those ages thirteen to eighteen to twelve hours. Adults worked even longer hours. When investigating commissions showed that women and young children, sometimes under age six, were hauling coal trucks through low, cramped passageways in coal mines, the British Parliament passed a Mines Act in 1842 prohibiting the employment of women and girls underground. In 1847, the Central Short Time Committee, one of Britain's many social reform organizations, successfully pressured Parliament to limit the workday of women and children to ten hours. Countries in continental Europe followed the British lead, but since most did not insist on government inspection, enforcement was lax.

The advance of industrialization in eastern Europe was slow, in large part because serfdom still survived there, hindering labor mobility and tying up investment capital: as long as peasants were legally tied to the land as serfs, they could not migrate to the new factory towns, and landlords felt little incentive to invest their income in manufacturing. The problem was worst in Russia, where industrialization had hardly begun and would not take off until the end of the nineteenth century. Nevertheless, even in Russia signs of industrialization could be detected: raw cotton imports (a sign of a growing textile industry) increased sevenfold between 1831 and 1848, and the number of factories doubled along with the size of the industrial workforce.

Urbanization and Its Consequences

Industrial development spurred urban growth wherever factories were located in or near cities, yet cities grew even with little industry. Here, too, Great Britain led the way: half the population of England and Wales lived in towns by 1850, while in France and the German states the urban population was only about a quarter of the total. In the 1830s and 1840s many European cities ballooned. In the 1830s, London grew by 130,000 people, and in the first half of the 1840s Paris expanded by 120,000. Everywhere critics complained of the consequences.

Massive rural emigration, rather than births to women already living in cities, accounted for this remarkable increase. Europe's population grew by nearly 100 percent between 1800 and 1850, yet agricultural yields increased only by 30 to 50 percent. City life and new factories beckoned those faced with hunger and poverty, including emigrants from other lands: thousands of Irish emigrated to English cities, Italians went to French cities, and Poles flocked to German cities. Since the construction of new housing could not keep up with population growth, overcrowding was inevitable. In 1847 in St. Giles, the Irish quarter of London, 461 people lived in just twelve houses. Men, women, and children huddled together on piles of filthy rotting straw or potato peels because they had no money for fuel to keep warm.

Severe crowding worsened already dire sanitation conditions. Residents dumped refuse into streets or courtyards, and human excrement collected in cesspools under apartment houses. At midcentury, London's approximately 250,000 cesspools were emptied only once or twice a year. Water was scarce and had to be fetched daily from nearby fountains. Despite the diversion of water from provincial rivers to Paris and a tripling of the number of public fountains, Parisians had enough water for only two baths annually per person (the upper classes enjoyed more baths; the lower classes, fewer). In London, private companies that supplied water turned on pumps in the poorer sections for only a few hours three days a week. In rapidly growing

British industrial cities such as Manchester, one-third of the houses contained no latrines. Human waste ended up in the rivers that supplied drinking water. The horses that provided transportation inside the cities left droppings everywhere, and city dwellers often kept chickens, ducks, goats, pigs, geese, and even cattle, as well as dogs and cats, in their houses. The result was, as one observer noted, a "universal atmosphere of filth and stink."

Such conditions made cities prime breeding grounds for disease; those with 50,000 people or more had twice the death rates of rural areas. Rumors and panic followed in the wakes of epidemics such as cholera. In Paris in April 1832, a crowd of workers attacked a central hospital, believing the doctors were poisoning the poor and using cholera as a hoax to cover up the conspiracy. Eastern European peasants burned estates and killed physicians and officials. Although devastating, cholera did not kill as many people as tuberculosis, Europe's number-one deadly disease. But tuberculosis took its victims one by one and therefore had less impact on social relations.

Raging epidemics spurred a growing concern for public health. When news of the cholera outbreak in eastern Europe reached Paris in 1831, the city set up commissions in each municipal district to collect information about lower-class housing and sanitation. In Great Britain, reports on sanitation conditions among the working class led to the passage of new public health laws.

But government intervention did little to ease the social tensions inspired by rapid urban growth. Reformers believed that overcrowding among the poor led to sexual promiscuity and illegitimacy. They depicted the lower classes as dangerously lacking in sexual self-control. A physician visiting Lille, France, in 1835 wrote of "individuals of both sexes and of very different ages lying together, most of them without nightshirts and repulsively dirty. . . . The reader will complete the picture."

Officials collected statistics on illegitimacy that seemed to bear out these fears: one-quarter to one-half of the babies born in the big European cities in the 1830s and 1840s were illegitimate, and alarmed medical men wrote about thousands of infanticides. Between 1815 and the mid-1830s in France, 33,000 babies were abandoned at foundling hospitals every year; 27 percent of births in Paris in 1850 were illegitimate, compared with only 4 percent of rural births. Sexual disorder seemed to go hand in hand with drinking and crime. Beer halls and pubs dotted the urban landscape. One London street boasted twenty-three pubs in three hundred yards. Police officials estimated that London had 70,000 thieves and 80,000 prostitutes. In many cities, nearly half the urban population lived at the level of bare subsistence, and increasing numbers depended on public welfare, charity, or criminality to make ends meet. A Swiss pastor said of the workers, "Their hearts seethe with hatred of the well-to-do; their eyes lust for a share of the wealth about them; their mouths speak unblushingly of a coming day of retribution."

■ **REVIEW:** *Why were cities seen as dangerous places?*

New Ideologies

Although traditional ways of life still prevailed in much of Europe, new modes of thinking about changes in the social and political order arose in the 1820s and 1830s. This was an era of "isms"—conservatism, liberalism, socialism, nationalism, and romanticism. The French Revolution had caused people to ask questions about the best possible form of government, and its effects had made clear that people acting together could change their political system. The events of the 1790s and the following decades, however, also produced enormous differences of opinion over what constituted the ideal government. Similarly, the Industrial Revolution posed fundamental questions about changes in society and social relations: How did the new social order differ from the earlier one, and who should control it? Should governments try to moderate or accelerate the pace of change? Answers to these questions about the social and political order were called ideologies, a word coined during the French Revolution. An **ideology** is a shared set of beliefs about the way a society's social and political order should be organized. New political and social movements organized around these ideologies.

Conservatism

The French Revolution and Napoleonic domination of Europe had shown contemporaries that government could be changed overnight, that the old hierarchies could be overthrown in the name of reason, and that even Christianity could be written off or at least profoundly altered with the stroke of a pen. The potential for rapid change raised many questions about the proper sources of authority. Kings and churches could be restored and former revolutionaries locked up or silenced, but the old order no longer commanded automatic obedience. The old order was now merely *old*, no longer "natural" and "timeless." It had been ousted once and therefore might fall again. People insisted on having reasons to believe in their "restored" governments. The political doctrine that justified the restoration was **conservatism**.

Conservatives benefited from the disillusionment that permeated Europe after 1815. In the eyes of most Europeans, Napoleon had become a tyrant who ruled in his own interests. Conservatives believed it was crucial to analyze the roots of such tyranny so established authorities could use their knowledge of history to prevent its recurrence. They saw a logical progression in recent history: the Enlightenment based on reason led to the French Revolution, with its bloody guillotine and horrifying Terror, which in turn spawned the authoritarian and militaristic Napoleon. Conservative intellectuals therefore either rejected Enlightenment principles or at least subjected them to scrutiny and skepticism.

The most influential spokesman of conservatism was Edmund Burke (1729–1799), the British critic of the French Revolution. He argued that the revolutionaries erred in thinking they could construct an entirely new government based on reason. Government, Burke said, had to be rooted in long experience, which evolved over generations. All change must be gradual and must respect national and historical traditions.

Like Burke, later conservatives believed that religious and other major traditions were an essential foundation for any society. Conservatives blamed the French Revolution's attack on religion on the skepticism and anticlericalism of such Enlightenment thinkers as Voltaire, and they defended both hereditary monarchy and the authority of the church, whether Catholic or Protestant. The "rights of man," according to conservatives, could not stand alone as doctrine based simply on nature and reason. The community, too, had its rights, more important than those of any individual, and established institutions best represented those rights. The church, the state, and the family would provide an enduring social order for everyone. Faith, sentiment, history, and tradition must fill the vacuum left by the failures of reason and excessive belief in individual rights. Across Europe, these views were taken up and elaborated by government advisers, professors, and writers. Not surprisingly, they had their strongest appeal in ruling circles and guided the politics of men such as Metternich in Austria and Alexander I in Russia.

Liberalism

The adherents of **liberalism** defined themselves in opposition to conservatives on one end of the political spectrum and revolutionaries on the other. Nineteenth-century liberals should not be confused with those of the present day. In the nineteenth century, liberals emphasized constitutionalism and free trade above all else. They generally applauded the social and economic changes produced by the Industrial Revolution, while opposing the violence and excessive state power promoted by the French Revolution. The leaders of the rapidly expanding middle class composed of manufacturers, merchants, and professionals favored liberalism.

The foremost exponent of early-nineteenth-century liberalism was the English philosopher and jurist Jeremy Bentham (1748–1832). He called his brand of liberalism utilitarianism because he held that the best policy is the one that produces "the greatest good for the greatest number" and is thus the most useful, or utilitarian. Bentham's criticisms spared no institution; he railed against the injustices of the British parliamentary process, the abuses of the prisons and the penal code, and the educational system. In his zeal for social engineering, he proposed elaborate schemes for managing the poor and model prisons that would emphasize rehabilitation through close supervision rather than corporal punishment.

Bentham and many other liberals joined the abolitionist, antislavery movement that intensified between the 1790s and 1820s. Agitation by such groups as the London Society for Effecting the Abolition of the Slave Trade succeeded in gaining a first victory in 1807 when the British House of Lords voted to abolish the slave

■ Anti–Corn Law League Demonstration

A contemporary engraving of an Anti–Corn Law League demonstration in London in the early 1840s makes the main point of the campaign: FREE TRADE. Supporters wanted to repeal the Corn Laws that set tariffs on grain in order to lower the price of food. Middle-class men can be identified by their top hats, working-class men by their caps or bare heads. The demonstrators are portrayed as vociferous, but not violent, a key to maintaining middle-class support.

(The Granger Collection, New York.)

trade. The abolitionists' efforts finally bore fruit in 1833 when Britain abolished slavery in all its colonies.

British liberals pushed for two major reforms in addition to the abolition of slavery: expansion of the electorate to give representation to a broader segment of the middle class and repeal of the **Corn Laws** or tariffs on foreign grain. They gained their first goal in the Reform Bill of 1832. When the Tories in Parliament resisted the proposed extension of the right to vote, liberals and their supporters organized mass demonstrations. The Reform Bill passed after the king threatened to create enough new peers to obtain its passage in the House of Lords. Although the number of male voters increased by about 50 percent, only one in five Britons could now vote, and voting still depended on holding property. Nevertheless, the bill gave representation to new cities in the industrial north for the first time and set a precedent for further widening suffrage.

When landholders in the House of Commons thwarted efforts to lower grain tariffs, two Manchester cotton manufacturers set up the Anti–Corn Law League. The league denounced the landlords as "blood-sucking vampires" and attracted working-class backing by promising lower food prices. The league established local branches, published newspapers and the journal *The Economist* (founded in 1843 and now one of the world's most influential periodicals), and campaigned in elections. They eventually won the support of the Tory prime minister Sir Robert Peel, whose government repealed the Corn Laws in 1846.

Liberalism had less appeal in continental Europe because industrial growth was slower and the middle classes smaller than in Britain. French liberals agitated for greater press freedoms and a broadening of the vote. Liberal reform movements also grew up in the pockets of industrialization in Prussia and the Austrian Empire. Some state bureaucrats, especially university-trained middle-class officials, favored economic liberalism. Hungarian count Stephen Széchenyi (1791–1860) personally campaigned for the introduction of British-style changes. He introduced British agricultural techniques on his own lands, helped start up steamboat traffic on the Danube, encouraged the importation of machinery and technicians for steam-driven textile factories, and pushed the construction of Hungary's first railway line, from Budapest to Vienna.

In the 1840s, however, Széchenyi's efforts paled before those of the flamboyant Magyar nationalist Lajos Kossuth (1802–1894). After spending four years in prison for sedition, Kossuth grabbed every opportunity to publicize American democracy and British political liberalism, all in a fervent nationalist spirit. In 1844, he founded the Protective Association, whose members bought only Hungarian products; to Kossuth, boycotting Austrian goods was crucial to ending "colonial dependence" on Austria. Born of a lesser landowning family without a noble title, Kossuth did not hesitate to attack "the cowardly selfishness of the landowner class."

Even in Russia, signs of liberal, even socialist, opposition appeared in the 1830s and 1840s. Small "circles" of young noblemen serving in the army or bureaucracy met in cities, especially Moscow, to discuss the latest Western ideas and to criticize the Russian state: "The world is undergoing a transformation, while we vegetate in our hovels of wood and clay," wrote one. Out of these groups came such future revolutionaries as Alexander Herzen (1812–1870), described by the police as "a daring free-thinker, extremely dangerous to society." Tsar Nicholas I (r. 1825–1855) banned Western liberal writings as well as all books about the United States. He sent nearly ten thousand people a year into exile in Siberia as punishment for their political activities.

Socialism and the Early Labor Movement

Socialism took up where liberalism left off: socialists believed that the liberties advocated by liberals benefited only the middle class, the owners of factories and businesses, not the workers. They sought to reorganize society totally rather than to reform it piecemeal through political measures. Many were utopians who believed that ideal communities are based on cooperation rather than competition. Like Thomas More, whose book *Utopia* (1516) gave the movement its name, the utopian socialists believed that society would benefit all its members only if private property ceased to exist.

Socialists criticized the new industrial order for dividing society into two classes: the new middle class, or capitalists, who owned the wealth; and the working class, their downtrodden and impoverished employees. Such divisions tore the social fabric, and, as their name suggests, the socialists aimed to restore harmony and cooperation through social reorganization. Three early socialists helped instigate the movement: Robert Owen, Claude Henri de Saint-Simon, and Charles Fourier. Robert Owen (1771–1858) founded British socialism. A successful Welsh-born manufacturer, Owen bought a cotton mill in New Lanark, Scotland, in 1800 and began to set up a model factory town, where workers labored only ten hours a day (instead of seventeen, as was common). He moved to the United States in the 1820s to establish in Indiana a community he named New Harmony. The experiment collapsed after three years, a victim of internal squabbling. Nonetheless, Owen's experiments and writings inspired the movement for producer cooperatives (businesses owned and controlled by their workers), consumer cooperatives (stores in which consumers owned shares), and a national trade union.

Claude Henri de Saint-Simon (1760–1825) and Charles Fourier (1772–1837) were Owen's contemporaries in France. Saint-Simon was a noble who had served as an officer in the War of American Independence and lost a fortune speculating in national property during the French Revolution. Fourier traveled as a salesman for a Lyon cloth merchant. Both shared Owen's alarm about the effects of industrialization on social relations. Saint-Simon coined the terms *industrialism* and *industrialist* to define the new economic order and its chief animators. He believed that work, the central element in the new society, should be controlled not by politicians but by scientists, engineers, artists, and industrialists. To correct the abuses of the new industrial order, Fourier urged the establishment of communities that were part garden city and part agricultural commune; all jobs would be rotated to maximize happiness. The emancipation of women was essential to Fourier's vision of a harmonious community: "The extension of the privileges of women is the fundamental cause of all social progress."

Women participated actively in the socialist movements of the day, even though socialist men often shared the widespread prejudice against women's political activism. In Great Britain, many women joined the Owenites and helped form cooperative societies and unions. They defended women's working-class organizations against the complaints of men in the new societies and trade unions. As one woman wrote, "Do not say the unions are only for men . . . 'tis a wrong impression, forced on our minds to keep us slaves!" As women became more active, Owenites agitated for women's rights, marriage reform, and popular education. In 1832, Saint-Simonian women founded a feminist newspaper in France, *The Free Woman*. Some followers of Saint-Simon's brand of socialism developed a quasi-religious cult with elaborate rituals and a "he-pope" and "she-pope," or ruling father and mother. They lived and worked together in cooperative arrangements and scandalized some by advocating free love.

The French activist Flora Tristan (1801–1844) devoted herself to reconciling the interests of male and female workers. She had seen the "frightful reality" of London's poverty and made a reputation reporting on British working conditions. Tristan published a stream of books and pamphlets urging male workers to address women's unequal status, arguing that "the emancipation of male workers is *impossible* so long as women remain in a degraded state." She advocated a Universal Union of Men and Women Workers.

Even though most male socialists ignored Tristan's plea for women's participation, like her they also worked to found working-class associations. French socialist Pierre-Joseph Proudhon (1809–1865) urged workers to form producers' associations so that the workers could control the work process and eliminate profits made by capitalists. His 1840 book *What Is Property?* argues that property is theft: labor alone is productive, and rent, interest, and profit are unjust.

After 1840, some socialists began to call themselves **communists**, emphasizing their desire to replace private property by communal, collective ownership. The Frenchman Étienne Cabet (1788–1856) first used the word *communist*. In 1840, he published *Travels in Icaria*, a novel describing a communist experiment in which a popularly elected dictatorship efficiently organized work, reduced the workday to seven hours, and made work tasks "short, easy, and attractive."

Out of the churning of socialist ideas of the 1840s emerged two men whose collaboration would change the definition of socialism and remake it into an ideology that would shake the world for the next 150 years. Karl Marx (1818–1883) and Friedrich Engels (1820–1895) were both sons of prosperous German-Jewish families that had converted to Christianity. Marx studied philosophy at the University of Berlin, edited a liberal newspaper until the Prussian government suppressed it, and then left for Paris, where he met Engels. While working in the offices of his wealthy family's cotton manufacturing interests in Manchester, England, Engels had been shocked into writing *The Condition of the Working Class in England in 1844* (1845), a sympathetic depiction of industrial workers' dismal lives. In Paris, where German and eastern European intellectuals could pursue their political interests more freely than at home, Marx and Engels organized the Communist League, in whose name they published the *Communist Manifesto* (1848). It eventually became the touchstone of Marxist and communist revolution all over the world.

Negligible as was the influence of Marx and Engels in the 1840s, they had already begun their lifework of scientifically understanding the "laws" of capitalism and fostering revolutionary organizations. Their principles and analysis of history were in place: communists, the *Manifesto* declared, must aim for "the downfall of the bourgeoisie [capitalist class] and the ascendancy of the proletariat [working class], the abolition of the old society based on class conflicts and the foundation of a new society without classes and without private property." Marx and Engels embraced industrialization because they believed it would eventually bring on the proletarian revolution and lead inevitably to the abolition of exploitation, private property, and class society.

Socialism accompanied, and in some places incited, an upsurge in working-class organization in western Europe. In 1824, the British government repealed laws prohibiting labor unions, though it maintained restrictions on strikes. Other European rulers forbade unions, though they tolerated cooperatives and societies for mutual aid. Working-class organization struck fear in the hearts of many in the upper classes. A British newspaper exclaimed in 1834, "The trade unions are, we have no doubt, the most dangerous institutions that were ever permitted to take root."

Many British workers joined in **Chartism**, a movement that aimed to transform Britain into a democracy. In 1838, political radicals drew up the People's Charter, which demanded universal manhood suffrage, vote by secret ballot, equal electoral districts, annual elections, and the elimination of property qualifications for and the payment of stipends to members of Parliament. Chartists denounced their opponents as seeking "to keep the people in social slavery and political degradation." Many women took part by founding female political unions, setting up Chartist Sunday schools, organizing boycotts of unsympathetic shopkeepers, and joining Chartist temperance associations. Nevertheless, the People's Charter refrained from calling for woman suffrage because the movement's leaders feared that doing so would alienate potential supporters.

The Chartists organized a massive campaign during 1838 and 1839, with large public meetings, fiery speeches, and torchlight parades. Presented with petitions for the People's Charter signed by more than a million people, the House of Commons refused to act. In response to this rebuff from middle-class liberals, the Chartists allied themselves in the 1840s with working-class strike movements in the manufacturing districts and associated with various European revolutionary movements. But at the same time, they—like their British and continental allies—distanced themselves from women workers. Chartists complained that workingwomen undermined men's manhood, taking men's jobs and turning the men into "women-men" or "eunuchs." Continuing agitation and organization prepared the way for a last wave of Chartist demonstrations in 1848.

Nationalism

Nationalists could be liberals, socialists, or even conservatives. In the nineteenth century, nationalism began as a radical or revolutionary movement and then evolved in a more conservative direction over time. **Nationalism** holds that all peoples derive their identities from their nations, which are defined by common language, shared cultural traditions, and sometimes religion. When such "nations" do not coincide with state boundaries, as they often did not in the nineteenth and twentieth centuries, nationalism can produce violence and warfare as different national groups compete for control over territory.

The French showed the power of national feeling in their revolutionary and Napoleonic wars, but they also provoked nationalism in the people they conquered. Once Napoleon and his satellite rulers departed, nationalist sentiment turned against other outside rulers—the Ottoman Turks in the Balkans, the Russians in Poland, and the Austrians in Italy. Intellectuals took the lead in demanding unity and freedom for their peoples. They collected folktales, poems, and histories and prepared grammars and dictionaries of their native languages (Map 17.3). Students,

Language Group

Romance
☐ French
☐ Italian
☐ Spanish
☐ Catalan
☐ Portuguese
☐ Corsican
☐ Romanian
☐ Walloon

Germanic
☐ English
☐ Dutch
☐ German
☐ Flemish
☐ Danish
☐ Norwegian
☐ Swedish

Slavonic
☐ Great Russian
☐ Ukrainian
☐ White Russian
☐ Polish
☐ Serbian
☐ Croatian
☐ Slovak
☐ Czech
☐ Bulgarian
☐ Macedonian
☐ Slovenian

Celtic
☐ Irish
☐ Gaelic
☐ Welsh
☐ Breton
☐ Cornish

Finno-Ugrian
☐ Finnish
☐ Estonian
☐ Magyar

Baltic
☐ Latvian
☐ Lithuanian

Basque
☐ Basque

Thraco-Illyrian
☐ Albanian

Hellenic
☐ Greek

Turkish-Tataric
☐ Turkish

☐ Mixed use
 of languages

■ **MAP 17.3 Languages of Nineteenth-Century Europe**
Even this detailed map of linguistic diversity understates the number of different languages and dialects spoken in Europe. In Italy, for example, few Italians spoke Italian as their first language. Instead, they spoke local dialects such as Piedmontese or Ligurian, and some might speak better French than Italian if they came from the regions bordering France. The map does underline the inherent contradictions of nationalism in eastern Europe, where many linguistic regions incorporated other languages and the result was constant conflict. But even in Spain, France, and Great Britain, linguistic diversity continued right up to the beginning of the 1900s.

middle-class professionals, and army officers formed secret societies to promote national independence and constitutional reform.

Nationalist aspirations were especially explosive for the Austrian Empire, which included a variety of peoples united only by their enforced allegiance to the Habsburg emperor. The empire included three main national groups: the Germans, who made up one-fourth of the population; the Magyars of Hungary (which included Transylvania and Croatia); and the Slavs, who together formed the largest group in the population but were divided into different nationalities such as Poles, Czechs, Croats, and Serbs. The empire also included Italians in Lombardy and Venetia and Romanians in Transylvania. Efforts to govern such diverse peoples preoccupied

Metternich, chief minister to the weak Habsburg emperor Francis I (r. 1792–1835). As a conservative, Metternich believed that the experience of the French Revolution proved the superiority of monarchy and aristocracy as forms of government and society. His domestic policy aimed to restrain nationalist impulses, and with the help of a secret police set up on the Napoleonic model, he largely succeeded until the 1840s. He insisted, for example, that "the Lombards [northern Italians] must forget that they are Italians."

The new Germanic Confederation set up by the Congress of Vienna had a federal assembly, but it largely functioned as a tool of Metternich's policies. The only sign of resistance came from university students, who formed nationalist student societies, or *Burschenschaften*. In 1817, they held a mass rally at which they burned books they did not like, including Napoleon's Civil Code. One of their leaders, Friedrich Ludwig Jahn, spouted such xenophobic (antiforeign) slogans as "If you let your daughter learn French, you might just as well train her to become a whore." Metternich was convinced that the Burschenschaften in the German states and the carbonari in Italy were linked in an international conspiracy. In 1820, when a student assassinated the playwright August Kotzebue because he ridiculed the student movement, Metternich convinced the leaders of the biggest German states to pass the Karlsbad Decrees dissolving the student societies and more strictly censoring the press. No evidence for a conspiracy was found.

Tsar Alexander faced similar problems in Poland, his "congress kingdom" (so called because the Congress of Vienna had created it), which in 1815 was one of Europe's most liberal states. The tsar reigned in Poland as a limited monarch, having bestowed a constitution that provided for an elected parliament, a national army, and guarantees of free speech and a free press. But by 1818, Alexander had begun retracting his concessions. Polish students and military officers responded by forming secret nationalist societies to plot for change by illegal means. In 1830, they rebelled against Alexander's successor Nicholas I. In reprisal, the tsar abolished the Polish constitution and ordered thousands of Poles executed or banished.

Most of the ten thousand Poles who fled took up residence in western European capitals, especially Paris, where they campaigned for public support. Their intellectual leader was the poet Adam Mickiewicz (1798–1855), whose mystical writings portrayed the Polish exiles as martyrs of a crucified nation with an international Christian mission. Mickiewicz formed a Polish Legion to fight for national restoration, but rivalries and divisions prevented united action until 1846, when Polish exiles in Paris tried to launch a coordinated insurrection for Polish independence. Plans for an uprising in the Polish province of Galicia in the Austrian Empire collapsed, however, when peasants instead revolted against their noble Polish masters. Slaughtering some two thousand aristocrats, a desperate rural population served the Austrian government's end by defusing the nationalist challenge.

One of those most touched by Mickiewicz's vision was Giuseppe Mazzini (1805–1872), a fiery Italian nationalist and republican journalist. Exiled in 1831 for his opposition to Austrian rule in northern Italy, Mazzini founded Young Italy, a secret society that attracted thousands with its message that Italy would touch off a European-wide revolutionary movement. In the 1830s and 1840s, nationalism spread among the many different peoples of the Austrian Empire. During the revolutions of 1848, however, it would become evident that these different ethnic groups disliked each other as much as they disliked their Austrian masters.

In most of the German states, economic unification took a step forward with the foundation in 1834, under Prussian leadership, of the *Zollverein*, or "customs union." Economist Friedrich List argued that the elimination of tariffs within the borders of the union would promote industrialization and cooperation and enable the union to compete with the rest of Europe. German nationalists sought a government uniting German-speaking peoples, but they could not agree on its boundaries. Austria was not part of the Customs Union. Would the unified German state include both Prussia and the Austrian Empire? If it included Austria, what about the non-German territories of the Austrian Empire? And could the powerful and conservative kingdom of Prussia coexist in a unified German state with other, more liberal but smaller states? These questions would vex German history for decades to come.

In Russia, nationalism took the form of opposition to Western ideas. Russian nationalists, or "Slavophiles" (lovers of the Slavs), opposed the "Westernizers," who wanted Russia to follow Western models of industrial development and constitutional government. The Slavophiles favored maintaining rural traditions infused by the values of the Russian Orthodox church. Only a return to Russia's basic historical principles, they argued, could protect the country against the corrosion of rationalism and materialism. Slavophiles sometimes criticized the regime, however, because they believed the state exerted too much power over the church. The conflict between Slavophiles and Westernizers continues to shape Russian cultural and intellectual life to the present day.

The most significant nationalist movement in western Europe could be found in Ireland. The Irish had struggled for centuries against English occupation, but Irish nationalists developed strong organizations only in the 1840s. In 1842, a group of writers founded the Young Ireland movement that aimed to recover Irish history and preserve the Irish Gaelic language (spoken by at least one-third of the peasantry). Daniel O'Connell (1775–1847), a Catholic lawyer and landowner who sat in the British House of Commons, hoped to force the British Parliament to repeal the Act of Union of 1801, which had made Ireland part of Great Britain. In 1843, London newspapers reported "monster meetings" that drew crowds of as many as 300,000 people in support of repeal of the union. In response, the British government arrested O'Connell and convicted him of conspiracy. More radical leaders, who preached insurrection against the English, replaced him.

Romanticism

More an artistic movement than a true ideology, romanticism glorified nature, emotion, genius, and imagination. It proclaimed these as antidotes to the

Enlightenment and to classicism in the arts, challenging the reliance on reason, symmetry, and cool geometric spaces. Classicism idealized models from Roman history; romanticism turned to folklore and medieval legends. Classicism celebrated orderly, crisp lines; romantics sought out all that was wild, fevered, and disorderly. Chief among the arts of romanticism were poetry, painting, and music, which captured the deep-seated emotion characteristic of romantic expression. George Gordon, Lord Byron (1788–1824), explained his aims in writing poetry:

> For what is Poesy but to create
> From overfeeling, Good and Ill, and aim
> At an external life beyond our fate,
> And be the new Prometheus of new man.

Prometheus was the mythological figure who brought fire from the Greek gods to human beings. Byron did not seek the new Prometheus among the men of industry; he sought him within his own "overfeeling," his own intense emotions.

Romantic poetry elevated the wonders of nature almost to the supernatural. Nature, wrote the English poet William Wordsworth (1770–1850), "to me was all in all." It allowed him to sing "the still, sad music of humanity." Like many poets of his time, Wordsworth greeted the French Revolution with joy; in his poem "French Revolution" (1809), he remembered his early enthusiasm: "Bliss was it in that dawn to be alive." But gradually he became disenchanted with the revolutionary experiment and celebrated British nationalism instead; in 1816, he published a poem to commemorate the "intrepid sons of Albion [England]" who died at the battle of Waterloo.

Their emphasis on authentic self-expression at times drew romantics to exotic, mystical, or even reckless experiences. Such transports drove one leading German poet to the madhouse and another to suicide. Some romantics depicted the artist as possessed by demons and obsessed with hallucinations. The aged German poet Johann Wolfgang von Goethe (1749–1832) denounced the extremes of romanticism, calling it "everything that is sick." Romanticism in painting often expressed anxiety about the coming industrial order while idealizing nature. These concerns came together in an emphasis on natural landscape. The German romantic painter Caspar David Friedrich (1774–1840) depicted scenes—often in the mountains, far from any factory—that captured the romantic fascination with the sublime power of nature. Friedrich hated the new modern world and considered industrialization a disaster. The English painter Joseph M. W. Turner (1775–1851) depicted his vision of nature in mysterious, misty seascapes, anticipating later artists by blurring the outlines of objects. The French painter Eugène Delacroix (1798–1863) chose contemporary as well as medieval scenes of great turbulence to emphasize light and color and break away from what he saw as "the servile copies repeated *ad nauseam* in academies of art." Critics denounced the new techniques as "painting with a drunken broom." To broaden his experience of light and color,

■ **Caspar David Friedrich,**
Wanderer above the Sea of
Fog **(1818)**
Friedrich, a German romantic painter,
captured many of the themes most dear
to romanticism: melancholy, isolation,
and individual communion with nature.
He painted trees reaching for the sky and
mountains stretching into the distance.
Nature to him seemed awesome, power-
ful, and overshadowing of human per-
spectives. The French sculptor David
d'Angers said of Friedrich, "Here is a
man who has discovered the tragedy of
landscape."
(Hamburger Kunsthalle, Hamburg/Bridgeman Art
Library.)

Delacroix traveled in the 1830s to North Africa and painted many exotic scenes in Morocco and Algeria.

Architects of the period sought to recapture a preindustrial world. When the British Houses of Parliament were rebuilt after they burned down in 1834, the architect Sir Charles Barry constructed them in a Gothic style reminiscent of the Middle Ages. This medievalism was taken even further by A. W. N. Pugin, who prepared the Gothic details for the Houses of Parliament. In his polemical book *Contrasts* (1836), Pugin denounced modern conditions and compared them unfavorably with those in the 1400s. To underline his view, Pugin wore medieval clothes at home.

The towering presence of the German composer Ludwig van Beethoven (1770–1827) in early-nineteenth-century music helped establish the direction for musical romanticism. His music, according to one leading German romantic, "sets in motion the lever of fear, of awe, of horror, of suffering, and awakens just that infinite longing which is the essence of Romanticism." Beethoven's symphonies conveyed the impression of growth, a metaphor for the organic process with an emphasis on the natural that was dear to the romantics. For example, his Sixth Symphony, the *Pastoral* (1808), used a variety of instruments to represent sounds heard in the country. Some of his work was explicitly political; his Ninth Symphony (1824) employed a chorus to sing the German poet Friedrich Schiller's verses in praise of universal human solidarity.

If any common political thread linked the romantics, it was support for nationalist aspirations, especially through the search for the historical origins of national identity. The Polish composer and pianist Frédéric Chopin (1810–1849) became a powerful champion for the cause of his native land with music that incorporated Polish folk rhythms and melodies. English poet Lord Byron died fighting for Greek independence. Romantic nationalism permeated *The Betrothed* (1825–1827), a novel by Alessandro Manzoni (1785–1873) that constituted a kind of bible for Italian nationalists. The career of the writer Sir Walter Scott (1771–1832) incorporated many of the strands of romanticism. He translated Goethe and published Scottish ballads that he heard as a child. After achieving immediate success with his poetry, he switched to historical novels, but he also wrote a nine-volume life of Napoleon and edited historical memoirs. His novels are almost all renditions of historical events, from *Rob Roy* (1817), with its account of Scottish resistance to the English in the early eighteenth century, to *Ivanhoe* (1819), with its tales of medieval England. The influence of Scott's historical novels was immense. One contemporary critic claimed that *Ivanhoe* was more historically true than any scholarly work: "There is more history in the novels of Walter Scott than in half of the historians."

■ **REVIEW:** *Why did ideologies have such a powerful appeal in the 1830s and 1840s?*

Reform or Revolution?

Europeans faced a daunting set of challenges in the 1830s and 1840s: the settlement devised by the Congress of Vienna was cracking under the pressure of unsatisfied nationalist and democratic aspirations, and industrialization and urbanization had produced dangerous social tensions made vivid by an outpouring of government reports, medical accounts, and novelistic depictions. Reformers of various stripes organized to meet these challenges, as well as new problems appearing in overseas colonies. Their efforts failed to stem the tide of revolution, which rose again in 1830 and 1848 and threatened to wash away the conservative regimes of the Vienna settlement.

Depicting and Reforming the Social Order

Lithographs, poetry, painting, and even booklets of jokes helped drive home the need for social reform, but novels proved to be the art form best suited to portraying the new society created by industrialization and urbanization. Thanks to increased literacy, the spread of reading rooms and lending libraries, and serialization in newspapers and journals, novels reached a large reading public and helped shape public awareness. Unlike the fiction of the eighteenth century, which had focused on individual personalities, the great novels of the 1830s and 1840s specialized in the description of social life in all its varieties. Manufacturers, financiers, starving students, workers, bureaucrats, prostitutes, underworld figures, thieves, and aristocratic men and women filled the pages of works by popular writers such as Honoré de Balzac and Charles Dickens. Pushing himself to exhaustion and a premature death to get out of debt, the French writer Balzac (1799–1850) cranked out ninety-five novels and many short stories. He aimed to catalog the social types that could be found in French society. Many of his characters, like himself, were driven by the desire to climb higher in the social order.

The English author Charles Dickens (1812–1870) worked with a similar frenetic energy and for much the same reasons. When his father was imprisoned for debt in 1824, the young Dickens took a job in a shoe-polish factory. In 1836, he published a series of literary sketches of daily life and then produced a series of novels that appeared in monthly installments and attracted thousands of readers. In them he paid close attention to the distressing effects of industrialization and urbanization. In *The Old Curiosity Shop* (1841), for example, he depicts the Black Country, the manufacturing region west and northwest of Birmingham, as a "cheerless region," a "mournful place," in which tall chimneys "made foul the melancholy air." In addition to publishing such enduring favorites as *Oliver Twist* (1838) and *A Christmas Carol* (1843), he ran charitable organizations and pressed for social reforms. For Dickens, the ability to portray the problems of the poor went hand in hand with a personal commitment to reform.

Novels by women often revealed the bleaker side of women's situations. *Jane Eyre* (1847), a novel by the English writer Charlotte Brontë, describes the difficult life of an orphaned girl who becomes a governess, the only occupation open to most single middle-class women. Although in an economically weak position, Jane Eyre refuses to achieve respectability and security through marriage, the usual option for women. The French novelist George Sand (Amandine-Aurore Dupin, 1804–1876) took her social criticism a step further. She announced her independence in the 1830s by dressing like a man and smoking cigars. Like many other women writers of the time, she published her work under a male pseudonym while creating female characters who prevail in difficult circumstances through romantic love and moral idealism. Sand's novel *Indiana* (1832), about an unhappily married woman, was read all over Europe. Her notoriety made the term George-Sandism a common expression of disdain for independent women.

Although women's professional opportunities were severely limited, they took a prominent role in charitable and reform work. Catholic religious orders, which by 1850 enrolled many more women than men, ran schools, hospitals, leper colonies, insane asylums, and old-age homes. New Catholic orders, especially for women, were established, and Catholic missionary activity overseas increased. Protestant women in Great Britain and the United States established Bible, missionary, and female reform societies by the hundreds. Many societies dedicated themselves to reforming prostitutes and castigating their male clients.

■ **George Sand**

In this lithograph by Alcide Lorentz of 1842, George Sand is shown in one of her notorious masculine costumes. Sand published numerous works, including novels, plays, essays, travel writing, and an autobiography. She actively participated in the revolution of 1848 in France, writing pamphlets in support of the new republic. Disillusioned by the rise to power of Louis-Napoleon Bonaparte, she withdrew to her country estate and devoted herself exclusively to her writing.

(The Granger Collection, NY.)

Religiously motivated reformers first had to overcome the perceived indifference of the working classes; less than 10 percent of the workers in the cities attended religious services. To combat such indifference, British religious groups launched the Sunday school movement, which reached its zenith in the 1840s. By 1851, more than half of all working-class children between five and fifteen were attending Sunday school, even though very few of their parents regularly went to religious services. The Sunday schools taught children how to read at a time when few working-class children could go to school during the week.

Catholics and Protestants alike promoted the **temperance movement** to fight the "pestilence of hard liquor." Many poor people drank alcoholic beverages because the water available to them was unsafe to drink. The first temperance societies had appeared in the United States as early as 1813, and by 1835 the American Temperance Society claimed 1.5 million members. Temperance advocates saw drunkenness as a sign of moral weakness and a threat to social order. Industrialists pointed to the loss of worker productivity, and efforts to promote temperance often reflected middle- and upper-class fears of the lower classes' lack of discipline. One German temperance advocate insisted, "One need not be a prophet to know that all efforts to combat the widespread and rapidly spreading pauperism will be unsuccessful as long as the common man fails to realize that the principal source of his degradation and misery is his fondness of drink." Yet temperance societies also attracted working-class people who shared the desire for respectability.

Social reformers saw education as one of the main prospects for uplifting the poor and the working class. In 1833, the French government passed an education law that required every town to maintain a primary school, pay a teacher, and provide free education to poor boys. As the law's author, François Guizot, argued, "Ignorance renders the masses turbulent and ferocious." Girls' schools were optional. By the late 1830s, 60 percent of children attended primary school in France, still less than in Protestant Prussia, where 75 percent of children went to school. Popular education remained woefully undeveloped in most of eastern Europe. Peasants were specifically excluded from the few primary schools in Russia, where Tsar Nicholas I blamed the Decembrist uprising of 1825 on education.

Above all else, the elite sought to impose discipline and order on working people. Organizations such as the Society for the Prevention of Cruelty to Animals tried to eliminate popular blood sports such as cockfighting and bear-baiting. By the end of the 1830s, bullbaiting had been abandoned in Great Britain. "This useful animal," rejoiced one reformer in 1839, "is no longer tortured amidst the exulting yells of those who are a disgrace to our common form and nature." Other blood sports died out more slowly, and efforts in other countries generally lagged behind those of the British.

When private charities failed to meet the needs of the poor, governments often intervened. Great Britain sought to control the costs of public welfare by passing a new poor law in 1834, called by its critics the "Starvation Act." The law required that all able-bodied persons receiving relief be placed in workhouses, with husbands separated from wives and parents from children. Workhouse life was designed to be as unpleasant as possible so that poor people would move on to regions of higher employment. British women from all social classes organized anti–poor law societies to protest the separation of mothers from their children in the workhouses.

Many women viewed charitable work as the extension of their domestic roles: they promoted virtuous behavior and morality and thus improved society. In one widely read advice book, Englishwoman Sarah Lewis suggested in 1839 that "women may be the prime agents in the regeneration of mankind." But women's social reform activities concealed a paradox. According to the set of beliefs that historians call the doctrine or ideology of **domesticity**, women should live their lives entirely within the domestic sphere; they should devote themselves to the home. The English poet Alfred, Lord Tennyson, captured this view in a popular poem published in 1847: "Man for the field and woman for the hearth; / Man for the sword and for the needle she. . . . All else confusion." Many believed that maintaining proper and distinct roles for men and women was critically important to maintaining social order in general.

Most women had little hope of economic independence. The notion of a separate, domestic sphere for women prevented them from pursuing higher education,

■ **Bearbaiting**

This colored engraving from 1821 of Charley's Theater in London shows that bearbaiting did not attract only the lower classes, as reformers often implied. Top hats were most often worn by middle-class men, who seem to be enjoying the spectacle of dogs taunting the bear as much as the working-class men present. At this time, bearbaiting, like bullbaiting, began to come under fire as cruel to animals. (Mary Evans Picture Library.)

work in professional careers, or participation in politics through voting or holding office—all activities deemed appropriate only to men. Laws everywhere codified the subordination of women. Many countries followed the model of Napoleon's Civil Code, which classified married women as legal incompetents along with children, the insane, and criminals. In Great Britain, which had no national law code, the courts upheld the legality of a husband's complete control.

Distinctions between men and women were most noticeable in the privileged classes. Whereas boys attended secondary schools, most middle- and upper-class girls still received their education at home or in church schools, where they were taught to be religious, obedient, and accomplished in music and languages. As men began to wear practical clothing—long trousers and short jackets of solid, often dark colors, no makeup (previously common for aristocratic men), and simply cut hair—women continued to dress for decorative effect, now with tightly corseted waists that emphasized the differences between female and male bodies. Middle- and upper-class women had long hair that required hours of brushing and pinning up, and they wore long, cumbersome skirts. Advice books written by women detailed the tasks that such women undertook in the home: maintaining household accounts, supervising servants, and organizing social events.

Scientists reinforced stereotypes. Once considered sexually insatiable, women were now described as incapacitated by menstruation and largely uninterested in sex, an attitude that many equated with moral superiority. Thus was born the "Victorian woman," a figment of the largely male medical imagination. Physicians and scholars considered women mentally inferior. In 1839, Auguste Comte, an influential early French sociologist, wrote, "As for any functions of government, the radical inaptitude of the female sex is there yet more marked . . . and limited to the guidance of the mere family."

Abuses and Reforms Overseas

Despite such attitudes, British women played a major role in the antislavery movement; as many as 350,000 women signed one major petition to Parliament demanding the abolition of slavery. Reformers gained one of their major objectives when Britain abolished slavery in its colonies in 1833. British missionary and evangelical groups condemned the conquest, enslavement, and exploitation of native African populations and successfully blocked British annexations in central and southern Africa in the 1830s. The new Latin American republics abolished slavery in the 1820s and 1830s after they defeated the Spanish with armies that included many slaves. In France, the government of Louis-Philippe (r. 1830–1848) took strong measures against clandestine slave traffic, virtually ending French participation during the 1830s. Slavery was abolished in the remaining French Caribbean colonies in 1848.

Slavery did not disappear immediately just because the major European powers had given it up. The transatlantic trade in slaves did not seriously diminish until 1850 (see Figure 14.1, page 571). Human bondage continued unabated in Brazil, Cuba (still a Spanish colony), and the United States. Some American reformers supported abolition, but it remained a minority movement. Like serfdom in Russia, slavery in the Americas involved a quagmire of economic, political, and moral problems that worsened over time.

As Europeans turned their interest away from the plantation colonies of the Caribbean toward colonies in Asia and Africa, they developed new forms of colonial rule. Colonialism became **imperialism**—a term first coined in the mid-nineteenth century. Colonialism most often led to the establishment of settler colonies, direct rule by Europeans, slave labor from Africa, and wholesale destruction of indigenous peoples. In contrast, imperialism usually meant more indirect forms of economic exploitation and political rule. Europeans still aimed to derive economic profit from their colonies, but now they also wanted to reform colonial peoples in their own image.

In the 1830s and 1840s, France and Britain continued to extend their influence across the globe. Using the pretext of an insult to its envoy, France invaded the north African country of Algeria in 1830 and after a long military campaign established political control over most of the region in the next two decades. By 1850, more than seventy thousand French, Italian, and Maltese colonists had settled there, often confiscating the lands of native peoples. The new French administration of the colony made efforts to balance native and settler interests, however, and eventually France would not only incorporate Algeria into France but also try to assimilate its native population to French culture. France also imposed a protectorate government over the South Pacific island of Tahiti.

Although the British granted Canada greater self-determination in 1839, they extended their dominion elsewhere by annexing Singapore (1819), an island off the Malay peninsula, and New Zealand (1840). They also increased their control in India through the administration of the East India Company, a private group of merchants chartered by the British crown. The British educated a native elite to take over much of the day-to-day business of administering the country and used native soldiers to augment their military control. By 1850, only one in six soldiers serving Britain in India was European.

The East India Company also tried to establish a regular trade with China in **opium**, a drug long known for its medicinal uses but increasingly bought in China as a recreational drug. The Chinese government did its best to keep the highly addictive drug away from its people, both by forbidding Western merchants to venture outside the southern city of Guangzhou (Canton) and by banning the export of precious metals and the import of opium. These measures failed. By smuggling opium grown in India into China and bribing local officials, British traders built up a flourishing market. When in 1839 the Chinese authorities expelled British merchants from southern China, Britain retaliated by bombarding Chinese coastal cities, beginning the First Opium War. In 1842, it dictated to a defeated China the Treaty of Nanking, by which the British forced the opening of four more Chinese ports to Europeans, took sovereignty over the island of Hong Kong, received a substantial war indemnity, and were assured of a continuation of the opium trade. In this case, reform took a backseat to economic interest, despite the complaints of religious groups in Britain.

The First Opium War, 1839–1842

The Revolutions of 1830 and 1848

Imperialist ventures abroad continued even as the revolutionary legacy revived again in Europe, first in 1830 and then in a more widespread series of upheavals in

1848. Given its revolutionary past, it is not surprising that France took the lead. In 1830, a revolution overthrew the French king, Charles X (r. 1824–1830), the younger brother and successor to Louis XVIII. Charles X brought about his own downfall by pushing through a Law of Indemnity in 1825 to compensate nobles for the loss of their lands during the revolution of 1789. At the same time, he insisted on a Law of Sacrilege imposing the death penalty for such offenses as stealing religious objects from churches. He then dissolved the legislature, removed many wealthy and powerful voters from the rolls, and imposed strict censorship. Spontaneous demonstrations in Paris led to fighting on July 26, 1830. After three days of street battles in which 500 citizens and 150 soldiers died, a group of moderate liberal leaders, fearing the reestablishment of a republic, agreed to offer the crown to Charles X's cousin Louis-Philippe, duke of Orléans.

Charles X went into exile in England, and the new king extended political liberties and voting rights. Although the number of voting men nearly doubled, it remained minuscule—approximately 170,000 in a country of 30 million, between 5 and 6 percent. Such reforms did little for the poor and working classes, who had manned the barricades in July. Dissatisfaction with the 1830 settlement boiled over in Lyon in 1831, when a silk-workers' strike over wages turned into a rebellion that died down only when the army arrived. Revolution had broken the hold of those who wanted to restore the pre-1789 monarchy and nobility, but it had gone no further this time than installing a more liberal, constitutional monarchy.

The success of the July Revolution in Paris ignited the Belgians, whose country had been annexed to the kingdom of the Netherlands in 1815. Differences in traditions, language, and religion separated the largely Catholic Belgians from the Dutch. King William of the Netherlands appealed to the great powers for help, but Great Britain and France opposed intervention and invited Russia, Austria, and Prussia to a conference that guaranteed Belgium independence in exchange for its neutrality in international affairs. Belgian neutrality would remain a cornerstone of European diplomacy for a century. After much maneuvering, the crown of the new kingdom of Belgium was offered to a German prince, Leopold of Saxe-Coburg, in 1831. Belgium, like France and Britain, now had a constitutional monarchy.

Political tensions boiled to the surface again in the late 1840s when crop failures across Europe threatened the food supply and food prices shot skyward. In the best of times, urban workers paid 50 to 80 percent of their income for a diet consisting largely of bread; now even bread was beyond their means. Overpopulation hastened famine in some places, especially Ireland, where an airborne blight destroyed the staple crop, potatoes, in 1846, 1848, and 1851. Out of a population of 8 million, as many as 1 million people died of starvation and disease. Corpses lay unburied on the sides of roads, and whole families were found dead in their cottages, half-eaten by dogs. Hundreds of thousands emigrated to England, the United States, and Canada.

■ **The Potato Blight and Irish Famine**
In this painting by Daniel McDonald, The Discovery of the Potato Blight *(1852), a family is shown digging up its potato crop only to find that the potatoes had rotted from blight. This discovery spelled disaster for this family and thousands like it. The airborne blight spores landed on the potato plants and killed the leaves, which fell to the ground. The spores were washed into the earth and infected the underground tubers. The crop could even look normal but still be infected.*

High food prices also drove down the demand for manufactured goods, resulting in increased unemployment. Industrial workers' wages had been rising—in the German states, for example, wages rose an average of 5.5 percent in the 1830s and 10.5 percent in the 1840s—but the cost of living rose about 16 percent each decade, canceling out wage increases. Seasonal work and regular unemployment were already the norm when the crisis of the late 1840s intensified the uncertainties of urban life. "The most miserable class that ever sneaked its way into history" is how Friedrich Engels described underemployed and starving workers in 1847.

The specter of hunger tarnished the image of established rulers and amplified voices critical of them. Louis-Philippe's government had blocked all moves for electoral reform, and in February 1848, a banquet campaign sponsored by the political opposition turned into a revolution. At first the police and the army dispersed the demonstrators who took to the streets on February 22, 1848. The next day, however, forty or fifty people died when panicky soldiers opened fire on the crowd. On February 24, faced with fifteen hundred barricades and a furious populace, Louis-Philippe abdicated and fled to England. A hastily formed provisional government declared France a republic once again.

The new republican government issued liberal reforms—an end to the death penalty for political crimes, the abolition of slavery in the colonies, and freedom of the press—and agreed to introduce universal adult male suffrage despite misgivings about political participation by peasants and unemployed workers. To address the gnawing problem of unemployment, the government allowed Paris officials to organize a system of "national workshops" to provide those out of jobs with construction work. When women protested their exclusion, the city set up a few workshops for women workers, albeit with wages lower than men's. To meet a mounting deficit, the provisional government then levied a 45 percent surtax on property taxes, alienating peasants and landowners.

The establishment of the republic politicized many segments of the population. Scores of newspapers and political clubs revived grassroots democratic fervor; meeting in concert halls, theaters, and government auditoriums, clubs became a regular attraction for the citizenry. Women also formed clubs, published women's newspapers, and demanded representation in national politics. Street-corner activism alarmed middle-class liberals and conservatives. To maintain control, the republican government paid some unemployed youths to join a mobile guard with its own uniforms and barracks. Tension between the government and the workers in the national workshops rose; the communist Étienne Cabet led one demonstration of 150,000 workers. Class warfare loomed like a thunderstorm on the horizon.

Faced with rising radicalism in Paris and other big cities, the voters elected a largely conservative National Assembly in April 1848, which immediately appointed a five-man executive committee to run the government and deliberately excluded known supporters of workers' rights. Suspicious of all demands for rapid change, the deputies dismissed a petition to restore divorce and voted down women's suffrage, 899 to 1. When the numbers enrolled in the national workshops in Paris rocketed from a predicted 10,000 to 110,000, the government ordered the workshops closed to new workers, and on June 21 it directed that those already enrolled move to the provinces or join the army.

The workers of Paris responded to these measures on June 23 by taking to the streets in the tens of thousands. In the June Days, as the following week came to be called, the government summoned the army, the National Guard, and the newly recruited mobile guard to fight the workers. Provincial volunteers came to help put down the workers, who had been depicted to them as lazy ruffians intent on destroying order and property. One observer breathed a sigh of relief: "The Red Republic [red being associated with demands for socialism] is lost forever; all France has joined against it. The National Guard, citizens, and peasants from the remotest parts of the country have come pouring in." The republic's army crushed the protesters; more than 10,000 were killed or injured, 12,000 were arrested, and 4,000 eventually were convicted and deported.

When the National Assembly adopted a new constitution calling for a presidential election in which all adult men could vote, the electorate chose Louis-Napoleon Bonaparte, nephew of the dead emperor. Bonaparte got more than 5.5 million votes out of some 7.4 million cast. He had lived most of his life outside of France, and the leaders of the republic expected him to follow their tune. In uncertain times, the Bonaparte name promised something to everyone. Even many workers supported him because he had no connection with the blood-drenched June Days.

In reality, Bonaparte's election spelled the end of the Second Republic, just as his uncle had dismantled the first one, established in 1792. In 1852, on the forty-eighth anniversary of Napoleon I's coronation as emperor, Louis-Napoleon declared himself Emperor Napoleon III (r. 1852–1870). (Napoleon I's son died and never became Napoleon II, but Napoleon III wanted to create a sense of legitimacy and so used the Roman numeral III.) Political division and class conflict had proved fatal to the Second Republic. Although the revolution of 1848 never had a period of terror like that in 1793–1794, it nonetheless ended in similar fashion, with an authoritarian government that played monarchists and republicans off against each other.

The Parisian uprising galvanized Italian nationalists. Armed demonstrators took on the Austrians in Milan and actually drove them out of Venice. Peasants in the south occupied their landowners' estates, while across central Italy the poor and unemployed rose up against local rulers. But class tensions and regional

The Divisions of Italy, 1848

differences still stood in the way of national unity. Property owners, businessmen, and professionals wanted liberal reforms and national unification under a conservative regime; intellectuals, workers, and artisans dreamed of democracy and social reforms. Some nationalists favored a loose federation; others wanted a monarchy under Charles Albert of Piedmont-Sardinia; still others urged rule by the pope. A few shared Mazzini's vision of a republic with a strong central government. Many leaders of national unification spoke Italian only as a second language; most Italians spoke regional dialects.

As king of the most powerful Italian state, Charles Albert played a central role. After some hesitation caused by fears of French intervention, he led a military campaign against Austria. It failed, partly because of dissension over goals and tactics among the nationalists. Although Austrian troops defeated Charles Albert in the north in the summer of 1848, democratic and nationalist forces prevailed at first in the south. In the fall, the Romans drove the pope from the city and in February 1849 declared Rome a republic. For the next few months republican leaders, such as Mazzini and Giuseppe Garibaldi (1807–1882), congregated in Rome to organize the new republic. These efforts faltered in July when foreign powers intervened. The new president of republican France, Louis-Napoleon Bonaparte, sent an expeditionary force to secure the papal throne for Pius IX (r. 1846–1878). Mazzini and Garibaldi fled. Although revolution had been defeated in Italy, the memory of the Roman republic and the commitment to unification remained, and they would soon emerge again with new force.

News of the revolution in Paris also provoked popular demonstrations in the German states. "My heart beat with joy. The monarchy had fallen. Only a little blood had been shed for such a high stake, and the great watchwords Liberty, Equality, Fraternity were again inscribed on the banner of the movement." So responded one Frankfurt woman to Louis-Philippe's overthrow. The Prussian army's efforts to clear the square in front of Berlin's royal palace on March 18, 1848, provoked panic and street fighting around hastily assembled barricades. The next day the crowd paraded wagons loaded with dead bodies under King Frederick William IV's window, forcing him to salute the victims killed by his own army. In a state of near collapse, the

Revolutions of 1848	
1848	
February	Revolution in Paris; proclamation of republic
March	Insurrections in Vienna, German cities, Milan, and Venice; autonomy movement in Hungary; Charles Albert of Piedmont-Sardinia declares war on Austrian Empire
May	Frankfurt parliament opens
June	Austrian army crushes revolutionary movement in Prague; June Days end in defeat of workers in Paris
July	Austrians defeat Charles Albert and Italian forces
November	Insurrection drives the pope out of Rome
December	Francis Joseph becomes Austrian emperor; Louis-Napoleon elected president in France
1849	
February	Rome declared a republic
April	Frederick William of Prussia rejects crown of united Germany offered by Frankfurt parliament
July	Roman republic overthrown by French intervention
August	Russian and Austrian armies combine to defeat Hungarian forces

king promised to call an assembly to draft a constitution and adopted the German nationalist flag of black, red, and gold.

The goal of German unification soon took precedence over social reform or constitutional changes within the separate states. In March and April 1848, most of the German states agreed to elect delegates to a federal parliament at Frankfurt that would attempt to unite Germany. Local princes and even the more powerful kings of Prussia and Bavaria seemed to totter. In Bavaria, students marched to the "Marseillaise" and called for a republic. Yet the revolutionaries' weaknesses soon became apparent. The eight hundred delegates to the Frankfurt parliament had little practical political experience: "a group of old women," one socialist called them; a "Professors Parliament" was the common sneer. These delegates had no access to an army, and they dreaded the demands of the lower classes for social reforms.

The German States, 1848

Unemployed artisans and workers smashed machines; peasants burned landlords' records and occasionally attacked Jewish moneylenders; women set up clubs and newspapers to demand their emancipation from "perfumed slavery."

The advantage lay with the princes, who retained legal authority and control over the armed forces. The most powerful German states, Prussia and Austria, expected to determine whether and how Germany should unite. While the Frankfurt parliament laboriously prepared a liberal constitution for a united Germany—one that denied self-determination to Czechs, Poles, and Danes within its proposed German borders—the Prussian king Frederick William IV (r. 1840–1860) recovered his confidence. First his army crushed the revolution in Berlin in the fall of 1848. Prussian troops then intervened to help other local rulers put down the last wave of democratic and nationalist insurrections in the spring. In April 1849, when the Frankfurt parliament finally concluded its work, offering the emperorship of a constitutional, federal Germany to the king of Prussia, Frederick William contemptuously refused this "crown from the gutter."

Events followed a similar course in the Austrian Empire. Just as Italians were driving the Austrians out of their lands in northern Italy and Magyar nationalists were demanding political autonomy for Hungary, on March 13, 1848, in Vienna, a student-led demonstration for political reform turned into rioting, looting, and machine-breaking. Metternich resigned, escaping to England in disguise. Emperor Ferdinand promised a constitution, an elected parliament, and the end of censorship. Beleaguered authorities in Vienna could not refuse Magyar demands for home rule, and Széchenyi and Kossuth both became ministers in the new Hungarian government. The Magyars were the largest ethnic group in Hungary but still did not make up 50 percent of the population, which included Romanians, Slovaks, Croats, and Slovenes, who preferred Austrian rule to domination by local Magyars.

The ethnic divisions in Hungary foreshadowed the many political and social divisions that would doom the revolutionaries. Fears of peasant insurrection prompted the Magyar nationalists around Kossuth to abolish serfdom. This measure alienated the largest noble landowners. In Prague, Czech nationalists convened a Slav congress as a counter to the Germans' Frankfurt parliament and called for a reorganization of the Austrian Empire that would recognize the rights of ethnic minorities. Such assertiveness by non-German peoples provoked German nationalists to protest on behalf of German-speaking people in areas with a Czech or Magyar majority.

The Austrian government slowly took advantage of these divisions. To quell peasant discontent and appease liberal reformers, it abolished all remaining peasant obligations to the nobility in March 1848. Rejoicing country folk soon lost interest in the revolution. Class conflicts flared in Vienna, where the middle classes had little sympathy for the starving artisans and workers. The new Hungarian government alienated the other nationalities when it imposed the Magyar language on them. Similar divisions sapped national unity in the Polish and Czech lands of the empire.

Military force finally broke up the revolutionary movements. The first blow fell in Prague in June 1848; General Prince Alfred von Windischgrätz, the military governor, bombarded the city into submission when a demonstration led to violence (including the shooting death of his wife, watching from a window). After another uprising in Vienna a few months later, Windischgrätz marched 70,000 soldiers into the capital and set up direct military rule. In December, the Austrian monarchy came back to life when the eighteen-year-old Francis Joseph (r. 1848–1916), unencumbered by promises extracted by the revolutionaries from his now-feeble uncle Ferdinand, assumed the imperial crown after intervention by leading court officials. In the spring of 1849, General Count Joseph Radetsky defeated the last Italian challenges to Austrian power in northern Italy, and his army moved east, joining with Croats and Serbs to take on the Hungarian rebels. In August, the Austrian army teamed up with Tsar Nicholas I, who marched into Hungary with more than 300,000 Russian troops. Hungary was put under brutal martial law. Széchenyi went mad, and Kossuth found refuge in the United States. Social conflicts and ethnic divisions weakened the revolutionary movements from the inside and gave the Austrian government the opening it needed to restore its position.

Aftermath to 1848

The revolutionaries of 1848 failed to achieve most of their goals, but their efforts left a profound mark on the political and social landscape. Between 1848 and 1851, the French served a kind of republican apprenticeship that prepared the population

■ **Revolution of 1848 in Eastern Europe**

This painting by an unknown artist shows Ana Ipatescu leading a group of Romanian revolutionaries in Transylvania in opposition to Russian rule. The Transylvanian provinces of Moldavia and Walachia had been under Russian domination since the 1770s and occupied directly since 1829. In April 1848, local landowners began to organize meetings. Paris-educated nationalists spearheaded the movement, which demanded the end of Russian control and various legal and political reforms. By August, the movement had split between those who wanted independence only and those who pushed for the end of serfdom and for universal manhood suffrage. In response, the Russians invaded Moldavia and the Turks moved into Walachia. By October, the uprising was over. Russia and Turkey agreed to control the provinces jointly. **For more help analyzing this image,** see the visual activity for this chapter in the ONLINE STUDY GUIDE at bedfordstmartins.com/huntconcise. (The Art Archive.)

for another, more lasting republic after 1870. No French government could henceforth rule without extensive popular consultation. In Italy, the failure of unification did not stop the spread of nationalist ideas and the rooting of demands for democratic participation. In the German states, the revolutionaries of 1848 turned nationalism from an academic idea into a popular movement. The very idea of a Frankfurt parliament and the insistence on brandishing a German national flag at demonstrations showed that German nationalism had become a practical reality. The initiation of artisans, workers, and journeymen into democratic clubs increased political awareness in the lower classes and helped prepare them for broader political participation. Almost all the German states had a constitution and a parliament after 1850. The spectacular failures of 1848 thus hid some important successes.

The absence of revolution in 1848 was just as significant as its presence. No revolution occurred in Great Britain, the Netherlands, or Belgium, three places where industrialization and urbanization had developed most rapidly. In Great Britain, the prospects for revolution actually seemed quite good: the Chartist movement took inspiration from the European revolutions in 1848 and mounted several gigantic demonstrations to force Parliament into granting all adult males the vote. But Parliament refused and no uprising occurred, in part because the government had already proved its responsiveness. The middle classes in Britain had been co-opted into the established order by the Reform Bill of 1832, and the working classes had won parliamentary regulation of children's and women's work.

The other notable exception to revolution among the great powers was Russia, where Tsar Nicholas I maintained a tight grip through police surveillance and censorship. The Russian schools, limited to the upper classes, taught Nicholas's three most cherished principles: autocracy (the unlimited power of the tsar), orthodoxy (obedience to the church in religion and morality), and nationality (devotion to Russian traditions). These provided no space for political dissent. Social conditions also fostered political passivity: serfdom continued in force, and the slow rate of industrial and urban growth created little discontent.

For all the differences between countries, some developments touched them all. European states continued to expand their bureaucracies. For example, in 1750 the Russian government employed approximately 10,500 functionaries; a century later it needed almost 114,000. New government agencies such as the British urban police forces (10,000 strong in the 1840s) intruded increasingly in ordinary people's lives. States wanted to take children out of the fields and factories where they worked with their families and educate them. In some German cities, the police reported people who cleared snow off their roofs after the permitted hour or smoked in the streets.

Although much had changed, the aristocracy remained the dominant power almost everywhere. As army officers, aristocrats put down revolutionary forces. As landlords, they continued to dominate the rural scene and control parliamentary bodies. They also held many official positions in the state bureaucracies. One Italian princess explained, "There are doubtless men capable of leading the nation . . . but their names are unknown to the people, whereas those of noble families . . . are in every memory." Aristocrats kept their authority by adapting to change: they entered the bureaucracy and professions, turned their estates into moneymaking enterprises, and learned how to invest shrewdly.

The reassertion of conservative rule hardened gender definitions. Women everywhere had participated in the revolutions, especially in the Italian states, where they joined armies in the tens of thousands and applied household skills toward making bandages, clothing, and food. Schoolgirls in Prague had thrown desks and chairs out of windows and helped build students' barricades. Many women in Paris had supported the new republic and seized the occasion of greater political openness to demand women's rights, only to experience isolation as their claims were denied by most republican men. Men in the revolutions of 1848 almost always defined universal suffrage as a male right. When workingmen gained the vote and women did not, the notion of separate spheres penetrated even into working-class life: political participation became one more way to distinguish masculinity from femininity. As conservatives returned to power, all signs of women's political activism disappeared. The French feminist movement, the most advanced in Europe, fell apart after the June Days when the increasingly conservative republican government forbade women to form political clubs and arrested and imprisoned two of the most outspoken women leaders for their socialist activities.

In May 1851, Europe's most important female monarch presided over a mid-century celebration of peace and industrial growth that helped dampen the still smoldering fires of revolutionary passion. Queen Victoria (r. 1837–1901), who herself

■ **The Crystal Palace, 1851**

George Baxter's lithograph shows the exterior of the main building for the Exhibition of the Works of Industry of All Nations in London. It was designed by Sir Joseph Paxton to gigantic dimensions: 1,848 feet long by 456 feet wide; 135 feet high; 772,784 square feet of ground-floor area covering no less than 18 acres. (Maidstone Museum and Art Gallery, Kent, UK/Bridgeman Art Library.)

IMPORTANT DATES

1814–1815	Congress of Vienna	1834	German customs union (Zollverein) established under Prussian leadership
1820	Revolt of liberal army officers against the Spanish crown; Karlsbad Decrees abolish German student societies and tighten press censorship	1839	Opium War between Britain and China begins
		1846	Famine strikes Ireland; England repeals Corn Laws; peasant insurrection in Austrian province of Galicia
1824	Ludwig van Beethoven composes his Ninth Symphony		
1825	Russian army officers demand constitutional reform in the Decembrist uprising	1847	Charlotte Brontë publishes Jane Eyre
1830	Liverpool and Manchester Railway opens in England; Greece gains independence from Ottoman Turks; France invades and begins conquest of Algeria; rebels overthrow Charles X of France and install Louis-Philippe; cholera epidemic begins in Europe	1848	Last great wave of Chartist demonstration in Britain; Karl Marx and Friedrich Engels write The Communist Manifesto; revolutions of 1848 throughout Europe; slavery abolished in French colonies; serfdom ended in Austrian Empire
		1851	Crystal Palace exhibition in London
1832	British Parliament passes Reform Bill		
1833	Factory Act regulates work of children in Great Britain; slavery abolished in the British Empire		

promoted the notion of domesticity as women's sphere, opened the international Exhibition of the Works of Industry of All Nations in London on May 1. A monument of modern iron and glass architecture had been constructed to house the display; the building was more than a third of a mile long and so tall that it was erected over the trees of its Hyde Park site. Soon people referred to it as the "Crystal Palace"; its nine hundred tons of glass created an aura of fantasy, and the abundant goods from all nations inspired satisfaction and pride. One German visitor described it as "this miracle which has so suddenly appeared to dazzle the inhabitants of our globe." In the place of revolutionary fervor, the Crystal Palace offered a government-sponsored spectacle of what industry, hard work, and technological imagination could produce.

■ **REVIEW:** *Why did the revolutions of 1848 fail?*

Legend:

- Major industrial areas
- No peasant emancipation before 1848
- Railroad development by 1850
- Iron ore fields
- Coalfields

SWEDEN AND NORWAY

St. Petersburg

North Sea

Baltic Sea

Glasgow

GREAT BRITAIN

Liverpool   Manchester

DENMARK

Birmingham

PRUSSIA

RUSSIA

N
W   E
S

Amsterdam

Berlin

POLAND   Warsaw

London

Brussels

GERMAN CONFEDERATION

Breslau

BELGIUM

Frankfurt

Saxony

Cracow

ATLANTIC OCEAN

FRANCE

Bohemia

Vienna

Munich   Buda Pest

AUSTRIAN EMPIRE

Danube R.

Lyon

Milan

Florence

OTTOMAN EMPIRE

Marseille

PORTUGAL

Madrid

Barcelona

Rome

Lisbon   SPAIN

Naples

Mediterranean Sea

0   200   400 miles
0   200   400 kilometers

■ **MAPPING THE WEST** Industrialization in Europe, c. 1850

Industrialization first spread across northern Europe in a band that included Great Britain, northern France, Belgium, the northern German states, the region around Milan in northern Italy, and Bohemia. Much of Scandinavia and southern and eastern Europe did not participate in this first phase of industrial development. Although railroads were not the only factor in promoting industrialization, the map makes clear the interrelationship between railroad building and the development of new industrial sites of coal mining and textile production. **For more help analyzing this map**, see the map activity for this chapter in the ONLINE STUDY GUIDE at bedfordstmartins.com/huntconcise.

Conclusion

Many of the six million people who visited the Crystal Palace display had not forgotten the threat of disease, fears of overpopulation, popular resentments, and political upheavals that had been so prominent in the 1830s and 1840s. Even though industrial growth brought railroads, cheaper clothing, and access to exhibitions like the Crystal Palace, it also produced urban overcrowding and miserable working conditions. The Crystal Palace presented the rosy view, but the housing shortages, inadequacy of water supplies, and recurrent epidemic diseases had not disappeared. Social reform organizations still drew attention to prostitution, child abandonment, alcohol abuse, and other problems associated with burgeoning cities.

Although the revolutions of 1848 brought to the surface the profound tensions within a European society in transition toward industrialization and modernization, they did not definitively resolve those tensions. Industrialization and urbanization continued, workers developed more extensive organizations, and liberals, conservatives, and socialists fought over the pace of reform. The revolutions made their most striking impact negatively rather than positively: confronted with the menace of revolution, elites sought alternatives that would be less threatening to the established order and still permit some change. This search for alternatives became immediately evident in the question of national unification in Germany and Italy. National unification would hereafter depend on what the Prussian leader Otto von Bismarck would call "blood and iron," not speeches and parliamentary resolutions.

■ **MAKING CONNECTIONS**

1. *Which of the ideologies of this period had the greatest impact on political events? How can you explain this?*

2. *In what ways might industrialization be considered a force for peaceful change rather than a revolution? (Hint: Consider the situation in Great Britain.)*

■ **FOR FURTHER EXPLORATION**

For further reading and online research ideas, see the Suggested References on page SR-9 at the back of the book.

For practice quizzes, a customized study plan, and other study tools, see the ONLINE STUDY GUIDE at bedfordstmartins.com/huntconcise.

For primary-source material from this period, see Chapter 17 in *Sources of THE MAKING OF THE WEST: A CONCISE HISTORY*, Second Edition.

Constructing the Nation-State

c. 1850–1880

I N 1859, THE NAME "VERDI" SUDDENLY APPEARED scrawled on walls across the disunited cities of the Italian peninsula. The graffiti seemed to celebrate the composer Giuseppe Verdi, whose operas thrilled crowds of Europeans. Verdi was a particular hero among Italians, however, for his stories of downtrodden groups struggling against tyrannical government seemed to refer specifically to their plight. As his operatic choruses thundered out calls to rebellion in the name of the nation, Italian audiences were sure that Verdi meant for them to throw off Austrian and papal rule and unite in a new version of the ancient Roman Empire. Yet the graffiti was doubly political, a call to arms in the days before mass media. For VERDI also formed an acronym for *Vittorio Emmanuele Re* ("king") *d'Italia*, and in 1859 it summoned Italians to unite immediately under Victor Emmanuel II, king of Sardinia and Piedmont—the one leader with a nationalist, modernizing profile. The graffiti was good publicity, for the very next year Italy united as a result of warfare, popular uprisings, and hard bargaining by political realists.

In the wake of the failed revolutions of 1848, European statesmen and the politically conscious public increasingly rejected the politics of idealism in favor of **Realpolitik**—a politics of tough-minded realism aimed at strengthening the state and tightening social order. Realpolitikers distrusted the romanticism and

■ *Aïda* **Poster**

Aïda, Giuseppe Verdi's opera of human passion and state power, became a staple of Western culture. As the opera played across Europe, it brought Europeans into a common cultural orbit. Written to celebrate the opening of the Suez Canal, Aïda also celebrated Europe's better access to Asian resources provided by the new waterway. As the poster shows, the opera ushered in another wave of Egyptomania—the craze for Egyptian styles and objects. (Madeline Grimoldi.)

high-minded ideologies of the revolutionaries and aimed to control nationalism. Instead they put their faith in power politics, a strong national economy, and the use of violence to attain their goals. Two particularly skilled practitioners of Realpolitik, the Italian Camillo di Cavour and the Prussian Otto von Bismarck, succeeded in unifying Italy and Germany, respectively, not by consensus but by war and diplomacy. Most leading figures of these decades, enmeshed like Verdi's operatic heroes in violent political maneuverings, advanced state power by harnessing the forces of nationalism and liberalism that had led to earlier romantic revolts.

Many ingredients went into making modern nation-states and empires during these momentous decades. Continued economic development was crucial, and entrepreneurs produced a host of new inventions, new procedures, and new ways of doing business. A growing sense of national identity and common purpose was forged by both culture and government policy. As productivity and wealth increased, governments took vigorous steps to improve the environment of their rapidly growing cities, monitor public health, and promote national sentiment. State support for cultural developments ranging from public schools to opera productions helped establish a common fund of knowledge and even shared political beliefs. Authoritarian leaders such as Bismarck and the new French emperor Napoleon III believed that a better quality of life would not only calm revolutionary impulses and build state power but also keep political liberals at bay.

Culture also built a sense of belonging. Reading novels, attending art exhibitions, keeping up-to-date at the newly fashionable world's fairs, and attending theater and opera created not only a greater sense of being French or German or British but also of being European. Cultural works increasingly rejected romanticism, featuring instead realistic aspects of ordinary people's lives. Artists painted nudes in shockingly blunt ways, eliminating romantic hues and poses. Verdi's celebrated opera *La Traviata* showed a frolicking courtesan menacing a middle-class family. The Russian author Leo Tolstoy depicted the bleak life of soldiers in the Crimean War that erupted in 1853 between the Russian and Ottoman Empires, while his countryman Fyodor Dostoevsky wrote of criminals and murders in urban neighborhoods. Realism in the arts paralleled that in politics.

Realpolitik focused on outcomes in state building with far less concern for the costs to people's lives. Advancing state power entailed global expansion and stamping out resistance to it. At home, governments uprooted neighborhoods in favor of constructing public buildings, roads, and parks. The process of nation building was often brutal, bringing war, arrests, protests, and outright civil war—all of these the centerpieces of Verdi's operas as well. In 1871, an uprising of Parisians challenged the central government's intrusion into everyday life and its failure to count the costs. For the most part, the powerful Western state did not spring up automatically or tranquilly during these years. Instead, its growth depended on shrewd policy, deliberate warfare, dislocation, and new inroads on the lives of people around the world. Realpolitik relied on all of these as well as a general climate of modern opinion that valued realism and hard facts.

The End of the Concert of Europe

The revolutions of 1848 had weakened the concert of Europe, driving out its architect Klemens von Metternich and allowing the forces of nationalism to flourish. It became more difficult for countries to control their competing ambitions and act together. In addition, the dreaded resurgence of Bonapartism in the person of Napoleon III (Louis-Napoleon, the nephew of Napoleon I) added to the volatility in international politics as France sought to reassert itself. One of Napoleon's targets was Russia, formerly a mainstay of the concert of Europe. To limit Russia's pursuit of further expansion, France helped engineer the Crimean War of 1853–1856. Taking a huge toll in human life, the war hurt Russia and Austria and made way for a shift in the distribution of European power.

Napoleon III and the Quest for French Glory

Louis-Napoleon Bonaparte encouraged the resurgence of French grandeur and the cult of his famous uncle as part of nation building. "There are certain men who are born to serve as a means for the march of the human race," he wrote. "I consider myself to be one of these." In deft political coups Louis-Napoleon converted himself from president of the Second Republic to emperor. Arresting opponents in towns and cities, he declared himself Emperor Napoleon III (r. 1852–1870) and proclaimed the Second Empire on December 2, 1852—the anniversary of Napoleon I's own ascension to power.

Napoleon III acted as Europe's schoolmaster, showing its leaders how to combine economic liberalism and nationalism with authoritarian rule. Cafés where men might discuss politics were closed, and a rubber-stamp legislature (the *Corps législatif*) reduced representative government to a façade. Imperial style replaced republican simplicity. Napoleon's opulent court dazzled the public, and the emperor cultivated a masculine image of strength and majesty by wearing military uniforms (like his namesake) and by conspicuously maintaining mistresses. Napoleon's wife, Empress Eugénie, however, followed middle-class conventions such as observing separate spheres for men and women by serving as a devoted mother to her only son and supporting many volunteer charities. The authoritarian, apparently old-fashioned order imposed by Napoleon satisfied the many peasants that urban radicalism was under control.

Yet Napoleon III simultaneously pushed for a modern economy, and he promoted industrial growth, public works programs, and jobs, which lured the middle and working classes away from radical politics. International trade fairs and the magnificent rebuilding of Paris helped sustain French prosperity as Europe

■ **Napoleon III and Eugénie Receive the Siamese Ambassadors**
At a splendid gathering of their court, Emperor Napoleon III, Empress Eugénie, and their son and heir greet ambassadors from Siam, whose exoticism and servility before the French imperial family are the centerpiece of this depiction. Amid the grandeur of the Napoleonic dynasty, the West towers above the East. (Bridgeman-Giraudon/Art Resource, NY.)

recovered from the hard times of the late 1840s. Empress Eugénie wore lavish gowns, encouraging French silk production and keeping Paris at the center of the lucrative fashion trade. The regime also reached a free-trade agreement with Britain and backed an innovative investment bank—the Crédit Mobilier. Such new institutions led the way in financing railroad expansion, and railway mileage increased fivefold during Napoleon III's reign. During the economic downturn of the late 1850s, he wooed support by allowing working-class organizations and introducing features of democratic government. Although some historians have judged Napoleon III to be enigmatic and shifty because of these abrupt changes, his maneuvers were pragmatic responses to economic change.

On the international scene, Napoleon III's main goals were to overcome the containment of France imposed by the Congress of Vienna and acquire international glory like a true Bonaparte. To realign European politics in France's favor, Napoleon pitted France first against Russia in the Crimean War, then against Austria in the War of Italian Unification, and finally against Prussia in the Franco-Prussian War of 1870. Beyond Europe, Napoleon's army continued to enforce French rule in Algeria and Southeast Asia and tried to install Habsburg emperor Francis Joseph's brother Maximilian as ruler of Mexico and ultimately of all Central America—an assault that displayed French weakness in 1867 when Mexican forces executed Maximilian. Napoleon's foreign policy transformed relations among the great powers by causing a breakdown in the international system of peaceful diplomacy established at the Congress of Vienna. While his encouragement of projects like the Suez Canal to connect the Mediterranean and the Red Sea proved visionary, his push for worldwide influence eventually destroyed him: the French overthrew him after Prussia easily defeated his army in 1870.

The Crimean War, 1853–1856: Turning Point in European Affairs

Napoleon first flexed his diplomatic muscle in the Crimean War (1853–1856), which began as a conflict between the Russian and Ottoman Empires. While professing to uphold the concert of Europe, Russia continued to build state power by making further inroads into Asia and the Middle East. In particular, Tsar Nicholas I wanted to absorb much of the Ottoman Empire, fast becoming known as "the sick man of Europe" because of its disintegrating political authority. Napoleon III maneuvered Tsar Nicholas to be more aggressive, and amid this increasing belligerence war erupted in October 1853 between the two eastern empires (Map 18.1).

The Crimean War drew in other states, and as the conflict widened it threatened Europe's balance of power as set in the Congress of Vienna. Napoleon III convinced Austria to remain neutral during the war, thus fracturing the conservative Russian-Austrian coalition that had quashed French ambitions since 1815. The Austrian government still resented its dependence on Russia in putting down Hungarian revolutionaries in 1849 and felt threatened by continuing Russian expansion into the Balkans. To protect their Mediterranean routes to Asia, the British prodded the Ottomans to stand up to Russia, but in the fall of 1853, the Russians blasted the wooden Turkish ships to bits at the Ottoman port of

■ **MAP 18.1 The Crimean War, 1853–1856**

The most destructive war in Europe between the Napoleonic Wars and World War I, this conflict drew attention to the conflicting ambitions around territories of the declining Ottoman Empire. Importantly for state building in these decades, it fractured the alliance of conservative forces from the Congress of Vienna, allowing Italy and Germany to come into being as unified states and permitting Napoleon III to pursue his ambitions for France. **For more help analyzing this map,** see the map activity for this chapter in the ONLINE STUDY GUIDE at **bedfordstmartins. com/huntconcise.**

Sinope on the Black Sea. In 1854, France and Great Britain, enemies in war for more than a century, declared war on Russia to defend the Ottoman Empire's sovereignty and territories. Their own interests were of course primary.

Faced with attacking the massive Russian Empire, the allies settled for limited military goals focused on capturing the Russian naval base at Sevastopol on the Black Sea in the Crimea. Even so, the Crimean War was spectacularly bloody. British and French troops landed in the Crimea in September 1854 and waged a long siege of the fortified city, which fell after a year of savage and costly combat. Generals on both sides demonstrated their incompetence, and governments failed to provide combatants with even minimal supplies, sanitation, or medical care. The war claimed a massive toll. Three-quarters of a million men died, more than two-thirds from disease and starvation.

In the midst of this unfolding catastrophe, Alexander II (r. 1855–1881) ascended the Russian throne after the death of his father, Nicholas I, in 1855. With casualties mounting, the new tsar asked for peace. As a result of the Peace of Paris, signed in March 1856, Russia lost the right to base its navy in the Straits of Dardanelles and the Black Sea, which were declared neutral waters. Moldavia and Walachia (which soon merged to form Romania) became autonomous Turkish provinces under the victors' protection.

Some historians have called the Crimean War one of the most senseless conflicts in modern history because competing claims in southeastern Europe could have been settled by diplomacy had it not been for Napoleon III's driving ambition. Yet the war was full of consequence. New technologies were introduced into warfare: the railroad, shell-firing cannon, breech-loading rifles, and steam-powered ships. The relationship of the home front to the battlefront was beginning to change with the use of the telegraph and increased press coverage. Home audiences received news from the Crimean front lines more rapidly and in more detail than ever before. However, reports of incompetence, poor sanitation, and the huge death toll outraged the public, inspiring some civilians, such as Florence Nightingale, to head for the front to help. Nightingale seized the moment to escape the confines of middle-class domesticity by organizing a battlefield nursing service to care for the British sick and wounded. Through her tough-minded organization of nursing units, she improved the sanitary conditions of the troops both during and after the war and pioneered nursing as a profession. More immediately, the war accomplished Napoleon III's goal of ending Austria's and Russia's direction of European affairs. The war thus undermined their ability to contain the forces of liberalism and nationalism.

Spirit of Reform in Russia

Defeat in the Crimean War not only thwarted Russia's territorial ambition but also forced Russia on the path of long-overdue reform. Hundreds of peasant insurrections had erupted during the decade before the Crimean War. Serf defiance ranged from malingering while at forced labor to boycotting vodka to protest its heavy taxation. "Our own and neighboring households were gripped with fear," one aristocrat reported, because everyone expected "a serf uprising at any minute." Although economic development spread in parts of eastern Europe, the Russian economy stagnated compared with western Europe. Old-fashioned farming techniques depleted soil and led to food shortages, and the nobility was often contemptuous of ordinary people. Works of art such as novelist Ivan Turgenev's sympathetic portrayals of serfs and frank depictions of brutal masters in *A Hunter's Sketches* (1852) contributed to a spirit of reform. A Russian translation of Harriet Beecher Stowe's antislavery novel *Uncle Tom's Cabin* (1852) also struck a responsive chord. When Russia lost the Crimean War, the educated public, including some government officials, found the poor performance of serf-conscripted armies a disgrace and the system of serf labor an intolerable liability.

Confronted with the need for change, Alexander proved more flexible than his father Nicholas I. Well educated and more widely traveled, he ushered in what came to be known as the age of Great Reforms, granting Russians new rights from above as a way of ensuring that violent action from below would not force change. The most dramatic reform was the emancipation of almost 50 million serfs beginning in 1861. By the terms of emancipation, communities of former serfs, headed by male village elders, received grants of land. The community itself, called a **mir**, had full power to allocate this land among individuals and to direct their economic activity. Thus, although emancipation partially laid the groundwork for a modern labor force in Russia, communal landowning and decision making prevented unlimited mobility and the development of a pool of free labor. The condition attached to these so-called land grants was that peasants were not *given* land along with their personal freedom: they were forced to "redeem" the land they farmed by paying the government through long-term loans, which in turn compensated the original landowners. The best land remained in the hands of the nobility, and most peasants ended up actually owning less land than they had tilled as serfs. These conditions, especially the huge burden of debt and communal regulations, blunted Russian agricultural development for decades. But idealistic reformers believed the emancipation of the serfs, once treated by the nobility practically as livestock, produced miraculous results. As one reformer put it, "The people are without any exaggeration transfigured from head to foot. . . . The look, the walk, the speech, everything is changed."

The state also reformed local administration, the judiciary, and the military. The government compensated the nobility for loss of peasant services and set up *zemstvos*—regional councils through which aristocrats could direct neglected local matters such as education and public health. Aristocratic dominance assured that zemstvos would remain a conservative structure, but they provided some balance at the local level to the autocratic central government. Simultaneously, judicial reform gave all Russians, even former serfs, access to modern civil courts, rather than leaving them at the mercy of a landowner's version of justice. The Western

VÉRITABLE EXTRAIT DE VIANDE LIEBIG.

Episodes de l'histoire de la Russie.
Abolition du servage par Alexandre II, le 3 Mars 1861.   6.

Voir l'explication au verso.

■ Emancipation of the Russian Serfs

This trading card was used as a marketing gimmick by businesspeople hoping to push their new products—in this case canned meat. They were given away by the thousands in stores and traded just as baseball cards are today. Historical scenes were popular subjects for the cards—this one shows the emancipation of the serfs in Russia, which was a major event to people across Europe. Note that the caption is in French, which was known by European upper classes including those in Russia, who would have consumed this product. The emancipation is presented as a wholly beneficial act with no strings attached, such as the immense debt imposed on former serfs. (Mary Evans Picture Library.)

principle of equality of all persons before the law, regardless of social rank, was introduced in Russia for the first time. Military reform followed in 1874 when the government replaced the twenty-five-year period of conscription with a six-year term and focused on educating Russian troops in an effort to match the efficiency of soldiers elsewhere in western Europe.

Alexander's reforms assisted modernizing and market-oriented landowners just as enclosures and emancipation had done much earlier in western Europe. At the same time, the changes diminished the personal prerogatives of the nobility, leaving their authority weakened and sparking intergenerational conflict. "An epidemic seemed to seize upon [noble] children . . . an epidemic of fleeing from the parental roof," one observer noted. Rejecting aristocratic leisure, youthful rebels from the upper class valued practical activity and sometimes identified with peasants and workers. Some formed communes where they hoped to do humble manual labor; others turned to higher education, especially the sciences. Rebellious daughters of the nobility flouted parental expectations by cropping their hair short, wearing black, and escaping from home through phony marriages so they could study in European universities. This repudiation of traditional society led Turgenev to label radical youth as *nihilists* (from the Latin for "nothing"), a term that meant a lack of belief in any values whatsoever. In fact, they showed a defiant spirit percolating in Russian society.

The atmosphere of nation building through reform also inspired resistance among Russian-dominated nationalities, including an uprising by aristocratic and upper-class nationalist Poles in 1863. By 1864, Alexander II's army regained control of the Russian section of Poland, while the government intensified repression and **Russification**—a tactic meant to reduce the threat of future rebellion by national minorities within the empire by forcing them to adopt Russian language and culture. In this era of the Great Reforms, the tsarist regime only partially succeeded in developing the administrative, economic, and civic institutions of the nation-state. The tsar and his inner circle tightly held the reins of government, allowing few to share in power. In imperial Russia the persistence of autocracy and the abuse of large numbers of the population hindered the development of the sense of citizenship forming elsewhere in the West.

■ **REVIEW:** *What were the main results of the Crimean War?*

War and Nation Building

Dynamic leaders in the German and Italian states used the opportunity offered by the weakened concert of Europe to unify their countries through warfare. When national disunity threatened, the United States also waged a bloody civil war to maintain its integrity, which opened the way for dynamic economic growth. Historians sometimes treat the rise of powerful nation-states such as Italy, Germany, and the United States as part of an inevitable process, but millions of individuals, especially those living in rural areas, maintained a local or regional sense of identity rather than a national one.

Cavour, Garibaldi, and the Process of Italian Unification

Despite the failed revolutions of 1848 in the Italian states, the issue of *Risorgimento* (literally meaning "rebirth," especially in the movement for Italian unification) continued to simmer, aided by the disintegration of diplomatic stability across Europe. This time the kingdom of Piedmont-Sardinia in the economically modernizing north of Italy drove the unification process. The kingdom rallied to the operas of Verdi, but its nationalizing spirit was fortified by railroads and a modern army. It allied with France to drive the Austrian Empire from its dominant role on the peninsula.

The architect of the new Italy was the pragmatic Camillo di Cavour (1810–1861), prime minister of the kingdom of Piedmont-Sardinia from 1852 until his death. A rebel in his youth, the young Cavour had conducted agricultural experiments on his aristocratic father's land. He organized steamship companies,

■ MAP 18.2 Unification of Italy, 1859–1870

The many states of the Italian peninsula had different languages, ways of life, and economic interests. In the north, the Kingdom of Sardinia, which included the commercially advanced state of Piedmont, had much to gain from a unified market and a more extensive pool of labor. Although King Victor Emmanuel's and Garibaldi's armies unified these states into a single country, it would take decades to construct a culturally, socially, and economically connected nation.

played the stock market, and inhaled the heady air of modernization during his travels to Paris and London. As prime minister, Cavour capitalized on favorable conditions to develop a healthy Piedmontese economy, a modern army, and a liberal political climate as the foundation for Piedmont's control of the unification process (Map 18.2).

To unify Italy, however, Piedmont would have to confront Austria, which governed the provinces of Lombardy and Venetia and exerted strong influence over most of the peninsula. Cavour turned for help to Napoleon III, who in the summer of 1858 promised French assistance in exchange for the city of Nice and the region of Savoy. Napoleon III expected that France rather than Austria would influence the peninsula thereafter. Sure of French help, Cavour provoked the Austrians to invade northern Italy in April 1859. Using the newly built Piedmontese railroad to move troops, the French and Piedmontese armies achieved rapid victories at Solferino and Magenta. The cause of Piedmont now became the cause of nationalist Italians everywhere, even those who had supported romantic republicanism in 1848. Political liberals in Tuscany and other central Italian states rose up on the side of Piedmont. Suddenly fearing Piedmontese force, Napoleon independently signed a peace treaty with Austria that gave Lombardy but not Venetia to Piedmont; the rest of Italy remained disunited.

Napoleon's plans for controlled liberation of Lombardy and Venetia and a partitioned Italy were derailed as support for Piedmont continued to swell inside Italy and as a financially strapped Austria stood by helplessly. Ousting their rulers, citizens of Parma, Modena, Tuscany, and the Papal States (except Rome, which French troops had occupied) elected to join Piedmont. In May 1860, Giuseppe Garibaldi (1807–1882), a committed republican, inspired guerrilla fighter, and veteran of the revolutions of 1848, set sail from Genoa with a thousand red-shirted volunteers (many of them teenage boys) to liberate Sicily, where peasant revolts against landlords and the corrupt government were under way. In the autumn of 1860, the forces of King Victor Emmanuel of Piedmont-Sardinia and Garibaldi finally met in Naples (see Map 18.2). Although some of his supporters still clamored for social reform and a republic, Garibaldi threw his support to the king. In 1861, the kingdom of Italy was proclaimed with Victor Emmanuel as ruler (r. 1861–1878).

 Seamstresses of the Red Shirts
Sewing uniforms and making battle flags, European women like these Italian volunteers saw themselves as contributors to the nation. Donating their domestic skills and raising the next generation of citizens to be patriotic, many nineteenth-century women participated in nation building as "republican mothers."

Exhausted by a decade of overwork, Cavour died within months of leading the unification, leaving lesser men to organize the new Italy. Consensus among Italy's elected political leaders was often elusive once the war was over, and admirers of Cavour, such as Verdi (who had been made senator), fled the heated political scene. The wealthy commercial north and impoverished agricultural south remained at odds over taxation and development, as they do even today. Finally, Italian borders did not yet seem complete because Venetia and Rome remained outside them, under Austrian and French control, respectively. Amidst these strains, the legend of an Italian struggle for freedom symbolized by the figure of Garibaldi and his Red Shirts became a powerful unifying force even though it sentimentalized the economic and military Realpolitik that had made unification possible. Many citizens of the new country took pride in the Italian nation based on Garibaldian and other national myths.

Bismarck and the Realpolitik of German Unification

The most momentous act of nation building for the future of Europe and of the world was the creation of a united Germany in 1871. This, too, was the product of Realpolitik, undertaken once the concert of Europe was smashed and the champions of the status quo defeated. Employing the old military order to wage war, yet with the support of economic modernizers who saw profits in a single national market, the Prussian state brought a vast array of cities and kingdoms under its control within a single decade. From then on, Germany prospered, continuing to consolidate its economic and political might. By the end of the century it would be the foremost continental power.

The architect of a unified Germany was Otto von Bismarck (1815–1898), the Prussian minister-president. Bismarck came from a traditional Junker (Prussian landed nobility) family on his father's side; his mother's family included high-ranking bureaucrats of the middle class. At university, the young Bismarck had gambled and womanized, interested only in a course on the economic foundations of politics. After failing in the civil service, he worked to modernize operations on his landholdings while leading an otherwise loutish life. His marriage to a pious Lutheran woman gave him new purpose. In the 1850s, his diplomatic service to the Prussian state made him increasingly angry at the Habsburg grip on German affairs and the roadblock it created to the full flowering of Prussia. Establishing Prussia as a respected and dominant power became his cause.

In 1862, William I (king of Prussia, r. 1861–1888; German emperor, r. 1871–1888) appointed Bismarck prime minister in hopes that he would quash the growing power of the liberals in the Prussian parliament. The liberals, representing the prosperous professional and business classes, had gained parliamentary strength at the expense of conservative landowners during the decades of industrial expansion. Indeed, the liberals' wealth was crucial to Prussia's growing power. Desiring Prussia to be like western Europe, Prussian liberals advocated the extension of political rights and increased civilian control of the military. William I, along with members of the traditional Prussian elite such as Bismarck, rejected the western European model. Bismarck simply rammed through programs to build the army and thwart civilian control. "Germany looks not to Prussia's liberalism, but to its power," he preached. "The great questions of the day will not be settled by speeches and majority decisions—that was the great mistake of 1848 and 1849—but by iron and blood."

After his triumph over the parliament, Bismarck led Prussia into a series of wars, against Denmark in 1864, against Austria in 1866, and finally, against France in 1870. Using war as a political tactic, he kept the disunited German states from choosing Austrian leadership and instead united them around Prussia. Bismarck drew Austria into a joint war with Prussia against a rebellious Denmark in 1864 over Denmark's proposed incorporation of the provinces of Schleswig and Holstein, with their partially German population. Their joint victory resulted in an agreement that Prussia would administer Schleswig, and Austria, Holstein. Such an arrangement stretched Austria's geographic interests far from its central European base.

Austria proved weaker than Prussia, as the Habsburgs lagged in economic development and suffered from a swelling national debt and the restlessness of its many national minorities. Bismarck, however, encouraged Habsburg pretensions to its former grandeur and influence. He simultaneously fomented disputes over the administration of Schleswig and Holstein, goading a puffed up and confident Austria into declaring war on Prussia itself. In the summer of 1866, Austria went to war with the support of most small states in the German Confederation. Within seven weeks, the modernized Prussian army, using railroads and fast breech-loading rifles against the outdated Austrian military, had won decisively. The masterful victory allowed Bismarck to drive Austria from the German Confederation, create a North German Confederation led by Prussia, and coordinate economic and political programs (see Map 18.3 on page 760).

To bring the remaining German states into the rapidly developing nation, Bismarck next moved to entrap France in a war with Prussia. During the Austro-Prussian War, Bismarck had suggested to Napoleon III that his neutrality would bring France territory, thus heating up nationalist sentiments in both France and Germany. The atmosphere became even more charged when Spain proposed a minor Prussian prince to fill its vacant royal throne. This candidacy threatened the French with Prussian rulers on two of their borders. Bismarck used the occasion to stir up nationalist journalism in both countries by editing a diplomatic communication (known as the Ems telegram) to make it look as if the king of Prussia had insulted France over the succession issue. Release of the revised version to journalists inflamed the French public into demanding war against Prussia. The parliament gladly declared it on July 19, 1870, setting in motion the alliances Prussia had created with the other German states. The Prussians captured Napoleon III

■ MAP 18.3 Unification of Germany, 1862–1871

In a complex series of diplomatic maneuvers, Otto von Bismarck welded disunited kingdoms and small states into a major continental power independent of the other dominant German dynasty, the Habsburg monarchy. Prussia's use of force unified Germany politically, and almost immediately that unity unleashed the new nation's economic potential. An aristocratic and agrarian elite remained firmly in power, but a rapidly growing working class would soon become a political force to be reckoned with.

with his army on September 2, 1870, and the Second Empire fell two days later. With Prussian forces still besieging Paris, in January 1871 in the Hall of Mirrors at Versailles, King William of Prussia was proclaimed the kaiser (or emperor) of a new, imperial Germany. The terms of the peace signed in May 1871 required France to cede the rich industrial provinces of Alsace and Lorraine to Germany and to pay a multibillion-franc indemnity. Without French protection for the papacy, Rome became part of Italy. Germany was now poised to dominate continental politics.

■ Emperor William I of Germany, 1871

The defeat of France in the Franco-Prussian War of 1870–1871 ended with the proclamation of the king of Prussia as emperor of a unified Germany. Otto von Bismarck, who had orchestrated the wars of unification, appropriately appears in this artistic rendering as the central figure attired in heroic white. The event in the French palace of Versailles symbolized the militaristic and antagonistic side of state building, especially the Franco-German rivalry that would disastrously motivate European politics in the future. (AKG-Images, London.)

Prussian military might served as the foundation for German state building, and a complex constitution ensured the continued political dominance of the aristocracy and monarchy despite the growing wealth of the business classes. The kaiser, who remained Prussia's king, controlled the military and appointed Bismarck to the powerful position of imperial chancellor. The German states balanced monarchical authority somewhat through the *Bundesrat,* a body composed of representatives from each state. The *Reichstag,* an assembly elected by universal male suffrage, ratified all budgets. In framing this constitutional settlement, Bismarck accorded rights such as suffrage in the belief that the masses would uphold autocracy out of their fear of "the domination of finance capital"—shorthand for "liberal power." He balanced this move, however, with an electoral system in which votes from the upper classes counted more than votes from the lower classes. He had little to fear from liberals, who, dizzy with German military success, came to support the blend of economic progress, constitutionalism, and militaristic nationalism that Bismarck represented.

Francis Joseph and the Creation of the Austro-Hungarian Monarchy

There was no blueprint for nation building. Just as the Crimean War left Russia searching for solutions to its social and political problems, so the confrontation with Cavour and Bismarck left the Habsburg Empire defeated and at bay. At first, the Habsburg Empire emerged from the revolutions of 1848 and 1849 renewed by the ascension of Francis Joseph (r. 1848–1916), who favored absolutist rule. A tireless worker, Francis Joseph enhanced his authority through stiff, formal court ceremonies, playing to the popular fascination with the trappings of power. Though the emperor stubbornly resisted change, official standards of honesty and efficiency improved, and the government promoted local education. The German language was used by the administration and taught by the schools, but the government respected the rights of national minorities—Czechs and Poles, for instance—to receive education and to communicate with officials in their native tongues. Above all, the government abolished most internal customs barriers, freed trade with Germany, fostered a boom in private railway construction, and attracted foreign capital. The capital city of Vienna underwent extensive rebuilding, and people found jobs as industrialization progressed, if unevenly.

In a fast-paced age, the absolutist emperor could not match Bismarck in advancing modernization and the power of the state. Too much of the old regime remained as a roadblock to reform. The Catholic church had nearly a free hand in education and in civil institutions such as marriage, and wealthy businessmen lacked representation in such important policy matters as taxation and finance. After Prussia's victory over Francis Joseph's armies in 1866, the most disaffected but wealthy part of the empire, Hungary, became the key to stability, even to the empire's existence. The leaders of the Hungarian agrarian elites forced the emperor

The Austro-Hungarian Monarchy, 1867

to accept a **dual monarchy**—that is, Magyar home rule over the Hungarian kingdom. This agreement restored the Hungarian parliament and gave it control of internal policy (including the right to decide how to treat Hungary's national minorities). Although the Habsburg emperor Francis Joseph was crowned king of Hungary and Austro-Hungarian foreign policy was coordinated from Vienna, the Hungarians mostly ruled themselves after 1867 and hammered out common policies such as tariffs in acrimonious negotiations with Vienna. The new political arrangement was an additional roadblock to strengthening and modernizing the empire as a whole.

The dual monarchy of Austria-Hungary, or Austro-Hungarian monarchy as the new arrangement was also called, was designed specifically to address Hungarian demands, but in so doing it strengthened the voices of Czechs, Slovaks, and at least half a dozen other national groups in the Habsburg Empire wanting the same kind of self-rule. Czechs who helped the empire advance industrially failed to gain Hungarian-style liberties, and for some of the dissatisfied ethnic groups, **Pan-Slavism**—that is, the transnational loyalty of all ethnic Slavs—became a rallying cry as the various Slav peoples saw themselves as linked through a common heritage. Instead of looking toward Vienna, they turned to the largest Slavic country— Russia—as a focal point for potential national unity. As the nation-state grew in strength, transnational movements like Pan-Slavism would emerge to provide alternative allegiances for those not recognized as equal citizens in their home countries.

Political Stability through Gradual Reform in Great Britain

In contrast to the turmoil in continental Europe, Britain appeared the epitome of liberal progress. By the 1850s, the monarchy symbolized domestic tranquility and stability. Unlike their predecessors, Queen Victoria (r. 1837–1901) and her husband, Prince Albert, were considered models of middle-class virtue. Britain's parliamentary system incorporated new ideas and steadily brought more men into the

■ **Queen Victoria and Prince Albert**

In the mid-nineteenth century, rulers started using the new photographic technology to portray themselves as respectable and distinguished figures. Queen Victoria and her husband were expert publicists, often posing as an ordinary middle-class couple and the epitome of domestic order in marked contrast to their often dissolute royal predecessors. Photos of them were sold or given away on small cards called cartes de visites, *which many leaders used to spread their fame.*
(The Royal Archives © 2005 Her Majesty Queen Elizabeth II.)

political process. Economic prosperity fortified peaceful political reform except for Ireland's continued suffering and thwarted demands for justice. An ever-changing and focused party system fostered smooth governmental decision making: the Tory Party evolved into the Conservatives, many of whose policies favored the aristocracy. Nonetheless, the Conservatives still went along with the developing liberal consensus around economic development and representative government. Skilled politician William Gladstone, who would serve four terms as prime minister, helped the Whigs and several other political groups become the Liberals. In 1867, the Conservatives, led by Benjamin Disraeli, passed the Second Reform Bill, which made a million more men eligible to vote.

Political parties supported reforms because pressure groups now influenced the party system. The Law Amendment Society and the Social Science Association, for example, lobbied for laws to improve social conditions, and women's groups advocated the Matrimonial Causes Act of 1857, which facilitated divorce, and the Married Women's Property Act of 1870, which allowed married women to own property and keep the wages they earned. Dissension over new policies was papered over by plush ceremonies that united critics and activists and, more important, different social classes. Whereas previous monarchs' sexual infidelities had incited mobs to riot, the monarchy of Queen Victoria and Prince Albert, with its newly devised celebrations of royal marriages, anniversaries, and births, drew respectful crowds. Promoting the monarchy in this way was so successful that the term *Victorian* came to symbolize almost the entire century and could refer to anything from manners to political institutions. Yet Britain's politicians were as devoted to Realpolitik as were those in Germany, Italy, or France, endorsing violence to expand their overseas empire and to control Ireland. The violence was far beyond the view of most British people, however, allowing them to imagine their nation as peaceful, advanced, and united.

Civil War and Nation Building in the United States and Canada

In North America, increasing nationalism and powerful economic growth characterized the nation-building experience. The United States experienced the mid-century as a period of unprecedented and destructive upheaval born of nation building. It had a far more democratic political culture than existed in Europe, including almost universal white male suffrage, a rambunctiously independent press, and mass political parties, all of which endorsed the accepted view that sovereignty derived from the people.

The United States continued to expand its territory to the west (Map 18.4). In 1848, victory in a war with Mexico almost doubled the size of the country: Texas was officially annexed, and large portions of California and the American Southwest extended the borders of the United States into former Mexican land. Politicians and ordinary citizens alike favored banning the native Indian peoples

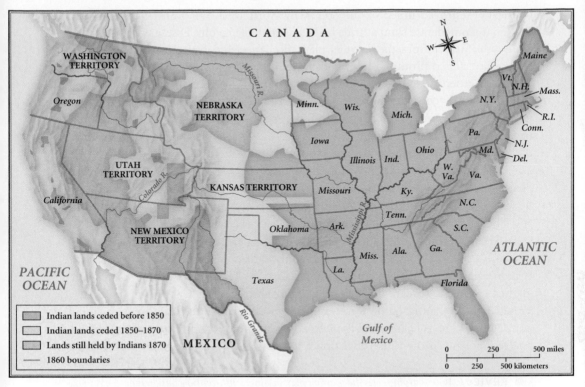

■ **MAP 18.4 U.S. Expansion, 1850–1870**

Like Russia, the United States expanded into adjacent regions to create a continental nation-state, conquering indigenous peoples and taking over their territories. The United States' treatment of those whose lands it took was different from that of Russia, however. Native American peoples were herded into small confined spaces called reservations so that settlers could acquire thousands of square miles for farming and other enterprises. Gradually some native Americans acquired the right to vote, and the U.S. government granted full citizenship for all in 1925.

from these western lands. Complicating matters, however, was the question of whether the U.S. West would be settled by free white farmers or whether southern slaveholders could bring in their slaves. The issue polarized the country. In the North, the new Republican Party emerged to demand "free soil, free labor, free men," although few Republicans endorsed the abolitionist demand to end slavery.

With the 1860 election of Republican Abraham Lincoln to the presidency, most of the slaveholding states of the South seceded to form the Confederate States of America. Under Lincoln's leadership, the North fought a civil war against the South to restore the Union. Lincoln did not initially aim to abolish slavery, but in January 1863 his Emancipation Proclamation came into force as a wartime measure, officially freeing all slaves in the Confederate states and turning the war into a fight not only for the Union but also for liberation from slavery. After the summer of 1863, the superior industrial strength and military might of the North overpowered and physically destroyed much of the South. By April 1865, the North had won even though a Confederate sympathizer had assassinated Lincoln. Distancing the United States still further from the colonial plantation model, constitutional amendments ended slavery and promised full political rights to African American men.

Northerners hailed their victory as the triumph of American values, but racism remained entrenched throughout the United States. By 1871, northern interest in promoting African American political rights was waning, and southern whites began regaining control of state politics, often by organized violence and intimidation. The end of northern occupation of the South in 1877 put on hold for nearly a century the promise of rights for blacks. Nonetheless, in ending slavery, the Union victory opened the way to more coherent national government and further economic advance beyond the old Atlantic system based on slave production.

The North's triumph had profound effects elsewhere in North America. It allowed the reunited United States to contribute to Napoleon III's defeat in Mexico in 1867. The United States also eyed the annexation of Canada in retribution for Britain's partiality to the Confederacy because of British dependence on cotton. To head off this threat, the British government allowed Canadians to form a united, self-governing dominion. According dominion status answered Canadian appeals for home rule, lessened domestic opposition to Britain's control of Canada, and still advanced the cause of national integration.

■ **REVIEW:** *What varying roles did warfare play in nineteenth-century nation building?*

Industry and Nation Building

Behind the growing power of European states lay the often dramatic development of economic and technological power. Industry turned out a cornucopia of products that improved people's material well-being. Paris, Vienna, and other cities experienced a frenzy of building, and the wages of many workers increased. Unpredictable downturns in business, however, threatened both entrepreneurs and the working class. Businesspeople sought remedies in new managerial techniques and innovative marketing, most visibly in the development of the department store. Governments played their part by changing business law and supporting the drive for global profits. The steady advance of industry and global trade and the rise of a consumer economy further transformed the work lives of millions of people.

Industrial Innovation

Industrial, technological, and commercial innovation abounded in nineteenth-century Europe. New products ranging from the bicycle, typewriter, and telephone to the internal combustion engine provided dizzying proof of industrial progress. Many independent tinkerers and inventor-manufacturers created new products, and sophisticated engineers—for example, Karl Benz of Germany and Armand Peugeot of France—invented revolutionary technologies such as the gasoline engine. Electricity began to provide the power to light everything from private drawing rooms to government office buildings. To fuel industrial growth, the leading industrial nations mined and produced massive quantities of coal, iron, and steel during the 1870s and 1880s. Production of iron increased from 11 million to 23 million tons. Steel output in the industrial nations grew just as impressively, increasing from 500,000 to 11 million tons in the 1870s and 1880s. Manufacturers used the metal to build the more than 100,000 locomotives that pulled trains during these years—trains that transported 2 billion people annually.

Historians used to contrast a "second" Industrial Revolution, with its concentration on heavy industrial products, to the "first" Industrial Revolution of the eighteenth and early nineteenth centuries, in which innovations in textile making and the use of steam energy predominated. But many historians now believe this distinction applies mainly to Britain. In countries where industrialization came later, the two stages occurred simultaneously. Numerous textile mills were installed on the European continent later than in Britain, for instance, at the same time as blast furnaces were constructed. Industrialization led to the decline of cottage production in traditional crafts like weaving. Domestic production—or outwork—persisted in garment making, metalwork, and "finishing trades" such as porcelain painting and button polishing. Urban families painted tin soldiers, wrapped chocolate, and made cheese boxes. Factory owners liked to employ outworkers because low piece rates made them desperate for work under any conditions, and they were willing to work extremely long days. A German seamstress at her new home sewing machine reported that she "pedaled at a stretch from six o'clock in the morning until midnight. . . . At four o'clock I got up and did the housework and prepared meals." Although joblessness and destitution always threatened, some city workers prospered in comparison to those left behind in rural areas even with the decline of traditional artisanal work. The coexistence of home and factory enterprise continued through all the changes in manufacturing to the present day.

Industrial innovations also changed agriculture. Chemical fertilizers boosted crop yields, and reapers and threshers mechanized harvesting. In the 1870s, Sweden produced a cream separator, a first step toward mechanizing dairy farming. Wire fencing and barbed wire replaced wooden fencing and stone walls, both of which were labor-intensive to create. Refrigeration, developed during this period, allowed fruits, vegetables, and meat to be transported long distances without spoiling, thus diversifying and increasing the urban food supply. Tin from colonial trade facilitated large-scale commercial canning, which made many foods available year-round to people in the cities.

During these decades, Britain's rate of industrial growth slowed as its entrepreneurs remained wedded to older, successful technologies. Two countries began surpassing Britain in technical education, innovation, and rate of growth:

Germany and the United States. Profiting from the acquisition of resource-rich Alsace and Lorraine, German businesses invested in research and began to mass-produce goods that other countries had originally manufactured. Germany also spent as much money on education as on its military in the 1870s and 1880s. This investment resulted in highly skilled engineers and technical workers whose productivity enabled Germany's electrical and chemical engineering capabilities to soar. The United States began an intensive exploitation of its vast natural resources, including coal, ores, gold, and oil. Whereas German accomplishments rested more on state promotion of industrial efforts, innovative entrepreneurs, such as Andrew Carnegie in iron and steel and John D. Rockefeller in oil, drove U.S. growth.

Most other countries trailed the three leaders in the pervasiveness of industry. French industry grew steadily, but French businesses remained smaller than businesses in Germany and the United States. Although France had some huge mining, textile, and metallurgical establishments, many French businessmen retired early to imitate the still-enviable aristocratic way of life. Industrial development in Spain, Austria-Hungary, and Italy was primarily a local phenomenon. Austria-Hungary had densely industrialized areas around Vienna and in Styria and Bohemia, but the rest of the country remained tied to traditional, unmechanized agriculture. Italy continued to industrialize in the north while remaining rural and agricultural in the south. The Italian government spent more on building Rome into a grand capital than it invested in economic growth. A mere 1.4 percent of Italy's 1872 budget went to education and science, compared with 10.8 percent in Germany. The commercial use of electricity helped Scandinavians, who were poor in coal and ore, to industrialize in the last third of the nineteenth century. Sweden and Norway became leaders in the use of hydroelectric power and the development of electrical products. Russia's road to industrialization was torturous, slowed partly by the terms of the serf emancipation, which prevented peasants from freely moving to jobs in the city. By the end of the century, however, the new railroad lines and development of metallurgy and mining advanced Russian industrialization.

Facing Economic Crisis

Although innovations and business expansion often conveyed a sense of optimism, economic health was far from steady. Sharp downturns occurred in the business cycle throughout these decades, and within two years of the end of the Franco-Prussian War, prosperity abruptly gave way to a severe economic depression in many industrial countries. The crisis of 1873 was followed by almost three decades of economic fluctuations, most alarmingly a series of sharp downturns whose severity varied from country to country. People of all classes lost their jobs or businesses and faced consequences ranging from long stretches of unemployment to bankruptcy. Economists of the day were stunned by the relentlessness and pervasiveness of the slump. Because economic ties bound industrialized western Europe to international markets, recession affected the economies of such diverse regions as Australia, South Africa, California, Newfoundland, and the West Indies.

By the 1870s, industrial and financial setbacks—not agricultural ones, as in the past—were sending businesses into long-term tailspins in a fundamentally new economic climate. First, the start-up costs of new enterprises skyrocketed. Textile mills had required relatively modest amounts of capital in comparison with factories producing steel and iron. Industrialization had become what modern economists call *capital-intensive* rather than *labor-intensive:* industrial growth required the purchase of expensive machinery, not merely the hiring of more workers. Second, the distribution and consumption of goods were inadequate to sustain industrial growth, in part because businessmen kept wages so low despite rising productivity that workers could afford little besides food. Industrialists had made their fortunes by emphasizing production, not consumption. The series of slumps refocused entrepreneurial efforts on enhancing sales and controlling markets and prices.

New laws and institutions helped raise capital. Development of the limited liability corporation protected businesspeople from personal responsibility for the firm's debt and thus encouraged their investment. Before limited liability, business owners drew the necessary capital primarily from their own family assets, and financial backers were individually responsible for a firm's financial difficulties. In one case in England, a former partner who failed to have his name removed from a legal document after leaving the business remained responsible to creditors when the company went bankrupt. He lost everything he owned except a watch and the equivalent of $100. Public financing in stocks also helped raise vast amounts of new capital. Early stock exchanges had dealt mainly in government bonds and in government-sponsored enterprises such as railroads. By the end of the century, stock markets traded heavily in industrial corporate stock, thus raising money from a larger pool of private capital than before.

In another adaptive move, firms in the same industry banded together in cartels and trusts to control prices and competition. Cartels flourished particularly in German chemical, iron, coal, and electric industries. For example, the Rhenish-Westphalian Coal Syndicate, founded in 1893, eventually dominated more than 95 percent of coal production in Germany. Although business owners continued to advocate free trade, cartels broke with free-trade practices by restricting output and setting prices. Smaller businesses and consumers had no effective means of resisting these new business techniques. Trusts appeared first in the United States. In 1882, John D. Rockefeller created the Standard Oil Trust by acquiring stock from many different oil companies and placing it under the direction of trustees. The trustees then controlled so much of the companies' stock that they could set prices for the entire industry and even dictate to the railroads the rates for transporting the oil.

Like the practices of cartels and trusts, government imposition of tariffs expressed declining faith in classical liberal economics. Much of Europe had adopted free trade after midcentury, but during the recessions of the 1870s, huge trade deficits—caused when imports exceed exports—had soured many Europeans on the concept. A country with a trade deficit had less capital available to invest internally; fewer jobs were created, and the chances of social unrest increased. Farmers in many European countries were hurt when improvements in transportation made it possible to import perishable food, such as cheaper grain from the United States and Ukraine. With broad popular support, governments approved tariffs throughout these decades to prevent competition from foreign goods.

Revolution in Business Practices

Industrialists tried to minimize the damage of economic downturns by revolutionizing the everyday conduct of their businesses. A generation earlier, a factory owner was directly involved in every aspect of his business and often learned to run the firm through trial and error. In the late 1800s, industrialists began to hire managers to run their increasingly complex day-to-day operations. Managers who specialized in sales and distribution, finance, and the purchase of raw materials made decisions and oversaw the implementation of their policies. Other managers changed the nature of ordinary people's work by determining formal skill levels, from the most knowledgeable machinist to the untrained carrier of supplies. On the one hand, the introduction of machinery "deskilled" some jobs—traditional craft ability was not a prerequisite for operating many new machines. Employers could increasingly use untrained workers, often women, and pay them less than they paid skilled workers. On the other hand, inventions always demanded new skills, especially for those who had to understand work processes or repair machinery. Managers used the concept of skill (based in the old craft traditions) to segment the labor force, but sometimes the designations were arbitrary. Already prevalent in such trades as garment making, the trend toward breaking down and separating work processes into discrete tasks advanced with the management revolution. For example, builders employed excavators, scaffolders, and haulers to do the "dirty work," hiring fewer highly paid carpenters. On the other end of the scale, foremen were no longer the most skilled workers but instead were supervisors chosen, as one worker complained, for the "pushing powers . . . of driving fellow men."

Simultaneously, the rise of management led to the emergence of a "white-collar" service sector of office workers such as secretaries, file clerks, and typists to guide the flow of business information. Banks, railroads, insurance companies, and government-run telegraph and telephone companies all needed armies of white-collar employees. Workers with mathematical skills and literacy acquired in the new public primary schools staffed this service sector, which provided clean work for educated, middle-class women. Whether to help pay the growing cost of raising and educating children or to support themselves, unmarried and a greater number of married women of the respectable middle class took jobs despite the dominant ideology of domesticity. Employers, as one put it, found in the new women workers

■ **The Great Staircase of the Bon Marché (c. 1880)**
The Bon Marché in Paris was one of the West's premier department stores. It centralized consumption in a single large place and in so doing became the object of wonder and excitement as well as criticism. The vast array of goods caused customers to flock to these stores and gape in amazement at the luxurious displays and sheer abundance. As a result, many small-scale shopkeepers were driven out of business as their customers defected. Consumption as a whole expanded with the birth of the department store shopper. (Snark/Art Resource, NY.)

a "quickness of eye and ear, and the delicacy of touch" essential to office work. By hiring women for newly created clerical jobs, business and government contributed to a dual labor market in which certain categories of jobs were predominantly male, and others were overwhelmingly female. White-collar work gradually became the domain of cheap female labor. In the absence of competition, businesses in the service sector saved significantly by paying women chronically low wages—much less than they would have had to pay men for the same work.

Finally, the rise of consumer capitalism magnified the scale of consumption the way industrial capitalism had revolutionized the scale of production. The principal institution of this change was the department store. Founded after midcentury in large cities, department stores gathered such an impressive variety of goods in one place that consumers popularly called them "marble palaces" or "the eighth wonder of the world." Created by daring entrepreneurs, department stores eventually replaced the single-item stores that people entered knowing clearly what they wanted to purchase. Instead, these modern palaces sought to stimulate consumer whims and desires with lavish displays spilling over railings and counters in glorious disarray. Shoppers no longer bargained rationally over prices; now they reacted to sales, a new marketing technique that could incite a buying frenzy. Because most men lacked the time for shopping expeditions, department stores appealed mostly to women, who came out of their domestic sphere into a new public role. Attractive salesgirls, another variety of service workers, were hired to inspire customers to buy. Glossy mail-order catalogs brought to rural households both necessities and exotic items from the faraway dream world of the city.

▪ **REVIEW:** *What were the major economic changes in the West between 1850 and 1880?*

Establishing Social Order

This age of nation building and economic expansion disturbed everyday life, often bringing chaos and sometimes dramatic public protest. Thus government officials sought ways to forge social unity and order, hoping to offset the violence and economic change by which the nation-state was expanding. Population rose dramatically and cities grew crowded, leading officials across Europe to attend to public health and safety. Many liberal theorists advocated a laissez-faire government that left social and economic life largely to private enterprise. Nevertheless, confident in the benefits of European institutions in general, bureaucrats and reformers paid more attention to citizens' lives and, with the help of missionaries and explorers, spread European influence to the farthest reaches of the globe. Some of these efforts met violent resistance both within Europe and outside it.

Bringing Order to the Cities

European cities became the backdrop for displays of state power and national solidarity; thus efforts to improve sanitation and control disease redounded to the state's credit. Governments focused their refurbishing efforts on their capital cities, although many noncapital cities acquired handsome parks, widened streets, and erected stately museums and massive city halls. In 1857, Francis Joseph ordered the destruction of the old Viennese city walls and replaced them with concentric boulevards lined with major public buildings such as an opera house and government offices. Such buildings were tangible displays of national wealth and power, and the broad boulevards allowed crowds to observe royal pageantry. These wider roads were also easier for troops to navigate than the twisted, narrow medieval streets that in 1848 had concealed insurrectionists in cities such as Vienna and Paris—an advantage that convinced some otherwise reluctant officials to approve the expense. Impressive parks and public gardens showed the state's control of nature, helped order people's leisure time, and inspired respect for the nation-state's achievements.

■ Vienna Opera House
The era of nation building saw the construction of architectural monuments in the center of capital cities to display cultural power and to bring music, art, and science to the people. Vienna's center was rebuilt around imposing façades like that of the Imperial Opera House, which opened in 1869. (Hulton Archive/Getty Images.)

One effect of refurbished cities was to highlight class differences. Construction first required destruction; buildings and entire neighborhoods of housing for the poor disappeared, and thousands of city dwellers were dislocated. The boulevards often served as boundaries marking rich and poor sections of the city. In Paris, the process of urban change was called **Haussmannization**, named for the prefect Georges-Eugène Haussmann, who implemented a grand design that included eighty-five miles of new city streets, many lined with showy dwellings for the wealthy. In London, planners believed that improved architectural taste including "Victorian" ornamentation would blot out the ugliness of commerce and industry. Moreover, the size and spaciousness of the many new banks and insurance companies built in London "help[ed] the impression of stability," as an architect put it, and this would foster social order. Civic pride was to be another result of urban renewal, replacing strikes and rebellions.

Yet amid redevelopment and beautification, serious problems loomed. The devastation caused by repeated epidemics of diseases such as cholera debilitated city dwellers and gave the strong impression of social decay. Poor sanitation allowed typhoid bacteria to spread through sewage and into water supplies, infecting rich and poor alike. In 1861, Britain's Prince Albert reputedly died of typhus, commonly known as a "filth disease." Unregulated urban slaughterhouses and tanneries; heaps of animal excrement in chicken coops, pigsties, and stables; human waste alongside buildings; open cesspools; and garbage everywhere facilitated the spread of disease. The stench, diseases, and "morbid air" of cities indicated such a degree of disorder that sanitation became a government priority.

Scientific research, increasingly undertaken in public universities and hospitals, provided the means to promote public health and control disease. France's Louis Pasteur, whose three young daughters had died of typhus, advanced the germ theory of disease. Seeking a method to prevent wine from spoiling, Pasteur began his work in the mid-1850s by studying fermentation. He found that the growth of living organisms caused fermentation, and he suggested that certain organisms— bacteria and parasites—might be responsible for human and animal diseases. Pasteur further demonstrated that heating foods such as wine and milk to a certain temperature, a process soon known as pasteurization, killed these organisms and made food safe. In the mid-1860s, English surgeon Joseph Lister applied the germ theory in medicine. He connected Pasteur's theory of bacteria to infection and developed antiseptics for treating wounds and preventing puerperal fever, a condition that was caused by the dirty hands of physicians and midwives and that killed innumerable women after childbirth.

Governments undertook projects to improve sewer and other sanitary systems, and citizens prized such urban improvements, often attributing them to national superiority. In Paris, huge underground collectors provided a watertight terminus for accumulated sewage. In addition, Haussmann piped in water from uncontaminated sources in the countryside to provide each household with a secure supply. Such ventures were imitated throughout Europe: the Russian Empire's port city Riga (now in Latvia), for example, organized its first water company in 1863. Improved sanitation testified to progress and a more active role for the state. Shopkeepers agitated for paved streets to end the difficulties of transporting goods along muddy or flooded roadways. When public toilets for men became a feature of modern cities, women petitioned governments for similar facilities. On the lookout for disease and sanitary dangers, the average person became more aware of smells and the foul air that had been an accepted part of daily life for thousands of years. To show that they were becoming more "civilized," the middle and lower-middle classes bathed more regularly, mirroring in their own lives the quest of governments for order.

Expanding the Reach of Bureaucracy

State bureaucracies expanded to direct the drive for social order. The nation-state required citizens to follow a growing catalog of regulations as government authority reached further into the realm of everyday life. The censuses that Britain, France, and the United States had begun early in the nineteenth century became routine in most other countries as well. Censuses provided the state with personal details of citizens' lives such as age, occupation, marital status, residential patterns, and fertility. Governments used these data for a variety of endeavors, ranging from setting quotas for military conscription to predicting needs for new prisons. Reformers like Florence Nightingale, who gathered statistics to support sanitary reform, believed that such quantitative information made government less susceptible to corruption, special deals, and inefficiency. In 1860, Sweden introduced income taxes, which opened an area of private life—one's earnings from work or investment—to government scrutiny.

To bring about their vision of social order, most governments, including those of Britain, Italy, Austria, and France, also expanded their regulation and investigation of prostitution. Venereal disease, especially syphilis, was a scourge that, like typhus, infected individuals and whole families. Officials blamed prostitutes, not their clients, for its spread. The police picked up suspect women and turned them over to public health doctors, who examined them for syphilis and incarcerated them for treatment. As states began monitoring prostitution and other social matters like public health and housing, they had to add departments and agencies. In 1867, Hungary's bureaucracy handled fewer than 250,000 individual cases, ranging from health to poverty issues; twenty years later, it handled more than a million. The middle classes recognized the potential for influential jobs in the expansion of bureaucratic agencies. They argued that civil service jobs should be awarded according to talent and skill rather than birth or political loyalty. In Britain, a civil service law passed in 1870 required competitive examinations to ensure competency in government posts—an idea in the air since the West had become familiar with the Chinese examination system in the sixteenth and seventeenth centuries. Citizens thus demanded that the state itself conform to middle-class ideas of fairness, competence, and opportunity.

Schooling and Professionalizing Society

Emphasis on empirical knowledge and objective standards changed the professions and raised their status. Growing numbers of middle-class doctors, lawyers, managers, and successful journalists employed solid information in their work. Governments began to allow professional people to influence policy and to determine rules for admission to "the professions." Such legislation had both positive and negative effects: groups could set their own standards, but some otherwise experienced people were prohibited from working because they lacked the established credentials. The German medical profession, for example, was granted authority to control licensing, which led to more rigorous university training for future doctors but also pushed out experienced midwives and other healers even when practices such as leeching were common to professionals and amateurs alike. Science, too, became the province of the trained specialist rather than the amateur genius. Scientists were likely to be employed by government-funded universities and institutes and provided with equipment and assistants. Like other members of the middle class, professors of science were intensely patriotic, often interpreting their work as part of an international struggle for prestige and excellence.

Nation building led to major improvements in the education of all citizens, professional or not. Government officials called for radical changes in the scope, curriculum, and personnel of schools—from kindergarten to university—to make the general population more fit for citizenship and useful in fostering economic progress. Ongoing expansion of the electorate along with lower-class activism prompted one British aristocrat to say of the lower classes, whose growing influence he feared, "We must now educate our masters!" The growth of commerce and the state was partly behind a craze for learning, which made traveling lecturers, public forums, reading groups, and debating societies popular among the middle and working classes. Governments also introduced compulsory schooling to reduce illiteracy (more than 65 percent in Italy and Spain in the 1870s and even higher in eastern than in western Europe; see "Taking Measure," below). Even a few hours of lessons each day were said to teach the average person important social habits and the responsibilities of citizenship, along with practical knowledge.

Accomplishing this goal was not easy. Initially, various religious denominations had supervised schools and charged tuition, making primary education an option chosen only by prosperous or religious parents. After the 1850s, many leaders felt that liberal rationalism should supplant religiosity as a guiding principle.

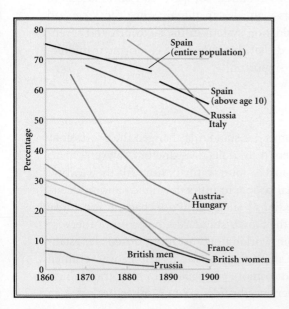

■ TAKING MEASURE Decline of Illiteracy, 1850–1900

The development of mass politics and the consolidation of the nation-state depended on building a cohesive group of citizens concerned with the progress of the nation. Increasing literacy was thus a national undertaking but one with national variations ranging from the low levels of illiteracy in Prussia to the high levels in Austria-Hungary and Russia. Even in regions of high illiteracy, however, governments successfully got people reading.

In 1861, an English commission on education concluded that, instead of the Bible, "the knowledge most important to a labouring man is that of the causes which regulate the amount of his wages, the hours of his work, the regularity of his employment, and the prices of what he consumes."

Supplanting religion was one challenge and enforcing school attendance another. Although the Netherlands, Sweden, and Switzerland had functioning primary school systems before midcentury, many parents resisted compulsory education. Farm families depended on children to perform chores and believed that work in the fields or the household provided the best education. Urban homemakers needed their children to help with domestic tasks such as fetching water, disposing of waste, tending the younger children, and scavenging for household necessities such as stale bread from bakers or soup from local missions. Secondary and university education was even more of a luxury, and Russia and some other countries saw modern subjects such as science and technology as potentially subversive.

Nonetheless, primary school systems grew, women's education developed, and the secondary school became more systematized, reflecting the demands of both an industrial society and a bureaucratic state. In Prussia, secondary schools (*Gymnasia*) offered a liberal arts curriculum that trained students for a variety of careers. In the 1860s, however, new *Realschulen*, less prestigious at the time, emphasized math, science, and modern languages for those who would not attain a Gymnasium degree or go on to attend the university. Reformers pushed for more advanced and more complex courses for young women as part of nation building. In France and Russia, for example, government leaders themselves saw that "public education has had in view only half the population—the male sex," as the Russian minister of education wrote to Tsar Alexander II in 1856. Both Napoleon III and Alexander II sponsored secondary- and university-level courses for women as part of their programs to control the modernization of society. Reformers from across the political spectrum concurred that women who knew some science, history, and literature would rear their children to be more rational and informed citizens. Even so, to some, religion, sewing, deportment, and writing appeared more than adequate areas of study for women.

Amidst heated controversy, young women in the 1860s began to attend universities in Zurich and Paris, where medical training was open to them. Despite criticism that they would undermine the system of separate gender spheres, women doctors thought their practice of medicine would protect female patients' modesty and bring feminine values to health care. In Britain, the founders of two women's colleges, Girton (1869) and Newnham (1871) at Cambridge University, believed that exacting standards in women's higher education would provide an example of a modern curriculum, reward merit, and thus raise the low standards of scholarship prevalent in the men's colleges of Cambridge and Oxford at the time.

The need for knowledgeable citizens offered opportunities for large numbers of women to enter teaching, a field once dominated by men. Hundreds of women founded nurseries, kindergartens, and primary schools based on the Enlightenment idea that developmental processes start at an early age. In Italy, women founded schools as a way to expand knowledge and teach civics lessons, thus providing a service to the fledgling state. Yet the idea of women teaching also aroused intense opposition: "I shudder at philosophic women," wrote one German critic of female kindergarten teachers. Seen as radical because it enticed middle-class women out of the home, the cause of early childhood education, or the "kindergarten movement," was as controversial as most other educational reforms.

Spreading Western Order beyond the West

In an age of nation building and industrial development, colonies took on new importance, adding political rule from the homeland to the economic role that global trade already played in national prosperity. After midcentury, Great Britain, France, and Russia revised their colonial policies by instituting direct rule, expanding colonial bureaucracies, and in many cases providing colonies with social and cultural services such as schools. For instance, in the 1850s and 1860s provincial governors and local officials promoted the extension of Russian borders to gain control over nomadic tribes in central and eastern Asia. As in areas like Poland and Ukraine, they instituted educational and religious programs to integrate these regions into the Russian social order.

Great Britain, the era's mightiest global power, made a dramatic change of course toward direct political rule as part of nation building during these decades. Before the 1850s, British liberals desired commercial gain from colonies, but believing in laissez-faire, they kept political involvement in colonial affairs minimal. In India, for example, an East India trading company ruled on Britain's behalf, and many regional rulers awarded the company commercial advantages. Since the eighteenth century, the East India Company had expanded its dominion over various kingdoms on the Indian subcontinent whenever a regional throne fell vacant and had built railroads throughout the countryside. Gradually, the British bureaucratic and economic presence expanded, allowing some Indian merchants to grow wealthy and send their children to British schools. Other local men enlisted in the British-run Indian army, despite resistance to British institutions.

European nation building was contested around the world, however. In 1857, Indian troops, both Muslim and Hindu, violently rebelled when, ignoring the Hindu ban on beef and the Muslim prohibition on pork, the British forced Indian soldiers to use ammunition cartridges greased with cow and pig fat. This was not their main grievance, though. The soldiers, angered at tightening British control, stormed and conquered the old Mughal capital at Delhi and declared the independence of the Indian nation—an uprising that became known as the Indian Rebellion of 1857.

Simultaneously, civil rebellions erupted among leaders who were being displaced and the general populace who backed them against "the tyranny and oppression of the infidel and treacherous English." The rani ("queen") Lakshmibai, widow of the ruler of the state of Jhansi in central India, led a separate military revolt when the East India Company tried to take over her lands after her husband died. As the British brutally crushed the rebels, the Indian Rebellion and the Jhansi revolt gave birth to Indian nationalism. Victorious, the British government issued the Government of India Act of 1858, by which Britain took direct control of India. In 1876, the British Parliament declared Queen Victoria the empress of India.

Indian Resistance, 1857

A system of rule emerged in which close to half a million Indians governed a region the British called *India* under the supervision of a few thousand British men. Indians also collected taxes and distributed patronage. Colonial rule meant both blatant oppression and more subtle intervention in everyday life. British production of cheap goods forced the impoverishment of such artisans as Indian handloom weavers who once dominated international markets. The British aimed to divert colonial populations into the production of cheap raw materials such as wheat, cotton, and jute to supply their industries. Meanwhile, enclaves of British civil servants enforced segregation and an inferior status on all classes of Indians. Nonetheless, some Indians benefited from improved sanitation and medicine and chose to accept British arguments against their own customs such as infanticide, child marriage, and *sati*—a widow's self-immolation on her husband's funeral pyre. Others found Europe's scientific values attractive and, ironically, also came to appreciate that British rule brought unity to what were once small, separate princedoms, thus laying the foundation for Indian nationalism.

French political expansion was a similarly complex phenomenon, riddled with paradox. The French government pushed to establish its dominion over Cochin China (modern southern Vietnam) in the 1860s. But missionaries in the area, ambitious French naval officers stationed in Asia, and even some local peoples pulled the French government further into the region. Like the British, the French brought improvements, such as the Mekong Delta project that increased the amount of cultivated land and spurred rapid growth of the food supply. Sanitation and public health programs proved a mixed blessing because they led to population growth that strained other resources. Furthermore, landowners and French imperialists siphoned off most of the profits from economic improvement.

The French also undertook a cultural mission to transform cities, such as Saigon, with tree-lined boulevards and other signs of Western urban life as they were doing in France itself. French literature, theater, and art diverted not only colonial officials but also upper-class Indochinese.

Strategic commercial and military advantages remained an important motivation for some European overseas ventures in this age of Realpolitik. The Crimean War had shown the great powers that the Mediterranean basin was pivotal and thus needed to be tamed. Napoleon III, remembering his uncle's campaign in Egypt, took an interest in building the Suez Canal, which would connect the Mediterranean with the Red Sea and the Indian Ocean and thus dramatically shorten the route to Asia. The canal was completed in 1869, and as "canal fever" spread, Verdi composed the opera *Aïda* (set in ancient Egypt) in celebration.

Great Britain and France were especially eager to do business with Egypt, where the combined value of imports and exports had jumped from 3.5 million Egyptian pounds in 1838 to 21 million in 1880 (and would grow to 60 million in 1913). European capital investment in the region also rose, first in ventures such as the Suez Canal in the 1860s and then in the laying of thousands of miles of railroad track and the creation of telegraph systems. Improvement-minded rulers in Asia and Africa paid dearly in 12 percent interest rates for modernization. The completion of harbors, dams, canals, and railroads increased the Middle East's desirability as a market for European exports and as an intermediate stop on the way to trade with Asia. Having invested in the Suez Canal and in other commercial development, the British and French soon took over the Egyptian treasury to secure their own financial investments, and after invading Egypt in 1882, the British effectively took over the government despite heated parliamentary opposition at home. Britain reshaped the Egyptian economy from a system based on multiple crops that maintained the country's self-sufficiency to one that emphasized the production of a few crops—mainly cotton, raw silk, wheat, and rice—that were especially useful to Europe. Local landowners and moneylenders also profited from these agricultural changes, while the bulk of the rural population barely eked out an existence.

The rest of the Mediterranean and the Ottoman Empire felt the heightened presence of the European powers. Driving into the North African hinterland, the French army occupied all of Algeria by 1870, and the number of European immigrants reached one-quarter million by then. There was also a draw: French rule in Algeria as elsewhere brought European goods, technology, and institutions to the local peoples. Merchants and local leaders cooperated in building railroads, sought bank loans and trade from the French, and sent their children to European-style schools. Many local peoples, however, resisted the invasions and died from European-spread diseases. By 1872, the native population in Algeria had declined by more than 20 percent from five years earlier. As a further guarantee of their Mediterranean claims, the French occupied neighboring Tunisia in 1881. Western businessmen flooded the region with cheap goods, driving artisans from their trades and into low-paid work building railroads or processing tobacco. Instead of basing wage rates on gender (as they did at home), Europeans used ethnicity and religion, paying Muslims less than Christians and Arabs less than other ethnic groups. Such practices, as well as contact with European technology and nationalism, planted the seeds for anticolonial movements, which flourished as the century drew to a close.

The vastness of China allowed it to escape complete takeover, but traders and Christian missionaries from European countries, carrying their message of Christian salvation, made inroads for the Western powers. Missionaries directed the Christian message to a population of 430 million, which had nearly doubled since the last century. Defeat in the Opium War, economic pressures from European trade, and contacts with the West helped generate the mass opposition movement known as the Taiping ("Heavenly Kingdom"). Headed by a leader who claimed to be the brother of Jesus, its millions of followers wanted an end to the ruling Qing dynasty, the elimination of foreigners, more equal treatment of women, and land reform. By the mid-1850s, the Taiping controlled half of China. The Qing regime, its dynasty threatened, promised the British and French greater influence in exchange for aid in defeating the Taiping. The result was a bloody civil war that lasted until 1864 and killed more than 20 million Chinese (compared with 600,000 dead in the U.S. Civil War). When peace finally came, Western governments controlled much of the Chinese customs service and had almost unlimited access to the country. The spreading influence of Western nation-states to eastern as well as southern Asia reverberated in these mass uprisings.

Japan alone was able to escape European domination but not its influence. Through Dutch traders at Nagasaki, the Japanese had become keenly aware of the industrial, military, and commercial innovations of European society. By 1854, when Americans claimed to be opening Japan to trade, contacts with Europe had already given the Japanese a healthy appetite for Western goods and knowledge and an interest in superior Western weaponry. Trade agreements with the United States and European nations followed. In 1867, the ruling Tokugawa shogun (the dominant military leader) abdicated under pressure from reformers, who subsequently restored the emperor to full power. The goal of the **Meiji Restoration** (1868) was to establish Japan as a modern, technologically powerful state free from Western control. The word *Meiji*, chosen by the new emperor to name his reign, meant "enlightened rule," and the regime professed to combine "Western science and Eastern values" as a way of "making new"—hence, a combination of restoration and innovation.

Contesting the Nation-State at Home

By and large, the urban working class was better informed and more connected to the progress of industry and the nation-state. After a period of repression in the 1850s, workers' organizations slowly reemerged as a political force in the West, directing their attention both to economic and political issues. Changes in technology eliminated outmoded jobs and often made the work of those who survived job cuts more difficult. Workers complained that new machinery sped up the pace of work to an unrealistic level. For example, new furnaces at a foundry in suburban Paris required workers to turn out 50 percent more metal per day than they had produced using the old furnaces. Stepped-up productivity demanded much more physical exertion to tend and repair machines, often at a faster pace, but workers did not receive additional pay for their extra efforts. Workers also grumbled about the proliferation of managers; many believed that foremen, engineers, and other supervisors interfered with their work. For women, supervision sometimes brought on-the-job harassment, as in the case of female workers in a German food-canning plant who kept their jobs only in return for granting sexual favors to the male manager.

Many of the most outspoken labor activists were artisans, struggling to survive in the new industrializing and modernizing urban environment, and influenced either by the ideas of former printer Pierre-Joseph Proudhon (1809–1865) or by anarchist thought. In the 1840s, Proudhon had coined the explosive phrase "Property is theft," suggesting that ownership robbed propertyless people of their rightful share of the earth's benefits. He opposed the centralized state and proposed that society be organized instead around natural groupings of men (but not women, who should work in seclusion at home for their husbands' comfort) in artisans' workshops. These workshops and a central bank crediting each worker for his labor would replace government and would lead to a *mutualist* social organization. **Anarchism** maintained that the existence of the state was the root of social injustice. According to Russian nobleman and anarchist leader Mikhail Bakunin (1814–1876), the slightest infringement on freedom, especially by the central state and its laws, was unacceptable. Anarchists thus advocated the destruction of all state power, and their numbers grew with the growth of the nation-state in the second half of the nineteenth century.

As workers' movements expanded, the political theorist and labor organizer Karl Marx constantly battled mutualism and anarchism. These doctrines, he insisted, were wrongheaded, lacking the sound, scientific basis of his own theory, subsequently called **Marxism**. Marx's analysis, expounded most notably in his book *Das Kapital* ("Capital"), adopted the liberal idea dating back to John Locke in the seventeenth century that human existence was defined by the requirement to work as a way of fulfilling basic needs such as food and shelter. Published between 1867 and 1894, *Das Kapital* was based on mathematical calculations of production and profit that would justify Realpolitik for the working classes. Marx held that the fundamental organization of any society, including its politics and culture, derived from the relationships arising from work or production. This idea, known as materialism, meant that the foundation of a society rested on class relationships—such as those between serf and medieval lord, slave and master, or worker and capitalist. Marx called the class relationships that developed around work the "mode of production"—for instance, feudalism, slavery, or capitalism. Rejecting the liberal focus on individual rights, he emphasized the unequal class relations caused by the capitalists or bourgeoisie—that is, those who took control of the "means of production" in the form of the capital, land, or factories necessary to fulfill basic human needs. Workers' awareness of their oppression would produce class consciousness among those in the same predicament and ultimately lead them to revolt against their exploiters. Capitalism would be overthrown by these workers—the proletariat—ushering in a socialist society.

Marx made what he considered tough-minded and realistic appraisals of the economy and working-class life, and indeed, conditions for ordinary workers remained harsh. A wave of strikes erupted in the late 1860s: in France alone, 40,000 workers participated in strikes in 1869, followed by more than 85,000 in 1870. The strikers included artisans and industrial workers who felt exploited because of the continuing pace of technological innovation. From the 1870s through the 1890s, sharp economic downturns aggravated the situation. More often than not, strikes focused on economic issues, but at times protesters questioned the system as a whole, including the intertwined growth of the nation-state and the industrial economy.

The Paris Commune in the spring of 1871 was one of those times. As the Franco-Prussian War ended, revolution and civil war erupted not only in Paris but other cities of France. One issue was the nation-state's takeover of city-life: the

Haussmannization of Paris, which had displaced tens of thousands of workers from their homes in the heart of the city, embittered many Parisians against the state. As the Prussians pressed on to Paris late in 1870, the besieged Parisians demanded new republican liberties, new systems of work, and a more balanced distribution of power between the central government and localities. By the winter of 1870–1871, the Parisian population

■ Woman Incendiary

The Paris Commune galvanized women activists, many of whom hoped to reform social conditions. After the fall of the Commune, women Communards were denigrated as half-clothed degenerates as a way of underscoring the disorderliness of the Commune's resistance to the state.

(Bibliothèque Nationale, Paris/Lauros/Giraudon/ Bridgeman Art Library.)

was suffering from the harsh weather and a Prussian siege that deprived them of sufficient food to feed more than 2 million people. Parisians demanded to elect their own local officials to handle the emergency and greeted troops sent to calm the strife with a call to insurrection. To counter what they saw as the despotism of the centralized government, they declared themselves a self-governing commune on March 28, 1871. Other French municipalities did the same in an attempt to form a decentralized nation of independent, confederated units.

In the Paris Commune's two months of existence, its forty-member council, its National Guard, and its many other improvised offices found themselves at cross-purposes. Trying to maintain "communal" instead of "national" values, Parisians quickly developed a wide array of political clubs, local ceremonies, and self-managed, cooperative workshops. Women workers, for example, banded together to make National Guard uniforms on a cooperative rather than on a profit-making basis. Beyond liberal political equality and industrial values, the Commune proposed to liberate the worker and ensure "the absolute equality of women laborers." Thus a *commune* in contrast to a *republic* was meant to entail a social revolution. But Communards often disagreed on what specific route to take to change society: mutualism, feminism, international socialism, and anarchism were but a few of the proposed avenues to social justice.

In the meantime, the provisional government that succeeded the defeated Napoleon III struck back to reinstitute national order. It quickly stamped out uprisings in other French cities. On May 21, the army entered Paris. In a week of fighting, both Communards and the army set the city ablaze (the Communards did so to slow the progress of government troops). Both sides executed hostages, and in the wake of victory the army shot tens of thousands of citizens found on the streets. Parisian insurgents, one citizen commented, "deserved no better judge than a soldier's bullet." The Communards had fatally promoted a kind of antistate in an age of growing national power. Soon a different interpretation of the Commune emerged: it was the work of the *pétroleuse*, or "woman incendiary"— a case of women run mad, crowding the streets in frenzy and fury. Within a year, writers were blaming the burning of Paris on women—"shameless slatterns, half-naked women, who kindled courage and breathed life into arson." Revolutionary men later became heroes in the history books, but women in political situations were characterized as "sinister females, sweating, their clothing undone, [who] passed from man to man." The Franco-Prussian War, the Commune, and the civil war were all horrendous blows from which the French state struggled to recover. Key to restoring order in France after 1870 were instilling family virtues, fortifying religion, and claiming that the Commune had resulted from the collapsed boundaries between the male political sphere and the female domestic sphere. Karl Marx disagreed: he analyzed the Commune as a class struggle of workers attacking bourgeois interests, which were embodied in the centralized state. In the struggle against the Commune the nation-state once again showed its strengthening muscle. Executions and deportations by the thousands also shut down the French labor movement, and fear of workers smoldered across Europe.

■ **REVIEW:** *How did nation-states expand their reach, and what resistance did they face?*

The Culture of Social Order

The reactions of artists and writers to the expanding nation-state were as complex as those of other Europeans and people around the world. In one way, however, the arts took a remarkable turn by adopting a realistic style in cultural works in the 1850s to 1870s that paralleled Realpolitik. After 1848, many artists and writers expressed profound grievances, notably about political repression, and economic growth. To some artists, daily life, infused with commercial values and organized by government officials, seemed tawdry and hardly bearable. Unlike the romantics of the first half of the century, artists of the second half often had difficulty depicting heroic ideals. "How tired I am of the ignoble workman, the inept bourgeois, the stupid peasant, and the odious priest," wrote the French novelist Gustave Flaubert, frustrated by his inability to romanticize these figures as previous generations had done. Such disenchantment promoted the literary and artistic style called realism. Similarly, intellectuals proposed theories called positivism and Darwinism, which offered hard-headed appraisals of social change and even political upheaval as part of human progress. It was a stark realism similar to that which statesmen applied to politics.

The Arts Confront Social Reality

The quest for national power enlisted culture in its cause. The reading public devoured biographies of political leaders, past and present, and credited heroes with creating the triumphant nation-state. As literacy spread, readers of all classes responded to the mid-nineteenth-century novel and to an increasing number of artistic, scientific, and natural history exhibitions. Whether reading the same novels or attending musical events together, citizens were schooled in the common artistic style called realism.

A well-financed press and commercially minded publishers produced an age of best sellers out of the craving for **realism**—or true-to-life portrayals of society without romantic or idealistic overtones. The novels of Charles Dickens appeared in serial form in newspapers, and each installment attracted buyers eager for the latest plot twist. His characters came from contemporary English society and included starving orphans, grasping lawyers, and ruthless opportunists. *Hard Times* (1854) depicted the grinding poverty and ill health of workers alongside the heartlessness of businessmen. The novelist George Eliot (the pseudonym of Mary Ann Evans) deeply probed private, "real-life" dilemmas in works such as *The Mill on the Floss* (1860) and *Middlemarch* (1871–1872). Depicting rural society—high and low—Eliot allowed Britons to see one another's predicaments, wherever they lived. She knew the pain of ordinary life from her own experience: she was a social outcast because she lived with a married man. Despite her fame, she was not received in polite society. These popular novels showed a hard reality and thus helped form a shared culture among people in distant parts of a nation much as state institutions did.

French writers also scorned dreams of political utopias and ideals of tran-scendent beauty. In *Madame Bovary* (1857), Gustave Flaubert told the story of a bored doctor's wife who acts out her romantic longings in one love affair after another and becomes so hopelessly indebted that she commits suicide. *Madame Bovary* scandalized French society for its frank picture of women's sexuality. The poet Charles-Pierre Baudelaire, called satanic and perverse by his critics, wrote explicitly about sex; in *Les Fleurs du mal* (*Flowers of Evil*, 1857), he expressed sex-ual passion and described drug- and wine-induced fantasies. French authorities fought these violations of social convention, successfully prosecuting Flaubert and Baudelaire on obscenity charges. At issue was social and artistic order: "Art with-out rules is no longer art," the prosecutor maintained.

During the era of the Great Reforms, Russian writers debated whether west-ern European values were insidiously transforming Russian culture. Rather than dividing the nation, this discussion about Russian culture united people around a national issue. From one viewpoint, Ivan Turgenev created a powerful novel of Russian life, *Fathers and Sons* (1862), a story of nihilistic children rejecting the older, romantic generation's spiritual values and espousing science instead. Popular in the West, Turgenev aroused anger in Russian readers for the way he criticized both romantics and the new generation of hardheaded "materialists." From another point of view, Fyodor Dostoevsky in *The Possessed* (1871–1872) and other works showed the dark, ridiculous, and neurotic side of nihilists, thus holding up Turgenev as a softheaded romantic. Dostoevsky's highly intelligent characters in *Notes from the Underground* (1864) and *Crime and Punishment* (1866) are often personally tormented and condemned to lead absurd, even criminal lives. He used these antiheroes to emphasize spirituality and traditional Russian values, but with a "realistic" spin by planting such values in ordinary, often seedy people.

Unlike writers, visual artists across Europe depended on government com-missions and government-sponsored exhibitions and drew a more limited set of buyers. Prince Albert of England was an active patron of the arts, purchasing works for official collections and for himself until his death in 1861. Having artwork cho-sen for display at government-sponsored exhibitions was the best way for an artist to gain prominence and earn a living. Officially appointed juries selected works of art to be exhibited and then chose prize winners from among them. Hundreds of thousands of people from all classes attended these exhibitions.

After 1848, artists began rejecting romantic conventions idealizing ordinary folk and grand historic events. Instead, French artist Gustave Courbet, for example, portrayed weary laborers at backbreaking work because he believed an artist

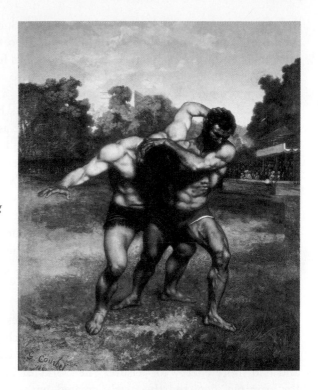

■ **Gustave Courbet,**
Wrestlers (1850)
Courbet painted his dirty, grunting
wrestlers in the realist style, which
rejected the hazy romanticism of
revolutionary Europe. These
muscular men summed up the
resort to physical struggle during
these state-building decades and
conveyed the art world's recogni-
tion that Realpolitik had taken
over the governance of society.
(Museum of Fine Arts, Budapest/Bridgeman
Art Library.)

should "never permit sentiment to overthrow logic." The city, artists found, had become a visual spectacle whose wide new boulevards served as a stage for displaying status and individual ambition. *Universal Exhibition* (1867) by Édouard Manet used the World's Fair of 1867 as the background; figures from all social classes in the foreground were separated from one another by the planned urban spaces as they promenaded, gazing at the Paris scene and watching one another to learn the new social rules of modern life. Manet also broke with romantic conventions of the nude. His *Olympia* (1865) depicted a white courtesan lying on her bed, attended by a black woman. This disregard for the classical traditions of showing women in mythical or idealized settings was too much for the critics: "a sort of female gorilla," one wrote of *Olympia*. Shocking at first, graphic portrayals that shattered comforting illusions were a feature of realism.

Artistic realism faced a challenge from photography—a challenge that found its response in the 1860s to 1890s in a new style called **impressionism**. Manet coined the term to reflect the artist's attempt to capture a single moment by focusing on the ever-changing light and color found in everyday vision. Using splotches and dots, impressionists moved away from the precise realism of earlier painters: Claude Monet, for example, was fascinated by the way light transformed an object, and he often portrayed the same place—a bridge or a railroad station—at different times of day. Dutch-born Vincent Van Gogh used vibrant colors in great swirls to capture sunflowers and the starry evening sky. Such distortions of reality made the impressionists' visual style seem outrageous to those accustomed to realism, but others enthusiastically greeted impressionism's luminous quality as more real than realism. Industry contributed to the new style, as factories produced paint in a wider, more intense spectrum of colors.

In both composition and style, impressionists borrowed heavily from Asian art, knowledge of which rapidly infiltrated Europe as the West extended its reach. The concept of the fleetingness of situations came from a centuries-old and well-developed Japanese concept—*mono no aware* (sensitivity to the fleetingness of life). The color, line, and delicacy of Japanese art (which many impressionists collected) is evident, for example, in Monet's later paintings of water lilies, his studies of wisteria, and even his re-creation of a Japanese garden at his home in France as the subject for artistic study. Similarly, the American expatriate Mary Cassatt used the two-dimensionality of Japanese art in her work. Other artists, such as Edgar Degas, imitated Asian art's use of wandering and conflicting lines to orchestrate space on a canvas, and Van Gogh filled the background of portraits with copies of intensely colored Japanese prints.

As artists chose to favor a realism of the senses instead of photographic realism, many nonetheless kept commenting on the changing economic scene, especially the fact that a growing segment of service workers did less physical work and had more energy for leisure. The works of French painter Georges Seurat, for example, depicted the newly created parks with their walking paths and Sunday bicyclists; white-collar workers carrying books or newspapers paraded in their store-bought clothing. Degas focused on portraying women—from ballet dancers to laundry women—in various states of exertion and fatigue. Van Gogh, avoiding the intense colors he typically used for the countryside, depicted the bleak outskirts of cities, where industries were often located and where the desperately poor lived.

Unlike most of the visual arts, opera was commercially profitable, accessible to most classes of society, and thus an effective means of reaching the nineteenth century public. Verdi used musical theater to contrast noble ideals with the corrosive effects of power, love of country with the inevitable call for sacrifice and death, and the lure of passion with the need for social order. The German composer Richard Wagner, the most flamboyant and musically innovative composer of this era, hoped to revolutionize opera by fusing music and drama to arouse the audience's fear, awe, and engagement. A gigantic cycle of four operas, *The Ring of the Nibelungen* (1854–1874), reshaped ancient German myths into a modern, nightmarish allegory of a world doomed by its obsessive pursuit of money and power and redeemable only through unselfish love. Another of his operas, *The Master Singer of Nürnberg* (1867), was a nationalistic tribute to German culture, and like the arts elsewhere, helped unite individuals into a public with a shared, if debated, cultural experience.

Religion and Secular Order

Organized religion formed one bulwark of traditional social and political order after the revolutions of 1848, but the expansion of state power set the stage for clashes over influence. Should religion have the same hold on government and public life as in the past, thus competing with national loyalty? Views were mixed and would remain so. In the 1850s, many politicians supported religious institutions and attended religious services because they were another source of order. Simultaneously, some nation builders, intellectuals, and economic liberals rejected the competing worldview and jurisdiction of established churches, particularly Roman Catholicism. Bismarck was one of these. Believing that the church impeded the development of nationalist sentiment, in 1872 he mounted a full-blown *Kulturkampf* ("culture war") against Catholic influence. Mercilessly attacking the church, the government expelled the Jesuits in 1872, increased state power over the clergy in Prussia in 1873, and introduced obligatory civil marriage in 1875. Bismarck, however, overestimated his ability to manipulate politics, for both conservatives and Catholics objected to religious repression in the name of state building.

The Catholic church felt assaulted by a growing rationalism that was supposed to supplant religious faith and by the state building in Italy and Germany that competed for people's traditional loyalty. In addition, nation building had resulted in the extension of liberal rights to Jews, whom many Christians considered enemies. Provocatively attacking reform and changing values, Pope Pius IX (r. 1846–1878) issued *The Syllabus of Errors* (1864), and in 1870, the First Vatican Council approved the dogma of papal infallibility. This teaching proclaimed that the pope spoke divinely revealed truth on issues of morality and faith. Eight years later, a new pontiff, Leo XIII (r. 1878–1903), began the process of reconciliation with modern politics by encouraging up-to-date scholarship in Catholic institutes and universities and by accepting aspects of democracy. Leo's ideas marked a dramatic turn, ending the Kulturkampf and fortifying beleaguered Catholics across Europe.

Religious doctrine continued to have powerful popular appeal, but the place of organized religion in society was changing. Church attendance declined among workers and artisans, but many people in the upper and middle classes and most of the peasantry remained faithful. The Orthodox church of Russia and eastern Europe with its Pan-Slavic appeal fostered nationalism among oppressed Serbs and became a rallying point. Women's spirituality intensified, and Roman Catholic and Russian Orthodox religious orders of women increased in size and number. Men, by contrast, were falling away from religious devotion. In 1858, an outburst of popular religious fervor, especially among women, followed a young peasant girl's visions of the Virgin Mary at Lourdes in southern France. Bernadette Soubirous said that Mary told her to drink from the ground, at which point a spring appeared. Crowds besieged the area to be cured of ailments by the waters of Lourdes. In 1867, less than ten years later, a railroad track was laid to Lourdes to enable millions of pilgrims to visit the shrine on church-organized trips. The Catholic church thus showed that it was up-to-date, willing to use modern means such as railroads and medical verification of miraculous cures to make Lourdes itself the center of a brisk commercial as well as religious culture.

At nearly the same time as Bernadette's vision, the English naturalist Charles Darwin published *On the Origin of Species* (1859), which challenged the Judeo-Christian worldview that humanity was a unique creation of God. Darwin argued that life had taken shape over countless millions of years before

humans existed and that human life was the result of this slow development, or evolution. As a young scientist on an expedition to South America, Darwin theorized that because of evolution, species of animals varied from one tropical island to another even though climate and other natural conditions were roughly the same: new biological forms arise from older ones as the most fit forms survive and reproduce. Instead of the Enlightenment vision of nature and society as harmonious, Darwin saw the constant clash of species, including humans, struggling to survive. In this fight, only the hardiest prevail

■ **Darwin Ridiculed, c. 1860**
Charles Darwin's theories claimed that humans evolved from animal species and rejected the long-standing explanation of a divine human origin. His scientific ideas so diverged from people's beliefs that cartoonists lampooned both the respectable Darwin and his theory. Despite the controversy, evolution withstood the test of further scientific study. **For more help analyzing this image,** see the visual activity for this chapter in the ONLINE STUDY GUIDE at **bedfordstmartins.com/ huntconcise.** (Hulton Archive/Getty Images.)

and in the selection of sexual partners pass their natural strength to the next generation. In a perpetual challenge to meet the forces of nature, Darwin suggested, some species die out and those with better-adapted characteristics survive.

Darwin's theories outraged adherents of traditional Christianity because the idea of evolution undercut the story of creation described in Genesis. According to the biblical account, God miraculously brought the universe and all life into being in six days. According to Darwin, life developed from lower forms through a primal battle for survival and through the sexual selection of mates—processes that Darwin called **natural selection**. An eminently respectable Victorian gentleman, Darwin announced that the Bible gave a "manifestly false history of the world." Darwin's theories also undermined certain liberal, secular beliefs. Enlightenment principles, for example, glorified nature as tranquil and noble and viewed human nature as essentially rational. The theory of natural selection—survival of the fittest—suggested that human society was one where combative individuals and groups constantly fight one another.

Innovative biological research influenced contemporary beliefs about society. In the 1860s, working in obscurity on pea plants in his monastery garden, Gregor Mendel discovered the principles of heredity from which the science of genetics later developed. Investigation into the female reproductive cycle led German scientists to discover the principle of spontaneous ovulation—the automatic release of the egg by the ovary whether sexual intercourse took place or not. This discovery caused theorists to conclude that men had aggressive and strong sexual drives because reproduction depended on their sexual arousal. In contrast, the spontaneous and cyclical release of the egg independent of arousal indicated that women were passive and lacked sexual feeling.

Darwin added to this social commentary. The legal, political, and economic privilege of white European men in the nineteenth century, he maintained, naturally derived from their being more highly evolved than white women or people of color. Despite his belief in a common ancestor for people of all races, Darwin held that people of color, or "lower races," were far behind whites in intelligence and civilization. As for women, "the chief distinction in the intellectual powers of the two sexes," Darwin declared, "is shewn by man's attaining to a higher eminence in whatever he takes up." A school of Social Darwinism developed its own version of evolutionary theory to lobby for racist, sexist, and nationalist policies. Their arguments were influential in the years to come.

From Natural Science to Social Science

Darwin's thought accelerated the search for alternatives to the religious understanding of social order as being divinely ordained. Simultaneously, the theories of the French social philosopher Auguste Comte, whose ideas formed the basis of a "positive science" of society and politics, also inspired a host of reform organizations. **Positivism** claimed that careful study of facts would generate accurate, or "positive," laws of society. Comte's *System of Positive Politics, or Treatise on Sociology* (1851) proposed that social scientists construct knowledge of the political order as they would construct understanding of the natural world—by means of informed investigation. This idea inspired people to believe they could solve the problems spawned by economic and social change. Comte also promoted women's participation in reform because he deemed "womanly" compassion and love and scientific public policy to be equally fundamental to social harmony. Positivism led not only to women's increased social and political activism but to the growth of the social sciences.

Comte's theories led English philosopher John Stuart Mill to espouse widespread reform and mass education and to support the complete enfranchisement of women. Mill's political treatise *On Liberty* (1859) couched his aspiration for general social improvement in a concern that superior people not be brought down or confined by the will of the masses. Influenced by his wife, Harriet Taylor Mill, he advocated the extension of rights to women and introduced a woman suffrage bill into the House of Commons after her death. The bill's defeat prompted Mill to publish *The Subjection of Women* (1869), which presented the family as maintaining an older kind of order devoid of modern concepts of rights and freedom. Mill also proposed that women's voluntary obedience and love in marriage made each woman deceptively appear "not a forced slave, but a willing one." Critiquing the century's basic beliefs about men's and women's roles, *The Subjection of Women* became a respected guide around the world for those committed to expanding women's basic rights.

The more progressive side of Mill's social thought was soon lost in the flood of Social Darwinist theories. Even before *Origin of Species*, Herbert Spencer's *Social Statics* (1851) advocated the study of society but also promoted laissez-faire and unadulterated competition, claiming that the "unfit" should be allowed to perish in the name of progress. Spencer's opposition to public education, social reform, and any other attempt to soften the harshness of the struggle for existence struck a receptive chord among the middle and upper classes and contributed to the surge of Social Darwinism in the next decades. Darwinism and Mill's liberalism, like the arts, religion, and science, would serve to shape the public, setting the subjects and terms of social and political thought. In an age of nation building, culture often enhanced the political call for realistic, hardheaded thinking about social order.

▪ **REVIEW:** *What were the results of applying the scientific method to social thought?*

■ **MAPPING THE WEST   Europe and the Mediterranean, c. 1880**

European nation-states consolidated their power by building unified state structures and by developing the means to foster social and cultural integration of the diverse peoples within their borders. They also were rapidly expanding outside their boundaries, extending the economic and political reach of the nation-state. North Africa and the Middle East—parts of the declining Ottoman Empire—had particular appeal for their resources and for their potential for further European settlement. They were one gateway to the rest of the world.

IMPORTANT DATES

1850s–1860s	Positivism and Darwinism become popular in social and political thought	1868	Meiji Restoration begins in Japan
1850s–1870s	Realism in the arts	1869–1871	Women's colleges founded at Cambridge University
1852	The Second Empire begins in France	1870	Bismarck manipulates the Ems telegram and sparks the Franco-Prussian War
1854–1856	Britain and France clash with Russia in the Crimean War	1871	Franco-Prussian War ends; German Empire proclaimed at Versailles; Parisians form Commune in March to oppose the central government; the French army crushes the Commune in May
1857	Indian Rebellion		
1860s–1890s	Impressionism flourishes in the arts often incorporating Asian influences		
1861	Victor Emmanuel declared king of a unified Italy; serfdom abolished in Russia	1872	Bismarck begins Kulturkampf against Catholic influence
1861–1865	Civil War in the United States	1873	Extended economic recession begins with global impact
1867	Second Reform Bill in England increases the number of male voters; Austro-Hungarian monarchy established	1876	Queen Victoria declared empress of India

Conclusion

Throughout modern history, the development of nation-states and the economic prosperity on which they depended has been neither inevitable nor uniform nor peaceful. This was especially true in the nineteenth century, when ambitious politicians, resilient monarchs, and determined bureaucrats transformed very different countries into various kinds of states by a variety of methods and policies. Nation building was most dramatic in Germany and Italy, where states unified through military force and where people of diverging political tendencies ultimately agreed that national unity trumped most other causes. Compelled by military defeat to shake off centuries of tradition, the Austrian and Russian monarchs instituted reforms as a way of keeping their systems in place. In eastern Europe, the middle class was far less powerful than in western Europe, and reform came from above to preserve autocratic power rather than from popular agitation to democratize it. In all cases, however, central governments expanded and took various steps to incorporate the growing population into stable national institutions.

After decades of romantic fervor, hardheaded realism in politics and the industrial economy became a much-touted norm, which spread to cultural matters as well, often with surprising results. Darwin and Marx breathed the air of realism, and their theories were disturbing to those who maintained an Enlightenment faith in social and political harmony. Realist novels and art jarred polite society; like the operas of Verdi, they also portrayed dilemmas of the times. The policies of the growing state apparatus that were meant to bring order often brought disorder and resistance, including the Taiping uprising, the Indian Rebellion, and the Paris Commune—all of them challenging the results of European nation building. When the ordinary people of the Paris Commune rose up to protest the loss of French power and prestige in the Franco-Prussian War, they also defied the trend toward economic modernity and state building. Their actions raised difficult questions. How far should the power of the state extend in both domestic and international affairs? Would nationalism be a force for war or for peace? As these issues ripened, the next decades would see continued economic advance, growing competition for global power, and unprecedented changes that ultimately would lead to a major war.

■ **MAKING CONNECTIONS**

1. *Some would call the decades between 1850 and 1880 a period of order, while others would call it a period of disorder. Which characterization would you choose and why?*

2. *What ingredients contribute to the "realism" historians see in the events and actions of this period?*

■ **FOR FURTHER EXPLORATION**

For further reading and online research ideas, see the Suggested References on page SR-9 at the back of the book.

For practice quizzes, a customized study plan, and other study tools, see the ONLINE STUDY GUIDE at bedfordstmartins.com/huntconcise.

For primary-source material from this period, see Chapter 18 in *Sources of THE MAKING OF THE WEST: A CONCISE HISTORY*, Second Edition.

Empire, Modernity, and the Road to War

c. 1880–1914

I N THE FIRST DECADE OF THE TWENTIETH CENTURY, a wealthy young Russian man traveled from one country to another to find relief from neurasthenia, a common malady in those days. Its symptoms included fatigue, lack of interest in life, depression, and sometimes physical sickness. In 1910, the young man encountered Sigmund Freud, a Viennese physician whose unconventional treatment—eventually called psychoanalysis—took the form of conversations about the patient's dreams, sexual experiences, and everyday life. Over the course of four years, Freud uncovered his patient's deeply rooted fear of castration disguised as a fear of wolves—thus the name Wolf-Man by which the young man is known to us. Often building his theories from information about colonized peoples and cultures, Freud worked his cure, as the Wolf-Man himself put it, "by bringing repressed ideas into consciousness." Freud's theories laid the groundwork for an

■ **Edvard Munch, *The Scream* (1893)**

In some of his paintings Norwegian artist Edvard Munch captured the spirit of the turn of the century using delightful pastel colors to convey the leisured life of people strolling in the countryside. But modern life at this time also had its tortured side, which Munch was equally capable of portraying. The Scream *is seen as emblematic of the torments of modernity as the individual turns inward, beset by neuroses, self-destructive impulses, and even madness. While some—like the two other figures in the painting—could react calmly to whatever modern life had to offer, others like the screamer were agonized at every turn of events. It can also be suggested that the screamer, like Europe, travels the road to World War I.*

(Scala/Art Resource, NY. © 2007 The Munch Museum/The Munch-Ellingsen Group/Artists Rights Society [ARS], NY.)

understanding of the human psyche that has endured, with modifications and some controversy, to our own time.

The Wolf-Man is evocative of the age. Born into a family that owned vast estates, he reflected the growing prosperity of Europeans, albeit on a grander scale than most. Countless individuals seemed, like him, anguished and mentally disturbed. Suicide was not uncommon. The Wolf-Man's own sister and father died from intentional drug overdoses. Throughout European society people engaged in agonized questioning about family life, gender relationships, empire, religion, and the consequences of technology. Conflict rattled the world as an array of powers, including Japan, fought their way into even more territories and took political control. Every sign of imperial wealth brought on an apparently irrational sense of Europe's decline. The British writer H. G. Wells saw in this era "humanity upon the wane . . . the sunset of mankind."

Governments expanded the male electorate during this period in the hope of making politics more harmonious and manageable. Ethnic chauvinists, anti-Semites, and militant nationalists, however, increasingly used violent rhetoric. Women suffragists along with politically disadvantaged groups such as the Slavs and Irish demanded full rights, but the liberal ethos of tolerance was swept away by a wave of political assassinations and public brutality. As the race for worldwide empire continued—most notably in Africa—colonized peoples developed a variety of liberation movements, many of them matching the progressive values but also the violence of the colonizing powers. While the great powers fought to dominate people around the world, the competition for empire fueled an arms race that threatened to turn Europe, the "most civilized" continent in the world according to its leaders, into a savage battleground.

Those were just some of the conflicts associated with **modernity**—a term often used to describe the accelerated pace of life, the rise of mass politics, and the decline of a rural social order that were so visible in the West from the late nineteenth century on. Modernity also refers to the response of artists and intellectuals to this rapid change. The celebrated "modern" art, music, science, and philosophy of this period still resonate for their brilliant, innovative qualities. Yet like modern technology, these same innovations were often considered offensive at the time: cries of outrage at the new music echoed in concert halls, and educated people were shocked at Freud's ideas that sexual drives motivate even the smallest children. Middle-class faith in artistic and scientific progress grew strained, and just as the Wolf-Man was finishing his treatment in June 1914, all the tensions that had been building nationally and internationally were coming to a head. Though the Wolf-Man rejoiced at the end of June that "he could now leave Vienna a healthy man," the political, social, and diplomatic discord that had been simmering for several decades was about to boil over in one of the most horrific wars the world had ever seen.

The Challenge of Empire

The quest for empire remained intense and became increasingly paradoxical. In a climate of ongoing boom and bust, colonies provided crucial markets for some businesses. Late in the century, for example, French colonies bought 65 percent of France's exports of soap, and imperialism provided huge numbers of jobs to people in European port cities. Yet Europeans did not benefit uniformly from the search for new markets, which often proved more costly than profitable. Whether they benefited or not, taxpayers in all parts of a nation paid for colonial armies, increasingly costly weaponry, and colonial administrators. As politicians debated the economic value of colonies, this period of "new imperialism" intensified distrust in international politics. Countries vied with one another for a share of world influence. In securing India's borders, for example, the British faced Russian expansion in Afghanistan and along the borders of China. Bringing conflict around the world, imperial competition made areas of Europe, such as the Balkans, more volatile than ever as states sought status and national security in the control of disputed territory.

Motives for imperialism were equally paradoxical. Goals such as fostering national might and Christianizing peoples often proved unattainable or difficult to measure. Governments worried that imperialism—because of its expense and the constant possibility of war—might weaken rather than strengthen them. The French statesman Jules Ferry (1832–1893) argued that France "must keep its role as the soldier of civilization." But it was unclear whether imperialists should emphasize soldiering—that is, conquest and conflict—or the more encompassing goal of exporting culture and religion. Hoping to Christianize colonized peoples, European missionaries ventured to newly secured areas of Africa and Asia. A woman missionary working among the Tibetans reflected a common view when she remarked that the native peoples were "going down, down into hell, and there is no one but me . . . to witness for Jesus amongst them." Europeans were confident of their religious and cultural superiority. In the judgment of many, Asians and Africans—variously characterized as lying, lazy, self-indulgent, or irrational—were a class beneath Europeans. One English official pontificated that "accuracy is abhorrent to the Oriental mind." Viewing other races as "degenerate" prompted missionaries and other "civilizers" to ignore brutal military measures used against local resistance to imperialism.

Scramble for Africa

After the British takeover of the Egyptian government in the 1880s, European influence in Africa turned into direct control as one sub-Saharan African territory after another fell to European military force. Europeans' principal objective was expanding trade in Africa's raw materials, such as palm oil, cotton, diamonds, cocoa, and rubber. Additionally, with its industrial and naval supremacy and its empire in

N
W · E
S

MADEIRA IS. (Port.)

CANARY IS. (Sp.)

RIO DE ORO

Tangier

2 Algiers

ALGERIA

TUNISIA

Tunis

MOROCCO
Marrakech

Tripoli

TRIPOLI

Mediterranean Sea

OTTOMAN
EMPIRE

4 Suez
Canal

Alexandria

Cairo

EGYPT

ARABIA

S   A   H   A   R   A

AHAGGAR MTS.

TIBESTI

Niger R.

Red Sea

2 SENEGAL

St. Louis

Timbuktu

GAMBIA

TUKULOR
EMPIRE

BORNU

WADAI

L. Chad

MAHDIST
STATE

White Nile R.

Blue Nile R.

Adowa

Gulf of Aden

BR.
SOMALIA

SOKOTO
SULTANATE

GUINEA

Freetown

SIERRA
LEONE

LIBERIA

SAMORI'S
EMPIRE

DAHOMEY

ASANTE

YORUBA

3

TOGO

GOLD
COAST

São Tomé
(Port.)

RABIH

Fashoda

ETHIOPIA

Addis
Ababa

CAMEROON

Ubangi R.

Congo R.

EQUATORIA

BUGANDA

GABON

CABINDA

CONGO
FREE
STATE

TIPPU
TIB'S
DOMAIN

L. Victoria

L. Tanganyika

Mombasa

SULTANATE OF
ZANZIBAR

INDIAN
OCEAN

ATLANTIC
OCEAN

Luanda

ANGOLA

CHOKWE
DOMAIN

MSIRI'S
KINGDOM

L. Nyasa

Mozambique

Madagascar

PORTUGUESE
EAST AFRICA
(MOZAMBIQUE)

Zambezi R.

GERMAN
SOUTH-WEST
AFRICA

WALVIS BAY

KALAHARI
DESERT

SOUTH
AFRICAN
REPUBLIC
(TRANSVAAL)

MERINA (HOVA)
KINGDOM

Pretoria

BRIT.
BECHUANALAND

1

Limpopo R.

Orange R.

ORANGE
FREE
STATE

ZULULAND

CAPE COLONY

NATAL

BASUTOLAND

Cape Town

Routes of Colonial Expansion

British

French

German

Italian

Portuguese

Spanish

Ottoman

Nominally Ottoman;
British controlled

Non-European regimes
(including Boer republics)

Boundary of the
Congo Free State

1 Route of Rhodes's British
S. African Company, 1890

2 French expansion into
West Africa, 1883–1896

3 British expansion into
Nigeria, 1880–1902

4 British invasion and
occupation of Egypt, 1882

0   500   1,000 miles
0   500   1,000 kilometers

■ **MAP 19.1 Africa, c. 1890**

The scramble for Africa entailed a real expansion of European trading practices, which until approximately 1880 generally were limited to the coastline. The effort to conquer, economically penetrate, and rule the interior would result in a map of the continent (see Map 19.2) that made sense only to the imperial powers, for it divided ethnic groups and created colonial entities that had nothing to do with Africans' sense of geography, patterns of settlement, or political organization.

India, Britain hoped to keep the southern and eastern coasts of Africa secure for stopover ports on the route to Asia. The British, French, Belgians, Portuguese, Italians, and Germans jockeyed to dominate peoples, land, and resources—"the magnificent cake of Africa," as King Leopold II of Belgium (r. 1865–1909) put it (Map 19.1). Driven by insatiable greed, Leopold claimed the Congo region of central Africa, thereby initiating competition with France for that territory and inflicting on local Africans unparalleled acts of cruelty. German chancellor Otto von Bismarck, who saw colonies mostly as political bargaining chips, sent out explorers in 1884 and established German control over Cameroon and a section of East Africa. Faced with competition, the British poured millions of pounds into preserving their position by dominating the continent "from Cairo to Cape Town," as the slogan went, and the French cemented their hold on large portions of western Africa.

Technological development of powerful guns, railroads, steamships, and medicines were central to the expansion of Western domination. The gunboats that forced the Chinese to open their borders to opium played a part in forcing African ethnic groups to give up their independence. Quinine and guns were also an important factor in African conquest. Before the development of medicinal quinine in the 1840s and 1850s, the deadly tropical disease malaria had threatened to decimate any European party embarking on exploration or military conquest, giving Africa the nickname the "White Man's Grave." The use of quinine, extracted from cinchona bark from the Andes, to treat malaria sent death rates among missionaries, adventurers, traders, and bureaucrats plummeting. While quinine saved white lives, technology to take lives was also advancing. Improvements to the breech-loading rifle and the development of the machine gun, or "repeater," between 1862 and the 1880s dramatically increased firepower. Europeans carried on a brisk trade selling inferior guns to Africans on the coast, but peoples of the interior used bows and arrows. Muslim slave traders and European Christians alike crushed African resistance with blazing gunfire: "The whites did not seize their enemy as we do by the body, but thundered from afar," claimed one local African resister. "Death raged everywhere."

Nowhere did this destructive capacity have greater effect than in southern Africa, where farmers of European descent and prospectors, rather than military personnel, battled African peoples for control of the frontier regions of Transvaal, Natal, the Orange Free State, and the Cape Colony. Although the Dutch originally settled the area in the seventeenth century, the British had gained control by 1815. Thereafter, descendants of the Dutch, called Boers (Dutch for "farmers"), were joined by British immigrants in their fight to wrest farmland and mineral resources from natives. British businessman and politician Cecil Rhodes (1853–1902) was sent to South Africa for his health just as diamonds were being discovered in 1870. He cornered the diamond market and claimed a huge amount of African territory with the help of official charters from the British government, all before he turned forty. Pushing hundreds of miles into the interior of southern Africa (a region soon to be named Rhodesia after him), Rhodes moved into gold mining, too (see Map 19.1). His ambition for Britain and for himself was boundless: "I contend that we are the finest race in the world," he explained, "and that the more of the world we inhabit the better it is."

While Europeans credited China and India with a scientific and artistic heritage, Africans were seen as valuable only for manual labor despite their many accomplishments such as dyeing, road building, and architecture. By confiscating Africans' land, Europeans forced native peoples to work for them to earn a living and to pay the taxes they imposed. Subsistence agriculture, often performed by women and slaves, thus declined in favor of mining and farming cash crops. Standards of living dropped for Africans who lost their lands without realizing the Europeans were claiming permanent ownership.

Almost immediately, the scramble for Africa escalated tensions in Europe itself, prompting Bismarck to call a conference of European nations at Berlin. The fourteen nations at the conference, held in a series of meetings in 1884 and 1885, decided that their settlements along the African coast guaranteed their rights to the interior territory as well. This agreement led to the strictly linear dissection of the continent; geographers and diplomats cut across indigenous boundaries of African culture and ethnic life (Map 19.2). The Berlin conference also banned the sale of alcohol and controlled the sale of arms to native peoples. The purpose of the meeting was supposed to be the reduction of bloodshed and the tempering of European ambitions in Africa, but greed-filled Europeans like King Leopold continued to plunder the continent and terrorize its people. The news from Berlin whetted the popular appetite for more imperialist ventures.

Skirmishes with the French in Africa and the Boer War soured British enthusiasm. Accustomed to crushing resistance, the British experienced a bloody defeat in 1896, when Cecil Rhodes, then prime minister of the Cape Colony in southern Africa, directed his right-hand man, Dr. Leander Jameson, to lead a raid into the neighboring territory of the Transvaal. The foray was intended to stir up trouble between the Boers and the more recent immigrants from Britain and elsewhere who had come to southern Africa in search of gold and other riches. Rhodes hoped the raid would justify a British takeover of the Transvaal and the Orange Free State, which the Boers controlled. The Boers, however, easily routed the raiders, striking a blow at British imperial pride. The British did not accept defeat: for the next three years they fought the Boer War directly against the Boer-controlled Transvaal and the Orange Free State. Britain finally annexed the area after defeating the Boers in 1902, but the cost of war—in money, destruction, and loss of life—horrified many Britons and caused them to see imperialism as a burden.

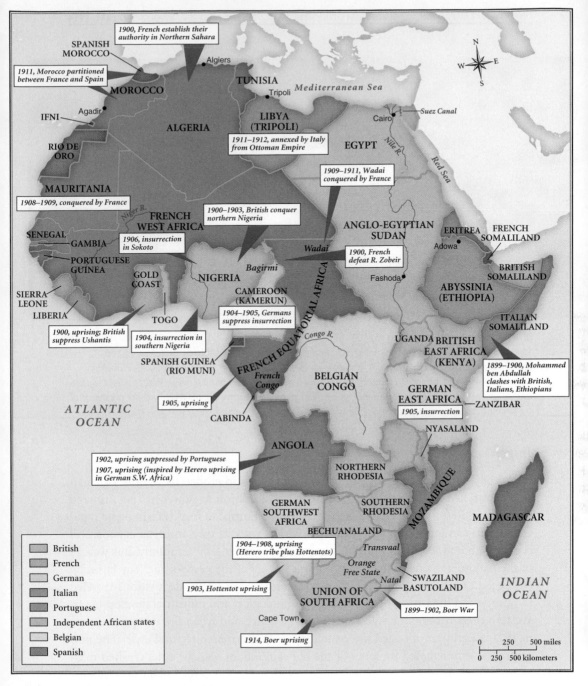

Map labels (within the map):

SPANISH MOROCCO

1900, French establish their authority in Northern Sahara

1911, Morocco partitioned between France and Spain

MOROCCO

IFNI

Agadir

RIO DE ORO

MAURITANIA

1908–1909, conquered by France

FRENCH WEST AFRICA

SENEGAL

GAMBIA

PORTUGUESE GUINEA

SIERRA LEONE

LIBERIA

1900, uprising; British suppress Ushantis

GOLD COAST

TOGO

1904, insurrection in southern Nigeria

SPANISH GUINEA (RIO MUNI)

1905, uprising

CABINDA

ATLANTIC OCEAN

1902, uprising suppressed by Portuguese
1907, uprising (inspired by Herero uprising in German S.W. Africa)

ANGOLA

Algiers

TUNISIA

Tripoli

LIBYA (TRIPOLI)

1911–1912, annexed by Italy from Ottoman Empire

ALGERIA

Mediterranean Sea

Cairo — Suez Canal

EGYPT

Nile R.

Red Sea

1909–1911, Wadai conquered by France

1900–1903, British conquer northern Nigeria

1906, insurrection in Sokoto

NIGERIA

Bagirmi

CAMEROON (KAMERUN)

1904–1905, Germans suppress insurrection

Wadai

ANGLO-EGYPTIAN SUDAN

1900, French defeat R. Zobeir

Fashoda

ERITREA

Adowa

FRENCH SOMALILAND

BRITISH SOMALILAND

ABYSSINIA (ETHIOPIA)

ITALIAN SOMALILAND

FRENCH EQUATORIAL AFRICA

French Congo

Congo R.

BELGIAN CONGO

UGANDA

BRITISH EAST AFRICA (KENYA)

1899–1900, Mohammed ben Abdullah clashes with British, Italians, Ethiopians

GERMAN EAST AFRICA

ZANZIBAR

1905, insurrection

NYASALAND

NORTHERN RHODESIA

SOUTHERN RHODESIA

MOZAMBIQUE

GERMAN SOUTHWEST AFRICA

BECHUANALAND

1904–1908, uprising (Herero tribe plus Hottentots)

Transvaal

Orange Free State

Natal

SWAZILAND

BASUTOLAND

1903, Hottentot uprising

UNION OF SOUTH AFRICA

1899–1902, Boer War

Cape Town

1914, Boer uprising

MADAGASCAR

INDIAN OCEAN

Legend:

- British
- French
- German
- Italian
- Portuguese
- Independent African states
- Belgian
- Spanish

0   250   500 miles
0   250   500 kilometers

■ **MAP 19.2 Africa in 1914**

Uprisings intensified in Africa in the early twentieth century as Europeans tried to consolidate their rule through bureaucratization and military action and to extract more wealth from the Africans. While the Europeans were putting down rebellions against their rule, a pan-African movement arose, attempting to unite Africans as one people. As in Asia and the Middle East, the more the colonial powers tried to impose their will, the greater the political forces—including the force of political ideas—that took shape against them. **For more help analyzing this map,** see the map activity for this chapter in the ONLINE STUDY GUIDE at bedfordstmartins.com/huntconcise.

■ **Modernization in Japan**

Japan modernized with breathtaking speed. As this view of a railroad station indicates, Japan borrowed from the West but did not abandon its own culture. In this woodcut by Ando Hiroshige II—son of an artist imitated by many in the West—many of the Japanese wear Western-style clothes, and others continue to wear traditional styles. Notice, too, the native cherry trees and the portrayal of traditional modes of transportation. The train schedule appears across the top. (Laurie Platt Winfrey Inc.)

Imperial Newcomers

Europeans' confident approach to imperialism was also eroded by the rise of Japan as a power. Led by the Satcho Hito clan, whose accession to power in 1868 ushered in the Meiji Restoration, Japan escaped the "new" European imperialism by its rapid transformation into a modern industrial nation with its own imperial agenda. "All classes high and low shall unite in vigorously promoting the economy and welfare of the nation," ran one of the first pronouncements of the new regime. The Japanese embraced knowledge from other countries, and in the 1870s, deputations traveled to Europe and the United States to study technological and industrial developments. Western dress became the rule at the imperial court, and when fire destroyed Tokyo in 1872 a European directed the rebuilding in Western architectural style. The new central government, led by some of the old samurai, or warrior elite, crushed massive rebellions by any who resisted modernization. It also merged older samurai traditions, such as spiritual discipline and the drive to excel, with a technologically modern military and sponsorship of trade. The state stimulated economic development by building railroads and shipyards, establishing financial institutions, and encouraging daring innovators like Iwasaki Yataro, founder of the Mitsubishi firm, to develop heavy industries such as mining and shipping. In Japan, unlike the rest of Asia, the adaptation of Western-style enterprises became a patriotic goal.

Like its Western models, Japan started intervening in Asia, ultimately provoking war with its powerful neighbors China and Russia. The Japanese began building an empire by invading the Chinese island of Formosa (present-day Taiwan) in 1874 and in 1894 by sparking the brief Sino-Japanese War, which in 1895 ended China's domination of Korea. Japan's growing imperial ambitions soon clashed with those of the great powers. Russian expansion to the east and south in Asia, the building of the Trans-Siberian Railroad through Manchuria, and fomenting anti-Japanese groups in Korea so angered the Japanese that they attacked tsarist forces at Port Arthur in 1904 (Map 19.3). The Russian military proved inept in

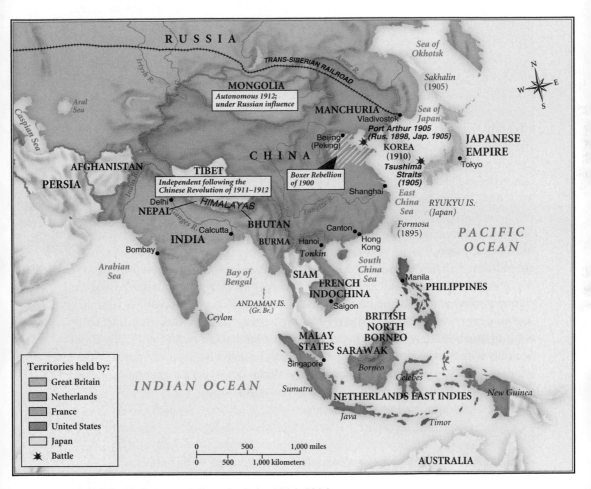

■ **MAP 19.3 Imperialism in Asia, 1894–1914**

Most of the modernizing states converged on Asia. The established imperialists came to blows in East Asia as they struggled for influence in China and encountered a formidable new rival—Japan. Simultaneously, liberation movements like that of the Boxers in China were taking shape, committed to throwing off restraints imposed by foreign powers. In 1911, Sun Yat-Sen overthrew the Qing dynasty and started the country along a different course.

the ensuing year-long Russo-Japanese War: in an astonishing display of poor leadership, Russia's Baltic Fleet sailed halfway around the globe only to be completely destroyed in the battle of Tsushima Straits (1905). Opening an era of Japanese domination in East Asian politics, the victory was the first by a non-European nation over a European great power in the modern age. As one English general ominously observed of the Russian defeat: "I have today seen the most stupendous spectacle it is possible for the mortal brain to conceive—Asia advancing, Europe falling back." Japan went on to annex Korea in 1910 and to eye other areas.

There were other troublesome newcomers to the imperial table. Almost simultaneously, Spain lost Cuba, Puerto Rico, and the Philippines following its defeat by the United States in the Spanish-American War of 1898. Urged on by the expansionist-minded Theodore Roosevelt (1858–1919), then assistant secretary of the navy, and an inflammatory daily press, the United States aimed to drive Spain out of these colonies. Even the triumphant United States, encouraged by the British poet Rudyard Kipling (1865–1936) to "take up the white man's burden" by bringing the benefits of Western civilization to those liberated from Spain, had to wage a bloody war against the Filipinos, who wanted independence, not another imperial ruler. Reports of American brutality in the Philippines further disillusioned the European public, who liked to imagine native peoples joyously welcoming the bearers of civilization. This war revealed the unpredictability of imperial fortunes.

Emerging powers had an emotional stake in gaining colonies. In the early twentieth century, Italian public figures aimed to restore Italy to its ancient position of world domination by conquering Africa. After a disastrous war against Ethiopia in 1896, Italy won a costly victory over Turkey in Libya. Germany likewise demanded an end to the virtual British-French monopoly of colonial power. Foremost among the new competitors for empire, German bankers and businessmen were ensconced throughout Asia, the Middle East, and Latin America. Colonial skirmishes Germany had once ignored became matters of utmost concern. Germany, too, instead of winning unalloyed glory, met humiliation and constant problems, especially in its dealings with Britain and France. As Italy and Germany aggressively pursued new territory, the rules set for imperialism at the Berlin conference a generation earlier gave way to increasingly heated rivalry and nationalist fury.

Growing Resistance to Colonial Domination

The Japanese military victory over two important dynasties—the Qing in China and the Romanov in Russia—within a single decade had global repercussions. Uprisings began in China after its 1895 defeat by Japan forced the ruling Qing to grant more economic concessions to Western powers. Humiliated by these events, peasants organized into secret societies to restore Chinese integrity. One organization was the Society of the Righteous and Harmonious Fists (or Boxers), whose members maintained that ritual boxing would protect them from a variety of evils, including

■ The Foreign Pig Is Put to Death

The Boxers sought to fortify the Chinese government against powerful threats to China's survival. They used brightly colored placards to spread information about their goals and their successes to build wide support among the Chinese population. They felt that the presence of foreigners had caused a series of disasters including the defection of the Chinese from traditional religion, the flow of wealth from the country, and natural disasters such as famine that seemed to be taking place with greater frequency. This depiction shows the harsh judgment of the Boxers toward foreigners and their Chinese allies—they are pigs to be killed. **For more help analyzing this image,** see the visual activity for this chapter in the ONLINE STUDY GUIDE at bedfordstmartins.com/ huntconcise. (Bridgeman Art Library.)

bullets. Encouraged by the Qing ruler and desperate because of spreading famine, the Boxers rebelled in 1900, massacring the missionaries and Chinese Christians to whom they attributed China's troubles. The forces of eight colonial powers put down the Boxer Rebellion and forced the Chinese to pay a huge indemnity and to allow more extensive foreign military occupation. The Boxer Rebellion thoroughly discredited the Qing dynasty; in 1911 a successful group of revolutionaries overthrew the dynasty and the next year declared China a republic. Their leader, Sun Yat-Sen (1866–1925), who had been educated in Hawaii and Japan, combined Western concepts with traditional Chinese values, including revival of the Chinese tradition of correctness in behavior between governors and the governed and modern economic reform. Sun's stirring leadership and changes brought by China's revolution seriously threatened Western channels of trade and domination.

In 1885, the Indian elite founded the Indian National Congress, which challenged Britain's right to rule, but the Japanese victory over Russia stimulated Indian politicians to take a more radical course. Anti-British Hindu leader B. G. Tilak (1856–1920) preached noncooperation: "We shall not give them assistance to collect revenue and keep peace. We shall not assist them in fighting beyond the frontiers or outside India with Indian blood and money." Tilak promoted Hindu customs, asserted Hindus' distinctiveness from British ways, and inspired violent rebellion in his followers. This brand of nationalism broke with that based on assimilating to British culture and promoting gradual change. Trying to repress Tilak, the British sponsored the Muslim League, a rival nationalist group favored for its restraint and its potential to divide Muslim nationalists from Hindus in the Congress. Britain made two concessions, however: voting rights based on property ownership and Indian representation in ruling councils. Because the independence movement had not fully reached the masses, these small concessions allowed the British to maintain power by appeasing influential dissidents among the upper and middle classes. But Britain's hold on India was weakening.

Revolutionary nationalism also sapped the Ottoman Empire, which for centuries had controlled much of the Mediterranean. In the nineteenth century, several rebellions had plagued Ottoman rule, and more erupted early in the twentieth century because of growing resistance to the empire and to European influence. Sultan Abdul Hamid II (r. 1876–1909) tried to revitalize the multiethnic empire by using Islam to counteract the rising nationalism of the Serbs, Bulgarians, and Macedonians. Instead, he unwittingly provoked the burgeoning Turkish nationalism in Constantinople itself. Turkish nationalists rejected the sultan's pan-Islamic solution and built their movement on the uniqueness of their culture, history, and language, changing the word *Turk* from one of derision to one of pride and purging their language of words from Arabic and Persian. Japan's victory over Russia electrified these nationalists with the vision of a modern Turkey becoming "the Japan of the Middle East," as they called it. In 1908, a group called the Young Turks took control of the government in Constantinople. Their triumph motivated others in the Middle East and the Balkans to demand an end to Ottoman domination in their regions as well. But the Young Turks, often aided by European powers with financial and political interests in the region, brutally tried to repress the uprisings in Egypt, Syria, and the Balkans that their own success had encouraged. By the early twentieth century, competition among the great powers, nationalist movements, and outright military resistance were upsetting the stable domination that European countries envisioned over the rest of the world.

■ **REVIEW:** *What changes occurred in Europe's relationships with the rest of the world between the early nineteenth and early twentieth centuries?*

Modern Life in an Age of Empire

As empire made the world an interconnected marketplace it transformed every-day culture and society. Success in manufacturing and foreign ventures created millionaires, and consumers in the West could purchase goods that poured in from around the world. Many Europeans grew healthier, partly because of improved diet and partly because of the efforts of reformers who sponsored government pro-grams aimed at promoting the fitness they saw as necessary for citizens of impe-rial powers. Opportunities for mobility arose as Europeans opened up markets across the globe. Working people's experience of the internationalizing force of imperialism was different from that of the middle class: increasingly from the mid-nineteenth century on, millions facing political or economic insecurity migrated to the United States, Canada, Australia, Argentina, Brazil, and Siberia and, as fre-quently, from country to city and back.

While European power grew, the accepted social order at home weakened. Western ideals of a comfortable family life flourished because of Europe's improved standard of living, but a falling birthrate, a rising divorce rate, and growing activism for marriage reform provoked intense debate about values. Homosexuality became acknowledged as a way of life and the topic of politics. Middle-class women took jobs and became active in public to such an extent that some feared the disappearance of distinct gender roles. Conflict over gender roles and private life contributed to rising social tensions.

Life in the "Best Circles"

Profits from empire and industrial expansion swelled the ranks of the upper class, or "best circles," so called at the time because of their members' wealth, education, and social status. Many people in the best circles came from the aristocracy, which retained much of its power. Increasingly, however, aristocrats had to socialize with new millionaires from the bourgeoisie. In fact, the very distinction between aristo-crat and bourgeois became blurred, as monarchs gratefully bestowed aristocratic titles on millionaire industrialists and businesspeople. Moreover, down-at-the-heels aristocrats were only too willing to offer their children in marriage into the families of the newly rich. Such arrangements brought much-needed infusions of funds to old, established families and the cachet of an aristocratic title to upstart families. Thus Jeanette Jerome, daughter of a wealthy New York financier, married England's Lord Randolph Churchill (their son Winston later became England's prime minister). Even millionaires without official connections to the aristocracy discarded the modest ways of a century earlier to build palatial villas, engage in conspicuous displays of wealth, and wall themselves off from the poor in suburbs or new sections of town. Social Darwinist principles assured the wealthy that their prosperity sprang from their natural superiority.

■ Tiger Hunting in the Punjab

Big-game hunting became the imperial sport of choice, as shown in this colorful Indian painting. European and American hunters adopted the sport from local Asians and Africans who had previously depended on the hunt for their livelihood. Now these Asians and Africans served the Western amateurs, many of whom were in wretched physical shape and inexperienced in hunting big game. Nonetheless, Western manliness was coming to depend on such feats, as imperialists saw those who continued the old aristocratic fox hunt as effeminate. Some Western women enjoyed hunting too. As a chivalrous gesture, men would let women issue the coup de grace, or death shot, should a tiger materialize during the hunt.
(© Victoria and Albert Museum, London/Art Resource, NY.)

Upper-class men bonded around hunting, a favorite leisure activity, which was reshaped by imperial contact. For centuries, aristocrats had pursued fox and bird hunting locally; now, big-game hunting in Asia and Africa became the rage. European hunters forced native Africans, who traditionally depended on hunting for income or food and for group unity, to work as guides, porters, and domestics on hunts. By mastering foreign games like polo (an Asian sport) or activities like big-game hunting, Europeans demonstrated that they could conquer not only territory but less tangible things like culture. Collectors on the hunts brought exotic specimens back to Europe for zoological exhibits and natural history museums, all of which flourished during this period.

Members of the upper class did their best to exclude others by controlling their children's social lives, especially by monitoring girls' sexual activity and relationships with the lower classes. Upper-class men had liaisons with lower-class women—a double standard judged promiscuity normal for men and immoral for women—but few thought of marrying them. Parents still arranged many marriages directly, and visiting days brought eligible young people together to help ensure correct matrimonial decisions.

Ritualistic visits filled the everyday lives of upper-class women. Instead of working for pay, upper-class women devoted themselves to having children, directing staffs of servants, and maintaining standards of social conduct. Furnishings in fashionable homes displayed imperial treasures such as Oriental carpets, bamboo furniture, and Chinese porcelains. With the importation of azaleas, rhododendrons, and other plants from around the world, lavish flower gardens replaced parks and lawns. Being an active consumer of fashionable clothing was also a time-consuming female activity. In contrast to men's plain garments, upper-class women's clothing was elaborate, ornate, and dramatic, featuring constricting corsets, long voluminous skirts, bustles, and low-cut necklines for evening wear. Women took their roles seriously by keeping detailed accounts of their expenditures and monitoring their children's religious and intellectual development. In addition, they tried to offset the drabness of industrial life with the rigorous practice of art and music. One Hungarian observer wrote, "The piano mania has become almost an epidemic in Budapest as well as Vienna." Some upper-class women also engaged in religious and philanthropic activities to aid lower-class women and children.

Although middle-class professionals could sometimes mingle with people at the apex of society, especially in charity work, their lives remained more modest. They employed at least one servant, which created the illusion of leisure for busy middle-class women performing the onerous duties of maintaining a home. Professional men working at home did so from the best-appointed room. Middle-class domesticity substituted cleanliness and polish for upper-class conspicuous consumption. The middle classes pointed to their bathing with soap, along with hard work, as a sign of racial superiority over colonized peoples who actually labored to produce such goods.

The "Best Circles" Transformed

Despite the well-being of the middle and upper classes, urgent concerns over population, marriage, and sexuality clogged the agendas of politicians and reformers from the 1880s on. The staggering population increases of the eighteenth century had continued through the nineteenth. At the turn of the twentieth century, cities looked chaotic, as population soared and crowded the urban landscape. Germany increased in size from 41 million people in 1871 to 64 million in 1910; tiny Denmark grew from 1.7 million in 1870 to 2.7 million in 1911. Such growth resulted from improvements in sanitation and public health that extended longevity and reduced infant mortality. To cope with their burgeoning populations,

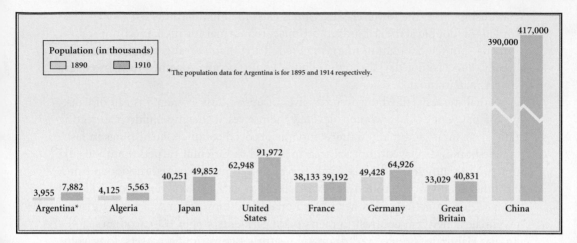

■ TAKING MEASURE Population Growth Worldwide, 1890–1910

Countries in the West underwent a demographic revolution in these decades as birthrates declined sharply. Nevertheless, population in many countries soared because of improved health, and nations such as Argentina and the United States received vast numbers of immigrants. Exceptions were China and other regions suffering the effects of imperialism, and France, where growth stagnated because the French had drastically curtailed reproduction early in the nineteenth century.

(B. R. Mitchell, *International Historical Statistics: Africa, Asia, and Oceania, 1750–1993*, 3d ed. [London: Macmillan Reference, 1998], 3, 56, 57; Mitchell, *International Historical Statistics: The Americas, 1750–1993*, 4th ed. [London: Macmillan Reference, 1998], 6, 24; Mitchell, *International Historical Statistics: Europe, 1750–1993*, 4th ed. [London: Macmillan Reference, 1998], 4, 8.)

Berlin, Budapest, and Moscow were torn apart and rebuilt, following the lead of Vienna and Paris. The German government reconstructed the capital with new roadways and mass-transport systems that helped push Berlin's population to over 4 million. Rebuilding was not confined to the capitals of the most powerful states: Balkan cities such as Sofia, Belgrade, and Bucharest gained tree-lined boulevards, public buildings, and improved sanitation.

While the absolute size of the population was rising in much of the West, the birthrate (measured in births per thousand people) was falling because of urbanization and industrialization. (See "Taking Measure," above.) The birthrate had been decreasing in France since the eighteenth century; other European countries began experiencing a decline late in the nineteenth century. The Swedish rate dropped from 35 births per thousand people in 1859 to 24 per thousand in 1911; even populous Germany went from 40 births per thousand in 1875 to 27 per thousand in 1913. In an age of agricultural industrialization, farm families needed fewer hands, and individual couples increasingly practiced birth control to limit family size. The spread of new birth-control practices that would encompass most of the globe by the end of the twentieth century mainly accounted for Europe's ebbing birthrate. In cities, pamphlets and advice books for those with enough money

■ **A Large German Family**
Improved medicine, hygiene, and diet at the turn of the century helped more people survive
infancy and childhood. Thus in many cases family size grew larger, as this photo from a working-
class apartment suggests. Even opponents of birth control were appalled that lower-class families
were becoming larger than families in the "best circles," where limitation of childbirth was
increasingly practiced. (AKG-Images, London.)

and education spread information about coitus interruptus—the withdrawal method of preventing pregnancy. Technology also played a role in curtailing repro- duction: condoms, improved after the vulcanization of rubber in the 1840s, proved fairly reliable in preventing conception. In the 1880s, Aletta Jacobs (1851–1929), a Dutch physician, opened the first birth-control clinic, which specialized in pro- moting the new, German-invented diaphragm. Abortions were not uncommon.

The wider use of birth control stirred controversy. Critics accused middle-class women, whose fertility was falling most rapidly, of holding a "birth strike." Anglican bishops, meeting early in the twentieth century, deplored family limitation as "demoralizing to character and hostile to national welfare." Politicians worried about a crisis in masculinity that would undermine military strength. In the United States, Theodore Roosevelt, now president, blamed middle-class women's selfishness for the population decline, calling it "one of the most unpleasant and unwholesome fea- tures of modern life." If the "best" classes had fewer children, politicians asked, what would society look like when peopled mostly by the "worst" classes? The decline in fertility, one German nationalist warned, would make the country a "conglomerate of alien peoples, above all Slavs and probably East European Jews as well." The Social Darwinist focus on these national perils inflamed the political climate.

Reformers focused on improving both the conditions within marriage and the quality of children born. The fear that one's nation or "race" was being polluted by the presence of foreigners and mental inferiors gave rise to eugenics, a pseudoscience popular among wealthy, educated Europeans at the turn of the century. As a famed Italian criminologist put it, such groups were not people but "orangutans." Eugenicists favored increased fertility for "the fittest" and limitations on the fertility of "degenerates," leading even to their sterilization or elimination. Women of the better classes, reformers felt, would be more inclined to reproduce if the shackles of the traditional system of marriage were removed and wives gained the legal right to their wages and to their own property. Sweden, which made men's and women's control over property equal in marriage, allowed women to work without their husbands' permission. Other countries legalized divorce and made it less complicated, and thus less costly, to obtain. Reformers believed that these legal changes would result in an upswing of the birthrate. Given the existing constraints of motherhood—no legal rights to their own children and no financial resources in the event of an abusive marriage—women were reluctant to have more than two or three, if any, children. Divorce would allow unhappy couples to separate and undertake a new, more loving, and thus more fertile marriage.

The conditions of marriage, motherhood, and other aspects of women's lives varied throughout Europe: women could get university degrees in Austrian universities long before they could at Oxford or Cambridge. A greater number of legal reforms occurred in western Europe, however. In much of rural eastern Europe, the father's power over the extended family remained almost absolute. According to a survey of family life in eastern Europe in the early 1900s, fathers married off their children so young that 25 percent of women in their early forties had been pregnant more than ten times. Yet reform of everyday customs occurred, as community control gave way to individual practice in some places. For instance, in some Balkan villages, a kind of extended-family system called the *zadruga* survived from earlier times: all the nuclear families shared a common great house, but now individual couples developed a degree of privacy by building one-room sleeping dwellings surrounding the great house. Among the middle and upper classes of eastern Europe, many grown children were coming to believe they had a right to select a marriage partner, not just to accept the spouse their parents chose for them.

The spread of empire and rapid social change set the stage for even bolder behaviors among some middle-class women. Adventurous women traveled the globe to promote Christianity, make money, or obtain knowledge of other cultures. The increasing availability of white-collar jobs for the educated meant that more European women could afford to adopt an independent way of life. The so-called **new woman** dressed more practically with fewer petticoats and looser

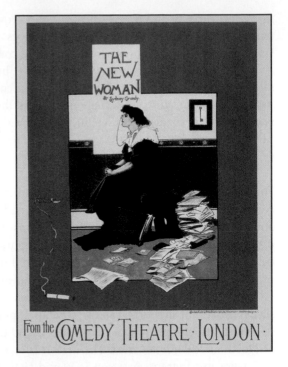

■ **Sydney Grundy, *The New Woman* (1900)**

By the opening of the twentieth century, the "new woman" had become a much-discussed phenomenon. Artists painted portraits of this independent creature, while playwrights such as Henrik Ibsen and novelists such as Nobel Prize winner Sigrid Undset depicted her ambition to throw off the wifely role— or at least to shape that role more to her own personality. The new woman was also well educated: she had been to university, or wrote as a journalist, or entered professions such as law and medicine.

(Private Collection/The Stapleton Collection/ Bridgeman Art Library.)

corsets, biked through city streets and down country lanes, lived apart from her family in a women's club or apartment, and supported herself. Italian educator Maria Montessori, for example, went to medical school and secretly gave birth to an illegitimate child. The growing number of women living on their own challenged accepted views of women's economic dependence. The "new woman," German philosopher Friedrich Nietzsche wrote, had led to the "uglification of Europe."

Sexual identity also fueled discussion. Among books in the new field of "sexology," which studied sex from a clinical and medical point of view, *Sexual Inversion* (1894) by Havelock Ellis was popular. Ellis, a British medical doctor, postulated a new personality type—the homosexual—identifiable by such traits as effeminate behavior and a penchant for the arts in males and physical passion for members of their own sex in both males and females. Homosexuals joined the discussion and asked to be recognized as a legitimate and natural "third sex"—not as people behaving sinfully. The press provoked debate on the other side: in the spring of 1895, reporters covered the trial of Irish playwright Oscar Wilde, who was sentenced to two years in prison for indecency—a charge that referred to his sexual affairs with young men. After Wilde's conviction, one newspaper rejoiced, "Open the windows! Let in the fresh air!" Between 1907 and 1909, German newspapers also publicized the courts-martial of men in Kaiser William II's closest circle who were condemned for homosexuality and transvestitism. Amid growing concern over population and family values, the public received assurances from the government itself that William's own family life "provides the entire country with a fine model." Sexuality thus took on patriotic overtones: the accused homosexual elite in Germany were said by journalists to be out to "emasculate our courageous master race." These cases paved the way for growing sexual openness in the next generations and established sexual issues as regular weapons in politics.

Working People's Strategies

For centuries, working people had migrated from countryside to city and from country to country to make a living. By the end of the nineteenth century, empire and economic change were spurring millions more to migrate. Older port cities of Europe, such as Riga, Marseille, and Hamburg, offered jobs in global trade; new colonies provided land, posts for soldiers and administrators, and the possibility of unheard-of wealth in diamonds, gold, and other natural resources.

Some Europeans moved far beyond their national borders because the land simply could not support a rapidly expanding population: Sicilians by the hundreds of thousands left the eroded soil of their island to find work in the industrial cities of North and South America. The British Isles, especially Ireland, sent one-third of all European emigrants between 1840 and 1920, first because of the potato famine and then because of uncertain farm tenancy and periodic economic crisis. Between 1886 and 1900, half a million Swedes out of a population of 4.75 million quit their country (Figure 19.1). Millions of rural Jews, especially in eastern Europe, left their villages for economic reasons. Russian Jews fled as vicious mobs attacked their communities, destroyed homes and businesses, and even murdered some of them.

As news of opportunity abroad reached Europe, migrants headed to North and South America, Australia, and New Zealand. The railroad and steamship made journeys across and then out of Europe more affordable and faster, though most migrants sailed in steerage, with few amenities. Once established elsewhere, migrants frequently sent money back home and thus remained part of the family economy. Nationalist commentators in Slovakia, Poland, Hungary, and other parts of eastern and central Europe bemoaned the loss of ethnic vigor, but peasants themselves welcomed the arrival of "magic dollars" from their kin. Migrants appreciated the chance to begin anew without the deprivation and social constrictions of the old world. One settler in the United States was relieved to escape the meager peasant meal of rye bread and herring: "God save us from . . . all that is Swedish," he wrote home sourly.

Migration out of Europe often meant the end of the old ways of life. Men and women seeking employment had to learn new languages and compete for jobs in unfamiliar cities, where they formed the cheapest pool of labor. Women who

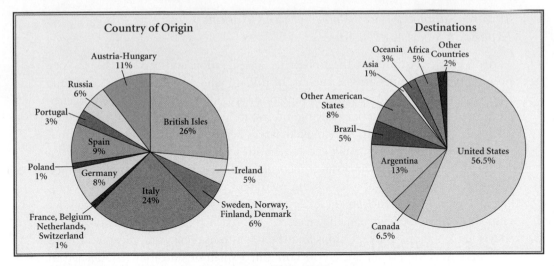

■ FIGURE 19.1 European Emigration, 1881–1910

The suffering caused by economic change and by political persecution motivated people from almost every European country to leave their homes for greater security elsewhere. North America attracted nearly two-thirds of these migrants, many of whom followed reports of vast quantities of available land in Canada and the United States. Both countries were known for following the rule of law and for economic opportunity in urban as well as rural areas.

worked in the home, however, tended to associate with others like themselves, preserving traditional ways. More insulated, they might never learn the new language or abandon their peasant dresses. Their husbands and children were more likely than they to put the past behind them as they faced the challenges of the factories and schools of the new world.

Internal migration from rural areas to European cities—more common than international migration—accelerated urbanization. The most urbanized countries at the start of the twentieth century were Great Britain and Belgium, followed by Germany, France, and the Netherlands. In Russia, only 7 percent of the population lived in cities of 10,000 or more; in Portugal the figure was 12 percent. Cities of more than 100,000 grew the most, but every urban area attracted migrants seeking employment. Nevertheless, more people lived in rural areas with under 2,000 people than lived in towns and cities, and migration back to rural areas occurred at harvest time. Temporary migrants to the cities worked as masons, horse-drawn cab drivers, or factory hands to supplement declining income from agriculture. In the winter, those remaining on the land turned to cottage industries, making bricks, pottery, sieves, shawls, lace, locks, and samovars. To maintain their status as independent artisans, handweavers sent their wives and daughters to towns to work in factories.

Toward National Fitness: Reforming the Working Class, Expanding Sports and Leisure

Two phenomena addressed the upheavals of migration and the stresses of economic modernization. One was the rise of middle- and upper-class reform organizations and charities to improve urban conditions. The other was the emergence of competitive sports and the growing interest in healthy recreation. Influenced by Social Darwinist thought, which associated health and fitness with national strength, governments generally endorsed both phenomena.

Settlement houses, clinics, and maternal and child wellness societies seemed to spring up overnight in cities. Young men and women, often from universities, eagerly took up residence in these centers in poor neighborhoods to study and help the people. Believing in the scientific approach to solving social problems, they sought the causes of social ills and their solutions. One group devoted to this enterprise was the Fabian Society in London, a small organization established in 1884. Committed to a socialism based on reform and state planning rather than revolution, the Fabians helped found the Labour Party in 1893 as a way of making social improvement a political issue. Religious fervor often added a moral component to reform efforts: some Protestants and Catholics countered growing secularization through increased missionary efforts among the urban poor at home. The church in Hungary, for example, channeled some of its efforts away from its traditional constituency in villages and toward ministering to workers in cities.

Impelled as well by a Social Darwinist fear that Europeans would lack the fitness to survive in a competitive world, philanthropists and government agencies intervened more and more in the lives of working-class families. They sponsored health clinics and milk centers to provide good medical care and food for children, and they instructed mothers in child-care techniques, including breast-feeding—an important way, reformers maintained, to promote infant health. Some schools distributed free lunches, medicine, and clothing. Some health care professionals began to make birth-control information available in the belief that small families were more likely to survive the rigors of urban life. But some reformers believed that the sexual exploitation of women would increase if the likelihood of pregnancy were overcome so easily. On the downside, government officials and private reformers deemed themselves the overseers of working-class families and entered apartments without being invited. Such intrusions pressured poor, overworked mothers to conform to standards for their children—such as finding them respectable shoes and other clothing—that they often could not afford.

Fearing that women were not producing healthy enough children and were stealing jobs from men, reformers pushed for "protective" legislation. Such legislation barred women across Europe from night work and from pottery and other "dangerous" trades, allegedly for health reasons even though medical statistics demonstrated that women became sick on the job less often than men. The new

■ Anglo-Indian Polo Teams

Team sports underwent rapid development during the imperial years, as spectators rooted for the success of their football team in the same spirit they rooted for their armies abroad. Some educators believed that team sports formed the male character so that men could be more effective soldiers against peoples of other races. Thus these mixed-race teams of polo players were uncharacteristic. In cricket, soccer, and other sports, city challenged city, nation challenged nation, and race often challenged race. (Hulton Archive/Getty Images.)

laws did not prevent women from earning their livelihood, but they made the task harder by blocking women's access to well-paid work.

Competitive sports and healthy leisure-time activities also served to enhance national fitness and provide some release from the stresses of daily life. As nations competed for territory and economic markets, male athletes banded together to organize team sports that eventually replaced village games. Soccer, rugby, and cricket drew mass followings and helped to integrate migrants as well as people from the lower and upper classes into a common national culture. Large audiences drawn from all classes backed their favorite teams, and competitive sports began to be seen as valuable promoters of national strength and spirit. Newspapers reported the results of all sorts of new contests, including the Tour de France bicycle race, sponsored by tire makers who wanted to prove the superiority of their products.

Team sports further differentiated male and female spheres and thus promoted social order based on distinctions between the sexes. Some team sports for women emerged—soccer, field hockey, and rowing—but women generally were encouraged to engage in individual sports. "Riding improves the temper, the spirits and the appetite," wrote one sportswoman. Rejecting the idea of women's natural frailty, reformers introduced exercise and gymnastics into schools for girls, often with the idea that they would strengthen young women for motherhood and thus help build the nation-state. A kind of aerobics called Swedish exercises for young women spread through respectable homes across Europe, while more cosmopolitan women practiced yoga.

The middle classes saw leisure pursuits like mountain-climbing as honing mental and physical skills. Working-class people adopted middle-class habits by joining clubs for bicycling, touring, and hiking. Laborers and their families also sought the benefits of fresh air and exercise by visiting the beach, taking the train into the countryside, and enjoying day trips on river steamships. Clubs that sponsored trips often had names such as "The Patriots" or "The Nationals," again associating physical fitness with national strength. The new emphasis on healthy recreation gave people a greater sense of individual freedom and power and thereby fostered a sense of citizenship based less on constitutions and rights than on an individual nation's exercise of raw power. A farmer's son in the 1890s boasted that with a bicycle "I was king of the road, since I was faster than a horse."

Sciences of the Modern Self

Scientists and Social Darwinists found cause for alarm not only in the condition of the working class but also in modern society's complaints about fatigue and irritability. Such illnesses originated in the "nerves," they reasoned, which were overstimulated by the pace and demands of urban living. A rash of books in the 1890s expounded on the subject of nervous illness. The most widely translated of them, *Degeneration*, written by Hungarian-born physician Max Nordau (1849–1923), saw increasingly bizarre modern art, male lethargy, and female hysteria as symptoms of overstimulation and signs of a general downturn in the human species. The Social Darwinist prescription for curing such mental decline was imperial adventure, renewed virility, and increased childbearing.

Some researchers attempted to quantify and classify mental characteristics. Scientific study of the origins of criminal traits created the field of criminology. The French psychologist Alfred Binet (1857–1911) designed intelligence tests that he claimed could measure the capacity of the human mind more accurately than schoolteachers could. In Russia, physiologist Ivan Pavlov (1849–1936) proposed that conditioning mental reflexes—that is, causing a subject to associate a desired response with a previously unrelated stimulus—could modify behavior. His experiments, especially his success in changing the behavior of a dog, formed the basis of modern psychology.

Sigmund Freud (1856–1939) devised an approach to treating modern anxieties that, he claimed, avoided traditional moral evaluations of human behavior. He became convinced that the human psyche was far from rational. Dreams, he

■ Freud's Office

Sigmund Freud's therapy room, where his patients experienced the "talking cure," was filled with imperial trophies such as Oriental rugs and African art objects. Freud himself was fascinated by cures brought about through shamanism, trances, and other practices of non-Western medicine as well as through drug-induced mental states. In 1938, Freud fled to England to escape the Nazis. This photo shows his office in London.

(Mary Evans Picture Library/Sigmund Freud copyrights.)

explained in *The Interpretation of Dreams* (1900), reveal a repressed part of personality—the "unconscious"—where all sorts of desires are more or less hidden. Freud also believed that the human psyche is made up of three competing parts: the *ego*, the part that is most in touch with external reality; the *id* (or libido), the part that governs instinctive drives and sexual energies; and the *superego*, the part that serves as the force of conscience. Like Darwin's ideas, Freud's notions challenged the widespread liberal beliefs in a rational self that peacefully acts in its own best interest.

Freud shocked many of his contemporaries by insisting that all children have sexual drives from the moment of birth. He believed that many of these sexual impulses have to be repressed for the individual to attain maturity and for society to remain civilized. Attaining one's adult sexual identity is always a painful process because it depends on repressing infantile urges, which include bisexuality and incest. Thus the Wolf-Man's nightmare of white wolves outside his window symbolized his unresolved sexual feelings for members of his family. Freud claimed that certain aspects of gender roles—such as motherhood—are normal and that throughout their lives women in general achieve far less than men do. At the same time, he believed that adult gender identity results not from anatomy alone (motherhood is not the only way to be female) but from inescapable mental processing of life experiences as well. He thus made gender more complicated than simple biology would suggest. Finally, Freud's psychoanalytic theory maintained that girls and women have powerful sexual feelings, an assertion that broke with ideas of women's passionlessness.

The influence of **psychoanalysis** became pervasive in the twentieth century, offering paradoxes and representing another turn toward global thinking. Two mainstays of psychoanalysis—free association of ideas and interpretation of dreams—derived from African and Asian influences on Freud's thought: the "talking cure," as it was quickly labeled, gave rise to a general acceptance of talking out one's problems. As psychoanalysis became a respected means of recovering mental health, terms such as *neurosis, unconscious,* and *libido* came into widespread use and could apply to anyone, not just the mentally ill. On the one hand, Freud was a meticulous scientist, examining symptoms, urging attention to the most minute evidence from everyday life, and demanding that sexual life be regarded with a rational rather than religious eye. On the other hand, he was a pessimistic visionary who abandoned the optimism of the Enlightenment and pre-Darwinian science and instead theorized that humans are motivated by irrational drives toward death and destruction and that these drives shape society's collective mentality. Freud would later interpret the devastation of World War I as bearing out his bleak conclusions.

■ **REVIEW:** *What social changes were transforming Europe at the start of the twentieth century?*

Modernity and the Revolt in Ideas

Although the intellectuals and artists who participated in the turmoil and triumph of turn-of-the-century society did not know it at the time, their rejection of accepted beliefs and artistic forms announced a new era. Scientific theories that time is relative and that energy and mass are interchangeable rocked established truths about time, space, matter, and energy. Philosophers emphasized the role of the irrational and accidental in everyday life. Art and music became unrecognizable. Artists and musicians who deliberately produced shocking, lurid works were, like Freud, heavily influenced by advances in science, critical thinking, and empire. Amid contradictions such as the blending of the scientific and the irrational, "West" and "non-West," intellectuals and artists helped launch the disorienting revolution in ideas and creative expression that we now identify collectively as **modernism.**

The Challenge to Positivism

Late in the nineteenth century, at the height of empire building and reform efforts, many philosophers and social thinkers rejected the century-old belief that scientific methods would lead to the discovery of enduring social laws. This belief, called positivism, had emphasized the permanent nature of fundamental laws and had motivated reformers' attempts to perfect legislation based on studies of society. Challenging positivism, the philosophers Wilhelm Dilthey (1833–1911) in Germany and John Dewey (1859–1952) in the United States declared that because human experience is ever changing, theories and standards cannot be constant or enduring. Just as scientific theory was modified over time, so must social theories and practice react pragmatically to the immediate conditions at hand. In the same vein, German political theorist Max Weber (1864–1920) maintained that the sheer number of factors involved in policy-making would thwart wise action by bureaucrats—especially in times of crisis. At such times, a charismatic leader might take power because of his ability to make flexible and instinctive decisions. Turn-of-the-century thinkers called relativists and pragmatists influenced thinking about society throughout the twentieth century.

The most radical scholar was the German philosopher Friedrich Nietzsche (1844–1900), who early in his career developed the challenging distinction between the "Apollonian," or rational, side of human existence and the "Dionysian" side, with its expression of more primal urges. Nietzsche believed that people generally cling to rational, Apollonian explanations of life because Dionysian ideas about nature, death, and love are too disturbing. He maintained that all assertions of scientific fact and theory are mere illusions, that knowledge of nature is only a mathematical, linguistic, or artistic representation. Truth, Nietzsche insisted, thus exists only in the representation itself, for humans can never experience unfiltered knowledge of nature or reality. This aspect of Nietzsche's philosophy powerfully questioned scientific certainty.

Much of Nietzsche's writing took the form of aphorisms—short, disconnected statements of truth or opinion—a form that broke with the logical rigor of traditional Western philosophy. Nietzsche used aphorisms to convey the impression that his ideas were a single individual's unique perspective, not universal truths that thinkers since the Enlightenment had claimed were attainable. Nietzsche was convinced that late-nineteenth-century Europe was witnessing the decline of dogmatic truth, most notably in religion—hence his announcement that "God is dead, we have killed him." Far from arousing dread, the death of God, according to Nietzsche, would give birth to a joyful quest for new "poetries of life" to replace worn-out religious and middle-class rules. Not the rulebound bourgeois but the untethered "superman" was Nietzsche's highly influential model. On his death, however, Nietzsche's sister edited his diatribes against middle-class values into attacks on Jews. She revised his complicated concepts about each individual's "will to power" and the "superman" so as to appeal to nationalists and to justify violent anti-Semitism and competition for empire.

Revolutionizing Science

While philosophers questioned the ability of science to provide timeless truths, scientific inquiry itself flourished, and the scientific method gained authority in history, psychology, and other fields beyond the traditional sciences. Around the turn of the century, however, discoveries by pioneering researchers shook the foundations of traditional scientific certainty and challenged accepted knowledge about the nature of the universe. In 1896, Antoine Becquerel (1852–1908) discovered radioactivity and suggested the mutability of elements by the rearrangement of their atoms. French chemist Marie Curie (1867–1934) and her husband Pierre Curie (1859–1906) isolated the elements polonium and radium, which are more radioactive than the uranium Becquerel used. From these and other discoveries, scientists concluded that atoms are composed of subatomic particles moving about a core. Instead of being solid, as scientists had believed since ancient times, atoms are largely empty space and act not as a concrete substance but as an intangible electromagnetic field. German physicist Max Planck (1858–1947) announced his influential quantum theorem in 1900; it demonstrated that energy is emitted in irregular packets, not in a steady stream.

In this atmosphere of innovation, physicist Albert Einstein (1879–1955) published his special theory of relativity. On his own, working in a Swiss patent office, he proclaimed in his 1905 paper that space and time are not absolute categories but instead vary according to the vantage point of the observer. Only the speed of light is constant. That same year, he also suggested that the solution to problems in Planck's quantum theorem lay in considering light both as little packets *and* as waves. These theories continued to undercut Newtonian physics as well as commonsense understanding. Einstein later proposed yet another blurring of two distinct physical properties, mass and energy. He expressed this equivalence in the formulation $E = mc^2$, or energy equals mass times the square of the speed of light. In 1916, his general theory of relativity connected the force, or gravity, of an object with its mass and postulated a fourth mathematical dimension to the universe. Much more lay ahead, once Einstein's theories of energy were developed: television, nuclear power, and, within forty years, nuclear bombs.

The revolutionary findings of Planck, Einstein, and others were not accepted immediately because power and time-honored beliefs were at stake. Einstein like Planck struggled against mainstream science and its professional institutions. As a female scientist, Marie Curie faced such resistance that even after she became the first person ever to receive a second Nobel Prize (1911), the prestigious French Academy of Science turned down her candidacy for membership that year.

■ **Marie Curie and Her Daughter**
Recipient of two Nobel Prizes, Marie Curie came from Poland to western Europe to study science. Curie's extraordinary career made her the epitome of the new womanhood; her daughter Irene Joliot-Curie followed her into the field and also won a Nobel Prize. Both women died of leukemia caused by their exposure to radioactive materials. Today a reconstruction of the Curie laboratory as a museum contains a display indicating the intense radioactivity that remains in the scientific instruments they used a century ago. (ACJC—Fund Curie et Joliot-Curie.)

Traditionalists, however, eventually gave way, and Max Planck institutes were established in German cities, streets across Europe were named after Marie Curie, and Einstein's name became synonymous with genius. These scientists achieved what historians call a paradigm shift—that is, in the face of staunch resistance they transformed the foundations of science.

Modern Art

Conflicts between traditional values and new ideas also raged in the arts, as artists distanced themselves from classical Western realism and from the conventions of polite society. Modernism in the arts not only fractured traditional standards but ushered in competing artistic styles and disagreement about art's relationship to society. Some modern artists tried both to challenge and to comfort urbanites caught up in the rush of modern life. Abandoning the soft colors of impressionism as too subtle for a dynamic industrial society, a group of Parisian artists exhibiting in 1905 combined blues, greens, reds, and oranges so intensively that they were called fauves, or "wild beasts." A leader of the short-lived fauvism, Henri Matisse (1869–1954) soon struck out in a new direction, targeting the expanding class of white-collar workers. Matisse dreamed of "an art . . . for every mental worker, be he businessman or writer, like an appeasing influence, like a mental soother, something like a good armchair in which to rest from physical fatigue."

In the work of the French artist Paul Cézanne (1839–1906), one of the most powerful and enduring trends in modern art took shape. Emphasizing structure, Cézanne used rectangular daubs of paint to capture a geometric vision of dishes, fruit, drapery, and the human body. Accentuating the lines and planes found in nature, Cézanne's art, like science, was removed from the realm of ordinary perception. Following in Cézanne's footsteps, Spanish artist Pablo Picasso (1881–1973) initiated cubism, a style whose radical emphasis on planes and surfaces portrayed people as bizarre, inhuman, almost unrecognizable forms. Picasso's painting *Les Demoiselles d'Avignon* (1907) depicted the bodies of the *demoiselles*, or young ladies (prostitutes in this case), as fragmented and angular, with their heads modeled on African masks. Continuing along the path of impressionism and fauvism, Picasso's work showed the profound influences of African, Asian, and South American arts, but his interpretation of these influences was less decorative and more brutal than those by Matisse, for example. Like explorers, botanists, and foreign journalists, he was bringing knowledge of the empire into the imperial homeland, this time in a distinctly disturbing form.

Across Europe, political critique also shaped art. "Show the people how hideous is their actual life, and place your hands on the causes of its ugliness" was the anarchist challenge at the time. Picasso, who had spent his youth in the heart of working-class Barcelona, a hotbed of anarchist thought, aimed to replace middle-class sentimentality in art with truth about industrial society. In 1912, Picasso and the French painter Georges Braque (1882–1963) devised a new kind of collage that incorporated bits of newspaper, string, and other artifacts. The effect was a canvas that appeared to be cluttered with refuse. The newspaper clippings Picasso included described battles and murders, suggesting the shallowness of Western pretensions to high civilization. In eastern and central Europe, artists criticized the growing nationalism that determined official purchases of sculpture and painting: "The whole empire is littered with monuments to soldiers and monuments to Kaiser William of the same conventional type," one German artist complained. Such groups as the Berlin Secession and the Vienna Workshop were at the forefront of depicting psychological complexity in experimental form.

Scandinavian and eastern European artists produced anguished works. Like the vision of Freud, their style of portraying inner reality—called expressionism— broke with middle-class optimism. Norwegian painter Edvard Munch (1863–1944) aimed "to make the emotional mood ring out again as happens on a gramophone." His painting *The Scream* (1895) used twisting lines and a depiction of tortured skeletal human form to convey the horror of modern life that many artists perceived (see page 796). The German avant-garde artist Gabriele Münter (1877–1962) and Russian painter Wassily Kandinsky (1866–1944) opened their "Blue Rider" exhibit in Munich in 1911 featuring "expressive" work that made use of geometric forms and striking colors. Artists of the Blue Rider group imitated the paintings of children and the mentally ill to achieve their depiction of psychological reality. Kandinsky, who employed these forms and colors to express an inner, spiritual truth, is often credited with producing the first fully abstract paintings. The expressionism of Austrian painter Oskar Kokoschka (1886–1980) was even more intense, displaying ecstasy, horror, and hallucinations. As a result, his work—like that of other expressionists and cubists before World War I—was a commercial failure in an increasingly complex marketplace that featured not only museum curators but professional dealers and art "experts" trading in art.

Only one innovative style emerged an immediate commercial success: **art nouveau** ("new style") won approval from government, critics, and the masses. Creating everything from dishes and advertising posters to streetlamps and even entire buildings in this new style, designers manufactured beautiful things for the general public. As one French official said about the first version of art nouveau coins issued in 1895, "Soon even the most humble among us will be able to have a masterpiece in his pocket." Adapted from Asian design, the organic and natural elements of art nouveau were meant to offset the fragmentation of factory and office work with images depicting the unified forms of nature. The impersonality of machines was replaced by intertwined vines and flowers and the softly curving bodies of female nudes that would psychologically soothe the individual viewer—an idea that directly contrasted with Picasso's artistic vision. Art nouveau was the notable exception to the public outcries over innovations in the visual arts.

Musical Iconoclasm

"Astonish me!" was the motto of modern dance and music, both of which shocked audiences in the concert halls of Europe. American dancer Isadora Duncan (1877–1927) took Europe by storm at the turn of the century when, draped in a flowing garment, she danced barefoot in the first performance of modern dance. Drawing on sophisticated Japanese practices, hers was nonetheless called a primitive style that one observer noted, "lifted from their seats people who had never left theater seats before except to get up and go home." Similarly, experimentation with forms of bodily expression animated the Russian Ballet's performance in 1913 of *Rite of Spring* by Igor Stravinsky (1882–1971), the tale of an orgiastic dance to the death performed to ensure a bountiful harvest. The choreography of its star, Vaslav Nijinsky (1890–1950), created a scandal when his troupe struck awkward poses and danced to rhythms intended to sound primitive. At the work's premiere in Paris,

■ **Léon Bakst, *Nijinsky in
"L'Après-Midi d'un Faune"*
("The Afternoon of a
Faun"), 1912**
*Theater sets, costume designs,
and performance itself resonated
with the experimental climate of
early-twentieth-century Europe.
Léon Bakst, a Russian painter
and set designer, used art
nouveau style to capture the
faun-like character of ballet star
Vaslav Nijinsky. Yet on the eve of
World War I, Nijinsky was part
of a revolution in ballet that
introduced jerky, awkward,
pounding movements to indicate
the primal nature of dance.*
(Wadsworth Atheneum Museum of Art,
Hartford, CT. The Ella Gallup Sumner
and Mary Catlin Sumner Collection
Fund.)

one journalist reported that "the audience began shouting its indignation . . . Fighting actually broke out among some of the spectators." Such controversy made *Rite of Spring* a box-office hit, although its choreographer was called a "lunatic" and the music itself "the most discordant composition ever written."

Music had been making this turn for several decades. Having heard Asian musicians at international expositions, French composers such as Claude Debussy (1862–1918) transformed their style to reflect non-European musical patterns and themes. The twentieth century opened with *Schéhérazade* by Frenchman Maurice Ravel (1875–1937) and *Madame Butterfly* by the Italian composer Giacomo Puccini (1858–1924), both with non-Western subject matter. Using non-Western tonalities, sound became jarring to many listeners. Austrian composer Richard Strauss (1864–1949) upset convention by using several keys simultaneously in his compositions. Like the fragmented representation of reality in cubism, atonality or several tonalities at once distorted familiar harmonic patterns for the audience. Strauss's operas *Salome* (1905) and *Elektra* (1909) reflected modern fascination with violence and obsessive passion. A newspaper critic claimed that Strauss's dissonant works "spit and scratch and claw each other like enraged panthers."

The early orchestral work of Austrian composer Arnold Schoenberg (1874–1951), who also wrote cabaret music to earn a living, shocked even Strauss. In his book *Theory of Harmony* (1911), Schoenberg proposed eliminating tonality altogether; a decade later he devised a new twelve-tone scale. "I am aware of having broken through all the barriers of a dated aesthetic ideal," Schoenberg wrote of his music. But new aesthetic models distanced artists like Schoenberg from their audiences, separating high from low culture even more and ending the support of many in the upper classes, who found this music not only incomprehensible but unpleasant. The artistic elite and the social elite parted ranks. "Anarchist! Nihilist!" shouted Schoenberg's audiences, showing their contempt for modernism and bringing the language of politics into the arts.

■ **REVIEW:** *What changes in intellectual life disrupted accepted cultural standards at the start of the twentieth century?*

The Birth of Mass Politics

The political atmosphere grew charged alongside the modernist disturbances in intellectual life, even as the advance of liberal ideals opened the door to expanded political representation. Networks of communication, especially the development of journalism, enhanced the trend toward universal male suffrage in Europe, leading to the creation of mass politics. Working-class people seemed to come into their own: even high-ranking politicians such as William Gladstone, the prime minister of Great Britain, had to campaign by railroad to win their support. Simultaneously, however, political activists were no longer satisfied with the liberal rights sought by reformers a century earlier. Militant nationalists, anti-Semites, socialists, suffragists, and others demanded changes that challenged liberal values. Traditional elites, resentful of the rising middle classes and urban peoples, aimed to stem constitutional processes and the development of modern life. Mass politics soon threatened social unity, especially in central and eastern Europe, where governments often answered reformers' demands with refusal and repression.

Mass Politics and the Growing Power of Labor

Mass politics arose from a combination of the right to vote accorded to men across Europe before World War I and the rise of popular activism, especially among working people. In the fall of 1879, William Gladstone (1809–1898), leader of the British Liberals, whose party was then out of power, waged an experimental electoral campaign across the country. Speaking before thousands of working men and women, he urged greater self-determination in India and Africa and advocated a way of life based on "honest, manful, humble effort" in the middle-class tradition of "hard work." Newspapers around the country highlighted his trip, further fueling public interest in politics and helping him become prime minister—testimonial to the trend toward expanded participation in political life. The Reform Act of 1884 doubled the British electorate to around 4.5 million men, enfranchising many urban workers and artisans and thus diminishing traditional aristocratic influence in the countryside. This move reflected the universal manhood suffrage already granted in France and in Germany; much of Europe would follow suit before World War I.

Journalism helped elite politicians forge a broad national community of up-to-date citizens by providing ready access to information (and misinformation) about politics and world events. The invention of mechanical typesetting and the production of newsprint from wood pulp lowered the costs of printing; the telephone allowed reporters to communicate news to their papers almost instantly. Once philosophical and literary in content, daily newspapers now emphasized the sensational, using banner headlines and gruesome or lurid details—particularly about murders, sexual scandals, and sagas of the empire—to sell papers as well as political points of view. In the hustle and bustle of industrial society, one editor wrote, "you must strike your reader right between the eyes." Elites grumbled that the sensational press was another sign of social decay. But a number of up-and-coming people from the working and middle classes got their start in politics working for daily newspapers.

Working-class solidarity in neighborhoods, shop-floor activism, the development of labor unions, and the rise of worker or socialist parties formed the other side of mass politics. Community bonds forged by homemakers and neighborhood groups were a necessary precondition for collective worker action. When landlords evicted tenants, women would gather in the streets and return household goods as fast as they were removed from the rooms of ousted families. Meeting on doorsteps or at fountains, laundries, pawnshops, and markets, women initiated rural newcomers into urban ways and developed class unity. Conditions of economic life also led workers to organize formal unions, which attracted the allegiance of millions. Unions demanded a say in working conditions and aimed, as one union's rule book put it, "to ensure that wages . . . always follow the rises in the price of basic commodities." Despite the worker turbulence of the Paris Commune, strong unions even appealed to some industrialists because a union could make strikes more predictable (or even prevent them) and present demands more coherently.

From the 1880s on, the pace of collective action for more pay, lower prices, and better working conditions accelerated. In 1888, for example, hundreds of young women who made matches, the so-called London matchgirls, struck to end the fining system, under which they could be penalized an entire day's wage for being a minute or two late to work. This system, the matchgirls maintained, helped companies reap profits of more than 20 percent. Newspapers and philanthropists picked up the strikers' story, helping them win their case. Soon after, London dock-workers and gasworkers protested their precarious working conditions. Across Europe, the number of strikes and demonstrations rose from 188 in 1888 to 289 in 1890. Housewives, who often demonstrated in support of strikers, carried out their own protests against high food prices. In keeping with centuries of women's protest, they confiscated merchants' goods and sold them at what they considered a just price. "There should no longer be either rich or poor," argued organized Italian peasant women. "All should have bread for themselves and for their children. We should all be equal." Fearing threats to industrial and agricultural productivity, governments increasingly responded with force, even though most strikes were about the conditions of everyday life for workers and not about political revolution.

From unions soon evolved working-class political parties. Craft-based unions of skilled artisans, such as carpenters and printers, were the most active and cohesive, but from the mid-1880s on, a new unionism attracted transport workers, miners, matchgirls, and dockworkers. These new unions were nationwide groups with salaried managers who could plan massive general strikes across the trades, focusing on such common goals as the eight-hour workday, and thus paralyze an entire nation. Large unions of the industrialized countries of western Europe, like cartels and trusts, increasingly influenced business practices. They were joined by working-class parties: the Labour Party in England, the Socialist Party in France, and the Social Democratic Parties of Sweden, Hungary, Austria, and Germany— most of them inspired by Marxist theories. Germany was home to the largest socialist party in Europe after 1890.

Workingwomen joined these parties, but in much smaller numbers than men. Not able to vote in national elections and usually responsible for housework in addition to their paying jobs, women had little time for party meetings. Furthermore, their low wages hardly allowed them to survive, much less to pay party or union dues. Many workingmen opposed their presence. Contact with women would mean "suffocation," one Russian workingman believed, and end male union members' sense of being "comrades in the revolutionary cause." The shortage of women's voices in unions and political parties paralleled women's exclusion from government; it helped make the middle-class belief in separate spheres part of a working-class ideology that glorified the heroic struggles of a male proletariat against capitalism. Marxist leaders continued to maintain that injustice to women was caused by capitalism and would disappear in socialist society. As a result, they downplayed women's concerns about lower wages and sexual coercion.

Socialist parties attracted workingmen because they promised that male voters would become a powerful collective force in national elections. Those who accepted Marx's assertion that "workingmen have no country," however, wanted an international movement that could address workers' common interests. In 1889, some four hundred socialists from across Europe (joined by many onlookers and unofficial participants) met in Paris to form the **Second International**, a federation of working-class organizations and political parties replacing the First International, founded by Marx before the Paris Commune. Growing strength, especially electoral victories, raised issues for socialists. Some felt uncomfortable sitting with the upper classes in parliaments. Others worried that their participation in cabinets would produce reform but compromise their ultimate goal of revolution. Often these deputies refused seats in the government. Between 1900 and 1904, the Second International wrestled with the issue of reformism—that is, a preference for evolutionary tactics rather than violent revolution to overthrow governments.

European leaders watched with dismay the rise of working-class political power late in the century. Some trade union members, known as syndicalists, along with anarchists kept Europe in a panic with their terrorist acts. Anarchism flourished in the less industrial parts of Europe—Russia, Italy, and Spain, where many rural people looked to the possibility of life without the domination of large landowners and government. Many advocated extreme tactics, including physical violence and even murder. "We want to overthrow the government . . . with violence since it is by the use of violence that they force us to obey," wrote one Italian anarchist. In the 1880s, anarchists bombed stock exchanges, parliaments, and businesses and by the 1890s were assassinating heads of state: Spanish premier Antonio Canovas del Castillo in 1897, Empress Elizabeth of Austria-Hungary in 1898, King Umberto of Italy in 1900, and President William McKinley of the United States in 1901, to name a few famous victims. Syndicalists advocated the use of direct action, such as general strikes and sabotage, to gain power by paralyzing the economy.

Much worker organization was highly sociable, intertwining community solidarity with activities of everyday life. The gymnastic and choral societies that had once united Europeans in nationalistic fervor now served working-class goals. Songs emphasized worker freedom, progress, and eventual victory. Socialist gymnastics, bicycling, and marching societies rejected competition and prizes as middle-class preoccupations, but they valued physical fitness for helping workers in the "struggle for existence"—a reflection of Darwinian thinking about "survival of the fittest." Workers also held festivals and gigantic parades, most notably on May 1, proclaimed by the Second International as a labor holiday. Like religious processions of an earlier time, parades were rituals that fostered unity. European governments at the time could not discriminate among the various worker organizations and frequently prohibited such gatherings as a public danger.

Another group of working-class parties operated in exile. The Russian government, for instance, outlawed political parties until 1905 and persecuted activists. The foremost Russian activist, V. I. Lenin (1870–1924), migrated to western Europe after his release from confinement in Siberia and earned his reputation among Russian Marxists there with his hard-hitting journalism and political intrigue. Lenin advanced the theory that a highly disciplined socialist elite would lead a lightly industrialized Russia immediately into socialism. Outmaneuvering the Mensheviks, who dominated Russian Marxism, Lenin's Bolsheviks, so named after the Russian word for "majority" (which they had briefly formed), constantly struggled to suppress other groups. Neither of these factions, however, had as large a constituency within Russia as the Socialist Revolutionaries, whose objective was to politicize peasants rather than industrial workers as the prelude to revolution. All these groups prepared for the revolutionary moment through study, propaganda efforts, and organizing—not through the electoral politics successfully employed elsewhere in Europe. Whether operating in representative or authoritarian countries, working-class organizations caused the upper and middle classes grave anxiety.

Rights for Women and the Battle for Suffrage

Singly or in groups, women continued to agitate against their exclusion from benefits of liberalism such as parliamentary representation. They usually could not vote, exercise free speech, or own property if married. Laws in France, Austria, and Germany curtailed women's political activism, including their attendance at political meetings. Influenced by the cultural ideal of *Bildung*—the belief that education can strengthen character and that individual development has public importance—German women sought better education for themselves and more opportunity to teach, instead of agitating for political reform. In several countries, women continued to monitor the regulation of prostitution. Their goal was to prevent prostitutes from being imprisoned on suspicion of having syphilis when men with syphilis faced no such incarceration. Other women took up pacifism as their special cause. Many of them were inspired by Bertha von Süttner's popular book *Lay Down Your Arms* (1889), which emphasized the terror inflicted on women and families by the ravages of war.

By the 1890s, however, many activists had concluded that only the right to vote would correct the problems caused by male privilege, which they were combating in piecemeal fashion. Thus major suffrage organizations with millions of activists, paid officials, and permanent offices emerged out of the earlier reform groups. Using skills gained from their charity work and from this organizing, British suffrage leader Millicent Garrett Fawcett (1847–1929) and other women pressured members of Parliament for the vote and participated in national and international congresses on behalf of suffrage. Similarly, American Susan B. Anthony (1820–1906) traveled throughout the United States, organized suffrage societies, raised money for the movement, and founded the International Woman Suffrage Association in 1904. The leadership argued that men had promised to protect disfranchised women but that this system of male chivalry had led to exploitation and abuse. Power and privilege—no matter how couched in expressions of goodwill—worked to the detriment of those without them. "So long as the subjection of women endures, and is confirmed by law and custom, . . . women will be victimized," a leading suffragist claimed. Other activists believed that women had the attributes needed to counterbalance masculine qualities in the running of society. The characteristics that came from women's work as mothers should shape a country's destiny as much as qualities that stemmed from work in industry, they asserted.

Women's rights activists were predominantly, though not exclusively, from the middle class. Enjoying conveniences like freestanding stoves, running water, and household help, they had more time than workingwomen to be activists, and a higher level of education allowed them to read the works of feminist theorists such as Harriet Taylor and John Stuart Mill. Many were influenced by such works as Norwegian playwright Henrik Ibsen's *A Doll's House* (1879), whose heroine Nora leaves a loveless and oppressive marriage. Some working-class women also participated, although many distrusted the middle class and saw suffrage for women as less important than economic concerns. Textile workers in Manchester, England, for example, put together a vigorous suffrage movement connecting the vote to improved working conditions.

In 1906 in Finland, suffragists achieved their first major victory when the Finnish parliament granted women the vote. But the failure of parliaments

■ Woman Suffrage in Finland

In 1906, Finnish women became the first women in Europe to receive the vote in national elections when the Socialist Party—usually opposed to feminism as a middle-class rather than a working-class project—supported woman suffrage. The Finnish vote elated activists in the West, now linked by many international organizations and ties, because it showed that more than a century of lobbying for reform could lead to gains.

(Mary Evans Picture Library.)

elsewhere in Europe to enact similar legislation provoked some suffragists to violence. Part of the British suffragist movement adopted a militant political style. Emmeline Pankhurst (1858–1928) and her daughters had founded the Women's Social and Political Union (WSPU) in 1903 in the belief that women would accomplish nothing unless they threatened men's property. In 1907, WSPU members began to stage parades in English cities, and in 1909 they began a campaign of violence, blowing up railroad stations, slashing works of art, and chaining themselves to the gates of Parliament. Easily disguising themselves as ordinary shoppers, they carried little hammers in their handwarmers to smash the plate-glass windows of department stores and shops. Parades and demonstrations made suffrage a public spectacle, provoking attacks on the marchers by outraged men. Arrested for disturbing the peace, the marchers went on hunger strikes in prison. Like striking workers, these women were willing to use confrontational tactics to obtain rights. As politicians continued to deny women the vote, militant suffragists added to the tensions of conflict-ridden urban life.

Liberalism Modified

Governments in western Europe, where liberal institutions seemed well entrenched, sought to control the conflicts of the late nineteenth century with pragmatic policies that often (and paradoxically) struck at liberalism's very foundations. Some ended laissez-faire trade policies by instituting protective tariffs; some politicians and reformers decided that government needed to intervene in more than economic matters and expand social welfare legislation. In 1905, the British Liberal Party won a solid majority in the House of Commons and seemed determined to enact social legislation to gain working-class support. "We are keenly in sympathy with the representatives of Labour," one Liberal politician announced. "We have too few of them in the House of Commons." The British government initiated a system of relief for the unemployed in the National Insurance Act of 1911, provided new taxes on the wealthy to fund the system, and eliminated the veto power of the House of Lords.

A modified liberalism advanced in Britain on social issues, but the Irish question tested British commitment to such values as self-determination and individual rights. British political reforms armed disaffected Irish tenant farmers with the secret ballot, but the political climate in Ireland remained explosive because of the repressive tactics of absentee landlords, many of them English and Protestant. These landlords evicted unsuccessful and prosperous tenants alike so they could raise the rents of newcomers. But Irish tenants elected a solid bloc of nationalist representatives to the British Parliament. The Irish members of Parliament, voting as a group, had sufficient strength to defeat legislation proposed by either the Conservatives or the Liberals in the House of Commons. Irish leader Charles Parnell (1846–1891) demanded support for home rule—allowing Ireland to have its own parliament—in return for Irish votes. The House of Lords, however, vetoed the bills.

Parnell's leadership ended because of scandal in his personal life, but in the 1890s, new groups formed to foster Irish culture. In 1901, the circle around the modernist poet William Butler Yeats (1865–1939) and the charismatic patriot and actress Maud Gonne (1865–1953) founded the Irish National Theater. Gonne took Irish politics into everyday life by opposing British efforts to woo the young. Every time an English monarch visited Ireland, he or she held special receptions for children. Gonne and other Irish volunteers sponsored competing events, handing out candies and other treats for patriotic youngsters. Speaking Gaelic instead of English, singing Gaelic songs, using Catholicism as a rallying point, and generally reconstructing an "Irish way of life," the promoters of Irish culture threw into question the educated class's preference for everything English. This cultural agenda took political shape with the founding in 1905 of Sinn Fein ("We Ourselves"), a group that strove for complete Irish independence. In 1913, Parliament approved home rule for Ireland, but the outbreak of World War I prevented the legislation from taking effect and cut short dreams of independence.

Liberal Italian nation builders, left with a towering debt from unification and with massive pockets of discontent, drifted more rapidly from liberalism's moorings. With little money being spent on education and sanitary improvements, the average Italian feared the devastating effects of national taxes and the military draft on the family economy. Corruption plagued Italy's constitutional monarchy, which had developed neither the secure parliamentary system of England nor the authoritarian monarchy of Germany to guide its growth. To forge a national consensus in the 1890s, prime ministers used patriotic rhetoric, bribes to gain support from the press, and imperial adventure, culminating in a second thwarted attempt to conquer Ethiopia in 1896. Riots and strikes, followed by armed government repression, erupted, until Giovanni Giolitti, who served as prime minister for three terms between 1903 and 1914, adopted a policy known as *trasformismo* (from the word for "transform"), by which he used bribes, public works programs, and other benefits to localities to influence their deputies in parliament. Political opponents called Giolitti the "Minister of the Underworld" and accused him of preferring to buy the votes of local bosses instead of spending money to develop the Italian economy. He hoped to appease unrest in the industrializing cities of Turin and Milan and in the depressed agrarian south by instituting social welfare programs and, in 1912, nearly complete manhood suffrage.

Anti-Semitism, Nationalism, and Zionism in Mass Politics

In the two decades leading up to World War I, anti-Semitism and nationalism suggested simplistic answers to complex questions. Leaders fueled these sentiments to maintain interest-group support, to direct hostility away from themselves, and to win elections. The public responded vehemently, coming to see Jews as villains responsible for the perils of modern society and the nation-state as the hero in the struggle to survive. In both republics and monarchies, anti-Semitism and nationalism played key roles in mass politics by providing a focus for the creation of a radical right increasingly committed to combating the radical left of social democracy. The right fundamentally changed the older notion of nationalism based on liberal ideas of rights by adopting the imperiled nation as its theme and using the Social Darwinist category of race to identify threats to the nation. Liberals had hoped that voting by the masses would make politics more harmonious as parliamentary debate and compromise smoothed out class differences. But anti-Semites and nationalists, scorning tolerant liberal values as weak, often preferred fights in the street to consensus building in parliaments.

The most notorious instance of anti-Semitism occurred in France, where the political compromise that had created the Third Republic after the French defeat in the Franco-Prussian War produced institutional fragility. An alliance of businessmen, shopkeepers, professionals, and rural property owners backed republican government, but during economic downturns, the press attributed these and any other problems to Jews. Despite an excellent system of primary education promoting literacy and rational thinking, the public was quick to agree. The clergy and monarchists also contributed to the belief that the republic was backed by a conspiracy of Jews.

Amid rising anti-Semitism, a Jewish French army captain, Alfred Dreyfus (1859–1935), was charged with spying for Germany in 1894. Dreyfus had attended elite schools and become an officer in the French military, whose upper echelons were traditionally aristocratic, Catholic, and monarchist. Dreyfus's conviction and harsh exile to Devil's Island failed to stop the espionage, but the government adamantly upheld his guilt. Then several newspapers received proof that the army had used perjured testimony and fabricated documents to convict Dreyfus. In 1898, the celebrated French novelist Émile Zola published "J'accuse" ("I accuse") on the front page of a Paris daily. Zola cited a list of military lies and cover-ups perpetrated by highly placed government officials to create an illusion of Dreyfus's guilt. The article was explosive because it revealed the names of conspirators and endorsed a government based on truth and tolerance. "I have but one passion, that of Enlightenment," wrote Zola. "J'accuse" led to public riots, quarrels among families and friends, and denunciations of the army, which eroded public confidence in the republic and in French institutions. The government finally pardoned Dreyfus in 1899, ousted from office the aristocratic and Catholic officers held responsible, and ended religious teaching orders to ensure a public school system that was secular and that taught liberal values of tolerance. Nonetheless, the Dreyfus Affair made anti-Semitism a standard political tool by producing hate-filled slogans that would shape mainstream politics.

The ruling elites in Germany also used anti-Semitism to gain political support from those who feared the consequences of Germany's sudden and overwhelming industrialization. After his failed culture war against Catholics, in 1882–1884 Bismarck tried to woo the working classes with an array of social programs such as accident and disability insurance while outlawing the Social Democratic Party. The agrarian elites, who controlled the highest reaches of government, lost ground economically as agriculture declined as a percentage of Germany's gross national product. The agrarian elites came to loathe both vibrant industry and the working class as better jobs lured rural people away from the land. As a Berlin newspaper noted, "The agrarians' hate for cities . . . blinds them to the simplest needs and the most natural demands of the urban population."

These conservatives and a growing radical right claimed that Jews, who made up less than 1 percent of the German population, were responsible for the disruption of traditional society and charged them with being the main beneficiaries of economic change. In the 1890s, nationalist and anti-Semitic pressure groups flourished, spewing diatribes against Jews and "new women" but also against Social Democrats, whom they branded as internationalist and unpatriotic. In the 1890s, the new Agrarian League played to the fears of small farmers by accusing Jews of causing agricultural booms and busts. Expressions of extremist hatred and violent feelings of nationalism rather than rational programs

■ Public Opinion in the Dreyfus Affair: "Ah! The Dirty Beast!"

The French army used forged documents and perjured testimony to convict Captain Alfred Dreyfus of espionage. In a climate of escalating anti-Semitism, the conviction of a Jew struck many in the public as yet another narrow escape for the country. Only intense detective work by pro-Dreyfus activists and lobbying by Dreyfus's family convinced republican leaders that the system of equal rights was imperiled not by Dreyfus but by the bigotry of the army and those right-wing politicians who had trumped up the case against him.

(© Photothèque des Musées de la Ville de Paris/Toumazet.)

to meet problems of economic change became regular features of political campaigns.

People in Austria-Hungary—the dual monarchy—also expressed their discontent in militantly nationalistic and anti-Semitic terms, but nationalism there felt the presence of many competing ethnic groups. From 1879 to 1893, Austrian prime minister Count Eduard von Taaffe favored Catholics and the Slavic parties in order to break the growing power of liberals. But every favor to one group brought protest from the others. Foremost among the nationalists were the Hungarians, who wanted autonomy for themselves while forcibly imposing Hungarian language and culture (called Magyarization, from Magyars, the dominant ethnicity) on all other ethnic groups working in Hungary. The demands for greater Magyar influence stemmed from Budapest's importance as a thriving industrial city and the massive export of Hungarian grain from the vast estates of the Hungarian nobility, which balanced the monarchy's foreign trade deficit. Political

Principal Ethnic Groups in Austria-Hungary, c. 1900

chaos ensued from Magyar domination, as Slovaks, Romanians, and Ruthenians protested horrendous labor conditions and tens of thousands of others demanded the vote. In the face of this resistance, Hungary intensified Magyarization, even decreeing that all tombstones be engraved in Magyar.

Hungarian policies changed the course of Habsburg politics by arousing other nationalists to intensify their demands for rights. Croats, Serbs, and other Slavic groups in the south organized and called for equality with the Hungarians. The central government gave more privileges to the Czechs and allowed them to increase the proportion of Czech officials in the government simply because growing industrial prosperity in their region gave them more influence. But every step toward recognition of Czech ethnicity provoked outrage from the traditionally dominant ethnic Germans, increasing tension in the empire. When Austria-Hungary decreed in 1897 that government officials in the Czech region of the empire would have to know Czech as well as German, the Germans rioted.

Tensions mounted as politicians in Vienna linked the growing power of Hungarian and Czech politicians to Jews. A prime instigator of this "politics of the irrational"—as historians often label this ultranationalist and anti-Semitic phenomenon—was Karl Lueger (1844–1910), whose newly formed Christian

Social Party attracted members from among the aristocracy, Catholics, artisans, shopkeepers, and white-collar workers. Lueger used hatred to appeal to those groups for whom modern life meant a loss of privilege and security. In 1895, he was elected mayor of Vienna after using rough language and verbal abuse against Jews and ethnic groups in his campaign. Lueger's ethnic nationalism and anti-Semitism destabilized the multinational coexistence on which Austria-Hungary was based. By the turn of the century, Jewishness became a symbol that politicians often attacked in their election campaigns, calling Jews the "sucking vampire" of modernity and blaming them for any and all problems. The realm of politics moved from parliaments to the streets, inflaming the atmosphere with racism.

The prevailing view in the West that Jews were inferior to Christians provoked varying responses from Jews themselves. Jews in western Europe had responded to the spread of legal tolerance by adopting liberal political and cultural values, inter-marrying with Christians, and in some cases converting to Christianity—practices known as assimilation. Many Jews also favored the German Empire because classical German culture seemed more appealing than the Catholic ritual promoted by Austria-Hungary. By contrast, Jews in Russia and Romania were increasingly singled out for persecution, legally disadvantaged, and forced to live in ghettos. If Jews wanted refuge, the cities of central and eastern Europe provided the best opportunity to succeed. They often adopted the cosmopolitan culture of Vienna or Magyar ways in Budapest. Despite escalating anti-Semitism, the celebrated composer Gustav Mahler, the budding writer Franz Kafka, and the pioneer of psycho-analysis Sigmund Freud flourished in Habsburg society. By 1900, Jews were prominent in cultural and economic affairs in many cities across the continent and discriminated against, even victimized, elsewhere.

Most Jews, however, were not so accomplished or prosperous as these cultural giants. Pogroms in Russia and economic persecution throughout Europe escalated Jewish migration to the United States and other countries. Amid this vast migration and continued persecution, a spirit of Jewish nationalism arose, as Jews began organizing resistance to pogroms and anti-Semitic politics, and intellectuals drew upon Jewish folklore and history to establish a national identity. In the 1880s, the Ukrainian physician Leon Pinsker, seeing the Jews' lack of national territory as fundamental to the persecution heaped on them, advocated the migration of Jews to Palestine—a goal known as **Zionism**. Strongly influenced by Pinsker, Theodor Herzl (1860–1904) called not simply for migration but for the creation of a Jewish nation-state. A Hungarian-born Jew, Herzl experienced anti-Semitism firsthand as a Viennese journalist and writer in Paris during the Dreyfus Affair. With the support of poorer eastern European Jews, he succeeded in calling the first International Zionist Congress in Basel, Switzerland (1897), which endorsed settlement in Palestine and helped gain financial backing from the Rothschild banking family. By 1914, some 85,000 Jews had resettled in Palestine.

Threats to Russian Empire

European domestic politics remained explosive and nowhere more so than in Russia, where anti-Semitism escalated and internal affairs were in disarray. Russia was almost the only European country without a constitutional government, and reform-minded Russian youth increasingly turned to revolutionary, even terrorist groups for solutions to political and social problems. Writers fueled an intense debate over Russia's future. Leo Tolstoy, author of the epic *War and Peace* (1869), opposed the revolutionaries' desire to overturn the social order, touting the cause of spiritual regeneration instead. In his novel *Anna Karenina* (1877), Tolstoy tells the story of an impassioned, adulterous love affair but also weaves in the spiritual quest of Levin, a landowner who, like Tolstoy himself, rejects modernization and idealizes the peasantry's stoic endurance. Radicals, however, sought to change Russia by violent action rather than by spiritual uplift, and in 1881, a group of them killed Tsar Alexander II in a bomb attack. His death failed to provoke the peasant uprising the terrorists expected because peasants thought the assassination of the "tsar liberator" was directed against them.

Alexander III (r. 1881–1894) rejected his father's legacy of liberal reform and unleashed a new wave of oppression against religious and ethnic minorities. He gave the police almost unchecked power. Intensified Russification further alienated oppressed nationalities such as the Poles; it also turned the once-loyal German middle and upper classes of the Baltic provinces against Russian rule, with serious long-term consequences. But the major victims were the five million Russian Jews, confined to the eighteenth-century Pale of Settlement (the name for the restricted territory in which they were permitted to live), against whom local officials instigated new pogroms. Distinctive language, dress, and isolation in ghettos made Jews easy targets in an age when the Russian government was enforcing cultural uniformity and national identity. Government officials also encouraged people to blame Jews for escalating taxes and living costs—though the true cause was the policy of raising taxes to force the peasantry to pay for industrialization and reform.

When Alexander III's son Nicholas II took the throne in 1894, the empire was trapped in the contradictions of European modernity. Taught as a child to hate Jews, Nicholas II (r. 1894–1917) stepped up the persecutions, and many high officials eagerly endorsed anti-Semitism to gain his favor. Pogroms became a regular feature of the Easter holiday in Russia, and Nicholas increasingly limited where Jews could live and how they could earn a living. Simultaneously, Russians settled much of Siberia, and the government sponsored industrialization, especially the growth of transport and manufacturing. Industrialization, however, produced onerous taxes and urban unrest as Marxist and union activists incited workers to demand better conditions. In 1903, skilled workers led strikes in Baku, where Armenians and Tatars united in a demonstration that showed how urbanization and Russification could actually facilitate political action that challenged the auto-cratic regime.

The situation exploded into revolution during the Russo-Japanese War. In January 1905, a crowd gathered outside the tsar's Winter Palace in St. Petersburg to try to make Nicholas aware of brutal working conditions. Instead of allowing the demonstration to pass, troops guarding the palace shot into the crowd, killing hundreds and wounding thousands. News of "Bloody Sunday" prompted turmoil across Russia, as workers struck over wages, hours, and factory conditions and demanded political representation in the government. They rejected the leadership of both Social Democrats and Social Revolutionaries and instead organized their own councils, called soviets. In June, sailors on the battleship *Potemkin* mutinied; in October, a massive railroad strike brought rail transportation to a halt and the Baltic states and Transcaucasia rebelled; and in November, uprisings broke out in Moscow. Professionals and the upper classes joined the assault on autocracy, demanding a constitutional monarchy and a representative legislature. They believed the reliance on censorship and the secret police that was characteristic of Romanov rule had relegated Russia to the ranks of the most backward states.

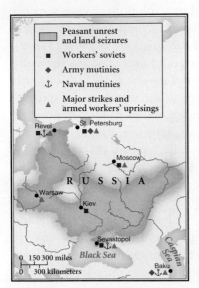

The Russian Revolution of 1905

Amid continuing violence, the tsar created a representative body—the Duma. Although very few could vote for representatives to the Duma, its mere existence, coupled with the right of public political debate, liberalized government and allowed people to present their grievances to a responsive body. Political parties took shape, and the Revolution of 1905 drew to an end. But people soon wondered whether anything had really changed. From 1907 to 1917, the Duma convened, but twice when the tsar disliked its recommendations, he sent the delegates home. Prime Minister Pyotr Stolypin (1863–1911), a successful administrator and landowner, was determined to eliminate one source of discontent by ending the mir system of communal farming, canceling the peasants' burden of redemption payments, and making loans available to peasants for the purchase of land. Although these reforms did not eradicate rural poverty, they did allow people to move to the cities in search of jobs, and they created a larger group of independent peasants. The industrial proletariat began another round of strikes, culminating in a general strike in St. Petersburg in 1914. Despite the creation of the Duma and other reforms, the imperial government and the conservative nobility had no solution to the social turmoil and felt little inclination to share power.

Their ineffectual responses to crises since the start of the century would foster an even greater revolution in 1917.

■ **REVIEW:** *What were the major changes in political life between 1880 and 1914?*

Roads to World War I

Unsettled internal politics kept nerves on edge, while imperial rivalries intensified antagonisms among European states. After centuries of global expansion, imperial adventure soured for Britain and France as the twentieth century opened, and being an imperial power proved difficult for such newcomers as Italy and Germany. As a result of imperial competition, one British economist wrote in 1902, "Diplomatic strains are of almost monthly occurrence between the Powers." Western nationalism swelled. In the spring of 1914, U.S. president Woodrow Wilson sent his trusted adviser Colonel Edward House abroad to assess the tensions among the European powers. "It is militarism run stark mad," House reported. Government spending on what people called the "arms race" stimulated European economies, but arms were not stockpiled only for economic growth. Europe was jittery, as it waged a growing number of wars to keep colonial peoples in line. In German East Africa, for example, colonial forces countered native resistance in 1905 with a scorched-earth policy, which eventually killed more than 100,000 Africans (see Map 19.2). The French closed the University of Hanoi, executed Indochinese intellectuals, and deported thousands of suspected nationalists to maintain a tenuous grip on Indochina (see Map 19.3). A French general stationed there noted "the growing hatred that our subjects show toward us more and more." By 1914, the air was even more charged, with militant nationalism in the Balkan states and conflicts in domestic politics taking Europeans down the road toward mass destruction.

Competing Alliances and Clashing Ambitions

As the twentieth century opened, an alliance system first established by Bismarck to ensure the peaceful consolidation of the new German Empire and to maintain European stability was changing rapidly. Anxious about the Balkans and Russian leadership of the Slavs, Austria-Hungary had entered a defensive alliance with Germany in 1879. The **Dual Alliance**, as it was called, offered protection against Russia, which appeared to threaten Hungarian control of its Slavic peasantry. In 1882, Italy joined this partnership (henceforth called the Triple Alliance), largely because of Italy's imperial rivalries with France, but Bismarck also signed the Reinsurance Treaty (1887) with Russia to stifle Habsburg illusions about having a free hand against rivals for Slavic loyalty. Bismarck intended these alliances to show that Germany was now a "satisfied" nation and one that hoped to prevent further destabilizing wars.

Bismarck's delicate alliance system started unraveling, however, when a blustering but deeply insecure young kaiser, William II, mounted the German throne in 1888. Advisers flattered the twenty-nine year old into thinking that his own personal talent made Bismarck a hindrance, even a rival. William II (r. 1888–1918) dismissed Bismarck in 1890 and, because he ardently supported German nationalism and thus the alliance with a supposedly kindred Austria-Hungary, he let the alliance with Russia lapse, driving the Russians to ally with the French. Next, Germany under William II became "dissatisfied" with its international status and inflamed rather than calmed the diplomatic atmosphere. William believed in British hostility toward France and used the opportunity presented by the defeat of France's ally Russia in the Russo-Japanese War to contest French claims in Morocco, brashly landing his own ship in Morocco in 1905 to challenge personally French predominance. To resolve what became known as the First Moroccan Crisis, an international conference met in Spain in 1906. Instead of awarding Germany new territory, the powers supported French rule. The French and British military, faced with German aggression in Morocco, drew closer together. When the French finally took over Morocco in 1911, Germany triggered the Second Moroccan Crisis by sending a gunboat to the port of Agadir and demanding concessions from the French (see Map 19.2). This time no power—not even Austria-Hungary—backed the German move.

William's brazen diplomatic demands were predicated on imperial rivalry between France and Britain, which seemed to preclude an alliance between these traditional enemies. Constant rivals in Africa, Britain and France had edged to the brink of war in 1898 at Fashoda in the Sudan (see Map 19.2). The French government, however, backed away, and both nations were frightened into getting along for mutual self-interest. To prevent another Fashoda, they entered into secret agreements, the first of which (1904) guaranteed British claims in Egypt and French claims in Morocco. This agreement marked the beginning of the British-French alliance called the **Entente Cordiale**. After the Moroccan incident, the British and French made binding military provisions for the deployment of their forces in case of war, strengthening the Entente Cordiale. Thus two opposing alliance systems were now in place.

Facing setbacks on the world stage, Germany refocused on its role in continental Europe. German statesmen began envisioning the creation of a **Mitteleuropa** that included central Europe, the Balkans, and Turkey under their sway. Russia, however, saw itself as the protector of Slavs in the region and wanted to replace the Ottomans as the dominant Balkan power, especially after Japan had crushed its hopes for expansion to the east. In 1877–1878, in the Russo-Turkish War, Russia had helped Bulgaria, Bosnia-Herzegovina, Serbia, and Montenegro in their revolts against the declining Ottoman Empire. Although Bulgarian independence was rolled back by the great powers, Serbia and Montenegro became fully independent. Austria's swift annexation of Bosnia-Herzegovina during the Young Turk revolt in 1908 enraged not only the Russians but the Serbs as well because these southern Slavs wanted Bosnia as part of an enlarged Serbia. The Balkans thus whetted many appetites, and the region was ripe for war (Map 19.4).

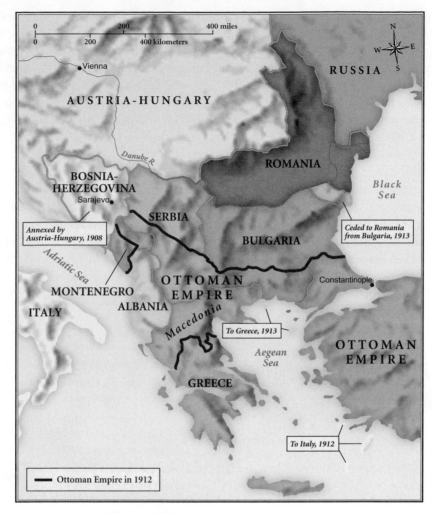

■ **MAP 19.4 The Balkans, 1908–1914**

Balkan peoples—mixed in religion, ethnicity, and political views—were successful in developing and asserting their desire for independence, especially in the First Balkan War, which claimed territory from the Ottoman Empire. Their increased autonomy sparked rivalries among them and continued to attract attention from the great powers. Three empires in particular—the Russian, Ottoman, and Austro-Hungarian—simultaneously sought greater influence for themselves in the region, which became a powder keg of competing ambitions.

Even without the greedy eyes cast on the Balkans by outside powers, the situation would have been extremely complex given the tensions created by the modern lure of ethnic independence. By the early twentieth century, the Balkan states, composed of several ethnicities as well as Orthodox Christians, Roman Catholics, and Muslims, sought more Ottoman and Habsburg territory that included their own ethnic group—a complicated desire given the mixed ethnicities of every region. In the First Balkan War, in 1912, Serbia, Bulgaria, Greece, and Montenegro joined forces to gain Macedonia and Albania from the Ottomans. The victors divided up their booty but soon turned against one another. Serbia, Greece, and Montenegro contested Bulgarian gains in the Second Balkan War in 1913. Much to Austrian dismay, these allies won a quick victory, though Austria-Hungary blocked Serbia from annexing parts of Albania. Grievances between the Serbs and the Habsburgs, who feared that any disturbance in the Balkan balance of power would encourage ethnic rebellion at home, now seemed irreconcilable, and angry Serbs looked to Russia for help.

The Race to Arms

In the nineteenth century, global rivalries and aspirations for national greatness made constant readiness for war seem increasingly necessary. On the seas and in foreign lands, the colonial powers battled to establish control, and they developed railroad, telegraph, and telephone networks everywhere to move troops as well as commerce. Governments began to conscript ordinary citizens for periods of two to

IMPORTANT DATES

1870s–1914	Vast emigration from Europe continues; age of new imperialism	1903	Emmeline Pankhurst founds the Women's Social and Political Union to fight for woman suffrage in Great Britain
1882	Triple Alliance formed among Germany, Austria-Hungary, and Italy	1904–1905	Japan defeats Russia in the Russo-Japanese War
1882–1884	Bismarck sponsors social welfare legislation in Germany	1905	Revolution erupts in Russia; violence forces Nicholas II to establish an elected body, the Duma; Albert Einstein publishes his special theory of relativity
1884	Reform Act doubles the size of the male electorate in Britain		
1884–1885	European nations carve up Africa at the Berlin conference	1906	Women receive the vote in Finland
1889	Socialists meet in Paris and establish the Second International	1907	Pablo Picasso launches cubism
1894–1899	Dreyfus Affair lays bare anti-Semitism in France	1908	Young Turks revolt against rule by the sultan in the Ottoman Empire
1899–1902	Boer War fought between Dutch descendants and the British in South African states	1911–1912	Revolutionaries overthrow the Qing dynasty and declare China a republic
1900	Sigmund Freud publishes *The Interpretation of Dreams*	1912–1913	First and Second Balkan Wars
1901	Irish National Theater established by Maud Gonne and William Butler Yeats		

six years into large standing armies, in contrast to smaller eighteenth-century forces that had served the more limited military goals of the time. By 1914, escalating tensions in Europe boosted the annual intake of conscripts: Germany, France, and Russia called up 250,000 or more troops each year; Austria-Hungary and Italy, about 100,000. Per capita expenditures on the military rose in all the major powers between 1890 and 1914; the proportion of national budgets devoted to defense in 1910 was lowest in Austria-Hungary at 10 percent and highest in Germany at 45 percent.

The modernization of weaponry also transformed warfare. Swedish arms manufacturer Alfred Nobel (1833–1896) patented dynamite and developed a kind of gunpowder that improved the accuracy of guns and produced a less cloudy battlefield environment by reducing smoke from the process of firing. The industrial revolution in chemicals affected long-range artillery, which by 1914 could fire on targets as far as six miles away. Military leaders devised strategies to protect their armies from overwhelming firepower. In the Russo-Japanese War, Chinese defenders dug trenches and strung barbed wire in an attempt to hold on to Port Arthur. In that conflict and in the Boer War, new weapons were used, including howitzers, Mauser rifles, and Hotchkiss machine guns. Munitions factories across Europe manufactured ever-growing quantities of these weapons.

Naval construction also played a major role in nationalist politics. In 1905, the English launched the H.M.S. *Dreadnought*, a warship with unprecedented firepower and the centerpiece of a program to update the British navy by constructing at least seven battleships per year. Germany followed British naval building step by step and made itself a force to be feared not just on land but also at sea. Grand Admiral Alfred von Tirpitz (1849–1930) encouraged the insecure William II to see the navy as the essential ingredient needed to make Germany a world power and oversaw an immense buildup of the fleet. Tirpitz admired the American naval theorist Alfred Thayer Mahan (1840–1914) and planned to build bases as far away as the Pacific, following Mahan's conclusion that command of the seas had historically been the key factor in determining international power. The German drive to build battleships further motivated Britain to ally with France in the Entente Cordiale. Britain raised its naval spending from $50 million per year in the 1870s to $130 million in 1900; Germany, from $8.75 million to $37.5 million; France, from $37 million to $62.5 million. The Germans announced the fleet buildup as "a peaceful policy," but like the British buildup, it led only to a hostile international climate and intense competition in weapons manufacture.

Military policy was made with the use of public relations campaigns and an eye on internal politics. When critics of the arms race suggested a temporary "naval holiday" to stop British and German shipbuilding, British officials opposed the moratorium by warning that it "would throw innumerable men on the pavement." Colonial leagues and nationalist groups lobbied for military spending, while enthusiasts in government publicized large navies as beneficial to trade and industry. To enlarge the German fleet, Tirpitz made sure the German press connected the

| | Triple Alliance, 1882–1915 |
| | Triple Entente, 1907–1917 |

■ MAPPING THE WEST Europe at the Outbreak of World War I, August 1914

All the powers expected a great, swift victory when war broke out. Many were convinced that war would bring them many advantages against their rivals for trade and empire, including the chance to expand their territories. But if the European powers appeared well prepared and invincible at the start of the war, relatively few would survive the conflict intact.

buildup to the cause of national power and pride. The press accused Social Democrats, who wanted an equitable tax system more proportionate to wealth, of being unpatriotic. The Conservative Party in Great Britain, eager for more battleships, made popular the slogan "We want eight and we won't wait." One military leader captured the enthusiasm for war at the time, even among the public at large. When asked in 1912 about his predictions for war and peace, he responded enthusiastically, "We shall have war. I will make it. I will win it." Everything was in place for war—alliances, stocks of armaments and war plans, mass armies, and a boiling cauldron of animosities and tensions—in the summer of 1914.

■ **REVIEW:** *What major factors made Europe prone to war by 1914?*

Conclusion

By 1914, Europe as a whole was ripe for a major conflagration and had feverishly prepared for it. Imperialism and the arms race had stimulated militant nationalism and brought many Europeans to favor war over peace. The rapid pace of change had helped blaze the path to war. Facing continuing violence in politics, incomprehensibility in the arts, and problems in the social order, Europeans had come to believe that war would set events back on course and save them from the perils of modernity. Disturbances in private life and challenges to tradition posed by new technologies and modern urban life would disappear, it was believed, in the crucible of war. "Like men longing for a thunderstorm to relieve them of the summer's sultriness," wrote one Austrian official, "so the generation of 1914 believed in the relief that war might bring." Such a possibility caused many Europeans to rejoice as war approached in 1914. But instead of bringing the refreshment of summer rain, the war that erupted in the summer of 1914 opened an era of political turmoil, widespread suffering, massive human slaughter, and even greater doses of modernity.

■ **MAKING CONNECTIONS**

1. *How did changes in society at the beginning of the twentieth century affect the development of mass politics?*

2. *How did cultural changes affect the world of politics between 1880–1914?*

■ **FOR FURTHER EXPLORATION**

For further reading and online research ideas, see the Suggested References on page SR-10 at the back of the book.

For practice quizzes, a customized study plan, and other study tools, see the ONLINE STUDY GUIDE at **bedfordstmartins.com/huntconcise**.

For primary-source material from this period, see Chapter 19 in *Sources of THE MAKING OF THE WEST: A CONCISE HISTORY*, Second Edition.

War, Revolution, and Reconstruction

1914–1929

JULES AMAR FOUND HIS TRUE VOCATION in World War I. A French expert on mak-ing industrial work more efficient, Amar switched focus after 1914 as hundreds of thousands of men returned from the battlefront missing body parts. Plastic sur-gery developed rapidly, as did the construction of masks and other devices to hide deformities. Amar, who designed artificial limbs and appendages in these trau-matic years, sought to devise prostheses that would allow the wounded soldier to return to normal life by "mak[ing] up for a function lost, or greatly reduced." So he designed arms that featured hooks, magnets, and other mechanisms with which the veteran could hold a cigarette, play a violin, and, most important, work with tools such as typewriters. Mangled by the weapons of modern technological war-fare, the survivors of World War I would be made whole, it was thought, by tech-nology such as Amar's.

Amar dealt with the human tragedy of the "Great War," so named by con-temporaries because of its staggering human toll—forty million wounded or killed in battle. The Great War was also what historians call a **total war**, meaning one built on full mobilization of soldiers, civilians, and the technological capacities of the most highly industrialized nations. The Great War did not settle problems or

■ **Grieving Parents**
Before World War I, the German artist Käthe Kollwitz gained her artistic reputation with wood-cuts of handloom weavers whose livelihoods were threatened by industrialization. From 1914 on, she depicted the suffering and death that swirled around her and never with more sober force than in these two monuments to her son Peter, who had died on the western front in the first months of battle. Today one can still travel to his burial place in Vladslo, Belgium, to see this father and mother mourning their loss, like millions across Europe in those heartbreaking days.
(© The John Parker Picture Library. © 2007 Artists Rights Society [ARS], NY/VG Bild-Kunst, Bonn.)

restore social order as the European powers hoped it would. Instead, the war produced political cataclysm, overturning the Russian, German, Ottoman, and Austro-Hungarian empires. The crushing burden of war on the European powers accelerated the rise of the United States, while service in the war intensified the demands of colonized peoples for autonomy.

For all the vast changes that the Great War ushered in, it also hastened transformations under way before it started. Nineteenth-century optimism, already on the decline, gave way to postwar cynicism. Many Westerners turned their backs on politics and attacked life with frenzied gaiety in the Roaring Twenties, snapping up new consumer goods, drinking in entertainment provided by films and radio, and enjoying personal freedoms that Victorianism had forbidden. Others found reason for hope in the new political systems the war made possible: Soviet communism and Italian fascism. Modern communication technologies such as radio gave politicians the means to promote a mass politics that ironically was often antidemocratic, militaristic, and eventually dictatorial.

Seen as a solution to the conflicts of modernity, a war that was long anticipated and even welcomed in some quarters destabilized Europe and the rest of the world far into the next decades. From statesmen to ordinary citizens, many Europeans like Amar would devote their peacetime efforts to making war-ravaged society function normally, while others saw that task as utterly futile, given the globally transformative force of the Great War.

The Great War, 1914–1918

June 28, 1914, began as an ordinary day for Austria's Archduke Francis Ferdinand and his wife, Sophie, as they ended a state visit to Sarajevo in Bosnia. Wearing full military regalia, the archduke was riding in a motorcade to bid farewell to various officials when a group of young Serb nationalists threw bombs in an unsuccessful assassination attempt. The full danger did not register, and after a stop the archduke and his wife set out again. In the crowd was another Serbian nationalist, Gavrilo Princip, who for several weeks had traveled clandestinely to reach this destination, dreaming of reuniting his homeland of Bosnia-Herzegovina with Serbia and smuggling weapons with him to accomplish his end. The unprotected and unsuspecting couple became Princip's victims, as he shot both dead. Within weeks, the assassination led to all-out war, for the ground had been prepared with long-standing alliances, the development of strategies for war, and the buildup of military technologies such as heavy artillery, machine guns, and the airplane. Seeing precedents in Prussia's rapid victories in the 1860s and 1870 and the swift blows that Japan dealt Russia in 1904–1905, most people felt the conflict would be short and decisive. But the unforeseen happened: the war lasted for more than four years, and it was a total war, mobilizing entire societies and producing the unprecedented horror that made it "great."

■ **Archduke Francis Ferdinand
and His Wife in Sarajevo,
June 1914**

*Archduke Francis Ferdinand, heir to the
Austro-Hungarian monarchy, was a thorn
in the side of many politicians because he
did not want to favor Hungarian interests
over other ethnic interests in his kingdom.
His own family life was also unusual for
royalty in those days: his wife, Sophie,
and he had married for love and did not
like to be apart. They were traveling
together to Bosnia in 1914. The double
assassination was the immediate prelude
to the outbreak of World War I.*
(Mary Evans Picture Library.)

War Erupts

Some in the Habsburg government saw the assassination as an opportunity to
defeat Serbia once and for all. Evidence showed that Princip had received arms
and information from Serbian officials who directed a terrorist organization from
within the government. German statesmen and military leaders agreed, urging the
Austrians to be unyielding and reiterating promises of support in case of war. The
Austrians sent an ultimatum to the Serbian government, demanding public disavowals
of terrorism, suppression of terrorist groups, and the participation of Austrian
officials in an investigation of the crime. The ultimatum was severe. "You are
setting Europe ablaze," the Russian foreign minister remarked of the humiliating
demands made upon a sovereign state. Yet the Serbs were conciliatory, accepting
all the terms except one—the presence of Austrian officials in the investigation.
Kaiser William was pleased: "A great moral success for Vienna! All reason for war
is gone." His relief proved unfounded. Confident of German backing, Austria-
Hungary used Serbia's resistance to that one demand as the pretext for declaring
war against it on July 28.

Complex and ineffectual maneuvering now consumed statesmen, some of
whom tried very hard to avoid war. The tsar and the kaiser sent pleading letters
to one another not to start a European war. The British foreign secretary proposed
an all-European conference, but to no avail. Germany displayed firm support for
Austria in hopes of convincing the French and British to shy away from the war.
The failure of either France or Britain to fight, German officials believed, would
keep Russia from mobilizing. At the same time, German military leaders had
become fixed on fighting a short, preemptive war that would provide territorial

gains leading toward the goal of a Mitteleuropa. Furthermore, martial law would justify the arrest of the leadership of the German Social Democratic Party, which posed a threat to conservative rule.

The European press caught the war fever of the expansionist, imperialist, and other pro-war organizations, even as many governments were torn over what to do. Likewise, military leaders, especially in Germany and Austria-Hungary, promoted mobilization rather than diplomacy in the last days of July. The Austrians declared war and then ordered mobilization on July 31, believing Russia would not dare intervene. But Nicholas II ordered the Russian army to mobilize in defense of Russia's Slavic allies, the Serbs. Encouraging the Austrians to attack Serbia, the German general staff mobilized on August 1.

German strategy was based on the Schlieffen Plan, named after its author, Alfred von Schlieffen, a former chief of the general staff. The plan outlined a way to combat antagonists on two fronts by concentrating on one foe at a time. First would come a rapid and concentrated German blow to the west against Russia's ally France, which would lead to France's defeat in six weeks; accompanying that strike would be a light holding action to the east. With France beaten, German armies in the west would then be deployed against Russia, which, German war planners believed, would be slow to mobilize. The attack on France was to proceed through Belgium, whose neutrality was guaranteed by the European powers. Events did not occur as the Germans hoped. The Belgian government rejected an ultimatum to allow the uncontested passage of the German army through the country, and Germany's subsequent violation of Belgium's neutrality brought Britain into the war on the side of Russia and France, which already was mobilizing in support of its ally Russia.

The Conflict Widens

World War I pitted two sets of opponents formed roughly out of the alliances developed during the previous fifty years. On one side stood the Central Powers (Austria-Hungary and Germany), which had evolved from Bismarck's Triple Alliance. On the other side stood the Allies (France, Great Britain, and Russia), which had emerged as a bloc from the Entente Cordiale between France and Great Britain and the 1890s treaties between France and Russia. In 1915, Italy, originally part of the Triple Alliance, joined the Allies in hopes of postwar gain. The two sides expanded globally almost from the start: in late August 1914, Japan, eager to extend its empire into China, went over to the Allies; in the fall the Ottoman Empire united with the Central Powers against its traditional enemy, Russia (see Map 20.1).

The antagonists fought with the same ferocious hunger for power, prestige, and prosperity that had inspired imperialism. Germany aspired to a far-flung empire to be gained by annexing Russian territory and incorporating parts of

Belgium, France, and Luxembourg. Some German leaders wanted to annex Austria-Hungary as well. Austria-Hungary hoped to retain its great-power status in the face of competing nationalisms within its borders. Among the Allies, Russia wanted to reassert its status as a great power and as the protector of the Slavs by adding a reunified Poland to the Russian Empire and by taking formal leadership of other Slavic peoples. The French, too, craved territory, especially the return of resource-rich Alsace and Lorraine, taken after the Franco-Prussian War. The British sought to cement their hold on Egypt and the Suez Canal and to secure the rest of the British world empire. By the Treaty of London (1915), France and Britain promised Italy territory in Africa, Asia Minor, the Balkans, and elsewhere in return for joining the Allies.

The colonies provided massive assistance and were also a battleground. Some one million Africans, another one million Indians, and more than a million members of the British commonwealth countries served on the battlefronts, while the imperial powers also conscripted still uncounted numbers of colonists as forced laborers both at home and on the battlefront. Fighting occurred across north and sub-Saharan Africa, with colonial troops playing a major role. Reliant on Arab, African, and Indian troops, the British waged successful war on Turkey and Germany, menacing Germany's longtime interests by taking Baghdad in 1917 and also taking Palestine, Syria, and Mesopotamia.

Unprecedented use of machinery also determined the course of war. In August 1914, machine guns and rifles, airplanes, battleships, submarines, and motorized transport—cars and railroads—were at the armies' disposal. New technologies like chlorine gas, tanks, and bombs developed between 1914 and 1918. Countries differed, however, in their experience with and quantities of weapons of war, with the British having full knowledge of the destructive capacity of these weapons because of their colonial wars and the Germans far more advanced in strategy and weaponry than either the Russians or the Austrians. The war itself became a lethal testing ground, as both new and old weapons were used, often ineffectively. Officers on both sides believed in a "cult of the offensive": they were sure that spirited attacks and high troop morale would be decisive. Despite the availability of the new, more powerful war technology, an old-fashioned vision of warfare made many officers unwilling to abandon sabers, lances, bayonets, and cavalry charges. In the face of massive firepower, the "cult of the offensive" would cost millions of lives.

Battlefronts

The first months of the war crushed hope of quick victory. All the major armies mobilized rapidly. Guided by the Schlieffen Plan, the Germans quickly reached Luxembourg and Belgium and expected unchallenged passage through them and into France. The Plan disintegrated when the Belgians unexpectedly resisted, slowing the German advance and allowing British and French troops to reach the northern front after the French had mistakenly fallen for German diversionary moves on the eastern border. In September, British and French armies engaged the Germans along the Marne River in France. Neither side could defeat the other, and the number of casualties was shocking: in the first three months of war, more than 1.5 million men fell on the western front alone. Firepower turned what was supposed to be an offensive war of movement into a stationary, defensive impasse along a line stretching from the North Sea through Belgium and northern France to Switzerland. Deep within parallel trenches dug along this western front, soldiers lived a nightmarish existence (Map 20.1).

On the eastern front, the "Russian steam-roller"—so named because of the number of men mobilized, some twelve million in all—drove far more quickly than expected into East Prussia. The Russians believed that no army could withstand their massive numbers, no matter how ill equipped and poorly trained Russian forces were. The Germans, however, crushed the tsar's army in East Prussia and turned south to Galicia. Victory boosted German morale and made heroes of military leaders Paul von Hindenburg (1847–1934) and Erich Ludendorff (1865–1937). Despite heartening victories, by year's end German triumphs in the east had failed to knock out the Russians and also had undermined the Schlieffen Plan, which called for only a light holding action in the east until the western front had been won.

War at sea proved equally indecisive. Confident in Britain's superior naval power, the Allies blockaded ports to prevent supplies from reaching Germany and Austria-Hungary. William II and his advisers planned a massive submarine, or U-boat (*Unterseeboot*, "underwater boat"), campaign against Allied and neutral shipping around Britain and France. In May 1915, German submarines sank the British passenger ship *Lusitania* and killed 1,198 people, including 124 Americans. Despite U.S. outrage, Woodrow Wilson (1856–1924; president 1913–1921) maintained a policy of U.S. neutrality; Germany, unwilling to provoke Wilson further, called off unrestricted submarine warfare. In May 1916, the navies of Germany and Britain finally clashed in the North Sea at the inconclusive battle of Jutland, which demonstrated that the German fleet could not master British seapower (see Map 20.1).

Ideas of a negotiated peace were discarded: "No peace before England is defeated and destroyed," the kaiser railed against his cousin King George V. "Only amidst the ruins of London will I forgive Georgy." French leadership called for a "war to the death." General staffs continued to prepare fierce attacks several times a year. Indecisive campaigns opened with heavy artillery pounding enemy trenches and gun emplacements. Troops then responded to the order to go "over the top," scrambling out of their trenches, usually to be mowed down by machine-gun fire from defenders secure in their own trenches. On the western front, throughout 1915 the French assaulted the enemy in the north to drive the Germans from industrial regions, but they accomplished little, and casualties of

■ MAP 20.1 The Fronts of World War I, 1914–1918

Fighting on all fronts destroyed portions of Europe's hard-won industrial and agricultural capacity. Because the western front remained relatively stationary, the devastation of land and resources in northern and eastern France was especially intense. Men engaged in trench warfare developed an intense camaraderie based on their mutual suffering and deprivation.

100,000 and more during a single campaign became commonplace. On the eastern front, Russian armies captured parts of Galicia in the spring of 1915 and lumbered toward Hungary. The Central Powers struck back in Poland later that year, bringing the front closer to Petrograd (formerly St. Petersburg), the Russian capital.

The next year was even more disastrous. To cripple French morale, the Germans launched massive assaults on the fortress at Verdun, firing as many as a million shells in a single day. Combined French and German losses totaled close to a million men. Nonetheless, the French held. Hoping to relieve their allies, the British unleashed an artillery pounding of German trenches in the Somme River region in June 1916. In several months of battle at the Somme, 1.25 million men were killed or wounded, but the final result was stalemate. By the end of 1916, the French had absorbed more than 3.5 million casualties. To help the Allies engaged at Verdun and the Somme, the Russians struck again, driving once more into the Carpathians, recouping territory, and menacing the Habsburg Empire. Only the German army stopped the Russian advance.

Had military leaders thoroughly dominated the scene, historians judge, all armies would have been demolished in nonstop offensives by the end of 1915. Yet ordinary soldiers in this war were not automatons in the face of what seemed to them suicidal orders. For long periods of time, some battalions experienced hardly any casualties. These low rates stemmed from agreements among troops to avoid battles. Enemies facing each other across the "no man's land" separating the trenches frequently ate their meals in peace even though the trenches were within hand grenade reach. Throughout the war, soldiers on opposing sides fraternized. During pauses in the fighting, they played an occasional game of soccer, shouted to each other across the battlefield, exchanged mementos, and made gestures of agreement not to fight. One British veteran of the trenches explained to a new recruit that the Germans "don't want to fight any more than we do, so there's a kind of understanding between us. Don't fire at us and we'll not fire at you." Burying enemy dead in common graves with their own fallen comrades, many ordinary soldiers came to feel more warmly toward enemies who shared the trench experience than toward uncomprehending civilians back home.

Newly forged bonds of male camaraderie alleviated some of the misery of trench life and aided survival. The danger of death and the deprivations of front-line experience weakened traditional class distinctions. Some upper-class officers and working-class draftees became friends in that "wholly masculine way of life uncomplicated by women," as one soldier put it. Soldiers picked lice from one another's bodies and clothes, revered section leaders who tended their blistered feet, and came to love one another, sometimes even passionately. Positive memories of this front-line sense of community survived the war and influenced postwar politics.

■ The Toll of Trench Warfare

On both sides, the war took an enormous toll in male lives, leaving politicians and citizens alike concerned about society's future. Depictions of bodies shattered by heavy firepower, however, rarely reached the home front, so the illusions that the war was about individual prowess and that individual soldiers had a fighting chance of survival remained intact. Troops from the colonies were often depicted as bringing an innate savagery to the battlefront, although these soldiers had even less chance of surviving because usually they were placed in the front lines.
(Left: Imperial War Museum, London; right: Robert Hunt Library.)

Troops of colonized soldiers from Asia and Africa had different experiences, especially because they were often put in the very front ranks where the risks were greatest. European observers noted that these soldiers suffered particularly from the rigors of a totally unfamiliar climate and strange food as well as from the ruin inflicted by Western war technology. Yet, like class divisions, racial barriers sometimes fell—for instance, whenever a European understood enough to alleviate the distress that cold inflicted. The perspectives of colonial troops changed, too: "What miserable crowned head was able to order such horrors?" wrote one corporal from West Africa. Colonial troops saw their "masters" completely undone and "uncivilized," for when fighting did break out, trenches became a veritable hell of shelling and sniping, flying body parts, rotting cadavers, and blinding gas. Some soldiers were reduced to hysteria or were shell-shocked by the violence of battle. Alienation and cynicism helped others to cope: "It might be me tomorrow," a young British soldier wrote his mother in 1916. "Who cares?" Soldiers who had gone to war to escape ordinary life in industrial society learned, as one German put it, "that in the modern war . . . the triumph of the machine over the individual is carried to its most extreme form." They took this hard-won knowledge into battle, pulling their comrades back when an offensive seemed lost or too costly.

The Home Front

World War I took place off the battlefield, too. Even before the war reached the stage of catastrophic impasse, it had become total. Total war meant the indispensable involvement of civilians in war industry, manufacturing the shells and machine guns, poisonous gases, bombs and airplanes, and eventually tanks that were the backbone of technological warfare. The increased production of coffins, canes, wheelchairs, and the artificial limbs devised by the likes of Jules Amar was also a wartime necessity. Civilians had to work overtime for, believe in, and sacrifice for victory. To keep the war machine operating smoothly, governments oversaw factories, transportation systems, and resources ranging from food to coal to textiles. Before the war, such tight government control would have outraged many liberals, but now it was accepted as a necessary condition for victory.

At first, political parties put aside their differences. Many socialists and working-class people who had criticized the military buildup announced their support for the war. For decades, socialist parties had preached that "the worker has no country" and that nationalism was mere ideology meant to keep workers disunited and subject to the will of their employers. In August 1914, however, the socialist rank and file, along with most of the party leaders, became as patriotic as the rest of society. Feminists divided over whether to maintain their traditional condemnation of militarism or to support the war. Although many feminists actively opposed the conflict, Emmeline Pankhurst and her daughter Christabel were among those who became militant nationalists, even changing the name of their suffrage paper to *Britannia*. Parties representing the middle classes shelved

■ War Propaganda, 1915

"Never Forget!" screams the headline of this propaganda poster depicting an assaulted woman in despair. Intended to incite sentiment against the Germans, the poster suggests what German passage through neutral Belgium came to be called—"the rape of Belgium." Propaganda offices for the Allies sent out reports of women attacked and children massacred as the German armies moved through Belgian territories. **For more help analyzing this image,** see the visual activity for this chapter in the ONLINE STUDY GUIDE at bedfordstmartins.com/huntconcise.
(Mary Evans Picture Library.)

their distrust of the socialists and working classes. In the name of victory, national leaders wanted to end political division of all kinds: "I no longer recognize [political] parties," William II declared on August 4, 1914. "I recognize only Germans." Ordinary people, even those who had been at the receiving end of discrimination, came to believe that a new day of unity was dawning. One rabbi proudly echoed the kaiser: "In the German fatherland there are no longer any Christians and Jews, any believers and disbelievers, there are only Germans."

Governments mobilized the home front with varying degrees of success. All countries were caught without ready replacements for their heavy losses of weapons and military equipment and soon also felt the shortage of food and labor. War ministries set up boards to allocate labor on the home front and the battlefront and give industrialists financial incentives to encourage productivity. In several countries emergency measures allowed the drafting of both men and women for military or industrial service, further blurring distinctions between military and civilian life. The Russian bureaucracy, however, only cooperated half-heartedly with industrialists and other groups that could aid the war effort. Desperate for factory workers, the Germans forced Belgian citizens to move to Germany, housing them in prison camps. In rural Russia, Austria-Hungary, Bulgaria, and Serbia, youths, women, and old men struggled to sustain farms without government help.

Governments throughout Europe passed sedition laws that made it a crime to criticize official policies. To ensure civilian acceptance of longer working hours and shortages of consumer goods, governments created propaganda agencies to tout the war as a patriotic mission to resist villainous enemies. British propagandists fabricated atrocities that the German "Huns" supposedly committed against Belgians, and German propaganda warned that French African troops would rape German women if Germany was defeated. In Russia, Nicholas II changed the German-sounding name of St. Petersburg to the Russian Petrograd in 1914.

Playing on fears and arousing hatred, propaganda rendered a compromise peace unlikely. Nonetheless, some individuals sought to shatter the nationalist consensus supporting the war. In 1915, activists in the international women's movement met in The Hague, site of late-nineteenth-century peace conferences, in their own effort to end the war. "We can no longer endure . . . brute force as the only solution of international disputes," declared Dutch physician Aletta Jacobs. Despite their lack of success, many spent the remainder of the war urging statesmen to work out a peace settlement. In Austria-Hungary, nationalist groups agitating for ethnic self-determination hampered the empire's war effort. The Czechs undertook a vigorous anti-Habsburg campaign at home, while exiled politicians in Paris established the Czechoslovak National Council to lobby Western governments for recognition of Czech rights. In the Balkans, Croats, Slovenes, and Serbs formed a committee to plan a South Slav state carved from Habsburg possessions and other Balkan territory. The Allies encouraged such independence movements as part of their strategy to defeat the Habsburgs.

■ A Woman Munitions Worker, England (1917)

*Many women had to work out of economic necessity during the war, and the military effort
needed them in manufacturing jobs. These jobs paid salaries far beyond traditional women's
jobs, which often brought accusations that extra money was making women frivolous and that
their cravings were needlessly sending men to their deaths. Others applauded women's energy,
patriotism, and sacrifice. Praise turned to dismay, however, when the armies began forming units
of women: "'She-Men,' who wished to be armed to the teeth," one aristocrat called them; and a
letter to a London newspaper in 1915 called them "ridiculous" and insulting to the dignity of the
nation. Gender issues remain highly debated even amid the crisis of war.*

(© Hulton-Deutsch Collection/Corbis.)

The war upset the social order as well as the political one. In the war's early
days, many women had lost their jobs when luxury shops, textile factories, and
other nonessential establishments closed. But governments and businesses soon
recognized the amount of labor it would take to wage technological war. As more
and more men left for the trenches, women who had lost their jobs in nonessential businesses as well as many low-paid domestic workers took over higher-paying
jobs in formerly restricted munitions and metallurgical industries. In Warsaw, they
drove trucks, and in London, they worked as streetcar conductors. Some young
women nursed the wounded near the front lines.

Women's assumption of men's jobs looked to many like the reversal of traditional gender roles. From the start, a steady flood of wounded and weakened men
returned home to women who had adapted resourcefully and taken full charge.
Workingmen commonly protested that women, in the words of one metalworker,

were "sending men to the slaughter." Men feared that when the war was over women would remain in the workforce, robbing them of their breadwinner role. Many people, even some women, objected to women's loss of femininity. "The feminine in me decreased more and more, and I did not know whether to be sad or glad about this," wrote one Russian nurse about learning to wear rough male clothing near the battlefield. Others criticized young female munitions workers for squandering their pay on ribbons and jewelry and revived prewar gender concerns about "new" women.

Although many soldiers from different social backgrounds felt bonds of solidarity in the trenches, wartime conditions increasingly pitted civilians against one another or against the government. Workers toiled longer hours eating less, while many in the upper classes bought abundant food and fashionable clothing on the black market (outside the official system of rationing). Governments allowed many businesses high rates of profit, a step that resulted in a surge in the cost of living and thus contributed to social strife. Shortages of staples like bread, sugar, and meat grew worse, while Germans called the brutal winter of 1916–1917 the "turnip winter" because turnips were often the only available food. A German roof workers' association pleaded for relief: "We can no longer go on. Our children are starving." Dredging up prewar hatred, some explained deprivation as the work of the Jews. Civilians in occupied areas and in the colonies suffered the most oppressive working conditions. The French forcibly transported some 100,000 Vietnamese to work in France for the war effort. Africans also faced grueling forced labor along with skyrocketing taxes and prices. All such actions further politicized ordinary people whether in the colonies or at home in Europe.

■ **REVIEW:** *What factors contributed to making World War I a total war?*

Protest, Revolution, and War's End: 1917–1918

By 1917, discontent on the home front started shaping the course of the war. Neither patriotic slogans before the war nor propaganda during it had prepared people for wartime suffering. Cities across Europe experienced civilian revolt; soldiers mutinied, and nationalist struggles continued to plague Britain and Austria-Hungary. Soon revolution was sweeping Europe, toppling the Russian dynasty for good and threatening not just war against external forces but civil war at home.

War Protest

On February 1, 1917, the German government, hard-pressed by public clamor over mounting casualties and by the military's growing control over decision making, resumed unrestricted submarine warfare. The military made the irresistible promise to end the war in six months by cutting off imported food and military supplies to Britain and thus forcing the island nation to surrender before the United States could come to its rescue. The British responded by mining harbors and the seas and by developing the convoy system of shipping, in which a hundred or more warships and freighters traveling the seas together could drive off the submarines. The Germans' submarine gamble failed to defeat the British. Moreover, unrestricted submarine warfare brought the United States into the war in April 1917, after German U-boats had sunk several American ships.

Political opposition increased in Europe, and deteriorating living conditions sparked outright revolt by civilians. "We are living on a volcano," warned an Italian politician in the spring of 1917. High prices and food shortages plagued everyday life. Food shortages in the cities of Italy, Russia, Germany, and Austria provoked riots by women who were unable to feed their families. As inflation mounted, tenants conducted rent strikes, factory hands and white-collar workers alike walked off the job, and female workers protested the skyrocketing cost of living and their fatigue from overwork. Amid protest, the new emperor of Austria-Hungary secretly asked the Allies for a negotiated peace to avoid a total collapse of his empire. In the summer of 1917, the German Reichstag made peace overtures. Woodrow Wilson further weakened civilian resolve in Germany and Austria-Hungary in January 1918 by issuing his Fourteen Points, a blueprint for a new international order that held out the promise of a nonvindictive peace settlement to war-weary citizens of the Central Powers. The Allies, too, faced dissent. On Easter Monday, 1916, a group of Irish nationalists attacked government buildings in Dublin in a poorly coordinated effort to wrest Irish independence from Britain. The rebels, a band of between one and two thousand, declared an independent Irish Republic and constituted themselves as the Irish Republican Army or IRA. They held out for some six days against government forces, which pounded away at the city of Dublin and the rebels in it. When the Easter Rebellion was over, the British, who could not tolerate sedition amidst the mounting problems of war, dealt harshly with the participants, executing fifteen and incarcerating many more. In the spring of 1917, French soldiers mutinied against further bloody and fruitless offensives. In Russia, wartime protest turned into outright revolution.

Revolution and Civil War in Russia

Of all the warring nations, Russia sustained the greatest number of casualties—7.5 million by 1917. Slaughter on the eastern front drove hundreds of thousands of peasants into the Russian interior, bringing hunger, homelessness, and disease. In March 1917, crowds of workingwomen swarmed the streets of Petrograd demanding relief from harsh conditions, and soon factory workers and other civilians joined them. Russia's comparative economic underdevelopment overwhelmed the government's ability to provide basic necessities on the home front. Instead of remaining loyal to the tsar, many in the army were embittered by the massive casualties caused by their inferior weapons and their leaders' foolhardy tactics.

Since the Revolution of 1905, the masses had become politicized, leading to rising protest against the government's incompetence and Nicholas II's stubborn resistance to change. Unlike other heads of state, Nicholas failed to unify the bureaucracy and his peoples in a concerted wartime effort. Grigori Rasputin, a combination of holy man and charlatan, held Nicholas and his wife, Alexandra, in his thrall by claiming to control the hemophilia of their son and heir. Rasputin's disastrous influence on state matters led prominent and educated leaders to withdraw their support. When riots erupted in March 1917, Nicholas abdicated, and the three-hundred-year-old Romanov dynasty came to an abrupt end.

Politicians from the old Duma formed a new ruling entity called the **Provisional Government**. At first, hopes were high that under the Provisional Government, as one revolutionary poet put it, "our false, filthy, boring, hideous life should become a just, pure, merry, and beautiful life." Composed essentially of moderate aristocrats and members of the middle class, the Provisional Government had to pursue the war successfully, manage internal affairs better, and set government on a firm constitutional footing to establish its credibility. However, it did not rule alone, for the Russian Revolution felt the tug of many different political forces. Spontaneously elected **soviets**—councils of workers and soldiers—competed with the government for political support. Born during the Revolution of 1905, the soviets campaigned to end the deference society usually paid the wealthy and officers, urged respect for workers and the poor, and temporarily gave an air of celebration and carnival to this political upheaval. The peasantry, another force competing for power, began to confiscate gentry estates and withhold produce from the market because of the lack of consumer goods for which to exchange food. Urban food shortages intensified.

In hopes of further destabilizing Russia, in April 1917 the Germans provided safe rail transportation for Lenin and other prominent Bolsheviks to return from exile through German territory. Lenin had devoted his entire existence to bringing about socialism through the force of his small band of Bolsheviks, and as a political exile he had no parliamentary experience. Upon his return to Petrograd, Lenin issued the April Theses, a radical document that called for Russia to withdraw from the war, for the soviets to seize power on behalf of workers and poor peasants, and for all private land to be nationalized. The Bolsheviks aimed to supplant the Provisional Government with the slogans "All power to the soviets" and "Peace, land, and bread."

Time was running out for the Provisional Government, which saw a battlefield victory as the only way to ensure its position. On July 1, the Russian army attacked the Austrians in Galicia but was defeated once again (see Map 20.1). The new prime minister, the Socialist Revolutionary Aleksandr Kerensky (1881–1970),

■ **Lenin Addressing the Second All-Russian Congress of Soviets**
In the spring of 1917, the German government craftily let Lenin and other Bolsheviks travel from their exile in Switzerland back to the scene of the unfolding revolution in Russia. A committed revolutionary instead of a political reformer, Lenin used oratory and skillful maneuvering to convince many in the soviets to follow him in overthrowing the Provisional Government, taking Russia out of the war, and implementing his brand of communism. (RIA Novosti.)

used commanding oratory to arouse patriotism but lacked the political skills to fashion an effective wartime government. In November 1917, the Bolshevik leadership, urged on by Lenin, seized power on behalf of a congress of soviets while simultaneously asserting its own right to form a government. When elections for a constituent assembly in January 1918 failed to give the Bolsheviks a plurality, the party used troops to disrupt the assembly and took over the government by force. They seized town and city administrations, closing down the zemstvos (local councils) and other institutions that might oppose them. In the winter of 1918–1919, the Bolshevik government, observing Marxist doctrine, abolished private property and nationalized factories in order to restore production, which had fallen off precipitously. The Provisional Government had allowed both men and women to vote in 1917; Russia was thus the first great power to legalize universal suffrage—a hollow privilege once the Bolsheviks limited electoral slates to candidates from the Communist Party.

■ MAP 20.2 The Russian Civil War, 1917–1922

Nationalists, aristocrats, middle-class citizens, and property-owning peasants tried to combine their interests to defeat the Bolsheviks, but they failed to create an effective political consensus. The result was more suffering for ordinary people, whose produce was confiscated to fight the civil war. The Western powers and Japan also sent in troops to put down this revolution that so threatened the economic and political order.

The Bolsheviks asked Germany for peace and agreed to the Treaty of Brest-Litovsk (March 1918), which placed vast regions of the old Russian Empire under German occupation (Map 20.2). The treaty partially realized the German ideal of a central European region, or Mitteleuropa, under German control. Because the loss of millions of square miles put Petrograd at risk, the Bolsheviks relocated the capital to Moscow and formally adopted the name Communists (taken from Marx's writings) to distinguish themselves from the socialists and Social Democrats who had voted for the disastrous war in the first place. "Obscene," Lenin called the catastrophic terms of the treaty, but he accepted them not only because he had promised to bring peace to Russia but also because he believed that the rest of Europe would soon rebel against war and overthrow the capitalist order.

Resistance to Bolshevik policies mushroomed into a civil war in which the pro-Bolsheviks (or "Reds") faced an array of antirevolutionary forces (the "Whites"). Among the Whites, the tsarist military leadership, composed of many landlords and supporters of aristocratic rule, fielded whatever troops it could muster. Dispossessed businessmen and the liberal intelligentsia soon lent their support. Many non-Russian nationality groups, formerly incorporated into the empire through force, fought the Bolsheviks because they saw their chance for independence. Before World War I ended, Russia's former allies, notably the United States, Britain, France, and Japan, landed troops in the country both to block the Germans and to stop Bolshevism. To compete effectively with the Bolsheviks, the counterrevolutionary groups desperately needed a strong leader and unified goals. Instead, the groups competed with one another: the pro-tsarist forces, for example, alienated those aspiring to nation-state status, such as the Ukrainians, Estonians, and Lithuanians. Ultimately, without a common purpose or unified command, the opponents of revolution could not win.

The civil war shaped communism. Leon Trotsky (1879–1940), Bolshevik commissar of war, built the highly disciplined Red Army by ending democratic procedures, such as the election of officers, which had originally attracted soldiers to Bolshevism. Lenin and Trotsky introduced the policy of war communism, whereby urban workers and troops moved through the countryside, brutally confiscating grain from the peasantry to feed the army and workforce. The Cheka (secret police) set up detention camps for political opponents and black marketeers and shot many of them without trial. The expansion of the size and strength of the Cheka and the Red Army—the latter would eventually number five million men— accompanied the expansion of the bureaucracy, making government more authoritarian and undermining the promise of Marxism that revolution would bring a "withering away" of the state.

As the Bolsheviks clamped down on opposition during the bloody civil war, they organized their supporters to foster revolutionary Marxism across Europe. In March 1919, they founded the Third International, also known as the Comintern (Communist International) for the explicit purpose of replacing the old International with a centralized organization dedicated to preaching communism. By mid-1921, the Cheka had shored up Bolshevism in Russia, and the Red Army had secured the Crimea, the Caucasus, and the Muslim borderlands. After ousting the Japanese from Siberia in 1922, the Bolsheviks were in charge of a state as multinational as the old Russian Empire had been (see Map 20.2).

The Russian Revolution led by the Bolsheviks promised bold experiments in social and political leadership at home and changed the balance of forces in the Great War. The revolution turned out the inept Romanovs and the privileged aristocracy, but the civil war turned Russia into a battlefield stalked by disease, hunger, and death. Moreover, the brutal way in which the Bolsheviks came to power—by crushing their opponents—ushered in a political style and direction far different from earlier socialist hopes. In the midst of war protest, the rest of Europe's leaders were left fearing that communism might lie in their future too.

Ending the War: 1918

In the spring of 1918, the Central Powers made one final attempt to smash through the Allied lines, but the offensive ground to a bloody halt within weeks. By then, the British and French had started making limited but effective use of tanks supported by airplanes. Although the first tanks were cumbersome, their ability to withstand machine-gun fire made offensive attacks possible. In the summer of 1918, the Allies, now fortified by the Americans, pushed back the Germans all along the western front and headed toward Germany. The German armies, suffering more than two million casualties between spring and summer, rapidly disintegrated.

By October 1918, the desperate German command helped create a civilian government to take over from its own dictatorial rule of the home front. It hoodwinked inexperienced politicians into accepting responsibility for the defeat and asking for peace. Deflecting blame from the military, generals proclaimed themselves still fully capable of winning the war. Weak-willed civilians, they claimed, had dealt the military a "stab in the back" that forced a surrender. Amid this blatant political deceit, naval officers called for a final sea battle, but the order triggered a sailors' mutiny against what they saw as a suicide mission. The sailors' revolt spread to the workers, who demonstrated in Berlin, Munich, and other major German cities. Social Democratic politicians stepped in to declare a German republic in an effort to prevent revolution. On November 9, 1918, Kaiser William II fled as the Central Powers collapsed on all fronts. At the end of October, Czechs and Slovaks had declared an independent state, and the Croatian parliament simultaneously announced Croatia's independence.

Finally, on November 11, 1918, at 5:00 A.M., an armistice was signed. The guns fell silent on the western front six hours later. In the course of four years, European civilization had been sorely tested, if not shattered. Conservative figures put the battlefield toll at a minimum of ten million deaths and thirty million wounded, incapacitated, or eventually to die of their wounds. In every European combatant country, industrial and agricultural production had plummeted, and much of the reduced output had been put to military use. Parts of Asia, Africa, and the Americas, which depended on European trade, also felt the impact of Europe's declining production. From 1918 to 1919, the weakened global population suffered an influenza epidemic that left as many as one hundred million more dead.

Moral questioning accompanied the suffering. Soldiers returning home in 1918 and 1919 flooded the book market with their memoirs, trying to give meaning to their experiences. Whereas many had begun by emphasizing heroism and glory, others were cynical and bitter by war's end. They insisted the fighting had been meaningless. Total war had drained society of resources and population and had inadvertently sown the seeds of future catastrophes.

■ **REVIEW:** *Why did people revolt during World War I, and what turned revolt into outright revolution in Russia?*

The Search for Peace in an Era of Revolution

The war was over, but revolutionary fervor swept the continent of Europe, especially in the former empires of Germany and Austria-Hungary. Until 1921, the triumph of socialism seemed plausible, as many of the newly independent peoples of eastern and central Europe fervently supported socialist principles. The revolutionary mood captured workers and peasants in Germany, too. In contrast, many liberal and right-wing opponents hoped for a political order based on military authority of the kind they had relied on during the war. Faced with a volatile mix of revolution and counterrevolution, diplomats from around the world arrived in Paris in January 1919 to negotiate the terms of peace, often without recognizing the magnitude of the changes brought about by war.

Europe in Turmoil

Urban people and returning soldiers ignited the protest that swept Europe in 1918 and 1919. In January 1919, the red flag of socialist revolution flew from city hall in Glasgow, Scotland, while in cities of the collapsing Austro-Hungarian Empire workers set up councils to direct factory production and influence politics. Many soldiers did not disband at the armistice but formed volunteer armies, making Europe ripe not for parliamentary politics but for revolution by force. Germany was politically unstable, partly because of the shock of defeat. Independent socialist groups and workers' councils vied with the dominant Social Democrats for control of the government, and workers and veterans took to the streets to demand food and back pay. Whereas in 1848 revolutionaries had marched to city hall or the king's residence, these protesters took over newspapers and telegraph offices, thus controlling the flow of information. Some were inspired by one of the most radical socialist factions, the Spartacists, led by cofounders Karl Liebknecht (1871–1919) and Rosa Luxemburg (1870–1919). Unlike Lenin, the two Spartacist leaders favored political uprisings that would give workers political experience and thus eliminate the need for an all-knowing party leadership. They shared Lenin's dislike for parliamentary politics, but they argued for *direct* worker control of institutions.

Social Democratic leader Friedrich Ebert (1871–1925), who headed the new government, shunned revolution and supported the creation of a parliamentary republic. Splitting with his former socialist allies, he called on the German army and the Freikorps—a roving paramilitary band of students, demobilized soldiers, and others—to suppress the workers' councils and demonstrators. He thus appeared to endorse the idea that political differences could be settled with violence. "The enthusiasm is marvelous," wrote one young soldier. "No mercy's shown. We shoot even the wounded. . . . We were much more humane against the French in the field." Members of the Freikorps hunted down Luxemburg and Liebknecht and murdered them.

Protest continued even as a constituent assembly meeting in the city of Weimar in February 1919 approved a constitution and founded a parliamentary republic called the **Weimar Republic**. The military leadership dreamed of a restored monarchy and rebelled: "As I love Germany, so I hate the Republic," wrote one officer. Facing a military coup by Freikorps officers, Ebert called for a general strike that abruptly averted a takeover by showing the lack of popular support for a military regime. In so doing, the Weimar Republic had replaced consensus building with street violence, paramilitary groups, and protests to solve political problems.

Revolutionary activism surged and was smashed. Late in the winter of 1919, leftists proclaimed soviet republics—governments led by workers' councils—in Bavaria and Hungary. These soon fell before the assault of the volunteer armies and troops. The Bolsheviks tried to establish a Marxist regime in Poland in the belief that its people wanted a workers' revolution. Instead, the Poles resisted and drove the Red Army back in 1920, while the Allied powers rushed supplies and advisers to Warsaw (see Map 20.2). Though this and other revolts failed, they provided further proof that total war had loosened political and social order.

The Paris Peace Conference, 1919–1920

As political turmoil engulfed peoples from Berlin to Moscow, the Paris Peace Conference opened in January 1919. Visions of communism spreading westward haunted the assembled statesmen, but the desperation of millions of war-ravaged citizens, the status of Germany, and the reconstruction of a secure Europe topped their agenda. Leaders such as French premier Georges Clemenceau had to satisfy their angry citizens, who demanded revenge or, at the very least, compensation for their suffering. France had lost 1.3 million people—almost an entire generation of young men; and more than a million buildings, six thousand bridges, and thousands of miles of railroad lines and roads had been destroyed while the war was fought on French soil. Great Britain's representative, Prime Minister David Lloyd George, caught the mood of the British public by campaigning in 1918 with such slogans as "Hang the kaiser." Italians arrived on the scene demanding the territory promised to them in the 1915 Treaty of London. Meanwhile, U.S. president Woodrow Wilson, head of the new world power that had helped achieve the Allied victory, had his own agenda. His **Fourteen Points**, on which the truce had been based, was steeped in the language of freedom and called for open diplomacy, arms reduction, and the right for nationalities to have their own government.

The Fourteen Points did not represent the mood of the victors, however. Allied propaganda had made the Germans seem like inhuman monsters, and many citizens demanded a harsh peace. Moreover, some military experts feared that Germany was using the armistice only to regroup for more warfare. Indeed, Germans widely refused to admit that their army had lost the war. Eager for army support, Ebert had given returning soldiers a rousing welcome: "As you return unconquered from the field of battle, I salute you." Thus, conservative leaders among Wilson's former allies campaigned to make him look naive and deluded. "Wilson bores me with his Fourteen Points," Clemenceau complained. "Why, the good Lord himself has only ten."

Nevertheless, Wilson's Fourteen Points appealed to European moderates and persuaded Germans that the settlement would not be vindictive. His commitment to *settlement* as opposed to *surrender* contained tough-minded stipulations, for Wilson wisely recognized that Germany was still the strongest state on the continent. He merely pushed for a treaty that balanced the strengths and interests of various European powers. Economists and other specialists accompanying Wilson to Paris agreed that, harshly dealt with and humiliated, Germany might soon become vengeful and chaotic—a lethal combination that could lead to the growth of unsavory political movements.

After six months, the statesmen and their teams of experts produced the **Peace of Paris** (1919–1920), composed of a cluster of individual treaties. These treaties shocked the countries that had to accept them, and in retrospect historians see how they destabilized eastern and east-central Europe (Map 20.3). The treaties separated Austria from Hungary, reduced Hungary by almost two-thirds of its inhabitants and three-quarters of its territory, broke up the Ottoman Empire, and treated Germany severely. They replaced the Habsburg Empire with a group of small, internally divided, and relatively weak states: Czechoslovakia, Poland, and the Kingdom of the Serbs, Croats, and Slovenes, soon renamed Yugoslavia. After a century and a half of partition, Poland was reconstructed from parts of Russia, Germany, and Austria-Hungary; one-third of its population was ethnically non-Polish. The statesmen in Paris also created a Polish Corridor that connected Poland to the Baltic Sea and separated East Prussia from the rest of Germany. Austria and Hungary were both left reeling at their loss of territory and resources. Many of the new states became rivals and were for the most part politically and economically weak.

The Treaty of Versailles with Germany was the centerpiece of the Peace of Paris, however. France recovered Alsace and Lorraine, and the victors would temporarily occupy the left, or western, bank of the Rhine and the coal-bearing Saar basin. Wilson accepted his allies' expectations that Germany would pay substantial reparations for civilian damage during the war. The specific amount was set in 1921 at the crushing sum of 132 billion gold marks. Germany also had to reduce

■ MAP 20.3 Europe and the Middle East after the Peace Settlements of 1919–1920

The political landscape of central, east, and east-central Europe changed dramatically as a result of the Russian Revolution and the Peace of Paris. The Ottoman, German, Russian, and Austro-Hungarian empires were either broken up altogether into multiple small states or reduced in size. The settlement bred resentment among Germans and Hungarians and created a group of weak, struggling nations in the heartland of Europe. The victorious powers took over much of the oil-rich Middle East. **For more help analyzing this map,** see the map activity for this chapter in the ONLINE STUDY GUIDE at bedfordstmartins.com/huntconcise.

its army, almost eliminate its navy, stop manufacturing offensive weapons, and deliver a large amount of free coal each year to Belgium and France. Furthermore, it was forbidden to have an air force and had to give up its colonies. The average German saw in these terms an unmerited humiliation that was compounded by Article 231 of the treaty, which described Germany's "responsibility" for damage "imposed . . . by the aggression of Germany and her allies." The outraged German people interpreted this as a "war guilt" clause, which allowed the victors to collect reparations from economically viable Germany rather than from decimated Austria. War guilt made Germany an outcast in the community of nations.

Besides redrawing the map of Europe, the Peace of Paris set up an organization called the **League of Nations**, whose responsibility for maintaining peace—a principle called collective security—was to replace the divisive secrecy of prewar power politics. As part of Wilson's vision, the league would guide the world toward disarmament, arbitrate its members' disputes, and monitor labor conditions around the world. Returning to prewar isolationism, the U.S. Senate, in a humiliating defeat for the president, failed to ratify the peace settlement and refused to join the league. Moreover, both Germany and Russia initially were excluded from the league and were thus blocked from acting in legal concert with other nations.

The covenant, or charter, of the League of Nations organized the administration of the former colonies and territories of Germany and the Ottoman Empire— such as Togo, Cameroon, Syria, and Palestine—through a system of mandates (see "Mapping the West," page 895). The European powers exercised political control over mandated territory, while local leaders retained limited authority. The league covenant justified the mandate system as providing governance by "advanced nations" over territories "not yet able to stand by themselves under the strenuous conditions of the modern world." However, colonized and other people of color who had served on the battlefield began to challenge the claims of their European masters. They had seen how savage and degraded these people who claimed to be racially superior, politically more advanced, and leaders of global culture could be. "Never again will the darker people of the world occupy just the place they had before," the African American leader W. E. B. Du Bois predicted in 1918. The mandate system kept imperialism alive, and like the Peace of Paris it aroused anger and resistance.

Economic and Diplomatic Consequences of the Peace

The financial and political settlement in the Peace of Paris had repercussions in the 1920s and beyond. Western leaders worried deeply about two intertwined issues in the aftermath of the war. The first was economic recovery. France, the hardest hit by wartime destruction and billions of dollars in debt to the United States, estimated that Germany owed it at least $200 billion. The British, by contrast, worried about maintaining their empire and restoring trade with Germany, not about exacting huge reparations. Nevertheless, both France and Britain depended on some monetary redress to pay their war debts to the United States because Europe's share of world trade had plunged during the war.

Germany claimed that the demand for reparations strained its government, already beset by political upheaval. But hardship was not the only result of the Peace of Paris. The kaiser had refused to raise taxes, especially on the rich, to pay for the war, so the new German republic had to pay reparations while also managing the staggering war debt. As an experiment in democracy, the Weimar Republic needed to woo the citizenry, not alienate it by hiking taxes. In 1921, when Germans refused to present a realistic payment scheme, the French occupied several cities in the Ruhr until a settlement was reached.

Embroiled with powers to the west, the German government deftly turned to eastern Europe. It reached an agreement to foster economic ties with Russia, desperate for western trade, in the Treaty of Rapallo (1922). Its relations with powers to the west, however, continued to deteriorate. In 1923, after Germany defaulted on coal deliveries, the French and Belgians sent troops into the Ruhr basin, planning to use its abundant resources to recoup their wartime expenditures. Urged on by the government, Ruhr citizens fought back, shutting down industry by staying home from work. The German government printed trillions of marks to support the workers and to pay its own war debts with practically worthless currency. Soon Germany was in the midst of a staggering inflation that demoralized its citizens and gravely threatened the international economy: at one point a single U.S. dollar cost 4.42 trillion marks, and wheelbarrows of money were required to buy a turnip. The spirit of the League of Nations demanded a resolution to this economic chaos through negotiations. The Dawes Plan (1924) and eventually the Young Plan (1929) reduced payments to the victors and restored the value of German currency. Nonetheless, the inflation had wreaked enduring psychological havoc, wiped out people's savings, and ruined those living on fixed incomes.

A second burning issue in addition to economic recovery involved ensuring that peace would last. Statesmen recognized that peace demanded disarmament, a return of Germany to the community of European nations, and security for the new countries of eastern Europe. It took hard diplomatic bargaining outside the league to produce two plans in Germany's favor. At the Washington Conference in 1921, the United States, Great Britain, Japan, France, and Italy agreed to reduce their number of battleships and to stop constructing new ones for ten years. Four years later, in 1925, the league sponsored a meeting of the great powers, including Germany, at Locarno, Switzerland. The Treaty of Locarno provided Germany with a seat in the League of Nations as of 1926. In return, Germany agreed not to violate the borders of France and Belgium and to keep the nearby Rhineland demilitarized—that is, unfortified by troops.

To the east, the door seemed open to a German attempt to regain territory lost to Poland, to form a merger with Austria, or to launch aggression against the states spun off from Austria-Hungary (see Map 20.3). To meet the threat, Czechoslovakia, Yugoslavia, and Romania formed the "Little Entente" in 1920–1921. This was a collective security agreement to protect themselves from their two powerful neighbors, Germany and Russia, and to guard against Hungarian expansionism. Then, between 1924 and 1927, France allied itself with the Little Entente and with Poland. The major European powers, Japan, and the United States also signed the Kellogg-Briand Pact (1928), which formally rejected international violence. The nations failed, however, to commit themselves to concrete action to prevent its outbreak.

The publicity and planning that yielded the international agreements during the 1920s sharply contrasted with old-style diplomacy, which was conducted in secret and subject to little public scrutiny or democratic influence. The development of a system of collective security and the new openness suggested a diplomatic revolution that would promote peace in international relations. Despite this promise, openness allowed diplomats of the era to feed the press reports calculated to arouse the masses. For example, much of the German populace was lashed into a nationalist frenzy by the press and opposing parties whenever Germany's diplomats compromised as they worked to undo the Treaty of Versailles. International meetings such as the one at Locarno promoting the goal of collective security exposed diplomatic processes to the nationalist press and to demagogues whose only goal was to rekindle political hatreds.

■ **REVIEW:** *What were the major outcomes of the postwar peacemaking process?*

A Decade of Recovery: Europe in the 1920s

The 1920s were devoted to coming to terms with the cultural and political legacy of the war. Towns and villages built their war monuments, and battlefield tourism sprang up for veterans and for families in search of a son's or father's resting place. The wartime spirit endured in words and phrases from the battlefield that punctuated everyday speech. Before the war, the word *lousy* had meant "lice-infested," but English-speaking soldiers returning from the trenches now applied it to anything bad. Raincoats became *trenchcoats*, and military terms like *bombarded* and *rank and file* entered peacetime usage. Maimed, disfigured veterans were present everywhere. Some used prostheses designed by Jules Amar; others without limbs were sometimes carried in baskets—hence the expression *basket case*. They overflowed hospitals and mental institutions, and family life centered on their care. Total war had generally strengthened military values, authoritarian government, and a controlled economy. A key question facing society was how to restore civilian

■ **Otto Dix, *The Sleepwalkers* (1928)**

Artists in the defeated countries were especially attuned to the tragic absurdity of the war. The German ex-soldier Otto Dix sketched smashed faces and corpses in varying states of decay, depicting people who survived as grotesque or benumbed "sleepwalkers" who picked their way through the postwar wreckage. The simple horror of death and disfigurement made painted whores of those seeking a return to ordinary life.

(© Erich Lessing/Art Resource, NY./VG Bild-Kunst, Bonn.)

government and put down the continuing violence. Although contemporaries referred to the 1920s as the "Roaring Twenties" and the "Jazz Age," the sense of cultural release masked the serious problem of restoring social stability and implementing democracy. Four autocratic governments— in Germany, Austria-Hungary, Russia, and the Ottoman Empire—had collapsed as a result of the war, but how newly empowered citizens would act politically remained a burning question.

Changes in the Political Landscape across Europe

The collapse of autocratic government and the widespread extension of suffrage to women brought political turmoil as well as a sense of democratic rebirth. Woman suffrage resulted in part from decades of activism; more immediately, many governments gave women the vote to reward them for their war efforts and to make revolution less tempting. In the first postwar elections, women were voted into parliaments, and the impression grew that they had also made extraordinary gains in the workplace. French men pointedly denied women the vote, insisting they would use their vote to bring back the rule of kings and priests. France and Italy did not extend suffrage to women until the end of World War II.

Women Gain Suffrage in the West	
1906	Finland
1913	Norway
1915	Denmark, Iceland
1917	Netherlands, Russia
1918	Czechoslovakia, Great Britain (limited suffrage)
1919	Germany
1920	Austria, United States
1921	Poland
1925	Hungary (limited suffrage)
1945	Italy, France
1971	Switzerland

Economic problems threatened the democratic trend, as cycles of boom and bust that had characterized the late nineteenth century reemerged. A short postwar boom prompted by rebuilding war-torn areas and filling consumer needs unsatisfied during the war was followed by an economic downturn that was most severe between 1920 and 1922. Skyrocketing unemployment led some to question the effectiveness of their governments and the fairness of society. By the mid-1920s, many of the economic opportunities for women had disappeared, and they made up a smaller percentage of the workforce than in 1913. Veterans were especially angered by economic insecurity after their years of enduring the war's horrors. Eastern and central Europe were filled with impoverished refugees, driven from their homes by ethnic majorities who took to heart the message that new nations should be as ethnically pure as possible.

National Minorities in Postwar Poland

Hard times especially corroded the new republics of eastern Europe, which were unprepared for independence in the sophisticated world market even as they flaunted ethnic nationalism and drove out minorities. None but Czechoslovakia had a mature industrial sector, and agricultural techniques were often primitive. The development of Poland exemplified the postwar political landscape in eastern Europe. Nationalism was increasingly defined in terms of ethnic purity, even though the reunified Poland consisted of one-third Ukrainians, Belorussians, Germans, and other ethnic minorities—many of whom had grievances against the dominant Poles. Moreover, varying religious, dynastic, and cultural traditions divided the Poles, who for 150 years had been split among Austria, Germany, and Russia. Polish reunification occurred without a common currency, political structure, or language—even the railroad tracks were not a standard size.

With practically no economic or other support from the Allies, a constitutional government nonetheless took shape in this new Poland. Under a constitution that professed equal rights for all ethnicities and religions, the new democratic government, run by the Sejm (parliament), tried to legislate the redistribution of large estates to the peasantry, but declining crop prices and overpopulation made life in the countryside difficult. Urban workers were better off than the peasantry (two-thirds of the population lived by subsistence farming) but worse off than laborers across Europe. The economic downturn brought strikes and violence in 1922–1923, and the inability of coalition parliaments to effect economic prosperity led to a coup in 1926 by strongman Jozef Pilsudski. Economic hardship and strong-arm solutions went hand in hand in east-central Europe.

Germany was a different case. The industrially sophisticated Weimar Republic confronted daunting challenges to making Germany democratic, even after putting down the postwar revolution. Although the German economy picked up and Germany became a center of experimentation in the arts, political life remained precarious because so many people felt nostalgia for imperial glory and loathed the Versailles treaty's restrictions. On the surface, Weimar's political system—a bicameral parliament and a chancellor responsible to the lower house—appeared similar to the parliamentary system in Britain and France, but extremist politicians heaped daily abuse on parliamentary politics. Anyone who cooperated with the parliamentary system, wrote the wealthy newspaper and film magnate Alfred Hugenberg, "is a moral cripple." Right-wing parties favored violence rather than consensus building, and nationalist thugs murdered democratic leaders and Jews. The Communists, feeling their muscle, plunged into street brawls too.

Support for the far right came from wealthy landowners and middle-class businessmen, white-collar workers whose standard of living had dropped during the war, and members of the lower-middle and middle classes hurt by inflation. Bands of disaffected youth and veterans proliferated, among them a group called Brown Shirts led by ex-soldier and political newcomer Adolf Hitler (1889–1945). In the wake of the Ruhr occupation of 1923, German military leader Erich Ludendorff and Hitler launched a coup d'état from a beer hall in Munich. Government troops suppressed the Beer Hall Putsch, but Hitler spent less than a year in jail and Ludendorff was acquitted. For conservative judges, as for former aristocrats and most of the prewar bureaucrats who remained in government, such men were national heroes.

In France and Britain, parties of the right had less effect than elsewhere because parliamentary institutions were better established and the upper classes were not plotting to restore an authoritarian monarchy. In France, politicians from the conservative right and moderate left successively formed coalitions and rallied general support to rebuild war-torn regions and to force Germany to pay for the reconstruction. Hoping to stimulate population growth after the devastating loss of life, the French parliament made distributing birth-control information illegal and abortion a severely punished crime.

Britain encountered postwar boom and bust and continuing strife in Ireland. Ramsay MacDonald, elected the first Labour prime minister in 1924, represented the newly formed political ambitions of the working masses. Like other postwar British leaders, he had to swallow the paradoxical fact that although Britain had the largest world empire, many of its industries were obsolete or in poor condition. A showdown came in the ailing coal industry, where prices fell and wages plummeted once the Ruhr mines reopened to offer tough competition to British mines. On May 3, 1926, workers launched a nine-day general strike against wage cuts and dangerous conditions in the mines. The strike prompted unprecedented middle-class resistance. University students, homemakers, and businessmen shut down the strike by driving trains, working on docks, and replacing workers in other jobs. Thus citizens from many walks of life revived the wartime spirit to defend the declining economy.

In Ireland, the British government met bloody confrontation over the issue of home rule, intensified by the wartime executions of the Easter Uprising rebels. In

January 1919, republican leaders announced Ireland's independence from Britain and created a separate parliament. The British government refused to recognize the parliament and sent in the Black and Tans, a volunteer army of demobilized soldiers so called for the color of their uniforms. Terror reigned in Ireland, as both the pro-independence forces and the Black and Tans waged guerrilla warfare, taking hostages, blowing up buildings, and even shooting into crowds at soccer matches. By 1921, public outcry forced the British to negotiate a treaty. It reversed the Irish declaration of independence and made the Irish Free State a self-governing dominion owing allegiance to the British crown. Northern Ireland, a group of six northern counties containing a majority of Protestants, gained a separate status: it was self-governing but still had representation in the British Parliament. Incomplete independence and the rights of religious minorities remained contentious issues.

The Irish Free State and Ulster, 1921

European powers encountered rebellion in overseas empires as well. Colonized peoples who had fought in the war expected more rights and even independence. Indeed, European politicians and military recruiters had actually promised the vote and many other reforms in exchange for support. But colonists' political activism, now enhanced by increasing education, trade, and experience with the West, mostly met a brutal response. Fearful of losing India, British forces massacred protesters at Amritsar in 1919 and put down revolts against the mandate system in Egypt and Iran in the early 1920s. The Dutch jailed political leaders in

Indonesia; the French punished Indochinese nationalists. For many Western governments, maintaining empires abroad was crucial to ensuring democracy at home, for any hint of declining national prestige fed antidemocratic forces.

In fact, the 1920s marked the high tide of imperialism and saw a fresh burst of imperialist activity. Britain and France, enjoying new access to Germany's colonies in Africa and the spoils of the fallen Ottoman Empire in the Middle East, were at the height of their global power despite their financial problems at home. These countries along with Holland, Belgium, Japan, and Australia took advantage of the growing profitability that enterprise around the world could bring. Most notably, Middle Eastern and Indonesian oil fueled the growing number of automobiles, airplanes, trucks, ships, and buses, and increasingly heated homes. Products like hot chocolate and tropical fruit from overseas became regular items in the European diet, thanks to the ongoing globalization of the economy.

Reconstructing the Economy

Worldwide economic competition was as big a challenge to recovery as were global political struggles. During the war, the European economy had lost many of its international markets to India, Canada, Australia, Japan, and the United States. Nonetheless, the war had forced European manufacturing to become more efficient and had expanded the demand for automotive and air transport, electrical products, and synthetic goods. The prewar pattern of mergers and cartels continued after 1918, giving rise to gigantic food-processing firms such as Nestlé in Switzerland and petroleum enterprises such as Royal Dutch Shell. Owners of these large manufacturing conglomerates wielded more financial and political power than entire small countries. By the late 1920s, Europe had overcome the wild economic swings of the immediate postwar years and was enjoying renewed economic prosperity.

Despite this growth, the United States had become the trendsetter in economic modernization. Many European businessmen made pilgrimages to Henry Ford's Detroit assembly line, which by 1929 produced a Ford automobile every ten seconds. Ford touted that the miracle of productivity resulted in a lower cost of living and increased purchasing power for workers. Indeed, whereas French, German, and British citizens in total had under two million cars, some seventeen million cars were on U.S. streets in 1925.

Scientific management, sometimes called the science of work, also aimed to raise productivity. American efficiency expert Frederick Taylor (1856–1915) developed methods to streamline workers' tasks and motions for maximum productivity. European industrialists adopted Taylor's methods during the war and after, but they were also influenced by European psychologists who emphasized the mental aspects of productivity and the need to balance work and leisure activities, such as moviegoing and sports. In theory, increased productivity not only would produce prosperity for all but also would bind workers and management together, avoiding Russian-style worker revolution. For many workers, however, the emphasis on efficiency seemed inhuman; in some workplaces, the restrictions on time and motion were so severe that workers were allowed to use the bathroom only on a fixed schedule. "When I left the factory, it followed me," wrote one worker. "In my dreams I was a machine."

The managerial sector in industry had expanded during the war and continued to do so thereafter. Workers' initiative became devalued; managers alone were considered to be creative and innovative. Managers reorganized work procedures and classified workers' skills. They categorized work that required less skill as "female jobs" that deserved lower wages, thus adapting the old segmentation of the labor market to the new working conditions. Because male workers' jobs were increasingly threatened by labor-saving machinery, unions usually agreed to hold down women's wages to keep women from competing with men for scarce high-paying jobs. Like the managerial sector, union bureaucracy had ballooned during World War I to help monitor labor's part in the war. Union bureaucrats became specialists: negotiators, membership organizers, educators and propagandists, and political liaisons. Unions played a key role in politics. They could mobilize masses of people, as they demonstrated when they blocked coups against the Weimar government in the 1920s and organized the 1926 general strike in Great Britain.

Restoring Society

Postwar society met the returning millions of brutalized, incapacitated, and shell-shocked veterans with combined joy and apprehension. Many veterans harbored hostility toward civilians, who had rebelled against wartime conditions, these soldiers charged, instead of patriotically enduring them. The world to which the veterans returned differed from the homes they had left: veterans often had no jobs, and some found that their wives and sweethearts had abandoned them—a wrenching betrayal of those who had risked their lives to protect the homeland. The war had blurred some class distinctions because massive battlefield casualties had made it possible for commoners to move into the ranks of officers—positions often monopolized by the prewar aristocracy. Members of all classes had rubbed shoulders in the trenches. The identical, evenly spaced crosses in military cemeteries implied that all the dead were equal, as did the mass "brothers' graves" at the battlefront, in which rich and poor lay side by side in a single burial pit or the tomb that overlooked Verdun. On the home front, many middle-class daughters worked outside the home, and their mothers did their own housework because their former servants could earn more money working in factories.

United by patriotism when the war erupted, civilians, especially women, sometimes felt estranged from these returning warriors, who had inflicted so much death and had lived daily with filth, rats, and decaying animal and human flesh. Civilian anxieties were often valid. Tens of thousands of German, central European, and Italian soldiers refused to disband; a few British veterans even vandalized university classrooms and assaulted women streetcar conductors and factory workers. Women who had served at the front could empathize with the soldiers' woes. But many suffragists in England, for instance, who had fought for an end to separate spheres before the war, now embraced gender segregation, so fearful were they of returning veterans.

Governments tried to improve civilian life to reintegrate men into society and to reduce the appeal of Bolshevism. Politicians believed in the stabilizing power of traditional family values and supported social programs such as pensions, benefits for out-of-work men, and housing for veterans to alleviate their pent-up anger. The new housing—"homes for heroes," as politicians called the program—was a vast improvement over nineteenth-century working-class tenements. In Vienna, Frankfurt, Berlin, and Stockholm, modern housing projects provided common laundries, day-care centers, and rooms for group socializing. They featured gardens, terraces, and balconies to provide a soothing, country ambiance. Inside they boasted modern kitchens, indoor plumbing, central heating, and electricity. Domestic architects avoided ornate moldings, plasterwork, and curlicues—now seen as "old-fashioned"—in favor of streamlined buildings.

■ **Le Corbusier's Paris of the Future**
While the war profoundly disillusioned many in the West, peace aroused utopian hopes for a better future. For modern architects like Swiss-born Le Corbusier (1887–1965), the "future city" and the "radiant city" would organize space, and thus life, for ordinary people. Horizontal windows, roof gardens, and very plain façades were hallmarks of this new design—a radical break with ornate prewar styles in building. (Fondation Le Corbusier/© 2007 Artists Rights Society [ARS], NY/ADAGP, Paris.)

Despite government efforts to restore traditional family values, war had dissolved many middle-class conventions, among them attempts to keep unmarried young men and women apart. Freer relationships and more open discussions of sex characterized the 1920s. Middle-class youth of both sexes visited jazz clubs and attended movies together. Revealing bathing suits, short skirts, and body-hugging clothing emphasized women's sexuality, seeming to invite men and women to join together and replenish the postwar population. Still, the context for sexuality remained marriage. In 1918, British scientist Marie Stopes published the best seller *Married Love*, and in 1927, the wildly successful *Ideal Marriage: Its Physiology and Technique* by Dutch author Theodor van de Velde appeared. Both described sex in rhapsodic terms and offered precise information about birth control and sexual physiology. Changing ideas about sex were not limited to the middle and upper classes. One Viennese reformer described working-class marriage as "an erotic-comradely relationship of equals" rather than the economic partnership of past centuries. The flapper, a sexually liberated workingwoman, vied with the dedicated housewife to represent the ordinary woman in the public's eyes. Meanwhile, such writers as the Englishman D. H. Lawrence and the American Ernest Hemingway glorified men's sexual vigor in, respectively, *Women in Love* (1920) and *The Sun Also Rises* (1926). Mass culture's focus on heterosexuality encouraged the return to traditional social norms after the gender disorder caused by independent women and troubled masculinity of the prewar and war years.

As images of men and women changed, people paid more attention to bodily improvement. The increasing use of toothbrushes and toothpaste, safety and electric razors, and deodorants reflected new standards of personal hygiene and grooming. A multibillion-dollar cosmetics industry sprang up almost overnight. Women went to beauty parlors regularly to have their short hair cut, set, dyed, conditioned, straightened, or curled. They also tweezed their eyebrows, applied makeup, and even submitted to cosmetic surgery. Ordinary women painted their faces as formerly only prostitutes had done and competed in beauty contests that judged physical appearance. Instead of wanting to look plump and prosperous, people aimed to become thin and tan. The proliferation of boxers, hikers, gymnasts, and tap dancers spurred people to exercise and to participate in amateur sports. Modern industry encouraged consumers' new focus on personal health, which coincided with the need for a physically fit workforce.

The strong economic upturn encouraged people to buy more and more consumer goods. Thanks to the gradual postwar increase in real wages, middle- and upper-class families snapped up sleek modern furniture, washing machines, and vacuum cleaners. Other modern conveniences such as electric irons and gas stoves appeared in better-off working-class households. Installment buying, popularized from the 1920s on, helped finance these purchases. Family intimacy increasingly depended on machines of mass communication such as radios and phonographs, and on automobiles. These new products that transformed private life also brought unforeseen changes in the public world of culture and mass politics.

■ **REVIEW:** *What were the major social and economic problems facing postwar Europe, and how did leaders address them?*

Mass Culture and the Rise of Modern Dictators

Wartime propaganda had aimed to unite all classes against a common enemy. In the 1920s, the merging of diverse groups into a homogeneous Western culture, increasingly seen as a "mass culture," continued. The homogenizing instruments— primarily radio, film, and newspapers—expanded their influence in the 1920s. Whereas some intellectuals urged elites to form an experimental avant-garde that refused to cater to "the drab mass of society," others wanted to use modern media and art to reach out to and even control the masses. The mass media had the potential for creating an informed citizenry and thus enhancing democracy. Paradoxically, it also provided the tools for dictatorship in the troubled postwar climate. Authoritarian rulers—Benito Mussolini, Joseph Stalin, and Adolf Hitler— were thus able to control the masses in unprecedented ways.

Culture for the Masses

An array of media had received a big boost from the war. Bulletins from the battlefront had whetted the public's craving for news and real-life stories, and sales of nonfiction books soared. After years of deprivation, people felt driven to achieve material success, and they devoured books that advised how to do so. Henry Ford's biography, a story of social mobility and technological accomplishment, became a best seller in Germany. With postwar readers avidly pursuing practical knowledge, institutes and night schools became popular, and school systems promoted reading in geography, science, and history. Photographs, the radio, and movies also contributed to the formation of national culture.

In the 1920s, filmmaking changed from an experimental medium to a thriving international business, in which large corporations set up theater chains and marketed films worldwide. The war years, when the U.S. film industry began to outstrip the European, gave rise to specialization: directors, producers, marketers, photographers, film editors, and many others subdivided the process. A "star" system turned film personalities into celebrities, promoted by professional publicity and living like royalty. Films of literary classics and political events developed people's sense of a common heritage. Thus Bolshevik leaders backed the innovative work of director Sergei Eisenstein (1898–1948), whose films *Potemkin* (1925) and *Ten*

Days That Shook the World (1927–1928) presented a Bolshevik view of history to Russian and international audiences.

Films incorporated familiar elements from other cultural forms and succeeded in earning viewers—some 100 million weekly, the majority of them women. The piano accompaniment that went along with the action of silent films derived from music halls; comic characters and slapstick humor were borrowed from street or burlesque shows. The popular comedies of the 1920s poked fun at men's and women's feckless attempts to achieve emotional intimacy or featured the flapper and made her more visible to the masses around the world. Cinematic portrayals also played to postwar fantasies and fears. In Germany, the influential hit *The Cabinet of Doctor Caligari* (1919) depicted frightening events in an insane asylum as horrifying symbols of state power. Popular detective and cowboy films portrayed heroes who could restore wholeness to the disordered world of murder, crime, and injustice. Depictions of the plight of gangsters appealed to veterans, whose combat experiences had raised questions about the value of life in the modern world. Charlie Chaplin (1889–1977), an English comedian, actor, and producer, created the character of the Little Tramp, who won international popularity as the defeated hero, the anonymous modern man, trying to preserve his dignity in a mechanized world. Films featured characters from around the world and were set in faraway deserts or mountain ranges; newsreels showed international sporting events like boxing and cricket.

Film remained experimental well into the 1920s, but radio was even more so. Developed from Guglielmo Marconi's wireless technology, radio broadcasts in the first half of the 1920s were heard by mass audiences in public halls (much like movie theaters) and featured orchestras and song followed by audience discussion. The radio quickly became an affordable consumer item, and public concerts and lectures could then penetrate the individual's private living space. (See "Taking Measure," page 887.) Specialized programming for men (such as sports reporting) and for women (such as advice on home management) soon followed. By the 1930s, radio allowed politicians to reach the masses wherever they might be—even alone at home.

Cultural Debates over the Future

Cultural leaders in the 1920s were either obsessed by the horrendous experience of war or—like the modernists before the war—held high hopes for creating a fresh utopian future that would have little relation to the past. Those haunted by the war produced bleak or violent visions—a common feature of postwar German art. Käthe Kollwitz (1867–1945), whose son died in the war, portrayed in her woodcuts bereaved parents, starving children, and other heart-wrenching, antiwar images (see page 850). Other artists used satire, irony, and flippancy to express postwar rage and revulsion at civilization's apparent failure. George Grosz (1893–1959), stunned by the carnage like so many other German veterans, joined

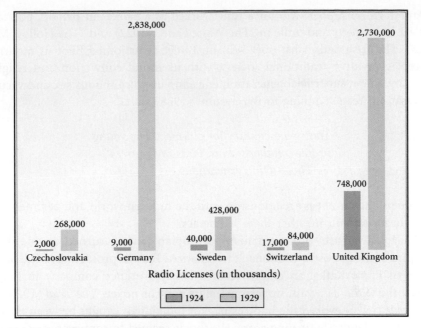

■ **TAKING MEASURE The Growth of Radio, 1924–1929**

The spread of radio technology, like the earlier development of printing, advanced the cultural and political unity of nation-states. The most rapid diffusion of radios occurred in the most industrially and commercially developed societies. At first, governments programmed and taxed radios. Because of this centralized control and the paperwork it created, historians can compare the country-by-country use of radio in Europe and in much of the rest of the world.

Dada, an artistic and literary movement that had emerged during the war. Dadaists produced works marked by nonsense and shrieking expressions of alienation. Grosz's paintings and cartoons of maimed soldiers and brutally murdered women reflected his psychic wounds and his self-proclaimed desire "to bellow back." In the postwar years, the modernist desire to shock audiences intensified. Avant-garde portrayals of seediness and perversion in everyday life flourished in cabarets and theaters in the 1920s and reinforced veterans' visions of civilian decadence.

The art world itself became a battlefield, especially in defeated Germany, where art mirrored the Weimar Republic's contentious politics. Popular writers such as Ernst Jünger glorified life in the trenches and called for the militarization of society to restore order. Erich Maria Remarque cried out for an end to war in his controversial novel *All Quiet on the Western Front* (1928). This international best seller depicted the life shared by enemies on the battlefield, thus aiming to dampen the national hatred stoked by wartime propaganda.

Poets reflected on postwar conditions in more general terms, using styles that rejected the comforting rhymes or accessible metaphors of earlier verse. T. S. Eliot, an American-born poet who for a time worked as a banker in Britain, portrayed postwar life as petty and futile in "The Waste Land" (1922) and "The Hollow Men" (1925). The Irish nationalist poet William Butler Yeats joined Eliot in mourning the replacement of traditional society, with its moral conviction and religious values, by a new, superficial generation engaging in promiscuous sex and vacuous conversation. Yeats's "Sailing to Byzantium" (1928) starts:

> *That is no country for old men. The young*
> *In one another's arms, birds in the trees*
> *— Those dying generations*

Both poets had an uneasy relationship with the modern world and at times advocated authoritarianism rather than democracy.

The postwar arts produced many a utopian fantasy turned upside down; dystopias of life in postrevolutionary, traumatized Europe proliferated. The bizarre stories of Franz Kafka, an employee of a large insurance company in Prague, showed the world as a vast, impersonal machine. His novels *The Trial* (1925) and *The Castle* (1926) evoked the hopelessness of individuals caught between the cogs of society's relentlessly turning gears. His theme seemed to capture for civilian life the helplessness that soldiers had felt at the front. As an old social order collapsed in the face of political and technological innovation, other writers depicted the complex, sometimes nightmarish inner life of individuals. French author Marcel Proust, in his multivolume novel *Remembrance of Things Past* (1913–1927), explored the workings of memory, the passage of time, and sexual modernity through the life of a narrator. At the beginning of the first volume, the narrator recalls a childhood obsession with his mother's absence as he tries to fall asleep at night. He witnesses progressively disturbing obsessions, such as violent sexuality and personal betrayals of love. The haunted inner life analyzed by Freud was infiltrating fiction: for Proust redemption lay in producing beauty from the raw material of life, not in promoting outmoded conventions of decency and morality.

The Irish writer James Joyce and the English writer Virginia Woolf shared Proust's vision of an interior self built on memories and sensations. Joyce in *Ulysses* (1922) and Woolf in *Mrs. Dalloway* (1925) illuminated the fast-moving inner lives of their characters in the course of a single day. In one of *Ulysses'* most celebrated passages, a long interior monologue traces a woman's lifetime of erotic and emotional sensations. The technique of using a character's thoughts to propel a story was called stream of consciousness. For Woolf the war had dissolved the solid society from which absorbing stories and fascinating characters were once fashioned. Her characters experience fragmented conversations, momentary sensations, and incomplete relationships.

There was another side to the postwar story—one based on the promise of technology and not the traumatized individual. Avant-garde artists before the war had

■ **Virginia Woolf**
Along with Marcel Proust and James Joyce, Virginia Woolf represented the peak of literary modernism with its emphasis on interior states of mind and disjointed, dreamlike slices of reality. Woolf's novels and essays also captured the unappreciated centrality of women, who provided an array of personal services to their more highly valued husbands. Woolf boldly announced that for a woman to be as creative as a man, she needed to be partially relieved of the burdens of family and to have "a room of [her] own."
(Time Life Pictures/Getty Images.)

celebrated the new, the futuristic, the utopian. After the war, like Jules Amar crafting prostheses for shattered limbs, they were optimistic that technology could make an entire society whole after the slaughter. The aim of art, observed one of them, "is not to decorate our life but to organize it." German architects and artists influenced by the Bauhaus school of design (after the idea of a craft association, or *Bauhütte*) created streamlined office buildings and designed functional furniture, utensils, and decorative objects, many of them inspired by forms from "untainted" East Asia and Africa. Russian artists, temporarily entranced by the Communist experiment, optimistically wrote novels about cement factories and created ballets about steel—an element common to artificial limbs and to advanced, utopian design.

Artists fascinated by technology and machinery were drawn to the most modern of all countries: the United States. Hollywood films and jazz, the improvisational music emanating from Harlem, attracted war-weary Europeans. African American jazz musicians showed a resiliency of spirit, and performers such as Josephine Baker (1906–1976) and Louis Armstrong (1900–1971) became international sensations when they toured Europe's capital cities. Like jazz, the skyscrapers rising in New York provided Europeans with a potent example of avant-garde expression that rejected a terrifying past and boldly embraced the future.

The Communist Utopia

Communists also promised a shining future and a modern, technological culture, but they encountered powerful obstacles to consolidating their rule. In the early

1920s, peasant bands called Green Armies revolted against the policy of war communism that permitted the government to seize agricultural produce. Industrial production stood at only 13 percent of prewar levels; the civil war had produced still more casualties; shortages of housing affected everyone; and millions of refugees clogged the cities and roamed the countryside. In the early spring of 1921, workers in Petrograd and sailors at the nearby naval base at Kronstadt revolted. They protested their short rations and the privileged standard of living that Bolshevik supervisors enjoyed, and they called for "soviets without Communists"— that is, a worker state minus the Bolsheviks.

The government had many of the rebels shot, but the Kronstadt revolt pushed Lenin to institute reform. His New Economic Policy (NEP) returned parts of the economy to the free market. This temporary compromise with capitalist methods allowed peasants to sell their grain freely and to profit from free trade in consumer goods. The state still controlled large industries and banking, but the NEP encouraged people to produce, sell, and even, in the words of one leading Communist, "get rich." Consumer goods and more food to eat soon became available. Some peasants and merchants did indeed get rich, but many more remained impoverished. The rise of "NEPmen," who bought and furnished splendid homes and who cared only about conspicuous consumption, belied the Bolshevik goal of a classless utopia.

Protest erupted within Communist ranks. At the 1921 party congress, a group called the Worker Opposition objected to the party's usurpation of economic control from worker organizations and pointed out that the NEP was an agrarian program, not a proletarian one. In response to charges of growing bureaucratization, Lenin suppressed the Worker Opposition faction and set up procedures for purging dissidents. Bolshevik leaders also tightened their grip on politics by making the Communist revolution a cultural reality that would inform people's daily lives and reshape their thoughts. Party leaders invaded the countryside to set up classes in a variety of political and social subjects, and volunteers harangued the public about the importance of literacy—only 40 percent on the eve of World War I. To facilitate social equality between men and women, which was part of the Marxist vision of the future, the state made birth control, abortion, and divorce readily available. The commissar for public welfare, Aleksandra Kollontai (1872–1952), promoted birth-control education and day-care programs for children of working parents.

The bureaucracy swelled to bring modern culture to every corner of life. *Hygiene* and *efficiency* became watchwords, as they were in the rest of Europe. Such agencies as the Zhenotdel (Women's Bureau) sought to teach women about their rights under communism and about modern sanitary practices. Efficiency experts aimed to replace tsarist backwardness with technological modernity based on American techniques. The short-lived government agency Proletkult tried to develop proletarian culture through such undertakings as workers' universities and a workers' theater. Russian artists experimented with blending high art and technology in mass culture, and composers punctuated their music with the sound of train or factory whistles.

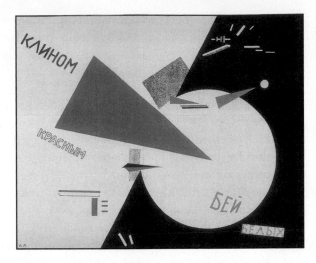

■ **El Lissitzky, *Beat the Whites with the Red Wedge* (1919)**

Russian artist El Lissitzky traveled Europe to bring news of Soviet experimentation. In particular, the Soviets were taken with the new physics, and their works of art surrounded the viewer with geometric forms. But abstract art was also political: in this 1919 painting, the "red" wedge uses the force of physical principles to defeat the objectively greater counterrevolutionary power of the "whites."

(David King Collection, London. © 2007 Artists Rights Society [ARS], NY/VG Bild-Kunst, Bonn.)

The poet Vladimir Mayakovsky wrote verse praising his Communist passport and essays promoting toothbrushing, and staged uproarious farces for ordinary citizens.

As with war communism, many resisted the reshaping of culture to "modern" or "Western" standards. Bolsheviks threatened everyday customs and the distribution of power within the family. As Zhenotdel workers moved into the countryside, for example, they attempted to teach women to behave as men's equals. Peasant families were still strongly patriarchal, however, and Zhenotdel activists threatened gender relations. In Islamic regions incorporated from the old Russian Empire into the new Communist one, Bolsheviks urged Muslim women to remove their veils and change their way of life, but fervent Muslims often attacked both Zhenotdel workers and women who followed their advice.

In the spring of 1922, Lenin suffered a debilitating stroke, and in January 1924, amid ongoing cultural experimentation, factional fighting, and repression, the architect of the Bolshevik Revolution died. The party congress declared the day of his death a permanent holiday, changed the name of Petrograd to Leningrad, and elevated the deceased leader into a secular god. After Lenin's death, no one was allowed to criticize anything associated with his name, a situation that paved the way for abuses of power by later Communist leaders.

Joseph Stalin (1879–1953), who held the powerful position of general secretary of the Communist Party, led the deification of Lenin, using the occasion to dispense an enormous amount of patronage. He claimed executive accomplishment for welding Russian and non-Russian regions into the Union of Soviet Socialist Republics (USSR) in 1923. Wary of Stalin's growing influence and ruthlessness, Lenin in his last will and testament had asked that "the comrades find a way to remove Stalin." Stalin, however, discredited Leon Trotsky, his chief rival, and prevented Lenin's will from being publicized. Bringing in several hundred thousand new party members who owed their positions in government and industry to him, by 1929 Stalin had achieved virtually complete control of the USSR.

Fascism on the March in Italy

The war's legacy and postwar discontent in Italy brought to power Benito Mussolini (1883–1945), who like the Bolsheviks promised an efficient utopia. Italians raged when the Allies at Paris refused to honor the territorial promises of the Treaty of London. Domestic unrest swelled when peasants and workers protested their economic plight, made worse by the slump of the early 1920s. Since the late nineteenth century, many Europeans had come to blame parliaments for their ills. So Italians were responsive when Mussolini, a socialist journalist who turned to the right, built a personal army (the Black Shirts) of veterans and the unemployed to overturn parliamentary government. In 1922, his supporters, known as Fascists, started a **march on Rome**, forcing King Victor Emmanuel III (r. 1900–1946) to make the dynamic Mussolini prime minister.

The Fascist movement flourished in the soil of poverty and wounded national pride. It attracted to its bands of Black Shirts many young men who felt cheated of glory by the Allies and veterans who missed the vigor of military life in the Great War. The *fasces*, an ancient Roman symbol depicting a bundle of sticks wrapped around an ax with the blade exposed, served as the movement's emblem; to Mussolini's supporters it represented both unity and force. Unlike Marxism, fascism scoffed at coherent ideology: "Fascism is not a church," Mussolini announced upon taking power in 1922. "It is more like a training ground." **Fascism** was thus defined by its political grounding in an instinctual male violence and its opposition to the "antinationalist" socialist movement and parliamentary rule.

Mussolini consolidated his power by criminalizing any criticism of the state and by violently steamrolling parliamentary opposition. Fascist bands demolished socialist newspaper offices, attacked striking workers, used their favorite tactic of forcing castor oil (which causes diarrhea) down the throats of socialists, and even murdered certain powerful opponents. Yet this brutality and the sight of the Black Shirts marching through the streets like disciplined soldiers signaled to many Italians that their country was ordered and modern. Large landowners and businessmen approved Fascist attacks on strikers and financially supported the movement. Their generous funding allowed Mussolini to build a large staff by hiring the unemployed and thus advancing the belief that Fascists could spark the economy when no one else could.

In addition to violence, Mussolini used mass propaganda and the media to foster support for a kind of military campaign to remake Italy. Peasant men huddled around radios to hear him call for a "battle of wheat" to enhance farm productivity. Peasant women, responding to his praise of maternal duty, adored him for appearing to value womanhood. In the cities, the government launched avant-garde

■ Mussolini and the Black Shirts

For movements like fascism, the best society was one controlled by militarized politics that killed its critics and political opponents. Fascism saw parliamentary democracies as effeminate and doomed in the modern world, which would need dictators and obedient warriors to make it strong, efficient, and machinelike. Thus, in the name of promoting state power, Mussolini gained adherents both within and outside of Italy. (Farabolafoto.)

architecture projects, designed new statues and public adornments, and used public relations promoters to advertise its achievements. Mussolini claimed that he made the trains run on time, and this one triumph of modern technology fanned people's hopes that he could restore order out of wartime and postwar chaos.

Mussolini added a strong dose of traditional values and prejudices to his modern order. Although he was an atheist, he recognized the importance of Catholicism to most Italians. In 1929, the Lateran Agreement between the Italian government and the church made the Vatican a state under papal sovereignty. The government recognized the church's right to determine marriage and family doctrine and endorsed its role in education. In return, the church ended its criticism of Fascist tactics. Mussolini also introduced a "corporate" state that denied individual political rights in favor of duty to the state. Corporatist decrees in 1926 organized employers, workers, and professionals into groups or corporations that

IMPORTANT DATES			
1914 August	World War I begins	**1919**	Constitution for German republic drawn up at Weimar
1914–1925	Woman suffrage expands		
1916	Irish nationalists stage Easter Uprising against British rule	**1919–1920**	Paris Peace Conference redraws the map of Europe
1917 March	Revolution in Russia overturns tsarist autocracy	**1922**	By Anglo-Irish treaty of 1921, Ireland divided into the independent Irish Free State in the south and British-affiliated Ulster in the north; Fascists march on Rome; Mussolini becomes Italy's prime minister; T. S. Eliot publishes "The Waste Land"; James Joyce publishes *Ulysses*
1917 April	The United States enters World War I		
1917 November	Bolshevik Revolution in Russia		
1918 March	Russia signs Treaty of Brest-Litovsk and withdraws from the war	**1924**	Lenin dies; Stalin and Trotsky contend for power
1918 November	Revolutionary turmoil throughout Germany; the kaiser abdicates; armistice ends fighting of World War I	**1924–1929**	Period of general economic prosperity and stability
1918–1922	Civil war in Russia	**1929 October**	Stock market crash in United States

would settle grievances and determine conditions of work. These decrees outlawed independent labor unions and peasant groups, effectively ending workplace activism. Mussolini drew more applause from business leaders when he announced cuts in women's wages; and then late in the 1920s he won the approval of civil servants, lawyers, and professors by banning women from those professions. Mussolini did not want women out of the workforce altogether but aimed to confine them to low-paying jobs as part of his scheme for reinvigorating men.

Mussolini's admirers were numerous across the West and included Adolf Hitler, who throughout the 1920s had been building a paramilitary group of storm troopers and a political organization called the National Socialist German Workers' Party, or Nazis. During his brief stint in jail for the Beer Hall Putsch in 1923, Hitler wrote *Mein Kampf* (*My Struggle*, 1925), which articulated both a vicious anti-Semitism

■ **MAPPING THE WEST Europe and the World in 1929**
This map reflects the partitions and nations that came into being as a result of war and revolution, while it obscures the increasing movement toward throwing off colonial rule. The year 1929 was the true high point of empire: the desire for empire would diminish after 1929 except in Italy, which still craved colonies, and in Japan, which continued searching for land and resources to fuel its rapid growth.

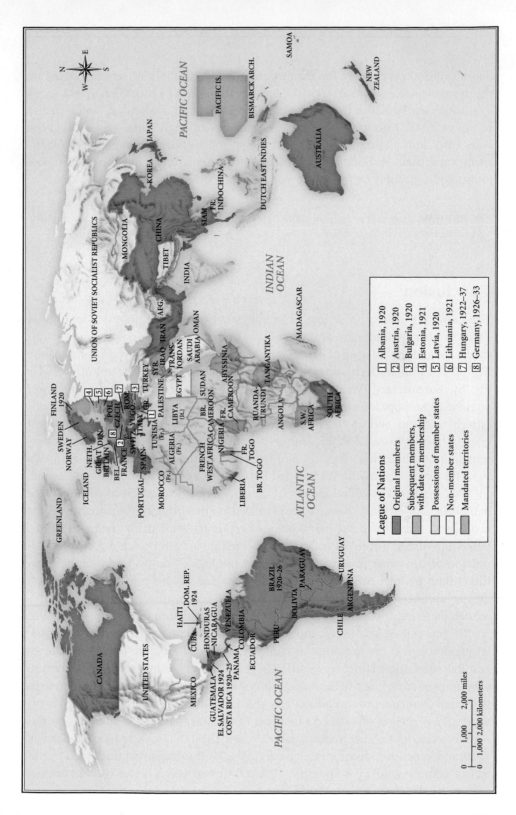

League of Nations

- Original members
- Subsequent members, with date of membership
- Possessions of member states
- Non-member states
- Mandated territories

1 Albania, 1920
2 Austria, 1920
3 Bulgaria, 1920
4 Estonia, 1921
5 Latvia, 1920
6 Lithuania, 1921
7 Hungary, 1922–37
8 Germany, 1926–33

PACIFIC OCEAN

SAMOA

BISMARCK ARCH.

NEW ZEALAND

AUSTRALIA

PACIFIC IS.

JAPAN

KOREA

CHINA

MONGOLIA

UNION OF SOVIET SOCIALIST REPUBLICS

TIBET

INDIA

AFG.

IRAN

IRAQ

SIAM

FR. INDOCHINA

DUTCH EAST INDIES

INDIAN OCEAN

MADAGASCAR

TANGANYIKA

ABYSSINIA

SAUDI ARABIA

OMAN

TRANS. JORDAN

EGYPT

PALESTINE

SUDAN

BR.

CAMEROON

FR. CAMEROON

RUANDA-URUNDI

ANGOLA

S.W. AFRICA

SOUTH AFRICA

SYR.

TURKEY

GR.

LIBYA (It.)

NIGERIA

FINLAND 1920

SWEDEN

NORWAY

ICELAND

4
5
6
7

POL.

CZECH

ROM.

3

GREAT BRITAIN

NETH.

DEN.

8

BEL.

SWITZ.

ITALY

YUGO.

1

2

FRANCE

SPAIN

PORTUGAL

TUNISIA

ALGERIA (Fr.)

MOROCCO (Fr.)

FRENCH WEST AFRICA

FR. TOGO

BR. TOGO

LIBERIA

ATLANTIC OCEAN

GREENLAND

CANADA

UNITED STATES

MEXICO

GUATEMALA

EL SALVADOR 1924

COSTA RICA 1920–25

PANAMA

COLOMBIA

ECUADOR

HONDURAS

NICARAGUA

VENEZUELA

HAITI

DOM. REP. 1924

CUBA

PERU

BOLIVIA

BRAZIL 1920–26

PARAGUAY

CHILE

ARGENTINA

URUGUAY

PACIFIC OCEAN

0   1,000   2,000 miles

0   1,000   2,000 kilometers

and a political psychology for manipulating the masses. Hitler was fascinated by the dramatic success of the Fascists' march on Rome and by Mussolini's legal accession to power. However, the austere conditions that had allowed Mussolini to rise to power in 1922 no longer existed in Germany. Although Hitler was welding the Nazi Party into a strong political instrument, the Weimar parliamentary government was actually working as the decade neared its end. It remained to be seen how events could possibly bring him to power.

■ **REVIEW:** *How did the postwar cultural atmosphere encourage both beneficial innovations and the trend toward dictatorship?*

Conclusion

The year 1929 was to prove just as fateful as 1914 had been. In 1914, an orgy of death had begun, leading to tens of millions of casualties, the destruction of major dynasties, and the collapse of aristocratic classes. For four years, war promoted the free play of military technology, virulent nationalism, and the control of everyday life by bureaucracy. While dynasties collapsed, the centralization of power increased the scope of the nation-state. The Peace of Paris in 1919 left Germans bitterly resentful, and in eastern and central Europe it created new states built on principles of nationalist ethnic unity—a settlement that, given the intense intermingling of ethnicities, religions, and languages in the area, failed to guarantee a peaceful future. The Great War shaped Europe throughout the 1920s and beyond.

War furthered the development of mass society. It leveled social classes on the battlefield and in the graveyard, standardized political thinking through wartime propaganda, and extended many political rights to women for their war effort. Peacetime turned improved techniques of wartime industry toward the mass production of consumer goods and directed technological innovations like the prostheses built by Jules Amar, air transport, cinema, and radio transmission to affect greater numbers of people. Modernity in the arts intensified, probing the nightmarish battering endured by all segments of the population during the Great War.

By the end of the 1920s, the legacy of war had so militarized politics that strongmen had come to power in Hungary, Poland, Romania, the Soviet Union, and Italy, and Adolf Hitler was waiting in the wings in Germany. Many Westerners were impressed by the tough, modern efficiency of the Fascists and Communists, who made parliaments and citizen rule seem out-of-date, even effeminate. People were so hardened to bloodshed as a result of the war that Fascist and Communist commitment to violence seemed tame. When the U.S. stock market crashed in 1929 and economic disaster circled the globe, authoritarian solutions and militarism continued to look appealing. What followed was a series of catastrophes even more devastating than World War I.

■ **MAKING CONNECTIONS**

1. *How was postwar mass politics shaped by the experience of World War I?*

2. *What social changes from World War I carried over into the postwar years and why?*

■ **FOR FURTHER EXPLORATION**

For further reading and online research ideas, see the Suggested References on page SR-10 at the back of the book.

For practice quizzes, a customized study plan, and other study tools, see the ONLINE STUDY GUIDE at **bedfordstmartins.com/huntconcise**.

For primary-source material from this period, see Chapter 20 in *Sources of* THE MAKING OF THE WEST: A CONCISE HISTORY, Second Edition.

An Age of Catastrophes

1929–1945

WHEN ETTY HILLESUM MOVED TO AMSTERDAM in the early 1930s to attend law school, an economic depression gripped the world. A resourceful young Dutch woman, Hillesum pieced together a living as a housekeeper and part-time language teacher. The pressures and pleasures of everyday life blinded her, however, to Adolf Hitler's spectacular rise to power in Germany on a platform demonizing her fellow Jews for the economic slump. World War II ruptured her world. The German conquest of the Netherlands in 1940 led to persecution of Dutch Jews and brought Hillesum to the shattering realization, noted in her diary: "What they are after is our total destruction." The Nazis started relocating Jews to camps in Germany and Poland. Hillesum went to work for Amsterdam's Jewish Council, which was compelled by the Nazis to organize the transportation of Jews to the east. Changing from self-absorbed student to heroine, she did what she could to help other Jews and minutely recorded the deportation. "I wish I could live for a long time so that one day I may know how to explain it." When she was taken prisoner, she smuggled out letters describing the brutal treatment in the transit camps. Etty Hillesum never fulfilled her ambition to become a professional writer: she died in the Auschwitz death camp in November 1943.

The U.S. stock market crash of 1929 opened a horrific era in world history when people, old or young like Etty Hillesum, first experienced economic distress

■ **Nazis on Parade**
By the time Adolf Hitler came to power in 1933, Germany was mired in economic depression. Hated by Communists, Nazis, and conservatives alike, the German republic had few supporters. To Germans still reeling from their defeat in World War I, the Nazis looked as though they would restore national power by defeating enemies both within and beyond Germany's borders. Hitler took his cue from Benito Mussolini by promising an end to democracy and tolerance. **For more help analyzing this image**, see the visual activity for this chapter in the ONLINE STUDY GUIDE at bedfordstmartins.com/huntconcise. (Hugo Jaeger/Time Life Pictures/Getty Images.)

and then felt the full horror of war and genocide. During the Great Depression of the 1930s, worldwide suffering intensified social grievances. In Europe, many people turned to military-style strongmen for answers. Adolf Hitler roused the German masses to pursue national greatness by scorning democratic rights and rooting out what he considered to be inferior, menacing people like Jews, Slavs, and gypsies. Simultaneously, authoritarian, militaristic, and fascist regimes spread to Portugal, Spain, Poland, Hungary, Japan, China, and elsewhere, trampling on representative institutions. Joseph Stalin oversaw the Soviet Union's rapid industrialization and justified the killing of millions of citizens as being necessary for Soviet growth.

The international scene was also perilous because elected leaders in the democracies reacted cautiously to both the depression and to fascist aggression. In an age of mass media, civilian leaders appeared timid and fearful of conflict, while dictators in uniform looked bold and decisive. Only the German invasion of Poland in 1939 finally roused the democracies to strong action, as World War II erupted in Europe. By the end of 1941, the war had spread to the rest of the world with the United States, Great Britain, and the Soviet Union allied in combat against Germany, Italy, and Japan. Tens of millions would perish in this war because technology and ideology had become more deadly than they had been just two decades earlier. Half the dead were civilians, among them Etty Hillesum, whose only crime was being a Jew.

The Great Depression

The depression triggered by the U.S. stock market crash of 1929 threw millions out of work and brought suffering to rural and urban folk alike. The whole world felt the depression's impact as commerce and investment in industry fell off, social life and gender roles were upset, and the birthrate plummeted. From peasants in Asia to industrial workers in Germany and the United States, the lives of large segments of the global population were ravaged.

Economic Disaster Strikes

In the 1920s, U.S. corporations and banks as well as millions of individual Americans had optimistically invested their money in the stock market or, more often, borrowed money to invest. Using easy credit, they bought shares in popular new companies based on electric, automotive, and other new technologies with full confidence in ever-rising stock prices. By the end of the decade, the Federal Reserve Bank—the nation's central bank, which controlled financial policy— tightened the availability of credit in an attempt to stabilize the market. To meet the new restrictions, brokers had to demand that their clients immediately repay the money they had borrowed to buy stock. When millions of shares of stock were sold to cover the borrowed funds, the market collapsed. Between early October

■ Italian Newspaper Depicts Crash on Wall Street
The collapse of the U.S. stock market was felt around the world, from Italian cities to the Asian countryside. Credit, the lifeblood of business, dried up. Governments greatly increased import tariffs to protect their nations' industries, thereby curtailing trade. At first, they also cut back on aid to unemployed people, reducing consumer purchasing, worsening financial hardship, and inflicting psychological pain. (Mary Evans Picture Library.)

and mid-November 1929, the value of businesses listed on the U.S. stock market dropped from $87 billion to $30 billion. For individuals and for the economy as a whole, it was the beginning of economic catastrophe.

The crash helped bring on a global depression because the United States, a leading international creditor, had financed the relative economic growth of the previous five years. Suddenly strapped for credit, U.S. financiers cut back on loans and called in debts, undermining banks and industry at home and abroad. Amid the credit crunch Europe faced a decline in consumer buying, overproduction, and competition from low-cost U.S. and Japanese goods, which further eroded the European economy, including the fledgling factories of eastern Europe.

The Great Depression left no sector of the world economy unscathed, and government actions made the situation worse. To spur their economies, governments used standard tools such as budget cuts and high tariffs against foreign goods. Part of accepted economic theory at the time, these policies further reduced individual spending and dampened trade. Great Britain, with its textile, steel, and coal industries near ruin because of out-of-date technology and foreign competition, had close to three million unemployed workers in 1932. By 1933, almost six million German workers, about one-third of the workforce, were unemployed, and many Germans were underemployed. France had a more self-sufficient economy, but big businesses such as the innovative Citroën car manufacturer began to fail, and by the mid-1930s more than 800,000 French people had lost their jobs.

In the agricultural sector, prices had been declining for several years because of abundant harvests and technological innovation. People in the countryside already faced ruin when creditors were forced to foreclose on farms and confiscate equipment. Millions of small farmers had no money to buy the chemical fertilizers and motorized machinery they needed to remain competitive; they, too, went under. In eastern and southern Europe, peasants who had pressed for the redistribution of land after World War I could not afford to operate their newly acquired farms. In Poland, many of the 700,000 new landowners fell into debt trying to make their farms viable. Eastern European governments often ignored the farmers' plight in order to direct available funds toward industrialization—a policy that increased tensions in rural society.

Social Effects of the Depression

The depression had complex effects on society. First, life was not uniformly bleak in the 1930s. Despite the slump, modernization proceeded. Bordering English slums, one traveler in the mid-1930s noticed, were "filling stations and factories that look like exhibition buildings, giant cinemas and dance halls and cafés, bungalows with tiny garages, cocktail bars, Woolworth's [and] swimming pools." Municipal and national governments continued road construction; running water, electricity, and sewage pipes were installed in many homes for the first time. New factories manufactured synthetic fabrics, electrical products such as stoves, and automobiles—all of them in demand. With government assistance, industry developed in eastern Europe. In Romania, for example, industrial production increased by 55 percent between 1929 and 1939.

Second, the majority of Europeans and Americans had jobs throughout the 1930s, and people with steady employment benefited from a drastic drop in prices. Many service workers, managers, and business leaders enjoyed considerable prosperity. People with jobs, however, worried about becoming unemployed and having to scrape, like thousands of others, for a bare existence. In towns with heavy industry, sometimes more than half the population was out of work. In England in the mid-1930s, close to 20 percent of the population lacked adequate food, clothing, or housing. In a 1932 school assignment, a German youth wrote: "My father has been out of work for two and a half years. He thinks that I'll never find a job." Despite pockets of prosperity, a dark cloud of fear and resentment settled over Western society.

Economic catastrophe upset social life and strained gender relations. Unemployed men sometimes stayed home all day, increasing the tension in small, overcrowded apartments. Women often found low-paying jobs doing laundry and cleaning houses. Men who stayed home sometimes took over the housekeeping chores but often felt that this "women's work" demeaned their masculinity. As many women became breadwinners, albeit at low wages, men could be seen standing on street corners begging—a rearrangement of gender expectations that fueled discontent. Young men in cities faced severe unemployment. Some loitered in parks, intruding in areas usually frequented by mothers and their children and old people. As the percentage of farmworkers decreased in many areas, rural men faced the erosion of patriarchal authority, once central in overseeing farm labor and allocating property among offspring. Demagogues everywhere berated parliamentary politicians for their failure to stop the collapse of traditional values, setting the stage for Nazi and fascist politicians who promised to restore prosperity and male dignity.

Politicians of all stripes forecast national collapse as declining birthrates (after a brief postwar upturn) combined with the economic decline. A stagnant population was less apt to increase consumption and thus restore prosperity, and in difficult economic times people chose to have fewer children. Mandatory education and more years of required schooling, enforced more strictly after World War I, resulted in greater expenses for parents, adding another reason to limit family size. Working-class children no longer earned wages to supplement the family income; instead, they cost the family money while they went to school. Family planning centers opened, receiving a warm reception, and knowledge of birth control spread to the working and lower-middle classes, who continued the half-century-long trend of cutting family size.

Many politicians used the population "crisis" to gain votes by igniting racism: "superior" peoples were selfishly failing to breed, they charged, and "inferior" peoples were poised to take their place. This racism took a violent form in eastern Europe, where the rural population was growing because of increased life expectancy despite an overall drop in the birthrate. The population increase compounded the burdens of eastern European farm families, who faced an unprecedented struggle for survival. Throughout eastern Europe, peasant political parties blamed Jewish bankers for farm foreclosures and Jewish civil servants (of whom there were actually very few) for new taxes and inadequate relief programs. Population issues along with economic misery fueled ethnic hatred and anti-Semitism.

Global Dimensions of the Crash

The effects of the depression extended beyond the West, further accelerating the pace of change and spread of discontent in the European colonial empires. World War I and postwar investment had generated economic development, a rising population, and explosive urbanization in Asia, Africa, and Latin America. Japan in particular had become a formidable economic rival, and between 1920 and

1940, Shanghai ballooned from 1.7 million to 3.75 million residents and Calcutta from 1.8 million to 3.4 million. The depression, however, cut the demand for copper, tin, and other raw materials and for the finished products made in urban factories beyond the West. Rising productivity drove down the price of foodstuffs such as rice and coffee, and this proved disastrous to people who had been forced to grow a single cash crop. However, the economic picture was uneven in the colonies as well as in Europe. Established industrial sectors of the Indian economy, for instance, gained strength. In textiles, India achieved virtual independence from British cloth. The colonial powers' response to the depression added to ordinary people's smoldering grievances: they insisted that all taxes and loans be paid and manipulated currency rates in favor of the mother country so that those taxes were even higher than before. The millions of African and Asian colonial veterans of World War I fortified their resolve to be free.

India was a prime example of visibly rising anger toward colonialism. In the 1930s hundreds of thousands of veterans and millions of working people joined the upper-class Indians who had organized to gain rights from Britain in the late nineteenth century. Mohandas K. Gandhi (1869–1948, called "Mahatma," or "great-souled"), emerged as the charismatic leader for Indian independence.

■ **A Historic Act of Civil Disobedience**
Mohandas Gandhi used nonviolent resistance to challenge British rule. Because of the British government's monopoly on salt, Indians were prohibited from gathering this natural product, and every Indian family had to pay a tax on salt. In 1930, Gandhi led his supporters on a 200-mile march to India's salt flats to protest the hated salt tax and to extract salt from seawater. Gandhi was arrested and jailed, but his followers continued their march to the sea.
(© Bettmann/Corbis.)

Trained in England as a Western-style lawyer, Gandhi embraced Hindu self-denial, rejecting the elaborate trappings of British life in favor of simple clothing made of thread he had spun. Gandhi advocated **civil disobedience**—the deliberate but peaceful breaking of the law—which he claimed to model on British suffragists' tactics and on the teachings of Jesus, Buddha, and other spiritual leaders. Boycotting British-made goods and disobeying British laws, he aimed to end the Indians' traditional deference toward the British. The British jailed Gandhi repeatedly and tried to split the independence movement by encouraging the rival Muslim League and promoting Hindu-Muslim conflict.

In the Middle East, Westernizer Mustafa Kemal (1881–1938), known as Atatürk ("first among Turks"), led the Turks to found the independent republic of Turkey in 1923 and to craft a capitalist economy. In an effort to nationalize and modernize Turkish culture, Kemal moved the national capital from Constantinople to Ankara in 1923, changed the ancient Greek *Constantinople* to the Turkish *Istanbul* in 1930, mandated Western dress for men and women, introduced the Latin alphabet, and abolished polygamy. In 1936, women received the vote and became eligible to serve in the Turkish parliament. Like Atatürk, nationalist leaders in Persia and Egypt sought to loosen the financial and political grip of Europeans on their countries.

France made few concessions to colonized peoples. The French were obsessed by rising trade barriers in Europe and by their own population decline. Trade with their colonies increased as their trade with Europe lagged, and the demographic surge in Asia and Africa bolstered French optimism. One French official remarked: "One hundred and ten million strong, France can stand up to Germany." Like other Western-educated native leaders, Ho Chi Minh, founder of the Indochinese Communist Party, contested his people's subjection, but in 1930 the French crushed a peasant uprising he led. Thus preoccupied with their empires, Britain and France fortified their positions around the world and let totalitarian forces spread unchecked throughout Europe during the crisis-ridden 1930s.

■ **REVIEW:** *How did the Great Depression affect society and politics?*

Totalitarian Triumph

Representative government collapsed under the sheer weight of social and economic crisis. After 1929, Italy's Benito Mussolini, the Soviet Union's Joseph Stalin, and Germany's Adolf Hitler were able to mobilize vast support for their violent regimes. Many people admired Mussolini and Hitler for the discipline they brought to social and economic life. In an age of crisis, utopian hopes led many to support political violence as a means of solving all their problems. Unity and obedience—not freedom and civil rights—were seen as keys to rebirth. The common use of violence has led some scholars to apply the term **totalitarianism** to the Fascist, Nazi, and

Communist regimes of the 1930s. The term refers to highly centralized systems of government that attempt to control society in its most private details and ensure conformity through a single party and police terror. Other historians find a single term too simplistic to embrace Fascism in Italy, Nazism in Germany, and Communism in the Soviet Union. But, forged in the crucible of war and its aftermath, these regimes all broke with the liberal principles of the rule of law and fundamental rights and eventually waged war on their own citizens.

The Rise of Stalinism

In the 1930s, Joseph Stalin led the astonishing transformation of the USSR from a rural society into a formidable industrial power. Having taken firm control against Lenin's express wishes, Stalin ended the New Economic Policy (NEP), Lenin's temporary compromise between Marxism and capitalism, with the first of several **five-year plans** presented in 1929. The first plan outlined a program for massive increases in the output of coal, steel, and industrial goods. Without an end to economic backwardness, Stalin warned, "the advanced countries . . . will crush us." He thus established central economic planning—a policy used on both sides in World War I and increasingly favored by economists and industrialists around the world. Between 1928 and 1940, the number of Soviet workers in industry, construction, and transport grew from 4.6 million to 12.6 million. From 1927 to 1937, production in metallurgy and machinery rose 1,400 percent. Stalin's first five-year plan helped make the USSR a leading industrial nation.

Central planning led to the creation of a new elite of bureaucrats and industrial officials. Mostly party officials and technical experts, these managers dominated Soviet workers by limiting their ability to change jobs or move from place to place. Nonetheless, skilled workers as well as bureaucrats benefited substantially from the redistribution of privileges that accompanied industrialism and central planning. Compared with people working the land, both managers and workers in industry had better housing and higher wages, and Communist officials enjoyed additional perquisites such as country homes and luxurious vacations.

Unskilled workers faced a grim plight, often with real dedication. Newcomers from the countryside were herded into barrack-like dwellings, even tents, and subjected to dangerous factory conditions. Many took pride in the skills they acquired: "We mastered this profession—completely new to us—with great pleasure," a female lathe operator recalled. More often, however, workers lacked the technical education and even the tools necessary to accomplish goals prescribed by the five-year plan. Because fulfilling the plan had top priority as a measure of progress toward the Communist utopia, official lying about productivity became ingrained in the economic system. Both the grim conditions and honest commitment to Communist goals turned the Soviet Union from an illiterate peasant society into an advanced industrial economy in a single decade. Intense suffering was tolerated because Soviet workers believed in the ethos of "constant struggle, struggle, and struggle" to achieve a Communist society, in the words of one worker. As another put it, "Man himself is being rebuilt."

In country and city alike, work was politicized. Stalin demanded more grain from peasants (who had prospered under the NEP), both to feed the urban workforce and to export as a way to finance industrialization. Peasants resisted government demands by cutting production or withholding produce from the market. Faced with such recalcitrance, Stalin announced a new challenge: "liquidation of the kulaks." The name *kulak* ("fist") was supposed to apply to prosperous peasants, and from late in the 1920s party workers scoured villages, forcing villagers to identify the kulaks in their midst. Anti-kulak propaganda was intense. One Russian remembered believing they were "bloodsuckers, cattle, swine, loathsome, repulsive: they had no souls; they stank." As "enemies of the state," whole families and even entire villages were robbed of their possessions, left to starve, or even murdered outright. Confiscated kulak land formed the basis of the *kolkhoz,* or collective farm, where peasants were to create a Communist agricultural system using cooperative farming and modern machinery.

Economic disaster followed and ushered in violent purges. The inexperience of workers and party officials with advanced industrialization often meant they were unable to meet quotas. Soviet citizens starved as the grain harvest declined from 83 million tons in 1930 to 67 million in 1934. Stalin blamed such failure on "wreckers," saboteurs of communism. To rid society of these villains, he instituted **purges**—state violence in the form of widespread arrests, imprisonment in labor camps, and executions. The purges touched nearly all segments of society, but "bourgeois" engineers were the first group condemned for causing low productivity. Trials of prominent figures followed. When Sergei Kirov, the popular first secretary of the Leningrad Communist Party, was murdered, Stalin used his death (which he may have instigated) as the pretext to try former Bolshevik leaders in a series of "show trials"—trials based on trumped-up charges, fabricated evidence, and coerced confessions. Tortured and coerced to confess in court, most of those found guilty were shot.

The spirit of purge swept society. One woman poet described the scene: "Great concert and lecture halls were turned into public confessionals. . . . People did penance for [everything]. . . . Beating their breasts, the 'guilty' would lament that they had 'shown political short-sightedness' and 'lack of vigilance' . . . and were full of 'rotten liberalism.'" In 1937 and 1938, military leaders were arrested and executed without public trials; some ranks were entirely wiped out. Simultaneously, the government centralized and vastly expanded the number of prison camps stretching several thousand miles from Moscow to Siberia. Called the Gulag—an acronym for the administrative arm of the camps—the system held millions of prisoners who served as slave laborers in the cause of Communist development. A million people died annually as a result of the harsh conditions. Insufficient food and housing, twelve- to sixteen-hour workdays at mining, digging canals, and other crushing labor, and regular beatings and murder of prisoners rounded out Gulag life, which became another aspect of Soviet violence.

Before the outbreak of World War II in 1939, casualties of the Soviet system far exceeded those in Nazi Germany. Some historians have seen the purges as a clear-headed attempt by Stalin to eliminate barriers to total control; others, as the machinations of a psychopath. More recently, historians have judged the purges as resulting from power struggles among party officials and fueled by those looking for a quick route to the top. Still other interpretations see many of the denunciations and confessions as sincere expressions of workers' commitment to rooting out enemies of their proletarian utopia. Finally, historians point out that the horrific toll in human life opened doors to better jobs for those who survived and built their loyalty to communism. We may be certain of still another outcome: ongoing arrests, incarcerations, and executions removed rivals to Stalin's power.

The 1930s also marked a sharp reversal of toleration in Soviet social life, as sexual freedom also retreated. Much like the rest of Europe, the Soviet Union experienced a rapid decline in its birthrate in the 1930s. This drop, combined with the need to replace the millions of people lost since 1914, motivated Stalin to end the reproductive freedom of the early revolutionary years in order to increase the birthrate. The state restricted access to birth-control information and abortion. More lavish wedding ceremonies came back into fashion, divorces became difficult to obtain, and the state criminalized homosexuality. Whereas Bolsheviks had once derided the family as a "bourgeois" institution, propaganda now referred to the family unit as a "school for socialism." Yet women in rural areas made gains in literacy and received improved health care. Positions in the lower ranks of the party opened to women as the purges continued, and women increasingly were accepted into the professions. However, the stress on women, particularly those in the industrial workforce, increased. After long hours in factories, they also waited in long lines to obtain scarce consumer goods, and they performed all household and child-care tasks under harsh conditions.

Cultural life was equally paradoxical under Stalin, for he brought an end to avant-garde experimentation even though he called artists and writers "engineers of the soul." The Communist Party controlled their work through the Union of Soviet Writers, which assigned housing, office space, equipment, and secretarial help and even determined the types of books authors could write. In return, the "comrade artist" adhered to the official style of "socialist realism," derived from the 1920s focus on the common worker as a type of social hero. Some artists, such as the poet Anna Akhmatova (1889–1966), refused to accept this system.

> Stars of death stood above us, and Russia,
> In her innocence, twisted in pain
> Under blood-spattered boots . . .

■ **N. J. Altman,** *Anna Akhmatova*
This modernist painting portrays the poet in 1914 when she was a centerpiece of literary salon life in Russia and the subject of several avant-garde portraits. In the 1930s and 1940s, Akhmatova gave poetic voice to Soviet suffering, recording in her verse ordinary people's endurance of purges, deprivation, and warfare. As she encouraged people to resist the Nazis during World War II, Stalin allowed her to revive Russian patriotism instead of socialist internationalism.
(State Russian Museum, St. Petersburg/ The Bridgeman Art Library. Art © Estate of Natan J. Altman/RAO, Moscow/VAGA, NY.)

wrote Akhmatova in those years. Many others, including the composer Sergei Prokofiev (1891–1953), found ways to accommodate their talents to the state's demands. Prokofiev composed scores for the delightful *Peter and the Wolf* and for Sergei Eisenstein's 1938 film *Alexander Nevsky*, a work that transparently compared Stalin with the towering medieval rulers of the Russian people. Aided by adaptable artists, workers, and bureaucrats, Stalin stood triumphant as the 1930s drew to a close.

Hitler's Rise to Power

Hitler ended German democracy. Since the early 1920s, he had been trying to rouse the German people to crush the fragile Weimar Republic. In his failed 1923 attempt to take over the government, in his influential book *Mein Kampf* ("My Struggle," 1925), and in his leadership of the Nazi Party, Hitler drummed at a message of anti-Semitism and the rebirth of the German "race." When the Great Depression struck Germany, his party began to outstrip its rivals in elections. Film and press mogul Alfred Hugenberg's newspapers helped, relentlessly slamming the Weimar government as responsible for the disastrous economy and inflaming wounded German pride over the defeat in World War I. Parliamentary government practically ground to a halt in the face of economic crisis. The Reichstag failed to approve emergency plans to improve the economy, and Hitler's followers made parliamentary government look even more inept by rampaging through the streets attacking Jews and jousting with young Communists who agitated on behalf of the Soviets. By targeting these different institutions and groups as a single, monolithic "Bolshevik" enemy, the Nazis won wide approval.

As a result of the depression, media publicity, and its own street tactics, Hitler's National Socialist German Workers' Party (NSDAP)—the Nazi Party—which had received little more than 2 percent of the vote in 1928, won almost 20 percent in the Reichstag elections of 1930 and more than doubled its representation in 1932. Many of Hitler's supporters, like Stalin's, were young and idealistic. In 1930, 70 percent of Nazi Party members were under forty, a stark contrast to the image of Weimar politicians as aged and ineffectual. To youth, the future looked bleak, and they were full of idealism that a better world was possible under Hitler's militaristic control. Germans of every class also supported the Nazis. The largest number of supporters came from the industrial working class, which had the most voters, but white-collar workers and members of the lower middle class joined the party in percentages out of proportion with their numbers in the population. The years of inflation that wiped out savings left them with especially bitter memories, and they, like middle-class businessmen, were ready for Hitler to lead them even if he did seem a little rough around the edges.

Hitler's modern propaganda techniques helped build his appeal. Thousands of recordings of Hitler's speeches and Nazi mementos circulated widely among the citizenry. Teenagers painted their fingernails with swastikas, a symbol used by the Nazis, and soldiers flashed metal match covers with Nazi insignia. Nazi rallies were masterpieces of political display in which Hitler mesmerized the crowds as their *Führer,* or leader—a strong, superior being. Frenzied and inspirational, he seemed neither a calculating politician nor a rational bureaucrat but "the creative element," as one poet put it. In actuality, however, Hitler viewed the masses as tools. In *Mein Kampf,* he explained his philosophy of how to deal with them:

> *The receptivity of the great masses is very limited, their intelligence is small. In consequence of these facts, all effective propaganda must be limited to a very few points and must harp on those in slogans until the last member of the public understands what you want him to understand.*

With Hitler, as with Stalin, mass politics reached terrifying and cynical proportions.

Nazi success along with Communist electoral strength in the 1932 Reichstag elections made the leader of one of those parties the logical choice as chancellor. Germany's conservative elites—from the military, industry, and the state bureaucracy—loathed the Communists and favored Hitler as a common type they thought they could easily manipulate. In January 1933, he was invited to become chancellor, and he accepted.

■ Toys Depicting Nazis

As a totalitarian ideology, Nazism permeated everyday life. Nazi insignia decorated clothing, dishes, cigarette lighters, and even toys. Men and women became husbands and wives in accordance with Nazi rules and sent their children to Nazi clubs and organizations. Nazi songs, Nazi parades and festivals, and Nazi radio filled leisure hours.
(Trustees of the Imperial War Museum, London.)

The Nazification of German Politics

Hitler took office amid jubilation in Berlin. Tens of thousands of storm troopers (SA) holding blazing torches paraded through the streets. Millions of Germans celebrated Hitler's ascent to power. One recalled: "My father went down to the cellar and brought up our best bottles of wine. . . . And my mother wept for joy." Instead of being easy to manipulate, Hitler took power brutally and closed down representative government.

Within a month of Hitler's taking power, the elements of Nazi political domination were in place. When the Reichstag building was gutted by fire in February 1933, Hitler blamed the Communists and used the fire as the excuse for suspending civil rights, imposing censorship of the press, and prohibiting meetings of the opposition. He had always claimed that *all* political parties except the NSDAP were his enemies. "Our opponents complain that we National Socialists, and I in particular, are intolerant and intractable," he declared. "They are right, we are intolerant! I have set myself one task, namely to sweep those parties out of Germany."

Storm troopers' political violence became a tool for suppressing parliamentary debate. At the end of March, intimidated Reichstag delegates let pass the **Enabling Act**, which suspended the constitution for four years and allowed Nazi laws to take effect without parliamentary approval. Solid middle-class Germans approved the Enabling Act as a way to advance the creation of a *Volksgemeinschaft* ("people's community") of like-minded, racially pure Germans—"Aryans" in Nazi terminology. Heinrich Himmler headed the elite SS (*Schutzstaffel*) organization that protected Hitler, and he commanded the government's political police system. The Gestapo, an internal security police force organized by Hermann Goering, also enforced complete obedience to Nazism. These organizations had vast powers to arrest, execute, or imprison people in concentration camps, the first of which opened at Dachau near Munich in March 1933. The Nazis filled it and later camps with socialists, homosexuals, Jews, and others said to interfere with the Volksgemeinschaft. As one Nazi leader proclaimed:

> [*National socialism*] *does not believe that one soul is equal to another, one man equal to another. It does not believe in rights as such. It aims to create the German man of strength, its task is to protect the German people, and all . . . must be subordinate to this goal.*

Hitler deliberately blurred authority in the government and party so that confusion and bitter competition reigned. He thus prevented the emergence of coalitions against him and allowed himself to arbitrate the confusion, often with violence. When Ernst Roehm, leader of the SA and Hitler's long-time collaborator, called for a "second revolution" to end the corrupt influence of the old business and military elites on the Nazi leadership, Hitler ordered Roehm's assassination. The bloody "Night of the Long Knives" (June 30, 1934), during which hundreds of SA leaders and innocent civilians were killed, enhanced Hitler's support among conservatives. Nazism's terroristic politics remained as the foundation of Hitler's "Third Reich"— a German empire succeeding the empires of Charlemagne and William II.

New economic and social programs, especially those that put people back to work, also bolstered Hitler's regime. Economic revival built popular support, strengthened military industries, and provided the basis for German expansion. The Nazi government pursued **pump priming**—that is, stimulating the economy through government spending on tanks and airplanes and the Autobahn highway system. From farms to factories, the government demanded high productivity, and unemployment declined from a peak of almost 6 million in 1932 to 1.6 million by 1936. When labor shortages appeared in some areas, the government conscripted single women into service as farmworkers and domestics. The Nazi Party closed down labor unions. Government bureaucrats classified jobs, determined work procedures, and set pay levels, rating women's jobs lower than men's regardless of the level of expertise required. Imitating Stalin, Hitler announced a four-year plan in 1936 with the secret aim of preparing Germany for war by 1940, and he instituted central planning. His programs produced large deficits, which the spoils of future conquests were supposed to eliminate.

Hitler exercised unprecedented power over the workings of everyday life, including gender roles. In June 1933, a bill took effect that encouraged Aryans to marry and have children. The bill provided for loans to Aryan newlyweds, but only to those couples in which the wife left the workforce. The loans were forgiven on the birth of a couple's fourth child. Nazi marriage programs enforced a nineteenth-century ideal of femininity; women were supposed to be subordinate so men would feel tough and industrious despite military defeat and economic depression.

Nazism impoverished ordinary life. Although 70 percent of households had "people's radios" by 1938, the programming that was broadcast was severely censored. In May 1933 a huge book-burning ceremony rid libraries of works by Jews, socialists, homosexuals, and modernist writers out of favor with the Nazis. Modern art in museums and in private collections was destroyed or confiscated, and laws took jobs from Jews and women and bestowed them on Nazi Party members. In the Hitler Youth organization, which boys and girls over age ten had to join, children learned to report to Nazi authorities any adults they suspected of disloyalty to the regime, even their own parents. Germans boasted that they could leave their bicycles outdoors at night without fear of robbery, but their world was filled with informers—some 100,000 of them on the Nazi payroll. In general, the improved economy led many to believe that Hitler was working an economic miracle while restoring pride in Germany and the harmonious community of an imaginary past. For hundreds of thousands if not millions of Germans, however, Nazi rule in the 1930s brought anything but community.

Nazi Racism

The Nazis defined Jews as an inferior "race" dangerous to the superior Aryan or Germanic "race" and responsible for most of Germany's problems, including the defeat in World War I and the intensity of the depression. Hitler attacked many ethnic and social groups, but he propelled the nineteenth-century politics of anti-Semitism to new and frightening heights. In the rhetoric of Nazism, Jews were "vermin," "abscesses," "parasites," and "Bolsheviks," whom the Germans would have to eliminate to create a true Volksgemeinschaft. By defining the Jews as evil financiers and businessmen and as working-class Bolsheviks, Hitler fashioned an enemy for many segments of the German population to hate.

Nazi racism led to laws against non-Aryans—a group that, like Aryans, was fuzzily defined. Racial classifications were made to appear scientific, however, by lists of physical and other characteristics that the Nazis claimed determined a person's "race." In 1935, the government enacted the **Nuremberg Laws**, legislation that specifically deprived Jews of citizenship, defined Jewishness according to a person's ancestry as opposed to religion, and prohibited marriage between Jews and other Germans. Whereas women classified as Aryan had increasing difficulty obtaining abortions or birth-control information, these were readily available to the outcast groups, including Jews, gypsies, Slavs, and people with mental or physical disabilities. In the name of improving the Aryan race, German doctors helped organize the T4 project, which used carbon monoxide poisoning and other means to kill large numbers of people—200,000 with disabilities and the elderly—late in the 1930s. This murder of those deemed harmful to the Aryan race prepared the way for the even larger mass exterminations that would occur later.

Jews were forced into slave labor, evicted from their apartments, and prevented from buying most clothing and food. In 1938, a Jewish teenager, reacting to the harassment of his parents, killed a German official. In retaliation, Nazis attacked some two hundred synagogues, smashed the windows of Jewish-owned stores, ransacked apartments of known or suspected Jews, and threw more than twenty thousand Jews into prisons and camps. The night of November 9–10 became known as *Kristallnacht*, the "Night of Broken Glass." Faced with relentless persecution, which some historians have called a "social death," by the outbreak of World War II in 1939 more than half of Germany's 500,000 Jews had emigrated. The confiscation of the emigrants' property enriched their neighbors and individual Nazis; the payment of enormous emigration fees helped finance Germany's revival.

■ **REVIEW:** *What role did violence play in the Soviet and Nazi regimes?*

Democracies on the Defensive

Nazism, communism, and fascism offered bold new approaches to modern politics and new kinds of economic and social policies. Their leaders' energetic, military style of mobilizing the masses made the democratic values of the United States, France, and Great Britain seem to be the effeminate and their parliamentary system of building consensus a waste of time. During the 1930s, democracies were on the defensive in a variety of arenas—economic, political, and cultural.

Confronting the Economic Crisis

As the depression wore on, some governments undertook notable experiments to solve social and economic crises and still maintain democratic politics. In the early days of the slump, U.S. president Herbert Hoover (1874–1964) opposed direct federal help to the unemployed and in the summer of 1932 even ordered the army to use tanks to break up a march of unemployed World War I veterans in Washington, D.C. With unemployment close to fifteen million, Franklin Delano Roosevelt, the wealthy, patrician governor of New York, defeated Hoover in the fall presidential election, promising innovation. Roosevelt (1882–1945) pushed through a torrent of legislation, known as the "New Deal," some of it inspired by the central control of the economy achieved during World War I: relief for businesses, price supports for hard-pressed farmers, and public works programs for unemployed youth. The Social Security Act of 1935 set up a fund to which

■ Fireside Chat with FDR

President Franklin Delano Roosevelt was a master of words, uttering many memorable phrases that inspired Americans during the depression and World War II. Here he addresses the nation on August 23, 1938, over a radio hookup while his wife Eleanor and his mother Sarah observe. Although Roosevelt was disabled by polio, wore leg braces, and could not walk unassisted, the press never showed or mentioned his impairment, even on the rare occasions when he used crutches or a wheelchair in public. (Getty Images.)

employers and employees contributed. It provided retirement benefits for workers, unemployment insurance, and payments to dependent mothers, their children, and people with disabling physical conditions.

Roosevelt's New Deal advanced the trend toward the **welfare state**—a society in which the government guarantees a certain level of economic well-being for individuals and businesses—across the West. The New Deal angered businesspeople and the wealthy, who considered it "socialist." But even though the depression remained severe, Roosevelt (quickly nicknamed FDR) maintained widespread support. Like other successful politicians of the 1930s, he made expert use of the mass media, especially in his "fireside chats" broadcast by radio to the American people. In sharp contrast to Mussolini and Hitler, however, Roosevelt aimed in his public statements to sustain—not denounce—faith in democratic rights and popular government. Eager to separate themselves from Hoover's position, First Lady Eleanor Roosevelt (1884–1962) rushed to greet the next group of veterans marching on Washington, and the president received a delegation of veterans at the

White House. The Roosevelts insisted that justice and human rights must not be surrendered in difficult times. "We Americans of today . . . are characters in the living book of democracy," FDR told a group of teenagers in 1939. "But we are also its author." Lynchings, racial violence, and harsh discrimination continued to cause enormous suffering in the United States during the Roosevelt administration, but the president's media success kept faith in democracy strong.

Sweden also developed a coherent program for solving economic and population problems that reconceived the government's role in promoting social welfare and economic democracy. Sweden industrialized later than western Europe and the United States but had a tradition of community responsibility for working through social and economic difficulties. Sweden succeeded in turning its economy around in the 1930s and instituted central planning of the economy and social welfare programs. It also devalued the currency to make Swedish exports more attractive on the international market. Thanks to pump-priming programs, Swedish productivity rose 20 percent between 1929 and 1935, a time when other democracies were still experiencing economic decline.

Sweden addressed the population problem with government programs but without racist and antidemocratic coercion. Alva Myrdal (1902–1986), a leading member of Sweden's parliament, believed fertility rates reflected economic conditions and individuals' sense of their personal well-being. Acting on her advice to promote "voluntary parenthood," the government of Sweden started a loan program for married couples in 1937 and introduced prenatal care, free childbirth in a hospital, a food relief program, and subsidized housing for large families. By the end of the decade, almost 50 percent of all Swedish mothers were receiving government aid. Long a concern of feminists and other social reformers in Sweden, care of families became an important task of the modern state, which now saw itself as responsible for citizen welfare in hard times.

The most powerful democracy, the United States, had withdrawn from world leadership by refusing to participate in the League of Nations, leaving Britain and France with virtually sole responsibility for maintaining international peace—a far greater task than their postwar resources could sustain. When the Great Depression hit, Britain was already mired in economic difficulties. Faced with falling government revenues, Prime Minister Ramsay MacDonald, though leader of the Labour Party, reduced payments to the unemployed, and Parliament effectively denied unemployment insurance to women even though they had contributed to the unemployment fund. To protect jobs, the government imposed huge protective tariffs that actually discouraged a revival of international trade. Only in 1933, when all else had failed to improve the economy, did the government turn to pump priming with massive programs of slum clearance, new housing construction, and health insurance for the needy.

Depression struck later in France, but the country endured a decade of public strife in the 1930s due to severe postwar demoralization, stagnant population growth, and wage cuts. Deputies with opposing views on the economic crisis frequently came to blows in the Chamber of Deputies, and governments were voted in and out with dizzying rapidity. Parisians took to the streets to protest the government's belt-tightening policies, and right-wing paramilitary groups mushroomed, attracting the unemployed, students, and veterans with promises to end representative government. In February 1934, the paramilitary groups joined Communists and other outraged citizens in riots around the parliament building. "Let's string up the deputies," chanted the crowd. "And if we can't string them up, let's beat in their faces, let's reduce them to a pulp." Hundreds of demonstrators were wounded and killed, but the antirepublican right lacked both substantial support outside Paris and a leader like Hitler or Mussolini capable of unifying its various groups. In France, as elsewhere, hard times menaced democracy.

Shocked into action by the force of fascism, French liberals, socialists, and Communists established an antifascist coalition known as the Popular Front. Until that time, such a merging of groups had been impossible in democratic countries because of Stalin's strict opposition to Communist collaboration with liberals and socialists. As fascism spread throughout Europe, however, Stalin reversed course and allowed Communists to join such efforts to protect democracy. For just over a year in 1936–1937 and again very briefly in 1938, the French Popular Front formed a government, with the socialist leader Léon Blum (1872–1950) as premier. Like the American New Dealers and the Swedish Social Democrats, the French Popular Front instituted long-overdue reforms. Blum extended family subsidies and welfare benefits, and he appointed women to his government (though women in France still were not allowed to vote). In June 1936, the government guaranteed workers two-week paid vacations, a forty-hour workweek, and the right to collective bargaining. Working people would long remember Blum as the man who improved their living standards and provided them with benefits and vacations. During its brief life, the French Popular Front offered the masses a youthful but democratic political culture. "In 1936 everyone was twenty years old," one man recalled, evoking the atmosphere of idealism. Local cultural centers sprang up, and to express their opposition to fascism, citizens celebrated Bastille Day and other democratic holidays with new enthusiasm. Powerful business elites thought differently about government spending and sent their capital out of the country, leaving France financially strapped. "Better Hitler than Blum" was the slogan of the upper classes. Blum's government fell when it also lost the left by refusing material support in the fight against fascism in Spain. As in Britain, memories of World War I caused leaders to block crucial support to foreign democratic forces, such as the republicans in Spain, and to keep domestic military budgets small. The collapse of the antifascist Popular Front in late June 1937 showed the difficulties that pluralistic and democratic societies faced in crisis-ridden times.

Fledgling democracies in central Europe, hit hard by the depression, also fought the twin struggle for economic survival and representative government, but less successfully. In 1932, Engelbert Dollfuss (1892–1934) came to power in Austria, dismissing the parliament and ruling briefly as a dictator. Despite his authoritarian stance, Dollfuss would not submit to the Nazis, who assassinated him in 1934. In Hungary, where outrage over the Peace of Paris remained intense, a crippled economy resulted in right-wing general Gyula Gömbös (1886–1936) taking over in 1932. Gömbös reoriented his country's foreign policy toward Mussolini and Hitler. He stirred up anti-Semitism and ethnic hatreds and left considerable pro-Nazi feeling after his death in 1936.

President Tomas Masaryk worked to maintain a democratic Czechoslovakia, welcoming refugees from Nazi Germany and pushing for further industrial growth. Meanwhile, the Slovaks, who were both poorer and less educated than the urbanized Czechs, built a strong Slovak Fascist Party, while the Communists attacked democratic government there: "when you are swept away," one young Communist leader announced to his fellow representatives in parliament, "there will be peace and order." The country clung to democracy nonetheless unlike Poland, Romania, Yugoslavia, and Bulgaria, where authoritarian leaders took power as ethnic tensions simmered. The appeal of fascism grew among rural people and unemployed workers across central and eastern Europe as the Great Depression lingered.

Cultural Visions in Hard Times

Cultural leaders now mobilized to meet the crisis of economic hard times and the antidemocratic political menace by making films, writing novels, and producing art that captured the spirit of everyday struggle. Some empathized with the situations of factory workers, homemakers, and shopgirls struggling to support themselves or their families; others, with the ever-growing numbers of the unemployed and destitute. In 1931, French director René Clair's film *À nous la liberté* ("Give Us Liberty") related prison life to work on a factory assembly line. In 1936, Charlie Chaplin's film *Modern Times* showed his hero the Little Tramp as a factory worker who was so molded by his monotonous job that he assumes that anything he can see, even a coworker's body, needs mechanical adjustment. This sympathetic representation of the modern factory worker in hard times made Chaplin a hit even in the Soviet Union.

Media sympathy poured out to victims of the crisis. Women were portrayed alternately as the cause of and as the cure for society's problems. *The Blue Angel* (1930), a German film starring Marlene Dietrich, showed how a vital, modern woman could destroy men—and civilization; it depicted a woman's power to dominate over the ineffectuality of an impractical professor. In comedies and musicals, by contrast, heroines behaved bravely, pulling their men out of the depths of despair and setting things right. For example, in *Keep Smiling* (1938) and other films, the British comedienne Gracie Fields portrayed spunky working-class women who remained cheerful despite hard times.

Ridiculed in the past, techniques of modern art became standard tools for popular culture and advertising. Graphic artists used montage, which overlaid two

■ **Paul Klee, *Dancing with Fear* (1938)**
Swiss-German artist Paul Klee (1879–1940) explored modern art's ability to evoke universal truths behind surface reality. Delightful shapes and colors often marked his work, although he was always concerned with how technology would affect people's values. As the danger of Nazism's triumph mounted, Klee grew depressed and produced dark visions of fear and death.
(Paul-Klee-Stiftung, Kunstmuseum Bern, photo: Peter Lauri. © 2007 Artists Rights Society [ARS], New York/VG Bild-Kunst, Bonn.)

or more photos or parts of photos, to grab visual attention in the cultural battles of the 1930s. Some intellectuals turned away from experimentation with nonrepresentational forms as they drove home their antifascist, pacifist, or pro-worker beliefs. Popular Front writers created realistic studies of human misery and the threat of war that haunted life in the 1930s. The British writer George Orwell described his experiences among the poor of Paris and London, wrote investigative pieces about the unemployed in the north of England, and published an account of atrocities committed by both sides during the Spanish Civil War (1936–1939). Art reaffirmed Western values such as rationalism, rights, and concern for the poor. German writer Thomas Mann, a Christian, went into exile when Hitler came to power and began a series of novels based on the Old Testament hero Joseph to convey the struggle between humanist values and barbarism. The fourth volume, *Joseph the Provider* (1944), eulogized Joseph's welfare state, in which the granaries were full and the rich paid taxes so the poor might live decent lives. One of the last works of English writer Virginia Woolf, *Three Guineas* (1938), rejected experimental forms such as interior monologues for a direct attack on militarism, poverty, and the oppression of women, claiming they were interconnected parts of a single, devastating ethos undermining Europe in the 1930s.

While writers rekindled moral concerns, scientists in research institutes and universities continued to point out limits to human understanding—limits that seemed at odds with the megalomaniacal pronouncements of dictators. Astronomer

Edwin Hubble in California determined in the early 1930s that the universe was an expanding entity. Czech mathematician Kurt Gödel maintained that any mathematical system contains some propositions that are undecidable. The German physicist Werner Heisenberg developed the "uncertainty," or "indeterminacy," principle in physics. Scientific observation of atomic behavior, according to this theory, actually disturbs the atom and thereby makes precise formulations impossible. Even scientists, Heisenberg asserted, had to settle for statistical probability. Limits to understanding and probability were not concepts employed by or welcome to dictators, and even people in democracies had a difficult time reconciling these new ideas with the certainty of which science and technology had once boasted.

Many religious leaders helped foster a spirit of resistance to dictatorship among the faithful. The Swiss theologian Karl Barth encouraged rebellion against the Nazis, teaching that religious people had to take seriously scriptural justifications of resistance to oppression. Pope Pius XI in his 1931 social encyclical (a letter addressed to the world on social issues) condemned the failure of modern societies to provide their citizens with a decent life and supported government intervention to create better moral and material conditions. The encyclical, *Quadragesimo Anno,* seemed to some an endorsement of the heavy-handed intervention of the fascists, and the Catholic leadership in the Vatican never condemned the lethal politics at work in Europe. Individual German Catholics frequently opposed Hitler, and religious commitment inspired many other individuals to contest the rising tide of fascism.

■ **REVIEW:** *How did the democracies work to maintain their values while facing the twin challenges of economic depression and the rise of fascism?*

The Road to Global War

In the wake of economic catastrophe, Hitler, Mussolini, and Japan's military leaders marched the world toward another catastrophic war. These leaders believed that their nations deserved to rule far larger territories. At first, many ordinary citizens and statesmen in Britain and France hoped that sanctions imposed by the League of Nations would work to contain aggression. Others, believing that the powers had rushed into World War I, counseled the appeasement of Hitler and Mussolini. The widespread desire for peace in the 1930s sprang from fresh and painful memories: the destruction of World War I and the economic turmoil of the Great Depression. But it left many people blind to Japanese actions in China, Hitler's outright expansionism, and the fascist attack on the Spanish republic. So brutal was the expansionism of the interwar years that some historians claim that along with World War I and World War II, they make up a "Thirty Years' War" of the twentieth century.

A Surge in Global Imperialism

The 1930s brought the last surge of global imperialism and one that ultimately led to a thoroughly global war. In the East, Japan's military leaders chafed to control more of Asia and saw China, the Soviet Union, and the other Western powers as obstacles to the empire's prosperity and the fulfillment of its destiny. By the 1930s the young emperor Hirohito and his advisers had successfully spread the idea that as a racially superior nation, Japan deserved an extensive empire. Renewed military vigor was seen as the key to pulling agriculture and small business from the depths of economic depression. The Japanese army took the lead in making these claims a reality. In September 1931, a train in the Chinese province of Manchuria blew up. Japanese officers used the explosion, which they had set, as an excuse to invade Manchuria, set up a puppet government, and push farther into China. The Japanese public agreed with journalistic calls for aggressive expansion in China and elsewhere to boost Japan's prestige, and businessmen wanted new markets and resources for their burgeoning but wounded industries. Advocating Asian conquest as part of Japan's "divine mission," the military extended its influence in the government. By 1936–1937, Japan was spending 47 percent of its budget on arms, and its claims to racial superiority and entitlement to the lands of inferior people linked it with Germany and Italy, setting the stage for a powerful global alliance.

The situation in East Asia had international repercussions. The League of Nations condemned the invasion of Manchuria but imposed no sanctions that would have enforced its condemnation. The rebuff alone outraged the Japanese public and goaded the government to ally with Hitler and Mussolini. In 1937, Japan attacked China again, justifying its offensive as a first step toward liberating the region from Western imperialism. Hundreds of thousands of Chinese were massacred in the "Rape of Nanjing"—an atrocity so named because of the brutality toward girls and women and the grim acts of torture perpetrated by the Japanese. President Roosevelt immediately announced an embargo on the U.S. export of airplane parts to Japan and later enforced stringent economic sanctions on the crucial raw materials that

The Road to World War II	
1929	Global depression begins with U.S. stock market crash
1931	Japan invades Manchuria
1933	Hitler comes to power in Germany
1935	Italy invades Ethiopia
1936	Civil war breaks out in Spain; Hitler remilitarizes the Rhineland
1937	Japan invades China
1938	Germany annexes Austria; European leaders meet in Munich to negotiate with Hitler
1939	Germany seizes Czechoslovakia; Hitler and Stalin sign nonaggression pact; Germany invades Poland; Britain and France declare war on Germany

drove Japanese industry. Nonetheless, the Western powers, including the Soviet Union, did not effectively resist Japan's territorial expansion in Asia and the Pacific.

Like Japanese leaders, Mussolini and Hitler called their countries "have-nots." Mussolini threatened "permanent conflict" to expand Italy's borders, and Hitler's agenda included breaking free from the Versailles treaty's military restrictions and gaining *Lebensraum* (living space) in which superior Aryans could thrive. This space would be taken from the "inferior" Slavic peoples and Bolsheviks, who would be moved to Siberia or serve as slaves. Both dictators portrayed themselves as peace-loving men who resorted to extreme measures only to benefit their countries and humanity. Their anticommunism appealed to statesmen across Europe, and Hitler's anti-Semitism found widespread support.

Both leaders' moves against the international status quo were open and audacious. In the autumn of 1933, Hitler announced Germany's withdrawal from the League of Nations. In 1935, Hitler loudly rejected the clauses of the Treaty of Versailles that limited German military strength; he reintroduced military conscription and publicly started rearming, although Germany had been rearming in secret for years. Mussolini also chose 1935 to invade Ethiopia, one of the few African states not overwhelmed by European imperialism. The attack was intended to demonstrate his regime's youth and vigor and to raise Italy's standing among the colonial powers. "The Roman legionnaires are again on the march," one soldier exulted. The poorly equipped Ethiopians resisted, but their capital, Addis Ababa, fell in the spring of 1936. The League of Nations voted sanctions against Italy; Britain and France, however, opposed an embargo with teeth in it—one on oil—and thus kept the sanctions from being effective while also suggesting a lack of resolve to fight aggression.

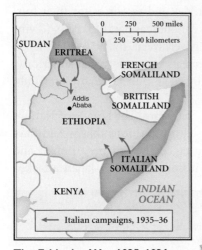

The Ethiopian War, 1935–1936

Profiting from the diversion of Italy's attack on Ethiopia, in March 1936 Hitler had defiantly sent his troops into what was supposed to be a permanently demilitarized zone in the Rhineland. The inhabitants greeted the Germans with wild enthusiasm. The French, whose security was most endangered by this action, protested to the League of Nations instead of countering with an invasion of their own as they had done in the Ruhr in 1923. The British, distracted with their own crises at home and abroad, accepted the remilitarization. The two dictators thus appeared as powerful military heroes forging, in Mussolini's muscular phrase, a "Rome–Berlin Axis." Next to them, the politicians of France and Great Britain looked timid and defeatable.

■ **MAP 21.1 The Spanish Civil War, 1936–1939**

Pro-republican and antirepublican forces fought one another to determine whether Spain would be a democracy or an authoritarian state. Germany and Italy sent opponents of the republic military assistance, notably airplanes to experiment with bombing civilians, while volunteers from around the world arrived to fight for the losing cause of the republic. Defeating these ill-organized groups, General Francisco Franco instituted a pro-fascist government that sent many to jail and into exile.

The Spanish Civil War, 1936–1939

Spain joined the wave of authoritarianism inundating Europe despite attempts to achieve democracy. In 1931 Spanish republicans overthrew their monarchy, which for centuries had fortified the grip of large landowners and the Catholic clergy over an impoverished peasantry. As Spain fitfully developed an industrial capacity in cities like Barcelona and Bilbao, these ruling elites failed to modernize the rural economy. Spanish republicans hoped to promote industry and efficient, independent farming, but they were so embroiled in battling one another that the republic had a hard time implementing a political program that would gain it widespread support in the countryside. Most important, the government they established failed to enact land redistribution, which might have ensured popular loyalty and diminished the power of landowners and the church. In 1936, pro-republican forces temporarily banded together in a Popular Front coalition to win elections and prevent the republic from collapsing under the weight of internal squabbling and growing monarchist opposition. With the Popular Front victory, euphoria swept Spain as coveted municipal jobs were doled out and unemployment abated.

In response, the forces of the right drew closer together, making use of their considerable wealth to undermine the government. In 1936, a group of army officers staged an uprising against the republican government in Madrid (Map 21.1). The rebellious officers soon found a determined leader, General Francisco Franco (1892–1975), who was able to make use of the right's considerable resources. The rebels—a mixture of monarchists, landowners, the clergy, and the fascist Falange

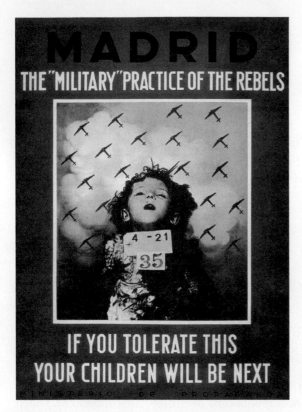

MADRID
THE "MILITARY" PRACTICE OF THE REBELS

IF YOU TOLERATE THIS
YOUR CHILDREN WILL BE NEXT

MINISTERIO DE PROPAGANDA

■ **The Spanish Republic Appeals for Aid**
The government of the Spanish republic sent out modern advertising and propaganda to attract support from the remaining democracies—especially Great Britain and France. Antiwar sentiment remained high among the British and French, however. Thus, despite the horrifying and deliberate bombing of civilians by Franco's German allies, aid for the republic failed to arrive.
(Imperial War Museum, London.)

Party—soon gained support from fascists in other parts of Europe, and the struggle in Spain became a rehearsal for World War II. Hitler and Mussolini sent military personnel to support the right under Franco, which allowed them to test new weapons and to practice the terror bombing of civilians. In 1937, low-flying German planes attacked the town of Guernica on market day, mowing down civilians in the streets. This gratuitous slaughter inspired Pablo Picasso's memorial mural to the dead, *Guernica* (1937), in which the intense suffering is starkly displayed in monochromatic grays and whites to capture a sense of moral decay as well as physical death.

The Spanish Republic appealed everywhere for assistance, but only the Soviet Union answered. Stalin withdrew his troops and tanks in 1938 as government ranks floundered. Britain and France showed their war-wariness by refusing to provide aid. Instead, a few thousand volunteers from a variety of countries—including students, journalists, and artists—fought for the republic. With Mussolini and Hitler on a rampage, "Spain was the place to stop fascism," these volunteers believed. The conflict was bitter and bloody with atrocities committed on both sides, but the splinter groups and citizen armies with which the Spanish Republic defended itself could not hold, while the aid Franco received ultimately proved decisive. His troops defeated the republicans in 1939, bringing another victory to the forces of authoritarianism in Europe. The ensuing dictatorship remained in place until 1975.

■ MAP 21.2 The Growth of Nazi Germany, 1933–1939

German expansion was rapid and surprising, as Hitler's forces and Nazi diplomacy brought about the annexation of the new states of central and eastern Europe. Though committed to defending the sovereignty of these states through the League of Nations, French and British diplomats were more interested in satisfying Hitler because they believed that doing so would prevent his claiming even more of Europe. They were mistaken, and Hitler proceeded to acquire the human and material resources of adjacent countries to support the Third Reich. **For more help analyzing this map,** see the map activity for this chapter in the ONLINE STUDY GUIDE at bedfordstmartins.com/huntconcise.

Hitler's Conquest of Central Europe, 1938–1939

The Nazi takeover of central Europe that ultimately led to World War II began with Hitler's annexation of Austria in 1938 (Map 21.2). Many Austrians actually wished for such a merger, or *Anschluss*, after the Paris peace settlement stripped them of their empire. So Hitler's troops easily entered Austria, and the enthusiasm of Nazi sympathizers among the Austrians made the Anschluss appear to support the Wilsonian idea of self-determination. The annexation began the unification of Aryan peoples into one greater German nation and marked the first step in Hitler's planned takeover of central and eastern Europe. Austria was declared a German province, and Hitler's thugs ruled once-cosmopolitan Vienna. An observer later commented on the scene: "University professors were obliged to scrub the streets with their naked hands, pious white-bearded Jews were dragged into the synagogue by hooting youths and forced to do knee-exercises and to shout 'Heil Hitler' in chorus." Nazis also generated support in Austria by building factories and housing and making Austrians feel that once again they were part of a great empire.

With Austria firmly in his grasp, Hitler turned to Czechoslovakia and its rich resources. Overpowering this democracy did not appear as simple a task as seizing Austria, however. Czechoslovakia had a large army and formidable border defenses and armament factories, and most Czech citizens were prepared to fight for their country. Hitler gambled correctly that the other Western powers would not interfere, especially as the Nazi propaganda machine poured tremendous abuse on Czechoslovakia for allegedly persecuting its German minority. By October 1, 1938, he warned, Czechoslovakia would have to grant autonomy (tantamount to Nazi rule) to the German-populated border region, the Sudetenland, or face German invasion.

As the October deadline approached, British prime minister Neville Chamberlain (1869–1940), Mussolini, and French premier Edouard Daladier (1884–1970) met with Hitler in Munich and agreed not to oppose Germany's claim to the Sudetenland. The strategy of preventing a war by making concessions for legitimate grievances (in this case, the alleged affront to Germans in the Peace of Paris) was called **appeasement**. At the time, it was widely seen as a positive act, and the agreement between Germany and Great Britain—the Munich Pact—prompted Chamberlain to announce that he had secured "peace in our time." Stalin, excluded from the Munich conference, learned from the deliberations that the democracies were not going to fight to protect eastern Europe. Having portrayed himself as a man of peace, Hitler waited until March 1939 to invade Czechoslovakia. Britain and France responded by promising military support to Poland, Romania, Greece, and Turkey in case of Nazi invasion. In May 1939, Hitler and Mussolini countered this agreement by signing a pledge of offensive and defensive support called the Pact of Steel.

Some historians have sharply criticized the Munich Pact because it bought Hitler time to build his army and seemed to give him the green light for further aggression. They believe that a confrontation might have stopped Hitler and that even if war had resulted, the democracies would have triumphed at less cost than they later did. According to this view, each military move by Germany, Italy, and Japan should have been met with stiff opposition, and the Soviet Union should have been made a partner to this resistance. Others counter that appeasement provided France and Britain precious time to beef up their own armies, which the Munich crisis prompted them to do, and to prepare their citizens for another war.

On August 23, 1939, to the astonishment of public opinion in the West, Germany and the USSR signed a nonaggression agreement. Despite Hitler's ambition to wipe the Bolsheviks off the face of the earth, Stalin needed time to reconstitute his military because he had destroyed his officer corps in the purges. The **Nazi-Soviet Pact** provided that if one country became embroiled in war, the other country would remain neutral. Moreover, the two dictators secretly agreed to divide Poland and the Baltic states—Latvia, Estonia, and Lithuania—at some future date. The Nazi-Soviet Pact ensured that if war came, the democracies would be fighting a Germany with no fear of attack on its eastern borders. Believing that Great Britain and perhaps even France would not fight because his aggression had met no resistance so far, Hitler now aimed his forces at Poland.

■ **REVIEW:** *How did the aggression of Japan, Germany, and Italy create the conditions for global war?*

World War II, 1939–1945

On September 1, 1939, Hitler launched an all-out attack on Poland opening the global catastrophe of World War II. In contrast to 1914, no jubilation in Berlin accompanied the invasion; when Britain and France declared war two days later, the mood in their capitals was similarly grim. Although Japan, Italy, and the United States did not join the battle immediately, their eventual participation spread the fighting throughout the world. By the time World War II ended in 1945, many Europeans were starving, much of the European continent lay in ruins, and systematic murder had killed six million Jews and six million Slavs, gypsies, homosexuals, and other civilian enemies of fascism.

The German Onslaught

German ground forces quickly defeated the ill-equipped Polish troops by launching an overpowering **Blitzkrieg** ("lightning war"). The Germans concentrated airplanes, tanks, and motorized infantry to encircle Polish defenders and capture the capital, Warsaw, with overwhelming speed. Allowing the German army to conserve supplies, Blitzkrieg lulled Germans at home into believing that the human costs of gaining Lebensraum would be low. On September 17, 1939, Soviet forces invaded Poland from the east. By the end of the month, the Polish army was in shambles, and the victors had divided Poland according to the Nazi-Soviet Pact. Hitler sold the war within the Third Reich as one of self-defense, especially from what Nazi propagandists called the "warlike menace" of world Jewry.

Hitler ordered an attack on France for November 1939, but his generals, who feared that Germany was ill prepared for total war, were able to postpone the offensive until the spring of 1940. In April 1940, the Blitzkrieg crushed Denmark and Norway; the battles of Belgium, the Netherlands, and France followed in May and June. On June 5, Mussolini, eyeing future spoils for Italy, invaded France from the southeast, as the French defense rapidly collapsed. Nor could the British army, allied with the French, withstand the German onslaught. Trapped on the beaches of Dunkirk in northern France, 370,000 British and French soldiers were rescued in a heroic effort by an improvised fleet of naval ships, fishing boats, and pleasure craft. The dejected French government surrendered on June 22, 1940, leaving Germany to rule the northern half of France, including Paris. In the south, known as Vichy France after the spa town where the government sat, Germany allowed the reactionary and aged World War I hero Henri Philippe Pétain to govern. Stalin used the diversion in western Europe to annex the Baltic states.

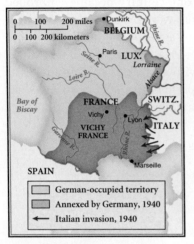

The Division of France, 1940

Britain now stood alone. Blaming Germany's rapid victories on Chamberlain's policy of appeasement, the British swept him out of office and installed as prime minister Winston Churchill (1874–1965), an early advocate of resistance to Hitler. After Hitler ordered the bombardment of Britain in the summer of 1940, Churchill rallied the nation by radio—now in more than nine million British homes—to protect the ideals of liberty with their "blood, toil, tears, and sweat." In the battle of Britain, or Blitz as the British called the bombing of their cities, the German air force (*Luftwaffe*) bombed public buildings and monuments, harbors and weapons depots, and industry. Using the wealth of their colonies, the British poured resources into anti-aircraft weapons, a highly successful code-breaking group called Ultra, and development of Britain's advantage in radar. At year's end, the British air industry was outproducing the Germans by 50 percent.

By the fall of 1940, German air losses forced Hitler to abandon his plan for a naval invasion of Britain. By forcing Hungary, Romania, and Bulgaria to join the Axis, Hitler gained access to more food and oil. He then made his fateful decision to attack what he called the "center of judeobolshevism"—the Soviet Union. In June 1941, the German army crossed the Soviet border, as Hitler broke the Nazi-Soviet Pact and promised to "raze Moscow and Leningrad to the ground." Deployed along a 2,000-mile front, 3 million German and other Axis troops quickly penetrated Soviet lines. Stalin disappeared for several days but then rallied to direct the defense. By July, the German army had rolled to within 200 miles of Moscow and eventually reached its suburbs. Using a strategy of rapid encirclement, German troops killed, captured, and wounded more than half the 4.5 million Soviet soldiers defending the borders. Amid success, Hitler blundered. Considering himself a military genius and the Slavic people inferior, he proposed attacking Leningrad, the Baltic States, and the Ukraine simultaneously, ignoring his generals' recommendation to concentrate on Moscow. Hitler's cumbersome strategy cost the German forces precious time. Driven by Stalin, local party members, and rising patriotic resolve, the Soviet people fought back. The onset of winter turned Nazi soldiers into frostbitten wretches because Hitler had feared that equipping his army for the harsh Russian winter would suggest to the German people that a prolonged campaign lay in store. His ill-supplied armies succumbed to the weather, disease, and ultimately a shortage of equipment. As the war spread worldwide, Germany faced another obstacle: fighting a global war from a strictly European base and with far less familiarity of the global terrain. What it did have was an inflated and poorly calculated view of its own might.

War Expands: The Pacific and Beyond

As the German army stalled in the Soviet Union, a dramatic attack ignited war in the Pacific. The outbreak of war in Europe had intensified U.S.-Japanese competition, as Japan took control of parts of the British Empire, bullied the Dutch in Indonesia, and invaded Indochina to procure raw materials for its expansion. The militarist Japanese government decided to settle matters with the West once and for all. On December 7, 1941, Japanese planes bombed American naval and air bases at Pearl Harbor in Hawaii and then decimated a fleet of U.S. airplanes in the Philippines. President Roosevelt summoned Congress to declare war on Japan. By spring 1942, the Japanese had conquered Guam, the Philippines, Malaya, Burma, Indonesia, Singapore, and much of the southwestern Pacific.

On December 11, 1941, Germany joined its ally in war on the United States—an appropriate enemy, Hitler proclaimed, as it was "half Judaized and the other half Negrified." Mussolini followed suit. The United States was initially not prepared for a prolonged struggle. Isolationist sentiment remained strong; U.S. armed forces numbered only 1.6 million, and no plan existed for producing the necessary guns, tanks, and airplanes. Also working against war-preparedness was U.S. ambivalence toward the Soviet Union even in the face of Hitler's attack, and Stalin himself reciprocated the mistrust. Nevertheless, Hitler's four enemies came together in the Grand Alliance of Great Britain, the Free French (an exile government led by General Charles de Gaulle and based in London), the Soviet Union, and the United States. Given the urgency of war and the partners' competing interests, the Grand Alliance and a larger coalition with twenty other countries—known collectively as the Allies—had much internal strife to overcome in their struggle against the Axis— Germany, Italy, and Japan. Yet in the long run, the Allies had distinct advantages: their vast potential for war in terms of manpower and resources and their experience in waging war on a global terrain.

The War against Civilians and the Holocaust

Everyone was a target in World War II, and the war killed far more civilians than soldiers. The Axis and the Allies alike bombed cities simply to destroy civilian will to resist—a debatable tactic that seemed to inspire defiance rather than surrender. Allied firebombing of Dresden and Tokyo were but two instances that killed tens of thousands of civilians, but Axis attacks far outweighed these. As the German army swept through eastern Europe, it slaughtered Jews, Communists, Slavs, and others whom the Nazis deemed "racial inferiors" and enemies. In Poland, the SS murdered hundreds of thousands of Polish citizens or relocated them to forced labor camps. Across Europe, the German army rounded up civilians to work on farms and in labor camps throughout the Reich—all to power the voracious Nazi war machine. The Nazis focused, however, on the extermination of the Jews, herding them first into urban ghettos with minimal provisions. Around captured Soviet towns, Jews were usually shot in pits, some of which they had been forced to dig themselves. After shedding their clothes and putting them in orderly piles for later Nazi use, ten thousand or more at a time were killed, often with the help of anti-Semitic villagers. The Japanese did the same to civilians in China, southeast Asia, and on the islands of the Pacific, killing at least 2.5 million Chinese civilians alone.

The "Final Solution"—the Nazis' diabolical plan to exterminate all of Europe's Jews—went into full effect with the implementation of a bureaucratically organized and efficient technological system for rounding up Jews and transporting them to extermination sites. On the eve of war in 1939, Hitler had predicted "the destruction of the Jewish race in Europe." Although no clear order written by Hitler exists, he discussed the Final Solution's progress, issued oral directives for it, and from the beginning made lethal anti-Semitism a basis for Nazism. Modern social and legal science and technology, managed by efficient scientists, doctors, lawyers, and government workers, also made the

■ Persecution of Warsaw Jews

Hitler was determined to exterminate Jews, Slavs, gypsies, homosexuals, and others he deemed "undesirable," and he often enlisted community leaders to cooperate in deportation and even executions. In the 1930s, people fled Germany and then countries the Nazis conquered. In the city of Warsaw, where Jews were crowded into ghettos and deprived of food and fuel, a Jewish uprising brought massive retaliation. (© Bettmann/Corbis.)

Holocaust work. Six camps in Poland were developed specifically for the purposes of mass murder, although some, like Auschwitz-Birkenau, served as both extermination and labor camps. Using techniques developed in the T4 project in the late 1930s, the camp at Chelmno first gassed Christian Poles and Soviet prisoners of war. Specially designed crematoria for the mass burning of corpses started functioning in 1943. By then, Auschwitz had the capacity to burn 1.7 million bodies per year. About 60 percent of new arrivals—particularly children, women, and the elderly—were selected directly for murder in the gas chambers. The other 40 percent labored until they were utterly used up; then they, too, were sent to their deaths.

Extermination camps received their victims from across the European continent. In the ghettos in various European cities, councils of Jewish leaders, such as the council in Amsterdam where Etty Hillesum worked, were ordered to identify those to be "resettled in the east." For weakened, poorly armed ghetto inhabitants, open resistance meant certain death. When defiant Polish Jews rose up against their Nazi captors in Warsaw in 1943, they were mercilessly butchered. The Nazis took pains to cloak their true purposes in the extermination camps. Bands played when trainloads of victims arrived; some were given postcards with reassuring messages to mail home. Those not chosen for immediate murder had their heads shaved, were disinfected, and then given prison garments. So began life in "a living hell," as one survivor wrote.

Camps were scenes of struggle for life in the face of torture and death. Overworked inmates usually took in less than five hundred calories per day, leaving them vulnerable to typhus and other diseases that swept through the camps. Surviving prisoners sometimes went mad, as did many of the guards. Inhumane medical experiments performed by doctors in the name of advancing "racial science" coexisted with prisoners' brave observance of religious holidays and celebrations of birthdays. Prisoners forged new friendships that helped in the struggle for survival. Thanks to those sharing a bread ration and doing him favors, wrote the Auschwitz survivor Primo Levi, "I managed not to forget that I myself was a man." Ordinary people drafted from civilian society committed these mass murders, but behind them lay the deliberate, bureaucratic organization of a vast and unspeakable crime.

Societies at War

Even more than World War I, World War II depended on industrial productivity geared totally toward war and mass murder. The Axis countries remained at a disadvantage throughout the war despite their vast conquests. Although the war accelerated economic production some 300 percent between 1940 and 1944 in all belligerent countries, the Allies produced more than three times the Axis output in 1943. Even with some of its land occupied and many of its cities besieged, the Soviet Union increased its production of weapons. Both Japan and Germany made the most of their lower capacity, most notably in the strategy of Blitzkrieg. Hitler had to avoid imposing wartime austerity because he had come to power promising to end economic suffering, not increase it. The use of millions of slave laborers and assets from occupied areas helped, but both Japan and Germany underestimated the resources and morale of their enemies.

Allied governments were overwhelmingly successful in generating civilian participation, especially among women. In the Axis countries, where government policy particularly exalted motherhood, women avoided paid work even though they were desperately needed in offices and factories. In contrast, women constituted more than half the Soviet workforce by war's end. They dug massive antitank trenches around Moscow and other threatened cities, and 800,000 volunteered for the military, even serving as pilots. As the Germans invaded, Soviet citizens moved entire factories eastward, and the Communist government encouraged renewed religious fervor for the Russian Orthodox church to inspire resistance.

Even more than in World War I, propaganda saturated society in movie theaters and on the radio. People were glued to their radios for war news, but much of it was tightly controlled. The dictatorships often withheld news of defeats and the number of casualties to keep civilian support. Films depicted aviation heroes and infantrymen as well as the workingwomen and wives left behind. Government agencies monitored filmmaking and allocated supplies to approved films. In the United States, military leaders loaned authentic props only if they could censor the scripts.

Between 1939 and 1945, governments organized many aspects of everyday life. Bureaucrats regulated the production and distribution of food, clothing, and household products, all of which were rationed and generally of low quality. They gave hints for preparing meals without meat, sugar, fat, and other staples and exhorted women and children to embrace deprivation so their fighting men would survive. Governments hired economists, statisticians, and other specialists to influence civilian thought and behavior. With governments standardizing such items as food, clothing, and entertainment, World War II furthered the development of mass society.

On both sides, propaganda and government policies promoted racial thinking. Since the early 1930s, the German government had drawn ugly caricatures of Jews, Slavs, and gypsies. Similarly, Allied propaganda during the war depicted Germans as sadists and perverts and the "Japs" as uncivilized, insect-like fanatics. The U.S. government forced citizens of Japanese origin into internment camps. In the Soviet Union, Muslims and minority ethnic groups were uprooted and relocated as potential Nazi collaborators. Simultaneously, colonized peoples were drawn into the war through conscription into the armies and forced labor. Some two million Indian men served the Allied cause, as did several hundred thousand Africans. As the Japanese swept through the Pacific and parts of East Asia, they, too, conscripted men into their army. Both sides bombarded colonized societies with propaganda, as radio stations and newspapers proliferated during the war. This propaganda, in the context of forced labor, energized colonized peoples to seek postwar liberation.

From Resistance to Allied Victory

Professional armies ultimately defeated the Axis powers, but civilian resistance in Nazi-occupied areas also contributed to the Allied triumph. General Charles de Gaulle (1890–1970) directed the Free French government and its forces from England; some 20 percent of these French troops were colonized Asians and Africans. Other French resisters fought in Communist-dominated groups, some of whom gathered information to aid a planned Allied landing on the French coast. Rural partisans across Europe plotted assassinations of German officers and civilian collaborators and bombed bridges, rail lines, and military facilities in

German-occupied areas. The spirit of resistance produced both group efforts such as the Warsaw uprising, and individual heroes, such as Swedish diplomat Raoul Wallenberg (1912–1947?), whose dealings with Nazi officials saved thousands of Hungarian Jews.

Ordinary people fought back through everyday activities. Homemakers circulated newsletters urging demonstrations at prisons where civilians were detained and in marketplaces where food was rationed. In central Europe, hikers smuggled Jews and others through dangerous mountain passes. Danish villagers created vast escape networks. Resisters played on stereotypes of femininity: women often carried weapons to assassination sites in the correct belief that the Nazis were not likely to suspect or search them; they also seduced and murdered enemy officers. Other actions subtly undermined the demands of fascist leaders. Couples in Germany and Italy limited family size in defiance of pro-birth policies. German teenagers danced the forbidden American jitterbug, thus defying the Nazis and forcing the police to monitor their groups. Resistance underscored the importance of the liberal ideal of individual political action and courage in the face of the totalitarian state's monopoly of power.

Amid civilian resistance, Allied forces started tightening a noose around the Axis in mid-1942 (Map 21.3). A major turning point came in August when the German army began a siege on Stalingrad, a city whose capture would give Germany access to Soviet oil. Months of ferocious fighting ended when the Soviet army captured the ninety thousand German survivors in February 1943. Allied victories in North Africa in 1942 were followed in July 1943 by an Allied landing in Sicily. However, the Germans came to Italy's aid and fought bitterly for the peninsula of Italy until April 1945, when Allied forces finally triumphed. After Italy's liberation, partisans shot Mussolini and his mistress and hung their dead bodies for public display.

The Soviet victory at Stalingrad marked the beginning of the costly Red Army drive westward—during which the Soviets bore the brunt of the Nazi war machine. As Stalin pressed for the opening of a western front, Roosevelt, Churchill, and Stalin met at Teheran, Iran, in November and December 1943 to coordinate their efforts. On June 6, 1944, the combined Allied forces under the command of U.S. general Dwight Eisenhower landed on the heavily fortified beaches of Normandy, France, and then fought their way through the German-held territory of western France. In late July, Allied forces broke through German defenses and a month later helped liberate Paris, where rebellion had erupted

■ **MAP 21.3 World War II in Europe and North Africa**
The Axis and Allied powers waged war in Europe and Africa, inflicting massive loss of life and destruction of property on civilians, armies, and infrastructure—including factories, equipment, and agriculture—needed to wage total war. The war swept the European continent as well as areas in Africa colonized by or allied with the major powers. Ultimately, the Allies crushed the Axis by moving from the east, west, and south to inflict a total defeat.

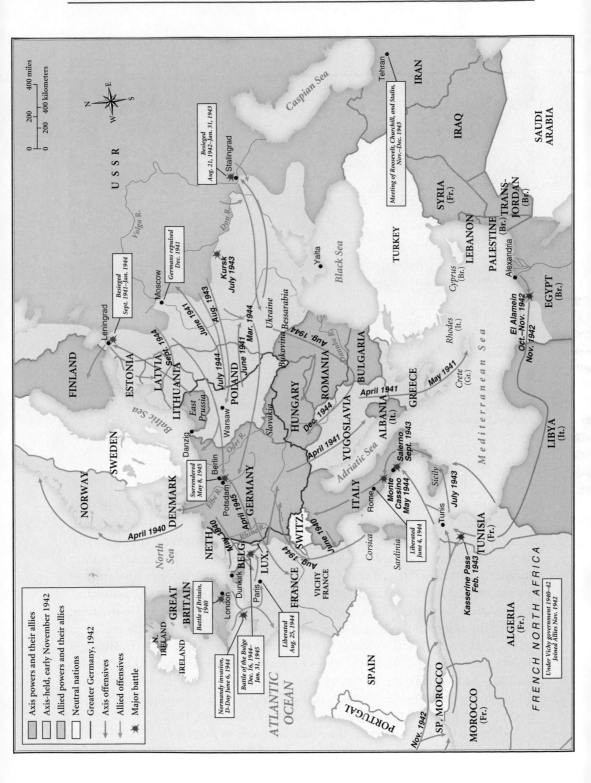

400 miles
0   200   400
0   200   400 kilometers

Tehran
IRAN
Meeting of Roosevelt, Churchill, and Stalin, Nov.–Dec. 1943
IRAQ
SAUDI ARABIA
SYRIA (Fr.)
LEBANON
TRANS-JORDAN (Br.)
PALESTINE (Br.)
Alexandria
EGYPT (Br.)
Caspian Sea
U S S R
Besieged Aug. 21, 1942–Jan. 31, 1943
Stalingrad
Volga R.
Don R.
Germans repulsed Dec. 1941
Moscow
Kursk July 1943
Aug. 1943
June 1941
Sept. 1944
Mar. 1944
July 1944
Ukraine
Bukovina Bessarabia
June 1941
Aug. 1944
Danube R.
Black Sea
Yalta
TURKEY
Cyprus (Br.)
Rhodes (It.)
Crete (Gr.)
May 1941
GREECE
April 1941
BULGARIA
ROMANIA
Dec. 1944
April 1941
YUGOSLAVIA
ALBANIA (It.)
HUNGARY
Slovakia
POLAND
Warsaw
Oder R.
East Prussia
Danzig
Besieged Sept. 1941–Jan. 1944
Leningrad
FINLAND
ESTONIA
LATVIA
LITHUANIA
Baltic Sea
SWEDEN
NORWAY
April 1940
North Sea
Mediterranean Sea
LIBYA (It.)
El Alamein Oct.–Nov. 1942
Nov. 1942
Adriatic Sea
Salerno Sept. 1943
Monte Cassino May 1944
Rome
ITALY
Liberated June 4, 1944
Sicily
July 1943
Tunis
Sardinia
Corsica
TUNISIA (Fr.)
Kasserine Pass Feb. 1943
FRENCH NORTH AFRICA
Under Vichy government 1940–42 Joined Allies Nov. 1942
ALGERIA (Fr.)
Nov. 1942
SP. MOROCCO
MOROCCO (Fr.)
SPAIN
PORTUGAL
ATLANTIC OCEAN
IRELAND
N. IRELAND
GREAT BRITAIN
Battle of Britain, 1940
London
Dunkirk
Paris
Normandy invasion, D-Day June 6, 1944
Liberated Aug. 25, 1944
Battle of the Bulge Dec. 16, 1944– Jan. 31, 1945
FRANCE
VICHY FRANCE
NETH.
BELG.
LUX.
SWITZ.
GERMANY
Berlin
Potsdam April 1945
Surrendered May 8, 1945
Elbe R.
Rhine R.
May 1940
June 1940
Aug. 1944
DENMARK

Axis powers and their allies
Axis-held, early November 1942
Allied powers and their allies
Neutral nations
Greater Germany, 1942
Axis offensives
Allied offensives
Major battle

■ **Battle of Leningrad**
In the face of Nazi invasion, Soviet citizens reacted heroically, moving entire factories to the inte-
rior of the country and building fortifications. Nowhere was their resolve so tested as in
Leningrad (now St. Petersburg). For more than two years, the German army besieged the city,
causing the deaths of hundreds of thousands. Before the Allied landing at Normandy in 1944, the
people of the USSR bore the brunt of Nazi military might in Hitler's attempt to defeat what he
called "judeobolshevism." (Sovfoto.)

against the Nazis. British, Canadian, U.S., and other Allied forces then fought their
way eastward to join the Soviets in squeezing the Third Reich to its final defeat.

In July 1944, a group of German military officers, fearing their country's military humiliation, attempted to assassinate, but only wounded, Hitler. As the Allies
advanced, Hitler maintained that Germans were proving themselves unworthy of
his greatness and deserved to perish in a cataclysmic conflagration. He refused all
negotiations that might have spared Germans further death and destruction.
Soviet armies took Poland, and then, facing more than twice as many troops as
on the western front, Stalin's forces withstood a fierce German defense in Hungary
during the winter of 1944–1945. Hitler's refusal to surrender resulted in massive
bombing of Germany. As the Soviet army took Berlin, Hitler and his wife, Eva
Braun, committed suicide. Although many German soldiers remained committed
to the Third Reich, Germany finally surrendered on May 8, 1945.

After the German surrender, the Allies were able to focus solely on the war in
the Pacific (Map 21.4). In 1940 and 1941, Japan had ousted the Europeans from

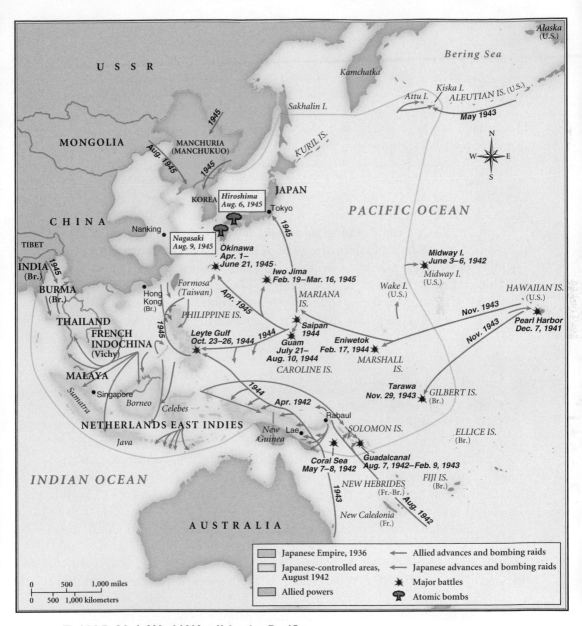

■ MAP 21.4 World War II in the Pacific

As in Europe, the early days of World War II gave the advantage to the Axis, as Japan took the offensive in conquering islands in the Pacific and territories in Asia—many of them colonies of the European states. Britain countered by mobilizing a vast Indian army. After the disastrous losses at Pearl Harbor and in the Philippines, the Allies gradually gained the upper hand by costly assaults, island by island. The Japanese strategy of fighting to the last person instead of surrendering when a loss was in sight was one factor in the decision to drop the atomic bomb in August 1945.

many of their colonial holdings in Asia. In 1942, the Allies turned the tide, despite their diminished forces, destroying some of Japan's formidable naval power in battles at Midway Island and Guadalcanal. Unlike the United States, Japan lacked the capacity to recoup losses of ships or manpower. The Allies stormed one Pacific island after another, gaining bases from which to cut off the import of supplies and to launch bombers toward Japan itself. Despite these losses and the firebombing of Tokyo, the Japanese ruled out surrender and resorted instead to kamikaze tactics, in which pilots deliberately crashed their planes into American ships, killing themselves in the process.

Meanwhile, a U.S.-based international team of more than 100,000 scientists, technicians, and other workers had developed the atomic bomb. The Japanese practice of dying almost to the man rather than surrender caused Allied military planners to calculate that defeating Japan with conventional weapons might cost hundreds of thousands of Allied lives and take many more months. Thus, on August 6 and 9, 1945, the U.S. government unleashed its new atomic weapons on Hiroshima and Nagasaki, respectively, instantly killing 140,000 people and causing tens of thousands of later deaths from burns, wounds, and other afflictions. Hardliners in the Japanese military wanted to continue the war, but on August 14, 1945, Japan surrendered.

An Uneasy Postwar Settlement

Envisioning a postwar settlement was a major priority throughout the war, and the Allies held critical meetings during the hostilities not only to plan strategy but also to set the terms for the postwar order. Unlike World War I, however, there was neither a celebrated peace conference nor a definitive, formal agreement among all the Allies about the final resolution of the war. The victorious Allies distrusted one another in varying degrees, and the United States and Soviet Union were poised on the brink of another war.

Wartime agreements among members of the Grand Alliance about the future reflected ongoing differences that roused intense postwar debate. In 1941, Roosevelt and Churchill had forged the Atlantic Charter, which condemned aggression, reaffirmed the ideal of collective security, and endorsed the right of all peoples to choose their governments. Not only had the Allies come to focus on these points, but so had colonized peoples to whom, Churchill had said, the charter was not meant to apply. In October 1944, Churchill and Stalin had agreed on the postwar distribution of territories. The Soviet Union would control Romania and Bulgaria, Britain would control Greece, and together they would oversee Hungary and Yugoslavia. These agreements were at odds with Roosevelt's preference for collective security, self-determination, and open doors in trade. In February 1945, the "Big Three"—as Roosevelt, Churchill, and

■ Hiroshima Victim

In early August 1945, the United States dropped atomic bombs on Hiroshima and Nagasaki, Japan, killing tens of thousands outright and leaving tens of thousands more to die from their wounds. A few days later, Japan surrendered. Controversy still swirls around the decision to drop the bomb. People who see it as a racist act point out that no atomic weapons were dropped on Germany. People who see it as a justified act of warfare point out that Japan's no-surrender policy increased the likelihood of countless more casualties.
(Tokyo/Fuji/Sumiko Kurita/Gamma.)

Stalin were known—had met in the Crimean town of Yalta. There Roosevelt had advocated the formation of the United Nations organization to replace the League of Nations as a global peace mechanism, and he had supported future Soviet influence in Korea, Manchuria, and the Sakhalin and Kurile Islands. At their last meeting, at Potsdam, Germany, in the summer of 1945, the Allied leaders had agreed to give the Soviets control of eastern Poland, to cede a large stretch of eastern Germany to Poland, and to adopt a temporary four-way occupation of Germany that would include France as one of the supervising powers. But as victory unfolded, the Allies scrambled to outmaneuver one another.

The Great Depression had inflicted global suffering. World War II left an estimated 100 million people dead and more than 50 million refugees without homes—one of the most tragic moral legacies in human history. Peacemaking proved a long and bitter process that did not end in 1945. Forced into armies or labor camps for war production, colonial peoples in Asia and Africa were in full rebellion or close to it. For the second time in three decades, they had seen Europeans killing one another, slaughtered by the very technology that Europeans had insisted made their civilization so superior. Deference to Europe was virtually finished, and independence was only a matter of time.

Western values at home were imperiled as well. Rational, democratic Europe had succumbed to continuous wartime values. It was this Europe that George Orwell captured in his novel *1984* (1949). Poor food and worn clothing, grimy streets and dwellings, people prematurely aged and careworn—all characterized London of the 1940s and Orwell's fictional state, Oceania. Orwell had worked for Britain's wartime Ministry of Information (called the Ministry of Truth in the novel) churning out propaganda and doctored news for wartime audiences. Information and truth hardly mattered: *disengagement* replaced *retreat*, *battle fatigue* substituted for *insanity*, and *liberating* a country could mean invading it and slaughtering its civilians. Millions rejoiced at the demise of Nazi evil in 1945, but Orwell saw as part of the war's legacy the end of prosperity, the deadening of creativity, and the intrusion of big government into everyday life. For Orwell, bureaucratic domination depended on the

IMPORTANT DATES

1929	U.S. stock market crashes; global depression begins; Soviet leaders launch war against the kulaks	1939	Germany invades Poland; World War II begins; Spanish Civil War ends
1930	Nationalist ruler Mustafa Kemal changes the name of Turkey's capital from Constantinople to Istanbul; French crush peasant uprising in Indochina; Marlene Dietrich stars in *The Blue Angel*	1940	France falls to the German army
		1940–1941	British air force fends off German attacks in the battle of Britain
1930s	Movement for Indian independence; Sweden constructs welfare state	1941	Germany invades USSR; Japan attacks Pearl Harbor; United States enters the war
1933	Hitler comes to power in Germany	1941–1945	The Holocaust
		1944	Allied forces land at Normandy, France
1936	Stalin starts purges of top Communist Party officials and later military leaders in show trials; Spanish Civil War begins	1945	Germany surrenders; United States drops atomic bombs on Hiroshima and Nagasaki; World War II ends
1938	Virginia Woolf publishes *Three Guineas*		

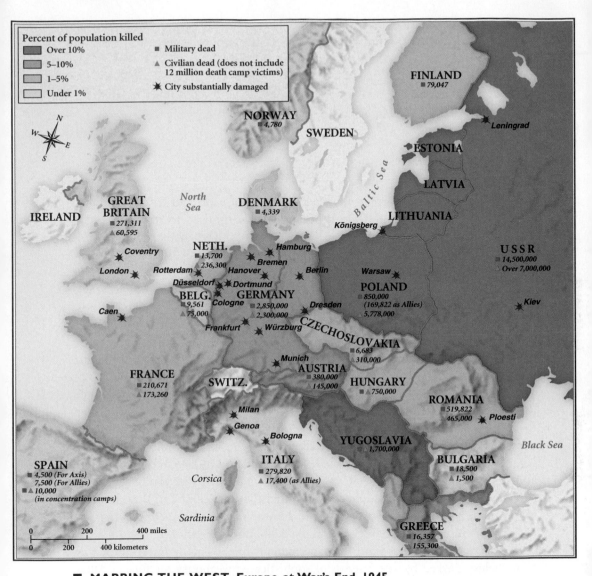

Percent of population killed

- Over 10%
- 5–10%
- 1–5%
- Under 1%

- ■ Military dead
- ▲ Civilian dead (does not include 12 million death camp victims)
- ✳ City substantially damaged

FINLAND
■ 79,047

NORWAY
■ 4,780

SWEDEN

ESTONIA

Leningrad

Baltic Sea

LATVIA

IRELAND

North Sea

GREAT BRITAIN
■ 271,311
▲ 60,595

DENMARK
■ 4,339

LITHUANIA

Königsberg

USSR
■ 14,500,000
Over 7,000,000

Coventry

NETH.
■ 13,700

Hamburg

London   Rotterdam
▲ 236,300   Hanover   Bremen   Berlin   Warsaw

Düsseldorf   Dortmund

BELG.   Cologne   GERMANY   Dresden
■ 9,561   ■ 2,850,000
▲ 75,000   2,300,000

POLAND
■ 850,000
(169,822 as Allies)
▲ 5,778,000

Kiev

Caen

Frankfurt   Würzburg   CZECHOSLOVAKIA
■ 6,683
▲ 310,000

Munich

FRANCE
■ 210,671
▲ 173,260

SWITZ.   AUSTRIA
■ 380,000
145,000

HUNGARY
■ ▲ 750,000

ROMANIA
■ 519,822
▲ 465,000   Ploesti

Milan

Genoa

Bologna

YUGOSLAVIA
■ ▲ 1,700,000

Black Sea

SPAIN
■ 4,500 (For Axis)
7,500 (For Allies)
■ ▲ 10,000
(in concentration camps)

Corsica

ITALY
■ 279,820
▲ 17,400 (as Allies)

BULGARIA
■ 18,500
▲ 1,500

Sardinia

GREECE
■ 16,357
▲ 155,300

0   200   400 miles
0   200   400 kilometers

■ MAPPING THE WEST Europe at War's End, 1945

All of Europe was severely shocked during the age of catastrophe, but wartime damage left scars that would last for decades. Major German cities were bombed to bits. The Soviet Union suffered an unimaginable toll of 25 to 40 million deaths due to the war alone. Everything from politics to family life needed rebuilding. The chaos fueled postwar tensions stemming both from the quest to punish those held responsible for such suffering and from the Allied powers' manipulation of recovery assistance to gain political advantage in the cold war.

(From *The Hammond Atlas of the Twentieth Century* [London: Times Books, 1996], 102.)

perpetuation of conflict, and fresh conflict was indeed brewing even before the war ended. As Allied powers competed for territory, a new struggle called the cold war was beginning.

■ **REVIEW:** *What were the major consequences of World War II?*

Conclusion

The Great Depression brought massive social dislocation and fear. It provided a setting in which dictators thrived because they promised to restore national greatness and economic prosperity. Enticed by the mass media, many people turned from representative institutions and toward dynamic, if brutal, leaders. Memories of World War I permitted Hitler and Mussolini to menace Europe unimpeded throughout the 1930s. When a coalition formed to stop them, it was an uneasy one among the imperial powers France and Britain, the Stalinist Soviet Union, and the industrial giant the United States. World War II ended European domination. Its economies were shattered, its population reduced, its colonies were on the verge of independence, and its peoples were starving and homeless.

The costs of a bloody war—waged against civilians as well as armies—taught these powers different lessons and raised different expectations. The United States, Britain, and France were convinced that at least some citizen well-being would be necessary to prevent a recurrence of fascism. Soviet citizens hoped their lives would become easier and less restricted. The devastation of the USSR's population and resources, however, made Stalin increasingly obsessed with national security and reparations. Britain and France confronted the final eclipse of their imperial might, underscoring Orwell's insight that the war had transformed society irrevocably. The militarization of society and the deliberate murder of millions of innocent citizens like Etty Hillesum left a permanent blight on the European legacy. Nonetheless, backed by vast arsenals of sophisticated weaponry the former Allies, the United States and the Soviet Union, threatened one another—and the world—with yet another war.

■ **MAKING CONNECTIONS**

1. *Compare fascist ideas about the individual with the idea of individual rights that drove the American and French Revolutions.*

2. *What are the major differences between World War I and World War II?*

■ **FOR FURTHER EXPLORATION**

For further reading and online research ideas, see the Suggested References on page SR-11 at the back of the book.

For practice quizzes, a customized study plan, and other study tools, see the ONLINE STUDY GUIDE at **bedfordstmartins.com/huntconcise**.

For primary-source material from this period, see Chapter 21 in *Sources of THE MAKING OF THE WEST: A CONCISE HISTORY*, Second Edition.

Remaking Europe in the Shadow of Cold War

c. 1945–1965

A FTER THE UNITED STATES DROPPED two atomic bombs on Japan in 1945, the Union of Soviet Socialist Republics raced to catch up with its rival in atomic weaponry. In late August 1949, the Soviet Union detonated its own atomic bomb. Two days after President Harry S. Truman announced the news of this test, Billy Graham, a young Baptist preacher, based his sermon at a revival meeting on the fearsome event. Graham warned that U.S. officials believed "we have only five to ten years and our civilization will be ended." He announced that Russia had aimed bombs to strike New York, Chicago, and Los Angeles, where the revival was taking place. "Time is desperately short. . . . Prepare to meet thy God," he warned. People flocked to hear Graham talk about the end of the world, launching the evangelist's astonishing career of spiritual and political influence in the United States and around the globe.

Graham's message—"We don't know how soon, but we do know this, that right now the grace of God can still save a poor lost sinner"—captured the extremes of postwar sentiment in an atomic age. At one extreme, the global postwar situation was tragic. One hundred million people had died; survivors in Europe and East Asia were starving; evidence of genocide and other inhumanity

■ **The Atomic Age**
The dropping of atomic bombs on Hiroshima and Nagasaki in 1945 was followed by several decades of increasingly powerful test detonations. The Soviet Union used underground testing, while the United States carried out atmospheric tests in the Pacific region. Protests against testing arose in the 1950s, many of them citing the hazards of radioactivity and the growing threat of nuclear annihilation. Simultaneously, nuclear power was converted to peacetime use, notably serving both as a source of energy and as a therapy for cancer. (© Corbis.)

was everywhere; the menace of nuclear annihilation loomed. It was to this menace that Graham referred. The old international order was gone, replaced by the rivalry of the United States and the Soviet Union for control of a devastated Europe. The nuclear arsenals of these two *superpowers*—a term coined in 1947—grew massively in the 1950s, but they were enemies who did not fight outright. Thus, their terrifying rivalry was called the **cold war**. The cold war divided the West and caused acute anxiety, even for someone like Graham from the victorious and wealthy United States.

At the other extreme, the defeat of Nazism inspired an upsurge of hope, a revival of religious feeling like Graham's, and a new commitment to humanitarian goals. Heroic effort had defeated fascism, and that defeat raised hopes that a new age would begin. Atomic science promised advances in medicine, and nuclear energy was trumpeted as a replacement for coal and oil. The creation of the United Nations heralded an era of international cooperation. Around the globe, colonial peoples won independence from European masters, while in the United States the civil rights movement gained new momentum. The welfare state expanded, and by the end of the 1950s economic rebirth, stimulated in part by the cold war, had made much of Europe more prosperous than ever before. Unbelievably, an "economic miracle" had occurred.

Extremes of hope and fear shaped the atomic age, as society, culture, and the international order were all transformed. Gone was the definition of a West comprising Europe and its cultural offshoots such as the United States and an East comprising Asian countries like India, China, and Japan. During the cold war, the word *West* came to stand for the United States and its client countries in western Europe, while *East* meant the Soviet Union and its tightly controlled bloc in eastern Europe. Still another terminology arose in the 1950s, one that divided the globe into the first world, or capitalist bloc of countries; the second world, or socialist bloc; and the **third world**, or countries emerging from imperial domination. Amid these changes, the superpowers took the world to the brink of nuclear disaster when the United States discovered Soviet missile sites on the island of Cuba. From the dropping of the atomic bomb on Japan in 1945 to the Cuban missile crisis of 1962, Graham's dread that "we are moving madly toward destruction" gripped much of the world, albeit in the midst of prosperity and Europe's rebirth.

World Politics Transformed

World War II ended the global leadership of Europe. Many countries lay in ruins by the summer of 1945, and conditions would deteriorate before they got better. In contrast, the United States, whose territory was virtually untouched in the war, emerged as the world's sole economic giant, and the Soviet Union, despite suffering immense destruction, retained formidable military might. The disagreement over what to do with postwar Germany was central to the growing East-West division of Europe. By the late 1940s, the USSR imposed Communist rule throughout most of eastern Europe and in the 1950s quashed rebellions against its dominance there. Western Europeans found themselves at least partially constricted by the very U.S. economic power that helped them rebuild, as the United States maintained air bases and nuclear weapons sites on their soil. The age of bipolar world politics had begun, with Europe as its testing ground.

Europe Prostrate

In contrast to World War I, when devastation was limited to the front lines around the trenches, armies in World War II had fought a war of movement and massive air strikes that leveled thousands of square miles of territory. Across the continent, homeless survivors wandered city streets clogged with rubble. In Sicily and on the Rhine River, almost no bridge remained standing; in the Soviet Union, seventy thousand villages and more than a thousand cities lay in shambles. Everywhere people were suffering. In the Netherlands, the severity of Nazi occupation left the Dutch population close to death, relieved only by a U.S. airlift of food. Italian bakers sold bread by the slice. When Allied troops passed through German towns, the famished inhabitants lined the roads in hopes that someone would toss them something to eat. "To see the children fighting for food," one British soldier noted, "was like watching animals being fed in a zoo." There was social disarray, even chaos, at the war's end but no mass uprisings as after World War I. Until the late 1940s, people were too exhausted by the struggle for bare survival.

The millions of refugees and homeless suffered the most. Many had been inmates of prisons and death camps, and, weakened and ill, they were now released into a world where resources were slim and old ways of living destroyed. Others, especially millions of ethnic Germans, fled westward, ejected from Czechoslovakia, Poland, and other eastern European countries. Many refugees ultimately found homes in countries that experienced little or no war damage, such as Denmark, Sweden, Canada, and Australia. Following the exodus of refugees from the east, western Europe, another of their destinations, became one of the world's most densely populated regions (see Map 22.1 on page 948). The USSR lobbied hard for the repatriation of several million Soviet prisoners of war and forced laborers, and the Allies transported the majority of the Russian refugees back to the Soviet Union. "Contaminated" by Western ideas, according to Soviet leaders, they faced execution until the Allies slowed the process.

Survivors of the concentration camps also discovered that their suffering had not ended with Germany's defeat. Many returned diseased and disoriented, while others often had no home to return to, as property had been confiscated and entire communities destroyed. Moreover, anti-Semitism—official policy under the Nazis—lingered in popular attitudes. In the summer of 1946, a vicious crowd in Kielce, Poland, rioted against 250 returning Jewish survivors, killing at least 40.

Legend:

- Lost by Germany to Poland, 1945
- Territory gained by Soviet Union
- Allied occupation of Germany and Austria, 1945–55
- Lost by Italy to Yugoslavia, 1945
- Lost by Romania to Bulgaria, 1940–47
- Zones of occupation
  - American
  - British
  - French
  - Soviet
  - Jointly occupied cities
- Refugee movements and repatriated armed forces
  - Germans
  - Finns
  - Baltic peoples
  - Russians
  - Poles
  - Czechs
- People settled by the International Refugee Organization

From Finland, 1940–56 410,000
From Romania, 1940–47
From Czechoslovakia, Ukraine
From Poland, 1940–47
From Czechoslovakia, 1940–47

40,000 100,000 80,000 2,300,000
60,000 50,000 90,000 1,500,000
1,950,000 3,000,000 5,500,000
1,900,000 850,000 3,250,000 1,950,000
1,000,000 2,900,000 250,000
200,000 50,000

Estonia To USSR, 1940
Latvia, 1940 To USSR, 1940
Lithuania, 1940 To USSR, 1940
Bessarabia
Ukraine

Leningrad
Helsinki
Stockholm
Oslo
Copenhagen
Gdańsk (Danzig)
Warsaw
Kielce
Berlin
Bremen
Prague
Vienna
Budapest
Bucharest
Belgrade
Munich
Bern
Milan
Rome
Amsterdam
Brussels
Paris
London
Madrid
Athens
Istanbul
Odessa
Yalta
Sofia

FINLAND USSR SWEDEN NORWAY DENMARK POLAND
EAST GERMANY WEST GERMANY NETH. BELG. LUX. FRANCE
SWITZ. AUSTRIA CZECHOSLOVAKIA HUNGARY ROMANIA BULGARIA
YUGOSLAVIA ITALY ALBANIA GREECE TURKEY CYPRUS
UNITED KINGDOM IRELAND SPAIN

Baltic Sea *North Sea* *Black Sea* *Adriatic Sea* *Mediterranean Sea* *ATLANTIC OCEAN*
Danube R. *Rhine R.* *Rhône R.* *Po R.*
Corsica (Fr.) *Sardinia (It.)* *Sicily* *Crete*

400 miles
400 kilometers
0 200
0 200

N E W S

■ MAP 22.1 The Impact of World War II on Europe

European governments, many of them struggling to provide food and other necessities for their populations, found themselves responsible for hundreds of thousands, if not millions, of new refugees. At the same time, millions of prisoners of war, servicemen, and slave laborers were returned to the Soviet Union, many of them by force. This situation unfolded amid political instability and even violence.

Elsewhere in eastern Europe, such violence was common. Meanwhile, some officials across Europe even denied that unprecedented atrocities had been committed and wanted to refuse Jews any help. Survivors crammed into the port cities of Italy and other Mediterranean countries, eventually to escape Europe for Palestine, where Zionists had been settling for half a century. Unwilling or unable to help Hitler's most abused victims, many European countries had simply lost the capacity for moral and economic leadership.

New Superpowers: The United States and the Soviet Union

Only two powerful countries were left in 1945: the United States and the Soviet Union. The United States was now the richest country in the world. Its industrial output had increased by a remarkable 15 percent annually between 1940 and 1944, a rate of growth that was reflected in workers' wages. By 1947, the United States controlled almost two-thirds of the world's gold bullion. It also controlled more than half of the commercial shipping, up from almost one-fifth of the total in the 1930s. Spending on industrial and military research continued, adding to prosperity and creating a confident mood. Casting aside the post–World War I policy of nonintervention, Americans embraced their position as global leaders. Many had learned about the world while tracking the war's progress; hundreds of thousands of soldiers, government officials, and relief workers had direct experience of Europe, Africa, and Asia. Although many shared Billy Graham's worries about nuclear annihilation, a wave of suburban housing development and consumer spending kept the economy buoyant. A baby boom exploded from the late 1940s through the early 1960s in response to the economic abundance.

The Soviets also emerged from the war with a well-justified sense of accomplishment. Withstanding horrendous losses, they had resisted the most massive onslaught ever launched against a nation. Instead of the international isolation dealt Russia after World War I, Soviet leadership expected equality in decision making with the United States. Ordinary Soviet citizens believed their wartime sacrifices would bring improvement to their lives and a continuation of the war's relatively relaxed politics. Rumors spread among the peasants that the collective farms would be disbanded and returned to them as individual property now that the war was won. "Life will become pleasant," one writer prophesied. "There will be much coming and going, and a lot of contacts with the West." The Stalinist goals of industrialization and defense against Nazism had been won, and thus many Soviets expected an end to decades of hardship, even an end to censorship and repressive government.

Stalin took a different view and moved ruthlessly to reassert control. In 1946, his new five-year plan set increased production goals and mandated more stringent collectivization of agriculture. For him, rapid recovery meant more work, not less, and more order, not greater freedom. Stalin cut back the army by two-thirds to beef up the labor force and also turned his attention to the low birthrate, a result of wartime male casualties and women's long, arduous working days, which discouraged them from adding child care to their already heavy responsibilities. He introduced an intense propaganda campaign emphasizing that women should hold down jobs and also fulfill their "true nature" by producing many children. A crackdown on freedom took place, and a new round of purges began. Jews were especially targeted, and in 1953 the government announced that doctors—most of them Jews— had long been assassinating Soviet leaders, murdering newborns and patients in hospitals, and plotting to poison water supplies. Hysteria gripped the nation, as people feared for their lives. "I am a simple worker and not an anti-Semite," one Moscow resident wrote, "but I say . . . it's time to clean these people out." In these ways, Stalinism was reborn and an atmosphere developed that was ripe for cold war.

Origins of the Cold War

In the immediate postwar years, the United States and the Soviet Union launched a cold war that would afflict the world for more than four decades. Its origins remain a matter of debate, with historians faulting both sides for starting this fearsome rivalry. Some point to consistent U.S., British, and French hostility to the Soviets that began as far back as the Bolshevik Revolution of 1917 and Russia's withdrawal from World War I. Others stress Stalin's aggressive policies, notably the Nazi-Soviet alliance in 1939 and his land grabs when World War II broke out. In this view, countries naturally feared unlimited Soviet expansionism.

During the war, suspicions ran deep: Stalin felt that Churchill and Roosevelt were deliberately letting the USSR bear the brunt of Hitler's onslaught on the continent as part of their anti-Communist policy. He rightly viewed Churchill in particular as committed to preserving Britain's imperial power, no matter what the cost in Soviet lives. Some Americans believed that dropping the atomic bomb on Japan would halt a frightened USSR's expansion, while the new U.S. president, Harry Truman, fueled Stalin's belief that the United States was aiming for his country's utter collapse by cutting off aid as the last gun was fired. Facing this menace, Stalin saw the USSR as needing not just a temporary military occupation but also a permanent "buffer zone" of European states loyal to the USSR as a safeguard. Across the Atlantic, Truman saw the Soviet occupation of eastern Europe as heralding an era of Communist takeovers around the world. By 1946, members of the U.S. State Department were describing Stalin as a dangerous tyrant fixated on world domination.

The cold war thus became a series of moves and countermoves by two very different countries who jointly occupied the rich European heartland. Between 1945 and 1949, the USSR repressed democratic coalition governments of liberals, socialists, Communists, and peasant parties in central and eastern Europe. It imposed Communist rule almost immediately in Bulgaria and Romania. In Romania, Stalin

The Cold War, to 1962			
1945–1949	USSR establishes satellite states in eastern Europe	**1950–1954**	U.S. senator Joseph McCarthy leads hunt for American Communists
1947	Truman Doctrine announces U.S. commitment to contain communism; U.S. Marshall Plan provides massive aid to rebuild Europe	**1953**	Stalin dies
		1955	USSR and Eastern bloc countries form military alliance, the Warsaw Pact
1948–1949	Soviet troops blockade Berlin; United States airlifts provisions to Berliners	**1956**	Khrushchev denounces Stalin in "secret speech" to Communist Party Congress; Hungarians revolt unsuccessfully against Soviet domination
1949	Western democracies form North Atlantic Treaty Organization (NATO); Soviet bloc establishes Council for Mutual Economic Assistance (COMECON); USSR tests its first nuclear weapon	**1959**	Fidel Castro comes to power in Cuba
		1961	Berlin Wall erected
		1962	Cuban missile crisis
1950–1953	Korean War		

cited citizen violence in 1945 as the excuse to oust all non-Communists from the civil service and cabinet. In Poland, the Communists rigged the elections in 1945 and 1946 to create the illusion of approval for communism. Nevertheless, the Communists had to share power between 1945 and 1947 with the popular Peasant Party, which had a large constituency of rural workers and peasant landowners. The Allies protested many of these moves by the Communists as the cold war advanced.

The United States put its new interventionist spirit to work. It acknowledged Soviet authority in areas it occupied but aimed to counter communism in western Europe where the party's leadership in the Resistance gave it a powerful allure. Both U.S. and British concern mounted when Communist insurgents had enough of a following to threaten the right-wing monarchy the British had installed in Greece in 1944. In March 1947, Truman reacted to the Communist threat by announcing what quickly became known as the **Truman Doctrine**—the use of economic and military aid to block communism. The president requested $400 million in military aid for Greece and Turkey, where the Communists were also exerting pressure. Fearing that Americans would balk at backing nondemocratic Greece, U.S. congressmen would agree to the program only if Truman would "scare the hell out of the country," as one put it. Truman thus publicized an expensive aid program as necessary to fortify the world against a tide of global Soviet conquest. The show of American support convinced the Communists to back off, and in 1949 the Greek rebels declared a cease-fire.

In 1947, the United States also devised the **Marshall Plan**—a program of massive postwar economic aid to Europe—to alleviate some of the hardships that were making ordinary people in western Europe find communism attractive. "The seeds of totalitarian regimes are nurtured by misery and want," the president warned in the same speech that introduced the Truman Doctrine. Named after Secretary of State George C. Marshall, the program's direct aid would immediately improve everyday life, while the loans and other financial credit aimed to restart the flow of international trade. The government claimed that the Marshall Plan was not directed "against any country or doctrine but against hunger, poverty, desperation, and chaos." By the early 1950s, the United States had sent Europe more than $12 billion in food, equipment, and services, and the Marshall Plan did its intended political work by reducing the appeal of communism in the countries of western Europe that received the aid.

Stalin saw the aid as a U.S. political ploy that caught him without similar largess to offer to his client countries in eastern and central Europe. He thus clamped down still harder on eastern European governments, eliminating the last remnants of democracy in Hungary and Poland and preventing governments in his sphere of influence from responding to the U.S. offer of assistance. In Czechoslovakia, which welcomed the Marshall Plan as the beginning of East-West reconciliation, Communists purged rival officials beginning in the autumn of 1947. By June 1948, Czechoslovakia's socialist president, Edouard Beneš, had resigned and been replaced by a Communist figurehead. The populace accepted the change so passively that Communist leaders said the takeover was "like cutting butter with a knife." The Soviet Union had successfully created a buffer of satellite states in eastern Europe directed by what it called people's governments.

The only exception to the Soviet sweep in eastern Europe came in Yugoslavia, under the Communist ruler known as Tito (Josip Broz, 1892–1980). During the war, Tito led the powerful anti-Nazi Yugoslav "partisans." After the war, he drew on support from Serbs, Croats, and Muslims to mount a Communist revolution. His revolution, however, was explicitly meant to modernize while avoiding Soviet influence. "We study and take as an example the Soviet system," Tito remarked, "but we are developing socialism in our country in somewhat different forms." Stalin was furious at Tito's disobedience. Nonetheless, Yugoslavia emerged from its Communist revolution as a culturally diverse federation of six republics and two independent provinces within Serbia. Holding diverse groups of south Slavs together until his death in 1980, Tito's forceful personality and strong organization also held the Soviets at bay.

Yugoslavia after the Revolution, 1948

■ MAP 22.2 Divided Germany and the Berlin Airlift, 1946–1949

Berlin, controlled by the United States, Great Britain, France, and the Soviet Union, was deep in the Soviet zone of occupation and became a major point of contention among the former allies. When the USSR blockaded the western half of the city, the United States responded with a massive airlift. To stop movement between the two zones, the USSR built a wall in 1961 and used troops to patrol it.

The Division of Germany

The cold war became most menacing in the struggle for control of Germany. The agreements reached at Yalta divided Germany into four occupied zones, each of which was controlled by one of the four principal victors in World War II—the United States, the Soviet Union, Britain, and France (Map 22.2). However, there was fundamental disagreement over how to treat Germany. Many in the United States had come to believe in an inherently flawed German character, responsible for two world wars and the Holocaust. After the war, the U.S. occupation forces undertook a reprogramming of German cultural attitudes by censoring all media in the U.S. zone to ensure that they did not express fascist or authoritarian values. In contrast, Stalin believed that Nazism was merely an extreme form of capitalism. His solution was to confiscate and redistribute the estates of wealthy Germans to ordinary people and supporters.

A second disagreement, this one over Germany's economic potential, led to that nation's partition. According to the American plan for coordinating the various segments of the German economy, surplus produce from the Soviet-occupied areas would feed urban populations in the western zones; in turn, industrial goods would be sent to the USSR. The Soviets upset this plan. Following the Grand Alliance agreement that the USSR would receive reparations from German resources, the Soviets seized German equipment and shipped it to the Soviet Union. They transported skilled workers, engineers, and scientists to the USSR to work virtually as slave laborers. The Soviets also manipulated the currency in their

■ **MAP 22.3 European NATO Members and the Warsaw Pact in the 1950s**

The two superpowers intensified their rivalry by creating large military alliances: NATO, formed in 1949, and the Warsaw Pact, formed in 1955 after NATO invited West German membership. The United States and Canada also were NATO members. International politics revolved around these two alliances, which faced off in the heart of Europe. Military planners on both sides devised war games to plan strategies for fighting a massive war in central Europe over control of Germany. **For more help analyzing this map**, see the map activity for this chapter in the ONLINE STUDY GUIDE at bedfordstmartins.com/huntconcise.

zone, enabling the USSR to buy German goods at unfairly low prices. The superpower struggle escalated as the western Allies merged their individual zones into a West German state, prompting the Soviets to form an East German state in their zone. Instead of curtailing German power, the United States began an economic buildup of the western zone of Germany under the Marshall Plan. By 1948, notions of a permanently weakened Germany came to an end, as the United States enlisted many former Nazi officials as spies and bureaucrats.

On July 24, 1948, Stalin retaliated by blockading Germany's capital, Berlin. Like Germany as a whole, the city had been divided into four occupation zones, even though it was located more than one hundred miles deep into the Soviet zone and was thus cut off from western territory. Expecting the United States and its allies to capitulate, the Soviets declared that Berlin was now part of their zone of occupation and refused to allow western vehicles to travel through the Soviet zone, including Berlin. The United States responded decisively, flying in millions of tons of provisions to the stricken city. During the winter of 1948–1949, the Berlin airlift— Operation Vittles, as U.S. pilots called it—even funneled in coal to warm some two million isolated Berliners. Pilots kept the plane engines on so they could turn around quickly to ensure the arrival of sufficient provisions. When Stalin lifted the ineffective blockade in May 1949, a divided Berlin became the symbol of the cold war.

Accelerating cold war tensions led to the formation of competing military alliances. The United States, Canada, and their allies in western Europe and Scandinavia formed the **North Atlantic Treaty Organization (NATO)** in 1949.

NATO provided a unified military force for its member countries. In 1955, after the United States forced France and Britain to invite West Germany to join NATO, the Soviet Union retaliated by establishing with its satellite countries the military organization commonly called the **Warsaw Pact**. By that time, both the United States and the USSR had accelerated their arms buildups. Each had tested highly destructive hydrogen bombs and increased its potential for annihilating the enemy with nuclear weapons. These two massive regional alliances, armed to the teeth, formed the military muscle for cold war politics and definitively replaced the individual might of the European powers (Map 22.3).

■ **REVIEW:** *What major events led to the cold war?*

Political and Economic Recovery in Europe

The cold war served as a background to the remarkable economic and political recovery that took place in Europe. The first order of business was a highly charged eradication of the Nazi past and the inauguration of peacetime governments. Western Europe revived its democratic political structures, its individualistic culture, and its productive capabilities. Eastern Europe restlessly endured a far less prosperous and far more repressive existence under Stalinism, although even there the conditions of everyday life improved as peasant societies were forced to modernize.

By 1965, people across the continent had escaped the poverty of the depression and war to enjoy a higher standard of living than ever before in their history. This rapid revival was even called the "economic miracle," especially in the case of West Germany's striking prosperity. As governments took increasing responsibility for the health and well-being of citizens, the cold war era also became the age of the welfare state.

Dealing with the Nazi Past

In May 1945, Europeans lived under a complex system in which local resistance leaders, Allied armies of occupation, international relief workers, and the remnants of bureaucracies—among them Nazi sympathizers—shared jurisdiction. Amid confusion, starvation, and a thriving black market, the goals of feeding civilians, dealing with millions of refugees, purging Nazis, and setting up new governments all competed for attention. Members of governments-in-exile returned to claim their rightful share of power, but they often met up with occupying armies that covered much of the continent and were often a law unto themselves. The Soviets were especially feared for inflicting rape and robbery—abuses they justified by pointing to tens of millions of Soviet deaths at the hands of the Nazis. The

■ The Punishment of Collaborators

Women who had romantic involvements with Germans were called "horizontal" collaborators to suggest that they were traitorous prostitutes. They were often forced to parade through cities and towns enduring verbal and other abuse with heads shaved and often stripped of their clothing. The public shaming of these women, a vivid part of the memory of the war, served as the background for the film Hiroshima Mon Amour, *which gripped audiences late in the 1950s.*
(© Robert Capa/Magnum Photos Inc.)

desire for revenge against Nazis hardened with the discovery of the death camps' skeletal survivors and the remains of the millions murdered there. Swift vigilante justice by civilians released pent-up rage and aimed to punish collaborators. In France, villagers often shaved the heads of women suspected of associating with Germans and made some of them parade naked through the local streets. Members of the resistance executed tens of thousands of Nazi officers and collaborators on the spot. These became the founding acts of a reborn European political community.

Allied representatives undertook a more systematic "denazification" that ranged from forcing German civilians to view the death camps to the Nuremberg trials in the fall of 1945. Although international law lacked a precedent for defining genocide as a crime, the judges at Nuremberg found sufficient evidence from the Nazis' own records to impose death sentences on half of the twenty-four defendants from the German leadership, among them Hitler's closest associates, and give prison terms to the remainder. The Nuremberg trials introduced current notions of prosecution for crimes against humanity and an international politics based on demands for human rights.

Prosecution of Nazi and fascist leadership varied. Some of the leaders most responsible for war crimes simply disappeared, while in Hungary some 3 percent of the population—including high ranking ministers—was called to account. Furthermore, many Germans were skeptical about denazification. As women in Germany were forced to clear rubble in bombed-out cities, the belief spread among Germans that they themselves were the main victims of the war. German civilians also interpreted the trials of Nazis as a characteristic retribution of victors rather than a well-deserved punishment of the guilty. Soon the new West German government proclaimed that the war's real casualties were the German prisoners of war held in Soviet camps. The Nazi past affected European cultural life and politics unevenly. While many were rightly horrified at the unprecedented murder and genocide, others to this day attempt to paper over these grim truths. Political expediency also led Westerners to forgive some Nazis and enlist them to serve in the cold war.

Rebirth of the West

Against all political and economic odds, Europe revived at an accelerated pace in the 1950s. In western Europe, reform-minded civilian governments reflected the broad coalitions that had opposed the Axis. They conspicuously emphasized democracy to show their rejection of the totalitarian regimes that had earlier attracted so many Europeans with such dire consequences.

Resistance leaders had the first claim on political office in post-fascist western Europe. In France, the leader of the Free French, General Charles de Gaulle, governed briefly as chief of state, and the French approved a constitution in 1946 that established the Fourth Republic and finally granted the vote to French women. Wanting a conservative political system that would grant him more authority, de Gaulle soon resigned in favor of left-wing and centrist forces. Meanwhile, Italy replaced its constitutional monarchy with a full parliamentary system that also allowed women the vote for the first time. As in France, a resistance-based government initially took control. Then, late in 1945, the socialist and labor politicians were replaced by a coalition headed by the conservative Christian Democrats, descended from the traditional Catholic centrist parties of the prewar period. As in Italy, other parts of Europe saw the growing influence of Christian parties because of their participation in the resistance.

The Communist Party also attracted the vocal loyalty of a consistently large segment of the western European population. Symbol of the common citizen, the ordinary Soviet soldier was a hero to many western Europeans outside occupied Germany, as were the resistance leaders—many of them Communist. People still remembered the common man's plight in the depression of the 1930s. Thus, in Britain, despite the wartime successes of Winston Churchill's Conservative Party leadership, British voters elected the Labour government of Clement Attlee, which seemed more likely to fulfill promises to share prosperity equitably among the classes through social welfare programs and the nationalization of key industries. Voters chose governments that would represent the millions of ordinary people who had suffered, fought, and worked incredibly hard during the war.

In West Germany, however, communism and the left in general had little appeal, so sure was the hold of the Western allies and so distasteful were the Communist takeovers going on to the east. In 1949, centrist politicians helped create a new state, the German Federal Republic, whose constitution aimed to prevent the emergence of a dictator, to guarantee individual rights, and to build a sound economy. West Germany's first chancellor was the seventy-three-year-old Catholic anti-Communist Konrad Adenauer, who allied himself with the economist Ludwig Erhard. Committed to the free market, Erhard had stabilized the postwar German currency so that commerce could resume. The economist and the politician successfully guided Germany away from both fascism and communism and restored the representative government that Hitler had overthrown.

Paradoxically, given its leadership in the fight against fascism, the United States was a country in which individual freedom and democracy were imperiled after the war. Two events—a successful test of an atomic bomb by the Soviet Union in 1949 and the Communist revolution in China—brought to the fore Joseph McCarthy, a U.S. senator foreseeing a reelection struggle. To strengthen his following in advance of the election, McCarthy warned of a great Communist conspiracy to overthrow the United States. As during the Soviet purges, people of all occupations including government workers, film stars, and union leaders were called before congressional panels to confess, testify against friends, and to reveal having held Communist thoughts or sympathies. The atmosphere was electric with confusion and a sense of betrayal, for only five years before the mass media had run glowing stories about Stalin and the Soviet system. During the war, Americans were told to think of Stalin as a friendly "Uncle Joe." By 1952, however, more than six million Americans had been investigated, imprisoned, or fired from their jobs. McCarthy had books like Thomas Paine's *Common Sense*, written in the eighteenth century to support the American Revolution, removed from government shelves, and he personally oversaw book burnings. Although the Senate finally voted to censure McCarthy in the winter of 1954, the assault on freedom had been devastating, and anticommunism dominated political life.

A surprising economic rebirth took place alongside the revival of democracy in western Europe. In the first months after the war, the job of rebuilding often involved menial physical labor that mobilized entire populations, including women. Initially governments diverted labor and capital into rebuilding infrastructure—transportation, communications, industrial capacity—and away from producing consumer goods. However, the scarcity of those goods sparked unrest and made communism politically attractive because it proclaimed less interest in the revival of big business than in the ordinary person's standard of living. The

■ TAKING MEASURE World Manufacturing Output, 1950–1970
During the "long boom" from the 1950s to the early 1970s, the world experienced increased industrial output, better agricultural production, and rising consumerism. This era of prosperity resulted from both the demand generated by the need to rebuild Europe and the adaptation of war technology to peacetime uses. The General Agreement on Trade and Tariffs (GATT) was also implemented after the war, lowering tariffs and thus advancing trade.

Marshall Plan countered by boosting recovery with American dollars; food became more plentiful; and demand for automobiles, washing machines, and vacuum cleaners accelerated economic growth. Increased production in all sectors wiped out most unemployment. (See "Taking Measure," above.)

The postwar recovery also featured the adaptation of wartime technology to consumer industry and the continuation of military spending. Civilian travel expanded as nations organized their own air systems based on improved airplane technology. Factories churned out a vast assortment of synthetics like nylon and plastic products, ranging from pipes to household goods to rainwear. In the climate of cold war, governments ordered bombs, fighter planes, tanks, and missiles and continued to sponsor military research. The outbreak of the Korean War in 1950, and the U.S. need for manufactured goods to wage that war, further sustained economic growth in Europe. Ultimately, the cold war prevented a repeat of the 1920s, when reduced military spending threw people out of jobs and thus fed the growth of fascism.

Large and small states alike developed prosperous, modern economies. In the twelve principal countries of western Europe, the annual rate of economic growth had been 1.3 percent per inhabitant between 1870 and 1913. Between 1950 and 1973 those countries almost tripled that rate, attaining an annual per capita growth rate of 3.8 percent. Among the larger powers, West Germany surprisingly became the economic leader by the 1960s. The smaller Scandinavian countries also achieved a notable recovery: Sweden developed successful automobile, truck, and shipbuilding industries. Finland modernized its industry in order to pay the reparations demanded by the Soviet Union for resisting its invasion; it also modernized the agricultural sector, which freed up farmers to move into factory work. Scandinavian women joined the workforce in record numbers, which also boosted economic growth and expanded prosperity. The thirty years after World War II were a golden age of European economic growth.

As a final ingredient in the postwar recovery, international cooperation and planning led to the creation of the Common Market and ultimately the European Union of the 1990s. In 1951, Italy, France, Germany, Belgium, Luxembourg, and the Netherlands formed the European Coal and Steel Community (ECSC). This organization managed joint production and prices and arranged for the abundant West German output of coal and steel to benefit all of western Europe. According to the ECSC's principal architect, Robert Schuman, this economic cooperation would make another war "materially impossible." Simply put, the bonds of common productivity and trade would keep France and Germany from another cataclysmic war.

In 1957, the six ECSC members took another major step toward regional prosperity when they signed the Treaty of Rome. The treaty provided for a more general trading partnership called the **European Economic Community (EEC)**, known popularly as the Common Market. The EEC reduced tariffs among the six partners and developed common trade policies. It brought under one cooperative economic umbrella more than 200 million consumers and would eventually add several hundred million more. According to one of its founders, the EEC aimed to "prevent the race of nationalism, which is the true curse of the modern world." The six members' rates of economic growth soared. Britain pointedly refused to join the partnership at first; membership would have required that it surrender certain imperial trading rights among its Commonwealth partners such as Australia, New Zealand, and Canada. Since 1945, British statesmen had shunned the developing continental trading bloc because, as one of them put it, participation would make Britain "just another European country."

Behind the move to the Common Market stood the wartime adoption of economic planning determined by specialists. Called technocrats after 1945, specialists were to base decisions on expertise rather than on personal interest; those working for the Common Market were to disregard the self-interest of any one nation and thus reduce the potential for irrationality and violence in politics, both domestic and international. Supervised by a commission in Brussels, experts working for the Common Market functioned beyond the confines of the nation-state and thus exceeded the power of elected politicians. Some critics insisted (and some insist today) that expert planning would diminish democracy by putting massive control in the hands of bureaucracy, not legislatures. Defenders were just as insistent that planning and cooperation would be the surest tools of prosperity and peace.

The Welfare State: Common Ground East and West

On both sides of the cold war, governments intervened forcefully to ameliorate social conditions with state-financed programs such as pensions and insurance. This system of intervention became known as the welfare state, indicating that states were no longer interested solely in maintaining order and augmenting their power. Veterans' pensions and programs were primary. Beyond that, almost all countries now desperately supported reproduction and family life with direct financial aid to offset population losses. Imitating the sweeping Swedish programs of the 1930s, nations expanded or created family allowances, health-care and medical benefits, and programs for pregnant women and new mothers. The French gave larger family allowances for each birth after the first; for many French families, this allowance provided as much as a third of the household income.

Aspects of the welfare state reflecting gender bias worked to the detriment of women. Britain's maternity benefits and child allowances, announced in a wartime report, provided little coverage of workingwomen. The West German government passed strict legislation that forced employers to give women maternity leaves, thus discouraging them from hiring women. It also cut back or eliminated pensions and benefits to married women. West Germans bragged about keeping women from the workforce, claiming that this distinguished democratic practices from Communist ones. West Germany's refusal to build day-care centers or to allow stores to remain open in the evening so that workingwomen could buy food for their families led it to have among the lowest rate of female employment of any industrial country and the highest rate of female poverty in old age.

By contrast, in eastern Europe and the Soviet Union, where wartime loss of life had been enormous, women worked nearly full time and usually outnumbered men in the workforce. Like many countries of western Europe, however, child-care programs, family allowances, and maternity benefits were designed to encourage pregnancies by working women. A national health program provided medical and health services, as in most countries to the west. There were marked differences in everyday life that undermined the drive to increase population, however. The scarcity of consumer goods, the housing shortages, and the lack of household conveniences in the eastern bloc discouraged workingwomen from having large families. Because women had sole responsibility for onerous domestic duties on top of their paying jobs, their already heavy workload increased with the birth of each additional child. As a result, the birthrate in Communist states stagnated.

■ Postwar Soviet Housing

Wartime devastation worsened the shortage of housing that had begun when resources were diverted to fight World War I and increased during the depression of the 1930s, when housing construction almost halted. In the post–World War II years, shortages were so grave that slapdash, cheap buildings with far less than one room per person went up from England to eastern Europe and the Soviet Union. Not until the 1960s did the Soviets begin building anywhere near the million or more housing units needed each year. (Time Life Pictures/Getty Images.)

Across Europe, welfare-state programs aimed to improve people's health. State-funded medical insurance, subsidized medical care, or nationalized health-care systems covered health-care needs in most industrial nations except the United States. Contributing to the overall progress, the number of doctors and dentists more than doubled between the end of World War I and 1950, and vaccines greatly reduced the death toll from such diseases as tuberculosis, diphtheria, measles, and polio. In England, schoolchildren stood on the average an inch taller than children the same age had a decade earlier. As people lived longer, governments began to establish programs for the elderly.

State initiatives in other areas played a role in the higher standard of living. A growing network of government-built atomic power plants brought more thorough electrification of eastern Europe and the Soviet Union. Governments legislated better conditions and more leisure time for workers. Beginning in 1955, Italian workers received twenty-eight paid holidays annually; in Sweden, they received twenty-nine vacation days, a number that grew in the 1960s. Planning also helped provide a more varied diet and more abundant food, with meat, fish, eggs, cheese, milk, and fresh fruit supplementing the older grain-based foods.

Housing shortages posed a daunting challenge after three decades of economic depression and destructive war. Postwar Europeans often lived with three generations sharing one or two rooms, and eastern Europeans faced the worst conditions. To rebuild, governments sponsored a postwar housing boom. New cities formed around the edges of major urban areas in both the East and West. Many buildings went up slapdash, and Westerners labeled many Eastern-bloc apartments environmentally horrible, meaning that they were a blight on cities and towns across the Soviet landscape.

Recovery in the East

To create a Soviet bloc according to Stalin's prewar vision of industrialization, Communists revived the harsh policies that had transformed peasant economies. In Hungary, for example, Communists reapportioned all estates over twelve hundred acres. Having gained support of the poorer peasants through this redistribution, Communists later dispossessed everyone of their prized lands and pushed them into cooperative farming. Only in Poland did a substantial number of private farms remain. The process of collectivization was brutal and slow everywhere, and rural people looked back on the 1950s as dreadful. But some among those in the countryside felt that ultimately their lives and their children's lives had improved. "Before we peasants were dirty and poor, we worked like dogs. . . . Was that a good life? No sir, it wasn't. . . . I was a miserable sharecropper and my son is an engineer," said one Romanian peasant. Despite modernization, government investment in agriculture was never high enough to produce the bumper crops of western Europe, and lack of motivation among farmers—even their outright hostility toward the new system—worked against the success of collective farming.

An admirer of American industrial know-how, Stalin prodded all the socialist economies in his bloc to match U.S. productivity and built on advances fostered by German investment during the war in local industry. The Soviet Union also formed regional organizations like those to the west, instituting the Council for Mutual Economic Assistance (COMECON) in 1949 to coordinate economic relations among the satellite countries and Moscow. The terms of the COMECON relationship ironically thwarted development of the satellite states, for the USSR was allowed to buy goods from its clients at bargain prices and sell to them at exorbitant ones. Nonetheless, these formerly peasant states became oriented toward technology and bureaucratically directed industrial economies. New technical and bureaucratic careers opened. Tired of the struggles on the land, rural people moved to cities, where they received better education, health care, and ultimately jobs, albeit at the price of repression. The Roman Catholic church, which often protested the imposition of communism, was crushed as much as possible or infiltrated by government agents. Communists discriminated against agrarian elites, intellectuals, and other members of the middle class or imprisoned them. Political prisoners in East German camps did hard labor in uranium and other dangerous mines.

Culture, along with science, was a building block of Stalinism in the satellite countries. State-instituted programs aimed to build loyalty to the modernizing regime; thus, citizens found themselves obliged to attend adult education classes, women's groups, and public ceremonies. An intense program of Russification and de-Christianization forced students in eastern Europe to read histories of the war that ignored their own country's resistance and gave the Red Army sole credit for fighting the Nazis. They replaced national symbols with Soviet ones. For example, Hungarians had to accept a new flag with a Soviet red star beaming rays onto a hammer and sickle; the Hungarian colors were reduced to a small band on the flag. Utter historical distortion, revivified anti-Semitism, and rigid censorship resulted in what one staunchly socialist writer in the USSR characterized as "a dreary torrent of colorless, mediocre literature." Stalin also purged prominent wartime leaders to ensure conformity. Marshal Zhukov, a popular leader of the Soviet armed forces, was shipped to a distant command, while Anna Akhmatova, the great poet whose widely admired writing had emphasized perseverance during the war, was confined to a crowded hospital room because she refused to glorify Stalin in her postwar poetry.

In March 1953, Stalin died, and it soon became clear that the old ways would not hold. Political prisoners in the labor camps who had started rioting late in the 1940s now pressed for reform. In the spring of 1953, more than a million people were released from the Gulag, or prison camp system, and returned home with horrific stories. At the other end of the social order, many Soviet officials had come to distrust Stalinism and were ready for some changes despite their privileges. A power struggle ensued within the Soviet government, and protests took place across the Soviet bloc. In response, the government beefed up the production of consumer goods—a policy ultimately called "goulash communism" after the Hungarian lead in providing more food for ordinary people. There was still lingering uncertainty, however, about the post-Stalin future.

In 1955, Nikita Khrushchev (1894–1971), an illiterate coal miner before the revolution, emerged as the undisputed leader of the Soviet Union, but he did so without the usual executions. Khrushchev listened to popular complaints in both city and countryside, and in 1956 he attacked Stalinism head on. At a party congress, Khrushchev denounced the "cult of personality" Stalin had built about himself and announced that Stalinism did not equal socialism. The problems within Soviet communism thus became the fault of a single individual. The "secret speech"—it was not published in the USSR but became widely known—was a sensation at home and abroad. People experienced, in the words of one writer, "a holiday of the soul." Debates broke out in public, and books appeared championing the ordinary worker against the party bureaucracy. The climate of relatively free expression was called "the thaw"; however, it proved an uneven Soviet policy.

Protest erupted when news of Stalin's crimes reached official communist gatherings in Poland, and in early summer 1956 discontented Polish railroad workers struck for better wages. Popular support for their cause ushered in a more liberal

■ **Re-creating Hungarian Youth**

"Forward for the Congress of the Young Fighters of Peace and Socialism," exhorts this poster informing Hungarian youth about a conference to be held in June 1950. After World War II, people across Europe focused on the well-being of young people, and regimes in the Soviet sphere took steps to provide education in Communist ways. Youth groups like those in the early Stalinist USSR served this end, and vivid posters in the Soviet realist style carried inspirational messages. **For more help analyzing this image,** see the visual activity for this chapter in the ONLINE STUDY GUIDE at **bedfordstmartins.com/ huntconcise.**

(Magyar Nemzeti Múzeum, Budapest [Hungarian National Museum].)

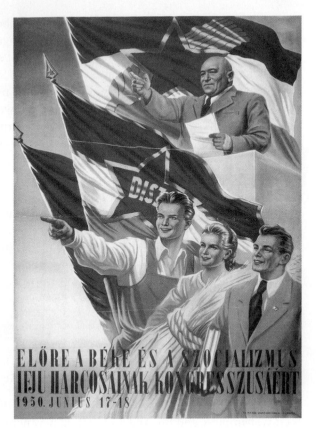

ELŐRE A BÉKE ÉS A SZOCIALIZMUS
IFJU HARCOSAINAK KONGRESSZUSÁÉRT
1950. JUNIUS 17-18

Communist program. Inspired by the Polish example, Hungarians rebelled against forced collectivization in October 1956. As in Poland, reports of Stalin's crimes and economic issues sparked outbreaks of violence, targeting the entire Communist system. Tens of thousands of protesters filled the streets of Budapest, and popular hero Imre Nagy returned to power. When Nagy announced that Hungary might leave the Warsaw Pact, Soviet troops moved in, killing tens of thousands and causing hundreds of thousands more to flee to the West. Nagy was hanged. Crushing the Hungarian Revolution vividly displayed the limits to the thaw, but the simultaneous U.S. refusal to intervene in Hungary showed that, despite a rhetoric of liberation, the United States would not risk World War III by militarily challenging the Soviet sphere of influence.

The failure of eastern European uprisings overshadowed significant changes since Stalin's death. Khrushchev ended the Stalinist purges and reformed the courts, which came to function according to procedures instead of staging the show trials of the past. The gates of the Gulag opened further, and the secret police lost many of its arbitrary powers. A new sense of security acquired from increased productivity, military buildup, and stunning successes in aerospace development helped promote reform. In 1957, the Soviets successfully launched the first artificial earth satellite, *Sputnik*; in 1961, they put the first cosmonaut, Yuri Gagarin, in orbit around the earth. The Soviets' edge in space technology shocked the Western bloc and motivated the United States to create the National Aeronautics and Space Administration (NASA).

Soviet successes advanced Stalin's goal of modernization. Nevertheless, Khrushchev alternately bullied dissidents and showed himself open to changing Soviet culture. For example, he forced Boris Pasternak to refuse the 1958 Nobel Prize in literature because his novel *Doctor Zhivago* (1957) cast doubt on the glory of the Communist revolution and affirmed the value of the individual. Yet in 1961, he allowed the publication of Aleksandr Solzhenitsyn's *One Day in the Life of Ivan Denisovitch*, a chilling account of life in the Gulag. Under the thaw, Khrushchev himself made several trips to the West and was more widely seen by the public than Stalin. More confident and more affluent, the Soviets took steps to reduce their diplomacy's paranoid style and concentrated their efforts on spreading socialism in emerging third world nations. Despite the USSR's more relaxed posture, both superpowers continued to move the world to the nuclear brink.

■ **REVIEW:** *What factors drove economic recovery in western Europe? In eastern Europe?*

Decolonization in a Cold War Climate

World War II dealt the final blow to the ability of European powers to maintain their vast empires, and the cold war allowed new nations to turn to the superpowers for help. Despite their postwar weakness, Britain, France, the Netherlands, and others futilely attempted to stamp out nationalist groups that had strengthened during the war. As before, colonized peoples had been on the front lines defending the West; and as before, they had experienced discrimination and witnessed the full barbarism of Western warfare. Moreover, the successive wars had allowed local industries to develop, as the imperial powers lost their ability to maintain their own consumer manufacturing. As a result of the war, people in Asia, Africa, and the Middle East, often led by individuals steeped in Western values and experienced in military and manufacturing technology, embraced the cause of independence.

The path to achieving independence—a process called **decolonization**—was treacherous and difficult. In Africa, a continent whose peoples spoke more than five thousand languages and dialects, the European conquerors' creation of convenient administrative units such as Nigeria and Rhodesia had obliterated living arrangements based on ethnic ties and local cultures. In addition, religion played a divisive role in independence movements. In India, Hindus and Muslims battled one another even though they shared the goal of eliminating British rule. In the Middle East and North Africa, pan-Arab and pan-Islamic movements might seem to have been unifying forces. Yet many Muslims were not Arab, not all Arabs were

Muslim, and Islam itself encompassed competing beliefs and sects. Despite these differences—often promoted by the colonizers—peoples in the third world succeeded in gaining independence while they offered a new field for competition between the United States and the Soviet Union in the cold war.

The End of Empire in Asia

At the end of World War II, leaders in Asia continued mobilizing the mass discontent that had intensified during the war and, often facing stiff resistance from white settlers, were able to drive out foreign rulers. Declining from an imperial power to a small island nation, Britain was the biggest loser. In 1947 it parted with India, whose independence it had promised in the 1930s. When the war broke out, independence was postponed and some two million Indian men fought for the British. Local industry became an important supplier of war goods, and Indian business leaders bought out local British entrepreneurs short of cash. The British honored their commitment after the war and decreed that two countries should emerge from the old colony. Given the legacy of mistrust, in 1947 India was created for Hindus and Pakistan—itself later divided into two parts—for Muslims. Yet during the independence year, tensions exploded among opposing members of the two religions, and hundreds of thousands were massacred. In 1948, a radical Hindu assassinated Gandhi, who though a Hindu himself had continued to champion religious reconciliation. Britain retained control of Hong Kong; but before two decades of the postwar era had passed, almost half a billion Asians had gained their freedom from the rule of fifty million British.

In 1949, a Communist takeover in China brought in a government led by Mao Zedong (1893–1976) that ended the influence of the traditional colonial powers. It nationalized commerce and industry and eliminated foreign privileges, causing tens of thousands of Western businesspeople, artisans, and refugees to flee. Chinese communism in the new People's Republic of China emphasized above all the welfare of the peasantry, yet it copied Soviet collectivization, rapid industrialization, and brutal repression.

The United States and the Soviet Union were deeply interested in East Asia—the United States because of the region's economic importance and the USSR because of its shared borders. Thus, the Communist victory spurred both superpowers to increase their involvement

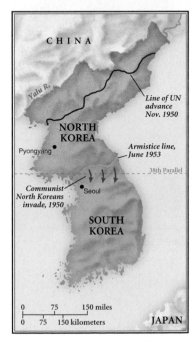

The Korean War, 1950–1953

in Asian politics. They faced off indirectly in Korea, which had been split at the thirty-eighth parallel after World War II. In 1950, North Korea's government, supported at the end of the war by the USSR, invaded U.S.-backed South Korea. The United States maneuvered the United Nations' Security Council into approving a "police action" against the North, and its forces quickly drove well into North Korean territory, where they were met by the Chinese army. After two and a half years of stalemate, the opposing sides finally agreed to a settlement in 1953: Korea would remain split at its prewar border, the thirty-eighth parallel. Some three million Koreans died in the war, while the United States lost more than fifty thousand troops and increased its military spending from $10.9 billion in 1948 to almost $60 billion in 1953. The expansion of the cold war to Asia prompted the creation of an Asian counterpart to NATO: the Southeast Asia Treaty Organization (SEATO), established in 1954. Another side effect of the Korean War was the rapid reindustrialization of Japan to provide the United States with supplies.

The cold war spread to Indochina, where nationalists struggled against the postwar revival of French imperialism. Their leader, the European-educated Ho

Chi Minh (1890–1969), built a powerful organization, the Viet Minh, to fight colonial rule. He advocated the redistribution of land held by big landowners, especially in the rich agricultural area in southern Indochina where some six thousand owners possessed more than 60 percent of the land. Viet Minh peasant guerrillas ultimately forced the technologically advanced French army, which was receiving aid from the United States, to withdraw from the country after the bloody battle of Dien Bien Phu in 1954. Later that year, the Geneva Convention divided Vietnam into North and South, each free from French control. The Viet Minh was ordered to retreat to an area north of the seventeenth parallel. But superpower intervention undermined the peace treaty. The United States, continuing to assist the corrupt government in the south, looked to some eyes like an imperialist power of the old school.

Indochina, 1954

The Struggle for Identity in the Middle East

Independence struggles in the Middle East gained in force because of the world's growing need for oil. The cold war also gave Middle Eastern leaders an opening to bargain with the superpowers, playing them against each other. Middle Eastern

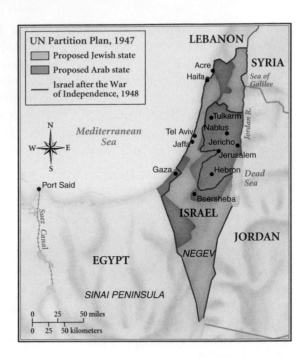

■ MAP 22.4 The Partition of Palestine and the Creation of Israel, 1947–1948

The creation of the Jewish state of Israel in 1948 against a backdrop of ongoing wars among Jews and indigenous Arab peoples made the Middle East a powder keg. The struggle for resources and for securing the borders of viable nation-states was at the heart of these bitter contests, threatening to pull the superpowers into a third world war.

countries, mandated to Britain and France after World War I, not only gained their full independence after the war but began building their economic clout by successfully renegotiating higher payment for drilling rights from Western companies. The legacy of the Holocaust, however, complicated the Middle Eastern political scene as the Western powers' commitment to secure a Jewish settlement in the Middle East further stirred up Arab determination not to be pushed out of their homeland.

When World War II broke out, 600,000 Jewish settlers and twice as many Arabs lived, in intermittent conflict, in British-controlled Palestine. In 1947, an exhausted Britain ceded the area to the United Nations (UN), which in the aftermath of the Holocaust voted to partition Palestine into an Arab region and a Jewish one (Map 22.4). Conflicting claims, however, led to war, and Jewish military forces prevailed. On May 14, 1948, the state of Israel came into being. "The dream had come true," Golda Meir, the future prime minister of Israel, remembered, but "too late to save those who had perished in the Holocaust." Israel opened its gates to immigrants, driving its expansionist ambitions against those of its Arab neighbors.

One of those neighbors, Egypt, had gained its independence from Britain at the end of the war despite Britain's continued control of the Suez Canal, which was owned by a British-run company. In 1952, Colonel Gamal Abdel Nasser (1918–1970) became Egypt's president on a platform of economic modernization and true national independence. A prime goal was reclaiming the Suez Canal, "where 120,000 of our sons had lost their lives in digging it [by force]," he stated. In July 1956, Nasser nationalized the canal, becoming a hero to fellow Arabs. In October, Britain, Israel, and France, following a secret plan, attacked Egypt while the Hungarian revolt was in full swing and the United States was preoccupied with presidential elections. As the USSR sent a warning, the Americans, outraged at being deceived by allies and concerned that Egypt would turn to the USSR, made the British back down. Nasser's triumph inspired confidence in the region, while it also showed the decline of the old imperial order.

New Nations in Africa

In sub-Saharan Africa, nationalist leaders roused their people to challenge Europe's domination. Disrupted in their traditional agricultural patterns, many Africans flocked to shantytowns in cities during the war, where they kept themselves alive through scavenging, making crafts, and doing menial labor for whites. "The European Merchant is my shepherd, and I am in want," went one African version of the Twenty-third Psalm. At war's end, Kwame Nkrumah (1909–1972) led the inhabitants of the West African Gold Coast in passive resistance against British rule. After years of arresting and jailing the protesters to no avail, the British withdrew, allowing the state of Ghana to form in 1957. Next, Nigeria, the most populous African region, became independent in 1960 after the leaders of its many regional groups agreed to a federal-style government. In these and other African states where the population was mostly black, independence came less violently than in mixed-race territory (Map 22.5).

The eastern coast and southern and central areas of Africa had numerous European settlers, who violently resisted independence movements. In British East Africa, where white settlers ruled in splendor and where blacks lacked both land and economic opportunity, violence erupted in the 1950s. African men formed rebel groups named the Land Freedom Army but nicknamed Mau Mau. With women serving as provisioners, messengers, and weapon stealers, Mau Mau bands, composed mostly of war veterans from the Kikuyu ethnic group, tried to recover land from whites. In 1964, Kenya gained formal independence, but only after the British had slaughtered at least one hundred thousand Kikuyus.

France, although eager to regain its great-power status after its humiliating defeat and occupation in World War II, easily granted independence to Tunisia, Morocco, and West Africa, where there were fewer white settlers and more limited economic stakes. However, in Algeria, with its million settlers of European descent, the French waged a vicious war when in 1954 the Front for National Liberation (FNL) rebelled against colonialism. In response, the French dug in, sending more than 400,000 troops. Neither side fought according to the rules of warfare: Algerian women, shielded by gender stereotypes, planted bombs in European cafés and carried weapons to assassination sites; the French savagely tortured Algerian Arabs.

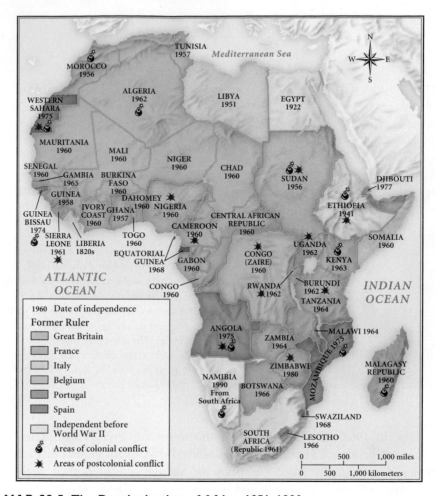

■ MAP 22.5 The Decolonization of Africa, 1951–1990

The liberation of Africa from European rule was an uneven process, sometimes occurring peace-fully and at other times demanding armed struggle to drive out European settlers, governments, and armies. After liberation, the difficult process of nation building—forming governments, edu-cating children, providing social services—began. Creating national unity also proved challenging, except in places where the struggle against colonialism had already brought people together.

Vastly outnumbered, the FNL took its struggle to the court of public opinion, leading the United States to urge a French withdrawal in the name of freedom and third world development. French military and settlers in Algeria terrorized the mainland with bombings and political assassinations in the name of keeping Algeria French.

France's Fourth Republic collapsed over Algeria, and Charles de Gaulle came back to power in 1958, demanding in exchange for his leadership the creation of a new republican government, one with a strong president. Amid escalating

■ **Jomo Kenyatta, First President of the New Kenyan Nation**
Educated in England, Kenyatta wrote Facing Mount Kenya, *a work that explained Kikuyu life as a distinct culture to Westerners. After a costly struggle during which he was imprisoned by the British, Kenyatta became president (1964–1978) of the new republic of Kenya. He stifled political debate by outlawing opposition parties. His one-party government brought social calm, which made Kenya a good place for Western investment.*
(© Bettmann/CORBIS.)

terrorism, in 1962, de Gaulle finalized the terms for French withdrawal and Algerian independence. Hundreds of thousands of *pieds noirs* ("black feet"), as the French condescendingly called Europeans in Algeria, as well as their Arab supporters fled to France. The Dutch and Belgian empires also disintegrated. Violent resistance to the reimposition of colonial rule led to the establishment of the large independent states of Indonesia (1949) and the Congo (1960—now known as the Democratic Republic of the Congo).

As independent nations emerged from colonialism, structures arose to promote international security and worldwide deliberations that included voices from the new states. Foremost among these, the **United Nations (UN)** convened for the first time in 1945. It had a greater chance of success than the League of Nations because of one notable change: both the United States and the Soviet Union were active members. The UN charter outlined a collective global authority that would adjudicate conflicts and provide military protection if any members were threatened by aggression. In 1955, Achmed Sukarno, who succeeded in wrenching Indonesian independence from the Dutch, sponsored the Bandung Convention of nonaligned nations to set a common policy for achieving modernization and facing the major powers. Both the UN and the meetings of emerging nations helped nudge issues of north-south inequities and human rights into public consciousness.

The Arrival of New Europeans

Amid wars of liberation and the struggles to achieve solid economic independence, people from the former colonies began migrating to Europe—a reversal of the nineteenth-century trend of migration out of Europe. The first influx of non-European newcomers came from Britain's Caribbean possessions right after the war. Next, labor shortages in northern Europe compelled governments to negotiate with southern European countries for temporary workers. The German situation was particularly dire because in 1950, the working-age population (people between the ages of fifteen and sixty-four) was composed of 15.5 million men and 18 million women. In an ideological climate that kept women out of the workforce, the government needed immigrant labor. After southern European reserves proved insufficient, Germany and France turned to North African and then to sub-Saharan countries in the 1960s. During the cold war, countries in the Soviet bloc took refugees from war-torn Southeast Asia. Then, in the late 1970s, clandestine workers from Africa and Asia began entering countries like Italy that had formerly exported labor. Scandinavia received immigrants from around the world who flocked there because of reportedly greater opportunity and social programs to integrate newcomers. Immigrants from Surinam and Indonesia headed toward the Netherlands. By the 1980s, some 8 percent of the European population was foreign-born, compared with 6 percent in the United States.

The agreements stipulated that immigrant workers would have only temporary resident status, with a regular process of emigration back to their homeland. Initially, these workers were housed in barracks-like dormitories, and few Europeans paid any attention to the quality of their lives. Instead of settling into community affairs, they created their own enclaves. Temporary workers made economic sense: virtually none of the welfare-state benefits applied to them; often their menial work was off the books. "As they are young," one French business publication explained, "the immigrants often pay more in taxes than they receive in allowances." Most immigrants did jobs that people in the West were not likely to want: they collected garbage, built roads, held factory jobs, and cleaned homes. Although men predominated among migrant workers, women performed similar chores for less pay.

Immigrants saw Europe as a land of relatively good government, wealth, and opportunity. Others simply appreciated the conditions of everyday existence. As one Chinese immigrant to Spain put it: "If you want to be a millionaire, you must go to Singapore; if you want to be rich, you must go to Germany; but if you want good weather and an easy life, go to Spain." As empires collapsed, the composition of the European population in terms of race, religion, and ethnicity began to change, becoming more multicultural and diverse. Many white Europeans looked

■ **The First "New" Europeans (1949)**
Many immigrants came to Europe after World War II in search of economic well-being. Some of the first people to arrive in the late 1940s were from the Caribbean (like the men in the photograph looking for work in Britain) and from South Asia. Expanding welfare states hired some of them to do menial work in hospitals, clinics, and construction, no matter what their qualifications. Race riots erupted, however, and immigration was so extensive that in the 1950s, the British House of Commons began debating the rights of these new Europeans. While the government and businesses in western Europe needed these new laborers to rebuild after the war, some Europeans questioned whether these workers—or their wives and children—should be allowed to become citizens.
(© Hulton Deutsch Collection/Corbis.)

back nostalgically on their imperial history and produced exotic films and novels about conquest and its pageantry, while the new nations coped with the costs of nation building, the legacy of colonial exploitation, and unaffordable government corruption.

■ **REVIEW:** *How did former imperial powers come to be dependent on temporary workers from the former colonies?*

Cultural Life on the Brink of Nuclear War

Both World War II and the cold war shaped postwar leisure and political culture. People engaged in heated debate over the responsibility for Nazism, the cause of ethnic and racial justice, and the merits of the two superpowers. During this period of intense self-scrutiny, they discussed the Americanization that seemed to accompany the influx of U.S. dollars, consumer goods, and cultural media. Were they becoming too materialistic like the Americans or too intolerant like the Soviets? As Europeans debated these issues, the leaders of the Soviet Union and the United States nearly provoked nuclear conflagration in 1962 over the issue of missiles on the island of Cuba. In hindsight, the existence of extreme nuclear threat in an age of unprecedented prosperity seems utterly bewildering, but for those who lived on the precipice of global annihilation, the dangers were all too real.

Restoring "Western" Values

After the depravity and inhumanity of Nazism, cultural currents in Europe and the United States reemphasized universal values and spiritual renewal. Some, like Billy Graham, saw the churches as central to the restoration of values through an active commitment to "re-Christianizing" Europe and the United States. Their success was only partial, however, as the trend toward a more secular culture continued. In the early postwar years, people in the U.S. bloc emphasized the triumph of a Western heritage over fascism, and they characterized the war as one "to defend civilization [from] a conspiracy against man." This definition of the West often emphasized the heritage of Greece and Rome and the rise of national governments in England, France, and western Europe as they encountered "barbaric" forces, be these nomadic tribes, Nazi armies, Communist agents, or national liberation movements in Asia and Africa. University courses in Western civilization flourished after the war to reaffirm those values.

Memoirs of the death camps were compelling reading material that showed those values struggling against barbarism. Rescued from the Third Reich in 1940, Nelly Sachs won the Nobel Prize in literature in 1966 for her poetry about the Holocaust. Anne Frank's *Diary of a Young Girl* (1947), the poignant record of a teenager hidden with her family in the back of an Amsterdam house, was emblematic of the survival of Western values in the face of Nazi persecution. Confronted with the small miseries of daily life and the grand evils of Nazism, Anne never stopped believing that "people are really good at heart." Governments erected permanent plaques at spots where resisters had been killed, organizations of resisters commemorated their role in winning the war, and their biographies filled magazines and bookstalls, hiding the fact of widespread collaboration in the mythical story of resistance.

Alongside the resistance story, **existentialism** became the rage among the cultural elites and students in postwar universities. It explored the meaning (or lack of meaning) of human existence in a world where evil flourished. Two of its leaders, Albert Camus (1913–1960) and Jean-Paul Sartre (1905–1980), had written for the resistance during the war, although Nazi censors had allowed the production of Sartre's plays. Existentialists confronted the question of "being," given what they perceived as the absence of God and the breakdown of morality. Their answer was that being, or existing, was not the automatic process either of God's creation or of birth into the natural world. One was not born with spiritual goodness in the image of a creator, but instead one created an "authentic" existence through action and choice. Camus's novels, such as *The Stranger* (1942) and *The Plague* (1947), dissected the evils of a corrupt political order and pondered human responsibility in such situations. Sartre's writings emphasized political activism and resistance under totalitarianism. Despite never having faced the enormous problems of making choices while living under fascism, young people in the 1950s found existentialism compelling and made it the most fashionable philosophy of the day.

In 1949, Simone de Beauvoir (1908–1986), Sartre's lifetime companion, published the twentieth century's most important work on the condition of women, *The Second Sex*. Beauvoir believed that most women had failed to take the kind of action necessary to lead authentic lives. Instead they lived in the world of biological necessity, devoting themselves exclusively to reproduction and motherhood. Failing to create an authentic self through considered action and accomplishment, they had become its opposite—an object, or "Other." Moreover, instead of struggling to define themselves and assert their freedom, women passively accepted their own "Otherness" and lived as defined by men. Beauvoir's classic book was a smash hit, in large part because people thought Sartre had written it. Both were celebrities, for the media spread the new commitment to humane values.

While Europeans debated decolonization, intellectuals spawned new theories of what their liberation would mean. The first half of the century had witnessed the rise of pan-Africanism, but it was in the 1950s that the immensely influential Frantz Fanon (1925–1961), a black psychiatrist from the French colony of Martinique, began analyzing liberation movements. He wrote that the mental functioning of the colonized person was "traumatized" by the violence and the brutal imposition of an outside culture as the only standard of value. Ruled by guns, the colonized person knew only violence and would thus naturally decolonize by means of violence. Translated into many languages, Fanon's *Black Skin, White Masks* (1952) and *The Wretched of the Earth* (1961) posed the question of how to decolonize one's mind.

Simultaneous with decolonization, in the 1950s the commitment to the civil rights cause of such long-standing organizations as the National Association for the Advancement of Colored People (NAACP, founded 1909) intensified. African Americans had fought in the war to defeat the Nazi idea of white racial superiority; as civilians, they now hoped to advance their ideals in the United States. In 1954, the U.S. Supreme Court declared segregated education unconstitutional in *Brown v. Board of Education*, a case initiated by the NAACP. On December 1, 1955, in Montgomery, Alabama, Rosa Parks, a part-time secretary for the local branch of the NAACP, boarded a bus and took the first available seat in the so-called white section at the front. When a white man found himself without a seat, the driver screamed at Parks, "Nigger, move back." Sitting in the front violated southern laws, which encompassed a host of inequitable, even brutal policies toward African Americans. Parks confronted that system through the studied practice of civil disobedience. She refused to move back, and her action led to a community-wide boycott of public transportation by African Americans.

As activists then boycotted a range of discriminatory businesses, talented leaders emerged, foremost among them the great orator Martin Luther King Jr. (1929–1968), a Baptist pastor from Georgia. He advocated nonviolent resistance and "soulforce"—Gandhi's *satyagraha*, or "holding to truth"—to counter aggression. The postwar culture of nonviolence would shape the civil rights movement for a few years. Soon, however, the voices of thinkers like Fanon came to revolutionize attitudes toward race and rights.

Rising Consumerism and Shifting Gender Norms

Government spending on reconstruction and welfare helped prevent the kind of upheaval that had followed World War I. Nor did the same tensions prevail among men and women: men returned from World War II much less frustrated than they had been in the 1920s because of the decisive result of World War II. A rising birthrate and bustling youth culture boosted consumer spending. Returning veterans had fewer worries about jobs. Nonetheless, the war affected men's roles and sense of themselves. Young men who had missed World War II adopted the rough, violent style of soldiers, and roaming gangs posed as tough military types. While Soviet youth admired aviator aces, elsewhere groups such as the "teddy boys" in England (named after their Edwardian style of dressing) and the *gamberros* ("hooligans") in Spain took their cues from pop culture in music and film.

The leader of rock-and-roll style and substance was the American singer Elvis Presley. Sporting slicked-back hair and an aviator-style jacket, Presley bucked his hips and sang sexual lyrics to screaming and devoted fans. Rock-and-roll concerts and movies galvanized youth across Europe, including the Soviet bloc, where teens demanded the production of blue jeans and leather jackets. In a German nightclub late in the 1950s, members of a rock group of Elvis fans called the Quarrymen performed, yelling at and fighting with one another as part of their show. They would soon become known as the Beatles. Rebellious young American film stars like James Dean in *Rebel Without a Cause* (1955) and Marlon Brando in *The Wild One* (1953) created the beginnings of a conspicuous postwar youth culture.

The rebellious masculine style appeared also in literature such as James Watson's autobiography, *The Double Helix* (1968), explaining how he and Francis

Crick had heroically discovered the structure of the gene by being bad boys, rifling people's desk drawers (among other dishonest acts). In the revival of West German literature, Heinrich Böll published *The Clown* (1963), a novel whose young middle-class hero takes to performing as a clown and begging in a railroad station. Böll protested that West Germany's postwar goal of respectability had allowed the resurgence of precisely those groups of people who had produced Nazism. Across the Atlantic, the American "Beat" poets affected a dirty, bearded, and sometimes crazy appearance to critique traditional ideals of the upright male achiever.

Both high and low culture revealed that two horrendous world wars had weakened the Enlightenment view of men as rational, responsible breadwinners. The 1953 inaugural issue of the American magazine *Playboy*, and the hundreds of magazines that came to imitate it, ushered in a startling depiction of a changed male identity. This segment of the media presented modern man as sexually aggressive and independent of dull domestic life—just as he had been in the war. Breadwinning for a family only destroyed a man's freedom and sense of self, this new male culture claimed. The notion of men's liberty came to include not just political rights but also sexual freedom outside the restrictions of the family.

In contrast, Western society promoted a postwar model for women that differed from their wartime experience. Instead of being essential workers and heads of families in the absence of their men, postwar women were made to symbolize the return to normalcy—a prewar domestic norm. Late in the 1940s, the fashion house of Christian Dior launched a clothing style called the "new look." It featured a pinched waist, tightly fitting bodices, and voluminous skirts, symbolizing a renewal of clear gender roles. Women's magazines publicized the new look and urged a return to domesticity. Even in the hard-pressed Soviet Union, recipes for homemade face creams passed from woman to woman, and beauty parlors did a brisk business.

However, new-look propaganda did not mesh with reality or even with all social norms. Dressmaking fabric was still being rationed in the late 1940s, and in countries where people had barely enough to eat, the underwear needed for new-look contours simply did not exist. In Spain, women were said to perform their role best by being religious and concerned with the spiritual well-being of their families. These values clashed with the quest for physical beauty available through consumption of cosmetics and clothing. European women continued to work outside the home after the war; indeed, mature women and mothers were working more than ever before—especially in the Soviet bloc. This constituted a profound revolution as the workforce gradually became less youthful and more populated by wives and mothers who would hold jobs all their lives despite the marketing of domesticity.

The advertising business presided over the creation of mass consumerism and the economic miracle. Guided by marketing experts, western Europeans were imitating Americans by driving some forty million motorized vehicles, including motorbikes, cars, buses, and trucks. They drank Coca-Cola and used American detergents, toothpaste, and soap. The number of radios in homes grew steadily— for example, by 10 percent a year in Italy between 1945 and 1950—and the 1950s marked a high tide of radio influence. Only in the 1960s did television become an important consumer item for most Europeans. In the 1950s, radio was still king and consumerism a growing mass phenomenon.

The Culture of Cold War

Radio was at the center of the cold war. As superpower rivalry heated up, radio's propaganda function remained at the fore, as it had in wartime. During the late 1940s and early 1950s, the Voice of America broadcast in thirty-eight languages from one hundred transmitters and provided an alternative source of news for people in eastern Europe. The Soviet counterpart broadcast in Russian around the clock but initially spent much of its wattage jamming U.S. programming. Russian programs stressed a uniform

■ **The "New Look"**
Immediately after the war, the French fashion industry swung into action to devise styles for the return to normal life in the West. Cinched or corseted waists and ample skirts brought to mind the nineteenth century rather than the depression and war years, when some women had started regularly wearing trousers. The elegant middle-class Western lifestyle implied by the "new look" contrasted sharply with the conditions facing most women in the Soviet Union, who had to work to rebuild their devastated country.
(Time Life Pictures/Getty Images.)

Communist culture and values; the United States, by contrast, emphasized diverse programming and promoted debate about current affairs. The contrast was meant to show commitment to socialist values versus commitment to choice and free speech.

Cold war media messages featured news of nuclear buildup. In school, children rehearsed for nuclear war, while at home families built bomb shelters in their backyards. Books like George Orwell's *1984* (1949) were claimed by ideologues on both sides as vindicating their beliefs. Ray Bradbury's popular *Fahrenheit 451* (1953), whose title indicated the temperature at which books would burn, condemned cold war curtailment of intellectual freedom. In the USSR, official writers churned out spy stories, and espionage novels topped best-seller lists in the West. *Casino Royale* (1953), by the British author Ian Fleming, introduced James Bond, who tested his wit and physical prowess against Communist and other political villains. Soviet pilots would not take off for flights when the work of Yulian Simyonov, the Russian counterpart of Ian Fleming, was playing on radio or television. Reports of Soviet- and U.S.-bloc characters—fictional or real—facing one another down became part of everyday life.

Culture as a whole came under the cold war banner. While many Europeans admired American innovation, the Communist Party in France led a successful campaign to ban Coca-Cola for a time in the 1950s. Soviet magazines carried fashion photos touted as decently attractive in contrast to the highly sexualized garments for women to the West. Both sides also poured vast sums into high culture, though the United States did it by secretly channeling government money into foundations to award fellowships to designated artists and writers. As leadership of the art world passed to the United States, art became part of the cold war. Abstract expressionism, practiced by American artists such as Jackson Pollock, produced nonrepresentational works by dripping, spattering, and pouring paint. Abstract expressionists spoke of the importance of the artist's self-discovery. "If I stretch my arms next to the rest of myself and wonder where my fingers are, that is all the space I need as a painter," commented Dutch-born Willem de Kooning on his relationship with his canvas. Said to exemplify Western freedom, such painters were given shows in Europe and awarded commissions at the secret direction of the U.S. Central Intelligence Agency (CIA).

The USSR openly promoted an official Communist culture. When a show of abstract art opened in the Soviet Union, Khrushchev yelled at the exhibition itself that it was "dog shit." Pro-Soviet critics focused on workers and the oppressed races in the United States. In Italy, the neorealist technique was developed by filmmakers such as Roberto Rossellini in *Open City* (1945) and Vittorio De Sica in *The Bicycle Thief* (1948). Such works challenged Hollywood-style sets and costumes by using ordinary characters living in devastated, impoverished cities. By depicting stark conditions, neorealist directors conveyed their distance both from middle-class prosperity and from fascist bombast. "We are in rags? Let's show everyone our rags," said

■ **Barbara Hepworth,** *Single Form* **(1961–1964)**

Like others in the West, British sculptor Barbara Hepworth was strangely buoyed by the war, hoping that it meant the dawn of a new age. Full of renewed energy, Hepworth believed that art should follow pure forms, which some called "primitive," as a way of expressing enduring values. Her twenty-one-foot abstract sculpture Single Form, *shown here as a plaster cast, was installed at the United Nations building in New York to commemorate the life of her friend Dag Hammarskjöld, who served as secretary-general of the United Nations from 1953 to 1961.*

(Photo: Morgan-Wells, London. © Bowness, Hepworth Estate.)

one Italian director. Many of these directors associated support for the suffering masses with the Communist cause. Seen or unseen, the cold war entered cultural life.

Kennedy, Khrushchev, and the Atomic Brink

In this pervasive climate of cold war, John Fitzgerald Kennedy (1917–1963) became U.S. president in 1960. Kennedy represented American affluence and youth but also the nation's commitment to cold war. Kennedy's media advisers played an articulate, good-looking president to the television audience. A war hero and early fan of the fictional cold war spy James Bond, Kennedy escalated the cold war perilously over the nearby island of Cuba, where in 1959 Fidel Castro had come to power and

IMPORTANT DATES			
1945	Cold war begins	1955	Soviet Union establishes the Warsaw Pact
1947	India and Pakistan win independence from Britain; U.S. President Harry Truman announces the "Truman Doctrine"	1956	Egyptian leader General Abdel Nasser nationalizes the Suez Canal; uprising in Hungary against USSR
1948	State of Israel established		
1949	Mao Zedong leads Communist revolution in China; Western allies establish NATO; Simone de Beauvoir publishes *The Second Sex*	1957	Boris Pasternak publishes *Doctor Zhivago*; USSR launches *Sputnik*; European Economic Community formed
1950	Korean War begins	1958	Fifth Republic begins in France
1953	Stalin dies; Korean War ends; first issue of *Playboy*	1961	East German workers begin to construct the Berlin Wall
1954	*Brown v. Board of Education* prohibits segregated schools in the United States; Vietnamese forces defeat the French at Dien Bien Phu	1962	United States and USSR face off in the Cuban missile crisis

allied his government with the Soviet Union after being rebuffed by the United States. In the spring of 1961, Kennedy, assured by the CIA of success, launched an invasion of Cuba at the Bay of Pigs to overthrow Castro. The invasion failed miserably and humiliated the United States. Cold war tensions increased.

In the summer of 1961, the government directed East German workers to stack bales of barbed wire across miles of the city's east-west border to begin construction of the Berlin Wall. The divided city had served as an escape route by which some three million people had fled to the West. Kennedy responded at home with a call for more weapons and an enhanced civil defense program. In October 1962, matters came to a head in the **Cuban missile crisis**, when the CIA reported the installation of launching sites for Soviet medium-range missiles in Cuba. Kennedy now acted forcefully, calling for a blockade of ships headed for Cuba and threatening nuclear war if the sites were not dismantled. For several days, the world stood on the brink of nuclear disaster. Then, between October 25 and 27,

■ MAPPING THE WEST The Cold War World, c. 1960

Superpower rivalry resulted in the division of much of the industrial world into cold war alliances. The United States and the Soviet Union also vied for the allegiance of the newly decolonized countries of Asia and Africa by providing military, economic, and technological assistance. Wars such as those in Vietnam and Korea were also products of the cold war.

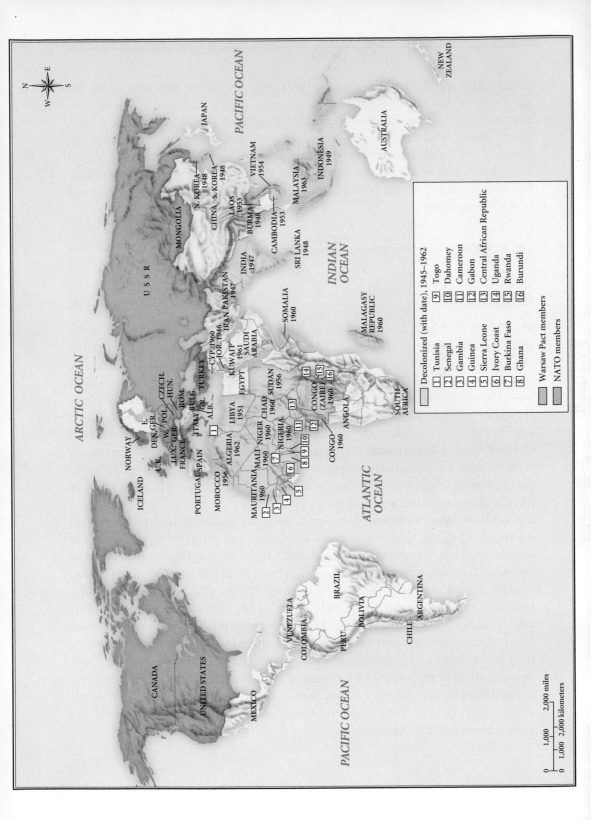

ARCTIC OCEAN

PACIFIC OCEAN

N. KOREA 1948
S. KOREA 1948
JAPAN
CHINA 1948
MONGOLIA
USSR
VIETNAM 1954
LAOS 1953
BURMA 1948
CAMBODIA 1953
MALAYSIA 1963
INDONESIA 1949
AUSTRALIA
NEW ZEALAND

SRI LANKA 1948
INDIA 1947
PAKISTAN 1947
IRAN 1946
JOR. 1946
CYP. 1960
TURKEY
GR.
ALB.
ITALY
BULG.
ROM.
HUN.
CZECH.
POL.
W. GER.
E. GER.
DEN.
NORWAY
ICELAND
U.K.
LUX.
FRANCE
PORTUGAL
SPAIN

INDIAN OCEAN

SOMALIA 1960
MALAGASY REPUBLIC 1960
SOUTH AFRICA

KUWAIT 1961
SAUDI ARABIA
EGYPT 1951
LIBYA
SUDAN 1956
CHAD 1960
NIGER 1960
MALI 1960
MAURITANIA 1960
MOROCCO 1956
ALGERIA 1962

1
2
3
4
5
6
7
8
9
10
11
12
13
14
15
16
NIGERIA 1960
CONGO 1960
CONGO (ZAIRE) 1960
ANGOLA

ATLANTIC OCEAN

BRAZIL
VENEZUELA
COLOMBIA
PERU
BOLIVIA
CHILE
ARGENTINA

CANADA
UNITED STATES
MEXICO

PACIFIC OCEAN

Decolonized (with date), 1945–1962
1 Tunisia   9 Togo
2 Senegal   10 Dahomey
3 Gambia   11 Cameroon
4 Guinea   12 Gabon
5 Sierra Leone   13 Central African Republic
6 Ivory Coast   14 Uganda
7 Burkina Faso   15 Rwanda
8 Ghana   16 Burundi
Warsaw Pact members
NATO members

0   1,000   2,000 miles
0   1,000   2,000 kilometers

Khrushchev and Kennedy negotiated an end to the crisis. Kennedy spent the remainder of his short life working to improve nuclear diplomacy; Khrushchev did the same. The two leaders, who had looked deeply into the nuclear future, clearly feared what they saw. In the summer of 1963, less than a year after the shock of the Cuban missile crisis, the United States and the Soviet Union signed a test-ban treaty outlawing the explosion of nuclear weapons in the atmosphere and in the seas and raising hopes that the cold war and its culture would give way to something better.

■ **REVIEW:** *How did the cold war affect everyday culture and social life?*

Conclusion

World War II began the atomic age and transformed international power politics. Two superpowers, the Soviet Union and the United States, each controlling atomic arsenals, replaced the former European leadership and engaged in a menacing cold war. The cold war saturated everyday life, giving birth to cold war religion in the preachings of the Reverend Billy Graham and to a postwar revival of religious faith. Radio broadcasts, spy stories, purges, and witch hunts kept people thinking that war was at hand. Postwar diplomacy created a cold war division of Europe into an eastern bloc dominated by the Soviets and a freer western bloc mostly allied with the United States. It was in this grim international atmosphere that starving, homeless, and refugee people faced the task of rebuilding a devastated Europe.

Yet both halves of Europe recovered almost miraculously in little more than a decade. The east, where wartime devastation was greatest, experienced less prosperity, while in western Europe wartime technology and planning served as the basis for new consumer goods. Spurred on by aid from the United States, western Europe formed a successful Common Market that became the foundation for greater European unity. As a result of the war, Germany recovered as two countries, not one, and the weakened European powers shed their colonies. Newly independent nations emerged in Asia and Africa, opening the possibility for a redistribution of global power. Often serving as pawns in the cold war, these new countries faced the problem of guaranteeing their economic future. As prosperity returned, cultural life focused paradoxically on rethinking Western values while enjoying mass consumerism. Above all, the world had to survive the atomic rivalry of the superpowers.

■ **MAKING CONNECTIONS**

1. *How did the political climate after World War II differ from the political climate after World War I?*

2. *Why did decolonization follow World War II so immediately?*

■ **FOR FURTHER EXPLORATION**

For further reading and online research ideas, see the Suggested References on page SR-11 at the back of the book.

For practice quizzes, a customized study plan, and other study tools, see the ONLINE STUDY GUIDE at bedfordstmartins.com/huntconcise.

For primary-source material from this period, see Chapter 22 in *Sources of THE MAKING OF THE WEST: A CONCISE HISTORY*, Second Edition.

Postindustrial Society and the End of the Cold War Order

1965–1989

I N JANUARY 1969, JAN PALACH, a twenty-one-year-old philosophy student, drove to a main square in Prague, doused his body with gasoline, and set himself ablaze. Before killing himself he left a statement in his coat—deliberately put to one side—demanding an end to Soviet-style repression in Czechoslovakia. It promised more such suicides unless the government lifted state censorship. The manifesto was signed: "Torch No. 1." Across a stunned nation, black flags were flown, close to a million people flocked to Palach's funeral, and shrines to his memory seemed to spring up overnight. In the next months, more Czech youth followed Palach's grim example and became torches for freedom.

Before his self-immolation, Jan Palach was an ordinary, well-educated citizen of the technological and postindustrial age. Having recovered from the war, the West was in the midst of still another astonishing transformation, shifting from a manufacturing economy based in heavy industry to a service economy that depended on technical knowledge in such fields as engineering, health care, and finance. To staff this new postindustrial society, institutions of higher education sprang up at a dizzying rate and drew in more students than ever before—among

■ **Shrine to Jan Palach**
Jan Palach was a martyr to the cause of an independent Czechoslovakia, free to pursue a non-Soviet destiny. His self-immolation on behalf of that cause roused the nation. As makeshift shrines sprang up and multiplied throughout the 1970s and 1980s, they served as common rallying points that ultimately contributed to the overthrow of Communist rule. Václav Havel, the future president of a liberated Czechoslovakia, was arrested early in the momentous year of 1989 for commemorating Palach's sacrifice at the shrine. In light of so many other deaths in the Soviet bloc, why did Jan Palach's death become so powerful a force? (© Marc Garanger/Corbis.)

them Jan Palach. But those young people—along with women, minorities, and many other activists in the 1960s and 1970s—struck out against war and cold war, inequality and repression, and even against knowledge and technology themselves. From Czechoslovakia to the United States and around the world, protests arose against the way in which postindustrial nations in general and the superpowers in particular were directing society. Before long, countries in both the Soviet and U.S. blocs were on the verge of political revolution.

While reformers questioned the values of technological and cold war society, whole nations challenged the superpowers' monopoly of international power. An agonizing war in Vietnam sapped the resources of the United States, and China confronted the Soviet Union with increasing confidence. The oil-producing states of the Middle East formed a cartel and reduced the flow of oil to the leading industrial nations in the 1970s. The resulting price increases helped bring on a recession, throwing the future of the postindustrial order into question. Others resorted to terrorism to achieve their ends, and all the wealth and military might of the superpowers could not guarantee that they would emerge victorious in this age of increasingly global competition. Soviet legitimacy eroded, and soon a reform-minded leader—Mikhail Gorbachev—directed the USSR to change course. It was too late: in 1989, the Soviet bloc collapsed, inspired by countless acts of protest, not least of them the individual heroism of Jan Palach and the other human torches.

The Revolution in Technology

The protests of the 1960s and after took place in the midst of incredible technological advance. These advances steadily boosted prosperity and changed daily life in the West, where people awoke to instantaneous radio and television news, worked with computers, and used revolutionary contraceptives to control reproduction. Satellites orbiting the earth reported weather conditions, relayed telephone signals, and collected military intelligence. Smaller gadgets—electric popcorn poppers, portable radios and tape players, automatic garage door openers—made life more pleasant. The reliance of humans on machines led one philosopher to insist that people were no longer self-sufficient individuals, but rather cyborgs—that is, humans who needed machines to sustain ordinary life processes.

The Information Age: Television and Computers

Information technology catalyzed social and political change in these postindustrial decades just as innovations in textile making and the spread of railroads had in the nineteenth century. This technology's ability to transmit knowledge, culture, and political information globally appeared even more revolutionary. Mass journalism, film, and radio had begun to forge a more homogeneous society based on shared information and images in the first half of the twentieth century; in the last third of the century, television, computers, and telecommunications made information even more accessible and, some critics said, made culture more standardized. Once-remote villages were linked to urban capitals on the other side of the world thanks to videocassettes, satellite television, and telecommunications.

Between the mid-1950s and the mid-1970s, Europeans rapidly adopted television as a major entertainment and communications medium. In 1954, just 1 percent of French households had television; by 1974, almost 80 percent did. With the average viewer tuning in about four and a half hours a day, the audience for newspapers and theater declined. "We devote more . . . hours per year to television than [to] any other single artifact," one sociologist commented in 1969. As with radio, European governments funded television broadcasting with tax dollars and controlled TV programming to avoid what they perceived as the substandard fare offered by American commercial TV; instead, they featured drama, ballet, concerts, variety shows, and news. Thus, the welfare state, in Europe at least, assumed a new obligation to fill its citizens' leisure time. It thereby gained more power to shape daily life.

With the emergence of communications satellites and video recorders in the 1960s, state-sponsored television encountered competition. Satellite technology allowed for the transmission of sports broadcasts and other programming to a worldwide audience. Feature films on videotape became readily available to television stations (although not yet to individuals) and competed with made-for-television movies and other programs. The competition increased in 1969 when the Sony Corporation introduced the first affordable color videocassette recorder to the consumer market. What critics considered the junk programming of the United States—soap operas, game shows, sitcoms—arrived dubbed in the native language, amusing a vast audience with the joys, sorrows, tensions, and aspirations of daily life. These commentators complained that, although TV provided more information than had ever been available before, the resulting shared culture represented the lowest common denominator.

East and West, television exercised a powerful political and cultural influence. Even in a rural area of the Soviet Union more than 70 percent of the inhabitants watched television regularly in the late 1970s; the rest continued to prefer radio. Educational programming united the far-flung population of the USSR by broadcasting shows designed to advance Soviet culture. At the same time, with travel impossible or forbidden to many, shows about foreign lands were among the most popular—as were postcards from these lands, which became household decorations. Heads of state could usually preempt regular programming. In the 1960s, French president Charles de Gaulle addressed his fellow citizens frequently, employing the grandiose gestures of an imperial ruler to stir patriotism. As electoral success in western Europe increasingly depended on cultivating a successful media image, political staffs came to rely on media experts as much as they did policy experts.

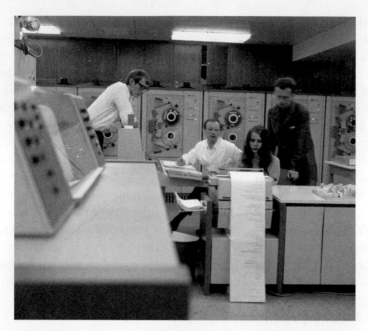

■ Advances in Computing

Robotron was the first mainframe computer in East Germany, and like many computers in 1970, it was huge. Within a decade, computing would be miniaturized due to the development of chip technology, and powerful computers would become small and lightweight. Robotron was run by a postindustrial workforce whose clean work took more technical knowledge than muscle power. As computing became miniaturized, the ability to manipulate computers became more widespread, and the postindustrial workforce itself became highly segmented. Technology was revolutionizing the way people worked, just as it had in the Industrial Revolution some two centuries earlier.
(AKG Images.)

The computer reshaped work in science, defense, and ultimately industry. Computers had evolved dramatically since the first electronic ones, among them the Colossus, which the British used in 1943 to decode Nazi military and diplomatic messages. With growing use in civilian industry and business after the war, computing machines shrank from the size of a gymnasium in the 1940s to that of an attaché case in the mid-1980s. They also became far less expensive and fantastically more powerful than the Colossus, thanks to the development of increasingly sophisticated digital electronic circuitry implanted on tiny silicon chips. Within a few decades, the computer could perform hundreds of millions of operations per second, and the price of the integrated circuit at the heart of computer technology would fall to less than a dollar, allowing businesses and individuals access to computing ability at a reasonable cost.

Computers changed the pace and patterns of work not only by speeding up and easing tasks but also by performing many operations that workers had once done themselves. In garment making, for example, experienced workers no longer painstakingly figured out how to arrange patterns on cloth for maximum efficiency and economy. Instead, a computer specified instructions for the optimal positioning of pattern pieces, and trained workers, usually women, followed the machine's directions. By the end of the 1970s, the miniaturization of the computer had made possible a renewal of the eighteenth-century cottage industry, and in 1981 the French phone company launched a public Internet server, the Minitel—a forerunner of the World Wide Web—through which one could make reservations, perform stock transactions, and gain information.

Did computers transform society for the better? Whereas the Industrial Revolution had seen physical power replaced by machine capabilities, the information revolution witnessed brainpower augmented by computer technology. Many believed that computers would profoundly expand mental life, providing, in the words of one scientist, "boundless opportunities . . . to resolve the puzzles of cosmology, of life, and of the society of man." Others maintained that computers programmed people, reducing human capacity for inventiveness, problem solving, and initiative.

The Space Age

The Soviet launch of the *Sputnik* satellite in 1957 marked the start of the space race. The U.S. drive to beat the Soviets in space by putting a man on the moon by the end of the 1960s prompted increasingly complex space flights that tested humans' ability to survive the process of space exploration, including weightlessness. Astronauts walked in space, endured weeks (and later, months) in orbit, fixed satellites, and carried out experiments for the military and private industry. Meanwhile, a series of unmanned rockets filled the earth's gravitational sphere with weather, television, intelligence, and other communications satellites. In July 1969, a worldwide television audience watched as U.S. astronauts Neil Armstrong and Edwin "Buzz" Aldrin walked on the moon's surface—the climactic moment in the space race.

The space race drove cultural developments. Astronauts and cosmonauts were perhaps the era's most admired heroes: Yuri Gagarin, John Glenn, and Valentina Tereshkova—the first woman in space—topped the list. Children's toys and games revolved increasingly around space. Films such as *2001: A Space Odyssey* (1968) portrayed space explorers answering questions about life that were formerly the domain of church leaders. Likewise, in the internationally popular television series *Star Trek*, members of the starship *Enterprise*'s diverse crew wrestled with the problems of maintaining humane values against less-developed, often menacing civilizations. In the Eastern bloc, Polish author Stanislaw Lem's popular novel *Solaris* (1971) similarly portrayed space age individuals engaged in personal quests and likewise drew readers into futuristic fantasy.

■ **Valentina Tereshkova, Russian Cosmonaut**
People sent into space were heroes, representing modern values of courage, strength, and well-honed skills. Insofar as the space age was part of the cold war race for superpower superiority, the USSR held the lead during the first decade. The Soviets trained both women and men, and the 1963 flight of Valentina Tereshkova—the first woman in space—supported Soviet claims of gender equality in contrast to the all-male superstar image of the early U.S. space program. The achievements of both countries led to the launching of communications satellites that produced the globalizing communications revolution of the next decades.
(Getty Images.)

The space age grew out of cold war concerns, but it also provided an opportunity for global political cooperation. From the 1960s on, U.S. spaceflights often involved the participation of other countries such as Great Britain and the Netherlands. In 1965, an international consortium headed by the United States launched the first commercial communications satellite, *Intelsat I*, and by the 1970s some 150 countries worked together at more than four hundred stations worldwide to maintain global satellite communications. Although half of all satellites were used for spying, the rest promoted international communication and were sustained by transnational collaboration.

Lunar landings and experiments in space advanced pure science in the midst of space-race hype. Mineral samples from the moon, for example, allowed astronomers to calculate the age of the solar system with unprecedented precision. Unmanned spacecraft provided data on cosmic radiation, magnetic fields, and infrared sources. Although the media touted the human conquerors of space, breakthroughs in space exploration and astronomy were utterly dependent on a range of technology, including the radiotelescope, which depicted space by receiving, measuring, and calculating nonvisible rays. These findings reinforced the so-called "big bang" theory of the origins of the universe, first posited in the 1930s by American astronomer Edwin Hubble and given crucial support in the 1950s by the discovery of a low level of radiation permeating the universe in all directions. Based on the earlier work of Albert Einstein and Max Planck, the big bang theory explains the development of the universe from a condition of extremely high density and temperature some ten billion years ago. Nuclei emerged when these conditions dissipated in a rapid expansion of space—the big bang.

Revolutions in Biology, Reproductive Technology, and Sexual Behavior

Sophisticated technologies extended to the life sciences, bringing dramatic new health benefits and ultimately changing reproduction itself. In 1952, scientists Francis Crick, an Englishman, and James Watson, an American, discovered the structure of **DNA**, the material in a cell's chromosomes that carries hereditary information. They showed how the double helix of the DNA molecule splits in cellular reproduction to form the basis of each new cell. This genetic material, biologists concluded, provides a chemical pattern for an individual organism's life. Beginning in the 1960s, genetics and the new field of molecular biology progressed rapidly. Growing understanding of nucleic acids and proteins advanced knowledge of viruses and bacteria that effectively ended the ravages of polio, tetanus, syphilis, tuberculosis, and such dangerous childhood diseases as mumps and measles in the West.

Understanding how DNA works allowed scientists to alter the makeup of plants and to bypass natural animal reproduction in a process called cloning—obtaining the cells of an organism and dividing or reproducing them (in an exact copy) in a laboratory. In 1997 one group of researchers produced a cloned sheep named "Dolly," though the breakthrough was marred by the fact that she suffered an array of disabilities and died six years later. Cloning raised the question of whether scientists should interfere with so basic and essential a process as reproduction. The possibility of genetically altering species and even creating new ones (for instance, to control agricultural pests) led to concern about how such actions would affect the balance of nature. In a related medical field, Dr. Christiaan Barnard of South Africa performed the first successful heart transplant in 1967, and U.S. doctors later developed an artificial heart. Commentators debated the selection process for these scarce, reusable organs and asked whether the enormous cost of new medical technology to save a few people would be better spent on helping the many who lacked even basic health care.

Technology also influenced the most intimate areas of human relations—sexuality and procreation. In traditional societies, community and family norms dictated marital arrangements and sexual practices, in large part because too many or too few children threatened the crucial balance between population size and agricultural productivity. With industrialization these considerations became less urgent while the availability of reliable birth-control devices permitted young people to begin sexual relations earlier, with less risk of pregnancy. These trends accelerated in the 1960s as the birth-control pill, first produced in the United States notes by the corresponding numbers in the ancient Chinese *I Ching* (Book of Changes). The development widened the gulf between the composer and the larger public: many listeners simply hated such music. Other composers, called minimalists, simplified music by featuring repetition and sustained notes as well as by rejecting the "masterpiece" tradition of lush nineteenth-century symphonies and piano music. Arvo Pärt, the famed Estonian composer, wrote minimalist pieces in the 1970s using only three or four notes in total; he called this style "starvation" music to underscore the lack of both freedom and goods in the Soviet bloc.

Some musicians stressed modern technology; they introduced tape recordings into vocal pieces and used computers and synthesizers to compose and perform their works. German composer Karlheinz Stockhausen introduced electronic music into classical composition in 1953; Cage also used it soon after. Influenced by his own travels, Stockhausen continued the modern style of fully exploring non-Western tonalities in such 1970s pieces as *Ceylon*. But even though this music echoed familiar electronic sounds, its concert audiences diminished because new music continued to seem dissonant and even shrill. At the same time, improved recording technology and mass marketing brought music of all varieties to a wider home audience than ever before.

The social sciences reached the peak of their prestige during these decades, often because of their increasing use of statistical models and predictions made possible by advanced electronic computations. Social scientists produced empirical studies that were more detailed than ever before and that purported to demonstrate rules for understanding behavior. Anthropology was among the most exciting of the social sciences, for it brought to the young university student information about societies that seemed immune to modern technology and industry. The sense of adventure was more vivid than ever before, as colorful ethnographic films captured alternative lifestyles and exotic practices. While studying people who came to be called "the other," the young had their sense of freedom reinforced by the vision of going back to nature.

Simultaneously, the social sciences undermined some of the foundations for the belief that individuals had true freedom. French anthropologist Claude Lévi-Strauss (b. 1908) developed a theory called structuralism, which insisted that all societies function within controlling structures—kinship and exchange, for example—that operate according to coercive rules similar to those of the unbreakable conventions in language. Structuralism challenged existentialism's tenet that humans could create a free existence and shook the social sciences' faith in the triumph of rationality. Lévi-Strauss's book *The Savage Mind* (1966) also demonstrated that people outside of the West had not a scientific but an improvisational style that could be extremely effective. In the 1960s and 1970s, the findings of the social sciences generally paralleled concerns that complex managerial systems would eradicate individualism and human freedom.

Church officials made an effort to bring religion up to date with the changing times, which tended to value toleration. Responding to what he saw as a crisis in faith caused by affluence and secularism, Pope John XXIII (r. 1958–1963) in 1962 convened the Second Vatican Council, known as **Vatican II**. The Council modernized the liturgy, democratized many church procedures, and at the last session in 1965 renounced church doctrine that condemned the Jewish people as guilty of killing Jesus. Vatican II promoted ecumenism—that is, mutual cooperation among the world's faiths. In the face of scientific advance, Pope John's successor, Paul VI (r. 1963–1978), kept Catholic opposition to artificial birth control alive, but he also became the first pontiff to demonstrate global concerns by visiting Africa, Asia, and South America. A succession of popes, most notably Polish-born John Paul II (r. 1978–2005), encouraged Catholicism in the Soviet bloc, strengthening religion as a primary focal point for anticommunism there.

In some parts of the West, there was a notable upsurge in postwar religious fervor. In the face of scientific advance, growing numbers of U.S. Protestants joined sects that stressed the literal truth of the Scripture and denied the validity of past scientific discoveries such as the age of the universe and the evolution of the species. In western Europe, however, Christian churchgoing remained at a low ebb. In the 1970s, for example, only 10 percent of the British population went to religious services—about the same number that attended live soccer matches. Most striking was the changing composition of the Western religious public. Citizens from former colonies and other parts of the world practiced non-Christian religions such as Islam and varieties of Hindu faiths. Cities and towns came to house mosques, Buddhist temples, and shrines to other creeds, sometimes mixing easily and sometimes tensely with European and U.S. cultures.

■ **REVIEW:** *What major changes took place in the formation of postindustrial society?*

Protesting Cold War Conditions

Affluence, scientific sophistication, and military might elevated the United States and the Soviet Union to the peak of their power in the 1960s. By 1965, however, the six nations of the Common Market had replaced the United States as the leader in worldwide trade, and they often acted in their own self-interest across the U.S.-Soviet divide. In 1973, Britain joined the Common Market, followed by Ireland and Denmark. The market's exports now amounted to almost three times those of the United States. Communist China, along with countries in eastern Europe, contested Soviet leadership, and many decolonizing regions refused to become pliable allies to the superpowers. The struggle for Indochinese independence had never ended, and by the mid-1960s a devastating war in Vietnam was under way. At the end of the 1970s, the USSR became embroiled in an equally devastating war in Afghanistan. Another serious challenge to the cold war order also came from rising citizen discontent and from dramatic protest like that of Jan Palach. From the 1960s until 1989, people rose up against the consequences of techno-logical development, the lack of fundamental rights, and the potential for nuclear holocaust latent in the cold war. Leaders of emerging nations in the Middle East also shook up the international political order of the cold war.

Cracks in the Cold War Order

Across the social and political spectrum there were calls for at least softening the effects of the cold war in this age of unprecedented progress and technological prowess. The new Soviet middle class of bureaucrats and managers demanded a better standard of living and a reduction in menacing cold war animosity. In western European countries, voters elected politicians in the late 1960s who promoted an increasing array of social programs central to the economic democracy of the welfare state. A significant minority shifted their votes away from the centrist Christian Democratic coalitions that supported U.S. political goals. In Germany, Social Democratic politicians pushed to reallocate funds from defense spending to domestic programs. Willy Brandt (1913–1992), the socialist mayor of West Berlin, became foreign minister in 1966 and pursued an end to frigid relations with Communist East Germany. This anti–cold war policy, known as **Ostpolitik**, gave West German business leaders what they wanted: "the depoliticization of Germany's foreign trade," as one industrialist put it, and an unlocking of Soviet-bloc consumerism. West German trade with eastern Europe grew rapidly; how-ever, it left the relatively poorer countries of the Soviet bloc strapped with mounting debt—some $45 billion annually by 1970.

To break the cold war stranglehold on international politics, French president Charles de Gaulle poured more money into French nuclear development, with-drew French forces from NATO, and signed trade treaties with the Soviet bloc. Communist China and France also drew closer. However, de Gaulle protected France's good relations with Germany to prevent further encroachments from the Soviet bloc. At home, de Gaulle's government sponsored construction of modern housing and mandated the exterior cleaning of all Parisian buildings to highlight civic, not cold war, values. With his haughty and stubborn pursuit of French grandeur, de Gaulle offered an alternative to submissively obeying the superpowers.

Brandt's Ostpolitik and de Gaulle's assertiveness had their echoes in Soviet-bloc reforms. Pushing de-Stalinization, Soviet premier Nikita Khrushchev took the dangerous course of trying to reduce Communist officialdom's privileges. Khrushchev's blunders—notably his humiliation in the Cuban missile crisis, his ineffectual schemes to improve Soviet agriculture, and his inability to patch the rift with China—were highly visible and led to his ouster in 1964. The new lead-ership of Leonid Brezhnev (1909–1982) and Alexei Kosygin (1904–1980) initially

■ **Leonid Sokov, *Project to Construct Glasses for Every Soviet Person*, 1976**
In the cold war era, the Soviets persecuted those who produced abstract or critical art. Dissident
artists were adept, however, at incorporating Soviet icons into works critical of the regime. They
might, for instance, depict Lenin's portrait, but with citizens turning their back on it instead of
being inspired by it. Or, as in this sculpture, they might create a Communist version of rose-
colored glasses. Strikingly, Sokov's red-star glasses paralleled the developments of pop art in the
U.S. bloc, which mocked the array of consumer items that filled people's lives.
(Collection of the Jane Voorhees Zimmerli Art Museum, Rutgers, The State University of New Jersey, The Norton and
Nancy Dodge Collection of Nonconformist Art from the Soviet Union. Photograph by Jack Abraham, 07809.)

continued boosting consumerism and reform such as cultural and scientific meetings with Westerners. The Soviet satellites in eastern Europe followed suit: Poland
facilitated private farming and Hungarian leader János Kádár introduced elements
of a market system into the national economy.

In the arts, Soviet-bloc writers continued for a time to thaw the frozen mono-
lith of socialist realism and slavish praise for the Soviet past. Ukrainian poet
Yevgeny Yevtushenko exposed Soviet complicity in the Holocaust in *Babi Yar*
(1961), a passionate protest against the slaughter of tens of thousands of Jews near
Kiev during World War II. Challenging the celebratory nature of socialist art, East
Berlin writer Christa Wolf showed a couple tragically divided by the Berlin Wall
in her novel *Divided Heaven* (1965). Repression returned later in the 1960s and
1970s, however, as the Soviet government took to bulldozing outdoor art shows,
thereby forcing visual artists to hold secret exhibitions in their apartments.
Dissident artists' paintings depicted Soviet citizens as worn and tired in grays and
other monochromatic color schemes instead of the brightly attired and heroic figures of socialist realism. For their part, writers relied on samizdat culture, a key

form of dissident activity in which uncensored publications were reproduced by hand and passed from reader to reader, thus building a foundation for the successful resistance of the 1980s.

In the United States, other issues challenged the cold war for front-page attention. The assassination of President John F. Kennedy in November 1963 shocked the nation and the world. While white segregationists murdered, maimed, and arrested activists for rights and freedom, Kennedy had introduced civil rights legislation and forced the desegregation of schools and universities because violent racism undercut America's claim to moral superiority in the cold war. Lyndon B. Johnson (1908–1973), Kennedy's successor, steered the Civil Rights Act through Congress in 1964. This legislation forbade segregation in public facilities and created the Equal Employment Opportunity Commission (EEOC) to fight job discrimination based on "race, color, national origin, religion, and sex." Modeling himself on his hero Franklin Roosevelt, Johnson envisioned what he called a Great Society that would arise from such programs as Project Head Start for disadvantaged preschool children and the Job Corps for training youth. Black novelist Ralph Ellison called Johnson "the greatest American president for the poor and the Negroes."

However, the cold war did not go away; in fact, the United States became increasingly embroiled in Vietnam (Map 23.1). After the Geneva settlement in 1954, the United States escalated its commitment to the corrupt and incompetent leaders in non-Communist South Vietnam. North Vietnam, China, and the Soviet Union backed the rebel Vietcong, or South Vietnamese Communists. The strength of the Vietcong seemed to grow daily, and by 1966 the United States had more than half a million soldiers in South Vietnam. Before the war ended in 1975, the United States would drop more bombs on North Vietnam than the Allies had launched on Germany and Japan combined during World War II. But after decades of anticolonial struggle, the insurgents rejected a negotiated peace even as Johnson's advisers regularly told Americans that the United States was winning the war. Confronting mounting casualties and declining popularity, President Johnson announced in March 1968 that he would not run for president again.

The Explosion of Civic Activism

People grew ever more eager for peace and social justice as the 1960s progressed. The U.S. civil rights movement broadened, joined by others demanding fair treatment. In 1965, César Chávez (1927–1993) led vulnerable Mexican American migrant workers in the California grape agribusiness to strike for better wages and working conditions. Deeply religious and ascetic, Chávez helped Hispanic Americans struggle against deportation, inferior schooling, and discrimination. The same year, urban riots erupted across the United States as angry activists changed their struggle into a militant celebration of their race under the banner

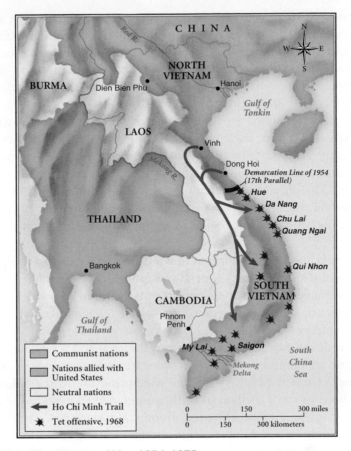

■ MAP 23.1 The Vietnam War, 1954–1975

The local peoples of Southeast Asia had long resisted incursions by their neighbors. They also resisted French rule from the end of the nineteenth century, never more fiercely than in the war that liberated them after World War II. Ill prepared by comparison with the French, the Vietnamese nonetheless triumphed in the battle of Dien Bien Phu in 1954. But the Americans soon became involved, trying to stem what they saw as the tide of Communist influence behind the Vietnamese liberation movement. The ensuing war in Vietnam in the 1960s and 1970s spread into neighboring countries, making the region the scene of vast destruction. How were the Vietnamese wars after 1945 related to the struggle between Japan and the United States for resources in the region in the 1930s and in World War II? Or were these two distinct contests?

"Black is beautiful." The issue they faced was one they felt they had in common with decolonizing people: how to shape an identity different from that of white oppressors. Separatism and "black power," not simple integration, became the goals of still others; small cadres of militants even took up arms, believing that, like decolonizing people elsewhere, they needed to protect themselves against the violent whites around them.

The 1960s also pulsated with white young people's activism. As a result of the new turn in black efforts for change, white American university students who had participated in the early stages of the civil rights movement found themselves excluded from leadership positions. Many of them soon joined the swelling protest against technological change, consumerism, and the Vietnam War. European youth were also feverish for reform. In the mid-1960s, university students in Rome occupied an administration building after right-wing opponents assassinated one of their number during a protest against the 200-to-1 student-teacher ratio. In 1966, Prague students held carnival-like processions, commemorated the tenth anniversary of the 1956 Hungarian uprisings, and took to chanting, "The only good Communist is a dead one." The "situationists" in France called on students to wake up from the slumbering pace of mass society and student life by jolting individuals to action with shocking graffiti and street theater.

Throughout the 1960s, students criticized the traditional university curriculum and flaunted their own countercultural values. They questioned how studying Plato or Dante would help them after graduation. "How to Train Stuffed Geese" was French students' satirical version of the teaching methods inflicted on them. "No professors over forty" and "Don't trust anyone over thirty" were powerful slogans of the day. Long hair, communal living, and a repudiation of personal hygiene announced students' rejection of middle-class values, as did their denunciation of sexual chastity. With the widespread use of the pill, abstinence became unnecessary as a method of birth control, and students made the sexual revolution explicit and public with open promiscuity. Marijuana use became common among students, and amphetamines and barbiturates added to the drug culture, which had its own rituals, songs, and gathering places. Scorned by students, businesses nonetheless made billions of dollars not only by selling blue jeans, dolls dressed as "hippies," natural foods, and drugs but also by packaging and managing the stars of the counterculture.

Women's activism erupted across the political spectrum. Working for reproductive rights, women in France helped end the ban on birth control in 1965. American journalist Betty Friedan, author of international best seller *The Feminine Mystique* (1963), pointed to the stagnating talents of many housewives and helped organize the National Organization for Women (NOW) in 1966 "to bring women into full participation in the mainstream of American society now." NOW advocated equal pay and a variety of other legal and economic reforms. In Sweden, women lobbied to make tasks both at home and in the workplace less gender-segregated, and in these same years a few Soviet women began speaking out against their low and unpaid work that kept the USSR running.

Those engaged in the civil rights and student movements soon realized that many of those protest organizations devalued women just as society at large did. Male activists adopted the leather-jacketed machismo style of their film and rock heroes, but women in the movements were often judged by the status of their male-protester lovers. "A woman was to 'inspire' her man," African American activist Angela Davis complained, adding that women aiming for equality supposedly "wanted to rob [male protesters] of their manhood." A speaker in Frankfurt, West Germany, interrupted a student meeting, demanding "that our problems be discussed substantively. It is no longer enough that women are occasionally allowed to say a few words."

Women also took to the streets on behalf of such issues as abortion rights or the decriminalization of gay and lesbian sexuality. Many flouted social conventions in their attire, language, and attitudes and spoke openly about taboo subjects such as their sexual feelings and recourse to illegal abortions. This brand of feminist activity was meant to shock polite society—and it did. West German women students tossed tomatoes at male protest leaders in defiance of standards for ladylike behavior. Many women of color, however, broke with feminist solidarity and spoke out against the "double jeopardy" of being "black and female." Concrete change followed: in Catholic Italy, feminists won the rights to divorce, to gain access to birth-control information, and to obtain legal abortions. Thousands of women's groups continued to demand equal pay; job opportunities; and protection from rape, incest, and battering into the 1970s and beyond.

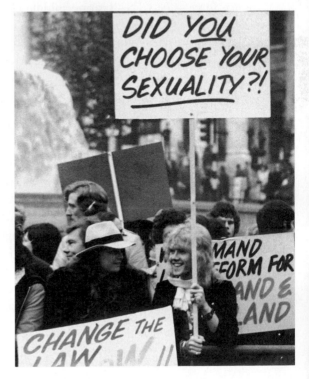

■ Gay Activists in London, 1974

The reformist spirit of the 1960s and 1970s changed the focus of homosexuals' activism. Instead of concentrating mostly on legal protection from criminal prosecution, gays and lesbians began affirming a special and positive identity. As other groups who had endured discrimination began making similar affirmations, "identity politics" was born. Critics charged that traditional universal values were sufficient and that homosexuals and others constituted special-interest groups. Gays, women, and ethnic or racial minorities countercharged that the universal values first put forth in the Enlightenment seemed to apply only to a privileged few. In what ways were gays' demonstrations similar to those of women, colonized people, union activists, and civil rights organizers over the past centuries? In what ways did they differ?

(© Hulton-Deutsch Collection/Corbis.)

1968: Year of Crisis

Protest and calls for reform finally boiled over in 1968. In January, on the first day of Tet, the Vietnamese New Year, the Vietcong and the North Vietnamese attacked more than one hundred South Vietnamese towns and American bases, inflicting heavy casualties. The Tet offensive, as it came to be called, caused many to conclude that the war might be unwinnable and fueled the antiwar movement globally. The war protest intersected with African American anguish and rage when on April 4, 1968, a white racist assassinated Martin Luther King Jr. More than a hundred cities in the United States erupted in strife. "Burn, baby, burn," chanted rioters who, rejecting King's message of nonviolent resistance, destroyed the grim inner cities around them. On campuses, strident confrontation over the intertwined issues of war, technology, racism, and sexism closed down classes.

Student dissent escalated everywhere, most dramatically in France. In January, students at Nanterre, outside of Paris, had gone on strike, invading administration offices to protest their inferior education and status. They called themselves a proletariat—an exploited working class—and, rejecting the Soviets, considered themselves part of a New Left. When students at the prestigious Sorbonne in Paris took to the streets in protest, police assaulted them. The Parisian middle classes reacted with unexpected sympathy to the student uprising because of their own resentment of bureaucracy. They were also horrified at seeing the elite and brutal police force—the CRS—beating middle-class students and supportive passersby alike.

French workers joined in: some nine million went on strike, occupying factories and calling for higher wages and participation in everyday decision making. To some, the revolt of youth and workers looked as if it might spiral into another French Revolution, so unified were the expressions of political alienation. President Charles de Gaulle sent tanks into Paris. In June, he announced a raise for workers, and businesses offered them a strengthened voice in decision making. Many citizens, having grown tired of the street violence, the destruction of so much private property, and the breakdown of services (for example, the garbage was not collected for weeks), began to sympathize with the government instead of the students. Although sporadic demonstrations continued, the revolutionary moment for students passed.

By contrast, the 1968 revolt in Prague began within the Czechoslovak Communist Party itself. In the autumn of 1967 at a party congress, Alexander Dubček, head of the Slovak branch of the party, had called for more social and political openness. Attacked as an inferior Slovak by the leadership, Dubček nonetheless struck a chord among frustrated party officials, technocrats, and intellectuals. Czechoslovaks began to dream of creating a new society—one based on "socialism with a human face." Party delegates elevated Dubček to the top position, where he quickly changed the Communist style of government, ending

■ **Prague Spring**
When the Soviet Union and other Warsaw Pact members cracked down on the Prague Spring, they met determined citizen resistance. People refused assistance of any kind to the invaders and many Czechs attacked Soviet tanks in the street, like the angry youth shown here. Indeed, despite dejection at the Soviet's repression of Dubček's government, protest on a small and large scale continued from 1968 until the final fall of Communist rule two decades later. How was the citizen confrontation that occurred in Prague similar to other protests around the world? (AFP/Getty Images.)

censorship, instituting the secret ballot for party elections, and allowing competing political groups to form. "Look!" one little girl in the street remarked as the new government took power. "Everyone's smiling today." The Prague Spring had begun—"an orgy of free expression," one Czech journalist called it. People bought uncensored publications, packed uncensored theater productions, and engaged in almost nonstop political debate.

Dubček faced the enormous problem of negotiating policies acceptable to the USSR, the entrenched party functionaries, and the reform-minded citizenry. Reforms were handed down with warnings about "discipline" and "wise behavior." Fearing change, the Polish, East German, and Soviet regimes threatened the reform government daily. When Dubček failed to attend a meeting of Warsaw Pact leaders, Soviet threats became intense. Finally, in August 1968, Soviet tanks rolled into Prague in a massive show of antirevolutionary force. Citizens tried to halt the return to Communist orthodoxy by using free expression as sabotage.

They painted graffiti on the tanks and confused invading troops by removing street signs. Merchants refused to sell food and other goods to Soviet troops. A determined Soviet leadership nonetheless removed reformers from power, and despite protests like Jan Palach's, the moment for reform-minded change passed here too.

Protest in 1968 challenged both domestic politics and superpower dominance but mostly yielded conservative solutions. In November 1968, the Soviets announced the Brezhnev Doctrine, which stated that reform movements, as a "common problem" of all socialist countries, would face swift repression. As the hard-liner Brezhnev clamped down on critics, dissident morale was at a low ebb. "The shock of our tanks crushing the Prague Spring . . . convinced us that the Soviet colossus was invincible," explained one pessimistic liberal. Other voices persisted, however. In 1974, Brezhnev expelled author Aleksandr Solzhenitsyn from the USSR after the publication of the first volume of *Gulag Archipelago* (1973–1976) in the U.S.-led bloc. Composed from myriad biographies and firsthand reports, Solzhenitsyn's story of the Gulag documented the brutal conditions endured by Soviet prisoners. More than any other single work, the *Gulag Archipelago* disillusioned many loyal Communists around the world.

The USSR also persecuted many ordinary people who did not have Solzhenitsyn's international reputation. Soviet psychologists, complying with the government, certified the "mental illness" of dissidents, who often wound up as virtual prisoners in mental institutions. The crudest Soviet persecutions, however, involved anti-Semitism: Jews were subject to educational and job discrimination and constant assault on their religious practice. A commonplace accusation by Soviet officials was that Jews were "unreliable, they think only of emigrating. . . . It's madness to give them an education, because it's state money wasted." Ironically, even dissidents blamed Jews for the Bolshevik Revolution and Stalinist terror. As attacks intensified in the 1970s, Soviet Jews sought to emigrate to Israel or the United States, often unsuccessfully.

The brain drain of eastern European intellectuals increased. Modernist composer Gyorgy Ligeti had left Hungary in 1956, after which his work was celebrated in concert halls and in such classic films as *2001: A Space Odyssey*. From exile in Paris, Czech writer Milan Kundera enthralled audiences with *The Book of Laughter and Forgetting* (1979) and *The Unbearable Lightness of Being* (1984). His novels chronicled his own descent from enthusiasm for communism to a despair characterized by bitter humor. Kundera claimed that Communist regimes depended on making people forget by erasing the memory of fallen leaders from history books, for instance. Individuals papered over a grim reality through sexual promiscuity. The presence of exiles and escapees in the West eroded any lingering support for communism, and newcomers—from noted intellectuals to industrial workers to dancers and artisans—enriched the culture of those countries that welcomed them.

In the United States the impulse to restore order also prevailed. Elected in 1968 to replace Johnson, the conservative Richard Nixon (1913–1994) promised to bring peace to Southeast Asia, but in 1970 he sent U.S. troops to invade Cambodia, the site of North Vietnamese bases. Campuses erupted again in protest, and on May 4 the National Guard killed four students and wounded eleven others at a demonstration at Kent State University in Ohio. Nixon called the victims "bums," and a growing reaction against the counterculture made many Americans agree with him. Mired in turmoil, the United States and North Vietnam continued to support hostilities until 1975, when South Vietnam collapsed under a determined North Vietnamese offensive, and Vietnam was forcibly reunified. The United States reeled from the defeat, having suffered the loss of young lives, turbulence at home, vast military costs, and a weakening of its reputation around the world. Yet a strong current of public opinion felt that activists, not the war or government corruption, had dealt the United States this blow. As in the United States, protesters like Jan Palach had opened all leadership to question, and their legacy was permanent—especially to those in eastern Europe who wanted political change.

■ **REVIEW:** *What were the main issues for protesters in the 1960s, and how did governments address them?*

The Erosion of Superpower Mastery Ends the Cold War

The 1970s brought a lessening of cold war tensions called détente. The major powers sought calm abroad in the face of instability at home, and limitations on the nuclear arms race followed. The two superpowers were further challenged by evidence of their own internal corruption and by their continuing attempts to control world politics. An eruption of terrorist violence also threw the superpowers and their allies off balance, and the oil-producing nations brought a crashing halt to postindustrial prosperity in the West. As economic hard times set in, reformers ranging from Margaret Thatcher (b. 1925) in Britain to Mikhail Gorbachev (b. 1931) in the USSR began implementing drastic new policies in the 1980s to keep their economies moving forward instead of backward. But in the Communist bloc, postindustrial prosperity was simply unattainable under the old system, and in 1989, astonishingly, that system collapsed.

The West, the World, and the Politics of Energy

In foreign policy, except for Vietnam, the 1970s opened well for the United States. In 1972, Henry Kissinger, Nixon's secretary of state, arranged for Nixon to visit China. The negotiations masterfully took advantage of an ongoing rivalry between

China and the Soviet Union, the Communist giants who skirmished along their shared borders and in diplomatic arenas. The visit linked, if only tentatively, two very different great nations that both faced internal challenges. Within China, the meeting helped stop the brutality and excesses of Mao's Cultural Revolution, during which Mao had incited students to decimate schools, destroy property, and injure and even kill "class enemies." The visit also helped advance the careers of Chinese pragmatists interested in technology, trade, and relations with the West who laid the groundwork for China's boom later in the century. For the United States, the diplomatic success advanced détente with the Soviet Union. Fearful of the Chinese diplomatic advantage and similarly confronted by popular protest, the Soviets agreed with the United States, as a result of the first Strategic Arms Limitation Talks (SALT I, 1972), to limit the number of antimissile defenses each country could have, and the Helsinki accords on human rights (1975), in which the Western bloc officially acknowledged Soviet territorial gains in World War II in exchange for the Soviet bloc's guarantee of basic human rights.

Despite these successes, rising purchases of military and imported goods brought inflation and made the United States a debtor nation that owed billions to other countries. In 1971, the Bretton Woods currency system, created during World War II to maintain stable international markets, collapsed. As Common Market countries united to prevent financial chaos, they forced the United States to relinquish its single-handed direction of Western economic strategy. Simultaneously, the enigmatic Nixon's reelection committee set out to undermine free elections by paying several men—caught in the act and arrested—to wiretap the telephones at the Democratic Party headquarters in Washington's Watergate building, which Nixon himself attempted to cover up. Between 1968 and 1972, Nixon had forged a powerful conservative consensus, but in the summer of 1974 the Watergate scandal forced Nixon to resign in disgrace—the first U.S. president ever to do so—and profoundly weakened U.S. superpower status.

Amid instability, the Middle East's oil-producing nations dealt Western dominance and postindustrial prosperity another major blow. In two wars in 1967 and 1973, U.S.-backed Israeli forces defeated Arab troops and seized Gaza and the Sinai peninsula from Egypt, the Golan Heights from Syria, and the West Bank from Jordan. Having failed militarily, the Arab nations turned decisively to economic clout. They struck at the West's weakest point—its dependence on

Israel after the Six-Day War, 1967

■ **FIGURE 23.1 Fluctuating Oil Prices, 1955–1985**

Colonization allowed the Western imperial powers to obtain raw materials at advantageous prices or even without paying at all. Even with decolonization, European and American firms often had such entrenched roots in newly independent economies that they were able to set the terms for trade. OPEC's oil embargo and price hikes of the 1970s were signs of change, which included the exercise of decolonized countries' control over their own resources. Not only did OPEC's action lead to a decade of painful economic downturn, but it also encouraged some European governments to improve public transportation, encourage the production of fuel-efficient cars, and impose policies that would make individual consumers cut back their dependence on oil.

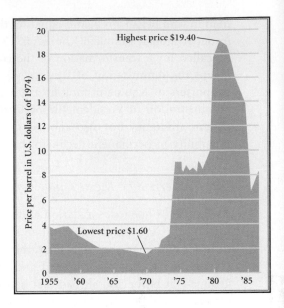

Middle Eastern oil for its industries and lifestyle. The **Organization of Petroleum Exporting Countries (OPEC)**, a relatively loose consortium before the 1973 Israeli war with Egypt, quadrupled the price of its oil and imposed an embargo, cutting off all exports of oil to the United States in retaliation for that country's support of Israel. For the first time since imperialism's heyday, the producers of raw materials— not the industrial powers—controlled the flow of commodities and set prices to their own advantage (Figure 23.1). The West was now mired in an oil crisis.

Throughout the 1970s, oil-dependent Westerners watched in astonishment as OPEC upset the balance of economic power and helped provoke a recession in the West. The oil embargo and price hike caused unemployment to rise by more than 50 percent in Europe and the United States and inflation to soar. By the end of 1973, the inflation rate jumped to over 8 percent in West Germany, 12 percent in France, and 20 percent in Portugal. Eastern-bloc countries, dependent on Soviet oil, fared little better because the West could no longer afford their products, and the Soviets boosted the price of their own oil. Skyrocketing interest rates discouraged both industrial investment and consumer buying. With prices, unemployment, and interest rates soaring—an unusual combination of economic conditions dubbed **stagflation**—western Europe drastically cut back on its oil dependence by undertaking conservation, enhancing public transportation, and raising the price of gasoline to encourage the development of fuel-efficient cars.

As the U.S. bloc reeled economically, a further crisis in the Middle East erupted late in the 1970s, when students, clerics, shopkeepers, and unemployed men in Iran began a religious agitation that brought to power the Islamic religious leader Ayatollah Ruhollah Khomeini. Using audiocassettes to spread his message, he called for a transformation of the country into a truly Islamic society, which meant the renunciation of Western ways. In the autumn of 1979, revolutionary supporters of Khomeini took hostages at the American embassy in Teheran. The administration of President Jimmy Carter was impotent in the face not only of Islamic militancy but also another round of OPEC price hikes, suggesting the possibility of permanent decline of the West.

The Western Bloc Meets Challenges with Reform

As the 1980s opened, stagflation and the realignment of global economic power forced non-Communist governments in the West to put their economic houses in order and change course. First, they had to face the growing phenomenon of **terrorism**—that is, coordinated and targeted political violence by opposition groups—at home and abroad that had actually begun in the West. In the 1970s, terrorist bands of disaffected youth in Europe responded to the restoration of political order and the worsening economic conditions with kidnappings, bank robberies, bombings, and assassinations. Eager to bring down the Social Democratic coalition that led West Germany throughout the 1970s, the Red Army Faction assassinated prominent businessmen, judges, and other public officials. Italy's Red Brigades kidnapped and then murdered the head of the dominant Christian Democrats in 1978. Advocates of independence for the Basque nation in northern Spain assassinated Spanish politicians and police officers.

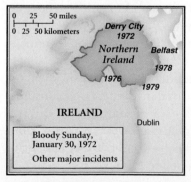

Nationalist Movements of the 1970s

In Britain, nationalist and religious violence in the 1970s pitted the Catholics in Northern Ireland against the dominant Protestants. Catholics experienced job discrimination and civil rights violations. Demonstrators urged union with the Irish Republic, and with protest escalating the British government sent in troops. On January 30, 1972, which became known as Bloody Sunday, British troops fired at demonstrators and killed thirteen, setting off a cycle of violence that left five hundred dead in that single year. Protestants fearful of losing their dominant position combated a reinvigorated Irish Republican Army (IRA), which carried out bombings and assassinations to achieve the union of the two Irelands in order to end the oppression of Catholics.

Terrorists failed in their goal of overturning the existing democracies, and sorely tried as it was, parliamentary government scored a few important successes in the 1970s. The Iberian Peninsula, suffering under dictatorship since the 1930s, regained its freedom and a measure of prosperity. The death of Spain's Francisco Franco in 1975 ended more than three decades of dictatorial rule. Franco's hand-picked successor, King Juan Carlos, surprisingly steered his nation to Western-style constitutional monarchy, facing down threatened military coups. Portugal and Greece also ousted right-wing dictators, thus paving the way for their integration into western Europe and for substantial economic growth. Despite democratic advances, the economies of the West still appeared to be troubled.

Into this breach stepped Margaret Thatcher, outspoken prime minister from Britain's Conservative Party (1979–1990), who reshaped the West's political and economic ideas to meet the crisis. Believing that only a resurgence of private enterprise could revive the sluggish British economy, Thatcher lashed out at union leaders, Labour Party politicians, and people who received welfare-state benefits as enemies. Her anti–welfare-state policies struck a revolutionary chord, and she called herself "a nineteenth-century liberal" in reference to the economic individualism of that age. In her view, business leaders and entrepreneurs were the key members of society, and immigrants, whose low wages contributed to corporate profits, were inferior ones. Under Thatcher, even workers blamed labor leaders or newcomers for Britain's trauma.

The policies of "Thatcherism" were based on monetarist, or supply-side, economic theories. Monetarists contend that inflation results when government pumps money into the economy at a rate higher than a nation's economic growth rate. Thus, they advocate a tight rein on the money supply to keep prices from rising rapidly. Supply-side economists maintain that the economy as a whole flourishes when businesses grow and their prosperity "trickles down" throughout the society. To implement such theories, the British government cut income taxes on the wealthy to spur new investment, increasing sales taxes to compensate for the lost revenue. The result was an increased burden on working people, who bore the brunt of the sales tax. Thatcher also sold publicly owned businesses and utilities such as British Airways, refused to prop up "outmoded" industries such as coal mining, and slashed education and health programs. As their influence spread through the West and the world, the package of economic policies came to be known as **neoliberalism**. The quality of universities, public transportation, highways, and hospitals deteriorated; leading scholars and scientists left the country in a renewal of the brain drain; and social unity fragmented, as blacks and Asians rioted in major cities. As Britain

■ **Margaret Thatcher at Conservative Party Conference (1983)**
As British prime minister for more than a decade, Margaret Thatcher profoundly influenced the course of modern government by rolling back the welfare state. Thatcher was convinced and convinced others that the welfare state did not advance society and its citizens but made them lazy when it rewarded useless people with handouts. Her tenure in office encouraged other politicians, from Ronald Reagan to Helmut Kohl, to execute similar cuts in social programs. More than any other head of state during this period, she set the course for domestic policy into the twenty-first century. (©Bettmann/Corbis.)

cut back on its welfare-state programs, its neoliberalism became a model for other leaders.

In the United States, President Ronald Reagan (1911–2004) followed a similar road to combat the economic crisis. Dividing citizens into the good and the bad, Reagan vowed to promote the values of the "moral majority," which included commitment to Bible-based religion, dedication to work, sexual restraint, and unquestioned patriotism. Those who disagreed were labeled immoral "liberals"—a confusing use of the word but effective political rhetoric. "Reaganomics" was his program of large income tax cuts for the wealthy combined with massive reductions in federal spending for student loans, school lunch programs, and mass transit because these "welfare" programs only encouraged bad Americans to be lazy. In foreign policy, Reagan labeled the Soviet Union an "evil empire" and demanded increased military budgets for programs such as the Strategic Defense Initiative (SDI), known popularly as Star Wars, a costly plan to put lasers in space to defend the United States against a nuclear attack. The combination of tax cuts and military expansion had pushed the U.S. federal budget deficit to $200 billion by 1986; Britain and the United States came to have the lowest longevity and highest infant mortality rates among the wealthy industrial nations. As in Britain, inflation came under control, and American prosperity returned.

Other western European leaders also limited welfare-state benefits in the face of stagflation, though without the socially divisive rhetoric of Thatcher and Reagan. West German leader Helmut Kohl, who took power in 1982, reduced welfare spending, froze government wages, and cut corporate taxes. By 1984, the inflation rate was only 2 percent, and West Germany had acquired a 10 percent share of world trade. Unlike Thatcher, Kohl did not fan class and racial hatreds. The politics of divisiveness was particularly unwise in Germany, where terrorism on the left and on the right continued to flourish. Moreover, the legacy of Nazism loomed menacingly. When an unemployed German youth said of immigrant Turkish workers, "Let's gas 'em," the revival of Nazi language appalled many in Germany's middle class rather than gaining their support.

France took a different political path, though by 1981 stagflation had put more than 1.5 million people out of work and reduced the economic growth rate to an anemic 1.2 percent. The French elected a socialist president, François Mitterrand (1916–1996), who nationalized banks and certain industries and stimulated the economy by wage increases and social spending—the opposite of Thatcherism. New public buildings like museums and libraries arose along with new subway lines and improved public transport. Financial leaders reacted by sending capital abroad rather than investing it at home. When in Mitterrand's second term conservatives captured the majority of seats in the assembly and subsequently won the presidency, their leader Jacques Chirac adopted many neoliberal policies. As unemployment remained high, divisive rhetoric came from outside the mainstream: the politically racist National Front Party won 10 percent of the popular vote with promises to deport African and Middle Eastern immigrants and cut diplomatic ties with nonwhite nations as part of a plan to ensure that whites remained dominant economically and politically.

Meanwhile, a cluster of smaller states without heavy defense commitments enjoyed increasing prosperity, though many slashed away at welfare programs. In Spain, tourist dollars helped rebuild the southern cities of Grenada and Córdoba, and the country joined the Common Market in 1986. In Ireland, a surge of investment in education for high-tech jobs combined with low wage rates attracted much new business to the country in the 1990s. Austria prospered, too, in part by reducing government pensions and aid to businesses. Austrian chancellor Franz Vranitsky summed up the changed focus of government: "In Austria, the shelter that the state has given to almost everyone—employee as well as entrepreneur—has led . . . a lot of people [to] think not only what they can do to solve a problem but what the state can do. . . . This needs to change." Almost alone, Sweden maintained a full array of social programs, including a wide choice of subsidized housing for immigrants. Such programs were expensive: the tax rate on income over $46,000 was 80 percent. Although the Swedes reduced their costly dependence on foreign oil by cutting consumption in half between 1976 and 1986, their welfare state came to seem extreme as Sweden's overall prosperity dropped. As elsewhere, immigrants were cast as a major threat to the country: "How long will it be before our Swedish children will have to turn their faces toward Mecca?" one politician asked, as commitment to the welfare state weakened in the 1980s.

Collapse of Communism in the Soviet Bloc

Beginning in 1985, real reform came to the Soviet Union as well. In that year, a new leader, Mikhail Gorbachev, unexpectedly opened an era of change. The son of peasants, Gorbachev had risen through the party ranks as an agricultural specialist and had traveled abroad to gain a firsthand glimpse of life in the West. He saw that economic stagnation had many ramifications. Ordinary people decided not to have children, and fertility fell below replacement levels throughout the Soviet bloc, except for the Muslim areas of Soviet Central Asia. The country was forced to import massive amounts of grain because 20 to 30 percent of the grain that was produced in the USSR rotted before it could be harvested or shipped to market, so great was the inefficiency of the state-directed economy. A massive and privileged party bureaucracy hobbled innovation and failed to achieve socialism's professed goal of a decent standard of living for working people. Alcoholism was rampant. To match American military growth, the Soviet Union diverted 15 to 20 percent of its gross national product (more than double the U.S. proportion) to armaments, further crippling the economy's chances of raising living standards. As this combustible mix of problems heated up, a new generation came of age: "They believe in nothing," a mother said of Soviet youth in 1984.

Gorbachev quickly proposed several programs to improve the woefully inadequate Soviet system. First, recognizing how severely the cold war arms race was draining Soviet resources, Gorbachev almost immediately began scaling back missile production. Second, a crucial economic reform, **perestroika** ("restructuring"), aimed to improve productivity, increase the rate of capital investment, encourage the use of up-to-date technology, and gradually introduce such market features as profits. Finally, the complement to economic change was the policy of **glasnost** (usually translated as "openness" or "publicity"), which called for disseminating "wide, prompt, and frank information" and for allowing Soviet citizens new measures of free speech. The pressing need for glasnost became most evident after the Chernobyl catastrophe in 1986, when a nuclear reactor exploded and spewed radioactive dust into the atmosphere. Bureaucratic cover-ups delayed the spread of information about the accident, with lethal consequences for people living near the plant. When officials complained that glasnost threatened their status, Gorbachev replaced more than a third of the Communist Party's leadership.

After Chernobyl, even the Communist Party and Marxism-Leninism were opened to public criticism. Party meetings suddenly included complaints about the highest leaders, and television shows adopted the outspoken methods of American investigative reporting, covering for instance the plight of Leningrad's homeless children. Instead of publishing made-up letters praising the great Soviet state, newspapers carried real ones complaining of shortages and abuse. One outraged "mother of two" protested that the cost-cutting policy of reusing syringes in hospitals was a source of AIDS. "Why should little kids have to pay for the criminal actions of our Ministry of Health?" she asked. Factions arose: in the fall of 1987, Gorbachev ally Boris Yeltsin quit the governing Politburo after denouncing perestroika as inadequate. Yeltsin's political daring inspired others, and by the spring of 1989, in a remarkably free balloting in Moscow's local elections, not a single Communist was chosen.

In early 1989, the year that ended the Soviet system and the cold war, Gorbachev withdrew his country's forces from the debilitating war in Afghanistan. Meanwhile, as Gorbachev's reforms in the USSR started spiraling out of his control, dissent had been rising across the Soviet bloc. Already in 1980, Poles had reacted furiously to government-increased food prices by going on strike and forming an independent union, **Solidarity**, led by electrician Lech Walesa and crane operator Anna Walentynowicz of the Gdańsk shipyards. The organization soon embraced much of the adult population, including a million members of the Communist Party, and its members waved Polish flags and paraded giant portraits of the Virgin Mary and Pope John Paul II—a Polish native. Tens of thousands of women marched in the streets crying "We're hungry!" and protesting working conditions. The police and the army, with Soviet support, imposed a military government under General Wojciech Jaruzelski and in the winter of 1981 outlawed Solidarity. Solidarity remained alive as a force both inside and outside of Poland, as poets read dissident verse to overflow crowds, and university professors lectured to Solidarity members on such forbidden topics as Polish resistance in World War II.

Ongoing activism in Poland set the stage for communism's downfall in 1989, but the global scene was active too. Inspired by Gorbachev's visit to China's capital, Beijing, in the spring of 1989, thousands of students massed in the city's Tiananmen Square, the world's largest public square, to demand democracy. They used telex machines and e-mail to rush their messages to the international community, and they effectively conveyed their goals through the cameras that Western television trained on them. China's aged Communist leaders, while pushing economic modernization and even allowing market operations, refused to consider the introduction of democracy. As workers began joining the pro-democracy forces, the government crushed the movement and executed as many as a thousand rebels.

The protests in Tiananmen Square were galvanizing. In June 1989, the Polish government, weakened by its own bungling of the economy and lacking Soviet support for further repression, held free parliamentary elections. Solidarity candidates won overwhelmingly, and in early 1990 Walesa became president, hastening Poland's rocky transition to a market economy. Gorbachev pointedly reversed the Brezhnev Doctrine, refusing to interfere in the political course of another nation. Communism collapsed next in Hungary. It too had introduced elements of a market economy three decades earlier, and Hungarian officials slowly realized that political democracy had to accompany economic freedom. Citizens lobbied against ecologically unsound projects like the construction of a new dam. They encouraged boycotts of Communist holidays, and on March 15, 1989, they commemorated instead the anniversary of the Hungarian uprising—the "battle of the holidays," it was called. Finally, in the fall of 1989 the Parliament dismissed the Communist Party as the official ruling institution, and people tore down Soviet and Communist symbols across the country.

The most potent symbol of a divided Europe—the Berlin Wall—stood in the midst of a divided Germany. East Germans had attempted to escape over the wall for decades, and since the early 1980s dissidents had held peace vigils in cities across East Germany. In the summer of 1989, crowds of East Germans flooded the borders of the crumbling Soviet bloc, and hundreds of thousands of protesters rallied throughout the fall against the regime. Satellite television brought them visions of postindustrial prosperity and of free and open public debate in West Germany. The crowds intensified in November, when Gorbachev, taken as a hero by many, visited the country. On November 9, an ambiguous statement from the government encouraged guards to allow free passage across the wall. Protest turned to festive holiday: As they strolled freely in the streets, East Berliners saw firsthand the goods available in a successful postindustrial society. Soon thereafter, citizens—east and west—released years of frustration by assaulting the Berlin Wall with sledgehammers; the government finished the wall's complete destruction in the fall of 1990.

In Czechoslovakia, which after 1968 had been firmly restored to Soviet-style rule, people also watched the progress of glasnost expectantly. Persecuted, dissidents had nonetheless maintained their critique of Communist rule, especially that it made people materialistic and indifferent to public life. In 1977, intellectuals and workers, including playwright Václav Havel, signed Charter 77, a public protest against the regime that resulted in the arrest of its signers. In the mid-1980s, these dissidents watched Gorbachev on television calling for free speech, and ordinary people took to the streets on behalf of democracy. Despite arrests, demonstrations such as commemorations of the death of Jan Palach continued. The turning point came in November 1989 when Alexander Dubček, leader of the Prague Spring of

■ Reunited Berliners Welcome the New Year
On New Year's Eve, 1989, Berliners—and indeed supporters from around the world—celebrated the fall of the Berlin wall and the prospect of a new Germany. The exuberant crowd tore the Communist seal from the flag and then hoisted it above the Brandenburg Gate as fireworks added to the intense emotion of the moment. Disposing of the remnants of communism lay in the future, and for many the transition would prove difficult. Rebuilding Berlin after communism, like the rebuilding of most of eastern Europe, lasted into the twenty-first century.
(Ullstein Bild, Berlin-Boening.)

1968, addressed the crowds in Prague's Wenceslas Square to call for the ouster of Stalinists from the government after the police had beaten students. Almost immediately, Communist leadership resigned. Capping the country's "velvet revolution," as it became known for its lack of bloodshed, the formerly Communist-dominated parliament elevated the dissident Havel to the presidency.

The world's attention now fastened on an unfolding political drama in Romania. From the mid-1960s on, Nicolae Ceauşescu had ruled as the harshest dictator in Communist Europe since Stalin. In the name of modernization, he destroyed whole villages; to build up the population, he outlawed contraceptives and abortions, a restriction that led to the abandonment of tens of thousands of children. He preached the virtues of a very slim body so that he could cut rations

IMPORTANT DATES

1962–1965	Vatican II reforms Catholic ritual and dogma	**1973–1976**	Aleksandr Solzhenitsyn publishes *Gulag Archipelago*
1963	Betty Friedan publishes *The Feminine Mystique*	**1978**	The first test-tube baby is born in England
1966	West German foreign minister Willy Brandt develops Ostpolitik, a policy designed to bridge tensions between the two Germanies	**1978–1979**	Islamic revolution in Iran; hostages taken at U.S. embassy in Teheran
1967	South Africa's Dr. Christiaan Barnard performs first successful human heart transplant	**1980**	An independent trade union, Solidarity, organizes resistance to Polish communism; Prime Minister Margaret Thatcher begins dismantling the welfare state in Britain
1968	Revolution in Czechoslovakia against communism; student uprisings throughout Europe and the United States	**Early 1980s**	AIDS epidemic strikes the West
1969	U.S. astronauts walk on the moon's surface	**1981**	Ronald Reagan becomes U.S. president
1972	SALT I results in antiballistic missile treaty between the United States and Soviet Union	**1985**	Mikhail Gorbachev comes to power in the USSR
1973	North Vietnam and the United States sign treaty ending war in Vietnam; OPEC raises oil prices and imposes oil embargo on the West	**1986**	Explosion at Soviet nuclear plant at Chernobyl
		1989	Chinese students revolt in Tiananmen Square and government suppresses them; Communist governments ousted in eastern Europe; fall of the Berlin Wall

and use the savings on his pet projects such as buying up private castles and building himself an enormous palace in Bucharest. To this end, he tore down entire neighborhoods and dozens of historical buildings, and so much did he torture any opponents that the gaudy project seemed to have unanimous support. Yet in early December 1989, an opposition movement rose up, and workers kept up a string of demonstrations against the dictatorial government. Most of the army rose up, too, and crushed the forces loyal to Ceauşescu. On Christmas Day, viewers watched on television as the dictator and his wife were tried by a military court and then executed. For many, the death of Ceauşescu meant that the very worst of communism was over.

■ **REVIEW:** *What factors led to the collapse of communism in the Soviet bloc?*

■ **MAPPING THE WEST** The Collapse of Communism in Europe, 1989–1990
*The 1989 overthrow of the Communist Party in the USSR satellite countries of eastern Europe
occurred with surprising rapidity. The transformation began in Poland when Polish voters tossed
out Communist Party leaders in June 1989 and then accelerated in September when thousands
of East Germans fled to Hungary, Poland, and Czechoslovakia. Between October and December,
Communist regimes were replaced in East Germany, Czechoslovakia, Bulgaria, and Romania.
Within three years, the Baltic States would declare their independence, the USSR itself would
dissolve, and the breakup of Yugoslavia would lead to war in the Balkans.* **For more help
analyzing this map,** *see the map activity for this chapter in the* ONLINE STUDY GUIDE *at*
bedfordstmartins.com/huntconcise.

Conclusion

The collapse of communism in the Soviet satellites was an utter surprise, for U.S.-bloc analysts had erroneously reported throughout the 1980s that the Soviet empire was in dangerously robust health. But no one should have been unaware of dissent or economic discontent. Since the 1960s, a surge of rebellion among youth, ethnic and racial minorities, and women condemned conditions across the West and criticized the threat posed by the cold war. By the early 1980s, wars in Vietnam and Afghanistan, protests against privations in the Soviet bloc, the power of oil-producing states, and the growing political force of Islam had weakened superpower preeminence. Reformers like Margaret Thatcher, Ronald Reagan, and Mikhail Gorbachev tried with varying degrees of success to put their postindustrial and cold war houses in order. Thatcher and Reagan succeeded, while Gorbachev brought on collapse by introducing glasnost and perestroika—each a policy aimed at political and economic change.

Reforms were supposed to bring about the high levels of postindustrial prosperity enjoyed outside the Soviet bloc, where unprecedented technological development had transformed businesses, the exploration of space, and the functioning of government. It also had an enormous impact on everyday life. Work changed, as society reached a postindustrial stage in which the service sector predominated. New patterns of family life, new relationships among the generations, and revised standards for sexual behavior also characterized these years. But it was only in the United States and western Europe that the consumer benefits of postindustrialization soared, for the attainment of a thoroughgoing consumer, service, and high-tech society demanded levels of efficiency, coordination, and cooperation that had not been reached in the Soviet bloc. There were complaints everywhere, nonetheless, about the dramatic changes that postindustrial society entailed. The protesters of the late 1960s addressed postindustrial society's stubborn problems: concentrations of bureaucratic and industrial power, social inequality, and environmental degradation. In the Soviet sphere, protests also materialized, but were never heeded until they brought the collapse of Soviet domination of eastern Europe in 1989. Soon communism would be overturned in the USSR itself, opening an era of painful adjustment, impoverishment, and even violence. Finally, the cold war ended, which accelerated the process of globalization, brought unexpected dilemmas, and opened a world of opportunity.

■ **MAKING CONNECTIONS**

1. *How was the industrial society of the late nineteenth century different from the postindustrial society of the late twentieth century?*

2. *Why were there so many protests, acts of terrorism, and uprisings across the West between 1960 and 1990?*

■ **FOR FURTHER EXPLORATION**

For further reading and online research ideas, see the Suggested References on page SR-12 at the back of the book.

For practice quizzes, a customized study plan, and other study tools, see the ONLINE STUDY GUIDE at bedfordstmartins.com/huntconcise.

For primary-source material from this period, see Chapter 23 in *Sources of THE MAKING OF THE WEST: A CONCISE HISTORY*, Second Edition.

The New Globalism: Opportunities and Dilemmas

1989 to the Present

O N JANUARY 1, 2002, PEOPLE IN TWELVE COUNTRIES OF THE EUROPEAN UNION (EU) woke up to find their centuries-old national currencies gone, replaced by a single unit of money—the **euro**. The bills were all standard, designed to reflect the EU's shared ideals, represented by the image of bridges. Supporters of the currency pointed to the savings on currency exchanges for businesses, consumers, and international travelers, while its detractors felt that a traditional bulwark of the nation-state—a controlled, independent monetary system—would be undermined, and perhaps national integrity with it. Thus, Britain, Sweden, and Denmark refused to join the currency system despite being members of the EU. For those adopting the euro, funds for industry and commerce moved unhampered. Having the new currency in their pockets also gave psychological advantages to EU citizens. "People with the same money don't go to war with one another," a French nuclear scientist remarked. An Italian student enthused that the euro provided "a sense of belonging to a European Union and I think it's beautiful that there's this big European country." For these people, the euro represented post–cold war

■ The Euro

These new bills went into public circulation on January 1, 2002. The design of the euro bills and coins, like everything else in the European Union, represented compromise and unity. The bills' designer used architectural imagery of windows and bridges, suggesting openness, light, connectedness, and boundary crossing. Reflecting the compromise between Europe and individual states, the head side of the coins bears a common image, while the tail sides contain symbols chosen by individual nations within the euro zone. Europeans were generally enthusiastic about the common currency for many reasons both idealistic and practical: it allowed for more effective bargain hunting, while it also represented yet another step in ending the divisive nationalism that had plagued the history of the West. Why might some Europeans object to the euro? (Royalty Free/Corbis.)

opportunity—an opportunity to start the new millennium with the risks of disastrous wars perhaps permanently diminished.

The end of the cold war rivalry among the superpowers and their allies paved the way for a more intimately connected world, and the euro was just one concrete example of weakening national boundaries. The collapse of communism in Europe spread after 1989 to Yugoslavia and then the Soviet Union itself—another major piece of the globalization puzzle. After that, the former Common Market transformed itself into the European Union and in 2004 admitted many states from the former Soviet Empire in eastern Europe. Instead of being forced to adhere to the demands of one superpower or the other, nations around the world had more opportunity to trade and interact with each other, and technology moved from region to region. Further advances in communication added to the potential for Europe-wide and global relationships; spurred by the fall of the Soviet realm, these advances paved the way for the West as a whole to enter the global age. The world was no longer divided in two with all the burdensome restrictions the cold war division implied. Rather, a denser web of economic and social ties bound peoples and cultures together.

The globalizing world brought challenges, opportunities, disasters, and astonishing accomplishments. Migration from eastern to western Europe accelerated in the 1990s as an unexpected consequence of the Soviet collapse. As the costs of the welfare state were cut across the West, governments increased subsidies and incentives for businesses facing global competition from the rising economic power of Japan, China, and other Asian countries. International business mergers accelerated from the 1990s on. The global age brought the vast migration of tens of millions of people; an expanding global marketplace; and an accelerated cultural exchange of popular music, books, films, and television entertainment. Less hopefully, it also encompassed the international impact of lethal disasters such as AIDS, environmental degradation, genocide, and terrorism. The global age was indeed one of golden opportunities and unprecedented dilemmas.

While the end of superpower rivalry made global exchange easier, it also resulted in the dominance of a single power, the United States, in world affairs. As the United States sought to exercise global power through warfare, however, the West itself seemed to fragment. European states, more interested in peace than war, started to resist the United States just as the Soviet satellites had pulled away from the USSR. As global events progressed, the West faced rivalry not only from the economic power of the Asian and Middle Eastern countries but also from the cultural might of Islam. Some observers predicted a huge "clash of civilizations" based on the incompatibility of Western civilization and cultures outside it. Others, however, saw a different clash—one between a nonmilitaristic Europe reborn after decades of disastrous wars and allied with other peace-seeking states confronting an imperial United States that, like Europe in the nineteenth century, increasingly waged war around the world. Instead of bringing connections and understanding, globalization in either of these scenarios looked far less hopeful.

For historians, understanding the recent past is a challenge. Every day since 1989 has been filled with news, and never more so than after September 11, 2001. This news receives virtually instantaneous reporting because of global communication technology. Unlike journalists, historians do not choose from this mass the most sensational story of the moment. Rather, they are interested in judging which items from the unfiltered mass of information are actually true and, of these, which will be important in the long run. Historians want to identify social, cultural, and political events that are uniquely important or generally significant for people's everyday lives, and they need time to collect facts from more than one national source of news. They make the most reliable evaluations when phenomena are no longer "news"—that is, after a good period of time has shown their staying power and influence.

When we first started writing this book, we held our breath in the face of rapidly changing events and judged that the fall of communism and the increasing interconnectedness of the world's peoples and cultures were the challenges not only of the moment but also of history. In this second edition, we persisted in that judgment although the fall of communism and coming of globalism had brought greater perils than we had seen only five or six years earlier. Other forces, such as the Internet, had missed our notice altogether despite the fact that the system had been around for several decades. Today, almost a decade after we made our first selections of important trends, we judge the gradual unification of the entire European continent as potentially momentous. We also see the forces of terrorism and possibly a new fragmentation of the West itself into U.S. and European blocs as events with historical staying power. As an experiment in history, you might note the important events of the months in which you take this course, put your list away for several years or more, and then see if they—along with the events discussed in this chapter—stand the test of time.

Soviet Collapse Releases Global Forces

Rejection of communism spread in the 1990s, turning events in unpredictable and ever more violent directions. Yugoslavia and then the Soviet Union itself fell apart. Like Hungarians and Czechs in the early-twentieth-century Habsburg Empire, nationality groups in the USSR began to demand political and cultural autonomy. The Soviet empire had held together more than one hundred ethnic groups, and the five republics of Soviet Central Asia were home to fifty million Muslims. The policy of Russification failed to build full allegiance but instead only improvised at holding the vast multiethnic empire together. The USSR fragmented quickly. In Yugoslavia, Communist rulers had also enforced unity among religious and ethnic groups, and intermarriage among them occurred regularly. During the unstable years of the early 1990s, ambitious politicians used ethnicity as their most effective political slogan, and ethnic violence became the major political tool. Alongside such human issues in post-Soviet society lay the questions of who would control the massive Soviet arsenal of nuclear weapons and how global politics would shape up without cold war guidelines.

The Breakup of Yugoslavia

Ethnic nationalism came to replace communism in Yugoslavia, driving political debate for the first time in decades. Tensions erupted in Yugoslavia in 1990 when a Serb Communist, Slobodan Milosevic, won the presidency of Serbia and began to assert Serb ascendancy in the Yugoslav federation as a whole. Other ethnic groups in Yugoslavia resisted Milosevic's militant pro-Serb nationalism and called for secession. "Slovenians . . . have one more reason to say they are in favor of independence," warned one of them in the face of mounting Serb claims to rule the other groups. Against Milosevic's desire to maintain a centralized state, Slovenia, Croatia, and Bosnia hoped for a confederation of independent republics (Map 24.1). In the spring of 1991, first Slovenia and then Croatia seceded, but Croatia soon lost almost a quarter of its territory when the Serb-dominated Yugoslav army, eager to enforce Serbian supremacy, invaded. An even more devastating civil war engulfed Bosnia-Herzegovina, where the republic's Muslim majority tried to create a multicultural and multiethnic state. Many Bosnian Serb men formed a guerrilla army and under Milosevic's leadership pursued a policy they called **ethnic cleansing**—that is, genocide—against the other nationalities. They raped women to leave them pregnant with Serb babies as a form of conquest, and in July 1995 in just a few days they took away some 7,000 men and boys from the small spa village of Srebrenica and murdered them. Croatian forces also murdered people of other ethnicities, and each competing force took aim at the cultural heritage of its opponent. Military units on all sides destroyed libraries and museums, architectural treasures like the Mostar Bridge, and cities rich with history such as Dubrovnik. Ethnic cleansing thus entailed eliminating both actual people and all traces of their complex past. Many in the West explained violence in the Balkans as part of "age-old" blood feuds typical of a backward, almost "Asian" society. Others saw ethnic rivalry using genocide to achieve national power as a modern phenomenon practiced by a variety of politicians, including Adolf Hitler.

Humane values were tested still further when, late in the 1990s, Serb forces, having withdrawn from Croatia, moved to attack Muslims of Albanian ethnicity living in the Yugoslav province of Kosovo. From 1997 to 1999, hundreds of thousands of Albanian Kosovars fled their homes as Serb militias, and the Yugoslav army slaughtered the civilian population. NATO pilots bombed the region in an attempt to drive back the army and Serb militias. Amid incredible violence and suffering, UN peacekeeping forces stepped in to enforce an interethnic truce, but

■ MAP 24.1 The Former Yugoslavia, c. 2000

After a decade of destructive civil war, UN forces and UN-brokered agreements attempted to protect the civilians of the former Yugoslavia from the brutal consequences of post-Communist rule. Ambitious politicians, most notably Slobodan Milosevic, used the twentieth-century Western strategy of fostering ethnic and religious hatred as a powerful tool to build support for themselves while making those favoring peace look softhearted and unfit to rule. What issues of national identity does the breakup of Yugoslavia indicate? Have these changed since the nineteenth century?

people throughout the world felt that this intervention came far too late, reflecting great-power self-interest rather than a true commitment to maintaining peace and protecting human rights. A new regime emerged in Serbia, and Milosevic was turned over to the International Court of Justice, or World Court, in the Netherlands to be tried for crimes against humanity. In 2003, Milosevic loyalists assassinated the new Serbian president. Across both western and eastern Europe, the language of racial, ethnic, and religious hatred shaped political agendas, especially in the former Communist states.

The Soviet Union Comes Apart

Amid the ongoing genocide in the former Yugoslavia, the Soviet Union came apart in 1992. By 1990, perestroika had failed to revitalize the Soviet economy; people confronted soaring prices, the specter of unemployment, and even greater scarcity of goods than they had endured in the past. Although Mikhail Gorbachev announced late that year that there was "no alternative to the transition to the market [economy]," his plan was too little, too late, and satisfied no one. After the Russian parliament elected Boris Yeltsin as president of the Russian Republic over a Communist candidate in 1991, a group of eight antireform hard-liners, from the Soviet vice president to the powerful head of the Soviet secret police, or KGB, tried to overthrow the reform government. As they held Gorbachev under house arrest, Boris Yeltsin, defiantly standing atop a tank outside the Russian Republic's parliament building, called for mass resistance. Hundreds of thousands of residents of Moscow and Leningrad filled the streets, and units of the army defected to protect Yeltsin's headquarters. People used fax machines and computers to coordinate internal resistance and send messages to the rest of the world. Citizen determination prevented a return to Soviet orthodoxy.

After the failed coup, the Soviet Union disintegrated. People tore down statues of Soviet heroes; Yeltsin outlawed the Communist Party newspaper, *Pravda*, and sealed the KGB's files. At the end of August 1991, the Soviet parliament suspended operations of the Communist Party itself. The Baltic states of Estonia, Latvia, and Lithuania declared their independence in September; other republics followed their lead. Bloody ethnic conflicts erupted in the disintegrating Soviet world. In the Soviet republic of Tajikistan, native Tajiks rioted against Armenians living there; in Azerbaijan, Azeris and Armenians clashed over contested territory; and in the Baltic states, anti-Semitism revived as a political tool. The USSR finally dissolved on January 1, 1992. Twelve of the fifteen former Soviet republics banded together in a Commonwealth of Independent States (CIS) (Map 24.2).

Gorbachev abandoned politics, but the change to a market economy under Yeltsin introduced new problems. Plagued by corruption, the Russian economy entered an ever-deepening crisis. Yeltsin's political allies bought up national resources cheaply, stripped them of their value, and sent billions of dollars out of the country. By 1999, Yeltsin's own family appeared to be deeply implicated in stealing the wealth once seen as belonging to all the people. Managers, military officers, and bureaucrats took whatever goods they could lay their hands on, including weaponry, and sold it. Ethnic and religious battles continued for the entire decade of the 1990s, and the government undertook disastrous policies. In an attempt to consolidate support, Yeltsin launched military action against Muslim dissenters in the province of Chechnya, inflicting destruction and massive casualties on both sides. The political right appealed to nationalist sentiments in Russia, and ethnic hatred became a standard tool in the new multiparty politics. Political disorder was matched by social disarray as organized criminals interfered in the

■ **MAP 24.2 Countries of the Former Soviet Union, c. 2000**

Following an agreement of December 1991, twelve of the countries of the former Soviet Union formed the Commonwealth of Independent States (CIS). Dominated by Russia and with Ukraine often disputing this domination, the CIS worked to bring about common economic and military policies. As nation-states dissolved rapidly in the late twentieth century, regional alliances and coordination were necessary to meet the political and economic challenges of the global age. What is the relationship between the breakup of the Soviet Union over the course of the 1990s and international events in the 1990s and early twenty-first century? **For more help analyzing this map,** see the map activity for this chapter in the ONLINE STUDY GUIDE at bedfordstmartins.com/huntconcise.

distribution of goods and services and assassinated legitimate entrepreneurs, legislators, and anyone who criticized them. As the Russian parliament pursued an investigation in the business dealings of Yeltsin, his family, and his allies, he resigned on December 31, 1999, appointing protégé Vladimir Putin as interim president.

Putin was a little-known functionary in Russia's new security apparatus, which had evolved from the old KGB. Though associated with the Yeltsin family corruption, he initially stressed legality: "Democracy," he announced, "is the dictatorship of law." The electorate voted him to a regular term in 2000, abandoning old Communist bosses, rabid nationalists, and new robber barons alike. With a solid mandate, Putin proceeded to drive from power the biggest figures in regional government, usually the henchmen of the robber barons, sent into exile Boris Berezovsky, who had gained his billions of dollars from wheedling control of the Russian media and oil, and in 2003 brought to trial the billionaire head of Yukos Oil, one of Russia's largest oil companies. As he denounced the influence of a "handful of billionaires with only egotistical concerns," Putin's popularity soared. The pillaging of the country—the source of ordinary citizens' recent suffering—was finally being punished. Putin's own commitment to democracy and the rule of law came into question when he dismissed his entire cabinet and adopted an increasingly authoritarian style of government.

An Elusive Market Economy

Developing a free market and a republican government brought misery to Russia and the rest of eastern Europe. The conditions of everyday life grew increasingly dire as salaries went unpaid, food remained in short supply, and essential services disintegrated. In 1994, inflation soared at a rate of 14 percent a month in Russia, while industrial production dropped by 15 percent. People took drastic steps to stay alive. Hotel lobbies became clogged with prostitutes because women were the first people fired as governments privatized industry and cut service jobs. Unpaid soldiers sold their services to the Mafia. Ordinary citizens stood on the sidewalks of major cities selling their household possessions. Simultaneously, a pent-up demand was unleashed for items never before available. An enormous underground economy existed in goods such as automobiles stolen from people in other countries and then driven or shipped to Russia.

There were, of course, many pluses: people were able to travel freely for the first time, and the media were more open than ever before in Russian history. Some workers, many of them young and highly educated, profited from contacts with technology and business. However, their frequent emigration to more prosperous parts of the world further depleted Russia's human resources. "I knew in my heart that communism would collapse," said one ex-dissident, commenting sadly on the exodus of youth from his country, "but it never crossed my mind that the future would look like this." At the same time, as the different republics that had once comprised the Soviet Union became independent, the hundreds of thousands of Russians who had earlier been sent there by the state as colonizers returned as refugees to put further demands on the chaotic Russian economy. Some 900,000 returned in 1993 alone. The dismantling of communism was thus more complicated and painful than anyone had imagined it would be.

For many in the former Soviet bloc, the first priority was getting economies running again—but on new terms. Replacing a government-controlled economy with a market one could not happen naturally or automatically but rather required government planning. Given the spiraling misery, however, many opposed the introduction of new market-oriented measures. With the farms up for sale, most collective farmers faced landlessness and starvation. The countries that experienced the most success were those in which administrators had introduced ingredients of free trade, such as allowing farmers to sell their produce on the open market or encouraging independent entrepreneurs or even government factories to deal in international trade. Hungary and Poland thus emerged from the transition with less strain because both had favored market elements early on and had hired advisers to speed the transformation of the economy. They set up business schools and other institutions to foster modern trade and industry with comparative

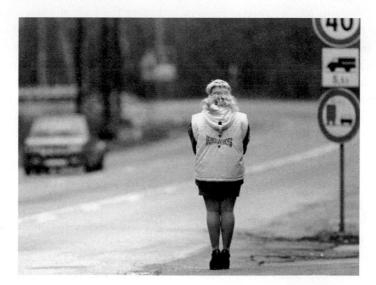

■ Czech Prostitute on German Border

The collapse of communism and the Soviet Union created financial disaster, particularly for women who represented more than two-thirds of all the unemployed. Communists advocated the belief that all people, regardless of gender, should work and that they should be paid equally. While this equality never worked in practice, it did provide jobs so that women could support themselves and their children. Under the free market system, women were eliminated from good jobs and given lower pay. Many resorted to prostitution, which often took place on borders with more prosperous countries such as Germany, as shown here. (Getty Images.)

ease. Foreign capital arrived as well, anchoring these two countries securely to the world economy.

Elsewhere, however, the transition happened differently. The former Soviet Union itself, in the words of one critic, became simply one vast "kleptocracy" in the 1990s as the country's resources—theoretically the property of all the people—were stolen for individual gain. In this regard, one Polish adviser noted, democracy and a successful transition went hand in hand, for unless the people were represented and institutionally powerful enough to prevent it, former administrators would operate as criminals, given the cancerous inheritance of corruption, tax evasion, and off-the-books dealing. Moreover, because the socialist leadership had removed their economies from global developments, they had not benefited from technological change, leaving plants and personnel hopelessly out of date, even worthless. In these countries, competition and free trade meant closing plants and firing all the workers.

A final element in post-Soviet economic difficulties stemmed from a brain drain that plagued the region. The fall of the Soviet empire and the economic chaos that followed brought a rush of migration from eastern Europe to western Europe, often involving those with marketable skills. The countries that received the most migrants were Austria and Germany, which bordered the former Soviet satellites. Migrants left for several reasons, including the lack of jobs, the upsurge of ethnic hatreds, and the availability of higher remuneration for well-educated workers in other countries. Escaping anti-Semitism also played a role: post-Communist politicians used the cruel rallying cry of hatred of Jews to build a following, just as Hitler and many others had done so effectively in the past. Finally, despite neoliberal budget cuts, western Europe provided citizens with better amenities such as safe water, decent housing, and social services than in formerly Communist countries where health care and regular pay had often vanished. In these circumstances, citizenship in western Europe appeared even more desirable.

Chechnya and Post-Soviet States: The Quest for Independence and Influence

Although Gorbachev had pulled the Soviet Union out of its disastrous war with Afghanistan, his successors opened another war to prevent the secession of oil-rich Chechnya (see Map 24.2) and to provide a nationalist rallying cry to shore up domestic support for the administration. For decades, Chechens had been integrated into the bureaucracy and military. The Soviets had effectively squashed ethnic hostility of and toward Chechens, deporting those who used ethnic politics and importing peoples to regions where ethnic concentrations needed diluting. In the fall of 1991, the National Congress of the Chechen People took over the government of the region from the USSR, moving toward the same kind of independence sought by the Baltic nations and other former Soviet states. In June 1992,

■ **Terrorist Attack on a Moscow Bus, 1996**

Terrorism became more widespread from the 1970s onward, taking many forms and espousing many causes. Although terrorists often targeted prominent individuals for kidnapping and assassination, they also engineered wider attacks on random citizens to increase the loss of life. Post-Soviet Russia experienced such attacks at the hands of breakaway Chechens, whose independence Russia violently resisted. But large-scale bombings occurred in the Paris subway, on London streets, and on Spanish railways, causing these countries to cover public wastebaskets and to train people to be vigilant about parcels in streets, public buildings, and train and subway stations. Terrorism instilled a generalized feeling of fear that the wartime targeting of civilians had become a regular threat in peacetime. (© Ivo Lorenc/Corbis Sygma.)

after the collapse of the Soviet Union, Chechen rebels got control of massive numbers of Russian weapons, including airplanes, tanks, and some forty thousand automatic weapons and machine guns.

In December 1994, the Russian government sealed the Chechen borders and invaded. A high Russian official defended the war as crucial to bolstering Yeltsin's position: "We now need a small victorious war. . . . We must raise the President's rating." In 1996, amid strong opposition to the war, the KGB assassinated the Chechen leader Dzhokhar Dudayev with a rocket as he spoke on his cell phone, but the war persisted. There was intense suffering among the Chechens themselves and retaliatory terrorist attacks in Russian cities, particularly Moscow. As the war dragged on, Chechnya's capital city of Grozny was pounded to bits, but Russian casualties mounted too—as did protest against continuing the conflict. In 2002, Chechen loyalists took hundreds of hostages in a Moscow theater; they were killed by nerve gas in a liberation attempt that also killed hundreds of the hostages. Bombings of apartment houses and suicide bombings of buses and airplanes compounded the problems of establishing a sound economy and credible post-Communist government.

As the war in Chechnya continued, the newly independent states of Central Asia became enmeshed in the politics of oil and Islam, as did much of the rest of the world. Led by strong men, if not dictators, the states of Kazakhstan and Uzbekistan became especially involved in the intertwined issues of terrorism, local political factionalism, and the global economy, particularly centered on issues of oil. Uzbekistan lent its territory to various groups of anti-Western radicals for the purposes of recruiting and training militant activists. Kazakhstan had huge resources to exploit, which allowed it to play Western oil companies off against Muslim interests in the region. As in some of the other newly independent nations of the former USSR, such as Ukraine, critics of the strongmen were murdered, and democracy did not exist. In 2004 in Ukraine, however, citizen protest over fraudulent results prompted a new election. Reformer Victor Yushchenko, whose campaign colors led the movement to be dubbed the "Orange Revolution," won the new election amid suspicions that supporters of former dictator Leonid Kuchma had poisoned him for his backing of democracy and a free market. By 2005 Yushchenko's government felt many of the same economic and political strains as post-Communist governments across the region.

■ **REVIEW:** *What were the major issues facing the former Soviet world in the 1990s and early 2000s?*

Global Opportunities Transcend the Nation-State

Although the end of the Soviet system fractured one large regional economy, it gave further impetus to European unification. The European Community was robust in marked contrast to the wars and civil strife that plagued many other regions of the world. The union's economic success provoked the formation of the North American Free Trade Agreement (NAFTA), which established a free-trade zone of the United States, Canada, and Mexico. As new forms of world governance and large regional blocs took shape in the 1990s, Europeans took immense strides to advance their institutions beyond those of the traditional nation-state.

Europe Looks beyond the Nation-State

In 1992, the twelve countries of the Common Market moved beyond a primary concern for economic policy by ending a variety of political and cultural distinctions such as passport controls at most of their common borders. Citizens of the member countries carried a common burgundy-colored passport, and governments, whether municipal or national, had to treat all member nations' firms the same. In 1994, by the terms of the **Maastricht Treaty**, the European Community became the **European Union (EU)**. In 1999, a common currency—the euro—

came into being, first for transactions among financial institutions and then in 2002 for general use by the public. Common policies governed everything from the number of American soap operas aired on television to pollution controls on automobiles to the health warnings on cigarette packages. The EU parliament convened regularly in Strasbourg, France, while subgroups met to negotiate further cultural, economic, and social policies. With the adoption of a common currency, an EU central bank came into being to guide interest rates and economic policy.

The EU continued to play a pacifying role in Europe. It was Greece that pushed for the admission of its traditional enemy Turkey despite the warnings of a former president of France that a predominantly Muslim country could never fit in with the Christian traditions of EU members. "Turkey has been a great European power since the sixteenth century," Greek prime minister Costas Simitis maintained in 2003, rejecting religious criteria to resolve political issues. Both Greece and Turkey, like France and Germany before them, stood to benefit by having their disputes adjudicated by the larger body of European members, principally by being able to cut that part of their defense budget used for weaponry against the other country.

Governments of eastern European nations clamored to join, working hard to meet not only the EU's fiscal requirements but also those pertaining to human rights and social policy. They saw the EU's attractions demonstrated in such member countries as Greece, long considered the poor relative of the other EU states. Greece joined the European Community in 1981; its per capita gross domestic product was 64 percent of the European average in 1985 and 58.5 percent in 1990. However, Greek leaders and the EU made a real effort during the 1990s to bring the country closer to EU norms. By the early twenty-first century, thanks to advice from the EU and an infusion of funds—8.3 percent of the total EU budget—Greece had reached 80 percent of the EU per capita gross domestic product.

In 2004, the EU admitted ten new members, mostly from central and eastern Europe (Estonia, Latvia, Lithuania, Poland, the Czech Republic, Slovakia, Hungary, Slovenia, Malta, and Cyprus) even though troubles were brewing in the EU itself (Map 24.3). On the eve of Poland's admission to the EU, its standard of living was 39 percent of EU standards, up from 33 percent in 1995. The Czech Republic and Hungary enjoyed 55 and 50 percent, respectively, but in all three cases these figures masked the discrepancy between the ailing countryside and thriving cities. On the eve of entering the EU, citizens in eastern Europe were not always happy at the prospect. "It's bad," a farmer in the Czech Republic maintained. "The European Union is already imposing various quotas and regulations on us." A retiree foresaw the cost of beer going up and added, "If I wanted to join anything in the West, I would have defected." Still others felt that having just established an independent national identity, it was premature to join yet another body that would swallow them up. People in older member states were having second

Original members of the European Economic Union

Became members 1973–1995

Became members in 2004

Applying for membership

■ **MAP 24.3 The European Union in 2004**

The European Union (EU) appeared to increase the economic health of its members despite the rocky start of its common currency: the euro. The EU helped end the traditional competition among its members and facilitated trade and worker migration by providing common passports and business laws, and open borders. But many critics feared a loss of cultural distinctiveness among peoples in an age of mass communications, if the economic union turned into a political one. What advantages does the expansion of the EU provide to Europe and to the world? What are the disadvantages?

thoughts too: in the spring of 2005, a majority of voters in France and the Netherlands rejected a complex draft constitution that would have strengthened EU ties. Commentators interpreted the rejection as a temporary setback to the EU dealt by people angry at the lack of popular participation in fundamental EU decision making.

The economic life of eastern Europe picked up considerably despite looming uncertainty. In contrast to the first bleak years of massive layoffs, soaring inflation, and unpaid salaries, in 2002 residents of Poland, Slovenia, and Estonia had purchasing power some 40 percent higher than in 1989. Latvia, Romania, and

■ **Prague Supermarket, 2002**
For people living in former eastern bloc countries daily life in the post-Communist world was one
of extremes. Within several years, entrepreneurs opened supermarkets filled with more goods than
most people had ever seen before, like the different irons available to this Prague shopper. But
along with the unprecedented array of goods, the collapse of communism brought new dangers as
well, such as bombings on public transportation and economic instability for those who did not
benefit from the uneasy transition to capitalism. (Getty Images.)

Bulgaria's economies were at the bottom of those of former Communist states. Even there, however, a greater number of residents enjoyed freezers, computers, and portable telephones. The shopping malls that rose mostly around capital cities testified to the urban nature of the benefits of the free economy. They also showed that eastern Europe was seen as a great new market consisting of 100 million customers for superstores like the Swedish furniture giant IKEA or the electronics firm Electroworld. "When Electroworld opened in Budapest [April 2002], it provoked a riot. Two hundred thousand people crowded to get in the doors," reported one observer. Critics worried that eastern Europeans had fallen prey to uncontrolled materialism and frenzied shopping, a Western disease they called "Consomania." However, people learned to read labels and to use the superstores, where prices were lower, and some saw joining the consumer world as a sign of belonging to a global community of those free and prosperous enough to consume.

Globalizing Cities and Fragmenting Nations

The West in the transitional period of the 1990s and early 2000s both fragmented into more nation-states and consolidated new forms—most notably the global city.

These were cities whose institutions, functions, and visions were overwhelmingly global rather than regional or national. They contained stock markets, legal firms, insurance companies, financial service organizations, and other enterprises that operated across local and national borders, linking to similar enterprises in other global cities. Within these cities, there came together high-level decision makers who interacted with one another primarily to set global economic policy and to enact global business. The high-powered and high-priced nature of such global business operatives made life in global cities extremely costly, driving middle managers and engineers to lower-priced living quarters in the suburbs that nonetheless provided good schools and other amenities for well-educated white-collar earners. However, living in very squalid conditions in the global cities and in segregated, less privileged suburbs were the very lowest paid of service providers—the maintenance, domestic, and other workers whose menial labor was essential around the clock to the needs and comfort of those at the top.

Global cities were those with the best transport or telecommunication facilities. They thus became centers for migration, whether of highly skilled or more modest workers. Paris, London, and New York were not just cosmopolitan but global; workers maintained direct and constant contact with people around the world. As a result, citizens of other cities who took pride in maintaining a distinctive national culture or way of life denounced them. Global cities also drew criticism for their very concentrated wealth, seen to be taken at the expense of poorer people in southern countries. In other cases, however, globalization produced intentional diasporas of willing migrants, such as the estimated ninety thousand Japanese in England in the mid-1990s who staffed Japan's global businesses. Because these migrants did not aim to become citizens, they made no economic or political claims on the adopted country and were thus sometimes said to be invisible migrants. Global cities were said to produce a "deterritorialization of identities"—meaning that many urbanites lacked both a national and a local sense of themselves, so much did they travel the world.

Ironically, as globalization took hold economically and culturally, political borders grew smaller. There were more nations in Europe in 2000 than there had been in 1945, as individual nation-states fragmented under the ideology of ethnic distinctiveness (Map 24.4). Despite two centuries aimed at Slavic unification and the trend toward larger nation-states, ethnic groups separated in the 1990s and early twenty-first century. In 1993, Czechoslovakia split into the Czech Republic and Slovakia. As noted earlier in this chapter, Yugoslavia came apart into several states, as did the Soviet Union. Activists launched movements for regional autonomy in places such as France, Italy, and Spain. Some Bretons and Corsicans demanded their independence from France, and Basque nationalists in northern Spain continued to assassinate tourists, police, and other public servants in an effort to gain autonomy. The push for an independent northern Italy began somewhat halfheartedly, but when politicians saw its attractiveness to voters, they

■ **MAP 24.4 Eastern Europe, c. 2000**

In the 1990s, the countries of eastern Europe tried to forge their own destiny free from the direction of either Russia or the United States. The transition, as the new situation came to be called, was far from easy. Old states like Czechoslovakia fragmented, and many state borders were contested. Turning definitively from Russia, the leadership of these countries began to look to western Europe, most of them eventually opting for membership in the European Union. Compare this map with the sharp divisions between eastern and western Europe shown in Map 22.3. What were the most significant changes to the region in the post–cold war era?

became adamant in their demands and the movement grew. The presence of global cities and fragmenting nations threw the status of the nation-state into question.

Global Organizations

Globalization spawned the proliferation of supranational organizations, many of them to regulate international finance and trade but others to address social issues. The **World Bank** and the International Monetary Fund had been in existence for several decades, but as national economies interacted more closely, these supranational organizations gained power and new ones such as the World Trade Organization came into being (1995). Raising money from individual governments, the International Monetary Fund made loans to developing countries but on the condition that they restructure their economies according to neoliberal principles. Other supranational organizations were charitable foundations, many of them based in Europe and the United States. Because some—the Rockefeller, Ford, and Open Society Foundations, for example—controlled so much money, these **nongovernmental organizations** (**NGOs**) often had considerable international power. After the fall of the Soviet bloc, NGOs used their resources to shape economic and social policy and the course of political reform. Some charitable and activist NGOs, like the French-based Doctors Without Borders, used money raised through global contributions to provide medical attention in such places as the war-torn former Yugoslavia. Small, locally based NGOs excelled at inspiring grass-roots activism, while the larger ones were sometimes criticized for exercising their power with no regard for democratic processes or citizens' own preferences.

While the World Bank, World Trade Organization, and International Monetary Fund forced poorer nations to adopt free trade in exchange for loans and financial aid, the European Union and the United States often enacted huge tariffs to prevent cheap goods from competing with their own products. In 2002, the U.S. government under George W. Bush, a staunch advocate of free trade, levied large tariffs on steel in order to win the votes of workers in this declining industry. The European Union threatened retaliation with its own list of U.S. goods to be taxed. The biggest threat, however, came from the financial help given to European and U.S. agribusiness by propping up prices, enacting tariffs, and providing outright subsidies—all of which artificially made them profitable in the world market even though poor countries with lower wages produced less expensive food. Tariffs and subsidized profits, it was estimated, diverted $100 billion worth of business away from poorer nations even though their goods were better bargains for consumers.

Activists began movements to attack globalization itself. In 1998, Bernard Cassen of France founded the Association for the Benefit of Citizens (or ATTAC, after its French name). The organization, which soon had adherents in forty different countries, stood against the control of globalization by the forces of high finance: "Commercial totalitarianism is not free trade." ATTAC took its major policy goal from U.S. economist and Nobel Prize winner James Tobin: to tax financial transactions (just as the purchase of household necessities were taxed) and to create with the tax a fund for people living in underdeveloped countries. Cassen sided with European integration and opposed the "balkanization" of regions and countries. The organization held well-attended conferences to show policy alternatives. ATTAC was but one of several antiglobalization movements, some of which organized mass demonstrations during international economic meetings.

■ **REVIEW:** *What trends suggest that the nation-state was a declining institution at the beginning of the twenty-first century?*

Global Challenges and Discontents

Despite prosperity for many, the post–cold war period was one of challenges. First, the health of the world's peoples and their environment came under a multipronged attack from nuclear disaster, acid rain, and surging population. Second, economic prosperity and physical safety continued to elude great masses of people, especially in the southern half of the globe. Third, as suprastate organizations developed, transnational allegiances and religious and ethnic movements also vied for power and influence. Growing prosperity in regions outside the West gave these movements not only financing but also confidence in the idea that it was time for the West to surrender some of its power.

Pollution and Population

Whereas industrialization and a growing population had once appeared wholly positive, people in the late twentieth century became concerned that technological development threatened the environment. The aftermath of the 1986 nuclear explosion at Chernobyl left thousands perishing slowly from the effects of radiation. Levels of radioactivity rose for hundreds of miles in all directions, and by the 1990s cancer rates in the region were soaring, particularly among children. Fossil-fuel pollutants such as those from natural gas, coal, and oil mixed with atmospheric moisture to produce acid rain, a poisonous brew that destroyed forests in industrial areas and inflicted ailments such as chronic bronchial disease on children. In less industrial areas, clearing the world's rain forests depleted the global oxygen supply and threatened the biological diversity of the entire planet. By the late 1980s, scientists determined that the use of chlorofluorocarbons (CFCs), chemicals found in aerosol and refrigeration products, had blown a hole in the earth's ozone layer, the part of the blanket of atmospheric gases that prevents harmful ultraviolet rays from reaching the planet. Simultaneously, automobile and industrial emissions of chemicals were adding to that thermal blanket. The result was **global warming**, an increase in the temperature of the earth's lower atmosphere. Changes in temperature and dramatic weather cycles of drought or drenching rain indicated that a greenhouse effect might be permanently warming the earth. Already in the 1990s the Arctic pack ice was breaking up, allowing Finland to ship oil along the once-iced-over route in 2002. Scientists predicted dire consequences: the rate of global ice melting, which had more than doubled since 1988, would raise sea levels 27 centimeters by 2100, flooding coastal areas, disturbing fragile ecosystems, and harming the fresh water supply.

Rising activism protesting unbridled industrial growth took decades to develop as an effective political force. An escapee from Nazi Germany, E. F. "Fritz" Schumacher, produced one of the bibles of the environmental movement, *Small Is Beautiful* (1973), which spelled out how technology and industrialization actually threatened the earth and its inhabitants. Behind him stood the legacy of American Rachel Carson, author of a powerful critique—*Silent Spring* (1962), which advocated the immediate rescue of rivers, forests, and the soil from the ravages of factories and chemical farming. In 1979, the Green Party was founded in West Germany, and across Europe Green Party candidates came to force other politicians to voice their concern for the environment. As the horrific effects of utterly unchecked pollution in eastern Europe became known, protest mounted and solutions began to unfold.

Europeans addressed pollution on both the local and global levels. Some European cities—Frankfurt, for example—developed car-free zones, and the city of Venice operated completely without the use of automobiles. In Paris, when pollution reached dangerous levels, cars were banned. The Smart, a very small and fuel-efficient car, became a fashionable way in Europe to reduce dependence on fossil fuels. Cities also developed bicycle lanes on major city streets. Some areas of Europe developed wind power to such an extent that 20 percent of Germany's electricity was generated by wind. Many cities in the West began to recycle waste materials. These were success stories, involving changing habits and dependencies,

■ **Windmills in the Netherlands**
The oil crisis of the 1970s upset the world economy and prompted many European states to development alternate sources of energy. Surprisingly, entrepreneurs turned to an older source of energy—wind power—and constructed these modern windmills that dot many coastal regions of northern Europe. Whereas windmills several centuries earlier had powered tools that ground grain, these mills generated energy that was stored and then sold to regional power companies. What made the windmill an attractive means of generating power?
(© Benoit Roland/The Image Works.)

by some of the most industrialized countries in the world. Many of these countries added their signatures to the Kyoto Protocol, an international treaty fashioned in 1997 to reduce the level of emissions and other pollutants around the world. But here, as in other policies, the West was fragmenting: the United States and Russia—among the world's top polluters—rejected the treaty, making cooperation on the environment a dead issue.

Population and Disease

Nations with less developed economies struggled with surging populations, while the global public health establishment confronted the spread of deadly disease. The cause of the population surge was complex. Whereas by 1995 Europe was actually experiencing negative growth (that is, more deaths than births), the less industrially developed countries accounted for 98 percent of worldwide population growth in part because the spread of Western medicine enabled people there to live much longer than before. By late 1999, the earth's population had reached six billion, with a doubling forecast for 2045 (see "Taking Measure," page 1050). In nonindustrial countries, birthrates were much higher than in the West, while life expectancy rose by an average of sixteen years between 1950 and 1980. The world's sole remaining superpower did not fare particularly well by this measure of social health: by 1995, the United States had fallen from the top twenty in longevity for both women and men. However, life expectancy in the Soviet Union and then in its successor states was catastrophic, falling steadily from a peak of seventy years for Russian men in the mid-1970s to fifty-three in 1995 and to fifty-one at the beginning of the twenty-first century. Meanwhile, birthrates were declining. They had been dropping in the West for decades. In the less economically developed world, they also began to fall noticeably by 1995 when some 58 percent of couples in these economies were estimated to use birth control.

Western medicine and better health found their way into the less developed world in the form of vaccines and drugs for diseases such as malaria and smallpox. However, half of all Africans did not benefit from basic public health facilities such as safe drinking water. Drought and poverty, along with the maneuvers of politicians in some cases, spread famine in regions like the Sudan, Somalia, and Ethiopia. In the West, specialists performed heart bypass surgery, transplanted organs, and treated cancer with radiation and chemotherapy, while preventive care for the masses received less attention. The poor and unemployed suffered more chronic illnesses than those who were better off, but they received less care. The distribution of health services became a hotly debated issue.

Disease, like population and technology, operated on a global terrain. In the early 1980s, both Western values and Western technological expertise were challenged by the spread of a global epidemic disease: acquired immunodeficiency syndrome (AIDS). A highly virulent killer that effectively shuts down the body's entire immune system,

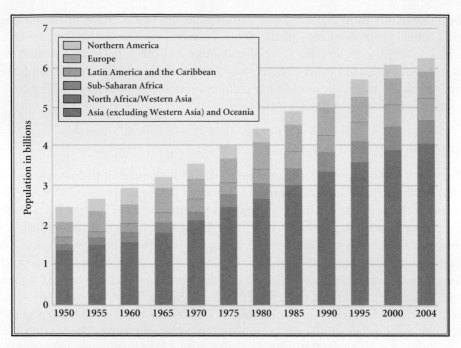

■ TAKING MEASURE World Population Growth, 1950–2004

In the twenty-first century, a major question is whether the global environment can sustain billions of people indefinitely. In the early modern period, local communities had lived according to unwritten rules that balanced population size with the productive capacities of individual farming regions. Centuries later, the same need for balance had reached global proportions. As fertility dropped around the planet because of contraception, population continued to grow because of improved health.

AIDS initially afflicted heterosexuals in central Africa; the disease later turned up in Haitian immigrants to the United States and in homosexual men worldwide. The disease spread especially quickly and widely among the heterosexual populations of Africa and Asia. By the late 1990s, no cure had yet been discovered, though pro-tease-inhibiting drugs helped alleviate the symptoms. The mounting death toll made some equate AIDS to a Black Death of the twentieth century, and as millions con-tracted the disease—some thirty-three million in 2000 had it—treatment was often not forthcoming because most of the ill were too poor, living in sub-Saharan Africa. On top of that, the deadly Ebola virus and dozens of other viruses smoldered like a global conflagration in the making. Interconnectedness via disease became all too real once again in 2003, when an unknown respiratory illness traveled the world: in the space of a month, severe acute respiratory syndrome (SARS) caused hundreds of deaths. Fortunately, it was rapidly brought under control through global medical cooperation. In 2005–2006, a virulent strain of avian flu quickly crossed borders, intensifying fears of a global pandemic.

North versus South?

During the 1980s and 1990s, world leaders tried to address the growing economic schism between the earth's northern and southern regions. Other than Australians and New Zealanders, southern peoples generally suffered lower living standards and measures of health than northerners. Recently emerging from colonial rule and economic exploitation by northerners, citizens in the southern regions could not yet count on their new governments to provide welfare services or education. Their funds generally coming from the wealth of the northern countries, for example, international organizations like the World Bank and the International Monetary Fund provided loans for economic development, but the conditions tied to them, such as cutting government spending, led to criticism that underprivileged citizens gained no real benefit if education and health care had to be cut as a result. Some twenty-first-century leaders from both regions advocated that wealthy countries simply give southern countries the money they needed in recognition of centuries of imperial pillage.

Southern regions experienced a variety of barriers to economic development. Latin American nations grappled with government corruption, multibillion-dollar debt, widespread crime, and grinding poverty, though some countries—prominent among them Mexico and Venezuela—began to strengthen their economies by marketing their oil and other natural resources more effectively. Sub-Saharan Africa suffered from drought, continuing famine, and civil war. In lands such as Rwanda, military rule, ideological factionalism, and ethnic antagonism encouraged under imperialism produced a lethal mixture of conflict and genocide in the 1990s. Millions perished; others were left starving and homeless due to a kleptocracy that drained resources.

Emerging economies in the Southern Hemisphere as a whole continued to increase their share of the world's gross domestic product during the 1980s and 1990s, and some achieved political gains as well. In South Africa, native peoples began winning the struggle for political rights when, in 1990, the moderate government of F. W. de Klerk released political leader Nelson Mandela, imprisoned for almost three decades because of his antiapartheid activism. De Klerk followed Mandela's release with a gradual dismantling of apartheid, including the desegregation of parks and beaches. In 1993, the government agreed to a democratic constitution that granted the vote to the nonwhite majority while guaranteeing whites and other minorities civil liberties. The next year, Mandela became the country's president in a landslide victory, formalizing the institution of a multiracial democracy in which international business made strides. In India, Rajiv Gandhi, the grandson of India's first prime minister, Jawaharlal Nehru, worked for education, women's rights, and an end to bitter local rivalries. Even after his assassination in 1991, India continued modernization despite Hindu nationalism that sought to obstruct, even through violence, India's global reach.

Islam Confronts the West

The Iranian hostage crisis that began in 1979 showed religion, nationalism, and the power of oil uniting to make the Middle East an arbiter of international order. The charismatic leaders of the 1980s and 1990s—Iran's Ayatollah Ruhollah Khomeini; Libya's Muammar Qaddafi; Iraq's Saddam Hussein; and Osama bin Laden, leader of the al-Qaeda transnational terrorist organization—variously promoted a pan-Arabic or pan-Islamic world order that gathered increasing support. Khomeini's program—"Neither East, nor West, only the Islamic Republic"—had wide appeal. Turning from the Westernization that had flourished under the shah, his regime in Iran required women once again to cover their bodies almost totally in special clothing, restricted their access to divorce, and eliminated a range of other rights. Islamic revolutionaries believed these restrictions would restore the pride and Islamic identity that imperialism had stripped from Middle Eastern men. By proclaiming the ascendancy of the Shi'ite clergy, Khomeini built widespread support among Shi'ite Muslims, who had long been ruled by the Sunnis.

Power in the Middle East remained dispersed, however, and Islamic leaders did not achieve their unifying goals (Map 24.5). Instead, war plagued the region, as Saddam Hussein of Iraq sought to make his country the dominant power and launched an attack on Iran in 1980. Hussein feared that Iraq's Shi'ite majority might be convinced by Iran's example to rebel against his regime, and he sought to channel their aggression through a patriotic crusade against the non-Arab Iranians. During this period of cold war, the United States provided Iraq with massive aid in the struggle against the power of Muslims in Iran. Eight years of combat produced only stalemate and extensive loss of life on both sides.

Simultaneously, the Soviet Union became entrenched in a bitter ten-year struggle with Muslim resisters in Afghanistan after it invaded the country in 1979 to prop up a failing Communist government. The United States, China, Saudi Arabia, and Pakistan aided the resistance movement that finally forced the Soviets to withdraw in 1989. Several groups of resistance fighters coalesced into the Islamic fundamentalist Taliban movement that took over in the 1990s and imposed a strict regime, creating millions of political and religious refugees.

His country mired in war debt, Saddam Hussein was the first to test the post–cold war waters by invading neighboring, oil-rich Kuwait in 1990. Contrary to Hussein's expectations that he would be left alone, the deployment of Iraqi troops on the Saudi Arabian border galvanized a UN coalition (joined by the USSR) whose forces pummeled the Iraqi army. But the Middle East remained in turmoil, as conflicts between the Israelis and the Palestinians and fruitless efforts to resolve them continued. As Israeli settlers began taking more Palestinian land, in the late 1990s, Palestinian suicide bombers began murdering Israeli civilians. The Israeli government retaliated with missiles, machine guns, and tanks, often killing Palestinian civilians in turn. Throughout the 1980s and 1990s, terrorists

■ **MAP 24.5 The Middle East, c. 2003**

Tensions among states in the Middle East, especially the ongoing conflict between the Palestinians and Israelis, became more complicated in the 1990s. As Islam took center stage in politics, Middle Eastern populations divided over such issues as the extent of religious determination of state policies, the rule of religion in everyday life, and access to human rights including freedom of speech and of movement. Conflicts erupted around some of these questions because, as elsewhere, they were also vehicles for political ambition. The increasing demands of globalization in the 1990s pulled other citizens in the direction of secularization, high-tech international partnerships, and reduced violence. In 2001, however, violence escalated among Arabs and Israelis, bringing tensions in the region close to the breaking point. In 2003, the situation in the Middle East grew more uncertain and violent when the United States and Britain led an invasion in Iraq to seize its weapons of mass destruction and to overthrow the government of the dictator Saddam Hussein.

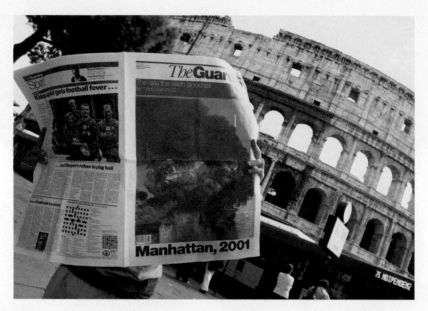

■ Europeans React to 9/11 Terror

On September 11, 2001, terrorists killed thousands of people from dozens of countries in airplane attacks on the World Trade Center in New York. Throughout the world, people expressed their shock and sorrow in vigils, and like this British tourist in Rome, they remained glued to the latest news. Terrorism, which had plagued Europeans for several decades, easily traveled the world in these days of more open borders, economic globalization, and cultural exchange, finally reaching the sole superpower left after the collapse of the Soviet Union. **For more help analyzing this image,** see the visual activity for this chapter in the ONLINE STUDY GUIDE *at* bedfordstmartins.com/huntconcise. (© Pizzoli Alberto/Corbis Sygma.)

from the Middle East and North Africa planted bombs in many European cities, blew up European airplanes, and bombed the Paris subway system—among other acts. These attacks, causing widespread destruction and loss of life, were said to be punishment for the West's support for both Israel and the repressive regimes in the Middle East.

On September 11, 2001, terrorism finally caught the full attention of the United States. In an unprecedented act, Muslim militants hijacked four planes in the United States and flew two of them into the World Trade Center in New York and one into the Pentagon in Virginia. The fourth plane crashed in Pennsylvania. The hijackers, most of whom were from Saudi Arabia, were inspired by the wealthy radical leader Osama bin Laden, who sought to end the presence of U.S. forces in Saudi Arabia. These hijackers trained in bin Laden's terrorist camps in Afghanistan and learned to pilot planes in the United States. The loss of more than three thousand lives led the United States to declare a "war against terrorism." The administration of U.S. president George W. Bush forged a multinational coalition, which included the vital cooperation of Islamic countries such as Pakistan. The coalition enjoyed quick successes in driving out the ruling Taliban party in Afghanistan, though it failed in its major goal of capturing bin Laden.

Global cooperation followed the September 11 attacks and other lethal bombings around the world. European countries rounded up terrorists and conducted the first successful trials of them in the spring of 2003. However, ultimately the West fragmented its efforts when the United States claimed that Iraq's Saddam Hussein had menacing weapons of mass destruction and suggested ties between Saddam Hussein and bin Laden's terrorist group. Great Britain, Spain, and Poland were among those who joined the U.S. invasion of Iraq in March 2003, but powerful European states, including Germany, Russia, and France, refused. Many people in the United States were furious, sporting bumper stickers with the demand "First Iraq, Next France" and joining happy hours to participate in "French bashing." U.S. war fever mounted with the suggestion that Syria and Iran should be invaded as well even as the rest of the world condemned what seemed a sudden American blood lust. Europeans in general, including the British public, accused the United States of becoming a world military dictatorship in order to preserve its only remaining value—wasteful consumerism. The United States countercharged that the Europeans were too selfish in their enjoyment of democracy and creature comforts to fund military defense of freedom under attack. This judgment seemed confirmed when the Spanish withdrew from the U.S. occupation of Iraq after al-Qaeda–linked terrorists bombed four Madrid commuter trains on March 11, 2004. The British reeled too, when terrorists left bombs in three subway cars and a bus in central London in July 2005. There was a sense that the West was vulnerable and coming apart.

The Rise of the Pacific Economy

Challenges to Western economic leadership came from the global diffusion of industry and technology in the last third of the twentieth century. Just as economic change in the early modern period had redirected European affairs from the Mediterranean to the Atlantic, so explosive productivity from Japan to Singapore in the 1980s and 1990s spread economic power from the Atlantic region to the Pacific. In 1982, the Asian Pacific nations accounted for 16.4 percent of global gross domestic product, a figure that had doubled since the 1960s. By 1989, the share of East Asia's world production was more than 25 percent, while production in the West declined comparatively. By the mid-1990s, China's economy alone was growing at a rate of 8 percent per year; after 2000, it was 9 percent. Japan and China joined the United States and Germany as the top trading nations.

South Korea, Taiwan, Singapore, and Hong Kong were the initial **Pacific tigers**, so named for the ferocity of their growth in the 1980s and 1990s. China, pursuing a policy of economic modernization and market orientation, saw phenomenal

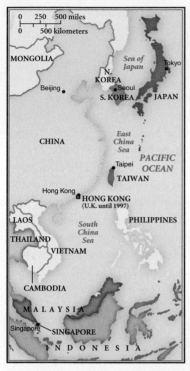

Tigers of the Pacific Rim, c. 1995

economic growth in the 1990s and thereafter, soon to be joined by India. Japan, however, led development of high-tech consumer industries. Thus, in 1982, Japan had 32,000 industrial robots to automate factory work in operation; western Europe employed only 9,000, and the United States had 7,000. In 1989, the Japanese government and private businesses invested $549 billion to modernize industrial capacity, a full $36 billion more than American public and private investment combined. Such spending paid off substantially, as buyers around the world snapped up automobiles, televisions, and computers from Japanese or other Asian Pacific companies. Low-paid Asian workers were also central to creating this wealth. For example, women in South Korea and Taiwan labored in sweatshops to produce clothing for such U.S.-based companies as J. C. Penney and Calvin Klein, attracted by the lure of a low-paid and docile female workforce. However, educational standards rose, along with access to birth control and other medical care, ranking some of the Pacific tigers high by UN standards for human development. As the United States poured vast sums into its cold war and post–cold war military budgets, the resulting profits from Asian Pacific industries went to purchase U.S. government bonds, thus financing America's national debt. Forty years after its total defeat in World War II, Japan was bankrolling its former conqueror, while in the twenty-first century China and Middle Eastern states joined in as major U.S. creditors.

Mounting economic difficulties plagued Japan and the other Pacific tigers in the 1990s and early twenty-first century. Financial scandals and widespread corruption, which governments refused to address, destabilized the Japanese and other economies. The Japanese stock market plunged; domestic consumers cut back, and a severe business crisis struck the Pacific rim as currency speculation and corrupt financial practices—labeled crony capitalism—first brought down the Thai currency in 1997 and then toppled politicians and industrial leaders in the region. By 2001, the economic downturn had spread to Europe and the United States, where widespread corruption similarly plagued business from Moscow to New York and Texas. European business additionally languished because of welfare costs and low levels of investment in economic growth. China, however, continued its expansion; India joined the "Tigers"; and in 2001, Japan finally selected a reform prime minister whose reelection in 2005 promised increased leadership for the entire region. The non-West became a powerful engine of economic development in the contemporary world.

■ **REVIEW:** *What were the most important challenges facing the West in the new millennium?*

Global Culture and Society in the New Millennium

As the final years of the millennium unfolded, thinkers began to debate the future, with scenarios changing as rapidly as global politics and economics did. Some saw the world's peoples rapidly absorbing Western cultural values with the adoption of the West's systems of technology, representative government, and the free market. An opposing view predicted a clash of civilizations in which increasingly incompatible religions and cultures would lead to future global strife. These thinkers believed that Islam, with more than one billion followers, would confront Western values rather than absorb them. Finally, there was the prediction of the collapse of the West itself because the United States continued to venture forth as the determining force in the world, opposed by much of Europe, which—as in the case of the Iraq invasion—suddenly refused to obey U.S. requests to join invasions of sovereign states.

There was much to argue against any group's claim to cultural purity, including that of the West. "Civilizations," as Nobel Prize winner Amartya Sen wrote after the terrorist attacks of September 11, "are hard to partition . . . , given the diversities within each society as well as the linkages among different countries and cultures." Increasing migration in the 1990s and thereafter changed Western society more rapidly than when it came into intense contact with the rest of the globe hundreds of years earlier. Moreover, national boundaries in the traditional European center of the West were weakening politically and economically, given the growing strength of the European Union and the simultaneous influx of migrants. East, West, North, and South became saturated with one another's cultural products as communications transcended national boundaries. Observers even labeled the new millennium an era of denationalization—meaning that national cultures as well as national boundaries were becoming less distinct. But there is no denying that the West continued to exercise not only economic influence but also hotly debated cultural influence over the rest of the globe.

Redefining the West: The Impact of Global Migration

The global movement of people was massive in the last third of the twentieth century and into the twenty-first. Uneven economic development, political persecution, and warfare (which claimed more than 100 million victims worldwide since 1945) sent tens of millions in search of opportunity and safety. In the 1970s

■ **The Headscarf Controversy**
In 2004, France banned all conspicuous religious attire in schools, including yarmulkes, crosses, and the headscarves worn by many Muslim women. The previous year, French high school student Alma Levy-Omari, shown here copying course lessons at home, was temporarily suspended from school for wearing a headscarf. The long-standing debate in Western countries over the relationship between religion and the nation-state has focused recently on the need for religiously neutral education to develop citizens with impartial judgment and undivided national loyalties. Critics see this religious garb in the schools as weakening the commitment to secular education. Such complex debates show how individual rights, born in the eighteenth and nineteenth centuries, have become open to intense questioning in the twenty-first century world. (AFP/Getty Images.)

alone, more than 4.7 million people moved to the United States. By 2001, France had some six million Muslims within its borders, and Europe as a whole had between thirty-five and fifty million. Tensions between European Muslims and non-Muslim populations flared in 2006 over the publication of cartoons showing the Prophet Muhammed. Muslims worldwide protested and some began to boycott Danish goods.

Other parts of the world were also full of people from other cultures on the move. The oil-producing nations of the Middle East employed millions of foreign workers, who generally constituted one-third of the labor force. The ongoing violence in Africa sent Rwandans, Congolese, and others to South Africa, as its government became dominated by blacks. War in Afghanistan increased the number of refugees to Iran to close to two million in 1995, while the Iraq-Iran war and successive attacks on Iraq by the West had sent still further millions fleeing. By 2000, there were some 120 million migrants worldwide.

Migrants often earned desperately needed income for family members who remained in the native country, and in some cases they propped up the economies of entire nations. In the southern African country of Lesotho, where the soil had been ruined by overuse during colonial rule, between 40 and 50 percent of national income came from migrant workers, particularly from those who toiled in the mines of South Africa. In countries as different as Yugoslavia, Egypt, Spain, and Pakistan, money sent home from abroad constituted up to 60 percent of national income. Illegal migrants, unprotected by law, risked exploitation and abuse of their human rights. At greatest risk were the eastern European and Asian prostitutes, many of whom were coerced into international sex rings that controlled their passports, wages, and lives. Political parties with racist programs successfully scapegoated migrants as responsible for unemployment. The West in particular remained a place of opportunity and hope despite all obstacles.

Among migrants to the West, women had little to say in decisions about leaving home; a patriarchal head of the household generally made such choices. Once abroad, migrant women suffered the most from unstable working conditions and usually obtained more menial, lower-paying jobs than migrant men or native Europeans. They were also more likely than men to be refused political asylum. Rape and other violence against them, even during civil war, were classified as part of everyday life, not politics. The offspring of immigrants often had a difficult time being accepted even when they became citizens. Unemployment hit them especially hard because "whites" received preference. They also struggled with questions of identity, sometimes feeling torn between two cultures. Young black immigrants in particular forged transnational identities, for example, when they created music combining elements of African, Caribbean, Afro-American, and European cultures. As tens of millions of people migrated, belief in a national identity based on a single, unique culture was losing credibility.

Global Networks and the Economy

Rapid technological change in electronic communications also made traditional national borders appear permeable, if not obsolete, and it made the world's economy far more global than ever before. In 1969, the U.S. Department of Defense developed a computer network to carry communications in case of nuclear war. This system and others like it in universities, government, and business grew into an unregulated system of more than ten thousand networks globally. These came to be known as the Internet—shorthand for *internetworking*. By 1995, users in more than 137 countries were connected to the Internet, creating new "communities" based on business needs and shared cultural interests that transcended citizenship in a particular nation-state. An online global marketplace emerged, offering goods and services ranging from advanced weaponry to organ transplants. While enthusiasts claimed that the Internet could promote world democracy, critics charged that communications technology favored elites and disadvantaged those without computer skills. Yet these skills advanced so quickly that in 2001, countries like Estonia, Hungary, and the Czech Republic as well as Morocco, India, and the Philippines were successfully luring businesses to employ their help desk and other call-center service workers. The Internet allowed some service industries to globalize as the manufacturing sector had done.

Globalization of the economy affected the West in complex ways. Those who worked in outsourcing enterprises were more likely than those in domestic firms to participate in the global consumer economy, much of it for Western goods. A twenty-one-year-old Indian woman, working for a service provider in Bangalore under the English name Sharon, was able to buy a cell phone from the Finnish

▪ **Call Center in Bangalore, India**
Modern communications now permits the outsourcing not just of manufacturing jobs, which began after World War II, but of service jobs to places like eastern Europe, Africa, and South Asia. In many countries, citizens are bi- and polylingual, enabling them to service customers in Europe and the United States, such as these workers in southern India, who are answering a customer service hotline. What are the advantages and disadvantages of a division of labor that operates internationally?
(© Jagadeesh/Reuters/Corbis.)

company Nokia and other consumer items with her salary. "As a teenager I wished for so many things," she said of her job. "Now I'm my own Santa Claus." The Irish and the eastern Europeans benefited from the booming global economy of the 1990s. Their new disposable income gave them access to luxury automobiles, CD players, and personal computers that would have been far beyond their means a decade before. The downside for ordinary Western workers was that this global revolution threatened their jobs. In Germany, where taxes for social security and other welfare-state financing comprised 42 percent of payroll costs in 2003, the incentive for business to move to countries with lower costs was strong. Globalization redistributed jobs and reworked economic networks.

The Global Diffusion of Culture

Culture has long transcended political boundaries, and in fact archaeologists point to its diffusion as a constant of tens of thousands of years of human history. In the postwar period, cultural exchange accelerated: tourism, for instance, became the largest single industry in Britain and in many other Western countries by the early 1990s. Chinese students in Tiananmen Square in 1989 had rallied around their own representation of the Statue of Liberty (which itself was a gift from France to the United States). In Japan, businesspeople wore Western-style clothing and watched soccer, baseball, and other Western sports using English terms, but the connections flew in many directions. Videotapes and satellite-beamed telecasts transported American television shows to Hong Kong and Japanese movies to Europe and

North America. American rock music sold briskly in Russia and elsewhere in the former Soviet bloc. When more than 100,000 Czechoslovakian rock fans, including President Václav Havel, attended a Rolling Stones concert in Prague in 1990, it was clear that despite half a century of supposedly insular Communist culture, Czechs and Slovaks had tuned in to the larger world. Sports stars like the Brazilian soccer player Pelé, the American basketball hero Michael Jordan, and Japanese baseball ace Ichiro Suzuki became better known to countless people than their own national leaders were. With their messages conveyed around the world, even today's moral leaders—the Nobel Peace Prize winners Nelson Mandela, former president of South Africa; the Dalai Lama, the spiritual leader of Tibet; and Aung San Suu Kyi, opposition leader in Burma—are global figures.

As it had done for centuries, the West continued to absorb material from other cultures—whether Hong Kong films, African textiles, Indian music, or Latin American pop culture. Global literature exerted a strong influence on European and North American readers and writers. The lush, exotic fantasies of Colombian-born Nobel Prize winner Gabriel García Márquez, for example, attracted a vast Western readership. His novels, including *One Hundred Years of Solitude* (1967) and *Love in the Time of Cholera* (1988), portray people of titanic ambitions and passions—a magical realism, the overall style has been called. Another Nobel Prize recipient who won high regard in the West was Egyptian writer Naguib Mahfouz. Having immersed himself in his youth in great Western literature, Mahfouz authored more than forty books. His celebrated *Cairo Trilogy*, written in the 1950s, describes a middle-class family—from its practice of Islam and seclusion of women to the business and cultural life of men as they struggle against British colonialism. To some Arab observers, Mahfouz won the Nobel Prize in 1988 precisely because he described European colonialism in novelistic form. "He borrowed the novel from Europe," charged one fellow Egyptian writer. "It's not an Egyptian art form. Europeans . . . like it very much because it is their own form." The globally read Egyptian Nawal el-Saadawi was also accused of producing exotic accounts of women's oppression to appeal to Western feminists. International conflict around artistic expression became dangerous. Salman Rushdie, an immigrant to Great Britain from India, produced the novel *The Satanic Verses* (1988), which ignited outrage among Muslims around the world because it appeared to blaspheme the prophet Muhammad. From Iran, the Ayatollah Khomeini promised both a monetary reward and salvation in the afterlife to anyone who would assassinate the writer. In a display of Western cultural unity, international leaders protected Rushdie until the threat was lifted a decade later.

Immigrants to the West described the experiences of the transnational person. The popular writer Buchi Emecheta, in her novel *In the Ditch* (1972) and her autobiography *Head above Water* (1986), detailed life as a newcomer to Britain. Her *Joys of Motherhood* (1979) was an imaginary foray back in time to probe the nature of mothering under colonial rule in her native Lagos, Nigeria. The lure of Western culture was powerful: Andrei Makine, who migrated to France from eastern-most

Siberia, described in his novels the fantasies of his protagonists created from French fiction and films. *Reading Lolita in Tehran* by Azar Nafisi (2003) and *Balzac and the Little Chinese Seamstress* by Dai Sijie (2000) detailed the power of Western literature under conditions of oppression. The narrator of *Reading Lolita*, having left her post at the university because of the repressive Iranian theocracy, brings together a group of young women to imbibe courage and values from their reading of forbidden Western works. The two young men in the work of Sijie, a Chinese refugee in Europe, are similarly exiled during China's Cultural Revolution and discover a cache of exhilarating Western classics, which they commit theft to obtain.

Within the West, the mainstream became fraught with conflict as groups outside the accepted circles engaged in artistic production. Novelist Toni Morrison, who in 1993 became the first African American woman to win the Nobel Prize in literature, described the nightmares, daily experiences, and dreams of the descendants of men and women who had been brought as slaves to the United States. But some parents objected to the inclusion of Morrison's work in school curricula, charging that, unlike Shakespeare's universal Western truth, the writing of African Americans, Native Americans, and women represented only a partial vision, not great literature. In both the United States and western Europe, politicians on the right saw the presence of multiculturalism as a sign of deterioration similar to that brought about by racial mixing. It was an era of culture wars—much like that ushered in by the Nazis and by the cold warriors of both the USSR and United States—focused on new kinds of thinking and writing.

The collapse of the Soviet Union put literary dissidents out of business and opened the question of post-Soviet art. Those who had helped bring down the Soviet regime had lost their subject matter—the critique of a tyrannical system. Tied as their work was to the

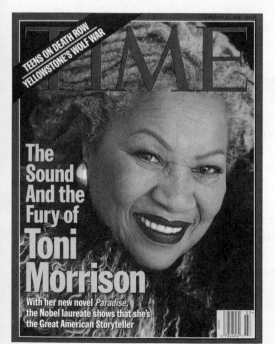

■ **Toni Morrison, Recipient of the Nobel Prize**
The first African American woman to receive the Nobel Prize, Toni Morrison has used her literary talent to depict the condition of blacks under slavery and after emancipation. Morrison also publishes cogent essays on social, racial, and gender issues in the United States.
(Time Life Pictures/Getty Images.)

drama of the Soviet empire, there was no drama left. Additionally, there was no consensus on what the post-Communist arts should be. Was everything that had appeared under the Soviets utterly worthless because it was produced by a corrupt system? Some seemed to think so, for in many cases the post-Soviet legacy was to look beyond the region itself for models to replace Communist ones.

However, much energy was spent on simply absorbing all the underground arts that had been hidden since 1917. The situation was utterly astonishing as the work of literally dozens of first-rate composers, for example, emerged. They had written their classical works in private for fear that they might contain phrasings, sounds, and rhythms that would be called subversive. Meanwhile, they had often earned a living writing for films, as did Giya Kancheli, who wrote immensely popular music for more than forty films. Other work could now become even better known. Alfred Schnittke (1934–1998) produced rich compositions—dozens of operas, symphonies, chamber music pieces, concertos, and other works—that were extremely sad, punctuated with anger in loud bursts of dissonance, and set in a somber bass register. The public also discovered virtually unknown composers, such as Galina Ustvolskaya, a protégé and lover of Soviet composer Dmitry Shostakovich. Ustvolskaya lived in poverty because she refused to join the Communist cultural system; her music surfaced for the public only after the USSR collapsed, as did unknown works of classical writers like Mikhail Bulgakov (1891–1940), famous for his novel *The Master and Margarita* (published 1966–1967). Dissident writers who formerly found success in the West seemed less heroic—and less talented—in the wide-open post-Soviet world. Milan Kundera's work, for example, lost its luster. It was, according to one critic, merely a phenomenon of the West's prosperous book contracts, not literature but merely a "line of business."

The political and economic power of the United States gave its culture an edge. U.S. success in "marketing" culture, along with the legacy of British imperialism, helped make English the dominant international language by the end of the twentieth century. Such English words as *stop, shopping, parking, okay, weekend,* and *rock* infiltrated dozens of non-English vocabularies. English operated in the European Union and united the scientific community as well as served travelers across the continent and around the world. In the 1960s, French president de Gaulle, fearing the corruption of the French language, had banned such new words as *computer* in government documents, and his path was followed by succeeding administrations; but such a directive did not stop the influx of English into television and pop culture, with such films as *Titanic* (1997) and *The Matrix Reloaded* (2003) earning hundreds of millions of dollars from global audiences. Simultaneously, however, films from around the world—whether the Chinese *Crouching Tiger, Hidden Dragon* (2000), the Mexican *Y Tu Mamá También* (2001), or "Bollywood" productions—happy, lavish films from the Indian movie industry—had a huge following in all Western countries.

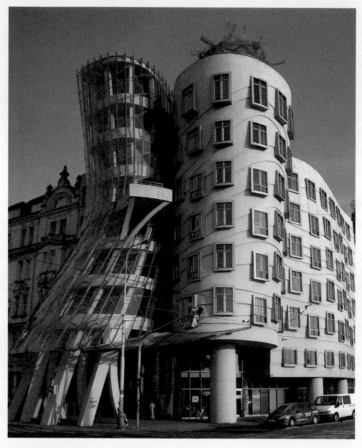

■ The "Dancing Building," Prague

This building—also nicknamed "Fred and Ginger" after the famed American dancers—rose in the 1990s on the site of an accidental bombing by U.S. forces in World War II. American architect Frank Gehry and Czech architect Vladimir Milunic hoped to achieve something light and pleasure-giving— a mark of postmodern style. Critics, however, felt that the building looked more like a crushed can of Coca-Cola and that it served as an ugly reminder of American militarism and consumerism. Defenders, however, pointed to the international cooperation of the design team and the fact that its eccentric look called attention to the destruction instead of simply papering over the wartime devastation with a mere restoration of the original building. (Ben R. Hays/brhphoto.com.)

Some have called the global culture of the late twentieth and early twenty-first centuries **postmodernism**, defined in part as intense stylistic mixing in the arts without a central unifying theme or privileged canon. Striking examples of postmodern art abounded in Western society, including the AT&T building in New York City, the work of architect Philip Johnson. Although the structure itself, designed in the late 1970s, looked sleek and modern, its entryway was a Roman arch, and its cloud-piercing top suggested eighteenth-century Chippendale furniture. The buildings of Johnson and other postmodernists appealed to the human past and drew from cultural styles that spanned millennia and continents without valuing one style above others. The Guggenheim Museum in Bilbao, Spain, designed by American Frank Gehry, was similarly bizarre by classical or even "modern" standards as it represented forms, materials, and perspectives that by rules of earlier decades did not belong together. The postunification rebuilding of Berlin was accomplished by architects from around the world in a variety of hybrid styles.

Other intellectuals defined the postmodern in political terms as an outgrowth of the demise of the eighteenth-century Enlightenment ideals of human rights, individualism, personal freedom, and their guarantor—the Western nation-state. A structure like the Bilbao Guggenheim was just an international tourist attraction that had no Spanish roots or purpose; consumption, global technology, mass communications, and international migration made citizenship, nationalism, and rights irrelevant to its meaning. It was a rootless structure, unlike the Louvre in Paris. For postmodernists of a political bent, computers had replaced the autonomous, free self, and bureaucracy had rendered representative government obsolete.

Another definition of the postmodern involved investigating the "unfreedom" or irrationality that shaped human life. Thus, French psychoanalyst Jacques Lacan, whose writing deeply influenced Western literary criticism in the 1990s, maintained that people operate in an unfree, predetermined world of language.

IMPORTANT DATES

1989	Chinese students revolt in Tiananmen Square and government suppresses them; fall of the Berlin Wall	1997	Collapse of Thai currency launches economic problems for Pacific tigers
1990s	Internet revolution	1999	Euro introduced in the European Union; world population reaches six billion
1990–1991	War in the Persian Gulf		
1991	Civil war erupts in the former Yugoslavia; failed coup by Communist hard-liners in the Soviet Union	2000	Vladimir Putin becomes president of Russia
		2001	Terrorist attack on the United States; United States declares "war against terrorism"
1992	Soviet Union is dissolved		
1993	Toni Morrison becomes the first African American woman to win the Nobel Prize	2003	United States–led coalition invades Iraq; the West divides on this policy; European Union constitution drafted
1994	Nelson Mandela elected president of South Africa; Russian troops invade Chechnya; European Union officially formed	2004	Ten countries join the European Union
		2005	Terrorist bombings at three sites in central London

In becoming social, communicating beings, we must bow to these laws, implanted in us at birth. Another prominent French thinker, Michel Foucault, deplored the easy acceptance of such liberal ideas as the autonomous self, the progressive march of history, and the advance of freedom. For him, the sexual revolution had not been liberating at all; rather, sexuality was merely a way in which humans expressed power over one another and through which society, by allowing greater sexual expression, actually controlled individuals. Some postmodern thinkers thus questioned the West's conviction that it had achieved freedom: even in the most intimate part of human experience, a grid of social and individual constraint determined people's lives. We can point to such critical rethinking—whatever its momentary conclusions—as itself a key ingredient in the making of the West.

■ **REVIEW:** *What social and cultural questions has globalization raised?*

Conclusion: The Making of the West Continues

Although some postmodernists have proclaimed an end to centuries of faith in progress, they themselves have worked within the modern Western tradition of constant criticism and reevaluation. Moreover, said their critics, the daunting problems of contemporary life—population explosion, resource depletion, North–South inequities, global pollution, ethnic hatred, and global terrorism—demanded, more than ever, the exercise of humanistic values and the renewal of a rational commitment to progress. Postmodernists and other philosophers countered with the question of "unintended consequences," that is, the question of whether one could begin to know the consequences of an act. Who would have predicted, for example, the human misery resulting from the fall of the Soviet Empire?

The years since 1990 have proved both sides correct. The collapse of communism signaled the eclipse of an ideology that was perhaps noble in intent but deadly in practice. Events from South Africa, for example, indicated that certain long-feuding groups were wearying of conflict and groping for peace, even as other peoples took up arms against their neighbors. Yet the unintended consequences of communism's fall were bloodshed, sickness, and hardship, while the global age, instead of being one of post–cold war peace has seen prosperous militants from Saudi Arabia, Egypt, Indonesia, and the Philippines unleashing unprecedented terrorism on the world.

■ **MAPPING THE WEST The World in the New Millennium**
By the twenty-first century, the Internet had transformed communications and economic organization into an interconnected global network. People in the so-called North had greater access to this network in 2004 and for the most part enjoyed greater wealth. Despite globalization, historians still find local and national conditions of political, social, and economic life important in telling the full story of peoples and cultures. In what ways does this map indicate a closely connected world?
(From www.mids.org. Austin: Matrix Information and Directory Services, Inc.)

Meanwhile, many in Africa and Asia also face disease and the dramatic social and economic change associated with the global age.

Western traditions of democracy, human rights, and economic equality have offered much for the world to consider and even the nation-state, which protected those values for privileged Westerners, is now being reappraised. The West faces questions of its own unity and cultural identity—an identity made from the far-flung cultural, natural, and human resources of Asia, Africa, and the Western Hemisphere. Non-Westerners have challenged, criticized, refashioned, and made enormous contributions to Western culture; they have also served the West's citizens as slaves, servants, and menial workers. Whether the West survives as a unit or not, one of the greatest challenges to the West and the world in this global millennium is to determine how peoples and cultures can live together on terms that are fair for everyone.

A final challenge to the West is living with the inventive human spirit. In the past five hundred years, the West has benefited from its scientific and technological advances. Longevity and improved material well-being have spread to many places. In the past century, communication and information technology have brought people closer to one another than ever before. Simultaneously, through the use of technology the period from the last century to the present one has become the bloodiest era in human history. War, genocide, and terrorism are among technology's hallmarks, posing perhaps the greatest challenge to the West and to the world. The making of the West has been a constantly inventive undertaking but also a deadly one. What mixture of peoples and cultures will face the paradoxical challenge of technology to protect the creativity of the human race in the century that now stretches before us?

■ MAKING CONNECTIONS

1. *How did global connections at the beginning of the twenty-first century differ from global connections at the start of the twentieth century?*

2. *How did the Western nation-state of the early twenty-first century differ from the Western nation-state at the opening of the twentieth century?*

■ FOR FURTHER EXPLORATION

For further reading and online research ideas, see the Suggested References on page SR-12 at the back of the book.

For practice quizzes, a customized study plan, and other study tools, see the ONLINE STUDY GUIDE at bedfordstmartins.com/huntconcise.

For primary-source material from this period, see Chapter 24 in SOURCES OF THE MAKING OF THE WEST: A CONCISE HISTORY, Second Edition.

Suggested References

CHAPTER I

Foundations of Western Civilization, to 500 B.C.E.

Archaeological excavation is our best resource for understanding the long period of history from the Stone Age to the rise of the Greek city-state.

Ancient Near Eastern sites: http://www.etana.org/abzu
Ancient Olympic Games: http://www.perseus.tufts.edu/Olympics
*Barnes, Jonathan. *Early Greek Philosophy*. 1987.
Brosius, Maria. *Women in Ancient Persia (559–331 B.C.)*. 1996.
Bryce, Trevor. *The Kingdom of the Hittites*. 1998.
*Dalley, Stephanie, trans. *Myths from Mesopotamia: Creation, the Flood, Gilgamesh, and Others*. 1991.
Ehrenberg, Margaret. *Women in Prehistory*. 1989.
Fisher, Nick, and Hans van Wees, eds. *Archaic Greece: New Approaches and Evidence*. 1998.
Hunt, Norman Bancroft. *Historical Atlas of Ancient Mesopotamia*. 2004.
Nigosian, S. A. *The Zoroastrian Faith: Tradition and Modern Research*. 1993.
Osborne, Robin. *Greece in the Making, 1200–479 B.C.* 1996.
Redford, Donald B., ed. *The Oxford Encyclopedia of Ancient Egypt*. 2000.
Van de Mieroop, Marc. *A History of the Ancient Near East c. 3000–323 B.C.* 2003.
Virtual Museum of Nautical Archaeology (including the Uluburun shipwreck):
   http://ina.tamu.edu/vm.htm

CHAPTER 2

The Greek Golden Age, c. 500–400 B.C.E.

A major challenge in studying the Greek Golden Age is to understand how the period's nearly constant wars affected every part of life.

Davidson, James. *Courtesans and Fishcakes: The Consuming Passions of Classical Athens*. 1998.
Easterling, P. E., and J. V. Muir, eds. *Greek Religion and Society*. 1985.
Ferguson, John. *Morals and Values in Ancient Greece*. 1989.
Fisher, N. R. E. *Slavery in Classical Greece*. 1995.
Greek daily life: http://www.museum.upenn.edu/Greek_World/index2.html

*Primary sources are indicated with an asterisk.

Green, Peter. *The Greco-Persian Wars.* 1996.

Hanson, Victor Davis. *The Other Greeks: The Family Farm and the Agrarian Roots of Western Civilization.* 1995.

Lazenby, J. F. *The Spartan Army.* 1985.

*Lefkowitz, Mary R., and Maureen B. Fant, eds. *Women's Life in Greece and Rome: A Source Book in Translation.* 1982.

Martin, Thomas R. *Ancient Greece: From Prehistoric to Hellenistic Times.* 2000.

Parthenon: http://www.perseus.tufts.edu/cgi-bin/vor?lookup=parthenon&collection=

Patterson, Cynthia B. *The Family in Greek History.* 1998.

Pollitt, J. J. *Art and Experience in Classical Greece.* 1972.

Samons II, Loren J. *What's Wrong with Democracy? From Athenian Practice to American Worship.* 2004.

*Strassler, Robert B., ed. *The Landmark Thucydides: A Comprehensive Guide to the Peloponnesian War.* 1996.

CHAPTER 3

From the Classical to the Hellenistic World, c. 400–30 B.C.E.

Research on the transition from the Classical to the Hellenistic Mediterranean world focuses on the imaginative ways in which rulers, thinkers, and artists combined the old and the new, the familiar and the foreign, in the multicultural environment that emerged from the conquests of Alexander the Great.

Ancient Alexandria in Egypt: http://ce.eng.usf.edu/pharos/alexandria

Barnes, Jonathan. *Aristotle.* 1982.

Chauveau, Michel. *Egypt in the Age of Cleopatra.* Trans. David Lorton. 2000.

Collins, John J. *Between Athens and Jerusalem: Jewish Identity in the Hellenistic Diaspora.* 2d ed. 2000.

Gosling, J. C. B. *Plato.* 1973.

Hamilton, J. R. *Alexander the Great.* 1973.

Pomeroy, Sarah B. *Women in Hellenistic Egypt: From Alexander to Cleopatra.* Rev. ed. 1990.

Rogers, Guy MacLean. *Alexander: The Ambiguity of Greatness.* 2004.

*Roisman, Joseph. *Alexander the Great: Ancient and Modern Perspectives.* 1995.

Sharples, R. W. *Stoics, Epicureans, and Sceptics: An Introduction to Hellenistic Philosophy.* 1996.

Shipley, Graham. *The Greek World after Alexander, 323–30 B.C.* 2000.

*Snyder, Jane M. *The Woman and the Lyre: Women Writers in Classical Greece and Rome.* 1989.

Witt, R. E. *Isis in the Greco-Roman World.* 1971.

*Xenophon. *The Persian Expedition.* Trans. Rex Warner. 1950.

CHAPTER 4

The Rise of Rome, c. 753–44 B.C.E.

Our knowledge of the political and economic changes in the Roman republic is being revised by archaeological research linked to close study of the ancient literary sources.

Beard, Mary, et al. *Religions of Rome.* 2 vols. 1998.

Bonfante, Larissa, ed. *Etruscan Life and Afterlife: A Handbook of Etruscan Studies.* 1986.

Bradley, Keith. *Slavery and Society at Rome.* 1994.

*Caesar. *The Civil War.* Trans. John Carter. 1997.

*Cicero. *Philippic Orations.* Trans. Walter C. Ker. 1969.

Daily life (and more): http://www.vroma.org/~bmcmanus/romanpages.html

Earl, Donald. *The Moral and Political Tradition of Rome.* 1967.

Forsyth, Gary. *A Critical History of Early Rome: From Prehistory to the First Punic War.* 2005.

Gardner, Jane. *Women in Roman Law and Society.* 1986.

Goldsworthy, Adrian. *The Punic Wars.* 2000.
Ladder of offices (*cursus honorum*): http://www.vroma.org/~bmcmanus/romangvt.html
Lancel, Serge. *Carthage: A History.* Trans. Antonia Nevill. 1995.
Rosenstein, Nathan. *Rome at War: Farms, Families, and Death in the Middle Republic.* 2004.
Strong, Donald. *Roman Art.* 2d ed. 1988.
Williams, Craig A. *Roman Homosexuality: Ideologies of Masculinity in Classical Antiquity.* 1999.

CHAPTER 5
The Roman Empire, c. 44 B.C.E.–284 C.E.

Modern scholarly work on the principate reveals how the emperors tried to create political legitimacy and social stability through a combination of military, religious, and artistic policy.

Doran, Robert. *Birth of a World View: Early Christianity in Its Jewish and Pagan Contexts.* 1999.
Futrell, Alison. *Blood in the Arena: The Spectacle of Roman Power.* 1997.
Galinsky, Karl. *Augustan Culture.* 1996.
Garnsey, Peter, and Richard Saller. *The Roman Empire: Economy, Society, and Culture.* 1987.
George, Michele, ed. *The Roman Family in the Empire: Rome, Italy, and Beyond.* 2005.
Jackson, Ralph. *Doctors and Diseases in the Roman Empire.* 1988.
*Kraemer, Ross Shephard. *Her Share of the Blessings: Women's Religion among Pagans, Jews, and Christians in the Greco-Roman World.* 1992.
MacMullen, Ramsay. *Christianizing the Roman Empire (A.D. 100–400).* 1984.
Potter, D. S., and D. J. Mattingly, eds. *Life, Death, and Entertainment in the Roman Empire.* 1999.
Roman emperors: http://www.roman-emperors.org
*Suetonius. *The Twelve Caesars.* Trans. Robert Graves. 2003.
Torjesen, Karen Jo. *When Women Were Priests: Women's Leadership in the Early Church and the Scandal of Their Subordination in the Rise of Christianity.* 1993.
Treggiari, Susan. *Roman Marriage: Iusti Coniuges from the Time of Cicero to the Time of Ulpian.* 1991.
Webster, Graham. *The Roman Imperial Army of the First and Second Centuries A.D.* 3d ed. 1985.
Wiedemann, Thomas. *Emperors and Gladiators.* 1995.

CHAPTER 6
The Transformation of the Roman Empire, c. 284–c. 600 C.E.

Recent research has deepened our appreciation of the complexity of the religious transformation of the Roman Empire and the emotional depths that the process stirred up for polytheists and Christians.

Brown, Peter. *The Body and Society: Men, Women, and Sexual Renunciation in Early Christianity.* 1988.
Burns, Thomas. *Barbarians within the Gates of Rome: A Study of Roman Military Policy and the Barbarians, ca. 375–425 A.D.* 1994.
Cavallo, Guglielmo, ed. *The Byzantines.* 1997.
Corcoran, Simon. *The Empire of the Tetrarchs: Imperial Pronouncements and Government, A.D. 284–324.* Rev. ed. 2000.
*Drew, Katherine Fischer. *The Laws of the Salian Franks.* 1991.
*Early Christian literature: http://www.voskrese.info/spl/index.html
Elsner, Jaś. *Imperial Rome and Christian Triumph: The Art of the Roman Empire, A.D. 100–450.* 1998.
Heather, Peter. *The Fall of the Roman Empire.* 2005.
MacMullen, Ramsay. *Christianity and Paganism in the Fourth to Eighth Centuries.* 1997.
Potter, David. *The Roman Empire at Bay A.D. 180–395.* 2004.
Rapp, Claudia. *Holy Bishops in Late Antiquity: The Nature of Christian Leadership in an Age of Transition.* 2005.

Rousseau, Philip. *Pachomius: The Making of a Community in Fourth-Century Egypt.* 1985.
Southern, Pat, and Karen R. Dixon. *The Late Roman Army.* 1996.
Ward-Perkins, Bryan. *The Fall of Rome: And the End of Civilization.* 2005.
Women in Byzantine history bibliography: http://www.wooster.edu/Art/wb.html

CHAPTER 7
The Heirs of the Roman Empire, 600–750

Haldon and Whittow are excellent guides to early Byzantine history; Wood and Geary emphasize different aspects of the Merovingian world. Sells's lyrical translations and commentaries illuminate the Qur'an, and the book includes an audio CD of Qur'an recitations.

Ahmed, Leila. *Women and Gender in Islam: Historical Roots of a Modern Debate.* 1992.
*Bede. *A History of the English Church and People.* Trans. Leo Sherley-Price. 1991.
The Byzantine Studies Page: http://www.fordham.edu/halsall/byzantium
Charles-Edwards, T. M. *Early Christian Ireland.* 2001.
*Fouracre, Paul, and Richard A. Gerberding, eds. *Late Merovingian France: History and Hagiography, 640–720.* 1996.
Geary, Patrick. *Before France and Germany: The Creation and Transformation of the Merovingian World.* 1988.
*Gregory of Tours. *The History of the Franks.* Trans. Lewis Thorpe. 1976.
Haldon, J. F. *Byzantium in the Seventh Century: The Transformation of a Culture.* 1990.
Islamic Sourcebook: http://www.fordham.edu/halsall/islam/islamsbook.html
Kennedy, Hugh. *The Prophet and the Age of the Caliphates: The Islamic Near East from the Sixth to the Eleventh Century.* 2d ed. 2004.
*Murray, Alexander C., ed. and trans. *From Roman to Merovingian Gaul: A Reader.* 2000.
Ousterhout, Robert, and Leslie Brubaker. *The Sacred Image East and West.* 1995.
*Sells, Michael, trans. *Approaching the Qur'an: The Early Revelations.* 1999.
Whittow, Mark. *The Making of Byzantium, 600–1025.* 1996.
Wood, Ian. *The Merovingian Kingdoms, 450–751.* 1994.

CHAPTER 8
Unity and Diversity in Three Societies, 750–1050

Compare Barbero's picture of Charlemagne with Nelson's view of Charles the Bald. Many primary sources for the Carolingian period are translated by Paul Dutton. Political disintegration used to be seen as a bad thing, but recent historians, such as Berkey, Duby, Head, Landes, and Glick, value the diversity and local developments that it permitted.

Barbero, Alessandro. *Charlemagne: Father of a Continent.* Trans. Allan Cameron. 2004.
Berkey, Jonathan P. *The Formation of Islam: Religion and Society in the Near East, 600–1800.* 2003.
Byzantine art: http://witcombe.sbc.edu/ARTHmedieval.html#Byzantine
Duby, Georges. *The Early Growth of the European Economy: Warriors and Peasants from the Seventh to the Twelfth Century.* Trans. H. B. Clark. 1974.
*Dutton, Paul Edward. *Carolingian Civilization: A Reader.* 2d ed. 2004.
Franklin, Simon, and Jonathan Shepard. *The Emergence of Rus, 750–1200.* 1996.
Garland, Lynda. *Byzantine Empresses: Women and Power in Byzantium, A.D. 527–1204.* 1999.
Glick, Thomas. *Islamic and Christian Spain in the Early Middle Ages: Comparative Perspectives on Social and Cultural Formation.* 1979.
Head, Thomas, and Richard Landes, eds. *The Peace of God: Social Violence and Religious Response in France around the Year 1000.* 1992.

Lawson, M. K. *Cnut: The Danes in England in the Early Eleventh Century.* 1993.

McCormick, Michael. *Origins of the European Economy: Communications and Commerce,*
    A.D. *300–900.* 2001.

Medieval and Renaissance manuscripts: http://www.columbia.edu/cu/libraries/indiv/rare/images

Nelson, Janet. *Charles the Bald.* 1987.

*Psellus, Michael. *Fourteen Byzantine Rulers: The Chronographia.* Trans. E. R. A. Sewter. 1966.

Reuter, Timothy. *Germany in the Early Middle Ages, c. 800–1056.* 1991.

Treadgold, Warren. *The Byzantine Revival, 780–842.* 1988.

CHAPTER 9
Renewal and Reform, 1050–1200

Clanchy is excellent on both Abelard and Heloise. The Hildegard of Bingen Web site offers numerous links to her work and works about her. Curiosity about the Crusades has never waned, but Holt shows that there is new interest in their impact.

Clanchy, Michael. *Abelard: A Medieval Life.* 1997.

*The Crusades: http://www.fordham.edu/halsall/sbook1k.html

Daniell, Christopher. *From Norman Conquest to Magna Carta: England, 1066–1215.* 2003.

Epstein, Steven. *Wage Labor and Guilds in Medieval Europe.* 1991.

Glick, Leonard B. *Abraham's Heirs: Jews and Christians in Medieval Europe.* 1999.

Hildegard of Bingen: http://www.healingchants.com/hvb_links.html

Hildegard von Bingen: Ordo virtutum, Deutsche Harmonia Mundi CD, 77394 (music from Hildegard's
    Scivias and the expanded play at its end).

Holt, P. M. *The Crusader States and Their Neighbours, 1098–1291.* 2004.

Hudson, John. *The Formation of the English Common Law: Law and Society in England from the Norman
    Conquest to Magna Carta.* 1996.

Letters of Abelard and Heloise. Trans. Betty Radice. 1974. Includes *History of My Calamities.*

Little, Lester K. *Religious Poverty and the Profit Economy in Medieval Europe.* 1978.

*Lopez, Robert S., and Irving W. Raymond, eds. *Medieval Trade in the Mediterranean World.* 1955.

*Miller, Maureen C., ed. and trans. *Power and the Holy in the Age of the Investiture Conflict: A Brief
    History with Documents.* 2005.

Moore, R. I. *The First European Revolution, c. 970–1215.* 2000.

*Otto of Freising. *The Deeds of Frederick Barbarossa.* Trans. C. C. Mierow. 1953.

Riley-Smith, Jonathan. *The Crusades. A Short History.* 1987.

CHAPTER 10
An Age of Confidence, 1200–1340

Bartlett and Christiansen take up the physical expansion of Europe, while Dante and Thomas Aquinas demonstrate its intellectual range. Bynum deftly ties together religious, theological, and gender issues. The politics of the period always had religious implications, and religious movements always had political ramifications, as Jordan, R. I. Moore, and John C. Moore show in different ways.

Bartlett, Robert. *The Making of Europe: Conquest, Colonization, and Cultural Change,*
    950–1350. 1993.

Boyle, John A. *The Mongol World Empire, 1206–1370.* 1977.

Bynum, Caroline Walker. *Holy Feast and Holy Fast: The Religious Significance of Food to Medieval
    Women.* 1987.

Christiansen, Eric. *The Northern Crusades.* 2d ed. 1997.

*Dante. *The Divine Comedy.* Many editions; recommended are translations by Mark Musa, John Ciardi,
    and Robert Pinsky.

*Fourth Lateran Council: http://www.fordham.edu/halsall/basis/lateran4.html

Jones, Philip J. *The Italian City-State: From Commune to Signoria.* 1997.

Jordan, William Chester. *The French Monarchy and the Jews: From Philip Augustus to the Last Capetians.* 1989.

Moore, John C. *Pope Innocent III (1160/61–1216): To Root Up and to Plant.* 2003.

Moore, R. I. *The Formation of a Persecuting Society: Power and Deviance in Western Europe, 950–1250.* 1987.

O'Callaghan, Joseph F. *The Cortes of Castile-León, 1188–1350.* 1989.

*Polo, Marco. *The Travels.* Trans. Ronald Latham. 1958.

Rubin, Miri. *Corpus Christi: The Eucharist in Late Medieval Culture.* 1991.

*Thomas Aquinas: http://www.fordham.edu/halsall/source/aquinas1.html (Questions 1 and 2 from the *Summa Theologiae*)

*William of Puylaurens. *The Chronicle of William of Puylaurens: The Albigensian Crusade and Its Aftermath*, trans. W. A. Sibly and M. D. Sibly. 2003.

CHAPTER 11
Crisis and Renaissance, 1340–1500

The old view associated the Renaissance primarily with Florence, but now the Renaissance is seen as a European movement (Kirkpatrick; *The Renaissance in Europe*) and even part of Ottoman culture (Jardine and Brotton). Similarly, the traditional view of "Europe discovering the world" has been replaced by a more nuanced and complex discussion that includes non-European views and uses Asian, African, and Mesoamerican sources.

Aberth, John. *From the Brink of the Apocalypse: Confronting Famine, War, Plague, and Death in the Later Middle Ages.* 2001.

Bisaha, Nancy. *Creating East and West: Renaissance Humanists and the Ottoman Turks.* 2004.

The Black Death. Ed. and trans. Rosemary Horrox. 1994.

Crabb, Ann. *The Strozzi of Florence: Widowhood and Family Solidarity in the Renaissance.* 2000.

Epstein, Steven A. *Speaking of Slavery: Color, Ethnicity, and Human Bondage in Italy.* 2001.

*Froissart, Jean. *Chronicles.* Trans. Geoffrey Brereton. 1968.

Jardine, Lisa, and Jerry Brotton. *Global Interests: Renaissance Art between East and West.* 2000.

Jordan, William Chester. *The Great Famine: Northern Europe in the Early Fourteenth Century.* 1996.

Kirkpatrick, Robin. *The European Renaissance, 1400–1600.* 2002.

Nirenberg, David. *Communities of Violence: Persecution of Minorities in the Middle Ages.* 1996.

Plague and public health in Renaissance Europe: http://jefferson.village.virginia.edu/osheim/intro.html

Renaissance art links: http://witcombe.sbc.edu/ARTHLinks2.html

The Renaissance in Europe: An Anthology. Eds. Peter Elmer, Nicholas Webb, and Roberta Wood. 2000.

Russell-Wood, A. J. R. *A World on the Move: The Portuguese in Africa, Asia, and America, 1415–1808.* 1992.

Thomas, Hugh. *Rivers of Gold: The Rise of the Spanish Empire, from Columbus to Magellan.* 2003.

CHAPTER 12
Struggles over Beliefs, 1500–1648

Painstaking archival research has enabled historians to reconstruct the demographic, economic, and social history of this period. Recently, attention has focused more specifically on women, the family, and the early history of slavery.

Ashton, Trevor H., ed. *Crisis in Europe.* 1965.

Bonney, Richard. *The Thirty Years' War.* 2002.

Bouwsma, William J. *John Calvin: A Sixteenth-Century Portrait.* 1988.

Carney, Jo Eldridge, ed. *Renaissance and Reformation, 1500–1620: A Biographical Dictionary*. 2001.
*Essential Works of Erasmus. Ed. W. T. H. Jackson. 1965.
The Galileo Project: http://galileo.rice.edu
*Hillerbrand, Hans J., ed. *The Protestant Reformation*. 1969.
Holt, Mack P. *The French Wars of Religion, 1562–1629*. 1995.
Hsia, R. Po-chia. *The World of the Catholic Renewal*. 1997.
Jacob, James. *The Scientific Revolution*. 1998.
Kamen, Henry. *Philip of Spain*. 1997.
Martin Luther's life and thought: http://www.luther.de/en
Mattingly, Garrett. *The Defeat of the Spanish Armada*. 2d ed. 1988.

CHAPTER 13
State Building and the Search for Order, 1648–1690

Recent studies have insisted that absolutism could never be entirely absolute because the king depended on collaboration to enforce his policies. Some of the best sources for Louis XIV's reign are the letters written by important noblewomen.

Barkey, Karen. *The Ottoman Route to State Centralization*. 1994.
*Beik, William. *Louis XIV and Absolutism: A Brief Study with Documents*. 2000.
Collins, James B. *The State in Early Modern France*. 1995.
Davis, Natalie Zemon. *Women on the Margins: Three Seventeenth-Century Lives*. 1995.
*Forster, Elborg, trans. *A Woman's Life in the Court of the Sun King: Elisabeth Charlotte, Duchesse d'Orléans*. 1984.
Gaunt, Peter, ed. *The English Civil War: The Essential Readings*. 2000.
Hill, Christopher. *The World Turned Upside Down: Radical Ideas during the English Revolution*. 1972.
Israel, Jonathan. *Dutch Primacy in World Trade, 1585–1740*. 1989.
Kivelson, Valerie A. *Autocracy in the Provinces: The Muscovite Gentry and Political Culture in the Seventeenth Century*. 1996.
*Pincus, Steven Carl Anthony. *England's Glorious Revolution and the Origins of Liberalism: A Documentary History of Later Stuart England*. 1998.

CHAPTER 14
The Atlantic System and Its Consequences, 1690–1740

Historians have become increasingly interested in the workings of the Atlantic system in recent years. The definitive study of the early Enlightenment is the book by Hazard, but many others have contributed biographies of individual figures, or, more recently, studies of women writers.

Age of Enlightenment: http://www.fordham.edu/halsall/mod/modsbook10.html
Blackburn, Robin. *The Making of New World Slavery: From the Baroque to the Modern, 1492–1800*. 1997.
Brewer, John. *The Sinews of Power: War, Money, and the English State, 1688–1783*. 1990.
Brockliss, Laurence, and Colin Jones. *The Medical World of Early Modern France*. 1997.
Bushkovitch, Paul. *Peter the Great*. 2001.
Handel's Messiah: The New Interactive Edition (CD-ROM). 1997.
Harms, Robert. *The Diligent: A Voyage Through the Worlds of the Slave Trade*. 2003.
Hazard, Paul. *The European Mind: The Critical Years, 1680–1715*. 1990.
*Hill, Bridget. *The First English Feminist: Reflections upon Marriage and Other Writings by Mary Astell*. 1986.
Hunt, Margaret R. *The Middling Sort: Commerce, Gender, and the Family in England, 1680–1780*. 1996.

CHAPTER 15

The Promise of Enlightenment, 1740–1789

The interpretive study by Gay remains useful, but the Kors volumes offer the most up-to-date views on the Enlightenment. Equiano, a freed slave, provides one of the earliest firsthand views of the experience of slavery, but some scholars now question whether he was born in Africa (and not in the New World).

Darnton, Robert. *The Great Cat Massacre and Other Episodes in French Cultural History.* 1984.
*Equiano, Olaudah. *The Interesting Narrative and Other Writings.* Ed. Vincent Carretta. 1995.
Gay, Peter. *The Enlightenment: An Interpretation.* 2 vols. 1966, 1969.
Goodman, Dena. *The Republic of Letters: A Cultural History of the French Enlightenment.* 1994.
Hull, Isabel V. *Sexuality, State, and Civil Society in Germany, 1700–1815.* 1996.
*Jacob, Margaret C. *The Enlightenment: A Brief History with Selected Readings.* 2000.
Kors, Alan Charles, ed. *Encyclopedia of the Enlightenment.* 4 vols. 2003.
McMahon, Darrin M. *Enemies of the Enlightenment: The French Counter-Enlightenment and the Making of Modernity.* 2001.
Mozart Project: http://www.mozartproject.org
Palmer, R. R. *The Age of Democratic Revolution: A Political History of Europe and America, 1760–1800.* Vol. 1, *The Challenge.* 1959.
*Rakove, Jack N. *Declaring Rights: A Brief History with Documents.* 1998.
Showalter, Dennis E. *The Wars of Frederick the Great.* 1996.
Slave movement during the eighteenth and nineteenth centuries: http://dpls.dacc.wisc.edu/slavedata
Thompson, E. P. *Whigs and Hunters: The Origin of the Black Act.* 1975.
Venturi, Franco. *The End of the Old Regime in Europe, 1768–1776: The First Crisis.* Trans. R. Burr Litchfield. 1989.
*Voltaire. *Candide.* Ed. and trans. Daniel Gordon. 1999.
Voltaire Foundation: http://www.voltaire.ox.ac.uk

CHAPTER 16

The French Revolution and Napoleon, 1789–1815

The most influential book on the meaning of the French Revolution is still the classic study by Tocqueville, who insisted that the Revolution continued the process of state centralization undertaken by the monarchy. Recent works on Napoleon show how powerfully his armies affected every European state.

*Arnold, Eric A., Jr., ed. *A Documentary Survey of Napoleonic France.* 1994.
Beaucour, Fernand Emile, Yves Laissus, and Chantal Orgogozo. *The Discovery of Egypt.* Trans. Bambi Ballard. 1990.
*Brunn, Geoffrey. *Napoleon and His Empire.* 1972.
Censer, Jack R., and Lynn Hunt. *Liberty, Equality, Fraternity: Exploring the French Revolution* (includes CD-ROM of images and music). 2001. See also the accompanying Web site: http://www.chnm.gmu.edu/revolution
Chartier, Roger. *The Cultural Origins of the French Revolution.* Trans. Lydia G. Cochrane. 1991.
Dubois, Laurent. *Avengers of the New World: The Story of the Haitian Revolution.* 2004.
Englund, Steven. *Napoleon: A Political Life.* 2004.
Furet, François. *Interpreting the French Revolution.* Trans. Elborg Forster. 1981.
Godineau, Dominique. *The Women of Paris and Their French Revolution.* Trans. Katherine Streip. 1998.
*Hunt, Lynn, ed. *The French Revolution and Human Rights: A Brief Documentary History.* 1996.
*Levy, Darline Gay, Harriet Branson Applewhite, and Mary Durham Johnson, eds. *Women in Revolutionary Paris, 1789–1795.* 1979.
Napoleon Foundation: http://www.napoleon.org
Palmer, R. R. *The Age of the Democratic Revolution: A Political History of Europe and America, 1760–1800.* Vol. 2, *The Struggle.* 1964.

Simms, Brendan. *The Impact of Napoleon: Prussian High Politics, Foreign Policy, and the Crisis of the Executive, 1797–1806.* 1997.

Tocqueville, Alexis de. *The Old Regime and the French Revolution.* Trans. Stuart Gilbert. 1955. Originally published 1856.

CHAPTER 17
Industrialization and Social Ferment, 1815–1850

The spread of industrialization has elicited much more historical interest than the process of urbanization because the analysis of industrialization occupied a central role in Marxism. The Web site Gallica, produced by the National Library of France, offers a wealth of imagery and information on French cultural history.

Davidoff, Leonore, and Catherine Hall. *Family Fortunes: Men and Women of the English Middle Class, 1780–1850.* 1987.

The Dickens Project: http://humwww.ucsc.edu/dickens

Gallica: Images and Texts from Nineteenth-Century French-Speaking Culture: http://gallica.bnf.fr

Hobsbawm, E. J. *The Age of Revolution, 1789–1848.* 1996.

Johnson, Paul. *The Birth of the Modern: World Society, 1815–1830.* 1991.

Kahan, Alan S. *Liberalism in Nineteenth-Century Europe: The Political Culture of Limited Suffrage.* 2003.

Kramer, Lloyd S. *Nationalism: Political Cultures in Europe and America, 1775–1865.* 1998.

Laven, David, and Lucy Riall, eds. *Napoleon's Legacy: Problems of Government in Restoration Europe.* 2000.

*Marx, Karl, and Frederick Engels. *The Communist Manifesto: With Related Documents.* Ed. John E. Toews. 1999.

More, Charles. *Understanding the Industrial Revolution.* 2000.

Murray, Christopher John, ed. *Encyclopedia of the Romantic Era, 1760–1850.* 2004.

*Pollard, S., and C. Holmes. *Documents of European Economic History.* Vol. 1, *The Process of Industrialization, 1750–1870.* 1968.

Romantic Chronology: http://english.ucsb.edu:591/rchrono

Schroeder, Paul W. *The Transformation of European Politics, 1763–1848.* 1994.

Sperber, Jonathan. *The European Revolutions, 1848–1851.* 1994.

Thompson, E. P. *The Making of the English Working Class.* 1964.

CHAPTER 18
Constructing the Nation-State, c. 1850–1880

Nation building has produced a varied literature ranging from studies of royalty as unifying figures to histories of the arts and industry.

Blackbourn, David. *Fontana History of Germany, 1780–1918: The Long Nineteenth Century.* 1997.

*Darwin, Charles. *Autobiography.* 1969.

Edgerton, Robert B. *Death or Glory: The Legacy of the Crimean War.* 1999.

Engel, Barbara Alpern. *Between the Fields and the City: Women, Work, and Family in Russia, 1861–1914.* 1994.

Good, David. *The Economic Rise of the Habsburg Empire.* 1984.

Homans, Margaret. *Royal Representations: Queen Victoria and British Culture, 1837–1876.* 1998.

Jordan, David. *Transforming Paris: The Life and Labor of Baron Haussmann.* 1995.

Kaufman, Suzanne. *Consuming Visions: Mass Culture and the Lourdes Shrine.* 2005.

Lebra-Chapman, Joyce. *The Rani of Jhansi: A Study in Female Heroism in India.* 1986.

Marks, Steven G. *Road to Power: The Trans-Siberian Railroad and the Colonization of Asian Russia, 1850–1917.* 1991.

Rappaport, Erika. *Shopping for Pleasure: Women in the Making of London's West End.* 2000.

*Seacole, Mary. *Wonderful Adventures of Mrs. Seacole in Many Lands.* 1857.
Stites, Richard. *Serfdom, Society, and the Arts in Imperial Russia.* 2005.
The Victorian Web: http://www.victorianweb.org

CHAPTER 19

Empire, Modernity, and the Road to War, c. 1880–1914

New studies of imperialism show increasing conquest, the creation of an international economy, and the social and cultural impulses behind it. The University of Pennsylvania's African studies Web site looks at African history, politics, and culture, including this era. New forms of art and philosophy and the rise of mass politics were central to the challenges Europe faced, but the question of why war broke out remains widely debated.

African Studies Center: http://www.sas.upenn.edu/African_Studies/AS.html
*Bonnell, Victoria, ed. *The Russian Worker.* 1983.
Conklin, Alice. *Mission to Civilize: The Republican Idea of Empire, 1895–1930.* 2000.
Duberman, Martin, Martha Vicinus, and George Chauncey Jr. *Hidden from History: Reclaiming the Gay and Lesbian Past.* 1989.
Headrick, Daniel R. *The Tools of Empire: Technology and European Imperialism in the Nineteenth Century.* 1981.
Hermann, David G. *The Arming of Europe and the Making of the First World War.* 1997.
Kornberg, Jacques. *Theodor Herzl: From Assimilation to Zionism.* 1993.
Koven, Seth. *Slumming: Sexual and Social Politics in Victorian London.* 2004.
Marchand, Suzanne, and David Lindenfeld, eds. *Germany at the Fin de Siècle: Culture, Politics, and Ideas.* 2004.
Moch, Leslie Page. *Moving Europeans: Migration in Western Europe since 1650.* 2003.
Nineteenth- and twentieth-century philosophy: http://www.epistemelinks.com/index.asp
Reeder, Linda. *Widows in White: Migration and the Transformation of Rural Italian Women, Sicily, 1880–1920.* 2003.
Roberts, Mary Louise. *Disruptive Acts: The New Woman in Fin-de-Siècle France.* 2002.
Sinha, Mrinalini. *Colonial Masculinity: The "Manly Englishman" and the "Effeminate Bengali" in the Late Nineteenth Century.* 1995.
Weeks, Theodore R. *Nation and State in Late Imperial Russia: Nationalism and Russification on the Western Frontier.* 1996.

CHAPTER 20

War, Revolution, and Reconstruction, 1914–1929

The most recent histories of the Great War consider its military, technological, psychic, social, and economic aspects. This vision of the war as a phenomenon occurring both on and off the battlefield characterizes the newest scholarship. Histories of the war's end show deprivation, ongoing mass slaughter, the eruption of revolution, and the complexities of peacemaking.

Echenberg, Myron. *Colonial Conscripts: The "Tirailleurs Sénégalais" in French West Africa, 1857–1960.* 1990.
Harsch, Donna. *German Social Democracy and the Rise of Nazism.* 1994.
*Hasek, Jaroslav. *The Good Soldier Schweik.* 1920.
Healy, Maureen. *Vienna and the Fall of the Habsburg Empire: Total War and Everyday Life in World War I.* 2004.
Kent, Susan. *Making Peace: The Reconstruction of Gender in Postwar Britain.* 1994.
*Kollontai, Alexsandra. *Love of Worker Bees.* 1923.
Liulevicius, Vejas Gabriel. *War Land on the Eastern Front: Culture, National Identity and German Occupation in World War I.* 2000.

Makaman, Douglas, and Michael Mays, eds. *World War I and the Cultures of Modernity.* 2000.

Nolan, Mary. *Visions of Modernity: American Business and the Modernization of Germany.* 1994.

Panchasi, Roxanne. "Reconstructions: Prosthetics and the Rehabilitation of the Male Body in World War I." *Differences.* 1995.

Robb, George. *British Culture and the First World War.* 2002.

Roshwald, Aviel. *Ethnic Nationalism and the Fall of Empires: Central Europe, Russia and the Middle East, 1914–1923.* 2001.

Smith, Leonard. *Between Mutiny and Obedience: The Case of the French Fifth Infantry Division during World War I.* 1994.

Winter, Jay, and Jean-Louis Robert, eds. *Capital Cities at War: Paris, London, Berlin, 1914–1919.* 1997.

World War I Documents Archive: http://www.lib.byu.edu/%7Erdh/wwi

CHAPTER 21

An Age of Catastrophes, 1929–1945

The vicious dictators Stalin, Hitler, and Mussolini and the intricacies of World War II are among the most popular subjects for historians and readers alike. Recent historical works have moved beyond this fascination to investigate their mobilization of art and the mass media and to consider people's own engagement with totalitarian regimes.

Ben-Ghiat, Ruth. *Fascist Modernities: Italy, 1922–1945.* 2001.

Burleigh, Michael. *The Third Reich: A New History.* 2000.

Chickering, Roger, et al., eds. *A World at Total War: Global Conflict and the Politics of Destruction, 1937–1945.* 2005.

*Dawidowicz, Lucy S., ed. *A Holocaust Reader.* 1976.

Engel, Barbara Alpern, and Anastasia Posadskaya-Vanderbeck, eds. *A Revolution of Their Own: Voices of Women in Soviet History.* 1998.

Fink, Carole. *Defending the Rights of Others: The Great Powers, the Jews, and International Minority Protection, 1878–1938.* 2004.

Helstosky, Carol. *Garlic and Oil: The Politics of Food in Italy.* 2004.

Petrone, Karen. *Life Has Become More Joyous, Comrades: Celebrations in the Time of Stalin.* 2000.

Rose, Sonya O. *Which People's War: National Identity and Citizenship, 1939–1945.* 2003.

Rothermund, Dietmar. *The Global Impact of the Great Depression, 1929–1939.* 1996.

Siegel, Mona L. *The Moral Disarmament of France: Education, Pacifism, and Patriotism, 1914–1940.* 2004.

South Asia and Gandhi: http://www.columbia.edu/cu/libraries/indiv/area/sarai

Stolzfus, Nathan. *Resistance of the Heart: Intermarriage and the Rosenstrasse Protest in Nazi Germany.* 1996.

U.S. Holocaust Museum: http://www.ushmm.org

Weinberg, Gerhard. *A World at Arms: A Global History of World War II.* 1994.

CHAPTER 22

Remaking Europe in the Shadow of Cold War, c. 1945–1965

In the past decade, the opening of Soviet archives and closer research in American records have allowed for more informed views of the diplomacy and politics of the cold war. The cold war Web site contains biographies of the main players, time lines, and miscellaneous details of cold war events.

Cold war: http://history.sandiego.edu/gen/20th/coldwar0.html

Cronin, James. *The World the Cold War Made: Order, Chaos, and the Return of History.* 1996.

De Grazia, Victoria. *Irresistible Empire: America's Advance through 20th-Century Europe.* 2005.

*Fanon, Frantz. *The Wretched of the Earth.* 1961.

Gaddis, John. *The Cold War: A New History.* 2006.

Heineman, Elizabeth D. *What Difference Does a Husband Make? Women and Marital Status in Nazi and Postwar Germany.* 1999.

Judt, Tony. *Postwar: A History of Europe Since 1945.* 2006.

McIntyre, W. David. *British Decolonization, 1946–1997: When, Why, and How Did the British Empire Fall?* 1999.

Milward, Alan S. *The United Kingdom and the Economic Community.* 2002.

Moeller, Robert, ed. *West Germany under Construction: Politics, Society, and Culture in the Adenauer Era.* 1997.

Naimark, Norman, and Leonid Gbianshii, eds. *The Establishment of Communist Regimes in Eastern Europe.* 1997.

*Pasternak, Boris. *Doctor Zhivago.* 1958.

Poiger, Uta. *Jazz, Rock, and Rebels: Cold War Politics and American Culture in a Divided Germany.* 2000.

Zubkova, Elena. *Russia after the War: Hopes, Illusions, and Disappointments, 1945–1957.* 1998.

CHAPTER 23

Postindustrial Society and the End of the Cold War Order, 1965–1989

Wartime technological development had profound consequences for the peacetime lives of individuals and for society. Technology created a postindustrial workplace, changing work and social life. The strains of an interlocked technological society along with citizen activism ultimately brought down the Soviet empire.

*Altbach, Edith Hoshino, et al., eds. *German Feminism: Readings in Politics and Literature.* 1984.

Bauer, Martin W., and George Gaskell, eds. *Biotechnology: The Making of a Global Controversy.* 2002.

*Dubček, Alexander. *Hope Dies Last: The Autobiography of Alexander Dubček.* 1993.

Fink, Carole, et al. *1968: The World Transformed.* 1998.

Green parties worldwide: http://www.greens.org

Hecht, Gabrielle. *The Radiance of France: Nuclear Power and National Identity after World War II.* 1998.

Kenney, Padraic. *Carnival of Revolution: Central Europe 1989.* 2002.

Koshar, Rudy. *Germany's Transient Pasts: Preservation and National Memory in the Twentieth Century.* 1998.

Kotkin, Steven. *Armageddon Averted: Soviet Collapse 1970–2000.* 2001.

The Martin Luther King Jr. Papers Project at Stanford University: http://www.stanford.edu/group/King

Reiton, Earl A. *The Thatcher Revolution: Margaret Thatcher, John Major, Tony Blair, and the Transformation of Modern Britain.* 2002.

Rosenfeld, Alla, and Norton T. Dodge. *From Gulag to Glasnost: Nonconformist Art from the Soviet Union.* 1995.

Suri, Jeremy. *Power and Protest: Global Revolution and the Rise of Detente.* 2003.

Varon, Jeremy. *Bringing the War Home: The Weather Underground, the Red Army Faction, and Revolutionary Violence in the Sixties and Seventies.* 2004.

Williams, Walter L., and Yolanda Retter. *Gay and Lesbian Rights in the United States: A Documentary History.* 2003.

CHAPTER 24

The New Globalism: Opportunities and Dilemmas, 1989 to the Present

Historians see the challenges since 1989 as enormously diverse, ranging from conditions in the environment to issues of leadership in international affairs to the safety of the world's citizens in a global age. However, as Rives and Yousefi show, challenges such as the globalization of work have benefits as well as costs.

Applegate, Celia. "A Europe of Regions: Reflections on the Historiography of Sub-National Places in Modern Times." *American Historical Review* 104 (1999): 1157–82.

Bales, Kevin. *Disposable People: New Slavery in the Global Economy.* 1999.

Bess, Michael. *The Light-Green Society: Economic and Technological Modernity in France.* 2003.

Engel, Barbara. *Women in Russian History, 1700–2000.* 2004.

Feshbach, Murray. *Ecological Disaster: Cleaning Up the Hidden Legacy of the Soviet Regime.* 1995.

*Gorbachev, Mikhail. *Memoirs.* 1996.

Hoerder, Dirk. *Cultures in Contact: World Migrations in the 2nd Millennium.* 2002.

Iriye, Akira. *Cultural Internationalism and World Order.* 1997.

Public Broadcasting Service: http://www.pbs.org

Rashid, Ahmed. *Jihad: The Rise of Militant Islam in Central Asia.* 2002.

Redmond, John, and Glenda S. Rosenthal. *The Expanding European Union: Past, Present, Future.* 1998.

Rives, Janet, and Mahmood Yousefi. *Economic Dimensions of Gender Inequality: A Global Perspective.* 1997.

Smith, Andrea, ed. *Europe's Invisible Migrants.* 2002.

UN population data: http://www.unfpa.org/swp/swpmain.htm

Wachtel, Andrew B. *Making a Nation, Breaking a Nation: Literature and Cultural Politics in Yugoslavia.* 1998.

Additional Acknowledgments

Chapter 1, page 18: Figure 1.2: Egyptian Hieroglyphs. Print of chart from *Detail of Book of the Dead–18th Dynasty. Tomb of Thutmosis III, Valley of the Kings.* Reproduced by permission of Bridgeman-Giraudon/Art Resource, NY.

Chapter 2, page 84: Taking Measure: Military Forces of Athens and Sparta at the Beginning of the Peloponnesian War. From *Ancient Greece: Using Evidence* by Pamela Bradley. Published 1990 by Edward Arnold Publishers.

Chapter 4, page 151: Taking Measure: Census Records of Adult Male Roman Citizens during the First and Second Punic Wars. From *An Economic Survey of Ancient Rome*, Vol. 1, by Frank Tenney. Originally published in 1959 by Pageant Books/Hamish Hamilton (Ltd). Reprinted by permission of The Johns Hopkins University Press.

Chapter 5, page 207: Taking Measure: The Value of Roman Imperial Coinage, 27 B.C.E–300 C.E. Print of Roman Imperial Silver Coinage chart. From *The Archeology of the Roman Empire* by Kevin Greene. Originally published by Salamander Books Limited (B. T. Batsford Ltd., 1986).

Chapter 8, page 321: Taking Measure: Viking Coin Hoards, c. 865–895. From *An Atlas of Anglo-Saxon England* by David Hill.

Chapter 9, page 376: Figure 9.2: Floor Plan of a Cistercian Monastery. Adaptation of three figures (8a, 8b, and 8c) from p. 75 in *Monasteries of Western Europe: The Architecture of the Orders* by Wolfgang Braunfels. Princeton University Press, 1972, p. 75. Reprinted courtesy of DuMont Literatur und Kunst Verlag.

Chapter 10, page 393: Taking Measure: Sentences Imposed by an Inquisitor, 1308–1323. From J. Given, "A Medieval Inquisitor at Work," in *Portraits of Medieval and Renaissance Living* by Samuel K. Cohn Jr. and Steven A. Epstein. Copyright © 1996. Reprinted with permission from the University of Michigan Press. **Page 417:** Figure 10.1: Elements of a Gothic Cathedral. From *Gothic Art: Glorious Visions* by Michael Camille. Abrams, 1996.

Chapter 11, page 429: Taking Measure: Population Losses and the Plague, 1340–1450. From *Fontana Economic History of Europe: The Middle Ages* edited by Carlo M. Cipolla. Originally published by HarperCollins/Fontana Books, 1974, p. 36.

Chapter 12, page 504: Taking Measure: The Rise and Fall of Silver Imports to Spain, 1550–1660. From *American Revolution and the Price Revolution in Spain, 1501–1650*, edited by Earl J. Hamilton. Courtesy of Harvard University Press.

Chapter 13, page 534: Taking Measure: The Seventeenth-Century Army. *Armées et societiés en Europe de 1494 à 1789* by André Corvisier. Universitaires de France, 1976, 126. Reprinted with permission of the publisher.

Chapter 14, page 571: Figure 14.1: African Slaves Imported into American Territories, 1701–1810. From *The Atlantic Slave Trade: A Census* by Philip D. Curtin. © 1969. Reprinted by permission of The University of Wisconsin Press. **Page 579:** Taking Measure: Relationship of Crop Harvested to Seed Used, 1400–1800. From *World Trade since 1431: Geography, Technology, and Capitalism* by Peter J. Hugill. © 1993. Reprinted with the permission of The Johns Hopkins University Press.

Chapter 17, page 708: Taking Measure: Railroad Lines, 1830–1850. From *European Historical Statistics, 1750–1970* by B. R. Mitchell. Columbia University Press, 1975. Reprinted by permission.

Chapter 18, page 776: Taking Measure: Decline of Illiteracy, 1850–1900. From *The Birth of New Europe: State and Society in the Nineteenth Century* by Theodore S. Hamerow. Copyright © 1983 by the University of North Carolina Press. Used by permission of the publisher.

Chapter 19, page 812: Taking Measure: Population Growth Worldwide, 1890–1910. From *International Historical Statistics: Africa, Asia, and Oceania 1750–1993*, 3rd ed. By B. R. Mitchell. Macmillan Reference, 1998. Reprinted with permission of the publisher. **Page 817:** Figure 19.1: European Emigration, 1881–1910. Adapted from *International Migrations*, Volume 1: Statistics edited by Walter F. Willcox. Gordon and Breach Science Publishers, 1969. Reprinted by permission.

Chapter 20, page 888: W. B. Yeats. Three lines from "Sailing to Byzantium." From *The Collected Poems of W. B. Yeats*, Volume 1: The Poems, Revised, edited by Richard J. Finneran. Copyright © 1928 by The Macmillan Company. Copyright renewed © 1956 by Georgie Yeats. Reprinted with permission.

Chapter 21, page 908: Anna Akhmatova. Three lines from "Requiem." From *Anna Akhmatova: Poems* by Anna Akhmatova, translated by Lyn Coffin. Copyright © 1983 by Lyn Coffin. Used by permission of W. W. Norton & Company, Inc.

Chapter 22, page 959: Taking Measure: World Manufacturing Output, 1950–1970. From *Hammond Atlas of the Twentieth Century.* Published by Times Books: London, 1987. Reproduced by permission.

Glossary of Key Terms

This glossary of key terms contains definitions of words and ideas that are central to your understanding of the material covered in this textbook. Each term in the glossary is in **boldface** in the text when it is first defined. We have also included the page number on which the full discussion of the term appears so that you can easily locate the complete explanation to strengthen your historical vocabulary.

For words not defined here, two additional resources may be useful: the index, which will direct you to many more topics discussed in the text, and a good dictionary.

Abbasids (296): The caliphal dynasty that came to power in 750. The Abbasids built their capital at Baghdad, where they exercised considerable power over the entire Islamic world until the late ninth century.

absolutism (524): A system of government in which the ruler claimed sole and uncontestable power.

agora (61): The central market square of a Greek city-state; a popular place to gather for conversation.

agricultural revolution (578): Increasingly aggressive attitudes toward investment in and management of land that increased production of food in the 1700s; this revolution developed first in England and then spread to the continent.

Anabaptists (479): Sixteenth-century religious dissenters who believed that humans have free will and that people must knowingly select the Christian faith through rebaptism as adults. They advocated radical separation from society; though originally pacifist, some chose violent paths to religious renewal.

anarchism (782): The belief that people should not have government; it was popular among peasants and workers in the last half of the nineteenth century and the first decades of the twentieth.

Anglo-Saxon England (286): England *after* the invasions of the Angles and Saxons (which began in the 440s) and *before* the Norman conquest in 1066.

apocalypticism (32): A religious belief about the end of the world; literally, "uncovering the future."

apostate (223): Literally, "renegade from the faith"; the emperor Julian (r. 361–363), who rejected Christianity and tried to restore traditional religion as the state religion, was given the nickname "the Apostate."

apostolic succession (201): The principle by which Christian bishops traced their authority back to Jesus' apostles.

appeasement (926): The strategy of preventing a war by making concessions for legitimate grievances.

Arianism (227): The Christian doctrine named after Arius, who argued that Jesus was "begotten" by God and did not have an identical nature with his Father.

art nouveau (827): A successful style in the arts, household and fashion design, and graphics that featured flowing, sinuous lines that contrasted with the mechanical influence of the early twentieth century. It borrowed many of its motifs from Asian and African art and was internationally popular.

asceticism (231): The practice of self-denial of pleasure (from the Greek *askesis*, "training"), as in the lives of monks; a doctrine for Christians emphasized by Augustine.

atheists (613): People who do not believe in the existence of God.

Atlantic system (568): The triangular pattern of trade established in the 1700s that bound together western Europe, Africa, and the Americas. Europeans sold slaves from western Africa and bought commodities such as coffee and sugar that were produced by the new colonial plantations in North and South America and the Caribbean.

auctoritas (175): Literally, "moral authority"; the authority derived from respect on which the Roman princeps' power rested.

Augustus (174): The title meaning "divinely favored" that Rome's Senate granted Octavian and that became shorthand for "Roman imperial ruler."

auto da fé (447): Literally, "demonstration of faith"; the ritual of public confession that was one of the punishments given to heretics by the Inquisition in the fifteenth century.

ban (326): The rights to collect taxes, hear court cases, levy fines, and muster men for defense. It was largely understood as a complex of royal rights, but around 1000, local rulers as well as kings began exercising the ban as well.

baroque (510): An artistic style of the seventeenth century that featured curves, exaggerated lighting, intense emotions, release from restraint, and even a kind of artistic sensationalism; like mannerism, it departed from the Renaissance emphasis on harmonious design, unity, and clarity.

Blitzkrieg (927): Literally, "lightning war"; a strategy for the conduct of war in which motorized firepower quickly and overwhelmingly attacks the enemy, leaving it in a state of shock and awe and unable to resist psychologically or militarily.

buccaneers (575): Pirates of the Caribbean who governed themselves and preyed on international shipping.

bureaucracy (529): A network of state officials carrying out orders according to a regular and routine line of authority.

Byzantine Empire (218): Historians' name for the eastern Roman Empire from about 500 to 1453, derived from Byzantium, the original name of Constantinople.

castellan (326): A person who controlled a castle. After around 1000, these castles were the seats of local power in France.

Chartism (720): The movement of supporters of the People's Charter (drawn up in Britain in 1838), which demanded universal manhood suffrage, vote by secret ballot, equal electoral districts, annual elections, and the elimination of property qualifications for and the payment of stipends to members of Parliament. Chartism attracted many working-class adherents.

chivalry (369): The proper, ideal comportment of a knight, who was constrained by a code of refinement, fair play, and piety.

cholera (699): An epidemic, usually fatal disease that appeared in the 1830s in Europe; it is caused by a waterborne bacterium that induces violent vomiting and diarrhea and leaves the skin blue, eyes sunken and dull, and hands and feet ice cold.

Christ (196): Greek for "anointed one" (the corresponding English word is *Messiah*); in apocalyptic religious thinking, the agent of God sent to conquer the forces of evil.

city-state (9): A state consisting of an urban center exercising political and economic control over the countryside around it.

Civil Code (685): The French legal code formulated by Napoleon in 1804 (hence also called the Napoleonic Code); it assured equal treatment under the law to all classes of men and guaranteed religious liberty but curtailed many of the rights of women.

civil disobedience (905): Deliberately but peacefully breaking the law, a tactic used by Mohandas Gandhi in India and earlier by British suffragists to protest oppression and obtain political change.

civilization (5): A way of life that includes political states based on cities with dense populations, large buildings constructed for communal activities, diverse economies, a sense of local identity, and some knowledge of writing.

classicism (558): A style of painting and architecture that reflected the ideals of the art of antiquity; in classicism, geometric shapes, order, and harmony of lines took precedence over the sensuous, exuberant, and emotional forms of the baroque.

cold war (946): The rivalry between the United States and the Soviet Union following World War II that led to massive growth in nuclear weapons on both sides.

Colosseum (187): Rome's giant amphitheater for gladiatorial shows and other spectacles.

commercial revolution (340): The economic transformation of Europe, especially western Europe, from rural to urban and from gift-based to cash-based.

commune (345): Sworn associations of citizens who formed a legal corporate body. Communes were the normal institution of self-government in many medieval towns.

communists (719): Those socialists who after 1840 (when the word was first used) advocated the abolition of private property in favor of communal, collective ownership.

conservatism (714): A political doctrine that emerged after 1815 and rejected much of the Enlightenment and the French Revolution, preferring monarchies over republics, tradition over revolution, and established religion over Enlightenment skepticism.

constitutionalism (524): A system of government in which rulers had to share power with parliaments made up of elected representatives.

consumer revolution (577): The rapid increase in consumption of new staples produced in the Atlantic system as well as of other items of daily life, such as mirrors, that were previously unavailable or beyond the reach of ordinary people.

Continental System (691): The system inaugurated by Napoleon's order in 1806 that France and its satellites boycott British goods; after some early successes in blocking British trade, the system was undermined by smuggling.

conversos (447): Jews in the Iberian peninsula who converted to Christianity in the fifteenth century.

Corn Laws (716): Tariffs on grain in Great Britain that benefited landowners by preventing the import of cheap foreign grain; after agitation by the Anti–Corn Law League, the tariffs were repealed by the British government in 1846.

Cuban missile crisis (982): The confrontation in 1962 between the United States and the USSR over Soviet installation of missiles off the American coast; both John F. Kennedy and Nikita Khrushchev backed down from using nuclear weapons to resolve the situation.

cuneiform (11): The earliest form of writing, invented in Mesopotamia and formed with wedge-shaped characters.

curials (220): The social elite in the Roman Empire's towns who were responsible for collecting taxes for the imperial government and paying for any shortfalls themselves.

debasement of coinage (206): Putting less silver in a coin without changing its face value; practiced during the third-century crisis in Rome, which contributed to inflation.

de-Christianization (667): The campaign of extremist republicans against organized churches; militants forced priests to give up their vocations and marry, sold off the buildings of the Catholic church, and set up festivals of reason to compete with Catholicism.

Declaration of the Rights of Man and of the Citizen (660): The preamble to the French constitution drafted in August 1789; it established the sovereignty of the nation and the equality of rights of citizens and granted freedom of religion, freedom of the press, equality of taxation, and equality before the law.

decolonization (966): The process—both violent and peaceful—by which colonies gained their independence from the imperial powers after World War II.

deists (613): Those who believe in God but who give God no active role in human affairs. Deists of the Enlightenment believed that a benevolent, all-knowing God had designed the universe and set it in motion but no longer intervened in the functioning of the universe. A deist might belong to no particular church (Catholic or Protestant).

Delian League (57): The naval alliance headed by Athens after the Persian Wars, and the basis of Athenian empire.

DNA (993): The genetic material that forms the basis of each cell; the discovery of its structure in 1952 revolutionized genetics, molecular biology, and other scientific and medical fields.

domesticity (729): The set of beliefs, prevailing in the early to mid-nineteenth century, purporting that women should live their lives within the domestic sphere and devote themselves to their families and the home.

dominate (215): Roman rule from Diocletian (r. 284–305) onward; a blatantly authoritarian style of rule; derived from dominus ("master"; "lord") and contrasted with principate (172).

Dual Alliance (843): A defensive alliance forged by German chancellor Otto von Bismarck between Germany and Austria-Hungary in 1879 as part of his system of alliances to prevent or limit war; after Italy joined in 1882, it was called the Triple Alliance.

dualism (96): The concept that spiritual being and physical being are separate.

dual monarchy (762): A shared power arrangement between the Habsburg Empire and Hungary after the Prussian defeat of the Austrian Empire in 1867.

Edict of Milan (221): Constantine and Licinius's proclamation of religious toleration that also expressed their favoring of Christianity.

empire (5): A political unit in which one or more formerly independent territories or peoples are ruled by a single sovereign power.

Enabling Act (911): The legislation passed in 1933 suspending constitutional government for four years in order to meet the crisis in the German economy.

enlightened despots (632): A political term that refers to rulers who tried to promote reform without giving up their own supreme political power; the best examples were Catherine the Great of Russia, Frederick the Great of Prussia, and Joseph II of Austria. Also called enlightened absolutists.

Enlightenment (600): The eighteenth-century intellectual movement whose proponents believed that human beings could apply a critical, reasoning spirit to every problem. Based on a popularization of scientific discoveries, the movement often challenged religious and secular authorities.

Entente Cordiale (844): An alliance between Britain and France that began with an agreement in 1904 to honor colonial holdings.

Epicureanism (116): The philosophy initiated by Epicurus of Athens to help people achieve pleasure (meaning an "absence of disturbance") in their lives.

epigrams (113): Short poems covering a variety of themes, especially love, and a favorite genre of Hellenistic women poets.

Estates General (655): A body of deputies from the three estates, or orders, of France; the clergy (First Estate), the nobility (Second Estate), and everyone else (Third Estate); disputes about procedures of voting in this body in 1789 opened the way to the French Revolution.

ethnic cleansing (1032): The mass murder—or genocide—of people of different ethnicities.

euro (1029): The common currency accepted by twelve of the fifteen members of the European Union. It went into effect gradually, becoming the denominator of business transfers in 1999 and entering public circulation in 2002.

European Economic Community (EEC or Common Market) (960): A consortium of six European countries established to promote free trade and economic cooperation among its members. Since its founding in 1957, it has expanded its membership and also its sphere of activity.

European Union (EU) (1040): Formerly the European Economic Community (EEC, or Common Market), and then the European Community; instituted in 1994 by the terms of the 1992 Maastricht Treaty. Its members have political ties through the European parliament as well as common economic, legal, and business mechanisms; as of 2005, it consists of twenty-five member countries.

existentialism (975): A philosophy prominent after World War II that stressed the importance of action in the creation of an authentic self.

Fascism (892): A doctrine advocated by Benito Mussolini that glorified the state over the people and their individual or civil rights. Beginning in the 1920s, Fascism was politically grounded in an instinctual male violence and opposed to the so-called antinationalist socialist movement and parliamentary rule.

fealty (325): The promise of faithfulness that a vassal made to his lord.

First Consul (683): The most important of the three consuls established by the French Constitution of 1800; the title, given to Napoleon Bonaparte, was taken from the ancient Roman republic.

First Triumvirate (164): The coalition formed in 60 B.C.E. by Gnaeus Pompey, Licinius Crassus, and Julius Caesar (the word *triumvirate* means "a group of three").

five-year plans (906): Centralized programs for long-range economic development first used by Joseph Stalin and copied by Adolf Hitler; these plans set production priorities and give production targets for individual industries and agriculture.

flagellants (446): A group of Christians who whipped themselves publicly as a form of penance during the fourteenth century.

Fourteen Points (871): A proposal by U.S. president Woodrow Wilson for peace during World War I. The Fourteen Points called for a peace based on settlement rather than on victory or a definitive conquest and thus helped bring about the surrender of the Central Powers.

Freemasons (623): Members of Masonic lodges, which were based on the rituals of stonemasons' guilds and provided a place where nobles and middle-class professionals (and even some artisans) shared interest in the Enlightenment and reform; lodges drew up constitutions and voted in elections. The movement began in Great Britain and spread eastward across Europe.

friars (379): "Brothers" of the mendicant orders, such as the Franciscans and Dominicans.

Fronde (525): A series of revolts in France, 1648–1653, that challenged the authority of young Louis XIV and his minister Mazarin.

gift economy (281): System of give-and-take that determined most seventh- and eighth-century economic transactions; kings and other powerful people amassed large treasuries and foodstuffs that they distributed at will to mark their power, boost their prestige, and demonstrate their generosity.

glasnost (1020): Literally, "openness" or "publicity"; a policy instituted in the 1980s by Soviet premier Mikhail Gorbachev calling for greater openness in speech and in thinking, which translated to the reduction of censorship in publishing, radio, television, and other media.

global warming (1047): An increase in the temperature of the earth's lower atmosphere resulting from a buildup of chemical emissions, causing a greenhouse effect.

Glorious Revolution (547): The events when the English Parliament deposed King James II in 1688 and replaced him with William, prince of Orange, and James's daughter Mary.

Golden Horde (397): The name for the Mongol Empire in Russia.

Gothic (416): A style of architecture characterized by pointed arches, ribbed vaults, and large stained-glass windows.

Great Fear (659): The term used by historians to describe the rural panic of 1789; fears of an aristocratic plot to pay beggars and vagrants to burn crops or barns sometimes turned into peasant attacks on aristocrats or on seigneurial records of peasants' dues.

Great Persecution (221): The violent program initiated by Diocletian in 303 to make Christians convert to traditional religion or risk confiscation of their property and even death.

Great Schism (348, 442): The term *Great Schism* refers to two different periods in the history of the Christian church. The first, in 1054, refers to the separation of the Latin Catholic church and the Greek Orthodox church; the second, to the period from 1378 to 1417, when the church had two separate popes, one in Rome and one in Avignon, France.

Gregorian reform (349): The movement for church reform—including clerical celibacy and an end to lay investiture—associated with Pope Gregory VII.

guilds (344): Religious, economic, and trade associations. They regulated, protected, and policed their membership, setting up standards for professional practices.

Hasidim (620): A religious group within Judaism whose members pray in a highly emotional fashion; founded by the Ba'al Shem Tov in the 1740s and 1750s, and especially important in Poland-Lithuania. (The word is Hebrew for "most pious.")

Haussmannization (773): The process of urban renewal followed by many governments after the middle of the nineteenth century and named after its prime practitioner, Georges-Eugène Haussmann.

heliocentrism (514): The view articulated by Polish clergyman Nicolaus Copernicus that the earth and planets revolve around the sun; Galileo Galilei was condemned by the Catholic church for supporting this view.

Hellenistic (92): An adjective meaning "Greek-like" that is today used as a chronological term for the period 323–30 B.C.E.

hierarchy (4): Social system that ranks certain people as more important and more dominant than others; the earliest evidence of social differentiation comes from the Paleolithic period.

Holocaust (931): A term used, after World War II, to name the mass murder of European Jews by the Nazis.

hubris (81): The Greek term for excessive arrogance, especially when an overconfident human being goes against the will of the gods.

Huguenots (489): The name given to Calvinists in France after 1560; its linguistic origin remains uncertain.

humanism (450): A literary and intellectual movement that arose in the early fifteenth century to valorize the writings of Greco-Roman antiquity; it was so named because its practitioners studied and supported the liberal arts, or humanities.

humanitas (154): Cicero's ideal of "humaneness," meaning generous and honest treatment of others based on natural law.

iconoclasm (267): Literally, "icon breaking"; the destruction of icons, or images of holy people (e.g., Christ, Mary, the saints). Byzantine emperors banned icons from 726 to 787; a modified ban was revived in 815 and lasted until 843.

ideology (714): A coherent set of beliefs (conservatism, liberalism, socialism, etc.) about the way the social and political order should be organized and changed; the word was coined during the French Revolution.

imperialism (731): European dominance of the non-West through economic exploitation and political rule (as distinct from the word *colonialism*, which usually implied establishment of settler colonies, often with slavery as the labor system); the word was coined in the mid-nineteenth century.

impressionism (787): A mid- to late-nineteenth-century artistic style that captured the sensation of light in images, derived from Japanese influences and from an opposition to the realism of photographs.

indulgences (474): In Roman Catholic doctrine, a remission of sin earned by performing certain religious tasks to avoid purgatory after death; indulgences were in use by the thirteenth century. The Catholic clergy's practice of selling indulgences came under fire during the Reformation.

industrialization (629): The process of economic transformation that began in Great Britain in the 1770s and 1780s; its most striking features were the introduction of steam engines to power machinery and the concentration of those machines in factories that mass-produced cloth from cotton grown in the British colonies.

Inquisition (392): The court of inquiry permanently set up by the church in 1233; its purpose was to ferret out and punish heretics.

Investiture Conflict (350): The conflict between Pope Gregory VII and Henry IV over the right of laymen to appoint bishops and install them in their office.

in vitro fertilization (994): A process developed in the 1970s by which eggs are fertilized by sperm outside the human body and then implanted in a woman's uterus.

Jacobin Club (663): The first and most influential of the political clubs formed during the French Revolution; the Paris Jacobin Club inspired the formation of a national network of Jacobin clubs whose members dominated the revolutionary government during the period known as the Terror.

Koine (120): The "common" or "shared" form of the Greek language that became the international language in the Hellenistic period.

ladder of offices (145): The series of Roman elective government offices from quaestor to consul.

laissez-faire (616): An economic doctrine developed by Adam Smith based on his reading of the French physiocrats who advocated freeing the economy from government intervention and control. (The term is French for "to leave alone.")

law of universal gravitation (555): Newton's law uniting celestial and terrestrial mechanics held that every body in the universe exerts over every other body an attractive force directly proportional to the product of their masses and inversely proportional to the square of the distance between them.

League of Nations (874): The international organization set up following World War I to maintain peace by arbitrating disputes and promoting collective security.

liberalism (715): An economic and political doctrine that emphasized free trade and the constitutional guarantees of individual rights such as freedom of speech and religion; liberals were favorable to the Enlightenment but critical of the violence of the French Revolution.

lithograph (699): A mass-produced print using an inked stone (the Greek *lithos* means "stone"); lithographs played a key role in social commentary and political discussion in the 1830s–1850s.

Maastricht Treaty (1040): The agreement among the members of the European Community to have a closer alliance, including the use of common passports and eventually the development of a common currency; by the terms of this treaty, the European Community became the European Union (EU) in 1994.

madrasa (309): A school located within or attached to a mosque.

mannerism (510): A late-sixteenth-century style of painting in which a distorted perspective created bizarre and theatrical effects that contrasted with the precise, harmonious lines of Renaissance painting.

manor (317): A great estate consisting (normally) of arable fields, vineyards, meadows, and woodland, ordinarily owned by a lord (which could as easily be a monastery or a church as a layperson) and cultivated by serfs.

march on Rome (892): The threat by Benito Mussolini and his followers in 1922 to take over the Italian government in a military convergence on Rome; the march forced

King Victor Emmanuel II to make Mussolini prime minister.

Marshall Plan (952): A post–World War II program funded by the United States to get Europe back on its feet economically and thereby reduce the appeal of communism. It played an important role in the rebirth of European prosperity in the 1950s.

martyr (200): Greek for "witness," designating someone who dies for his or her religious belief.

Marxism (782): A body of thought about the organization of production, social inequality, and the processes of revolutionary change as devised by the philosopher and economist Karl Marx.

materialism (116): The philosophical doctrine that only things made of matter truly exist and thus deny the existence of the soul or any nonmaterial phenomena.

Meiji Restoration (781): A change in the Japanese government in 1867 that reinstalled the emperor as legitimate ruler in place of the military leader, or shogun.

mercantilism (529): The doctrine that governments must intervene to increase national wealth by whatever means possible.

Merovingian dynasty (285): The dynasty that ruled as kings of the Franks from about 486 to 751.

mestizos (574): People born to Spanish fathers and native American mothers.

metaphysics (96): Ideas about the ultimate nature of reality beyond the reach of human senses.

Methodism (621): A religious movement founded by John Wesley that broke away from the Anglican church in Great Britain and insisted on strict self-discipline and a "methodical" approach to religious study and observance. Wesley emphasized an intense personal experience of salvation and a life of thrift, abstinence, and hard work.

metic (72): A foreigner granted a permanent residency permit in a Greek city-state in return for obligations to pay taxes and do military service.

mir (753): A Russian farm community fortified by the emancipation of the serfs in 1861 that provided for holding the land in common and regulating the movements of any individual by the group. The mir hindered the free movement of labor and individual agricultural enterprise, including modernization.

Mitteleuropa (844): Literally, "central Europe," but used by influential military leaders in Germany before World War I to refer to land in both central and eastern Europe that they hoped to acquire as a substitute for vast colonial empires in Africa and Asia. This territory ultimately became a war aim in World War I and for Hitler thereafter.

modernism (822): Changes in the arts at the end of the nineteenth century that featured a break with realism in art and literature and with lyricism in music.

modernity (798): The accelerated pace of life, the rise of mass politics, the spread of industrial production, and the decline of a rural social order that were visible in the West from the late nineteenth century onward.

monotheism (22): The belief in only one god, as in Judaism, Christianity, and Islam.

mos maiorum (131): Literally, "the way of the ancestors"; the set of Roman traditional values.

motet (415): A two- or three-part polyphonic song that interweaves vernacular and sacred texts.

multinational corporation (995): A business that operates in many foreign countries by sending large segments of its manufacturing, finance, sales, and other business components abroad.

mystery cult (66): A set of prayers, hymns, ritual purification, sacrifice, and other forms of worship undertaken to gain divine protection; each cult was connected to a particular divinity and centered on initiation into secret knowledge about the divine and human worlds.

nationalism (720): A political doctrine that holds that all peoples derive their identities from their nations and should have states to express their common language and shared cultural traditions.

natural selection (791): Theory developed by Charles Darwin that life developed from lower forms through a primal battle for survival and through the sexual selection of mates.

Nazi-Soviet Pact (927): The agreement reached in 1939 by Germany and the Soviet Union in which both agreed not to attack the other in case of war. The agreement secretly divided up territory that would later be conquered.

neoliberalism (1017): A theory promoted by Margaret Thatcher, Britain's prime minister from 1979 to 1990, and those who followed her calling for a return to liberal principles of the nineteenth century, including the reduction of welfare-state programs and the cutting of taxes for wealthy people in order to promote economic growth.

Neoplatonism (204): The spiritual philosophy developed by Plotinus (c. 205–270) that was based on Plato's ideas, and was very influential for Christian intellectuals.

new woman (814): A woman of the turn of the twentieth century, often from the middle class, who dressed practically, moved about freely, lived apart from her family, and supported herself.

nongovernmental organizations (NGOs) (1046): Charitable foundations and activist groups such as Doctors Without Borders that often work internationally on political, economic, and relief issues; also, organizations such as the Rockefeller, Ford, and Open Society Foundations that shape economic and social policy and the course of political reform.

North Atlantic Treaty Organization (NATO) (954): The security alliance formed in 1949 to provide a unified military force for the United States, Canada, and their allies in western Europe and Scandinavia. The corresponding alliance of the Soviet Union and its allies was known as the Warsaw Pact.

Nuremberg Laws (913): Legislation in 1935 that deprived Jewish Germans of their citizenship and imposed many other hardships on them.

opium (732): An addictive drug derived from the heads of poppy plants; it was imported to Europe from the Ottoman Empire and India, available in various forms, and often used by ordinary people until restricted by governments after the 1860s.

Organization of Petroleum Exporting Countries (OPEC) (1015): A consortium that regulated the supply and export of oil and that acted with more unanimity after the United States supported Israel against the Arabs in the wars of the late 1960s and early 1970s.

Ostpolitik (1004): A policy initiated by Willy Brandt in the late 1960s in which West Germany sought better economic relations with the Communist countries of eastern Europe.

ostracism (59): Athenian democracy's annual procedure to block tyranny by sending a citizen into exile for ten years by a vote of six thousand citizens in the assembly.

Pacific tigers (1055): Countries of East Asia so named because of their massive economic growth, much of it from the 1970s and 1980s on; foremost among these were Japan and China.

Pan-Slavism (763): A movement in the nineteenth century that called for the unity of all Slavs across national and regional boundaries.

parlements (525): High courts in France (the term comes from the French *parler*, "to speak"). Each region had its parlement; the parlements could not propose laws, but they could review laws presented by the king and refuse to register them (the king could also insist on their registration).

patria potestas (134): Literally, "father's power"; the legal right of a father in ancient Rome to own the property of his children and slaves and to control their lives.

patriarchy (10): Social system in which men exert control over political, social, and economic life.

patron-client system (132): The interlocking network of mutual obligations between Roman patrons (social superiors) and clients (social inferiors).

Pax Romana (172): The period of "Roman peace" under the principate in the first and second centuries C.E.

Peace of God (328): A movement begun by bishops in the south of France first to limit the violence done to property and later (with the Truce of God) to limit fighting between warriors.

Peace of Paris (872): The series of peace treaties that provided the settlement of World War I. These treaties were resented, especially by Germany and Hungary, as well as by states of the Middle East in which England and France took over the government.

perestroika (1020): Literally, "restructuring"; an economic policy instituted in the 1980s by Soviet premier Mikhail Gorbachev calling for the introduction of market mechanisms and the achievement of greater efficiency in manufacturing, agriculture, and services.

philosophes (610): Public intellectuals of the Enlightenment who wrote on subjects ranging from current affairs to art criticism with the goal of furthering reform in society. (The word in French means "philosophers.")

physiocrats (639): French economists who advocated deregulation of the grain trade and a more equitable tax system to encourage agricultural productivity.

Pietism (586): A Protestant revivalist movement that emphasized deeply emotional individual religious experience.

plantations (529): Large tracts of land producing staple crops such as sugar, coffee, and tobacco; farmed by slave labor; and owned by a colonial settler who emigrated from western Europe.

plebiscites (144): Laws passed by the Plebeian Assembly in the Roman republic.

polis (38): The Greek term for an independent city-state based on citizenship.

politiques (490): Political advisers during the French Wars of Religion who argued that compromise in matters of religion—limited toleration for the Calvinists—would strengthen the monarchy.

polyphony (415): Music that consists of two or more melodies performed simultaneously.

polytheism (10): The worship of multiple gods.

pop art (1000): A style in the visual arts that mimicked advertising and consumerism and that used ordinary objects as a part of paintings and other compositions.

positivism (791): A theory, developed in the mid-nineteenth century, stating that the study of facts would generate accurate, or "positive," laws of society; these laws could, in turn, help formulate policy and legislation.

postmodernism (1064): A term applied in the late twentieth century to both an intense stylistic mixture in the arts and a critique of Enlightenment and scientific beliefs in rationality and the possibility for precise knowledge.

praetorian guard (175): The group of soldiers stationed in Rome under the emperor's control; first formed by Augustus.

predestination (480): John Calvin's doctrine that God preordained salvation or damnation for each person before creation; those chosen for salvation were considered the "elect."

primogeniture (328): The right to inheritance of the firstborn.

principate (172): The political system invented by Augustus as a disguised monarchy with the *princeps* ("first man") as emperor.

proletarians (144): In the Roman republic, the mass of people so poor that males were not eligible to serve in the army.

Protestants (473): Members of the Christian branch that formed when Martin Luther and his followers broke from the Catholic church in 1517; the name was first used in 1529 in an imperial diet by German princes who protested Emperor Charles V's edict to repress religious dissent.

Provisional Government (865): The initial government to take control in Russia after the overthrow of the Romanov empire in 1917.

The government was composed of aristocrats and members of the middle class, often deputies in the Duma—the assembly created after the Revolution of 1905.

psychoanalysis (822): Sigmund Freud's theory of human mental processes and his method for treating their malfunctioning.

pump priming (912): An economic policy used by governments to stimulate the economy through public works programs and other infusions to public funds.

purges (907): The series of attacks instituted by Joseph Stalin on citizens of the USSR in the 1930s and later. The victims were accused of being "wreckers," or saboteurs of communism, while the public grew hysterical and pliable because of its fear.

Puritans (495): Strict Calvinists who opposed all vestiges of Catholic ritual in the Church of England.

radical democracy (59): The ancient Athenian system of democracy, established in the 460s and 450s B.C.E., that extended direct political power and participation in the court system to the mass of adult male citizens.

raison d'état (503): French for "reason of state." The political doctrine, first proposed by Cardinal Richelieu of France, that held that the state's interests should prevail over those of religion; Richelieu, for example, allied with the Lutheran king of Sweden even though he himself was a leading official of the Catholic church.

rationalism (46): The philosophic idea that people must justify their claims by logic and reason.

realism (785): An art style that arose in the mid-nineteenth century and was dedicated to depicting society realistically without romantic or idealistic overtones.

Realpolitik (747): Policies associated initially with nation building that are said to be based on hard-headed realities rather than the romantic notions of earlier nationalists. The term has come to mean any policy based on considerations of power alone.

reconquista (348): The Christian reconquest of Spain.

redistributive economy (10): A system in which state officials control the production and distribution of goods.

rococo (583): A style of painting that emphasized irregularity and asymmetry, as well as movement and curvature, but on a smaller, more intimate scale than the baroque.

Romanesque (374): The term for the art and architecture in western Europe of the period before around 1150, characterized by monumentality and solidity enlivened by sculpture and painting.

Romanization (190): The spread of Roman law and culture in the provinces of the Roman Empire.

Roman republic (140): A system of government based on shared political decision making and the election of male officials by assemblies organized by social hierarchy; the republic lasted from 509 to 287 B.C.E.

romanticism (619): An artistic movement of the early nineteenth century that glorified nature, emotion, genius, and imagination.

ruler cults (121): Cult that involved worship of a Hellenistic ruler as a savior god.

Russification (755): A program for the integration of Russia's many nationality groups involving the forced acquisition of Russian language and the practice of Russian orthodoxy as well as the settlement of ethnic Russians among other nationality groups.

salons (612): Informal gatherings, usually sponsored by middle-class or aristocratic women, that provided a forum for new ideas and an opportunity to establish new intellectual contacts among supporters of the Enlightenment; works that could not be published officially were read aloud. (The word in French means "living rooms.")

sans-culottes (663): French for "without breeches"; the name given to politically active men from the lower classes. They worked with their hands and wore the long trousers of workingmen rather than the knee breeches of the upper classes.

Sassanid Empire (261): The empire of the Sassanid dynasty of Persia, which lasted from 224 until its conquest by Islamic armies from 637 to 651.

scholasticism (411): The body of theological and philosophical thought of the scholastics, the scholars of the medieval universities.

scientific method (516): A combination of experimental observation and mathematical deduction to determine the laws of nature; it became the secular standard of truth and as such challenged the hold of both the churches and popular beliefs.

Second International (832): A transnational organization of workers established in 1889, mostly committed to Marxian socialism.

Seljuk Turks (353): A Sunni Muslim Turkic group whose migration westward, into areas that had been controlled by Byzantium and various local Muslim rulers, set off the First Crusade.

serfs (325): Semi-free peasants. Serfs could not legally leave the land they tilled; they owed labor services and either produce or money to their lord. Yet they were not slaves: they had the right to marry, to keep part of their produce, and to remain on the land.

simony (347): Derived from the name of Simon Magus, a magician in the New Testament who offers St. Peter money to have the power to confer the Holy Spirit (Acts 8:9–24), the term came to mean the giving of gifts or money for church offices.

social contract (553): The doctrine found in the writings of Hobbes and Locke that all political authority derives not from divine right but from an implicit contract between citizens and their rulers.

Socratic method (77): Socrates' method of conversation, in which he asked probing questions to make his listeners examine their most cherished assumptions before drawing conclusions.

Solidarity (1021): An outlawed Polish labor union of the 1980s that contested

Communist Party programs and eventually succeeded in ousting the party from the Polish government.

Sophists (65): Competitive intellectuals and teachers who offered a new form of education and new philosophical and religious ideas beginning about 450 B.C.E.

soviets (865): Councils of workers and soldiers first formed in Russia during the Revolution of 1905; they took shape to represent the people in the early days of the 1917 Russian Revolution. These groups saw themselves as a more legitimate political force than the Provisional Government.

stagflation (1015): The combination of a stagnant economy and soaring inflation; a period of stagflation occurred in the West in the 1970s as a result of an OPEC embargo on oil.

Stoicism (116): The most influential Hellenistic philosophy, which taught the goal of living a virtuous life in harmony with nature.

struggle of the orders (143): Turmoil between elite Roman families (patricians) and the rest of Rome's population (plebeians) that centered on social and economic issues and resulted in greater sharing of political power between 509 and 287 B.C.E.

subjectivism (74): The belief, especially associated with the Sophist Protagoras, that there is no absolute reality behind and independent of appearances.

successor kings (106): Alexander's commanders (Antigonus, Seleucus, and Ptolemy) who took over portions of his empire to create personal monarchies after his death.

summa (412): A scholastic treatise. These characteristically took up a topic and explored it exhaustively, resulting in a "summary" of all opinions and their resolution.

symposium (plural: symposia) (71): A drinking party for Greek men with entertainment ranging from philosophical conversation to hired female companions.

temperance movement (728): A movement in the United States and Europe begun in the early nineteenth century to discourage consumption of alcohol.

Terror (665): The emergency government established under the direction of the Committee of Public Safety during the French Revolution; the government aimed to establish a republic of virtue, but to do so it arrested hundreds of thousands of political suspects and executed thousands of ordinary people.

terrorism (1016): Coordinated and targeted political violence by opposition groups.

tertiaries (410): Laypeople who affiliated themselves with the friars and adopted many of their pious practices while living in the world.

tetrarchy (216): Literally, "rule by four"; devised by Diocletian to put into practice his principle of subdivision of power in ruling the Roman Empire.

Thermidorian Reaction (674): The violent backlash against the rule of Robespierre that began with his arrest and execution; most of the instruments of the Terror were dismantled, and supporters of the Jacobins were harassed or even murdered.

third world (946): A term devised after World War II to designate those countries outside either the capitalist world of the U.S. bloc or the socialist world of the Soviet bloc— most of them emerging from imperial domination.

tithe (326): A tax, taken by the church, equivalent to one-tenth of the parishioner's annual income.

totalitarianism (905): Highly centralized systems of government that attempt to control society in its most private details and ensure conformity through police terror and single-party rule.

total war (851): A war built on full mobilization of soldiers, civilians, and the technological capacities of the nations involved. The term also refers to a highly destructive war and one that is both a physical war and a war for ideas and ideologies.

Truman Doctrine (951): The U.S. policy to limit communism after World War II by countering political crises with economic and military aid.

tsar (439): The Russian imperial title first taken by Muscovite prince Ivan III (r. 1462–1505); also spelled *czar*, from *Caesar*.

Umayyad caliphate (274): The successors of Muhammad who traced their ancestry to Umayyah, a member of Muhammad's tribe. The dynasty lasted from 661 to 750.

ummah (269): The community of believers in Islam.

United Nations (UN) (972): An organization for collective security and deliberation set up as World War II closed; it replaced the ineffective League of Nations and has proved active in resolving international conflicts both through negotiation and by the use of force.

vassals (324): Free warriors who pledged homage and fealty to a lord, thereby creating a bond that implied mutual obligations, among them to fight for one another.

Vatican II (1003): A Catholic Council held between 1962 and 1965 to modernize some aspects of church teachings (such as condemnation of Jews), update the liturgy, and promote cooperation among the faiths (i.e., ecumenism).

Warsaw Pact (955): Military alliance established in 1955 by the Soviet Union with its satellite countries in response to the formation of the North Atlantic Treaty Organization.

Weimar Republic (871): The parliamentary republic established in 1919 in Germany to replace the imperial form of government.

welfare state (915): A system comprising state-sponsored programs for citizens, including veterans' pensions, social security, health care, family allowances, and disability insurance. Most highly developed after World War II, the welfare state intervened in society to bring economic democracy (to supplement political democracy) by setting a minimum standard of well-being.

wergild (244): Under Frankish law, money or goods a murderer had to pay as compensation for his crime; most went to the victim's kin, but the king received about one-third.

Westernization (592): The effort, especially in Peter the Great's Russia, to make society and social customs resemble counterparts in western Europe, especially France, Britain, and the Dutch Republic.

World Bank (1045): An international institution of credit created in the 1940s. With the globalization of finances and of national economies from the 1980s on, it became increasingly powerful.

Zionism (840): A movement that began in the late nineteenth century among European Jews to found a Jewish state in Palestine.

Index

A note about the index:

Names of individuals appear in boldface; biographical dates are included for major historical figures.

Letters following pages refer to:
(*i*)   illustrations, including photographs and artifacts
(*f*)   figures, including charts and graphs
(*m*) maps
n   footnote

Aachen (A kuhn), 311, 312, 314
Abandonment of children. *See* Infanticide
Abbasid Caliphate (AB a sid) (750–c. 950),
    303–307, 306(*m*), 336–337
  Carolingians and, 296, 309, 317
Abd al-Rahman (caliph; r. 912–961), 306
Abdul Hamid II (Ottoman sultan;
    r. 1876–1909), 808
Abelard, Peter (AH beh lard) (1079–1142), 370,
    372–373, 411–412
Abolitionist movement (antislavery movement),
    554, 680, 715–716, 731
Abortion, 265, 629, 813. *See also* Reproductive rights
  in 1920s, 879
  Napoleonic code and, 686
  in Russia, 890
Abraham (Hebrew patriarch), 31, 250
Absolutism
  in France, 524–533, 537, 540, 546, 568,
    587, 588(*m*), 600–601
  in Germany, 533–535
  in Russia, 533, 537–539
Absolutism (absolute authority), 513, 524–540, 565
  in central and eastern Europe (1648–1699),
    532–540, 535(*m*)
    Austrian Habsburgs and Ottoman Turks,
    533, 535–537

    Brandenburg-Prussia, 532–534
    Poland-Lithuania, 533, 539–540
    Russia, 533, 537–539
    Sweden, 534–535
  in eighteenth century, 632, 638
  the Enlightenment and, 640
  in France, 615
  Hobbes on, 553–554
  Louis XIV and, 524–533, 568, 587,
    589, 600–601
  in Russia, 592–594
Abstract expressionism, 980
Académie française (French Academy), 526
Academy (Athens), 95–97, 96(*i*), 224
  closing of (530), 255
Accius (c. 170–80 B.C.E.), 138
Achilles, 37
Achilles Tatius, 192
Acid rain, 1047
Acropolis (Athens), 58(*i*), 62(*m*), 63(*i*)
Actium, battle of (AK tee uhm) (31 B.C.E.),
    173, 183
Activism, 988, 1008–1009, 1046–1047, 1048
Act of Supremacy (1529), 495
Act of Union (United Kingdom; 1707),
    589–590
Act of Union (United Kingdom; 1801), 723

Adam and Eve, 230, 231
Adam, Robert, 624(*i*)
Adams, John, 653
Addison, Joseph (1672–1719), 583
Adenauer, Konrad (1876–1967), 958
Administration (administrative structure).
    See also Bureaucracy; Law(s)
  of Alexander the Great, 103, 105
  in ancient Egypt, 20–21
  in Byzantine Empire, 248–249, 250
  under Carolingian emperors, 311–313
  in France
    under Louis IX, 399–401, 400(*m*), 409
    under Philip Augustus (r. 1180–1223),
      398–400
  in Hellenistic Kingdoms, 108
  in Ottoman Empire, 437
  papal (curia), 352, 441, 443
  in Persian Empire, 28–29
  in Roman Empire, 189–190, 216–217
Adrianople, battle of (378), 238
Adrianople, Treaty of (1829), 706
Adultery, 180, 252, 265, 686
Advancement of Learning, The (Bacon), 516
Advertising, 978–979
Aediles (EE dilz), 145
Aegean Sea, 33, 33(*m*), 39(*m*), 57
Aeneas, 176(*f*), 183
Aeneid (Virgil), 183, 189
Aerospace development, Soviet, 965–966
Aeschines (ES kin eez) (c. 397–322 B.C.E.), 105
Aeschylus (ES kil us) (525–456 B.C.E.), 80
Affair of the Placards (1534), 480
Afghanistan, 92, 121, 799, 1021, 1052, 1054–1055
Africa (Africans), 5, 15, 468(*i*), 798, 1050, 1051
  c. 1890, 801(*m*)
  in 1914, 803(*m*)
  Catholic church in, 485–486
  decolonization and new nations in
      (1951–1990), 966, 970–973, 971(*m*)
  exploration and colonies in, 426, 463, 465,
      465(*m*), 466, 471, 485–486, 492, 493(*m*)
  German colonialism in, 843, 881
  independence in, 970–973
  influence on art of, 826, 889
  missionaries in, 485–486
  scramble for, 799–803, 801(*m*), 803(*m*)
  slaves and. *See* Slaves and slavery
  World War I and, 855, 859, 861, 863
African Americans, 765, 766, 1010
Afterlife, Egyptian belief in, 6, 20, 23, 23(*i*)
Afyeh, 17
Agbar (Osrhoëne; r. 179–216), 229(*i*)
Agincourt, battle of (1415), 431, 432(*m*)

Agnosticism, 74
Agora (ag OH ra), 61, 62(*m*)
Agrarian League (Germany), 838
Agrarian reform, in Rome, 158–159
Agribusiness, 997
  subsidies for, 1046
Agriculture. *See also* Farming; Peasants; Serfs;
      Plantations
  in 1960s and 1970s, 997
  in Byzantine Empire, 265, 299
  in Carolingian period, 317–318
  collectivization of, 949
  colonialism and, 780, 802
  in early Middle Ages, 280
  Egyptian, 16
  in eighteenth century, 578–581, 579(*f*),
      615, 622, 631, 638–639
  increased production and, 340–343, 377
  industrial innovations in, 767, 768
  invention of (Neolithic Revolution), 3–4, 6–8
  in post-Carolingian age, 325
  seventeenth-century economic crisis and,
      504–506, 507(*i*), 508
  three-field system, 318, 325
Agrippa, Marcus (ah GRIP ah), 174(*i*), 178
Ahura Mazda (ah HOOR uh MAZ duh), 29–30
AIDS (acquired immune deficiency syndrome),
      1049–1050
Airbus, 996
Aix-la-Chapelle, Treaty of
      (AYKS la shah PELL) (1668), 530
Akhenaten (ahk hen AH ten) (**Amenhotep IV**)
      (Egyptian pharaoh; fourteenth century
      B.C.E.), 22
Akhmatova, Anna (1889–1966), 908–909,
      909(*i*), 964
Akkadia (uh KAY dee uh) (Akkadian Empire), 5,
      12–14
Alaric (AHL uhr ihk), 230, 231, 239
Albania (Albanians), 8*n*, 846, 1032
Albert, Prince (Great Britain), 763, 763(*i*),
      764, 774, 786
Alberti, Leon Battista (1404–1472), 455
Albertus Magnus (c. 1200–1280), 412
Albigensian Crusade (1209–1229), 391–393, 404
Albigensians (al bee JENS ee uhns), 381
Alcibiades (al si BI ah deez)
      (c. 450–404 B.C.E.), 85
Alcuin (AL kwin) (c. 732–804), 314–315
Aldrin, Edwin "Buzz," 991
Alexander I (Russia; r. 1801–1825), 689, 690–691,
      692–693, 703, 705, 715, 722
Alexander II (Russia; r. 1855–1881), 752, 753,
      754, 755, 777, 841

Alexander III (pope; r. 1159–1181), 367
Alexander III (Russia; r. 1881–1894), 841
Alexander III (the Great) (Macedonia;
    r. 336–323 B.C.E.), 52, 94, 97, 102–106,
    103(m), 117, 130, 215(i), 695
Alexander IV (pope; r. 1254–1261), 385
Alexander V (antipope), 443
Alexander VI (pope; r. 1492–1503), 447, 466
Alexandria (al ek ZAN dree ah) (Egypt), 103–104,
    109, 112, 118, 120, 122–123, 192,
    245, 255
Alexei (Russia; r. 1645–1676), 538
Alexiad (Anna Comnena), 359–360
Alexius (claimant to Byzantine throne), 389
Alexius I (Byzantine emperor; r. 1081–1118),
    353(m), 354, 359
Alfonso IX (Castile-León; r. 1188–1230), 408
Alfonso X (Castile-León; r. 1252–1284), 408
Alfred (the Great) (Wessex; r. 871–899), 321,
    330(m), 330–331, 331(i)
Algebra, 307
Algeria, 731–732, 780, 970–972
Ali (caliph; c. 600–661), 274
Ali al-Hasan (Alhazen) (d. 1038), 307–308
Allah, 269
Alliances (alliance systems)
    before World War I, 843–846
    in World War I, 852, 854–855
All Quiet on the Western Front (Remarque), 887
Almohades, 388(m), 390–391
Almoravids, 390
Alphabets. See also Writing
    Canaanite, 24, 25, 37
    Cyrillic, 302
    Roman, 142
Al-Qaeda, 1052
Alsace (AHL says), 501, 760, 768, 855, 872
Altar of Augustan Peace, 174(i), 184(i)
Amar, Jules, 851, 852, 860, 876, 889, 896
Ambrose (AM broz) (bishop of Milan;
    c. 339–397), 230, 253
American Revolution (War of Independence)
    (1775–1783), 554, 615, 644–648, 645(i), 675
    Dutch and, 653
    French involvement in, 652, 655, 659
American Temperance Society, 728
Americas, the (New World; Western Hemisphere),
    511. See also Latin America; North America;
    South America; Spain, American colonies of
    Christianity in, 467–470
    English colonies in, 548, 551–552
    European exploration and conquests in
    (sixteenth century), 426, 463, 465(m),
    466–471

French colonies in. See also North America
    France's retreat from America (1803),
    688(m), 689
    French and Indian War (1756–1763), 634
    French Revolution and, 678(m),
    678–680, 679(i)
    Louis XIV and, 530, 551
    slavery in, 606
    Spanish colonies in, 477, 485–486, 551
Amiens, Treaty of (1802), 689
Amritsar massacre (1919), 880
Amsterdam, 508, 653
Amun-Re, cult of, 22
Anabaptists, 473, 479–480, 480(f), 491
Anarchism, 782, 826
Anarchists, 832
Anatolia (an ah TOL ee ah), 4, 51, 86(m),
    88(m), 102, 106, 107(m), 109, 121, 299,
    537, 564(m)
    Hittite kingdom in, 15, 22, 24–26
    King's Peace (386 B.C.E.) and, 98
Anatomy, 120, 514–516
Anaxagoras of Clazomenae (an ak SAG or as), 75
Anaximander of Miletus (an ak si MAND er)
    (c. 610–540 B.C.E.), 46
Andalusia (an da LOOTH yuh) (al-Andalus),
    305–307, 306(m), 311, 319(m), 322,
    335(m), 348, 367
Angela of Foligno, 411
Angevin kings of England, 362n
Anglican church (Church of England), 495–496,
    496(i), 541–543, 590
    in seventeenth century, 544–547
Anglo-Saxon language (Old English), 362
Anglo-Saxons, 240–241, 286(m), 286–288,
    321(f), 331
    churchmen, 289, 293, 310, 314
    Norman conquest of England and (1066),
    360–362
Angola, 575
Animals. See also Hunting
    Aristotle and, 98
    blood sports and, 729
    domestication of, 8
    in Egypt, 19
    livestock raising, in Great Britain, 578
    sacrifice of, 66–67
Anjou, 398(m), 398–399
Anna Comnena (1083–c. 1148),
    359–360
Anna Karenina (Tolstoy), 841
Annals (Ennius), 154
Annals (Tacitus), 193
Anne (Great Britain; r. 1702–1714), 589

Anne, grand princess of Kiev, 303
Anne of Austria (r. 1056–1075), 500, 525
Anno (archbishop of Cologne) (r. 1056–1075), 357
Anschluss, 925–926
Anselm, St. (archbishop of Canterbury; 1033–1109), 362, 377
Anthony, Susan B. (1820–1906), 833
Anticlericalism, 444–446, 474, 476–478
Anti-Corn Law League, 716
Antigone (an TIG on ee) (Sophocles), 81
Antigonids, 106
Antigonus (an TIG on uhs) (c. 382–301 B.C.E.), 106, 121
Antioch (AN ti ok) (Syria), 192, 297, 298(m), 355
Antiochus I (an TI ok uhs) (Seleucid king; c. 324–261 B.C.E.), 108
Antiochus IV (Seleucid king; r. 175–164 B.C.E.), 124–125, 196
Anti-Semitism, 540, 798, 824, 964
    in 1930s, 903, 909, 913–914, 918, 930–932
    as basis for Nazism, 930
    in eleventh and twelfth centuries, 356–358
    in fourteenth and fifteenth centuries, 444(i), 446–448, 471
    Hitler and, 894
    in late nineteenth and early twentieth centuries, 836–840, 838(i)
    mass politics and, 829
    Soviet persecutions and, 1012
    after World War II, 947
Antoninus Pius (an to NI nuhs PI uhs) (Roman emperor; r. 138–161), 187
Antony (Christian ascetic) (c. 251–356), 232, 233
Antony, Mark (83–30 B.C.E.), 173
Antwerp, 494, 494(m), 508, 512(i)
Apartheid, 1051
Aphrodite (af ro DI tee), 66, 113, 114
Apocalypticism (uh pahk uh LIHP tih sihzuhm), 32, 196, 197
Apollinaris, Sidonius (ap o LOH nahr uhs) (c. 430–479), 239
Apollo, 66, 224(i), 526
    Oracle at Delphi and, 118
Apollonis (Pergamum; r. c. 165 B.C.E.), 111
Apostate, 223
Apostles, Jesus', 197, 201–202
Apostolic succession (ahp uh STAHL ihk), 201
Appeasement, 926–927, 928
Apprenticeships, 344, 453
"April Theses" (Lenin), 865
Apuleius (ahp yuh LEE uhs) (c. 125–170), 180, 193, 203
Aqueducts, Roman, 148, 149(i), 177

Aquinas, St. Thomas (ah KWIE nehs) (c. 1225–1274), 411(i), 412–414
Aquitaine (A kwi tayn), 276(m), 398, 398(m), 430, 433(m)
Arabia, in Muhammad's lifetime, 269(m)
Arabic language and literature, 273, 274, 275, 307, 367, 371, 808
Arabic numerals, 308, 333, 593
Arabs. *See also* Islam
    Byzantine Empire and, 259, 260, 262–263, 267, 273, 290, 292
    Roman Empire and, 259
Aragon, 368(i), 388(m), 390–391, 391(m), 396, 459
Aramaeans (ah rah MAY anz), 26
Aramaic language (a rah MAY ic), 26
Arawaks, 467
Arcadius, 218
Archaic Age (Greece; c. 750–500 B.C.E.). *See* Greece, Ancient
Archilochus of Paros (ahr KI lo kuhs) (early seventh century B.C.E.), 46
Archimedes of Syracuse (ar kih MEE deez) (287–212 B.C.E.), 118
Architecture. *See also* Building(s); Housing; Palaces; Pyramids, in ancient Egypt; Temples
    in 1920s, 883, 883(i), 889, 893
    ancient, 4, 8, 22, 27, 34, 35
    Athenian, 52, 61–65, 62(m), 63(i), 64(f)
    column styles, 63, 64(f)
    Gothic, 414(i), 415–421, 417(i)
    Renaissance (fifteenth century), 455–456
    Roman, 129(i), 192(i)
    Romantic, 725
Areopagitica (Milton), 557
Areopagus Council (ay ree O pah guhs), 59
Ares, 45(i), 66
Aretê (ar e TAY) (excellence), 36–37, 108
Argos, 98
Arianism, 228, 242, 288–290
Aristarchus (ar is TAHRK uhs) (Socrates' friend), 93
Aristarchus of Samos (third century B.C.E.), 118–119
Aristides (ar is TI deez) (c. 525–465 B.C.E.), 56, 60–61
Aristocracy (nobility). *See also* Hierarchy; Upper classes
    Austrian Habsburgs and, 535–537
    in Brandenburg-Prussia, 533
    Carolingian, 310, 313, 315, 316–317, 317
    democracy and, 646
    in eighteenth century, 621–623, 638–640, 642
    in England (Great Britain), 622

in France, 332, 399, 622–623
  eighteenth century, 652, 654–657, 659
  Louis XIV and, 524–528
French Revolution and, 660, 662, 664(i),
    671, 672, 676, 683, 685
in Germany, 333
as government, 513
manners and (seventeenth century), 559–562
Merovingian, 278, 280–285, 310
in Poland, 539–540, 622
post-Carolingian, 323–328
in Prussia, 622
after revolution of 1848, 739, 741
Roman, 145
in Russia, 539, 592–594, 593(i), 622, 623, 642, 753
in Spain, 622, 623
in Sweden, 534
in twelfth century, 360, 362, 367–369
Aristophanes (ar i STOF ah neez)
    (c. 455–385 B.C.E.), 77, 82, 83(i)
Aristotelian philosophy, in the Middle Ages,
    412–414
Aristotle (AR is taw tuhl) (384–322 B.C.E.), 93,
    97–98, 105, 255
  on the city-state, 40, 41
  in Middle Ages, 307, 360, 371, 412–414
  on slaves, 41
  teachings of, 514–516, 604
Arius (uh RIH uhs) (c. 260–336), 228
Arles (France), amphitheater at, 277(i)
Armed forces. *See also* War; Warriors; Weapons
    and military technology
  Abbasid, 305
  in ancient Greece, 40–41, 43
  in Byzantine Empire, 265, 297
  colonialism and, 780
  conscription in, 775
  eighteenth-century, 598, 632
  English, 534(f), 541, 543
  French, 530–532, 605(m)
    1790s, 666, 672
    late eighteenth century, 652
    under Napoleon, 680, 688–690, 691, 695
    national draft and, 665–666, 671, 676, 688,
      690, 691
    under Republic, 675–679
  German unification and, 758, 759, 761
  in Hellenistic kingdoms, 108
  Macedonian, 101
  in Peloponnesian War (431–404 B.C.E.), 84(f)
  Prussian, 595–596, 632, 634–635, 636
  Roman Empire, 219, 220
    under Augustus, 175
    Christianity and, 225

economic factors, 205–206
  in Golden Age (96–180 C.E.), 189
Roman Republic, 142, 156
  first client armies, 160–161, 162, 165
Russian, 534(f), 538, 592, 595(m)
Sassanid, 261–262
seventeenth-century, 533–537, 534(f), 565
Thirty Years' War and, 501, 503, 520, 541
Arms race, before World War I, 843, 846–849
Arnolfo di Cambio (d. 1302), 404(i)
Arsinoe II (ahr SI no ee) (c. 316–270 B.C.E.),
    110, 111(i)
Art and artists. *See also* Painting(s); Sculpture
  in 1920s, 885–889, 896
  in ancient Greece, 37, 45
  Carolingian renaissance, 309, 314(i),
    314–315
  Dutch, 548–550, 550(i)
  Egyptian, 21
  Flemish school of, 454–456, 456(i)
  French Revolution and, 667
  in Golden Age Athens, 52, 65
  Hellenistic, 112–115
  under Hitler, 913
  in late nineteenth and early twentieth
    centuries, 825–827
  under Louis XIV, 526–527
  modern, 918–919
  in nineteenth century, 785–788
  Paleolithic and Neolithic, 6, 6(i), 8
  postindustrial, 1000–1001
  postmodern, 1064–1065
  post-Soviet, 1062–1063
  in Renaissance (fifteenth century),
    452–457, 471
  Roman, 155–156
  in seventeenth century, 556–559
  in Soviet Union, 908–909, 1005, 1005(i)
Artemia, 285
Artemisia (ar tuh MIHZH ee uh), 55–56
Arthur, King, legend of, 369, 414
Articles of Confederation (1777), 646
Artisans, 344, 382, 782, 783
Art nouveau, 827
Art of Love (Ovid), 183
Art of Measurable Song (Franco of Cologne), 415
Aryan people, 912, 926
Asceticism, Christian, 232–234
  Augustine's view of, 231
Asclepius (uh SKLEE pee uhs), 121, 122, 137
Ashoka (ah SOK ah) (Afghanistan;
    r. c. 268–232 B.C.E.), 121
Ashurbanipal (a shur BA nuh pal) (Neo-Assyria;
    r. 680–626 B.C.E.), 27

Asia
  Alexander the Great's conquests in, 103, 103*(m)*
  decolonization of, 967–968
  economies of (1980 to present), 1055–1057
  imperialism in, 804–808, 805*(m)*
  music and, 826, 827
  trade and, 439, 463, 466, 574
Asia Minor, Romans and (first century B.C.E.),
        137, 151, 152, 161, 162, 201*(m)*
Aspasia (ah SPAY zhuh), 72
Assemblies, Roman, 144, 161
Assembly of Notables (France), 655
Assembly of the Land (Russia; 1649), 538
Assignats, 661
Assyria (uh SIHR ee uh) (Assyrians), 13–14
  Neo-Assyrian Empire (c. 900–650 B.C.E.),
        26*(m)*, 26–27
Astarte, 142
Astell, Mary (1666–1731), 604
Astrolabes (AHS truh laybs), 308
Astrology, 204*(i)*
  in Hellenistic period, 121
  in Mesopotamia, 15
Astronauts, 991
Astronomy, 15, 514–515, 554–555, 600*(i)*, 601,
        619, 992
  Babylonian, 46
  Chaldean (Neo-Babylonian), 27–28
  in Hellenistic period, 118–119, 119*(i)*, 121
Asturlabi, al-, 308
Atatürk (Mustafa Kemal) (1881–1938), 905
Aten, cult of, 22
Athaulf (Visigoth king; r. 410–415), 244
Atheists, 601, 613
Athena, 62–65, 66, 67, 137
Athens. *See also* Greece, ancient
  alliances in, 56–58
  democracy in, 44, 52, 54, 57, 59–61, 73–75, 85,
        86–87, 93, 97, 98
  disunity of Greece after Peloponnesian War
        and, 93–95
  economy of, 44, 58
  Golden Age and Classical period
        (c. 500–323 B.C.E.)
    decline of Classical Greece
        (c. 400–350 B.C.E.), 93–99
    democracy, 73–75, 85, 86–87, 97, 98
    education and intellectual innovation,
        52, 73–78
    end of the Golden Age (431–404 B.C.E.),
        83–87
    establishment of the Athenian Empire
        (479–c. 460 B.C.E.), 56–59
    historical writing, 78

  medicine, 78
  Peloponnesian War (431–404 B.C.E.), 84–86, 93
  Persian wars (499–479 B.C.E.), 52, 53*(m)*,
        54–56
  radical democracy and Pericles' leadership
        (461–445 B.C.E.), 59–61
  religion, 66–68
  Socrates, 75–78
  sophists, 74–75
  Thirty Tyrants period (404–403 B.C.E.),
        86–87, 93, 95
  tragic drama and comedy, 79–83, 80*(i)*, 83*(i)*
  urban architecture and art, 61–65, 62*(m)*,
        63*(i)*, 64*(f)*
  women, 43, 65, 68–72, 77, 82–83, 93
  Philip II of Macedonia and, 99–101
  Sparta and, 51
Atlantic Charter, 938
Atlantic revolutions, 653
Atlantic system, 507–508, 568–577, 570*(m)*,
        578, 606
  slave trade and, 552, 568–575
  world trade and settlement and, 552, 574–577
Atomic bomb. *See* Nuclear weapons
Atomic theory of matter, 75, 116, 154
Attalid kingdom, 107, 107*(m)*, 159
Attalus I (Pergamum; r. 241–197 B.C.E.), 115*(i)*
Attalus III (Attalid king; d. 133 B.C.E.), 152
Attila (AT i lah) (Hun leader; r. c. 440–453), 238
Attlee, Clement, 957
Augustine (missionary; archbishop of
        Canterbury) (r. 601–604), 286
Augustine, St. (bishop of Hippo; 354–430), 225,
        230–232, 255, 286, 287, 290, 311, 330
Augustinian order, 476
Augustinus (Jansen) (609 B.C.E.), 528
Augustus (Octavian) (aw GUHS tuhs)
        (Roman emperor; 63 B.C.E.–14 C.E.),
        110, 129*(i)*, 168*(m)*, 172–177, 184*(i)*,
        188*(m)*, 196, 203, 209*(m)*, 223
  arts and literature under, 182–184
  life in Rome under, 177–182
  principate and, 172–177, 184–185
  public expenditures under, 175
Aurelian (aw REE lee an) (Roman emperor;
        r. 270–275), 208, 209*(m)*
Auschwitz-Birkenau concentration camp, 899, 931
Austerlitz, battle of (1805), 689
Australia, 769, 816, 881
Austrasia (aw STRAY zhuh), 276*(m)*, 285, 310, 311
Austria (1918–1938, 1955–present), 917, 1019
  German annexation of (1938), 925–926
Austria-Hungary (1867–1918), 768
  in 1867, 762*(m)*

anti-Semitism in, 839–840
in early twentieth century (before World
    War I), 843, 844
establishment of dual monarchy in,
    762–763
ethnic groups in, 839(m), 839–840
Peace of Paris (1919–1920) and, 872
World War I and, 847, 852–854, 855, 856, 861,
    863–864, 869, 870, 877
Austrian Empire (to 1867), 395, 535(m), 535–537,
    536(i), 558, 564(m), 705, 762–763. See also
    Austria-Hungary; individual emperors
Congress of Vienna (1814–1815) and,
    700–701, 703
conquest of Hungary (1657–1730), 596(m),
    596–597
Crimean War (1853–1856) and, 751
eighteenth-century reforms, 636–640
French Revolution and, 662, 666, 672,
    676–678
German unification and, 758–761
Habsburgs and, 477, 493(m), 501, 502(m),
    519(m), 605(m)
Italian unification and, 736, 747, 750, 755,
    757, 758
Napoleon and, 681, 688–690, 693
nationalism and, 721–723, 739
Ottoman Empire and (eighteenth century), 596
partition of Poland-Lithuania and, 636, 636(m)
partitions of Poland and, 675(m), 675–676
Prussian wars with and against (1860s),
    759–760
revolution of 1848 and, 738–739
Seven Years' War (1756–1763) and,
    634–636, 635(m)
War of Austrian Succession (1740–1748),
    632–634, 633(m)
Austrian Netherlands (present-day Belgium
    and Luxembourg), 632, 633(m), 653,
    702, 702(m)
French invasion of (1790s), 666, 672
French Revolution and, 676–677, 681, 688
political unrest in (late eighteenth century),
    654–655
Austro-Prussian War, 759
Auto da fé, 447
Avars, 261, 261(m), 262, 263, 311
Avian flu, 1050
Avicenna (Ibn Sina) (980–1037), 308
Avignon papacy (ah vee NYON) ("Babylonian
    Captivity"; 1309–1378), 405–406,
    440–443, 442(m), 450
Azerbaijan, 1034
Aztecs, 469–470

Ba'al Shem Tov (Israel ben Eliezer) (bal shehm
    TOHV) (c. 1700–1760), 620
Babi Yar (Yevtushenko), 1005
Babylon (Babylonia), 24, 27, 28, 105, 109. See also
    Neo-Babylonian Empire
Hammurabi's code, 13–15
"Babylonian Captivity." See Avignon papacy
Bach, Johann Sebastian (1685–1750), 567,
    577, 585
Bacon, Sir Francis (1561–1626), 516
Bactria, 103, 107
Badr, battle of (624), 269(m), 271
Baghdad, 353, 396
as Abbasid capital, 296, 304, 306(m), 307, 336
Bahamas, 467
Baker, Josephine (1906–1976), 889
Bakst, Léon, 828(i)
Balance of power
doctrine of, 597
in eastern Europe (eighteenth century),
    594–597
Baldwin of Flanders (Latin emperor of
    Constantinople; r. 1204–1205), 390
Balkans, the, 7n, 298(m), 487(m), 564(m), 636,
    705, 751, 808
c. 850–950, 302(m)
Byzantine Empire and, 260, 262, 263, 359
in early twentieth century (before World War I),
    799, 812, 814, 843, 844, 845(m)
nationalistic movements in (1815–1830), 705(m)
Ottomans and, 436(m), 436–437, 537
World War I and, 855, 861
Ball, John, 435
Balthild (BALT hild) (Frankish queen;
    d. c. 680), 284(i)
Baltic region, 534, 587, 591, 594, 595(m)
Hanseatic League in, 406–407
Northern Crusades in, 386, 387, 388(m)
Balzac, Honoré de (BAWL zahk)
    (1799–1850), 727
Banks and bankers, 439–440, 457, 458
Dutch Republic, 653
England, 591
France, 589, 684
seventeenth-century, 505, 548
sixteenth-century, 489
Baptists, 543
Barbados, 551, 574
Barcelona, 500
Barnard, Christiaan (1922–2001), 993
Baroque style (ba ROWK), 510–511, 511(i),
    512(i), 537, 557(i), 557–558, 558(i),
    583–584, 624, 626
Barry, Sir Charles (1795–1860), 725

Barth, Karl (1886–1968), 920
Basil I (Byzantine emperor; r. 867–886), 299
Basil II (Byzantine emperor; r. 976–1025), 302, 303
Basil (the Great) of Caesarea (c. 330–379), 234
Basset, Ralph, 364(i)
Bassi, Laura (1711–1778), 600(i)
Bastille prison (bah STEEL), fall of (1789), 652,
        656(i), 658(i), 658(m), 658–659, 667
Batavian Republic, 678
Bathing, 599
Baths, public, in Rome, 178, 207
Baudelaire, Charles-Pierre (bo DLAYR), 786
Bauhaus school of design, 889
Bavaria, 501, 675(m), 689, 871
Baxter, George, 742(i)
Bayeux (by YOO) "tapestry," 361(i)
Bayle, Pierre (1647–1706), 561, 601
Bay of Pigs invasion (1961), 982
Beatles, the, 977, 1000(i)
"Beat" poets, 978
Beaumarchais, Pierre-Augustin Caron de
        (1732–1799), 644
Beauvoir, Simone de, 976
Beccaria, Cesare (1738–1794), 618, 636–637
Becket, Thomas (1118–1170), 365, 382
Beckford, William (1760–1844), 572
Becquerel, Antoine (1852–1908), 824
Bede (673–735), 288, 314
Bedouins (BEHD oo ihnz), 268, 271, 282, 292, 468
Beer Hall Putsch (1923), 879, 894
Beethoven, Ludwig van (1770–1827), 626, 725
Beguines (be GEENS), 379, 410
Behn, Aphra (1640–1689), 561
Belarus, 438
Belgium, 277, 316, 654, 708–709, 733, 801, 874,
        928. *See also* Austrian Netherlands
    in 1920s, 881
    in World War I, 854, 855, 856, 860(i)
Benedict XIII (pope; r. 1394–1417), 443
Benedict Biscop (c. 630–690), 287, 288, 314
Benedictine rule, 234, 310, 315–316, 373, 376,
        376(i), 379
Benedict of Aniane (an YAHN) (c. 750–821), 315
Benedict of Nursia (c. 480–553), 234
Benefices, 428, 440–441, 445
Beneš, Edouard (ben ESH) (1884–1948), 952
Benevento, Duchy of, 289, 289(m), 290–291
Benignus, St., 280
Bentham, Jeremy (1748–1832), 715
Berbers, 305, 390
Berlin, 577, 581, 700
    1848 unrest in, 737–738
    blockade and airlift (1948–1949), 953,
        953(m), 954

Berlin conference (1884–1885), 802, 806
Berlin Wall, 982, 1022, 1023(i)
Bern, 407, 407(m)
Bernard, St. (c. 1090–1153), 362, 371(i), 375,
        377, 382, 387
Bernini, Gian Lorenzo (1598–1680), 557, 557(i)
Bes, 23
Bible. *See also* New Testament;
        Old Testament; Torah
    English-language, 481, 496
    the Enlightenment and, 601
    Latin Vulgate, 314, 481
    vernacular translations of, 481, 483
"Big bang" theory, 992–993
Big Three, 938–939
Bill of Rights (England; 1689), 547
Bill of Rights (United States), 646
Binet, Alfred (bee NAY) (1857–1911), 820
Bin Laden, Osama (b. 1957), 1052–1055
Biology, twentieth-century revolution in, 993
Birth control, 812–813, 879, 890, 903, 908,
        993–995, 1008, 1049. *See also*
        Reproductive rights
Birthrates, 812–813, 1049
    in 1960s and 1970s, 999
    in Communist states, 908, 950, 961
    in eighteenth century, 629
    during Great Depression, 903
Bishops, 328, 332, 333, 345–346
    in Byzantine Empire, 266
    early Christian church and, 201–202, 226–227
    in early Middle Ages, 282–283, 285, 286,
        288, 290
    German, 333
    monasteries and, 235
    Nestorian, 228
    reforms of 1050–1150 and, 346–352, 357
Bismarck, Otto von (BIZ mark, OT to fahn)
        (1815–1898), 745, 748, 761(i), 838
    alliance system and, 843–844
    colonial policy, 801, 802
    German unification and, 758–761, 760(m)
    Roman Catholic church and, 789
Black and Tans, 880
Black Death. *See* Plague
Black Shirts (Italy), 892, 893(i)
Blitz, 928
Blitzkrieg, 927, 928, 932
"Blood libel," 358
Blood sports, 729
Bloody Sunday (1972), 1016
Blum, Léon (1872–1950), 917
Boccaccio, Giovanni (bo KAH cho, jo VAH nee)
        (1313–1375), 428, 448–449, 450

Bodin, Jean (1530–1596), 512–513, 517
Boers, 801, 802
Boer War (1899–1902), 802, 847
Boethius, 242
Bohemia (boh HEE mee uh) (Bohemians),
 333–334, 437, 469(m), 768
 religious dissent and popular revolt in
  (fifteenth century), 443, 445–446
 in seventeenth century, 535–536
  religious conflicts, 498–499
 Thirty Years' War and, 498–499, 501,
  502, 502(m)
Boleslaw the Brave (Poland; r. 992–1025),
 334, 336
Boleyn, Anne (boh LIHN) (1507–1536), 495
Bolívar, Simon (1783–1830), 706–707
Böll, Heinrich (bohl) (1917–1985), 978
Bologna (Italy), law education at, 370–372, 402
Bolsheviks, 833, 865–869, 867(m), 871, 883,
 890–891, 907, 908, 922
Bonaparte, Caroline (BOH nuh part), 685
Bonaparte, Jerome, 689
Bonaparte, Joseph, 685, 691, 693
Bonaparte, Louis (Holland; r. 1806–1810),
 685, 690
Bonaparte, Louis-Napoleon. *See* Napoleon III
Bonaparte, Lucien, 683
Bonaparte, Napoleon. *See* Napoleon Bonaparte
Boniface, Bishop (680–754), 310
Boniface VIII (pope; r. 1294–1303), 401, 404(i),
 404–405, 407, 422
Boniface IX (pope; r. 1389–1404), 436
Book of Common Prayer, 542, 544, 545
Book of Psalms, 265
Book of the City of Ladies, The
 (Christine de Pisan), 449
Book of the Dead (Egypt), 23
Books and publishing industry. *See also* Literature
 in Augustan Rome, 183
 in Byzantine Empire, 253–254
 in eighteenth century, 583, 585, 618–619, 621,
  626–627
 in fifteenth century, 451–452
Bora, Katharina von (1499–1550), 484
Borodino, battle of (1812), 693
Bosnia-Herzegovina, 7n, 844, 1032
Bossuet, Bishop Jacques-Benigne (baws WAY)
 (1627–1704), 528, 561, 601–602
Boston (Massachusetts), 508, 628, 644
Boston Tea Party (1773), 645
Boucher, François (boo SHAY, frahn SWAH)
 (1703–1770), 584
Bourbon dynasty (France), 489–490,
 588(m), 704

Bourgeoisie. *See* Middle class(es)
Bouvines, battle of (boo VEEN) (1214), 398(m),
 399, 401
Boxer Rebellion (China; 1900), 805(m),
 806–807, 807(i)
Brahe, Tycho (bra) (1546–1601), 514–515
Brandenburg Gate, 1023(i)
Brandenburg-Prussia, 501, 502(m), 529, 532–534,
 535(m), 539, 555, 564(m)
Brandt, Willy (1913–1992), 1004
Braque, Georges (1882–1963), 826
Brasidas (BRA sid as) (d. 422), 86(m)
Braun, Eva, 936
Brazil, 466, 468, 470, 486, 691, 707
 slavery and slave trade in, 569, 570(m), 571(f),
  572–575, 731
Brest-Litovsk, Treaty of (1918), 867
Brezhnev, Leonid (1906–1982), 1004
Brezhnev Doctrine, 1012, 1022
Britain (British Isles). *See also* England;
  Great Britain
 Anglo-Saxon invasion of, 240
 early Middle Ages, 286–288
 Viking invasions (eighth to tenth centuries),
  319(m), 320–321, 330
British East India Company, 574, 577
Brittany, 362, 363(m), 398, 398(m), 400(m)
Brontë, Charlotte (BRAHN tee) (1816–1855), 727
Bronze Age, 5, 12
Brothers of St. Francis, 379–380, 383
Brown Shirts, 879
Brown v. Board of Education (1954), 976
Bruges (broozh), 439
Brunelleschi, Filippo (1377–1446), 456
Bruno of Cologne (c. 1030–1101), 339–340, 355,
 375, 379, 381, 383
Brunswick Manifesto (1792), 663
Brussels, 456(i), 654, 672
Brutus, Lucius Junius (sixth century B.C.E.),
 143, 167
Brutus, Marcus Junius (85–42 B.C.E.), 167
Bubonic plague. *See* Plague
Buccaneers, 575
Building(s) (construction). *See also*
  Architecture; Housing
 in twelfth century, 374, 375(i), 376(i), 378(i)
Bulgakov, Mikhail, 1063
Bulgaria (Bulgarians; Bulgars), 8n, 261, 261(m),
 262, 296–297, 298(m), 301–303, 302(m),
 322, 436, 808, 950
 World War I and, 844, 845, 846, 861
 World War II and, 929, 938
Bureaucracy. *See also* Administration

(continued)

under Louis XIV, 529–530, 532
in nineteenth century, 741, 774–775
in Russia, 537–538
in Soviet Union, 906
Thirty Years' War and, 503
Weber on, 823
Burgundofara, 283–284
Burgundy (Burgundians), 276(*m*), 285, 431–433,
    433(*m*), 435, 437, 456, 459
Burgundy, duke of, 425(*i*), 431–433, 433(*m*)
Burial practices
    Egyptian, 20, 23(*i*), 23–24
    Mesopotamian, 10
    Paleolithic (hunter-gatherer societies), 6
    Roman, 137, 181, 182(*i*)
Burke, Edmund (1729–1799), 714–715
Burma, 929
Burschenschaften, 722
Bush, George W., 1046, 1054
Business and commerce, 13–14. *See also*
        Management; Trade
    in 1920s, 881–882
    revolution in (eleventh and twelfth centuries)
        business arrangements, 343–344
        centers of commerce, 340–346
        self-government of towns, 345–346
        trade routes, 341(*m*)
    revolution in (nineteenth century),
        770–772
Byblos (BIHB luhs), 24
Byron, Lord (George Gordon) (1788–1824),
    724, 726
Byzantine Empire (Byzantium), 214, 218, 243(*m*),
    245–255, 272(*m*). *See also specific emperors*
    c. 600, 254(*m*), 261(*m*), 292–293
    c. 700, 263(*m*)
    c. 750, 336–337
    Christianity and Christians in, 245–246, 248
        classical literature and, 245, 251, 265
        icons and iconoclasm, 266(*i*), 266–267,
            290–291, 293, 299, 315
        ninth and tenth centuries, 301–303
    classical literature and education in, 252–255,
        260, 265, 266
    Islam (Muslims) and, 268, 275, 296–297
    Leo IX and, 347–348
    Magyars and, 319(*m*), 322
    Ottomans and, 436(*m*), 436–437
    pope and, 290–291, 310–311, 312(*m*)
    renewed strength and influence of (750–1050),
        296–303
        expansion of (860–1025), 297–303, 298(*m*)
        Macedonian renaissance (c. 870–c. 1025),
            297, 299–300, 301(*i*), 307, 314(*i*), 315

new states under the influence of Byzantium,
    301–303
Roman identity in, 246, 247
Sassanid Persia and, 250, 261(*m*), 261–262,
    262(*i*), 269(*m*), 272(*m*), 273, 274(*i*),
    296–297
society in, 245–249, 248
urban decline in, 263–265
wars against invaders (c. 570–750), 261–263, 359

Cabet, Étienne (1788–1856), 719, 735
Cabot, John (c. 1450–1499?), 464(*m*), 470
Cabral, Pedro Alvares (kuh BRAL) (1467–1520),
    466, 470
Caesar, Julius (SEE zahr, JOOL yuhs)
    (100–44 B.C.E.), 153(*m*), 172, 173, 176(*f*)
    coin portrait of, 165(*i*)
    downfall of republic and, 159, 163–167, 168(*m*)
Calas, Jean, 614
Calendar, 593*n*
    Egyptian, 22
    French Revolution and, 669, 674
    Islamic, 271
    Muslim, 308(*i*)
    Roman, 167
    Russian, 593
Caligula (ca LIG yoo lah) (Roman emperor;
        r. 37–41 C.E.), 185–186
Caliphs, 268, 272(*m*), 273–275, 293, 322. *See also*
    specific caliphs
    Abbasids and, 296, 303–307
Calvin, John (1509–1564), 479–481, 480(*f*)
Calvinism (Calvinists), 519(*m*). *See also* Puritans
    in Brandenburg-Prussia, 533
    in England, 481, 486, 542
    in France (Huguenots), 480–481, 489–491,
        490(*m*), 528–529, 614
    in Netherlands (Dutch Republic), 481, 493–494,
        494(*m*), 551
    Peace of Augsburg (1555) and, 491
    Scottish, 481, 497
    Thirty Years' War and, 498–499, 501–502
Cambodia, 1013
Cambyses (kam BI seez) (Persia;
        r. 529–522 B.C.E.), 55(*m*)
Cameroon, 801
Camus, Albert (1913–1960), 975
Canaanite alphabet, 24, 25, 37
Canada, 470, 509, 634, 635(*m*)
    in 1920s, 881
    dominion status, 766
    French, 530, 574, 588(*m*)
Cannae (KAN eye), battle of (216 B.C.E.), 150
Canon law, 347, 348, 352, 371, 403–404, 443, 483

Canon of Medicine (Avicenna), 308
Canterbury, 286, 288
Canterbury Tales (Chaucer), 449
Cape of Good Hope, 465, 570(*m*), 575
Capetian kings (cap EE shuhn), 332, 392, 398–401
Capital-intensive industrialization, 769
Capitalism, 615, 631, 717
    class struggle and, 783
    women's rights and, 831
Capitals, Greek, 64(*f*)
Caracalla (ca rah KAH lah) (Roman emperor;
        r. 211–217), 207–208
Carbonari, 691, 705, 722
Carchemish (KAR kuh mihsh), battle of
        (605 B.C.E.), 27
Cardinals, 441–443
Caribbean colonies
    French, 678(*m*), 678–680, 679(*i*). *See also*
        Americas, the, French colonies in
    slavery and slave trade in, 568, 569–575,
        570(*m*), 571(*f*), 573(*i*)
    trade and, 630, 691
Caribbean region, 464(*m*), 467, 469, 508–509, 551
Caribs, 467, 509, 575
Caroline minuscule, 315
Carolingian Empire (Carolingians)
        (kar oh LIN jee un), 285, 295,
        296, 309–315, 312(*m*), 332, 343
    economy, 317–318
    invasions by Vikings, Muslims, and Magyars,
        309, 318–323, 319(*m*)
Carolingian renaissance (c. 790–c. 900), 309,
        314(*i*), 314–315
Carrier, Jean-Baptiste, 671, 674
Cartels, 769, 881, 988
Carter, Jimmy (b. 1924), 1016
Carthage (KAR thij), 55, 88, 142, 148–152, 166,
        241(*i*)
Carthusian order (kar THOO zhuhn), 339, 339(*i*),
        355, 375, 383
Cartier, Jacques (1491–1557), 470
Cartoons of Prophet Muhammed, 1058
Cartwright, Edmund, 630
Casimir III (Poland; r. 1333–1370), 437–438
Cassatt, Mary (ka SAHT) (1845–1926), 788
Cassen, Bernard, 1046
Cassiodorus (cas i o DOH ruhs) (c. 490–585),
        242, 245
Cassius Dio (c. 164–230), 174
Castellans (CAS tel ens), 326–327, 332,
        345, 357, 392
Castiglione, Baldassare (1478–1529), 504
Castile (kas TEEL), 368(*i*), 388(*m*), 390–391,
        391(*m*), 442, 456(*i*)

Castile-León (kas TEEL lay ON), 391(*m*),
        394(*m*), 408
Castlereagh, Robert (KAHS uhl ray)
        (1769–1822), 701–703
Castles, 323, 326–327, 328, 332, 363, 366, 387.
        See also Castellans
Castor and Pollux, Temple of (Rome), 129(*i*)
Castro, Fidel (b. 1926), 981–982
Catacombs, 199(*i*)
Catalonia (Catalans), 500
Cateau-Cambrésis (kah TO kahm bray SEE),
        peace treaty of (1559), 488
Catena, Vincenzo, 473(*i*)
Cathars, 381, 383, 392
Catherine II (the Great) (Russian empress;
        r. 1762–1796), 608(*i*), 609–610, 613,
        618, 622, 624, 634, 637(*i*), 641–642
    Poland and, 675
    reforms under, 636–638, 640, 648, 654–655, 691
Catherine of Alexandria (saint; fourth
        century C.E.?), 233(*i*)
Catherine of Aragon (d. 1536), 495
Catherine de Medicis (duh MEHD ih chee)
        (1519–1589), 489–490
Catherine of Siena (see YEN ah)
        (1347–1380), 443
Catholic church. *See* Roman Catholic church
Catholic League (France), 490
Cato, Marcus Porcius (KAY toh) (234–149 B.C.E.),
        135, 150, 154, 166
Catullus (kuh TUL uhs) (c. 84–54 B.C.E.), 154
Cavaliers, 542–543
Cavendish, Margaret, 556
Cavour, Camillo di (kah VOOR,
        kah MEEL lo dee), 748, 755–756, 758, 762
Ceauçescu, Nicolae (chow SHES koo), 1023–1024
Celibacy, clerical, 202, 232, 283, 290, 347, 351–352,
        372, 382
Celts (kelts), in Britain, 240
Censors, 145
Censuses, 151(*f*), 459, 775
Central Powers, 854–855, 858, 864, 869
Centuriate Assembly, 144
Cervantes, Miguel de (suhr VAHN teez)
        (1547–1616), 497, 585
Ceuta (SYOO tuh), 465
Cézanne, Paul (say ZAHN) (1839–1906), 826
Chaeronea (ki ron AY ah), battle of
        (338 B.C.E.), 101
Chalcedon, Council of (451), 229, 252
Chaldeans (kal DEE ans), 27–28
Chamberlain, Neville (1869–1940), 926, 928
Chandragupta (India; r. 323–299 B.C.E.), 107
Chaplin, Charlie (1889–1977), 886, 918

Chariots, 24, 26, 120, 181, 246

Charities (charitable organizations), 505–506, 562–564, 598, 628, 686, 729, 749, 818

Chariton (second century C.E.), 192

Charlemagne (SHAR luh mayn) (Frankish king; r. 768–814), 295, 296, 304, 311–315, 311–317, 312(m), 365
  successors of (814–911), 315–317, 332

Charles I (England; r. 1625–1649), 541–545, 664

Charles I (the Bald) (Frankish king and Carolingian emperor; r. 843–877), 295, 296, 312(m), 316

Charles II (England; r. 1660–1685), 545–546, 552, 553–554

Charles II (Spain; r. 1665–1700), 587

Charles IV (Holy Roman emperor; r. 1347–1378), 444–445, 446

Charles IV (Spain; r. 1788–1808), 691

Charles V (France; r. 1364–1380), 442–443, 487–489

Charles V (Holy Roman emperor and Spain as Charles I; r. 1520–1558), 477–478, 480(f), 487–489, 491–492, 492, 492(i), 495

Charles VI (Holy Roman emperor; r. 1685–1740), 632

Charles VII (France; r. 1422–1461), 431, 433, 435

Charles IX (France; r. 1560–1574), 489, 490, 492

Charles X (France; r. 1824–1830), 733

Charles XII (Sweden; r. 1697–1718), 594, 595

Charles Albert (Piedmont-Sardinia; r. 1831–1849), 705, 736, 737

Charles of Anjou (Naples and Sicily; r. 1266–1285), 396

Charles Martel (mayor of palace in Merovingian kingdom; 715–741), 310

Charles the Simple (or Straightforward) (Carolingian king; r. 893–923), 321

Charter 77 (Czechoslovakia), 1022

Charter of the Nobility (Prussia; 1785), 622

Chartist movement (Great Britain), 720, 741

Chartres (SHAHR truh) cathedral, 416, 420

Chartreuse, La (shar TROOZ), 339, 339(i)

Chateaubriand, François-René de (sha to bree AHND) (1768–1848), 687–688

Châtelet, Émilie du (1706–1749), 612

Chaucer, Geoffrey (CHAW suhr) (c. 1342–1400), 448–449, 450

Chávez, César (1927–1993), 1006

Chechnya, 1034, 1038–1040

Cheka (secret police), 868

Chelmno, labor camp at, 931

Cheops (KEE ahps) (Egypt; 2590–2567 B.C.E.), 19–20

Chernobyl nuclear power plant explosion (1986), 1020–1021, 1047

Chiefdoms, Germanic, 237

Childbearing
  in Florence (fifteenth century), 460(i), 460–462
  in Golden Age Athens, 68, 71
  in Roman Empire, 194

Childbirth, 68, 506, 599, 994–995
  in Roman Empire, 194

Child care, in the Renaissance (fifteenth century), 460–462

Child labor, 710–712, 741

Children. See also Education; Family; Infanticide; Schools
  in eighteenth century, 627
  in Golden Age Athens, 69, 71, 72
  in Hellenistic kingdoms, 110–111
  Napoleon's Civil Code and, 686
  in nineteenth century, 728, 735, 741, 777–778, 818
  in Rome, 180, 183, 194–195
  in Sparta, 43–44

China, 4, 245, 304, 427, 451
  1980s to present, 1021–1022, 1055–1057
  Christian missionaries in, 486
  Communist takeover in, 967
  Cultural Revolution in, 1014
  European powers and (nineteenth century), 781, 799, 802
  Europeans in, 571(m), 575, 648(m)
  Great Britain and (nineteenth century), 732, 801
  Japan and, 805, 920–922
  Mongol conquest of, 385, 397(m), 397–398, 463
  Nixon's visit to (1972), 1013–1014
  resistance to colonial domination, 806–807
  trade and, 385(i), 397(m), 397–398, 470, 570(m), 583
  travel literature in 1700s and, 603

Chingiz Khan (c. 1162–1227), 385, 396, 397(m)

Chirac, Jacques (b. 1932), 1019

Chivalry, 369, 401, 430, 435, 449, 497

Chlorofluorocarbons (CFCs), 1047

Chocolate, 568, 577

Cholera, 699(i), 713

Chopin, Frédéric (shoh PAHN) (1810–1849), 726

Chosroes II (koss ROH) (Sassanid king; r. 591–628), 262

Chrétien de Troyes (KRAY tyahn duh TRWAH) (c. 1150–1190), 369

Christ. See Jesus

Christian IV (Denmark; r. 1596–1648), 499

Christian church ("the church"). See also Bishops; Christianity, Roman Empire and; Roman Catholic church

Carolingian renaissance and, 309, 314(i), 314–315
humanism and, 451
orthodoxy and heresies, 228–229
reform of (1050–1150), 346–358
  beginnings of, 346–348
  early crusades and crusader states, 352–356
  Gregorian reform and Investiture Conflict (1073–1085), 349(m), 349–351, 366–367, 382
  Jews and, 356–358
  sacraments and, 351, 443–445
Christian Democrats (Italy), 957
Christianity (Christians). See also Christian church; Monasticism; Protestantism
in Americas, 467–470, 574–575
in British Isles, 286–288
in Byzantine Empire, 245–246, 248
  classical literature and, 252–255, 265
  icons and iconoclasm, 266(i), 266–267, 290–291, 293, 299, 315
  Kievan Russia, 302–303
  ninth and tenth centuries, 301–303
classical literature and, 282, 309, 311
colonialism and, 799
conversion to
  in American colonies, 574–575
  Czechs and Poles, 333
  Magyars, 335
  Russians, 302–303
  Scandinavia, 322
  in the sixteenth century, 484–486
  Vikings, 320–322, 330
early, 195–205, 214, 225
  Jews and, 195–205
Hellenistic period and, 92–93
influences on, 30, 32, 122, 125
in Ireland, 286–288
Islam and, 268, 269, 272, 273–275, 388(m), 390–391, 391(m), 394
Jews and (twelfth century), 356–358, 380(m), 383
in late third century C.E., 201(m)
Napoleon and, 683–684, 687
in Poland, 636
poverty and, 562–563
Roman Empire and, 171, 195–205, 222–235
  appeal of religious and social values, 225
  Constantine's conversion, 214, 221
  development as new religion, 199–202
  Jesus and spread of his teachings, 196–198
  Jews and, 224–225
  the military and, 225
  persecution of Christians, 200, 208–210, 221

polytheism and, 202–204, 221, 222(i), 222–224, 226(m)
  spread of (300–600), 222–227, 226(m)
  as state religion, 224, 225
science and, 514, 791
in twelfth and thirteenth centuries, 373–383, 380(m)
Voltaire on, 613
women and, 295(i), 604
  early Christianity, 198, 202, 225–226
  monasteries, 234, 280, 283–285, 284(i), 286, 288, 333
  virginity and sexual renunciation, 232
Christian missionaries, 704
Arianism and, 228
in China, 575, 781
in England, 286–288, 293, 310
Jesuit, 484–486, 485(i)
in Scandinavia, 322
thirteenth-century, 392
Christian Social Party (Austria-Hungary), 839–840
Christina (Sweden; r. 1632–1654), 534
Christine de Pisan (pee ZAHN) (1364–c. 1430), 449(i), 449–450
Chrysippus (kris IP uhs) (c. 280–206 B.C.E.), 116
Church, the. See Christian church
Churches (buildings)
Byzantine, 245, 263
Gothic, 386, 414(i), 416–421, 417(i)
Italian, 329
Ottonian dynasty and (Germany), 333
in post-Carolingian age, 325–326
Romanesque, 374, 375(i), 376, 378(i), 414(i)
Churchill, Winston (1874–1965), 809, 928, 934, 957
postwar settlement and, 938–942
Church of England (Anglican church), 495–496, 496(i), 508, 541–543, 703
in seventeenth century, 544–547
Church of the Holy Wisdom (Hagia Sophia), 250, 251(i), 437
Cicero (SIHS uh roh) (106–43 B.C.E.), 135, 136, 139, 147, 154–155, 182, 253, 278, 450
Circumcision, 198
Cisalpine Republic, 678
Cistercians (sih STUR shuhnz), 362, 375–379, 376(i), 378(i), 383
Cîteaux (see TOH), 375
Cities. See also Towns; Urbanization
in Byzantine Empire, 260, 263–265, 273, 281, 292
in colonies, 780

(continued)

in eighteenth century, 577, 578, 581–583,
    598–599, 606
in Hellenistic kingdoms, 108–109, 118
in Italy, 323, 329–330, 341, 341(*m*), 343, 395,
    408. *See also* Florence; Milan; Rome; Venice
    communes and, 345–346, 350, 366–367,
    406, 457
Mesopotamian, 8–13, 14–15
of Roman Empire, 292–293
trade and, 339–340, 342(*i*), 382
urban renewal in, 773
Citizenship
    in ancient Greece, 39–41, 44, 60–61, 70, 72
    Roman, 133(*i*), 139–140, 148, 159, 166, 189
        under Caracalla, 207–208
        slaves and, 180
        Social War (91–87 B.C.E.), 160
    Stoicism and, 117
City of God (Augustine), 230, 231, 311
City-states
    Greek (*polis*), 38–47. *See also* Athens; Sparta
        Alexander the Great and, 104–105
        citizenship in, 39–44
        disunity after Peloponnesian War, 98–99
        Hellenistic period (323–30 B.C.E.), 92,
            107(*m*), 108
        Philip II of Macedonia and, 99–101
    Mesopotamian, 8–13, 9
Civil Code (Napoleonic Code), 683, 685–686, 690,
    704, 722, 730
Civil Constitution of the Clergy (1790), 661–662
Civil disobedience, 904(*i*), 905, 977
Civilizations, early (to 1000 B.C.E.), 3–25
Civil rights, 759, 814. *See also* Religious
    tolerance/intolerance; Voting rights
Civil Rights Act (1964), 1006
Civil rights movement (United States), 946,
    976–977, 1006–1009
Civil war(s)
    in England
        1139–1153, 362
        1460–1485 (War of the Roses), 435
        1642–1646, 541–545, 542(*m*), 556
        thirteenth century, 409
    in France (1790s), 671, 673
    in Germany (1075–1122), 346, 350, 366
    Islamic (seventh and eight centuries), 274,
        304–305
    in Roman Empire
        305–324, 218, 219, 221
        first century C.E., 186
        second and third centuries C.E., 172, 173,
            205–206, 208–210, 209(*m*), 214
    in Roman Republic (49–45 B.C.E.), 159, 161–163

in Russia (1917–1922), 867(*m*), 868–869,
    889–890
in Spain (1936–1939), 923–924
in United States (1861–1865), 755, 764–766
Clair, René, 918
Clairvaux (monastery of), 375
Clans, Germanic, 237
Clare, St., 379
Class differences. *See* Hierarchy
Classical literature and learning, 483, 666
    in Byzantine Empire, 252–255, 265, 359–360
    Carolingian renaissance and, 309, 311, 314(*i*),
        314–315
    in England and Ireland, 287–288
    Islam and, 307–309, 371
    Macedonian renaissance (c. 870–c. 1025) and,
        297, 299–300, 301(*i*), 314(*i*)
    in Renaissance (fifteenth century), 425–426,
        448–451, 471
    in sixth century, 282
Classical music, 625–626
Classicism, 583, 724
    French, 557–558, 558(*i*)
Claudius (KLAW dee uhs) (Roman emperor;
    r. 41–54 C.E.), 186
Cleisthenes (KLYS then eez) (c. 508 B.C.E.),
    44, 59, 60
Clemenceau, Georges (klehm uhn SOH)
    (1841–1929), 871, 872
Clement VII (pope; r. 1523–1534), 442–443, 495
Clement XIV (pope; r. 1769–1774), 637
Cleon (KLEE ahn) (d. 422 B.C.E.), 82
Cleopatra VII (klee o PAT rah) (69–30 B.C.E.), 92,
    110, 124(*m*), 166, 173, 203
Clergy (priests and priestesses). *See also* Bishops;
    Christian missionaries; Papacy
    in American colonies, 574–575
    anti-Semitic persecutions and, 446–448
    celibacy of, 283, 290, 347, 351–352, 372, 382
    Roman, 139, 174(*i*)
    Roman Catholic
        in Bohemia, 445–446
        Fourth Lateran Council and (1215), 389(*i*),
            403–404
        taxation of, 404(*i*), 404–405
Climate (climate change)
    ancient Egypt, 21
    fourteenth century, 426–427
    global warming, 1047
    Neolithic Revolution and, 7
    seventeenth century, 505
Cloning, 993
Clothar II (Austrasia; r. 613–623), 285
Clothing

in Byzantine Empire, 247
in eighteenth century, 582
in nineteenth century, 730, 811
after World War II, 978
Clotilda (Frankish queen; d. 545), 242
Clovis (KLOH vis) (Frankish king; r. 485–511), 242, 244, 288
Cluny, 322
Benedictine monastery of, 339(i), 346–347, 370, 373
Cnidos, 114
Cnut (k NOOT) (**Canute**) (England, Denmark, and Norway; r. 1017–1035), 322, 331
Cochin China, 779–780
Codex (Byzantine legal code), 251, 254–255
Coffee, 567(i), 567–569, 576, 577, 606
Coffeehouses, 567(i), 567–568, 577, 583, 610, 626, 647
Coins (coinage)
Arabic, 274, 274(i)
Carolingian economy and, 317
debasement of, 206, 207(f)
invention of, 10
Roman, 165(i), 175, 206, 207(f), 219
Viking coin hoards (c. 865–895), 321(f)
Colbert, Jean-Baptiste (kohl BEHR) (1619–1683), 529–530, 556
Cold war, 942, 982(m)
cracks in consensus of, 1004–1006
culture of, 979–981
decolonization during, 966–974
origins of, 946, 950–952
Coligny, Gaspard de, 489
Collection in 74 Titles (canon law textbook), 348
Collective farms, 907, 1037
Collective security, 874, 876, 938
Collectivization, 963, 965
in China, 967
Colleges and universities, 422
in postindustrial society, 998
sixteenth-century, 483, 484
thirteenth-century, 370–372, 387, 401, 409–413
Colloquies (Erasmus), 475
Collot, Jacques (koh LOH, zhahk), 500(i)
Cologne (kuh LOHN), 357, 430, 452
Coloni (tenant farmers), 219, 236–237
Colonies (colonialism; colonized peoples), 798, 799. *See also* Americas, the; North America, English (British) colonies in; North America, French colonies in; Spain, American colonies of
in 1920s, 880–881, 894(m)
in Africa, 465, 465(m)
Alexander the Great and, 103

competition for (seventeenth century), 507–509, 568
consumer society and (eighteenth century), 577
decolonization, 966–974, 971(m)
in early twentieth century, 843
the Enlightenment and, 614–615, 618, 620, 640, 642, 644–648
Great Depression (1930s) and, 903–905
Greek, 38–39
League of Nations and, 874
mercantilism and, 508, 530
resistance to, 803(m), 807–808, 940, 970–973
Roman, 148, 159–160, 166, 173
Western social order in, 778–781
World War I and, 852, 855, 859, 863, 874
Colosseum (Rome), 187
Colossus (computer), 990
Columbanus, St. (d. 615), 282–283
Columbus, Christopher (1451–1506), 464(m), 466–467
COMECON (Council for Mutual Economic Assistance), 963
Comedies
Athenian, 81–82, 83(i)
Hellenistic, 113–114
Roman, 153–154, 155(i)
Comintern (Communist International), 868
Commenda, 343
Commerce. *See* Business and commerce; Mercantilism; Trade
Committee of Public Safety (France), 665–667, 671–672, 674
Common law, English, 364(i)
Common Market, 960–961, 1014, 1019, 1040
Common Sense (Paine), 958
Commonwealth of Independent States, 1034, 1035(m)
Communes
Italian, 345–346, 350, 366–367, 382, 406, 457
Swiss, 407, 407(m)
Communism (Communists), 615, 618, 719, 906
in 1920s, 879, 889–892
collapse of Soviet communism, 1020–1025, 1025(m), 1030
breakup of Yugoslavia, 1032–1033
disintegration of Soviet Union, 1034–1036, 1035(m)
in Poland, 1021–1022
revolutions of 1989, 1020–1025
in Germany, 911
in Russia and Soviet Union, 865–869
Communist Manifesto (Marx and Engels), 719

Communist Party (Soviet Union), 867
Comnena, Anna (1083–c. 1148), 359–360
Comnenian dynasty (Byzantine; 1081–1185), 359
Compagnia (kohm PAHN yuh), 343, 382
Companions, in Athens, 71–72
Computers, 990(*i*), 990–991
Comte, Auguste (kawmt) (1798–1857), 731, 792
Concentration camps, Nazi, 912, 947
Concert of Europe. *See* Congress of Vienna
Conciliarists, 443, 458
Concordance of Discordant Canons (Decretum)
   (Gratian), 352
Concordat of Worms (1122), 350
Confederation of the Rhine, 689(*m*), 690, 693
Confessions (Augustine), 231
Confessions (Rousseau), 620
Confraternities, 563
Confucianism, 486
Congo, 801, 972
Congregationalism, 542
Congress of Vienna (concert of Europe;
   1814–1815), 700–703, 701(*i*), 702(*m*),
   704, 707, 726, 750, 751
Conservatism (conservatives) 714–715, 741–742
Conservative Party (Tories; Great Britain), 764,
   848, 1017
Constantine (brother of Alexander I of Russia), 705
Constantine (Byzantine emperor; r. 306–337),
   215(*i*), 215–218, 219, 220, 222, 224(*i*)
   Arianism and, 228
   conversion to Christianity, 214, 221
Constantine VII Porphyrogenitos (Byzantine
   emperor; r. 913–959), 297–298, 299–300,
   300(*i*), 301(*i*)
Constantine Palaeologus (Byzantine emperor;
   r. 1449–1453), 437
Constantinople, 218, 221, 238, 245, 290, 292,
   299, 353(*m*), 599
   conquest of (1204), 386–390, 388(*m*), 422
   cultural renaissance in, 296–297, 300(*i*),
      301(*i*), 307
   in eleventh and twelfth centuries, 359–360
   under Justinian, 249–252
   Latin empire of (1204–1261), 390, 394(*m*)
   Ottoman conquest of (1453), 425, 425(*i*),
      436(*m*), 436–437, 451
   walls of, 264(*i*), 275
Constantius II (Roman emperor; r. 337–361), 228
Constitution(s)
   French
      1790s, 657, 659–660, 662–663, 674, 681, 683
      1946, 957
   German, 761
   Spanish (1812), 704

United States, 644, 646, 653
Constitutionalism, 514, 524, 565, 715
   in Dutch Republic, 548–552
   in England (Great Britain), 540–547, 552–554,
      590, 615
      civil war of 1642–1646, 540–545, 542(*m*)
      Cromwell and, 543–545, 545(*i*)
      Glorious Revolution of 1688, 545–547
   the Enlightenment and, 618, 623, 652
   in Poland-Lithuania, 539–540
Constitutions of Melfi (Frederick II), 395
Consuls, 144, 145, 160, 161, 163, 175
Consumerism (consumer society; consumer
      capitalism), 600, 606, 631, 769, 771–772
   in 1920s, 884–885
   1945–1960, 977–979
   in eighteenth century, 577, 578
Contado, 343, 346
Continental Congress (American colonies), 646
Continental System, 691
Contraception. *See* Birth control
Contracts, 344
Contrasts (Pugin), 725
Conversations on the Plurality of Worlds
      (de Fontenelle), 600–601
Conversos (Jewish converts to Christianity), 447–448
Copernicus, Nicolaus (koh PUR nih kuhs)
      (1473–1543), 514–515, 554, 600
Corday, Charlotte, 670
Córdoba, 391, 391(*m*)
   emirate (caliphate) of, 306–307
Corinne (de Staël), 687
Corinth, 56, 83–84, 98, 152, 166
Corneille, Pierre (cor NAY) (1606–1684), 527,
      532, 561
Corn Laws (Great Britain), 716, 716(*i*), 717
Corporatist state (Italy), 893–894
Corsica, 148, 150
Cortés, Hernán (1485–1547), 469–470
Cortes (KOR tez), Spanish, 408
Cossacks, 538–540, 641, 642(*i*)
Cottage industries. *See* Putting-out system
Cotton industry and trade, 621, 629–631, 630(*i*),
      691, 709–710
Council for Mutual Economic Assistance
      (COMECON), 963
Council of 500 (Athens), 59–61, 73
Council of Chalcedon (451), 229, 252
Council of Clermont (1095), 354
Council of Constance (1414–1418), 443–444, 446
Council of Fifteen, 409
Council of Five Hundred (France), 683
Council of Lyon (1245), 395
Council of Nicaea (325), 228

Council of Pisa (1409), 443
Council of Reims (1049), 348
Council of Soissons (1121), 373
Council of Trent (1545–1563), 484
Counterculture, 1008, 1013
Counter-Reformation, 484–486, 498, 507, 510
Counts, 323–328, 332, 398–399
Courbet, Gustave (koor BAY, goos TAHV)
        (1819–1877), 786–787, 787(i)
Court culture
    under Louis XIV, 523–528
    twelfth-century, 367–369
Courtly love, 368–369
Court of Star Chamber (England), 542
Court system. See Judicial system
Covenant with God, Hebrew, 31–32
Cranmer, Thomas (1489–1556), 495
Crassus, Marcus Licinius (c. 115–53 B.C.E.), 163,
        164, 165
Crécy, battle of (1346), 432(m)
Crédit Mobilier, 750
Crete, 33(m), 33–36, 35(i), 297, 298(m)
Crick, Francis (1916–2004), 977–978, 993
Crimea, 427, 427(m), 868
Crime and Punishment (Dostoevsky), 786
Crimean War (1853–1856), 748, 749, 750, 751(m),
        753, 762, 780
Crimes against humanity, 956–957
Criminology, 820
Critias, 95
Critique of Pure Reason, The (Kant), 619
Croatia (Croats), 7n, 301, 302(m), 535, 537, 869,
        872, 1032
    World War I and, 861
Croesus, 45(i)
Cromwell, Oliver (1599–1658), 543–545, 545(i)
Cromwell, Thomas (1485–1540), 495
Crusader states, 352–356, 355(m), 380(m),
        388(m), 465
Crusades, 352–356, 354(i), 355(m), 370, 380(m),
        382, 383, 386, 400, 422
    1150–1300, 386–391, 388(m), 389(i)
    Albigensian (1209–1229), 391–393
    First (1096–1099), 353(m), 353–355, 357, 359
    Fourth (1202–1204), 387–390, 388(m), 393
    Northern, 387, 388(m)
    against Ottomans, 436, 436(m)
    Second (1147–1149), 356, 362, 387, 399
    Third (1189–1192), 356, 387, 388(m)
Crystal Palace (London), 742(i), 743, 745
Ctesibius of Alexandria (te SIB ee uhs)
        (b. c. 310 B.C.E.), 119
Ctesiphon (TES e fon), 272(m), 273, 304
Cuba, 731, 806, 981

Cuban missile crisis (1962), 946, 982
Cubism, 826, 828
Cult(s)
    in Hellenistic period, 121–123
    imperial (emperor worship), 186–187, 190,
        199, 201
    mystery
        Athenian, 66–68
        Hellenistic, 121, 122
    of relics, 233, 279(i), 279–280, 284(i), 287,
        290, 325, 329, 336, 348, 374, 377, 389,
        410, 414(i), 416, 477(i), 562, 586
    in Roman Empire, 137, 139, 202–204
    ruler, 121
Cult of Reason, 667
Cultural Revolution (China), 1014
Culture(s) (cultural factors). See also Art and
        artists; Education; Intellectuals;
        Language(s); Literature; Philosophy
    in 1930s, 918–920
    in 1960s, 974–984
        restoring "Western" values, 975–977
    cold war, 979–981
    Communist, 980–981
    court
        under Louis XIV, 523–528
        twelfth-century, 367–369
    in eighteenth century, 578–586
        agricultural revolution, 578–581
        cities, 578, 581–583
        public, 582–586
    the Enlightenment and. See Enlightenment, the,
        society and culture and
    French Revolution and, 667–669
    global diffusion of, 1060–1067
    Hellenistic, 112–125
        the arts, 112–115
        languages, 120, 121, 123
        philosophy, 115–118
        religion, 121–125
        the sciences, 118–120
    in nineteenth century, 747–749
        social order, 785–788
    popular. See Popular culture
    postindustrial, 1000–1003
    Roman society and, 130–139
        education for public life, 136
        family, 134–136
        in the Golden Age (96–180 C.E.), 189–195
        Greek influence on literature and art, 130,
            153–156
        patron-client system, 132–134
        religion, 137–139, 142

(continued)

Romanization of provinces, 190–195, 191(m), 192, 192(i)
Cuneiform writing (kyu NEE e form), 11–13, 12(i), 13(f)
Curia (papal government), 352, 441, 443
Curials (curiales), 190, 193, 220, 225, 227, 264, 265, 293
Curie, Marie (koo REE) (1867–1934), 825, 825(i)
Curie, Pierre (1859–1906), 824
Currency. *See also* Coins
in Roman Empire, 206, 219
Cybele, 137
Cynicism (philosophy), 117–118
Cyril (Byzantine missionary), 302
Cyrillic alphabet, 302
Cyrus (SY ruhs) (Persia; r. 559–530 B.C.E.), 28, 29(m), 32, 104
Czartoryska, Zofia (Polish-Lithuanian princess; eighteenth century), 613
Czechoslovakia (chehk uh sluh VAH kee uh), 872, 876, 918, 1022–1023
under Communist rule, 952, 987–988
1968 revolt, 1010–1012
EU and, 1041
German invasion of (1939), 926
Czechs (chehks), 333–334, 445–446, 536, 739, 762, 763, 839, 861, 869
religious conflicts and
fifteenth century, 477
seventeenth century, 498–499

Dachau concentration camp, 912
Dacia (DA shee uh), 187
Dada, 887
Da Gama, Vasco (dah GAM uh, VAHSH koh) (1460?–1524), 464(m), 465
Daladier, Edouard (dah lah DYAY, ay doo AHR) (1884–1970), 926
Dalai Lama, 1061
Dalmatia (Croatia), 215
Damascus, 245, 259(i), 262, 272(m), 274–275, 296, 304, 357, 396
Damian, Peter (1007?–1072), 348
Damis, 105
Danegeld, 321
Danelaw, 321, 321(m)
Danes. *See* Vikings
Dante Alighieri (DAHN tay ah lee GYE ree) (1265–1321), 413–414, 420, 448
Danton, Georges-Jacques (1759–1794), 672
Darius I (da RY us) (Persia; r. 522–486 B.C.E.), 28–29, 29(m), 51, 52, 53(m), 54, 262
Darius III (Persia; r. 336–330 B.C.E.), 102, 104(i), 114

Dark Age, in ancient Greece (c. 1000–750 B.C.E.), 25, 33, 36–38
Darwin, Charles (1809–1882), 790–791, 791(i), 795, 821
Darwinism, 785, 792
Das Kapital (Marx), 782
David (Michelangelo), 454, 455(i)
David, Jacques-Louis (da VEED) (1748–1825), 667, 682(i)
Davis, Angela, 1009
Dawes Plan (1924), 875
Dean, James, 977
Debussy, Claude (duh BOO see, clawd) (1862–1918), 828
Decameron (Boccaccio), 449
Decembrist uprising (1825), 705, 729
De-Christianization
French Revolution and, 667–668
Stalinism and, 964
Decius (DEE shus) (Roman emperor; r. 249–251), 208
Declaration of Independence (United States), 610, 646–647, 660
Declaration of Indulgence (1673), 546
Declaration of the Rights of Man and of the Citizen (France), 660, 668(i)
Declaration of the Rights of Women (France), 660
Decline and Fall of the Roman Empire, The (Gibbon), 240
Decolonization, 966–974
Decretum (*Concordance of Discordant Canons*) (Gratian), 352
Decurions (curiales), 190, 193
Defender of the Peace, The (Marsilius), 441
Defenestration (Prague; 1618), 498
Defoe, Daniel (1660?–1731), 585
Degas, Edgar (duh GAH) (1834–1917), 788
De Gaulle, Charles (1890–1970), 930, 933, 957, 971–972, 989, 1004, 1010, 1063
Deir el Bahri (Egypt), 22
Deists, 613
Deities. *See* Gods and goddesses
De Klerk, F. W. (b. 1936), 1051
De Kooning, Willem (1904–1997), 980
Delacroix, Eugène (duh la KRWAH) (1798–1863), 724–725
Delian League, 57, 57(m), 59–61, 62, 83
Delos, 57, 110
Demeter, 66–68, 203
Demetrius (c. 336–283 B.C.E.), 121
Democracy. *See also* Legislative bodies
art and, 888
Athenian, 44, 54, 73–75, 79, 85, 86–87, 97–98, 98

radical democracy and Pericles' leadership
(461–445 B.C.E.), 59–61, 82, 83, 84, 85
resistance movement in, 87
economic, 878
the Enlightenment and, 610, 652
Napoleon III and, 750
natural law and, 513–514
Rousseau and, 615, 617
Democritus of Abdera (dee MOK rit uhs), 75
Demosthenes (384–322 B.C.E.), 100, 101
Denazification, 956–957
Denmark, 303, 322, 508, 591, 594, 703, 759, 811,
928
mercantilism and, 508
Denmark-Norway, absolutism in, 534
Department stores, 766, 771(i), 771–772
Depression, economic. *See* Great Depression
Descartes, René (day CART, re NAY)
(1596–1650), 516–517, 604, 611
Des Prez, Josquin (day PRAY, zhos KIHN)
(1440–1521), 456
De-Stalinization, 1004
Détente, 1013
Dewey, John (1859–1952), 823
Dhuoda (doo OH duh), 295, 296, 316–317
Dia, Contessa de (fl. c. 1160), 368
Diary of a Young Girl (Frank), 975
Dias, Bartholomeu, 464(m), 465
Diaspora, Jewish, 32, 198
Dickens, Charles (1812–1870), 727, 785
Dictatorship, 652, 885, 896, 924. *See also*
Totalitarianism
Diderot, Denis (dee duh ROH, duh NEE)
(1713–1784), 611–612, 614, 618, 619,
625, 625(i), 638
Didymus (DID im uhs) (c. 80–10 B.C.E.), 113
Dien Bien Phu, battle of (1954), 968
Diet of Regensburg (1541), 491
Diet of Worms, 477
Digest (Byzantine legal code), 251
Diggers, 543
Dilthey, Wilhelm (1833–1911), 823
Diocletian (di o KLEE shuhn) (Roman emperor;
r. 284–305), 172, 210, 214–218, 217(m),
219, 220–221
Diogenes (dy AW jen eez) (d. 323 B.C.E.), 117
Dionysius of Halicarnassus, 137
Dionysus (dy o NY sus), theater of (Athens), 66,
67(i), 79, 80(i), 100(i), 122
Diplomatic Revolution (1756), 632, 634
Diplomatic service
eighteenth-century, 587, 597–598, 606
Renaissance (fifteenth-century),
458–459

Directory government (France), 674, 678,
680–683
Disarmament, in the 1920s, 875
Discrimination. *See* Race
Diseases and epidemics, 599, 699(i), 713,
1049–1050. *See also* Medicine; Plague
in Athens (430–426 B.C.E.), 85
in Augustan Rome, 178
in Byzantine Empire (540s), 250
colonialism and, 780
early Middle Ages, 280
in eighteenth century, 598–599
in nineteenth century, 713, 773–774
seventeenth-century economic crisis and,
505–506, 509
Disraeli, Benjamin (1804–1881), 764
Divine Comedy (Dante Alighieri), 413–414, 420, 448
Divine right of kings, 28–29, 503, 523, 524, 528,
553–554, 615, 646
Division of labor by gender, 8, 14, 237
Divorce, 484, 556
in Babylon, 14
in Byzantine Empire, 265
in France, 669, 685–686
in nineteenth century, 814
Dix, Otto, 877(i)
DNA, 977, 993
Dollfuss, Engelbert (1892–1934), 917–918
Domesday Book (DOOMZ day), 361–362
Domestication of animals, 3–4, 8
Domesticity
doctrine or ideology of, 729, 743, 749, 752,
770, 772, 811, 978
social order and, 784
Domestic servants, 440, 581, 582, 629
in Florence (fifteenth century), 459, 462
slaves as, 459, 462, 467–468, 468(i)
Dominate, Roman, 215–216
Dominic, St. (1170–1221), 380–381, 392
Dominicans (Dominican order), 380–381, 383,
392, 409, 411(i), 411–412, 441, 443
Domitian (do MI shuhn) (Roman emperor
r. 81–96), 187, 205, 236(m)
Donatello (don uh TEL oh) (1386–1466), 453
Donation of Constantine, 313
Donation of Pippin (756), 310–311
Donatism, 228–229
Donatus, 229
Don Quixote (don kee HO tay) (Cervantes),
497, 585
Dostoevsky, Fyodor (1821–1881), 748, 786
Dowry, 43, 69, 272, 281, 282, 458, 461, 462
Drama. *See also* Comedies; Theater
in Golden Age Athens, 52, 79–80, 81–84

Dresden, firebombing of, 930
Dreyfus, Alfred (DRY foos) (1859–1935), 837
Dreyfus Affair, 840
Drugs (drug culture), 1008
Dual Alliance, 843
Dualists (dualism), 381, 391. *See also* Albigensians
    Plato's concept of, 96–97
Dual monarchy, 762
Du Barry, Madame, 639
Dubček, Alexander, 1010–1012, 1022–1023
Duchies, in Germany, 333, 366
Dudayev, Dzhokhar, 1039
Dufay, Guillaume (doo FAY, gee YOHM)
    (1400–1474), 455–456
Duma (Russian parliament), 842, 865
Duncan, Isadora (1877–1927), 827
Dunkirk (France), battle of, 928
Duns Scotus, John (c. 1266–1308), 413
Dürer, Albrecht (1471–1528), 468(i)
Dutch East India Company, 549(m), 567–568
Dutch Patriots, 653–655
Dutch Republic (United Provinces), 494,
    702, 702(m)
  Atlantic system and, 569
  constitutionalism in, 524, 548–551, 565
  economy (seventeenth century), 505–508,
    509, 521
  in eighteenth century, 578, 579(f), 580, 587,
    589, 591–592, 605(m)
  English war against (1652–1654), 544, 546,
    550–551
  French Revolution and, 666, 678
  Louis XIV and, 530–532, 531(m)
  political unrest in (late eighteenth century),
    653–655, 659
  in seventeenth century, 548–551, 549(m), 575
  Thirty Years' War and, 499–500, 501
Dutch West India Company, 551
Du Tertre, Father, 574
Dystopias, 888

Easter, date of, 286–287
Eastern Europe, 260, 946, 947, 1045(m)
  in 1920s, 878
  balance of power in (eighteenth century),
    594–597
  under Communist rule (Soviet bloc), 950–951
    1968 protests, 1010–1012
    economic recovery, 963–966
    welfare-state programs, 961–963
  in fifteenth century, 437–439, 438(m)
  industrialization in, 712
  peasants in, 580–581, 606, 648
  population growth and, 577, 581

  rise of Russia, 568
  under Stalinism, 955
  state building in (1648–1699), 532–540,
    535(m). *See also* Absolutism, in central
    and eastern Europe
Easter Rebellion (Ireland; 1916), 864, 880
East Germany, 1022
East India Company
  British, 574, 577, 732, 778
  Dutch, 549(m), 567–568
East Indies, 571(m), 576
Eberbech, 378(i)
Ebert, Friedrich (1871–1925), 870–871, 872
Ebla, 12–13
Economic democracy, 878
Economics, the Enlightenment and, 615–616, 619
Economy (economic conditions). *See also*
    Business and commerce; Industry;
    Inflation; Taxes; Trade
  1870s–1890s fluctuations, 766, 768–770
  in 1920s, 876, 878, 892, 896
  1950–1970 manufacturing output, 959(f)
  in 1970s, 1016–1020
  Byzantine Empire, 250
  Carolingian, 317–318
  early Middle Ages, 280–282, 324
  eighteenth century, 627–628
  in fourteenth and fifteenth centuries, 440–441
  German unification and, 758, 759
  gift, 281–282, 343, 374
  global, 881, 1059–1060
  Great Depression (1930s), 900–905, 914–917
  Greek, after Peloponnesian War, 94–95
  industrialization and, 629–631
  laissez-faire approach to, 616, 772, 778, 792, 835
  market, in Russia and eastern Europe, 1034,
    1036–1038
  Minoan, 34, 36
  Nazi Germany, 912–913
  in Neolithic Revolution, 8
  Pacific Rim, 1055–1057, 1056(m)
  profit-based, 340–343, 347, 375
  service sector, 770, 771, 987, 995, 996–997
  seventeenth-century crisis, 504–509, 524
  western European (1945–1960), 957–961
  after World War II, 949, 951–952, 957–961
ECSC (European Coal and Steel
    Community), 960
Edessa, 229(i), 355, 355(m)
Edgar (England; r. 959–975), 331
Edict of Milan (313), 221
Edict of Nantes (1598), 490–491, 528–529, 533,
    568, 614
Edict of Restitution (1629), 499

Edict on Maximum Prices (301), 219
Education. *See also* Colleges and
        universities; Schools
    in ancient Athens, 52, 73–78
    in Byzantine Empire, 252–253, 260, 265, 266
    Carolingian renaissance and, 309,
        314–315, 315*(i)*
    in eighteenth century, 582–583, 585–586, 632, 638
    the Enlightenment and, 610–611, 612, 614, 618,
        627, 642, 646–647
    French Revolution and, 667–668, 695
    in nineteenth century, 729–730, 775–778
    in postindustrial society, 997–998
    of women, 136, 485, 556, 585, 600*(i)*, 604,
        638, 777–778, 815*(i)*
Edward (the Confessor) (England;
        r. 1042–1066), 360
Edward I (England; r. 1272–1307), 404, 409
Edward III (England; r. 1327–1377), 430, 439
Edward IV (England; r. 1461–1483), 435
Edward VI (England; r. 1547–1553), 495
Egalitarianism 6, 40, 44, 60–61, 75
Egypt (Egyptian civilization), 4, 969–970,
        1014, 1015
    in 1920s, 880
    ancient, 15–25, 17*(m)*
        Alexander the Great and, 103
        Hebrews in, 31
        Hellenistic period (323–30 B.C.E.), 106
        Hyksos invasion and rule
            (c. 1670–1567 B.C.E.), 21–22
        Middle Kingdom (c. 2050–1786 B.C.E.), 21
        New Kingdom
            (c. 1567–1085 B.C.E.), 15–16, 22–25
        Old Kingdom (c. 3100–2181 B.C.E.), 16–21
        Ptolemaic kingdom, 107–111, 111*(i)*, 113,
            121–122, 123, 123*(i)*, 135, 166, 173
        pyramids, 16, 19–20, 20*(i)*
        religion in, 16–24
        Roman Empire and, 166, 173, 188*(m)*
Einhard (EYN hahrt) (c. 770–840), 311, 313
Einstein, Albert (1879–1955), 824, 825, 992
Eisenhower, Dwight (1890–1969), 934
Eisenstein, Sergei (1898–1948), 885–886, 909
Elba, 12, 694, 700
Eleanor of Aquitaine (A kwi tayn)
        (c. 1122–1204), 362, 363*(m)*, 367, 369
Elections, Roman, 144–145, 166
Electricity, 767, 768
Elements of the Philosophy of Newton
        (Voltaire), 602
Elephants, war, 150, 152*(i)*
Eleusis, 68
El Greco (c. 1541–1614), 510, 511*(i)*

Eliezer, Israel ben (Ba'al Shem Tov)
        (c. 1700–1760), 620
Eliot, George (Mary Ann Evans) (1819–1880), 785
Eliot, T. S. (1888–1965), 887–888
Elisabeth of Hungary (1207–1231), 410
Elisabeth de Valois (1545–1568), 492
Elizabeth (Austria-Hungary), 832
Elizabeth (Russia; r. 1741–1762), 634
Elizabeth I (England; r. 1558–1603),
        495–497, 496*(i)*, 510, 541
Ellison, Ralph (1914–1994), 1006
Elstob, Elizabeth, 604
Emancipation Proclamation
        (United States; 1863), 765
Emecheta, Buchi (b. 1944), 1061
Émile (Rousseau), 616, 627
Emperor worship (imperial cult), Roman, 186,
        187, 190, 199, 201
Empire, 5
Empiricism, 116, 619
Ems telegram, 759
Enabling Act (1933), 911
Enclosure movement (Great Britain), 579
Encomium Moriae (Erasmus), 475*n*
Encyclopedia, 611, 614, 623
Energy, politics of, 1013–1016
Engels, Friedrich (1820–1895), 719, 734
England. *See also* Britain; Great Britain; *individual*
        monarchs, political leaders, and specific
        events and topics
    civil war(s) in
        1139–1153, 362
        1642–1646, 541–545, 542*(m)*, 556
        thirteenth century, 409
    constitutionalism in, 524, 540–547, 552–554,
        565, 590, 615
    French wars with (seventeenth century),
        530, 532
    Hundred Years' War (1337–1453) and, 430–435,
        432*(m)*, 433*(i)*
    Magna Carta and, 401–402, 402*(i)*, 407–408
    medieval poetry in, 448–449
    in Middle Ages
        Anglo-Saxon, 286*(m)*, 286–288, 293,
            321*(f)*, 331
        ninth to eleventh centuries, 323, 326,
            329–332, 330*(m)*
        Norman conquest (1066), 360*(m)*,
            360–362, 361*(i)*
        twelfth and thirteenth centuries, 401–402
        Vikings, 319*(m)*, 320–321, 321*(f)*, 330–331
    monarchy in. *See* Monarchy, in England
    Parliament, 408–409, 435

(continued)

population growth in (eighteenth century), 627
religion and church in, 365, 540. *See also*
   Church of England
   Catholicism, 287, 494–497, 541–542,
      544–547, 589, 602
   English-language Bibles, 481
   Lollardy, 444–445
   new sects, 543–544
   Protestant Reformation, 482(*m*), 492,
      494–497, 529
   Puritans, 495–496, 509, 541–545, 556, 562
   seventeenth century, 541–547
   Test Act (1673), 546
seventeenth-century economy, 504–509, 521
women in. *See* Women, in England
English language, 362, 1063
Enheduanna, 12
Enlightened despots, 632
Enlightenment, the, 568–569, 600–606,
      609–649, 795
   American Revolution and, 634, 640, 644
   Catherine the Great and, 609–610
   church-state conflicts and, 613–615
   education and, 610–611, 612, 614, 618, 627,
      642, 646–647
   French Revolution and, 655, 659–660, 666, 669
   individual-society relationship and, 615–618,
      646–647
   at its height, 610–621
   philosophes and, 610–612, 614–615, 618–620,
      623, 637–638, 648
   popularization of science and, 600–602
   reason and, 652, 687–688
   reforms and, 611, 614–615, 618, 621, 623,
      632–640, 646–647, 648, 654, 676, 690–691
   religion and, 601–602, 611, 613–614, 618–621
   society and culture and, 621–629
      lower classes and poor people, 627–629
      middle class, 610, 618, 621–627
      nobility's reassertion of privilege, 621–623
      roots of industrialization, 610, 616, 621,
         629–632
   spread of, 618–621
   travel literature and, 602–603, 606
   women and, 604–605
Enlil, 10, 13
Ennius (EN ee us) (d. 169 B.C.E.), 153, 154
Entente Cordiale, 844, 847, 854
Entertainment. *See also* Popular culture
   in Byzantine Empire, 246
   in eighteenth century, 620, 628
   in Rome, 181, 187
Environment, 8, 1047
Environmental movement, 1030, 1047–1049

Ephesus (EF us sus), 263
Ephialtes (ef ee ALT eez), 59
Epic of Creation (Mesopotamia), 3, 10–11, 37
Epic of Gilgamesh (Mesopotamia), 10–11, 27
Epic poetry, 367, 448
Epicureanism, 116
Epicurus (e pi KEW rus) (341–270 B.C.E.),
      116, 154
Epidemics. *See* Diseases and epidemics
Equal Employment Opportunity Commission
      (EEOC), 1006
Equites (EK wih teez) (equestrians), 160, 180
Equity, in Roman law, 193–194
Erasmus, Desiderius (e RAS moos,
      deh sih DAY ree oos) (c. 1466–1536),
      475, 476, 481
Eratosthenes of Cyrene (er a TAWS then eez)
      (c. 275–194 B.C.E.), 119
Erhard, Ludwig (AYR hahrt) (1897–1977), 958
Eriksen, Vigilius, 609(*i*)
Ermengard (wife of Louis the Pious), 316
Essay Concerning Human Understanding
      (Locke), 554
Essay in Defence of the Female Sex
      (Anonymous), 604
Estates General (France), 407, 408*n*, 655–657, 656*i*
Estonia, 387, 388(*m*), 499, 534, 595, 927, 1034, 1041
Eszterházy family, 626
Ethics
   Aristotle's views on, 98
   Hellenistic, 116
   Jewish, 30–32
   Plato's views on, 95–97
   Socrates and, 75–76
Ethiopia, 806, 836, 922, 922(*m*)
Ethnic cleansing, 1032. *See also* Genocide
Ethnic groups, 798. *See also* Race
   in Austria-Hungary, 839–840
   in Balkans, 845
   colonialism and, 781, 801(*m*)
   nationalism and, 878
   in Rome, 140
   in Russia and Soviet Union, 841
Etiquette. *See also* Manners
   court, 367–369, 504, 526, 562
Etruscans, 47(*m*), 141(*m*), 141–142, 143(*i*)
Eucharist (holy communion), 358, 377, 403, 411
   Czech dissenters and, 445–446
   Luther and Zwingli's views of, 479
   transubstantiation and, 403, 414, 479, 484
Euclid (yew KLID) (fourth century B.C.E.), 118
Eugenics, 814
Eugénie (yew JE nee) (consort of Napoleon III),
      749, 750(*i*)

Eulalius, count, 284
Eunuchs, 297, 720
Euphrates River, 4, 8
Euripides (yoo RIP i deez) (c. 485–406 B.C.E.),
        68, 80, 81
Euro (European Currency Unit or ECU), 1029,
        1029(i), 1040–1041
Europe
    c. 400 B.C.E., 88(m)
    c. 600, 254(m), 261(m)
    c. 750, 291(m)
    c. 1050, 335(m)
    c. 1340, 420(m)
    c. 1500, 469(m)
    c. 1715, 588(m)
    in 1740, 605(m)
    c. 1780, 648(m)
    c. 1880, 793(m)
    in 1929, 895(m)
    after Congress of Vienna (1815), 702(m)
    at the end of seventeenth century, 564(m)
    immigrant labor in, 973–974
    industrialization in, 744(m)
    languages of (nineteenth-century), 721(m)
    under Napoleonic domination (1812), 696(m)
    after Peace of Paris (1919–1920), 873(m)
    religious divisions of (c. 1648), 519(m)
    thirteenth-century, 394(m)
    trade patterns (c. 1740), 571(m)
    twelfth-century, 363(m)
    as the West, 4
    witchcraft trials in, 517(i), 517–520
    at World War II's end, 941(m)
European Coal and Steel Community (ECSC), 960
European Economic Community (EEC; Common
        Market), 960–961, 1040
European Union (EU), 1029, 1030,
        1040–1042, 1042(m)
Eusebius (yoo SEE bee us) (c. 260–340), 221
Evans, Sir Arthur (1851–1941), 34
Evelyn, John, 546(i)
Everard, Count, 328
Evolution, Darwin's theory of, 790–791
Exarchate (EKS ar kate) of Ravenna, 262,
        289(m), 291
Exclusion Crisis (1678), 546
Exhibition of the Works of Industry of All
        Nations (London), 742(i), 743
Existentialism, 975–976
Exodus (Ezechiel), 114
Exodus, book of, 31
Exposure (abandonment), 72, 111, 134,
        194–195
Expressionism, 826–827

Eyres, 364
Ezechiel (ih ZEE kee uhl), 114

Fabian Society, 818
Fabius Pictor, 152
Fable of the Bees (Mandeville), 577
Factories, 709–712
    in eighteenth century, 629–631
Factory Act (Great Britain; 1833), 711
Faithfulness (fides), Roman view of, 131–132, 139
Falange Party, 923–924
Family (family life)
    in 1920s, 882–884
    in ancient Greece, 41, 82
    in Byzantine Empire, 265
    in Carolingian period, 295(i), 295–296,
        317–318
    eighteenth century, 604, 625, 625(i)
    in Florence (fifteenth century), 460(i), 460–463
    French Revolution and, 669
    in Islam, 269
    under Napoleon, 686
    in nineteenth century, 711, 814–815
    patrilineal, 328
    in post-Carolingian age, 327–328, 329
    in postindustrial society, 998–999
    Roman, 134–136
    seventeenth-century economic crisis and,
        506–507, 507(i)
    in Sweden, 916
Fanon, Frantz (1925–1961), 976, 977
Farming (farmers). See also Agriculture; Peasants
    in 1960s and 1970s, 997
    in Byzantine Empire, 265
    foreclosure on, 902, 903
    in Hellenistic kingdoms, 110
    Roman, 156–158, 160
    tenant, in Roman Empire, 219, 237
Fascism, 852, 892–896, 900, 905, 906
Fashoda crisis (1898), 844
Fathers. See Patriarchy
Fatimah (FAT im uh) (Muhammad's daughter),
        274, 305
Fatimids (FAT uh midz), 305, 306(m),
        307, 335(m)
Fauvism, 825, 826
Fawcett, Millicent Garrett (1847–1929), 833
Fealty, 316, 325, 327, 331, 395, 403
Federal Reserve Bank (U.S.), 900
Feiken, Hille, 473, 473(i), 480
Female Spectator, The, 585
Feminism (feminists), 718–719, 742
    in 1960s, 1009

(continued)

in 1970s, 1008–1009
Paris Commune (1871) and, 784
women of color and, 1009
World War I and, 860
Ferdinand I (Austria; r. 1835–1848), 738, 739
Ferdinand I (Holy Roman emperor;
    r. 1558–1564), 492
Ferdinand II (Aragon; r. 1479–1516), 447,
    467, 495
Ferdinand II (Bohemia, Holy Roman emperor;
    r. 1619–1637), 498, 499
Ferdinand VII (Spain; r. 1808 and 1814–1833),
    704–705
Ferrer, Vincent (1350–1419), 443
Ferry, Jules (1832–1893), 799
Fertile Crescent, 6–7, 8
Festivals, Athenian, 66–68, 79–83
Feudalism, 324
Ficino, Marsilio (fee CHEE no, mahr SEE lyo)
    (1433–1499), 451
Fideles, 309, 324
Fiefs, 324, 327, 348, 355, 361
    French monarchy and, 399, 430
Film industry. *See* Movies
Finland, 387, 534, 703, 960
    woman suffrage in, 834, 834(i), 878(f)
Fire, 186
    used for cooking, 6
Fire department, first, 178
Fireside chats (FDR), 915, 915(i)
First Balkan War (1912), 845
First Consul, 683
First Continental Congress, 646
First Crusade (1096–1098), 353(m), 353–355,
    357, 359
First Estate, 656, 656(i)
First International, 832
First Moroccan Crisis (1905–1906), 844
First Punic War (264–241 B.C.E.), 149–150, 151(f)
First Triumvirate (tree UHM ver et), 164, 165
First Vatican Council (1870), 789
Five-year plans (Stalin), 906
Flagellants, 446
Flamininus (flam ih NY nus), 151
Flanders, 341(m), 342, 345–346, 362,
    398–399, 431, 465
Flaubert, Gustave (flo BAYR, goos TAHV)
    (1821–1880), 785, 786
Fleming, Ian (1908–1964), 980
Fleurs du mal, Les (Baudelaire), 786
Fleury, Cardinal Hercule de (1653–1743), 589
Floods
    in Egypt, 16–18, 19, 21, 203, 233
    in Mesopotamia, 8

Florence
    Renaissance (fifteenth century), 450–451, 453,
        454(i), 455(i), 456–462
Flour War (France; 1775), 641
Flying shuttle, 630
Fontenelle, Bernard de (1657–1757), 600
Food (food supply), 640–641. *See also* Agriculture
    in eighteenth century, 581–582
    in France (1788–1789), 657–659
    in hunter-gatherer societies, 5–6
    in late 1840s, 733–735
    in Minoan Civilization, 34
    in post-Carolingian age, 325
    in postwar Athens, 94
    in Rome, 157, 159, 178–179, 191(m), 208
    seventeenth-century economic crisis and,
        505–507, 507(i)
Food riots
    eighteenth-century, 640–641
    French Revolution and, 670
Ford, Henry (1863–1947), 881, 885
Formosa (present-day Taiwan), 805
Forum of Augustus, 175, 176(f)
Foucault, Michel (foo KOH) (1926–1984), 1067
Fouché, Joseph (foo SHAY) (d. 1820), 684
Fourier, Charles (FOOR ee ay) (1772–1837), 718
Fourteen Points, 864, 871–872
Fourth Crusade (1202–1204), 387–390, 388(m), 393
Fourth Lateran Council (1215), 389(i), 403–404,
    409, 422
France, 277, 316, 973. *See also* Gaul(s); *individual
    monarchs, political leaders, and specific
    events and topics*
    in 1920s, 877, 879
    in 1930s, 916–917, 922
        Nazi Germany, 926–927
    1968 revolt in, 1010
    1980s to present, 1019
    Atlantic system and, 569
    beggar houses in, 628
    Catholic church in, 618, 637–638, 703
        French Revolution and, 655–657, 656(i),
            661–663, 667–669, 671, 672–673
        Inquisition, 386, 392–393, 393(f)
        under Louis IX, 400–401
        under Louis XIV, 528–529, 602
        Napoleon and, 678, 683–684, 687
        seventeenth century, 562–564
        taxing the clergy, 404(i), 404–405
        wars of religion (sixteenth century), 489–491
    colonialism and imperialism, 574, 627, 660,
        731–732, 778, 779–780, 799, 801, 843. *See
        also specific colonies*
    in the 1930s, 905

in Africa, 803(m)
New World colonies of. See Americas, the,
    French colonies in; North America,
    French colonies in
after World War II, 970–972
Congress of Vienna (1814–1815) and, 700, 701,
    702, 702(m)
Crimean War (1853–1856) and, 749–752, 751(m)
in early twentieth century (before World
    War I), 844, 847
education in, 612, 777
in eighteenth century, 605(m), 606. See also
    French Revolution
  American Revolution and, 646–648, 652,
    655, 659
  culture, 582, 583–585
  diplomatic service, 597
  the Enlightenment, 618, 623–625
  Flour War (1775), 641
  reforms, 639–640, 648
  Seven Years' War (1756–1763), 632,
    634, 635(m)
  War of the Austrian Succession (1740–1748),
    632–634, 633(m)
  War of the Polish Succession
    (1733–1735), 596
Fourth Republic, 957, 971
Franco-Prussian War (1870–1871) and, 761(i)
Great Depression (1930s), 916–917
Hundred Years' War (1337–1453) and, 429(f),
    430–435, 432(m), 433(i)
industrialization, 768
Italian unification and, 757, 758
Jews in, 357–358, 398, 400–401, 403, 448, 638
  anti-Semitism, 837
literacy in, 583, 628, 663, 668, 776(f)
monarchy in. See Monarchy, in France
under Napoleon Bonaparte, 674–696. See also
    Napoleon Bonaparte
nobility of, 652, 654–657, 656(i)
Paris Commune (1871), 783–784
peasant rebellion in, 434–435
political parties in, 831
Popular Front, 917
population growth in, 577, 812
Protestants (Huguenots) in, 480–481, 489–491,
    490(m), 492, 528–529, 614, 638, 655
Renaissance in, 456, 456(i)
revolution of 1830, 733
revolution of 1848, 735–736, 739–740
in seventeenth century, 506–509
  economy of, 507, 509
in sixteenth century, 487(m), 487–492,
    490(m)

church reform and, 481
religious wars, 489–491
in thirteenth and fourteenth centuries,
    398–401, 399(m), 400(m)
Thirty Years' War and, 497, 499–503, 502(m),
    506, 521, 525
Versailles Treaty (1919) and, 872, 873(m), 874
women in, 612–613, 623, 625, 735, 833, 877,
    878(f), 957
  seventeenth century, 560–561, 563
World War I and, 853, 854, 856–859, 857(m),
    863, 864, 868, 871
World War II and, 928, 928(m), 933
Francis I (Austria; r. 1792–1835), 722
Francis I (France; r. 1515–1547),
    487–489, 503
Francis I (Holy Roman emperor;
    r. 1745–1765), 633
Francis II (France; r. 1559–1560), 489, 496
Francis Ferdinand (archduke; 1863–1914),
    852, 853(i)
Francis Joseph (Austria, Austria-Hungary;
    r. 1848–1916), 739, 750, 762, 772
Francis of Assisi, St. (c. 1182–1226), 370,
    379–381, 411
Francis Xavier, St., 486
Franco, Francisco (1892–1975), 923–924, 1017
Franco of Cologne, 415
Franco-Prussian War (1870–1871), 750, 751,
    759–760, 761(i)
Franco-Turkish alliance (sixteenth century), 488
Frank, Anne (1929–1945), 975
Frankfurt-am-Main, 452
  1848 parliament at, 738, 740
Frankfurt Book Fair, 452
Franklin, Benjamin (1706–1790), 621
Franks (Frankish kingdoms), 242, 276–280,
    284(i), 286, 288, 289, 291(m), 292, 295,
    296, 309, 311, 312(m), 313, 319(m),
    320–322, 324, 332
Frederick (the Wise) (Prince of Saxony;
    r. 1486–1525), 477
Frederick I (Prussia; r. 1688–1713), 534–535
Frederick I Barbarossa (Germany and Holy
    Roman emperor; r. 1152–1190), 356,
    363(m), 366–367, 393
Frederick II (Sicily and Germany, Holy Roman
    emperor; r. 1212–1250), 391, 393–396,
    394(m), 405
Frederick II (the Great) (Prussia; r. 1740–1786),
    622, 623, 624
  reforms under, 638–640
  wars and expansion, 632–634, 633(m), 635(m),
    636, 637(i), 638

Frederick V of the Palatinate (Bohemia; r. 1616–1623), 498
Frederick William (Great Elector of Brandenburg-Prussia; r. 1640–1688), 555
Frederick William I (Prussia; r. 1713–1740), 595–596, 598, 634
  intervention in Dutch Republic, 653–654
Frederick William III (Prussia; r. 1797–1840), 690
Frederick William IV (Prussia; r. 1840–1860), 737, 738
Frederick William of Hohenzollern (Great Elector of Brandenburg-Prussia; r. 1640–1688), 533
Free Corps (Dutch Republic), 653–654
Free French, 930, 933
Free love, 718
Freemasons (Masonic lodges), 610, 621, 623–624, 626, 691
Free Spirits, 444
Free trade (free markets, free market economy), 615–616, 639–641, 666, 715, 716(i), 750, 769–770
Free will, Stoic view of, 116–117
Free Woman (newspaper), 718
Freikorps (Germany), 871
French and Indian War (1756–1763), 634
French Revolution (1789–1799), 573, 614, 618, 624, 632, 651–674, 658(m), 661(m), 714
  Catholic church and, 671, 672–673
  colonies and, 678(m), 678–680
  Committee of Public Safety and, 665–667, 671–672
  cultural changes, 667–669
  de-Christianization campaign, 667–668
  Directory government, 674, 678, 680–683
  origins of (1787–1789), 655–659
  republic
    end of, 674–675, 680–683
    establishment of (1792), 659, 662–663, 695
  "Republic of Virtue," 665–669
  the Terror, 665–674
  war with Austria (1792), 662, 666, 672
  women and, 651(i), 651–652, 660, 662, 669–670, 671–672
French Wars of Religion (1562–1598), 489–491
Freud, Sigmund (froyd, ZIG moond) (1856–1939), 797, 798, 820–822, 821(i), 840
Friars (Franciscans and Dominicans), 379–381, 383, 392, 409–410, 411(i)
Friedan, Betty (1921–2006), 1008
Friedrich, Caspar David (1774–1840), 724, 725(i)
Froissart, Jean (frwah SAHR) (1333?–c. 1405), 433(i), 434, 449, 450

Fronde (1648–1653), 525, 525(m)
Front for National Liberation (FNL) (Algeria), 970–971
Fugger, Jakob (the Rich) (FOO ger) (1459–1525), 489
Fugger bank, 489
Fulbert, 372
Fulk Nera, count of Anjou (987–1040), 326–327
Funerals. *See* Burial practices
Fur trade, 530, 548

Gaelic language, 836
Gagarin, Yuri (1934–1968), 966, 991
Galen (130?–200?), 515
Galicia, 722, 8056, 858, 865
Galileo Galilei (1564–1642), 255, 515, 554
Gallo-Romans, 278–279
Game laws, in Great Britain, 622
Gandhi, Mohandas K. (Mahatma) (1869–1948), 904(i), 904–905, 967, 977
Gandhi, Rajiv (1944–1991), 1051
García Márquez, Gabriel (gahr SEE ah mahr KEZ, gah bree EL) (b. 1928), 1061
Garden of Eden, 230, 231
Garibaldi, Giuseppe (ga ri BOL dee, joo SEP pee) (1807–1882), 737, 756(m), 757, 758
GATT (General Agreement on Trade and Tariffs), 959(f)
Gaul(s), 114, 115(i)
  Franks and Frankish kingdoms in, 276
  Germanic peoples and kingdoms in, 242, 288, 289, 293
  Rome and, 147, 152, 164, 165, 166, 186, 189
Gays and lesbians, 1009, 1009(i). *See also* Homosexuality
Gaza, 1014
Gehry, Frank, 1064(i), 1065
Gender differences (gender roles). *See also* Men; Women
  in 1920s, 884
  division of labor by, 8, 14, 237
  in Dutch society, 549–550
  following World War II, 977–978
  during Great Depression, 902–903
  in nineteenth century, 729–731
  postindustrial workforce and, 997
  in postwar Athens, 94
  in Renaissance (fifteenth century), 461–463
  Roman children and, 195
  Roman values and, 134, 234–235
  team sports and, 819–820
General Agreement on Trade and Tariffs (GATT), 959(f)
Generation gap, postindustrial, 998

Genetics, 791, 993
Geneva
    Calvinism in, 479–481, 480(f), 486
    religious intolerance in, 617
Geneva Convention (1954), 968
Genius of Christianity (Chateaubriand), 688
Genocide, 956, 957, 1032. *See also*
        Ethnic cleansing
Geoffrin, Marie-Thérèse (zhoff RAHN)
        (1699–1777), 612, 612(i), 613
Geometry, 118
George I (Great Britain; r. 1714–1727), 589, 590
George II (Great Britain; r. 1727–1760),
        590, 591(i)
George III (Great Britain; r. 1760–1820), 643,
        645(i), 646
George V (Great Britain; r. 1910–1936), 856
Gérard, François, 687(i)
Gerbert (Sylvester II), 333
German Federal Republic, 958
Germanic Confederation, 702(m), 703, 722,
        759, 760(m)
Germanic peoples and kingdoms, 277–278,
        311, 318
    Roman Empire and, 187, 205, 208
Germany (German states), 322, 323, 326. *See also*
        individual monarchs, political leaders, and
        specific events and topics
    in 1920s, 876, 879
    Carolingians and, 310, 312(m), 316, 332
    civil war in (1075–1122), 346, 350, 366
    denazification of, 956–957
    division of, after World War II, 953(m), 953–955
    in early twentieth century (before World
        War I), 843–844, 847, 852
    the Enlightenment and, 619, 620, 623
    Hohenstaufen dynasty and, 366
    industrialization in, 768, 769
    Jews in, 357–358, 446–447, 619, 840
        anti-Semitism, 838–839
        during Nazi era, 912–914, 926
    militaristic absolutism in, 533–535
    monarchy in
        eleventh and twelfth centuries, 366–367
        tenth and eleventh centuries, 331–335,
            332(m), 334(i), 335(m), 337
        thirteenth century, 394–396
    Napoleon and, 689(m), 690, 691, 693,
        694, 696(m)
    nationalism in, 723
    nation-building and, 794
    Nazi, 909–914, 921, 922. *See also* Hitler, Adolf;
        Nazis; World War II
        annexation of Austria (1938), 925–926

    central European conquests (1938–1939),
        925(m), 925–927
    the Holocaust, 930–932, 931(i)
    nazification of politics, 911–913
    Nazi-Soviet Pact (1939), 927
    racism of, 913–914
    Peace of Paris and, 871, 872, 873(m), 874
    reunification of (1989), 1022
    revolution of 1848, 737–738, 738(m), 740–741
    in seventeenth century, 506, 508, 533–534
    Thirty Years' War in, 499, 501, 502(m), 518
    unification of (1862–1871), 738, 748,
        758–761, 760(m)
    Weimar Republic, 871, 875, 879, 887, 909
    women in, 461–462
    workhouses in, 628
    World War I and, 852, 853, 854, 855–859,
        860(i), 863–864, 869, 870, 877
    World War II and, 927–929
Gerson, Jean (ger SOHN) (1363–1429), 443
Gestapo, 912
Geta, 207
Ghana, 970
Ghent, 341(m), 345, 427(m), 430
Gibbon, Edward (1737–1794), 240
Gibraltar, 587
Gift economy, 281–282, 343, 374
Gilbert (bishop of Poitiers; d. 1154),
        371(i), 419(i)
Gilbert of Liège, 370
Gilgamesh, Epic of, 10–11
Gillray, James, 677(i)
Giolitti, Giovanni (jee oh LEE ti), 836
Giotto (JOT oh) (1266–1337), 419(i), 421, 453
Girondins, 664–665, 666, 670, 672
Gla, palace at, 36
Gladiators, 146, 181, 182(i)
Gladstone, William (1809–1898), 829–830
Glanvill (treatise), 364
Glasnost, 1020
Globalization, 881, 1030, 1043–1044, 1046–1047,
        1059–1067
Global warming, 1047
Glorious Revolution (1688), 545–547, 554
Gödel, Kurt (1906–1978), 920
Gods and goddesses. *See also* Polytheism; Religion
    Athenian, 63, 63(i), 64–65, 66–68, 79, 81
    Babylonian, 27–28
    Chaldean (Neo-Babylonian), 27
    Christian God, 196, 205, 228
        disputes about the nature of, 228
        divine right doctrine and, 503
        Newton's view of, 554–555

(continued)

scholastics and, 412–414
  Spinoza's view of, 550
Egyptian, 18–19, 23
the Enlightenment and, 613, 619
Greek, 42(i), 46–47, 52, 79
Hebrew (Yahweh), 31–32, 124
Hittite, 24
in Homer and Hesiod, 37
in Islam, 269–272
Mesopotamian, 3, 13
Persian, 30
polytheism and, 202–204
Roman, 131, 132, 137–139, 138(i), 208, 209, 221
  Julian's restoration of (361–363), 223
  Roman imperialism and, 147
Sumerian, 10–11
Goering, Hermann (GEH ring), 912
Goethe, Johann Wolfgang von (GEH tuh)
      (1749–1832), 620, 724
Golan Heights, 1014
Gold, 465(m), 465–469, 470, 492, 504–505,
      504(f), 616
Golden Ass, The (Apuleius), 193, 203
Golden Horde, 397
Gole, Jacob (c. 1660–1723), 600(i)
Gömbös, Gyula (1886–1936), 918
Gonne, Maud (1865–1953), 836
Gonzaga Palace, 455
Gonzaga tapestries, 453
Gorbachev, Mikhail (b. 1931), 988, 1013,
      1020–1025, 1034
Gordion, 102
Gordon, Lord George, 643
Gordon riots (1780), 643
Gospels, Christian, 197
  Lindisfarne Gospels, 287(i)
Gothic architecture, sculpture, and painting, 409,
      414(i), 415–421, 417(i), 448
Gouges, Olympe de (1748–1793), 660, 666
Government (the state). See also Absolutism;
      Administration; Legislative bodies;
      Monarchy; State power
  Augustine's City of God and, 230, 231
  authoritarian, Napoleon Bonaparte and,
      683–685
  Machiavelli on, 457
  religious conflict and (1500–1618), 486–497
  Roman Empire, 172
  Roman Republic
    early republic (509–287 B.C.E.), 143–146
    religion and, 139
    Senate, 140, 145–146, 150, 152, 159–160, 161,
      162, 164, 167, 172, 175, 180, 185
    social elite and, 158–160

Thirty Years' War and growth, 503–505
Government of India Act (1858), 779
Goya, Francisco (1746–1828), 692(i)
Gracchus, Gaius Sempronius (GRAK us)
      (d. 121 B.C.E.), 135, 158–160
Gracchus, Tiberius (d. 133 B.C.E.), 135, 158–160
Graham, Billy (b. 1918), 945–946, 949, 975
Granada, 391, 391(m), 447, 447(m)
Grand Alliance, 930, 938, 953
Gratian (GRAY shun) (Roman emperor;
      r. 375–383 in the west), 223
Gravitation, law of (Newton), 554–555
Great Awakening
  first (1730s–1740s), 620
  second (1790s), 704
Great Britain (United Kingdom), 705
  in 1930s, 916, 922
    appeasement policy and Munich Pact,
      926–927
  Act of Union (1707), 589–590
  Catholic church in. See Roman Catholic
      church, in England
  China and (nineteenth century), 732
  colonialism and imperialism, 574, 576, 576(i),
      596, 731–732. See also North America,
      English (British) colonies in; and
      specific colonies
    1850s–1880s, 778–779
    in Africa, 799, 801, 802, 803(m)
    in India, 808
  Congress of Vienna (1814–1815) and, 701, 703
  Crimean War (1853–1856) and, 751–752
  in early twentieth century (before World
      War I), 844, 847, 852
  in eighteenth century, 587–592, 605(m), 606
    agriculture in, 578–580, 579(f)
    American Revolution (1775–1783), 634,
      640, 644
    enclosure movement, 579
    French Revolution, 671, 676–677(i), 678–679
    Industrial Revolution, 629–631
    landed gentry, 622
    wars, 632–634, 633(m), 635(m)
  Great Depression (1930s), 916
  industrialization in, 708–709, 767–768
  liberalism in, 715–717
  Napoleon and, 681, 688–689, 691–692, 693–694
  Parliament, 408–409, 642
    American Revolution and, 644–645
    Charles II and, 545–546
    in the eighteenth century, 589–590
    Exclusion Crisis (1678), 546
    Glorious Revolution (1688), 547
    in the nineteenth century, 710–711

rebuilding of Houses of Parliament
(1830s), 725
in the seventeenth century, 541–547, 556
in the sixteenth century, 495, 497
Wilkes affair (1763), 643–645, 648
politics in
Chartist movement, 720, 741
liberalism, 835–836
mass politics of late nineteenth and early
twentieth centuries, 829–831
reforms of 1850s–1870s, 763–764
Thatcher and, 1017–1018
after World War II, 957–958
railroads in, 708–709, 708(f)
revolution of 1848 and, 741
Seven Years' War and, 655
urbanization in, 712–713, 817
working class of, 709–711
after World War I, 875
World War I and, 853, 854, 855, 856–859,
862(i), 863, 864, 868
World War II and, 927, 928–929, 933, 936
Great Depression (1930s)
economic aspects of, 900–905
global dimensions of, 903–905
social effects of, 902–903
in United States, 914–916
Great Fear (1789), 659
Great Northern War (1700–1718), 495(m), 594–495
Great Persecution (303), 221
Great Pyramid at Giza (Egypt), 19, 20, 20(i)
Great Schism (1054), 348, 352
Great Schism (1378–1417), 426, 442(m),
442–443, 458
"Great Society" programs (United States), 1006
Greece, ancient (Greek civilization). See also
Athens; Sparta
c. 1500 B.C.E., 33(m)
c. 400 B.C.E., 88(m)
Aegean Sea and, 33(m), 34
Archaic Age (c. 750–500 B.C.E.), 38–47, 39(m)
citizenship in, 39–41
Dark Age (c. 1000–750 B.C.E.), 36–38
Etruscans and, 141–142
Golden Age and Classical period
(c. 500–323 B.C.E.), 51–89. See also Athens,
Golden Age and Classical period
decline of Classical Greece
(c. 400–350 B.C.E.), 83–87, 93–99
Persian wars (499–479 B.C.E.), 54–56
in Hellenistic period (323–30 B.C.E.), 107–110
Persian wars (499–479 B.C.E.), 51, 53(m)
philosophy, 45–47
Socrates, 75–78

sophists, 74–75
polis (city-states), 108. See also Athens; Sparta
Alexander the Great and, 104–105
citizenship (political rights), 38–44, 39(m)
disunity after Peloponnesian War, 98–99
Hellenistic period (323–30 B.C.E.), 92, 108
Philip II of Macedonia and, 99–101
religion, 42(i), 42–43, 121–125
Golden Age Athens, 66–68
Minoan and Mycenaean period, 37
Roman literature and art and, 152–156
Rome and, 151–152
slavery and, 41–42
women in
Athens, 65, 68–72, 82–83
comedies, 82–83
companions, 71–72
legal and political status, 40, 43
Olympics and, 38
after Peloponnesian War, 93–94
religious functions of, 42(i), 42–43
social and economic roles, 40, 42–44, 68–72
Spartan, 44
Greece, modern, 845, 938, 1017
under Byzantine rule, 260, 301, 302(m)
Communism and, 951
in EU, 1041
independence from Turks, 705–706
Greek culture, 152–156
in Byzantine Empire, 265
in eastern provinces of Roman Empire, 192
in Rome, 141
Greek language, 92, 108, 120, 121, 123, 288,
450–451
in Byzantine Empire, 247
in eastern provinces of Roman Empire,
191(m), 192
Greek Orthodox Church, 355, 380(m), 440,
519(m)
Great Schism (1054) and, 348, 352
Greeks
in ancient Italy, 141
Archaic Age settlements, 38–39, 41
in Hellenistic kingdoms, 92–93, 103, 108–110,
109(i), 115, 120
Greenhouse effect, 1047
Greenland, Viking settlement of, 319(m), 320
Green Party (West Germany), 1048
Gregorian calendar, 593n
Gregorian reform, 349
Gregory (bishop of Tours; r. 573–c. 594),
278–281, 283, 285
Gregory I (the Great) (pope; r. 590–604), 286,
290, 310, 330

Gregory VII (Hildebrand) (pope; r. 1073–1085), 346, 348, 349–350, 351
Gregory XI (pope; r. 1371–1378), 441
Gregory XII (pope; r. 1406–1415), 443
Greuze, Jean-Baptiste (groozh) (1725–1805), 625, 625(i)
Grosz, George (grohs) (1893–1959), 886–887
Grotius, Hugo (GROH shee uhs) (1583–1645), 512–514
Guadalcanal, battles at (World War II), 938
Guam, 929
Guangzhou (Canton, China), 574
Guarino of Verona, 450
Guernica (Picasso), 924
Guilds, 334–335, 344–345, 357, 372, 382, 386, 387, 402(i), 406, 416, 430, 530, 623, 631, 639
Guillotin, J. I., 664(i)
Guillotine, 664(i), 664–665, 666, 672, 674, 682(i)
Guinea, 465
Guizot, François, 729
Gulag, 907–908, 964, 1012
Gustavus Adolphus (guhs TAY vuhs ah DOHL foos) (Sweden; r. 1611–1632), 499, 503, 534
Gustavus III (guhs TAY vuhs) (Sweden; r. 1771–1792), 643, 676
Gustavus IV (Sweden; r. 1792–1809), 676–677
Gutenberg, Johannes (c. 1400–1470), 451
Gutians, 13
Guyon, Jeanne Marie (1648–1717), 586
Gymnasia, 73
Gymnasia, Protestant, 483
Gynaeceum, 318
Gypsies, murder of, 927

Habsburgs (Habsburg dynasty), 395, 407, 437, 588(m), 596(m), 750, 758, 759. *See also* Austria; Holy Roman Empire
  Louis XIV and, 530–532
  in seventeenth century, 533–537, 535(m)
  in sixteenth century, 477, 487(m), 487–489, 488(i), 492–493, 493(m)
  Thirty Years' War and, 498, 501–502, 502(m)
Hadrian (HAY dree uhn) (Roman emperor; r. 117–138), 187, 188(m), 203, 205, 224
Hadrian I (pope; r. 772–795), 313
Hagia Sophia. *See* Church of the Holy Wisdom
Haiti
  independence movement in, 679(i), 691
  slave revolt in, 652, 678(m), 678–680, 679(i)
Hajj, 271
Hamlet (Shakespeare), 510

Hammurabi (hah moo RAH bee) (Babylon; r. c. 1792–1750 B.C.E.), 14–15, 31
Handel, George Frederick (1685–1759), 585
Hannibal (247–182 B.C.E.), 150, 152(i), 159
Hanover, House of, 589
Hanseatic League, 406–407
Hanukkah, 124
Hard Times (Dickens), 785
Hargreaves, James, 630(i)
Harold (earl of Wessex; mid-eleventh century), 360, 360(m)
Harun al-Rashid (Abbasid caliph; r. 786–809), 304–305
Harvey, William (1578–1657), 516
Hasidic sect (Hasidim), 620
Hastings, battle of (1066), 360, 360(m)
Hatshepsut (Egypt; fifteenth century B.C.E.), 22
Hattusili III (Hittite king; c. 1286–c. 1265 B.C.E.), 25
Haussmann, Georges-Eugène (HOUS mahn) (1809–1891), 773, 774
Haussmannization, 773, 783
Havel, Václav (HAH vehl, VAHTS lahv) (b. 1936), 987(i), 1022–1023, 1061
Haydn, Franz Joseph (1732–1809), 626
Haywood, Eliza (1693?–1756), 585
Headscarf controversy (France), 1058(i)
Health care
  in eighteenth century, 598–599, 606
  welfare-state programs and, 961–962
Heavenly Kingdom (Taiping), 781
Hebrew Bible (Old Testament), 123, 197, 198, 225. *See also* Torah
  Luther's translation of, 481
  monotheism and, 30–32
  translated into Greek (the Septuagint), 123
Hebrew language, 281, 367
Hebrews (Israelites), 25. *See also* Jews; Judaism
  exile of, 32
  monotheism and, 30–32
Heisenberg, Werner, 920
Heliocentrism, 118, 514–515, 600–601
Hellenic League, 54–56
Hellenistic period (323–30 B.C.E.), 91–126, 107(m), 124(m)
  culture in, 112–125
    the arts, 112–115
    languages, 120, 121, 123
    philosophy, 115–118
    religion, 121–126
    the sciences, 118–120
  kingdoms, structure of, 106–110, 107(m)
  society in, 110–112
Hellespont, 54

Heloise (EHL uh weez) (c. 1100–c. 1163/1164), 372–373

Helots (HE lots), 43, 44, 98

Helsinki accords (1975), 1014

Helvetic Republic, 678

Hemingway, Ernest (1899–1961), 884

Henry (the Navigator) (prince; 1394–1460), 465

Henry I (England; r. 1100–1135), 362

Henry I (Germany; r. 919–936), 332

Henry II (England; r. 1154–1189), 357, 362–365, 363(*m*), 382, 398–399, 401, 408

Henry II (France; r. 1547–1559), 489

Henry II (Germany and Holy Roman emperor; r. 1002–1024), 333

Henry III (England; r. 1216–1272), 396, 408–409

Henry III (France; r. 1574–1589), 490, 492

Henry III (Germany and Holy Roman emperor; r. 1039–1056), 347, 349

Henry IV (Germany and Holy Roman emperor; r. 1056–1106), 346, 349–350, 357

Henry IV (Henry of Navarre) (France; r. 1589–1610), 489–491, 529

Henry V (England; r. 1413–1422), 431

Henry V (Germany; r. 1106–1125), 366

Henry VI (England; r. 1422–1461), 435

Henry VII (Henry Tudor) (England; r. 1485–1509), 435

Henry VIII (England; r. 1509–1547), 475, 480(*f*), 494–495

Henry the Younger, 362

Hephaestus (heh FEHS tuhs), 66

Hera, 38, 66, 137

Heracles (Hercules), 68

Heraclius (her uh KLIH uhs) (Byzantine emperor; r. 610–641), 259, 262, 265

Herculaneum (hur kyuh LAY nee uhm), 179(*i*), 187

Heresies (heretics), Christian, 202, 359, 371(*i*), 379, 380(*i*), 381, 383, 426. *See also* Inquisition, Catholic

anti-heretic campaigns (1150–1300), 391–393

Arianism, 228

in Bohemia, 443, 445–446

in Byzantine Empire, 248

Catholic church and, 481, 528

Donatism, 228–229

early church and, 227–229

fourteenth and fifteenth centuries, 441, 443–445

Free Spirits, 444

Hussitism, 443–446

Justinian and, 253

Monophysite, 229

Nestorianism, 228

thirteenth-century, 386, 391–395

Albigensian Crusade, 391–393, 404

Fourth Lateran Council (1215), 389(*i*), 403–404, 422

penitent heretics, 393

Hero (Alexandrian scientist), 119

Hero cults, Athenian, 66, 67

Herod Antipas, 197

Herodotus (c. 485–425 B.C.E.), 28, 78

Herod the Great (Judea; r. 37–4 B.C.E.), 196

Herophilus of Chalcedon (b. c. 300 B.C.E.), 120

Herzen, Alexander (HERT sen) (1812–1870), 717

Herzl, Theodor (hertsl, TAY o dor) (1860–1904), 840

Hesiod (HEE see ud), 36–37

Hierapolis (hy uh RAP uh lihs), 111

Hierarchy (social status; class differences), 4. *See also specific social classes*

in 1920s, 882, 885

in Byzantine Empire, 248, 249

in Egypt, 20–21

in Florence (fifteenth century), 459–463

in France, Napoleon and, 685

in hunter-gatherer societies, 4, 6

in Neolithic Revolution, 8

religion and, 789

in Roman Empire, 180, 193–194

in Roman Republic, 143, 144, 157

in Sumerian society, 9–10

Hieroglyphs, Egyptian, 17, 18, 18(*f*), 91(*i*)

Hijra, 270, 271, 273

Hildegard of Bingen (1098–1179), 373

Hillesum, Etty, 899, 900, 931

Himmler, Heinrich (1900–1945), 912

Hindenburg, Paul von (1847–1934), 856

Hindus, 576, 778, 808, 966, 967

Hipparchia (hip AHR kee ah), 117–118

Hippias (Athenian tyrant; 527–510 B.C.E.), 54

Hippocrates (hip OK rah teez) (c. 460–377 B.C.E.), 78, 122

Hirohito (Japan; r. 1926–1989), 921

Hiroshima, atomic bombing of (1945), 938, 939(*i*)

Hispanic Americans, 1006

Hispaniola, 467, 678

Historia calamitatum (Abelard), 372

Historical and Critical Dictionary (Bayle), 601

Histories (Gregory), 279

Histories (Herodotus), 78

History of the Peloponnesian War (Thucydides), 78

Hitler, Adolf (1889–1945), 693, 879, 885, 894, 896, 899, 899(*i*), 900, 905, 909–914, 920, 921, 922, 924

central European conquests, 925(*m*), 925–927

(continued)

rise to power, 909–910
  Spanish Civil War (1936–1939) and, 923–924
  World War II and, 927–929, 932, 936
Hitler Youth, 913
Hittite kingdom (Anatolia), 15–16, 22–25
Hiung-nu people, 238
Hobbes, Thomas (1588–1679), 553–554
Ho Chi Minh (1890–1969), 905, 968
Hohenstaufen dynasty, 366
Hohenzollern dynasty, 501, 533
Holocaust, 930–932, 931(i)
  denial of, 949
Holstein, 759, 760(m)
Holy Alliance, 703
Holy Land. *See* Levant
Holy Roman Empire. *See also individual emperors*
  c. 1273, 395
  c. 1340, 405, 420(m), 427(m), 443, 445, 446
  in fifteenth century, 458, 459, 469(m)
  in seventeenth century, 531(m), 531–532, 533,
    535(m), 535–536
  in sixteenth century, 476–479, 482(m), 490(m),
    492, 493(m)
  Thirty Years' War and, 498–502, 502(m),
    518, 536
Holy Synod (Russia), 593
Homage, 327, 334(i)
Homer (fl. 850 B.C.E.), 36–37, 79
  Iliad, 37, 102, 183, 255
  Odyssey, 37, 152–153, 183, 255
Homo sapiens, 5
Homosexuality (homosexuals), 815–816, 995,
    1009, 1009(i)
  in ancient Greece, 43–44, 73–74
  in Byzantine Empire, 252
  in eighteenth century, 629
  in Florence (fifteenth century), 462
Hong Kong, 732, 967, 1055
Honor, Roman view of, 131–132, 145, 161, 162
Honorius (ho NAW ri uhs) (Roman emperor;
    r. 395–423 in the west), 213(i), 214, 218,
    239, 247
Hoover, Herbert (1874–1964), 914
Hoplites (HOP lytz), 40–41, 41(i), 51(i),
    55(i), 84(f)
  Persian Wars and (499–479 B.C.E.), 54–55, 56
Horace (65–8 B.C.E.), 112, 183
Horatius (ho RAY shus), legend of, 143
Horses, in warfare (ninth to eleventh
    centuries), 327
Hospitals
  in eighteenth century, 598–599, 629, 658(m)
  in seventeenth century, 563–564
House, Edward, 843

Housing (dwellings)
  in 1920s, 883
  in Athens, 61
  in Augustan Rome, 177–178
  in eighteenth century, 581–582
  postwar Soviet, 962(i), 962–963
Hubble, Edwin (1889–1953), 920, 992
Hubris, 81
Hugenberg, Alfred, 879, 909
Hugh Capet (France; r. 987–996), 332
Hugh of St. Victor, 351
Huguenots (HYOO geh nots) (French
    Protestants), 480, 489–491, 490(m),
    528–529, 533, 601
Humanism, 426
  Christian, 474–475, 498, 520
  Renaissance, 448–452, 471
Humanitas, Cicero's doctrine of, 154–155
Humbert of Silva Candida, 348
Hume, David (1711–1776), 613–614
Humors, medical theory of, 78
"Hundred Days" (1815), 694, 700, 701–702
Hundred Years' War (1337–1453), 426, 429(f),
    430–435, 432(m), 433(i), 439, 449
Hungary, 301, 303, 335(m), 335–336, 436, 437,
    438(m), 469(m), 487(m), 488, 488(i),
    519(m), 751, 775.
    See also Austria-Hungary
  1848 revolution and, 738–739
  Austrian conquest of (1657–1730), 596(m),
    596–597, 762
  Communist collapse and, 1022
  under Communist rule, 952, 963, 964, 965(i)
    1956 uprising in, 965
  Mongol invasion of, 385, 396, 397(m)
  Ottoman Turks and, 535, 535(m), 537, 564(m)
  after World War I, 871, 872, 876, 896
  World War I and, 858
  World War II and, 918, 929, 938
Huns, 235–238, 236(m)
Hunter-gatherers, 3, 5–6
Hunting
  in Neo-Assyrian kingdom, 26–27
  by upper-class Europeans, 810, 810(i)
Hus, Jan (hoos, yon) (d. 1415), 443–446, 477, 499
Hussein, Saddam, 1052–1055
Hussites (Hussitism), 443–446
Hyksos, 21–22

Iaroslav the Wise (Russian prince;
    r. 1019–1054), 303
Ibn Sina (Avicenna) (980–1037), 308
Ibsen, Henrik (IHB suhn) (1828–1906), 834
Iceland, Viking settlement of, 319(m), 320

Icons and iconoclasm, 266(*i*), 266–267, 274, 290–291, 293, 299, 315, 539
Idealism, Kant's doctrine of, 619
Identity
  deterritorialization of, 1044
  transnational, 1059
Identity politics, 1009(*i*)
Ideologies, 714–726
Idylls (Theocritus), 113
Ignatius (ig NAY shus) (bishop of Antioch; c. 35–107 C.E.), 200
Ignatius of Loyola (1491–1556), 484
Île-de-France (eel duh FRAHNS), 332, 358, 365, 392, 398, 398(*m*)
Iliad (IL ee ad) (Homer), 37, 102, 183, 255
Illegitimate children
  in Florence (fifteenth century), 462
  overcrowding and, 713
Illidius, St., 280
Illiteracy
  in eighteenth century, 582–583, 628
  in nineteenth century, 776, 776(*f*)
Illyrians, 101
Immigrants. *See* Migrations
Immortality, in ancient Egypt, 15
Imperial cult, 202
  Roman, 186–187, 190
Imperialism, 731, 799–808, 801(*m*), 803(*m*), 805(*m*), 921–922. *See also* Colonies
  culture and society and, 808
  missionary activity and, 704
  Roman (fifth to second centuries B.C.E.)
    expansion in Italy, 146–148
    social consequences of wars, 156–158
    wars with Carthage, 148–152
  World War I and, 849, 854
Impressionism, 787–788, 825, 826
Inanna (Ishtar), 10, 12, 27
Incas (IHN kuhs), 469–470
Income tax, 775, 1018
India, 245, 464(*m*), 465–466, 492, 493(*m*), 632, 634, 635(*m*), 704, 855, 1056
  in 1920s, 880, 881
  Alexander the Great in, 104
  British rule in, 732, 778–779, 779(*m*), 904–905, 966
    end of, 967
    resistance to, 808
  Europeans in, 574, 576(*i*), 576–577, 648(*m*), 799
  religious practices of, 576–577
Indiana (Sand), 727
Indian National Congress, 808
Indian Ocean, 463, 464(*m*), 465, 549(*m*)

Indian Rebellion (1857), 778–779, 779(*m*), 795
Indians, American. *See* Native Americans
Individual, the Enlightenment and, 615–618, 646–647
Indochina, 843, 881, 929, 968, 968(*m*)
  Communist Party in, 905
Indo-European languages, 24
Indonesia, 881, 929, 972
Indulgences, sale of, 474–475, 476
Industrial Revolution, 629–630, 691, 707, 715
Industry (industrialization), 707–713, 718, 744(*m*). *See also specific industries and countries*
  in 1920s, 880
  economic fluctuations of 1870s–1890s and, 766, 768–770
  in eighteenth century, 610, 616, 621, 629–633
  in nineteenth century, innovations, 766–768
  in Russia and Soviet Union, 841, 906
  World War I and, 857(*m*), 861, 869
Indus Valley, 28
Infanticide, 272, 460, 629, 686, 713
  by exposure (abandonment), 72, 111, 134, 194–195, 462
Infant mortality, 711, 1019
Inflation
  in 1970s, 1014, 1015
  in eighteenth century, 636, 640
  in Germany (1920s), 875
  in Roman Empire, 205–206, 219–220
  in seventeenth century, 503, 504–505
Information technology, 988–991
Ingria, 595
Inheritance, 328, 329, 332–333, 337, 355, 461, 483
  in ancient Greece, 43, 69
  French Revolution and, 669
  Islamic women and, 272, 281
  in Merovingian period, 281–284
  in non-Roman societies, 237
  in northern Europe (fifteenth century), 461–462
Innocent III (pope; r. 1198–1216), 387, 389(*i*), 390, 392, 393, 402–403, 404(*i*)
Inquisition, Catholic, 386, 392–393, 393(*f*), 404, 515, 618
  in Germany, 444
  in Spain, 447–448
Institutes (ins tih TOO tays) (Byzantine law textbook), 251
Institutes of the Christian Religion, The (Calvin), 480
Institutions (Cassiodorus), 245
Instruction (Catherine II of Russia), 636
Instruction of Ptahhotep, 21

Insulae (IN sool eye) (Roman apartment
        buildings), 177
Intellectuals (intellectual life)
    in 1950s and 1960s, 976
    the Enlightenment and, 610–621.
        See also Philosophes
    Napoleon and, 686–688, 691
Intelligence tests, 820
Interim (Germany) (1548), 491
Intermarriage, in American colonies, 574–575
International Monetary Fund, 1045–1046, 1051
International Woman Suffrage Association, 833
International Zionist Congress (1897), 840
Internet, 1031, 1059
Internment camps, United States, 933
Interpretation of Dreams, The (Freud), 821
Investiture Conflict (c. 1070–1122), 349(m),
        349–351, 366, 367
In vitro fertilization, 994–995
Ionia (ee OH nee uh), 37, 46, 46(m), 47, 51, 52, 54
Ionian Revolt (499–490 B.C.E.), 52–54, 53(m)
Iran, 7, 8n, 28, 934, 1052–1055. *See also* Persia
    in 1920s, 880
    hostage crisis (1979–1980), 1016
    Islam and, 307
    as Islamic Republic, 1016
    Mongol invasion of, 396, 397(m)
Iraq, 7, 261, 304, 306(m), 1052–1055
Ireland, 589, 590, 798, 864, 1019
    Catholic church and Catholics in, 547, 590
    Christianity in, 286–288
    French Revolution and, 676
    home rule and independence, 835–836, 880
    Napoleon and, 681
    nationalism in, 723
    potato famines in (1846, 1848, and 1851), 733,
        734(i), 816
    in seventeenth century, 544, 545(i), 547
    Vikings in, 319(m), 320
Irish Free State, 880, 880(m)
Irish missionaries, in England, 286
Irish Republican Army (IRA), 864, 1016(m), 1017
Iron metallurgy, 38
Irrigation, 8–9
    in Mesopotamia, 8
Isabella I (Castile; r. 1474–1504), 447–448, 467, 495
Isabella of Bavaria (consort of Charles VI of
        France), 449(i)
Ishtar (Inanna), 10, 27
Isis (EYE sis), 19, 121, 122–123, 123(i), 193, 223
    cult of, 203
Islam (is LAHM or is LAM) (Muslims), 30, 32,
        260, 261, 268–275, 272(m), 291(m),
        303–309, 380(m), 808, 966, 967

c. 1000, 306(m)
    Abbasid Caliphate (750–c. 950), 303–307,
        306(m), 336–337
    Christianity and, 268, 269, 272, 273–275,
        306–307, 422
        crusades against, 352–357, 353(m),
            383, 488
    classical literature and learning and,
        307–309, 371
    Muhammad's successors (632–750),
        273–275, 293
    non-Muslim tension and, 1058
    Ottoman Empire and, 436(m), 436–439,
        438(m), 442(m)
    Qur'an, 269, 270(i), 273, 275, 287, 292
    regional diversity in, 305–307
    renaissance of (c. 790–c. 1050), 307–309, 314
    rise and development of (c. 610–632), 268–273,
        292–293, 298(m)
    Roman Empire and, 259, 274(i), 275, 281
    Shi'ite, 274, 304, 305, 1016, 1052
    since 1970s, 1052–1055
    in Spain, 268, 273, 289, 291(m), 305–307,
        306(m), 371, 426, 466
        Christian reconquest *(reconquista)*, 348, 386,
            388(m), 390–391, 391(m), 447–448
        Moriscos, 492–493
    Sunni, 274, 305, 353, 356, 1052
Isolationism, United States, 874
Israel, 7, 8n, 16, 969, 969(m), 1052–1054,
        1053(m). *See also* Jerusalem
    ancient, 32
    wars against Arab countries (1960s–1970s),
        1014(m), 1014–1015
Istanbul, 218, 581. *See also* Constantinople
Italian language, 414
Italy, 316, 871. *See also* Etruscans; Roman Empire;
        Roman Republic; Rome
    1848 divisions of, 736(m)
    in 1930s, 921, 922
    African colonies of, 803(m), 806
    ancient, 140–141, 141(m)
    Byzantine Empire and, 260, 359
    under Diocletian, 216–217
    in early twentieth century (before World
        War I), 843
    Enlightenment ideas in, 618, 623
    fascism in, 892–896, 893(i)
    fifth century B.C.E., 147(m)
    Justinian and, 249, 250
    in late nineteenth and early twentieth
        centuries, 836
    Lombards in. *See* Lombardy
    in Middle Ages, 311, 312(m), 313

business agreements, 343–344
communes, 406
early medieval kingdoms, 289(*m*), 289–293
at end of thirteenth century, 395(*m*)
Frederick I Barbarossa, 363(*m*), 366–367
Investiture Conflict and, 349–351
papal-imperial conflicts, 393–396,
    394(*m*), 395(*m*)
peasants, 326, 343
post-Carolingian age, 319(*m*), 322, 323,
    326, 329–330
urban self-government, 345–346
Napoleon and, 680–681, 685, 689(*m*), 690,
    691, 696(*m*)
nationalism in, 722–723
nationalist revolution in (1848–1849),
    736–737, 740
nation-building and, 794
Renaissance in, 425–426
Social War (91–87 B.C.E.), 161
unification of (Risorgimento), 747,
    750, 755–758
women in, 778, 877, 878(*f*), 957
before World War I, 847
World War I and, 852, 854, 855, 864
World War II and, 927, 928, 934, 957
Ivan III (ee VAHN) (Muscovite tsar;
    r. 1462–1505), 439
Ivan IV (the Terrible) (Russia; r. 1533–1584), 499
Iwasaki Yataro, 804

Jacobins (Jacobin Clubs), 633(*m*), 663–664,
    668(*i*), 670(*i*), 674, 675, 676–677,
    680–681, 684
Jacobitism, 588(*m*), 589–590
Jacobs, Aletta (1851–1929), 813, 861
Jacquerie (1358), 434–435
Jagiellonian dynasty, 438
Jahn, Friedrich Ludwig (yahn), 722
Jamaica, 572–573
James Edward (pretender to British throne), 589
James I (England; r. 1603–1625), 496–497, 503,
    541, 589
James II (England; r. 1685–1688), 546–547,
    552, 589–590
Jameson, Leander, 802
Jane Eyre (Brontë), 727
Janissaries (JAHN ih sehr ees), 437, 488(*i*)
Jan of Leiden (yahn uv LY den) (1626–1679),
    479
Jansen, Cornelius (1585–1638), 528
Jansenists (Jansenism), 528, 586
Japan, 876, 903, 968
    in 1920s, 881, 894(*m*)
    in 1930s, 920–922
    Christian missionaries in, 485(*i*), 486
    economy of (1980s to present), 1055–1057
    imperialism of, 798, 805–806, 894(*m*)
    modernization of, 804, 804(*i*)
    in nineteenth century, 781
    World War I and, 852, 854
    World War II and, 929–930, 933, 937(*m*),
        938, 939(*i*)
Japanese art, 788
Jaruzelski, Wojciech (yah roo ZEL skee,
    VOY chek), 1021
Java, 568, 571(*m*), 576
Jazz, 889
Jefferson, Thomas (1743–1826), 646, 647,
    653, 660
Jerome (theologian; c. 345–420), 151, 230,
    234, 255
Jerome, St., 287
Jerome of Prague (d. 1416), 445
Jerusalem, 123, 188, 197
    crusades and, 353(*m*), 354, 355, 355(*m*), 356,
        380(*m*), 388, 388(*m*)
    Muslims and, 271
    as Roman colony, 188, 196–197, 224
    temple in, 31, 32, 124, 163, 196, 198
Jesuits (JEHZH oo ihts) (Society of Jesus),
    484–486, 485(*i*), 498, 637–638, 703, 789
    in North America, 530
Jesus (Christ) (c. 4 B.C.E.–30 C.E.), 196–198,
    224, 562
    depictions of, 224(*i*), 253, 512
    disputes about nature of, 228–229
    twelfth- and thirteenth-century views of, 377,
        379, 411, 421
Jewish law, 196–198, 225
Jews, 814, 816. *See also* Anti-Semitism; Judaism
    in 1920s, 879
    Byzantine Empire and, 259, 299
    in Dutch Republic, 494, 550, 601
    in early Middle Ages, 281
    in eleventh and twelfth centuries, 342, 355–358,
        357(*i*), 380(*m*), 383
    emergence of Christianity and, 195–205
    in fourteenth and fifteenth centuries, 446–448
    Fourth Lateran Council and (1215), 403
    in France, 357–358, 398, 400–401, 448, 660, 837
    in Germany, 357–358, 446–447, 619, 838–839,
        912–914, 926
    Hasidic, 620
    in Hellenistic kingdoms, 109, 123–125
    Holocaust and, 927, 928, 930–932, 931(*i*), 947,
        949

(continued)

Islam and, 268, 269, 270–272, 275, 306, 307
nationalism (Zionism), 840
persecution of, 444(i), 446–448, 899
reforms of late eighteenth century and, 638
Roman Empire and, 163, 195–205, 224–225
in Russia and Soviet Union, 302, 638, 654,
    840, 841, 1012
in Spain, 426, 447–448
in thirteenth century, 422
World War I and, 861, 863
Jhansi revolt (India; 1857), 779
Jihad (jih HAD), 271, 273
Joan of Arc (1412?–1431), 431–433,
    432(m), 434(i)
Jogaila (yo GAY lo) (Jagiellon) (Lithuanian
    prince; fourteenth century), 438
John (England; r. 1199–1216), 399, 401–402,
    402(i), 422
John II (Portugal; r. 1481–1495), 465
John XXII (pope; r. 1316–1334), 441
John XXIII (antipope; r. 1410–1415), 443
John XXIII (pope; r. 1958–1963), 1003
John of Damascus, St., 267
John Paul II (pope; r. 1978–2005), 1003
Johnson, Lyndon B. (1908–1973), 1006, 1013
Johnson, Philip (1906–2005), 1064
John the Baptist, 197
Jolliet, Louis (zhoh LYAY) (1645–1700), 530
Jordan, 7, 16, 1014(m), 1014–1015
Joseph (biblical figure), 31
Joseph II (Austria and Holy Roman emperor;
    r. 1780–1790), 636–638, 637(i),
    639–640, 654
Josephine (France), 685
Journal des Dames, Le, 643
Journalism, 829. See also Newspapers
    mass, 988–989
Joyce, James (1882–1941), 888
Juan Carlos (Spain; b. 1938), 1017
Judaea, 195, 196
Judah, 32
Judah the Maccabee, 124
Judaism, 225. See also Jews
    early Christianity and, 195, 196, 199, 200
    Hebrew Bible and, 30
    in Hellenistic period, 123–125
    monotheism and, 25, 30–32, 292
Judicial system (court system)
    Athenian, 59–61
    eighteenth-century reforms in, 632,
        636–637, 654
    in England, 363–365, 364(i)
    in France, 398–401
    Roman, 145, 146, 160

in Russia, 753–754
Judith (consort of Louis I; early ninth century),
    316
Julia (Julius Caesar's daughter), 164, 165, 185
Julian (Roman emperor; r. 361–363), 223, 249
Julio-Claudians, 185, 193
Julius II (pope; r. 1503–1513), 495, 510
Julius Nepos, 241
July Revolution (France; 1830), 733
June Days (France), 735–736
Jünger, Ernst, 887
Junkers (YUN kers), 533, 639
Juno, 137
Jupiter, 137, 139, 189, 203, 216
Justice
    in ancient Greece, 37, 44, 96, 97
        Socrates' views of, 75–78
    divine, 196
    Roman, 144
Justin (c. 100–165), 200
Justinian (Byzantine emperor; r. 527–565), 233(i),
    243(m), 245, 246(i), 249–252, 254(m), 260,
    300, 312, 437
Justinian II (Byzantine emperor; r. 685–711),
    289–290
Jutland, battle of (1916), 856
Juvenal (JOO vuh nuhl) (c. 65–130), 177, 178, 193

Kadesh (KAY desh), battle of (c. 1274 B.C.E.), 25
Kafka, Franz (1883–1924), 840, 888
Kamikaze, 938
Kandinsky, Wassily (kan DIN skee, vah SEE lee)
    (1866–1944), 827
Kant, Immanuel (1724–1804), 611, 619
Karelia, 595
Karlowitz, Treaty of (1699), 537
Karlsbad Decrees (1820), 722
Kay, John, 630
Kazakhstan, 1040
Kellogg-Briand Pact (1928), 876
Kemal, Mustafa (Atatürk) (AHT uh turk)
    (1881–1938), 905
Kennedy, John F. (1917–1963), 981–984, 1006
Kent, 286, 286(m)
Kenya, 970
Kenyatta, Jomo (1894–1978), 972(i)
Kepler, Johannes (1571–1630), 515, 554–555
Kerensky, Aleksandr (1881–1970), 865
Khadija, 269, 270
Khomeini, Ayatollah Ruhollah (koh MAY nee)
    (1900?–1989), 1016, 1052, 1061
Khrushchev, Nikita (KROOSH cheff)
    (1894–1971), 964–966, 980, 984, 1004
Khwarizmi, al- (KWAR ihz mee) (c. 780–850), 308

Kiev, 396, 539
Kievan Russia, 302–303, 335*(m)*
King, Martin Luther, Jr. (1929–1968), 977, 1010
King James Bible, 496
King Lear (Shakespeare), 510
King Philip's War (1675–1676), 552
King's Peace (386 B.C.E.), 98
Kipling, Rudyard (1865–1936), 806
Kirov, Sergei (1888–1934), 907
Kissinger, Henry (b. 1923), 1013
Klee, Paul (klay) (1879–1940), 919*(i)*
Knights, 325, 327, 329, 335, 355, 359, 361*(i)*, 364, 368*(i)*, 369, 399, 401, 430–431, 435, 440, 444*(i)*
Knights, The (Aristophanes), 82
Knights Templar, 355, 356*(i)*
Knossos (NAHS uhs), 34, 35
Kohl, Helmut (b. 1930), 1019
Koine (koy NAY) (Greek language), 120
Kokoschka, Oskar (ko KOSH kah) (1886–1980), 827
Kolkhoz (collective farm), 907
Kollontai, Aleksandra (kahl uhn TY) (1872–1952), 890
Köllwitz, Käthe (KOHL wihts) (1867–1945), 851*(i)*, 886
Kore (KOR ay) (Persephone), 68
Korea, 805, 806, 939. *See also* North Korea; South Korea
Korean War (1950–1953), 959, 967*(m)*, 968
Kosciuszko, Tadeusz (kosh CHOOSH ko, TAH day oosh) (1746–1817), 675, 675*(m)*
Kosovo (KOSS oh voh), 436, 436*(m)*, 1032
Kossuth, Lajos (kaw SOOTH, LAH yosh) (1802–1894), 717, 738, 739
Kotzebue, August, 722
Krak-des-Chevaliers, 356*(i)*
Kristallnacht, 914
Kronstadt revolt (Russia; 1921), 890
Krum, Khagan (Bulgaria; r. c. 803–814), 301–302
Kuchma, Leonid, 1040
Kulaks (koo LAHKS), 907
Kulturkampf (kool TOOR kahmpf), 789
Kundera, Milan (b. 1929), 1012, 1063
Kurile Islands, 939
Kuwait, 1052
Kyoto Protocol, 1049

Labadie, Jean de, 559
Labadists, 559
Labor camps, 907, 930, 931
Labor force. *See* Workers
Labor unions (labor movement), 710, 717–720

in 1920s, 882, 894
early nineteenth-century, 717–720
mass politics of late nineteenth and early twentieth centuries, 829–833
in nineteenth century, 782, 783, 785
in Russia and Soviet Union, 841, 842
Labour Party (Great Britain), 818, 1017
Lacan, Jacques (1901–1981), 1065
Ladder of offices, 145
Lafayette, Madame de (Marie-Madeleine de La Vergne), 526, 561
Lafayette, marquis de, 659
Laissez-faire (lehs ay FAIR), 616, 772, 778, 792, 835
Lancelot, 369
Lancelot (Chrétien de Troyes), 367
Land Freedom Army, 970
Landownership (landowners; landlords). *See also* Tenant farmers
    Byzantine, 297, 299
    Carolingian economy and, 317–318
    in England (Great Britain), 331, 579–580
    Huns and, 238
    Merovingian economy and, 288, 310, 317–318
    in post-Carolingian age, 324–327, 337
    Roman, 140, 148, 156–158
Language(s). *See also specific languages*
    in Byzantine Empire, 247
    in Hellenistic period, 108, 122
    of nineteenth-century Europe, 721*(m)*
    of Roman world, 191*(m)*
    vernacular, 330, 331*(i)*, 367–369, 511, 515
        Renaissance (fifteenth-century), 448–450
Languedoc (lang DAWK), 381, 392, 393*(f)*, 400
Lares (LAHR eez), 137, 138*(i)*
La Salle, Sieur de (1643–1687), 530
Las Casas, Bartolomé de (lahs KAH sahs, bahr toh loh MAY day) (1474–1566), 486
Las Navas de Tolosa, battle of (1212), 388*(m)*, 391, 391*(m)*
Lateran Agreement (1929), 893
Latifundia (la tih FUN dee ah), 158
Latin America, 1051. *See also* Spain, American colonies of
    abolition of slavery in, 731
    independence movements in (1804–1830), 706–707, 707*(m)*
Latin language, 141, 148, 153, 154, 191*(m)*, 255, 278–279, 281, 282, 288, 323, 367, 370–371, 450–451, 475, 511, 515. *See also* Classical literature and learning
    in Byzantine Empire, 247–248, 262
    in England, 330
Latin literature

(continued)

Byzantine Empire and, 252
comedies, 153, 155(i)
in late first and early second centuries C.E., 193
Latin Vulgate, 314, 481
Latium (LAY shum), 140, 141
Latvia, 499, 534, 927, 1034, 1041
Laud, William (lawd) (archbishop of Canterbury; 1573–1645), 542
Law(s) (law codes), 753–754. *See also* Judicial system
    canon (church law), 347, 348, 352, 371, 403–404, 443, 483
    Constitutions of Melfi (Frederick II), 395
    Egyptian reforms (late eighteenth century), 681
    eighteenth-century reforms, 632, 636–637
    in England
        King Alfred, 330
        Magna Carta, 401–402, 402(i), 408, 422
    French Revolution and, 661(m)
    Hammurabi's, 14–15, 31
    Hebrew (Pentateuchal), 31
    Jewish, 196–198, 225
    Lombard, 289
    Napoleonic Code (Civil Code), 683, 685–686, 690, 695, 704, 722, 730
    Roman, 144–146, 159, 193–194, 216, 243, 244, 371
        Germanic kings and, 238, 244
    schools of, 371
    women and (nineteenth century), 730
Law, John (1671–1729), 589
Law Amendment Society (Great Britain), 764
Law of Indemnity (France; 1825), 733
Law of universal gravitation, 555
Lawrence, D. H. (1885–1930), 884
League of Nations, 874, 875, 895(m), 916, 920, 921, 922
Lebensraum (living space), 922, 928
Lechfeld, battle of (955), 319(m), 322, 332(m)
Le Corbusier (luh kawr boo ZYAY) (**Charles Édouard Jeanneret**) (1887–1965), 883(i)
Lefèvre d'Étaples, Jacques (leh FEHV day TAPL) (c. 1455–1536), 481
Legion of Honor (France), 685
Legislative Assembly (France), 663, 678
    1790s, 662
Legislative bodies (representative institutions). *See also* Democracy; *specific legislative bodies*
    in ancient Greece, 59–61
    in colonial North America, 509, 552, 615
    in Eastern Europe (seventeenth century), 533–534, 537, 539–540
    Roman, 144–145
    in thirteenth and fourteenth centuries, 407–409

Legnano (leh NYAH no), battle of (1176), 363(m), 367
Leibniz, Gottfried Wilhelm (LYB nihts) (1646–1716), 555–556, 612
Leisure activities, 818–820, 962, 989
Lem, Stanislaw, 991
Lenin, V. I. (1870–1924), 832–833, 865–868, 866(i), 890, 891, 906
Leningrad, battle of, 936(i)
Leo III (pope; r. 795–816), 313
Leo III the Isaurian (r. 717–741), 267, 290
Leo IX (pope; r. 1049–1054), 347–348
Leo X (pope; r. 1513–1521), 494
Leo XIII (pope; r. 1878–1903), 789
León (lay OHN), 388(m), 390, 391(m), 408. *See also* Castile-León
Leonardo da Vinci (1452–1519), 452–453
Leontion (le ON tee on), 116
Leopold I (Belgium; r. 1831–1865), 733
Leopold I (Holy Roman emperor; r. 1658–1705), 533, 535–537, 587
Leopold II (Belgium; r. 1865–1909), 801, 802
Leopold II (Holy Roman emperor; r. 1790–1792), 638, 654, 662
Leopold of Austria, 355
Leovigild (Visigothic king; r. 569–586), 288
Lepanto, battle of (1571), 492–493, 493(m), 497
Lepidus (LEP ih dus), 173
Lesbia, 154
Lessing, Gotthold (1729–1781), 619
Letters Concerning the English Nation (Voltaire), 602
Leucippus of Miletus (loo KIP us) (c. 500–400 B.C.E.), 75
Levant (luh VAHNT) (modern Syria, Lebanon, and Israel), 16, 16(m), 16n, 17, 17(m), 107, 142
    crusader states in, 353, 355(m), 356, 356(i), 380(m), 388(m)
    Hittite expansion in, 24
    Romans in, 153(m), 163
Levellers, 543–544, 643
Levi, Primo (LAY vee, PREE mo) (1919–1987), 932
Leviathan (luh VY uh thun) (Hobbes), 553
Lévi-Strauss, Claude (b. 1908), 1002
Levy-Omari, Alma, 1058(i)
Lewes, battle of (1264), 409
Liberal arts, 370–371, 450, 776–777
Liberalism, 798
    in early twentieth century, 835–836
    in Great Britain, 763, 764
    Mill's, 792
    in nineteenth century, 715–717

Realpolitik and, 748
Liberal party (Great Britain), 764, 835
Liberty, figure of, in French Revolution, 667,
    668(i), 670(i), 677(i)
Libraries, 112, 166
Libya, 806
Liebknecht, Karl (LEEB knekt) (1871–1919),
    870, 871
Life expectancy, 711, 903, 1049
Life sciences, 993
Ligeti, Gyorgy, 1012
Limited liability corporations, 769
Lincoln, Abraham (1809–1865), 765, 766
Lindisfarne Gospels, 287(i)
Linear A and B (Mycenaean script), 35
Lippi, Filippo (LEE pee, fee LIHP po)
    (1457–1504), 453
Lisbon, 388(m), 391, 391(m), 465
List, Friedrich, 722
Lister, Joseph, 774
Literacy/illiteracy, 770
    in eighteenth century, 582–583, 585–586, 606,
        626–627, 628, 663, 668, 726
    in nineteenth century, 776, 776(f), 785
Literature. *See also* Books and publishing
        industry; Drama; Novels; Poetry;
        individual authors
    in 1920s, 884, 888, 889
    in 1930s, 919
    1945–1960, 980
    1980s to present, 1061–1063
    in ancient Egypt, 21
    Byzantine, 245, 252–255, 260
    Chaldean (Neo-Babylonian; wisdom
        literature), 27
    Christian, 252–255
    classical. *See* Classical literature and learning
    cold war, 980
    courtly (twelfth century), 367–369
    eighteenth-century, 578, 583, 585–586,
        602–603, 606, 610, 613, 620, 621,
        626–627
    fifteenth-century (Renaissance), 448–450
    Greek, 153, 192
    Hellenistic, 113–114
    Latin
        Byzantine Empire and, 252
        comedies, 153, 155(i)
        in late first and early second
            centuries C.E., 193
    Mesopotamian, 12–13
    nineteenth-century, 785–786
        novels, 726–727
        romanticism, 723–726

novels, 192, 193, 687(i)
    of the 1830s and 1840s, 726–727
    in the 1920s, 884, 888, 889
    eighteenth-century, 578, 583, 585–586, 606,
        610, 620, 626–627
    seventeenth-century, 561
    Renaissance (fifteenth-century), 448–450
    Roman, 152–155, 183, 245. *See also* Classical
        literature and learning
    seventeenth-century, 561
    Soviet-bloc, 1005–1006, 1012
    thirteenth-century, 413–415
    travel (eighteenth century), 602–603, 606
    women authors, 561, 585, 613, 626, 727
Lithograph, 698(i), 699
Lithuania, 387, 388(m), 437, 438, 438(m), 636,
    927, 1034
    EU and, 1041
    Russian Revolution and, 868
Little Entente, 876
Liutprand (LYOOT prahnd) (bishop of
    Cremona), 297–298, 322
Livestock
    domestication of, 8
    in Great Britain, 578
Livius Andronicus, 153
Livonia (Livs), 387, 388(m), 393, 595
Livy (LIHV ee) (59 B.C.E.–17 C.E.), 140, 142, 143,
    144, 151, 183, 450
Lloyd George, David (1863–1945), 871
Local government
    in post-Carolingian age, 323–337
    of towns, 345–346
Locarno (loh KAR noh), Treaty of (1925), 875
Locke, John (1632–1704), 513, 553–554, 602,
    619, 782
Lodi, Treaty of (1454), 459
Logic, 46, 47, 370–373, 516. *See also* Reason
    Abelard and, 372–373
    Aristotle on, 97–98, 411–414
    in Hellenistic philosophy, 116
Lollardy, 444–445
Lombard League, 367
Lombardy (Lombards; Lombard kingdom),
    254(m), 261, 261(m), 262, 289(m),
    289–291, 291(m), 332, 458, 703, 756, 757
    Charlemagne and, 311
    papacy and, 290–293, 310–311
London, 509, 542, 597
    in eighteenth century, 577, 581–582, 583, 584
    Gordon riots (1780), 643
    Great Fire of (1666), 545, 546(i)
    in nineteenth century, 712–713
    Treaty of (1915), 855

London Corresponding Society, 676
London Society for Effecting the Abolition of the Slave Trade, 715
Looms, 345. *See also* Weaving
Lope de Vega (1562–1635), 509
Lorentz, Alcide, 728(i)
Lorrain, Claude (loh RAYN) (1600–1682), 558
Lorraine, 531(m), 532, 596, 760, 768, 855, 872
Lorris, Guillaume de, 414
Lothar I (Carolingian emperor; r. 840–855), 312(m), 316
Louis, A., 664(i)
Louis I (the Pious) (Carolingian emperor; r. 814–840), 295, 315–316
Louis VI (the Fat) (France; r. 1108–1137), 365–366, 382, 398, 416
Louis VII (France; r. 1137–1180), 362
Louis IX (St. Louis) (France; r. 1226–1270), 399–401, 400(m), 405, 414(i), 416
Louis XIII (France; r. 1610–1643), 499–500, 503, 525
Louis XIV (France; r. 1643–1715), 500, 523(i), 527(i), 548, 596, 677, 684
  absolutism and, 524–533, 537, 540, 546, 568, 587, 588(m), 589, 600–601
    bureaucracy, 529–530
    colonies and territorial holdings, 530–532, 531(m)
    court culture, 523–528
    the Fronde (1648–1653), 525, 525(m)
    mercantilism, 529–530
    religious orthodoxy, 528–529, 546, 586, 601
  reform of popular culture and, 562–564
  wars of, 597
Louis XV (France; r. 1715–1774), 587, 596, 613, 639
Louis XVI (France; r. 1774–1792), 638–640, 644, 655, 657–659, 662, 687(i), 694
  execution of, 663–664, 665, 671, 695
Louis XVII (France; d. 1795), 694
Louis XVIII (France; r. 1814–1824), 694, 704
Louisiana Territory, 530, 686, 688(m), 689
Louis of Bavaria (emperor), 441
Louis-Philippe (France; r. 1830–1848), 731, 733, 734, 735, 737
Louis the Child (Germany; r. 900–911), 332
Louis the German (Carolingian emperor; r. 843–876), 312(m), 316
Lourdes (France), 789–790
Louvre palace, 527–528, 557
Lower classes. *See also* Peasants; Poor, the; Serfs; Workers
  education of, 776
  in eighteenth century, 610, 614, 621, 627–629, 638, 640–642, 676

nineteenth-century health and sanitation conditions, 712–713
Lübeck, 406
Lucerne (loo SERN), 407, 407(m)
Lucian (LOO shun) (c. 117–180), 192–193
Lucretia (loo KREE shah), 142–143
Lucretius (loo KREE shus) (c. 94–55 B.C.E.), 154
Luddites, 710
Ludendorff, Erich (LOO den dorff) (1865–1937), 856, 879
Lueger, Karl (LOO gher) (1844–1910), 839–840
Luftwaffe (German Air Force), 928
Lupercalia festival, 137–138
Lusitania (ship), 856
Luther, Martin (1483–1546), 473, 474, 476–480, 477(i), 480(f), 481, 483, 495, 511
Lutherans (Lutheran church), 519(m)
  ninety-five theses and, 476
  in Norway, 562
  spread of, 476–479, 480(f), 483, 486, 491
  Thirty Years' War and, 498–499, 501–502
Lützen, battle of (1632), 499, 502(m)
Luxembourg, 276(m), 277, 316, 855. *See also* Austrian Netherlands
Luxemburg, Rosa (1870–1919), 870, 871
Lyceum (ly SEE um) (Peripatetic School; Athens), 97
Lydus, John, 248, 249
Lyon (France), 381, 395, 670, 673
Lyre, 3(i), 45–46, 157(i)
Lyric poetry, Greek, 45–46
Lysias (c. 445–380 B.C.E.), 66, 86–87
Lysimachus (ly SIM uh kus) (Egypt; c. 355–281 B.C.E.), 110
Lysippus (ly SIP us) (c. 400–300 B.C.E.), 114
Lysistrata (Aristophanes), 82–83

Maastricht Treaty (1994), 1040
Ma'at (supernatural force), 19
Macbeth (Shakespeare), 510
McCarthy, Joseph (1908–1957), 958
McDonald, Daniel, 734(i)
MacDonald, Ramsay (1866–1937), 880, 916
Macedonia (mass ih DOH nee uh), 7n, 93, 151, 152, 808, 846
  rise of (359–323 B.C.E.), 99–106
    under Alexander the Great (r. 336–323 B.C.E.), 102–106, 103(m)
    under Philip II (r. 359–336 B.C.E.), 99–101, 101(m)
Macedonian renaissance (c. 870–c. 1025), 297, 299–300, 301(i), 307, 314(i)
Macedonians (mass ih DOH nee uhns)

in Hellenistic kingdoms, 92
in territory conquered by Alexander
   the Great, 103
Machiavelli, Niccolò (mah kyah VEL lee,
   nee koh LOH) (1469–1527),
   457, 512, 553
McKinley, William, 832
Macrina, 234
Macrinus (muh KRY nus) (Roman emperor;
   r. 217–218), 208
Madame Bovary (Flaubert), 786
Madeira, 467
Madrasa, 309
Madrid, 509, 597, 692(*i*)
Magellan, Ferdinand (muh JEL un)
   (1480?–1521), 464(*m*), 465
Magic
   in Ancient Greece, 67(*i*)
   in Egypt, 23
   in Mesopotamia, 15
   in sixteenth and seventeenth centuries, 516–517
Magna Carta, 401–402, 402(*i*), 408, 422
Magyarization, 839
Magyars, 309, 318, 319(*m*), 322–323, 332, 335,
   537, 721, 839
   1848 revolution and, 738–739
Mahan, Alfred Thayer (1840–1914), 847
Mahfouz, Naguib (mah FOOZ) (b. 1911), 1061
Mahler, Gustav (1860–1911), 840
Maieul (may OOL) (abbot of Cluny), 322
Maintenon, marquise de (man tuh NOHN,
   mahr KEEZ duh) (**Françoise d'Aubigné**)
   (1635–1719), 528
Mainz, 357, 677
Majority rule, in Athenian radical democracy, 59
Malaria, 801
Malaya, 929
Malta, 148, 1041
Mamluks, 305, 692(*i*)
Management (managers), 770, 782
   in 1920s, 881, 882
Manchester (England), 710, 711, 713
Manchuria (man CHOOR ee uh), 805, 921, 939
Mandate system, after World War I, 873(*m*), 874
Mandela, Nelson (b. 1918), 1051, 1061
Mandeville, Bernard, 577
Manet, Édouard (mah NAY, ay DWAR)
   (1823–1883), 787
Manius Curius (MAN ee us KYOO ree us)
   (d. 270 B.C.E.), 158
Mann, Thomas (1875–1955), 919
Mannerism, 510, 511(*i*)
Manners. *See also* Etiquette
   in seventeenth century, 559–562

Manors, 317–318, 325–326, 328, 434
Manses, 343
   Carolingian, 317–318
Mantegna, Andrea (man TAY nyah, an DRAY ah)
   (1431–1506), 453, 455
Mantinea, battle of (man tin EE ah)
   (362 B.C.E.), 99
Manzikert, battle of (1071), 353(*m*), 354, 359
Mao Zedong (MOW dzeh DONG) (1893–1976),
   967, 1014
Mapmaking, 15
Marat, Jean-Paul (1743–1793), 670
Marathon, battle of (490 B.C.E.), 52, 53(*m*), 54
Marcel, Étienne (mar SEL, ay TYEHN), 434
March on Rome (Italy; 1922), 892, 896
Marcian, 229
Marconi, Guglielmo (1874–1937), 886
Marcus Aurelius (Roman emperor; r. 161–180),
   187, 188, 203, 205
Marduk (mythical king), 3, 4, 27–28
Marguerite de Valois (mahr guh REET duh
   vahl WAH) (1553–1615), 489
Maria Theresa (Holy Roman empress;
   r. 1740–1780), 632–633, 633(*m*), 636, 638
Marie-Antoinette (muh REE an twuh NET)
   (France; r. 1774–1793), 644, 655, 662, 666
Marie-Louise (consort of Napoleon Bonaparte),
   685, 694
Marius, Gaius (MAIR ee uhs) (c. 157–86 B.C.E.),
   159–161, 160, 162
Mark Antony, 110, 173
Markets
   in eleventh and twelfth centuries,
      340–343, 341(*m*)
   in ninth and tenth centuries, 329
Marquette, Jacques (1637–1675), 530
Marriage. *See also* Adultery; Divorce; Dowry
   in ancient Greece, 43, 69
   Christianity and, 231–232, 351–352, 483–484,
      893
   clerical, 290, 351–352
   early Middle Ages, 282–283
   in eighteenth century, 604
   in Florence (fifteenth century), 460–462
   interracial, in American colonies, 574–575
   nation-state and, 789
   in nineteenth century, 811, 814
   in postindustrial society, 999
   Protestant Reformation and, 483(*i*),
      483–484
   in Ptolemaic Egypt, 110–111, 111(*i*)
   Roman, 134, 136, 180, 194
   in seventeenth century, 506–507
   in twelfth century, 354(*i*)

Marriage of Figaro, The (Beaumarchais), 644
Married Women's Property Act (Great Britain;
    1870), 764
Mars, Roman Temple to, 175, 176(*f*)
"Marseillaise, La," 667
Marseilles (France), 276(*m*), 278, 428
Marshall, George C., 952
Marshall Plan, 952, 954, 959
Marsilius of Padua (mar SIL ee us)
    (c. 1290–1343), 441
Martin of Tours, St. (c. 316–397), 234,
    279–280, 283
Martin V (pope; r. 1417–1431), 443
Martyrdom, 200
    monasticism as, 232
    virginity and sexual renunciation as, 232
Marx, Karl (1818–1883), 618, 719, 782–783,
    784, 795
    working-class organizations and political
        parties and, 831, 832
Marxism, 782–783, 831, 841
    Russian Revolution and, 866, 867, 868
Mary, Virgin (mother of Jesus), 228, 266(*i*),
    295(*i*), 377, 414, 416, 418(*i*), 421, 494,
    562, 669, 789–790, 1021
Mary I (**Mary Tudor**) (England; r. 1553–1558),
    492, 495–496
Mary II (England; r. 1689–1694), 547–548,
    552, 589
Maryland, 508, 573
Mary of Oignies (1177–1213), 379
Mary Stuart (Mary, Queen of Scots)
    (1542–1587), 497
Masaccio (muh SAH chee oh) (1401–1428),
    453, 454(*i*)
Masaryk, Tomas (president; Czechoslovakia), 918
Masinissa (mah sin IS ah) (Numidian king;
    r. second century B.C.E.), 152
Masonic lodges (freemasons), 610, 621, 623–624,
    626, 691
Mass, sacrament of, 351, 375, 415, 416, 445, 475,
    480, 511, 562, 680. *See also* Eucharist
    Fourth Lateran Council and (1215), 403
Massachusetts Bay Company, 508
Mass culture. *See* Popular culture
Mass politics, 829–843, 852, 896
Masturbation, 627
Materialism, 116, 782
Mathematics, 516, 555, 601, 612
    in Ancient Greece, 46
    in Hellenistic period, 118–119
    Islam and, 308–309
    in Mesopotamia, 12–15
    Pythagoras and, 46

Matisse, Henri (1869–1954), 825–826
Matrimonial Causes Act (Great Britain; 1857), 764
Matthew, St., 314(*i*)
Matthias Corvinus (muh THY us kohr VY nus)
    (Hungary; r. 1456–1490), 437
Mau Mau, 970
Maurice (Duke of Saxony), 491
Mauryan dynasty, 107
Maxentius, 221
Maximianus (bishop of Ravenna), 246(*i*)
Maximilian (Mexico; r. 1864–1867), 750
Maximilian I (Holy Roman emperor;
    r. 1493–1519), 458, 489
Mayakovsky, Vladimir (may yuh KAWF skee)
    (1893–1930), 891
Mayflower, 508
Mazarin, Cardinal (maz uh RAN) (1602–1661),
    500, 525–526, 529
Mazzini, Giuseppe (maht SEE nee) (1805–1872),
    722, 736, 737
Mecca, 268, 270–271, 307
Medea (Euripides), 68, 81
Medes (meedz), 27
Medici, Cosimo de' (MEH dih chee)
    (1388–1464), 451, 453, 457
Medici, Lorenzo de' (the Magnificent)
    (1449–1492), 456–457
Medici family, 440, 456–457, 458, 461
Medicine, 774, 950, 1049–1050
    in ancient Egypt, 23
    colonialism and, 779
    in eighteenth century, 598–599
    in Hellenistic period, 120, 122
    Hippocrates and, 78
    Mesopotamian, 15
    professionalization of, 775–776
    Roman, 194
    in sixteenth and seventeenth centuries, 514–516
    in twentieth century, 993
    women in, 777
Medievalism, 725
Medina (mih DEE nuh), 268, 270–271
Meditations (Marcus Aurelius), 203
Mediterranean polyculture, 34
Mediterranean Sea and region, 7*n*
    c. 500 B.C.E., 4, 47(*m*)
    c. 400 B.C.E., 88(*m*)
    c. 750, 291(*m*)
    c. 1050, 335(*m*)
    c. 1350, plague and, 427(*m*), 428
    in fifteenth century, 463–465
    Greek settlements during Archaic Age, 38–39
    Rome and, 152, 188(*m*), 190
Megarons, 35

Mehmed II (the Conqueror) (Ottoman sultan; r. 1451–1481), 425, 436–437, 706(i)
Meiji Restoration (MAY jee) (1868), 781, 804
Mein Kampf (Hitler), 894, 909, 910
Meir, Golda (1898–1978), 969
Memphis (Egypt), 19
Men (men's roles and status). *See also* Patriarchy
  in ancient Egypt, 21
  in ancient Greece, 36, 38, 76
    Athenian, 59–61
    education and physical fitness, 73–74
    paternalism, 42, 43, 44
    sexual activity, 43–44, 74–75, 81–82
  Bedouin concept of manliness, 268
  eighteenth-century view of women, 604–605
  faithfulness in, 131–132
  as gladiators, 181
  during Great Depression, 902–903
  Hebrew, 31
  in hunter-gatherer societies, 5–6
  as Islamic warriors, 271, 273
  Macedonian, 99, 100(i)
  manners and (seventeenth century), 560
  Napoleon's Civil Code and, 685–686
  Neo-Assyrian, 26–27
  Paleolithic and Neolithic, 5–8
  Roman, 131, 132, 134, 140, 144, 145
    education of, 183
  after World War II, 977–978
Menander (meh NAN der) (c. 342–289 B.C.E.), 113, 114
Mendel, Gregor (1822–1884), 791
Mendelssohn, Moses (MEN dl sun) (1729–1786), 619
Menes (MEE neez) (Egypt; c. 3100– c. 3040 B.C.E.), 16
Mennonites, 480
Mental illness, late-nineteenth-century views on, 820–822
Mentuhotep II, 21
Mercantilism, 508, 615
  English, 544
  French, 529–530, 556
Mercenaries
  in Ancient Greece, 92
  Carthaginian, 149
Merchants. *See also* Trade
  Hanseatic League, 406–407
Merian, Maria Sibylla (1646–1717), 558–559, 559(i)
Mérida, battle of (1230), 391, 391(m)
Merovingian kingdoms (mer oh VIN jee un) (Merovingian society) (c. 485–751), 242, 244, 276(m), 276–286, 293. *See also* Franks

powerful people in, 281–285, 317–318
Mesmer, Franz (MEZ muhr) (1734–1815), 620
Mesopotamia (Mesopotamian civilization), 187, 188(m). *See also* Akkadia; Assyria; Babylon; Sumer
  Bronze Age, 5
  cities in, 8–13, 14–15
  cuneiform writing, 11–13, 13(f)
  emergence of civilization in, 4
  empire building in, 12
  Epic of Creation, 3
  Hammurabi's laws, 14–15, 31
  religion and mythology in, 3, 4, 10–11
  Sassanid Empire and, 261
  Sumerian (southern Mesopotamian) society, 8–13
  World War I and, 855
Messiah, 196, 197, 198
Messiah (Handel), 585
Mestizos, 486, 574–575
Metacomet (King Philip), 552
Metals and metallurgy
  agriculture and, 8
  in ancient Egypt, 16
  in ancient Greece, 38, 39
  Assyrian, 26
  demand for, 904
  Hittite, 24
  in Mesopotamia (Bronze Age), 12
  in Middle Ages, 344
Metamorphoses (Ovid), 183
Metaphysics, 96
Methodism, 621
Methodists (Wesleyans), 703–704
Methodius (Byzantine missionary), 302
Metics (noncitizens), 42, 72–73
Metric system, 669
Metternich, Prince Klemens von (MET uhr nik) (1773–1859), 701, 701(i), 705, 706, 715, 722, 738, 749
Metz (Germany), 357
Meulen, Adam Frans van der, 523(i)
Meun, Jean de, 414
Mexico, 486, 504, 750, 764, 766, 1051
Michelangelo Buonarroti (mik el AN jeh loh, bwo nah ROT tee) (1475–1564), 454, 455(i), 510
Mickiewicz, Adam (mits KYAY vich) (1798–1855), 722
Middle Ages
  commercial revolution and, 344–345, 369, 377, 379, 382
  early medieval kingdoms, 275–293, 276(m)
  use of term, 260n

Middle class(es) (bourgeoisie)
  in 1920s, 880
  in Byzantine Empire, 265
  domesticity and, 752
  education and, 775–776
  in eighteenth century, 567(i), 568, 581–584,
    586, 590, 610, 623–628, 655, 677
  the Enlightenment and, 610, 618, 621–627
  in fourteenth and fifteenth centuries, 430–431,
    448, 454
  German unification and, 761
  in Great Britain, 763(i)
  liberalism and, 715, 716, 716(i), 717
  mass politics and, 829
  modernity and, 798
  in nineteenth century, 719, 741, 749, 774, 775,
    809, 811
    leisure activities and sports, 818–820
  philosophy and, 823
  population decline and, 813–814
  Russian Revolution and, 865
  in seventeenth century, 491, 505, 524–525, 543,
    548–550, 560
  Social Darwinism and, 792
  socialism and, 717
  sports and, 820
  woman suffrage and, 834
  women of, 770, 778
Middle-Class Gentleman, The (Molière), 560
Middle East, 966. See also Near East
  in 1920s, 881
  in 1930s, 905
  1945–1960, 968–970
  1970s, 1052–1055
  1980–1991, 1053(m)
  Arab-Israeli conflict in, 1014–1015
  Byzantine Empire and, 260, 273, 296
  meaning of term, 7n
  oil-producing nations in, 1014–1015
  Peace of Paris and, 873(m), 874
  Russia and, 751
Middle Kingdom (Egypt; c. 2061–1665 B.C.E.),
    17(m), 21–22
Midrash, 225
Midway Island, battles at (World War II), 938
Midwives, 195(i), 599
Mieszko I (MYESH ko) (prince of Poland;
    r. 963–992), 334
Migrations. See also Refugees
  to American colonies, 575
  in Ancient Greece, 72
  economic consequences of, 1058
  from Europe, 733
  Germanic, in fourth century, 235–243, 236(m)

  global (1980s to present), 1030, 1038,
    1057–1059
  of Jews, 840
  in late nineteenth and early twentieth centuries,
    816–817, 817(f)
  population growth and, 812(f), 816
  rural, 712
  women and, 1058–1059
Milan, 327, 329, 345–346, 349, 451, 456
  Visconti dynasty and, 450, 453,
    458–459
Military. See Armed forces; War; Weapons and
    military technology
Mill, Harriet Taylor, 792, 834
Mill, John Stuart (1806–1873), 792, 834
Milo (athlete), 38
Milosevic, Slobodan (mih LOH seh vich)
    (1941–2006), 1032, 1033
Milton, John (1608–1674), 556–557
Milunic, Vladimir, 1064(i)
Milvian Bridge, battle of the (312), 221
Minerva, 137, 203
Mines Act (Great Britain; 1842), 711
Ming dynasty (China), 463
Minimalists, 1002
Mining, 711, 767. See also Metals and metallurgy
Minoan civilization (Minoans; Cretans), 33–36,
    34(m), 35(i)
Minoan Wall Painting (Thera), 35(i)
Minorities
  German unification and, 759
  Habsburg Empire and, 762
Minos (MY nus) (Crete), 34, 36
Minotaur, 34, 36
Mir, 753
Missi dominici (MEE see doh MIN ih kee),
    312–313, 316, 336
Missionaries, Christian, 422, 704, 772
  in Africa, 801
  Arianism and, 228
  in Balkans, 302
  in China, 397–398, 575, 603, 781, 807
  colonialism and, 799
  in England, 286
  in Frisia, 310
  Jesuit, 484–486, 485(i), 637
  Portugal and, 485(i), 486
  reform and, 818
  in Scandinavia, 322
  thirteenth-century, 392
Missy, Jean Rousset de, 593(i)
Mithras (MITH rus) (Mithraism), 204(i)
Mithridates VI (mith rih DAY teez)
    (Pontus; 120–63 B.C.E.), 161–162

Mitteleuropa, 844, 854, 867

Mitterrand, François (1916–1996), 1019

Mode of production, 782

Modern art, 825–827, 896

Modernism (modernity), 797(*i*), 798, 822–829
  in arts, 896
  the Enlightenment and, 615
  World War I and, 849, 852

Modernization
  during Depression, 902
  German unification and, 758, 759
  of Japan, 804, 804(*i*)

Modern Times (film), 918

Moero of Byzantium, 113

Mohács (MO hahch), battle of (1526), 487(*m*),
  488, 488(*i*)

Moldavia, 752

Molecular biology, 993

Molière (mohl YAYR) (1622–1673),
  560–561, 593

Monarchy (kings; queens; emperors). *See also*
    specific monarchies and empires
  absolute. *See* Absolutism
  in ancient Near East, 7(*m*)
  Byzantine, 245–249, 296–300. *See also*
    specific emperors
  in Central and Eastern Europe (tenth and
    eleventh centuries), 332–336, 335(*m*)
  constitutional, 733
  Danish, 322
  divine right of, 28–29, 503, 513, 523, 524, 528,
    553–554, 615, 646
  in Eastern Europe
    fourteenth and fifteenth century,
      437–439, 438(*m*)
  in Egypt, 18–20
  in England (Great Britain), 323, 327, 329–331,
    345, 457
    abolition of (1649), 544–545
    eleventh and twelfth centuries,
      360–365, 363(*m*)
    fourteenth and fifteenth centuries, 437, 439,
      447, 457
    Hundred Years' War and, 430–435, 433(*m*)
    King Alfred's law code, 330
    nineteenth century, 763–764
    restoration of (1660), 545–546
    sixteenth and seventeenth centuries, 494–497
    in twelfth and thirteenth centuries, 394(*m*),
      401–402, 402(*i*), 404–405, 407–409, 422
  in France, 331–332, 457, 643–644, 704. *See also*
    Louis XIV, absolutism and
    abolishing, 676
    absolute, 540, 546, 615

Capetian kings, 332, 392, 394(*m*),
  398–401, 422
  courtiers in the sixteenth century, 503–504
  eighteenth century, 603
  eleventh and twelfth century, 361, 365–366
  the Enlightenment and, 618–619, 639–640
  fourteenth and fifteenth century, 437, 440,
    442, 447, 457, 459
  French Revolution and, 651–665, 659–665
  Hundred Years' War and, 430–435, 433(*m*)
  limits of absolutism (eighteenth
    century), 587
  post-Carolingian, 326, 326(*m*), 331–332
  sixteenth and seventeenth century, 490–491
  thirteenth century, 398–401, 400(*m*), 404–405
  twelfth century, 361, 365–366
  in Germany
    eleventh and twelfth century, 366–367
    post-Carolingian, 332–333, 334(*i*)
    tenth and eleventh centuries, 323, 332–335
    thirteenth century, 394–396
  Hellenistic period, 92–93, 106–112, 107(*m*),
    110–112, 111(*i*)
  Hittite, 24
  Lombard Italy and, 299–293
  Macedonian, 99–101
  Merovingian, 276(*m*), 281–282, 285, 288, 310
  in Neo-Assyrian Empire, 26–27
  papal
    fourteenth and fifteenth centuries, 440–443
    thirteenth and fourteenth centuries, 402–406
  Persian, 28–29, 30(*i*)
  in Poland, 654–655
  in post-Carolingian age, 323–327, 331–337, 343
  public opinion and (eighteenth century), 643–644
  revival of (eleventh and twelfth centuries)
    Byzantium, 358–367
    courtly culture, 367–369
    England, 360–365
    France, 365–366
    Germany, 366–367
  Roman (c. 753–509 B.C.E.), 139–142
  Roman principate, 172, 173, 175, 176,
    184–188, 190
    Caesar, 166
  in Russia, 594
  in Spain, 405, 407–408, 447–448, 458
  Sumerian, 10

Monasticism (mo NAS tih sizum) (monasteries
    and convents), 232–235, 233(*i*), 245,
    281–283, 284(*i*), 285, 324, 328, 339–340,
    342. *See also specific monastic orders*
  in Austria, 638, 654

(continued)

in Byzantine Empire, 265, 266–267
coenobitic, 233–234
communities of, 232
crusaders and, 355, 356(i)
in eleventh and twelfth centuries, 370, 373–383
in England, 286–288, 331
in France, 661–662
in Frankish kingdoms, 277(i)
Irish (Columbanian), 282–283, 286, 310
in Italy, 289, 411(i)
Luther and, 476, 477(i)
reforms and, 315–316, 340, 346–347, 445
women in, 234, 280–281, 283–285, 284(i), 286, 288, 410
Monegund (nun), 280
Monet, Claude (mo NAY, clawd) (1840–1926), 787
Monetarist policies, 1017
Mongols (Tatars or Tartars), 385–386, 396–398, 397(m), 420(m), 422, 438(m), 438–439, 463, 466, 469(m)
Mono no aware (sensitivity to fleetingness of life), 788
Monophysites (muh NAHF uh syts), 229, 233(i), 246, 252, 273
Monotheism, 228, 270, 292
  in ancient Egypt, 22
  Byzantine Empire and, 260
  Hebrew, 25, 30–32
  Zoroastrianism and, 30
Monroe, James (1758–1831), 707
Monroe Doctrine, 707
Montagu, Lady Mary Wortley (MAHN tah gyoo) (1689–1762), 599
Montaigne, Michel de (mahn TAYN, mih shel de) (1533–1592), 512–513, 516, 518
Montenegro, 844, 845, 846
Montesquieu, baron de (mahn tess KYOO) (**Charles-Louis de Secondat**) (1689–1755), 603–604, 613, 615, 636, 655, 666
Montessori, Maria (mahn teh SO ree) (1870–1952), 815
Monteverdi, Claudio (mahn tuh VAYR dee) (1567–1643), 512
Morality (moral values), 230, 231.
    See also Virtue(s)
  dualism in, 30
  law codes and, 244
  Plato and, 96–97
  relativism in, 75, 823
  Roman, 130–132, 134, 136, 137, 139, 142, 145–146, 203, 205
    loss of, 158, 161, 162, 163
    males and, 234

Socrates and, 76–78, 95
  sophists and, 75
"Moral majority," 1018
Moravia, 535
More, Thomas (1478–1535), 475–476, 495, 717
Moriscos, 492–493
Morocco, 844, 970
Morrison, Toni (b. 1931), 1062, 1062(i)
Mortality rates, 713
  infant, 711, 1019
Mosaics
  Alexander the Great at battle of Issus, 104(i)
  Christ as Sun God, 224(i)
  family from Edessa, 229(i)
  Hagia Sophia, 251(i)
  Justinian and his court in Ravenna, 246(i), 250
  mosque at Damascus, 259(i)
  Plato's Academy, 96(i)
  Roman, 171(i)
  Theodora and her court in Ravenna, 247(i)
  upper-class country life (fourth century), 241(i)
Moscow, 581, 594, 693
Moses, 31, 233(i)
Mos maiorum ("the way of the ancestors"), 131, 146
Motets (mo TETS), 415
Mountain, the (France), 664
Movies (film industry), 989
  in 1920s, 885–886, 896
  in 1930s, 918
  1980s to present, 1063
Mozarabs, 306
Mozart, Wolfgang Amadeus (1756–1791), 626, 644
Muhammad (muh HAHM id) (prophet; c. 570–632), 268, 269–274, 272(m), 292
  cartoons of, 1058
  Fatima and, 274, 305
  hadith literature and, 275
  successors of (632–750), 273–275, 293
Muhammad ibn Musa (d. 850), 308
Mühlberg, battle of (1547), 491
Multinational corporations, 995–996
Mummification, 19, 23, 121
Munch, Edvard (moongk, ed VAHRT) (1863–1944), 797(i), 826
Munich, 462
Munich Pact (1938), 926–927
Münster (MOON stuhr), Anabaptists in, 473, 473(i), 479–480, 480(f)
Münter, Gabriele (1877–1962), 827
Müntzer, Thomas (1468?–1525), 478, 480(f)
Murat, General, 685
Mursili II (Hittite king; r. 1321–1295 B.C.E.), 24

Muscovy (MUS kuh vee), 426, 438(m), 438–439, 469(m), 505, 508
Music, 46
eighteenth-century, 567, 578, 584–585, 606, 621, 625–626, 628
Gregorian chant (plainchant), 373–374, 383
jazz, 889
in late nineteenth and early twentieth centuries, 827–829
modern (postindustrial), 1001–1002, 1063
in nineteenth century, 811
romanticism, 725–726
polyphonic, 415, 452, 455
Renaissance (fifteenth century), 452, 455–457
seventeenth-century, 511–512, 527
thirteenth-century, 386, 415
written notation, 368(i), 374
Muslim calendar, 308(i)
Muslim League (India), 808, 905
Mussolini, Benito (moo suh LEE nee) (1883–1945), 174(i), 885, 892, 893, 893(i), 894, 899(i), 905, 920, 921, 922, 924, 926, 928, 929, 934
Mutualism, 782
Mycenaean civilization (my seh NEE an), 33–36
Myrdal, Alva, 916
Mystery cults, 66–68, 121, 122
Mythology, 3, 4
Greek, 11, 34, 36, 37, 105
Mesopotamian, 10–12

Nabonidus (nah bo NEE dus) (Babylon; r. c. 555–539 B.C.E.), 28
Naevius (NEE vee us) (d. 201 B.C.E.), 153
NAFTA (North American Free Trade Agreement), 1040
Nagasaki, atomic bombing of (1945), 938, 939(i)
Nagy, Imre (nodj, IM reh), 965
Nanking, Treaty of (1842), 732
Nantes (nahnts), 577
massacre of 1793, 671
Naples, 141, 322
kingdom of, 685, 705
Napoleon Bonaparte (Napoleon I) (BO nuh part) (1769–1821), 532, 620, 682(i), 683–691, 700, 701, 714
as authoritarian ruler, 683–685
Catholic church and, 678, 683–684
Civil Code (Napoleonic Code), 683, 685–686, 690, 704, 722, 730
Egyptian campaign, 681, 685
in exile, 694–695

fall of, 691–695
as First Consul, 683–684
Italian campaigns of 1796–1797, 680–681
military conquests, 688–690, 696(m)
paternalism of, 685–688
revolt in Spain and, 692(i)
rise of, 652, 674–683
science and intellectual life under, 686–688
Napoleonic Code (Civil Code), 683, 685–686, 690, 704, 722, 730
Napoleon III (Louis-Napoleon Bonaparte) (r. 1852–1870), 736, 737, 748, 749–751, 750(i), 757, 759, 766, 777, 780
Naram-Sin (Akkadia; r. c. 2250 B.C.E.), 12–13
NASA (National Aeronautics and Space Administration), 966
Naseby, battle of (1645), 542(m), 543
Nasser, Gamal Abdel (1918–1970), 969–970
National Assembly (France), 657–662, 661(m), 664(i), 735, 736
National Association for the Advancement of Colored People (NAACP), 976
National Convention (France), 663–665, 667–669, 671–672, 674, 677, 679
National Front Party (France), 1019
National Guard (France), 659, 671, 674
National Insurance Act (Great Britain; 1911), 835
Nationalism (nationalist movements), 706, 720–723, 795, 798. See also specific nations
in 1970s, 1016(m), 1016–1017
colonialism and, 779, 781
Crimean War and, 752
ethnic purity and, 878
French intellectuals and, 720
German unification and, 761
Jewish, 837, 839, 840
mass politics and, 829
modern art and, 826
in nineteenth century, 691, 695, 696(m)
philosophy and, 824
Realpolitik and, 748, 749
romantic, 726
sports and, 819–820
working class and, 832
World War I and, 849, 855, 860–861, 896
National Organization for Women (NOW), 1008
National workshops (France), 735
Nation building (national unification). See also Germany, unification of; Italy, unification of
in nineteenth century, 748–749, 755–766
Nations, Battle of the (1813), 693
Nation-states. See also Nation building
1980s to present, 1040–1046

(continued)

nineteenth-century, 747–795, 748–749
  World War I and, 896
Native Americans (Indians), 467–470, 530, 552,
    572, 603, 614, 632, 764, 765(m)
  conversion to Christianity, 485–486, 574–575
NATO (North Atlantic Treaty Organization),
    954(m), 954–955
Natural History of Religion, The (Hume), 613
Natural law, 611
  Grotius's conception of, 513–514
Natural rights, 514, 611, 616
Natural selection, 791
Navigation. *See* Ships and navigation
Navigation Act (1651), 544
Navy (naval warfare)
  battle of Lepanto (1571), 492–493, 493(m), 497
  Byzantine, 265
  Delian League and Athens, 56–57, 58(i), 59, 61,
    84, 85, 86(m), 98
  Great Britain and, 591, 634, 635(m), 688
  Persian wars and, 55, 56
  Roman, 173
    First Punic War (264–241 B.C.E.), 149, 150
  Spanish Armada, 497, 505
  before World War I, 847
  in World War I, 856, 869
Nazis (National Socialist German Workers' Party),
    894, 899(i), 909–914, 975, 1019
  denazification, 956–957
  German politics and, 911–913
  after World War II, 955–957
Nazi-Soviet Pact (1939), 927–929
Near East, 37. *See also* Middle East
  ancient, 7(m), 7n, 8n
    empires in (to 500 B.C.E.), 25–32
    science and religion in, 28
  Dark Age (1200–1000 B.C.E.), 25, 38
  Greek art and literature and, 45
  Greek migration to, 92–93
  Hellenistic kingdoms in, 92
  influence of, 45
  knowledge from, 46
  Neolithic Revolution in
    (c. 10,000–4000 B.C.E.), 6–8
Nebuchadnezzar II (neh boo kud NEZ ur) (Neo-
    Babylonian king; r. 605–562 B.C.E.), 27, 32
Necker, Jacques (NEHK uhr) (1732–1804),
    658, 687(i)
Nefer-ka-Re (Egypt; r. c. 2300 B.C.E.), 20
Nefertiti (nef ur TEE tee) (Egyptian queen;
    r. fourteenth century B.C.E.), 22
Nehru, Jawaharlal (1889–1964), 1051
Nelson, Horatio (1758–1805), 681, 689
Neo-Assyrian Empire, 25–27, 26(m)

Neo-Babylonian Empire, 27–28
Neoclassical style, 624, 624(i)
Neoliberalism, 1017
Neolithic period (Neolithic Revolution;
    New Stone Age), 3–4, 5–8, 33
Neoplatonism (nee oh PLAY tuh nizum),
    204–205, 255, 307, 359–360
Neorealism, 980–981
Nepos, Julius, 241
Nero (Roman emperor; r. 54–68), 185, 186, 200
Nerva (Roman emperor; r. 96–98), 187
Nestorianism (Nestorian Christians), 228
Nestorius (bishop of Constantinople; d. 451), 228
Netherlands, 310, 316, 700, 703, 733, 928. *See also*
    Austrian Netherlands; Dutch Republic;
    Spanish Netherlands
  Calvinists in, 493–494
  colonies of, 805(m), 880–881
  education in, 777
  German conquest of, 899
  Napoleon and, 690, 693, 694
  under Spanish rule, 492–494, 493(m), 494(m),
    496–497, 513
  urbanization in, 817
  War of Spanish Succession and, 587, 588(m)
Neustria (NEW stree ah), 276(m), 285, 310
New Deal (United States), 914, 915
New Economic Policy (NEP), 890, 906
New England, 481, 552, 571, 583
Newfoundland, 470, 587
New Harmony, 718
New Heloise, The (Rousseau), 617(i)
New Kingdom (Egypt; c. 1569–1081 B.C.E.),
    15–16, 17(m), 22, 24, 25
"New look," 978, 979(i)
New Model Army, 543
New Plymouth Colony, 508
News from the Republic of Letters (Bayle), 601
Newspapers, 610, 829
  in 1920s, 876, 885, 892
  eighteenth-century, 583, 606, 626, 642–643
  in France, 657, 684
  nineteenth-century mass politics and, 831
  pre–World War I arms race and, 847–848
  Spanish-American War and, 806
  in United States, 764
  after World War I, 870
New Testament, 197, 198, 227, 475, 481
Newton, Isaac (1642–1727), 524, 554–556,
    602, 612, 613, 615
New woman, 814–815, 815(i)
New World. *See* Americas, The
New Zealand, 732, 816
NGOs (nongovernmental organizations), 1046

Nicaea (ny SEE uh), Council of (325), 228
Nice, 488, 677, 757
Nicephorus I (ny SEF uh rus) (Byzantine
    emperor; r. 802–811), 301, 302
Nicetius (Merovingian bishop), 282, 285
Nicholas I (Russia; r. 1825–1855), 705, 717,
    722, 729, 739, 741, 753
    Crimean War (1853–1856) and, 751
Nicholas II (Russia; r. 1894–1917), 841–842,
    854, 861, 865
Nicholas V (pope; r. 1447–1455), 465
Nicolaitism, 347
Nicomedia, 218
Nicopolis, battle of (1396), 436, 436(m)
Nietzsche, Friedrich (NEET chuh, FREE drikh)
    (1844–1900), 815, 823–824
Nigeria, 970
Nightingale, Florence (1820–1910), 752, 775
"Night of the Long Knives," 912
Nihilism, 754, 786
Nijinsky, Vaslav (1890–1950), 827, 828(i)
Nijmegen, Treaty of (NY may ghen) (1678–1679),
    531, 531(m)
Nika Riot (532), 249
Nile River, 16, 17, 17(m), 19, 21, 203, 233
Nîmes, aqueduct at, 149(i)
1984 (Orwell), 940, 980
Nineveh (NIN uh vuh), 27
Nine Years' War (War of the League of Augsburg)
    (1689–1697), 587
Nippur (nih POOR), 15
Nixon, Richard (1913–1994), 1013, 1014
Nkrumah, Kwame (1909–1972), 970
Nobel, Alfred (1833–1896), 847
Nobility. See Aristocracy
Nominalism, 413
Nongovernmental organizations (NGOs), 1046
Nordau, Max (1849–1923), 820
Normandy (Normans), 321–322, 348, 359,
    398(m), 398–399, 399n
    conquest of England (1066), 360(m),
        360–362, 361(i)
    Hundred Years' War (1337–1453) and,
        431, 432(m)
    landing on (World War II), 934
North Africa, 8n, 966
    Arabs and, 263
    Byzantine Empire and, 260
    city-states in, 55
    Donatism in, 228–229
    Islam and, 268, 305–307, 306(m), 390, 391(m),
        488, 493
    Ottoman Empire and, 436(m)
    Vandals in, 240

North America. See also Native Americans
    colonies in, 570(m), 574, 576, 590, 596
    constitutionalism in, 524, 548, 552, 565
    eighteenth-century wars and, 632, 634, 635(m)
    English (British) colonies in, 508–509, 548, 568,
        615, 618, 645, 648(m)
        American War of Independence,
            644–648, 645(i)
        Caribbean, 551, 678, 678(m)
        French and Indian War (1756–1763), 634
        representative government, 509, 552, 565, 615
        settlement patterns, 574–575
        slavery and slave trade, 548, 551–552, 568–569,
            570(m), 571, 571(m), 571(f), 573, 731
    exploration and settlements (fifteenth and
        sixteenth centuries), 470
    French and Indian War, 634
    French colonies in, 509, 568, 587, 588(m), 596
        Canada, 530, 574
    Great Awakening in, 620
North American Free Trade Agreement
    (NAFTA), 1040
North Atlantic Treaty Organization (NATO),
    954(m), 954–955
Northern Crusades, 387, 388(m), 406, 422
Northern Ireland, 880, 1016, 1016(m)
North German Confederation, 759, 760(m)
North Korea, 968
North Vietnam, 1013
Northwest passage, 470
Norway, 303, 322, 562, 703, 768, 928
Nossis of Locri, 113
Nova Scotia, 587
Novels, 192, 193
    of 1830s and 1840s, 726–727
    in 1920s, 884, 888, 889
    eighteenth-century, 578, 583, 585–586, 606,
        610, 620, 626–627
    seventeenth-century, 561
Novgorod (NAHV guh rahd), 428, 438(m), 439
Nubia (NOO bee uh), 16–17, 17(m), 22
Nuclear power, 962
    Chernobyl, 1020–1021, 1047
Nuclear weapons (nuclear warfare), 937(m), 938,
    939(i), 945, 945(i), 946, 955, 980
    Cuban Missile Crisis and, 982
Nur al-Din, 356
Nuremberg, 446, 452, 453
Nuremberg Laws, 913
Nuremberg trials, 956
Nystad, Treaty of (1721), 595, 595(m)

Oblation, 234, 283
Occitan, 366–367

Ockham, William of (c. 1285–1349), 413, 441
Ockham's razor, 413
O'Connell, Daniel (1775–1847), 723
Octavian. *See* Augustus
Odoacer (oh doh AH ser) (c. 434?–493), 241, 242
Odyssey (Homer), 37, 153, 183, 255
Ogodei (OH guh day) (Great Khan; 1186–1241), 396
Oil (petroleum), 968–969, 1013–1016, 1015(f), 1040
Old Believers (Russia), 538
Oldenburg, Claes (b. 1929), 1001
Old English (Anglo-Saxon language), religious works in, 330, 331(i)
Old Kingdom (Egypt; c. 2687–2190 B.C.E.), 16–21
Old Testament (Hebrew Bible), 30–32, 123, 198, 225, 481. *See also* Torah
Oleg (Russian chief; r. c. 900), 302
Oligarchy (AW lih gahr kee), 40, 44, 130
Oliver Twist (Dickens), 727
Olympia (Manet), 787
Olympic Games, in ancient Greece, 38
Olympus, Mount, 66
On Agriculture (Cato), 154
On Architecture (Alberti), 455
On Crimes and Punishments (Beccaria), 636–637
One Day in the Life of Ivan Denisovitch (Solzhenitsyn), 966
On Germany (de Staël), 687
On Liberty (Mill), 792
On the Caesars (Victor), 217(m)
On the Church (Wycliffe), 444
On the Construction of the Human Body (Vesalius), 515
On the Manner of Negotiating with Sovereigns (Callières), 597
On the Nature of Things (Lucretius), 154
On the Origin of Species (Darwin), 790–791
On the Revolution of the Celestial Spheres (Copernicus), 514
On the Rivers of Europe (Callimachus), 113
OPEC (Organization of Petroleum Exporting Countries), 1015, 1016
Open Society Foundation, 1046
Opera, 511–512, 521, 527, 584–585, 626, 788
Opium War (1839–1842), 732, 732(m), 781, 801
Optimates (op tee MAHT ays), 160, 161, 167
Oracles, 102, 118
Orange Free State, 801, 802
Orange, princes of, 493
Orange Revolution, 1040
Oratory. *See* Rhetoric
Order. *See* Social order
Order of Christ, 465

Order of Sword Brothers, 387
Oresteia (aw res TY uh) (Aeschylus) (458 B.C.E.), 80–81
Orestes (aw RES teez), 81, 241
Orfeo (Monteverdi), 512
Organization of Petroleum Exporting Countries (OPEC), 1015, 1016
Origen (OH rih jen) (c. 185–255), 203
Original sin, doctrine of, 230
Origins, The (Cato), 154
Orléans, duke of (or lay AHN) (1674–1723), 589
Orléans, siege of, 431, 432(m)
Oroonoko (Behn), 561
Orthodoxy, 741
    Christian, 202, 227, 228, 229, 230.
        See also Heresies
    Justinian and, 251–252
Orvieto, cathedral at, 418
Orwell, George (1903–1950), 919, 940, 980
Osiris (oh SY ris), 24, 123(i), 203
Osman I (Ottoman emperor; r. 1280–1324), 436
Ospedale degli Innocenti (Florence), 462
Osrhoëne, 229(i)
Ostpolitik, 1004
Ostracism (AHS trah siz um), 59–60
Ostrogoths, 242, 249, 254(m), 289
Oswy (Northumbria; r. c. 665), 287
Otto I (German king and Holy Roman emperor; r. 936–973), 322–323, 332(m), 332–333
Otto I (Greece; r. 1832–1862), 706
Otto II (German king and Holy Roman emperor; r. 973–983), 333
Otto III (German king and Holy Roman emperor; r. 983–1002), 332(m), 333, 334(i)
Ottoman Empire (Ottoman Turks), 420(m), 426, 436, 463, 466, 564(m), 648(m), 692, 751(m), 751–752, 808, 845(m), 872. *See also* Turkey
    Balkans and, 705
    colonialism and, 801(m), 881
    at Constantinople, 425, 425(i), 458
    Crimean War (1853–1856) and, 748, 751–752
    in early twentieth century (before World War I), 844
    eighteenth century, 636
    expansion in fourteenth and fifteenth centuries, 436(m), 437–438, 438(m), 457, 459, 467–468, 469(m), 471
    Greece and, 705, 706
    Hungary and (1657–1730), 596, 596(m)
    Jews in, 448
    Napoleon and, 689
    Peace of Westphalia and, 519(m)

revolutionary nationalism in, 808
Russia and, 654, 706
in seventeenth century, 533, 535(m), 535–537, 536(i), 540
in sixteenth century, 486–488, 487(m), 488(i), 492–493
Spain and, 692(i)
World War I and, 852, 854, 872, 874, 877
Ottonian dynasty (Germany), 332(m), 332–333, 334(i), 335(m)
Outwork. See Putting-out system
Ovid (AHV id) (43 B.C.E.–17 C.E.), 183
Ovism, doctrine of, 604–605
Owen, Robert (1771–1858), 718
Owenites, 718
Oxford University, 413, 444
Ozone layer, 1047

Pachomius, 233
Pacific Rim economies (Pacific tigers), 1055–1057, 1056(m)
Pact of Steel (1939), 926
Paganism, 202
Paine, Thomas (1737–1809), 958
Painted Stoa (Athens), 61, 116
Painting(s)
1848 Revolution, 740(i)
catacomb, 199(i)
Dutch, 548–550, 550(i), 559
in eighteenth century, 583–584, 606, 625, 625(i), 627
Greek Independence, 706(i)
Hellenistic, 114
portraiture and, 583
red-figure, 42(i), 55(i)
Renaissance (fifteenth century), 452–455, 454(i), 456(i)
romanticism in, 724–725, 725(i)
in sixteenth and seventeenth centuries, 510–511, 558(i), 558–559, 559(i)
vase, 42(i), 51(i), 69(i), 71(i), 94(i)
wall, 141, 157(i), 204(i)
Pakistan, 967
Palaces
Cretan (Minoan), 34
Mycenaean, 35
Persian, 30(i)
Sumerian, 10
Palach, Jan, 987(i), 987–988, 1004, 1012, 1013
Paleolithic period (Old Stone Age), 5–8
Palestine, 198, 225. See also Jerusalem; Levant
30 C.E., 197(m)
ancient, 22, 31, 32, 109, 123, 124
conflict in, 969

partition of (1948), 969, 969(m)
World War I and, 855, 874
Palestinians, 1052–1054, 1053(m)
Pan-Africanism, 803(m)
Panathenaia, 67
Pankhurst, Emmeline (1858–1928), 835, 860
Pan-Slavism, 763
Papacy (popes). See also individual popes
at Avignon (1309–1378; "Babylonian Captivity"), 405–406, 440–443, 442(m), 450
battle of Lepanto (1571) and, 492
Byzantium and, 290–292
Carolingians and, 310–311, 313
church reform and 1050–1150, 346–358, 365, 379–382
Fourth Lateran Council, 403–404, 422
curia (papal government), 352, 441, 443
Eastern Europe and, 334–336
English monarchs and, 495–496
in fourteenth and fifteenth centuries, 436, 440–443, 456, 458–459, 471
Great Schism (1378–1417), 426, 442(m), 442–443, 458
French Revolution and, 669
Germany and, 366–367, 387, 393–396
Italy and, 311, 393–396, 394(m), 395(m)
Lombard kings and, 290–293, 310–311
Luther and, 476–477
Napoleon and, 678, 684, 687
Ottonian Empire and, 333
patronage of, 510, 557
Protestantism and, 490–491
Papal States, 441, 469(m), 626, 638, 678, 757, 760
Paper (papermaking), 309, 451
Paracelsus (pah rah SEL sus) (Theophrastus Bombastus von Hohenheim) (1493–1541), 515–517
Paradigm shift, in science, 825
Paradise Lost (Milton), 557
Parallel Lives (Plutarch), 193
Parenti, Marco, 461
Parenti, Parente, 461
Paris, 285, 366, 407, 415, 584, 598, 602, 772, 774
1968 student revolt in, 1010
economic development and, 766
in eighteenth century, 628, 631, 641
in fourteenth and fifteenth centuries, 440, 456
French parlement in, 399, 400, 401
during French Revolution, 651–652, 655, 657–659, 658(m), 660, 662–666, 668(i), 670, 672, 674, 676, 678, 680
Haussmannization of, 773, 783
Jacquerie in, 434

(continued)

Napoleon and, 681, 684, 687(i)
Peace of (1856), 752
population growth in, 577
public health in, nineteenth century, 712–713
salons of, 612(i), 612–613, 616, 687
Treaty of (1763), 634
University of, 370, 371, 402
World War II and, 934–935
Paris Commune (1871), 783(i), 783–784, 795, 830, 832
Paris peace conference (1919–1920), 871–874
Parks, Rosa (1913–2005), 976–977
Parlements (France), 399, 408n, 525, 528, 529, 589, 614, 639–640, 642–643
Louix XIV and, 655
Parliament(s), 407–409, 435, 715, 716
constitutionalism and, 524
English (British), 408–409, 408n, 642, 763
American Revolution and, 644–645
Charles II and, 545–546
in the eighteenth century, 589–590
Exclusion Crisis (1678), 546
in the nineteenth century, 710–711
rebuilding of Houses of Parliament (1830s), 725
in the seventeenth century, 541–547, 556
in the sixteenth century, 495, 497
Wilkes affair (1763), 643–645, 648
German (1920s), 879
Hungarian, 537
Irish, 590
Russian (Duma), 842, 865
Parnell, Charles (1846–1891), 835–836
Pärt, Arvo, 1002
Parthenon (Athens), 62–65, 224
Parthians (Parthian Empire), 107, 165, 184(i), 205
Partnerships, 343–344
Pascal, Blaise (1623–1662), 528, 556
Pasternak, Boris (1890–1960), 966
Pasteur, Louis (1822–1895), 774
Pasteurization, 774
Pasti, Matteo de, 425, 437
Pastoral Care (Gregory the Great), 331(i)
Pastoralists, 8
Pastoral Rule (Gregory the Great), 290
Paternalism, in ancient Greece, 42–43, 44
Patria potestas (PAH tree ah poh TES tuz) ("power of a father"), 134
Patriarchy (patriarchal society)
Babylonian, 14
in Byzantine Empire, 248
European, 430
in Florence (fifteenth century), 461–462
Germanic, 237

Islamic, 272
Sumerian, 10
Patricians, 143, 144, 145, 148, 460–462
Patrick, St. (c. 389–461), 286
Patrilineal families, 328, 329, 332–333, 337, 461
Patriots
Dutch Republic, 653–655
Poland, 654–655
Patristic authors, 230
Patron-client system, Roman, 132, 133, 176
armed forces and, 161, 162
Paul (Russia; r. 1796–1801), 690
Paul III (pope; r. 1534–1549), 484
Paul VI (pope; r. 1963–1978), 1003
Paul of Tarsus (c. 10–65 C.E.), 196, 198
Pavia, 289
battle of, 487, 487(m)
Pavlov, Ivan (1849–1936), 820
Pax Romana (PAHKS roh MAHN ah) (Roman peace), 172–195
Paxton, Sir Joseph (1801–1865), 742(i)
Peace movement, in post-Carolingian age, 328–329
Peace of Aix-la-Chapelle (1748), 633
Peace of Augsburg (1555), 491, 498, 501
Peace of God, 328–329
Peace of Paris (Versailles Treaty; 1919–1920), 872, 873(m), 874, 896
economic and diplomatic consequences of, 874–876
Peace of Rijswijk (RICE vike) (1697), 531(m), 532
Peace of Utrecht (1713–1714), 587, 588(m), 597
Peace of Westphalia (1648), 501–503, 502(m), 519(m), 597
Pearl Harbor, attack on (1941), 929
Peasants. See also Serfs
in 1920s, 879, 892, 894
in Austrian Netherlands, 654
in Byzantine Empire, 299
in Carolingian estates, 317–318
in early Middle Ages, 278–281
in Eastern Europe, 580–581, 606, 648
in eighteenth century, 580–581, 606, 610, 622, 628
in Austrian Empire, 632, 638
food riots and uprisings, 640–642
Prussia, 634–635, 639
in eleventh and twelfth centuries, 340–342, 356(i)
in England, 360–361
in fourteenth and fifteenth centuries, 440
in France, 749
French Revolution and, 655–657, 659–661, 671, 673, 676
in Germany, 333, 533

in Hellenistic kingdoms, 112
Hundred Years' War (1337–1453) and,
    431, 435
in Ireland, 590
in Italy, 329, 892, 894
in Merovingian period, 278–279, 280–281
plague and, 426–429
in Poland, 540, 722
popular culture and, 561–562
in post-Carolingian age, 322–328
in Prussia, 634–635, 639, 690
revolution of 1848 and, 735, 736, 738
in Roman Empire, 220
in Russia and Soviet Union, 538, 539(i), 677,
    752–754, 841, 842, 864–869, 890, 907
in seventeenth century, 538, 539(i), 540
    economic crisis and, 497, 503, 505–507, 507(i)
in sixteenth-century Holy Roman Empire, 478
in Spain, 691
in Switzerland, 407
textile production and, 631
Thirty Years' War and, 500, 501
after World War I, 870
Peasants' War (1525), 478, 478(m), 480(f)
Peel, Sir Robert (1788–1850), 717
Pelletier, Fernande, 997
Peloponnese (pel oh poh NEES), 34, 38, 43(m)
Peloponnesian League, 56, 57(m), 61, 84
Peloponnesian War (431–404 B.C.E.), 78, 83,
    84–86, 84(f), 86(m), 88(m), 92, 93, 94–95
    Golden Age and, 52, 93
Penance, sacrament of, 474
Penates (spirits of the household), 137
Penitent heretics, 393
Pensées (Pascal), 556
Pentateuch (Torah), 31, 32
People's Charter (Great Britain), 720
Perestroika, 1020, 1021, 1034
Pergamum (PUR gah mum), 107, 114, 159
Pericles (PEHR ih kleez) (c. 495–429 B.C.E.),
    59–61, 62, 72, 74, 82, 83–85
Peripatetic School (Athens), 97
Persephone (Kore), 68, 203
Persepolis, 28, 30(i)
Persia (Persian Empire), 28–30, 29(m), 47(m),
    51, 53(m), 463. *See also* Iran
    Alexander the Great and, 92, 102
    European attitudes toward, 603
    Greece and, 51–56
        Delian League, 57
        invasion of Greece (480–479 B.C.E.),
            54–56, 63(i)
        King's Peace (386 B.C.E.), 98
        Peloponnesian War (431–404 B.C.E.), 85

wars (499–479 B.C.E.), 51–56, 53(m), 55(i),
    86(m), 101
in Hellenistic period (323–30 B.C.E.), 107
in India, 576
Islam and, 268, 272(m), 273–275, 292
Philip II of Macedonia and, 101
Sassanid, 205, 261, 296–297
Persian language, 808
Persian Letters (Montesquieu), 603–604
Perspective, 454–455, 471, 510, 511(i)
Pétain, Henri Philippe (1856–1951), 928
Peter (Portuguese regent; r. 1440–1448), 465
Peter, St. (apostle), 227, 287, 290
Peter I (the Great) (Russia; r. 1689–1725), 568,
    592–595, 593(i), 595(m)
Peter III (Russia; r. 1762), 609(i), 634, 641
Petition of Right (1628), 541
Petra, 109(i)
Petrarch, Francesco (1304–1374), 440,
    448, 450
Petronius (d. 66 C.E.), 182
Petronius Probus, 213(i)
Petty, William, 598
Peugeot, Armand, 767
Pharmacology, 514, 516. *See also* Medicine
Pharos (Alexandria), 120
Pharsalus (far SAY lus), battle of (48 B.C.E.), 166
Philip I (France; r. 1052–1108), 365
Philip II (Augustus) (France; r. 1180–1223), 356,
    358, 366, 398–401, 400(m), 422
Philip II (Macedonia; r. 359–336 B.C.E.),
    99–101, 101(m)
Philip II (Spain; r. 1556–1598), 490, 492–494,
    493(m), 495–497, 511(i)
Philip III (Spain; r. 1598–1621), 493–494
Philip IV (Spain; r. 1621–1665), 504
Philip IV (the Fair) (r. 1285–1314), 404(i),
    404–405, 407
Philip V (Macedonia; 238–179 B.C.E.), 150, 151
Philip V (Spain; r. 1700–1746), 587, 588(m)
Philip VI (France; r. 1328–1350), 430
Philippines, 806, 929
Philoponus, John (fil uh PAHN us)
    (c. 490–570), 255
Philosophes, 610–612, 614–615, 618–620, 623,
    637–638, 648
*Philosophical and Political History of European
    Colonies and Commerce in the Two Indies*
    (Raynal), 614
Philosophical Dictionary (Voltaire), 613
Philosophy
    existentialist, 975–976
    Greek, 45–47, 93

(continued)

Aristotle, 97–98
Plato, 95–97, 116
Socrates, 75–78
sophists, 74–75
Hellenistic, 115–118
rationalist, 46–47
Roman, 154–155
Philoxenus of Eretria, 114
Phoebe (early church deacon), 198
Phoenicians, 47(m)
Photography, 787, 788, 885, 974(i)
Phrygia (Asia Minor), 137
Physical fitness, 73, 818–820
Physics, 612, 824
in Ancient Greece, 46
in Hellenistic philosophy, 116
Newtonian, 554–556
Physiocrats, 639–640
Piacenza (Italy), 406
Picasso, Pablo (1881–1973), 826, 827, 924
Piedmont-Sardinia, kingdom of, 703, 705, 755,
756, 756(m), 757
Pietism, 586, 620, 703
Pilgrimage (pilgrims), 370, 377, 382, 410,
416, 475, 508, 562
to Holy Land, 352–353, 354(i), 355
to Mecca, 268, 271
to Rome, 278, 476
Pilsudski, Jozef (1867–1935), 879
Pinsker, Leon, 840
Pippin (son of Louis the Pius), 316
Pippin III (the Short) (Carolingian king;
r. 751–768), 291–292, 310
Pirates, 575
in Mediterranean, 163, 322, 463
Muslim, 322, 463
in North Africa, 488
Viking, 320
Pisano, Nicola (c. 1220–1278?), 421
Pius II (pope; r. 1458–1464), 457
Pius VI (pope; r. 1775–1799), 662
Pius VII (pope; r. 1800–1823), 684, 703
Pius IX (pope; r. 1846–1878), 737, 789
Pius XI (pope; r. 1922–1939), 920
Pizarro, Francisco (c. 1475–1541), 469–470
Placita, 329
Plague, 426–430, 427(m), 429(f), 444(i),
445–447, 449
of 1628–1632, 505–506, 508
in 1665 (London), 545
disappearance of, 577
in Germany, 501
Plague, The (Camus), 976
Plainchant (Gregorian chant), 373–374, 383

Planck, Max (1858–1947), 824, 825, 992
Plantagenets, 362n
Plantations (plantation economy), 467–468, 509,
548, 559, 568–574, 570(m), 571(f), 573(i),
629, 648(m), 678–680
Plataea (plah TEE uh), battle of (479 B.C.E.), 53(m)
Plato (PLAY toh) (c. 429–348 B.C.E.), 76–77, 93,
95–97, 116, 117, 204, 224, 253, 359–360
Academy established by, 95, 96(i)
Renaissance and (fifteenth century), 451
Platonic Academy (Florence), 451
Plautus (d. 184 B.C.E.), 153
Playboy (magazine), 978
Plebeian (pleh BEE in) Assembly, 144, 159
Plebeians, 143, 144, 145, 148, 175
Plebiscites (PLEB ih syts), 144, 162
Pliny (PLIN ee) (61–113 C.E.), 194
Pliska, battle of (811), 301, 302(m)
Plotinus (plah TY nuhs) (c. 205–270), 204
Plutarch, 666
Plutarch (PLOO tahrk) (c. 50–120),
159, 193
Podestà, 367, 406
Poetry. *See also* Literature; *individual poets*
in 1920s, 887–888
Akkadian, 12
Bedouin, 268, 273
Chaldean, 27
Greek, 36–37, 45–46, 81
Hellenistic, 113–114
Islamic, 275
lyric, 45–46
in Renaissance, 448–450, 449(i)
Roman, 154, 183, 282
romantic, 724, 726
in twelfth and thirteenth centuries, 367–369,
386, 409, 413–415
Poisson, Jeanne-Antoinette (PWAH sohn)
(Marquise de Pompadour)
(1721–1764), 613
Poitiers (pwah tee AY), battle of (1356), 433(m)
Poitou, 362, 398(m), 398–399, 400
Poland, 303, 437–438, 438(m), 594, 689, 702,
702(m), 722, 755, 871, 872, 899, 902
in 1920s, 878(m), 878–879
colonization and, 778
under Communist rule, 951, 952, 964–965,
1005, 1021–1022
Habsburg Empire and, 762
Jews in, 447, 539–540, 620, 947
migration from, 816, 817(f)
Mongol attacks on, 385, 396
nationalism in, 722
parliaments in, 407

partitions of (1772–1795), 636, 636(m), 637(i), 654, 675(m), 675–676
peasants in, 580–581
political unrest and reforms in (late eighteenth century), 652–655
Reformation in, 481, 482(m), 486
Roman Catholicism in, 333–334, 438, 443
in sixteenth century, 508
World War I and, 855, 858
World War II and, 900, 927, 928, 930, 931–932, 936, 939
Poland-Lithuania, 438, 438(m), 469(m)
in eighteenth century, 594, 595(m), 596, 605(m), 613, 620, 623
partition of, 632, 636, 636(m), 637(i)
Protestantism in, 499
in seventeenth century, 524, 533, 564(m)
siege of Vienna and, 537, 540
Polanians, 334
Police force, first, 178
Polis (Greek city-state), 38–43, 39(m), 108. See also Athens; Sparta
Alexander the Great and, 104–105
citizenship (political rights), 39–43
disunity after Peloponnesian War, 98–99
Hellenistic period (323–30 B.C.E.), 92, 108
Philip II of Macedonia and, 99–101
Polish Corridor, 872
Polish Legion, 722
Politics (political parties). See also Democracy; specific political parties
in 1920s, 877–881
mass (late nineteenth and early twentieth centuries), 829–843
modern music and, 829
Roman, 159–160
in seventeenth century, 512–514
working-class, 704, 831
World War I and, 860–861
Politiques, 490–491, 502–503, 512
Polke, Sigmar, 1001
Pollock, Jackson, 980, 1001(i)
Polo, Maffeo, 385
Polo, Marco (1254–1324), 385, 386, 398, 463, 466
Polo, Niccolò, 385
Polo family, 397
Poltava, battle of (1709), 594, 595(m)
Polyphony, 415, 452, 455
Polytheism, 230. See also Gods and goddesses
in Byzantine Empire, 251, 252, 253
in Golden Age Greece, 66
Hellenistic, 121
Islam and, 270
Mesopotamian, 10

in Roman Empire, 202–204, 221, 222(i), 222–224, 226(m)
Pompeii, 187
religious shrine from, 138(i)
Pompey, Gnaeus (POMP ee, NEE us) (106–48 B.C.E.), 153(m), 159, 163–167, 173
Poniatowski, Stanislaw August (Poland; r. 1764–1795), 654
Pontius Pilate (governor of Judea; r. 26–36), 197
Poor, the (poverty). See also Lower classes
in ancient Greece, 41
in Augustan Rome, 177, 179, 180, 181, 186
in Byzantine Empire, 248–249
Christianity and, 225
in eighteenth century, 581–582, 627–629
monastic orders and, 375–376, 379–381, 409–411, 411(i)
mothers and, 700
Protestant reformers and, 562–563
in Ptolemaic Egypt, 112
punishments of, 216
Roman, 156–159, 163, 182
in seventeenth century, 562–565
economic crisis and, 505–506, 507(i)
temperance movement and, 728
Poor Laws
England (1597), 505
Great Britain (1834), 729
Pop art, 1000–1001
Pope, Alexander (1688–1744), 555
Popolo, in Italian communes, 406
Popular culture (mass culture). See also Entertainment; Movies; Radio; Television
in 1920s, 884, 885–889
1945–1960, 977–979
in seventeenth century, 561–564
Populares (poh puh LAHR es), 160
Popular Front (France), 917, 919
Popular Front (Spain), 923–924
Population (population growth or decline). See also Migrations
in 1920s, 879
in Archaic Age, 40
census and, 459
in China, 781
in colonial America, 645
colonialism and, 779
in Dark Age, 33, 40
economic development and, 772
in eighteenth century, 577, 578, 581, 623, 627, 629, 630–631, 640

(continued)

in Great Britain, 710
in late twentieth and early twenty-first
    centuries, 1049–1050, 1050(f)
in Minoan civilization, 34
Neolithic Revolution and, 7, 9, 34
in nineteenth century, 811–814, 812(f)
overcrowding and, 712
plague and (1340–1450), 426–429, 429(f)
Roman Empire, 130, 140, 164, 194, 208
    under Augustus, 177
Rome and Italy (300 B.C.E.), 148, 156–157
in sixteenth and seventeenth centuries,
    474, 504–507
in twelfth century, 340–343
Poquelin, Jean-Baptiste. See Molière
Porphyry (POR fih ree) (c. 234–305), 223
Port Arthur, 805, 847
Portugal, 456(i), 1017
    Catholic church in, 637
    colonies of, 492, 493(m), 508, 549(m), 574–576,
        801. See also Brazil
        in Africa, 575, 803(m)
    exploration and settlements (fifteenth and
        sixteenth centuries), 426, 463–466, 464(m),
        465(m), 468, 468(i), 470, 485(i), 486
    Muslims in, 388(m), 390–391, 391(m)
    Napoleon and, 691–693
    slave trade and, 551, 569, 570(m), 574–575
    Thirty Years' War and, 500
    urbanization in, 817
Positivism, 785, 792, 823–824
Postindustrial society and culture, 989–990,
    995–1003
    multinational corporations and, 995–996
    workers, 996–997
Postmodernism, 1064–1067
Potemkin (film), 885
Potemkin (Russian battleship), 842
Poulain de la Barre, François (1647–1723), 561
Poussin, Nicolas (1594–1665), 558, 558(i)
Praetorian guard, 175
Praetors (PREE tohrz), 144, 145
Pragmatic Sanction of 1713, 632
Pragmatism, 823
Prague
    1648 sack of, 501
    defenestration in (1618), 498
    Hus in, 443, 445
    revolution of 1848 and, 739
Prague Spring (1968), 1011(i), 1011–1012
Praise of Folly, The (Erasmus), 475
Praxagoras of Cos (fourth century B.C.E.), 120
Praxiteles (prak SIT uh leez)
    (fourth century B.C.E.), 114

Predestination, doctrine of, 480–481
Pregnancy, 232, 994–995
Presbyterianism (Presbyterians), 496, 542–544,
    547, 583, 676
Presley, Elvis (1935–1977), 977
Press, the. See Newspapers
Price, Richard, 676
Priests and priestesses. See also Clergy
    in Athens, 43, 63
    influence of, 10
    ordaining of, 202, 227
    Roman, 139
Primogeniture, 328, 355
Prince, The (Machiavelli), 457
Princeps. See Principate
Princess of Clèves, The (Lafayette), 526, 561
Princip, Gavrilo, 852, 853
Principate (PRIN sih payt), Roman, 172, 173, 175,
    176, 177, 184–188, 190, 215
Principia Mathematica (Newton), 555
Printing
    Dutch Republic and, 550, 583, 603, 618–619
    in fifteenth century, 448, 451–452
    Reformation and, 477(i), 481
Professionalization, 775–776
Prokofiev, Sergei (1891–1953), 909
Proletariat (proletarians), 719, 783. See also Workers
    Roman, 144, 161
Propaganda
    in 1920s, 892, 896
    in World War I, 861, 863, 872
    in World War II, 933, 940
Property (property rights), 717, 719. See also
        Inheritance; Landownership
    in ancient Greece, 43–44, 68–69
    in Germanic society, 237
    Hammurabi's code, 14
    in Rome, 134, 136
    woman suffrage and, 833
Proscription, 162, 166
Prostitution, 440, 563, 700, 833
    in Byzantine Empire, 248, 252
    collapse of Communism and, 1036, 1037(i)
    in Florence (fifteenth century), 462
    in France, 686
    in Golden Age Athens, 71(i), 72–73
    in London, 713
    migrations and, 1058–1059
    in nineteenth century, 727, 775
    in Rome, 136, 157, 180
Protagoras, 74–75
Protestantism (Protestants). See also Calvinism;
        Lutherans; Presbyterianism; Protestant
        Reformation; Puritans

in Austrian Empire, 654
education and, 582–583, 586
in England (Great Britain), 492, 494–497, 529,
   589, 590
  Methodism, 621
  Toleration Act (1689), 547
French (Huguenots), 480, 489–491, 490(*m*),
   509, 528–529, 568, 614, 638, 655, 660, 667
in Germany, 476–479, 480(*f*), 481, 487, 499
in Holy Roman Empire (sixteenth century),
   476–479, 482(*m*), 490(*m*), 518, 519(*m*)
music and, 511
in Northern Ireland, 1016–1017
in Poland-Lithuania, 539–540, 636
popular religious practices of seventeenth
   century and, 562–563
revivalism and, 620–621
in sixteenth century, 473–497, 482(*m*)
Thirty Years' War and, 498, 499, 501–502
in United States, 1003
Protestant Reformation, 473–486, 482(*m*), 498
Anabaptists and, 473, 479–480, 480(*f*), 491
Calvin and, 479–481, 480(*f*)
in England, 492, 494–497
Luther and, 476–480, 477(*i*), 480(*f*)
marriage and, 483(*i*), 483–484, 507
social changes and, 481, 483–484
vernacular translations of Bible and, 481, 483
violence of, 512–513, 520–521
Zwingli and, 479–480, 480(*f*)
Proudhon, Pierre-Joseph (proo DOHN,
   pyayr zho ZEF) (1809–1865), 719, 782
Proust, Marcel (1871–1922), 888
Provincial Letters (Pascal), 528
Provisional Government (Russia), 865–866
Prussia, 387, 388(*m*), 568, 569, 591, 595(*m*),
   595–596, 624, 705, 750, 751
canton system and, 634
Congress of Vienna (1814–1815) and,
   700–701, 703
education in, 777
in eighteenth century, 605(*m*), 619, 627,
   632–636, 633(*m*), 635(*m*), 638–640
French Revolution and, 662–663, 666
German unification and, 758–761
intervention in Dutch Republic (1787),
   653–654
landholders in, 580
liberalism and, 717
Napoleon and, 678, 688–690, 693–694
partitions of Poland and, 675(*m*), 675–676
reforms in, 634–635, 636, 638–640
religion in, 789
wars and expansion of, 632–636, 633(*m*), 635(*m*)

World War I and, 852, 856, 872
Psychoanalysis (psychoanalytic theory), 797,
   820–822
Psychology, 820–822
Ptahhotep, 21
Ptolemaic Egypt (tawl eh MAY ik), 107–111, 111(*i*),
   112, 113, 121–122, 123, 123(*i*), 135, 166, 173
Ptolemy (TAW luh mee) (astronomer; fl. second
   century), 308(*i*), 514–515
Ptolemy I (Egypt; c. 367–282 B.C.E.), 106, 122, 123
Ptolemy II (Egypt; r. 282–246 B.C.E.), 111, 113, 123
Ptolemy III (Egypt; d. 221 B.C.E.), 122
Ptolemy V (Egypt; r. 203–180 B.C.E.), 91(*i*)
Ptolemy XIII (Egypt; 63–47 B.C.E.), 166
Public baths, in Rome, 178, 207
Public health, 1049–1050
  in eighteenth century, 598–599
  industrialization and, 713
  in nineteenth century, 727–729, 748, 818
  population growth and, 811, 813(*i*)
  in Russia, 753
  welfare-state programs and, 961–962
Public opinion
  in eighteenth century, 636, 640, 642–644,
   655–656
  the Enlightenment and, 610, 612
  in Rome, 144
Public sanitation, in the eighteenth century,
   598–599, 606
Public works
  under Louis XIV, 527–528
  in Roman Republic and Empire, 133, 146, 159,
   166, 190, 219, 220
Publishing industry. *See* Books and publishing
   industry
Publius Claudius Pulcher, 139
Puccini, Giacomo (1858–1924), 828
Puerto Rico, 806
Pugachev, Emelian (1742–1775), 641–642, 642(*i*)
Pugachev rebellion (1773), 641(*m*), 641–642
Pugin, A. W. N., 725
Pulcheria (puhl KER ee uh) (Byzantine emperor;
   r. 414–453), 229
Pump priming, 912, 916
Punic (PEW nik) Wars, 148–152
Purges (Russia), 907–908
Puritans, 495–496, 508, 509, 541–545, 556, 562
Putin, Vladimir (b. 1952), 1036
Putting-out system (domestic system; cottage
   industries), 631, 711, 767
Pyramids, in ancient Egypt, 15, 19–20, 20(*i*)
Pyrrho (PIHR ro) (c. 360–270 B.C.E.), 117
Pythagoras (py THAG or as) (sixth century
   B.C.E.), 46, 117

Qaddafi, Muammar, 1052
Qing (CHEENG) dynasty, 781, 805(*m*),
    806–807
Quadragesimo Anno (Pius XI), 920
Quadrivium, 371
Quaestor (KWES tohr), 145
Quakers, 543–544
Quantum theorem, 824
Quebec, French settlement of, 530
Quest of the Holy Grail, 414
Quietism, 586
Qur'an, 32, 269, 270(*i*), 273, 275, 287, 292, 307,
    308–309
Quraysh tribe, 268, 269, 270, 271

Race (racial discrimination; racism). *See also*
        Anti-Semitism; Civil Rights movement
    in 1930s, 903, 916
    in American colonies, 574–575
    colonialism and, 799
    Nazi, 903, 913–914, 930, 932
    Roman Catholic church and (sixteenth
        century), 485(*i*), 486
    in United States, 766, 976, 1006
    World War I and, 859
Racine, Jean-Baptiste (1639–1699), 527, 561
Radetsky, Count Joseph, 739
Radical democracy, 59–61
Radio, 884, 886, 887(*f*), 892, 896
    cold war and, 979
Rahman III, Abd al- (caliph; r. 912–961), 306
Railroads, 708–709, 708(*f*), 750, 816, 846
    colonialism and, 778, 780, 781
    Crimean War and, 752
    industrialization and, 767, 768
    Japanese modernization and, 804
    nation-building and, 755, 757, 759, 762,
        769, 790
    Russia and, 805
Raimon de Miraval (fl. 1191–1229), 368(*i*)
Rain forests, destruction of, 1047
Rainsford, Marcus, 679(*i*)
Raison d'état ("reason of state"), 503
Rákóczi, Ferenc (RAH kot see, FER ents)
        (1676–1735), 596
Ramadan, 271
Ramesses II (RAM uh seez) (Egypt; thirteenth
        century B.C.E.), 25
Ranters, 543
Rapallo, Treaty of (1922), 875
Rape, 462–463, 1032, 1059
Rape of Nanjing (1937), 921
Rape of the Sabine Women, 129
Rasputin, Grigori (1872–1916), 865

Rationalism (rationality), 46–47, 789.
    See also Logic; Reason
Rauschenberg, Robert (b. 1925), 1000
Ravenna, 218, 242, 312
    Exarchate of, 262, 289(*m*), 291
    Justinian and his Court in, 246(*i*)
    Theodora and her court in, 247(*i*)
Raymond VI (count of Toulouse), 392
Raymond VII (count of Toulouse), 392
Raynal, Abbé Guillaume (1713–1796), 614
Razin, Stenka (d. 1671), 538, 539(*i*)
Reagan, Ronald (1911–2004), 1018–1019
Reaganomics, 1018
Realism, 785–788, 794–795
Realpolitik, 747–749, 758, 764, 780, 782, 787(*i*)
Reason. *See also* Logic; Rationalism
    Cult of, in French Revolution, 667
    Descartes and, 516–517, 604
    the Enlightenment and, 601–602, 610–611, 613,
        615, 619–620, 627, 652, 687–688
    French Revolution and, 661(*m*), 666
    scholastics and, 411–413
Reccared (REK a red) (Visigothic king;
        r. 586–601), 288
Recession
    in fourteenth and fifteenth centuries, 440–441
    in sixteenth and seventeenth centuries,
        504–507
Reconquista (ray con KEE stuh) (Christian
        reconquest of Spain), 348, 386, 388(*m*),
        390–391, 391(*m*), 408, 447–448
Redistributive economies, 10, 14, 34–36, 37
Red Shirts (Italy), 757, 757(*i*), 758
Reflections upon Marriage (Astell), 604
Reform (reform movements), 700, 703, 710–712,
        818–820. *See also specific reforms and*
        reform movements
    Catholic Church (1050–1300), 346–358, 370
        beginnings of, 346–348
        early crusades and crusader states, 352–356
        Fourth Lateran Council and, 403–404
        Gregorian reform and Investiture Conflict
            (1073–1085), 349(*m*), 349–351,
            366–367, 382
    in Dutch Republic, 653–654
    the Enlightenment and, 611, 614–615, 618, 621,
        623, 632–640, 648, 676, 690–691
    in fourteenth and fifteenth centuries, 445
    in Great Britain (1850s–1870s), 763–764
    Napoleonic code and, 683, 685–686, 690, 695
    in nineteenth century, 726–732
        overseas, 731–732
    Protestant (sixteenth century), 473–486, 477(*i*),
        480(*f*), 482(*m*)

in Russia, 690–691
state power and, 632–640
limits of, 638–640
state-sponsored, 636–640
war and diplomacy and, 632–636
women and, 727
Reform Act of 1884 (Great Britain), 830
Reform Bill of 1832 (Great Britain), 716, 741
Refrigeration, 767
Refugees
1980s to present, 1032, 1058
from World War II, 947
Regensburg, Diet of (1541), 491
Regulus, Marcus Atilius (REG yoo lus) (Roman
general; d. c. 250 B.C.E.), 156
Reichstag, 909, 910
Reims, 370
Cathedral of, 431–432
Council of (1049), 348
Reinsurance Treaty (1887), 843
Relativism, 75, 823
Relics, cult of, 233, 279(i), 279–280, 284(i), 287,
290, 325, 329, 336, 348, 374, 377, 389, 410,
414(i), 416, 477(i), 562, 586
Religion(s), 25, 715, 784, 789, 823. *See also* Cult(s);
Gods and goddesses; Reform;
specific religions
in 1930s, 920
Assyrian, 27
in early Middle Ages, 280–283
Egyptian, 18–24
the Enlightenment and, 601–602, 611, 613–614,
618–621
Greek, 121
Golden Age Athens, 66–68
Minoan and Mycenaean period, 37
sophists and, 74–75
Hebrew, 30–32
in Hellenistic period, 121–125
Hittite, 24
major (c. 1200), 380(m)
Mesopotamian, 3–4, 5
in nineteenth century
reform movements, 727–728
revivalist movements, 703–704
schools, 776–777
secular order and, 789–791
in North Africa, 263
Paleolithic, 6
Persian, 28, 30
in postindustrial society, 1003
Roman, 131, 137
Etruscans and, 142
government and, 139

in Roman Empire. *See also* Christianity,
Roman Empire and
reforms of fourth century C.E., 220–221
seventeenth-century conflicts over, 473–474, 565
Sumerian, 10–11
in thirteenth and fourteenth centuries, 409–413
women's role in, 42–43
Religious revivals (revivalism), 620–621
eighteenth-century, 586
nineteenth-century, 703–704
Religious tolerance/intolerance (religious
freedom), 512–514, 601–602
Archduke Ferdinand's curtailment of, 498
Constantine and, 221
in Dutch Republic, 494, 540, 550, 611
Edict of Nantes (1598) and, 490–491,
528–529, 533, 614
in eighteenth century, 610–611, 613, 614, 619,
638, 643, 654, 678
in England, 540, 545–547
French Revolution and, 660, 695
Napoleon and, 681, 685
in sixteenth century, 474, 489–491, 494
Theodoric and, 242
Remarque, Erich Maria (1898–1970), 887
Rembrandt van Rijn (REM brant van RINE)
(1606–1669), 511, 548, 559
Remegius, St., 348
Remembrance of Things Past (Proust), 888
Renaissance
Carolingian (c. 790–c. 900), 309, 314(i),
314–315
fifteenth-century, 448–471, 469(m)
art and music, 452–457
classical literature and learning of, 425–426,
453, 455(i), 471
humanism, 448–452, 471
in Italy, 425, 457–459
Islamic (c. 790–c. 1050), 307–309, 314
Macedonian (c. 870–c. 1025), 297, 299–300,
301(i), 307, 314(i)
Reparations after World War I, 872, 874–875
Reproduction, 604–605. *See also* Birth control;
Childbearing; Sex and sexuality
in Ancient Greece, 43
in Roman Empire, 194–195
Reproductive rights, 908, 913, 961, 1008, 1009
Republic, The (Plato), 97
Republican party (United States), 765
"Republic of Virtue" (France), 665–669
Research, in postindustrial society, 997–998
Resistance, in Nazi-occupied areas, 934, 936(i),
956, 957, 975

(continued)

Revenues. *See* Taxes

Revivalist movements. *See* Religious revivals

Revolution(s) (revolutionary movements).
    See also French Revolution; Russian
    Revolution
  in 1820s, 704–707, 705(*m*), 706(*i*), 707(*m*)
  of 1830 and 1848, 732–739, 737(*f*), 747, 749,
    755, 757, 762, 772, 789
    aftermath of, 739–743
  Chinese Communist, 967

Rhetoric (public speaking)
  in Byzantine Empire, 253
  Roman, 136, 182, 183

Rhineland, 381, 444, 875, 922
  Jews in, 357

Rhode Island, 508

Rhodes, Cecil (1853–1902), 802

Rich, the. *See also* Upper classes
  in Ancient Greece, 36, 57–58, 61, 70, 72
  in Byzantine society, 248–249
  in Hellenistic Kingdoms, 108
  Persian, 28
  Roman, 134, 144, 148, 157–158, 177, 179, 180,
    182, 183, 195

Richard I (the Lion-Hearted) (England;
    r. 1189–1199), 401

Richard II (England; r. 1377–1399), 356, 435, 443

Richard III (England; r. 1483–1485), 435

Richardson, Samuel (1689–1761), 626–627

Richelieu, Cardinal (1585–1642), 499–500, 503

Risorgimento (Italy), 747, 750, 755–758

Rite of Spring (Stravinsky), 827–828

Roads, Roman, 148, 148(*m*)

Roaring Twenties, 852, 877

Robert (Naples; r. 1309–1343), 450

Robespierre, Maximilien (1758–1794), 665–667,
    670(*i*), 671–674

Robinson Crusoe (Defoe), 585

Rock-and-roll, 977

Rockefeller, John D. (1874–1960), 768, 769

Rococo style, 583–584, 584(*i*), 624–625

Roehm, Ernst (1887–1934), 912

Rollo (Viking leader; c. 860–931), 321

Roman Catholic church (Catholicism), 202.
    See also Bishops; Heresies, Christian;
    Monasticism; Papacy; Sacraments
  astronomy and, 514–515
  Augustine and, 230
  clergy
    in Bohemia, 445–446
    Fourth Lateran Council and (1215), 389(*i*),
      403–404
    taxation of, 404(*i*), 404–405
  Counter-Reformation and, 484–486, 510

  crusades and, 352–356, 354(*i*), 355(*m*), 380(*m*),
    383, 386
  in Dutch Republic, 494
  in Eastern Europe, 303
  in eighteenth century, 586, 637–638
  in England (Great Britain), 287, 494–497,
    541–542, 544–547, 602, 638, 643
  the Enlightenment and, 603, 613–614, 618–619
  in France, 618–619, 637–638, 703
    French Revolution and, 655–657, 656(*i*),
      661–663, 667–669, 671, 672–673
    Inquisition, 392–393, 393(*f*)
    under Louis IX, 400–401
    under Louis XIV, 528–529, 557, 562–564
    Napoleon and, 678, 683–684, 687
    seventeenth century, 562–563
    taxing the clergy, 404(*i*), 404–405
    wars of religion (sixteenth century),
      489–491
  in Germany, 789
  Great Schisms and
    1054, 348, 352
    1378–1417, 426, 442(*m*), 442–443, 458
  in Holy Roman Empire (sixteenth century),
    476–479, 482(*m*), 490(*m*),
    493(*m*), 518, 519(*m*)
  Inquisition and, 386, 392–393, 393(*f*), 404, 444,
    447–448, 618
  in Ireland, 547, 590, 676, 836
  in Italy, 289–290, 893
    conversion of Lombards, 289–290
  Jansenism and, 528, 586
  in Lithuania, 438
  marriage and, 351–352, 483–484
  missionaries, 484–486, 485(*i*)
  in Poland, 333–334, 438, 443
  in Poland-Lithuania, 540, 636
  Protestant Reformation and, 475–486,
    482(*m*), 498
    violence of, 512–513, 520–521
  secular order and (nineteenth century), 789–790
  in sixteenth and seventeenth centuries
    Africa and the New World, 485–486
    Counter-Reformation, 484–486, 498, 507
    popular religious practices, 562–563
    religious wars, 487–497
  in Spain, 288–289, 637, 691–692
    reconquista, 447–448
  Thirty Years' War and, 498–503
  women and, in nineteenth century, 727

Romance of the Rose, The, 414–415

Romances, 369, 448

Roman Empire, 130, 139, 171–211. *See also*
    specific emperors

Arabs and, 259, 289, 292
under Augustus, 177–182
Byzantine Empire and, 260, 281, 289–293
Carolingian kingdoms and, 317–318, 323
Christianity and, 171, 181, 195–205, 222–235
    appeal of religious and social values, 225
    Constantine's conversion, 214, 221
    development as a new religion, 199–202
    Jesus and the spread of his teachings,
        196–198
    Jews and, 225
    the military and, 225
    persecution of Christians, 200, 208–210, 221
    polytheism and, 202–204, 221, 222(i),
        222–224, 226(m)
    spread of Christianity (300–600),
        222–227, 226(m)
    state religion, Christianity as, 224, 225
    women and, 225–226
expansion of
    c. 500–44 B.C.E., 153(m)
    30 B.C.E.–117 C.E., 188(m)
Germanic peoples and, 187, 205, 208
Golden Age of (96–180), 189–195
    armed forces, 189
    financial factors, 189–190
    law, 193–194
    literature, 193
    natural features and languages, 191(m)
    reproduction and marriage, 194–195
    Romanization of provinces, 190–195
Justinian's plan to reunite eastern and western
    empires, 249–252
Merovingian kingdoms and, 276–280,
    281, 285, 286, 288
natural features and languages of, 191(m)
Pax Romana (Roman peace)
    creating, 172–184
    maintaining, 184–195, 205
peoples and kingdoms of (c. 526),
    235–245, 243(m)
principate, 172, 176, 184–188, 193
reorganization of (fourth century C.E.)
    administrative structure, 214–221,
        217(m), 218(m)
    the dominate, 215–216
    financial reform and social consequences,
        219–220
    laws, 216
    religious reform, 220–221
slaves, 147, 156, 158, 180–181, 208
    citizenship, 140
    education and, 136
    ex-slaves, 133(i), 133–134

third-century crisis (c. 284 C.E.), 205–210,
    209(m), 214
    defense of frontiers, 205
    natural disasters, 208–210
    Severan emperors, 206–210
    "Year of the Four Emperors" (69 C.E.), 186
Romanesque churches, 374, 375(i), 376,
    378(i), 414(i)
Roman Forum, 129(i), 133
Romania (Romanians), 6(i), 8n, 537, 752, 839,
    876, 902, 929, 938, 950–951, 1023–1024
    dictatorship in, 896
    Jews in, 840
Romanization, 190–195, 191(m), 192(i)
Roman law, 144–146, 193–194, 216, 244, 292, 371
    traditions of, 276, 281, 285, 289, 398
    Umayyad caliphate and, 274(i)
Roman literature, 152–155, 183, 245. See also
        Classical literature and learning
Roman peace. See Pax Romana
Roman republic, 140
    c. 44 B.C.E., 168(m)
    c. 30 B.C.E., 124(m)
    Augustus's "restoration" of (27 B.C.E.–14 C.E.),
        158–168, 172, 174–177, 185
    early (509–287 B.C.E.), 142–146
    fifth century B.C.E., 147(m)
    imperialism and (fifth to second
        centuries B.C.E.), 146–158
        expansion in Italy, 147–148
        social consequences of wars, 147, 156–158
        wars with Carthage, 148–152
    late republic (c. 133–44 B.C.E.), 158–168
        downfall of, 163–167
        Gaius Marius and the first client armies,
            160–161
        Gracchi brothers and factional politics,
            158–160
        Sulla and civil war, 161–163
    social and moral values in, 130–132
Roman society and culture, 130–139
    education for public life, 136
    family, 134–136
    in Golden Age (96–180 C.E.), 189–195
    hierarchy in, 132
    influences on, 92–93, 152–156
    patron-client system, 132
    religion, 137–139, 142
    Romanization of provinces, 190–195,
        191(m), 192(i)
Romanticism, 619–620, 621, 723–726,
    747–748, 757
Romanus IV (Byzantine emperor; r. 1068–1071),
    353–354

Rome, 597, 760, 768
    under Augustus, 177–182
    bishops of, 227
    classicism and, 558
    under Diocletian, 218
    Etruscan influence on, 142
    family dynasties and, 184–185
    fifth century B.C.E., 147(m)
    foundation legend, 129–130
    geographical advantages of, 140
    Italian unification and, 758
    as kingdom (c. 753–509 B.C.E.), 130, 139–142
    living conditions in, 164
    papacy in, 313, 440–443
    pilgrimage to, 278, 476
    Pope Sixtus's renewal of, 455
    as republic (1849), 737
    sack of (410), 239
    sack of (1527), 487
    Sassanid Empire and, 262(i)
    St. Peter's Basilica, 557
    Sulla and, 162
    Treaty of (1957), 960
    Vandal plunder of (455), 240
Romulus, 129, 130, 176(f)
Romulus Augustulus (Roman emperor;
        r. 475–476), 241
Roosevelt, Eleanor (1884–1962), 915, 915(i)
Roosevelt, Franklin Delano (1882–1945),
        914–916, 915(i), 921, 929, 934
    postwar settlement and, 938–942
Roosevelt, Theodore (1858–1919), 806, 813
Rosetta stone, 91(i), 681
Rossbach, battle of (1757), 634, 635(m)
Rothari (Lombardy; r. 636–652), 2889
Roundheads, 542
Rousseau, Jean-Jacques (roo SO, zhohn zhahk)
        (1712–1778), 610, 612, 612(i), 615–618,
        617(i), 619–620, 623, 627, 655, 666, 707
Rouvroy, Louis de (duc de St.-Simon), 526
Roxane (Bactrian princess; fourth century B.C.E.),
        104, 105
Royal Academy of Sciences (France), 556
Royal African Company (England), 554, 569–570
Royalists (England), 553–554
    seventeenth century, 542, 542(m), 544
Royal Society (England), 556, 602
Rubens, Peter Paul (1577–1640), 510–511, 512(i)
Rudolph (Holy Roman emperor; r. 1273–1291), 395
Ruler cults, 121, 122
Rump Parliament (England; 1648–1653), 544–545
Rural areas. See also Agriculture; Peasants
    in Byzantine Empire, 263–265
    Hellenistic poetry and, 113

Rushdie, Salman (b. 1947), 1061
Russia, 322, 763. See also Soviet Union; individual
        tsars and political leaders
    1820s political events, 705–706
    absolutism in, 533, 537–539, 592–594
    anarchism in, 832
    Baltic trade and, 591
    Byzantine Empire and, 260, 299
    Catherine the Great and, 601–610, 609(i)
    civil war (1917–1922), 867(m), 868–869
    colonialism and, 778, 799
    Congress of Vienna (1814–1815) and, 700–701
    corruption in modern, 1038
    Cossacks in, 642(i)
    Crimean War and, 748, 749, 751(m),
        751–752, 762
    in early twentieth century (before World
        War I), 844, 846, 847
    education in, 776(f), 777
    in eighteenth century, 605(m), 632, 634,
        635(m), 636–638
        balance of power in eastern Europe, 594–597
        emergence as European power, 587,
            592–595, 595(m)
        Great Northern War (1700–1718),
            594–595, 595(m)
        partition of Poland-Lithuania, 636
        westernization, 592–594, 593(i), 723
    Enlightenment ideas in, 618
    expansion to Siberia of, 499
    industrialization in, 712, 768
    Japan and, 805–806
    Jews in, 302, 638, 840, 841
    Kievan, 302–303, 335(m)
    in late nineteenth and early twentieth centuries,
        841–843
    liberalism in, 717
    Mongols and, 385, 396–397, 397(m), 438–439
    Muslims in, 302, 641
    Napoleon and, 688–689, 690, 692–693, 696(m)
    Napoleon III and, 749
    nationalism in, 723
    nation-building and, 794
    nineteenth-century literature of, 786
    in ninth and tenth centuries, 301–303
    partitions of Poland and, 636, 637(i), 675(m),
        675–676
    peasant unrest in, 677
    Peter the Great and, 568
    political parties in, 832–833
    Provisional Government, 865, 866
    reforms in, 690–691
        of 1850s–1860s, 752–755
        eighteenth century, 636–638

Revolution of 1905, 842, 842(*m*), 865
Revolution of 1917, 864–869
revolutions of 1848 and, 741
rise of, 296
serfs in, 538, 539(*i*), 580(*i*), 581, 641–642,
    712, 752–754, 754(*i*)
urbanization in, 817
water supply in, 774
working-class parties in, 832–833
World War I and, 852, 853, 854, 858, 861, 863, 877
Russian Academy of Sciences, 593, 594
Russian Orthodox church, 439, 538, 592–593,
    609(*i*), 723, 789, 932
Russian Revolution (1905), 842, 842(*m*), 865
Russian Revolution (1917), 864–869
Russification, 755, 841, 964
Russo-Japanese War (1905), 805–806, 842,
    844, 847, 852
Russo-Polish war (1654–1667), 539
Russo-Turkish War (1877–1878), 844
Ruysch, Rachel, 559
Rwanda, 1051

Saar basin, 872
Sachs, Nelly, 975
Sacraments, 443–445, 474. *See also*
    specific sacraments
  eleventh-century church reforms and, 351
  Fourth Lateran Council and (1215), 403
Sacrifice
  in ancient Greece, 10, 66–67
  infant, 149
  Roman, 139, 171, 223, 224
Sacrosanctity, 145
St. Bartholomew's Day massacre (1572), 490
St. Catherine, Monastery of (Mount Sinai), 233(*i*)
St. Denis, church of, 365, 416
St. Domingue (present-day Haiti), 678(*m*),
    678–680, 679(*i*), 689
St.-Germain-des-Prés, monastery of, 317–318
St. Helena, Napoleon on, 695
St. Peter Baptizing (Masaccio), 453, 454(*i*)
St. Peter's Basilica (Rome), 476, 557
St. Petersburg, 593–594, 705
St.-Savin-sur-Gartempe, 378(*i*), 414(*i*)
St.-Simon, Claude Henri de (sahn see MOHN)
    (1760–1825), 718
St.-Simon, duc de (Louis de Rouvroy)
    (1675–1755), 526, 587
Saint-Phalle, Niki de (b. 1930), 1001, 1001(*i*)
Saints, 279(*i*), 279–280, 329. *See also* Relics,
    cult of; *individual saints*
Saisset, Bernard (bishop of Pamiers),
    404(*i*), 405

Sakhalin Island, 939
Saladin (sultan of Egypt and Syria;
    1138–1193), 356
Salamis, island of, 53(*m*), 55
Salem (Massachusetts), witchcraft trials in, 520
Salons, 560–561, 628
  in Berlin, 619
  eighteenth century, 647
  in Paris, 612(*i*), 612–613, 616
  in Russia, 594
Salt, importance of, 904(*i*)
SALT I (Strategic Arms Limitation Treaty), 1014
Samarra, minaret of the Great Mosque at,
    304(*i*)
Samizdat culture, 1005–1006
Samurai (Japanese warrior class), 804
Sand, George (Amandine Dupin) (1804–1876),
    727, 728(*i*)
Sanitation (hygiene), 775
  in Augustan Rome, 177–178
  colonialism and, 779
  in nineteenth century, 712–713, 773–774
  population growth and, 811, 812, 813(*i*)
  in Russia, 890
Sans-culottes, 663, 669, 671
Sappho (SAH foh) (fl. c. 600 B.C.E.), 46
Saracens, 305, 395
Sarapis (sar AH pis), 122, 123(*i*)
Sardinia, 148, 150, 596, 666, 756(*m*)
Sardis, 51, 52, 109
Sargon (Akkadia; fl. c. 2350 B.C.E.), 12–13
SARS (severe acute respiratory syndrome), 1050
Sartre, Jean-Paul (1905–1980), 975
Sassanids (Sassanid Empire) (Persia), 205, 208,
    209(*m*), 245, 250, 261(*m*), 261–262, 262(*i*),
    269(*m*), 273, 274(*i*), 296–297, 304
Satellites, 966
  communications, 989, 991, 992
Saturn, 222(*i*)
Saturnalia (sat ur NAYL ee uh) festival, 138
Satyricon (Petronius), 182
Satyrs, 79, 100(*i*)
Saudi Arabia, 1054
Savage Mind, The (Lévi-Strauss), 1002
Saxons. *See also* Anglo-Saxons
  Charlemagne and, 311
Saxony, 326, 332, 332(*m*), 387, 477, 491, 594,
    634, 635(*m*), 700, 703
Scandinavia, 302, 303, 548, 583, 586.
    See also Vikings
  agriculture in, 579(*f*), 580
  Anglo-Saxons and, 321(*f*), 331
  Christianity in, 319
  Reformation in, 482(*m*), 486

Schiller, Friedrich (1759–1805), 725
Schleswig, 759
Schlieffen, Alfred von (1833–1913), 854
Schlieffen Plan, 854, 855, 856
Schmalkaldic League, 491
Schnittke, Alfred, 1063
Schoenberg, Arnold (1874–1951), 829
Scholars (scholarship)
    Byzantine, 309, 360
    Carolingian renaissance and, 309, 314(i),
        314–315
    Islamic, 308–309, 371
    Renaissance, 450–452
    in twelfth century, 369–373, 382
Scholastica, 234
Scholastics (Scholasticism), 411–416, 418
Schools. *See also* Education
    Carolingian, 314–315
    Islamic, 309, 315
    in nineteenth century, 729, 775–778
    Protestant reformers and, 481, 483
    twelfth-century, 369–373, 382
Schott, Johann, 477(i)
Schumacher, E. F. "Fritz," 1048
Schuman, Robert (SHOO mahn)
        (1886–1963), 960
Science(s). *See also specific sciences*
    in 1930s, 919–920
    Alexander the Great and, 105
    Aristotle and, 97–98
    bureaucracy and, 998
    the Enlightenment and, 600–602, 616, 647
    in Hellenistic period, 118–120
    Islam and, 308
    in late nineteenth and early twentieth centuries,
        820–825
    Napoleon and, 686–687
    in postindustrial society, 992, 997–998
    professionalization of, 776
    rationalism and, 46
    in sixteenth and seventeenth centuries, 474,
        509, 514–521, 554–556
    in thirteenth and fourteenth centuries, 412
Scientific management, 881
Scientific method, 514, 516–517, 521
Scientific revolution, 514–521, 524
Scipio Africanus (SKIP ee oh ahf ree KAHN us)
        (fl. c. 200 B.C.E.), 150
Scipio Nasica (SKIP ee oh nah SEE kah), 159
Scivias (Hildegard), 373
Scotland, 320, 583, 870
    British incorporation of, 589–590
    Calvinists in, 497
    Christianity in, 286, 442

seventeenth-century religious conflicts and,
    542, 544
Scott, Sir Walter (1771–1832), 726
Scream, The (Munch), 797(i), 826
Scribes, 11–12, 13(f), 253
Script. *See* Writing
Scriptoria, 451
Sculpted Tomb, 133(i), 182(i)
Sculpture, 21, 25, 76(i), 83(i), 111
    Gothic, 418(i), 419–421, 448
    Greek, 45, 45(i), 64–65, 64(f)
    Hellenistic, 114, 115(i)
    modern, 981(i), 1005(i)
    in Neo-Assyrian Empire, 26–27
    Persian, 28, 30(i)
    relief, 58(i), 115, 174(i), 182(i), 222(i), 361
    Renaissance (fifteenth century), 454, 455(i)
    Roman, 123(i), 135(i), 155–156, 184,
        184(i), 215(i)
    Romanesque, 374, 374(i), 375(i)
    Sassanid Empire and, 262(i)
    seventeenth-century, 557, 557(i)
Sea Peoples (c. 1200–1000 B.C.E.), 25, 36
SEATO (Southeast Asia Treaty Organization), 968
Second Balkan War (1913), 846
Second Continental Congress, 646
Second Crusade (1147–1149), 356, 362, 387, 399
Second Empire (France), 749
Second Estate, 656(i), 656–657
Second International, 832
Second Moroccan Crisis (1911), 844
Second Punic War (218–201 B.C.E.), 150, 151(f)
Second Reform Bill (Great Britain; 1867), 764
Second Sex, The (de Beauvoir), 976
Second Triumvirate, 173
Second Vatican Council (1962), 1003
Secularization, 509, 521
    the Enlightenment and, 615
Seekers, 543
Segregation, 976, 1006
Seigneurial dues, 622, 656, 659, 677, 690
Sejm (Polish parliament), 540
Seleucid (seh LOO sid) kingdoms, 106–107,
        107(m), 121, 123, 124, 163, 196
Seleucus (se LEWK uhs) (c. 358–281 B.C.E.), 106
Self-government of towns, 345–346, 351
Seljuk Turks, 353–355, 355(m), 359
Senate (senators), Roman, 140, 145–147, 150, 152,
        156, 158, 161, 162, 164, 167, 180
    Augustus and, 172, 173, 177
    Gaius Marius and, 160
    Julius Caesar and, 165
    taxes and, 219
Seneca (SEN ek ah) (4 B.C.E.–65 C.E.), 203

Sennacherib (sen AHK uh rib) (Neo-Assyrian
      king; r. 704–681 B.C.E.), 27
Septimius Severus (Roman emperor; r. 193–211),
      181, 206, 207, 208, 218
Serbs (Serbia), 301–303, 322, 436–437, 438(m),
      537, 705, 808, 839, 845, 846, 1033
   nationalism of, 1032
   rise of, 296
   World War I and, 852, 853, 854, 861, 872
Serfs (serfdom), 325, 435, 508, 594, 606, 635,
      638–639, 680, 739, 740(i), 741
   abolition of, 478, 540, 654, 659
   industrialization and, 712, 768
   Jews as, 357
   Napoleon and, 690
   in Russia, 538, 539(i), 580(i), 581, 641–642,
      712, 752–754
      emancipation, 753–754, 754(i)
   uprising of, 610
Sergius I (pope; r. 687 or 689–701), 290
Serious Proposal to the Ladies, A (Astell), 604
Servetus, Michael (1511–1553), 481
Service sector, 770, 771, 987, 995, 996–997
Seurat, Georges (1859–1891), 788
Seven Years' War (1756–1763), 632, 634–636,
      635(m), 645, 655
Sévigné, Marie de (say vee NYAY) (1626–1696),
      523, 524, 526, 561
Seville, 391, 391(m), 508, 509
Sex and sexuality. *See also* Adultery; Celibacy;
      Homosexuality
   in 1920s, 884
   in ancient Greece, 43–44, 71–74, 81, 100(i)
   Augustine's view of, 231–232
   birth control and, 812–813, 995
   Christian view of, 231–232
   Cynics and, 117
   Darwinism and, 791
   in eighteenth century, 617(i), 619, 620,
      627, 629
   Foucault on, 1067
   Justinian and, 252
   in nineteenth century, 731, 810–813, 815–816
   Plato's view of, 97
   in Renaissance (fifteenth century), 462–463
   in Roman poetry, 154
   in seventeenth century, 506–507
   in twentieth century, 993–995, 1008
Sexual Inversion (Ellis), 815
Seymour, Jane (England; r. 1536–1537), 495
Seymour, Robert, 699(i)
Sforza, Bianca Maria (SFOR tsa), 458
Sforza, Francesco (1401–1466), 458–459
Sforza, Ludovico, 458

Shaftesbury, Earl of, 554
Shakespeare, William (1564–1616), 193, 510–511
Shamash, 14
Shapur I (Sassanid king; r. c. 240–270 C.E.),
      208, 209(m)
Shi'ite Muslims, 274, 304, 305, 1052
Ships and navigation
   in fifteenth century, 466
   Greek, 58(i)
   Vikings and, 320, 320(i)
Shostakovich, Dmitry, 1063
Shrines, Roman, 137, 138(i)
Shtetls, 540
Siberia, 499, 717, 805, 868
Sic et Non (Abelard), 372, 411
Sicily, 39, 86(m), 88(m), 150, 428, 757
   city-states in, 55
   Islam and, 306, 322, 371
   in thirteenth century, 386, 394(m),
      394–396, 395(m)
   in twelfth century, 363(m)
Sidonius Apollinaris (c. 430–479), 239
Siege tactics and weapons, 26. *See also* Weapons
      and military technology
   Alexander the Great and, 102
   in Hellenistic period, 120
Sigismund (Holy Roman emperor; r. 1410–1437),
      443, 446
Signoria, 406
Sikhs, 576
Silesia, 535, 632–634, 633(m)
Silk trade and industry, 189, 299, 427, 548, 575, 576
Silver, 616, 684
   Carolingian economy and, 317
   imports to Spain, 504–505, 504(f)
   Italian economy and, 439
   Kutnà Hora mine, 445
   in Roman coins, 206, 207(f)
Simitis, Costas, 1041
Simon de Montfort (c. 1208–1265), 409
Simon IV de Montfort l'Amaury
      (1165?–1218), 392
Simons, Menno (1469–1561), 480
Simony, 346, 347, 348, 476
Simyonov, Yulian, 980
Sinai, Mount, 31, 233(i)
Sinai peninsula, 1014
Singapore, 732, 929, 1055
Sinn Fein, 836
Sino-Japanese War (1894–1895), 805
Sisters of St. Francis, 379
Sistine Chapel, 510
Situationists, 1008
Six Acts, 710–711

Six Books of the Republic, The (Bodin), 513
Six-Day War (1967), 1014(*m*), 1014–1015
Sixtus IV (pope; r. 1471–1484), 455
Sixtus V (pope; r. 1585–1590), 497
Skeptics (Skepticism), 117, 513, 516, 568,
    601, 603
Slaves and slavery, 31, 231, 488, 802, 932. *See also*
    Slave trade
  abolition of, 554, 646, 700, 715–716, 731
  African, 465, 465(*m*), 467–468, 468(*i*), 576(*i*), 801
  in ancient Egypt, 20
  in ancient Greece, 41, 41(*i*), 42, 43, 51(*i*), 72–73,
    85, 95, 98
  in Brazil, 569, 570(*m*), 571(*f*), 572–575
  in Caribbean, 652
  the Enlightenment and, 614
  in Florence (fifteenth century), 459, 462, 463
  in fourteenth and fifteenth centuries, 437, 440
  in French colonies, 678(*m*), 678–680, 679(*i*)
  French Revolution and, 660
  in Hellenistic kingdoms, 110, 116
  Islamic society and, 307
  Mamluks and, 305
  in Merovingian period (c. 485–751), 277–278,
    279, 281, 283, 317–318
  in New World, 538, 548, 551–552,
    588(*m*), 606
  in Roman Republic and Empire, 147, 148, 156,
    158, 180–181, 186, 193, 208
    citizenship, 140
    education and, 136
    ex-slaves, 133(*i*), 133–134, 138
    rebellion of, 163
  Rousseau on, 617
  in Sparta, 43
  in Sumerian society, 9–10
  in United States, 765–766
Slave trade, 465(*m*), 467–468, 614
  1701–1810, 571(*f*)
  abolishment of, 703
  Atlantic system and, 552, 568–575
  in eighteenth century, 568–575, 571(*m*),
    571(*f*), 648(*m*)
    conditions on slave ships, 572
  in nineteenth century, 731
  in seventeenth century, 548, 551–552
Slavophiles, 723
Slavs (Slavic peoples and states), 261, 262, 263,
    322, 332, 445, 468, 763, 798, 844, 855
  Byzantine Empire and, 297, 301–303
  World War II and, 927
Slovaks (Slovakia), 816, 839, 918, 1041
Slovenia, 7*n*, 861, 872, 1032, 1041
Smallpox, 599

Smith, Adam (1723–1790), 615–616, 618, 619,
    639, 640
Sobieski, Jan (sob YES kee, yahn) (Poland-
    Lithuania; r. 1674–1696), 536(*i*), 540
Social classes. *See also* Hierarchy; Lower classes;
    Middle class(es); Upper classes
  curiales, 190, 220, 225, 264, 265, 293
  in eighteenth century, 581–583
  in Florence (fifteenth century), 457, 459–463
  racial discrimination and, 486
Social Contract, The (Rousseau), 616–618
Social contract theory, 553–554, 646
Social Darwinism, 791–792, 809, 814, 818, 820,
    832, 837
Social Democratic party (Germany), 838, 848,
    854, 870
Social Democrats (Sweden), 917
Social elites. *See* Upper classes
Socialism (Socialists), 717–720, 784, 818, 997
  mass politics and, 829
  parties, 831
  Russian Revolution and, 865
  World War I and, 861
Socialist realism, 908
Social order
  Augustine's view of, 231
  Justinian and, 249
  in nineteenth century, 772–785
    bureaucracy, 774–775
    cities, 772–774
    colonial policies, 778–781
    culture, 785–788
    religion and, 789–791
    social sciences, 791–792
  in seventeenth century, 552–565
    the arts, 556–559
    reforming popular culture, 561–564
    social contract theory, 553–554
    women and manners, 559–561
Social Science Association (Great Britain), 764
Social sciences, 791–792, 1002
Social Security Act (United States; 1935), 914
Social Statics (Spencer), 792
Social War (91–87 B.C.E.), 161
Society for the Prevention of Cruelty to Animals
    (SPCA), 729
Society of Jesus. *See* Jesuits
Society of Revolutionary Republican Women
    (France), 671
Society of Supporters of the Bill of Rights, 643, 644
Society of United Irishmen, 676
Socrates (SAW krah teez) (469–399 B.C.E.), 65,
    75–78, 76(*i*), 93, 95
Socratic method, 77

Sogdiana (sog dee AH nah), 104

Solar system, Hellenistic models of, 118–119

Soldiers. *See* Armed forces

Solidarity (Poland), 1021

Solomon (Israel; r. c. 961–922 B.C.E.), 31, 32

Solon (SOHL on) (c. 638–559 B.C.E.), 44

Solzhenitsyn, Aleksandr (SAWL zhen EET sin)
        (b. 1918), 966, 1012

Somme, battle at the (1916), 858

Sophia (daugher of Tsar Alexei), 538

Sophists, 65, 74–75

Sophocles (SOF o kleez) (c. 496–406 B.C.E.), 80, 81

Soranus (sor AH nus), 194

Sorrows of Young Werther, The (Goethe), 620

Soubirous, St. Bernadette, 789–790

South Africa, 769, 1051

South America
    African slaves in, 569
    colonies in, 570(*m*), 574, 648(*m*)
        Dutch, 559, 559(*i*)
        Spanish, 504, 508, 551, 568
    exploration of (sixteenth century), 465(*m*)

Southeast Asia Treaty Organization (SEATO), 968

South Korea, 968, 1055

South Vietnam, 1006

Soviets, 842, 865, 866

Soviet Union (Union of Soviet Socialist Republics;
        USSR). *See also* Cold war; Russia;
        individual Soviet leaders
    in 1920s, 889–892
    in 1950s and 1960s, 961–66
    in 1970s, 1014
    1991 attempted coup in, 1034–1036
    aerospace development in, 965–966
    Afghanistan and, 1021, 1038, 1052
    collapse of communism in, 1020–1025, 1030,
        1031–1040
    dictatorship in, 896
    disintegration of, 1034–1036
    eastern Europe and. *See* Eastern Europe, under
        Communist rule
    as evil empire, 1018
    expansionism of, 950
    former, 1035(*m*)
    industrialization in, 900
    purges and show trials in, 907, 964
    Stalinism in, 906–909, 964
    as superpower, 949–950
    World War I and, 852
    World War II and, 927, 929, 955
        postwar settlement, 938–942

Space age (space exploration), 966, 991–993, 992(*i*)

Spain, 39, 509, 596, 832, 1017, 1019
    1820–1823 revolt in, 705

American colonies of, 477, 485–486, 492,
        493(*m*), 508, 511, 568, 646
    settlement patterns, 574–575
    silver imports, 504–505, 504(*f*)
    slavery and, 551

American Revolution and, 646

baroque style and, 558

Bismarck and, 759

Catholic church in, 288–289, 637, 691–692
    reconquista, 447–448

Charlemagne and, 311, 312(*m*)

colonialism and, 801(*m*), 803(*m*)

in eighteenth century, 605(*m*)

exploration and settlements (fifteenth and
        sixteenth centuries), 426, 463, 464(*m*),
        466–470

French Revolution and, 666, 677, 679

illiteracy in, 776(*f*)

industrialization in, 768

Inquisition in, 618

Jews in, 358, 403, 426

Louis XIV and, 525, 530–532

monarchy in
    fifteenth century, 447–448
    thirteenth century, 405, 407–408

Muslims (Moors) in, 289, 291(*m*), 305–307,
        306(*m*), 371, 422, 426
    Christian reconquest (*reconquista*), 348, 386,
        388(*m*), 390–391, 391(*m*), 408, 447–448
    Moriscos, 492–493

Napoleon and, 689, 691–692, 692(*i*), 693, 696(*m*)

Netherlands and, 492–494, 493(*m*), 494(*m*),
        496–497, 513, 548, 549(*m*)

Roman Empire and, 148, 150, 166, 220

in sixteenth century, 477, 487, 487(*m*), 490,
        492–497, 493(*m*)

slave trade and, 467–468, 468(*i*), 569, 570(*m*),
        571(*f*), 574

Thirty Years' War and, 499–501, 503

unification of (late fifteenth century),
        447, 447(*m*)

Visigothic, 239(*i*), 240, 288–290, 293

War of Spanish succession and, 587, 588(*m*)

Spanish-American War (1898), 806

Spanish Armada, 497, 505

Spanish Civil War (1936–1939), 919, 923(*m*),
        923–924, 924(*i*)

Spanish Fury (1576), 494

Spanish Netherlands, 510–511, 530–531, 531(*m*)

Sparta, 51
    c. 750–500 B.C.E., 43(*m*)
    c. 400 B.C.E., 88(*m*)
    alliances in, 56–58

(continued)

citizenship (political rights) in, 44
disunity of Greece and (390s to 370s B.C.E.),
    93, 98–99
homosexuality and, 43–44
Peloponnesian League and, 56, 57(m), 61
Peloponnesian War (431–404 B.C.E.) and,
    84–86, 84(f), 86(m), 93
Persian invasion and (480–479 B.C.E.), 55, 56–58
Thirty Tyrants period in Athens and, 86–87,
    93, 95
Spartacists, 870
Spartacus (SPAHRT ah kus) (d. 71 B.C.E.), 163
Spectator, The (magazine), 583
Spencer, Herbert (1820–1903), 792
Speyer (Germany), 357
Spice trade, 189, 245, 341(m), 342, 398, 427, 465,
    466, 548, 549(m), 571(m), 575–576
Spinoza, Benedict (1633–1677), 550
Spirit of the Laws (Montesquieu), 603, 615
Spoleto, Duchy of, 289, 289(m),
    290–291, 335(m)
Sports
    in 1920s, 810, 884, 886
    in eighteenth century, 628
    in nineteenth century, 819–820
    Olympic Games, 38
Sputnik (1957), 966, 991
Srebrenica (sreh breh NEET sah), ethnic cleansing
    in, 1032
Staël, Madame de (stayl) (1766–1817), 687,
    687(i), 692
Stagflation, 1015, 1016, 1019
Stalin, Joseph (1879–1953), 885, 891–892, 900,
    905, 917, 926, 927, 949–950, 963, 964
    eastern Europe and, 952
    postwar settlement and, 938–942
    Stalinism and, 906–909, 965
    World War II and, 929, 930, 934, 938–939
Stalingrad, siege and battle of (1943), 934
Stamp Act (1765), 645
Standard Oil Trust, 769
Star Wars (Strategic Defense Initiative), 1018
State. See Government
State power, in eighteenth century, 632–649
    food riots and peasant uprisings, 640–642
    limits of reform, 638–640
    public opinion and political opposition, 636,
        640, 642–644
    rebellions against, 640–648
    revolution in North America, 644–648
    state-sponsored reform, 636–640, 646–648
    war and diplomacy, 632–636
Statues. See Sculpture
Ste.-Chapelle, 414(i)

Steam-powered machinery and engines, 629–630,
    708–709, 717
Steele, Sir Richard (1672–1729), 583
Steen, Jan (1626?–1679), 550(i)
Stephen I (Magyar king; r. 997–1038), 335–336
Stephen II (pope; r. 752–757), 292
Stephenson, George, 708
Stigmata, 379
Stoas, 61
Stock exchanges, 769
Stockhausen, Karlheinz (b. 1928), 1002
Stock markets, 769
    crash of 1929 (United States), 899–902, 901(i)
Stoicism (STO ih sizum), 116–117, 154, 202,
    203, 223
Stolypin, Pyotr (1863–1911), 842
Stone Age, 3–4
Stopes, Marie, 884
Story of Sinuhe, The (Egypt), 21
Stowe, Harriet Beecher (1811–1896), 753
Stranger, The (Camus), 976
Strasbourg, 484
    cathedral in, 418(i)
    Louis XIV's seizure of (1681), 532
    printing in, 452, 477(i)
Strategic Arms Limitation Treaty (SALT I), 1014
Strategic Defense Initiative (Star Wars), 1018
Strauss, Richard (shtrows, REE kahrd)
    (1864–1949), 828–829
Stravinsky, Igor (1882–1971), 827–828
Strozzi, Alessandra (STROT zee), 461
Strozzi, Caterina, 461
Strozzi, Filippo, 461
Strozzi family, 453, 461
Struggle of the orders, 143
Structuralism, 1002
Stuart dynasty (Great Britain), 589–590
Students
    clerical status of (thirteenth and fourteenth
        centuries), 411–413
    protests (1960s), 1008, 1010
    in twelfth century, 369–373
Styria, 535, 768
Subjection of Women, The (Mill), 792
Subjectivism, 74–75
Submarine warfare, in World War I, 856, 864
Successor kings, 106
Sudan, 22
Sudetenland, 926
Suetonius (swee TOH nee us) (c. 70–130),
    173, 186, 217(m), 314
Suez Canal, 747(i), 751, 780, 855, 969–970
Suffrage. See Voting rights
Sufi, al-, 308(i)

Sugar production and trade, 467–468, 509, 548, 551, 559, 568–572, 570(m), 573, 573(i), 577, 592
Suger (abbot of St. Denis; 1081–1152), 365–366, 382, 416
Suicide bombers. *See* Terrorists
Sukarno, Achmed (1901–1970), 972
Suleiman I (the Magnificent) (Ottoman sultan; r. 1520–1566), 488
Sulla, Lucius Cornelius (SUHL uh) (c. 138–78 B.C.E.), 161–163
Sumer (Sumerians), 8–13
Summa, 412
Summa Theologiae (Thomas Aquinas), 412–413
Sunday School Movement, 728
Sunni Muslims, 274, 305, 353, 356, 1052
Sun Yat-Sen (1866–1925), 805(m), 807
Superpowers, 946, 949–950
   in 1970s, 1013–1026
Superstition
   the Enlightenment and, 611, 613, 614
   seventeenth-century campaign against, 562
Supply-side policies, 1017
Surinam, 559, 559(i)
Süttner, Bertha von, 833
Swabia, 367
Sweden, 322, 634, 635(m), 692, 693, 703, 768, 775, 814
   1980s to present, 1019–1020
   absolutist consolidation in, 533–535
   economic recovery in, 960
   education in, 777
   in eighteenth century, 597, 605(m), 643
      decline, 587, 591, 593, 594, 595, 595(m)
   French Revolution and, 676–677
   French wars with, 432, 530
   mercantilism and, 508
   Poland-Lithuania and, 539–540
   political parties in, 831
   population growth in, 812
   social welfare programs in, 916
   Thirty Years' War and, 499, 501–503, 502(m), 534
Swiss Confederation, 407, 407(m), 501
Switzerland, 277, 279(i), 316, 597, 619, 678
   Bolsheviks and, 866(i)
   education in, 583, 777
   religious reform and, 479–480, 482(m)
   World War I and, 856
Syllabus of Errors, The (Pius IX), 789
Sylvester II (pope; r. 999–1003), 333
Symeon the Stylite (390–459), 232
Symmachus, Aurelius (c. 340–402), 223, 230
Symposia, in Athens, 71, 71(i), 73

Synagogues, 225
Syndicalists, 832
Synod of Sutri (1046), 347
Synod of Whitby (664), 287
Syracuse, 55
Syria, 12, 16, 22, 163, 208, 681, 1014(m), 1014–1015, 1055
   Arabs and, 263, 292
   colonialism and, 808
   in Hellenistic period (323–30 B.C.E.), 106
   Islam and, 272(m), 273–275, 274(i), 305, 308
   trade and, 281
   World War I and, 855, 874
Széchenyi, Count Stephen (SAY chen yee) (1791–1860), 717, 738, 739

T4 project, 913–914, 931
Taaffe, Count Edouard von, 839
Table of Ranks (1722), 592
Taborites, 446
Tacitus (TAS ih tuhs) (c. 56–120 C.E.), 177, 187, 193, 200, 450, 666
Taifa, 307, 348, 390
Taiping (Heavenly Kingdom; China), 781, 795
Taiwan, 1055
Tajikistan, 1034
Taliban, 1052, 1055
Talmud, 225
Tarquin the Proud (Rome; r. late sixth century B.C.E.), 143
Tartars. *See* Mongols
Taxes (revenues)
   Abbasid, 305
   in Byzantine Empire, 249–250, 290, 297, 359
   colonialism and, 799, 802
   Delian League and, 62
   in early Middle Ages, 283, 285, 289, 325–326
   in Egypt, 21
   in eighteenth century, 622, 636, 638, 639, 655–657, 658(m)
   in England, 321, 331, 361, 401
      Hundred Years' War (1337–1453) and, 435
      seventeenth century, 541–542, 545, 547
   in France, 366, 399, 503, 622, 639
      eighteenth century, 655–657, 658(m)
      French Revolution and, 659, 660
      Louis XIV, 525, 529, 531–532
   in Germany, 367, 395, 533
   Habsburg Empire and, 762
   Hebrew, 32
   in Hellenistic kingdoms, 103, 108–109
   in Islam, 271, 273, 274(i), 275, 293
   in Italy, 406, 459

                                    (continued)

on Jews, 357–358
in Mesopotamia, 10
Mongol system of, 397
in Ottoman Empire, 437
papal, 441
Peace of Paris and, 875
on peasants, 343
in Persian Empire, 28
pre-World War I arms race and, 848
protests against, 445, 640, 645
in Prussia, 596
Roman Catholic clergy and, 404(i), 404–405, 478
in Roman Empire, 148, 175, 189–190, 208, 219, 220
in Roman Republic, 161
in Russia and Soviet Union, 538, 592, 841
in seventeenth century, 538, 541–542, 545, 547, 565
social welfare and, 835
in Spain, 407
Thirty Years' War and, 505, 520, 524
Taylor, Frederick (1856–1915), 881
Taylor, Harriet, 834
Tea Act (1773), 645
Teachers, women as, 777–778
Tea trade, 548, 568, 575, 577, 606
Technocrats, 960
Technology (technological advances)
in 1920s, 893, 896
art and, 888–889, 890
birth control and, 813
colonialism and, 781
communications, 852, 989, 991, 992
Crimean War and, 752
economic development and, 766
Japanese modernization and, 804
mass politics and, 830
metallurgical, 4
migration and, 816
trade and, 6
workers and, 781–782, 783
World War I and, 851, 852, 855
after World War II, 988–995
life sciences, 993–995
space exploration, 991–993
Teenagers, in postindustrial society, 999
Telegraph, 752, 780, 846
Telephone, 830, 846
Television, 979, 988–989
Tell, William, legend of, 407
Temperance movement, 700, 720, 728
Temples. *See also* Architecture
Egypt, 22
Etruscan, 142

Greek, 62–65, 63(i), 64–65
Israelite, 31, 32
Mesopotamia, 9, 10, 11(i)
Roman, 137, 158
Tenant farmers
in England, 580, 622
in Roman Empire, 219, 237, 244
Ten Commandments, 31, 32, 233(i)
Tennyson, Alfred, Lord (1809–1892), 729
Tenochtitlán, 470
Terence (c. 190–159 B.C.E.), 153
Tereshkova, Valentina (teh resh KOH vah) (b. 1937), 991, 992(i)
Terror, the (France), 664(i), 665–674, 680, 682(i), 684, 695
end of (1794–1799), 671–674
Terrorists (terrorism), 970, 1052–1055
in 1970s, 1016–1017
September 11, 2001, attacks, 1031, 1054(i), 1054–1055
Tertiaries, 410
Tertullian (tur TUHL ee an) (c. 160–240), 181, 200
Test Act (1673), 546
Tet Offensive (Vietnam War), 1010
Tetradia, 284
Tetrarchy, 216, 218
Teutonic Knights, 387, 406, 438, 469(m)
Textiles (textile industry), 398, 505, 548, 606, 711, 769. *See also* Cotton industry and trade
in ancient Greece, 94
in Byzantine Empire, 264
Dutch Republic and, 591
in eighteenth century, 629–631
in fourteenth century, 429–430, 458
in France, 530, 657
in India, 574, 576(i), 576–577, 691, 709–710
industrialization and, 621, 629–631, 630, 630(i), 691, 767
in Middle Ages, 344, 345
Thales (thay LEEZ) (c. 625–545 B.C.E.), 46
Thalidomide, 994(i)
Thamugadi, arch at, 192(i)
Thatcher, Margaret (b. 1925), 1013, 1017–1018, 1018(i)
Thatcherism, 1017
alternatives to, 1019–1020
Theater. *See also* Comedies; Drama; Tragedy
in Golden Age Athens, 65, 79–83, 80(i)
Hellenistic, 113–114
under Louis XIV, 527
in sixteenth and seventeenth centuries, 509–510, 521, 538
Thebes, 22, 93, 98, 101, 102
Themes (military districts), 297, 359

Themistocles of Athens (theh MIS toh kleez) (c. 528–462 B.C.E.), 55

Theocracy, Sumerian, 10

Theocritus (thee OK rit us) (c. 300–260 B.C.E.), 113

Theodora (thee uh DOH ruh) (Byzantine empress; d. 548), 247(i), 249

Theodore (archbishop; r. 669–690), 287

Theodoric the Great (Ostrogothic king; r. 493–526), 242, 246(i)

Theodorus the Atheist, 117–118

Theodosius (Roman emperor; r. 379–395 in the east), 224, 238

Theodosius II (Roman emperor; r. 408–450), 264(i)

Theophrastus (c. 370–285 B.C.E.), 116, 118

Theopompus of Chios, 101

Theotokopoulos, Domenikos. *See* El Greco

Thera (Santorini), 35(i)

Thermidorian Reaction, 674

Thermopylae (ther MAH pill ee), battle of (480 B.C.E.), 55

Theseus of Athens (THEE see us), 36

Thessalonika, 436, 436(m), 448

Theuderic, 279(i)

Third Council of Toledo (587), 288

Third Crusade (1189–1192), 356, 387, 388(m)

Third Estate (France), 656(i), 656–657, 664(i)

Third International (Comintern), 868

Third Punic War (149–146 B.C.E.), 150

Third Reich, 912, 925(m)

Third world, defined, 946

Thirty-Nine Articles of Religion (Church of England; 1563), 496

Thirty Tyrants period (Athens), 86–87, 95

Thirty Years' War (1618–1648), 473–474, 498–505, 500(i), 516, 525, 533, 534, 535(m), 536, 541, 920
    Germany and, 499, 501, 502(m), 518
    origins and course of, 498–503
    peace negotiations and treaty, 501–503, 502(m)
    recession after, 504–508, 520–521, 524
    Sweden and, 594

Thrace, 28, 29(m)

Three-field system, 318, 325

Thucydides (thoo SID ih deez) (c. 455 399 B.C.E.), 57, 85
    on Peloponnesian War, 78, 84(f)

Thuringia (Germany), 429, 478

Tiamat, 3

Tiananmen Square (China), 1989 demonstrations in, 1021–1022, 1060

Tiberius (Roman emperor; r. 14–37 C.E.), 185, 190

Tibet, 799

Tiglathpileser III (Assyria; r. 745–727 B.C.E.), 32

Tigris River, 4, 8

Tilak, B. G. (1856–1920), 808

Timbuktu (Africa), 307

Tinguely, Jean (1925–1991), 1001

Tirpitz, Alfred von (1849–1930), 847

Tithe, 326

Titian (1477–1576), 492(i)

Tito (Josip Broz), 952

Titus (TY tus) (Roman emperor; r. 79–81 C.E.), 187

Tobacco, 509, 548, 569, 573, 577, 592

Tobin, James, 1046

Tocqueville, Alexis de (1805–1859), 711

Toledo, 288

Toleration Act (1689), 547

Tolstoy, Leo (1828–1910), 748, 841

Tombs and graves, 143(i), 229(i). *See also* Burial practices
    ancient Egyptian, 22, 23
    Etruscan, 141
    Mycenaean, 34, 36
    Roman, 182(i)
    Sumerian, 10

Topkapi Saray Palace, 425, 437

Torah (Pentateuch), 31, 32, 50. *See also* Hebrew Bible

Tordesillas (tor day SEE yahs), Treaty of (1494), 464(m), 466

Tories, 547, 590, 677(i), 716

Torture, 513, 515, 520, 592
    Enlightenment ideals and, 610, 614, 636–637, 643, 681

Totalitarianism, 695
    in 1930s, 905–914
    defined, 905–906
    French Revolution and, 652, 666

Total war, 851, 852, 860, 870, 871, 876

Tours, 278–280, 283

Toussaint L'Ouverture, François-Dominique (too SAHN loo vehr TOOR) (1743–1803), 679(i), 679–680

Towns
    medieval, walled, 340, 342(i)
    self-government of, 345–346

Trade. *See also* Business and commerce; Mercantilism
    Adam Smith on, 615–616
    in ancient Egypt, 16
    ancient trade routes, 22, 24
    with Asia, 439, 463, 466
    Assyrian, 26
    Atlantic system and, 507–508, 552, 568–577, 570(m), 578

(continued)

Byzantine Empire, 264, 299, 302
Carolingian, 317
with China, 245, 304, 385, 385(i), 397(m),
    397–398, 470, 732, 807
colonialism and, 780, 781, 799, 801(m)
Continental System and, 691
Dutch, 507–508, 530, 544, 548–551, 549(m),
    575, 589, 591–592
in early Middle Ages, 281
in eighteenth century, 627, 631, 632, 639–641
Etruscan, 141–142
free, 641, 716(i), 750, 769
Greek, 37, 39
    Athens, 44, 61
    Minoan and Mycenaean period, 33–35
Habsburg Empire and, 762
Hanseatic league and, 406–407
Hittite, 24
India, 576(i), 576–577
international, 766, 769–770
Iraqi, 304
iron metallurgy and, 37–38
Islamic, 307, 317
with Japan, 781
medieval routes in eleventh and twelfth
    centuries, 340–342, 341(m), 382
Mediterranean (fifteenth century), 463–465
Neolithic, 4, 5, 6, 7–8
in North American colonies, 530
silk, 189, 427
sixteenth and seventeenth centuries, 493(m),
    494, 544, 548, 549(m), 551
slave. See Slave trade
spice, 189, 245, 341(m), 342, 398, 427, 465, 466,
    548, 549(m), 571(m), 575–576
Sumerian, 9–10
tariffs and, 716, 716(i), 1046
in textiles, 398
thirteenth century, 422
Vikings and, 321
Trade deficits, 770
Trafalgar, battle of (1805), 689
Tragedy, Greek, 79–81
Trajan (Roman emperor;
    r. 98–117 C.E.), 187, 188(m),
    190, 192(i), 193
Transportation, in the eleventh century, 342
Trans-Siberian Railroad, 805
Transubstantiation, doctrine of, 403, 414,
    479, 484
Transvaal, 801, 802
Transylvania, 488(i), 535(m), 539, 596, 721, 740(i)
Trasformismo, 836
Travel, in Merovingian period (c. 485–751), 277–278

Travel literature, eighteenth-century, 602–603, 606
Travels of Marco Polo, The (Polo), 466
Treaties of Tilsit, 689
Treaty of London (1915), 871, 892
Trench warfare, in World War I, 856, 857(m), 858,
    859, 859(i)
Triangular Trade, 570(m)
Tribunes, Roman, 144, 145, 159, 175
Tricolor, revolutionary (France), 668
Triennial Act (1694), 590
Trier, 278
Triple Alliance, 843, 848(m), 854
Triple Entente, 848(m)
Triremes (TRY reemz), 57, 58(i), 84(f)
Tristan, Flora (1801–1844), 718–719
Trivium, 370–371
Trojan War, 37, 80
Trotsky, Leon (TROT skee) (1879–1940),
    868, 891
Troubadours, 368(i), 368–369, 448
Truce of God, 329
Truman, Harry S. (1884–1972), 945, 950–951
Truman Doctrine, 951
Trusts, 769
Truth (Protagoras), 74–75
Tsar, defined, 439
Tsushima Straits, 806
Tuberculosis, 713
Tullia (TUHL ee ah) (c. 79–45 B.C.E.), 135
Tunis, battle of (1535), 487(m), 488
Tunisia, 142, 305, 780, 970
Turgenev, Ivan (1818–1883), 753, 754, 786
Turgot, Jacques (1727–1781), 639–641
Turkey, 7, 8n, 806, 808, 905. *See also*
    Ottoman Empire
    Byzantine Empire and, 260
    EU and, 1041
    World War I and, 855
    after World War II, 951
Turks
    Ottoman. *See* Ottoman Empire
    Seljuk, crusades and, 353–355, 355(m), 359
Turner, Joseph M. W. (1775–1851), 724
Tuscany, 459–460, 757
Tustari brothers, 307
Tutankhamun (r. 1361–1352 B.C.E.), 22
Twelve Tables, 144
Two Treatises of Government (Locke), 554
Tyche (TY kee) (Chance), 121
Tyndale, William (1495–1536), 481
Tyranny, 40
    in ancient Greece, 44
Tyre, 24, 109
    capture of (332 B.C.E.), 102

Ubayd Allah, 305
Ugarit (OO gah reet), 24
Ukraine, 302, 438, 538, 539, 642(i), 770,
    778, 868, 1040
Ulster, 544, 880(m)
Ultras (ultraroyalists) (France), 704
Ulysses (Joyce), 888
Umayyad dynasty (oo MAY ahd) (Umayyad
    period), 272(m), 273–275, 274(i),
    287, 291(m)
  overthrow of, 296, 304, 306
Ummah (OO ma), 269, 308
Unam Sanctam (1302), 405
Underclass, in the fourteenth and fifteenth
    centuries, 440. See also Lower classes
Undset, Sigrid, 815(i)
Unemployment, 734
  in 1930s, 902–903, 912, 914–915
Union of Soviet Socialist Republics.
    See Soviet Union
United Kingdom. See Great Britain
United Nations (UN), 939, 946, 968, 972
United Provinces. See Dutch Republic
United States, 764–766, 769. See also Cold war;
    individual presidents
  in 1920s, 881
  in 1970s, 1013–1016
  in Asia, 805(m)
  civil rights movement, 976–977
  expansion of (1850–1870), 764–765, 765(m)
  French Revolution and, 676
  imperialism of, 1030–1031
  industrial growth in, 768
  Latin America and, 707
  Louisiana Territory and, 689
  Peace of Paris and, 874, 875, 876
  population in, 775, 812(f)
  post–World War II politics in, 958
  railroads and, 709
  religious revival in, 704
  slavery in, 710
  Spanish-American War and, 806
  stock market crash in, 896
  as superpower, 949–950
  terrorist attacks against (September 11, 2001),
      1031, 1054(i), 1054–1055
  World War I and, 852, 856, 864
  World War II and, 929–930
    postwar settlement, 938–942
Universal Exhibition (Manet), 787
Universities. See Colleges and universities
University of Bologna, 370–372, 600(i)
University of Leiden, 550
University of Paris, 370, 371, 412, 413, 441, 443

University of Wittenberg, 476
Upper classes. See also Aristocracy; Hierarchy
  in ancient Greece, 36, 56, 57–58, 59, 80, 86
  in Byzantine Empire, 260, 264
  Christian missionaries and, 486
  in Florence (fifteenth century), 450, 460–462
  in France, 489–490
  gender differences in (nineteenth century),
      730–731
  German unification and, 759, 760(m), 761
  in Hellenistic kingdoms, 92, 108–109,
      110–112, 114
  in Italian cities, 323, 450, 460–462
  in late nineteenth and early twentieth centuries,
      809–811
  Macedonian renaissance (c. 870–c. 1025)
      and, 299
  manners and (seventeenth century), 553,
      559–563
  modern music and, 829
  mosaic of country life
      (fourth century), 241(i)
  in Muslim society, 308–309
  Persian Wars and, 56, 57
  in Roman Republic and Empire, 140, 142,
      143, 157–158, 180, 189–190, 192–193, 220,
      223, 244–245
  in Russia, 754
  Social Darwinism and, 792
  Visigoths and, 239
  women of, 754
Ur (oor), 3, 9, 10, 31
  Ziggurat of, 11(i)
Urban II (pope; r. 1088–1099), 354–355, 359
Urban V (pope; r. 1360s), 436, 444
Urban VI (pope; r. 1378–1389), 441–443
Urban areas. See Cities
Urbanization, 273–274, 707–713, 812, 817, 841
Ur-Nammu (Ur; r. 2112–2095 B.C.E.), 11(i)
Ursula, St., Company of (Ursulines), 485
Uruk, 9, 10
USSR. See Soviet Union
Ustvolskaya, Galina, 1063
Usury, 344, 357, 411(i)
Uthman (caliph; r. 644–656), 273–274
Utilitarianism, 715
Utopia (More), 475–476, 717
Utopias, 97, 717
Utraquists (OO truh kwists), 445–446
Uzbekistan, 1040

Vaccination, 599
Václav (duke of Bohemia; r. 920–929), 333–334
Valencia, 388(m), 390, 391(m)

Valens (Roman emperor; r. 364–378), 238
Valerian (Roman emperor; r. 253–260),
    208, 209(m)
Vallain, Jeanne-Louise, 667
Valois (vahl WAH), 487(m), 487–490
Vandals, 240, 241(i), 244, 249, 254(m)
Van de Velde, Theodor, 884
Van de Venne, Adriaen Pietersz, 507(i)
Van Gogh, Vincent (1853–1890), 787–788
Vassals (vassalage), 324–329, 353(m), 355, 398
    Carolingians and, 316
    in England, 361, 362, 401
    in France, 332, 359, 365–366, 369, 399
    in Germany, 333, 366, 395
    oath of fealty and, 316, 325, 327, 395, 403
    in Ottoman Empire, 437
    in Sicily, 348, 395
    in Spain, 390
Vatican, 224(i), 458, 920. *See also* Papacy
Vatican II (1962), 1003
Vendée region, resistance to French Revolution in,
    671, 673, 674
Venetia, 756, 757, 758
Venezuela, 1051
Venice (Venetians), 291, 298(m), 299, 355, 440,
    508, 584, 597
    Battle of Lepanto (1571) and, 492
    in fourteenth and fifteenth centuries, 451,
        457–458, 462, 469(m)
    Fourth Crusade (1202–1204) and, 388(m),
        388–390
    in seventeenth century, 564(m)
    trade and, 385, 385(i), 397, 425
    Turks and, 457, 463
"Venus" figurines, 6(i)
Verdi, Giuseppe (1813–1901), 747(i), 748, 755,
    758, 780, 788, 795
Verdun, battle of (1916), 858
Verdun, Treaty of (843), 312(m), 316, 333
Vernacular languages and literature, 330, 331(i),
    367–369, 515
    music and, 511
    Renaissance (fifteenth-century), 448–450
    translations of Bible into, 481, 483
Versailles
    Estates General at, 657–658
    palace at, 523(i), 527(i), 527–528
    Treaty of (1919–1920), 872, 873(m),
        874–876, 896, 922
    women's march to (1789), 651(i),
        651–652, 660
Vesalius, Andreas (vih SAY lee us)
    (1514–1564), 515
Vesconte, Pietro, 385(i)

Vespasian (ves PAY shun) (Roman emperor;
    r. 69–79 C.E.), 178, 186, 187
Vespucci, Amerigo, 464(m), 467
Vesta, shrine of, 137
Vestal Virgins, 137
Vesuvius, Mount (veh SOO vee us), 179(i), 187
Veterans, World War I, 870, 876, 878, 879,
    882–883, 886, 892, 914
Veto, in Rome, 145
Vibia Perpetua, 171, 171(i), 172
Vichy France, 928
Victor, Sextus Aurelius, 217(m)
Victor Emmanuel II (Italy; r. 1861–1878), 747,
    756(m), 757
Victor Emmanuel III (Italy; r. 1900–1946), 892
Victoria (Great Britain; r. 1837–1901), 742–743,
    763(i), 763–764, 779
Vienna, 437, 597, 762, 766, 768, 772
    Imperial Opera House, 773(i)
    Jews in, 403
    Napoleon in, 689
    siege of (1683), 536(i), 537, 540
Vienna Workshop, 826
Vietcong, 1006
Viet Minh, 968
Vietnam, 779, 780, 843, 863, 968, 1006
Vietnam War, 988, 1006, 1007(m), 1013
    antiwar movement and, 1010
Vigée-Lebrun, Marie-Louise-Elizabeth
    (1755–1842), 625
Vikings (Danes), 317, 387
    coin hoards (c. 865–895), 321(f)
    in England, 319(m), 320–321, 321(f), 330–331
    invasions of ninth and tenth centuries, 302,
        309, 318–323, 319(m), 330–331
Villages
    early medieval, 278–279
    post-Carolingian, 325–326
Villani, Matteo, 430
Villeneuve St.-Georges, 317–318
Villiers, George, 541
Violence
    against civilians, 924, 924(i)
    efforts to contain, in post-Carolingian age,
        328–329
    Roman, 159, 162, 165, 166, 209, 249
    as entertainment, 181
Virgil (70–19 B.C.E.), 183, 189, 193, 282, 314, 414
Virginia, 508, 573
Virginity, Christianity and, 232, 234
Virgin Mary (mother of Jesus), 228, 266(i),
    295(i), 377, 414, 416, 418(i), 421, 494, 562,
    669, 789–790, 1021
Virtue(s). *See also* Morality

Plato on, 96
Roman view of, 132
Socrates on, 77, 95
Stoic view of, 116–117
Visconti dynasty (vees KON tee), 450, 458–459
Visigoths (VIS ih gawths), 238–240, 254(m), 261(m), 293, 311
in Spain, 288–289
Visual perspective, 454–455, 471, 510, 511(i)
Vitry, Jacques de, 379
Vladimir (grand prince of Kiev and all Russia; r. c. 980–1015), 303
Voice of America, 979
Volksgemeinschaft, 911–912
Voltaire (vohl TAYR) **(François-Marie Arouet)** (1694–1778), 602, 609–612, 612(i), 613–614, 618, 636, 637, 707, 715
Voting rights (suffrage), 716, 735, 740(i), 741, 742
anti-Semitism and, 837
German unification and, 761
in Great Britain, 764, 829, 830
in India, 808
Irish home rule and, 835–836
in Italy, 836
mass politics and, 830
nineteenth-century reforms, 720
restricted, 704
in Russia, 842, 866
in United States, 764
women's, 720, 798, 833–835, 877, 878(f), 957
Vranitsky, Franz, 1019
Vulgate (bible translation), 314, 481

Wagner, Richard (VAHG ner) (1813–1883), 788
Walachia (vuh LAY kee uh), 752
Waldensians, 381
Waldo, 381
Walentynowicz, Anna, 1021
Wales, 286, 544, 589
Walesa, Lech (vuh WEN zuh, lek) (b. 1943), 1021–1022
Walid, al- (Umayyad caliph), 259(i)
Wallenberg, Raoul (1912–1947?), 934
Wallenstein, Albrecht von (1583–1634), 499
Walpole, Sir Robert (1676–1745), 590, 591(i)
War (warfare). *See also* Armed forces; Weapons and military technology; *specific wars*
Alexander the Great and, 103(m), 105
in ancient Near East, 7(m)
cultural interaction and, 13
in eighteenth century, 632–636
in fourteenth and fifteenth centuries, 440
influence of, 4

Louis XIV and, 533–532, 591
Mongols' military tactics, 396
Neo-Assyrian kingdom, 26, 27
New Kingdom (Egypt), 22, 24
in ninth to eleventh centuries, 327–329
between Persians and Greeks, 28, 51–56
Roman, 140, 144, 146, 147, 150, 156–158, 159, 161
in twelfth-century poetry, 369
War, and communism, 868, 890, 891
Warhol, Andy (1927?–1987), 1000
War of Independence (American). *See* American Revolution
War of the Austrian Succession (1740–1748), 632–634, 633(m)
War of the League of Augsburg (Nine Years' War) (1689–1697), 587
War of the Polish Succession (1733–1735), 596
War of the Roses (1460–1485), 435
War of the Spanish Succession (1701–1713), 587, 588(m)
Warriors (warrior class)
crusaders as, 388, 392
Islam and, 271, 273
Japanese, 804
knights as, 367, 434
in Merovingian period, 280, 282
Mongolian, 385
in post-Carolingian age, 323, 327–329
Warsaw, 581, 613, 675(m), 927
duchy of, 689, 700, 702, 702(m)
Jewish uprising in (1943), 931(i), 931–932
Warsaw Pact, 954(m), 955
Washington, George (1732–1799), 646
Washington Conference (1921), 875
Watergate scandal, 1014
Waterloo, battle of (1815), 694
Water power, 344–345
Water supply, 148, 149(i), 774
Watson, James (b. 1928), 977, 993
Watt, James (1736–1819), 630
Watteau, Antoine (1684–1721), 584, 584(i)
Wealth of Nations, An Inquiry into the Nature and Causes of the (Smith), 615
Wealthy, the. *See* Rich, the; Upper classes
Weapons and military technology. *See also* Nuclear weapons; War
African colonies and, 799, 801
Alexander the Great and, 102
in Ancient Greece, 56
artillery, 488(i), 488–489
battering rams, 26
gender roles and, 12

(continued)

in Golden Age Greece, 58
in Hellenistic kingdoms, 108, 120
Hittite, 24
of mass destruction, 1055
in Mesopotamia (Bronze Age), 12
Neo-Assyrian kingdom, 26
in ninth to eleventh centuries, 327
under Philip II, 101
before World War I, 847
in World War I, 855, 859, 869, 896
Weaving, 94, 345, 630(i), 630–631. See also Textiles
Weber, Max (1864–1920), 823
Wedgwood, Josiah (1730–1795), 624
Weimar Republic, 871, 879, 882, 887, 909
Welfare (social welfare programs), 483–484, 713, 729, 835, 836
Welfare state, 915, 946, 955, 961–963, 1017–1018
Wellington, duke of (Sir Arthur Wellesley) (1769–1852), 694
Wergild (VER gilt), 244
Wesley, John (1703–1791), 621, 703–704
Wesleyans (Methodists), 703
Wessex, 321, 330, 330(m)
West, the, idea of, 4
West Africa, 970
West Bank, 1014
Western Europe, 260, 275
   c. 600, 254(m), 261(m)
   c. 750, 291(m)
   Byzantine Empire and, 262, 295–296, 310, 312(m)
   Charlemagne's conquests in, 311–312, 312(m)
   early medieval kingdoms, 275–293
      British isles, 286–288
      economic activity in a peasant society, 280–282
      Frankish kingdoms, 275–280, 317, 319(m), 320–322
      Italy, 289–291
      Merovingian society, 281–285
      Spain, 288–289
   Frankish kingdoms, 276–280, 317, 319(m), 320–322, 332
   local rule in post-Carolingian society, 323–337
      public power and private relationships, 323–328
   profit economy and, 340–343, 347, 375
   Russia and, 303
   Viking, Muslim, and Magyar invasions of ninth and tenth centuries, 318–323, 319(m)
   after World War II, 947, 951
      economic rebirth in, 957–961
      political rebirth in, 955
Westernization of Russia, 592–594, 593(i), 723

"Western" values, restoring, after World War II, 975–977
West Germany, 953–955, 978, 1019, 1022
   economy of, 958, 960
   environmental movement, 1048
West Indies, 509, 632, 634, 635(m), 769
Westphalia, kingdom of, 689
Weyden, Rogier van der (c. 1400–1464), 454, 456(i)
What Is Property? (Proudhon), 719
Whigs, 547, 554, 590, 644, 764
Whitby, Synod of (664), 287
Whitefield, George (1714–1770), 704
White Mountain, Battle of (1620), 498–499, 502(m)
Why God Became Man (St. Anselm), 377
Wilde, Oscar (1854–1900), 815
Wilkes, John (1727–1797), 643, 644, 648
Wilkes affair, 643–645, 648
William (prince of Orange; d. 1584), 494
William I (Netherlands; r. 1815–1840), 733
William I (Prussia; r. 1861–1888; German emperor, r. 1871–1888), 758–759, 761(i)
William I (the Conqueror) (England; 1027–1087), 360(m), 360–362, 361(i)
William II (Germany; r. 1888–1918), 815–816, 844, 847, 853, 856, 861, 869
William III (prince of Orange, king of England and Scotland; r. 1689–1702), 547–548, 552, 587, 589–591
William IX (duke of Aquitaine; 1071–1126), 367–368
Wilson, Woodrow (1856–1924), 843, 856, 864
   Paris peace conference and, 871–872, 874
Winchester Cathedral (England), 362
Windischgrätz, Prince Alfred von, 739
Wind power, 1048, 1048(i)
Windsor, House of, 599
Wisdom literature, Egyptian, 21, 22, 27, 32
Witches and witchcraft, 517(i), 517–520
Wladyslaw II (Poland; r. 1386–1434), 438
Wolf, Christa, 1005
Wolf-Man, 797–798, 821
Women, 643, 838. See also Divorce; Family; Feminism; Gender differences; Marriage; Prostitution; Sex and sexuality
   in 1920s, 882–884, 886, 890, 892, 894, 896
   in 1930s, 902–903, 908, 916, 917, 918
   activism of (1960s), 1008–1009
   Alexander the Great and, 102
   in American colonies, 575
   in ancient Egypt, 21
   in ancient Greece, 38, 98
      Athens, 43, 60–61, 65, 67, 68–72, 73, 82–83

comedies, 82–83
companions, 71–72
fetching water, 94(i)
legal and political status of, 40, 42, 43
after Peloponnesian War, 93–94
religious functions of, 42(i), 42–43
roles of, 42, 42(i)
social and economic roles of, 44, 68–72
Sparta, 44
Asian, 781, 1056
in Byzantine Empire, 249, 265, 267
Christianity and, 295(i), 604
early Christianity, 202, 225–226
monasteries, 234, 280–281, 283–285, 284(i),
286, 288, 333
virginity and sexual renunciation, 232
in city-states, 40
as collaborators, 956, 956(i)
colonialism and, 802
division of labor by gender, 8, 14, 237
domesticity ideology and, 729, 743, 752, 770,
811, 978
as domestic servants, 440, 459, 462, 467, 468(i)
economic independence and, 729–730
education of, 485, 556, 600(i), 604, 776(f)
eighteenth century, 585, 604, 638
nineteenth century, 777–778
in Rome, 136
in eighteenth century, 629
novels and, 585, 626–627
emancipation of, 718, 738
in England (Great Britain), 461–462, 543–544,
556, 582, 585, 711–712, 764
social reform and charitable work, 729–730
the Enlightenment and, 600, 600(i), 604–605,
609–610, 612–613, 623, 625–627, 626
in Florence (fifteenth century), 459–463
in France, 612–613, 623, 625, 735
Civil Code (Napoleonic Code), 685–686
French Revolution, 651(i), 651–652, 660,
662, 669–670
French Revolution and, 651(i), 651–652, 660
seventeenth century, 560–561, 563
Freud on, 821–822
guilds and, 334–335, 430
Hebrew, 31
in Hellenistic kingdoms
medical view of, 120
philosophy and, 116–117, 118
poetry and, 113
social and economic status, 110–111
Indo-European, 24
inheritance and, 272, 281, 329, 632
in Iran, 1052

Islam and, 269, 272
Jewish, 613
in labor force, 767, 770, 771, 772, 782, 818–819,
830, 831, 882
in sweatshops, 1056
in late nineteenth and early twentieth
centuries
in labor force, 830, 831
reformers and, 814–815, 815(i)
sports and leisure, 818–820
suffrage (voting rights), 833–835, 834(i)
unions and working-class political parties,
830, 831
upper-class women, 810–811
in Mesopotamia, 12, 14
in Middle Ages
Carolingian period, 295(i), 318
commercial revolution and, 344–345
courtly literature, 368–369
crusades and, 355
early Middle Ages, 280–285, 284(i)
fourteenth and fifteenth centuries, 430,
437, 440
monastic orders, 373, 375–376, 379, 382
post-Carolingian age, 324, 328, 333
religion, 410–411
migration and, 816–817, 1059
in Nazi Germany, 912–913, 913
Neo-Assyrian kingdom, 27
in nineteenth century
Great Britain, 711–712, 729–731, 764
John Stuart Mill's views, 792
in labor force, 767, 770, 771, 772, 782
nation building and, 757(i)
Paris Commune (1871), 783(i), 783–784
positivism and, 792
reform movements and, 727–730
religion and, 789–790
after revolutions of 1848, 741–742
as teachers, 777–778
in northern Europe (fifteenth century), 461–462
novels and, 561, 585, 626–627, 687(i), 889(i)
in Paleolithic and Neolithic periods, 5–6, 6(i), 7
in patriarchal society. See Patriarchy
Plato's view of, 97
Protestant Reformation and, 483(i), 483–484
radio and, 886
reproductive technologies and, 993–995
as republican mothers, 757(i)
in Roman Republic and Empire
childbearing, 194–195
education, 136
family and household, 134–136
(continued)

gladiators, 181
independence of, 134–135
moral values, 131–132, 135
property, 135(i), 136
reproduction, 194–195
as slaves, 180
Vestal Virgins, 137
in Russia and Soviet Union, 594, 754,
890, 891, 908
in science, 308
in seventeenth century, 549–550, 556
artists, 558–559, 559(i)
authors, 561
manners, 559–561
novels, 561
salons, 560–561
Social Darwinism and, 791
socialist movements and, 718–719, 720
suffrage (voting rights) for, 720, 798, 833–835,
866, 877, 878, 878(f), 957
as terrorists, 970
welfare state and (1945–1960), 961
witches (witchcraft) and, 517(i), 517–520
World War I and, 860(i), 861–863, 862(i), 864
after World War II, 950, 976, 978
World War II and, 932–933, 934
Women's Social and Political Union (WSPU), 835
Wonders of the World, The (Callimachus), 113
Woolen industry, 362, 430, 629, 631.
See also Textiles
Wooley, Hannah, 561
Woolf, Virginia (1882–1941), 888, 889(i), 919
Wordsworth, William (1770–1850), 680, 724
Worker Opposition (Soviet Union), 890
Workers (working class), 717–718. See also Labor
unions; Unemployment
in 1920s, 879, 880, 881–882, 892
in ancient Egypt, 23
Asian (1980s to present), 1056
education and, 729
in eighteenth century, 629–631
factory work and, 709–712
in France, 686
Popular Front, 917
revolution of 1848, 735–736
German unification and, 760(m)
in late nineteenth and early twentieth centuries
mass politics, 829–843
migrations (1881–1910), 816–817
reform and, 818
mechanization and, 770
Napoleon III and, 749, 750
nation-state and, 781–785
in nineteenth century, 733

changes in worklife, 781–782
formation of working class, 709–712
Marxism and, 782–783
religiously motivated reformers, 728
political participation of, 740–741
in postindustrial society, 996–997
in Roman Empire, 219–220
Russian Revolution and, 864–869
in Soviet Union, 906–907
women, 830, 831, 834
nineteenth century, 767, 770, 771, 772, 782
World War I, 861–863
after World War I, 870
World War I and, 861–862, 863
Workhouses, 628, 686, 729
Works and Days (Hesiod), 37
World Bank, 1045–1046, 1051
World Trade Center (New York City), terrorist
attacks against (September 11, 2001),
1031, 1054(i), 1054–1055
World Trade Organization, 1046
World War I (1914–1918), 797(i), 851–870
alliances in, 852, 854–855
armistice (1918), 869
battlefronts in, 855–859
events and conditions leading to, 843–849
competing alliances, 843–846
home front in, 860–863
Irish home rule and, 836
outbreak of, 848(m), 852–854
protests against, 863–864
protests and unrest after, 870–871
trench warfare in, 857(m), 858, 859, 859(i)
World War II (1939–1945), 927–942
Allies in, 930, 932, 936–938
Axis in, 930
in Europe and North Africa, 934(m)
events and conditions leading to, 899–927
Holocaust, 930–932, 931(i)
home front in, 932–933
impact on Europe, 948(m)
in Pacific, 937(m)
postwar settlement, 938–942
resistance in Nazi-occupied areas, 934
Worms, 357
Concordat of (1122), 350
Diet of, 477
Writing (script), 5. See also Alphabets
Arabic, 270(i), 275
cuneiform, 11–13, 13(f)
demotic, 18
Greek, 36, 37
hieroglyphs, 17, 18, 18(f), 91(i)
Kufic, 270(i)

Linear A and B, 35
Roman, 183
Wycliffe, John (c. 1330–1384), 444–445

Xenophanes (zen OFF uh neez)
    (c. 580–480 B.C.E.), 47
Xenophobia, 722
Xenophon (ZEN uh fun) (c. 430–355 B.C.E.),
    72–73, 99
Xerxes I (ZUHRK seez) (r. 486–465 B.C.E.),
    53(m), 54–55, 262

Yahweh, 31–32, 124
Yalta Conference (1945), 939, 953
Yangzhou (China), 397, 427
Year of the Four Emperors (69 C.E.), 186
Yeats, William Butler (1865–1939), 836, 888
Yeltsin, Boris (b. 1931), 1021, 1034–1036, 1039
Yevtushenko, Yevgeny (b. 1933), 1005
Young Ireland movement, 723
Young Italy, 722
Young Plan (1929), 875
Young Turks, 808, 844
Ypres (EE pruh), 341(m), 345, 427(m), 430
Yuan dynasty (China), 463
Yugoslavia, 8n, 537, 872, 876, 938, 952, 952(m)
    breakup of, 1031–1033, 1033(m), 1044
Yushchenko, Victor, 1040

Zachary (pope; r. 741–752), 291–292, 310
Zama, battle of (202 B.C.E.), 150
Zara, 388(m), 389
Zarathustra (ZAR uh THOO struh) (**Zoroaster**)
    (sixth century B.C.E.), 30
Zell, Katharina, 484
Zell, Matthew, 484
Zemstvos, 753, 866
Zengi (Seljuk chieftain; fl. 1145), 355
Zeno (philosopher) (335–263 B.C.E.),
    116–117, 203
Zeno (Roman emperor; r. 474–491), 241, 242
Zenobia (Palmyra; r. 269–272), 208
Zeus, 37, 38, 66, 105, 123(i), 137
Zhenotdel (Women's Bureau), 890, 891
Zhukov, Marshall (ZHOO kof), 964
Ziggurat of Ur in Sumer (ZIG uh rat), 10, 11(i)
Zionism (Zionists), 949
Zographos, Panagiotis, 706(i)
Zola, Émile (1840–1902), 837
Zollverein, 723
Zoroastrianism (zohr oh AHS tree uh nizum), 30
Zurich, 407, 479
Zwingli, Huldrych (TSVING lee, HOOLD rik)
    (1484–1531), 479–480, 480(f)

80 N

Greenland
(Den.)

Alaska

60 N

ICELAND

CANADA

UNITED
KINGDOM

IRELAND

40 N

UNITED STATES

FRANCE

SPAIN

PORTUGAL

Azores
(Port.)

ATLANTIC
OCEAN

MOROCCO

Canary Is.
(Sp.)

Hawaii

20 N

MEXICO

BAHAMAS

DOMINICAN
REPUBLIC

HAITI

Puerto Rico (U.S.)

Western Sahara
(Mor.)

MAURITANIA

CUBA

JAMAICA

BELIZE

ST. KITTS AND NEVIS

ANTIGUA AND BARBUDA

DOMINICA

CAPE
VERDE

Guadeloupe (Fr.)

GUATEMALA

HONDURAS

Martinique (Fr.)

ST. VINCENT AND THE GRENADINES

SENEGAL

MALI

EL SALVADOR

NICARAGUA

ST. LUCIA

BARBADOS

GRENADA

GAMBIA

GUINEA-BISSAU

GUINEA

COSTA RICA

TRINIDAD AND TOBAGO

GUYANA

SIERRA LEONE

PANAMA

VENEZUELA

SURINAME

LIBERIA

French Guiana (Fr.)

CÔTE D'IVOIRE

COLOMBIA

BURKINA FASO

GHANA

PACIFIC OCEAN

0

Equator

Galápagos Is.
(Ec.)

ECUADOR

SAMOA

PERU

BRAZIL

20 S

TONGA

BOLIVIA

Easter I.
(Chile)

PARAGUAY

CHILE

URUGUAY

ATLANTIC
OCEAN

ARGENTINA

0		1,500		3,000 miles
0	1,500		3,000 kilometers	

40 S

Falkland Is.
(U.K.)

60 S

80 S

160 W   140 W   120 W   100 W   80 W   60 W   40 W   20 W